The Future of Business

THE ESSENTIALS

4th Edition

Lawrence J. Gitman

San Diego State University

Carl McDaniel

University of Texas, Arlington

SOUTH-WESTERN
CENGAGE Learning

Australia • Brazil • Japan • Korea • Mexico • Singapore • Spain • United Kingdom • United States

SOUTH-WESTERN
CENGAGE Learning™

The Future of Business: The Essentials,
Fourth Edition

**Lawrence J. Gitman,
Carl McDaniel**

VP/Editorial Director:
Jack W. Calhoun

Editor-in-Chief:
Melissa S. Acuña

Acquisitions Editor:
Erin Joyner

Developmental Editor:
Daniel Noguera

Editorial Assistant:
Danny Bolan

Executive Marketing Manager:
Kimberly Kanakes

Marketing Manager:
Mike Cloran

Senior Marketing Coordinator:
Sarah Rose

Marketing Communications Manager:
Sarah Greber

Art Director:
Stacy Jenkins Shirley

Internal Designer:
Craig Ramsdell

Cover Designer:
Craig Ramsdell

Cover Image:
©Getty Images/Image Bank

Director, Content and Media Production:
Barbara Fuller-Jacobsen

Content Project Manager:
Emily Nesheim

Rights Acquisition Account Manager:
Mollika Basu

Text Permissions Researcher:
James Reidel

Senior Permissions Image Manager:
Deanna Ettinger

Photo Permissions Researcher:
Terri Miller

Media Editor:
Kristen Meere

Senior Print Buyer:
Beverly Breslin

Production Service:
Pre-Press PMG

For product information and technology assistance, contact us at
Cengage Learning Customer & Sales Support, 1-800-354-9706
For permission to use material from this text or product,
submit all requests online at **www.cengage.com/permissions**
Further permissions questions can be emailed to
permissionrequest@cengage.com

Library of Congress Control Number: 2008930406

Student Edition

PKG ISBN-13: 978-0-324-59076-0
PKG ISBN-10: 0-324-59076-8
ISBN-13: 978-0-324-59075-3
ISBN-10: 0-324-59075-X

South-Western Cengage Learning
5191 Natorp Boulevard
Mason, OH 45040
USA

Cengage Learning products are represented in Canada by Nelson Education, Ltd.

For your course and learning solutions, visit **www.cengage.com**

Purchase any of our products at your local college store or at our preferred online store **www.ichapters.com**

Printed in the United States of America
1 2 3 4 5 6 7 12 11 10 09 08

Dedicated to the memory of my mother, Dr. Edith Gitman, who instilled in me the importance of education and hard work.

—Lawrence J. Gitman

To Michelle, Mimi, and Eric.

—Carl McDaniel

Lawrence J. Gitman

Lawrence J. Gitman is an emeritus professor of finance at San Diego State University. He received his bachelor's degree from Purdue University, his M.B.A. from the University of Dayton, and his Ph.D. from the University of Cincinnati. Professor Gitman is a prolific textbook author and has over 50 articles appearing in *Financial Management, Financial Review, Financial Services Review, Journal of Financial Planning, Journal of Risk and Insurance, Journal of Financial Research, Financial Practice and Education, Journal of Financial Education*, and other publications.

His singly authored major textbooks include *Principles of Managerial Finance: Brief*, Fifth Edition, *Principles of Managerial Finance*, Twelfth Edition, and *Foundations of Managerial Finance*, Fourth Edition. Other major textbooks include *Personal Financial Planning*, Eleventh Edition, and *Fundamentals of Investing*, Tenth Edition, both co-authored with Michael D. Joehnk. Gitman and Joehnk also wrote *Investment Fundamentals: A Guide to Becoming a Knowledgeable Investor*, which was selected as one of 1988's 10 best personal finance books by *Money* magazine. In addition, he co-authored *Introduction to Finance* with Jeff Madura and *Corporate Finance*, Second Edition, with Scott B. Smart and William L. Meggison.

An active member of numerous professional organizations, Professor Gitman is past president of the Academy of Financial Services, the San Diego Chapter of the Financial Executives Institute, the Midwest Finance Association, and the FMA National Honor Society. In addition he is a Certified Financial Planner (CFP®) and a Certified Cash Manager (CCM). Gitman served as vice-president, Financial Education of the Financial Management Association, as a director of the San Diego MIT Enterprise Form, and on the CFP® Board of Standards. He and his wife have two children and live in La Jolla, California, where he is an avid bicyclist.

Carl McDaniel

Carl McDaniel is a professor of marketing at the University of Texas—Arlington, where he is currently on leave. He served as chairman of the marketing department for 30 years. He has also been an instructor for more than 30 years and is the recipient of several awards for outstanding teaching. McDaniel has also been a district sales manager for Southwestern Bell Telephone Company. He served as a board member of the North Texas Higher Education Authority, a $1.5 billion organization that provides financing for student loans across America. He has also held the position of senior trade advisor for the International Trade Center (ITC) in Geneva, Switzerland. The ITC is jointly funded by the World Trade Organization and the United Nations. Currently, McDaniel is teaching in Executive MBA programs in both the United States and China.

In addition to this text, McDaniel has also co-authored a number of textbooks in marketing. McDaniel's research has appeared in such publications as *Journal of Marketing, Journal of Business Research, Journal of the Academy of Marketing Science*, and *California Management Review*.

McDaniel is a member of the American Marketing Association, Academy of Marketing Science, and the Society for Marketing Advances.

Besides his academic experience, McDaniel has business experience as the co-owner of a marketing research firm. The research firm has grown into one of the largest specialty marketing research companies in America. He has a bachelor's degree from the University of Arkansas and his master's degree and doctorate from Arizona State University.

ONLINE RESOURCES

Online Enrichment Chapter: Managing Your Personal Finances
Online Enrichment Chapter: Using the Internet for Business Success
Online Appendix: Managing Risk and Insurance
www.cengage.com/introbusiness/gitman

© PhotoAlto / Getty Images

brief contents

contents

© PhotoAlto / Getty Images

Contents

Contents

Contents

YOUR FUTURE IS OUR BUSINESS

What is in your future?

The Future of Business: The Essentials prepares you for a successful career in business by equipping you with the knowledge, skills, and competencies you need to prepare for tomorrow's competitive workplace. The authors present business principles and highlight emerging business trends in fields such as management, leadership, production, marketing, and finance.

Advanced learning tools such as the Integrated Learning System help build business competencies. This system provides learning goals at the beginning of each chapter to outline the key concepts that will be discussed throughout the chapter. The authors designed this approach to anchor chapter concepts, provide a framework for study, and help you learn quickly and study more efficiently. Your future is our business!

This edition is packed with updated features and cases to help you stay excited about the business world. Each feature, case, or activity is designed to help you understand how real business problems are solved, determine what business careers are right for you, and evaluate how ethics come into play. All of these are in place to prepare you for the future business world.

New Building Your Career Booklet This lively, concise booklet on career planning and study skills is the perfect complement to the Fourth Edition of *The Future of Business: The Essentials*. The *Building Your Career Booklet* covers career planning and study strategies to ensure success, not only in class but in your careers.

NEW BizFlix Videos These video clips show the world of business from a new perspective. Taken from popular Hollywood films, the videos offer a unique and tangible way to present business principles. You can draw the connections and articulate the relationship between the movie and the chapter concepts.

THE FUTURE WITH THE

Apple, Inc. Continuing Case Apple Computer, Inc. is featured in a continuing case at the end of each part, providing an in-depth look at the company's tumultuous evolution and demonstrating how chapter concepts are applied in an actual business. By presenting the strategies that helped Apple rebound from a business slump in the mid-80s to success today, you will understand management and organizational problems and solutions over an extended period of time.

Exploring Business Careers Videos End-of-chapter "Exploring Business Careers" vignettes and videos highlight the careers of successful business leaders from a variety of service and manufacturing firms. In addition to providing insight into a variety of business careers, the end-of-chapter vignettes and videos help reinforce an interest in the chapter topics through professionally produced videos.

Concept in Action Photo Essays "Concept in Action" photo essays help illustrate chapter concepts using interesting companies and business leaders. Each photo is accompanied by descriptive captions that provide detailed information about the person or business profiled and is followed by a critical-thinking question.

Ethics Activities Ethics activities at the end of each chapter present real-world ethical challenges and prompt you to choose the most ethical course of action. Scenarios include the Enron collapse, teenage obesity and fast food, executive compensation, outsourcing jobs to foreign countries, whistle-blowing, and more.

ESSENTIALS' FEATURES

Expanding Around the Globe As you enter today's workplace, you are very likely to conduct business with colleagues, clients, and vendors from around the world. This feature offers insights into the global economy and highlights the strategies firms employ to expand their business and improve their productivity by using global resources.

SCANS Integration To help you develop high-performance workplace skills, the Secretary's Commission on Achieving Necessary Skills (SCANS) recommends developing five workplace competencies: using and allocating resources, working with others, acquiring and using information, understanding systems, and working with technology. The "Preparing for Tomorrow's Workplace" activities are designed to develop these workplace skills and are included in the homework section of each chapter.

THE FUTURE WITH

Business & Company Resource Center (BCRC) Through Cengage Learning's Business & Company Resource Center, you can get access to a dynamic database of information and resources that will keep you up-to-date and continually interacting with the business world. BCRC supplies online access to a wide variety of global business information, including competitive intelligence, career and investment opportunities, business rankings, company histories, and much more. View a guided tour of the Business & Company Resource Center at http://www.cengage.com/bcrc.

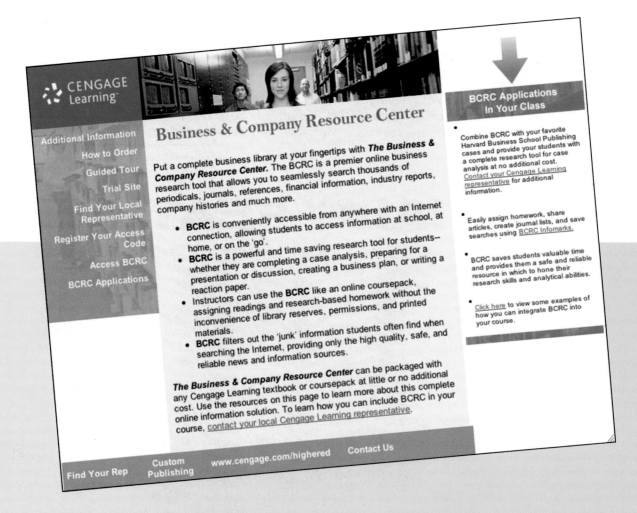

ONLINE LEARNING TOOLS

The Future of Business: The Essentials, 4e is supported with many options for extra study.

Web Site When you use the Fourth Edition, you will have access to a rich array of learning resources that you won't find anywhere else. This outstanding site features chapter-by-chapter online tutorial quizzes, a final exam, chapter outlines, chapter review, chapter-by-chapter weblinks, flashcards, and more!

YOUR FUTURE IS OUR BUSINESS

The future is coming at you at warp speed! Yes, your future and all of the excitement and challenges it entails. The story that we are about to tell you is all about your future. If you plan to be an engineer, medical doctor, social worker, or any other type of professional person, business will impact you. Even though a doctor will devote the bulk of her day to treating patients, she also needs the skills and understanding of business to make her office run smoothly and profitably. What you choose to do in life will also have a big impact on your lifestyle as well. A doctor, for example, may have a good income but a limited amount of free time. Our point is this: you will be in business one way or another!! So enjoy reading this exciting, easy-to-read, story-filled book because it will help you navigate the tricky waters that make up the future of business and prepare you for success!

Features that Help You Learn

We are thrilled that you have joined us on the journey to the future of business. We have made many changes in the Fourth Edition that make it by far the best ever. In this preface, we describe the hallmark features that make this text a success with both students and instructors. We also spotlight the new features and content of this dynamic edition.

Each Chapter Continues to Offer Both Business Principles and Business Trends

You told us that you wanted a crisp, innovative chapter structure, and that's what we deliver in the Fourth Edition. With the dual coverage of business principles and business trends in every chapter, *The Future of Business: The Essentials* prepares you for tomorrow's business world.

Principles of Business
Each chapter delivers a comprehensive overview of current business principles and practices. You will learn what is happening in today's businesses with examples from the largest global corporate giants, such as General Electric and Procter & Gamble, to the smallest family start-ups.

Trends in Business
The last learning goal of every chapter explores new business trends and how they are reshaping today's business and altering tomorrow's competitive environment. Technology and the global economy are covered extensively in every trends section. We expose you to the fundamental factors that are reshaping the business world in which you will soon begin professional careers. With this preview of the future, you gain a keen advantage when entering the workplace.

The Integrated Learning System Ties Everything Together

The Integrated Learning System helps you learn quickly by driving home key chapter concepts and providing a framework for studying. We tie all instructor and student materials to each chapter's learning goals. The learning goals provide a common link to the text and all of the great supplements that accompany the Fourth Edition. Learning goals are listed at the beginning of each chapter and then repeated throughout the chapter in the margins of the text. After reading each section, you can test your retention by answering the questions in the Concept Checks. Every learning goal is further reinforced by the chapter summary.

The Integrated Learning System also helps instructors easily prepare their lectures. Learning goals at the beginning of each chapter outline the key concepts in the chapter and provide structure for lesson plans and help in exam preparation. Test questions, the PowerPoint Slides, and the Instructor's Manual lecture outline are all organized by the Integrated Learning System.

Hundreds of Business Examples Bring Business Concepts to Life

This book is about you—the typical student. We have done a lot of research about your needs, abilities, experiences, and interests and then shaped the text around them. We have used our vast experience both inside and outside the classroom to create a book that is both readable and enjoyable. We believe that the real business applications that are found throughout every chapter set the standard for readability and understanding of key concepts.

BizFlix Video Cases Offer an Excellent Tool for Generating Excitement and Interest in Both the Printed Textbook and Online Book Companion Site

The online BizFlix Video Cases enable the instructor to launch the chapter with student excitement and enthusiasm for the concepts and principles to come. It is all real-world and is what is happening right now! At the end of each chapter a second video, including such firms as BP, Harley Davidson, JP Morgan Chase, and Caterpillar, explores business careers and highlights the main ideas from each chapter. Learning is made fun and interesting through the study of real business issues and strategies implemented by a variety of America's best-known service and manufacturing firms.

Learning Business Terminology Is Made Easy

As you begin your study of business, you will begin to explore new words and concepts like entrepreneurship, venture capital, competitive advantage, relationship management, the European Union, strategic alliance, and more. To help you learn this language of business, we define each new term in the chapter, print them in blue type, list the word and its definition in the margin, and offer a complete glossary at the end of the book. When you finish this book, you will be able to speak the language of business!

Activities and Cases Put Knowledge to Work

The Future of Business: The Essentials, Fourth Edition helps you develop a solid grounding in skills like those you will apply in the workplace. These skill-building activities and resources help you build and polish competencies that your future employer will value.

- **Preparing for Tomorrow's Workplace and Team Activities.** These activities are designed to help build your business skills and practice teamwork. These highly practical exercises give you a meaningful advantage over fellow graduates in the workplace. New team activities in every chapter give you an opportunity to work with other students, building communication skills and interpersonal skills.
- **Ethics Activities Explore Right and Wrong.** Ethics activities at the end of each chapter present real-world ethical challenges and prompt students to choose the most ethical course of action. Scenarios include the Enron collapse, teenage obesity and fast food, executive compensation, outsourcing jobs to foreign countries, whistle-blowing, and more. Each activity gives you a chance to decide the most ethical course of action in these challenging situations.
- **Working the Net Activities.** These activities guide you through a step-by-step analysis of actual e-business practices and give you opportunities to build online research skills.
- **Creative Thinking Cases.** The creative thinking cases invite you to explore business strategies of various companies, analyze business decisions, and prepare comments.
- **Exploring Business Careers.** This feature offers an inside look at successful people in business. Students end each chapter by reading the stories of these successful business leaders in the *Exploring Business Careers* feature and watching the professionally produced, fast-paced video to gain quick insight into business careers and the chapter topic.

Student-Friendly Writing Makes *The Future of Business: The Essentials*, Fourth Edition, Accessible

Our objective is for you to finish this text and feel like this is absolutely the best college textbook that you have ever read! You will find that our writing style is friendly and very conversational—like two friends speaking together. Instead of formal language that can often be stilted, chapter titles, headings, and chapter text are written in a relaxed, inviting manner.

New Features in the Fourth Edition

The Fourth Edition has been thoroughly updated with new learning tools and content to offer a complete, creative learning experience.

The Apple, Inc. Continuing Case Has Been Fully Updated

What company could be more exciting and fun than Apple? Apple, Inc. is featured in a continuing case at the end of each part, providing an in-depth look at the company's tumultuous evolution and demonstrating how chapter concepts are applied in a real business. By presenting the strategies that helped Apple rebound from a business slump in the mid-1980s to success today, you gain an insider's look at the organizational problems and solutions of one of America's most creative companies!!

BizFlix Video Cases

This new and engaging feature uses scenes from current Hollywood films in the beginning of every chapter and closes with critical thinking questions. The powerful and memorable scenes explore the essential business concept, while case questions foster student class participation. The BizFlix Video Cases are available in the PowerPoint presentation and the written case description is conveniently located at the beginning of every chapter.

Fully Updated Concept in Action Photo Essays Demonstrate Concepts at Work

In each chapter you will find interesting companies and business leaders profiled in our "Concept in Action" photo essays. The photos and accompanying essays are fun, contemporary, insightful, and a super learning tool for the visual learner. Each photo essay concludes with a critical thinking question to spark further discussion and study about a business topic.

Building Your Career Booklet

This lively, concise booklet on career planning and study skills, bundled with the text is the perfect complement to *The Future of Business: The Essentials*, Fourth Edition. The *Building Your Career* booklet covers career planning and study skills strategies to ensure the success of the student, not only in class but in their careers as well.

This booklet can also be easily customized to meet specific campus needs or bundled with any Cengage Learning text. This booklet is also perfect for professors who do not use a conventional text for the student success course and want information on career planning.

We Have Retained the Most Popular Features from the Third Edition

This edition has been completely updated so that you are prepared for tomorrow's competitive workplace. However, we have retained those features that instructors and students tell us they really enjoy.

Chapter 1 (Understanding Economic Systems and Business) has been updated to reflect the latest economic conditions and structured to present more thorough coverage of the economic, political and legal, demographic, social, competitive, global, and technological sectors of the business environment. New material includes knowledge as a potential fifth factor of production, a fully updated discussion of baby boomers and their economic impact, and the critical importance of America's petroleum shortage.

Chapter 2 (Making Ethical Decisions and Managing a Socially Responsible Business) contains new material on ethics as a two-way street between buyer and seller. It stresses the notion that the purchaser has ethical responsibilities as well. The discussion on irresponsible but legal behavior has been completely rewritten. You will find a description of Warren Buffett's views of corporate philanthropy. There is a new major section on checking on how charities spend their money and a second section on cause-related marketing.

Chapter 3 (Competing in the Global Marketplace) contains completely updated trade statistics. The sections on NAFTA and the European Union have been rewritten and there is a new section on the importance of the European Union to the United States. There is a new section on the growing trend of government's blocking foreign investment.

Chapter 4 (Forms of Business Ownership) offers new student-friendly examples, and boxes on Pizza Hut's rapid expansion in India and Crocs' explosive growth in the United States illustrate the relative merits of sole proprietorships, partnerships, corporations, and other alternative forms of business organization. Updated information on mergers and acquisitions keeps students abreast of this current trend.

Chapter 5 (Entrepreneurship: Starting and Managing Your Own Business) invites students to put themselves in the shoes of entrepreneurs like Tory Burch, fashion designer; Elon Musk, serial entrepreneur who founded PayPal, Tesla, and SpaceX; Tom Szaky, who started Terracycle, the organic plant food; Bob Cramer of Nimbit, the band management company; and more. Students will be inspired by the fascinating stories of these dynamic young—and not-so-young—entrepreneurs.

Chapter 6 (Management and Leadership in Today's Organizations) features new examples throughout. We offer a new section on the importance of listening to employees.

Chapter 7 (Designing Organizational Structures) offers new insights on formal organizations. This chapter has new material on how many organizations are moving away from traditional organization structures to teams. The material on virtual teams has been completely rewritten. There are new examples throughout the chapter.

Chapter 8 (Managing Human Resources and Labor Relations) has been thoroughly revised. You will find new sections on hiring freezes, using social networking for recruiting, realistic job previews, online performance reviews, and the importance of employee benefits to working mothers. We also discuss the critical importance of successful recruiting. The section on recruitment branding has also been thoroughly revised.

Chapter 9 (Motivating Employees) discusses the relationship between employee satisfaction and customer service. The material on telecommuting has been completely rewritten as has the discussion of absenteeism. There is a new section on employee praise. There are new examples throughout the chapter.

Chapter 10 (Achieving World-Class Operations Management) focuses on the way technology and robotics, competitive forces, and changes in consumer expectations are shaping production and operations management. The trend section highlights a looming U.S. workforce crisis, a challenging domestic business environment, and how U.S. companies are using business process management to keep their edge.

Chapter 11 (Creating Products and Pricing Strategies to Meet Customers' Needs) begins with a new discussion on the consequences of not following the marketing concept. We present the highly popular concept of the "net promoter score" and its relationship to customer satisfaction. There is new material on the critical importance of correctly defining the target market. The gender segmentation material has been thoroughly revised. Two new trends are presented: brand/product line extension and private-label branding.

Chapter 12 (Distributing and Promoting Products and Services) offers new material on the supply chain. The "new promotional media" are discussed as well as their impact on traditional advertising. The material on point-of-purchase displays and event marketing is new. We also discuss the new trend of viral, or buzz, marketing.

Chapter 13 (Using Technology to Manage Information) presents the latest developments in information technology and knowledge management, including networking trends and advances in software-on-demand services. The chapter also discusses digital forensics, a new field that provides tools for cyber-sleuthing; the shift to a distributed workforce model; and the rise in grid computing.

Chapter 14 (Using Financial Information and Accounting) provides updates on the latest issues in accounting. These include the collaboration between U.S. and international accounting boards to develop global accounting standards; the costs, challenges, and effects of implementing the provisions of the Sarbanes-Oxley Act; and the changing relationship between accountants and their clients. The chapter also discusses the new XBRL tagging of financial documents and its challenges and opportunities.

Chapter 15 (Understanding Money and Financial Institutions) highlights the changing structure of the financial services industry. Financial institutions face new regulatory and compliance issues while striving to maintain and increase market share. Tightening credit is creating opportunity for microlenders and alternate models of lending, like formalizing lending relationships between family members, and retailers like Wal-Mart opening bank branches abroad. Students will also read about electronic banking tools, like direct banking, mobile banking, remote deposit capture, and automated clearinghouses.

Chapter 16 (Understanding Financial Management and Securities Markets) highlights the shift in finance from a relatively isolated, inward-looking function to a unit that is heavily involved in shaping and implementing a company's overall strategic objectives. CFOs are taking a more visible, active role, and financial managers must work closely with other business units. The chapter explains the significant changes happening in broker and dealer markets around the world and how trade-cycle automation and electronic algorithms help markets stay on the edge of an intensely competitive business.

Key Themes that Highlight Today's Latest Topics

Ethics

The business world has been rocked in recent years by ethics scandals that led to bankruptcies for major organizations and jail terms for top executives. Well-publicized scandals have touched off a wave of reform and renewed emphasis on ethical business behavior. A paramount theme of this text will always be that business must be conducted in an ethical and socially responsible manner.

Chapter 2 (Making Ethical Decisions and Managing a Socially Responsible Business) is completely devoted to business ethics and social responsibility. We discuss techniques for setting personal ethical standards, how managers influence organizational ethics, tools for creating employee ethical awareness, and the concept of social responsibility. The Fourth Edition features new ethics activities at the end of each chapter. All ethical dilemmas are taken right out of today's business world!

Customer Satisfaction and Quality

We believe that delivering superior customer value, satisfaction, and quality is essential to attracting and keeping customers. Because customer satisfaction and quality are the foundation of all business principles, we have addressed these important topics in most chapters. Each chapter stresses that satisfied customers who experience quality products and services become loyal customers. We offer boxes throughout the book called Customer Satisfaction and Quality that demonstrate how these concepts are applied in actual companies.

Managing Change

If there is one truth in the business world it is that it is constantly changing. Failure to keep up with change can create huge problems such as those experienced by Ford, General Motors, Pier 1, and Radio Shack. On the other hand, change can offer great opportunities for firms such as Apple, Inc. and ExxonMobil. Our Managing Change boxes describe how companies have recognized and responded to changes in technology, competition, economic forces, demographics, and culture.

Entrepreneurship and Small-Business Management

Because many of you will either open your own businesses or go to work for small organizations, entrepreneurship and small-business principles are covered throughout the text. Chapter 5 (Entrepreneurship: Starting and Managing Your Own Business) delivers interesting discussions on starting and managing a small business, including the advantages and disadvantages of small-business ownership.

In addition, a boxed feature called Catching the Entrepreneurial Spirit appears throughout the book and offers practical insights into the challenges and rewards of actually owning and managing a small business.

Global Business Economy

Chapter 3 (Competing in the Global Marketplace) offers a thorough and exciting picture of competition in the global marketplace. We discuss why global trade is important to the United States, why nations trade, barriers to international trade, how companies enter the global marketplace, and a host of other international concepts and topics.

Because globalization impacts all of us today, it is covered throughout the text. The Trends section of each chapter frequently includes a discussion of how globalization will affect specific business activities. In addition, our Expanding Around the Globe boxes appearing throughout the book demonstrate how businesses are expanding their workforce, products, and customer base throughout the world in order to grow.

Careers in Business

Many of you will launch your business careers in the near future. It is our responsibility to help you find the field that is right for you. The Fourth Edition is a rich source of career guidance. As mentioned before, all business people know that the only thing certain about business is that it always changes. The Fourth Edition along with the *Building Your Career* booklet features the following valuable career information:

- **Fast Forward to the Future.** Strategies for Success in School and Business explores the interpersonal, time management, and planning skills every student needs for success in school. In the *Building Your Career* booklet, we also offer career advice and recommendations for finding and landing that first professional job. The booklet addresses how to use the Internet to jump-start a job search, prepare a cyber résumé, and research potential employers. In addition, the *Building Your Career* booklet shows you how to discover economic, demographic, and climatic information about cities in which you might work. We close the booklet with tips on interviewing and winning that first promotion.
- **Career Material for Each Part.** You can explore the career opportunities in small businesses, management, marketing, technology and information, and finance at the companion Web site. This career material describes the different types of employment available, positions in demand, skills required, salary expectations, and employment outlook through the next several years.
- **Exploring Business Careers.** Videos highlight the careers of successful business leaders from a variety of service and manufacturing firms. In addition to giving you insight into a variety of business careers, the end-of-chapter videos help spark an interest in the topics through professionally produced videos.

The Best Instructor Resources Available

Our research tells us that you want a comprehensive, easy-to-use instructor resource package that helps you bring the text concepts and principles to life. You also want a great test bank and attention-grabbing videos. For us, these were just "starters." We place all the necessary tools in your hands to help you save time and be a great instructor!

Each component of the comprehensive supplements package has been carefully crafted by outstanding teachers, with guidance from the textbook authors, to ensure this course is a rewarding experience for instructors and students. The supplements package includes excellent time-tested teaching tools as well as new supplements designed for the electronic classroom.

Comprehensive Instructor's Manual. (*Available on the Instructor's Web site*: www.cengage.com/introbusiness/gitman *and Instructor's Resource Guide CD-ROM*: ISBN: 0–324–59644–8.) At the core of the integrated learning system for *The Future of Business: The Essentials* is the instructor's manual. Developed in response to numerous suggestions from instructors teaching this course, each chapter is designed to provide maximum guidance for delivering the content in an interesting and dynamic manner. Each chapter begins with learning goals that anchor the integrated learning system. The instructor's manual also includes an in-depth lecture outline that is interspersed with lecture "tidbits" that allow instructors to add timely and interesting enhancements to their lectures. In addition, we know that it's hard to generate class discussion. So the lecture outline also includes questions to be asked of the class to generate discussion and debate. A comprehensive video guide includes the running time of each video, concepts illustrated in the video, teaching objectives for the case, and solutions for video case study questions.

Teaching SCANS Competencies. Not long ago the Department of Labor created the Secretary's Commission on Achieving Necessary Skills (SCANS) to encourage a high-skills, high-wage economy. From this came the SCANS competencies, which define know-how that students need for workplace success. Many colleges and universities are now charged with teaching to these competencies. We make your job easier by identifying those skills in the Preparing for Tomorrow's Workplace activities. The core SCANS competencies are resource skills (allocating time, money, etc.), interpersonal skills (teamwork, negotiating), information ability (acquiring and evaluating data, using computers), systems understanding (operating within an organization or social system), and technology ability (selecting equipment, tools, and applying technology to specific tasks).

Certified Test Bank and ExamView Testing Software. (*Available on the Instructor's Resource Guide CD-ROM*: ISBN: 0–324–59644–8.) To ensure your total confidence in the accuracy of the test bank, it has been certified for accuracy. The comprehensive test bank is organized by learning goal to support the integrated learning system. With nearly 2,000 true/false, multiple-choice, fill-in-the-blank, and short-answer questions, tests can be customized to support a variety of course objectives. The test bank is available in both Word and ExamView Testing software formats. This test bank is just one more way the Gitman author team is making instructors feel comfortable and at ease with their support materials. Custom tests can be ordered through the Cengage Learning Customer Service Center (1–800–824–5179) between 8:00 A.M. and 6:00 P.M., EST.

PowerPoint Slides Lecture. (*Available on the Instructor's Web site*: **www.cengage. com/introbusiness/gitman** *and Instructor's Resource Guide CD-ROM*: ISBN: 0–324–59644–8.) The PowerPoint Lecture System comes in two forms, with BizFlix and without BizFlix, to accommodate your specific needs. The PowerPoint Lecture System includes hundreds of slides that illustrate key chapter concepts and explain business vocabulary. As part of the integrated learning system, each slide is identified by the appropriate learning goal. These professionally designed slides help improve lecture organization and reduce classroom preparation time.

Instructor Web Site. (**www.cengage.com/introbusiness/gitman**) Designed to support your course objectives, the Instructor Web site is a source of downloadable supplements and other valuable resources. **Intro to Business News**, for example, provides summaries of the latest business news stories, indexed by topic for your convenience. Each Intro to Business News summary contains a headline, subject category, key words, a three- to five-paragraph summary of a news article, article source line, and questions to spur further thought. In addition, an Online Instructor's Resource Guide provides a guide for using all of *The Future of Business* resources to teach your course.

Instructor's Resource CD-ROM. (ISBN: 0–324–5944–8) For maximum convenience, the Instructor's Manual, Test Bank, ExamView Testing System, and PowerPoint Lecture System are all available on CD.

Resources for Students

Companion Web Site (**www.cengage.com/introbusiness/gitman**) Developed to maximize your success in the course and build online skills, the student portion of the text's Web site includes quizzes for each chapter, links to related Web sites, online enrichment chapters, Intro to Business News, and career information.

Acknowledgments

We are exceedingly grateful to the many reviewers who have offered suggestions and recommendations for enhancing the coverage, pedagogy, and support package of *The Future of Business: The Essentials*. The insightful feedback from these instructors helped guide our efforts and ensured that this text surpassed expectations for customer satisfaction and quality.

We are deeply appreciative of the insight from the following reviewers of the current and past editions of this textbook:

Maria Zak Aria
Camden County College

Joseph H. Atallah
Devry Institute of Technology

Herm Baine
Broward Community College

Dennis R. Brode
Sinclair Community College

Harvey Bronstein
Oakland Community College

Mark Camma
Atlantic Cape Community College

Bonnie R. Chavez
Santa Barbara City College

M. Bixby Cooper
Michigan State University

Evelyn Delaney
Daytona Beach Community College

Kathryn E. Dodge
University of Alaska, Fairbanks

Jonas Falik
Queensborough Community College

Janice M. Feldbauer
Austin Community College–Northridge

Dennis Foster
Northern Arizona University

James Giles
Bergen Community College

Mary E. Gorman
University of Cincinnati

Carnella Hardin
Glendale College

Elizabeth Hastings
*Business Department,
Middlesex Community College*

Frederic H. Hawkins
Westchester Business Institute

Melvin O. Hawkins
Midlands Technical College

Charlane Bomrad Held
Onondaga Community College

Merrily Joy Hoffman
San Jacinto College

Ralph F. Jagodka
Mt. San Antonio College

Andrew Johnson
Bellevue Community College

Connie Johnson
Tampa College

Jerry Kinskey
Sinclair Community College

Raymond T. Lamanna
Berkeley College

Carol Luce
Arizona State University

Tom McFarland
Mt. San Antonio College

Carl Meskimen
Sinclair Community College

Andrew Miller
Hudson Valley Community College

H. Lynn Moretz
Central Piedmont Community College

Linda M. Newel
Saddleback College

Joseph Newton
Bakersfield College

David Oliver
Edison College

Teresa Palmer
Illinois State University

Jude A. Rathburn
University of Wisconsin–Milwaukee

Robert F. Reck
Western Michigan University

Carol Rowey
Community College of Rhode Island

Ann Squire
Blackhawk Technical College

Richard E. T. Strickler Sr.,
McLennan Community College

Susan Thompson
Palm Beach Community College

David L. Turnipseed
Indiana-Purdue University

Ron Weidenfeller
Grand Rapids Community College

We wish to thank Kimberly Hurns, Washtenaw Community College, for her creative work on the Instructor's Manual and online quizzes; Deb Baker, Texas Christian University, for developing highly comprehensive, professionally designed PowerPoint™ slides; Aubrey Fowler, University of Nebraska–Lincoln, for his upstanding and creative work adapting Hollywood movie scenes to the business environment and making them into BizFlix; and David Folsom, University of South Carolina, for designing a highly accurate and extensive variety of test bank questions. A word of thanks is also due to Jamie Bryant of B-books Ltd. for her research and writing assistance.

A special word of appreciation goes to the project team at South-Western, including Melissa Acuña, Editor-in-Chief; Erin Joyner, Acquisitions Editor; Daniel Noguera, Developmental Editor; Danny Bolan, Editorial Assistant; Kimberly Kanakes, Executive Marketing Manager; Mike Cloran, Marketing Manager; Sarah Greber, Marketing Communications Manager; Emily Nesheim, Content Project Manager; Kristen Meere, Media Editor; Deanna Ettinger, Photo Permissions Manager; James Reidel, Text Permissions Researcher; Stacy Jenkins Shirley, Art Director; and Beverly Breslin, Senior Manufacturing Coordinator.

Lawrence J. Gitman
Carl McDaniel

The Business Environment

PART 1

Understanding Economic Systems and Business

Learning Goals

After reading this chapter, you should be able to answer these questions:

1 How do businesses and not-for-profit organizations help create our standard of living?

2 What are the sectors of the business environment, and how do changes in them influence business decisions?

3 What are the primary features of the world's economic systems, and how are the three sectors of the U.S. economy linked?

4 How do economic growth, full employment, price stability, and inflation indicate a nation's economic health?

5 How does the government use monetary policy and fiscal policy to achieve its macroeconomic goals?

6 What are the basic microeconomic concepts of demand and supply, and how do they establish prices?

7 What are the four types of market structure?

8 Which trends are reshaping the business, micro-, and macroeconomic environments and competitive arena?

"Mapping Enemy Territory"

Intolerable Cruelty/Corbis

We sometimes tend to think of competition as something that takes place in a football stadium every Saturday or Sunday in the fall; however, competition is also something that helps to drive private enterprise within a capitalist culture. In such a culture, firms compete with one another in order to provide goods and services to customers at the highest price possible while keeping costs low. To be able to do so requires that each firm possess an understanding of the environment in which this competition takes place. Furthermore, each firm must also be able to anticipate the resources available to them as well as those available to their competitor as demonstrated in the clip from the 2003 movie *Intolerable Cruelty*.

Miles Massey is one of the most successful divorce attorneys in the United States and has built a stellar reputation based on his ability to win seemingly unwinnable cases. Take Bonnie's case for instance. She was caught by her husband in the arms of the pool cleaner, and during the ensuing melee, she stabbed him in the buttocks with a lifetime achievement award. After recounting the details in his office, Miles takes a moment to assess the situation before beginning to spin the details into a story that works to Bonnie's benefit, actually managing to make her sound like the victim instead of the betrayer after he has finished the story. After agreeing to take her case, he ushers her out of the office, explaining to her that he would need information on her husband's net worth and a map of enemy territory, as well as promising that her husband's silly little television was about to be hers.

Though this scene from *Intolerable Cruelty* concerns divorce proceedings, it does contain certain elements that are common in the business environment. First of all, Miles has performed a very basic analysis of the situation presented to him by acknowledging his own strengths and weaknesses as well as examining the opportunities and threats inherent within the environment. He knows that a strength of his is that he will be able to make the story "equally transparent to any jury"; however, he also acknowledges that he is not omniscient, a clear weakness. The opportunity he sees is that the case is winnable because Bonnie's husband acted upon certain "assumptions" he could not prove; but he also notes the threats to the case, the fact that the husband "showed incredible foresight in taking those pictures" and that the absence of a swimming pool does make the "presence of a pool man a bit suspicious."

Miles is simply doing what any manager, entrepreneur, or CEO would do in a situation where there is opportunity to be assessed. He has developed an understanding of the competitive business environment that will allow him to take advantage of the opportunity for his, and his client's, mutual gain; and he seeks to further develop that understanding so that he ultimately reduces the amount of risk that he and his client will undertake. As such, he will then be able to move forward with this particular divorce case armed with the tools it will take to succeed.

This chapter is designed to provide you with the basic building blocks of business so that you too can begin the process of analyzing and understanding the competitive environment. Like Miles, you will be presented with various opportunities throughout your career ranging from recognizing a potential new marketing opportunity for your employer to developing and running your own small business. To do so, you will need to know how business functions as well as what influences those functions. Such knowledge comes with a need to understand both macro- and microeconomic goals in order to fully take advantage of the opportunities presented to you. In other words, like Miles, you will need the tools it takes to make as accurate a map of "enemy" territory as possible.

Discussion Questions
- What is the nature of Miles Massey's business, and what factors of production are at play here?
- What elements of the business environment most likely play a part in this case and why?
- What trend in the business environment is most likely on display within this film clip?

The Nature of Business

1 How do businesses and not-for-profit organizations help create our standard of living?

business
An organization that strives for a profit by providing goods and services desired by its customers.

goods
Tangible items manufactured by businesses.

services
Intangible offerings of businesses that can't be held, touched, or stored.

standard of living
A country's output of goods and services that people can buy with the money they have.

quality of life
The general level of human happiness based on such things as life expectancy, educational standards, health, sanitation, and leisure time.

risk
The potential to lose time and money or otherwise not be able to accomplish an organization's goals.

revenue
The money a company receives by providing services or selling goods to customers.

costs
Expenses incurred from creating and selling goods and services.

profit
The money left over after all costs are paid.

Take a moment to think about the many different types of businesses you come into contact with on a typical day. As you drive to class, you may stop at a gas station that is part of a major national oil company and grab lunch from a fast-food chain like Taco Bell or McDonald's or the neighborhood pizza place. Need more cash? You can do your banking while you are grocery shopping, at an in-store branch that your bank opened. You don't even have to visit the store anymore: online shopping brings the stores to you, offering everything from clothes to food, furniture, and concert tickets.

A **business** is an organization that strives for a profit by providing goods and services desired by its customers. Businesses meet the needs of consumers by providing movies, medical care, autos, and countless other goods and services. **Goods** are tangible items manufactured by businesses, such as desks. **Services** are intangible offerings of businesses that can't be held, touched, or stored. Physicians, lawyers, hairstylists, car washes, and airlines all provide services. Businesses also serve other organizations, such as hospitals, retailers, and governments, by providing machinery, goods for resale, computers, and thousands of other items.

Thus, businesses create the goods and services that are the basis of our **standard of living**. The standard of living of any country is measured by the output of goods and services people can buy with the money they have. The United States has one of the highest standards of living in the world. Although several countries such as Switzerland and Germany have higher average wages than the United States, their standard of living isn't higher because prices are so much higher. As a result, the same amount of money buys less in those countries. For example, in the United States we can buy a "Real Meal Deal" at McDonald's for less than $4, while in another country, a similar meal might cost as much as $10!

Businesses play a key role in determining our quality of life by providing jobs and goods and services to society. **Quality of life** refers to the general level of human happiness based on such things as life expectancy, educational standards, health, sanitation, and leisure time. Building a high quality of life is a combined effort of businesses, government, and not-for-profit organizations. Zurich and Geneva, Switzerland, rank highest in quality of life, followed by Vienna, Austria, and Vancouver, Canada. It may come as a surprise that the world's top cities for quality of life are not in the United States. Of the top 25 cities in the survey, 68 percent are in Europe, whereas Canada and Australia/New Zealand have 20 percent each. At the other end of the scale, Baghdad is the city scoring lowest on the survey.[1]

Creating a quality of life is not without risks, however. **Risk** is the potential to lose time and money or otherwise not be able to accomplish an organization's goals. Without enough blood donors, for example, the American Red Cross faces the risk of not meeting the demand for blood by victims of disaster. Businesses like Microsoft face the risk of falling short of their revenue and profit goals. **Revenue** is the money a company receives by providing services or selling goods to customers. **Costs** are expenses for rent, salaries, supplies, transportation, and many other items that a company incurs from creating and selling goods and services. For example, some of the costs incurred by Microsoft in developing its software include expenses for salaries, facilities, and advertising. If Microsoft has money left over after it pays all costs, it has a **profit**. A company whose costs are greater than revenues shows a loss.

When a company like Microsoft uses its resources intelligently, it can often increase sales, hold costs down, and earn a profit. Not all companies earn profits, but that is the risk of being in business. In American business today, there is generally a direct relationship between risks and profit: the greater the risks, the greater the potential for profit (or loss). Companies that take too conservative a stance may lose out to more nimble competitors who react quickly to the changing business environment.

Take Sony, for example. The electronics giant, once a leader with its Walkman music players and Trinitron televisions, steadily lost ground—and profits—to other consumer technology companies by not embracing new technologies like the MP3 digital music format and flat-panel television screens. Sony misjudged what the market wanted and stayed with proprietary technologies such as MiniDiscs rather than create cross-platform options. Apple—an upstart in personal music devices—quickly grabbed the lion's share of the digital music market with its iPod players and iTunes music service. "The world in which this company operates has

CONCEPT in action

© AP Images/Paul Sakuma

Apple's revolutionary iPhone can be characterized as both a good and a service. The iPhone handset, with its three-part functionality as mobile phone, digital media player, and Internet communications device, is a tangible good. However, to use the handset customers must enter into a two-year phone service agreement with AT&T, Apple's exclusive wireless carrier. The cleverly designed gadget was named *Time* magazine's Invention of the Year in 2007. What other products are a mix of both goods and services?

undergone seismic change," said Sony's chief executive officer Howard Stringer, as he announced a major restructuring plan designed to revitalize the company's electronics business. [2]

Not-for-Profit Organizations

Not all organizations strive to make a profit. A **not-for-profit organization** is an organization that exists to achieve some goal other than the usual business goal of profit. Charities such as Habitat for Humanity, the United Way, the American Cancer Society, and the Sierra Club are not-for-profit organizations, as are most hospitals, zoos, arts organizations, civic groups, and religious organizations. Over the last 20 years, the number of not-for-profit organizations—and the employees and volunteers who work for them—has increased considerably. Government is our largest and most pervasive not-for-profit group. In addition, more than 1.4 million nongovernmental not-for-profit entities operate in the United States today and account for more than 28 percent of the country's economic activity.

Like their for-profit counterparts, these groups set goals and require resources to meet those goals. However, their goals are not focused on profits. For example, a not-for-profit organization's goal might be feeding the poor, preserving the environment, increasing attendance at the ballet, or preventing drunk driving. Not-for-profit organizations do not compete directly with one another in the same manner as, for example, Ford and Honda, but they do compete for talented employees, people's scarce volunteer time, and donations.

The boundaries that formerly separated not-for-profit and for-profit organizations have blurred, leading to a greater exchange of ideas between the sectors. As we will learn in Chapter 2, for-profit businesses are now addressing social issues. Successful not-for-profits apply business principles to operate more effectively. Not-for-profit managers are concerned with the same concepts as their colleagues in for-profit companies: developing strategy, budgeting carefully, measuring performance, encouraging innovation, improving productivity, and demonstrating accountability.

The Empire State Building glowed red for an evening. Niagara Falls ran red for a day. And female newscasters wore red dresses. It's all part of a campaign to remind women of heart disease risks that has drawn employees at thousands of companies to hand out Red Dress pins plugging the American Heart Association's National Wear Red Day. Activities such as the above require extensive business planning. Millions of people have now participated in the "Wear Red" movement. Public support for the American Heart Association is now more than $500 million annually.[3]

Factors of Production: The Building Blocks of Business

To provide goods and services, regardless of whether they operate in the for-profit or not-for-profit sector, organizations require inputs in the form of resources called factors of production. Four traditional **factors of production** are common to all productive activity: natural resources, labor, capital, and entrepreneurship. Many experts now include knowledge as a fifth factor, acknowledging its key role in business success. By using the factors of production efficiently, a company can produce more goods and services with the same resources.

Commodities that are useful inputs in their natural state are known as natural resources. They include farmland, forests, mineral and oil deposits, and water. Sometimes natural resources are simply called land, although, as you can see, the term means more than just land. Companies use natural resources in different ways. International Paper Company uses wood pulp to make paper, and Pacific Gas & Electric Company may use water, oil, or coal to produce electricity. Today urban sprawl, pollution, and limited resources have raised questions about resource use. Conservationists, ecologists, and government bodies are proposing laws to require land-use planning and resource conservation.

Labor refers to the economic contributions of people working with their minds and muscles. This input includes the talents of everyone—from a restaurant cook to a nuclear physicist—who performs the many tasks of manufacturing and selling goods and services.

The tools, machinery, equipment, and buildings used to produce goods and services and get them to the consumer are known as **capital**. Sometimes the term capital is also used to mean the money that buys machinery, factories, and other production and distribution facilities. However, because money itself produces nothing, it is not one of the basic inputs. Instead, it is a means of acquiring the inputs. Therefore, in this context, capital does not include money.

Entrepreneurs are the people who combine the inputs of natural resources, labor, and capital to produce goods or services with the intention of making a profit or accomplishing a not-for-profit

not-for-profit organization
An organization that exists to achieve some goal other than the usual business goal of profit.

factors of production
The resources used to create goods and services.

capital
The inputs, such as tools, machinery, equipment, and buildings, used to produce goods and services and get them to the customer.

entrepreneurs
People who combine the inputs of natural resources, labor, and capital to produce goods or services with the intention of making a profit or accomplishing a not-for-profit goal.

goal. These people make the decisions that set the course for their firms; they create products and production processes or develop services. Because they are not guaranteed a profit in return for their time and effort, they must be risk takers. Of course, if their firms succeed, the rewards may be great.

Today, many Americans want to start their own businesses. They are attracted by the opportunity to be their own boss and reap the financial rewards of a successful firm. Many start their first business from their dorm rooms, like Michael Dell of Dell Computers, or while living at home, so their cost is almost zero. Entrepreneurs include people like Bill Gates, the founder of Microsoft, who is now one of the richest people in the world; and Sergey Brin and Larry Page, Google's founders. Many thousands of individuals have started companies that, while remaining small, make a major contribution to America's economy. Entrepreneurship is a global activity, as we'll see in the Catching the Entrepreneurial Spirit box on the next page. We'll meet many more enterprising business people throughout this book, especially in Chapter 5 and other Catching the Entrepreneurial Spirit boxes.

A number of outstanding managers and noted academics are beginning to emphasize a fifth factor of production—knowledge. **Knowledge** refers to the combined talents and skills of the workforce and has become a primary driver of economic growth. The new competitive environment places a premium on knowledge and learning over physical resources. For example, the Organization for Economic Co-operation and Development (OECD) estimates that knowledge-based industries added about 50 percent in total value to the economies of Germany and Great Britain from 1985 to 1997. Companies that want to reap similar benefits are investing more heavily in areas that emphasize knowledge, such as research and development, licensing, and marketing.[4]

"**Knowledge workers** are going to be the primary force determining which economies are successful and which aren't," says Thomas Davenport, Babson College professor of information technology and management. "They are the key source of growth in most organizations. New products and services, new approaches to marketing, new business models—all these come from knowledge workers." Davenport estimates that knowledge workers, whom he defines as "people whose primary job is to do something with knowledge: to create it, distribute it, apply it," already comprise between 25 percent and 33 percent of the U.S. workforce. [5]

knowledge
The combined talents and skills of the workforce.

knowledge workers
Workers who create, distribute, and apply knowledge.

CONCEPT check

Explain the concepts of revenue, costs, and profit.

What are the five factors of production?

What is the role of an entrepreneur in society?

Understanding the Business Environment

2 What are the sectors of the business environment, and how do changes in them influence business decisions?

Businesses do not operate in a vacuum but rather in a dynamic environment that has a direct influence on how they operate and whether they will achieve their objectives. This external business environment is composed of numerous outside organizations and forces that we can group into seven key subenvironments, as Exhibit 1.1 depicts: economic, political and legal, demographic, social, competitive, global, and technological. Each of these sectors creates a unique set of challenges and opportunities for businesses.

Business owners and managers have a great deal of control over the internal environment of business, which covers the day-to-day business decisions. They choose the supplies they purchase, which employees they hire, the products they sell, and where they sell those products. They use their skills and resources to create goods and services that will satisfy existing and prospective customers. However, the external environmental conditions that affect a business are generally beyond the control of management and change constantly. To compete successfully, business owners and managers must continuously study the environment and adapt their businesses.

Other forces, such as acts of nature, also have a major impact on businesses. For example, in September 2005, Hurricane Katrina devastated large areas of Louisiana and Mississippi. The city of New Orleans suffered major damage as its levees broke. Businesses in the affected areas experienced tremendous losses, with many destroyed completely. Residents were left homeless and without jobs. In the aftermath of the storm, which left behind damages estimated at $60 billion, many corporations reported additional costs directly attributable to the storm. For instance, Walgreen Co., the leading drugstore chain in the United States, suffered many store closures related to the storm. Other businesses, however, will benefit from the disaster. Manufacturers of recreational vehicles (RVs) such as Thor Industries and Fleetwood Enterprises supplied RVs to use as temporary shelters. Demand rose significantly for manufactured homes from Champion Enterprises and Palm Harbor Enterprises, because of the quick construction time.

W00t World

Merriam-Webster, the dictionary-publishing company, just announced its 2007 word of the year, selected via the company's online poll. And that word is . . . w00t. That's right: a *w*, followed by two zeroes, and a *t*. Pronounced "*woot*." An exclamation of joy or triumph. Perhaps the most joyous w00t lover is Matt Rutledge. Matt founded woot.com in 2004 and pioneered deal-a-day Web sites. The idea is simple—sell one product a day in limited quantities. Once they are gone, they're gone. If the item is not sold out, the sale stops at 11:59 P.M. and a new product goes up at 12:01 A.M. Insomniacs and techies anxiously wait for the stroke of midnight, anticipating what new wonder product w00t will offer next.

W00t has sold everything from Roomba robot vacuum cleaners to MP3 players to TiVo HD DVRs. Rockford Corporation of Tempe, Arizona, manufactures a device that streams digital content to home stereos. As it turned out, not every consumer felt a strong need to own one of these gadgets at $800 a pop. The company turned to w00t and sold out its entire inventory at $199!

Now W00t has more than 800,000 members. W00t sales typically exceed $1 million a day! In 2006, the company opened wine.w00t, which offers one wine each week. The following year Rutledge created shirt.w00t, offering original designed shirts. Each week shirt designs are submitted by the public. Accepted designs are posted in a contest blog. The design receiving the most votes is offered for sale the following Friday.

The w00t format has been very successful, but also has a downside as well. If a product sells out by 8:00 AM, that means that there is no revenue for the rest of the day. The only way to generate additional sales is to sell other merchandise. W00t does offer T-shirts and a separate wine.w00t site that offers a wine a week. Both sites sell a limited amount of advertising space. Sometimes, both sites will offer a side deal. For example, wine.w00t recently offered "Gourmet Almond Toffee" as a side deal.[6]

Critical Thinking Questions

- Do you think that w00t has a viable long-term business model?
- There are now more than a hundred "deal-a-day" Web sites. Currently there are no deal-a-day sites for luggage, personal-care items, tools, or office supplies. Which category, if any, would make a good deal-a-day Web site?
- Go to the woot.com Web site. What are some things that you see that may contribute to the firm's success?

EXHIBIT 1.1   The Dynamic Business Environment

External Environment

- Technological
- Economic
- Global
- Political/legal
- Competitive
- Demographic
- Social

Internal Environment:
Entrepreneurs
Managers
Workers
Customers

External Environment

Chapter 1: Understanding Economic Systems and Business

No one business is large or powerful enough to create major changes in the external environment. Thus, managers are primarily adapters to, rather than agents of, change. Global competition is basically an uncontrollable element in the external environment. In some situations, however, a firm can influence external events through its strategies. For example, efforts by the major U.S. pharmaceutical companies were successful in getting the Food and Drug Administration to speed up the approval process for new drugs. Google has opened a lobbying office in Washington, DC, to focus on the Internet and telecommunications and copyright laws. Let's now take a brief look at these varied environmental influences.

Economic Influences

This category is one of the most important external influences on businesses. Fluctuations in the level of economic activity create business cycles that affect businesses and individuals in many ways. When the economy is growing, for example, unemployment rates are low and income levels rise. Inflation and interest rates are other areas that change according to economic activity. Through the policies it sets, such as taxes and interest rate levels, a government attempts to stimulate or curtail the level of economic activity. In addition, the forces of supply and demand determine how prices and quantities of goods and services behave in a free market.

Political and Legal Influences

The political climate of a country is another critical factor for managers to consider. The amount of government activity, the types of laws it passes, and the general political stability of a government are three components of political climate. For example, a multinational company such as General Electric will evaluate the political climate of a country before deciding to locate a plant there. Is the government stable, or might a coup disrupt the country? How restrictive are the regulations for foreign businesses, including foreign ownership of business property and taxation? Import tariffs, quotas, and export restrictions also must be taken into account. We'll return to this important topic in Chapter 3.

CONCEPT in action

The federal government is pushing America's Big 3 automakers to manufacture eco-friendly automobile fleets. In 2007, the president and Congress passed the Energy Independence and Security Act, which requires automakers to boost fleetwide gas mileage to 35 miles per gallon by the year 2020. The significantly higher fuel-economy standard will force General Motors to produce more Chevy Aveos and fewer best-selling Chevy Tahoes, since even the hybrid version of the popular SUV can't achieve government-mandated fuel efficiency. How might the changing political-legal environment affect GM's business and profits?

In the United States, too, laws passed by Congress and the many regulatory agencies cover such areas as competition, minimum wages, environmental protection, worker safety, and copyrights and patents. For example, Congress passed the Telecommunications Act of 1996 to deregulate the telecommunications industry. As a result, competition increased and new opportunities arose as traditional boundaries between service providers blurred. Today we have telephone companies offering Internet services and cable television companies offering phone and Internet services.

Federal agencies play a significant role in business operations. When Pfizer wants to bring a new medication for heart disease to market, it must follow the procedures set by the Food and Drug Administration (FDA) for testing and clinical trials and secure FDA approval. Before issuing stock, Pfizer must register the securities with the Securities and Exchange Commission. The Federal Trade Commission will penalize Pfizer if its advertisements promoting the drug's benefits are misleading. These are just a few ways the political and legal environments affect business decisions.

States and local governments also exert control over businesses—imposing taxes, issuing corporate charters and business licenses, and setting zoning ordinances and similar regulations. We'll discuss the legal environment in greater detail in the Appendix to Chapter 2.

Demographic Factors

demography
The study of people's vital statistics, such as their age, gender, race and ethnicity, and location.

Demographic factors are an uncontrollable factor in the business environment and extremely important to managers. **Demography** is the study of people's vital statistics, such as their age, gender, race and ethnicity, and location. Demographics help companies define the markets for their products and also determine the size and composition of the workforce. You'll encounter demographics as you continue your study of business. For example, later in this chapter and in Part 3, we'll examine the challenges of managing a diverse workforce. In Part 4, you'll learn how marketers use demographics to segment markets and select target markets.

Demographics are at the heart of many business decisions. Businesses today must deal with the unique shopping preferences of different generations, which each require marketing approaches and goods and services targeted to their needs. For example, the more than 72 million members of Generation Y, also called echo boomers or the Millennium Generation, were born between about 1978 and 1997. The marketing impact of Generation Y has been immense. These are computer-literate and prosperous young people, with hundreds of billions of dollars to spend. And spend they do—freely, even though they haven't yet reached their peak income and spending years. Other age groups such as Generation X, people born between 1964 and 1977, and the baby boomers, born between 1946 and 1964, have their own spending patterns. Many boomers nearing retirement have money and are willing to spend it on their health, their comforts, leisure pursuits, and cars. As the population ages, businesses are offering more products that appeal to middle-aged and elderly markets.

In addition, by 2010 minorities will represent 35 percent of the total U.S. population. Today, there are 44 million Hispanics, 40 million blacks, and 14 million Asians. To put this into perspective, there are more minorities in the United States today than there were people in the entire country in 1910.[7] California has the largest minority population, followed by Texas. By 2011, minority shoppers are expected to spend $1.9 trillion. As a result, more and more retailers are catering to this growing market. K-mart, for example, recently rolled out nearly four dozen types of ethnic dolls.[8]

Social Factors

Social factors—our attitudes, values, and lifestyles—influence what, how, where, and when people purchase products. They are difficult to predict, define, and measure because they can be very subjective. They also change as people move through different life stages. Several social trends are currently influencing businesses. People of all ages have a broader range of interests, defying traditional consumer profiles. They also experience a "poverty of time" and seek ways to gain more control over their time. Changing gender roles have brought more women into the workforce. This development is increasing family incomes, heightening demand for timesaving goods and services, and changing family shopping patterns.

Technology

The application of technology can stimulate growth under capitalism or any other economic system. **Technology** is the application of science and engineering skills and knowledge to solve production and organizational problems. New machines that improve productivity and reduce costs can be one of a firm's most valuable assets. **Productivity** is the amount of goods and services one worker can produce. Our ability as a nation to maintain and build wealth depends in large part on the speed and effectiveness with which we use technology—to invent and adapt more efficient machines to improve manufacturing productivity, to develop new products, and to process information and make it instantly available across the organization and to suppliers and customers.

American business is becoming better at using technology to create change. Many high-tech companies already showcase a whole new breed of miniaturized inventions with capabilities well beyond today's computer chips, called microelectromechanical systems (MEMS). Complete systems on a chip that can be manufactured at relatively low costs, MEMS are beginning to replace more expensive components in computer hardware, automobile engines, factory assembly lines, and dozens of other processes and products.

technology
The application of science and engineering skills and knowledge to solve production and organizational problems.

productivity
The amount of goods and services one worker can produce.

economic system
The combination of policies, laws, and choices made by a nation's government to establish the systems that determine what goods and services are produced and how they are allocated.

economics
The study of how a society uses scarce resources to produce and distribute goods and services.

CONCEPT check

Define the components of the internal and the external business environments.

What factors within the economic environment affect businesses?

Why do demographic shifts and technological developments create both challenges and new opportunities for business?

How Business and Economics Work

A business's success depends in part on the economic systems of the countries where it is located and where it sells its products. A nation's **economic system** is the combination of policies, laws, and choices made by its government to establish the systems that determine what goods and services are produced and how they are allocated. **Economics** is the study of how a society uses scarce resources to produce and distribute goods and services. The resources of a person, a firm, or a nation are limited. Hence, economics is the study of choices—what people, firms, or nations choose from among the available resources. Every economy is concerned with what types and amounts of goods and services should be produced, how they should be produced, and for whom. These decisions are

3 What are the primary features of the world's economic systems, and how are the three sectors of the U.S. economy linked?

made by the marketplace, the government, or both. In the United States, the government and the free-market system together guide the economy.

You probably know more about economics than you realize. Every day many news stories deal with economic matters: a union agrees to health care concessions at General Motors; the Federal Reserve Board lowers interest rates; Wall Street has a record day; the president proposes a cut in income taxes; consumer spending rises as the economy grows; or retail prices are on the rise, to mention just a few examples.

Global Economic Systems

Businesses and other organizations operate according to the economic systems of their home countries. Today the world's major economic systems fall into two broad categories: free market, or capitalism; and planned economies, which include communism and socialism. However, in reality many countries use a mixed market system that incorporates elements from more than one economic system.

The major differentiator among economic systems is whether the government or individuals decide how to:

- Allocate limited resources—the factors of production—to individuals and organizations to best satisfy unlimited societal needs
- Choose what goods and services to produce, and in what quantities
- Determine how and by whom to produce these goods and services
- Distribute goods and services to consumers

Managers must understand and adapt to the economic system or systems in which they operate. Companies that do business internationally may discover that they must make changes in production and selling methods to accommodate the economic system of another country. Exhibit 1.2 summarizes key factors of the world's economic systems.

Capitalism In recent years, more countries have shifted toward free-market economic systems and away from planned economies. Sometimes, as was the case of the former East Germany,

EXHIBIT 1.2	The Basic Economic Systems of the World			
	Capitalism	**Communism**	**Socialism**	**Mixed Economy**
Ownership of Business	Businesses are privately owned with minimal government ownership or interference.	Government owns all or most enterprises.	Basic industries, such as railroads and utilities, are owned by government. Very high taxation as government redistributes income from successful private businesses and entrepreneurs.	Private ownership of land and businesses but government control of some enterprises. The private sector is typically large.
Control of Markets	Complete freedom of trade. No or little government control.	Complete government control of markets.	Some markets are controlled and some are free. Significant central-government planning. State enterprises are managed by bureaucrats. These enterprises are rarely profitable.	Some markets such as nuclear energy and the post office are controlled or highly regulated.
Worker Incentives	Strong incentive to work and innovate because profits are retained by owners.	No incentive to work hard or produce quality products.	Private-sector incentives are the same as capitalism and public-sector incentives are the same as in a planned economy.	Private-sector incentives are the same as capitalism. Limited incentives in the public sector.
Management of Enterprises	Each enterprise is managed by owners or professional managers with little government interference.	Centralized management by the government bureaucracy. Little or no flexibility in decision making at the factory level.	Significant government planning and regulation. Bureaucrats run government enterprises.	Private-sector management similar to capitalism. Public sector similar to socialism.
Forecast for 2020	Continued steady growth.	No growth and perhaps disappearance.	Stable with probable slight growth.	Continued growth.
Examples	United States	Cuba, North Korea	Finland, India, Israel	Great Britain, France, Sweden, Canada

the transition to capitalism was painful but fairly quick. In other countries, such as Russia, the movement has been characterized by false starts and backsliding. **Capitalism**, also known as the private enterprise system, is based on competition in the marketplace and private ownership of the factors of production (resources). In a competitive economic system, a large number of people and businesses buy and sell products freely in the marketplace. In pure capitalism all the factors of production are owned privately, and the government does not try to set prices or coordinate economic activity.

A capitalist system guarantees certain economic rights: the right to own property, the right to make a profit, the right to make free choices, and the right to compete. The right to own property is central to capitalism. The main incentive in this system is profit, which encourages entrepreneurship. Profit is also necessary for producing goods and services, building plants, paying dividends and taxes, and creating jobs. The freedom to choose whether to become an entrepreneur or to work for someone else means that people have the right to decide what they want to do on the basis of their own drive, interest, and training. The government does not create job quotas for each industry or give people tests to determine what they will do.

Competition is good for both businesses and consumers in a capitalist system. It leads to better and more diverse products, keeps prices stable, and increases the efficiency of producers. Companies try to produce their goods and services at the lowest possible cost and sell them at the highest possible price. But when profits are high, more firms enter the market to seek those profits. The resulting competition among firms tends to lower prices. Producers must then find new ways of operating more efficiently if they are to keep making a profit and stay in business.

CONCEPT in action

Since joining the World Trade Organization in 2001, China has continued to embrace tenets of capitalism and grow its economy. China is the world's largest producer of mobile phones, PCs, and cameras, and the country's more than 1 billion citizens constitute a gargantuan emerging market. Viruslike expansion of McDonald's and KFC franchises epitomizes the success of American-style capitalism in China. Do you think China's capitalistic trend can continue to thrive under the ruling Chinese Communist Party that opposes workers' rights, free speech, and democracy?

Communism   The complete opposite to capitalism is **communism**. In a communist economic system, the government owns virtually all resources and controls all markets. Economic decision making is centralized: the government, rather than the competitive forces in the marketplace, decides what will be produced, where it will be produced, how much will be produced, where the raw materials and supplies will come from, who will get the output, and what the prices will be. This form of centralized economic system offers little if any choice to a country's citizens. Earlier in the twentieth century, countries such as the former Soviet Union and China that chose communism believed that it would raise their standard of living. In practice, however, the tight controls over most aspects of people's lives, such as what careers they could choose, where they could work, and what they could buy, led to lower productivity. Workers had no reasons to work harder or produce quality goods, because there were no rewards for excellence. Errors in planning and resource allocation led to shortages of even basic items.

These factors were among the reasons for the 1991 collapse of the Soviet Union into multiple independent nations. Recent reforms in Russia, China, and most of the eastern European nations have moved these economies toward more capitalistic, market-oriented systems. North Korea and Cuba are the best remaining examples of communist economic systems.

Socialism   **Socialism** is an economic system in which the basic industries are owned by the government or by the private sector under strong government control. A socialist state controls critical, large-scale industries such as transportation, communications, and utilities. Smaller businesses and those considered less critical, such as retail, may be privately owned. To varying degrees the state also determines the goals of businesses, the prices and selection of goods, and the rights of workers. Socialist countries typically provide their citizens with a higher level of services, such as health care and unemployment benefits, than do most capitalist countries. As a result, taxes and unemployment may also be quite high in socialist countries. For example, the top individual tax rate in France is 48 percent, compared to 35 percent in the United States. These high rates have, however, dropped considerably and further rate reductions are anticipated as many socialist countries seek to stimulate their economies.

Many countries, including Great Britain, Denmark, Israel, and Sweden, have socialist systems, but the systems vary from country to country. In Denmark, for example, most businesses are privately owned and operated, but two-thirds of the population is sustained by the state through government welfare programs.

Socialism is proving to be surprisingly resilient in Western Europe. France inched toward a capitalistic form of government after the presidency of François Mitterrand ended in 1995 and Jacques Chirac assumed the top office. It shifted back toward socialism under Lionel Jospin, who wanted more government control and intervention in the workplace. The reelection of Jacques Chirac in 2002 moved the country back toward capitalism again. In July 2005, Chirac's prime minister Dominique de Villepin spearheaded the public sale of 20 percent of the shares of Gaz de France, the nationalized gas utility, and planned to follow with a similar privatization of Electricité de France later in the year. Nicolas Sarkozy, elected president in 2007, appointed Christine Lagarde as the new finance minister. Lagarde and Sarkozy have laid out a detailed plan to roll back government spending and to unravel the tangle of rules that hinder business. Lagarde is a strong supporter of free markets and has traveled around the country urging people not to fear them. She has also spoken frankly about how France has discouraged investment by foreign corporations by forcing employers to pay for costly social programs.[9]

mixed economies
Economies that combine several economic systems; for example, an economy where the government owns certain industries but others are owned by the private sector.

macroeconomics
The subarea of economics that focuses on the economy as a whole by looking at aggregate data for large groups of people, companies, or products.

microeconomics
The subarea of economics that focuses on individual parts of the economy, such as households or firms.

circular flow
The movement of inputs and outputs among households, businesses, and governments; a way of showing how the sectors of the economy interact.

Mixed Economic Systems Pure capitalism and communism are extremes; real-world economies fall somewhere between the two. The U.S. economy leans toward pure capitalism, but it uses government policies to promote economic stability and growth. Also, through policies and laws, the government transfers money to the poor, the unemployed, and the elderly. American capitalism has produced some very powerful organizations in the form of huge corporations, such as General Motors and Microsoft. To protect smaller firms and entrepreneurs, the government has passed legislation that requires that the giants compete fairly against weaker competitors.

Canada, Great Britain, and Sweden, among others, are also called **mixed economies**; that is, they use more than one economic system. Sometimes, the government is basically socialist and owns basic industries. In Canada, for example, the government owns the communications, transportation, and utilities industries, as well as some of the natural-resource industries. It also supplies health care to its citizens. But most other activity is carried on by private enterprise, as in a capitalist system.

The few factors of production owned by the government in a mixed economy include some public lands, the postal service, and some water resources. But the government is extensively involved in the economic system through taxing, spending, and welfare activities. The economy is also mixed in the sense that the country tries to achieve many social goals—income redistribution and social security, for example—that may not be attempted in purely capitalist systems.

Macroeconomics and Microeconomics

The state of the economy affects both people and businesses. How you spend your money (or save it) is a personal economic decision. Whether you continue in school and whether you work part-time are also economic decisions. Every business also operates within the economy. Based on their economic expectations, businesses decide what products to produce, how to price them, how many people to employ, how much to pay these employees, how much to expand the business, and so on.

Economics has two main subareas. **Macroeconomics** is the study of the economy as a whole. It looks at aggregate data for large groups of people, companies, or products considered as a whole. In contrast, **microeconomics** focuses on individual parts of the economy, such as households or firms.

Both macroeconomics and microeconomics offer a valuable outlook on the economy. For example, Ford might use both to decide whether to introduce a new line of cars. The company would consider such macroeconomic factors as the national level of personal income, the unemployment rate, interest rates, fuel costs, and the national level of sales of new cars. From a microeconomic viewpoint, Ford would judge consumer demand for new cars versus the existing supply, competing models, labor and material costs and availability, and current prices and sales incentives.

Economics as a Circular Flow

Another way to see how the sectors of the economy interact is to examine the **circular flow** of inputs and outputs among households, businesses, and governments as shown in Exhibit 1.3. Let's review the exchanges by following the red circle around the

© Alex Wong/Getty Images

CONCEPT in action

United States currency is becoming more colorful and secure, as the Bureau of Engraving and Printing has redesigned $10, $20, and $50 bills with enhanced design and security flourishes. The newest $10 bill issued by the Federal Reserve features the first treasury secretary, Alexander Hamilton, emblazoned in American symbols against a background tinged with orange, yellow, and red. The note's color-shifting ink, watermark, and security thread are especially difficult to counterfeit. How often does the Fed issue currency and why?

EXHIBIT 1.3   Economics as a Circular Flow

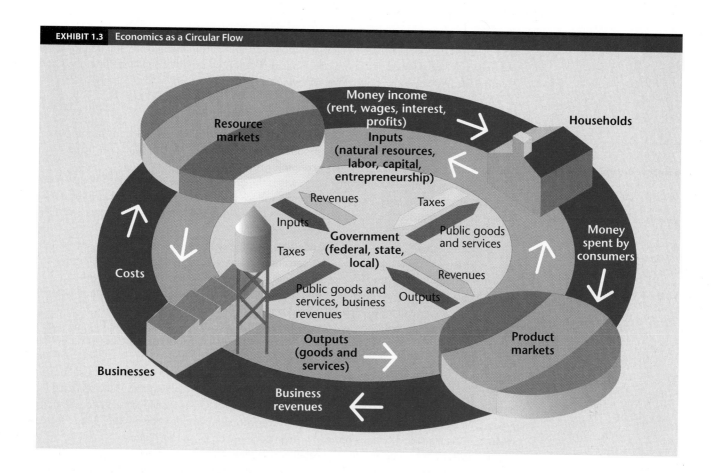

inside of the diagram. Households provide inputs (natural resources, labor, capital, entrepreneurship, knowledge) to businesses, which convert these inputs into outputs (goods and services) for consumers. In return, households receive income from rent, wages, interest, and ownership profits (blue circle). Businesses receive revenue from consumer purchases of goods and services.

The other important exchange in Exhibit 1.3 takes place between governments (federal, state, and local) and both households and businesses. Governments supply many types of publicly provided goods and services (highways, schools, police, courts, health services, unemployment insurance, Social Security assistance) that benefit consumers and businesses. Government purchases from businesses also contribute to business revenues. When a construction firm repairs a local stretch of state highway, for example, government pays for the work. As the diagram shows, government receives taxes from households and businesses to complete the flow.

Changes in one flow affect the others. If government raises taxes, households have less to spend on goods and services. Lower consumer spending causes businesses to reduce production, and economic activity declines; unemployment may rise. In contrast, cutting taxes can stimulate economic activity. Keep the circular flow in mind as we continue our study of economics. The way economic sectors interact will become more evident as we explore macroeconomics and microeconomics.

CONCEPT check

What is economics, and how can you benefit from understanding basic economic concepts?

Compare and contrast the world's major economic systems. Why is capitalism growing, communism declining, and socialism still popular?

What is the difference between macroeconomics and microeconomics?

Macroeconomics: The Big Picture

Have you ever looked at CNN's Headline News on the Internet or turned on the radio or television and heard something like, "Today the Labor Department reported that for the second straight month unemployment declined"? Statements like this are macroeconomic news. Understanding the national economy and how changes in government policies affect households and businesses is a good place to begin our study of economics.

4 How do economic growth, full employment, price stability, and inflation indicate a nation's economic health?

Let's look first at macroeconomic goals and how they can be met. The United States and most other countries have three main macroeconomic goals: economic growth, full employment, and price stability. A nation's economic well-being depends on carefully defining these goals and choosing the best economic policies for achieving them.

Striving for Economic Growth

Perhaps the most important way to judge a nation's economic health is to look at its production of goods and services. The more the nation produces, the higher its standard of living. An increase in a nation's output of goods and services is **economic growth**.

The most basic measure of economic growth is the **gross domestic product (GDP)**. GDP is the total market value of all final goods and services produced within a nation's borders each year. The Bureau of Labor Statistics publishes quarterly GDP figures that can be used to compare trends in national output. When GDP rises, the economy is growing.

The rate of growth in real GDP (GDP adjusted for inflation) is also important. Recently, the U.S. economy has been growing at between 3 percent and 5 percent annually. The forecasted rate for 2008 was around 3.5 percent, if the economy did not slide into a recession. This growth rate has meant a steady increase in the output of goods and services and relatively low unemployment. When the growth rate slides toward zero, the economy begins to stagnate and decline.

One country that continues to grow more rapidly than most is China, whose GDP has been growing at 8 to 9 percent per year. Today few things in the global marketplace are not or cannot be made in China. The downside of China's rapid economic growth has been pollution. Only 1 percent of the country's 560 million city dwellers breathe air considered safe.[10] Adding a thousand new cars a day to the overcrowded streets will only make matters worse. Beijing frantically searched for a magic formula to clear the skies before the 2008 Olympics. Other individuals and corporations around the globe are seeking ways to improve the environment and to preserve the globe's scarce resources. The Managing Change box on the next page examines one such effort.

The level of economic activity is constantly changing. These upward and downward changes are called **business cycles**. Business cycles vary in length, in how high or low the economy moves, and in how much the economy is affected. Changes in GDP trace the patterns as economic activity expands and contracts. An increase in business activity results in rising output, income, employment, and prices. Eventually, these all peak, and output, income, and employment decline. A decline in GDP that lasts for two consecutive quarters (each a three-month period) is called a **recession**. It is followed by a recovery period when economic activity once again increases. A recent recession was in 2001 and 2002. As this book went to print, there was a possibility of a recession in 2008.

Businesses must monitor and react to the changing phases of business cycles. When the economy is growing, companies often have a difficult time hiring good employees and finding scarce supplies and raw materials. When a recession hits, many firms find they have more capacity than the demand for their goods and services requires. During the housing downturn in 2007–2008, many large builders cut their new housing starts 80 percent or more. When plants use only part of their capacity, they operate inefficiently and have higher costs per unit produced. Let's say that Mars Corp. has a huge plant that can produce 1 million Milky Way candy bars a day, but because of a recession Mars can sell only half a million candy bars a day with large, expensive machines. Producing Milky Ways at 50 percent capacity does not efficiently utilize Mars's investment in its plant and equipment.

Keeping People on the Job

Another macroeconomic goal is **full employment**, or having jobs for all who want to and can work. Full employment doesn't actually mean 100 percent employment. Some people choose not to work for personal reasons (attending school, raising children) or are temporarily unemployed while they wait to start a new job. Thus, the government defines full employment as the situation when about 94 to 96 percent of those available to work actually have jobs. During the late 2000s, the economy operated at less than full employment.

Maintaining low unemployment levels is of concern not just to the United States but also to countries around the world. A contributing factor to the riots in France in the fall of 2005 was extremely high youth unemployment. The French government has made jobless and health benefits a higher priority than job creation. As a result, almost 22 percent of French youths under 25 were unemployed, compared to 13 percent in the United States and 11 percent in Great Britain. When jobs are limited and competition for jobs intense, discrimination is more likely to occur. One 21-year-old rioter of

economic growth
An increase in a nation's output of goods and services.

gross domestic product (GDP)
The total market value of all final goods and services produced within a nation's borders each year.

business cycles
Upward and downward changes in the level of economic activity.

recession
A decline in GDP that lasts for at least two consecutive quarters.

full employment
The condition when all people who want to work and can work have jobs.

Making "Green Gold" Green

Global food and consumer goods companies are backing a plan to certify palm oil—the vegetable oil used in products ranging from margarine to cosmetics, and, increasingly, biodiesel—to ensure that its soaring production doesn't spur greater destruction of tropical rain forests.

The push for "green" palm oil has been joined by Unilever, Johnson & Johnson, Nestlé SA, and H. J. Heinz Co. The companies have signed up with a consortium of 200 oil producers, commercial buyers, and environmental groups to improve the industry's image and avert a consumer backlash. Almost 90 percent of all palm oil is produced in Indonesia and Malaysia, which have seen widespread deforestation in recent years, much of it from illegal land clearing and logging. The development of oil-palm plantations is causing the loss of forests in Indonesia, putting the survival of animals like the orangutan at risk, the United Nations Environmental Program said in a report last year.

Environmental groups fear that destruction will accelerate as the price of crude palm oil—called "green gold" by some producers—hits records.

More and more, palm oil is also being sought as a feedstock for biodiesel, pushing its price even higher in line with crude oil's increase in price. To improve palm oil's tarnished image, the Malaysia-based Roundtable on Sustainable Palm Oil (RSPO)—as the industry consortium is known—plans to introduce a system soon to certify palm-oil operations that meet strict environmental criteria. The RSPO, which was created in 2003, hopes newly certified palm-oil refiners will start selling oil produced from "sustainable" plantations. Only operations that can prove they don't harm the environment will get its seal of approval, the RSPO says.

Still, some environmental groups criticize the RSPO's plans as unworkable. One problem, they say, is that palm fruit is typically collected by traders from a number of different plantations, large and small, and sold in bulk to companies. That makes it difficult to tell what portion is from sustainable sources.

"Buyers are simply using the RSPO as a front to cover up the fact they don't have control over their purchasing," says Pat Venditti, head of Greenpeace International's forest campaign. He wants companies to boycott all palm oil produced from areas of Indonesia where rain forests are being destroyed.

Another concern is that plantation owners with poor environmental records could get one palm-oil operation certified while continuing to raze forests elsewhere.[11]

Critical Thinking Questions
- Should multinational companies boycott all palm oil produced in Indonesia?
- What is meant by "green products"? If only a few firms sell green products, isn't it basically just a way to sell more goods and only have a tiny effect on the environment?

© Stockbyte / Getty Images

Moroccan origin described his life as "violence, unemployment, discrimination." Large numbers of idle youth, discontented and with no productive outlets for their energy, were easily angered and willing to participate in destructive activities.[12]

Some economists point to the very different situation in the United States, where economic growth has contributed to low unemployment. Young workers get to know people of other races and ethnicities in the workplace, reducing the barriers between them and promoting tolerance and understanding.

Measuring Unemployment

To determine how close we are to full employment, the government measures the **unemployment rate**. This rate indicates the percentage of the total labor force that is not working but is actively looking for work. It excludes "discouraged workers," those not seeking jobs because they think no one will hire them. Each month the Department of Labor releases statistics on employment. These figures help us understand how well the economy is doing. In the past two decades, unemployment rose as high as 9.7 percent in 1982, which was a recession year. It then declined steadily through the remainder of the 1980s and most of the 1990s. In 2000, the rate fell to under 4 percent, which was the lowest rate in almost 30 years, but the 2001–2002 recession drove unemployment to over 6 percent. Unemployment then declined steadily, but rose in early 2008 to 5 percent.

Types of Unemployment

Economists classify unemployment into four types: frictional, structural, cyclical, and seasonal. The categories are of small consolation to someone who is unemployed, but they help economists understand the problem of unemployment in our economy.

Frictional unemployment is short-term unemployment that is not related to the business cycle. It includes people who are unemployed while waiting to start a better job, those who are reentering the job market, and those entering for the first time such as new college graduates. This type of unemployment is always present and has little impact on the economy.

unemployment rate
The percentage of the total labor force that is not working but is actively looking for work.

frictional unemployment
Short-term unemployment that is not related to the business cycle.

CONCEPT in action

The strength of the U.S. labor market over the past decade has surprised many observers, especially since challenges ranging from globalization and political instability to unionization have been ongoing. Yet despite 10-year lows in the U.S. unemployment rate, not all industries have fared well. Energy and Internet firms have thrived in recent years, but banks, automakers, and newspaper businesses continue to announce massive layoffs. What type of unemployment is common to slumping industries?

© Bill Pugliano/Getty Images

structural unemployment
Unemployment that is caused by a mismatch between available jobs and the skills of available workers in an industry or region; not related to the business cycle.

cyclical unemployment
Unemployment that occurs when a downturn in the business cycle reduces the demand for labor throughout the economy.

seasonal unemployment
Unemployment that occurs during specific seasons in certain industries.

inflation
The situation in which the average of all prices of goods and services is rising.

purchasing power
The value of what money can buy.

demand-pull inflation
Inflation that occurs when the demand for goods and services is greater than the supply.

Structural unemployment is also unrelated to the business cycle but is involuntary. It is caused by a mismatch between available jobs and the skills of available workers in an industry or a region. For example, if the birthrate declines, fewer teachers will be needed. Or the available workers in an area may lack the skills that employers want. Retraining and skill-building programs are often required to reduce structural unemployment.

Cyclical unemployment, as the name implies, occurs when a downturn in the business cycle reduces the demand for labor throughout the economy. In a long recession, cyclical unemployment is widespread, and even people with good job skills can't find jobs. The government can partly counteract cyclical unemployment with programs that boost the economy.

In the past, cyclical unemployment affected mainly less-skilled workers and those in heavy manufacturing. Typically, they would be rehired when economic growth increased. Since the 1990s, however, competition has forced many American companies to downsize so they can survive in the global marketplace. These job reductions affected workers in all categories, including middle management. Firms continue to reevaluate workforce requirements and downsize to stay competitive to compete with Asian, European, and other U.S. firms. The Detroit 3 (Ford, Chrysler, and General Motors) and their suppliers are shedding U.S. jobs far faster than their foreign-based competitors are creating them. The U.S. auto industry employs nearly 25 percent fewer people today than it did seven years ago in manufacturing. In 2008, 985,000 people were employed in motor vehicle and equipment manufacturing in the United States. The tally includes cars, all trucks and buses, recreational vehicles, and all parts. That number is down from 1.3 million in 2000. U.S. auto industry employment peaked that year at levels it hadn't seen since the late 1970s.[13]

The last type is seasonal unemployment, which occurs during specific seasons in certain industries. Employees subject to **seasonal unemployment** include retail workers hired for the Christmas buying season, lettuce pickers in California, and restaurant employees in Aspen during the summer.

Keeping Prices Steady

The third macroeconomic goal is to keep overall prices for goods and services fairly steady. The situation in which the average of all prices of goods and services is rising is called **inflation**. Inflation's higher prices reduce **purchasing power**, the value of what money can buy. Purchasing power is a function of two things: inflation and income. If incomes rise at the same rate as inflation, there is no change in purchasing power. If prices go up but income doesn't rise or rises at a slower rate, a given amount of income buys less and purchasing power falls. For example, if the price of a basket of groceries rises from $30 to $40 but your salary remains the same, you can buy only 75 percent as many groceries ($30 ÷ $40) for $30. Your purchasing power declines by 25 percent ($10 ÷ $40). If incomes rise at a rate faster than inflation, then purchasing power increases! So you can, in fact, have rising purchasing power even if inflation is increasing. Typically, however, inflation rises faster than incomes, leading to a decrease in purchasing power.

Inflation affects both personal and business decisions. When prices are rising, people tend to spend more—before their purchasing power declines further. Businesses that expect inflation often increase their supplies, and people often speed up planned purchases of cars and major appliances.

From the late 1990s to 2004, inflation in the United States was in the 1.5 to 4 percent range. Because of a spike in energy prices, inflation for 2007 was 4.1 percent.

These levels are generally considered fairly low. In the 1980s we had periods of inflation in the 12 to 13 percent range. Some nations have had high double- and even triple-digit inflation in recent years. Countries with the highest inflation rates are: Zimbabwe at 385 percent, Angola at 77 percent, Burma at 50 percent, and Haiti at 38 percent.[14]

CONCEPT in action

What could have been more disappointing for New England Patriots fans than watching their team lose Super Bowl XLII after a perfect 18–0 season? How about higher ticket prices at Gillette Stadium? Days after the crushing world championship defeat, football's most domineering franchise upped the expense of Pats' games as much as 51 percent. The price hike on premium seats didn't sit well with Foxboro fans, who already pay the highest average ticket price in the NFL. What economic forces influence the cost of seats at sporting events?

Types of Inflation There are two types of inflation. **Demand-pull inflation** occurs when the demand for goods and services is greater than the supply. Would-be buyers have more money to spend than the amount needed to buy available goods and services. Their demand, which exceeds the supply, tends to pull prices up. This situation is sometimes described as "too much money chasing too few goods." The higher prices lead to greater supply, eventually creating a balance between demand and supply.

Cost-push inflation is triggered by increases in production costs, such as expenses for materials and wages. These increases push up the prices of final goods and services. Wage increases are a major cause of cost-push inflation, creating a "wage–price spiral." For example, assume that America's fastest growing union, the Service Employees International Union (SEIU), negotiates a three-year labor agreement that raises wages 5 percent per year and increases overtime pay. Hospitals and long-term care facilities raise their prices to cover their higher labor costs. Also, the higher wages will give the service workers, such as nurses and lab technicians, more money to buy goods and services. This increased demand may pull up other prices. Workers in other industries will demand higher prices to keep up with the increased prices, and the cycle will push prices even higher.

How Inflation Is Measured
The rate of inflation is most commonly measured by looking at changes in the **consumer price index (CPI)**, an index of the prices of a "market basket" of goods and services purchased by typical urban consumers. It is published monthly by the Department of Labor. Major components of the CPI, which are weighted by importance, are food and beverages, clothing, transportation, housing, health, recreation, and education. There are special indexes for food and energy. The Department of Labor collects about 80,000 retail price quotes and 5,000 housing rent figures to calculate the CPI.

The CPI sets prices in a base period at 100. The base period, which now is 1982–1984, is chosen for its price stability. Current prices are then expressed as a percentage of prices in the base period. A rise in the CPI means prices are increasing. For example, the CPI was 203.5 in July 2006, meaning that prices more than doubled since the 1982–1984 base period.

Changes in wholesale prices are another important indicator of inflation. The **producer price index (PPI)** measures the prices paid by producers and wholesalers for various commodities such as raw materials, partially finished goods, and finished products. The PPI, which uses 1982 as its base year, is actually a family of indexes for many different product categories, including crude goods (raw materials), intermediate goods (which become part of finished goods), and finished goods. For example, the PPI for finished goods was 170.6 in December 2007. In 2007, finished-goods prices moved up 6.3 percent compared with a 1.1 percent advance in 2006. The faster rate of increase in 2007 was due to food and energy prices. Examples of other PPI indexes include processed foods, lumber, containers, fuels and lubricants, metals, and construction. Because the PPI measures prices paid by producers for raw materials, energy, and other commodities, it may foreshadow subsequent price changes for businesses and consumers.

The Impact of Inflation
Inflation has several negative effects on people and businesses. For one thing, inflation penalizes people who live on fixed incomes. Let's say that a couple receives $1,000 a month retirement income beginning in 2008. If inflation is 10 percent in 2009, then the couple can buy only about 91 percent ($100 \div 110$) of what they could purchase in 2008. Similarly, inflation hurts savers. As prices rise, the real value, or purchasing power, of a nest egg of savings deteriorates.

Achieving Macroeconomic Goals

To reach macroeconomic goals, countries must often choose among conflicting alternatives. Sometimes political needs override economic needs. For example, bringing inflation under control may call for a politically difficult period of high unemployment and low growth. Or, in an election year, politicians may resist raising taxes to curb inflation. Still, the government must try to guide the economy to a sound balance of growth, employment, and price stability. The two main tools it uses are monetary policy and fiscal policy.

Monetary Policy

Monetary policy refers to a government's programs for controlling the amount of money circulating in the economy and interest rates. Changes in the money supply affect both the level of economic activity and the rate of inflation. The **Federal Reserve System (the Fed)**, the central banking system of the United States, prints money and controls how much of it will be in circulation. The money supply is also controlled by the Fed's regulation of certain bank activities.

cost-push inflation
Inflation that occurs when increases in production costs push up the prices of final goods and services.

consumer price index (CPI)
An index of the prices of a "market basket" of goods and services purchased by typical urban consumers.

producer price index (PPI)
An index of the prices paid by producers and wholesalers for various commodities such as raw materials, partially finished goods, and finished products.

CONCEPT check

What is a business cycle? How do businesses adapt to periods of contraction and expansion?

Why is full employment usually defined as a target percentage below 100 percent?

What is the difference between demand-pull and cost-push inflation?

5 How does the government use monetary policy and fiscal policy to achieve its macroeconomic goals?

monetary policy
A government's programs for controlling the amount of money circulating in the economy and interest rates.

Federal Reserve System (the Fed)
The central banking system of the United States.

As chairman of the Board of Governors of the Federal Reserve System for two decades, Alan Greenspan was the face of U.S. monetary policy. But when Greenspan stepped down in 2006, Ben Bernanke (pictured above), the head of the U.S. President's Council of Economic Advisers, took over as chairman. As a White House chief economist and former chair of Princeton's economics department, Bernanke earned a reputation for being scholarly and independent-minded. What are the responsibilities of the chairman of the Board of Governors of the Federal Reserve System?

contractionary policy
The use of monetary policy by the Fed to tighten the money supply by selling government securities or raising interest rates.

expansionary policy
The use of monetary policy by the Fed to increase, or loosen, the growth of the money supply.

fiscal policy
The government's use of taxation and spending to affect the economy.

crowding out
The situation that occurs when government spending replaces spending by the private sector.

When the Fed increases or decreases the amount of money in circulation, it affects interest rates (the cost of borrowing money and the reward for lending it). The Fed can change the interest rate on money it lends to banks to signal the banking system and financial markets that it has changed its monetary policy. These changes have a ripple effect. Banks, in turn, may pass along this change to consumers and businesses that receive loans from the banks. If the cost of borrowing decreases, the economy grows because interest rates affect consumer and business decisions to spend or invest. The housing industry, business, and investments react most to changes in interest rates.

In 2007 and early 2008, the U.S. housing market had basically collapsed and availability of credit was very tight. The housing market was characterized by vacant houses, depressed property values, and foreclosures. Home foreclosures are where a lending institution, such as a bank, takes possession of a property because of nonpayment by the borrower. Many of the foreclosures were due to lenders not being careful about to whom they loaned money. That is, borrowers were not carefully screened to make certain that they could afford the home and make timely payments.

Problems in the credit and housing markets ultimately led to a decline in global stock markets because of fears of a worldwide recession. Stock markets around the world shed nearly $7 trillion in value in January 2008.[15] On January 22, with global stock markets in a free fall, the Federal Reserve cut the rate it charges banks by three-quarters of a percent.[16] It was the largest single rate cut in 20 years. Because banks usually borrow for shorter terms than they lend, the reduction in rates will make lending more profitable and thus appealing. Major banks immediately lowered their prime rates (rates charged to the best customers) to 6.5 percent from 7.25 percent. As rates charged to consumers and businesses fall, they tend to borrow and spend more, thus stimulating the economy.

As you can see, the Fed can use monetary policy to contract or expand the economy. With **contractionary policy**, the Fed restricts, or tightens, the money supply by selling government securities or raising interest rates. The result is slower economic growth and higher unemployment. Thus, contractionary policy reduces spending and, ultimately, lowers inflation. With **expansionary policy**, the Fed increases, or loosens, growth in the money supply. An expansionary policy stimulates the economy. Interest rates decline, so business and consumer spending go up. Unemployment rates drop as businesses expand. But increasing the money supply also has a negative side: more spending pushes prices up, increasing the inflation rate.

Fiscal Policy

The other economic tool used by the government is **fiscal policy**, its program of taxation and spending. By cutting taxes or by increasing spending, the government can stimulate the economy. Look again at Exhibit 1.3. The more government buys from businesses, the greater the business revenues and output. Likewise, if consumers or businesses have to pay less in taxes, they will have more income to spend for goods and services. Tax policies in the United States therefore affect business decisions. High corporate taxes can make it harder for U.S. firms to compete with companies in countries with lower taxes. As a result, companies may choose to locate facilities overseas to reduce their tax burden.

Nobody likes to pay taxes, although we grudgingly accept that we have to. Although most U.S. citizens complain that they are overtaxed, we pay lower taxes per capita (per person) than citizens in many countries similar to ours. In addition, our taxes represent a lower percentage of gross income and GDP compared to most countries.

Taxes are, of course, the major source of revenue for our government. Every year the president prepares a budget for the coming year based on estimated revenues and expenditures. Congress receives the president's report and recommendations and then, typically, debates and analyzes the proposed budget for several months. The president's original proposal is always modified in numerous ways. Exhibit 1.4 shows the sources of revenue and expenses for the U.S. budget.

Whereas fiscal policy has a major impact on business and consumers, continual increases in government spending raise another important issue. When government takes more money from business and consumers (the private sector), a phenomenon known as **crowding out** occurs. Here are three examples of crowding out:

EXHIBIT 1.4   Revenues and Expenses for the Federal Budget

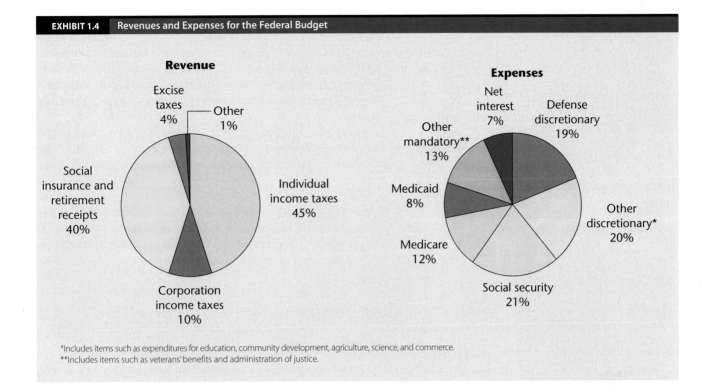

*Includes items such as expenditures for education, community development, agriculture, science, and commerce.
**Includes items such as veterans' benefits and administration of justice.

1. The government spends more on public libraries, and individuals buy fewer books at bookstores.
2. The government spends more on public education, and individuals spend less on private education.
3. The government spends more on public transportation, and individuals spend less on private transportation.

In other words, government spending is crowding out private spending.

If the government spends more for programs (social services, education, defense) than it collects in taxes, the result is a **federal budget deficit**. To balance the budget, the government can cut its spending, increase taxes, or do some combination of the two. When it cannot balance the budget, the government must make up any shortfalls by borrowing (just like any business or household).

In 1998, for the first time in a generation, there was a federal budget surplus (revenue exceeded spending) of about $71 billion. By 2002, there was once again a deficit ($159 billion), and for fiscal year 2007 the deficit was more than $163 billion. Whenever the government finds itself with a surplus, Congress begins an often-heated debate about what to do with the money. Some members of Congress, for example, want to spend more on social programs or for defense. Others say that this money belongs to the people and should be returned in the form of tax cuts. Another alternative is to reduce the national debt.

The U.S. government has run budget deficits for many years. The accumulated total of these past deficits is the **national debt**, which now amounts to about $9.2 trillion or about $30,220 for every man, woman, and child in the United States. Total interest on the debt is more than $430 billion a year.[17] To cover the deficit, the U.S. government borrows money from people and businesses in the form of Treasury bills, Treasury notes, and Treasury bonds. These are federal IOUs that pay interest to their owners.

The national debt is an emotional issue debated not only in the halls of Congress, but by the public as well. Some believe that deficits contribute to economic growth, high employment, and price stability. Others have the following reservations about such a high national debt:

- *Not Everyone Holds the Debt*: The government is very conscious of who actually bears the burden of the national debt and keeps track of who holds what bonds. If only the rich were bondholders, then they alone would receive the interest payments and could end up receiving

federal budget deficit
The condition that occurs when the federal government spends more for programs than it collects in taxes.

national debt
The accumulated total of all of the federal government's annual budget deficits.

more in interest than they paid in taxes. In the meantime, poorer people, who held no bonds, would end up paying taxes that would be transferred to the rich as interest, making the debt an unfair burden to them. At times, therefore, the government has instructed commercial banks to reduce their total debt by divesting some of their bond holdings. That's also why the Treasury created **savings bonds**. Because these bonds are issued in relatively small denominations, they allow more people to buy and hold government debt.

- *Crowding Out Private Investment*: The national debt also affects private investment. If the government raises the interest rate on bonds to be able to sell them, it forces private businesses, whose corporate bonds (long-term debt obligations issued by a company) compete with government bonds for investor dollars, to raise rates on their bonds to stay competitive. In other words, selling government debt to finance government spending makes it more costly for private industry to finance its own investment. As a result, government debt may end up crowding out private investment and slowing economic growth in the private sector.

Microeconomics: Zeroing in on Businesses and Consumers

6 What are the basic microeconomic concepts of demand and supply, and how do they establish prices?

Now let's shift our focus from the whole economy to microeconomics, the study of households, businesses, and industries. This field of economics is concerned with how prices and quantities of goods and services behave in a free market. It stands to reason that people, firms, and governments try to get the most from their limited resources. Consumers want to buy the best quality at the lowest price. Businesses want to keep costs down and revenues high to earn larger profits. Governments also want to use their revenues to provide the most effective public goods and services possible. These groups choose among alternatives by focusing on the prices of goods and services.

As consumers in a free market, we influence what is produced. If Mexican food is popular, the high demand attracts entrepreneurs who open more Mexican restaurants. They want to compete for our dollars by supplying Mexican food at a lower price, of better quality, or with different features such as Santa Fe Mexican food rather than Tex-Mex. This section explains how business and consumer choices influence the price and availability of goods and services.

CONCEPT in action

© AP Images/E.J. Flynn

Pop diva Britney Spears may have perplexing issues of self-worth, but when it comes to the U.S. economy the Grammy Award–winning megastar is worth an estimated $120 million annually—and that's when she's not touring. Record companies, promotion firms, tabloids, and paparazzi are but a few of the businesses that earn millions off of Britney, Inc. Even ex-hubby K-Fed collects big coin, simply from his association with Spears's soap opera–like meltdowns. What market forces control the frenzied demand for all things Britney?

demand
The quantity of a good or service that people are willing to buy at various prices.

demand curve
A graph showing the quantity of a good or service that people are willing to buy at various prices.

The Nature of Demand

Demand is the quantity of a good or service that people are willing to buy at various prices. The higher the price, the lower the quantity demanded, and vice versa. A graph of this relationship is called a **demand curve**.

Let's assume you own a store that sells jackets for snowboarders. From past experience you know how many jackets you can sell at different prices. The demand curve in Exhibit 1.5 depicts this information. The x-axis (horizontal axis) shows the quantity of jackets, and the y-axis (vertical axis) shows the related price of those jackets. For example, at a price of $100, customers will buy (demand) 600 snowboard jackets.

In the graph the demand curve slopes downward and to the right, because as the price falls, people will want to buy more jackets. Some people who were not going to buy a jacket will purchase one at the lower price. Also, some snowboarders who already have a jacket will buy a second one. The graph also shows that if you put a large number of jackets on the market, you will have to reduce the price to sell all of them.

Understanding demand is critical to businesses. Demand tells you how much you can sell and at what price—in other words, how much money the firm will take in that can be used to cover costs and hopefully earn a profit. Gauging demand is difficult even for the very largest corporations, but particularly for small firms.

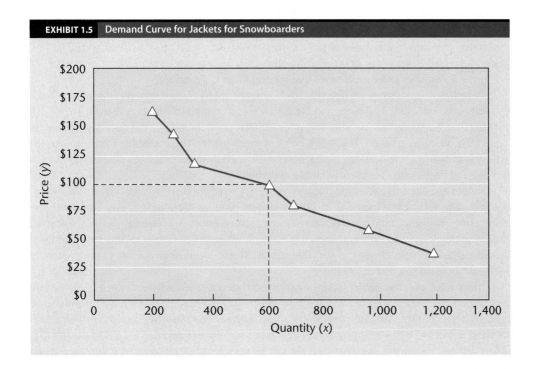

EXHIBIT 1.5   Demand Curve for Jackets for Snowboarders

The Nature of Supply

Demand alone is not enough to explain how the market sets prices. We must also look at **supply**, the quantity of a good or service that businesses will make available at various prices. The higher the price, the greater the number of jackets a supplier will produce, and vice versa. A graph of the relationship between various prices and the quantities a business will supply is a **supply curve**.

We can again plot the quantity of jackets on the x-axis and the price on the y-axis. As Exhibit 1.6 shows, 800 jackets will be available at a price of $100. Note that the supply curve slopes upward and to the right, the opposite of the demand curve. If snowboarders are willing to pay higher prices, suppliers of jackets will buy more inputs (Gore-Tex® fabric, dye, machinery, labor) and produce more jackets. The quantity supplied will be higher at higher prices, because manufacturers can earn higher profits.

supply
The quantity of a good or service that businesses will make available at various prices.

supply curve
A graph showing the quantity of a good or service that businesses will make available at various prices.

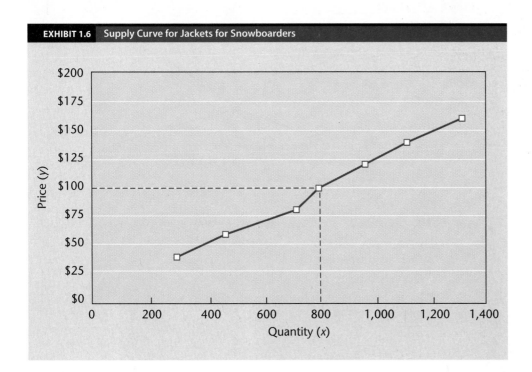

EXHIBIT 1.6   Supply Curve for Jackets for Snowboarders

How Demand and Supply Interact to Determine Prices

In a stable economy, the number of jackets that snowboarders demand depends on the jackets' price. Likewise, the number of jackets that suppliers provide depends on price. But at what price will consumer demand for jackets match the quantity suppliers will produce?

To answer this question, we need to look at what happens when demand and supply interact. By plotting both the demand curve and the supply curve on the same graph in Exhibit 1.7, we see that they cross at a certain quantity and price. At that point, labeled E, the quantity demanded equals the quantity supplied. This is the point of **equilibrium**. The equilibrium price is $80; the equilibrium quantity is 700 jackets. At that point there is a balance between the quantity consumers will buy and the quantity suppliers will make available.

Market equilibrium is achieved through a series of quantity and price adjustments that occur automatically. If the price increases to $160, suppliers produce more jackets than consumers are willing to buy, and a surplus results. To sell more jackets, prices will have to fall. Thus, a surplus pushes prices downward until equilibrium is reached. When the price falls to $60, the quantity of jackets demanded rises above the available supply. The resulting shortage forces prices upward until equilibrium is reached at $80.

The number of snowboarder jackets supplied and bought at $80 will tend to rest at equilibrium unless there is a shift in either demand or supply. If demand increases, more jackets will be purchased at every price, and the demand curve shifts to the right (as illustrated by line D_2 in Exhibit 1.8). If demand decreases, less will be bought at every price, and the demand curve shifts to the left (D_1). When demand decreased, snowboarders bought 500 jackets at $80 instead of 700 jackets. When demand increased, they purchased 800.

Changes in Demand A number of things can increase or decrease demand. For example, if snowboarders' incomes go up, they may decide to buy a second jacket. If incomes fall, a snowboarder who was planning to purchase a jacket may wear an old one instead. Changes in fashion or tastes

equilibrium
The point at which quantity demanded equals quantity supplied.

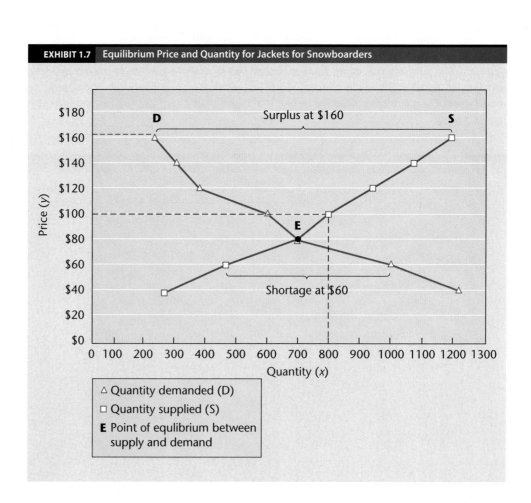

EXHIBIT 1.7 Equilibrium Price and Quantity for Jackets for Snowboarders

△ Quantity demanded (D)
□ Quantity supplied (S)
E Point of equlibrium between supply and demand

EXHIBIT 1.8   Shifts in Demand for Jackets for Snowboarders

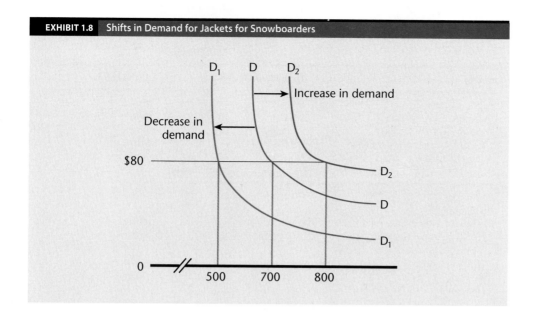

can also influence demand. If snowboarding were suddenly to go out of fashion, demand for jackets would decrease quickly. A change in the price of related products can also influence demand. For example, if the average price of a snowboard rises to $1,000, people will quit snowboarding and jacket demand will fall.

Another factor that can shift demand is expectations about future prices. If you expect jacket prices to increase significantly in the future, you may decide to go ahead and get one today. If you think prices will fall, you will postpone your purchase. Finally, changes in the number of buyers will affect demand. Snowboarding is a young person's sport, and the number of teenagers will increase in the next few years. Therefore, the demand for snowboarding jackets should increase.

Changes in Supply   Other factors influence the supply side of the picture. New technology typically lowers the cost of production. For example, North Face, a supplier of ski and snowboarder jackets, purchased laser-guided pattern-cutting equipment and computer-aided pattern-making equipment. Each jacket was cheaper to produce, resulting in a higher profit per jacket. This provided an incentive to supply more jackets at every price. If the price of resources such as labor or fabric goes up, North Face will earn a smaller profit on each jacket, and the amount supplied will decrease at every price. The reverse is also true. Changes in the prices of other goods can also affect supply.

Let's say that snow skiing becomes a really hot sport again. The number of skiers jumps dramatically and the price of ski jackets soars. North Face can use its machines and fabrics to produce either ski or snowboard jackets. If the company can make more profit from ski jackets, it will produce fewer snowboarding jackets at every price. Also, a change in the number of producers will shift the supply curve. If the number of jacket suppliers increases, they will place more jackets on the market at every price. If any suppliers stop making jackets available, the supply will naturally decrease. Taxes can also affect supply. If the government decides, for some reason, to tax the supplier for every snowboard jacket produced, then profits will fall and fewer jackets will be offered at every price. Exhibit 1.9 on the next page summarizes the factors that can shift demand and supply curves.

To better understand the relationship between supply and demand across the economy, consider the impact of 2005's Hurricane Katrina on U.S. energy prices. Oil and gas prices were already at high levels before Hurricane Katrina disrupted production in the Gulf Coast. Most U.S. offshore drilling sites are located in the Gulf of Mexico, and almost 30 percent of U.S. refining capacity is in Gulf States that were hit hard by the storm. Prices rose almost immediately as supplies fell, while demand remained at the same levels.

CONCEPT check

What is the relationship between prices and demand for a product?

How is market equilibrium achieved? Describe the circumstances under which the price for gasoline would have returned to equilibrium in the United States after Hurricane Katrina.

Draw a graph that shows an equilibrium point for supply and demand.

Chapter 1: Understanding Economic Systems and Business

EXHIBIT 1.9   Factors That Cause Demand and Supply Curves to Shift

	Shift Demand	
Factor	To the Right If	To the Left If
Buyers' incomes	increase	decrease
Buyers' preferences/tastes	increase	decrease
Prices of substitute products	increase	decrease
Expectations about future prices	will rise	will fall
Number of buyers	increases	decreases
	Shift Supply	
Technology	lowers cost	increases cost
Resource prices	fall	rise
Changes in prices of other products that can be produced with the same resources	profit of other product falls	profit of other product rises
Number of suppliers	increases	decreases
Taxes	decreased	increased

The storm drove home the vulnerability of the U.S. energy supply to not only natural disasters but also terrorist attacks and price increases from foreign oil producers. Many energy policy experts questioned the wisdom of having such a high concentration of oil facilities—about 25 percent of the oil and natural gas infrastructure—in hurricane-prone states. Refiners were already almost at capacity before Katrina's devastation.

Competing in a Free Market

7 What are the four types of market structure?

market structure
The number of suppliers in a market.

One of the characteristics of a free-market system is that suppliers have the right to compete with one another. The number of suppliers in a market defines the **market structure**. Economists identify four types of market structures: (1) perfect competition, (2) pure monopoly, (3) monopolistic competition, and (4) oligopoly. Exhibit 1.10 summarizes the characteristics of each of these market structures.

Perfect Competition

perfect (pure) competition
A market structure in which a large number of small firms sell similar products, buyers and sellers have good information, and businesses can be easily opened or closed.

Characteristics of **perfect (pure) competition** include:

- A large number of small firms are in the market.
- The firms sell similar products; that is, each firm's product is very much like the products sold by other firms in the market.
- Buyers and sellers in the market have good information about prices, sources of supply, and so on.
- It is easy to open a new business or close an existing one.

In a perfectly competitive market, firms sell their products at prices determined solely by forces beyond their control. Because the products are very similar and each firm contributes only a small amount to the total quantity supplied by the industry, price is determined by supply and demand. A firm that raised its price even a little above the going rate would lose customers. In the wheat market, for example, the product is essentially the same from one wheat producer to the next. Thus, none of the producers has control over the price of wheat.

Perfect competition is an ideal. No industry shows all its characteristics, but the stock market and some agricultural markets, such as those for wheat and corn, come closest. Farmers, for example, can sell all of their crops through national commodity exchanges at the current market price.

Pure Monopoly

pure monopoly
A market structure in which a single firm accounts for all industry sales of a particular good or service, and in which there are barriers to entry.

barriers to entry
Factors, such as technological or legal conditions, that prevent new firms from competing equally with an existing firm.

At the other end of the spectrum is **pure monopoly**, the market structure in which a single firm accounts for all industry sales of a particular good or service. The firm is the industry. This market structure is characterized by **barriers to entry**—factors that prevent new firms from competing equally with the existing firm. Often the barriers are technological or legal conditions. Polaroid, for example, has held major patents on instant photography for years. When Kodak tried to market its

EXHIBIT 1.10 Comparison of Market Structures

Characteristics	Perfect Competition	Pure Monopoly	Monopolistic Competition	Oligopoly
Number of firms in market	Many	One	Many, but fewer than perfect competition	Few
Firm's ability to control price	None	High	Some	Some
Barriers to entry	None	Subject to government regulation	Few	Many
Product differentiation	Very little	No products that compete directly	Emphasis on showing perceived differences in products	Some differences
Examples	Farm products such as wheat and corn	Utilities such as gas, water, cable television	Retail specialty clothing stores	Steel, automobiles, airlines, aircraft manufacturers

own instant camera, Polaroid sued, claiming patent violations. Polaroid collected millions of dollars from Kodak. Another barrier may be one firm's control of a natural resource. DeBeers Consolidated Mines Ltd., for example, controls most of the world's supply of uncut diamonds.

Public utilities, such as gas and water companies, are pure monopolies. Some monopolies are created by a government order that outlaws competition. The U.S. Postal Service is currently one such monopoly.

Monopolistic Competition

Three characteristics define the market structure known as **monopolistic competition**:

- Many firms are in the market.
- The firms offer products that are close substitutes but still differ from one another.
- It is relatively easy to enter the market.

Under monopolistic competition, firms take advantage of product differentiation. Industries where monopolistic competition occurs include clothing, food, and similar consumer products. Firms under monopolistic competition have more control over pricing than do firms under perfect competition because consumers do not view the products as perfect substitutes. Nevertheless, firms must demonstrate product differences to justify their prices to customers. Consequently, companies use advertising to distinguish their products from others. Such distinctions may be significant or superficial. For example, Nike says "Just Do It," and Tylenol is advertised as being easier on the stomach than aspirin.

Sometimes companies facing monopolistic competition attempt to enhance their product or service offerings to justify higher prices. Several innovative firms have extended this to the men's barber shop, as discussed in the Customer Satisfaction and Quality box on the next page.

monopolistic competition
A market structure in which many firms offer products that are close substitutes and in which entry is relatively easy.

Oligopoly

An **oligopoly** has two characteristics:

- A few firms produce most or all of the output.
- Large capital requirements or other factors limit the number of firms.

Boeing and Airbus Industries (aircraft manufacturers) and USX (formerly U.S. Steel) are major firms in different oligopolistic industries.

With so few firms in an oligopoly, what one firm does has an impact on the other firms. Thus, the firms in an oligopoly watch one another closely for new technologies, product changes and innovations, promotional campaigns, pricing, production, and other developments. Sometimes they go so far as to coordinate their pricing and output decisions, which is illegal. Many antitrust cases—legal challenges arising out of laws designed to control anticompetitive behavior—occur in oligopolies.

The market structure of an industry can change over time. Take, for example, telecommunications. At one time, AT&T had a monopoly on long-distance telephone service nationwide. Then the U.S. government divided the company into seven regional phone companies in 1984,

oligopoly
A market structure in which a few firms produce most or all of the output and in which large capital requirements or other factors limit the number of firms.

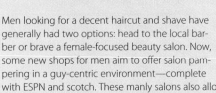

customer **satisfaction** AND

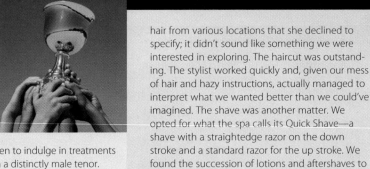

A Game of Pool with That Manicure?

Men looking for a decent haircut and shave have generally had two options: head to the local barber or brave a female-focused beauty salon. Now, some new shops for men aim to offer salon pampering in a guy-centric environment—complete with ESPN and scotch. These manly salons also allow men to indulge in treatments once taboo, such as manicures and facials—but all with a distinctly male tenor. Instead of pastel-colored walls, there are wood floors, black leather couches, and pool tables. Some also offer private areas for more blush-inducing services, such as hair coloring and body waxing.

Primping comes at a price. A haircut, shave, and manicure can cost $65 to $135. Add other services like facials or massages, and you can easily spend a few hundred dollars. To find out if the grooming indulgence was worth the price, the *Wall Street Journal* sent a reporter out to experience one of these new-style barbershops. His report is below.

The Mark Matthew Fine Gentlemen's Grooming Club in Studio City certainly aims for a "man's man" ambience. Inside, it's all guy stuff: flat-panel TVs turned to business news and Spike TV; posters of jazz musicians and single-malt scotches on the wall. But the atmosphere was undercut severely by the fact that, during our two-hour appointment, we were the only customers. It was a bit sad to be the only patrons for the whole afternoon.

We found the manicure—with a hand massage, creams, and a paraffin wax treatment—to be more than we needed. The manicurist also offered to trim body hair from various locations that she declined to specify; it didn't sound like something we were interested in exploring. The haircut was outstanding. The stylist worked quickly and, given our mess of hair and hazy instructions, actually managed to interpret what we wanted better than we could've imagined. The shave was another matter. We opted for what the spa calls its Quick Shave—a shave with a straightedge razor on the down stroke and a standard razor for the up stroke. We found the succession of lotions and aftershaves to be overkill. Worse, we still ended up with stubble on parts of our face.

All in all, the spa had a friendly staff working in an unfortunately tomb-like atmosphere. The haircut was great, but the shave was mediocre and the manicure was more than we needed. That didn't cut it for a $135 tab.[18]

Critical Thinking Questions
- If you were the owner of the above "Grooming Club," what might you do to improve the customer's service experience?
- What are some other service businesses that have attempted to differentiate by going upscale? Have they been successful? Why or why not?

© Digital Vision / Getty Images

CONCEPT check

What is meant by market structure?

Compare and contrast perfect competition and pure monopoly. Why is it rare to find perfect competition?

How does an oligopoly differ from monopolistic competition?

opening the door to greater competition. Other companies such as MCI and Sprint entered the fray and built state-of-the-art fiber-optic networks to win customers from the traditional providers of phone service. The 1996 Telecommunications Act changed the competitive environment yet again by allowing local phone companies to offer long-distance service in exchange for letting competition into their local markets. Today, the broadcasting, computer, telephone, and video industries are converging as companies consolidate through merger and acquisition.

Trends in the Business Environment and Competition

8 Which trends are reshaping the business, micro-, and macroeconomic environments and competitive arena?

Trends in the business and economic environment occur in many areas. As noted in earlier sections, today's workforce is more diverse than ever, with increasing numbers of minorities and older workers. Competition has intensified. Technology has accelerated the pace of work and the ease with which we communicate. Let's look at how companies are meeting the challenges of the graying of the workforce, the growing demand for energy, and competition.

Not Over the Hill Yet

As the huge baby boomer generation ages, so does the workforce. Today baby boomers make up 42 percent of the workforce, and by 2010, 25 percent of all employees will be of retirement age. Although many older workers will retire at the traditional age of 65, a surprisingly large percentage plan to keep working beyond the typical retirement age of 65, often into their 70s and beyond. No longer is retirement an all-or-nothing proposition, and the older boomers and postboomers are taking a more positive attitude toward their later years. A surprising number of Americans expect to work full- or part-time after "retirement," and most would work longer if phased retirement programs were available at their companies. Financial reasons motivate some of these older workers, who worry that their longer life expectancies will mean outliving their money. For many others, however, the

Plugging the Brain Drain

At the National Energy Technology Laboratory in Morgantown, West Virginia, Hugh Guthrie is a full-time technical adviser to other chemical engineers. "My experience gives me a perspective on questions, which may not always be right but nearly always will be different," he says. "The greatest service I provide is in stimulating the thinking of people involved in a project." And at 86, Guthrie has lots of experience to share.

The government, like scores of other organizations, recognizes the need to transfer Guthrie's knowledge to younger employees. But what about the millions of workers who decide to retire, instead of staying on like Guthrie? Much of their collective knowledge will leave along with them and could be forever lost. A recent study revealed that almost half of the companies surveyed had no strategies for preserving essential technological, procedural, and practical knowledge, placing them at a significant competitive disadvantage.

"Most of American business is totally in denial," warns David DeLong, author of *Lost Knowledge: Confronting the Threat of an Aging Workforce* and a leading researcher at MIT's AgeLab. "The situation is scary. People don't know what to do. But we can't give up just because it looks hard." Some recommended techniques include succession planning, mentoring initiatives, training and education, phased-retirement programs, and creating a culture of retention that supports knowledge sharing.

One company that is ahead of the curve in preparing for the "brain drain" is Johnson & Johnson Co. (J&J), which has a strong culture supporting knowledge sharing and retention. For example, it documents effective operating procedures so they can benefit all employees. Teamwork facilitates knowledge transfer. "We work in concert with others on projects, so knowledge is shared rather than hoarded by any individual," explains Robert J. Darretta, chief financial officer at the drug and health care products corporation. Unlike companies where employees follow specialized career paths, J&J moves employees around to different departments every few years. This provides a pool of flexible generalists who can take jobs in various areas of the organization as the need arises.

Darretta emphasizes leadership development and succession planning in his finance organization. He and other J&J executives review key positions annually, ensuring that the department has well-trained employees ready to step in as vacancies occur. "You don't want knowledge to simply reside with the individual; you want knowledge to reside with the organization," he says. "We make sure that knowledge is a consequence of the way we do things."[19]

Critical Thinking Questions

- What potential problems do companies need to address as large numbers of employees reach retirement age?
- You are a human resources manager at a large financial services corporation on a task force that is developing programs to prevent knowledge loss. Provide the details for two programs you would recommend. Would your recommendations differ, and how, if you worked at a large technology company? At a small retail business?

satisfaction of working and feeling productive is more important than money alone. As a result, this generation's extended work careers and rising productivity are expected to contribute 9 percent—about $3 trillion in today's dollars—to the economy by 2045. In addition, the number of new entrants to the labor market is not sufficient to replace the retirees, creating resource shortages.

These converging dynamics create several major challenges for companies today. Today's workforce spans four generations. Recent college graduates, people in their 30s and 40s, baby boomers (the first of which are of retirement age), and traditionals (the generation that preceded the baby boomers) work together in most businesses in greater numbers than before. It's not unusual, therefore, to find a worker who is 50, 60, or even 70 working for a manager who is not yet 30. Although older workers have always been part of the workforce, their presence is increasing as people who retired are returning to work. People in their 60s and 70s offer their vast experience of "what's worked in the past," whereas those in their 20s and 30s tend to be experimental, open to options, and greater risk takers. The best managers will be ones who recognize these generational differences and use them to the company's advantage.[20]

Many companies are developing special programs such as flexible hours to retain older workers and benefit from their practical knowledge and problem-solving skills. In addition, companies must track where employees fall in their career life cycles, to know when they are approaching retirement, and determine whether and how to replace them. Replacing employees is only part of the problem. A bigger issue is how the company continues to tap the vast store of knowledge that retiring employees possess. The issue is discussed in more detail in the Managing Change box above.

The aging of the huge baby boomer population provides other unique challenges and opportunities facing America. These include:

- *Health Care*: The higher patient volume with the aging of America will affect payers and providers, pharmaceutical research and development (R&D), prescription assistance programs, age-defying products, elder and hospice care, and assisted-living facilities.
- *Financial Services*: With $17 trillion to $20 trillion in wealth, boomer retirement will significantly affect financial planning, asset liquidation, risk aversion, estate and inheritance settlements, and an overall shift to income over capital growth.

- *Government*: Key considerations include the stress on Social Security and Medicare, lower income tax receipts, the burden on younger workers for payroll taxes, and entitlement program reform.
- *Society*: Boomers are forecasted to engage in more travel, hobbies and activities, remarriage and new relationships, home and online computing, and increased personal insurance, and to demand new and repackaged products and services to address their evolving needs.[21]

Running Out of Gas

As standards of living improve worldwide, the demand for energy continues to rise. Emerging economies such as China and India need energy to grow. Their demands are placing pressure on the world's supplies and driving up prices, as the laws of supply and demand would predict. By 2005, Chinese energy consumption had already moved beyond the U.S. Department of Energy's projections for 2010. State-supported energy companies in China, India, Russia, Saudi Arabia, Venezuela, and other countries will place additional competitive pressure on privately owned oil companies such as BP, Chevron, ExxonMobil, and Shell.[22]

Countries worldwide worry about relying too heavily on one source of supply for energy. The United States imports a large percentage of its oil from the Mideast and South America. Europeans get 25 percent of their natural gas from Russia's state-controlled gas utility OAO Gazprom. This gives foreign governments the power to use energy as a political tool. For example, in 2005 a disagreement over pricing caused Russia to stop supplying the Ukraine with gas. European gas supplies flow through Ukrainian pipelines, and Gazprom believed much of the gas was diverted and never made it to European customers, who reported shortages of as much as 50 percent. "Thirty percent of our gas comes from Russia at the moment. That should be increased," said Germany's Economy Minister Michael Glos. "But it can only be increased if we know that deliveries from the east are dependable."

Added U.S. State Department spokesman Sean McCormack, "Such an abrupt step creates insecurity in the energy sector in the region and raises serious questions about the use of energy to exert political pressure."[23]

Here are four myths about energy independence:

1. Energy independence will reduce or eliminate terrorism.

   In a 2007 speech, former CIA Director James Woolsey told American motorists: "The next time you pull into a gas station to fill your car with gas, bend down a little and take a glance in the side-door mirror. . . . What you will see is a contributor to terrorism against the United States." Woolsey is known as a conservative, but plenty of liberals also eagerly adopted the mantra that America's foreign oil purchasers are funding terrorism.

   But the hype doesn't match reality. Remember, the two largest suppliers of crude to the U.S. market are Canada and Mexico—neither exactly known as a belligerent terrorist haven.

   Terrorism is an ancient tactic that predates the oil era; it does not depend on petrodollars. And even small amounts of money can underwrite spectacular plots; as the 9/11 Commission Report noted, "The 9/11 plotters eventually spent somewhere between $400,000 and $500,000 to plan and conduct their attack."

2. A big push for alternative fuels will break our oil addiction.

   The new energy bill requires that the country produce 36 billion gallons of biofuels per year by 2022. That sounds like a lot, but the United States uses more than *320 billion* gallons of oil per year, of which nearly 200 billion gallons are imported.

   So biofuels alone cannot wean the United States off oil. Let's say the country converted all the soybeans grown by U.S. farmers into biodiesel; that would provide only about 1.5 percent of total annual U.S. oil needs. If the entire U.S. corn crop were devoted to producing ethanol, it would supply only about 6 percent of U.S. oil needs.

CONCEPT in action

© AP Images/Kiichiro Sato

From the president of the United States to presidents of big energy companies, national leaders are talking about alternative fuels. The push for energy independence, along with sky-high oil prices, has sparked renewed interest in homegrown fuels such as corn-based ethanol. The corn crop from which ethanol is produced is so abundant and renewable that some analysts predict cornstalks will replace imported foreign oil as a top fuel source. How might fluctuations in the price of oil and corn affect the viability of alternative fuels like ethanol?

Part 1: The Business Environment

What about cellulosic ethanol, the much-hyped biofuel that can be produced from grass, wood, and other plant sources? Its commercial viability is a bit like the tooth fairy: many believe in it, but no one ever actually sees it.

Even with heavy federal subsidies, it took 13 years before the corn-ethanol sector was able to produce 1 billion gallons of fuel per year. Two and a half decades elapsed before annual corn-ethanol production reached 5 billion gallons, as it did in 2006. But now Congress is demanding that the cellulosic-ethanol business produce many times that volume of fuel in just 15 years. It won't happen.

3. Energy independence will let America choke off the flow of money to countries working against the United States.

Fans of energy independence argue that if the United States stops buying foreign energy, it will deny funds to petro-states such as Iran and Hugo Chavez's Venezuela. But the world marketplace doesn't work like that. Oil is a *global* commodity. Its price is set globally, not locally. Oil buyers are always seeking the lowest-cost supplier. So any Iranian crude being loaded at an Iranian port that doesn't get purchased by a refinery in Corpus Christi or Houston will instead wind up in Singapore or Shanghai.

4. Energy independence will mean a more secure U.S. energy supply.

Think back to 2005: After hurricanes ravaged the Gulf Coast, chewing up refineries as they went, several southeastern U.S. cities were hit with gasoline shortages. Thankfully, they were short-lived. The reason? Imported gasoline, from refineries in Venezuela, the Netherlands, and elsewhere.

Throughout the first nine months of 2005, the United States imported about 1 million barrels of gasoline per day. By mid-October 2005, just six weeks after Hurricane Katrina, those imports soared to 1.5 million barrels per day.

So we're woven in with the rest of the world—and going to stay that way. Today, in addition to gasoline imports, the United States is buying crude oil from Angola, jet fuel from South Korea, natural gas from Trinidad, coal from Colombia, and uranium from Australia. Those imports show that the global energy market is just that: *global*. Anyone who argues that the United States will be more secure by going it alone on energy hasn't done the homework.[24]

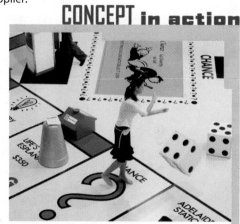

CONCEPT in action

© AP Images/Rick Rycroft

Fans of Parker Brother's *Monopoly* are cheering a new strategic partnership between toymaker Hasbro, Inc. and Universal Studios. The six-year deal between the No. 2 toymaker and the American motion-picture giant is set to entertain moviegoers with multiple big-screen films, including a full-length action-comedy featuring the world's most popular board game, directed by filmmaking legend Ridley Scott. How does each company benefit from this strategic alliance?

Meeting Competitive Challenges

Companies are turning to many different strategies to remain competitive in the global marketplace. One of the most important is **relationship management**, which involves building, maintaining, and enhancing interactions with customers and other parties to develop long-term satisfaction through mutually beneficial partnerships. Relationship management includes both supply chain management, which builds strong bonds with suppliers, and relationship marketing, which focuses on customers. (We'll discuss supply chain management in greater detail in Chapter 10 and return to relationship marketing in Chapter 11.) In general, the longer a customer stays with a company, the more that customer is worth. Long-term customers buy more, take less of a company's time, are less sensitive to price, and bring in new customers. Best of all, they require no acquisition or start-up costs. Good long-standing customers are worth so much that in some industries, reducing customer defections by as little as five points—from, say, 15 percent to 10 percent per year—can double profits.

Another important way companies stay competitive is through **strategic alliances** (also called strategic partnerships). The trend toward forming these cooperative agreements between business firms is accelerating rapidly, particularly among high-tech firms. These companies have realized that strategic partnerships are more than just important—they are critical. Strategic alliances can take many forms. Some companies enter into strategic alliances with their suppliers, who take over much of their actual production and manufacturing. Nike, the largest producer of athletic footwear in the world, does not manufacture a single shoe. Gallo, the largest wine company on earth, does not grow a single grape.

relationship management
The practice of building, maintaining, and enhancing interactions with customers and other parties to develop long-term satisfaction through mutually beneficial partnerships.

strategic alliance
A cooperative agreement between business firms; sometimes called a strategic partnership.

What steps can companies take to benefit from the aging of its workers and to effectively manage a multigenerational workforce?

Why is the increasing demand for energy worldwide a cause for concern?

Describe several strategies that companies can use to remain competitive in the global economy.

Others with complementary strengths team up. For example, computer manufacturer Hewlett-Packard (H-P) and retail giant Wal-Mart partnered to improve sales at both. H-P provided Wal-Mart with low-cost electronic products. The two companies worked together to develop special products for Wal-Mart, such as desktop and notebook computers for about $400, digital cameras for $100, and all-in-one printers for $50. H-P was eager to satisfy Wal-Mart, one of its biggest retail partners. For Wal-Mart, H-P's products would lure customers, who might otherwise shop for electronics at Best Buy and Circuit City, into Wal-Mart where they could spend more of their holiday gift dollars.[25]

Summary

Summary of Learning Goals

1 How do businesses and not-for-profit organizations help create our standard of living?

Businesses attempt to earn a profit by providing goods and services desired by their customers. Not-for-profit organizations, though not striving for a profit, still deliver many needed services for our society. Our standard of living is measured by the output of goods and services. Thus, businesses and not-for-profit organizations help create our standard of living. Our quality of life is not simply the amount of goods and services available for consumers but rather the society's general level of happiness.

Economists refer to the building blocks of a business as the factors of production. To produce anything, one must have natural resources, labor, capital, and entrepreneurship to assemble the resources and manage the business. Today's competitive business environment is based on knowledge and learning. The companies that will succeed in this new era will be those that learn fast, use knowledge efficiently, and develop new insights.

2 What are the sectors of the business environment, and how do changes in them influence business decisions?

The external business environment consists of economic, political and legal, demographic, social, competitive, global, and technological sectors. Managers must understand how the environment is changing and the impact of those changes on the business. When economic activity is strong, unemployment rates are low and income levels rise. The political environment is shaped by the amount of government intervention in business affairs, the types of laws it passes to regulate both domestic and foreign businesses, and the general political stability of a government. Demographics, or the study of people's vital statistics, are at the heart of many business decisions. Businesses today must deal with the unique shopping preferences of different generations, each of which requires different marketing approaches and different goods and services. The population is becoming increasingly diverse: by 2010 minorities will represent 35 percent of the total U.S. population. Minorities' buying power has increased significantly as well, and companies are developing products and marketing campaigns that target different ethnic groups. Social factors—our attitudes, values, and lifestyles—influence what, how, where, and when people purchase products. They are difficult to predict, define, and measure because they can be very subjective. They also change as people move through different life stages.

3 What are the primary features of the world's economic systems, and how are the three sectors of the U.S. economy linked?

Economics is the study of how individuals, businesses, and governments use scarce resources to produce and distribute goods and services. Today there is a global trend toward capitalism. Capitalism, also known as the private enterprise system, is based on marketplace competition and private ownership of the factors of production. Competition leads to more diverse goods and services, keeps prices stable, and pushes businesses to become more efficient.

In a communist economy, the government owns virtually all resources, and economic decision making is done by central government planning. Governments have generally moved away from communism because it is inefficient and delivers a low standard of living. Socialism is another centralized economic system in which the basic industries are owned by the government or by the private sector under strong government control. Other industries may be privately owned. The state is also somewhat influential in determining the goals of business, the prices and selection of products, and the rights of workers. Most national economies today are a mix of socialism and capitalism.

The two major areas in economics are macroeconomics, the study of the economy as a whole, and microeconomics, the study of households and firms. The individual, business, and government sectors of the economy are linked by a series of two-way flows. The government provides public goods and services to the other two sectors and receives income in the form of taxes. Changes in one flow affect the other sectors.

A nation's economy is growing when the level of business activity, as measured by gross domestic product (GDP), is rising. GDP is the total value of all goods and services produced in a year. The goal of full employment is to have a job for all who can and want to work. How well a nation is meeting its employment goals is measured by the unemployment rate. There are four types of unemployment: frictional, structural, cyclical, and seasonal. With price stability, the overall prices of goods and services are not moving very much either up or down. Inflation is the general upward movement of prices. When prices rise, purchasing power falls. The rate of inflation is measured by changes in the consumer price index (CPI) and the producer price index (PPI). There are two main causes of inflation. If the demand for goods and services exceeds the supply, prices will rise. This is called demand-pull inflation. With cost-push inflation, higher production costs, such as expenses for materials and wages, increase the final prices of goods and services.

4 How do economic growth, full employment, price stability, and inflation indicate a nation's economic health?

Monetary policy refers to actions by the Federal Reserve System to control the money supply. When the Fed restricts the money supply, interest rates rise, the inflation rate drops, and economic growth slows. By expanding the money supply, the Fed stimulates economic growth. The government also uses fiscal policy—changes in levels of taxation and spending—to control the economy. Reducing taxes or increasing spending stimulates the economy; raising taxes or decreasing spending does the opposite. When the government spends more than it receives in tax revenues, it must borrow to finance the deficit. Some economists favor deficit spending as a way to stimulate the economy; others worry about our high level of national debt.

5 How does the government use monetary policy and fiscal policy to achieve its macroeconomic goals?

Demand is the quantity of a good or service that people will buy at a given price. Supply is the quantity of a good or service that firms will make available at a given price. When the price increases, the quantity demanded falls but the quantity supplied rises. A price decrease leads to increased demand but a lower supply. At the point where the quantity demanded equals the quantity supplied, demand and supply are in balance. This equilibrium point is achieved by market adjustments of quantity and price.

6 What are the basic microeconomic concepts of demand and supply, and how do they establish prices?

Market structure is the number of suppliers in a market. Perfect competition is characterized by a large number of buyers and sellers, very similar products, good market information for both buyers and sellers, and ease of entry and exit into the market. In a pure monopoly, there is a single seller in a market. In monopolistic competition, many firms sell close substitutes in a market that is fairly easy to enter. In an oligopoly, a few firms produce most or all of the industry's output. An oligopoly is also difficult to enter and what one firm does will influence others.

7 What are the four types of market structure?

To remain competitive, businesses must identify and respond to trends in the various sectors of the business environment. As the population ages, large numbers of baby boomers are approaching retirement age. Companies must plan for this mass exodus of employees and find ways to retain the vast amounts of knowledge they represent. Many older workers are choosing to continue working after traditional retirement age, creating a four-generation workforce.

8 Which trends are reshaping the business, micro-, and macroeconomic environments and competitive arena?

Worldwide demand for energy, especially from China and India, is challenging oil companies to increase supplies. U.S. vulnerability to disruptions in energy supply became painfully apparent when Katrina put Gulf Coast refineries and offshore drilling rigs out of commission. Companies are using relationship management and strategic alliances to compete effectively in the global economy.

Key Terms

barriers to entry 24	knowledge workers 6
business 4	macroeconomics 12
business cycles 14	market structure 24
capital 5	microeconomics 12
capitalism 11	mixed economies 12
circular flow 12	monetary policy 17
communism 11	monopolistic competition 25
consumer price index (CPI) 17	national debt 19
contractionary policy 18	not-for-profit organization 5
cost-push inflation 17	oligopoly 25
costs 4	perfect (pure) competition 24
crowding out 18	producer price index (PPI) 17
cyclical unemployment 16	productivity 9
demand 20	profit 4
demand curve 20	purchasing power 16
demand-pull inflation 16	pure monopoly 24
demography 8	quality of life 4
economic growth 14	recession 14
economic system 9	relationship management 29
economics 9	revenue 4
entrepreneurs 5	risk 4
equilibrium 22	savings bonds 20
expansionary policy 18	seasonal unemployment 16
factors of production 5	services 4
federal budget deficit 19	socialism 11
Federal Reserve System (the Fed) 17	standard of living 4
fiscal policy 18	strategic alliance 29
frictional unemployment 15	structural unemployment 16
full employment 14	supply 21
goods 4	supply curve 21
gross domestic product (GDP) 14	technology 9
inflation 16	unemployment rate 15
knowledge 6	

Preparing for Tomorrow's Workplace: SCANS

1. Select a not-for-profit organization whose mission interests you. What are the organization's objectives? What resources does it need to achieve those goals? Select a for-profit business that provides a similar service and compare the differences between the two organizations. How does each use the factors of production? (**Resources, Information, Systems**)

2. **Team Activity** Form seven teams. Each team is responsible for one of the sectors of the external business environment discussed in the chapter (economic, political/legal, demographic, social, competitive, global, and technological). Your boss, the company president, has asked each team to report on the changes in that area of the external environment and how they will affect the firm over the next five years. The firm is the Boeing Company. Each team should use the library, Internet, and other data sources to make its projections. Each team member should examine at least one data source. The team should then pool the data and prepare its response. A spokesperson for each team should present the findings to the class. (**Interpersonal, Resources, Information**)

3. If a friend claimed, "Economics is all theory and not very practical," how might you counter this claim? Share your rationale with the class. (**Interpersonal, Information**)

4. **Team Activity** Create two teams of four people each. Have one side choose a communist economy and the other capitalism. Debate the proposition that "capitalism/a command economy is good for developing nations." (**Interpersonal, Information**)

5. What are the latest actions the federal government has taken to manage the economy? Has it used monetary policy or fiscal policy to achieve its macroeconomic goals? Summarize your findings. Choose one of the following industries and discuss how the government's actions will affect that industry: airlines, automobile manufacturers, banking, biotechnology, chemical manufacturing, home building, oil and gas, publishing, retail stores, telecommunication equipment, and telecommunication services. (**Information, Systems**)

6. As a manufacturer of in-line roller skates, you are questioning your pricing policies. You note that over the past five years, the CPI increased an average of 3 percent per year, but the price of a pair of skates increased an average of 8 percent per year for the first three years and 2 percent per year for the next two years. What does this information tell you about demand, supply, and other factors influencing the market for these skates? (**Resources, Information**)

Ethics Activity

As top executives at Enron, Kenneth Lay (who died in July 2006) and Jeffrey Skilling often were in the public eye, discussing the energy company's dynamic growth and climbing profits. Underneath the surface, however, the company was engaging in multiple schemes to manipulate financial data and inflate profits. In December 2001, Enron filed bankruptcy, sending shock waves through corporate America. Among the big losers were the company's employees, whose jobs and retirement savings disappeared, and investors in the company's stock, which became worthless. Many Enron executives, including Andrew Fastow, Enron's former chief financial officer, pleaded guilty to conspiracy and other charges and were sentenced to prison terms.

The trial of Kenneth Lay, Enron's former chief executive, began in Houston in January 2006. He was charged with multiple counts of fraud and conspiracy to deceive investors and employees about Enron's financial troubles. Lay continued to maintain that he was unaware of the crimes and placed major blame on Fastow, saying he could not be expected to know everything that was happening at Enron. In late May 2006, a jury determined that Lay was guilty of all Enron-related charges in two trials. Skilling was found guilty on 19 of 28 counts. Before their scheduled sentencing, Kenneth Lay died at age 64 on July 5, 2006.

Using a Web search tool, locate articles about this topic and then write responses to the following questions. Be sure to support your arguments and cite your sources.

ETHICAL DILEMMA: Do you agree with the verdict in the Lay and Skilling cases, and on what do you base your opinion? Was ignorance a valid defense for Kenneth Lay? How much can top executives be expected to know about the details of their companies' operations?

Sources: Alexei Barrionuevo, "Two Enron Chiefs Are Convicted in Fraud and Conspiracy Trial," *New York Times,* May 26, 2006, **http://www.nytimes.com**; Alexei Barrionuevo, "Witness Says Enron Hid Huge Loss From Investors," *New York Times,* February 3, 2006, p. C3(L); Greg Burns, "Enron Case Big Test of the 'Idiot Defense': Ex-Chief Vows to Say He Was Blind to Crimes," *Chicago Tribune,* January 2, 2006, p. 1; Anthony Bianco, "Ken Lay's Audacious Ignorance," *Business Week,* February 6, 2006, p. 58; Kate Murphy, "Ken Lay's Very Public Appeal," *Business Week Online,* December 15, 2005, **http://www.businessweek.com.**

Working the Net

1. The Bureau of Labor Statistics compiles demographic data. Visit its site, **http://www.bls.gov/bls/demographics.htm,** and describe the different types of information it provides. What kinds of changes are likely to occur in the United States over the next 25 years? Click on Time Use and read about the American Time Use Survey, which shows how people spend their time. What trends can you identify?

2. Go to either the Red Herring (**http://www.redherring.com**) or Wired (**http://www.wired.com**) site and research technology trends. Compile a list of three trends that sound most promising to you and describe them briefly. How will they affect businesses? What impact, if any, will they have on you personally?

3. Use the Bureau of Labor Statistics site, **http://stat.bls.gov,** to determine the current trends in GDP growth, unemployment, and inflation. What do these trends tell you about the level of business activity and the business cycle? If you owned a personnel agency, how would this information affect your decision making?

4. What's the latest economic news? Go to the ABC News site's Business section (**http://abcnews .go.com/business/**). Read the various articles. Prepare a summary of what you learned and use it to discuss where you think the economy is headed for in the next 6 to 12 months.

5. How would you spend the national budget if you were president? Here's your chance to find out how your ideas would affect the federal budget. The National Budget Simulator, at **http://www.econedlink.org/lessons/index.cfm?lesson=EM306**, lets you see how government officials make trade-offs when they prepare the federal budget. Experiment with your own budget ideas at the site. What are the effects of your decisions?

Creative Thinking Case

Nordstrom Plays a New Tune

Long known for traditional quality clothing and unsurpassed customer service, upscale department store chain Nordstrom is "going interactive" as a way to reach younger customer demographics. "The goal," says Linda Finn, executive vice president for marketing at Nordstrom, "is to build the relationship with our multi-channel shopper, primarily women in their 30's and 40's who buy at the Nordstrom Web site, **http://www.nordstrom.com**, as well as at the company's stores."

Nordstrom sent e-mail messages to 2.5 million customers, inviting them to download Nordstrom Silverscreen software from the Internet. Developed by Nordstrom's advertising agency Fallon Worldwide, the media player offers customers a branded entertainment channel, with video clips of popular music groups, a "mixing room" to create a personalized remix of the song with different fashions, merchandise previews, and, of course, opportunities to shop online. Customers who do not wish to download the software can enjoy a less elaborate version at a separate Silverscreen Web site. Those who download the software will receive messages alerting them to new content each month.

"We've been talking to some of Nordstrom's online users, who are very, very important customers, and they talk about how when they go online sometimes they shop and sometimes they look for fashion inspiration," said Rob White, president of Fallon.

"This [campaign] isn't going to be judged on whether we sell a lot of tops over the Web for the holiday season," he said. "It will be judged on long-term feedback and bringing more people into Nordstrom stores, as well as [to] the Web site. And there is always the hope that Nordstrom customers will invite their friends and family to download the Silverscreen software too."

What began as a single downtown Seattle shoe store in 1901 has grown into a nationwide fashion specialty chain with renowned services, generous size ranges, and a selection of the finest apparel, shoes, and accessories for the entire family. And despite tapping into today's trends, Nordstrom never loses sight of its original philosophy, which has remained unchanged since its establishment by John W. Nordstrom more than 100 years ago: offer customers the best possible service, selection, quality, and value.

Critical Thinking Questions

- Why did Nordstrom take the dramatic step of designing a branded entertainment channel? What risks are there to this strategy?
- What impact is Nordstrom's new media player likely to have on customer demographics and sales?
- What unique philosophy and features have helped Nordstrom survive and thrive for more than 100 years in the notoriously difficult world of department store retailing?

Sources: Stuart Elliott, "Eager Retailers Can't Wait for Thanksgiving; They're Starting Christmas Now," *New York Times,* November 12, 2005, **http://www.nytimes.com**; Nordstrom corporate Web site, **http://www.nordstrom.com** (August 11, 2006); Nordstrom Silverscreen Web site, **http://www.nordstromsilverscreen.com** (August 12, 2006); John Vomhof Jr., "Fallon Takes Nordstrom to the Silverscreen," *Minneapolis/St. Paul Business Journal,* November 3, 2005, **http://www.bizjournals.com/twincities**.

Exploring Business Careers

Karen Beal
Urban Gateways

Accounting for more than one-fourth of all economic activity in the United States, not-for-profits are an undeniable force in the business world, even though their focus on goals other than profit falls outside the traditional model of a for-profit business. But it is this shift away from a focus on profit that allows them to pursue missions of social improvement. To be truly effective in a not-for-profit organization, a person must share the organization's vision. Karen Beal, who has worked with several not-for-profit organizations as a volunteer, board member, even executive director, recognizes this: "I cannot stress enough the importance of the mission. You have to be in it for the mission—that has to be your reason for choosing this organization and not the one just down the block. Without that connection, there cannot be success."

Beal often begins her relationship with a not-for-profit as a volunteer because it allows her to get a feel for an organization without the level of commitment required by board membership. "Being a volunteer is an excellent way to determine firsthand if you espouse the mission of an organization. By volunteering for a committee or two, I am able to determine whether the organization and I are a good fit. This may lead to a more involved commitment, and frequently does, but that spark of connection needs to exist first."

Urban Gateways is one organization where she felt that spark immediately. Beal began working on a planning committee for a gala fund-raising event, and quickly recognized that the organization was something special. Soon, the organization asked her to join its board, and she readily agreed. "When you are engaged with an organization for the mission, you can sell it better, you can talk about it, make it come to fruition. With Urban Gateways, I felt that way. I loved Urban Gateways because it was created by the community to fulfill a need they saw."

Indeed, Urban Gateways, like many not-for-profits, grew out of the community it serves. Its mission, posted clearly on their Web site **http://www.urbangateways.org,** is simply: "To use art to educate and change children's lives." Created in 1961 as a response to inequities in arts education, especially in inner-city schools, Urban Gateways strove to expose children to the arts in an effort to awaken their potential to recognize the beauty and power of both creating and experiencing the arts. This awareness of the surrounding social trends and forces is important to any organization's success, whether it is for-profit or not. For organizations such as Urban Gateways, however, Beal feels it is even more critical. "You need to be intimately aware of the community you serve—much as in the for-profit world, you seek to please your shareholders. In a not-for-profit, community members are your shareholders, and they pay not with money but with their happiness, their opportunities to succeed, their time and commitment, and often their quality of life. In the end, their stake in what you are doing is so incredibly high that to disregard them would be a huge disservice both to them and to the organization." Urban Gateways actively engages the community in every level of their organization, from volunteer to board, and in every step of the process, from planning to implementation, to ensure they are keenly aware of their community's needs.

The not-for-profit world may not be for everyone, but if its growth within the overall economy is any indication, it does appeal to many. Undoubtedly some of you will choose that path. Beal's advice for you? "Recognize your responsibility to make things happen. Want to impact change. Learn from your work and share and exchange ideas with others. Always see the full spectrum to mobilize a wide range of resources and expertise to connect to new relationships as you build your organization. As an ambassador for your organization, love it enough to talk about it all of the time. Live the mission."

This chapter provided the basic structures upon which the business world is built: how it is organized, what outside forces influence it, and where it is heading. This chapter also explored the world's economies and government's role in shaping economic activity. Each day in America thousands of new businesses are born. Only a rare few will become the next Microsoft, Google, or eBay. Unfortunately, many others will never see their first anniversary. The survivors are those that understand that change is the one constant in the business environment. Those organizations pay attention to the business environment in which they operate and the trends that affect all businesses and then successfully adapt to those trends. Throughout this book, we will meet many businesses, both large and small, profit and not-for-profit, that prosper because they track trends and use them to identify potential opportunities. This ability to manage change is a critical factor in separating the success stories from the tales of business failure.

We began our study of business by introducing you to the primary functions of a business, the relationship between risk and profits, and the importance of not-for-profit organizations. We also examined the major components of the business environment and how changing demographic, social, political and legal, and competitive factors affect all business organizations. This chapter explored how economies provide jobs for workers and also compete with other businesses to create and deliver products to consumers. You also learned how governments attempt to influence economic activity through policies such as lowering or raising taxes. We also discussed how supply and demand determine prices for goods and services. Finally, we concluded by examining key trends in the business environment, economic systems, and competition.

Learning Goals

After reading this chapter, you should be able to answer these questions:

1 What philosophies and concepts shape personal ethical standards?

2 How can organizations encourage ethical business behavior?

3 What is social responsibility?

4 How do businesses meet their social responsibilities to various stakeholders?

5 What are the trends in ethics and social responsibility?

Appendix: Understanding the Legal and Tax Environment

6 How does the legal system govern business transactions and settle business disputes?

7 What are the required elements of a valid contract; and what are the key types of business law?

8 What are the most common taxes paid by businesses?

CHAPTER 2
Making Ethical Decisions and Managing a Socially Responsible Business

The Emperor's Club /Corbis

"The Real World"

Ethical decision making often plays a part in how business is conducted, and in fact, we all make a variety of ethical decisions in our daily lives. For instance, when each of us goes to the store, we make a decision as to whether or not we purchase the item we wish to obtain or to simply steal that item. I'm sure most people would agree that stealing the item is morally wrong and is, in fact, against the law; however, depending on the circumstances, there are some people who may actually come down on the side of the shoplifter. We could say similar things about a variety of other morally questionable activities such as illicit music downloading, insider trading, kickbacks and bribes, as well as lying and cheating. The movie *The Emperor's Club* explores these latter two activities from two perspectives.

William Hundert spent much of his life teaching at a private school for boys where he instructed his students to live lives of virtue and honor. One such student, Sedgewick Bell, proved to be a challenge that shook even his own seemingly unshakeable integrity. In order to help Sedgewick, he bent a grade on his behalf, a move that haunted him after he discovered that Sedgewick had in fact cheated his way into Mr. Hundert's good graces. Years later, after William has retired and the adult Sedgewick has initiated his own political campaign, the two are reunited at a retirement party the latter has set up on William's behalf, inviting all his former classmates to attend. During the highlight of the reunion, a contest pitting the former students against one another and their recollection of historical facts and figures, William discovers that Sedgewick, true to form, still cheats.

He then confronts Sedgewick in a restroom where he chastises the man for failing to live a life of virtue and ethics and blames himself for failing him as a teacher. Sedgewick, on the other hand, takes a very Machiavellian approach to his own sense of ethics. "I live in the real world," he states, "where people do what they need to do to get what they want; and if it's lying and it's cheating, then so be it." Sedgewick then claims that he will do what it takes to win his election and that he will worry about his contribution later. The scene is essentially a debate between a deontology and utilitarianism.

The utilitarian perspective basically looks at the consequences of an action, gauges its effect on the majority of people, and then determines whether the action is morally right or wrong. For instance, suppose it takes a bribe to finalize a business deal that will ultimately result in thousands of new jobs in a depressed economy. The utilitarian perspective would hold that the thousands of jobs are in fact indicative of the bribe's moral rightness. The deontological perspective is one that argues that the individual should follow the rules and obligations put forth by the society. Purveyors of this perspective will look at the action itself as morally wrong, since bribery is in fact illegal in many countries including the United States.

This chapter focuses on how businesses are involved in ethical and socially responsible decision making, examining the various responsibilities businesses have to their various stakeholders as well as addressing the influence organizations and firms have on the ethical conduct of its employees. Like Sedgewick, you may be faced with a variety of ethical issues during your careers, and as a result of the decisions you make, you may find yourself looking in the mirror and gauging whether or not you've acted in a moral fashion. This chapter is designed in such a way as to assist you on that path.

Discussion Questions

- William Hundert feels an overwhelming sense of responsibility to his stakeholders. Who are his stakeholders, and how is he responsible to them?
- Researchers at Brigham Young University have identified a number of categories of unethical business activities. What categories have both William Hundert and Sedgewick Bell violated and how?
- Suppose Sedgewick wins the election and eventually rides that election to the White House where he enacts a treaty that brings about peace in the Middle East. Put yourself in Mr. Hundert's shoes and imagine how you would feel then. What would your perspective of Sedgewick be then and why?

Understanding Business Ethics

Every day, managers and business owners make business decisions based on what they believe to be right and wrong. Through their actions, they demonstrate to their employees what is and is not acceptable behavior and shape the moral standard of the organization. **Ethics** is a set of moral standards for judging whether something is right or wrong. As you will see in this chapter, personal and professional ethics are important cornerstones of an organization that shape its ultimate contributions to society. First, let's consider how individual business ethics are formed.

The first step in understanding business ethics is learning to recognize an **ethical issue**. An ethical issue is a situation where someone must choose between a set of actions that may be ethical or unethical. Many times ethical issues are very clear-cut. Recently, United Kingdom defense manufacturer, BAE Systems, launched an independent review of its business ethics policies following reports that the firm made illegal payments to secure an arms deal from Saudi Arabia.[1] Few people would call that ethical behavior. But consider the actions of the stranded, hungry people in New Orleans who lost everything in the aftermath of Hurricane Katrina. They broke into flooded stores, taking food and bottled water without paying for them. Was this unethical behavior? Or what about the small Texas plastics manufacturer that employed more than 100 people and specialized in the Latin American market? The president was distraught because he knew the firm would be bankrupt by the end of the year if it didn't receive more contracts. He knew that he was losing business because he refused to pay bribes. Bribes were part of the culture in his major markets. Closing the firm would put many people out of work. Should he start paying bribes in order to stay in business? Would this be unethical? Let's look at the next section to obtain some guidance on recognizing unethical situations.

Recognizing Unethical Business Activities

Researchers from Brigham Young University tell us that all unethical business activities will fall into one of the following categories:

1. *Taking things that don't belong to you*. The unauthorized use of someone else's property or taking property under false pretenses is taking something that does not belong to you. Even the smallest offense, such as using the postage meter at your office for mailing personal letters or exaggerating your travel expenses, belongs in this category of ethical violations.

2. *Saying things you know are not true*. Often, when trying for a promotion and advancement, fellow employees discredit their coworkers. Falsely assigning blame or inaccurately reporting conversations is lying. Although "This is the way the game is played around here" is a common justification, saying things that are untrue is an ethical violation.

   In 2007, some 25 percent of nearly 2,000 U.S. employees said that they had observed their colleagues or their companies lying to customers, suppliers, workers, or the public, up from 19 percent in 2005. The industries in which people are most likely to bend the truth are hospitality and food (with 34 percent of employees observing falsehoods), arts, entertainment, and recreation (also 34 percent), and wholesalers (32 percent).[2]

3. *Giving or allowing false impressions*. The salesperson who permits a potential customer to believe that cardboard boxes will hold the customer's tomatoes for long-distance shipping when the salesperson knows the boxes are not strong enough has given a false impression. A car dealer who fails to disclose that a car has been in an accident is misleading potential customers.

4. *Buying influence or engaging in a conflict of interest*. A conflict of interest occurs when the official responsibilities of an employee or government official are influenced by the potential for personal gain. Suppose a company awards a construction contract to a firm owned by the father of the state attorney general while the state attorney general's office is investigating that company. If this construction award has the potential to shape the outcome of the investigation, a conflict of interest has occurred.

ethics
A set of moral standards for judging whether something is right or wrong.

ethical issue
A situation where a person must choose between a set of actions that may be ethical or unethical.

CONCEPT in action

© AP Images/Pablo Martinez Monsivais

Illegal steroid use has become a public relations nightmare for Major League Baseball. Home run kings Barry Bonds and Mark McGwire disappointed fans by their murky association with performance-enhancing drugs, and congressional investigations have implicated other top stars, including Andy Pettitte and seven-time Cy Young award winner Roger Clemens. Baseball's doping scandal raises troubling ethics questions about the fairness of the sport, the safety of players, and the impact on young fans. What can league officials do to restore the integrity of the game?

5. *Hiding or divulging information.* Failing to disclose the results of medical studies that indicate your firm's new drug has significant side effects is the ethical violation of hiding information that the product could be harmful to purchasers. Taking your firm's product development or trade secrets to a new place of employment constitutes the ethical violation of divulging proprietary information.

6. *Taking unfair advantage.* Many current consumer protection laws were passed because so many businesses took unfair advantage of people who were not educated or were unable to discern the nuances of complex contracts. Credit disclosure requirements, truth-in-lending provisions, and new regulations on auto leasing all resulted because businesses misled consumers who could not easily follow the jargon of long, complex agreements.

7. *Committing improper personal behavior.* Although the ethical aspects of an employee's right to privacy are still debated, it has become increasingly clear that personal conduct outside the job can influence performance and company reputation. Thus, a company driver must abstain from substance abuse because of safety issues. Even the traditional company Christmas party and picnic have come under scrutiny due to the possibility that employees at and following these events might harm others through alcohol-related accidents.

8. *Abusing another person.* Suppose a manager sexually harasses an employee or subjects employees to humiliating corrections in the presence of customers. In some cases, laws protect employees. Many situations, however, are simply interpersonal abuse that constitutes an ethical violation.

9. *Permitting organizational abuse.* Many U.S. firms with operations overseas, such as Levi Strauss, The Gap, and Esprit, have faced issues of organizational abuse. The unfair treatment of workers in international operations appears in the form of child labor, demeaning wages, and excessive work hours. Although a business cannot change the culture of another country, it can perpetuate—or stop—abuse through its operations there.

10. *Violating rules.* Many organizations use rules and processes to maintain internal controls or respect the authority of managers. Although these rules may seem burdensome to employees trying to serve customers, a violation may be considered an unethical act.

11. *Condoning unethical actions.* What if you witnessed a fellow employee embezzling company funds by forging her signature on a check that was to be voided? Would you report the violation? A winking tolerance of others' unethical behavior is itself unethical.[3]

After recognizing that a situation is unethical, the next question is what do you do? The action that a person takes is partially based on their ethical philosophy. The environment in which we live and work also plays a role in our behavior. This section describes personal philosophies and legal factors that influence the choices we make when confronting an ethical dilemma.

Justice—The Question of Fairness

Another factor influencing individual business ethics is **justice**, or what is fair according to prevailing standards of society. We all expect life to be reasonably fair. You expect your exams to be fair, the grading to be fair, and your wages to be fair, based on the type of work being done.

Today, we take justice to mean an equitable distribution of the burdens and rewards that society has to offer. The distributive process varies from society to society. Those in a democratic society believe in the "equal pay for equal work" doctrine, in which individuals are rewarded based on the value the free market places on their services. Because the market places different values on different occupations, the rewards, such as wages, are not necessarily equal. Nevertheless, many regard the rewards as just. A politician who argued that a supermarket clerk should receive the same pay as a physician, for example, would not receive many votes from the American people. At the other extreme, communist theorists have argued that justice would be served by a society in which burdens and rewards were distributed to individuals according to their abilities and their needs, respectively.

Utilitarianism—Seeking the Best for the Majority

One of the philosophies that may influence choices between right and wrong is **utilitarianism**, which focuses on the consequences of an action taken by a person or organization. The notion that "people should act so as to generate the greatest good for the greatest number" is derived from utilitarianism. When an action affects the majority adversely, it is morally wrong. One problem with this philosophy is that it is nearly impossible to accurately determine how a decision will affect a large number of people.

Another problem is that utilitarianism always involves both winners and losers. If sales are slowing and a manager decides to fire 5 people rather than putting everyone on a 30-hour workweek, the 20 people who keep their full-time jobs are winners, but the other 5 are losers.

A final criticism of utilitarianism is that some "costs," although small relative to the potential good, are so negative that some segments of society find them unacceptable. Reportedly, the backs of up to 3,000 animals a year are deliberately broken so that scientists can conduct spinal cord research that could someday lead to a cure for spinal cord injuries. To a number of people, however, the "costs" are simply too horrible for this type of research to continue.

Following Our Obligations and Duties

The philosophy that says people should meet their obligations and duties when analyzing an ethical dilemma is called **deontology**. This means that a person will follow his or her obligations to another individual or society because upholding one's duty is what is considered ethically correct. For instance, people who follow this philosophy will always keep their promises to a friend and will follow the law. They will produce very consistent decisions, because they will be based on the individual's set duties. Note that this theory is not necessarily concerned with the welfare of others. Say, for example, a serviceman for Orkin Pest Control has decided that it's his ethical duty (and very practical!) to always be on time to meetings with home owners. Today he is running late. How is he supposed to drive? Is the serviceman supposed to speed, breaking his duty to society to uphold the law, or is he supposed to arrive at the client's home late, breaking his duty to be on time? This scenario of conflicting obligations does not lead us to a clear ethically correct resolution, nor does it protect the welfare of others from the serviceman's decision.

deontology
The philosophy that says people should meet their obligations and duties when analyzing an ethical dilemma.

Individual Rights

In our society, individuals and groups have certain rights that exist under certain conditions regardless of any external circumstances. These rights serve as guides when making individual ethical decisions. The term human rights implies that certain rights—to life, to freedom, to the pursuit of happiness—are conveyed at birth and cannot be arbitrarily taken away. Denying the rights of an individual or group is considered to be unethical and illegal in most, though not all, parts of the world. Certain rights are guaranteed by the government and its laws, and these are considered legal rights. The U.S. Constitution and its amendments, as well as state and federal statutes, define the rights of American citizens. Those rights can be disregarded only in extreme circumstances, such as during wartime. Legal rights include the freedom of religion, speech, and assembly; protection from improper arrest and searches and seizures; and proper access to counsel, confrontation of witnesses, and cross-examination in criminal prosecutions. Also held to be fundamental is the right to privacy in many matters. Legal rights are to be applied without regard to race, color, creed, gender, or ability.

CONCEPT check

How are individuals' business ethics formed?

What is utilitarianism?

How can you recognize unethical activities?

How Organizations Influence Ethical Conduct

People choose between right and wrong based on their personal code of ethics. They are also influenced by the ethical environment created by their employers. Consider the following newspaper headlines:

2 How can organizations encourage ethical business behavior?

- James Beard Foundation president forced to resign after spending hundreds of thousands of dollars on excessive salaries and meals.
- Dennis Kozlowski, former top executive of Tyco, International, convicted of grand larceny, conspiracy, securities fraud, and falsifying business records and sentenced to 25 years in prison.
- Bernie Ebbers, ex-WorldCom chief executive, also sentenced to 25 years in prison for his role in corporate fraud.
- Ex-Adelphia CEO, John Rigas, sentenced to 15 years for looting the company and cheating investors.[4]

As these actual headlines illustrate, poor business ethics can create a very negative image for a company, can be expensive for the firm and/or the executives involved, and can result in bankruptcy and jail time for the offenders. Organizations can reduce the potential for these types of liability claims by educating their employees about ethical standards, by leading through example, and through various informal and formal programs.

CONCEPT in action

While the unethical conduct of a few nefarious individuals has tarnished the reputation of business in recent years, some prominent corporate chiefs are restoring confidence in America's corporations. Apple's Steve Jobs and Google's Eric Schmidt forgo annual salaries, opting instead to receive stock awards aligned with shareholder interests and company performance. Angelo Mozilo of Countrywide Financial turned down a $37.5 million severance package when the mortgage company hit financial rock bottom. How else might individuals demonstrate ethical leadership?

Leading by Example

Employees often follow the examples set by their managers. That is, leaders and managers establish patterns of behavior that determine what is and isn't acceptable within the organization. While Ben Cohen was president of Ben & Jerry's ice cream, he followed a policy that no one could earn a salary more than seven times the lowest-paid worker. He wanted all employees to feel that they were equal. At the time he resigned, company sales were $140 million and the lowest-paid worker earned $19,000 per year. Ben Cohen's salary was $133,000 based on the "seven times" rule. A typical top executive of a $140 million company might have earned 10 times Cohen's salary. Ben Cohen's actions helped shape the ethical values of Ben & Jerry's.

Offering Ethics-Training Programs

In addition to providing a system to resolve ethical dilemmas, organizations also provide formal training to develop an awareness of questionable business activities and to practice appropriate responses. Many American companies have some type of ethics-training program. The ones that are most effective, like those created by Levi Strauss, American Express, and Campbell Soup Company, begin with techniques for solving ethical dilemmas such as those discussed earlier. Next, employees are presented with a series of situations and asked to come up with the "best" ethical solution. One of these ethical dilemmas is shown in Exhibit 2.1. Some companies have tried to add a bit of excitement and fun to their ethics-training programs by presenting them in the form of games. Citigroup, for example, has created The Work Ethic, a board game in which participants strive to correctly answer legal, regulatory, policy-related, and judgment ethics questions.

Establishing a Formal Code of Ethics

code of ethics
A set of guidelines prepared by a firm to provide its employees with the knowledge of what the firm expects in terms of their responsibilities and behavior toward fellow employees, customers, and suppliers.

Most large companies and thousands of smaller ones have created, printed, and distributed codes of ethics. In general, a **code of ethics** provides employees with the knowledge of what their firm expects in terms of their responsibilities and behavior toward fellow employees, customers, and suppliers. Some ethical codes offer a lengthy and detailed set of guidelines for employees. Others are not really codes at all but rather summary statements of goals, policies, and priorities. Some companies have their codes framed and hung on office walls or printed on cards to be carried at all times by executives. The code of ethics for Costco Wholesale, the chain of membership warehouse clubs, is shown in Exhibit 2.2.

Do codes of ethics make employees behave in a more ethical manner? Some people believe that they do. Others think that they are little more than public relations gimmicks. If senior management abides by the code of ethics and regularly emphasizes the code to employees, then it will likely have a positive influence on behavior.

EXHIBIT 2.1	An Ethical Dilemma Used for Employee Training

Bill Gannon was a middle manager of a large manufacturer of lighting fixtures in Newark, New Jersey. Bill had moved up the company ladder rather quickly and seemed destined for upper management in a few years. Bill's boss, Dana Johnson, had been pressuring him about the semiannual reviews concerning Robert Talbot, one of Bill's employees. Dana, it seemed, would not accept any negative comments on Robert's evaluation forms. Bill had found out that a previous manager who had given Robert a bad evaluation was no longer with the company. As Bill reviewed Robert's performance for the forthcoming evaluation period, he found many areas of subpar performance. Moreover, a major client had called recently complaining that Robert had filled a large order improperly and then had been rude to the client when she called to complain.

Discussion Questions
1. What ethical issues does the situation raise?
2. What courses of action could Bill take? Describe the ethics of each course.
3. Should Bill confront Dana? Dana's boss?
4. What would you do in this situation? What are the ethical implications?

EXHIBIT 2.2   Costco Wholesale's Code of Ethics

CODE OF ETHICS

By Jim Sinegal

OBEY THE LAW

The law is irrefutable! Absent a moral imperative to challenge a law, we must conduct our business in total compliance with the laws of every community where we do business.

Comply with all statutes.

Cooperate with authorities.

Respect all public officials and their positions.

Avoid all conflict of interest issues with public officials.

Comply with all disclosure and reporting requirements.

Comply with safety and security standards for all products sold.

Exceed ecological standards required in every community where we do business.

Comply with all applicable wage and hour laws.

Comply with all applicable anti-trust laws.

Protect "inside information" that has not been released to the general public.

TAKE CARE OF OUR MEMBERS

The member is our key to success. If we don't keep our members happy, little else that we do will make a difference.

Provide top-quality products at the best prices in the market.

Provide a safe shopping environment in our warehouses.

Provide only products that meet applicable safety and health standards.

Sell only products from manufacturers who comply with "truth in advertising/packaging" standards.

Provide our members with a 100% satisfaction guaranteed warranty on every product and service we sell, including their membership fee.

Assure our members that every product we sell is authentic in make and in representation of performance.

Make our shopping environment a pleasant experience by making our members feel welcome as our guests.

Provide products to our members that will be ecologically sensitive.

> Our member is our reason for being. If they fail to show up, we cannot survive. Our members have extended a "trust" to Costco by virtue of paying a fee to shop with us. We can't let them down or they will simply go away. We must always operate in the following manner when dealing with our members:
> Rule #1– The member is always right.
> Rule #2– In the event the member is ever wrong, refer to rule #1.
>
> "There are plenty of shopping alternatives for our members. We will succeed only if we do not violate the trust they have extended to us. We must be committed at every level of our company, with every ounce of energy and grain of creativity we have, to constantly strive to bring goods to market at a lower price."

If we do these four things throughout our organization, we will realize our ultimate goal, which is to REWARD OUR SHAREHOLDERS.

TAKE CARE OF OUR EMPLOYEES

To claim "people are our most important asset" is true and an understatement. Each employee has been hired for a very important job. Jobs such as stocking the shelves, ringing members' orders, buying products and paying our bills are jobs we would all choose to perform because of their importance. The employees hired to perform these jobs are performing as management's "alter egos." Every employee, whether they are in a Costco warehouse or whether they work in the regional or corporate offices, is a Costco ambassador trained to give our members professional, courteous treatment.

Today we have warehouse managers who were once stockers and callers and vice presidents who were once in clerical positions for our company. We believe that Costco's future executive officers are currently working in our warehouses, depots, buying offices and accounting departments, as well as in our home offices.

To that end, we are committed to these principles:

Provide a safe work environment.

Pay a fair wage.

Make every job challenging, but make it fun!

Consider the loss of any employee as a failure on the part of the company and a loss to the organization.

Teach our people how to do their jobs and how to improve personally and professionally.

Promote from within the company to achieve the goal of a minimum of 80% of management positions being filled by current employees.

Create an "open door" attitude at all levels of the company that is dedicated to fairness and listening.

RESPECT OUR VENDORS

Our vendors are our partners in business, and for us to prosper as a company, they must prosper with us. It is important that our vendors understand that we will be tough negotiators but fair in our treatment of them.

Treat all vendors and their representatives as you would expect to be treated if visiting their places of business.

Pay all bills within the allocated time frame.

Honor all commitments.

Protect all vendor property assigned to Costco as though it were our own.

Always be thoughtful and candid in negotiations.

Provide a careful review process with at least two levels of authorization before terminating business with an existing vendor of more than two years.

Do not accept gratuities of any kind from a vendor.

> These guidelines are exactly that - guidelines, some common sense rules for the conduct of our business. Intended to simplify our jobs, not complicate our lives, these guidelines will not answer every question or solve every problem. At the core of our philosophy as a company must be the implicit understanding that not one of us is required to lie or cheat on behalf of Costco. In fact, dishonest conduct will not be tolerated. To do any less would be unfair to the overwhelming majority of our employees who support and respect Costco's commitment to ethical business conduct.
>
> If you are ever in doubt as to what course of action to take on a business matter that is open to varying ethical interpretations, take the high road and do what is right.
>
> If you want our help, we are always available for advice and counsel. That's our job, and we welcome your questions or comments.
>
> Our continued success depends on you. We thank each of you for your contribution to our past success and for the high standards you have insisted upon in our company.

All of the "Top 100 Best Corporate Citizens" listed by *Business Ethics* magazine, in a recent year, had formal codes of ethics. The top corporate citizens in 2007 were:

1. Green Mountain Coffee Roasters, Inc.
2. Advanced Micro Devices, Inc.
3. NIKE, Inc.
4. Motorola, Inc.
5. Intel Corporation
6. International Business Machines Corporation
7. Agilent Technologies, Inc.
8. Timberland Company (The)
9. Starbucks Corporation
10. General Mills Incorporated[5]

Cummins, Inc. is one of 19 companies to be named every year since the list was created in 2000.

Making the Right Decision

In many situations, there may be no simple right or wrong answers. Yet there are several questions that you can ask yourself to help you make the right ethical decision. First, ask yourself, "Are there any legal restrictions or violations that will result from the action?" If so, take a different course of action. If not, ask yourself, "Does it violate my company's code of ethics?" If so, again find a different path to follow. Third, ask "Does this meet the guidelines of my own ethical philosophy?" If the answer is "yes," then your decision must still pass two important tests.

The Feelings Test You must now ask, "How does it make me feel?" This enables you to examine your comfort level with a particular decision. Many people find that after reaching a decision on an issue they still experience discomfort that may manifest itself in a loss of sleep or appetite. Those feelings of conscience can serve as a future guide in resolving ethical dilemmas.

CONCEPT in action

Better known as trustworthy gatekeepers than purveyors of scandal, news organizations rarely face scrutiny over internal ethical lapses. But in a spectacular journalistic misstep during a presidential campaign, CBS News anchor Dan Rather delivered a potentially election-swaying report based on spurious, unauthenticated documents. The event drew harsh criticism from *60 Minutes* colleague Andy Rooney and led to executive firings and Rather's early retirement from CBS. How might the "front page of the newspaper" test help journalists make ethical decisions?

Front Page of the Newspaper Test The final test is the "front page of the newspaper" test. The question to be asked is how a critical and objective reporter would report your decision in a front-page story. Some managers rephrase the test for their employees: how will the headline read if I make this decision? This test is helpful in spotting and resolving potential conflicts of interest.

A Two-Way Street Just as businesses have an obligation to act in an ethical manner, so do consumers. Consider these two questions and answers sent to the "Ethics Guy." The "Ethics Guy" is Dr. Bruce Weinstein, a renowned professional ethicist.

Dear Ethics Guy: I enjoy going to the local megabookstore and spending the afternoon there reading the books and magazines they have. The store has big, comfortable chairs, and the clerks never bother me or ask me to leave. Unlike my local library, this place has all the latest publications. I even bring my own lunch to eat if I know I'm going to be there all day. A friend of mine told me that it's unethical of me to do this. I don't think it is, since the store obviously allows the practice (and you can bet I'm not the only one who does it). What do you say? We have dinner riding on it.

I say get ready to shell out some cash for the first time in a while, because I agree with your friend. You take without giving, and that's wrong. Just because you have a right to do something doesn't mean it's right to do it. I can't imagine the management of the store looking kindly on what you're doing. After all, they're running a business, not a public charity. The philosopher Immanuel Kant said that a distinguishing feature of right conduct is whether an action can be universalized. Applied here, what he means is that the bookstore couldn't survive if everyone behaved as you do. Why should you get preferential treatment? It's one thing to peruse reading material before making a purchase. It's another thing to take advantage of the store, whose clerks are too busy helping true customers to have time to shoo you away. If this argument isn't persuasive to you, consider this: If you were the manager of the bookstore, and you knew that someone treated your store as his personal book and magazine collection, wouldn't you be angry—and rightly so?

Dear Ethics Guy: I frequent an electronics store that has a liberal policy for returns: If you have the receipt, you can get a full refund for any item you buy, as long as you bring the merchandise

Part 1: The Business Environment

back in good shape and within 30 days. Accordingly, I have been able to take home various cameras, video equipment, and even some high-end stereos, and I don't risk losing a nickel. I basically treat the store as though it were a rental house, without having the burden of actually having to pay for what I use. You can't accuse me of being unethical, since the store itself allows me to do this.

I can't? Well, I will anyway. The reason stores have generous return policies is that they want to create goodwill with genuine customers. No store could stay in business for very long if everyone acted as you did, and as we saw above, Kant's dictum of treating one's actions as though they could be universalized is a useful way of deciding whether one is acting ethically or not. It's one thing to buy an item in good faith, expecting or hoping to keep it, but discovering that it's not quite what you wanted. It's another thing entirely to take that item home with the intention of using it only for 30 days and then returning it. The difference is between good intentions and purely selfish ones. Certainly you must know that if the store got wind of what you're doing, they wouldn't want you as a customer. Could you blame them? Of course, strictly speaking, you're not really a customer at all. You're a freeloader posing as a customer.[6]

CONCEPT check

What is the role of top management in organizational ethics?

What is a code of ethics?

Managing a Socially Responsible Business

Acting in an ethical manner is one of the four components of the pyramid of corporate social responsibility. **Social responsibility** is the concern of businesses for the welfare of society as a whole. It consists of obligations beyond those required by law or union contract. This definition makes two important points. First, social responsibility is voluntary. Beneficial action required by law, such as cleaning up factories that are polluting air and water, is not voluntary. Second, the obligations of social responsibility are broad. They extend beyond investors in the company to include workers, suppliers, consumers, and communities.

Exhibit 2.3 on the next page portrays economic responsibility as the foundation for the other three responsibilities. At the same time that a business pursues profits (economic responsibility), however, it is expected to obey the law (legal responsibility); to do what is right, just, and fair (ethical responsibility); and to be a good corporate citizen (philanthropic responsibility). These four components are distinct but together constitute the whole. Still, if the company doesn't make a profit, then the other three responsibilities are moot.

Many companies are already working to make the world a better place to live. Consider these examples:

- Starbucks sponsors literacy programs as well as a holiday gift drive for seriously ill children.
- Each year, the accounting firm PricewaterhouseCoopers sends at least 20 partners to the developing world, for several months, to help local aid programs.
- Home Depot refuses to purchase wood from endangered forests and actively works to protect the South American rain forest.

3 What is social responsibility?

social responsibility
The concern of businesses for the welfare of society as a whole; consists of obligations beyond those required by law or contracts.

Understanding Social Responsibility

Peter Drucker, the late globally-respected management expert, said that we should look first at what an organization does to society and second at what it can do for society. This idea suggests that social responsibility has two basic dimensions: legality and responsibility.

Illegal and Irresponsible Behavior The idea of social responsibility is so widespread today that it is hard to conceive of a company continually acting in illegal and irresponsible ways. Nevertheless, such actions do sometimes occur. Of course, the acts of managers of Enron, WorldCom, and Tyco created financial ruin for their organizations, extreme financial hardships for many former employees, and general hardships for the communities in which they operated. Yet top executives walked away with millions. Some, however, have been sentenced to jail and will ultimately pay large fines. Federal, state, and local laws determine whether an activity is legal or not. The laws that regulate business are discussed in the appendix to this chapter.

CONCEPT in action

British cosmetics company The Body Shop is proof that businesses can make money and make a difference at the same time. With over 2,000 locations in more than 50 countries, The Body Shop is one of the world's largest cosmetics franchises. The L'Oreal-owned business is also a model of social responsibility. Through its charitable foundation, The Body Shop has sponsored rain forest initiatives, championed human rights causes, and opposed animal testing. The retail stores are designed with eco-friendly hemp panels and recycled marble and glass. How do companies balance social responsibility and profitability?

© AP Images/Rachel Miller

EXHIBIT 2.3 The Pyramid of Corporate Social Responsibility

Philanthropic Responsibilities
The highest level of the triangle, philanthropic responsibilities can be considered only after economic, legal, and ethical responsibilities.

Legal Responsibilities
Corporations must, of course, follow the law. The second level of the pyramid recognizes that legal considerations are also necessary for a corporation's success.

Ethical Responsibilities
Resting on the foundation set by economic and legal responsibilities are ethical responsibilities. A corporation can turn its attention to ethical matters only after ensuring its economic and legal position.

Economic Responsibilities
Because a corporation must be profitable to survive, its economic responsibilities form the base of the pyramid.

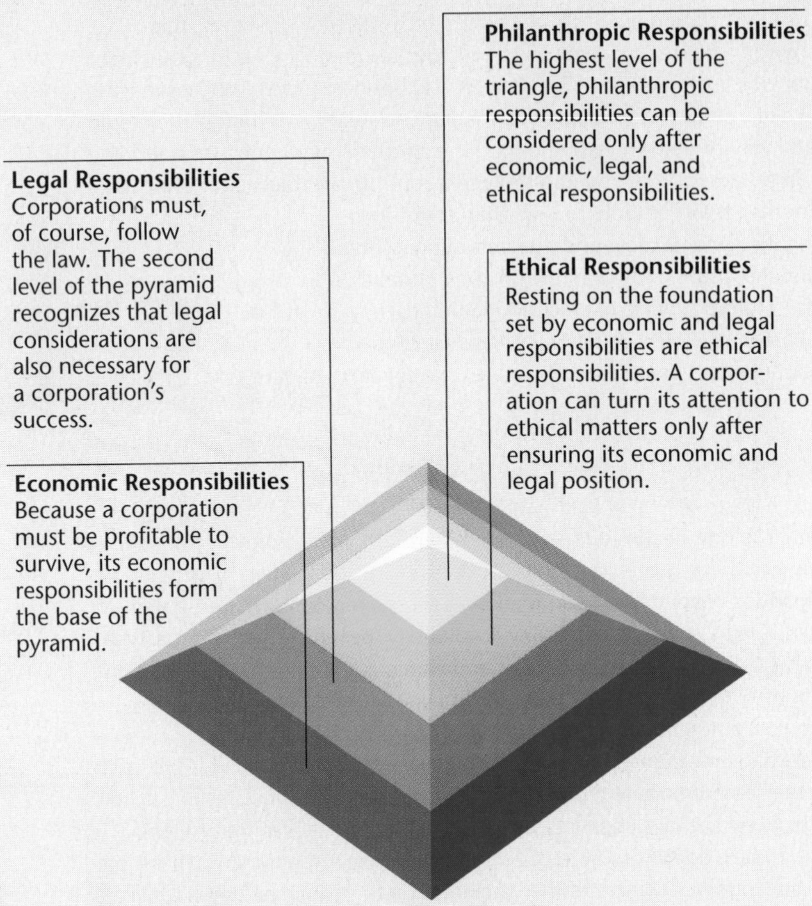

Irresponsible but Legal Behavior Sometimes companies act irresponsibly, yet their actions are legal. J.D. Byrider Systems is a national organization of used-car stores that serves customers with credit problems. Sometimes sales are made entirely on credit to very low-income individuals. Often these consumers quickly end up with more debt than they can handle at sky-high interest rates. For example, a Saturn with 103,000 miles sold for $7,922 completely on credit with a 24.9 percent interest rate. The customer made $900 in payments before falling behind and having the vehicle repossessed. This meant Byrider could sell it again. Byrider doesn't set prices on cars like traditional showrooms. Salesmen calculate what a person can pay and then set the total price, down payment, and interest rate.[7] A few other examples are Jackson Hewitt Tax Service, which offers a $4,351 "quick refund" but charges $453 or 10.4 percent in preparation and loan fees; and CompuCredit offers subprime credit cards such as an Aspire Visa with $199 in fees and initial payment and a $300 line of credit.[8]

Legal and Responsible Behavior The vast majority of business activities fall into the category of behavior that is both legal and responsible. Most firms act legally, and most try to be socially responsible. Research shows that consumers, especially those under 30, are likely to buy brands that have excellent ethical track records and community involvement. Target, for example, gives approximately $2 million a week to various causes. "Our guests feel good shopping with us because they know they're contributing to many great causes as they shop," says John Remington, Target's vice president of event marketing and communications.[9]

CONCEPT check

What are the four components of social responsibility?

Give an example of legal but irresponsible behavior.

Responsibilities to Stakeholders

What makes a company admirable or perceived as socially responsible? Such a company meets its obligations to its stakeholders. **Stakeholders** are the individuals or groups to whom a business has a responsibility. The stakeholders of a business are its employees, its customers, the general public, and its investors.

Responsibility to Employees

An organization's first responsibility is to provide a job to employees. Keeping people employed and letting them have time to enjoy the fruits of their labor is the finest thing business can do for society. Enron is an example of a company that violated this responsibility. Beyond this fundamental responsibility, employers must provide a clean, safe working environment that is free from all forms of discrimination. Companies should also strive to provide job security whenever possible.

Enlightened firms are also empowering employees to make decisions on their own and suggest solutions to company problems. Empowerment contributes to an employee's self-worth, which, in turn, increases productivity and reduces absenteeism.

Each year *Fortune* magazine conducts an extensive survey of the best places to work in America. The top 10 are shown in Exhibit 2.4. Some companies offer unusual benefits to their employees. CMP Media gives employees $30,000 for infertility treatments and adoption aid. FedEx allows free rides in the jump seats of company planes. Steelcase has a 1,200-acre camping and recreational area for employee use.

4 How do businesses meet their social responsibilities to various stakeholders?

stakeholders
Individuals or groups to whom a business has a responsibility; include employees, customers, the general public, and investors.

EXHIBIT 2.4	America's Top Ten Best Places to Work
Rank Company **Headquarters (Number of U.S. sites)** **Web site**	**What makes it so great?**
1. Google Mountain View, CA (27) **http://www.google.com**	Back in our No. 1 spot, Google continued to mint millionaires as the stock cracked $700. The company gives stock options to 99 percent of employees.
2. Quicken Loans Livonia, MI (16) **http://www.quickenloans.com**	"Ethically driven" is what one employee calls the online mortgage lender. It avoided the subprime crisis by sticking with plain-vanilla loans.
3. Wegmans Food Markets Rochester, NY (90) **http://www.wegmans.com**	Shopping is theater at this family-owned 71-store chain. It was named the nation's top supermarket by the Food Network in 2007.
4. Edward Jones St. Louis (8,953) **http://www.edwardjones.com**	Some 70 percent of employees in the St. Louis home office got a 6.5 percent raise last year as the brokerage firm opened 1,000 new offices in the United States.
5. Genentech South San Francisco (9) **http://www.gene.com**	Legendarily perk-heavy biotech firm (doggie day care, onsite farmers' market) bumped up 401(k) match in 2007 (100 percent up to 5 percent of pay).
6. Cisco Systems San Jose (136) **http://www.cisco.com**	Though the stock market flatlined in 2007, CEO John Chambers won praise for his leadership and his new blog, On My Mind, which solicits employee ideas.
7. Starbucks Seattle (6,302) **http://www.starbucks.com**	Rapid expansion led to a difficult year, but the stock rose 9 percent on January news that founder Howard Schultz is taking over the CEO post.
8. Qualcomm San Diego (19) **http://www.qualcomm.com**	New employees get stock options and 100 percent health insurance coverage. The popular onsite primary-care clinic is quadrupling in size.
9. Goldman Sachs New York (41) **http://www.gs.com**	It was a rough year for Wall Street, but Goldman had record sales and profits. Comp and benefits rose 23 percent from the previous year, to $10.19 billion.
10. Methodist Hospital System Houston (11) **http://www.methodisthealth.com**	Last year Methodist added a new program called "No One Dies Alone," in which employees volunteer time with terminally ill patients.

Source: Robert Levering and Milton Moskowitz, "The 100 Best Companies to Work For," *Fortune* (February 4, 2008), p. 75.
© 2008 Time Inc. All rights reserved.

Responsibility to Customers

A central theme of this text is that to be successful today a company must satisfy its customers. A firm must deliver what it promises. It must also be honest and forthright with its clients. We will discuss this in the Customer Satisfaction and Quality boxes in most chapters. We begin in this chapter with the story of the "Mexican Maverick," Ricardo Salinas Pliego, who offers customer satisfaction and opportunities to Mexico's poor. It is discussed in the Expanding Around the Globe box on the next page.

Responsibility to Society

A business must also be responsible to society. A business provides a community with jobs, goods, and services. It also pays taxes that go to support schools, hospitals, and better roads. Most companies, such as Target as previously discussed, try to be good citizens in their communities.

Responsibility to society doesn't end at our shores. Global enterprises are attempting to help around the public world as explained in the Expanding Around the Globe box.

Environmental Protection
Business is also responsible for protecting and improving the world's fragile environment. The world's forests are quickly being destroyed. Every second, an area the size of a football field is laid bare. Plant and animal species are becoming extinct at the rate of 17 species per hour. A continent-size hole is opening up in the earth's protective ozone shield. Each year we throw out 80 percent more refuse than we did in 1960; as a result, more than half of the nation's landfills are filled to capacity.

To slow the erosion of the world's resources, many companies are becoming more environmentally responsible. Toyota is now using renewable energy sources to power its facilities, making it the largest single user of clean power in the world. Toyota's first step in the United States was to turn to renewable sources such as solar, wind, geothermal, and water power for the electricity at its headquarters in Torrance and Irving, California.

An Israeli entrepreneur is now leading an effort to end the era of gas-powered autos. His story is presented in the Managing Change box on page 51.

CONCEPT in action

© 2007 Dave M. Benett / Getty Images

The Live Earth concert for global warming awareness has come and gone, but the carbon footprint left by the event's jet-setting performers, arena energy bills, and mountains of waste could set back the environment for years to come. Despite advocating severe cuts to energy use and development worldwide, the event itself produced an ecological footprint estimated at 31,500 tons of carbon emissions and 1,000 tons of garbage waste. A-list performers like Madonna contributed tons of carbon pollution in jet flights alone. Is the entertainment industry serious about going green?

Corporate Philanthropy
Companies also display their social responsibility through corporate philanthropy. **Corporate philanthropy** includes cash contributions, donations of equipment and products, and support for the volunteer efforts of company employees. Corporate philanthropy totals about $13 billion a year.[10] American Express is a major supporter of the American Red Cross. The organization relies almost entirely on charitable gifts to carry out its programs and services, which include disaster relief, armed-forces emergency relief, blood and tissue services, and health and safety services. The funds provided by American Express have enabled the Red Cross to deliver humanitarian relief to victims of numerous disasters around the world.

When Hurricane Katrina hit the Gulf Coast, Bayer sent 45,000 diabetes blood glucose monitors to the relief effort. Within a week of the disaster, Abbott, Alcoa, British Petroleum, Dell, Disney, Intel, Motorola, UPS, Walgreens, and other major corporations had contributed more than $100 million for hurricane relief. Headlines detailing major philanthropic efforts typically focus on big companies such as those mentioned above. Yet countless small business also do their part to make the world a better place. Several examples are given in the Catching the Entrepreneurial Spirit box on page 50.

corporate philanthropy
The practice of charitable giving by corporations; includes contributing cash, donating equipment and products, and supporting the volunteer efforts of company employees.

Responsibilities to Investors

Companies' relationships with investors also entail social responsibility. Although a company's economic responsibility to make a profit might seem to be its main obligation to its shareholders, some investors increasingly are putting more emphasis on other aspects of social responsibility.

Some investors are limiting their investments to securities that fit within their beliefs about ethical and social responsibility. This is called **social investing**. For example, a social investment fund might eliminate from consideration the securities of all companies that make tobacco products or liquor, manufacture weapons, or have a history of polluting. Not all social investment strategies are alike. Some ethical mutual funds will not invest in government securities because they help to fund the military; others freely buy government securities, with managers noting that federal

social investing
The practice of limiting investments to securities of companies that behave in accordance with the investor's beliefs about ethical and social responsibility.

© Digital Vision/Getty Images

Making a Fortune by Busting Monopolies and Selling to the Poor

Ricardo Salinas Pliego is the third-richest man in Mexico. He has turned a modest family business into a $5 billion conglomerate by forcing new competition on monopolistic industries. He also targets a booming market that competitors have ignored—Mexico's poor. About 20 percent of Mexico's 108 million people live on less than $2 per day.

Salinas got his start by taking over his family's discount retailer, Grupo Elektra, in 1987. (It had 59 stores then, and now has 1,600.) In 1993 he launched his television network, TV Azteca, to steal viewers from the country's leading channel, Televisa; he uses TV Azteca to air Elektra ads. Then, in 1999, he introduced a low-cost mobile carrier, Unefon, to undercut the dominant player, América Móvil, controlled by Carlos Slim Helú, who now rivals Bill Gates as the world's richest person. Now Salinas is pushing hard into banking. His Elektra chain was the first retailer to enter the business when it opened Banco Azteca in 2002. Now it has more than 900 minibranches in Elektra stores and almost 700 at other outlets. In 2007, Azteca took in $1.1 billion from 7 million low-income clients—a quarter of Mexico's 28 million "unbanked" people.

To reach the poor, Banco Azteca employs a fleet of 4,000 loan officers who hop on motorcycles to crisscross the poorest neighborhoods of Mexico's crowded cities and rural towns. The denizens lack any credit history, so Azteca's lenders assess creditworthiness by inspecting the customers' homes and interviewing their neighbors. They enter the data on handheld electronic devices that zap the info—over Salinas's lusacell network—back to their bosses.

The fleet processes 14,000 new loans at an average sum of $257 apiece. Borrowers make their payments at Elektra stores. Grupo Elektra is a big-box retailer that sells 60 percent of its goods on credit and now exceeds $3 billion in annual revenue. But the bank claims only 10 percent of its loans are for Elektra purchases; the rest are for clothing, food, medical expenses, and other necessities. Banco Azteca has a 90 percent collection rate overall, and it has been growing 42 percent a year since starting in 2002.[11]

Critical Thinking Questions

- Would the Banco Azteca model work in selling to America's poor? Why or why not?
- Elektra stores' prices are listed by weekly payment requirement. A refrigerator is tagged at $13—that is $13 a week for 78 weeks. That comes to $1,014 for a fridge that can be bought for $596 up front. Elektra says they take the risk by providing credit and must cover losses from nonpayment. Also, without the weekly payments most could never afford a new appliance. Is Elektra right or are they just exploiting the poor?

funds also support the arts and pay for AIDS research. Today, about $100 billion is invested in social investment funds.

This decade has been among the worst ever, in modern times for companies failing to meet responsibilities to investors. Scandals at WorldCom, Krispy Kreme, HealthSouth, Enron, and others so disturbed the investment community that they had a negative impact on the stock market. Investigators found companies claiming huge assets that never existed; falsified financial statements; huge loans by companies that could not be justified (or paid back); executives selling massive amounts of stock at high prices, then announcing several months later that the earnings were being restated at a much lower level, thus sending the stock crashing; and analysts making "buy" recommendations to the public while sending internal e-mails to coworkers stating that the stock was worthless. The Securities and Exchange Commission and many state attorneys general (particularly the attorney general of New York, which is America's financial center) are working to enact new laws to curb these abuses.

CONCEPT check

How do businesses carry out their social responsibilities to consumers?

What is corporate philanthropy?

Is a company's only responsibility to its investors to make a profit? Why or why not?

Trends in Ethics and Social Responsibility

Three important trends related to ethics and social responsibility are changes in corporate philanthropy, a new social contract between employers and employees, and the growth of global ethics and social responsibility.

5 What are the trends in ethics and social responsibility?

Changes in Corporate Philanthropy

Corporate philanthropy has typically involved seeking out needy groups and then giving them money or company products. Today, the focus is shifting to **strategic giving**, which ties philanthropy more closely to the corporate mission or goals and targets donations to regions where a company operates.

Stan Litow, IBM's vice president of corporate community relations, notes that the company knows it takes more than just money—checkbook philanthropy (the old model)—to have a successful giving program. "With checkbook philanthropy you could contribute a lot of money and accomplish very little," he says. "I think that in the new model, being generous is incredibly important, but the most important aspect of this new model is using our many resources to achieve something of lasting value in the communities where we live, work and do business."[12]

strategic giving
The practice of tying philanthropy closely to the corporate mission or goals and targeting donations to regions where a company operates.

Small Companies but Big Hearts

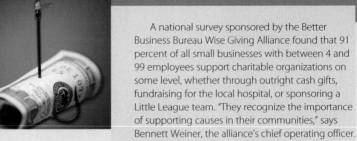

In the wake of the deadly Asian tsunami in December 2004, New York restaurateur William Jack Degel felt compelled to help with the massive relief effort in any way he could. So the owner of Uncle Jack's Steakhouses decided to donate the proceeds from all his January and February dessert sales to benefit survivors. Alone, he expected to give about $20,000. But eventually, he began reaching out to other restaurants, and Sweet Relief was born. Now 50 restaurants in eight states have earmarked between 25 percent and 50 percent of their dessert sales in an effort to raise $250,000 for CARE, a global poverty group. "A big company can afford to give $30 million," Degel says. "But if small businesses collaborated as a whole throughout the U.S., we could beat out the big business donations."

When tragedy strikes, giving tends to strike back even harder. At large corporations, there are deep pockets to tap. Following the tsunami, corporate donations—among them, Pfizer's $10 million, ExxonMobil's $5 million, and Cisco's $2.5 million—threatened to outpace the U.S. government's initial pledge of $35 million, which was later bumped up to at least $350 million.

But away from the headline-making multimillion-dollar checks—as well as the headline-making tragedies—small-business owners continue to dream up their own creative ways to contribute. Without their own foundations, employee gift-matching plans, and in some cases, entire philanthropy departments, individual small businesses cannot flex the same kind of charitable muscle as corporate giants. But their collective impact does make a difference, particularly within the communities where they operate. Countless small businesses in the South gave food, money, and merchandise to the victims of Hurricane Katrina in New Orleans. Most of them have found such acts of kindness to be an important part of doing business. Besides engendering goodwill among clients and employees, it helps raise visibility, burnish reputations, and can even bring in new business.

A national survey sponsored by the Better Business Bureau Wise Giving Alliance found that 91 percent of all small businesses with between 4 and 99 employees support charitable organizations on some level, whether through outright cash gifts, fundraising for the local hospital, or sponsoring a Little League team. "They recognize the importance of supporting causes in their communities," says Bennett Weiner, the alliance's chief operating officer.

One of the most traditional ways that small businesses have contributed is by giving their time and expertise. Owen Cleaners, a family drycleaning business in Paducah, Kentucky, started collecting used winter coats 18 years ago, cleaning them for free, and then distributing them to needy children. "We've probably cleaned more than 84,000 coats," says David Perry, who owns and operates the 85-year-old company, which boasts eight locations and 55 employees. "It's like an annual ritual here." Perry estimates that he spends about $7,500 a year on the Cal's Coats for Kids coat drive. Some employees volunteer their time while others get paid overtime. But, he says, "I don't really consider the tax deduction as part of the equation." His philosophy? "Every gift obviously adds up."[13]

Critical Thinking Questions
- Do small businesses have the same social responsibilities as large corporations?
- Should the federal government change tax laws and offer other incentives to encourage small businesses to be more socially responsible?

© Rubberball/Getty Images

CONCEPT in action

An impassioned debt-relief advocate and rock star extraordinaire, U2 front man Bono has joined forces with corporate America to fight AIDS through a branding program called Product RED. As part of the charitable program, companies such as American Express, Converse, and Gap develop and market "red-themed" products while donating the proceeds to disease-prevention agencies in Africa. In what ways does the creation of global brand Product RED exemplify trends in corporate philanthropy?

© AP Images/M. Spencer Green

Recently, Bayer Corporation refocused one of its four areas of strategic giving. Bayer USA Foundation's four giving areas include Arts and Culture; Education and Workforce Development; Environment and Sustainability; and Health and Human Services. The new category, Environment and Sustainability, replaces Civic and Social Service programs, which will now be incorporated into the Health and Human Services sector. According to the Bayer USA Foundation, its strategic mission to: "support programs that enhance the quality of life; provide unique and enriching opportunities that connect diverse groups; and ensure preparedness for tomorrow's leaders—thereby, resulting in sustainable partnerships that continually improve communities in which Bayer employees live and work, as well as society, at large."[14]

The biggest event in corporate philanthropy in recent years had nothing to do with a foundation giving but rather receiving. Warren Buffett announced that he was leaving his fortune to the Bill and Melinda Gates Foundation. His gift of more than $30 billion boosts the Foundation to over $70 billion. The Gates Foundation has already made a big difference in global health by giving to programs that fight malaria, polio, AIDS, and a host of other ills. But Mr. Gates is smart enough to know that simply giving money away is not enough. Bill Gates has come up with an idea he calls "creative capitalism." Companies will be encouraged to design products and establish businesses that help the poor while making profits at the same time. Gates noted, "If we can spend the early decades of the 21st century finding approaches that meet the needs of the poor in ways that generate profits for business, we will have found a sustainable way to reduce poverty in the world."[15]

As Patty Stonesifer, chief executive of the Gates Foundation, put it in the Foundation's latest report: "Giving away money isn't hard. Giving it away effectively sure is."[16] Think for a moment. When a foundation gives money away to, say, a charity, it becomes a customer of the charity. It spends money

Reducing Pollution with an Electric Car Network

Renault SA, France's second-largest carmaker, and affiliate Nissan Motor Co. said they will develop an electric-car network in Israel in a venture with entrepreneur Shai Agassi as a first step toward global mass-marketing. Renault plans to supply the vehicles, which will be powered entirely by electricity, while Agassi's Project "Better Place" will construct and operate a battery-recharging network. The vehicles would be available starting in 2011.

Israel's small size makes it an optimal market for electric cars, which have a limited range, said Carlos Ghosn, chief executive officer of Renault and Nissan. The country, not counting the occupied West Bank or Golan Heights, covers about 21,000 square kilometers, an area roughly the size of New Jersey. "In Israel, where 90 percent of the people drive less than 70 kilometers [42 miles] a day, a car with 100-killometre [60 mile] range would satisfy most of the population's transportation needs," Ghosn said.

According to Ghosn, Israeli tax breaks will lower the cost of an electric car to the price of a gasoline-powered vehicle and over the life of the car, the cost of ownership will be "significantly lower" than a conventional vehicle. The Renault-built cars will use lithium-ion batteries developed by Japan's NEC Corp. and Nissan, and will perform similarly to a gas-powered vehicle with a 1.6-liter engine. The cars will produce no emissions, the companies said. Lithium-ion batteries are standard in mobile phones and laptop computers.

Agassi contends that Israel is just the start. He hopes to expand his business into several other countries over the next few years, with China, France, and Britain among the potential markets. Ultimately, he believes that his company and others like it could shake two pillars of the global economy, the $1.5 trillion-a-year auto industry and the $1.5 trillion-a-year market for gasoline. "If what I'm saying is right,

this would be the largest economic dislocation in the history of capitalism," says Agassi.

The trouble with traditional electric cars is that they can go only 50 to 100 miles before they need to stop for hours to recharge their batteries. Hybrids overcome the mileage limitations, but only by burning gasoline. One of Agassi's unconventional ideas is to separate the battery from the car. That will allow drivers to pull into a battery-swapping station, a car-wash-like contraption, and wait for 10 minutes while their spent batteries are lowered from the car and fully charged replacements are hoisted into place. "Better Place" will build the service stations, as well as hundreds of thousands of charging locations, which look similar to parking meters.[17]

Critical Thinking Questions

- Do you think that Agassi's idea will work? Why or why not?
- Agassi plans to operate something like a mobile-phone carrier. He plans to sell electric cars to consumers at a relatively low price and then charge them monthly operating fees. The total cost of ownership is expected to be less than conventional ownership. What is your opinion of this concept?

© Stockbyte/Getty Images

and wants something in return, just like you and I. The foundation, or corporation, may simply want the charity to efficiently perform its function, such as provide hot lunches to underprivileged schoolchildren. By looking at the donor as a customer, we realize that they, like us, want satisfaction for the dollar spent. The Customer Satisfaction and Quality box on the next page shows how individuals and corporations can use certain tools to increase their chances of becoming satisfied customers (donors).

Cause-Related Marketing

A sometimes controversial subset of social responsibility is *cause-related marketing*. Sometimes referred to as simply "cause marketing," it is the cooperative efforts of a for-profit firm and a not-for-profit organization for mutual benefit. Cause-related marketing is sometimes used as any marketing effort for social or other charitable causes. Cause marketing differs from corporate giving (philanthropy), as the latter generally involves a specific donation that is tax deductible, while cause marketing is a marketing relationship not based on a straight donation.

Cause-related marketing is highly popular in America. It is estimated to generate around $7 billion a year in revenue.[18] It creates good public relations for the firm and will often stimulate sales of the brand.

Examples of cause-related marketing abound. Starwood Hotels has announced for every Westin Heavenly Bed, Sheraton Sweet Sleeper Bed, and Four Points by Sheraton Four Comfort bed sold through Starwood retail channels, the firm will donate $50 to the Special Olympics. Avaya recently publicized that it will donate $5 to the American Cancer Society for each pink desk phone faceplate it sells. The money is to be used to raise breast cancer awareness. Starbucks donates 5¢ of every sale of Ethos Water to help children around the world get access to clean drinking water. American Express launched a campaign to restore the Statue of Liberty and Ellis Island. The company contributes 1¢ each for card transaction and $1 for every new card issued. American Express collected $1.7 million for the restoration effort.[19]

Cause-related marketing is not without controversy. The Gap has been criticized for The Gap (Product) Red campaign. Thanks to the Gap and others, more

CONCEPT in action

Clothing retailer Gap, Inc. continues to struggle with its overseas manufacturing partners. In 2007 a British newspaper reported that a New Delhi, India, subcontractor was using child labor to produce Gap brand fashion apparel. The exposé offered video documentation of preteens working in squalid sweatshop conditions often for 16-hour days without pay or acceptable quarters. Underage labor trafficking is rampant in New Delhi's teeming garment industry and in other parts of the world. What can multinational corporations do to ensure that their outsourcing partners uphold human rights?

© AP Images/Richard Drew

Checking on Charities

Over the past couple of years, the nonprofit watchdogs that help donors have added more information to their sites, and they've increased the number of organizations they follow. Moreover, information about thousands of charities—including Internal Revenue Service (IRS) returns and governance details—is now available free on the Web. And it's in an easy-to-read format that even a layperson can understand.

The first stop when researching a charity should be a watchdog site. These groups offer information about nonprofits and often rate their efforts. Remember, though, that these sites come with some important caveats. Many of them rely on information in charities' IRS returns, called Form 990s. And that information can be quite old by the time the watchdogs get it. Charities file their returns as much as 11 months after the end of the fiscal year, and then it can take months for the IRS to process the form and make it available. Meanwhile, if the charities aren't forthcoming on their IRS return, the watchdogs' data and analysis will end up skewed. With that in mind, here's a look at some of the best information sources out there.

CharityNavigator.org, provided by the nonprofit group Charity Navigator in Mahwah, New Jersey, rates more than 5,000 U.S.-based charities, using information in their Form 990s. The site is free to people who register. For an idea of how the rankings work, consider the group's take on United Way of America. The charity, which is based in Alexandria, Virginia, gets three stars out of four for "Efficiency," in part because 90 percent of its budget went to programs, and it cost only 2¢ for the

program to raise a dollar. The organization also gets three stars of four for "Capacity," or its ability to sustain itself over time. The group had annualized revenue growth of 21 percent from 2002 through 2005 and had enough working capital to operate for about eight months without any income.

If you want to look at raw data, GuideStar.org, a product of Philanthropic Research Inc., in Williamsburg, Virginia, is the go-to organization for copies of a charity's Form 990. It covers 1.7 million groups and has about 3.1 million Form 990 images, many of which are available free to people who register.

Give.org, operated by the BBB Wise Giving Alliance in Arlington, Virginia, reports on whether the approximately 1,200 charities it has evaluated meet the alliance's 20 "Standards for Charitable Accountability." It doesn't do ratings or rankings.[21]

Critical Thinking Questions
- Would high executives' salaries necessarily be a reason not to give to a particular charity? What about high administrative expenses? Fund-raising expenses?
- Pick a charity that you have given money to and evaluate it using the three sources cited above. Are you surprised at the outcome? Why?

© Digital Vision/Getty Images

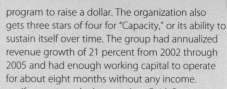

than $25 million has been raised to fight HIV/AIDS, tuberculosis, and malaria. The Gap has stated that 50 percent of (Product) Red products are being directed to the cause. Yet the promotional expenditures for the (Product) Red campaign were $100 million![20]

Yet, in the end, does the promotional expenditure really matter as long as $25 million was raised for a good cause? Gap probably saw an incremental increase in sales and increased brand loyalty. It is Gap's management that must ultimately decide if the $100 million expenditure was worthwhile.

Global Ethics and Social Responsibility

When American businesses expand into global markets, they must take their corporate codes of ethics and policies on social responsibility with them. As a citizen of several countries, a multinational corporation has many responsibilities. These include respecting local practices and customs, ensuring that there is harmony between the organization's staff and the host population, providing management leadership, and developing a cadre of local managers who will be a credit to their community. When a multinational corporation makes an investment in a foreign country, it should commit to a long-term relationship. That means involving all stakeholders in the host country in decision making. Finally, a responsible multinational corporation will implement ethical guidelines within the organization in the host country. By fulfilling these responsibilities, the company will foster respect for both local and international laws.

Multinational corporations often must balance conflicting interests of stakeholders when making decisions regarding social responsibilities, especially in the area of human rights. Questions involving child labor, forced labor, minimum wages, and workplace safety can be particularly difficult. A recent study by the National Labor Committee, a human rights organization, found that Christmas tree ornaments sold at Wal-Mart and other major retailers were made in a Chinese sweatshop employing workers as young as 12 and others who work more than 100 hours a week.[22]

CONCEPT check

Describe strategic giving.

What role do employees have in improving their job security?

How do multinational corporations demonstrate social responsibility in a foreign country?

Summary of Learning Goals

Ethics is a set of moral standards for judging whether something is right or wrong. A utilitarianism approach to setting personal ethical standards focuses on the consequences of an action taken by a person or an organization. According to this approach, people should act so as to generate the greatest good for the greatest number. Every human is entitled to certain rights such as freedom and the pursuit of happiness. Another approach to ethical decision making is justice, or what is fair according to accepted standards.

1 What philosophies and concepts shape personal ethical standards?

Top management must shape the ethical culture of the organization. They should lead by example, offer ethics-training programs, and establish a formal code of ethics.

2 How can organizations encourage ethical business behavior?

Social responsibility is the concern of businesses for the welfare of society as a whole. It consists of obligations beyond just making a profit. Social responsibility also goes beyond what is required by law or union contract. Companies may engage in illegal and irresponsible behavior, irresponsible but legal behavior, or legal and responsible behavior. The vast majority of organizations act legally and try to be socially responsible.

3 What is social responsibility?

Stakeholders are individuals or groups to whom business has a responsibility. Businesses are responsible to employees. They should provide a clean, safe working environment. Organizations can build employees' self-worth through empowerment programs. Businesses also have a responsibility to customers to provide good, safe products and services. Organizations are responsible to the general public to be good corporate citizens. Firms must help protect the environment and provide a good place to work. Companies also engage in corporate philanthropy, which includes contributing cash, donating goods and services, and supporting volunteer efforts of employees. Finally, companies are responsible to investors. They should earn a reasonable profit for the owners.

4 How do businesses meet their social responsibilities to various stakeholders?

Today, corporate philanthropy is shifting away from simply giving to any needy group and is focusing instead on strategic giving, in which the philanthropy relates more closely to the corporate mission or goals and targets donations to areas where the firm operates. Corporate philanthropy is coming under increasing attacks from special-interest groups, however.

A second trend is toward a new social contract between employer and employee. Instead of the employer having the sole responsibility for maintaining jobs, now the employee must assume part of the burden and find ways to add value to the organization.

As the world increasingly becomes a global community, multinational corporations are now expected to assume a global set of ethics and responsibility. Global companies must understand local customs. They should also involve local stakeholders in decision making. Multinational corporations must also make certain that their suppliers are not engaged in human rights violations.

5 What are the trends in ethics and social responsibility?

Appendix: Understanding the Legal and Tax Environment

Laws are the rules governing a society's conduct that are created and enforced by a controlling authority. The U.S. court system governs the legal system and includes both federal and state courts, each organized into three levels. The courts settle disputes by applying and interpreting laws. Most cases start in trial courts. Decisions can be appealed to appellate courts. The U.S. Supreme Court is the nation's highest court and the court of final appeal. To avoid the high costs of going to court, many firms now use private arbitration or mediation as alternatives to litigation.

6 How does the legal system govern business transactions and settle business disputes?

A contract is an agreement between two or more parties that meets five requirements: mutual assent, capacity, consideration, legal purpose, and legal form. If one party breaches the contract terms, the remedies are damages, specific performance, or restitution. Tort law settles disputes involving civil acts that harm people or their property. Torts include physical injury, mental anguish, and defamation. Product liability law governs the responsibility of manufacturers and sellers for product defects. Bankruptcy law gives businesses or individuals who cannot meet their financial obligations a way to be relieved of their debts. Some laws are designed to keep the marketplace free from influences that would restrict competition such as price fixing and deceptive advertising. Laws protecting consumer rights are another important area of government control.

7 What are the required elements of a valid contract; and what are the key types of business law?

Chapter 2: Making Ethical Decisions and Managing a Socially Responsible Business

53

Income taxes are based on the income received by businesses and individuals. Congress determines the income taxes that are to be paid to the federal government. In addition to income taxes, individuals and businesses also pay property taxes (assessed on real and personal property), payroll taxes (the employer's share of Social Security taxes and federal and state unemployment taxes), sales taxes (levied on goods), and excise taxes (levied against specific products such as gasoline, alcoholic beverages, and tobacco).

Key Terms

code of ethics 42	social investing 48
corporate philanthropy 48	social responsibility 45
deontology 41	stakeholders 47
ethical issue 39	strategic giving 49
ethics 39	utilitarianism 40
justice 40	

Preparing for Tomorrow's Workplace: SCANS

1. Many CEOs have sold shares of their company's stock when prices were near their high points. Even though their actions were legal, it soon became apparent that they knew that the stock was significantly overpriced. Was the CEO ethically obligated to tell the public that this was the case—even knowing that doing so could cause the stock price to plummet, thereby hurting someone who bought the stock earlier that day? (**Systems**)

2. Jeffrey Immelt, chairman and CEO of General Electric, the world's most admired company according to *Fortune* magazine, says that execution, growth, and great people are required to keep the company on top. Immelt said that these are predictable, but a fourth factor is not—virtue; and virtue was at the top of his list. Using BCRC or another articles database, find articles on what GE is doing to enhance its corporate citizenship. Report your findings to the class. Could GE do more or are they already doing too much? Why? (**Systems, Technology**)

3. The Boeing Company makes business ethics a priority, asking employees to take refresher training every year. It encourages employees to take the Ethics Challenge with their work groups and to discuss the issues with their peers. You can take your own ethics challenge. Go to **http://www.ethics.org/resources/articles-organizational-ethics.asp?aid=948** and click on the "Ethics Effectiveness Quick Test." Summarize your findings. Were there any answers that surprised you? (**Information**)

4. Identify the potential ethical and social responsibility issues confronting the following organizations: Microsoft, Pfizer, Nike, American Cancer Society, and R.J. Reynolds. Make recommendations on how these issues should be handled. (**Systems**)

5. **Team Activity** Divide the class into teams. Debate whether the only social responsibility of the employer to the employee is to provide a job. Include a discussion of the employee's responsibility to bring value to the firm. Also, debate the issue of whether the only social responsibility of a firm is to earn a profit. (**Interpersonal**)

Ethics Activity

Too Delicious to Resist

We are constantly bombarded with media reports claiming that as a nation, Americans are becoming dangerously overweight. A recent medical study also just classified obesity as a disease in its own right, unconnected to such symptoms as high blood pressure, cholesterol, or heart problems. So perhaps it is not surprising that a recent lawsuit claimed that McDonald's is responsible for the obesity of two teenagers by "getting them hooked" on their burgers and fries.

You are the attorney approached by the teens' parents to bring suit against McDonald's. You ask yourself some soul-searching questions. Does McDonald's market and sell food in such a manner that it poses a health danger to unsuspecting consumers? And what about personal accountability? Shouldn't the teens and/or their parents be held responsible for their food choices? You wonder if this were a local mom-and-pop restaurant, would the teens' parents be suing? Or are the deep pockets of McDonald's too delicious to resist?

Using a Web search tool, locate articles about this topic and then write responses to the following questions. Be sure to support your arguments and cite your sources.

ETHICAL DILEMMA: Do you tell the teens' parents to go home, cook healthy, and put their kids on a diet? Or do you take the case, believing that McDonald's has not acted in a socially responsible way and recognizing the potential for some serious money?

Sources: Dave Carpenter, "DIET: McDonald's to post nutrition facts on packaging next year," *The America's Intelligence Wire,* October 26, 2005, **http://galenet.thomsonlearning.com**; Pallavi Gogoi, "McDonald's New Wrap," *Business Week Online,* February 17, 2006, **http://www.businessweek.com**; Richard Martin, "Revived McD Obesity Lawsuit Still Suggests Personal-Responsibility Defense—for Now," *Nation's Restaurant News,* February 14, 2005, **http://galenet.thomsonlearning.com**; Wendy Melillo, "Bringing Up Baby: Where's the Line, and Who Should Draw It, In Advertising to Children?" *ADWEEK,* February 13, 2006, p.14+; Libby Quaid, "House Votes to Block Lawsuits Blaming Food Industry for Obesity," *The America's Intelligence Wire,* October 19, 2005, **http://galenet.thomsonlearning.com**.

Working the Net

1. You'll find a comprehensive list of business ethics sites at **http:www.web-miner.com/busethics .htm**. Once at the site, go to the section on Corporate Codes of Ethics. Look at three examples of codes in different industries. What elements do they have in common? How are they different? Suggest how one of the codes could be improved.

2. Richard S. Scrushy, former CEO of HealthSouth Corporation, was charged with $1.4 billion in fraud. He was acquitted. Bernie Ebbers, former CEO of WorldCom, was found guilty of helping mastermind an $11 billion accounting fraud. Go to the Internet and read several articles about the charges against both men. Find articles on why one was guilty on all counts and the other acquitted on all counts. Explain the ethical issues involved with each. Were they completely different or the same? Also, read about the latest charges against Scrushy and comment on them. Begin your search at **http://money.cnn.com** and **http://www.forbes.com**. You can find more articles on **http://www.google.com**.

3. Visit the Fur Is Dead Web site of the People for the Ethical Treatment of Animals (PETA), **http://furisdead.com**. Read about PETA's view of the fur industry. Do you agree with this view? Why or why not? How do you think manufacturers of fur clothing would justify their actions to someone from PETA? Would you work for a store that sold fur-trimmed clothing? Explain your answer.

4. Green Money Journal, **http://www.greenmoneyjournal.com**, is a bimonthly online journal that promotes social responsibility investing. What are the current topics of concern in this area? Visit the archives to find articles on socially responsible investing and two areas of corporate social responsibility. Summarize what you have learned.

5. A global resource for not-for-profit professionals is **http://www.onphilanthropy.com**. The site lists trends and best practices in corporate giving. Read several articles, then report to the class on trends in corporate giving. Also, give an example of a "best practice" in philanthropy.

Timbuk2 Gets the Message

Creative Thinking Case

It all started in 1989 with one product: a custom messenger bag designed for San Francisco's bicycle couriers. That unique carrier became popular with not just cyclists, but also students and professionals who loved its stylish yet durable features. Today Timbuk2 manufactures 30 products, including messenger bags, computer cases, totes, duffles, iPod sleeves, and yoga bags that generate more than $10 million in annual revenues. Loyal customers buy Timbuk2 cases at REI, EMS, Apple, and 1,200 independent specialty retail stores. The messenger bags cost from $60 to $90, depending on size; for $10 more, customers can select custom color combinations.

Although other companies have shifted production to low-cost manufacturing centers overseas, Timbuk2 still produces its messenger bags at its original San Francisco factory. To preserve its local presence and retain jobs while maintaining a financially sound company, Timbuk2 took steps to boost the plant's productivity. Originally Timbuk2 made its bags "on demand" as customer orders came in. Converting to predetermined color combinations allowed the factory to operate independent of demand and to build inventory, greatly improving productivity. "That change alone saved our San Francisco factory from going out of business," says Mark Dwight, Timbuk2's president and chief executive officer. "There is value in the made-in-USA products, and locally produced bags can be customized to customer requests on a very short lead time. That quick response is a unique advantage."

The company discovered, however, that the manufacturing of its new lines was more complex than that of the messenger bags and called for specialized machinery. These factors and the resulting high labor costs led Timbuk2 to explore offshore manufacturing options. Keeping the headquarters operation and design team in San Francisco but shifting production to a carefully selected factory in China enabled Timbuk2 to continue offering top-quality products while keeping prices affordable.

Timbuk2 is proud of its commitment to ethical working conditions and fair wages at all its facilities. Executives visit the China factory every month or two to monitor the work environment and make sure that product quality remains high. The new products have been well-received, increasing Timbuk2's reputation as a lifestyle brand. As a result of its higher sales volume, the company has expanded the San Francisco factory, doubled its production staff, and added employees in all departments. It continues to roll out new products. "Our goal is to create a solid growth company, to continue delighting our customers with great products, to contribute to our local community, and to make the Timbuk2 swirl as recognizable as the Nike swoosh," says Dwight.[23]

Critical Thinking Questions

- Mark Dwight faced considerable resistance from existing managers when he assumed control of Timbuk2 and wanted to move the production of new products overseas. He has asked for your help in preparing a presentation to win their support. Summarize the arguments in favor of offshore production.
- Now list the arguments against using foreign manufacturers and develop answers to help Dwight counter charges that it is not socially responsible to take jobs outside the United States.
- How did Dwight's decision to manufacture new products in China support the company's desire to be a good corporate citizen for San Francisco?

Lord John Browne BP

Exploring Business Careers

Although stories of greedy and unscrupulous business executives have dominated the business news during the last few years, one innovative leader for British Petroleum (BP) has been at the forefront of social responsibility by demonstrating a commitment to preserving the world's fragile environment. Lord John Browne, group chief executive to the world's second-largest company, is consistently recognized as one of the 100 most influential British executives, according to the British newspaper *The Times*. But there's a good reason he's so newsworthy: Browne is keenly aware of BP's responsibility to protect and preserve the environment, and he uses his influence and position to make BP more environmentally responsible.

Environmental issues are a growing concern among businesses worldwide. In particular, energy companies face tough scrutiny by their customers and stakeholders to make socially and ethically responsible decisions. Recognizing a rapidly increasing demand for energy worldwide, Browne is

© South-Western, *Exploring Business Careers*

committed to taking BP "beyond petroleum," although the burden of this increased demand still falls to hydrocarbon-based sources, such as oil and natural gas. And although Browne has confidence that the world's oil and natural gas supplies are sufficient, his concerns are clear: "The real challenge is the potential impact of burning ever greater volumes of hydrocarbons on the world's climate."

However, he is not satisfied simply to state the problem and head home. "Business is at heart of the process of taking scientific advances and transforming them into technology . . . which can alter the lives of individuals and whole communities, and which can protect the environment." And he is putting his—and BP's—money where his mouth is.

The Kyoto Protocol, a 1997 United Nations treaty on climate change, seeks to reduce the levels of carbon dioxide (CO_2), a harmful by-product of hydrocarbon use, by 5.2 percent below a 1990 baseline. BP immediately sought to reduce their emissions by twice that amount, a goal they reached by 2002. At the same time, BP increased profitability by almost $650 million, dispelling the belief that environmental concerns cannot coincide with good business sense. They did this by increasing efficiency and eliminating waste in their manufacturing processes.

Additionally, BP has begun several innovative initiatives to help preserve the environment:

- BP built China's first natural gas terminal and pipeline for distribution, which will save approximately 16 million tons of CO_2 emissions over coal.
- In Algeria, BP has started to use a process called carbon sequestration in which carbon, produced by natural gas production, is trapped before it can be released into the atmosphere. It is then injected back into reservoirs below the ground where it does not harm the environment. BP estimates this project will prevent the release of 17 million tons of CO_2.

This chapter examined further how ethical and socially responsible decisions, such as those concerning the environment, are a part of every business and discussed the role of ethics in a successful business career.

Understanding the Legal and Tax Environment

6 How does the legal system govern business transactions and settle business disputes?

Our legal system affects everyone who lives and does business in the United States. The smooth functioning of society depends on the law, which protects the rights of people and businesses. The purpose of law is to keep the system stable while allowing orderly change. The law defines which actions are allowed or banned and regulates some practices. It also helps settle disputes. The legal system both shapes and is shaped by political, economic, and social systems. As Judge Learned Hand wrote in The Spirit of Liberty, "Without [the law] we cannot live; only with it can we insure the future which by right is ours."

laws
The rules of conduct in a society, created and enforced by a controlling authority, usually the government.

In any society **laws** are the rules of conduct created and enforced by a controlling authority, usually the government. They develop over time in response to the changing needs of people, property, and business. The legal system of the United States is thus the result of a long and continuing process. In each generation new social problems occur, and new laws are created to solve them. For instance, in the late 1800s corporations in certain industries, such as steel and oil, merged and became dominant. The Sherman Antitrust Act was passed in 1890 to control these powerful firms. Eighty years later, in 1970, Congress passed the National Environmental Policy Act. This law dealt with pollution problems, which no one had thought about in 1890. Today new areas of law are developing to deal with the Internet and the recent financial scandals.

The Main Sources of Law

common law
The body of unwritten law that has evolved out of judicial (court) decisions rather than being enacted by a legislature; also called case law.

Common law is the body of unwritten law that has evolved out of judicial (court) decisions rather than being enacted by legislatures. It is also called case law. It developed in England and came to America with the colonists. All states except Louisiana, which follows the Napoleonic Code inherited from French settlers, follow the English system. Common law is based on community customs that were recognized and enforced by the courts.

statutory law
Written law enacted by a legislature (local, state, or federal).

Statutory law is written law enacted by legislatures at all levels, from city and state governments to the federal government. Examples of statutory law are the federal and state constitutions, bills passed by Congress, and ordinances, which are laws enacted by local governments. Statutory law is the chief source of new laws in the United States. Among the business activities governed by statutory law are securities regulation, incorporation, sales, bankruptcy, and antitrust.

administrative law
The rules, regulations, and orders passed by boards, commissions, and agencies of government (local, state, and federal).

Related to statutory law is **administrative law**, or the rules, regulations, and orders passed by boards, commissions, and agencies of federal, state, and local governments. The scope and influence of administrative law have expanded as the number of these government bodies has grown. Federal agencies issue more rulings and settle more disputes than all the courts and legislatures combined. Some federal agencies that issue rules are the Civil Aeronautics Board, the Internal Revenue Service, the Securities and Exchange Commission, the Federal Trade Commission, and the National Labor Relations Board.

Business Law

business law
The body of law that governs commercial dealings.

Business law is the body of law that governs commercial dealings. These laws provide a protective environment within which businesses can operate. They serve as guidelines for business decisions. Every businessperson should be familiar with the laws governing his or her field. Some laws, such as the Internal Revenue Code, apply to all businesses. Other types of business laws may apply to a specific industry, such as Federal Communications Commission laws that regulate radio and TV stations.

Uniform Commercial Code (UCC)
A model set of rules that apply to commercial transactions between businesses and individuals; has been adopted by all states except Louisiana, which uses only part of it.

In 1952 the United States grouped many business laws into a model that could be used by all the states. The **Uniform Commercial Code (UCC)** sets forth the rules that apply to commercial transactions between businesses and between individuals and businesses. It has been adopted by 49 states; Louisiana uses only part of it. By standardizing laws, the UCC simplifies the process of doing business across state lines. It covers the sale of goods, bank deposits and collections, letters of credit, documents of title, and investment securities. Many articles of the UCC are covered later in this appendix.

The Court System

judiciary
The branch of government that is responsible for settling disputes by applying and interpreting points of law; consists of the court system.

The United States has a highly developed court system. This branch of government, the **judiciary**, is responsible for settling disputes by applying and interpreting points of law. Although court

decisions are the basis for common law, the courts also answer questions left unanswered by statutes and administrative rulings. They have the power to assure that these laws do not violate the federal or state constitutions.

Trial Courts

Most court cases start in the **trial courts**, also called courts of general jurisdiction. The main federal trial courts are the U.S. district courts. There is at least one federal district court in each state. These courts hear cases involving serious federal crimes, immigration, postal regulations, disputes between citizens of different states, patents, copyrights, and bankruptcy. Specialized federal courts handle tax matters, international trade, and claims against the United States.

trial courts
The lowest level of courts, where most cases begin; also called courts of general jurisdiction.

Appellate Courts

The losing party in a civil (noncriminal) case and a losing defendant in a criminal case may appeal the trial court's decision to the next level in the judicial system, the **appellate courts (courts of appeals)**. There are 12 U.S. circuit courts of appeals. Cases that begin in a federal district court are appealed to the court of appeals for that district. These courts may also review orders from administrative agencies. Likewise, the states have appellate courts and supreme courts for cases tried in state district or superior courts.

No cases start in appellate courts. Their purpose is to review decisions of the lower courts and affirm, reverse, or modify the rulings.

appellate courts (courts of appeals)
The level of courts above the trial courts; the losing party in a civil case and the defendant in a criminal case may appeal the trial court's decision to an appellate court.

The Supreme Court

The U.S. Supreme Court is the highest court in the nation. It is the only court specifically established by the U.S. Constitution. Any cases involving a state or in which an ambassador, public minister, or consul is a party are heard directly by the Supreme Court. Its main function is to review decisions by the U.S. circuit courts of appeals. Parties not satisfied with a decision of a state supreme court can appeal to the U.S. Supreme Court. But the Supreme Court accepts only those cases that it believes will have the greatest effect on the country, only about 200 of the thousands of appeals it gets each year.

Administrative Agencies

Administrative agencies have limited judicial powers to regulate their special areas. These agencies exist at the federal, state, and local levels. For example, in 1998 the Federal Trade Commission enacted the "Federal Universal Service Fund," which subjects each pager phone to an 18¢ fee. This fund was created by the Federal Trade Commission to ensure that all citizens, schools, libraries, and hospitals in rural areas have access to telecommunications service (like the Internet) at prices comparable to those charged in urban and suburban areas. A list of selected federal agencies is shown in Exhibit 2A.1 on the next page.

CONCEPT in action

Big Three pharmaceutical firm Merck & Co. pulled Vioxx off the market after studies linked the drug to increased heart attacks and strokes. An osteoarthritis painkiller with annual sales of $2.5 billion, Vioxx is alleged to have caused up to 160,000 health failures nationwide. Merck originally opted to defend Vioxx in state courts, where corporate liability was estimated at $50 billion; the company eventually reached a $4.85 billion settlement with plaintiffs in federal court. What is the appeals process for product liability cases filed in U.S. courts?

© TOM MIHALEK/AFP/Getty Images

Nonjudicial Methods of Settling Disputes

Settling disputes by going to court is both expensive and time consuming. Even if the case is settled prior to the actual trial, sizable legal expenses can be incurred in preparing for trial. Therefore, many companies now use private arbitration and mediation firms as alternatives to litigation. Private firms offer these services, which are a high-growth area within the legal profession.

With **arbitration**, the parties agree to present their case to an impartial third party and are required to accept the arbitrator's decision. **Mediation** is similar, but the parties are not bound by the mediator's decision. The mediator suggests alternative solutions and helps the parties negotiate a settlement. Mediation is more flexible than arbitration and allows for compromise. If the parties cannot reach a settlement, they can then go to court, an option not available in most arbitration cases.

In addition to saving time and money, corporations like the confidentiality of testimony and settlement terms in these proceedings. Arbitration and mediation also allow businesses and medical professionals to avoid jury trials, which can result in large settlements in certain types of lawsuits, such as personal injury, discrimination, medical malpractice, and product liability.

arbitration
A method of settling disputes in which the parties agree to present their case to an impartial third party and are required to accept the arbitrator's decision.

mediation
A method of settling disputes in which the parties submit their case to an impartial third party but are not required to accept the mediator's decision.

EXHIBIT 2A.1 Federal Regulatory Agencies

Agency	Function
Federal Trade Commission (FTC)	Enforces laws and guidelines regarding unfair business practices and acts to stop false and deceptive advertising and labeling.
Food and Drug Administration (FDA)	Enforces laws and regulations to prevent distribution of adulterated or misbranded foods, drugs, medical devices, cosmetics, veterinary products, and hazardous consumer products.
Consumer Products Safety Commission (CPSC)	Ensures compliance with the Consumer Product Safety Act and seeks to protect the public from unreasonable risk of injury from any consumer product not covered by other regulatory agencies.
Federal Communications Commission (FCC)	Regulates wire, radio, and TV communication in interstate and foreign commerce.
Environmental Protection Agency (EPA)	Develops and enforces environmental protection standards and researches the effects of pollution.
Federal Energy Regulatory Commission (FERC)	Regulates rates and sales of natural gas products, thereby affecting the supply and price of gas available to consumers; also regulates wholesale rates for electricity and gas, pipeline construction, and U.S. imports and exports of natural gas and electricity.
Federal Aviation Administration (FAA)	Oversees the policies and regulations of the airline industry.
Federal Highway Administration (FHA)	Regulates vehicle safety requirements.

Contract Law

7 What are the required elements of a valid contract; and what are the key types of business law?

contract
An agreement that sets forth the relationship between parties regarding the performance of a specified action; creates a legal obligation and is enforceable in a court of law.

Linda Price, a 22-year-old college student, is looking at a car with a sticker price of $16,000. After some negotiating, she and the salesperson agree on a price of $15,000, and the salesperson writes up a contract, which they both sign. Has Linda legally bought the car for $15,000? The answer is yes, because the transaction meets all the requirements for a valid contract.

A **contract** is an agreement that sets forth the relationship between parties regarding the performance of a specified action. The contract creates a legal obligation and is enforceable in a court of law. Contracts are an important part of business law. Contract law is also incorporated into other fields of business law, such as property and agency law (discussed later in this appendix). Some of the business transactions that involve contracts are buying materials and property, selling goods, leasing equipment, and hiring consultants.

A contract can be an *express contract*, which specifies the terms of the agreement in either written or spoken words, or an implied contract, which depends on the acts and conduct of the parties to show agreement. An example of an express contract is the written sales contract for Linda Price's new car. An implied contract exists when you order and receive a sandwich at Jason's Grill. You and the restaurant have an implied contract that you will pay the price shown on the restaurant's menu in exchange for an edible sandwich.

Contract Requirements

Businesses deal with contracts all the time, so it's important to know the requirements of a valid contract. For a contract to be legally enforceable, all of the following elements must be present:

- *Mutual assent.* Voluntary agreement by both parties to the terms of the contract. Each party to the contract must have entered into it freely, without duress. Using physical or economic harm to force the signing of the contract—threatening injury or refusing to place another large order, for instance—invalidates a contract. Likewise, fraud—misrepresenting the facts of a transaction—makes a contract unenforceable. Telling a prospective used-car buyer that the brakes are new when in fact they have not been replaced makes the contract of sale invalid.

- *Capacity*. Legal ability of a party to enter into contracts. Under the law, minors (those under 18), mental incompetents, drug and alcohol addicts, and convicts cannot enter into contracts.
- *Consideration*. Exchange of some legal value or benefit between the parties. Consideration can be in the form of money, goods, or a legal right given up. Suppose that an electronics manufacturer agrees to rent an industrial building for a year at a monthly rent of $1,500. Its consideration is the rent payment of $1,500, and the building owner's consideration is permission to occupy the space. But if you offer to type a term paper for a friend for free and your offer is accepted, there is no contract. Your friend has not given up anything, so you are not legally bound to honor the deal.
- *Legal purpose*. Absence of illegality. The purpose of the contract must be legal for it to be valid. A contract cannot require performance of an illegal act. A contract to smuggle drugs into a state for a specified amount of money would not be legally enforceable.
- *Legal form*. Oral or written form, as required. Many contracts can be oral. For instance, an oral contract exists when Bridge Corp. orders office supplies by phone from Ace Stationery Store and Ace delivers the requested goods. Written contracts include leases, sales contracts, and property deeds. Some types of contracts must be in writing to be legally binding. In most states, written contracts are required for the sale of goods costing more than $500, for the sale of land, for contract performance that cannot be carried out within a year, and for guarantees to pay the debts of someone else.

As you can see, Linda Price's car purchase meets all the requirements for a valid contract. Both parties have freely agreed to the terms of the contract. Linda is not a minor and presumably does not fit any of the other categories of incapacity. Both parties are giving consideration, Linda by paying the money and the salesperson by turning over the car to her. The purchase of the car is a legal activity. And the written contract is the correct form because the cost of the car is over $500.

Breach of Contract

A **breach of contract** occurs when one party to a contract fails (without legal excuse) to fulfill the terms of the agreement. The other party then has the right to seek a remedy in the courts. There are three legal remedies for breach of contract:

- *Payment of damages*. Money awarded to the party who was harmed by the breach of contract, to cover losses incurred because the contract wasn't fulfilled. Suppose that Ajax Roofing contracts with Fred Wellman to fix the large hole in the roof of his factory within three days. But the roofing crew doesn't show up as promised. When a thunderstorm four days later causes $45,000 in damage to Wellman's machinery, Wellman can sue for damages to cover the costs of the water damage because Ajax breached the contract.
- *Specific performance of the contract*. A court order requiring the breaching party to perform the duties under the terms of the contract. Specific performance is the most common method of settling a breach of contract. Wellman might ask the court to direct Ajax to fix the roof at the price and conditions in the contract.
- *Restitution*. Canceling the contract and returning to the situation that existed before the contract. If one party fails to perform under the contract, neither party has any further obligation to the other. Because Ajax failed to fix Wellman's roof under the terms of the contract, Wellman does not owe Ajax any money. Ajax must return the 50 percent deposit it received when Wellman signed the contract.

breach of contract
The failure by one party to a contract to fulfill the terms of the agreement without a legal excuse.

Warranties

Express warranties are specific statements of fact or promises about a product by the seller. This form of warranty is considered part of the sales transaction that influences the buyer. Express warranties appear in the form of statements that can be interpreted as fact. The statement "This machine will process 1,000 gallons of paint per hour" is an express warranty, as is the printed warranty that comes with a computer or a telephone answering machine.

Implied warranties are neither written nor oral. These guarantees are imposed on sales transactions by statute or court decision. They promise that the product will perform up to expected standards. For instance, a man bought a used car from a dealer, and the next day the transmission

© Charley Gallay/WireImage for 944/Getty Images

Gangsta rapper 50 Cent, aka Curtis James Jackson, was embroiled in controversy when a copyright lawsuit alleged that the Jamaica, Queens, New York, recording artist stole lyrics for his chart-topping hit "In Da Club." According to legal briefs, lyrics to "In Da Club" originally appeared in "It's Your Birthday," a song by former 2 Live Crew front man Luther Campbell. What legal protections are offered to songwriters and composers in the United States and why?

patent
A form of protection established by the government for inventors; gives an inventor the exclusive right to manufacture, use, and sell an invention for 17 years.

copyright
A form of protection established by the government for creators of works of art, music, literature, or other intellectual property; gives the creator the exclusive right to use, produce, and sell the creation during the lifetime of the creator and for 50 years thereafter.

trademark
A design, name, or other distinctive mark that a manufacturer uses to identify its goods in the marketplace.

servicemark
A symbol, name, or design that identifies a service rather than a tangible object.

tort
A civil or private act that harms other people or their property.

fell out as he was driving on the highway. The dealer fixed the car, but a week later the brakes failed. The man sued the car dealer. The court ruled in favor of the car owner because any car without a working transmission or brakes is not fit for the ordinary purpose of driving. Similarly, if a customer asks to buy a copier to handle 5,000 copies per month, she relies on the salesperson to sell her a copier that meets those needs. The salesperson implicitly warrants that the copier purchased is appropriate for that volume.

Patents, Copyrights, and Trademarks

The U.S. Constitution protects authors, inventors, and creators of other intellectual property by giving them the rights to their creative works. Patents, copyrights, and registration of trademarks and servicemarks are legal protection for key business assets.

A **patent** gives an inventor the exclusive right to manufacture, use, and sell an invention for 17 years. The U.S. Patent Office, a government agency, grants patents for ideas that meet its requirements of being new, unique, and useful. The physical process, machine, or formula is what is patented. Patent rights—pharmaceutical companies' rights to produce drugs they discover, for example—are considered intangible personal property.

The government also grants copyrights. A **copyright** is an exclusive right, shown by the symbol ©, given to a writer, artist, composer, or playwright to use, produce, and sell her or his creation. Works protected by copyright include printed materials (books, magazine articles, lectures), works of art, photographs, and movies. Under current copyright law, the copyright is issued for the life of the creator plus 50 years after the creator's death. Patents and copyrights, which are considered intellectual property, are the subject of many lawsuits today.

A **trademark** is a design, name, or other distinctive mark that a manufacturer uses to identify its goods in the marketplace. Apple Computer's multicolored apple logo (symbol) is an example of a trademark. A **servicemark** is a symbol, name, or design that identifies a service rather than a tangible object. The Travelers Insurance umbrella logo is an example of a servicemark.

Most companies identify their trademark with the ® symbol in company ads. This symbol shows that the trademark is registered with the Register of Copyrights, Copyright Office, Library of Congress. The trademark is followed by a generic description such as Fritos corn chips, Xerox copiers, Scotch brand cellophane tape, Kleenex tissues.

Trademarks are valuable because they create uniqueness in the minds of customers. At the same time, companies don't want a trademark to become so well known that it is used to describe all similar types of products. For instance, Coke is often used to refer to any cola soft drink, not just those produced by the Coca-Cola Company. Companies spend millions of dollars each year to keep their trademarks from becoming generic words, terms used to identify a product class rather than the specific product. Coca-Cola employs many investigators and files 70 to 80 lawsuits each year to prevent its trademarks from becoming generic words.

Once a trademark becomes generic (which a court decides), it is public property and can be used by any person or company. Names that were once trademarked but are now generic include aspirin, thermos, linoleum, and toll house cookies.

Tort Law

A **tort** is a civil or private act that harms other people or their property. The harm may involve physical injury, emotional distress, invasion of privacy, or defamation (injuring a person's character by publication of false statements). The injured party may sue the wrongdoer to recover damages for the harm or loss. A tort is not the result of a breach of contract, which would be settled under contract law. Torts are part of common law. Examples of tort cases are medical malpractice, slander (an untrue oral statement that damages a person's reputation), libel (an untrue written statement that damages a person's reputation), product liability (discussed in the next section), and fraud.

A tort is generally not a crime, although some acts can be both torts and crimes. (Assault and battery, for instance, is a criminal act that would be prosecuted by the state and also a tort because of the injury to the person.) Torts are private wrongs and are settled in civil courts. Crimes are violations of public law punishable by the state or county in the criminal courts. The purpose of criminal law is to punish the person who committed the crime. The purpose of tort law is to provide remedies to the injured party.

For a tort to exist and damages to be recovered, the harm must be done through either negligence or deliberate intent. Negligence occurs when reasonable care is not taken for the safety of others. For instance, a woman attending a New York Mets baseball game was struck on the head by a foul ball that came through a hole in the screen behind home plate. The court ruled that a sports team charging admission has an obligation to provide structures free from defects and seating that protects spectators from danger. The Mets were found negligent. Negligence does not apply when an injury is caused by an unavoidable accident, an event that was not intended and could not have been prevented even if the person used reasonable care. This area of tort law is quite controversial, because the definition of negligence leaves much room for interpretation.

Product Liability Law

Product liability refers to manufacturers' and sellers' responsibility for defects in the products they make and sell. It has become a specialized area of law combining aspects of contracts, warranties, torts, and statutory law (at both the state and federal levels). A product liability suit may be based on negligence or strict liability (both of which are torts) or misrepresentation or breach of warranty (part of contract law).

An important concept in product liability law is **strict liability**. A manufacturer or seller is liable for any personal injury or property damage caused by defective products or packaging—even if all possible care was used to prevent such defects. The definition of defective is quite broad. It includes manufacturing and design defects and inadequate instructions on product use or warnings of danger.

Product liability suits are very costly. More than 100,000 product liability suits were filed against hundreds of companies that made or used asbestos, a substance that causes lung disease and cancer but was once used widely in insulation, brake linings, textiles, and other products. Eighteen companies were forced into bankruptcy as a result of asbestos-related lawsuits, and the total cost of asbestos cases to defendants and their insurers exceeds $10 billion (most of which was paid not to the victims but to lawyers and experts).

CONCEPT in action

© AP Images/Reed Saxon

Canada's Menu Foods, Inc. recalled 60 million containers of pet food in 2007 after thousands of dogs and cats became deathly ill from eating the company's high-end brands, such as Iams and Purina. A lengthy investigation by the Food and Drug Administration found that China-based suppliers had tainted the company's cuts-and-gravy product with melamine, a toxic chemical commonly found in cleansers and plastics. The massive recall was the first of many product scares that raised questions about the safety of goods made in China. Who was liable in this case?

Bankruptcy Law

Congress has given financially distressed firms and individuals a way to make a fresh start. **Bankruptcy** is the legal procedure by which individuals or businesses that cannot meet their financial obligations are relieved of their debts. A bankruptcy court distributes any assets to the creditors.

Bankruptcy can be either voluntary or involuntary. In a voluntary bankruptcy, the debtor files a petition with the court, stating that debts exceed assets and asking the court to declare the debtor bankrupt. In an involuntary bankruptcy, the creditors file the bankruptcy petition.

The Bankruptcy Reform Act of 1978, amended in 1984 and 1986, provides for the resolution of bankruptcy cases. Under this act, two types of bankruptcy proceedings are available to businesses: Chapter 7 (liquidation) and Chapter 11 (reorganization). Most bankruptcies, an estimated 70 percent, use Chapter 7. After the sale of any assets, the cash proceeds are given first to secured creditors and then to unsecured creditors. A firm that opts to reorganize under Chapter 11 works with its creditors to develop a plan for paying part of its debts and writing off the rest.

The Bankruptcy Abuse Prevention and Consumer Protection Act went into effect October 17, 2005. Under the new law Americans with heavy debt will find it difficult to avoid meeting their financial obligations. Many debtors will have to work out repayment plans instead of having their obligations erased in bankruptcy court under the new law. "Bankruptcy should always be a last resort in our legal system," President Bush said. "If someone does not pay his or her debts, the rest of

product liability
The responsibility of manufacturers and sellers for defects in the products they make and sell.

strict liability
A concept in product liability law under which a manufacturer or seller is liable for any personal injury or property damage caused by defective products or packaging even though all possible care was used to prevent such defects.

bankruptcy
The legal procedure by which individuals or businesses that cannot meet their financial obligations are relieved of their debt.

society ends up paying them. The act will protect those who legitimately need help, stop those who try to commit fraud, and bring greater stability and fairness to our financial system."[24]

The new law would require people with incomes above a certain level to pay some or all of their credit card charges, medical bills, and other obligations under a court-ordered bankruptcy plan. Supporters of the new law argue that bankruptcy frequently is the last refuge of gamblers, impulsive shoppers, the divorced or separated, and fathers avoiding child support. Now there is an objective, needs-based bankruptcy test to determine whether filers should be allowed to cancel their debts or be required to enter a repayment plan. Generally, people with incomes above the state median income would be required to use a plan to repay their debts. People with special circumstances, such as serious medical conditions, would be allowed to cancel debts despite this income guideline.

Also, companies will need a lot more cash to enter into a bankruptcy than in the past. Before the new law, utilities could not discontinue service as a result of a bankruptcy filing. But under the new act, the filing company must post a cash deposit or equivalent in order to continue their service. Sellers also have priority over other claims with regard to merchandise distributed to the debtor within 20 days prior to the bankruptcy filing.

The act limits the debtor's exclusivity period, which was a real boon of filing for bankruptcy. Past law allowed for indefinite extensions, which served to drag out the time before bondholders and other creditors received any money. But now that period is capped at 18 months, with no room for extension. For large corporations with complicated bankruptcies, such a quick turnaround may not be possible, and if a plan is not filed at the end of 18 months, the company must put itself at the mercy of creditors.

Laws to Promote Fair Competition

antitrust regulation
Laws that prevent companies from entering into agreements to control trade through a monopoly.

Many measures have been taken to try to keep the marketplace free from influences that would restrict competition. These efforts include **antitrust regulation**, laws that prevent companies from entering into agreements to control trade through a monopoly. The first act regulating competition was the Sherman Antitrust Act, passed in 1890 to prevent large companies from dominating an industry and making it hard for smaller firms to compete. This broad act banned monopolies and contracts, mergers, or conspiracies in restraint of trade. In 1914 the Clayton Act added to the more general provisions of the Sherman Antitrust Act. It outlawed the following:

- *Price discrimination*. Offering a customer discounts that are not offered to all other purchasers buying on similar terms.
- *Exclusive dealing*. Refusing to let the buyer purchase a competitor's products for resale.
- *Tying contracts*. Requiring buyers to purchase merchandise they may not want in order to get the products they do want.
- *Purchase of stock in competing corporations so as to lessen competition*. Buying competitors' stock in such quantity that competition is reduced.

The 1950 Celler-Kefauver Act amended the Clayton Act. It bans the purchase of one firm by another if the resulting merger decreases competition within the industry. As a result, all corporate acquisitions are subject to regulatory approval before they can be finalized. Most antitrust actions are taken by the U.S. Department of Justice, based on federal law. Violations of the antitrust acts are punishable by fines, imprisonment, or civil damage payments that can be as high as three times the actual damage amount. These outcomes give defendants an incentive to resolve cases.

The Federal Trade Commission Act, also passed in 1914, bans unfair trade practices. This act created the Federal Trade Commission (FTC), an independent five-member board with the power to define and monitor unfair trade practices, such as those prohibited by the Sherman and Clayton Acts. The FTC investigates complaints and can issue rulings called cease-and-desist orders to force companies to stop unfair business practices. Its powers have grown over the years. Today the FTC is one of the most important agencies regulating the competitive practices of business.

Regulation of Advertising and Pricing

A number of federal laws directly affect the promotion and pricing of products. The Wheeler-Lea Act of 1938 amended the Federal Trade Commission Act and gave the FTC authority to regulate advertising. The FTC monitors companies' advertisements for false or misleading claims.

The most important law in the area of pricing is the Robinson-Patman Act, a federal law passed in 1936 that tightened the Clayton Act's prohibitions against price discrimination. An exception

is made for circumstances like discounts for quantity purchases, as long as the discounts do not lessen competition. But a manufacturer cannot sell at a lower price to one company just because that company buys all its merchandise from the manufacturer. Also, if one firm is offered quantity discounts, all firms buying that quantity of goods must get the discounts. The FTC and the antitrust division of the Justice Department monitor pricing.

Consumer Protection Laws

Consumerism reflects the struggle for power between buyers and sellers. Specifically, it is a social movement seeking to increase the rights and powers of buyers vis-à-vis sellers. Sellers' rights and powers include the following:

- To introduce into the marketplace any product, in any size and style, that is not hazardous to personal health or safety, or if it is hazardous, to introduce it with the proper warnings and controls.
- To price the product at any level they wish, provided they do not discriminate among similar classes of buyers.
- To spend any amount of money they wish to promote the product, so long as the promotion does not constitute unfair competition.
- To formulate any message they wish about the product, provided that it is not misleading or dishonest in content or execution.
- To introduce any buying incentives they wish.

Meanwhile, buyers have the following rights and powers:

- To refuse to buy any product that is offered to them.
- To expect products to be safe.
- To expect a product to be essentially as the seller represents it.
- To receive adequate information about the product.

Many laws have been passed to protect consumer rights. Exhibit 2A.2 on the next page lists the major consumer protection laws.

consumerism
A social movement that seeks to increase the rights and powers of buyers vis-à-vis sellers.

Deregulation of Industries

During the 1980s and 1990s, the U.S. government has actively promoted **deregulation**, the removal of rules and regulations governing business competition. Deregulation has drastically changed some once-regulated industries (especially the transportation, telecommunications, and financial services industries) and created many new competitors. The result has been entries into and exits from some industries. One of the latest industries to deregulate is the electric power industry. With almost 200 investor-owned electric utilities, it is the largest industry to be deregulated so far.

Consumers typically benefit from deregulation. Increased competition often means lower prices. Businesses also benefit because they have more freedom to operate and can avoid the costs associated with government regulations. But more competition can also make it hard for small or weak firms to survive.

deregulation
The removal of rules and regulations governing business competition.

Regulation of the Internet

Although more than 200 million Americans are signing onto the Web regularly, only a minority do so to purchase products. The majority of electronic commerce remains business-to-business transactions. Americans are still far more likely to get the latest news, rather than the latest fashions, in cyberspace. Yet there are clear successes: Amazon.com is America's biggest bookstore. EBay is a hugely successful auction site.

Piracy of music through peer-to-peer networks is now a major problem for some artists and corporations. The Justice Department has seized computers and software in raids on homes and businesses. These actions have targeted the illegal distribution of copyright-protected movies, software, games, and music. In addition to actions by the federal government, the Recording Industry Association of America has filed lawsuits against a number of individuals who were sharing music illegally.

The government has also become concerned over losing control over telecommunications services (and resultant revenue) because of VOIP (voice over Internet protocol). VOIP is simply using the Internet to transfer voice messages through services such as SKYPE. Some legislators are calling

Mail Fraud Act (1872)	Makes it a federal crime to defraud consumers through use of the mail.
Pure Food and Drug Act (1906)	Created the Food and Drug Administration (FDA); protects consumers against the interstate sale of unsafe and adulterated foods and drugs.
Food, Drug, and Cosmetic Act (1938)	Expanded the power of the FDA to cover cosmetics and therapeutic devices and to establish standards for food products.
Flammable Fabrics Act (1953)	Prohibits sale or manufacture of clothing made of dangerously flammable fabric.
Child Protection Act (1966)	Prohibits sale of harmful toys and gives the FDA the right to remove dangerous products from the marketplace.
Cigarette Labeling Act (1965)	Requires cigarette manufacturers to put labels warning consumers about health hazards on cigarette packages.
Fair Packaging and Labeling Act (1966)	Regulates labeling and packaging of consumer products.
Consumer Credit Protection Act (Truth-in-Lending Act) (1968)	Requires lenders to fully disclose to borrowers the loan terms and the costs of borrowing (interest rate, application fees, etc.).
Fair Credit Reporting Act (1971)	Requires consumers denied credit on the basis of reports from credit agencies to be given access to their reports and to be allowed to correct inaccurate information.
Consumer Product Safety Act (1972)	Created the Consumer Product Safety Commission, an independent federal agency, to establish and enforce consumer product safety standards.
Equal Credit Opportunity Act (1975)	Prohibits denial of credit on the basis of gender, marital status, race, religion, age, or national origin.
Magnuson-Moss Warranty Act (1975)	Requires that warranties be written in clear language and that terms be fully disclosed.
Fair Debt Collection Practice Act (1978)	Makes it illegal to harass or abuse any person, to make false statements, or to use unfair methods when collecting a debt.
Alcohol Labeling Legislation (1988)	Provides for warning labels on liquor saying that women shouldn't drink when pregnant and that alcohol impairs our abilities.
Nutrition Labeling and Education Act (1990)	Requires truthful and uniform nutritional information labeling on every food the FDA regulates.
Children's Television Act (1990)	Limits the amount of advertising to be shown during children's television programs to not more than 10.5 minutes per hour on weekends and not more than 12.0 minutes per hour on weekdays.
Americans with Disabilities Act (ADA) (1990)	Protects the rights of people with disabilities; makes discrimination against the disabled illegal in public accommodations, transportation, and telecommunications.
Brady Law (1998)	Imposes a five-day waiting period and a background check before a gun purchaser can take possession of the gun.
Children's Online Privacy Protection Act (2002)	Regulates the collection of personally identifiable information (name, address, e-mail address, phone number, hobbies, interests, or other information collected through cookies) online from children under age 13.
Can-Spam Anti-Spam Law (2004)	Requires marketers to remove customers from their lists when requested, and provide automated opt-out methods as well as complete contact information (address and phone) with alternate means of removal. It also bans common practices such as false headers and e-mail harvesting (the use of software that spies on Web sites to collect e-mail addresses). Subject lines must be truthful and contain a notice that the message is an ad.

for VOIP taxes to fund E-911 (emergency 911 for cell phones) and CELA (Communications Assistance for Law Enforcement). The Internet environment is extremely dynamic, so what, if any, taxation and further regulation of VOIP will occur remains to be seen.

Taxation of Business

8 What are the most common taxes paid by businesses?

Taxes are sometimes seen as the price we pay to live in this country. Taxes are assessed by all levels of government on both businesses and individuals, and they are used to pay for the services provided by government. The federal government is the largest collector of taxes, accounting for 54 percent of all tax dollars. States are next, followed closely by local government taxes. The average American family pays about 37 percent of its income for taxes, 28 percent to the federal government and 9 percent to state and local governments.

Income Taxes

Income taxes are based on the income received by businesses and individuals. The income taxes paid to the federal government are set by Congress, regulated by the Internal Revenue Code, and collected by the Internal Revenue Service. These taxes are progressive, meaning that rates increase as income increases. Most of the states and some large cities also collect income taxes from individuals and businesses. The state and local governments establish their own rules and tax rates.

income taxes
Taxes that are based on the income received by businesses and individuals.

Other Types of Taxes

Besides income taxes, individuals and businesses pay a number of other taxes. The four main types are property taxes, payroll taxes, sales taxes, and excise taxes.

Property taxes are assessed on real and personal property, based on the assessed value of the property. They raise quite a bit of revenue for state and local governments. Most states tax land and buildings. Property taxes may be based on fair market value (what a buyer would pay), a percentage of fair market value, or replacement value (what it would cost today to rebuild or buy something like the original). The value on which the taxes are based is the assessed value.

property taxes
Taxes that are imposed on real and personal property based on the assessed value of the property.

Any business that has employees and meets a payroll must pay **payroll taxes**, the employer's share of Social Security taxes and federal and state unemployment taxes. These taxes must be paid on wages, salaries, and commissions. State unemployment taxes are based on the number of employees in a firm who have become eligible for unemployment benefits. A firm that has never had an employee become eligible for unemployment will pay a low rate of state unemployment taxes. The firm's experience with employment benefits does not affect federal unemployment tax rates.

payroll taxes
The employer's share of Social Security taxes and federal and state unemployment taxes.

Sales taxes are levied on goods when they are sold and are a percentage of the sales price. These taxes are imposed by states, counties, and cities. They vary in amount and in what is considered taxable. Some states have no sales tax. Others tax some categories (such as appliances) but not others (such as clothes). Still others tax all retail products except food, magazines, and prescription drugs. Sales taxes increase the cost of goods to the consumer. Businesses bear the burden of collecting sales taxes and sending them to the government.

sales taxes
Taxes that are levied on goods when they are sold; calculated as a percentage of the price.

Excise taxes are placed on specific items, such as gasoline, alcoholic beverages, cigarettes, airline tickets, cars, and guns. They can be assessed by federal, state, and local governments. In many cases, these taxes help pay for services related to the item taxed. For instance, gasoline excise taxes are often used to build and repair highways. Other excise taxes—like those on alcoholic beverages, cigarettes, and guns—are used to control practices that may cause harm.

excise taxes
Taxes that are imposed on specific items such as gasoline, alcoholic beverages, airline tickets, and guns.

Competing in the Global Marketplace

CHAPTER 3

"Teach Him Properly"

Trades are as much a part of baseball as strikeouts and homeruns. In fact, the period leading up to the July 31st trading deadline imposed by Major League Baseball is a time of much speculation and even hope for baseball teams that are on the fringes of putting together a championship run. A few such trades, though much less publicized than a trade between teams in the major leagues, actually occur in the global marketplace, particularly between Japan and America. *Mr. Baseball* is a movie that tells the story of just such a trade, a fictional account of an American-born baseball player adjusting and adapting to a country, a culture, and a style of play to which he is not accustomed.

Jack Elliot is traded to the Chunichi Dragons by the New York Yankees, and he goes begrudgingly, carrying on his shoulder a chip the size of the Bronx. Once there, he begins to alienate himself from his teammates, his manager, and even the other American-born player on the team; and much of this alienation occurs in his clashes with the different cultural norms and expectations that he must learn to navigate. In one scene, something as simple as sitting down to dinner proves to be a monumental exercise in culture clash in which he manages to make his discomfort with sitting on the ground very noticeable. He also manages to offend his hosts by exaggerating the slurping noise that is deemed polite, and he insults the daughter of his manager by not acknowledging that her father is served first. Finally, he brings bad luck upon the group by sticking his chopsticks abruptly into the noodles and leaving them there. Uchiyama, his manager and host, then extols his daughter to "Teach him properly."

Mr. Baseball is a case study in entering the global marketplace. As Jack first begins to conduct his business in Japan, he has no understanding of the cultural differences between his country and that of his new team. Instead of learning more about these differences and adapting to them, he insists on doing things his way, which results in his alienation, poor performance, and, finally, his suspension. In a very real way, because he has not attempted to explore the differences between American and Japanese baseball, he is no longer able to conduct the business that he traveled there to do. It is only once he begins to understand and embrace these differences that he sets himself up to succeed.

Jack's story should be a lesson to any business attempting to engage in the global marketplace. Entrepreneurs who see an opportunity in another country would do well to examine the differences between the countries of origin and opportunity in order to adapt the marketing plan and business strategy to the new cultural environment. This may include something as simple as personal etiquette and appropriate greeting rituals or something as complex as the political environment, the various trade agreements that the country of opportunity has with other nations, and the differing regional norms and customs that exist within the country.

The following chapter provides you with an overview of various considerations you need to be aware of as you think about the global marketplace. It ranges from how we measure trade between nations to why nations conduct trade in the first place. Along the way, the chapter outlines the barriers to trade as well as how governments can knock down some of those barriers. Ultimately, this chapter examines the benefits inherent within the global marketplace to the nations and institutions that engage in global trade as well as to you and your community. Furthermore, it provides you with an understanding of how the global marketplace might change those institutions that like baseball, are embedded within various cultures.

Discussion Questions

- Jack is a "product" that has been exported to Japan by the United States. Do you agree with this statement? Why or why not?
- How does Jack's trade to the Chunichi Dragons involve the principle of comparative advantage?
- How is Jack participating in the global marketplace? How are the New York Yankees? How are the Chunichi Dragons?

BIZ FLIX

Chapter 3 examines the business world of the global marketplace. It focuses on the processes of taking a business global (such as licensing agreements and franchisees), the challenges that are encountered, and the regulatory systems governing the world market of the 21st century. Global revolutions are under way in many areas of our lives: management, politics, communications, technology. The word global has assumed a new meaning, referring to a boundless mobility and competition in social, business, and intellectual arenas. No longer just an option, having a global vision has become a business imperative. Having a **global vision** means recognizing and reacting to international business opportunities, being aware of threats from foreign competitors in all markets, and effectively using international distribution networks to obtain raw materials and move finished products to the customer.

U.S. managers must develop a global vision if they are to recognize and react to international business opportunities, as well as remain competitive at home. Often a U.S. firm's toughest domestic competition comes from foreign companies. Moreover, a global vision enables a manager to understand that customer and distribution networks operate worldwide, blurring geographic and political barriers and making them increasingly irrelevant to business decisions. The purpose of this chapter is to explain how global trade is conducted. We also discuss the barriers to international trade and the organizations that foster global trade. The chapter concludes with trends in the global marketplace.

global vision
The ability to recognize and react to international business opportunities, be aware of threats from foreign competition, and effectively use international distribution networks to obtain raw materials and move finished products to customers.

Global Trade in the United States

1 Why is global trade important to the United States and how is it measured?

Over the past two decades, world trade has climbed from $200 billion a year to more than $11 trillion. U.S. companies play a major role in this growth in world trade. Gillette, for example, derives two-thirds of its revenue from its international division. The William Wrigley Jr. Company, makers of Wrigley's spearmint, Juicy Fruit, Altoids, Life Savers, and other products, has global sales of over $4.7 billion.[1]

Go into a Paris McDonald's and you may not recognize where you are. There are no Golden Arches or utilitarian chairs and tables and other plastic features. The restaurants have exposed brick walls, hardwood floors, and armchairs. Some French McDonald's even have faux marble walls. Most restaurants have TVs with continuous music videos. You can even order an espresso, beer, and chicken on focaccia bread sandwich. It's not America.

Global business is not a one-way street, where only U.S. companies sell their wares and services throughout the world. Foreign competition in the domestic market used to be relatively rare but now occurs in almost every industry. In fact, U.S. makers of electronic goods, cameras, automobiles, fine china, tractors, leather goods, and a host of other consumer and industrial products have struggled to maintain their domestic market shares against foreign competitors. Toyota now has passed GM in global sales.[2] Nevertheless, the global market has created vast, new business opportunities for many U.S. firms.

CONCEPT in action

General Motors outsold Japanese rival Toyota by a slim margin in 2007, maintaining its position as the world's top automaker. However, both companies say that emerging markets like China and India will determine who holds that title in the years ahead. GM sells 1 million vehicles annually in China, but in India all eyes are on Mumbai's Tata Motors, which promises to upgrade a billion people from rickshaws to rear wheel drive with the world's cheapest car, the Nano. Can U.S. automakers compete in India?

The Importance of Global Business to the United States

Many countries depend more on international commerce than the United States does. For example, France, Great Britain, and Germany all derive more than 19 percent of their gross domestic product (GDP) from world trade, compared to about 12 percent for the United States. Nevertheless, the impact of international business on the U.S. economy is still impressive:

- The United States exports about a fifth of its industrial production and a third of its farm products.
- One of every five jobs in the United States is directly or indirectly supported by exports.[3]
- U.S. businesses export more than $800 billion in goods to foreign countries every year, and almost a third of U.S. corporate profits is derived from international trade and foreign investment.
- Exports account for almost 25 percent of America's economic growth.

These statistics might seem to imply that practically every business in the United States is selling its wares throughout the world, but most is accounted for by big business. About 85 percent of all U.S. exports of manufactured goods are shipped by 250 companies. Yet, 97 percent of all exporters are small and medium-size firms.[4]

The Impact of Terrorism on Global Trade

The terrorist attacks on America on September 11, 2001, changed forever the way the world conducts business. The immediate impact was a short-term shrinkage of global trade. Globalization will continue, however, because the world's major markets are too vitally integrated for globalization to stop. Nevertheless, terrorism caused the growth to be slower and costlier.

Companies are paying more for insurance and to provide security for overseas staff and property. Heightened border security slows movements of cargo, forcing companies to stock more inventory. Tighter immigration policies curtail the liberal inflows of skilled and blue-collar workers that allowed companies to expand while keeping wages in check. Meanwhile, greater concern about political risk (such as multinational petroleum companies in Venezuela) is causing some firms to greatly narrow their horizons when making new investments. The impact of terrorism may lessen over time, but multinational firms will always be on guard.

Measuring Trade Between Nations

International trade improves relationships with friends and allies, helps ease tensions among nations, and—economically speaking—bolsters economies, raises people's standard of living, provides jobs, and improves the quality of life. This section takes a look at some key measures of international trade: exports and imports, the balance of trade, the balance of payments, and exchange rates.

Exports and Imports

The developed nations (those with mature communication, financial, educational, and distribution systems) are the major players in international trade. They account for about 70 percent of the world's exports and imports. **Exports** are goods and services made in one country and sold to others. **Imports** are goods and services that are bought from other countries. The United States is both the largest exporter and the largest importer in the world.

Each year the United States exports more food, animal feed, and beverages than the year before. A third of U.S. farm acreage is devoted to crops for export. The United States is also a major exporter of engineering products and other high-tech goods, such as computers and telecommunications equipment. For more than 40,000 U.S. companies (the majority of them small), international trade offers exciting and profitable opportunities. Among the largest U.S. exporters are Boeing Co., General Motors Corp., General Electric Co., Ford Motor Co., and IBM.

Despite our impressive list of resources and great variety of products, imports to the United States are also growing. Some of these imports are raw materials that we lack, such as manganese, cobalt, and bauxite, which are used to make airplane parts, exotic metals, and military hardware. More modern factories and lower labor costs in other countries make it cheaper to import industrial supplies (like steel) and production equipment than to produce them at home. Most of Americans' favorite hot beverages—coffee, tea, and cocoa—are imported. Lower manufacturing costs have resulted in huge increases in imports from China.

Balance of Trade

The difference between the value of a country's exports and the value of its imports during a specific time is the country's **balance of trade**. A country that exports more than it imports is said to have a favorable balance of trade, called a **trade surplus**. A country that imports more than it exports is said to have an unfavorable balance of trade, or a **trade deficit**. When imports exceed exports, more money from trade flows out of the country than flows into it.

Although U.S. exports have been booming, we still import more than we export. We have had an unfavorable balance of trade throughout the 1990s and 2000s. America's exports continue to grow but not as fast as our imports: the export of goods, such as computers, trucks, and airplanes, is very strong. The sector that is lagging in significant growth is the export of services. Although America exports many services—including airline trips, international phone calls, movie royalties, tourism in the United States by foreigners, education of foreign students, and legal advice—part of the problem is piracy. Hollywood estimates that it loses about $3 billion a year from international movie piracy.

Balance of Payments

Another measure of international trade is called the **balance of payments**, which is a summary of a country's international financial transactions showing the difference between the country's total payments to and its total receipts from other countries. The balance of payments includes

exports
Goods and services produced in one country and sold to other countries.

imports
Goods and services that are bought from other countries.

balance of trade
The difference between the value of a country's exports and the value of its imports during a specific time.

trade surplus
A favorable balance of trade that occurs when a country exports more than it imports.

trade deficit
An unfavorable balance of trade that occurs when a country imports more than it exports.

balance of payments
A summary of a country's international financial transactions showing the difference between the country's total payments to and its total receipts from other countries.

imports and exports (balance of trade), long-term investments in overseas plants and equipment, government loans to and from other countries, gifts and foreign aid, military expenditures made in other countries, and money transfers in and out of foreign banks.

From 1900 until 1970, the United States had a trade surplus, but in the other areas that make up the balance of payments, U.S. payments exceeded receipts, due in major part to the large U.S. military presence abroad. Hence, almost every year since 1950, the United States has had an unfavorable balance of payments. And since 1970, both the balance of payments and the balance of trade have been unfavorable. What can a nation do to reduce an unfavorable balance of payments? It can foster exports, reduce its dependence on imports, decrease its military presence abroad, or reduce foreign investment. In 2006, our exports totaled $1.438 trillion, yet our imports were $2.201 trillion. Thus, we had an unfavorable balance of trade of $763 billion.[5]

CONCEPT in action

Discontented by its enormous trade deficit with China, the United States is pressuring the Chinese government to raise the value of its currency, a move that would make U.S. goods more affordable relative to Chinese exports. The Chinese central bank has responded by threatening to liquidate its vast holding of U.S. dollars if Washington forces the yuan's revaluation with trade sanctions. China's so-called "nuclear option" could cause the dollar's value to collapse entirely. How does China benefit from the low valuation of its currency?

floating exchange rates
A system in which prices of currencies move up and down based on the demand for and supply of the various currencies.

devaluation
A lowering of the value of a nation's currency relative to other currencies.

The Changing Value of Currencies

The exchange rate is the price of one country's currency in terms of another country's currency. If a country's currency appreciates, less of that country's currency is needed to buy another country's currency. If a country's currency depreciates, more of that currency will be needed to buy another country's currency.

How do appreciation and depreciation affect the prices of a country's goods? If, say, the U.S. dollar depreciates relative to the Japanese yen, U.S. residents have to pay more dollars to buy Japanese goods. To illustrate, suppose the dollar price of a yen is $0.012 and that a Toyota is priced at 2 million yen. At this exchange rate, a U.S. resident pays $24,000 for a Toyota ($0.012 × 2 million yen = $24,000). If the dollar depreciates to $0.018 to one yen, then the U.S. resident will have to pay $36,000 for a Toyota.

As the dollar depreciates, the prices of Japanese goods rise for U.S. residents, so they buy fewer Japanese goods—thus, U.S. imports decline. At the same time, as the dollar depreciates relative to the yen, the yen appreciates relative to the dollar. This means prices of U.S. goods fall for the Japanese, so they buy more U.S. goods—and U.S. exports rise.

Currency markets operate under a system called **floating exchange rates**. Prices of currencies "float" up and down based on the demand for and supply of each currency. Global currency traders create the supply of and demand for a particular currency based on that currency's investment and trade potentials, and economic strength. If a country decides that its currency is not properly valued in international currency markets, the government may step in and adjust the currency's value. In a **devaluation**, a nation lowers the value of its currency relative to other currencies. This makes that country's exports cheaper and should, in turn, help the balance of payments.

In other cases, a country's currency may be undervalued, giving its exports an unfair competitive advantage. Many believe that China's huge trade surplus with the United States is partially because China's currency was undervalued. In 2005, a bill was introduced in the United States Senate to place a tariff (tax) of 27.5 percent on all China's exports to the United States if China failed to raise the value of its currency.

CONCEPT check

What is global vision, and why is it important?

What impact does international trade have on the U.S. economy?

Explain the impact of a currency devaluation.

On July 20, 2005, China said that it would allow its currency to fluctuate and strengthened the yuan's value. Since October 2007, the yuan has climbed at an annual rate of 13 percent against the dollar. This is the fastest rate of increase since July 2005 when China stopped pegging to the dollar. The reason for the increase is that Chinese policymakers believe that the benefits of a rising yuan outweigh the costs. China's main concern now is inflation, and a rising yuan will help reduce imported inflation, especially on food and raw materials.[6]

Why Nations Trade

2 Why do nations trade?

One might argue that the best way to protect workers and the domestic economy is to stop trade with other nations. Then the whole circular flow of inputs and outputs would stay within our borders. But if we decided to do that, how would we get resources like cobalt and coffee beans? The United States simply can't produce some things, and it can't manufacture some products, such as steel and most clothing, at the low costs we're used to. The fact is that nations—like people—are good at producing different things: you may be better at balancing a ledger than repairing a car. In that case you benefit by "exporting" your bookkeeping services and "importing" the car repairs you need from a good mechanic. Economists refer to specialization like this as advantage.

Part 1: The Business Environment

Absolute Advantage

A country has an **absolute advantage** when it can produce and sell a product at a lower cost than any other country or when it is the only country that can provide a product. The United States, for example, has an absolute advantage in reusable spacecraft and other high-tech items.

Suppose that the United States has an absolute advantage in air traffic control systems for busy airports and that Brazil has an absolute advantage in coffee. The United States does not have the proper climate for growing coffee, and Brazil lacks the technology to develop air traffic control systems. Both countries would gain by exchanging air traffic control systems for coffee.

Comparative Advantage

Even if the United States had an absolute advantage in both coffee and air traffic control systems, it should still specialize and engage in trade. The **principle of comparative advantage** states that each country should specialize in the products that it can produce most readily and cheaply and trade those products for goods that foreign countries can produce most readily and cheaply. This specialization ensures greater product availability and lower prices.

For example, India and China have a comparative advantage in producing clothing because of low labor costs. Japan has long held a comparative advantage in consumer electronics because of technological expertise. America has an advantage in computer software, airplanes, some agricultural products, heavy machinery, and jet engines.

Thus, comparative advantage acts as a stimulus to trade. When nations allow their citizens to trade whatever goods and services they choose without government regulation, free trade exists. **Free trade** is the policy of permitting the people and businesses of a country to buy and sell where they please without restrictions. The opposite of free trade is **protectionism**, in which a nation protects its home industries from outside competition by establishing artificial barriers such as tariffs and quotas. In the next section, we'll look at the various barriers, some natural and some created by governments, that restrict free trade.

The Fear of Trade and Globalization

The continued protests during meetings of the World Trade Organization and the protests during the convocations of the World Bank and the International Monetary Fund (the three organizations are discussed later in the chapter) show that many people fear world trade and globalization. What do they fear? The negatives of global trade are as follows:

- Millions of Americans have lost jobs due to imports or production shifts abroad. Most find new jobs, but those jobs often pay less.
- Millions of others fear losing their jobs, especially at those companies operating under competitive pressure.
- Employers often threaten to export jobs if workers do not accept pay cuts.
- Service and white-collar jobs are increasingly vulnerable to operations moving offshore.

Sending domestic jobs to another country is called **outsourcing**, a topic you will explore more in Chapter 8. Many American companies, such as Dell, IBM, and AT&T, have set up call service centers in India, Ireland, and other countries. Now even engineering and research and development jobs are being outsourced. Infineon Technologies recently eliminated 40 high-paying engineering jobs at its San Jose research facility and transferred the work to India.

So is outsourcing good or bad? For those who lose their jobs to outsourcing, it's obviously bad. However, some economists say it leads to cheaper goods and services for U.S. consumers because costs are lower. Also, it should stimulate exports to fast-growing countries. No one knows how many jobs will be lost to outsourcing in coming years. Alan Blinder, former Federal Reserve vice chairman, says as many as 40 million jobs may be shipped out of the country in the next decade or two.[7] That is more than double the total of workers employed in manufacturing today! Dr. Blinder notes that new communications technology allows services to be delivered from afar. His list of "most highly offshorable jobs" are: accounting and auditing clerks, computer programmers, data entry clerks, graphic designers, and financial analysts.[8]

absolute advantage
The situation when a country can produce and sell a product at a lower cost than any other country or when it is the only country that can provide the product.

principle of comparative advantage
The concept that each country should specialize in the products that it can produce most readily and cheaply and trade those products for those that other countries can produce more readily and cheaply.

free trade
The policy of permitting the people and businesses of a country to buy and sell where they please without restrictions.

protectionism
The policy of protecting home industries from outside competition by establishing artificial barriers such as tariffs and quotas.

outsourcing
Sending work functions to another country resulting in domestic workers losing their jobs.

CONCEPT in action

Anti-globalization groups oppose America's free-trade stance, arguing that corporate interests are hurting the U.S. economy and usurping the power of the American people. The "Stocks and Stripes" flag is a powerful anti-free-trade statement expressing the idea that multinational corporations wield too much power over the United States and its policies. Are fears expressed by anti-globalization activists and nationalists justified?

© Stefan Zaklin/Getty Images

Benefits of Globalization

A closer look, however, reveals that globalization has been the engine that creates jobs and wealth. Benefits of global trade include the following:

- Productivity grows more quickly when countries produce goods and services in which they have a comparative advantage. Living standards can improve faster.
- Global competition and cheap imports keep prices down, so inflation is less likely to arrest economic growth.
- An open economy spurs innovation with fresh ideas from abroad.
- The United States buys about $2 trillion a year from other countries or 16 percent of the gross domestic product. This is up from 8.5 percent in 1995.[9]
- Since 1997, prices for many heavily-traded goods have actually fallen: 86 percent for computers and peripherals, 68 percent for video equipment, 36 percent for toys, 20 percent for women's outerwear, and 17 percent for men's shirts and sweaters. Prices of goods and services not subject to foreign competition have fared less well: college tuition and fees, up 53 percent; cable and satellite television, up 41 percent; dental services, up 38 percent; and prescription drugs and medical supplies, up 37 percent.[10]
- Income from U.S. foreign subsidiaries of firms such as Pepsi, American Express, and Microsoft is over $200 billion a year, and many are enjoying record profits.[11]

CONCEPT check

Describe the policy of free trade and its relationship to comparative advantage.

Why do people fear globalization?

What are the benefits of globalization?

Barriers to Trade

3 What are the barriers to international trade?

International trade is carried out by both businesses and governments—as long as no one puts up trade barriers. In general, trade barriers keep firms from selling to one another in foreign markets. The major obstacles to international trade are natural barriers, tariff barriers, and nontariff barriers.

Natural Barriers

Natural barriers to trade can be either physical or cultural. For instance, even though raising beef in the relative warmth of Argentina may cost less than raising beef in the bitter cold of Siberia, the cost of shipping the beef from South America to Siberia might drive the price too high. Distance is thus one of the natural barriers to international trade.

Language is another natural trade barrier. People who can't communicate effectively may not be able to negotiate trade agreements or may ship the wrong goods.

Tariff Barriers

tariff
A tax imposed on imported goods.

A **tariff** is a tax imposed by a nation on imported goods. It may be a charge per unit, such as per barrel of oil or per new car; it may be a percentage of the value of the goods, such as 5 percent of a $500,000 shipment of shoes; or it may be a combination. No matter how it is assessed, any tariff makes imported goods more costly, so they are less able to compete with domestic products.

protective tariffs
Tariffs that are imposed in order to make imports less attractive to buyers than domestic products are.

Protective tariffs make imported products less attractive to buyers than domestic products. The United States, for instance, has protective tariffs on imported poultry, textiles, sugar, and some types of steel and clothing. On the other side of the world, Japan imposes a tariff on U.S. cigarettes that makes them cost 60 percent more than Japanese brands. U.S. tobacco firms believe they could gain as much as a third of the Japanese market if there were no tariffs on cigarettes. With tariffs, they have under 2 percent of the market.

Arguments for and against Tariffs
Congress has debated the issue of tariffs since 1789. The main arguments for tariffs include the following:

- Tariffs protect infant industries. A tariff can give a struggling new domestic industry time to become an effective global competitor.
- Tariffs protect American jobs. Unions, among others, say tariffs keep foreign labor from taking away U.S. jobs.
- Tariffs aid in military preparedness. Tariffs should protect industries and technology during peacetime that are vital to the military in the event of war.

© Stockbyte/Getty Images

Antigua Free to Violate U.S. Copyrights

In an unusual World Trade Organization ruling, the tiny Caribbean nation of Antigua won the right to violate copyright protections on goods like films and music from the United States—worth up to $21 million—as part of a dispute between the two countries over online gambling. The award comes after a WTO decision that Washington has wrongly blocked online-gambling operators on the island from the American market at the same time it permitted online wagering on horse racing.

Antigua and Barbuda had claimed annual damages of $3.44 billion. That makes the relatively small amount awarded in the case, $21 million, something of a setback for Antigua, which had been struggling to preserve its booming gambling industry. The United States had claimed that its behavior had caused only $500,000 of damage to the Antiguan economy.

Yet the ruling is significant in that it grants a rare form of compensation: the right of one country, in this case, Antigua, to violate intellectual-property laws of another—the United States—by allowing them to distribute copies of American music, movie, and software products, among other items.

"That has only been done once before and is, I believe, a very potent weapon," said Mark Mendel, a lawyer representing Antigua, after the ruling. "I hope that the United States government will now see the wisdom in reaching some accommodation with Antigua over this dispute."

Though Antigua is best known for its pristine beaches and tourist attractions, the dozens of online casinos now based there are vital to the island's economy, serving as its second-largest employer. By pressing its claim trade, lawyers said, Antigua could set a precedent for other countries to sue the United States for unfair trade practices, potentially opening the door to electronic piracy and other dubious practices around the world.[16]

Critical Thinking Questions
- Do you think the WTO ruling is fair? Why or why not?
- What might have been a more traditional remedy that the WTO could have used?

loans, the World Bank is a major source of advice and information for developing nations. The United States has granted the organization millions of dollars to create knowledge databases on nutrition, birth control, software engineering, creating quality products, and basic accounting systems.

The **International Monetary Fund (IMF)** was founded in 1945, one year after the creation of the World Bank, to promote trade through financial cooperation and eliminate trade barriers in the process. The IMF makes short-term loans to member nations that are unable to meet their budgetary expenses. It operates as a lender of last resort for troubled nations. In exchange for these emergency loans, IMF lenders frequently extract significant commitments from the borrowing nations to address the problems that led to the crises. These steps may include curtailing imports or even devaluing the currency.

Some global financial problems do not have a simple solution. One option would be to pump a lot more funds into the IMF, giving it enough resources to bail out troubled countries and put them back on their feet. In effect, the IMF would be turned into a real lender of last resort for the world economy.

The danger of counting on the IMF, though, is the "moral hazard" problem. Investors who would assume that the IMF would bail them out would therefore be encouraged to take bigger and bigger risks in emerging markets, leading to the possibility of even deeper financial crises in the future.

International Monetary Fund (IMF)
An international organization, founded in 1945, that promotes trade, makes short-term loans to member nations, and acts as a lender of last resort for troubled nations.

CONCEPT check

Describe the purpose and role of the WTO.

What are the roles of the World Bank and the IMF in world trade?

International Economic Communities

Nations that frequently trade with each other may decide to formalize their relationship. The governments meet and create agreements for a common economic policy. The result is an economic community or, in other cases, a bilateral trade agreement (an agreement between two countries to lower trade barriers). For example, two nations may agree upon a **preferential tariff**, which gives advantages to one nation (or several nations) over others. When members of the British Commonwealth trade with Great Britain, they pay lower tariffs than do other nations. In other cases, nations may form free-trade associations. In a **free-trade zone**, few duties or rules restrict trade among the partners, but nations outside the zone must pay the tariffs set by the individual members.

North American Free Trade Agreement (NAFTA)

The **North American Free Trade Agreement (NAFTA)** created the world's largest free-trade zone. The agreement was ratified by the U.S. Congress in 1993. It includes Canada, the United States, and Mexico, with a combined population of 360 million and an economy of over $6 trillion.

preferential tariff
A tariff that is lower for some nations than for others.

5 What are international economic communities?

free-trade zone
An area where the nations allow free, or almost free, trade among each other while imposing tariffs on goods of nations outside the zone.

North American Free Trade Agreement (NAFTA)
A 1993 agreement creating a free-trade zone including Canada, Mexico, and the United States.

Canada, the largest U.S. trading partner, entered a free-trade agreement with the United States in 1988. Thus, most of the new long-run opportunities opened for U.S. business under NAFTA are in Mexico, America's third-largest trading partner. Before NAFTA, tariffs on Mexican exports to the United States averaged just 4 percent, and most goods entered the United States duty-free, so NAFTA's primary impact was to open the Mexican market to U.S. companies. When the treaty went into effect, tariffs on about half the items traded across the Rio Grande disappeared. Since NAFTA came into effect, U.S.–Mexican trade has increased from $80 billion to $275 billion annually. The pact removed a web of Mexican licensing requirements, quotas, and tariffs that limited transactions in U.S. goods and services. For instance, the pact allows U.S. and Canadian financial-services companies to own subsidiaries in Mexico for the first time in 50 years.

The real test of NAFTA will be whether it can deliver rising prosperity on both sides of the Rio Grande. For Mexicans, NAFTA must provide rising wages, better benefits, and an expanding middle class with enough purchasing power to keep buying goods from the United States and Canada. That scenario seems to be working. At the Delphi Corp. auto parts plant in Ciudad Juárez, just across the border from El Paso, Texas, the assembly line is a cross section of working-class Mexico. In the years since NAFTA lowered trade and investment barriers, Delphi has significantly expanded its presence in the country. Today it employs 70,000 Mexicans, who every day receive up to 70 million U.S.-made components to assemble into parts. The wages are modest by U.S. standards—an assembly line worker with two years' experience earns about $1.90 an hour. But that's triple Mexico's minimum wage, and Delphi jobs are among the most coveted in Juárez.

In August 2007, the three NAFTA member countries met in Canada to "tweak" the agreement but not make substantial changes. For example, the members agreed to further remove trade barriers on hogs, steel, consumer electronics, and chemicals. They also directed the North American Steel Trade Committee, which represents the three governments, to focus on subsidized steel from China. Most Canadians (73 percent) and Americans (77 percent) felt that NAFTA has played a key role in North American prosperity.[17] The survey was not conducted in Mexico.

The largest new trade agreement is **Mercosur**, which includes Peru, Brazil, Argentina, Uruguay, and Paraguay. The elimination of most tariffs among the trading partners has resulted in trade revenues that currently exceed $16 billion annually. Recent recessions in Mercosur countries have limited economic growth, even though trade among Mercosur countries has continued to grow.

Central America Free Trade Agreement

The newest free trade agreement is the Central America Free Trade Agreement (CAFTA), which was passed in 2005. Besides the United States, the agreement includes Costa Rica, the Dominican Republic, El Salvador, Guatemala, Honduras, and Nicaragua. The United States is already the principal exporter to these nations, so economists don't think that it will result in a major increase in U.S. exports. It will, however, reduce tariffs on exports to CAFTA countries. Already, some 80 percent of the goods imported into the United States from CAFTA nations are tariff-free. CAFTA countries may benefit from the new permanent trade deal if U.S. multinational firms deepen their investment in the region.

The European Union

In 1993, the member countries of the European Community (EC) ratified the Maastricht Treaty, which proposed to take the EC further toward economic, monetary, and political union. Although the heart of the treaty deals with developing a unified European Market, Maastricht was also intended to increase integration among **European Union (EU)** members.

EU27 Member States:

			Candidate Countries:
• Austria	• Germany	• The Netherlands	• Croatia
• Belgium	• Greece	• Poland	• Macedonia
• Bulgaria	• Hungary	• Portugal	• Turkey
• Cyprus	• Ireland	• Romania	
• Czech Republic	• Italy	• Slovakia	
• Denmark	• Latvia	• Slovenia	
• Estonia	• Lithuania	• Spain	
• Finland	• Luxembourg	• Sweden	
• France	• Malta	• United Kingdom	

Mercosur
Trade agreement between Peru, Brazil, Argentina, Uruguay, and Paraguay.

European Union (EU)
Trade agreement among 27 European nations.

The EU has helped increase this integration by creating a borderless economy for the 27 European nations, shown on the map in Exhibit 3.1.

European Union member states have set up common institutions to which they delegate some of their sovereignty so that decisions on specific matters of joint interest can be made democrati-cally at the European level. This pooling of sovereignty is also called **European integration**.

One of the principal objectives of the European Union is to promote economic progress of all member countries. The EU has stimulated economic progress by eliminating trade barriers, differences in tax laws, and differences in product standards, and by establishing a common currency. A new European Community Bank was created along with a common currency called the euro. The European Union's single market has created 2.5 million new jobs since it was founded and has generated more than $1 trillion in new wealth.[18] The opening of national EU markets has brought down the price of national telephone calls by 50 percent since 1998. Under pressure of competition, the prices of airfares in Europe have fallen significantly. The removal of national restrictions has enabled more than 15 million Europeans to go to another EU country to work or spend their retirement.

The EU is a very tough antitrust enforcer; some would say tougher than the United States. The EU, for example, blocked a merger between General Electric and Honeywell (both American companies) even after U.S. regulators had approved the deal. Unlike the United States, the EU can

European integration
The delegation of limited sovereignty by European Union member states to the EU so that common laws and policies can be created at the European level.

EXHIBIT 3.1   The European Union

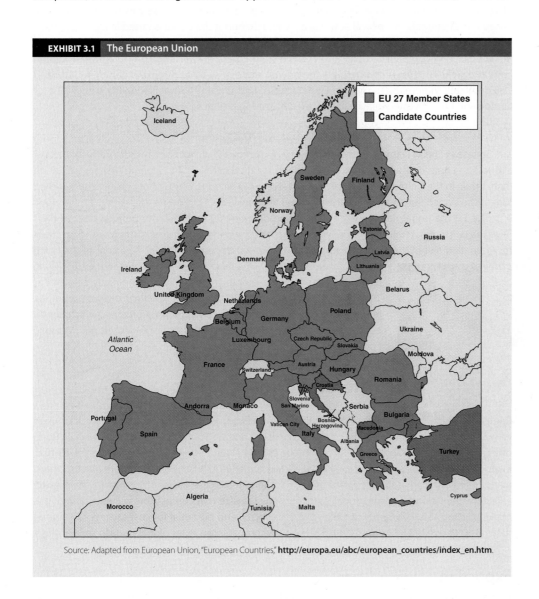

Source: Adapted from European Union, "European Countries," **http://europa.eu/abc/european_countries/index_en.htm**.

seal off corporate offices for unspecified periods to prevent destruction of evidence and enter the homes, cars, yachts, and other personal property of executives suspected of abusing their companies' market power or conspiring to fix prices. In 2005, the European offices of Intel were raided by EU antitrust officials seeking information about monopoly power abuse. Advanced Micro Devices (AMD) claimed that Intel had achieved its 90 percent of global market share through threats and kickbacks.[19]

Microsoft has been fighting the European Court since 2002, with no quick end in sight. The Court fined Microsoft for monopolizing Internet access by offering Internet Explorer with its Windows software. The company is also appealing a Court decision requiring it to share code with "open source" companies. Another big U.S. company, Coca-Cola, settled a six-year antitrust dispute with the European Court by agreeing to strict limits on its sales tactics. Coke can't sign exclusive agreements with retailers that would ban competing soft drinks or give retailers rebates based on sales volume. Furthermore, it must give rivals, like Pepsi, 20 percent of the space in Coke coolers so Pepsi can stock its own brands. If Coke violates the terms of the agreement, it will be fined 10 percent of its worldwide revenue (over $2 billion).[20]

An entirely different type of problem facing global businesses is the possibility of a protectionist movement by the EU against outsiders. For example, European automakers have proposed holding Japanese imports at roughly their current 10 percent market share. The Irish, Danes, and Dutch don't make cars and have unrestricted home markets; they are unhappy at the prospect of limited imports of Toyotas and Hondas. Meanwhile, France has a strict quota on Japanese cars to protect its own Renault and Peugeot. These local automakers could be hurt if the quota is raised at all.

Interestingly, a number of big U.S. companies are already considered more "European" than many European companies. Coke and Kellogg's are considered classic European brand names. Ford and General Motors compete for the largest share of auto sales on the continent. IBM and Dell dominate their markets. General Electric, AT&T, and Westinghouse are already strong all over Europe and have invested heavily in new manufacturing facilities there.

The Importance of the EU to the United States

The European Union is the largest economy in the world. It has a gross domestic product of about $18 trillion compared with around $11.5 trillion for the United States. Unemployment, although higher than in the United States, is at its lowest level in 15 years. In 2006, labor productivity matched that of the United States, again for the first time in many years.[21]

The EU is a huge market, with a population of nearly 500 million. The United States and EU have the largest bilateral trade and investment relationship in world history. Together they account for more than half of the global economy, while bilateral trade accounts for 7 percent of the world total. U.S. and EU companies have invested an estimated $2 trillion in each other's economies, employing directly and indirectly as many as 14 million workers. Nearly every U.S. state is involved with exporting to, importing from, or working for European firms. California, which has an economy tied closely to Asia, has roughly 1 million workers connected to European investment or trade.[22]

CONCEPT check

Explain the pros and cons of NAFTA.

What is the European Union? Will it ever be a United States of Europe?

Participating in the Global Marketplace

6 How do companies enter the global marketplace?

Companies decide to "go global" for a number of reasons. Perhaps the most urgent reason is to earn additional profits. If a firm has a unique product or technological advantage not available to other international competitors, this advantage should result in major business successes abroad. In other situations, management may have exclusive market information about foreign customers, marketplaces, or market situations not known to others. In this case, although exclusivity can provide an initial motivation for going global, managers must realize that competitors will eventually catch up. Finally, saturated domestic markets, excess capacity, and potential for cost savings can also be motivators to expand into international markets. A company can enter global trade in several ways, as this section describes.

Exporting

exporting
The practice of selling domestically produced goods to buyers in another country.

When a company decides to enter the global market, usually the least complicated and least risky alternative is **exporting**, or selling domestically produced products to buyers in another

A Big Cheese in Exporting

French cheese is easy to find in America. Creamy Camembert, soft Muenster: it's all made in the USA. Farmers are producing handcrafted chevre—goat cheese—right here in the United States. But there's a difference between French cheese and cheese produced in France. France has 400 varieties of cheese; the average resident eats 50 pounds a year; "terroir," the soil and region from which a cheese comes, holds a distinct magic; revered "affi-neurs," or cheese-agers, practice their art in underground cheese caves. The French are pretty serious about their cheese.

So what does a Portland, Maine, advertising agency know about marketing cheese from France? More than you might think, the French have decided. They signed a three-year, $3 million contract with Swardlick Marketing Group to sell cheese from France in the United States. It's the first time the industry has chosen someone outside France to directly market their cheese. And this is its first organized foray into the United States, where the appetite for specialty cheese seems to be growing. The French cheese contract really has its roots in a 15-year campaign to elevate the lowly wild blueberry from a frozen commodity to a high-profile health food. More on this below.

The cheese opportunity emerged in 2005 when a Swardlick manager went with Gov. John Baldacci on a Maine trade mission to France, organized by the Maine International Trade Center. The initial thought was to cultivate travel connections for America-bound tourists, but business went in a different direction. Swardlick had been working with the Mission Economique, part of the French embassy in New York City. That got the company a seat at the table to make a proposal to CNIEL—Centre National Interprofessionnel de l'Economie Laitire—which represents the milk industry in France.

Cheese is a multibillion industry in the United States. Sales have been growing by double digits as Americans who didn't know brie from Velveeta started to expand their cheese-eating horizons. The French want a slice of that action. They see the United States as a primary growth market for them. But dairy states like Wisconsin already make high-quality, French-inspired cheeses. Why should American consumers buy cheese made in France when there's good domestic cheese in the dairy case? That's where Swardlick's experience with the wild blueberry comes in.

Swardlick started working 15 years ago with the Wild Blueberry Association of North America. Wild blueberries, grown in Maine and eastern Canada, had been a cyclical commodity product. Swardlick developed a campaign to brand the wild blueberry and turn its image into a healthy, antiaging super-food. Prices and sales have skyrocketed, and wild blueberries are found in everything from cereal to yogurt. "We didn't change the berry," John Sauve, managing director, noted, "just the way people thought about it." Sauve was director of the world blueberry group for 12 years before coming to Swardlick. When the French learned how Sauve and Swardlick had transformed the wild blueberry, they saw the potential for their cheese. "We showed them a different way of thinking about how we would promote their product," Sauve said. "So our job is not to market French cheese. It's to market cheese from France."

Since then, Sauve and Paul Bonneau, the agency's creative director, have traveled to key cheese-making regions of France. This "tour de fromage" took them to small farms and large cheese-making operations. It helped them appreciate the rich history of a food that, like wine, is so closely tied to French culture and identity. "Our goal is to take the romance and translate it for the U.S. market," Bonneau said.[23]

Critical Thinking Questions
- Do you think that we could successfully export American cheese to France? Why or why not?
- What will Swardlick have to say to get Americans to eat French cheeses?

© Rubberball/Getty Images

country. A company, for example, can sell directly to foreign importers or buyers. Exporting is not limited to huge corporations such as General Motors or Westinghouse. Indeed, small companies typically enter the global marketplace by exporting. The United States is the world's largest exporter. Many small businesses claim that they lack the money, time, or knowledge of foreign markets that exporting requires. The U.S. Small Business Administration (SBA) now offers the Export Working Capital Program, which helps small and medium-size firms obtain working capital (money) to complete export sales. The SBA also provides counseling and legal assistance for small businesses that wish to enter the global marketplace. Companies such as American Building Restoration Products of Franklin, Wisconsin, have benefited tremendously from becoming exporters. American Building is now selling its chemical products to building restoration companies in Mexico, Israel, Japan, and Korea. Exports account for more than 5 percent of the firm's total sales.

Plenty of governmental help is available when a company decides to begin exporting. Export Assistance Centers (EACs) provide a one-stop resource place for help in exporting. Over 700 EACs are placed strategically around the country. Often the SBA is located in the same building as the EAC. The SBA can guarantee loans of $50,000 to $100,000 to help an exporter grow its business. Online help is also available at **http://www.export.gov.** The site lists international trade events, offers international marketing research, and has practical tools to help with every step of the exporting process. Companies considering exporting for the first time can get answers to questions such as "What's in it for me?", "Am I ready for this?", and "What do I have to do?"

One small company has played an important role in France exporting cheese to the United States. The story is told in the Catching the Entrepreneurial Spirit box above.

Licensing and Franchising

licensing
The legal process whereby a firm agrees to allow another firm to use a manufacturing process, trademark, patent, trade secret, or other proprietary knowledge in exchange for the payment of a royalty.

Another effective way for a firm to move into the global arena with relatively little risk is to sell a license to manufacture its product to a firm in a foreign country. **Licensing** is the legal process whereby a firm (the licensor) agrees to let another firm (the licensee) use a manufacturing process, trademark, patent, trade secret, or other proprietary knowledge. The licensee, in turn, agrees to pay the licensor a royalty or fee agreed on by both parties.

International licensing is a multibillion dollar–a–year industry. Entertainment, with DVD movies and character licensing, such as Batman, is the largest single category. Trademarks are the second-largest source of licensing revenue. Caterpillar licenses its brand for both shoes and clothing, which is very popular in Europe.

U.S. companies have eagerly embraced the licensing concept. For instance, Philip Morris licensed Labatt Brewing Company to produce Miller High Life in Canada. The Spalding Company receives more than $2 million annually from license agreements on its sporting goods. Fruit-of-the-Loom lends its name through licensing to 45 consumer items in Japan alone, for at least 1 percent of the licensee's gross sales.

The licensor must make sure it can exercise sufficient control over the licensee's activities to ensure proper quality, pricing, distribution, and so on. Licensing may also create a new competitor in the long run, if the licensee decides to void the license agreement. International law is often ineffective in stopping such actions. Two common ways that a licensor can maintain effective control over its licensees are by shipping one or more critical components from the United States and by locally registering patents and trademarks in its own name.

Franchising, covered in Chapter 4, is a form of licensing that has grown rapidly in recent years. Over 350 U.S. franchisors operate more than 32,000 outlets in foreign countries, bringing in sales of $6 billion. More than half of the international franchises are for fast-food restaurants and business services. The international division of McDonald's is responsible for over 50 percent of the chain's sales and 60 percent of its profits.

Having a big-name franchise doesn't always guarantee success or mean that the job will be easy. In China, franchises such as A&W, Chili's Grill & Bar, Dunkin' Donuts, and Rainforest Café closed up shop. When Subway opened its first sandwich shop, locals stood outside and watched for a few days. Patrons were so confused that the franchisee had to print signs explaining how to order. They didn't believe the tuna salad was made from a fish because they couldn't see the head or tail. And they didn't like the idea of touching their food, so they would hold the sandwich vertically, peel off the paper wrap, and eat it like a banana. Most of all, the Chinese customers didn't want sandwiches.

It's not unusual for Western food chains to have trouble selling in China. McDonald's, aware that the Chinese consume more chicken than beef, offered a spicy chicken burger. KFC got rid of coleslaw in favor of seasonal dishes such as shredded carrots, fungus, or bamboo shoots.

CONCEPT in action

Cold Stone Creamery recently opened its first ice cream store in Dubai Festival City, a vast entertainment district in the United Arab Emirates. The grand opening was part of the franchise's Middle East expansion, which will deliver the company's trademark Ultimate Ice Cream Experience to millions of customers throughout the region. In addition to serving up gooey signature creations like the Mud Pie Mojo, Cold Stone will offer menu items suited to the region's unique tastes, such as watermelon-flavored sorbet and coffee drinks. What challenges do franchisees face in foreign countries?

Contract Manufacturing

contract manufacturing
The practice in which a foreign firm manufactures private-label goods under a domestic firm's brand name.

In **contract manufacturing**, a foreign firm manufactures private-label goods under a domestic firm's brand. Marketing may be handled by either the domestic company or the foreign manufacturer. Levi Strauss, for instance, entered into an agreement with the French fashion house of Cacharel to produce a new Levi's line called "Something New" for distribution in Germany.

The advantage of contract manufacturing is that it lets a company "test the water" in a foreign country. By allowing the foreign firm to produce a certain volume of products to specification, and put the domestic firm's brand name on the goods, the domestic firm can broaden its global marketing base without investing in overseas plants and equipment. After establishing a solid base, the domestic firm may switch to a joint venture or direct investment, explained below.

Joint Ventures

joint venture
An agreement in which a domestic firm buys part of a foreign firm or joins with a foreign firm to create a new entity.

Joint ventures are somewhat similar to licensing agreements. In a **joint venture**, the domestic firm buys part of a foreign company or joins with a foreign company to create a new entity. A joint venture is a quick and relatively inexpensive way to enter the global market. It can also be very risky. Many joint ventures fail. Others fall victim to a takeover, in which one partner buys out the other.

Sometimes countries have required local partners in order to establish a business in their country. China, for example, had this requirement in a number of industries until recently. Thus, a joint venture was the only way to enter the market. Joint ventures help reduce risks by sharing costs and technology. Often in joint ventures, each member will bring different strengths to the partnership.

GM has a 50–50 joint venture with the Shanghai Automotive Corporation, owned by the Shanghai city government. The joint venture, founded in 1997, makes Buicks, Cadillacs, and Chevrolets. It has created hundreds of millions of dollars of profit for GM. Now the Chinese company, using the technology and the money earned from selling joint-venture cars, is becoming a serious competitor to GM. The Roewe is said to be bigger and more luxurious than the Buick. The chairman of Shanghai Automotive says, "We now want to build a global Chinese brand."[24]

Direct Foreign Investment

Active ownership of a foreign company or of overseas manufacturing or marketing facilities is **direct foreign investment**. Direct investors have either a controlling interest or a large minority interest in the firm. Thus, they stand to receive the greatest potential reward but also face the greatest potential risk. A firm may make a direct foreign investment by acquiring an interest in an existing company or by building new facilities. It might do so because it has trouble transferring some resources to a foreign operation or obtaining that resource locally. One important resource is personnel, especially managers. If the local labor market is tight, the firm may buy an entire foreign firm and retain all its employees instead of paying higher salaries than competitors.

Sometimes firms make direct investments because they can find no suitable local partners. Also, direct investments avoid the communication problems and conflicts of interest that can arise with joint ventures. IBM, in the past, insisted on total ownership of its foreign investments because it did not want to share control with local partners.

General Motors has done very well in China by building a $5,000 minivan that gets 43 miles to the gallon in city driving. The minivans have one-fourth the horsepower of American minivans, weak acceleration, and a top speed of 81 miles per hour. The seats are only a third of the thickness of seats in Western models but look plush compared to similar Chinese cars. The minivans have made GM the largest automotive seller in China and the biggest center of profit for GM in the world.[25]

Wal-Mart now has more than 2,000 stores located outside the United States. In 2007, international sales accounted for 20 percent of total sales. About one-third of all new Wal-Mart stores are opened in global markets.

However, not all of its global investments have been successful. In Germany, Wal-Mart bought the 21-store Wertkauf hypermarket chain and the 74 unprofitable and often decrepit Interspar stores. Problems in integrating and upgrading the stores resulted in at least $200 million in losses. Like all other German stores, Wal-Mart stores in Germany are required by law to close at 8 P.M. on weekdays and 4 P.M. on Saturdays and they cannot open at all on Sundays. And costs were astronomical. In 2006, Wal-Mart left the German market.

Wal-Mart does seem to be turning the corner on its international operations. It is pushing operational authority down to country managers in order to respond better to local cultures. Wal-Mart enforces certain core principles such as "everyday low prices," but country managers handle their own buying, logistics, building design, and other operational decisions.

Countertrade

International trade does not always involve cash. Today, countertrade is a fast-growing way to conduct international business. In **countertrade**, part or all of the payment for goods or services is in the form of other goods or services. Countertrade is a form of barter (swapping goods for goods), an age-old practice whose origins have been traced back to cave dwellers. The U.S. Commerce Department says that roughly 30 percent of all international trade involves countertrade. Each year about 300,000 U.S. firms engage in some form of countertrade. American companies, including General Electric, Pepsi, General Motors, and Boeing, barter billions of dollars in goods and services every year. Recently, the Malaysian government bought 20 diesel-powered locomotives from China and paid for them with palm oil.

direct foreign investment
Active ownership of a foreign company or of manufacturing or marketing facilities in a foreign country.

countertrade
A form of international trade in which part or all of the payment for goods or services is in the form of other goods and services.

CONCEPT check

Discuss several ways that a company can enter international trade.

Explain the concept of countertrade.

The Atwood Richards Co. is the world's largest countertrade organization. Atwood reviews a client's unsold products and issues trade credits in exchange. The credits can be used to obtain other products and services Atwood has acquired—everything from hotel rooms and airline tickets to television advertising time, forklift trucks, carpeting, pulp, envelopes, steel castings, and satellite tracking systems.

Threats and Opportunities in the Global Marketplace

7 What threats and opportunities exist in the global marketplace?

To be successful in a foreign market, companies must fully understand the foreign environment in which they plan to operate. Politics, cultural differences, and the economic environment can represent both opportunities and pitfalls in the global marketplace.

Political Considerations

We have already discussed how tariffs, exchange controls, and other governmental actions threaten foreign producers. The political structure of a country may also jeopardize a foreign producer's success in international trade.

nationalism
A sense of national consciousness that boosts the culture and interests of one country over those of all other countries.

Intense nationalism, for example, can lead to difficulties. **Nationalism** is the sense of national consciousness that boosts the culture and interests of one country over those of all other countries. Strongly nationalistic countries, such as Iran and Venezuela, often discourage investment by foreign companies. In other, less radical forms of nationalism, the government may take actions to hinder foreign operations. France, for example, requires that pop music stations play at least 40 percent of their songs in French. This law was enacted because the French love American rock and roll. Without airtime, American CD sales suffer. In another example of nationalism, it was rumored that Pepsico was planning a takeover of the French food and drink company Danone. There was a chorus of opposition from French politicians to the idea of a foreign takeover of Danone, the bottler of Evian water and Danone yogurts. The government warned that it would move to defend Danone from a hostile takeover attempt. Pepsico later denied that it was even interested in Danone. A week later Pernod Ricard, the French beverage company, bought British rival Allied Domecq. The head of Pernod Ricard strongly criticized the French government. He said, "You cannot be pleased when Pernod Ricard buys a British company, but then say that the foreigners do not have the right to take over French companies."[26] By fall 2005, the French government had announced 10 industries that it would protect from foreign takeover, including casino gambling and biotechnology.

In a hostile climate, a government may expropriate a foreign company's assets, taking ownership and compensating the former owners. Even worse is confiscation, when the owner receives no compensation. This happened during rebellions in several African nations during the 1990s and 2000s and also in Russia and Venezuela in the petroleum industry.

CONCEPT in action

Despite its politically correct business approach, Starbucks occasionally bumps up against powerful nationalistic sensibilities, especially in China where it operates more than 250 outlets. The Seattle-based coffee company recently left Beijing's Forbidden City after Chinese lawmakers declared the brand a threat to traditional Chinese culture. The Forbidden City, which served as the imperial palace during the Ming and Qing dynasties, is China's top tourist stop, attracting more than 7 million visitors annually. How should global companies address the issue of nationalism?

Cultural Differences

Central to any society is the common set of values shared by its citizens that determine what is socially acceptable. Culture underlies family, educational systems, religion, and social class systems. The network of social organizations generates overlapping roles and status positions. These values and roles have a tremendous effect on people's preferences and thus on marketers' options. In China, Wal-Mart holds live fishing contests on the premises, and in Korea the firm hosts a food competition with variations on a popular dish, kimchee.

Language is another important aspect of culture. Marketers must take care in selecting product names and translating slogans and promotional messages so as not to convey the wrong meaning. For example, Mitsubishi Motors had to rename its Pajero model in Spanish-speaking countries because the term refers to a sexual activity. Toyota Motors' MR2 model dropped the number 2 in France because the combination sounds like a French swearword. The literal translation of Coca-Cola in Chinese characters means "bite the wax tadpole." Perdue Farms' translation of its slogan "It takes a tough man to make a tender chicken" into Spanish means "It takes a sexually aroused man to make a chicken affectionate."

Each country has its own customs and traditions that determine business practices and influence negotiations with foreign customers. For example, attempting to do business in Western Europe during the first two weeks in August is virtually impossible. Businesses close and everyone goes on vacation at the same time. In many countries, personal relationships are more important than financial considerations. For instance, skipping social engagements in Mexico may lead to lost sales. Negotiations in Japan often include long evenings of dining, drinking, and entertaining; only after a close personal relationship has been formed do business negotiations begin. Exhibit 3.2 presents some cultural "dos and don'ts."

When Disney opened its new park in Hong Kong it found that long-term success required greater cultural sensitivity. The story unfolds in the Customer Satisfaction and Quality box on page 87.

Economic Environment

The level of economic development varies considerably, ranging from countries where everyday survival is a struggle, such as the Sudan and Eritrea, to countries that are highly developed, such as Switzerland and Japan. In general, complex, sophisticated industries are found in developed countries, and more basic industries are found in less developed nations. Average family incomes are higher in the more developed countries than in the least developed markets. Larger incomes mean greater purchasing power and demand not only for consumer goods and services but also for the machinery and workers required to produce consumer goods. Exhibit 3.3 on the next page provides a glimpse of global wealth.

Business opportunities are usually better in countries that have an economic infrastructure in place. **Infrastructure** is the basic institutions and public facilities on which an economy's development depends. When we think about how our own economy works, we tend to take our infrastructure for granted. It includes the money and banking system that provides the major investment loans to our nation's businesses; the educational system that turns out the incredible varieties of skills and basic research that actually run our nation's production lines; the extensive transportation

Overcoming language barriers can be tricky. International marketers must be careful to ensure that the promotional messages they send do not convey the wrong meaning to audiences. Advertisers behind the ever-popular "Got Milk?" campaign were forced to drop a Spanish-language version of the slogan because the translation posed the odd question, "Are you lactating?" What can global marketers do to avoid cross-cultural blunders?

infrastructure
The basic institutions and public facilities on which an economy's development depends.

EXHIBIT 3.2	Cultural Dos and Don'ts

DO:

- Always present your business card with both hands in Asian countries. It should also be right-side up and print-side showing so that the recipient can read it as it is being presented. If you receive a business card, accept it with gratitude and examine it carefully. Don't quickly put it into your pocket.
- Dress to the culture. If you are in Switzerland, always wear a coat and tie. In other countries, a coat and tie may be viewed as overdressing and snobbish.
- Use a "soft-sell" and subtle approach when promoting a product in Japan. Japanese do not feel comfortable with America's traditional hard-selling style.
- Understand the role of religion in business transactions. In Muslim countries, Ramadan is a holy month when most people fast. During this time everything slows down, particularly business.
- Have a local person available to culturally and linguistically interpret any advertising that you plan to do. When American Airlines wanted to promote its new first-class seats in the Mexican market, it translated the "Fly In Leather" campaign literally, which meant "Fly Naked" in Spanish.

DON'T:

- Glad-hand, back-slap, and use first names on your first business meeting in Asia. If you do, you will be considered a lightweight.
- Fill a wineglass to the top if dining with a French businessperson. It is considered completely uncouth.
- Begin your first business meeting in Asia talking business. Be patient. Let your clients get to know you first.
- Kiss someone on the cheek or pat them on the shoulder in Spain before you get to know them. In Chile, expect women to greet you with a kiss on the cheek even if you are a stranger. Do offer a kiss on both cheeks after you become friends with a French woman (even if you are a woman). In Switzerland, offer three kisses.
- Be on time for your appointment in some Latin American countries, but always be on time in Germany.

Chapter 3: Competing in the Global Marketplace

EXHIBIT 3.3   Where the Money Is

The Top 20	Gross National Income Per Capita*
Qatar	$80,900
Luxembourg	$80,500
Bermuda	$69,900
Jersey	$57,000
Malta	$53,400
Norway	$53,000
Brunei	$51,000
Singapore	$49,700
Cyprus	$46,900
United States	$45,800
Guernsey	$44,600
Cayman Islands	$43,800
Ireland	$43,100
Hong Kong	$42,000
Switzerland	$41,100
Kuwait	$39,300
Andorra	$38,800
Iceland	$38,800
Netherlands	$38,500
British Virgin Islands	$38,500
The Bottom Five	
Guinea-Bissau	$500
Burundi	$400
Liberia	$400
Democratic Republic of Congo	$300
Zimbabwe	$200

*__Gross Domestic Product__ is the total market value of all final goods and services produced within a nation's borders within a year.

__Final goods__ are the goods that are ultimately consumed rather than used in the production of another good. For example, a car sold to a consumer is a final good; the components such as tires sold to the car manufacturer are not; they are intermediate goods used to make the final good. The same tires, if sold to a consumer, would be a final good.

Source: **https://www.cia.gov/library/publications/the-world-factbook/rankorder/2004rank.html**

CONCEPT check

Explain how political factors can affect international trade.

Describe several cultural factors that a company involved in international trade should consider.

How can economic conditions affect trade opportunities?

and communications systems—interstate highways, railroads, airports, canals, telephones, Internet sites, postal systems, television stations—that link almost every piece of our geography into one market; the energy system that powers our factories; and, of course, the market system itself, which brings our nation's goods and services into our homes and businesses.

The Impact of Multinational Corporations

8 What are the advantages of multinational corporations?

multinational corporations
Corporations that move resources, goods, services, and skills ac ross natio nal boundaries without regard to the country in which their headquarters are located.

Corporations that move resources, goods, services, and skills across national boundaries without regard to the country in which their headquarters are located are **multinational corporations**. Some are so rich and have so many employees that they resemble small countries. For example, the sales of both ExxonMobil and Wal-Mart are larger than the GDP of all but a few nations in the world. Multinational companies are heavily engaged in international trade. The successful ones take political and cultural differences into account.

Many global brands sell much more outside the United States than at home. Coca-Cola has 80 percent of its sales outside the United States; Philip Morris's Marlboro brand, 67 percent; Pepsi, 42 percent; Kellogg's, 50 percent; Pampers, 65 percent; Nescafe, 50 percent; and Gillette, around 62 percent.[27]

© Digital Vision/Getty Images

Disney Localizes Mickey in Hong Kong

Hao Zhi met a character at Disneyland-Hong Kong that might seem kind of odd for Main Street, USA, but the civil servant from Inner Mongolia didn't find it "Goofy" at all. "This is terrific," said Mr. Hao, as he posed for a picture with his new friend, Cai Shen Ye, the bearded Chinese god of wealth, who was decked out in silk robes and an oversize belt. "It makes me so happy to see the god of wealth here."

That's just the reaction Walt Disney Co. is counting on following a marketing makeover designed to make a classic American theme park look a lot more Chinese. It transformed China's year of the rat (2007) into the "Year of the Mouse." Since it opened in 2005, Disney's Hong Kong park, the flagship for the booming Chinese Kids' market, has struggled to connect with consumers. The park, a joint venture with the Hong Kong government, missed public targets of 5.6 million visitors for its first year of operation, and attendance dropped nearly 30 percent to about 4 million in the second year.

The Disneyland Chinese New Year campaign features a logo with the kind of visual pun that only the Chinese might appreciate: the Chinese character for "luck" flipped upside-down (a New Year tradition), with mouse ears added on top. Inside the park, vendors hawk deep-fried dumplings and turnip cakes. The parade down Main Street, USA, is being joined by the "Rhythm of Life Procession," featuring a dragon dance and puppets of birds, flowers, and fish, set to traditional Chinese music. And of course there's the god of wealth, a relative newcomer to the regular Hong Kong Disneyland gang, joined by the gods of longevity and happiness, all major figures in Chinese New Year celebrations.

One aspect of Mr. Mouse's personality that's harder to make Chinese: his love of cheese, which isn't popular in Chinese cuisine. A showcase inside the kitchen of "Mickey's House," a new attraction at the Hong Kong park, displayed his favorite cheese from Europe and North America—and a steamed rice flour cake from China.[28]

Critical Thinking Questions

- Do you think that Disney was right to localize the park to the Chinese culture? Or should Disney expect the Chinese consumer to understand Disney's traditional stories and characters?
- Part of Mickey Mouse's personality emphasizes family and friends. Do you think this aspect of his personality should be emphasized in the Hong Kong part? Why?

In slow-growing, developed economies like Europe and Japan, a weaker dollar helps, because it means cheaper products to sell into those markets, and profits earned in those markets translate into more dollars back home. Meanwhile, emerging markets in Asia, Latin America, and Eastern Europe are growing steadily. General Electric expects 60 percent of its revenue growth to come from emerging markets over the next decade. For Brown-Forman, the spirits company, a fifth of its sales growth of Jack Daniels, the Tennessee whiskey, is coming from developing markets like Mexico and Poland. IBM had rapid sales growth in emerging markets such as Russia, India, and Brazil.

The largest multinational corporations in the world are shown in Exhibit 3.4 on page 88.

Despite the success of American multinationals abroad, there is some indication that preference for American brands may be slipping. The growth of competing global brands is discussed in the Customer Satisfaction and Quality box above.

The Multinational Advantage

Large multinationals have several advantages over other companies. For instance, multinationals can often overcome trade problems. Taiwan and South Korea have long had an embargo against Japanese cars for political reasons and to help domestic automakers. Yet Honda USA, a Japanese-owned company based in the United States, sends Accords to Taiwan and Korea. In another example, when the environmentally conscious Green movement challenged the biotechnology research conducted by BASF, a major German chemical and drug manufacturer, BASF moved its cancer and immune-system research to Cambridge, Massachusetts.

Another advantage for multinationals is their ability to sidestep regulatory problems. U.S. drugmaker SmithKline and Britain's Beecham decided to merge in part so that they could avoid licensing and regulatory hassles in their largest markets. The merged company can say it's an insider in both Europe and the United States. "When we go to Brussels, we're a member state [of the European Union]," one executive explains. "And when we go to Washington, we're an American company."

Multinationals can also shift production from one plant to another as market conditions change. When European demand for a certain solvent declined, Dow Chemical instructed its German plant to switch to manufacturing a chemical that had been imported from Louisiana and Texas. Computer models help Dow make decisions like these so it can run its plants more efficiently and keep costs down.

Multinationals can also tap new technology from around the world. Xerox has introduced some 80 different office copiers in the United States that were designed

CONCEPT in action

© MARVEL/SONY PICTURES/THE KOBAL COLLECTION

Spider-Man 3 received a superhero's welcome from international audiences, as the third installment of the billion-dollar franchise featuring Tobey Maguire and Kirsten Dunst set opening-weekend records in Japan, China, Italy, and elsewhere. The radioactive comic-book character captured the No.1 slot in 107 territories and earned a record-breaking single-weekend gross of $382 million worldwide. Sony Pictures premiered the film in Tokyo, a move that underscored the importance of overseas markets. How might film studios leverage their multinational advantage to achieve box-office success?

EXHIBIT 3.4	The World's Largest Multinational Corporations		
Rank	Company	Country	Revenues ($ millions)
1	Wal-Mart Stores	U.S.	351,139.0
2	ExxonMobil	U.S.	347,254.0
3	Royal Dutch Shell	Netherlands	318,845.0
4	BP	Britain	274,316.0
5	General Motors	U.S.	207,349.0
6	Toyota Motor	Japan	204,746.4
7	Chevron	U.S.	200,567.0
8	DaimlerChrysler	Germany	190,191.4
9	ConocoPhillips	U.S.	172,451.0
10	Total	France	168,356.7
11	General Electric	U.S.	168,307.0
12	Ford Motor	U.S.	160,126.0
13	ING Group	Netherlands	158,274.3
14	Citigroup	U.S.	146,777.0
15	AXA	France	139,738.1
16	Volkswagen	Germany	132,323.1
17	Sinopec	China	131,636.0
18	Credit Agricole	France	128,481.3
19	Allianz	Germany	125,346.0
20	Fortis	Belgium/Netherlands	121,201.8
21	Bank of America Corp.	U.S.	117,017.0
22	HSBC Holdings	Britain	115,361.0
23	American International Group	U.S.	113,194.0
24	China National Petroleum	China	110,520.2
25	BNP Paribas	France	109,213.6

Source: "World's Largest Corporations," *Fortune*, July 23, 2007, 133. ©2007 Time Inc. All rights reserved.

and built by Fuji Xerox, its joint venture with a Japanese company. Versions of the superconcentrated detergent that Procter & Gamble first formulated in Japan in response to a rival's product are now being sold under the Ariel brand name in Europe and under the Cheer and Tide labels in the United States. Also, consider Otis Elevator's development of the Elevonic 411, an elevator that is programmed to send more cars to floors where demand is high. It was developed by six research centers in five countries. Otis's group in Farmington, Connecticut, handled the systems integration, a Japanese group designed the special motor drives that make the elevators ride smoothly, a French group perfected the door systems, a German group handled the electronics, and a Spanish group took care of the small-geared components. Otis says the international effort saved more than $10 million in design costs and cut the process from four years to two.

Finally, multinationals can often save a lot in labor costs, even in highly unionized countries. For example, when Xerox started moving copier-rebuilding work to Mexico to take advantage of the lower wages, its union in Rochester, New York, objected because it saw that members' jobs were at risk. Eventually, the union agreed to change work styles and to improve productivity to keep the jobs at home.

CONCEPT check

What is a multinational corporation?

What are the advantages of multinationals?

Trends in Global Competition

9 What are the trends in the global marketplace?

In this section we will examine several underlying trends that will have an impact in world trade in the future. These trends are market expansion, blocking foreign investment, and the emergence of China and India.

Market Expansion

The need for businesses to expand their markets is perhaps the most fundamental reason for the growth in world trade. The limited size of domestic markets often motivates managers to seek markets beyond their national frontiers. The economies of large-scale manufacturing demand big markets. Domestic markets, particularly in smaller countries like Denmark and the Netherlands, simply can't generate enough demand. Nestlé was one of the first businesses to "go global" because its home country, Switzerland, is so small. Nestlé was shipping milk to 16 different countries as early as 1875. Today, hundreds of thousands of businesses are recognizing the potential for rich rewards to be found in international markets.

Blocking Foreign Investment

A new backlash against multinational corporations is that governments from China to Canada are placing restrictions on foreign purchases of factories, land, and companies in their countries. This has a major impact on U.S. multinationals because they serve foreign markets primarily through sales in their foreign affiliates and not through export from the United States. The foreign affiliates manufacture and sell goods locally and rely on local labor and distribution to reach nearby customers.

These new barriers to ownership are partially due to a backlash against globalization. Perhaps more important is the view that the United States is erecting barriers to foreign investment. In 2006, a Dubai-owned company tried to buy operations at five American ports and the year before, the state-owned Chinese oil company Cnooc Ltd. tried to buy California-based oil giant Unocal Corp. Both deals were ultimately voided amid the uproar, which prompted Congress to pass legislation to subject foreign investments to closer scrutiny by the Committee on Foreign Investment in the United States, or CFIUS, an interagency council that screens foreign purchases of U.S. assets with national-security implications.[29]

Now China's new regulations let government officials block a local purchase by a multinational corporation if it is a danger to "economic security." Russia is considered blocking foreign ownership in 39 "strategic sectors" of its economy. If more countries begin to block foreign investment by multinationals, it will definitely have a noticeable impact on global trade.

The Emergence of China and India

China and India—two of the world's hottest economic powerhouses—are impacting businesses around the globe, in very different ways. The boom in China's worldwide exports—up 125 percent in four years—has left few sectors unscathed, be they garlic growers in California, clothing manufacturers in Mexico, or plastic-mold manufacturers in South Korea. India's impact has altered how hundreds of service companies from Texas to Ireland compete for billions of dollars in contracts.

Tommy Hilfiger, Gucci, and Calvin Klein have long been popular with American consumers, and soon India's upwardly mobile classes may begin exchanging traditional saris for such hip Western fashions. Murjani Group, a decades-old apparel manufacturer in Mumbai, recently signed exclusive licensing partnerships with the world-renowned brands after spotting opportunities in India's emerging economy. The group is opening dozens of retail outlets to sell clothes, watches, shoes, and fragrances to Indian shoppers. Why might partnering with an established Indian business be an appealing strategy for international fashion designers?

The causes and consequences of each nation's growth are somewhat different. China's exports have boomed largely thanks to foreign investment: lured by low labor costs, big manufacturers have surged into China to expand their production base and push down prices globally. Now manufacturers of all sizes, making everything from windshield wipers to clothing, are scrambling either to reduce costs at home or to outsource more of what they make in cheaper locales.

Indians are playing invaluable roles in the global innovation chain. Motorola, Hewlett-Packard, Cisco Systems, and other tech giants now rely on their Indian teams to devise software platforms and multimedia features for next-generation devices. Google principal scientist Krishna Bharat is setting up a Bangalore lab complete with colorful furniture, exercise balls, and a Yamaha organ—like Google's Mountain View (Calif.) headquarters—to work on core search-engine technology. Indian engineering houses use 3-D computer simulations to tweak designs of everything from car engines and forklifts to aircraft wings for such clients as General Motors Corp. and Boeing Co. Barring unforeseen circumstances, within three decades India should have vaulted over Germany as the world's third-biggest economy. By midcentury, China should have overtaken the United States as No. 1. By then, China and India could account for half of global output.

An accelerating trend is that technical and managerial skills in both China and India are becoming more important than cheap assembly labor. China will stay dominant in mass manufacturing and is one of the few nations building multibillion-dollar electronics and heavy-industrial plants. India is a rising power in software, design, services, and precision industry.

China and India have the world's two largest populations, two of the world's largest geographical areas, greater linguistic and sociocultural diversity than any other country—and among the highest levels of income disparity in the world. Some people are extremely poor whereas others are very rich.[30] Given this scale and variety, there is no "average Chinese customer" or "average Indian customer." In each country, even the middle of the income pyramid consists of more than 300 million people encompassing significant diversity in incomes, geographic climates, cultural habits, and even language and religious beliefs. Because of this diversity, market success in China and India is rarely possible without finely segmenting the local market in each country and developing a strategy tailored to the needs of the targeted segments.

Haier Group, China's leading appliance maker, has proved to be particularly adept at fine market segmentation. The company's line of washing machines for the Chinese market includes a washing machine for rural peasants that can clean not only clothes but also sweet potatoes and peanuts. Haier also sells a tiny washing machine designed to clean a single change of clothes, which has proved to be a hit with the busy urban customers in Shanghai.[31]

CONCEPT check

What trends will foster continued growth in world trade?

Describe some of the ways businesses can take advantage of these trends to "go global."

Summary of Learning Goals

1 Why is global trade important to the United States and how is it measured?

International trade improves relations with friends and allies, eases tensions among nations, helps bolster economies, raises the standard of living, and improves the quality of life. The United States is still the largest importer and exporter in the world. We export a fifth of our industrial production and about a third of our farm crops. One out of every 10 jobs in the United States is supported by exports.

Two concepts important to global trade are the balance of trade (the difference in value between a country's exports and its imports over some period) and the balance of payments (the difference between a country's total payments to and total receipts from other countries). The United States now has both a negative balance of trade and a negative balance of payments. Another import concept is the exchange rate, which is the price of one country's currency in terms of another country's currency. Currencies float up and down based upon the supply of and demand for each currency. Sometimes a government steps in and devalues its currency relative to the currencies of other countries.

2 Why do nations trade?

Nations trade because they gain by doing so. The principle of comparative advantage states that each country should specialize in the goods it can produce most readily and cheaply and trade them for those that other countries can produce most readily and cheaply. The result is more goods at lower prices than if each country produced by itself everything it needed. Free trade allows trade among nations without government restrictions.

3 What are the barriers to international trade?

The three major barriers to international trade are natural barriers, such as distance and language; tariff barriers, or taxes on imported goods; and nontariff barriers. The nontariff barriers to trade include import quotas, embargoes, buy-national regulations, and exchange controls. The main argument against tariffs is that they discourage free trade and keep the principle of comparative advantage from working efficiently. The main argument for using tariffs is that they help protect domestic companies, industries, and workers.

4 How do governments and institutions foster world trade?

The World Trade Organization created by the Uruguay Round has dramatically lowered trade barriers worldwide. For the first time, a trade agreement covers services, intellectual property rights, and exchange controls. The World Bank makes loans to developing nations to help build infrastructures. The International Monetary Fund makes loans to member nations that cannot meet their budgetary expenses. Despite efforts to expand trade, terrorism can have a negative impact on trade growth.

International economic communities reduce trade barriers among themselves while often establishing common tariffs and other trade barriers toward nonmember countries. The best-known economic communities are the European Union, NAFTA, CAFTA, and Mercosur.

5 What are international economic communities?

There are a number of ways to enter the global market. The major ones are exporting, licensing, contract manufacturing, joint ventures, and direct investment.

6 How do companies enter the global marketplace?

Domestic firms entering the international arena need to consider the politics, economies, and culture of the countries where they plan to do business. For example, government trade policies can be loose or restrictive, countries can be nationalistic, and governments can change. In the area of culture, many products fail because companies don't understand the culture of the country where they are trying to sell their products. Some developing countries also lack an economic infrastructure, which often makes it very difficult to conduct business.

7 What threats and opportunities exist in the global marketplace?

Multinational corporations have several advantages. First, they can sidestep restrictive trade and licensing restrictions because they frequently have headquarters in more than one country. Multinationals can also move their operations from one country to the next depending on which location offers more favorable economic conditions. In addition, multinationals can tap into a vast source of technological expertise by drawing upon the knowledge of a global workforce.

8 What are the advantages of multinational corporations?

Global business activity will continue to escalate due to several factors. Firms that desire a larger customer base or need additional resources will continue to seek opportunities outside their country's borders. China and India are emerging as global economic powerhouses.

9 What are the trends in the global marketplace?

Key Terms

absolute advantage 73
balance of payments 71
balance of trade 71
buy-national regulations 75
contract manufacturing 82
countertrade 83
devaluation 72
direct foreign investment 83
dumping 75
embargo 75
European integration 79
European Union (EU) 78
exchange controls 75
exporting 80
exports 71
floating exchange rates 72
free trade 73
free-trade zone 77
global vision 70
import quota 75
imports 71

infrastructure 85
International Monetary Fund (IMF) 77
joint venture 82
licensing 82
Mercosur 78
multinational corporations 86
nationalism 84
North American Free Trade Agreement (NAFTA) 77
outsourcing 73
preferential tariff 77
principle of comparative advantage 73
protectionism 73
protective tariffs 74
tariff 74
trade deficit 71
trade surplus 71
Uruguay Round 76
World Bank 76
World Trade Organization (WTO) 76

Preparing for Tomorrow's Workplace: SCANS

1. How can a country's customs create barriers to trade? Ask foreign students to describe such barriers in their country. American students should give examples of problems that foreign businesspeople might experience with American customs. (**Information**)
2. Should Great Britain be admitted to NAFTA? Why might Britain not wish to join? (**Systems**)
3. Do you think that CAFTA will have a major impact on the U.S. economy? Why? (**Systems**)
4. What do you think is the best way for a small company to enter international trade? Why? (**Information**)
5. How can America compete against China and India in the long run? (**Information**)
6. Identify some U.S. multinational companies that have been successful in world markets. How do you think they have achieved their success? (**Information**)
7. **Team Activity** Divide the class into teams. Each team should choose a country and research its infrastructure to determine how it will help or hinder trade. Include a variety of countries, ranging from the most highly developed to the least developed. (**Resources, Interpersonal, Information, Technology**)

Ethics Activity

The executives of a clothing manufacturer want to outsource some of their manufacturing to more cost-efficient locations in Indonesia. After visiting several possible sites, they choose one and begin to negotiate with local officials. They discover that it will take about six months to get the necessary permits. One of the local politicians approaches the executives over dinner and hints that he can speed up the process, for an advisory fee of $5,000.

Using a Web search tool, locate articles about this topic and then write responses to the following questions. Be sure to support your arguments and cite your sources.

ETHICAL DILEMMA: Is paying the advisory fee a bribe or an acceptable cost of doing business in that area of the world? What should the executives do before agreeing to pay the fee?

Sources: Jane Easter Bahls, "Illicit Affairs? If You Do Business Overseas, Be Certain Your 'Administrative Fees' Aren't Really Illegal Bribes," *Entrepreneur*, September 2004, p. 80; Paul Burnham Finney, "Shaking Hands, Greasing Palms," *New York Times*, May 17, 2005, p. C10; Phelim Kyne, "Freeport-McMoRan Indonesia Payments Not Graft: Official," *FWN Financial News*, January 18, 2006.

Working the Net

1. Go to the Trade Compliance Center site at **http://tcc.export.gov**. Click on "Research Your Country Market" and then "Search Reports." Pick a country that interests you from the index, and read the most current available reports for that country. Would this country be a good market for a small U.S. motor scooter manufacturer interested in expanding internationally? Why or why not? What are the main barriers to trade the company might face?
2. While still at the Trade Compliance site, **http://tcc.export.gov**, click on "Trade Agreements" and then "List All Agreements." Select one that interests you and summarize what you learn about it.
3. Review the historical data about exchange rates between the U.S. dollar and the Japanese yen available at **http://www.x-rates.com**. Pull up charts comparing the yen to the dollar for several years. List any trends you spot. What years would have been best for a U.S. company to enter the Japanese marketplace? Given current exchange rate conditions, do you think Japanese companies are increasing or decreasing their exporting efforts in the United States?
4. Visit Foreign Trade Online, **http://www.foreign-trade.com**, and browse through the resources of this international business-to-business trade portal. What types of information does the site provide? Which would be most useful to a company looking to begin exporting? To a company who already exports and wants to find new markets? Rate the usefulness of the site and the information it offers.

5. Go to the Federation of International Trade Associations site at **http://www.fita.org**. Click on "Really Useful Links for International Trade." Follow five of those links and explain how they would help an American manufacturer that wanted to "go global."

6. Go to the World Trade Organization site at **http://www.wto.org**. Next, click on "WTO News." Inform the class of on current activities and actions at the WTO.

7. Go to **http://www.worldbank.org** and then to **http://www.imf.org**. Compare the types of information available on each Web site. Pick one example from each site and report your findings to the class.

Creative Thinking Case

We Want our MTV (International)

MTV, a mainstay of American pop culture, is just as popular in Shanghai as it is in Seattle and in Sydney, Australia, or in Lagos (Nigeria) as it is in Los Angeles. London-based MTV Networks International (MTVNI), the world's largest global network, has taken its winning formula to 167 foreign markets on six continents, including urban and rural areas. It broadcasts in 18 languages to 430 million homes, or about 1.3 billion people, through locally programmed and operated TV channels and Web sites. While the United States currently generates about 80 percent of MTV's profits, 80 percent of the company's subscriber base lives outside the U.S. "Now a large part of our future will be what happens outside the United States, and that is exciting," says Tom Freston, co-president of parent company Viacom and head of MTV Networks.

The MTV brand has evolved beyond its music television roots into a multimedia lifestyle entertainment and culture brand for all ages. In addition to MTV and MTV2, its channel lineup includes Nickelodeon, VH1, Comedy Central, LOGO, TMF (The Music Factory), Game One, and several European music, comedy, and lifestyle channels. Adding to the complexity is MTV's multimedia and interactive nature, with gaming, texting, and Web sites as well as television. Another challenge is integrating acquisitions of local companies such as European competitor Viva, which it purchased in 2004.

The company prefers to hire local employees rather than import staff. According to Brent Hansen, president and chief executive of MTV Networks Europe, getting the local perspective is invaluable in helping the network understand its markets, whether in terms of musical tastes or what children like. For example, Alex Okosi, a Nigerian who went to college in the United States, is chief executive for MTV Base, which launched in sub-Saharan Africa in 2005. Okosi recommended that MTV consider each country as an individual market, rather than blending them all together.

One reason for MTVNI's success is "glocalization"—its ability to adapt programs to fit local cultures while still maintaining a consistent, special style. "When we set a channel up, we always provide a set of parameters in terms of standards of things we require," Hansen explains. "Obviously an MTV channel that doesn't look good enough is not going to do the business for us, let alone for the audience. There's a higher expectation." Then the local unit can tailor content to its market. MTV India conveys a "sense of the colorful street culture," explains Bill Roedy, MTV International's president, while MTV Japan has "a sense of technology edginess; MTV Italy, style and elegance." In Africa, MTV Base will feature videos from top African artists as well as from emerging African music talent. The goal, according to Brent Hansen, is to "provide a unique cultural meeting point for young people in Africa, using the common language of music to connect music fans from different backgrounds and cultures."

Critical Thinking Questions

- Do you agree with Tom Freston that MTV's future lies mostly in its international operations? Why?
- What types of political, economic, and competitive challenges does MTV Networks International face by operating worldwide?
- How has MTVNI overcome cultural differences to create a world brand?

Sources: MTV International Web site, **http://www.mtv.com/mtvinternational/** (January 18, 2006); "Africa gets its MTV - but will the continent's musicians benefit?" International Herald Tribune, February 25, 2005, **http://www.iht.com/articles/2005/02/24/features/mtv.php**, Sharon LaFraniere; Johnnie L. Roberts, "World Tour," Newsweek, June 6, 2005, pp.34–35; and Robin D Rusch, "MTV Networks Internationally," Brandchannel.com, July 26, 2004, **http://www.brandchannel.com**.

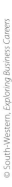

**Mike Lawton
Domino's Pizza**

Exploring Business Careers

Domino's Pizza has more than 8,000 stores worldwide. As executive vice president of Domino's International division, Mike Lawton is in charge of every store outside of the United States. In 1983, Domino's opened its first international store in Canada and by the time Lawton joined Domino's in 1999, there were over 1,500 stores beyond the U.S. borders. Today, there are over 3,000 stores in over 55 countries, almost half of all that Domino's operates. Given that Domino's delivers more than 400 million pizzas a year, that's a lot of dough he's responsible for!

Such an international scope might seem unusual for someone who has spent much of his life in a single state: Lawton was born in Michigan, went to school at Michigan State University, and today lives in Ann Arbor, Michigan. However, he was never one to turn down an opportunity. A broad base of accounting and financial skills opened a chance early in his career to work on some international projects, and he took it. "Since the work interested me, I jumped into international business." And from there, he's never looked back. "My career goal has always been to hold interesting and challenging positions. I never focused on attaining a particular level or position in a company, but sought to broaden my experiences so I was prepared when opportunities arose." Along with a strong financial and business background, he has direct international experience in Europe, Latin America, and Asia—experience that he is able to bring to his work heading Domino's International division.

Luckily, too, he doesn't have to do it alone. As he readily admits, "When we look at what has created success in our markets, we have to credit the people who take the responsibility of running our stores with excellence very seriously."

The people Lawton refers to are the master franchisees (see Chapter 5) of Domino's international business. In this case, master franchisees are individuals or entities who, under a specific licensing agreement with Domino's, control all operations within the country. They operate their own stores, set up a distribution infrastructure to transport materials into and throughout the country, and create sub-franchisees. One particular benefit of master franchisees is their local knowledge. As discussed in this chapter, a major challenge when opening a business on foreign soil is negotiating the political, cultural, and economic differences of that country. According to Lawton, master franchisees allow Domino's, and the franchisee, to "take advantage of their local expertise in dealing with marketing, political, and regulatory issues, as well as the local labor markets." It takes local experience to know, for example, that only 30 percent of the people in Poland have phones, so carryout needs to be the focus of the business; or that Turkey has changed their street names three times in the past 30 years so delivery is much more challenging; or even that, in Japanese, there is no word for pepperoni, the most popular topping worldwide. These are just a few of the challenges that Domino's has had to overcome on the road to becoming the worldwide leader in the pizza delivery business. Under the leadership of people like Lawton and with the help of dedicated, local master franchisees, Domino's has been able to not only compete in but lead the global pizza delivery market.

Apple, Inc.
continuing case
Part 1: The Evolution of Apple, Inc.

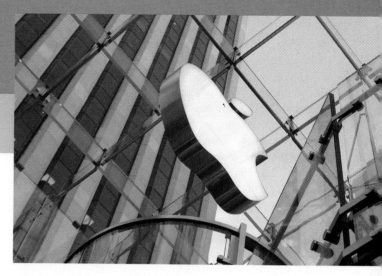

In the 1970s, the U.S. business environment was volatile, with unpredictable swings in inflation and recession. The political and social environments were unstable due largely to the country's continued presence in Vietnam. Price controls, oil embargos, high unemployment, highly publicized labor disputes, and rapid rates of change in consumer prices all contributed to a decade of pessimism. Such economic issues contributed to the productivity slowdown of the 1970s. The largest slowdowns were in pipelines, motor vehicles, oil/gas extraction, utilities, and air transportation—all industries affected by the energy crisis of the 1970s. Interestingly, this environment proved ripe for innovation and was the backdrop for the inception of Apple, Inc. and a new product category that would ultimately become a way of life in society.

Apple created a new product category when it offered the first personal computer to truly meet the market's needs. This new product category was the result of a unique combination of entrepreneurial energy, innovative technical skills, and financial wizardry. Steve Jobs provided the entrepreneurial energy, Stephen Wozniak imparted the innovative technical skills, and Mike Markkula bestowed his financial expertise upon the product effort. As Apple Computer, these three individuals started an evolution from hobbyist to technical hacker to a mass consumer-marketed personal computer.

A frequently overlooked precursor of Apple's start, however, was the creation and later miniaturization of integrated circuits. The first integrated circuit was introduced in the early 1960s at Texas Instruments and led to the invention of the handheld calculator. The ability to miniaturize electronic circuitry, and a group of "geeks" who could foresee a computer revolution are key components in the development of our computerized society.

The Homebrew Computer Club

In March 1975, the Homebrew Computer Club met for the first time in one of the members' garages. Members of the club were hobbyists who had electrical engineering or programming backgrounds. Initially, the typical discussion centered around the Altair 8800, a personal computer based on the Intel 8080 microprocessor. But the real intent of the club meetings was for attendees to trade parts, devices, and information. According to Stephen Wozniak, the Apple I was designed for fun to take to the Homebrew Computer Club meeting, not to be a product for a company. Diagrams of the Apple I were shared at the club meetings. Thus, the Apple computer was being demonstrated as it was being developed. In this manner, the product was receiving critical technical review from experts who were dabbling in computers as a hobby. The Homebrew Computer Club was one of the first steps in the development of today's multibillion-dollar personal computer industry.

The Wozniak and Jobs Duo

Stephen Wozniak and Steve Jobs met in 1969 and developed their first commercial product in 1971. Unfortunately, their first invention was not a viable product offering. The two had developed and packaged a "blue box" that could hack into the phone system. Product development was shut down, however, when the developer of the original phone hacking concept was convicted in 1972 of phone fraud charges.

Wozniak was employed at Hewlett-Packard in the mid-1970s when he was developing the early stages of the computer product that was shown regularly at the Homebrew Computer Club meetings. He discussed the computer with his employers at Hewlett-Packard, but they had no interest in the personal computer marketplace and provided him with a legal release. This legal release provided Wozniak ownership rights to the computer he was building while still employed at Hewlett-Packard. Whereas Wozniak was interested in the technical development of the computer, Jobs was more interested in its commercialization. This combination of technical and commercial expertise enabled the two entrepreneurs to begin developing and selling the Apple I computer on a very small scale.

The Rapid Growth of the Personal Computer Industry

Intel was the first company to use miniaturization in the development of a microprocessor in 1971. This particular microprocessor was intended for calculators and watches. The Altair 8800, the first personal computer, was introduced in 1975, and the now famous Bill Gates got his start by writing the software for the Altair. Wozniak and Jobs introduced the Apple II, an improved prototype of the Apple I, in 1977. When International Business Machines (IBM) released the IBM PC in 1981, the world of personal computers truly began to open up. IBM used its established brand name to capture a huge chunk of the evolving personal computer marketplace. In the early 1980s, Apple Computer introduced its Macintosh. This user-friendly computer had a mouse that allowed users to point and click on icons to execute demands. Although there were several early computer manufacturers, such as Commodore, Atari, and Radio

Shack, the battle for market share tended to be fought between IBM and Apple Computer. Because Apple was so user friendly, it found a natural niche as a home and educational computer. IBM's PC, on the other hand, was considered to be the more serious computer for business and computer enthusiasts. In this rapidly expanding marketplace, Apple was the only first-generation personal computer manufacturer in the United States to survive against the IBM PC.

By the beginning of 2000, the PC industry was exhibiting signs of maturation. This led to less distinction among competitors and price competition, with Dell Computer at the forefront of the pricing battle. Just as Apple had revolutionized desktop publishing, it was also an early pioneer in the use of electronic communications with its proprietary online services, and it opted to innovate along these communications lines rather than fight a head-to-head battle with Dell. Innovating along the company's strengths with its Macintosh, Apple focused on its digital communications hub. This focus on communications brought the world the iPod, the iTunes Music Store, and the Web-enabled iPhone. By the start of the twenty-first century, Apple remained at the forefront of electronic communications. Throughout its company life cycle, Apple has helped transform the personal computer industry from a hobby marketplace to a necessity in day-to-day living—this necessity in the worldwide marketplace for flash-based and hard disk drive-based MP3 players is expected to reach 275 million units sold annually by 2011.

Critical Thinking Questions

- How was the development of the Apple computer different from traditional product development? What are the risks inherent in this type of development process?
- What was technology's role in the development of the personal computer marketplace?
- What market segments existed in the personal computer marketplace, and who were the dominant product providers to these segments?
- What social trends are likely to impact Apple in the future?
- How has Apple been an innovator in the communications marketplace?

Sources: Roy A. Allan, *A History of the Personal Computer* (London, Ontario, Canada: Allan Publishing, 2001); Stephanie Ethier, "Worldwide Demand Remains Strong for MP3 and Portable Media Players," In-Stat Online, August 27, 2007, **http://www.instat.com**, accessed on February 7, 2008; DigiBarn Computer Museum, **http://www.digibarn.com**; IEEE Virtual Museum, **http://www.ieee-virtual-museum.org**; Carlos Lozada, "The Productivity Slowdown of the 1970s," *National Bureau of Economic Research*, June 2005, **http://www.nber.org**; Steve Ranger, "IPod and MP3 Player Ownership Soars," *Personal Computer World*, February 17, 2005, **http://www.pcw.co.uk**; Thomas R. Schori and Michael L. Garee, "Does Your Company Make Things Happen?" *Marketing News*, January 5, 1998, p. 4; Albert Schwenk, "Compensation in the 1970s," *Compensation and Working Conditions Online*, January 30, 2003, **http://stats.bls.gov**; Jason Snell, Steven Levy, Guy Kawasaki, Adam Engst, Roger Ebert, Andy Ihnatko, John Dvorak, and Pamela Pfiffner, "20 Years of the Mac," *Macworld*, February 2004, pp. 68–72; Joel West, "Apple Computer: The iCEO Seizes the Internet," Center for Research on Information Technology and Organizations, Paper 348, 2002, **http://repositories.cdlib.org**; Stephen Wozniak, "Homebrew and How the Apple Came to Be," **http://atariarchives.org**.

Business Ownership

PART 2

Chapter 4
Forms of Business Ownership

Chapter 5
Entrepreneurship: Starting and Managing Your Own Business

Forms of Business Ownership

Learning Goals

After reading this chapter, you should be able to answer these questions:

1 What are the advantages and disadvantages of the sole proprietorship form of business organization?

2 What are the advantages of operating as a partnership, and what downside risks should partners consider?

3 How does the corporate structure provide advantages and disadvantages to a company, and what are the major types of corporations?

4 What other options for business organization does a company have in addition to sole proprietorships, partnerships, and corporations?

5 What makes franchising an appropriate form of organization for some types of business, and why does it continue to grow in importance?

6 Why are mergers and acquisitions important to a company's overall growth?

7 What current trends will affect the business organizations of the future?

© iStockphoto.com/Rich Yasick

"I'm Not Trying to Tell You Your Business"

BIZ FLIX

Part of the American dream is to own one's home. In much the same way, an offshoot of the American dream is to own one's own business. As such, the two share much in common. The respective owners must devote a variety of resources to manage and maintain both or else they will fall into disrepair, and those same owners must have an understanding of how various ownership relationships may impact each. In Tom Hanks's movie, *The Money Pit,* these relationships are explored in comedic fashion.

Walter Fielding and Anna Crowley, his girlfriend, have recently purchased a house that they expected to be their dream home. However, the couple was swindled by con artists and what they have actually purchased is a house in need of major renovations . . . a detail they discover within minutes of moving in as the front door frame disintegrates, both the stairway and the chimney collapse, and the bathtub falls through the floor. Adding insult to injury, the couple finds that the plumbing is an absolute disaster that produces more rust-colored muck than it does water. The couple, both of whom have shared the cost of the house, continue to share the cost of making the necessary renovations. As such, they hire Art Shirk to oversee those renovations. Art recommends his brother, Brad, as a plumbing contractor, and the two work together to complete what was originally deemed to be a two-week project over the ensuing four months.

As Walter initially negotiates with Brad Shirk for the plumbing renovation, we actually see two forms of business ownership at work with the possibility of a third. The first is a partnership between Walter and his girlfriend where both have contributed equally to the endeavor in terms of their financial contributions. This is one of the main advantages of a partnership in that it allows for greater financial flexibility and availability of capital since both partners' financial resources can be drawn from. Given the nature of the partnership, Walter can actually respond very quickly to Brad's demands for a $5,000 deposit for plumbing repairs. In many ways, partnerships are comparable to marriages—or, as in Walter and Anna's case, long-term romantic relationships—in that both parties share the risks and rewards that come with the terrain navigated by the partnership.

We also see a sole proprietorship at work. Brad is an independent contractor who owns his own business, and that business is plumbing. As such, he has direct control of his business and the profits he reaps ultimately belong to him. Furthermore, he can operate the business as he sees fit, allowing him to charge Walter what he wants, accept or deny potential jobs like Walter's, and even assess the costs associated with a particular job—and consequently what he will charge—based on his own set of criteria. Unlike Walter and Anna, who share the risk and responsibility as well as the potential reward based on their partnership, Brad has accepted sole responsibility for the risk associated with the jobs he accepts, but he also is the sole recipient of the reward.

The following chapter further explores the issues of business ownership explored via *The Money Pit.* It begins with an overview of various types of ownership such as sole proprietorship and partnership, described above, as well as the notion of incorporation. It then continues with an exploration of specialized forms of business organization such as cooperatives and franchises, and then it discusses the hows and whys of mergers and acquisitions before outlining some of the current trends and issues in business ownership. All in all, you should emerge from this chapter with an understanding of the advantages and disadvantages of the various forms of business organizations that will carry you forward into issues of entrepreneurship.

The Money Pit/Corbis

Discussion Questions

- What are some of the potential disadvantages that Walter and Anna face with their particular partnership, considering that the two are not married?
- What are some of the potential disadvantages that Brad faces as sole proprietor of his plumbing business and how might he ease these disadvantages?
- As mentioned, there is a possibility of a third type of business organization described here between Brad's company and his brother's contracting business. What is that third type of business organization and what are its advantages and disadvantages?

Chapter 4 discusses sole proprietorships, as well as several other forms of business ownership, including partnerships and corporations, and compares the advantages and disadvantages of each. With a good idea and some cash in hand you decide to start a business. But before you get going you need to ask yourself some questions that will help you decide what form of business organization will best suit your needs.

Would you prefer to go it alone as a *sole proprietorship*, or do you want others to share your burdens and challenges in a *partnership*? Or would the limited liability protection of a *corporation*, or perhaps the flexibility of a *limited liability company (LLC)*, make more sense?

There are other questions you need to consider too: Will you need financing? How easy will it be to obtain? Will you attract employees? How will the business be taxed, and who will be liable for the company's debts? If you choose to share ownership with others, how much operating control would they want, and what costs would be associated with that?

As Exhibit 4.1 illustrates, sole proprietorships are the most popular form of business ownership, accounting for 72 percent of all businesses, compared with 9 percent for partnerships and 19 percent for corporations. Because most sole proprietorships and partnerships remain small, corporations generate approximately 84 percent of total business sales and 64 percent of total profits.

Most start-up businesses select one of these major ownership forms. In the following pages we will discover the advantages and disadvantages of each form of business ownership and the factors that may make it necessary to change from one form of organization to another, as the needs of the business change. As a company expands from small to midsize or larger, the form of business structure selected in the beginning may no longer be appropriate.

Going It Alone: Sole Proprietorships

1 What are the advantages and disadvantages of the sole proprietorship form of business organization?

When Kim Beattie entered the Clarkston Mini Storage, his one goal was to make Rick Detowski an offer he couldn't refuse. Beattie wanted to sell Detowski the buildings that housed his company, Moon Valley Rustic Furniture, liquidate his inventory, and go out of business. Because Detowski already owned eight buildings in the same office park as Moon Valley, Beattie considered him a perfect buyer for the properties.

Detowski was intrigued by Beattie's offer and immediately calculated that he could probably buy the properties for up to $1 million below market value. But instead of buying only the buildings, Detowski said impulsively, "Tell you what. If you sell me the company operations, too, then I'll buy the properties." After paying $1.8 million, Detowski became the sole proprietor of Moon Valley Rustic Furniture. The **sole proprietorship** is a form of business organization that is established, owned, operated, and often financed by one person. It is also the easiest to set up, an important consideration for Detowski after his spontaneous offer to buy the business.[1]

sole proprietorship
A business that is established, owned, operated, and often financed by one person.

EXHIBIT 4.1	Comparison of Forms of Business Organization		
Form	**Number**	**Sales**	**Profits**
Sole Proprietorships	72 percent	4 percent	14 percent
Partnerships	9 percent	12 percent	22 percent
Corporations	19 percent	84 percent	64 percent

Source: Internal Revenue Service, as reported in Table 721, U.S. Bureau of the Census, *Statistical Abstract of the United States, 2008,* **http://www.census.gov/compendia/statab/tables/08s0721.pdf**.

Advantages of Sole Proprietorships

Sole proprietorships have several advantages that make them popular:

- *Easy and inexpensive to form.* Sole proprietorships have few legal requirements (local licenses and permits) and are not expensive to form, making them the business organization of choice for many small companies and start-ups.
- *Profits all go to the owner.* The owner of a sole proprietorship obtains the start-up funds and gets all the profits earned by the business. The more efficiently the firm operates, the higher the company's profitability.
- *Direct control of the business.* All business decisions are made by the sole proprietorship owner without having to consult anyone else.
- *Freedom from government regulation.* Sole proprietorships have more freedom than other forms of business with respect to government controls.
- *No special taxation.* Sole proprietorships do not pay special franchise or corporate taxes. Profits are taxed as personal income as reported on the owner's individual tax return.
- *Ease of dissolution.* With no co-owners or partners the sole proprietor can sell the business or close the doors at any time, making this form of business organization an ideal way to test a new business idea.

Disadvantages of Sole Proprietorships

Along with the freedom to operate the business as they wish, sole proprietors face several disadvantages:

- *Unlimited liability.* From a legal standpoint, the sole proprietor and the company he or she owns is one and the same, making the business owner personally responsible for all debts the company incurs, even if they exceed the company's value. The owner may need to sell other personal property—his or her car, home, or other investments—to satisfy claims against his business.
- *Difficulty raising capital.* Business assets are unprotected against claims of personal creditors, so business lenders view sole proprietorships as high risk due to the owner's unlimited liability. Owners must often use personal funds—borrowing on credit cards, second-mortgaging their homes, or selling investments—to finance their business. Expansion plans can also be affected by an inability to raise additional funding. Indeed, when Rick Detowski began to look for $3 million in working capital to get Moon Valley back on track, several banks refused to finance his loans under usual terms, citing his lack of experience in the furniture business, and even asked for significant cash down payments.
- *Limited managerial expertise.* The success of a sole proprietorship rests solely with the skills and talents of the owner, who must wear many different hats and make all decisions. Owners are often not equally skilled in all areas of running a business. A graphic designer may be a wonderful artist but not know bookkeeping, how to manage production, or how to market his or her work.
- *Trouble finding qualified employees.* Sole proprietors often cannot offer the same pay, fringe benefits, and advancement as larger companies, making them less attractive to employees seeking the most favorable employment opportunities.
- *Personal time commitment.* Running a sole proprietorship business requires personal sacrifices and a huge time commitment, often dominating the owner's life with 12-hour workdays and seven-day workweeks.
- *Unstable business life.* The life span of a sole proprietorship can be uncertain. The owner may lose interest, experience ill health, retire, or die. The business will cease to exist unless the owner makes provisions for it to continue operating, or puts it up for sale.
- *Losses are the owner's responsibility.* The sole proprietor is responsible for all losses, although tax laws allow them to be deducted from other personal income.

The sole proprietorship may be a suitable choice for a one-person start-up operation with no employees and little risk of liability exposure.

CONCEPT check

What is a sole proprietorship?

Why is this a popular form of business organization?

What are the drawbacks to being a sole proprietor?

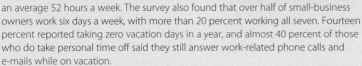

Work–Life Balance Important in Small Business

According to a recent survey released by the Wells Fargo/Gallup Small Business Index, about two-thirds of small-business owners are satisfied with how they balance their personal lives and work schedules, despite the fact that they work an average 52 hours a week. The survey also found that over half of small-business owners work six days a week, with more than 20 percent working all seven. Fourteen percent reported taking zero vacation days in a year, and almost 40 percent of those who do take personal time off said they still answer work-related phone calls and e-mails while on vacation.

Nonetheless, 67 percent of small-business owners said they were satisfied with their personal life–work balance and almost 90 percent said they were satisfied with being a small-business owner in general.

It's "not just a willingness" to work more hours, said Laine Caspi, who regularly logs in about 50 hours a week at work as owner of Parents of Invention (**http://www.parentsofinvention.com**), a manufacturer of baby accessories. "It's more like you want to do it. It's a choice, as opposed to someone else saying that you have to be there." Dennis Jacobe, chief economist at the Gallup Organization, agrees. "People see the benefits more closely tied to them when they're the owner," he says. "Working hard and long is a natural aspect of the kind of people willing to start their own business."

But if employees have trouble balancing work and life, odds are they will have less confidence in you as a leader, a recent study shows. The study, which polled more than 50,000 U.S. workers from various markets including professional services, consumer goods, and financial services, found that employees who strike a positive balance

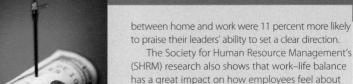

between home and work were 11 percent more likely to praise their leaders' ability to set a clear direction.

The Society for Human Resource Management's (SHRM) research also shows that work–life balance has a great impact on how employees feel about their leaders. Jennifer Schramm, a manager in SHRM's workplace trends and forecasting research department, predicts that as companies try to maximize the productivity of each employee, work–life balance will become increasingly more important.

"As other factors that contribute to job satisfaction become harder for employees to control—health care benefits, job security, and feeling safe in the workplace—work–life balance is something the business owner can offer," Schramm said. "Understanding your workforce is key to ensuring employee satisfaction." And research shows that happy employees can yield happy returns for businesses.[2]

Critical Thinking Questions

- Many small-business owners expect their employees to be as committed and to work as hard as they do. How would you avoid falling into that trap while still demanding the best from your workers?
- As a small-business owner, consider some strategies to ensure an appropriate work–life balance for your employees.

© Rubberball/Getty Images

For many sole proprietors, however, this is a temporary choice and as the business grows the owner may be unable to operate with limited financial and managerial resources. At this point he or she may decide to take in one or more partners to ensure that the business continues to flourish.

As you will see from the Catching the Entrepreneurial Spirit box above, small-business owners must work hard at balancing their professional and personal lives.

Partnerships: Sharing the Load

2 What are the advantages of operating as a partnership, and what downside risks should partners consider?

partnership
An association of two or more individuals who agree to operate a business together for profit.

Can a **partnership**, an association of two or more individuals who agree to operate a business together for profit, be hazardous to a business's health? Let's assume partners Ron and Liz own a stylish and successful beauty salon. After a few years of operating the business they find they have contrasting visions for their company. Liz is happy with the status quo, while Ron wants to expand the business by bringing in investors and opening salons in other locations.

How do they resolve this impasse? By asking themselves some tough questions. Whose view of the future is more realistic? Does the business actually have the expansion potential Ron believes it does? Where will he find investors to make his dream of multiple locations a reality? Is he willing to dissolve the partnership and start over again on his own? And who would have the right to their clients?

Ron realizes that expanding the business in line with his vision would require a large financial risk, and that his partnership with Liz offers many advantages he would miss in a sole proprietorship form of business organization. After much consideration he decides to leave things as they are.

For those individuals who do not like to "go it alone," a partnership is relatively simple to set up. Offering a shared form of business ownership, it is a popular choice for professional-service firms such as lawyers, accountants, architects, stockbrokers, and real estate companies.

The parties agree, either orally or in writing, to share in the profits and losses of a joint enterprise. A written partnership agreement, spelling out the terms and conditions of the partnership, is recommended to prevent later conflicts between the partners. Such agreements typically include the name of the partnership, its purpose, and the contributions of each partner (financial, asset, skill/talent). It also outlines the responsibilities and duties of each partner and their compensation structure (salary, profit sharing, etc.). It should contain provisions for the addition of new partners, the sale of partnership interests, and procedures for resolving conflicts, dissolving the business, and distributing the assets.

There are two basic types of partnerships: general and limited. In a **general partnership**, all partners share in the management and profits. They co-own the assets and each can act on behalf of the firm. Each partner also has unlimited liability for all the business obligations of the firm. A **limited partnership** has two types of partners: one or more **general partners** who have unlimited liability, and one or more **limited partners** whose liability is limited to the amount of their investment. In return for limited liability, limited partners agree not to take part in the day-to-day management of the firm. They help to finance the business but the general partners maintain operational control.

Advantages of Partnerships

Some advantages of partnerships come quickly to mind:

- *Ease of formation*. Like sole proprietorships, partnerships are easy to form. The partners agree to do business together and draw up a *partnership agreement*. For most partnerships, applicable state laws are not complex.
- *Availability of capital*. Because two or more people contribute financial resources, partnerships can raise funds more easily for operating expenses and business expansion. The partners' combined financial strength also increases the firm's ability to raise funds from outside sources.
- *Diversity of skills and expertise*. Partners share the responsibilities of managing and operating the business. Combining partner skills to set goals, manage the overall direction of the firm, and solve problems increases the chances for the partnership's success. To find the right partner you must examine your own strengths and weaknesses, and know what you need from a partner. Ideal partnerships bring together people with complementary backgrounds rather than those with similar experience, skills, and talents. In Exhibit 4.2 you'll find some advice on choosing a partner.
- *Flexibility*. General partners are actively involved in managing their firm and can respond quickly to changes in the business environment.
- *No special taxes*. Partnerships pay no income taxes. A partnership must file a partnership return with the Internal Revenue Service, reporting how profits or losses were divided among the partners. Each partner's profit or loss is then reported on the partner's personal income tax return, with any profits taxed at personal income tax rates.
- *Relative freedom from government control*. Except for state rules for licensing and permits, the government has little control over partnership activities.

general partnership
A partnership in which all partners share in the management and profits. Each partner can act on behalf of the firm and has unlimited liability for all its business obligations.

limited partnership
A partnership with one or more general partners who have unlimited liability, and one or more limited partners whose liability is limited to the amount of their investment in the company.

general partners
Partners who have unlimited liability for all of the firm's business obligations and who control its operations.

limited partners
Partners whose liability for the firm's business obligations is limited to the amount of their investment. They help to finance the business, but do not participate in the firm's operations.

EXHIBIT 4.2	**Perfect Partners**

Picking a partner is both an art and a science. Someone may have all the right credentials on paper, but does that person share your vision and the ideas you have for your company? Are they a straight shooter? Honesty, integrity, and ethics are important, because you may be liable for what your partner does. Be prepared to talk about everything and trust your intuition and your gut feelings—they're probably right. Ask yourself and your potential partner the following questions—then see how well your answers match up:

1. Why do you want a partner?
2. What characteristics, talents, and skills does each person bring to the partnership?
3. How will you divide responsibilities—from long-range planning to daily operations? Who will handle such tasks as marketing, sales, accounting, customer service?
4. What is your long-term vision for the business—its size, life span, financial commitment, etc.?
5. What are your personal reasons for forming this company? Are you looking to create a small company, or build a large one? Are you seeking a steady paycheck, or financial independence?
6. Will all parties put in the same amount of time, or is there an alternative arrangement that is acceptable to everyone?
7. Do you have similar work ethics and values?
8. What requirements will be in the partnership agreement?

© AP Images/Chris Pizzello

When Brad Pitt and Jennifer Aniston called it quits in one of Hollywood's most over-publicized splits ever, many hoped the magic would live on through the couple's joint-owned production company, Plan B Entertainment—the firm behind such blockbusters as *Troy* and *Charlie and the Chocolate Factory.* But Aniston exited the business relationship a year later, leaving Pitt to go solo on apocalyptic thrillers like *World War Z.* What are the pros and cons of forming a business partnership with a spouse?

Disadvantages of Partnerships

Business owners must consider the following disadvantages of setting up their company as a partnership:

- *Unlimited liability.* All general partners have unlimited liability for the debts of the business. In fact, any one partner can be held personally liable for all partnership debts and legal judgments (like malpractice)—regardless of who caused them. As with sole proprietorships, business failure can lead to a loss of the general partners' personal assets. To overcome this problem many states now allow the formation of *limited liability partnerships (LLPs),* which protect each individual partner from responsibility for the acts of other partners, and limit their liability to harm resulting from their own actions.

- *Potential for conflicts between partners.* Partners may have different ideas about how to run their business, which employees to hire, how to allocate responsibilities, and when to expand. Differences in personalities and work styles can cause clashes or breakdowns in communication, sometimes requiring outside intervention to save the business.

- *Complexity of profit-sharing.* Dividing the profits is relatively easy if all partners contribute equal amounts of time, expertise, and capital. But if one partner puts in more money and others more time it might be more difficult to arrive at a fair profit-sharing formula.

- *Difficulty exiting or dissolving a partnership.* As a rule, partnerships are easier to form than to leave. When one partner wants to leave, the value of his or her share must be calculated. To whom will that share be sold and will that person be acceptable to the other partners? If a partner who owns more than 50 percent of the entity withdraws, dies, or becomes disabled, the partnership must reorganize or end. To avoid these problems, most partnership agreements include specific guidelines for transferring partnership interests, and buy–sell agreements that make provision for surviving partners to buy a deceased partner's interest. Partners can also purchase special life insurance policies designed to fund such a purchase.

Business partnerships are often compared to marriages. As with a marriage, choosing the right partner is critical. So if you are considering forming a partnership, allow plenty of time to evaluate your and your potential partner's goals, personality, expertise, and working style before joining forces.

CONCEPT check

How does a partnership differ from a sole proprietorship?

Describe the three main types of partnerships and explain the difference between a limited partner and a general partner.

What are the main advantages and disadvantages of a partnership?

Corporations: Limiting Your Liability

3 How does the corporate structure provide advantages and disadvantages to a company, and what are the major types of corporations?

corporation
A legal entity with an existence and life separate from its owners, who are not personally liable for the entity's debts. A corporation is chartered by the state in which it is formed and can own property, enter into contracts, sue and be sued, and engage in business operations under the terms of its charter.

When people think of corporations they typically think of major, well-known companies like IBM, Microsoft, and General Electric. But corporations range in size from large multinationals with thousands of employees and billions of dollars in sales, to midsize or even smaller firms with few employees and revenues under $25,000.

A **corporation** is a legal entity subject to the laws of the state in which it is formed, where the right to operate as a business is issued by state charter. A corporation can own property, enter into contracts, sue and be sued, and engage in business operations under the terms of its charter. Unlike sole proprietorships and partnerships, corporations are taxable entities with a life separate from its owners, who are not personally liable for its debts.

When launching her company, Executive Property Management Services, Inc., 32-year-old Linda Ravden realized she needed the liability protection of the corporate form of business organization. Her company specialized in providing customized property management services to mid- and upper-level corporate executives on extended work assignments abroad, often for three to five years or longer. Taking care of substantial properties in the $1 million range and above was no small responsibility for Ravden's company. Therefore the protection of a corporate business structure, along with carefully detailed contracts outlining the company's obligations, were crucial in providing Ravden with the liability protection she needed—and the peace of mind to focus on running her business without constant worry.[3]

Crocs Runs with the Bulls

When Chris Haunold started selling Crocs in 2003, many of his customers thought the brightly colored shoes were a joke. Until they put them on and liked them, that is. Crocs are arguably the biggest shoe innovation in recent memory, and for a shoe that even the company embraces as "ugly," that's no small feat. The company founders developed the shoe for boating and made it out of lightweight, nonslip foam. The now-ubiquitous shoe debuted at the Fort Lauderdale boat show in November 2002, and within a year, the shoe had generated $1 million in sales. By 2008, Crocs had 50 designs in roughly 25,000 stores worldwide that generated nearly $850 million dollars in annual sales.

During the company's explosive beginnings, the founders focused on maintaining quality and operational control. They bought Finproject NA, the Canadian company that produced the footwear and owned the formula for the shoe's foam, and Foam Creations, a maker of spa pillows and products for boating. In 2006, the company sold 9.9 million shares in an initial public offering of stock to become a publicly held corporation. Revenue generated from the purchase (9.9 million shares at $21 per share) allowed Crocs to continue growing and also to purchase another related company—Jibbitz LLC, the company that pioneered the charms that Crocs wearers snap into the shoes' holes for decoration.

Many analysts believe that diversification is the key to Crocs's future success, Even though sales of Jibbitz rose from $200,000 to $2 million per month after the Crocs acquisition, some still see Jibbitz as an accessory for one style of Crocs. And even though nearly one in four people around the world own Crocs, a small but vocal backlash is growing against what is perhaps the ugliest shoe to win Brand of the Year by *Footwear News*. Still, if imitation is the sincerest form of flattery, the number of people wearing Crocs or Croc-inspired shoes could be much higher, as knockoffs and imitators have begun to appear in droves.[4]

Critical Thinking Questions

- What kind of diversification strategy can help Crocs continue on its path of astronomical growth?
- Do you think vertical or horizontal mergers and acquisitions (see page 115) are more important to Crocs as it tries to sustain growth and fend off imitations?

As Crocs's business grew, its form of business organization needed to adjust, too. In the Managing Change box above, you'll learn how it managed a very successful transition from a single (ugly) product developed by two avid boaters into a line of more than 50 designs that generate nearly $850 million in annual revenue.

Corporations play an important role in the U.S. economy. As Exhibit 4.1 demonstrated, corporations account for only 19 percent of all businesses, but generate 84 percent of all revenues and 64 percent of all profits. A list of the 10 largest U.S corporations, shown in Exhibit 4.3, includes many familiar names that affect our daily lives.

The Incorporation Process

Setting up a corporation is more complex than starting a sole proprietorship or partnership. Most states base their laws for chartering corporations on the Model Business Corporation Act of the American Bar Association, although registration procedures, fees, taxes, and laws that regulate corporations vary from state to state.

A firm does not have to incorporate in the state where it is based and may benefit by comparing the rules of several states before choosing a state of incorporation. Although Delaware is a small state with few corporations actually based there, its pro-corporate policies make it the

EXHIBIT 4.3	The 10 Largest U.S. Corporations (ranked by 2007 sales)	
	Company	**Revenues ($ millions)**
1	Wal-Mart Stores	378,799
2	ExxonMobil	372,824
3	ChevronTexaco	210,783
4	General Motors	182,347
5	ConocoPhillips	178,558
6	General Electric	176,656
7	Ford Motor	172,468
8	Citigroup	159,229
9	Bank of America Corp.	119,190
10	AT&T	118,928

Source: "The 2008 Fortune 500", *Fortune*, **http://money.cnn.com/magazines/fortune**. (May 2008). 2008 © Time Inc. All rights reserved.

© Justin Sullivan/Getty Images

Incorporated in 1902, the Target Corporation is one of America's most popular retail stores. Known early on as Goodfellows and the Dayton Dry Goods Company, Target launched into discount retailing in the 1960s and quickly established a strong brand image. Today, youthful shoppers seek out fashionably affordable merchandise at the company's more than 1,500 stores, and the Target bullseye is among the most recognizable trademarks in all of business—more recognizable than even the Nike swoosh. What steps must companies take to become incorporated?

stockholders (or shareholders)
The owners of a corporation who hold shares of stock that provide them with certain rights.

board of directors
A group of people elected by the stockholders to govern and handle the overall management of a corporation, such as setting major corporate goals and policies, hiring corporate officers, and overseeing the firm's operations and finances.

state of incorporation for many companies, including about half the Fortune 500. Incorporating a company involves five main steps:

- Selecting the company's name
- Writing the *articles of incorporation* (see Exhibit 4.4) and filing them with the appropriate state office, usually the secretary of state
- Paying required fees and taxes
- Holding an organizational meeting
- Adopting bylaws, electing directors, and passing the first operating resolutions

The state issues a corporate charter based on information in the articles of incorporation. Once the corporation has its charter, it holds an organizational meeting to adopt bylaws, elect directors, and pass initial operating resolutions. Bylaws provide legal and managerial guidelines for operating the firm.

The Corporate Structure

As Exhibit 4.5 shows, corporations have their own organizational structure with three important components: stockholders, directors, and officers.

Stockholders (or shareholders) are the owners of a corporation, holding shares of stock that provide them with certain rights. They may receive a portion of the corporation's profits in the form of dividends, and they can sell or transfer their ownership in the corporation (represented by their shares of stock) at any time. Stockholders can attend annual meetings, elect the board of directors, and vote on matters that affect the corporation in accordance with its charter and bylaws. Each share of stock generally carries one vote.

The stockholders elect a **board of directors** to govern and handle the overall management of the corporation. The directors set major corporate goals and policies, hire corporate officers, and oversee the firm's operations and finances. Small firms may have as few as 3 directors, whereas large corporations usually have 10 to 15.

The boards of large corporations typically include both corporate executives and outside directors (not employed by the organization) chosen for their professional and personal expertise. Outside directors often bring a fresh view to the corporation's activities because they are independent of the firm.

Hired by the board, the officers of a corporation are its top management, and include the president and chief executive officer (CEO), vice presidents, treasurer, and secretary, who are responsible for achieving corporate goals and policies. Officers may also be board members and stockholders.

Advantages of Corporations

The corporate structure allows companies to merge financial and human resources into enterprises with great potential for growth and profits:

- *Limited liability.* A key advantage of corporations is that they are separate legal entities that exist apart from their owners. An owner's (stockholder's) liability for the obligations of the firm is limited to the amount of the stock he or she owns. If the corporation goes bankrupt, creditors can look only to the assets of the corporation for payment.

EXHIBIT 4.4	**Articles of Incorporation**

Articles of incorporation are prepared on a form authorized or supplied by the state of incorporation. Although they may vary slightly from state to state, all articles of incorporation include the following key items:

- Name of corporation
- Company's goals
- Types of stock and number of shares of each type to issue
- Life of the corporation (usually "perpetual," meaning with no time limit)
- Minimum investment by owners
- Methods for transferring shares of stock
- Address of the corporate office
- Names and addresses of the first board of directors

EXHIBIT 4.5 Organizational Structure of Corporations

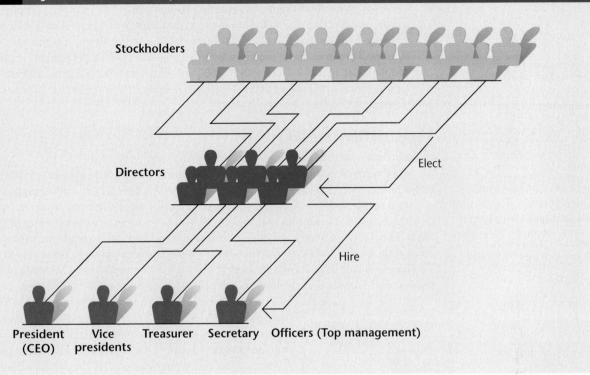

- *Ease of transferring ownership.* Stockholders of public corporations can sell their shares at any time without affecting the status of the corporation.
- *Unlimited life.* The life of a corporation is unlimited. Although corporate charters specify a life term, they also include rules for renewal. Because the corporation is an entity separate from its owners, the death or withdrawal of an owner does not affect its existence, unlike a sole proprietorship or partnership.
- *Tax deductions.* Corporations are allowed certain tax deductions, such as operating expenses, which reduces their taxable income.
- *Ability to attract financing.* Corporations can raise money by selling new shares of stock. Dividing ownership into smaller units makes it affordable to more investors, who can purchase one or several thousand shares. The large size and stability of corporations also helps them get bank financing. All these financial resources allow corporations to invest in facilities and human resources and expand beyond the scope of sole proprietorships or partnerships. It would be impossible for a sole proprietorship or partnership to make automobiles, provide nationwide telecommunications, or build oil or chemical refineries.

Disadvantages of Corporations

Although corporations offer companies many benefits, they have some disadvantages:

- *Double taxation of profits.* Corporations must pay federal and state income taxes on their profits. In addition, any profits (dividends) paid to stockholders are taxed as personal income, although at a somewhat reduced rate.
- *Cost and complexity of formation.* As outlined earlier, forming a corporation involves several steps, and costs can run into thousands of dollars, including state filing, registration, and license fees, as well as the cost of attorneys and accountants.

CONCEPT in action

When Walt Disney cast his now-famous mouse as Steamboat Willie back in the 1920s, he had little idea that his animation project would turn into one of the largest entertainment companies in the world. The house that Walt built, with its magical theme parks, movie studios, and product lines, is overseen today by visionary directors with accomplished backgrounds in media, technology, and government. What important tasks and responsibilities are entrusted to Disney's board of directors?

© AP IMAGES

C corporation
A conventional or basic form of corporate organization.

S corporation
A hybrid entity that is organized like a corporation, with stockholders, directors, and officers, but taxed like a partnership, with income and losses flowing through to the stockholders and taxed as their personal income.

limited liability company (LLC)
A hybrid organization that offers the same liability protection as a corporation but may be taxed as either a partnership or a corporation.

CONCEPT check

What is a corporation? Describe how corporations are formed and structured.

Summarize the advantages and disadvantages of corporations. Which features contribute to the dominance of corporations in the business world?

Why do S corporations and limited liability companies (LLCs) appeal to small businesses?

- *More government restrictions.* Unlike sole proprietorships and partnerships, corporations are subject to many regulations and reporting requirements. For example, corporations must register in each state where they do business, and must also register with the Securities and Exchange Commission (SEC) before selling stock to the public. Unless it is closely held (owned by a small group of stockholders), a firm must publish financial reports on a regular basis, and file other special reports with the SEC and state and federal agencies. These reporting requirements can impose substantial costs, and published information on corporate operations may also give competitors an advantage.

Types of Corporations

Three types of corporate business organization provide limited liability.

The **C corporation** is the conventional or basic form of corporate organization. Small businesses may achieve liability protection through S corporations or limited liability companies (LLCs).

An **S corporation** is a hybrid entity, allowing smaller corporations to avoid double taxation of corporate profits as long as they meet certain size and ownership requirements. Organized like a corporation with stockholders, directors, and officers, an S corporation is taxed like a partnership. Income and losses flow through to the stockholders and are taxed as personal income. S corporations are allowed a maximum of 100 qualifying shareholders and one class of stock. The owners of an S corporation are not personally liable for the debts of the corporation.

A newer type of business entity, the **limited liability company (LLC)**, is also a hybrid organization. Like S corporations, they appeal to small businesses because they are easy to set up and not subject to many restrictions. LLCs offer the same liability protection as corporations as well as the option of being taxed as a partnership or a corporation. First authorized in Wyoming in 1977, LLCs became popular after a 1988 tax ruling that treats them like partnerships for tax purposes. Today all states allow the formation of LLCs.

Exhibit 4.6 summarizes the advantages and disadvantages of each form of business ownership.

Specialized Forms of Business Organization

4 What other options for business organization does a company have in addition to sole proprietorships, partnerships, and corporations?

cooperative
A legal entity typically formed by people with similar interests, such as suppliers or customers, to reduce costs and gain economic power. A cooperative has limited liability, an unlimited life span, an elected board of directors, and an administrative staff; all profits are distributed to the member-owners in proportion to their contributions.

buyer cooperative
A group of cooperative members who unite for combined purchasing power.

seller cooperative
Individual producers who join together to compete more effectively with large producers.

In addition to the three main forms, several specialized types of business organization also play an important role in our economy. We will look at cooperatives and joint ventures in this section and take a detailed look at franchising in the following section.

Cooperatives

When you eat a Sunkist orange or spread Land O'Lakes butter on your toast, you are consuming foods produced by cooperatives. A **cooperative** is a legal entity with several corporate features, such as limited liability, an unlimited life span, an elected board of directors, and an administrative staff. Member-owners pay annual fees to the cooperative and share in the profits, which are distributed to members in proportion to their contributions. Because they do not retain any profits, cooperatives are not subject to taxes.

There are currently 750,000 cooperatives with 760 million members in more than 100 countries worldwide.[5] Cooperatives operate in every industry including agriculture, child care, energy, financial services, food retailing and distribution, health care, insurance, housing, purchasing and shared services, and telecommunications, among others. They range in size from large enterprises like Fortune 500 companies to small local storefronts, and fall into four distinct categories: consumer, producer, worker, and purchasing/shared services.

Cooperatives are autonomous businesses owned and democratically controlled by their members—the people who buy their goods or use their services—not by investors. Unlike investor-owned businesses, cooperatives are organized solely to meet the needs of the member-owners, not to accumulate capital for investors. As democratically controlled businesses, many cooperatives practice the principle of "one member, one vote," providing members with equal control over the cooperative.

There are two types of cooperatives. **Buyer cooperatives** combine members' purchasing power. Pooling buying power and buying in volume increases purchasing power and efficiency,

	Sole Proprietorship	Partnership	Corporation
Advantages			
	Owner receives all profits.	More expertise and managerial skill available.	Limited liability protects owners from losing more than they invest.
	Low organizational costs.	Relatively low organizational costs.	Can achieve large size due to marketability of stock (ownership).
	Income taxed as personal income of proprietor.	Income taxed as personal income of partners.	Receives certain tax advantages.
	Independence.	Fund-raising ability is enhanced by more owners.	Greater access to financial resources allows growth.
	Secrecy.		Can attract employees with specialized skills.
	Ease of dissolution.		Ownership is readily transferable.
			Long life of firm (not affected by death of owners).
Disadvantages			
	Owner receives all losses.	Owners have unlimited liability; may have to cover debts of other, less financially sound partners.	Double taxation because both corporate profits and dividends paid to owners are taxed, although the dividends are taxed at a reduced rate.
	Owner has unlimited liability; total wealth can be taken to satisfy business debts.	Dissolves or must reorganize when partner dies.	More expensive and complex to form.
	Limited fund-raising ability can inhibit growth.	Difficult to liquidate or terminate.	Subject to more government regulation.
	Proprietor may have limited skills and management expertise.	Potential for conflicts between partners.	Financial reporting requirements make operations public.
	Few long-range opportunities and benefits for employees.	Difficult to achieve large-scale operations.	
	Lacks continuity when owner dies.		

resulting in lower prices. At the end of the year, members get shares of the profits based on how much they bought. Obtaining discounts to lower costs gives the corner Ace Hardware store the chance to survive against retailing giants like Home Depot Inc. and Lowe's.

Founded in 1924, Ace Hardware is one of the nation's largest cooperatives and is wholly owned by its independent hardware retailer members in stores spanning all 50 states and 70 countries. The typical Ace store consistently outperforms its non-Ace competitors with annual sales that are 85 percent higher, net profits before taxes that are 146 percent higher, and a return on investment that is 42 percent greater.[6]

Seller cooperatives are popular in agriculture, wherein individual producers join to compete more effectively with large producers. Member dues support market development, national advertising, and other business activities. In addition to Sunkist and Land O'Lakes, other familiar cooperatives are Calavo (avocados), Ocean Spray (cranberries and juices), and Blue Diamond (nuts). Farmland Industries, the largest cooperative in the United States, sells feed, fertilizer, petroleum, and grain.

Cooperatives empower people to improve their quality of life and enhance their economic opportunities through self-help. Throughout the world, cooperatives are providing members with credit and financial services, energy, consumer goods, affordable housing, telecommunications, and other services that would not otherwise be available to them. Exhibit 4.7 on the next page outlines the basic principles of operation cooperatives follow.

CONCEPT in action

Riding the international fame of NBA stars like Yao Ming and LeBron James, the National Basketball Association recently launched NBA China in joint venture with ESPN, the Li Ka Shing Foundation, and three other Chinese companies. The newly formed subsidiary is expanding the league's Asian presence through regular season play in NBA-caliber arenas, as well as through business dealings with Chinese broadcasters and merchandisers. Basketball is currently the No. 2 sport in China. Why is a joint venture necessary for the NBA's overseas expansion?

© Andrew D. Bernstein/NBAE via Getty Images

Joint Ventures

joint venture
Two or more companies that form an alliance to pursue a specific project usually for a specified time period.

In a **joint venture** two or more companies form an alliance to pursue a specific project, usually for a specified time period. There are many reasons for joint ventures. The project may be too large for one company to handle on its own, and joint ventures also afford companies access to new markets, products, or technology. Both large and small companies can benefit from joint ventures.

To compete more successfully in the online and mobile entertainment industry dominated by iTunes, Sony BMG Music Entertainment recently joined with Dada, a provider of Web and mobile entertainment services, to create a new company called Dada Entertainment. Sony BMG will provide its full catalog of music and movies, as well as its massive distribution networks, to the joint venture, and Dada will provide the underlying software platform and the billing technology. Each venture partner owns a 50 percent stake in the newly formed Dada Entertainment and has an equal number of representatives on its board of directors.[7]

CONCEPT check

Describe the two types of cooperatives and the advantages of each.

What are the benefits of joint ventures?

Franchising: A Popular Trend

5 What makes franchising an appropriate form of organization for some types of business, and why does it continue to grow in importance?

With only seven years before retirement, Richard Rocco was laid off from his job. Over the 27 years Rocco had spent in graphic arts sales, he had steadily watched the industry contract, so finding a new job with suitable pay was proving impossible. Rocco spent five frustrating months looking for a new job, but then he decided to pursue his dream of owning his own business. Rather than research all the options, he concentrated on opportunities that best matched his experience. Finally, he found a company called PostNet, which specializes in printing, shipping, and graphics services.[8]

Choosing the right franchise can be challenging. Franchises come in all sizes and demand different skills and qualifications. And with somewhere around 2,500 different franchised businesses in the United States, Rocco had a lot to choose from—from cookie-bouquet peddlers and dog trainers to acupuncture specialists. Exhibit 4.8 shows *Entrepreneur* magazine's top 10 franchises for 2008.

Looking at these franchise start-up costs, it is easy to see that an important factor in picking a franchise is money. PostNet requires a total investment of approximately $200,000 with start-up costs of around $50,000, so Rocco used his home equity and his 401(k) to finance his entry into franchising.

franchising
A form of business organization based on a business arrangement between a *franchisor*, which supplies the product or service concept, and the *franchisee*, who sells the goods or services of the *franchisor* in a certain geographic area.

franchisor
In a franchising arrangement, the company that supplies the product or service concept to the *franchisee*.

franchisee
In a franchising arrangement, the individual or company that sells the goods or services of the franchisor in a certain geographic area.

Chances are you recognize some of the names listed in Exhibit 4.8 and deal with franchise systems in your neighborhood every day. When you have lunch at Taco Bell or Jamba Juice, make copies at FedEx Kinko's, change your oil at Jiffy Lube, buy candles at Wicks 'n' Sticks, or mail a package at The UPS Store, you are dealing with a franchised business. These and other familiar name brands mean quality, consistency, and value to consumers. Over 760,000 franchised businesses provide about 18 million jobs and generate $1.53 trillion in annual economic output.[9]

Franchising is a form of business organization that involves a **franchisor**, the company supplying the product or service concept, and the **franchisee**, the individual or company selling the goods or services in a certain geographic area. The franchisee buys a package that includes a proven product or service, proven operating methods, and training in managing the business. Offering a way to own a business without starting it from scratch, and to expand operations quickly into new geographic areas with limited capital investment, franchising is one of the fastest-growing segments of the economy. Food companies represent the largest number of franchises, as the industry segmentation in Exhibit 4.9 shows.

A **franchise agreement** is a contract that allows the franchisee to use the franchisor's business name, trademark, and logo. The agreement also outlines rules for running the franchise, services provided by the franchisor, and financial terms. The franchisee agrees to follow the franchisor's operating rules by keeping inventory at certain levels, buying a standard equipment package, keeping up sales and service levels, taking part in franchisor promotions, and maintaining a relationship with the franchisor. In return, the franchisor provides the use of a proven company name and symbols, help in finding a site, building plans, guidance and training, management assistance, managerial and accounting systems and procedures, employee training, wholesale prices for supplies, and financial assistance.

franchise agreement
A contract setting out the terms of a franchising arrangement, including the rules for running the franchise, the services provided by the *franchisor*, and the financial terms. Under the contract, the franchisee is allowed to use the franchisor's business name, trademark, and logo.

EXHIBIT 4.8	Top 10 Franchises for 2008	
Franchise Name		**Total Investment**
1. 7-Eleven Inc. (convenience store)		Varies
2. Subway (sandwiches and salads)		$76,100–$227,800
3. Dunkin' Donuts (donuts and baked goods)		Varies
4. Pizza Hut (quick-service pizza restaurant)		$1,100,000–$1,170,000
5. McDonald's (fast-food hamburger restaurant)		$506,000–$1,600,000
6. Sonic Drive-In Restaurants (drive-in hamburger restaurants)		$820,000–$2,300,000
7. KFC Corp. (fast-food chicken restaurant)		$1,100,000–$1,700,000
8. InterContinental Hotels Group (middle-market lodging)		Varies
9. Domino's Pizza LLC (pizza)		$118,500–$460,300
10. RE/MAX Int'l. Inc. (real estate)		$35,000–$191,000

Source: Top 10 Franchises in 2008 excerpted from "2008 Franchise 500 Rankings". Reprinted from **http://entrepreneur.com/franchises/rankings/franchise500-115608/2008,.html** with permission of Entrepreneur.com, Inc. © Entrepreneur.com, Inc. All rights reserved.

EXHIBIT 4.9	Franchises by Industry Segment

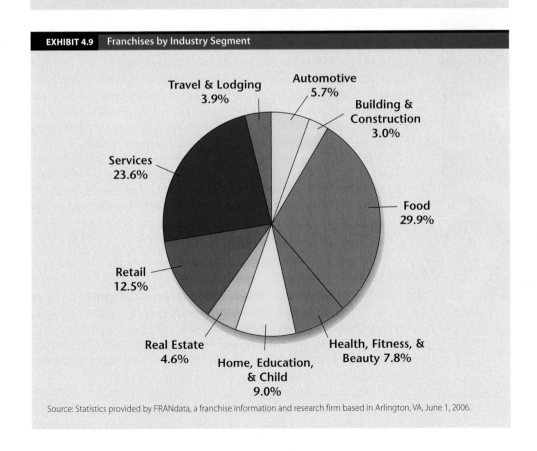

Source: Statistics provided by FRANdata, a franchise information and research firm based in Arlington, VA, June 1, 2006.

CONCEPT in action

Countless franchise opportunities exist for entrepreneurs with access to start-up capital. Despite the broad range of franchise opportunities available, lists of the fastest-growing franchises are heavily weighted with restaurant chains and cleaning services. Start-up costs for a Quiznos franchise can be pricey; expenses associated with opening a Jani-King or a CleanNet cleaning service are significantly lower. How do entrepreneurs evaluate which franchising opportunity is right for them?

CONCEPT in action

With nearly 600 restaurants, booming shares, and double-digit same-store-sales growth, Chipotle Mexican Grill is one of America's hottest fast-food chains. Yet despite out-the-door demand for its foil-concealed signature burritos bulging with rice, marinated steak, cilantro, and guacamole, Chipotle refuses to franchise its stores. The chain's top management eschew advertising, disparage fast-food franchises, and boast of serving "food with integrity." Why might some restaurants reject franchising as a means of growth?

Advantages of Franchises

Like other forms of business organization, franchising offers some distinct advantages:

- *Increased ability for franchisor to expand.* Because franchisees finance their own units, franchisors can grow without making a major investment.
- *Recognized name, product, and operating concept.* Consumers know they can depend on products from franchises like Pizza Hut, Hertz, and Holiday Inn. As a result, the franchisee's risk is reduced and the opportunity for success increased. The franchisee gets a widely known and accepted business with a proven track record, as well as operating procedures, standard goods and services, and national advertising.
- *Management training and assistance.* The franchisor provides a structured training program that gives the new franchisee a crash course in how to start and operate their business. Ongoing training programs for managers and employees are another plus. In addition, franchisees have a peer group for support and sharing ideas.
- *Financial assistance.* Being linked to a nationally known company can help a franchisee obtain funds from a lender. Also, the franchisor typically gives the franchisee advice on financial management, referrals to lenders, and help in preparing loan applications. Many franchisors also offer short-term credit for buying supplies, payment plans, and loans to purchase real estate and equipment. Although franchisors give up a share of profits to their franchisees, they receive ongoing revenues in the form of royalty payments.

Disadvantages of Franchises

Franchising also has some disadvantages:

- *Loss of control.* The franchisor has to give up some control over operations and has less control over its franchisees than over company employees. For example, in 2008, a group of Dairy Queen franchisees sued the franchisor American Dairy Queen to prevent the franchisor from forcing them to convert their existing franchises to either the DQ Grill & Chill or DQ Orange Julius format. Conversions, the franchisees argued, would cost too much and destroy their profitability and the value of their franchises.[10]
- *Cost of franchising.* Franchising can be a costly form of business. Costs will vary depending on the type of business, and may include expensive facilities and equipment. The franchisee also pays fees and/or royalties, which are usually tied to a percentage of sales. Fees for national and local advertising and management advice may add to a franchisee's ongoing costs.
- *Restricted operating freedom.* The franchisee agrees to conform to the franchisor's operating rules and facilities design, as well as inventory and supply standards. Some franchises require franchisees to purchase from only the franchisor or approved suppliers. The franchisor may also restrict the franchisee's territory or site, which could limit growth. Failure to conform to franchisor policies could mean the loss of the franchise.

Franchise Growth

Many of today's major franchise brands, such as McDonald's and KFC, started in the 1950s. Through the 1960s and 1970s more types of businesses—clothing, convenience stores, business services, and many others—used franchising to distribute their goods and services. Growth comes from expansion of established franchises—for example, Subway, Pizza Hut, and Curves, as well as new entrants such as those in Exhibit 4.10.

Changing demographics drive franchise industry growth in terms of who, how, and what experiences the most rapid growth. The continuing growth and popularity of technology and personal computing is responsible

| Exhibit 4.10 | Fast-Growing and Top New Franchises, 2008 |

Rank	Fastest-Growing Franchises, 2008	Top New Franchises, 2008
1	Jan-Pro Franchising Int'l. Inc. (commercial cleaning)	Instant Tax Service (retail tax preparation and electronic filing)
2	7-Eleven Inc. (convenience store)	Massage Envy (therapeutic massage services)
3	Subway (sandwiches and salads)	Snap Fitness Inc. (24-hour fitness center)
4	Jani-King (commercial cleaning)	System4 (commercial cleaning)
5	Dunkin' Donuts (donuts and baked goods)	One Hour Air Conditioning & Heating (HVAC replacement & services)
6	Jackson Hewitt Tax Service (tax preparation services)	Super Suppers (do-it-yourself home meal preparation)
7	Bonus Building Care (commercial cleaning services)	Mathnasium Learning Centers (math learning center)
8	Instant Tax Service (retail tax preparation and electronic filing)	The Growth Coach (small-business coaching & mentoring)
9	Liberty Tax Service (retail tax preparation and electronic filing)	Play N Trade Franchise Inc. (new & used video games)
10	RE/MAX Int'l. Inc. (real estate)	N-Hance (wood floor & cabinet renewal systems)

Source: "Top 10 Fastest-Growing Franchises for 2008". Reprinted from **http://entrepreneur.com/franzone/fastestgrowing** with permission of Entrepreneur.com, Inc. All rights reserved; and "Top 10 New Franchises for 2008." Reprinted from **http://entrepreneur.com/franchises/topnew** with permission of Entrepreneur.com, Inc.

for the rapidly multiplying number of eBay drop-off stores, and tech consultants like Geeks on Call are in greater demand than ever. Other growth franchise industries are the specialty coffee market, children's enrichment and tutoring programs, senior care, weight control, and fitness franchises.

And the savviest franchisees see multiunit development as a great way to further expand franchise systems and increase profits. Multiunit buyers tend to be white-collar workers who have been laid off from middle-management jobs. They are well qualified financially, and bring management skills, financial resources, business acumen, and a lot of drive to their franchise ventures.

The Next Big Thing in Franchising

All around you people are talking about the next big thing—Subway is the new miracle weight-loss solution, the half-hour workout at Curves is the answer to America's fitness needs—and you are ready to take the plunge and buy a trendy franchise. But consumers' desires can change with the tide, so how do you plan an entrance and exit strategy when purchasing a franchise that's a big hit today but could be old news by tomorrow? Exhibit 4.11 on the next page outlines some franchise purchase tips offered by Michael H. Seid, managing director of Michael H. Seid & Associates, a West Hartford, Connecticut–based management consulting firm specializing in the franchise industry.

International Franchising

Like other forms of business, franchising is part of our global marketplace economy. As international demand for all types of goods and services grows, most franchise systems are already operating internationally or planning to expand overseas. Restaurants, hotels, business services, educational products, car rentals, and nonfood retail stores are popular international franchises.

CONCEPT in action

© ARMANDO ARORIZO/Bloomberg News /Landov

Pinkberry is making it cool again to eat frozen yogurt. Founded in 2005 by Shelly Hwang and Young Lee, the upscale dessert franchise has become a cultural phenomenon, winning financial backing from Starbucks founder Howard Schultz and celebrity kudos from Paris Hilton and Ellen DeGeneres. Dubbed "crackberry" for its irresistible citrus flavors and exotic toppings, Pinkberry operates approximately 50 stores, each of which draws 1,500 customers daily. To open a shop, franchisees pay a $40,000 fee plus 7 percent of monthly sales. Is Pinkberry the next hot franchise or a risky fad?

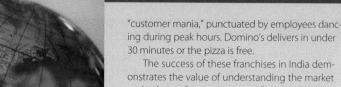

Slicing the Pizza Market in India

Thousands of miles from their Midwest head-quarters, two American franchises are vying to be the number one pizzeria in India. Although Domino's and Pizza Hut have had stores in India for more than 10 years, both companies have launched aggressive expansion plans to court India's swelling middle class. Competition started heating up when Domino's, self-proclaimed leader in pizza delivery, began adding in-store seating, and Pizza Hut, self-proclaimed leader in casual dining, announced it would double its number of stores by 2012.

What makes these two pizza giants so bullish on India? Unlike other ethnic cuisines, pizza is somewhat similar to some of India's native cuisine. Indians eat leavened bread called *naan,* and in some regions *naan* is prepared with butter and garlic. Cheese, tomatoes, and numerous sauces are also prevalent in many kinds of traditional dishes, so when combined American style into pizza, the tastes feel familiar. In addition, pizza is a good fit with India's primarily vegetarian culture.

Even though the basics are the same, both Domino's and Pizza Hut recognize the need to develop recipes for very different tastes. Ketchup and chili flakes are popular condiments at both, a pan pizza could be topped with chicken tikka or pepperoni, and mango ice cream and tomato soup—two things definitely *not* on the American menu of either chain—can be part of a four-course pizza dinner. The recipe isn't the only thing that makes pizza restaurants successful. India has a very social and family-oriented culture, so Pizza Hut restaurants cultivate a loud, chaotic, family atmosphere, called

"customer mania," punctuated by employees dancing during peak hours. Domino's delivers in under 30 minutes or the pizza is free.

The success of these franchises in India demonstrates the value of understanding the market and culture of an international franchise location. Neither Pizza Hut nor Domino's has grafted their American restaurant concept onto India. Rather, both companies know their core business and how to adapt it to meet the needs of their growing Indian customer base. The fact that Pizza Hut ranks as the most trusted food-service brand in India is a testament to that approach. According to a recent study by McKinsey Global Institute, the Indian middle class of 50 million people is expected to grow to 583 million by 2025. Any way you slice it, that could be a lot of pizza.[11]

Critical Thinking Questions

- How can franchises adapt when the main disadvantages of franchising involve lack of franchisee control and restricted operating freedom?
- Are some types of franchises better suited to international expansion than others? Are there some types of franchising that could not succeed on a global level? Which ones and why?

EXHIBIT 4.11 Franchise Purchase Tips

Act fast, yet proceed with caution. Normal trends tend to have a five-year life span, so it's important to get in early. Commit to a shorter term when the investment is not so secure.

Put the franchisor to the test. When you get into a franchise system that needs to be nimble, make certain it can respond quickly to change.

Know what you're getting into. Ask the franchisor what product(s) they plan to add if trends change. If they don't have an answer or aren't talking about research and development, you still might be able to buy into the trend but not with that franchisor.

Don't invest more than you can afford to lose. Bank your money and look at other investments.

Don't fall in love with a trend. Trends are fickle. Adored one day, they can become one-hit wonders the next. Buy on business sense not on emotions.

Source: Franchise Purchase Tips excerpted from "All the Rage—Tech & eBay." Reprinted from **http://entrepreneur.com/magazine/entrepreneur/2005/january/74990-2.html** with permission of Entrepreneur.com, Inc.

Franchisors in foreign countries face many of the same problems as other firms doing business abroad. In addition to tracking markets and currency changes, franchisors must understand local culture, language differences, and the political environment. Franchisors in foreign countries also face the challenge of aligning their business operations with the goals of their franchisees, who may be located half a globe away. In the Expanding Around the Globe box above, you will learn how two American fast-food giants are locked in fierce competition for market share in India.

Is Franchising in Your Future?

Are you ready to be a franchisee? Before taking the plunge ask yourself some searching questions: Are you excited about a specific franchise concept? Are you willing to work hard and put in long hours? Do you have the necessary financial resources? Do you have prior business experience? Do your expectations and personal goals match the franchisors?

Qualities that rank high on franchisors' lists are passion about the franchise concept, desire to be your own boss, willingness to make a substantial time commitment, assertiveness, optimism, patience, and integrity. Prior business experience is also a definite plus, and some franchisors prefer or require experience in their field.

So what can you do to prepare when considering the purchase of a franchise? When evaluating franchise opportunities, professional guidance can prevent expensive mistakes, so interview advisers to find those that are right for you. Selecting an attorney with franchise experience will hasten the review of your franchise agreement. Getting to know your banker will speed up the loan process if you plan to finance your purchase with a bank loan, so stop by and introduce yourself. The proper real estate is a critical component for a successful retail franchise, so establish a relationship with a commercial real estate broker to begin scouting locations. Doing your homework can make the difference between success and failure, and some early preparation can help lay the groundwork for the successful launch of your franchised business.

If the franchise route to business ownership seems right for you, begin educating yourself on the franchise process by investigating various franchise opportunities. You should research a franchise company thoroughly before making any financial commitment. Once you've narrowed your choices, ask for the Uniform Franchise Offering Circular (UFOC) for that franchisor, and read it thoroughly. The Federal Trade Commission (FTC) requires franchisors to prepare this document, which provides a wealth of information about the franchisor including its history, operating style, management, past or pending litigation, the franchisee's financial obligations, and any restrictions on the sale of units. Interviewing current and past franchisees is another essential step. And most franchise systems use computers so if you are not computer literate, take a class in the basics.

Would-be franchisees should also check recent issues of small-business magazines such as *Franchise Zone, Entrepreneur, Inc., Business Start Ups,* and *Success* for industry trends, ideas on promising franchise opportunities, and advice on how to choose and run a franchise. The International Franchise Association Web site at **http://www.franchise.org** has links to *Franchise World* magazine and other useful sites. (For other franchise-related sites, see the "Working the Net" questions.)

Mergers and Acquisitions

A **merger** occurs when two or more firms combine to form one new company. In a well-established industry, mergers can produce winning results in terms of improved efficiency and cost savings. They can also help struggling firms compete against stronger competitors. For example, in 2008, the Indy Racing League and the Champ Car Series merged to form one open-wheel racing league. (Open-wheel race cars have their wheels outside the body of the car.) During the 12 years that the two leagues coexisted, many Indy-car drivers defected to NASCAR, as did television ratings for open-wheel races, including the perennial Indianapolis 500. Executives of the new league hope to consolidate their fan base and reenergize the sport.[12]

In an **acquisition**, a corporation or investor group finds a target company and negotiates with its board of directors to purchase it. In 2008, Staples bid $3.6 billion for Corporate Express, a Dutch rival; Microsoft bid $41.6 billion for Yahoo!; and Electronic Arts, maker of Madden NFL video games, bid $2 billion for Take-Two Interactive, makers of the Grand Theft Auto series of video games. None of the bids were solicited, and Staples, Microsoft, and Electronic Arts were in the role of acquirer, while Corporate Express, Yahoo!, and Take-Two Interactive were their respective target companies.[13]

Worldwide merger activity in 2007 totaled $4.5 trillion for both completed and announced deals, an increase of 24 percent compared to 2006. The number of announced deals totaled an amazing 42,364.[14] Exhibit 4.12 on the next page lists the top 10 U.S. merger deals in 2007. We will discuss the increase in international mergers later in this chapter.

Types of Mergers

The three main types of mergers are horizontal, vertical, and conglomerate. In a **horizontal merger**, companies at the same stage in the production or sales process in the same industry combine to reduce costs, expand product offerings, or reduce competition. Many of the largest mergers are horizontal mergers to achieve economies of scale. The three takeover bids described above were horizontal in nature.

In a **vertical merger**, a company buys a firm in its same industry, often involved in an earlier or later stage of the production or sales process. Buying a supplier of raw materials, a distribution company, or a customer, gives the acquiring firm more control. Some good examples of this include

6 Why are mergers and acquisitions important to a company's overall growth?

merger
The combination of two or more firms to form one new company.

acquisition
The purchase of a target company by another corporation or by an investor group, typically negotiated with the target company board of directors.

horizontal merger
A merger of companies at the same stage in the production or sales process in the same industry; done to reduce costs, expand product offerings, or reduce competition.

vertical merger
A merger of companies at different stages in the same industry; done to gain control over supplies of resources or to gain access to different markets.

Toyota's purchase of a hybrid-battery manufacturer, Bridgestone Tire's purchase of a rubber plantation in Indonesia, and Armor Holdings's purchase of a North Carolina Textile manufacturer that supplies the super-strong fibers the company uses to make armored cars.[15]

conglomerate merger
A merger of companies in unrelated businesses; done to reduce risk.

A **conglomerate merger** brings together companies in unrelated businesses to reduce risk. Combining companies whose products have different seasonal patterns or respond differently to business cycles can result in more stable sales. The Philip Morris Company, now called Altria, started out in the tobacco industry but diversified as early as the 1960s with the acquisition of Miller Brewing Company. It diversified into the food industry with its subsequent purchase of General Foods, Kraft Foods, and Nabisco, among others. Current product categories include confectionery, cookies, snack foods, powdered soft drinks, convenience foods, cheese, and coffee.

leveraged buyout (LBO)
A corporate takeover financed by large amounts of borrowed money; can be initiated by outside investors or the corporation's management.

A specialized, financially motivated type of merger, the **leveraged buyout (LBO)**, became popular in the 1980s but is less common today. LBOs are corporate takeovers financed by large amounts of borrowed money—as much as 90 percent of the purchase price. LBOs can be initiated by outside investors or the corporation's management. For example, Freescale Semiconductor began as a division of Motorola that was spun off into a distinct public company. After a few years, the Blackstone group, a private equity firm, used a leveraged buyout to take Freescale private. Freescale now has the freedom to innovate and explore new markets without the pressure of having to meet artificial Wall Street revenue and growth targets.[16]

Often a belief that a company is worth more than the value of all its stock is what drives an LBO. They buy the stock and take the company private, expecting to increase cash flow by improving operating efficiency or selling off units for cash to pay off debt. Although some LBOs do improve efficiency, many do not live up to investor expectations or generate enough cash to pay their debt.

CONCEPT in action

© AP Images/Mark Lennihan

Media mogul Rupert Murdoch, formerly an Internet naysayer, now believes the Web is the future of media. The News Corp. CEO and wizard behind Fox News recently acquired the social networking site MySpace and has committed billions for additional Net-targeted purchases. Murdoch claims to be shopping for "sticky" sites—ones with popular features such as community networking, music file sharing, instant messaging, and photo publishing. What factors are driving the new wave of Internet-based acquisitions?

Merger Motives

Although headlines tend to focus on mega-mergers, "merger mania" affects small companies too, and motives for mergers and acquisitions tend to be similar regardless of the company's size. The goal is often strategic: to improve overall performance of the merged firms through cost savings, elimination of overlapping operations, improved purchasing power, increased market share, or reduced competition. Less than two years after Macy's acquired May company stores across the United States, the retail behemoth began consolidating operations and closing poorly performing stores. The strategy has yielded noteworthy results, including a two-for-one stock split and a leaner organization.[17]

Company growth, broadening product lines, acquiring technology or management skills, and the ability to quickly acquire new markets, are other motives for acquiring a company. News Corp.'s $6 billion purchase of the *Wall Street Journal* enabled the company to move into serious reporting in both world and business news. The purchase also fit well with News Corp.'s strategy of generating revenue from online content.[18]

Purchasing a company can also offer a faster, less risky, less costly option than developing products or markets in-house, or expanding internationally. EBay's purchase of Skype Technologies, an Internet phone provider based in Luxembourg, for $2.6 billion in cash and stock, is a move to boost trading on its online auction site.[19]

Another motive for acquisitions is financial restructuring—cutting costs, selling off units, laying off employees, and refinancing the company to increase its value to stockholders. Financially motivated mergers are based not on the potential to achieve economies of scale, but rather on the acquirer's belief that the target has hidden value to be unlocked through restructuring. Most financially motivated mergers involve larger companies. Financier Eddie Lampert nursed ailing retailer Kmart out of bankruptcy before orchestrating its recent acquisition of retailing giant Sears for $11 billion.[20]

Emerging Truths

Along with the technology boom of the late 1990s, merger activity also soared. Total annual transactions averaged $1.6 trillion a year. Companies were using their stock, which had been pushed to unrealistically high levels, to buy each other. When the technology bubble burst in 2000, the level of merger activity dropped as well. It fell even further after the United States was attacked on September 11, 2001. Then massive corporate wrongdoing began to surface. Stocks plummeted in reaction to these events, and merger transactions, which generally track stock market movements, fell as a result.

Soon, however, merger activity was once again on the rise. Propelled by a strong economy, low interest rates, good credit, rising stock prices, and stockpiles of cash, U.S. merger activity reached $4.5 trillion in 2007, up 24 percent from the year before. Despite a softening economy in late 2007 and early 2008, merger activity was sustained on one hand by bargain hunters surveying declining stock prices, and on the other by a desire to conclude deals before George W. Bush left office.[21]

Size is definitely an advantage when competing in the global marketplace, but bigger does not always mean better in the merger business. Study results show that heady mega-mergers can, in fact, be a bust for investors who own those shares. So companies are wise to consider their options before stuffing their dollars in the biggest merger slot machine they can find. In their eagerness to snare a deal, many buyers pay a premium that wipes out the merger's entire potential economic gain. Often managers envision grand synergies that prove illusory or unworkable, or buy a company that isn't what it seems—not fully understanding what they are getting.

Integrating acquisitions is both an art and a science. Acquirers often underestimate the costs and logistical nightmare of consolidating the operations of merged companies with very different cultures. As a result, they may fail to keep key employees aboard, keep sales forces selling, and customers happy.

Companies will always continue to seek out acquisition candidates, but the fundamental business case for merging will have to be strong. So what should companies look for to identify mergers with a better-than-even chance of turning out well?

- A purchase price that is low enough—a 10 percent premium over market as opposed to 50 percent—so the buyer doesn't need heroic synergies to make the deal work.
- A target that is significantly smaller than the buyer—and in a business the buyer understands. The more "transformational" the deal, such as entering a new business arena, the bigger the risk.
- A buyer who pays in cash and not overinflated stock.
- Evidence that the deal makes both business and financial sense and isn't purely the brainchild of an empire-building CEO. Mergers are tough—culturally, commercially, and logistically. The most important quality a company can bring to a merger may be humility.

Trends in Business Ownership

As we learned in Chapter 1, an awareness of trends in the business environment is critical to business success. Many social, demographic, and economic factors affect how businesses organize. When reviewing options for starting or organizing a business or choosing a career path, consider the following trends.

© Alessandro Abbonizio/AFP/Getty Images

Mergers and acquisitions are on the rise again in various industries. Financial woes in the mortgage-banking sector spurred Bank of America to acquire Countrywide at a bargain-basement price. Soaring fuel costs are pressuring airline carriers to merge into larger entities. A heat-up in online advertising has sparked merger mania among Internet giants—as with Google's staggering $1.65 billion purchase of video-sharing phenomenon YouTube. What are the motives behind mergers and acquisitions?

Differentiate between a merger and an acquisition.

What are the most common motives for corporate mergers and acquisitions?

Describe the different types of corporate mergers.

7 What current trends will affect the business organizations of the future?

Eccentric film actor Dennis Hopper has recently been cast in one of the most unusual roles of his career: spokesperson for Ameritrade Financial. The famed anti-hero of such iconic films as *Apocalypse Now* and *Easy Rider* may be an unlikely pitchman for responsible planning for one's golden years, but Hopper speaks for his generation when he looks into the television camera and says, "Dreams are what make you say, 'When I'm 64 I'm going to start a new business.'" In what ways are the Baby Boomers redefining traditional retirement?

"Baby Boomers" Drive Franchise Trends

We all hear and read a great deal about the "graying of America," which refers to the "baby boomer" generation heading toward retirement age. As we learned in Chapter 1, this unprecedented demographic phenomenon—in 2006 the first of 78 million members of the baby boom generation turned 60—is driving the ongoing battle to stay young, slim, and healthy. Boomers have transformed every life stage they've touched so far, and their demographic weight means that business opportunities are created wherever they go.

With their interest in staying fit, boomers are contributing to the growth of fitness and weight-loss franchises. In just the past year, this category in *Entrepreneur*'s Franchise 500 has grown from 8 to 17 franchisors. And according to the International Health, Racquet & Sportsclub Association, 39.4 million Americans belong to a health club—up from 24.1 million 10 years ago—so there are plenty of consumers feeding this growing trend. Among the over-55 age group, about one-quarter belong to health clubs.[22]

Another area of boomer-driven franchise growth is elder care. Founded in 1994, Home Instead Senior Care is recognized as one of the world's fastest-growing franchise companies in the elder care market, with a network of over 600 independently owned and operated franchises in six countries. And as the world's population continues to age, the need for these unique services will continue to increase.

Home Instead Senior Care provides a meaningful solution for the elderly who prefer to remain at home. Compared with the annual cost for a nursing home placement ($60,000), home care at around $45,000 a year is somewhat more affordable. Elder quality of life is enhanced by Home Instead Senior Care's part-time, full-time, and around-the-clock services, designed for people who are capable of managing their physical needs but require some assistance and supervision. Home Instead Senior Care provides meal preparation, companionship, light housekeeping, medication reminders, incidental transportation, and errands. These services make it possible for the elderly to remain in the familiar comfort of their own homes for a longer period of time.[23]

But the best deal yet may be adult day services, one of the top 10 fastest-growing franchises and "still one of the best-kept secrets around" according to *Entrepreneur* magazine. Based on the concept of day-care services for children, Sarah Adult Day Services, Inc. offers a franchising opportunity that meets the two criteria for a successful and socially responsible business: a booming demographic market with great potential for growth, and excellent elder care. Programs like SarahCare centers are highly affordable for its clients, ranging from $10,000 to $15,000 a year. The SarahCare franchise allows entrepreneurs to become part of an expanding industry while restoring a sense of dignity and vibrancy to the lives of older adults.[24]

Mergers and Foreign Investment Boom, Too

After shunning big deals for more than three years, corporate America has launched a new merger wave. From January 2005 through the end of 2007, worldwide merger activity was tremendous. For each quarter of 2007, more than 10,000 deals were announced, and even when levels tapered off a bit in early 2008, deal activity was at historic record levels. In 2007, the three largest leveraged buyouts in history occurred.[25] Non–U.S. companies accounted for about two-thirds of the transactions. European companies' cross-border transactions led the way, with deals totaling $1.8 trillion.[26] Much of this boom in mergers and acquisitions was driven by private equity groups, like KKR, Blackstone, and Cerberus, and foreign investment, but corporate buyers are in a strong cash position and may be able to propel the boom forward. With low interest rates and stock values lower than in recent years, companies may be able to afford deals that may have seemed out of reach previously.[27]

This current boom in mergers feels different from earlier mergermania, however. New players are entering the arena, and the number of U.S. and foreign companies making cross-border acquisitions has increased. Whether these new mergers will be good for the global economy remains to be seen. Transactions that lead to cost savings, streamlined operations, and more funding for research and capital investment in new facilities will have positive effects on profitability. Many deals, however, may fail to live up to the acquirers' expectations.

Foreign investment in U.S. companies has also increased dramatically. Between 1985 and 2004, annual foreign direct investment climbed from $185 billion to almost $1.5 trillion.[28] The jump is the result of a worldwide boom in mergers and acquisitions and the need to finance America's growing trade deficit, as well as the continued attraction of the U.S. economy to investors worldwide.

And what about American investment in foreign economies? It is skyrocketing as U.S. businesses seek out opportunities in developing countries. The U.S. Department of Commerce reports that outflows from the United States into foreign countries now exceeds $2 trillion a year.[29] In addition to the attraction of cheap labor and resources, American companies of all sizes are beginning to tap the intellectual capital of developing economies such as China and India, outsourcing such functions as payroll, information technology (IT), Web/e-mail hosting, customer relationship management (CRM), and human resources (HR) to keep costs under control and enhance profitability.

CONCEPT check

What are some of the demographic trends currently impacting American business?

As a prospective business owner what could you do to capitalize on these trends?

What other economic trends are influencing today's business organizations?

Summary of Learning Goals

The advantages of sole proprietorships include ease and low cost of formation, the owner's rights to all profits, the owner's control of the business, relative freedom from government regulation, absence of special taxes, and ease of dissolution. Disadvantages include owner's unlimited liability for debts and personal responsibility for all losses, difficulty in raising capital, limited managerial expertise, difficulty in finding qualified employees, large personal time commitment, and unstable business life.

The advantages of partnerships include ease of formation, availability of capital, diversity of managerial skills and expertise, flexibility to respond to changing business conditions, no special taxes, and relative freedom from government control. Disadvantages include unlimited liability for general partners, potential for conflict between partners, sharing of profits, and difficulty exiting or dissolving the partnership. Partnerships can be formed as either general or limited partnerships. In a general partnership the operations of the business are controlled by one or more general partners with unlimited liability. The partners co-own the assets and share the profits. Each partner is individually liable for all debts and contracts of the partnership. In a limited partnership the limited partners are financial partners whose liability is limited to their investment; they do not participate in the firm's operations.

A corporation is a legal entity chartered by a state. Its organizational structure includes stockholders who own the corporation, a board of directors elected by the stockholders to govern the firm, and officers who carry out the goals and policies set by the board. Stockholders can sell or transfer their shares at any time, and are entitled to receive profits in the form of dividends. Advantages of corporations include limited liability, ease of transferring ownership, unlimited life, tax deductions, and the ability to attract financing. Disadvantages include double taxation of profits, the cost and complexity of formation, and government restrictions.

Businesses can also organize as limited liability companies, cooperatives, joint ventures, and franchises. A limited liability company (LLC) provides limited liability for its owners, but is taxed like a partnership. These two features make it an attractive form of business organization for many small firms. Cooperatives are collectively owned by individuals or businesses with similar interests that combine to achieve more economic power. Cooperatives distribute all profits to their members. Two types of cooperatives are buyer and seller cooperatives. A joint venture is an alliance of two or more companies formed to undertake a special project. Joint ventures can be set up in various ways, through partnerships or special-purpose corporations. By sharing management expertise, technology, products, and financial and operational resources, companies can reduce the risk of new enterprises.

Franchising is one of the fastest-growing forms of business ownership. It involves an agreement between a franchisor, the supplier of goods or services, and a franchisee, an individual or company that buys the right to sell the franchisor's products in a specific area. With a franchise the business owner does not have to start from scratch, but buys a business concept with a proven product or service and operating methods. The franchisor provides use of a recognized brand-name product and operating concept, as well as management training and financial assistance. Franchises can be costly to start, and operating freedom is restricted because the franchisee must conform to the

1 What are the advantages and disadvantages of the sole proprietorship form of business organization?

2 What are the advantages of operating as a partnership, and what downside risks should partners consider?

3 How does the corporate structure provide advantages and disadvantages to a company, and what are the major types of corporations?

4 What other options for business organization does a company have in addition to sole proprietorships, partnerships, and corporations?

5 What makes franchising an appropriate form of organization for some types of business, and why does it continue to grow in importance?

franchisor's standard procedures. The growth in franchising is attributed to its ability to expand business operations quickly into new geographic areas with limited capital investment.

6 Why are mergers and acquisitions important to a company's overall growth?

In a merger, two companies combine to form one company. In an acquisition, one company or investor group buys another. Companies merge for strategic reasons to improve overall performance of the merged firm through cost savings, eliminating overlapping operations, improving purchasing power, increasing market share, or reducing competition. Desired company growth, broadened product lines, and the rapid acquisition of new markets, technology, or management skills are other motives. Another motive for merging is financial restructuring—cutting costs, selling off units, laying off employees, and refinancing the company to increase its value to stockholders.

There are three types of mergers. In a horizontal merger, companies at the same stage in the production or sales process in the same industry combine for more economic power, to diversify, or to win greater market share. A vertical merger involves the acquisition of a firm that serves an earlier or later stage of the production or sales process, such as a supplier or sales outlet. In a conglomerate merger, unrelated businesses come together to reduce risk through diversification.

7 What current trends will affect the business organizations of the future?

Americans are getting older but continue to open new businesses, from sole proprietorships to partnerships, corporations to franchise operations. The service sector is booming in efforts to meet the demand for fitness, health, and elder care.

Other key trends include an escalation of worldwide foreign investment through the number of mergers taking place. All forms of business organization can benefit from outsourcing, tapping into the intellectual capital of developing countries.

key terms

Key Terms

acquisition 115
board of directors 106
buyer cooperative 108
conglomerate merger 116
cooperative 108
corporation 104
C corporation 108
franchise agreement 111
franchisee 110
franchising 110
franchisor 110
general partners 103
general partnership 103

horizontal merger 115
joint venture 110
leveraged buyout (LBO) 116
limited liability company (LLC) 108
limited partners 103
limited partnership 103
merger 115
partnership 102
S corporation 108
seller cooperative 108
sole proprietorship 100
stockholders (or shareholders) 106
vertical merger 115

PREPARING

Preparing for Tomorrow's Workplace: SCANS

1. Suppose you are considering two job offers for a computer programming position at: a two-year-old consulting firm with 10 employees owned by a sole proprietor, or a publicly traded software developer with sales of $500 million. In addition to comparing the specific job responsibilities, consider the following:
   • Which company offers better training? Do you prefer the on-the-job training you'll get at the small company, or do you want formal training programs as well?
   • Which position offers the chance to work on a variety of assignments?
   • What are the opportunities for advancement? Employee benefits?
   • What happens if the owner of the young company gets sick or decides to sell the company?
   • Which company offers a better working environment for you?
   Answering these and similar questions will help you decide which job meets your particular needs. (**Resources, Information**)
2. Before starting your own company you should know the legal requirements in your area. Call the appropriate city or county departments, such as licensing, health, and zoning, to find

out what licenses and permits you need, and any other requirements you must meet. Do the requirements vary depending on the type of company? Are there restrictions on starting a home-based business? Contact your secretary of state or other agency that handles corporations to get information on how to incorporate. (**Information**)

3. Bridget Jones wants to open her own business selling her handmade chocolates over the Internet. Although she has some money saved and could start the business on her own, she is concerned about her lack of bookkeeping and management experience. A friend mentions he knows an experienced businessman seeking involvement with a start-up company. As Bridget's business consultant, prepare recommendations for Bridget regarding an appropriate form of business organization, outlining the issues she should consider and the risks involved, supported by reasons for your suggestions. (**Interpersonal, Information**)

4. You and a partner co-own Swim-Clean, a successful pool supply and cleaning service. Because sales have tapered off, you want to expand your operations to another town 10 miles away. Given the high costs of expanding, you decide to sell Swim-Clean franchises. The idea takes off and soon you have 25 units throughout the region. Your success results in an invitation to speak at a local Rotary Club luncheon. Prepare a brief presentation describing how you evaluated the benefits and risks of becoming a franchisor, the problems you encountered, and how you established good working relationships with your franchisees. (**Information**)

5. Do you have what it takes to be a successful franchisee? Start by making a list of your interests and skills, and do a self-assessment using some of the suggestions in this chapter. Next you need to narrow the field of thousands of different franchise systems. At Franchise Handbook Online (**http://www.franchise1.com**), you'll find articles with checklists to help you thoroughly research a franchise and its industry, as well as a directory of franchise opportunities. Armed with this information, develop a questionnaire to evaluate a prospective franchise. (**Resources, Interpersonal, Information**)

6. Find news of a recent merger using an online search or a business periodical like *Business Week*, *Fortune*, or the *Wall Street Journal*. Research the merger using a variety of sources including the company's Web site and news articles. Discover the motives behind the merger, the problems facing the new entity, and the company's progress toward achieving its objectives. (**Information**)

7. **Team Activity** After pulling one too many all-nighters, you realize your college needs an on-campus coffee/food delivery service, and decide this might be a good business opportunity for you and some friends. Split the class into small groups. Start by outlining the management, technical, and financial resources that are needed to start this company. Then evaluate what resources your group brings to the table, and what you will need from partners. Using Exhibit 4.2 as a guide, develop a list of questions for potential partners. After each group presents its findings to the class, it should pair up with another group that seems to offer additional resources. Interview the other group's members using your questions to decide if the teams could work together and if you would proceed with this venture. (**Resources, Interpersonal**)

Ethics Activity

After seeing a Quiznos franchise recruitment infomercial to recruit franchisees, you are tempted to apply to open your own Quiznos sub shop. However, your research on the company turns up some disturbing information. Many current franchisees are unhappy with the company's management and practices, among them excessive food costs, lack of promised support, and selling new franchise locations that are too close to existing stores. A group of New Jersey franchisees has sued Quiznos for selling them franchises but not providing locations 18 months after taking their franchise fees. Some franchise owners question Quiznos's purchasing tactics, choosing food and beverage suppliers based on the referral fees it receives instead of the lowest-cost provider. Other franchisees have suffered major financial losses.

Quiznos, which owns or operates more than 4,000 sub shops, disputes the various claims. President Steve Shaffer points out that in a franchise operation, there will always be unhappy franchisees and those who can't make a success of their units. Besides, Quiznos's franchise offering materials clearly state that the company may open stores in any location it selects.

Using a Web search tool, locate articles about this topic and then write responses to the following questions. Be sure to support your arguments and cite your sources.

ETHICAL DILEMMA: What are Quiznos's obligations to its franchisees? Is it ethical for the company to open new franchises very close to existing units and to choose vendors based on fees to the parent company rather than the cost to franchisees?

Sources: Kristi Arellano, "Quiznos' Success Not Without Problems," *Denver Post*, June 19, 2005, p. K1; Dina Berta, "Quiznos Denies Franchisees' Charges of Cost Gouging, Encroachment Problems," *Nation's Restaurant News*, June 20, 2005, p. 1+; "Quiznos Denies Fraud Suit Charges by 17 Franchisees," *Nation's Restaurant News*, May 16, 2005, p. 102; Quiznos' Web site, **http://www.quiznos.com** (May 23, 2006).

Working the Net

1. Consult Entrepreneur.com's Business Structure page at **http://www.entrepreneur.com/ startupbasics/businessstructure/archive166108.html**. There, you can read articles about S corporations and LLCs. If you were starting a company, which would you choose, and why?

2. Research how to form a corporation and LLC in your state using search engines to find relevant sites. Here are two to get you started: **http://www.incorporate.com** and **http://www. usa-corporate.com**. Find out what steps are necessary to set up a corporation in your state. How do the fees compare with other states? If you were incorporating a business, what state would you choose and why?

3. The Federal Trade Commission is the government agency that monitors and regulates franchises. Visit the FTC site (**http://www.ftc.gov**) and explore the links to its resources on franchising, including details on the legal responsibilities of franchisors and franchisees. What kinds of problems should a prospective franchisee look out for when considering a franchise? What kinds of scams are typical in the franchise industry?

4. Go to **http://www.entrepreneur.com/franchises/buyingafranchise/franchisebasics/ article70494.html**. In the article, "Are You Suited to Be a Franchisee?" at *Entrepreneur's* FranchiseZone, take the first section (questions 1–33) of the quiz. What did you discover about yourself? Were you surprised at the results?

5. Select three franchises that interest you. Research them at sites such as the Franchise Handbook Online (**http://www.franchise1.com**), *Entrepreneur* magazine's Franchise 500 (**http://www.entrepreneur.com**), and Be the Boss (**http://www.franchiseexpo.com**). Prepare a chart comparing your selections, including history, number and location of units, financial requirements (initial franchise fee, other start-up costs, royalty and advertising fees), and any other information that would help you evaluate the franchises.

6. *Inc.* magazine (**http://www.inc.com**) has many franchising articles in its section on Buying and Selling a Business. They offer insights into how franchisors and franchisees can better manage their businesses. Using the site's resources, discuss ways the owner of a franchise can motivate employees. What specific revenue items and expenses should you monitor daily in a franchise restaurant business to insure that you are profitable?

Creative Thinking Case

Organic Farmers Protect Their Turf

With more and more small family farms being threatened with extinction, a group of seven farmers decided in 1988 to create a solution, one that has grown into the largest organic farming cooperative in America, and one of the largest organic brands in the nation. Under the leadership of George Siemon, the farmers founded Organic Valley, a farming cooperative wholly owned and operated by organic farmers who shared a belief that a sustainable approach to agriculture could help rural farm communities survive.

Over the years, those original founding farmers have been joined by 682 others in states ranging from California to Maine—producing milk, eggs, meat, soy, juice, and produce—and the cooperative continues to grow, family farm by family farm. As a result, Organic Valley has become the most successful organic farmer-owned cooperative in the world.

What attracts these farmers to the cooperative style of doing business? First, the support and resources of a large and successful farming cooperative comes in handy in an industry where large corporations have swallowed more than 600,000 family farms since 1960. Second, it provides its farmer-owners with independence for their families and their way of life because the farmers know they can rely on a stable income.

The farmers participate in all aspects of the production process, such as selecting the plants, testing the quality and flavor of their products, and approving packaging and transportation. They also decide how to allocate profits and, most important, establish pricing. A quarterly newsletter makes sure members are kept informed and up-to-date on legislative and other changes affecting the organic food industry. Organic farmers are required by law to manage their property in an environmentally conscious manner. Crops and animals are isolated from pesticides and herbicides, and land and livestock health is enhanced by means of natural inputs. They shun antibiotics, growth hormones, and steroids in favor of other more holistic methods of managing crops and animals.

So why pay more for organic food products? You are contributing to something that is once again a viable part of the American landscape and culture—small family farms and sustainable rural farming communities in America. When you buy from the Organic Valley Farming Cooperative, more of your dollar goes directly to the farming families who are bringing pure high-quality products to market, farmers who might not otherwise be able to continue farming with their commitment to humane animal treatment, responsible stewardship of the environment, and the safeguarding of our critically important natural resources—soil, air, and water.[30]

Critical Thinking Questions
- Why is the cooperative form of business organization appropriate for Organic Valley?
- Describe how the Organic Valley Farming Cooperative has impacted America's small farmers. What effect has it had on the American cultural landscape?
- Is it worth paying more for organic products so that small family farmers can continue to focus on environmentally conscious and socially responsible farming? Why is this important?

Exploring Business Careers

Jessica MacLean
Sole Proprietor

In most any elementary school classroom, at least one child's answer to the question, "What do you want to do with your life?" will be, "A lawyer." One of the most popular careers, lawyers are powerful figures in society, shaping our laws and ensuring that we adhere to them. Their prominence and power have led to the stereotype of rich, career-driven lawyers, often leaving no room in our minds for those who truly want to bring justice to the world. However, Jessica MacLean, a lawyer focusing primarily on women's rights, is quick to say that, as with many stereotypes, that is only one side of the story. "I know because I lived that—I was on my way to being a successful corporate lawyer. But I realized what I was doing and how different that was from why I'd started practicing. So I walked away from it all to start my own practice."

Nervous about the prospect of private practice, she has chosen to operate as a sole proprietorship for now. Sole proprietorships are easy to set up for people who want to work on their own, prefer direct control of the business, and desire the flexibility to sell the business or close the doors at any time. "For me, it's the best choice because I am not responsible for or to anyone else. I can easily dissolve the business if I find it is not proceeding how I'd planned. More positively, too, if it does succeed, I know that success is due to my hard work."

Indeed MacLean's law career was not always in corporate law. She turned her sights toward law after a Gender and Communications professor at DePaul University suggested her argumentative style might be an asset in that profession. "She said I needed to tone it down for class—that the other students seemed afraid to speak up—but then asked if I'd ever considered being a lawyer." MacLean, who had always been interested in issues of justice and legality surrounding women, took her professor's advice and made the leap into law.

While in law school, she clerked for the City of Chicago in their Department of Personnel's Sexual Harassment Office and volunteered for the Cook County State's Attorney's Office in the Domestic Violence Division. The cases she worked on were emotionally trying. Despite the difficulty of the cases, she was drawn to them, compelled by the people she helped and the change she was able to affect. After school, she continued in related practice, working first for the Cook County State's Attorney's Office.

After several years with the State's Attorney's Office, she needed a change. It was then that MacLean decided to work for a corporation, a form of business that you learned about in this chapter. "Why did I switch to corporate law? I think I was burnt out, to some extent. It's so hard to work on those cases, day after day. I needed to see if I would be better somewhere else."

Today, MacLean enjoys the rewards of being a sole proprietor. As the needs of her business change, the form of business ownership may change also. In the meantime, the sole proprietorship structure is ideal for fulfilling her career goals.

Entrepreneurship: Starting and Managing Your Own Business

CHAPTER 5

Learning Goals

After reading this chapter, you should be able to answer these questions:

1 Why do people become entrepreneurs, and what are the different types of entrepreneurs?

2 Which characteristics do successful entrepreneurs share?

3 How do small businesses contribute to the U.S. economy?

4 What are the first steps to take if you are starting your own business?

5 Why does managing a small business present special challenges for the owner?

6 What are the advantages and disadvantages facing owners of small businesses?

7 How does the Small Business Administration help small businesses?

8 What trends are shaping entrepreneurship and small-business ownership?

© Hemera Technologies/AbleStock.com/Jupiterimages

124

"People Will Come"

The United States is a country filled to brimming with entrepreneurs, and in many ways, the country was founded in an entrepreneurship fashion. A bunch of risk takers saw an opportunity in the innovative ideas that were floating around the colonies and, almost overnight, a new nation was born. Since then, millions of Americans have sought their own opportunities and taken their own risks to bring something new to the marketplace, providing products and services to fill the various needs of the population. And in so doing, the entrepreneurial spirit thrives within this nation even today as the Bill Gates and Warren Buffets of the world make way for the Sergey Brins and the Mark Zuckerbergs. One could even say that the entrepreneurial spirit is as American as Mom's apple pie and baseball, and nowhere is that sentiment more evident than in the movie, *Field of Dreams*.

Ray Kinsella is a farmer who has heard voices telling him that "if you build it, he will come." He interprets those voices as directing him to build a baseball field in the middle of his cornfield, an activity that he undertakes with gusto. As he plows the corn under, he is heckled by friends and neighbors alike, but with the support of his wife and daughter, he presses on until he finishes the field of dreams. His brother-in-law warns him that he will go bankrupt if he continues to chase this madness, but ghost baseball players show up and start playing the game. After enlisting the aid of recluse author Terance Mann, Ray is again cajoled by his brother-in-law, telling him that he will lose the mortgage on the house and the land unless he sells. However, before signing over the deed to his property, Ray's daughter raises her voice.

"People will come," she says. People will come to Iowa City on vacation. They will come, and they will want to pay Ray so that they can watch the game. And then Terance pipes in, saying that people will come to relive their childhoods, not exactly knowing why but more than willing to hand over 20 dollars for a ticket. And those people will "find that they have reserved seats somewhere along one of the baselines . . . where they sat when they were children, and cheered their heroes." Listening to this, Ray decides not to sell the farm, taking the ultimate risk that he will lose everything to the bank but still believing that he will ultimately succeed. And at the end of the day, he does succeed as a long line of cars approaches the farm, all of them carrying people that have come to watch the game.

Field of Dreams, along with exploring the spiritual side of baseball, also examines the mind of the individual entrepreneur who has an innovative idea and then turns that idea into some kind of marketable entity, be it a product, a service, or a company. There is usually an amount of risk associated with this activity; in Ray's case, he risks the family farm and, in fact, his family's well-being, for what seems like, to some, a pipe dream. But he presses on, and eventually, people do come to him. They come to partake in the dreams that he is selling, and from this, we are led to believe that the risk was worth it. That he starts his own business, which sustains him and his family well into the future.

The following chapter continues to explore the nature of the entrepreneur, providing an overview of entrepreneurship today including an overview of the differing types of entrepreneurs and the characteristics that guide them. The authors then take you through the process of starting and managing a small business, from finding the idea to developing the business plan and even on to finding the financing and hiring employees. The chapter closes with an exploration of current trends in entrepreneurship. And underneath all of the discussion of entrepreneurship and entrepreneurs is that guiding mantra that each entrepreneur, like Ray, must be aware of: If you build it, people will come.

Discussion Questions

- Is Ray Kinsella an entrepreneur or a small-business owner? Explain your answer.
- The chapter explores various types of entrepreneurs. Assuming that Ray is in fact an entrepreneur, which type of entrepreneur is he, and why did you choose that type?

Field of Dreams/Corbis

- To make a going concern of his Field of Dreams, what steps should Ray take from this initial idea to a self-sustaining entity?
- If Ray decides to expand his Field of Dreams, how might he go about doing so?

This chapter examines the characteristics and potential of entrepreneurship in the business world. Those who catch the entrepreneurial bug come from all age groups and backgrounds. Teenagers are starting fashion-clothing companies and high-tech firms. College graduates are shunning the "jacket and tie" corporate world to head out on their own. Downsized employees, midcareer executives, and retirees who have worked for others all their lives are forming the companies they have always wanted to own.

Companies started by entrepreneurs and small-business owners make significant contributions to the U.S. and global economies. Hotbeds of innovation, they take leadership roles in technological change and the development of new goods and services. Just how important are small businesses (for our purposes, those with fewer than 500 employees) to our economy? Exhibit 5.1 provides insight into the role of small business in today's economy.

You may be one of the millions of Americans who's considering joining the ranks of business owners. As you read this chapter, you'll learn why entrepreneurship continues to be one of the hottest areas of business activity. Then you'll find the information and tools you need to help you decide whether owning your own company is the right career path for you. Next you'll discover what characteristics you'll need to become a successful entrepreneur. Then we'll look at the importance of small businesses in the economy, guidelines for starting and managing a small business, the many reasons small businesses continue to thrive in the United States, and the role of the Small Business Administration. Finally, the chapter explores the trends that shape entrepreneurship and small-business ownership today.

Entrepreneurship Today

1 Why do people become entrepreneurs, and what are the different types of entrepreneurs?

When Tom Szaky was a junior a Princeton University, the last thing he wanted to do was drop out. That is, until he and his roommate came up with the idea of making plant food—out of worm poop. After seeing a friend feed food waste to some worms that he had put in the soil of a potted plant, Tom Szaky became fascinated with garbage. Soon, he and his roommate had created a business plan based on converting the food waste from their university dining hall into organic plant food.

The numbers in the plan were so compelling that Szaky dropped out of school to make, bottle, and sell liquid plant fertilizer made from worm poop. Only five years later, Szaky's company, TerraCycle, Inc., was named the "Coolest Little Start-Up in America" by *Inc.* magazine. Today, Terracycle employs 30 workers, generates $5 million in annual sales, and enjoys 300 to 400 percent annual growth. The liquid fertilizer, packaged in used 20-ounce beverage containers, is now a regular

---

EXHIBIT 5.1   The Economic Impact of Small Business

Today's small businesses:

- Represent 99.7 percent of all employer firms.
- Employ about half of all private-sector employees.
- Pay more than 45 percent of total U.S. private payroll.
- Have generated 60 to 80 percent of net new jobs annually over the last decade.
- Create more than half of nonfarm private gross domestic product (GDP).
- Supplied 22.8 percent of the total value of federal prime contracts in FY 2006.
- Hire 40 percent of high-tech workers (such as scientists, engineers, and computer workers).
- Are 52 percent home-based businesses and 2 percent franchises.
- Made up 97 percent of all identified exporters and produced 28.6 percent of the known export value in FY 2004.
- Small, innovative firms produce 13 times more patents per employee than large patenting firms, and their patents are twice as likely as large firm patents to be among the 1 percent most cited.

Sources: U.S. Department of Commerce, Bureau of the Census; Advocacy-funded research by Kathryn Kobe, 2007, **www.sba.gov/advo/research/rs299tot.pdf**; Federal Procurement Data System; Advocacy-funded research by CHI Research, 2003, **www.sba.gov/advo/research/rs225tot.pdf**; U.S. Dept. of Labor, Bureau of Labor Statistics, Current Population Survey; U.S. Dept. of Commerce, International Trade Administration.

product on the shelves of Home Depot, Target, and Wal-Mart. More remarkable, the company has enlisted the help of schools and nonprofits to form a Bottle Brigade, which has collected more than 2 million used bottles at over 3,600 locations around the country. Terracycle has developed three additional products made from waste and recycled bottles, and Szaky remains committed to making a difference. "It's the power of a big idea," he says. "That's why I left school."[1]

The United States is blessed with a wealth of entrepreneurs such as Szaky. According to research by the Small Business Administration, two-thirds of college students intend to be entrepreneurs at some point in their careers, aspiring to become the next Bill Gates or Jeff Bezos, founder of Amazon.com, or Tom Szaky. But before you put out any money or expend energy and time, you'd be wise to check out Exhibit 5.2 for some preliminary questions.

The desire to be one's own boss cuts across all age, gender, and ethnic lines. Results of a 2002 U.S. Census Bureau survey of business owners released on July 28, 2005, shows that minority groups and women are becoming business owners at a much higher rate than the national average. Exhibit 5.3 demonstrates these minority-owned business demographics.

Why has entrepreneurship remained such a strong part of the foundation of the U.S. business system for so many years? Because today's global economy rewards innovative, flexible companies that can respond quickly to changes in the business environment. Such companies are started by **entrepreneurs**, people with vision, drive, and creativity, who are willing to take the risk of starting and managing a business to make a profit.

entrepreneurs
People with vision, drive, and creativity, who are willing to take the risk of starting and managing a business to make a profit, or greatly change the scope and direction of an existing firm.

Entrepreneur or Small-Business Owner?

The term entrepreneur is often used in a broad sense to include most small-business owners. The two groups share some of the same characteristics, and we'll see that some of the reasons for becoming an entrepreneur or a small-business owner are very similar. But there is a difference between entrepreneurship and small-business management. Entrepreneurship involves taking a risk, either to

---

EXHIBIT 5.2   Innovator's Inventory

Here are some questions would-be entrepreneurs should ask themselves:

1. What is new and novel about your idea?
2. Are there similar products/services out there? If so, what makes yours better?
3. Who is your target market? How many people would use your product or service?
4. What about production costs? How much do you think the market will pay?
5. How defensible is the concept? Is there good intellectual property?
6. Is this innovation strategic to my business?
7. Is the innovation easy to communicate?
8. How might this product evolve over time? Would it be possible to expand it into a product line? Can it be updated/enhanced in future versions?
9. Where would someone buy this product?
10. What are the challenges involved in developing this product?

Source: Adapted from Mike Collins, "Before You Start—Innovator's Inventory," *Wall Street Journal*, May 9, 2005, p. R4. Copyright 2005 by Dow Jones & Company, Inc.. Reproduced with permission of Dow Jones & Company, Inc. in the format Textbook via Copyright Clearance Center.

EXHIBIT 5.3   Increases in Minority-Owned Businesses

A recent survey shows minority-owned businesses increasing at a rapid rate from 1997 to 2002:

- 6.5 million women-owned businesses in 2002 represents an increase of 20 percent from 1997.
- 1.6 million Hispanic-owned businesses in 2002 represents an increase of 31 percent from 1997.
- 1.2 million black-owned businesses in 2002 represents an increase of 45 percent from 1997.
- 1.1 million Asian-owned businesses in 2002 represents an increase of 24 percent from 1997.
- 201,000 Native American-owned businesses in 2002 represents an increase of 2 percent from 1997.
- 32,299 Hawaiian/Pacific Islander–owned businesses in 2002 represents an increase of 67 percent from 1997.

Source: "Minorities in Business: A Demographic Review of Minority Business Ownership," Office of Advocacy, U.S. Small Business Administration, April 10, 2007, **http://www.sba.gov/advo/research/rs298tot.pdf**.

© Toby Canham/Getty Images

If there is one person responsible for the mainstream success of everything hip-hop in the past 25 years, it's Russell Simmons, founder and CEO of Rush Communications. Since the 1980s when he founded Def Jam Recordings and launched the careers of the Beastie Boys, LL Cool J, and Run-DMC, Simmons has pioneered countless urban companies and brands from Phat Farm apparel and DefCon3 energy drink to the Russell Simmons Presents Yoga Live video series. What entrepreneurial type best describes Russell Simmons?

© AP Images/Chitose Suzuki

As a young girl, Helen Greiner loved tech gadgets. But when a spunky droid named R2-D2 helped Luke Skywalker stick it to the Empire in the movie *Star Wars*, Greiner's love became an obsession. Today, Greiner is the co-founder and chairman of iRobot Corporation, a multimillion-dollar robotics firm that creates real-life R2-D2s that do everything from vacuuming household floors to sniffing out terrorist's bombs. How might a person's interests and passions lead to a life of successful entrepreneurship?

multipreneurs
Entrepreneurs who start a series of companies.

create a new business or to greatly change the scope and direction of an existing one. Entrepreneurs typically are innovators who start companies to pursue their ideas for a new product or service. They are visionaries who spot trends.

Although entrepreneurs may be small-business owners, not all small-business owners are entrepreneurs. Small-business owners are managers, or people with technical expertise, who started a business or bought an existing business and made a conscious decision to stay small. For example, the proprietor of your local independent bookstore is a small-business owner. Jeff Bezos, founder of Amazon.com, also sells books. But Bezos is an entrepreneur: he developed a new model—a Web-based book retailer—that revolutionized the bookselling world and then moved on to change retailing in general. Entrepreneurs are less likely to accept the status quo and generally take a longer-term view than the small-business owner.

Types of Entrepreneurs

Entrepreneurs fall into three categories: classic entrepreneurs, multipreneurs, and intrapreneurs.

Classic Entrepreneurs
Classic entrepreneurs are risk takers who start their own companies based on innovative ideas. Some classic entrepreneurs are micropreneurs who start small and plan to stay small. They often start businesses just for personal satisfaction and the lifestyle. Miho Inagi is a good example of a micropreneur. On a visit to New York City with college friends, Inagi fell in love with the city's bagels. "I just didn't think anything like a bagel could taste so good," she said. Her passion for bagels led the young office assistant to quit her job and pursue her dream of one day opening her own bagel shop in Tokyo. Although her parents tried to talk her out of it, and bagels were virtually unknown in Japan, nothing deterred her. Other trips to New York followed, including an unpaid six-month apprenticeship at Ess-a-Bagel, where Inagi took orders, cleared trays, and swept floors. On weekends, owner Florence Wilpon let her make dough.

Six years after that first trip to New York, using $20,000 of her own savings and a $30,000 loan from her parents, Inagi finally opened tiny Maruichi Bagel. The timing was fortuitous as Japan was about to experience a bagel boom. After a slow start, a favorable review on a local bagel Web site brought customers flocking for what are now considered the best bagels in Tokyo. Inagi earns only about $2,300 a month after expenses, the same amount she was making as a company employee. "Before I opened this store I had no goals," she says, "but now I feel so satisfied."[2]

In contrast, growth-oriented entrepreneurs want their business to grow into a major corporation. Most high-tech companies are formed by growth-oriented entrepreneurs, but that doesn't mean that growth is reserved for tech fields. New York socialite Tory Burch recognized that by planning for growth, she could build a fashion empire. To start, she created 15 product categories and made 50 of each item she designed. When she opened her store, everything sold out on the first day. Her most astounding success has been the Reva flat, which she intentionally designed as a stylish, practical, and comfortable ballet flat priced well below similarly styled shoes by well-known designers. The first year the shoe was in the collection, Burch sold 250,000 pairs in more than a dozen different colors at $195 a pair. Her first-year sales were $2 million, and now, after only four years in business, her collection contains 1,000 styles available online or at one of her 12 boutiques; she's opening more stores; she's launching a perfume; and her annual revenue is $115 million.[3]

Multipreneurs
Then there are **multipreneurs**, entrepreneurs who start a series of companies. They thrive on the challenge of building a business and watching it grow. In fact, over half of the chief executives at Inc. 500 companies say they would start another company if they sold their current one. Elon Musk is a good example of a multipreneur. Even though Musk's name might not be well known, his first start-up was PayPal. After he sold that to eBay for $1.5 billion, he founded Zip2, a dot-com media company, which he sold for $307 million. Flush with cash, Musk now juggles three businesses simultaneously: Tesla, an electric car that's more Ferrari than Prius; SolarCity, a solar panel installer in Southern California; and SpaceX, an aerospace startup that plans to provide some

The Juice of Success

By their mid-30s, Tom Scott and Tom First were ready to retire. They had sold a majority stake in the business they had started from the back of their boat to Ocean Spray, and when Cadbury Schweppes bought the entire business for $100 million, the two men realized they would never have to work again. But it wasn't easy giving up their moniker "The Juice Guys" even if they were satisfied with the sale price of Nantucket Nectars. Rather than spend their afternoons boating, golfing, or doing some other retirement activity, the men are both involved in new entrepreneurial ventures—a line of flavored waters, a company that operates television channels in historic, affluent towns, and a beverage-distribution software company.

Scott and First are part of a group of entrepreneurs called multipreneurs, or people who are able to bring two, three, or even more ideas and products to market. Sometimes multipreneurs undertake ventures in the same basic field; for example, Steve Jobs is a multipreneur in technology. Other times, multipreneurs start companies in distinctly different industries. Elizabeth Cogswell Baskin started a company that provided wellness materials to corporate human resource departments, an ad agency, and a book-packaging company called Airplane Books.

Whether they are well known, as Steve Jobs, or relatively obscure, like Elizabeth Cogswell Baskin, multipreneurs share some common traits. According to a study by Wayne Stewart, a professor of management at Clemson University, multipreneurs have a higher propensity for risk, innovation, and achievement, lower fear of failure, and a tendency to be resilient. They are also able to draw on their experience with their previous entrepreneurial venture to help them map out their current venture. Tom Scott sums up the drive of the multipreneur this way: "I think the best entrepreneurs are like artists and painters. It's about creating. It's not about business."[4]

Critical Thinking Questions
• Other than those listed above, what qualities do you think would be necessary to become a multipreneur?
• Do you think multipreneurs in the same industries are more successful than those who try their hand in different industries? Explain.

© Rubberball/Getty Images

---

of the spacecraft shuttling astronauts back and forth to the International Space Station.[5] Read more about multipreneurs in the Catching the Entrepreneurial Spirit box above.

Intrapreneurs Some entrepreneurs don't own their own companies but apply their creativity, vision, and risk taking within a large corporation. Called **intrapreneurs**, these employees enjoy the freedom to nurture their ideas and develop new products, while their employers provide regular salaries and financial backing. Intrapreneurs have a high degree of autonomy to run their own mini-companies within the larger enterprise. They share many of the same personality traits as classic entrepreneurs but take less personal risk. According to Gifford Pinchot, who coined the term intrapreneur in his book of the same name, large companies provide seed funds that finance in-house entrepreneurial efforts. These companies include Intel, IBM, Texas Instruments (a pioneering intrapreneurial company), Eastman Kodak, and Xerox. One of IBM's most recent ventures is the creation of a 3D avatar that can be used to map a patient's medical history. The technology is like Google Earth for the body and will help doctors better organize all the relevant information about a patient in one, easily accessible place. For example, to see everything that a patient has in his or her history related to back pain, the doctor can simply click on the avatar's spine. Two different divisions of IBM collaborated on this intrapreneurial development.[6]

intrapreneurs
Entrepreneurs who apply their creativity, vision, and risk taking within a large corporation, rather than starting a company of their own.

Why Become an Entrepreneur?

As the examples in this chapter show, entrepreneurs are found in all industries and have different motives for starting companies. The most common reason cited by CEOs of the Inc. 500, *Inc.* magazine's annual list of fastest-growing private companies, is the challenge of building a business, followed by the desire to control their own destiny. Other reasons include financial independence and frustration working for someone else. Two important motives mentioned in other surveys are a feeling of personal satisfaction with your work, and creating the lifestyle that you want. Do entrepreneurs feel that going into business for themselves was worth it? The answer is a resounding yes. Most say they would do it again.

CONCEPT check

Describe several types of entrepreneurs.

What differentiates an entrepreneur from a small-business owner?

What are some major factors that motivate entrepreneurs to start businesses?

Characteristics of Successful Entrepreneurs

Do you have what it takes to become an entrepreneur? Having a great concept is not enough. An entrepreneur must be able to develop and manage the company that implements his or her idea. Being an entrepreneur requires special drive, perseverance, passion, and a spirit of adventure, in

2 Which characteristics do successful entrepreneurs share?

addition to managerial and technical ability. Entrepreneurs are the company; they tend to work longer hours, take fewer vacations, and cannot leave problems at the office at the end of the day. They also share other common characteristics as described in the next section.

The Entrepreneurial Personality

Studies of the entrepreneurial personality find that entrepreneurs share certain key traits. Most entrepreneurs are:

- *Ambitious.* They are competitive and have a high need for achievement.
- *Independent.* They are individualists and self-starters who prefer to lead rather than follow.
- *Self-confident.* They understand the challenges of starting and operating a business, and are decisive and confident in their ability to solve problems.
- *Risk taking.* Although they are not averse to risk, most successful entrepreneurs favor business opportunities that carry a moderate degree of risk where they can better control the outcome—over highly risky ventures where luck plays a large role.
- *Visionary.* Their ability to spot trends and act upon them sets entrepreneurs apart from small-business owners and managers.
- *Creative.* To compete with larger firms, entrepreneurs need to have creative product designs, bold marketing strategies, and innovative solutions to managerial problems.
- *Energetic.* Starting and operating a business takes long hours. Even so, some entrepreneurs start their companies while still employed elsewhere full-time.
- *Passionate.* Entrepreneurs love their work, as Miho Inagi demonstrated by opening a bagel shop in Tokyo despite the odds against it being a success.
- *Committed.* Because they are so committed to their companies, entrepreneurs are willing to make personal sacrifices to achieve their goals. As the Customer Satisfaction and Quality box on the next page describes, Apollonia Poilâne makes huge sacrifices to maintain her family's business after tragedy struck.

Most entrepreneurs combine many of the above characteristics. Sarah Levy, 23, loved her job as a restaurant pastry chef but not the low pay, high stress, and long hours of a commercial kitchen. So she found a new one—in her parents' home—and launched Sarah's Pastries and Candies. Part-time staffers now help her fill pastry and candy orders to the soothing sounds of music videos playing in the background. Cornell University graduate Conor McDonough started his own Web design firm, OffThePathMedia.com, after becoming disillusioned with the rigid structure of his job. "There wasn't enough room for my own expression," he says. "Freelancing keeps me on my toes," says busy graphic artist Ana Sanchez. "It forces me to do my best work because I know my next job depends on my performance."[7]

CONCEPT in action

Celebrity super-twins Mary-Kate and Ashley Olsen are more than just a couple of pretty faces. The actors-cum-media-moguls are co-owners of Dualstar Entertainment Group, operating a Mary-Kate-and-Ashley entertainment empire estimated in the billions of dollars. From hawking their teen adventures in movies and books to creating grown-up lines of perfume and fashion apparel, the twins know how to mature their brand with their ever-maturing fan base. What personality traits are common to successful young entrepreneurs like the Olsens?

Managerial Ability and Technical Knowledge

A person with all the characteristics of an entrepreneur might still lack the necessary business skills to run a successful company. Entrepreneurs need the technical knowledge to carry out their ideas and the managerial ability to organize a company, develop operating strategies, obtain financing, and supervise day-to-day activities. Jim Crane, who built Eagle Global Logistics from a start-up into a $250 million company, addressed a group at a meeting saying, "I have never run a $250 million company before so you guys are going to have to start running this business."[8] Recall from Chapter 4 how when Rick Detowski purchased Moon Valley Rustic Furniture, he had no previous experience in the furniture industry. To resuscitate the business, he relied on people who had worked there for years.

Good interpersonal and communication skills are important in dealing with employees, customers, and other business associates such as bankers, accountants, and attorneys. As we will discuss later in the chapter, entrepreneurs believe they can learn these much-needed skills. Joel Spolsky's company, Fog Creek Software, had a great product to help software developers identify and track bugs in their programs, but nobody knew about it. To get the word out, Spolsky organized his office team and began to plan a world tour. They identified 34 cities to visit, booked conference rooms in upscale hotels in each, and invited sales prospects to a software demonstration. At each session, Spolsky began the day with time for developers to network with him and each other.

© Digital Vision/Getty Images

Let Them Eat Bread

How does Harvard University student Apollonia Poilâne spend her time between classes? Running one of the best French bakeries in the world—in Paris. When people asked her father, baker Lionel Poilâne, what his daughter wanted to do when she grew up, Apollonia would announce she planned to take over the bakery. Then when her parents were killed in a 2002 helicopter crash, France lost its most celebrated baker, and Poilâne did just that. Because the name Poilâne has earned a place with a very small group of prestige bakers, the 18-year-old determined to continue the tradition of customer satisfaction and quality her grandfather established in 1932.

With organization and determination Poilâne, who is studying economics, manages the Paris-based business from her apartment in Cambridge, Massachusetts. "I usually wake up an extra two hours before my classes so I can make sure I get all the phone calls done for work. After classes I check on any business regarding the company and then do my homework," she says. "Before I go to bed, I call my production manager in Paris to check the quality of the bread." In fact, she receives a shipment of fresh Poilâne bread each week as a flavorful and welcome change from cafeteria food.

"Apollonia is definitely passionate about her job," says Juliette Sarrazin, manager of the successful Poilâne Bakery in London, the only Poilâne shop outside of Paris. "She really believes in the work of her father and the company, and she is looking at the future, which is very good."

Experiments with sourdough distinguished Poilâne products from bread produced by Paris's other bakers and it soon evolved into the crusty loaf that has remained the company's signature product. It is baked with a "P" carved into the crust, a throwback to the days when the use of communal ovens forced bakers to identify their loaves. But it was her father, Lionel Poilâne, who turned the family's scrumptious bread into a globally recognized brand, shipped daily via FedEx to upscale restaurants and wealthy clients in the United States, Japan, and elsewhere.

Poilâne has retained control of important decisions, strategy, and business goals, describing herself as the "commander of the ship," determining the company's overall direction. Each day is a juggling act, with Poilâne solving problems in Paris while other students sleep. Is it worth it? After surviving numerous changes in consumer tastes over the years, the company is now profiting from a growing interest in healthy eating. "More people understand what makes the quality of the bread, what my father spent years studying, so I am thrilled about that," she says. And this young woman understands the importance of keeping customers happy, albeit from a long way away.[9]

Critical Thinking Questions
- What type of entrepreneur is Apollonia Poilâne?
- How does she ensure that customer satisfaction and quality are being maintained after her parents' death?

Then he started his demonstration promptly and moved through it clearly but swiftly to keep attendees from getting bored. He always allowed more time for questions and answers than for the demonstration. That way, he had time to work with the attendees and ensure that all their concerns and questions were resolved. The world tour allowed Spolsky to meet and develop a personal connection with thousands of potential Fog Creek customers.[10]

CONCEPT check

Describe the personality traits and skills characteristic of successful entrepreneurs.

What does it mean when we say that an entrepreneur should work on the business, not in it?

Small Business: Driving America's Growth

Although large corporations dominated the business scene for many decades, in recent years small businesses have once again come to the forefront. Corporate greed and fraud have given large corporations a bad name. Downsizings that accompany economic downturns have caused many people to look toward smaller companies for employment, and they have plenty to choose from. Small businesses play an important role in the U.S. economy, representing about half of U.S. economic output, employing about half the private-sector workforce, and giving individuals from all walks of life a chance to succeed.

3 How do small businesses contribute to the U.S. economy?

What Is a Small Business?

How many small businesses are there in the United States? Estimates range from 5 million to over 22 million, depending on the size limits government agencies and other groups use to define a small business. So what makes a business "small"? The Small Business Administration classifies all companies with under 500 employees as a small business. In addition, a **small business** has the following characteristics. It is:

- Independently managed
- Owned by an individual or a small group of investors
- Locally based (although the market it serves may be widespread)
- Not a dominant company (thus it has little influence in its industry)

Exhibit 5.4 on the next page provides a more detailed look at small-business owners.

small business
A business with under 500 employees that is independently managed, is owned by an individual or a small group of investors, is based locally, and is not a dominant company in its industry.

EXHIBIT 5.4 Snapshot of Small-Business Owners

Recent data provides a look at small-business owners:

- 10.1 million adults are attempting to create new businesses at any one time, about 5.6 million potential new businesses.
- Two-thirds of owners reported their business as their primary source of income.
- African Americans are 50 percent more likely to engage in start-up activities than whites.
- 14 percent are veterans.
- 49 percent spend more than 40 hours per week managing or working in their business, with 19 percent devoting 60 hours or more.
- 74 percent of businesses with employees are owned by men, 26 percent by women.
- 24 percent of small-business owners have a bachelor's degree and 19 percent have a graduate degree.

Sources: "Panel Study on Entrepreneurial Dynamics," *Ewing Marion Kauffman Foundation Entrepreneurial Research Portal 2005*, **http://research.kauffman.org**.

CONCEPT check

What are the criteria the Small Business Administration uses to define a small business?

What social and economic factors have prompted the rise in small business?

Small businesses in the United States can be found in almost every industry, including services, retail, construction, wholesale, manufacturing, finance and insurance, agriculture and mining, transportation, and warehousing. Home-based businesses represent 53 percent of the small-business population. Of these, 91 percent have no paid employees. About two-thirds of all sole proprietorships, partnerships, and S corporations are home based. They, too, represent a broad range of industries, as shown in Exhibit 5.5.

Ready, Set, Start Your Own Business

4 What are the first steps to take if you are starting your own business?

You have decided that you'd like to go into business for yourself. What is the best way to go about it? Start from scratch? Buy an existing business? Or buy a franchise? About 75 percent of business start-ups involve brand-new organizations, with the remaining 25 percent representing purchased companies or franchises. Franchising was discussed in Chapter 4, so we'll cover the other two options in this section.

Getting Started

The first step in starting your own business is a self-assessment to determine whether you have the personal traits you need to succeed and, if so, what type of business would be best for you. Exhibit 5.6 provides a checklist to consider before starting your business.

Finding the Idea Entrepreneurs get ideas for their businesses from many sources. It is not surprising that about 80 percent of *Inc.* 500 executives got the idea for their company while working in the same or a related industry. Starting a firm in a field where you have experience improves your chances of success. Other sources of inspiration are personal experiences as a consumer; hobbies and personal interests; suggestions from customers, family, and friends; and college courses or other education.

An excellent way to keep up with small-business trends is by reading entrepreneurship and small-business magazines and visiting their Web sites. With articles on everything from idea

EXHIBIT 5.5 Home-Based Businesses, by Industry

Industry	Percentage of Home-Based Businesses
Services	60%
Construction	16
Retail	14
Manufacturing, finance, transportation, communications, wholesale	10

Source: "The Small Business Economy 2004," *United States Government Printing Office*, **http://www.sbaonline.sba.gov** (March 21, 2006).

generation to selling a business, they provide an invaluable resource. Check out Exhibit 5.7 for some of the entrepreneurs who made Entrepreneur.com's (**http://www.entrepreneur.com**) 2005 list of young millionaires. These dynamic individuals, who are already so successful in their 20s and 30s, came up with unique ideas and concepts and found the right niche for their businesses.

Interesting ideas are all around you. Many successful businesses get started because someone identifies a need and then finds a way to fill it. Do you have a problem that you need to solve? Or a product that doesn't work as well as you'd like? Raising questions about the way things are done, and seeing opportunity in adversity is a great way to generate ideas.

When Mort Rosenthal realized that buying a wireless plan had become nearly as complicated and time-consuming as shopping for a house, he saw a business opportunity. "Every time I've purchased a wireless phone I've experienced frustration," he says. Rosenthal, the founder of

EXHIBIT 5.7 *Entrepreneur*®'s Young Millionaires 2007 Listed by Project Sales

Name and Age	Company and Description	Sales
Brad Sugars, 36	ActionCOACH (executive business coaching)	$220 million
Tim Vanderhook, 26 Chris Vanderhook, 28 Ryan Vanderhook, 30	Specific Media (online advertising, promotional, private-label, and licensed items)	$70 million
Herman Flores, 34 Myles Kovacs, 33 Haythem Haddad, 31	*DUB* (publisher of automotive magazine *DUB*)	$50 million
Kelly Flately, 28 Brendan Synnott, 29	Bear Naked (manufacturer of all-natural granola products)	$50 million
Jacob De Hart, 25 Jake Nickell, 27	Threadless (online T-shirt design company)	$25 million
Bob Shallenberger, 37 John Cavanagh, 38	Highland Homes (green residential builder)	$22 million
Amy Smilovic, 39	Tibi (clothing design)	$21 million
John Vechey, 28 Brian Fiete, 29 Jason Kapalka, 37	PopCap Games (creator of downloadable games)	$20 million
Ryan Black, 32 Ed Nichols, 32 Jeremy Black, 34	Sambazon (manufacturer of Brazilian acai berry products)	$15 million
Nathan Jones, 37	Xlear, Inc. (manufacturer of xylitol products)	$13 million
Devon Rifkin, 33	The Great American Hanger Company (clothes hangers)	$10 million
Jim Wetzel, 38 Lance Lawson, 36	Jake (luxury fashion retailer for men and women)	$7 million
Megan Duckett, 35	Sew What? (custom theatrical draperies and flame-retardant fabric)	$4.6 million

Travelers will soon make voyages to outer space, thanks to a futuristic idea from Virgin Galactic owner Sir Richard Branson and aerospace guru Burt Rutan. The duo's commercial suborbital spacecraft, dubbed "SpaceShipTwo," will transport ordinary air-travel passengers 60,000 feet above Earth to catch an astronaut's view of the blue planet—for a mere $200,000 per ticket. How do entrepreneurs generate ideas for their businesses?

Corporate Software, at one time the world's largest PC software distributor, had a simple idea: offer customers a one-stop retail outlet for all their wireless needs. His new company, called "imo" (short for independent mobile), sells all U.S. carriers' plans and phones in one store. The company began rolling out its stores in 2005, with the goal of taking the business nationwide.[11]

Choosing a Form of Business Organization
A key decision for a person starting a new business is whether it will be a sole proprietorship, partnership, corporation, or limited liability company. As discussed in Chapter 4, each type of business organization has advantages and disadvantages. The choice depends on the type of business, number of employees, capital requirements, tax considerations, and level of risk involved.

Developing the Business Plan
Once you have the basic concept for a product or service, you must develop a plan to create the business. This planning process, culminating in a sound **business plan**, is one of the most important steps in starting a business. It can help to attract appropriate loan financing, minimize the risks involved, and be a critical determinant in whether a firm succeeds or fails. Many people do not venture out on their own because they are overwhelmed with doubts and concerns. A comprehensive business plan lets you run various "what if" analyses and "operate" your business as a dry-run, without any financial outlay or risk. You can also develop strategies to overcome problems well before the business actually opens.

business plan
A formal written statement that describes in detail the idea for a new business and how it will be carried out; includes a general description of the company, the qualifications of the owner(s), a description of the product or service, an analysis of the market, and a financial plan.

Taking the time to develop a good business plan pays off. A venture that seems sound at the idea stage may not look so good on paper. A well-prepared, comprehensive, written business plan forces entrepreneurs to take an objective and critical look at their business venture and analyze their concept carefully; make decisions about marketing, production, staffing, and financing; and set goals that will help them manage and monitor the business's growth and performance.

The business plan also serves as the initial operating plan for the business, and writing a good business plan can take several months. But many businesspeople neglect this critical planning tool in their eagerness to begin doing business, getting caught up in the day-to-day operations instead.

The key features of a business plan are a general description of the company, the qualifications of the owner(s), a description of the product or service, an analysis of the market (demand, customers, competition), and a financial plan. The sections of a business plan should work together to demonstrate why the business will be successful, while focusing on the uniqueness of the business and why it will attract customers. Exhibit 5.8 provides an outline of what to include in each section of a business plan.

The most common use of a business plan is to persuade lenders and investors to finance the venture. The detailed information in the plan helps them assess whether to invest. Even though a business plan may take months to write, it must capture potential investors' interest within minutes. For that reason, the basic business plan should be written with a particular reader in mind. Then you can fine-tune and tailor it to fit the investment goals of the investor(s) you plan to approach.

Launched in 2004 as a communication tool for Harvard students, Facebook has become one of the most highly trafficked social-networking sites on the Web. The friend-finding brainchild of founder Mark Zuckerberg became an overnight success after attracting the interest and investment dollars of famed angel investor Peter Thiel. Today, Facebook is surging to the top of the Net, and the 20-something Zuckerberg is the world's youngest billionaire. Which sections of Facebook's business plan would you expect to be of greatest interest to investors?

But don't think you can set aside your business plan once you obtain financing and begin operating your company. Entrepreneurs who think their business plan is only for raising money make a big mistake. Business plans should be dynamic documents, reviewed and updated on a regular basis—monthly, quarterly, or annually, depending on how the business progresses and the particular industry changes.

Owners should adjust their sales and profit projections up or down as they analyze their markets and operating results. Reviewing your plan on a constant basis will help you identify strengths and weaknesses in your marketing and management strategies, and help you evaluate possible opportunities for expansion in light of both your original mission and current market trends.

EXHIBIT 5.8 Outline for a Business Plan

Title page: Provides names, addresses, and phone numbers of the venture and its owners and management personnel; date prepared; copy number; and contact person.

Table of contents: Provides page numbers of the key sections of the business plan.

Executive summary: Provides a one- to three-page overview of the total business plan. Written after the other sections are completed, it highlights their significant points and, ideally, creates enough excitement to motivate the reader to continue reading.

Vision and mission statement: Concisely describes the intended strategy and business philosophy for making the vision happen.

Company overview: Explains the type of company, such as manufacturing, retail, or service; provides background information on the company if it already exists; and describes the proposed form of organization—sole proprietorship, partnership, or corporation. This section should be organized as follows: company name and location, company objectives, nature and primary product or service of the business, current status (start-up, buyout, or expansion) and history (if applicable), and legal form of organization.

Product and/or service plan: Describes the product and/or service and points out any unique features; explains why people will buy the product or service. This section should offer the following descriptions: product and/or service; features of the product or service that provide a competitive advantage; available legal protection—patents, copyrights, and trademarks; and dangers of technical or style obsolescence.

Marketing plan: Shows who the firm's customers will be and what type of competition it will face; outlines the marketing strategy and specifies the firm's competitive edge. This section should offer the following descriptions: analysis of target market and profile of target customer; methods of identifying and attracting customers; selling approach, type of sales force, and distribution channels; types of sales promotions and advertising; and credit and pricing policies.

Management plan: Identifies the key players—active investors, management team, and directors—citing the experience and competence they possess. This section should offer the following descriptions: management team, outside investors and/or directors and their qualifications, outside resource people and their qualifications, and plans for recruiting and training employees.

Operating plan: Explains the type of manufacturing or operating system to be used, and describes the facilities, labor, raw materials, and product-processing requirements. This section should offer the following descriptions: operating or manufacturing methods, operating facilities (location, space, and equipment), quality-control methods, procedures to control inventory and operations, sources of supply, and purchasing procedures.

Financial plan: Specifies financial needs and contemplated sources of financing, and presents projections of revenues, costs, and profits. This section should offer the following descriptions: historical financial statements for the last three to five years or as available; pro forma financial statements for three to five years, including income statements, balance sheets, cash flow statements, and cash budgets (monthly for first year and quarterly for second year); breakeven analysis of profits and cash flows; and planned sources of financing.

Appendix of supporting documents: Provides materials supplementary to the plan. This section should offer the following descriptions: management team biographies, any other important data that support the information in the business plan, and the firm's ethics code.

Source: From *ACP-ECollege—Small Business Management: An Entrepreneurial Emphasis*, 13th edition, by Longenecker/Moore/Petty/Palich. © 2006. Reprinted with permission of South-Western, a division of Cengage Learning: **http://www.thomsonrights .com**, Fax 800-730-2215.

Many resources are available to help you prepare your business plan. Later in the chapter we will examine the role of one of these, the Small Business Administration (SBA), which offers sample business plans and online guidance for business plan preparation.

Financing the Business

Once the business plan is complete, the next step is to obtain financing to set up your company. The funding required depends on the type of business and the entrepreneur's own investment. Businesses started by lifestyle entrepreneurs require less financing than growth-oriented businesses, and manufacturing and high-tech companies generally require a large initial investment.

Who provides start-up funding for small companies? Like Miho Inagi and her Tokyo bagel shop, 94 percent of business owners raise start-up funds from personal accounts, family, and friends. Personal assets and money from family and friends are important for new firms, whereas funding

© Ray Tamarra/Getty Images

FUBU started when a young entrepreneur from Hollis, Queens, began making tie-top skullcaps at home with some friends. With funding from a $100,000 mortgage and a later investment from the Samsung Corporation, CEO Daymond John turned his home into a successful sportswear company. The FUBU brand tops the list for today's fashionistas who don everything from FUBU's classic Fat Albert line to swanky FUBU suits and tuxedos. How do start-ups obtain funding?

from financial institutions may become more important as companies grow. Three-quarters of Inc. 500 companies have been funded on $100,000 or less.[12]

The two forms of business financing are **debt**, borrowed funds that must be repaid with interest over a stated time period, and **equity**, funds raised through the sale of stock (i.e., ownership) in the business. Those who provide equity funds get a share of the business's profits. Because lenders usually limit debt financing to no more than a quarter to a third of the firm's total needs, equity financing often amounts to about 65 to 75 percent of total start-up financing.

Two sources of equity financing for young companies are angel investors and venture-capital firms. **Angel investors** are individual investors or groups of experienced investors who provide financing for start-up businesses by investing their own funds. This gives them more flexibility on what they can and will invest in, but because it is their own money angels are careful. Angel investors often invest early in a company's development, and they want to see an idea they understand and can have confidence in. Exhibit 5.9 offers some guidelines on how to attract angel financing.

Venture capital is financing obtained from venture capitalists, investment firms that specialize in financing small, high-growth companies. Venture capitalists receive an ownership interest and a voice in management in return for their money. They typically invest at a later stage than angel investors and often provide larger sums to start-up ventures. Bob Cramer, the CEO of Nimbit, knows this. Nimbit is a band management company that helps indie bands with their online-sales business. Often sites that sell MP3s, CDs, merchandise, and concert tickets are all different, so bands have a difficult time managing their fragmented distributors. Nimbit helps bands coordinate and monitor all of these activities. Early on, Nimbit secured $1 million in angel funding, but Cramer thought the idea was larger than that, so he wanted to pursue venture capital (VC). Cramer says, "I don't like angel funding. Angels are for small ideas. [Nimbit] needs VC money . . . And the process of raising VC money is all about making entrepreneurs jump through hoops. That's how they learn about you. They want to see what kind of stick-to-itiveness you've got."[13] We'll discuss venture capital in greater detail in Chapter 16.

Buying a Small Business

Another route to small-business ownership is buying an existing business. Although this approach is less risky, many of the same steps for starting a business from scratch apply to buying an existing company. It still requires careful and thorough analysis. The potential buyer must answer several

debt
A form of business financing consisting of borrowed funds that must be repaid with interest over a stated time period.

equity
A form of business financing consisting of funds raised through the sale of stock (i.e., ownership) in a business.

angel investors
Individual investors or groups of experienced investors who provide financing for start-up businesses by investing their own funds.

venture capital
Financing obtained from venture capitalists, investment firms that specialize in financing small, high-growth companies and receive an ownership interest and a voice in management in return for their money.

| EXHIBIT 5.9 | Making a Heavenly Deal |

You need financing for your start-up business. How do you get angels interested in investing in your business venture?

- Show them something they understand, ideally a business from an industry they've been associated with.
- Have respect for your prospective investors. They know things you don't.
- Hone your vision. Be able to describe your business—what it does and who it sells to—in less than a minute.
- Angels can always leave their money in the bank, so an investment must interest them. It should be something they're passionate about. And timing is important—knowing when to reach out to an angel can make a huge difference.
- They need to see management they trust, respect, and like. Present a mature management team with a strong, experienced leader who can withstand the scrutiny of the angel's inquiries.
- Angels prefer something to which they can bring added value. Those who invest could be involved with your company for a long time, or perhaps take a seat on your board of directors.
- They are more partial to deals that don't require huge sums of money or additional infusions of angel cash.
- Emphasize the likely exits for investors and have a handle on who the competition is, why your solution is better, and how you are going to gain market share.

Sources: Rhonda Abrams, "What Does It Take to Impress an Angel Investor?" *Inc.com*, **http://www.inc.com**, March 2001. Copyright © *Inc.com*; Stacy Zhao, "9 Tips for Winning Over Angels," **http://www.inc.com**, June 2005.

important questions: Why is the owner selling? Does he or she want to retire or move on to a new challenge, or are there problems with the business? Is the business operating at a profit? If not, can this be corrected? On what basis has the owner valued the company, and is it a fair price? What are the owner's plans after selling the company? Will he or she be available to provide assistance through the change of ownership of the business? And depending on the type of business it is, will customers be more loyal to the owner than to the product or service being offered? They could leave the firm if the current owner decides to open a similar business. To protect against this, many purchasers include a "noncompete clause" in the contract of sale.

You should prepare a business plan that thoroughly analyzes all aspects of the business. Get answers to all your questions, and determine, via the business plan, whether the business is a sound one. Then you must negotiate the price and other terms of purchase and obtain appropriate financing. This can be a complicated process, and may require the use of a consultant or business broker.

Risky Business

Running your own business may not be as easy as it sounds. Despite the many advantages of being your own boss, the risks are great as well. Nearly 600,000 small businesses fail every year, according to data from the Small Business Administration (SBA) and the Census Bureau.[14]

Businesses close down for many reasons—and not all are failures. Some businesses that close are financially successful and close for nonfinancial reasons. But the causes of business failure can be interrelated. For example, low sales and high expenses are often directly related to poor management. Some common causes of business closure are:

- Economic factors—business downturns and high interest rates
- Financial causes—inadequate capital, low cash balances, and high expenses
- Lack of experience—inadequate business knowledge, management experience, and technical expertise
- Personal reasons—the owners may decide to sell the business or move on to other opportunities

Inadequate early planning is often at the core of later business problems. As described earlier, a thorough feasibility analysis, from market assessment to financing, is critical to business success. Yet even with the best plans, business conditions change and unexpected challenges arise. An entrepreneur may start a company based on a terrific new product only to find that a larger firm with more marketing, financing, and distribution clout introduces a similar item.

The stress of managing a business can also take its toll. The business can consume your whole life. Owners may find themselves in over their heads and unable to cope with the pressures of business operations, from the long hours to being the main decision maker. Even successful businesses have to deal with ongoing challenges. Growing too quickly can cause as many problems as sluggish sales. Growth can strain a company's finances when additional capital is required to fund expanding operations, from hiring additional staff to purchasing more raw material or equipment. Successful business owners must respond quickly and develop plans to manage its growth.

So how do you know when it is time to quit? "Never give up" may be a good motivational catchphrase but it is not always good advice for a small-business owner. Howard Shaffer retired from the U.S. Air Force and moved to Taiwan where he spearheaded Nike's establishment of manufacturing facilities in China. When he left Nike to start his own shoe company, he expected his experience in shoe manufacturing to help ensure his success. Determined to revive a dying shoe manufacturing industry in the United States, Shaffer was soon making shoes that cost $450 a pair in his Pompano Beach, Florida, factory. After more than a dozen years watching the number of imported shoes rise to 99 percent of the total, he reluctantly closed his business.

What surprised him about the failure of his business was the unexpected reason for it. It wasn't that he couldn't compete with low-cost Chinese labor. It was that there were no suppliers left in the United States to provide him component parts (eyelets, laces, soles) in the

© AP Images/Pat Wellenbach

CONCEPT in action

With over 10,000 locations, Curves International is the largest fitness franchise in the world. The club's all-female clientele and trademark 30-minute workout have generated astounding membership growth in little over a decade. But success didn't come easy for Curves founder Gary Heavin. The premed dropout launched a conventional fitness chain during his 20s, became a millionaire by age 30, and soon thereafter declared bankruptcy when his gym business imploded. Undaunted, Heavin went on to launch Curves. Why do small businesses often fail?

CONCEPT check

How can potential business owners find new business ideas?

Why is it important to develop a business plan? What should such a plan include?

What financing options do small-business owners have? What risks do they face?

quantities he needed and no mechanics to repair his specialty equipment when it broke down. Shaffer spent $20 million of his own money before calling it quits and selling his machinery.[15]

Managing a Small Business

5 Why does managing a small business present special challenges for the owner?

Managing a small business is quite a challenge. Whether you start a business from scratch or buy an existing one you must be able to keep it going. The small-business owner must be ready to solve problems as they arise and move quickly if market conditions change. In the adjacent Managing Change box on the next page, you will see how one company grew from a young girl's hobby into a Web presence more popular than Oprah's.

A sound business plan is key to keeping the small-business owner in touch with all areas of his or her business. Hiring, training, and managing employees is another important responsibility because over time the owner's role may change. As the company grows, others will make many of the day-to-day decisions while the owner focuses on managing employees and planning for the firm's long-term success. The owner must constantly evaluate company performance and policies in light of changing market and economic conditions and develop new policies as required. He or she must also nurture a continual flow of ideas to keep the business growing. As the firm grows, the types of employees needed may also change. For instance, a larger firm may need more managerial talent and technical expertise.

Using Outside Consultants

One way to ease the burden of managing a business is to hire outside consultants. Nearly all small businesses need a good certified public accountant (CPA) who can help with financial record keeping and decision making, and tax planning. An accountant who works closely with the owner to help the business grow is a valuable asset. An attorney who knows about small-business law can provide legal advice and draw up essential contracts and documents. Consultants in areas such as marketing, employee benefits, and insurance can be used on an as-needed basis. Outside directors with business experience are another way for small companies to get advice. Resources like these free the small-business owner to concentrate on medium- and long-range planning, and day-to-day operations.

Some aspects of business can be outsourced or contracted out to specialists. Among the more common departments that use outsourcing are information technology, customer service, order fulfillment, payroll, and human resources. Hiring an outside company—in many cases another small business—can save money because the purchasing firm buys just the services it needs and makes no investment in expensive technology. Management should review outsourced functions as the business grows because at some point it may be more cost effective to bring them in-house. For 28 years, Richard Jepsen and Anthony Sandberg ran the O.C. Sailing Club (OCSC), one of the largest sailing schools in the United States, but all in that time, the company never generated more than a modest profit. Because the founders were approaching retirement age, they needed the business to be more profitable and quickly. They hired a consultant and joined a CEO roundtable group where they could get proven management ideas. The outside advisers identified areas where the company could tighten its financials and redirected the activities of the founders to areas where they could add more value. For example, Jepsen and Sandberg delegated the hiring of instructors to an employee and began organizing more club events themselves. They also found that public-speaking engagements brought in more clients than expensive advertisement, so they stopped advertising and invested in public-speaking classes. The advice of the outside consultants and advisers has helped OCSC increase its profit by 30 percent.[16]

Hiring and Retaining Employees

It is important to identify all the costs involved in hiring an employee to make sure your business can afford it. Help-wanted ads, extra space, taxes, and employee benefits will easily add about 10 to 15 percent to their salary. And having an employee may mean more work for you in terms of training and management. It's a catch-22: to grow you need to hire more people, but making the shift from solo worker to boss can be stressful.

Attracting good employees is more difficult for a small firm, which may not be able to match the higher salaries, better benefits, and advancement potential offered by larger firms. Small companies need to be creative to attract the right employees and convince applicants to join their firm. Once they hire an employee, small-business owners must make employee satisfaction a top priority in

Hiring Friends Can Be—Whatever

When Ashley Qualls was offered $1.5 million and a $100,000 car for her company, her e-mail reply was simple: Whatever. At the time, she didn't even have a driver's license. Qualls's company, Whateverlife, started as a hobby creating wallpaper for MySpace pages that she gave away for free. Qualls enlisted her friends to help design backgrounds and write articles for Whateverlife magazine, a section of the site. As MySpace grew in popularity, so did the number of people looking for layouts to use on their pages. The traffic at Whateverlife began to grow exponentially. For the seeming simplicity of its product offering, Whateverlife.com was soon attracting more viewers than sites of Oprah, TeenVogue, CosmoGirl, Martha Stewart, VH1, and FoxNews. Even though the 2,600 wallpaper downloads are still free, today the company generates $50,000 to $70,000 a month in ads posted by Google AdSense on the site.

As that revenue increased, latent family problems surfaced, and Qualls ultimately ended up in Wayne County Probate Court, where a judge determined that neither Ashley nor her parents could adequately manage the business's finances. The judge appointed a conservator until Qualls turned 18. The conservator put Qualls on a strict monthly budget. Anything she wants to spend over that amount, she has to ask first. When her lawyer realized Qualls was running the company solo (at 16), he encouraged her to hire Robb Lippitt, former chief operations officer at ePrize, as a consultant to help her navigate the explosive growth her company was experiencing and the problems that went with it. For example, as the company grew, so did Qualls's need to make sure employees, including her mother, were doing work. When it looked like her friends' productivity was dipping, Qualls drew up employee guidelines that spelled out her expectations: a minimum of 25 layouts a week to get paid.

Rapid growth has been fueled by an ever-growing audience of site visitors. When Qualls launched her series of Web tutorials on how to build and maintain MySpace pages, Lippitt expected modest results, but 28,000 users signed up the first week. Traffic like that prompted Qualls to begin working with offshore developers in India to build other Web applications. Her site debuted a unique video tool called Nabbr that music companies use—successfully—to launch viral marketing campaigns. And Qualls plans to start selling cell phone wallpapers that match the MySpace designs on Whateverlife. Lippitt is also pushing her to cultivate direct relationships with advertisers rather than rely exclusively on AdSense.

Building Whateverlife has been a tumultuous, yet valuable, undertaking. Brad Greenspan, cofounder of MySpace, offered Qualls $1.5 million for her company. When she declined, he came back with a second offer of $700,000, a car, and a $2 million budget to create her own Internet show. Qualls still declined. She wants to see how far she can take her business on her own.[17]

Critical Thinking Questions
- Do you think rapid change is a natural outcome of entrepreneurial activities? Explain.
- Should Qualls consider bringing Lippitt in-house? Lippitt is self-employed. Should he consider becoming an employee of Whateverlife if Qualls makes him an offer? Why or why not?

order to retain good people. Comfortable working conditions, flexible hours, employee benefit programs, opportunities to help make decisions, and a share in profits and ownership are some ways to do this.

Duane Ruh, 49, figured out how to build a $1.2 million business in a town with just 650 residents. It's all about treating employees right. The log birdhouse and bird feeder manufacturer, Little Log Co., located in Sargent, Nebraska, boasts employee-friendly policies you read about but rarely see put into practice. Ruh offers his 32 employees a flexible schedule that gives them plenty of time for their personal lives. During a slow period last summer, Ruh cut back on hours rather than lay anyone off. There just aren't that many jobs in that part of Nebraska that his employees could go to, so when he received a buyout offer that would have closed his facility but kept him in place with an enviable salary, he turned it down. Ruh also encourages his employees to pursue side or summer jobs if they need to make extra money, assuring them that their Little Log jobs are safe.[18]

Going Global with Exporting

More and more small businesses are discovering the benefits of looking beyond the United States for markets. As we learned in Chapter 3, the global marketplace represents a huge opportunity for U.S. businesses, both large and small. In fact, according to a recent survey, a third of U.S. small businesses are currently involved in international trade, and another survey projects that proportion to rise to half of U.S. small businesses by 2018.[19] Small businesses' decision to export is driven by many factors, one of which is the desire for increased sales and higher profits. U.S. goods are less expensive for overseas buyers when the value of the U.S. dollar declines against foreign currencies, and this creates opportunities for U.S. companies to sell globally. In addition, economic conditions such as a domestic recession, foreign competition within the United States, or new markets opening up in foreign countries may also encourage U.S. companies to export.

Like any major business decision, exporting requires careful planning. Small businesses may hire international-trade consultants to get started selling overseas. These specialists have the time, knowledge, and resources that most small businesses lack. Export trading companies (ETCs) buy goods at a discount from small businesses and resell them abroad. Export management companies

(EMCs) act on a company's behalf. For fees of 5 to 15 percent of gross sales and multiyear contracts, they handle all aspects of exporting, including finding customers, billing, shipping, and helping the company comply with foreign regulations.

Many online resources are also available to identify potential markets for your goods and services, and decipher the complexities of preparing to sell in a foreign country. The Small Business Administration's Office of International Trade (**http://www.sba.gov/ oit**) has links to many valuable sites. The Department of Commerce offers services for small businesses that want to sell abroad. Contact its Trade Information Center (**http://www.export.gov/exportbasics/ ticredirect.asp** or 1-800-USA-TRADE) or its Export Center (**http:// www.export.gov**).

CONCEPT check

How does the small-business owner's role change over time?

How does managing a small business contribute to its growth?

What are the benefits to small firms of doing business internationally, and what steps can small businesses take to explore their options?

Small Business, Large Impact

6 What are the advantages and disadvantages facing owners of small businesses?

An uncertain economy has not stopped people from starting new companies. The National Federation of Independent Businesses reports that 85 percent of Americans view small businesses as a positive influence on American life. This is not surprising when you consider the many reasons why small businesses continue to thrive in the United States:

- *Independence and a better lifestyle.* Large corporations no longer represent job security or offer the fast-track career opportunities they once did. Midcareer employees leave the corporate world—either voluntarily or as a result of downsizing—in search of new opportunities that self-employment provides. Many new college and business school graduates shun the corporate world altogether to start their own companies or look for work in smaller firms.
- *Personal satisfaction from work.* Many small-business owners cite this as one of the primary reasons for starting their companies. They love what they do.
- *Best route to success.* Business ownership provides greater advancement opportunities for women and minorities, as we will discuss later in this chapter. It also offers small-business owners the potential for profit.
- *Rapidly changing technology.* Technology advances and decreased costs provide individuals and small companies with the power to compete in industries that were formerly closed to them.
- *Major corporate restructuring and downsizing.* These force many employees to look for other jobs or careers. They may also provide the opportunity to buy a business unit that a company no longer wants.
- *Outsourcing.* As a result of downsizing, corporations may contract with outside firms for goods and services they formerly provided in-house. "Outsourcing" creates opportunities for smaller companies that offer these specialized goods and services.
- *Small businesses are resilient.* They are able to respond fairly quickly to changing economic conditions by refocusing their operations.

Pack your bags! Exhibit 5.10 lists the 10 hottest cities for entrepreneurs.

EXHIBIT 5.10	The 10 Hottest Cities for Entrepreneurs
1.	Phoenix-Mesa, AZ
2.	Charlotte-Gastonia-Rock Hill, NC-SC
3.	Raleigh-Durham-Chapel Hill, NC
4.	Las Vegas, NV-AZ
5.	Austin-San Marcos, TX
6.	Washington-Baltimore, DC-MD-VA-WV
7.	Memphis, TN-AR-MS
8.	Nashville, TN
9.	Norfolk-Virginia Beach-Newport News, VA-NC
10.	San Antonio, TX

Source: "Hot Cities for Entrepreneurs," *Entrepreneur*, October 2005, **http://www.entrepreneur.com**. Copyright © *Entrepreneur Magazine*. All rights reserved. Reproduced by permission.

Why Stay Small?

Owners of small businesses recognize that being small offers special advantages. Greater flexibility and an uncomplicated company structure allows small businesses to react more quickly to changing market forces. Innovative product ideas can be developed and brought to market more quickly, using fewer financial resources and personnel than would be needed in a larger company. And operating more efficiently keeps costs down as well. Small companies can also serve specialized markets that may not be cost effective for large companies. Another feature is the opportunity to provide a higher level of personal service. Such attention brings many customers back to small businesses like gourmet restaurants, health clubs, spas, fashion boutiques, and travel agencies.

Steve Niewulis played in baseball's minor leagues before an injury to his rotator cuff cut short his career. Niewulis, 32, decided to combine his love of the game with a clever idea that has elevated him to the big leagues. The fact that players had trouble keeping their hands dry while batting inspired his big idea, a sweat-busting rosin bag attached to a wristband so a player can dry the bat handle between pitches. In less than two years, Niewulis's Fort Lauderdale, Florida, company, Tap It! Inc., has sold thousands of Just Tap It! wristbands. The product, which retails for $12.95, is used by baseball players, basketball players, tennis players, golfers, and even rock climbers. His secret to success? Find a small distribution network that allows small companies, with just one product line, to succeed.[20]

On the other hand, being small is not always an asset. The founders may have limited managerial skills, or encounter difficulties obtaining adequate financing, both potential obstacles to growing a company. Complying with federal regulations is also more expensive for small firms. Those with fewer than 20 employees spend about twice as much per employee on compliance than do larger firms. In addition, starting and managing a small business requires a major commitment by the owner. Long hours, the need for owners to do much of the work themselves, and the stress of being personally responsible for the success of the business can take a toll.

That's why Kim Kleenan tries to create a "mental air bag" between herself and "the craziness of the day." She started Shakespeare Squared, a company that creates lesson plans, discussion guides, and activity books for large publishers. In three years, her company has grown 800 percent and now she has 10 employees. To manage growth-related stress, she has her assistant color-code her agenda and holds weekly staff meetings, department meetings, manager meetings, and even project team meetings. Most important, she leaves her BlackBerry in her car overnight and doesn't give her home number to employees. She says, "My managers can deal with emergencies."[21]

CONCEPT in action

The home theater concept is hot, and nobody helps customers create a high-definition big-screen experience at home like The Little Guys Home Electronics. Founded by three entrepreneurs with backgrounds in the electronics industry, the local Chicagoland venture made it big by staying small. The partners agreed early on that they preferred expert service and personalized customer contact to the prepackaged sales pitches of the big-box chains. What are the advantages and limitations of operating as a small business?

© Design Pics Inc./Alamy

CONCEPT check

Why are small businesses becoming so popular?

Discuss the major advantages and disadvantages of small businesses.

The Small Business Administration

Many small-business owners turn to the **Small Business Administration (SBA)**, a U.S. government agency, for assistance. The SBA's mission is to speak on behalf of small business, and through its national network of local offices it helps people start and manage small businesses, advises them in the areas of finance and management, and helps them win federal contracts. Its toll-free number—1-800-U-ASK-SBA (1-800-827-5722)—provides general information, and its Web site at **http://www .sba.gov** offers details on all its programs.[22]

Financial Assistance Programs

The SBA offers financial assistance to qualified small businesses that cannot obtain financing on reasonable terms through normal lending channels. This assistance takes the form of guarantees on loans made by private lenders. (The SBA no longer provides direct loans.) These loans can be used for most business purposes, including purchasing real estate, equipment, and materials. The SBA has been responsible for a significant amount of small-business financing in the United States. In the fiscal year ended September 30, 2005, the SBA backed more than $19 billion in loans to almost 98,000 small businesses, including about $6 billion to minority-owned firms and $3.3 billion in loans to businesses owned by women. It also provided more than $9 billion in rebuilding loans for victims of the fall 2005 Gulf Coast hurricanes Katrina, Rita, and Wilma—a new record for SBA disaster relief loans.[23]

7 How does the Small Business Administration help small businesses?

Small Business Administration (SBA)

A U.S. government agency that speaks on behalf of small business; specifically it helps people start and manage small businesses, advises them in the areas of finance and management, and helps them win federal contracts.

The SBA's New Markets Venture Capital Program promotes economic development and job opportunities in low-income geographic areas. Other SBA programs offer export financing and assistance to firms that suffer economic harm after natural or other disasters.

More than 300 SBA-licensed **Small Business Investment Companies (SBICs)** provide about $2.5 billion each year in long-term financing for small businesses. The SBA's Angel Capital Electronic Network (ACE-Net, **http://acenet.csusb.edu**) offers an Internet-based matching service for small businesses seeking funding of up to $5 million from individual investors. These privately owned and managed investment companies hope to earn a substantial return on their investments as the small businesses grow.

SCORE-ing with Management Assistance Programs

The SBA also provides a wide range of management advice. Its Business Development Library has publications on most business topics. Its "Starting Out" series offers brochures on how to start a wide variety of businesses—from ice cream stores to fish farms.

Business development officers at the Office of Business Development and local Small Business Development Centers counsel many thousands of small-business owners each year, offering advice, training, and educational programs. The SBA also offers free management consulting through two volunteer groups, the Service Corps of Retired Executives (SCORE) and the Active Corps of Executives (ACE). Executives in these programs use their own business backgrounds to help small-business owners. SCORE has expanded its outreach into new markets by offering e-mail counseling through its Web site (**http://www.score.org**). The SBA also offers free online resources and courses for small-business owners and aspiring entrepreneurs in its E-Business Institute (**http://www.sba.gov/training**).

Assistance for Women and Minorities

The SBA is committed to helping women and minorities increase their business participation. It offers a minority small-business program, micro-loans, and the publication of Spanish-language informational materials. It has increased its responsiveness to small businesses by giving regional offices more decision authority and creating high-tech tools for grants, loan transactions, and eligibility reviews.

The SBA offers special programs and support services for socially and economically disadvantaged persons, including women, Native Americans, and Hispanics through its Office of Minority Enterprise Development. It also makes a special effort to help veterans go into business for themselves.

CONCEPT check

What is the Small Business Administration (SBA)?

Describe the financial and management assistance programs offered by the SBA.

Trends in Entrepreneurship and Small-Business Ownership

8 What trends are shaping entrepreneurship and small-business ownership?

Entrepreneurship has changed since the heady days of the late 1990s, when starting a dot-com while still in college seemed a quick route to riches and stock options. In fact, today, a growing group of entrepreneurs is pursuing entrepreneurial ideas that will benefit the public good. Much entrepreneurial opportunity comes from major changes in demographics, society, and technology, and at present there is a confluence of all three. A major demographic group is moving into a significantly different stage in life, and entrepreneurs at both ends of the age spectrum are letting their passions drive their perceptions of business opportunities.

Social Entrepreneurship

Traditionally, entrepreneurs strike out on their own because they want more control over their work life, think their idea is the next big thing, or assume they'll make more money. Increasingly, however, today's young entrepreneurs are launching companies in the interest of social justice, environmental action, or generally bettering the world. Unlike so-called cause marketing, like Gap's (PRODUCT) Red AIDS awareness campaign, among others, these social entrepreneurs create entire businesses around their social passion. The result is a blending of charity and for-profit work that goes beyond shorter-lived marketing campaigns. For example, Ron Gonen developed RecycleBank to offer incentive to people to use curbside recycling. RecycleBank bins contain microchips that allow municipal collection trucks to scan a household's bin and determine the amount of recycled material. The amount recycled is credited to an online account in the form of points the consumer can redeem at participating merchants, like Starbucks and Whole Foods. Even though Gonen hasn't turned a profit yet, the former senior consultant at Deloitte has left the corporate grind behind. He says, "Professionally, I was doing well, but I wasn't satisfied or fulfilled."[24]

One of the downsides of social entrepreneurship can be difficulty raising money. Financial institutions are more likely to loan money to ventures that have a stated goal of making a profit. With social entrepreneurship, the entrepreneur may focus more on the social aspects of the organizational mission than on its profitability, and so lenders might consider the organization more of a charity than an investment.[25] Nonetheless, many individuals are pursuing social entrepreneurship. Ashoka is an organization that supports social entrepreneurs, and its CEO Bill Drayton says that "such people neither hand out fish nor teach people to fish; their aim is to revolutionize the fishing industry."[26] For more on social entrepreneurship, read *The Power of Unreasonable People: How Social Entrepreneurs Create Markets That Change the World,* by John Elkington and Pamela Hartigan.

Changing Demographics Create Entrepreneurial Diversity

As we have seen in Chapters 1 and 4, today's baby boomers will indulge in much less knitting and golf. The AARP predicts silver-haired entrepreneurs will rise in the coming years. According to the Bureau of Labor Statistics, roughly 10 million Americans are self-employed, and that figure continues to grow every year.[27] Of those who are self-employed, people ages 55 to 64 make up the fastest-growing group of self-employed workers, and not surprisingly, boomers are the largest component of the self-employed workforce. Roughly 7 million self-employed workers are over the age of 50.[28] That percentage increases with age. Of the 2 percent of all U.S. workers over the age of 80, nearly all are self-employed.[29] Either out of desire or necessity, many boomers will work beyond the traditional retirement age, according to John Challenger. "A growing number of these baby boomers are abandoning traditional employment for self-employment." As the labor market for educated workers tightens, boomer entrepreneurs may find that their "biggest customers are their former employers, who have no choice but to outsource certain functions to those with the most relevant experience."[30]

The growing numbers of baby boomer entrepreneurs has prompted some forward-thinking companies to recognize business opportunities in technology. At one time there was a concern that the aging of the population would create a drag on the economy. Conventional wisdom said that the early parenthood years were the big spending years, that as we aged we would spend less, and because boomers are such a big demographic group, this was going to create a long-term economic decline. Now it appears this is not true. The boomer generation has built sizable wealth, and they are not afraid to spend it to make their lives more comfortable.

"In the future, everything from cell phones to computers will be redesigned for users with limited manual dexterity, poor eyesight, and compromised hearing. Intel, MIT, and other research centers are working on sensor-rich environments that can monitor inhabitants, helping people remember to complete tasks, and watching for sudden behavioral or physical changes," says Jeff Cornwall, who holds the Jack C. Massey Chair in Entrepreneurship at Belmont University in Nashville, Tennessee. "This could be a huge entrepreneurial pot of gold for the next 40 years."[31]

Minorities are also adding to the entrepreneurial mix. As we saw in Exhibit 5.3, minority groups and women are increasing business ownership at a much faster rate than the national average, reflecting their confidence in the U.S. economy. These overwhelming increases in minority business ownership paralleled the demand for U.S. Small Business Administration loan products. Loans to minorities increased by 27 percent in 2005 compared to 2004, and loans to women in 2005 jumped almost 50 percent. The SBA loan budget for 2006 included more than $21 billion available to small businesses, which turned to the SBA in record numbers throughout 2005.[32]

The latest Kauffman Foundation Index of Entrepreneurial Activity found that immigrants and Latinos have swelled the growing numbers of self-employed

CONCEPT in action

Rapper by night, entrepreneur by day, Shawn Carter possesses an equal amount of street smarts and business savvy. Narrowly escaping gang-related violence during his teen years, Carter turned to music, founding Roc-A-Fella Records to promote his alter ego, Jay-Z. Multiple Grammys and a dozen hit songs later, Jay-Z is one of the most recognized names in music. After a three-year stint as CEO of Def Jam Recordings, Carter now juggles numerous ventures ranging from luxury watches to high-end clothing. What factors are driving the rapper-as-entrepreneur phenomenon?

© AP Images/Damian Dovarganes

Though rock 'n' roll has traditionally been a male-dominated art form, Tish Ciravolo's fast-growing company, Daisy Rock Guitars, is helping girls everywhere to shatter rock's glass ceiling. As founder and president of Daisy Rock Guitars, the music-loving Ciravolo has put more hot humbucklers in the hands of female guitarists than any other manufacturer in recent years. Daisy Rock's affordable line of electric and acoustic instruments ranges from heart- and star-shaped guitars for tweens to hot-colored axes for women. What unique perspectives do women business owners bring to the marketplace?

CONCEPT check

What significant trends are occurring in the small-business arena?

How is entrepreneurial diversity impacting small business and the economy?

How is technology affecting small business?

Americans in recent years, increasing the diversity of the country's entrepreneurial class. The SBA notes that the number of Latino-owned businesses has increased 400 percent since 1979 to more than 1 million and now represents about 7 percent of the total U.S. workforce.[33]

"These newly-released census estimates and our own loan figures validate what I see in the communities I have visited all across the country," said SBA administrator Hector V. Barreto. "Minority and women entrepreneurs are leading the way in business growth and are making important contributions to [the] nation's economic strength."[34]

The Growth of "Web-Driven Entrepreneurs"

Technology, of course, plays a large role in the U.S. economy, and a recent study found that a new generation of American businesses, "Web-driven entrepreneurs," now make up 25 percent of all U.S. small businesses. According to a survey of 400 small businesses conducted by MasterCard International and Warrillow & Co., a small-business consulting firm, Web-driven entrepreneurs are 25 percent more likely to be women and 25 percent more likely to be university educated.

The study found that Web-savvy companies are also more focused on expansion than their traditional counterparts. "Web-driven entrepreneurs are more growth-focused," said Yoela Harris, director of the Small Business Advisors System at Warrillow & Co. "Internet-based small businesses have a 14 percent growth rate and are 10 years old on average, while traditional small businesses have a 7 percent growth rate and are 14 years old on average."

Over the next five years, 54 percent of Web-driven entrepreneurs plan to access new domestic markets, versus 36 percent of traditional small businesses, 52 percent versus 38 percent plan to introduce new products or services, and 18 percent versus 8 percent plan to access international markets. Thanks to these Web-driven entrepreneurs, the technology growth trend doesn't look ready to slow down anytime soon.[35]

Summary of Learning Goals

1 Why do people become entrepreneurs, and what are the different types of entrepreneurs?

Entrepreneurs are innovators who take the risk of starting and managing a business to make a profit. Most want to develop a company that will grow into a major corporation. People become entrepreneurs for four main reasons: the opportunities for profit, independence, personal satisfaction, and lifestyle. Classic entrepreneurs may be micropreneurs, who plan to keep their businesses small, or growth-oriented entrepreneurs. Multipreneurs start multiple companies, while intrapreneurs work within large corporations.

2 Which characteristics do successful entrepreneurs share?

Successful entrepreneurs are ambitious, independent, self-confident, creative, energetic, passionate, and committed. They have a high need for achievement and a willingness to take moderate risks. Good managerial, interpersonal, and communication skills, as well as technical knowledge are important for entrepreneurial success.

3 How do small businesses contribute to the U.S. economy?

Small businesses play an important role in the economy. They account for over 99 percent of all employer firms and produce about half of U.S. economic output. Most new private-sector jobs created in the United States over the past decade were in small firms. The Small Business Administration defines a small business as independently owned and operated, with a local base of operations, and not dominant in its field. It also defines small business by size, according to its industry. Small businesses are found in every field, but they dominate the service, construction, wholesale, and retail categories.

After finding an idea that satisfies a market need, the small-business owner should choose a form of business organization. Preparing a formal business plan helps the business owner analyze the feasibility of his or her idea. The written plan describes in detail the idea for the business and how it will be implemented and operated. The plan also helps the owner obtain both debt and equity financing for the new business.

At first, small-business owners are involved in all aspects of the firm's operations. Hiring and retaining key employees and the wise use of outside consultants can free up an owner's time to focus on planning, strategizing, and monitoring market conditions, in addition to overseeing day-to-day operations. Expanding into global markets can be a profitable growth strategy for a small business.

Because of their streamlined staffing and structure, small businesses can be efficiently operated. They have the flexibility to respond to changing market conditions. Small firms can serve specialized markets more profitably than large firms, and provide a higher level of personal service. Disadvantages include limited managerial skill, difficulty in raising capital needed for start-up or expansion, the burden of complying with increasing levels of government regulation, and the major personal commitment that is required by the owner.

The Small Business Administration is the main U.S. government agency serving small businesses. It provides guarantees of private-lender loans for small businesses. The SBA also offers a wide range of management assistance services, including courses, publications, and consulting. It has special programs for women, minorities, and veterans.

Entrepreneurship is starting to be seen as an avenue for social change as well as for freedom, innovation, and wealth creation. Social entrepreneurship is starting to blend charity with for-profit enterprise. Changes in demographics, society, and technology are shaping the future of entrepreneurship and small business in America. More than ever, opportunities exist for entrepreneurs of all ages and backgrounds. The numbers of women and minority business owners continues to rise, and older entrepreneurs are changing the small-business landscape. Catering to the needs of an older population and a surge in "Web-based" companies, fuel continued technology growth.

4 What are the first steps to take if you are starting your own business?

5 Why does managing a small business present special challenges for the owner?

6 What are the advantages and disadvantages facing owners of small businesses?

7 How does the Small Business Administration help small businesses?

8 What trends are shaping entrepreneurship and small-business ownership?

Key Terms

angel investors 136
business plan 134
debt 136
entrepreneurs 127
equity 136
intrapreneurs 129
multipreneurs 128

small business 131
Small Business Administration
(SBA) 141
Small Business Investment Companies
(SBICs) 142
venture capital 136

1. After working in software development with a major food company for 12 years, you are becoming impatient with corporate "red tape" (regulations and routines). You have an idea for a new snack product for nutrition-conscious consumers and are thinking of starting your own company. What entrepreneurial characteristics do you need to succeed? What other factors should you consider before quitting your job? Working with a partner, choose one to be the entrepreneurial employee and one to play the role of his or her current boss. Develop notes for a script. The employee will focus on why this is a good idea and reasons he or she will succeed, while the employer will play devil's advocate to convince him or her that staying on at the large company is a better idea. Then switch roles and repeat the discussion. **(Information, Interpersonal)**

2. What does it really take to become an entrepreneur? Find out by interviewing a local entrepreneur, or researching an entrepreneur you've read about in this chapter or in the business press. Get answers to the following questions, as well as any others you'd like to ask:
   - How did you research the feasibility of your idea?
   - How did you develop your vision for the company?
   - How long did it take you to prepare your business plan?
   - Where did you obtain financing for the company?
   - Where did you learn the business skills you needed to run and grow the company?
   - What are the most important entrepreneurial characteristics that helped you succeed?
   - What were the biggest challenges you had to overcome?
   - What are the most important lessons you learned by starting this company?
   - What advice do you have for would-be entrepreneurs? **(Information, Interpersonal, Systems)**

3. A small catering business in your city is for sale for $150,000. The company specializes in business luncheons and small social events. The owner has been running the business for four years from her home but is expecting her first child and wants to sell. You will need outside investors to help you purchase the business. Develop questions to ask the owner about the business and its prospects, and a list of documents you want to see. What other types of information would you need before making a decision to buy this company? Summarize your findings in a memo to a potential investor that explains the appeal of the business for you and how you plan to investigate the feasibility of the purchase. **(Information, Interpersonal)**

4. Research various types of assistance available to women and minority business owners. Call or visit the nearest SBA office to find out what services and resources it offers. Contact trade associations such as the National Foundation for Women Business Owners (NFWBO), the National Alliance of Black Entrepreneurs, the U.S. Hispanic Chamber of Commerce, and the U.S. Department of Commerce's Minority Business Development Agency (MBDA). Call these groups or use the Web to develop a list of their resources and how a small-business owner could use them. **(Information, Interpersonal, Technology)**

5. Do you have what it takes to be an entrepreneur or small-business owner? You can find many online quizzes to help you figure this out. The Hampton Roads Small Business Development Center site offers a quiz for "Measuring the Ingredients of a Successful Entrepreneur" at **http://www.hrsbdc.org/start/quiz/**. What did your results tell you, and were you surprised by what you learned? **(Information, Technology)**

6. **Team Activity** Your class decides to participate in a local business plan competition. Divide the class into small groups and choose one of the following ideas:
   - A new computer game based on the stock market
   - A company with an innovative design for a skateboard
   - Travel services for college and high school students

   Prepare a detailed outline for the business plan, including the objectives for the business and the types of information you would need to develop product, marketing, and financing strategies. Each group will then present its outline for the class to critique. **(Information, Interpersonal, Systems)**

Ethics Activity

As the owner of a small factory that makes plastic sheeting you are constantly seeking ways to increase profits. As the new year begins, one of your goals is to find additional funds to offer annual productivity and/or merit bonuses to your loyal, hardworking factory personnel.

Then a letter from a large national manufacturer of shower curtains seems to provide an answer. As part of a new "supplier diversity" program it is putting in place, it is offering substantial purchase contracts to minority-owned suppliers. Even though the letter clearly states that the business must be minority owned to qualify for the program, you convince yourself to apply for it based on the fact that all your employees are Latino. You justify your decision by deciding they will benefit from the increased revenue a larger contract will bring, some of which you plan to pass on to them in the form of bonuses later in the year.

Using a Web search tool, locate articles about this topic and then write a response to the following question. Be sure to support your arguments and cite your sources.

ETHICAL DILEMMA: Is it wrong for this business owner to apply for this program even though it will end up benefiting his employees as well as his business?

Sources: "Kodak Achieves Supplier Diversity Goals," *M2 Presswire*, April 28, 2005, **http://www.Kodak.com** (May 22, 2006); "Xerox Supplier Diversity Program Celebrates 20 Years of Success," *M2 Presswire*, December 12, 2005, **http://www.gale.cengage.com**.

Working the Net

1. Visit Sample Business Plans at **http://www.bplans.com** to review examples of all types of business plans. Select an idea for a company in a field that interests you, and using information from the site, prepare an outline for its business plan.
2. Find a business idea you like or dislike at the American Venture Capital Exchange site, **http://www.avce.com**. Explain why you think this is a good business idea or not. List additional information the entrepreneur should have to consider for this business, and research the industry on the Web using a search engine.
3. Evaluate the export potential of your product idea at the Small Business Exporters Network Web site, **http://www.exporters.sbdc.com.au**. Explore three information areas, including market research, export readiness, and financing. Select a trade link site from government, university, or private categories. Compare them in terms of the information offered to small businesses that want to venture into overseas markets. Which is the most useful, and why?
4. Explore the SBA Web site at **http://www.sba.gov**. What resources are available to you locally? What classes does the E-Business Institute offer? What about financing assistance? Do you think the site lives up to the SBA's goal of being a one-stop shopping resource for the small-business owner? Why or why not?
5. You want to buy a business but don't know much about valuing small companies. Using the "Business for Sale" column available online at **http://www.inc.com**, develop a checklist of questions to ask when buying a business. Also summarize several ways that businesses arrive at their sale price ("Business for Sale" includes the price rationale for each profiled business).

Creative Thinking Case

180s Gives Old Products New Spin

People laughed when Ron Wilson and Brian Le Gette quit solid investment banking jobs with six-figure salaries to build a better earmuff. The buddies, both engineers, shared a vision based on a simple strategy: to innovate mundane products with redefined style and function.

It all started with the humble earmuff. Walking across campus at Virginia Tech in two feet of snow, Ron Wilson mused about keeping his ears warm without looking like a dork, conceptualizing what would later become the company's signature product, the Ear Warmer. Seven years later he and Wharton Business School buddy, Brian Le Gette (they both earned MBAs in Entrepreneurial Management), designed and developed prototypes of an expandable, collapsible, fleece-covered ear warmer that wraps around the back of the head.

They charged $7,500 in start-up expenses to credit cards, and the following fall sold their first ear warmers on the University of Pennsylvania campus—for $20 a piece. Two classmates interning at QVC persuaded Wilson and Le Gette to hawk their product on QVC's home shopping network, and the rest, as they say, is history. Their QVC debut sold 5,000 Ear Warmers in 8.5 minutes, and three years later home shoppers had bought 600,000 Ear Warmers. Their product was a winner.

Launched by this momentum, their business quickly grew into a booming product design and development company, a creator and marketer of innovative performance wear with 71 employees worldwide. The company's headquarters, known as the 180s Performance Lab, is situated on Baltimore's Inner Harbor and includes an interactive storefront where consumers can test new products. The building's architecture—"floating" conference rooms, a sailcloth roof, four huge windows to the sky—inspires the creative process taking place inside. World-class product design and development teams are constantly working on new innovations, the very core of the 180s culture. And nearly every product has multiple design and utility patents that reflect the unique design solutions the company creates.

Although both founders have now left the company to pursue other interests, it was recently named one of America's Most Innovative Companies by *Inc.* magazine, earned *Fortune* magazine's award for Top Outdoor Products of 2003 for its Exhale gloves, and is number nine on the 2005 Inc. 500 list of fastest-growing private companies. 180s' products posted record sales of over $45 million in 2004, and its products are now available through 18,000 retail stores in more than 40 countries. Wilson and Le Gette are the ones laughing now—all the way to the bank.

Critical Thinking Questions

*   What characteristics made Ron Wilson and Brian Le Gette successful entrepreneurs?
*   How did their partnership and shared vision serve their business goals?
*   Is their departure from the company likely to affect its growth? Why or why not?

Sources: Julekha Dash, "180s CEO Le Gette Departs," *Baltimore Business Journal*, July 15, 2005, **http://www.bizjournals.com**; "Winners Announced for Maryland's Business International Leadership Awards," World Trade Center Institute press release, March 9, 2004, "Brian Le Gette, CEO and co-founder, and Tim Hodge, Chief Legal Officer, of 180s, LLC," World Trade Center Institute, **www.wtci.org/events/awards/leadership2004/legette.htm** (November 9, 2005); 180s corporate Web site, **http://www.180s.com** (March 15, 2006).

**Natalie Tessler
Spa Space**

Exploring Business Careers

If you happen to catch her, Natalie Tessler will be trying simultaneously to find the company checkbook, prepare for a 100-person party, and talk to several employees about clients they are assisting. Her first career, as a lawyer for some of the country's most prestigious firms, required a great deal of educational training. None of that training, however, prepared her for running her own business. "People think that, owning a spa, I'm able to live this glamorous lifestyle," she says with a laugh. "Owning a spa is nothing like going to one—my nails always are broken from fixing equipment; my back is usually in pain from sitting hunched over a computer trying to figure out the budget or our next marketing promotion." President and founder of Spa Space, Tessler is a true entrepreneur, embodying the spirit and drive necessary to see her vision become a reality.

She always knew she wanted to start her own business, a place where she could express herself and highlight her own interests. Not until one night, though, when she was having dinner with a friend who recently had begun a writing career, did she realize it was time. "I was listening to her talk about how much she loved her job. Her passion and excitement—I wanted that. I wanted something that grabbed me and propelled me through the day—and being a lawyer wasn't it."

She began searching for what "it" was. Although she didn't see herself as an artistically creative person, she did find that she had a tremendous passion and talent for hospitality, entertaining others, and presentation. Seeking an outlet for that flair, she found the spa industry, an industry where attending to the client is key to success. And after much research, the idea for Spa Space was born.

Tessler wanted to design a spa that focused on something new: creating a comfortable, personalized environment of indulgence while not neglecting the medical technology of proper skin care. "My father's a dermatologist, so we discussed the importance of making this more than a spa where you can get a frou-frou, smell-good treatment that might actually harm your skin. We both thought it was important to create an experience that is as beneficial for people's skin as it is for their

Part 2: Business Ownership

emotional well-being." To address this need, Spa Space has a medical advisory board that helps with product selection, treatment design, and staff training.

Armed with a vision and a plan, Tessler turned her sights toward making it a reality. Spa Space opened in 2001 and has received a great deal of national recognition for its service excellence and unique treatments. Today, Tessler speaks of where she wants to take the business next. She has ideas of expanding to other locations and focusing on specific aspects that have proven successful, such as catering to women and men and providing a range of group services. Wherever she takes Spa Space next, however, one thing is certain. Through persevering entrepreneurship, she has found her passion and is able to live it every day.

Apple, Inc.
continuing case
Part 2: Ownership at Apple, Inc.

The Apple computer was the brainchild of two people—Stephen Wozniak and Steve Jobs. Wozniak was the self-taught master of electronics, and Jobs was the master of cross-functionality who intertwined electronics expertise with business skills. They needed a third party in the relationship, someone who would bring the money to the venture. This third party was A. C. "Mike" Markkula. Who were these three men, and why did it take all three of them to found Apple?

The Apple I—The Initial Partnership

Stephen Wozniak

Born with a keen interest in anything electronic and nurtured at the GTE Sylvania computer facility, Wozniak was a student at the University of Colorado in Boulder for only one year. While a student, he polished his FORTRAN and ALGOL programming skills using the university's computer. But he failed to meet the academic requirements of the university and returned home to California. In 1969, Wozniak and friend Bill Fernandez scavenged computer parts from a variety of sources and built the "Cream Soda Computer," named because of the amount of cream soda consumed during the development of the machine. At that time, Wozniak worked as an engineer for Hewlett-Packard on the HP 35 calculator. While he worked for Hewlett-Packard, he became a member of the Homebrew Computer Club.

Using a large employee discount from Hewlett-Packard, Wozniak purchased a Motorola MC6800 microprocessor from HP. He used this microprocessor to develop the first prototype of the Apple I board that he was constantly taking to the computer club meetings. In March 1976, Wozniak had built a computer board that he could interface with his video terminal and a keyboard. Wozniak was the sole designer of the computer part that led to the Apple computer. Although he was working at Hewlett-Packard at the time of the design, HP had relinquished any hold on what Wozniak was doing in his free time.

Steve Jobs

Although Steve Jobs had an interest in electronics, this interest was along the lines of commercialization rather than technical development. He was essentially obsessed with the user's experience with products, always trying to determine what captivated consumers. Jobs pursued this interest at Atari Computer, where he worked on their video games. After meeting Wozniak in the late 1960s and staying in close contact with him throughout the subsequent years, it was Jobs's drive and vision that convinced Wozniak of the commercial viability of his microcomputer board.

Essentially, it was Steve Jobs who made the key decisions that shaped Apple Computer and, because of those decisions, the launch of the personal computer industry. It was Jobs who wanted to name the product (and company) after a fruit, just as it was Jobs who wanted world-class public relations and marketing firms to represent the company. Jobs took personal responsibility for what Apple was making and for how the product felt to the user. Some have described Jobs as a master of hardware (not software), a trailblazer (not follower), a creator (not cloner), and an iconoclast (not an adherer to industry standards). He has been referred to as a perpetual innovation machine, a cultural inspiration, and an entrepreneurial icon.

The Partnership

When Wozniak and Jobs formed a partnership, they had to select a name for their partnership. As entrepreneurs in the heart of a countercultural time period, they thought that "Apple" was a fun and interesting name. Their vision for the company was that people would find their computer useful at home, using it for things such as balancing checkbooks, keeping address lists, and typing letters. An apple was the perfect fruit, representing something found in the home and the company's personal and healthy environment. The partnership gave Wozniak and Jobs equal ownership of 90 percent of Apple Computer. The remaining 10 percent went to Ron Wayne, who drew the diagrams of the Apple I board and designed the company logo. Fifty boards were sold to a local retailer and the commercial enterprise began in 1975. As the company sought financing to build more boards in 1976, Ron Wayne ended his relationship with the company due to concerns about his financial obligations. At the same time, Wozniak was improving on the Apple I and moving toward the Apple II.

Before the Apple II was introduced to the market, Wozniak and Jobs showed a prototype to Commodore Computer. Commodore had announced plans to enter the microcomputer market, and the Apple II would have eased the company's entry. However, Commodore and Jobs could not agree on the terms of the sale. Thus, Wozniak and Jobs continued to search for funding to bring the Apple II to market.

The Apple II—Expanding the Ownership Team

A. C. "Mike" Markkula

An electrical engineer by training, Markkula retired from Intel when he was in his late 30s. As marketing manager at Intel, he had accumulated stock options that made him a multimillionaire. Markkula agreed to provide the early funding for the Apple II.

In addition to securing a $250,000 line of credit for the company, Markkula invested around $90,000 of his own money into the business. He bought one-third of Apple Computer, with Wozniak and Jobs having equal one-third shares of the business. One stipulation by Markkula was that Wozniak leave his job at Hewlett-Packard and devote full time to the Apple II, something that Wozniak had been hesitant to do. Apple Computer, Inc. was thus created in early 1977. Wozniak was the computer designer, Jobs focused on product appearance and presentation to the public, and Markkula was in charge of marketing and business affairs.

Initial Public Offering

By the end of 1979, Apple Computer had net sales of close to $50 million and was the dominant player in the personal computer marketplace. The initial founders had maintained tight control over the company's shares. But in December of 1980, 4.5 million shares of Apple common stock were offered at $22. By the end of that year, each of the original investors of the company was a multimillionaire.

Critical Thinking Questions

- Describe the entrepreneurial styles of Wozniak, Jobs, and Markkula.
- What role did each of the three founders play in the development of Apple Computer?
- Why didn't Commodore Computer want to buy the Apple II from Wozniak and Jobs?
- Ron Wayne resigned from his role as one of the original Apple partners, forgoing millions in earnings as the company grew. Why do you think he hesitated to make the long-term commitment to Apple? What advice would you have given him at the time? What would you say to him today?
- What form(s) of business ownership existed at Apple Computer?

Sources: Anonymous, "A Design, a Dream," *U.S. News & World Report,* October 13, 2005, p. 54; **http://www.woz.org**, accessed on March 21, 2006; Roy A. Allan, *A History of the Personal Computer* (London, Ontario, Canada: Allan Publishing, 2001); Robert X. Cringely, "Because We Like to Be Seduced," *Inc. Magazine,* April 2004, p. 122; Phillip Elmer-DeWitt, "Steve Jobs: Apple's Anti-Gates," *Time,* December 7, 1998, p. 205; Terry Semel, "Steve Jobs," *Time,* April 18, 2005, p. 78; Stephen Wozniak, "Homebrew and How the Apple Came to Be," **http://atariarchives.org**, accessed on March 20, 2006; Steve Wozniak, "How We Failed Apple," *Newsweek,* February 1996, **http://www.woz.org**, accessed on March 21, 2006; Jason Zasky, "The Failure Interview: Apple Computer Co-Founder Steve Wozniak," **http://www.failuremag.com**, accessed on March 21, 2006.

Managing Organizations

PART 3

Management and Leadership in Today's Organizations

CHAPTER 6

Learning Goals

After reading this chapter you should be able to answer these questions:

1 What is the role of management?

2 What are the four types of planning?

3 What are the primary functions of managers in organizing activities?

4 How do leadership styles influence a corporate culture?

5 How do organizations control activities?

6 What roles do managers take on in different organizational settings?

7 What set of managerial skills is necessary for managerial success?

8 What trends will affect management in the future?

"A Mighty and Terrible Thing"

Lt. Andrew Tyler is the executive officer of the *S-33*, an American submarine in service during World War II. As such, he is second in command of the vessel and is responsible for many of the more mundane activities on board the submarine such as managing maintenance schedules and keeping things running smoothly. He ensures that the sub and its crew operate in tip-top shape, allowing the captain to focus on overall strategy and the tactical nuances of the mission at hand. Lt. Tyler, in short, is a manager who is responsible for developing the crew, maintaining the ship, and otherwise allocating resources in order to meet the goals set by the captain and those in the military above him.

At the onset of their current mission, Lt. Tyler believes that he is ready to be a submarine captain; however, his advancement has been curtailed by Capt. Dahlgren, his commanding officer. When he approaches the captain about this, the captain acknowledges that Tyler is a first-rate executive officer and a "damn good submariner" but then challenges him on whether or not he'd be willing to sacrifice the men under his command to suit the needs of the overall mission. When Lt. Tyler fails to respond, Capt. Dahlgren says, "You see you hesitate, and as a captain, you can't. You have to act. If you don't, you put the entire crew at risk." And as a captain, Dahlgren continues, "You have to be able to make hard decisions based on imperfect information, asking men to carry out orders that may result in their deaths."

It is doubtful that any of you, in your capacity as a manager of a company, will ever have to direct someone to do something that will lead to his or her death; however, Lt. Tyler's shortcoming as a leader also prevents the advancement of many middle managers into the upper-management echelons. Leaders must maintain an overall vision of the direction that the company is taking, including the goals of the organization, the strategies for attaining those goals, and ultimately the resources available for reaching those goals. As such, a manager may be called upon to make certain sacrifices that he or she may not want to carry out such as laying off individuals or cutting ties with a longtime supplier. Though it may not be in the best interest of the individual who is laid off or the supplier who is suddenly without a customer, the manager has to recognize that such activities are in the better interest of the overall structure of the organization, at least in most cases.

Lt. Tyler is, at this point, unable to maintain that overall vision, unlike Capt. Dahlgren. However, after the mission goes horribly wrong, resulting in the captain's death, Lt. Tyler must take up the mantle of leadership and press onward to complete the mission. The *S-33* has been sunk, and he and a small crew of sailors have captured the German submarine, *U-571*. As the crew looks to him for guidance and leadership, he admits to not knowing what to do, prompting the Chief Petty Officer to take him aside. "This is the Navy," he tells Tyler, "where a commanding officer is a mighty and terrible thing." He then challenges him to take up the mantle of leadership, informing him that he's "the skipper now, and the skipper always knows what to do whether he does or not." Following this admonition, Lt. Tyler does take up the challenge and proves that he is capable of keeping focused on the overall mission.

The following chapter continues to explore the issues of management and leadership that are raised within *U-571*, outlining the role of management in organizations and providing an overview of each of those roles. Managers at varying levels of the organization take part in strategic planning; organizing activities; leading, guiding, and motivating others; as well as controlling those activities. Furthermore, the chapter outlines the various roles that managers must undertake as well as the various skills necessary to become an effective manager. As such, the chapter should help you to understand how you too can be an effective manager and how you can learn from those who guide Lt. Tyler.

U-571/Corbis

- In the clip, we see three types of managers: Capt. Dahlgren, Lt. Tyler, and CPO Klough. What type of planning do you think each is involved in and why?
- Both Capt. Dahlgren and CPO Klough speak to Lt. Tyler about the power that comes with leadership. What types of power do you believe the two men are discussing, and which type of power do you think Lt. Tyler may have used before this mission?
- What type of leadership styles do you see in the film clip, and what type of managerial roles are at play?
- The chapter outlines the three basic sets of skills that managers require to be successful. Assess Lt. Tyler based on these skills.

The Role of Management

1 What is the role of management?

management
The process of guiding the development, maintenance, and allocation of resources to attain organizational goals.

Management is the process of guiding the development, maintenance, and allocation of resources to attain organizational goals. Managers are the people in an organization responsible for developing and carrying out this management process. Management is dynamic by nature and evolves to meet needs and constraints in the organization's internal and external environments. In a global marketplace where the rate of change is rapidly increasing, flexibility and adaptability are crucial to the managerial process. This process is based in four key functional areas of the organization: planning, organizing, leading, and controlling. Although these activities are discussed separately in the chapter, they actually form a tightly integrated cycle of thoughts and actions.

From this perspective, the managerial process can be described as (1) anticipating potential problems or opportunities and designing plans to deal with them, (2) coordinating and allocating the resources needed to implement plans, (3) guiding personnel through the implementation process, and (4) reviewing results and making any necessary changes. This last stage provides information to be used in ongoing planning efforts, and thus the cycle starts over again. The four functions are highly interdependent, with managers often performing more than one of them at a time and each of them many times over the course of a normal workday.

efficiency
Using the least amount of resources to accomplish the organization's goals.

effectiveness
The ability to produce the desired result or good.

The four management functions can help managers increase organizational efficiency and effectiveness. **Efficiency** is using the least possible amount of resources to get work done, whereas **effectiveness** is the ability to produce a desired result. Managers need to be both efficient and effective in order to achieve organizational goals. For example, for many years, General Motors' productivity lagged behind its Japanese rivals, but after the turnaround plans of CEO Rick Wagoner took hold, GM's most efficient plant in Ontario began making a car every 15.68 hours. To put this in perspective, the automaker with the highest productivity overall prior to this was Honda, which averaged 21.13 hours to assemble a car. That means GM is able to do the same work—or more—with fewer people and less money.[1] Unfortunately, however, the Ontario plant has been efficiently turning out cars that are not on GM's top list of sellers, which means that even though the plant was operating efficiently, it was not operating effectively. As a result, GM chose to close the Ontario plant.[2]

When Rick Wagoner took the CEO position at GM, he outlined an agenda for turning around the North America division (planning) which was built around four main goals: build great cars, revitalize sales, cut costs, and fix health care. Because Wagoner framed the plan in a simple, direct way, employees throughout the company now know the direction of the turnaround strategy, and his methodical personality and focus on achievement have inspired loyalty in his subordinates (leading). For years, GM had talked about the need to be competitive, but not much ever seemed to change (poor leadership) until Wagoner set clear and easily understood performance targets that employees and the company must meet (control). So even though the Ontario plant met performance targets for productivity, management closed the plant because it wasn't helping the company achieve its sales targets (control). To make sure that GM builds car models that customers want to buy (effectiveness), Wagoner redirected capital spending and engineering resources toward the development of more fuel-efficient vehicles (organizing).

© David Paul Morris/Getty Images/Newscom

CONCEPT in action

To create greater collaboration between the visual-effects and computer-gaming divisions of LucasFilm Ltd., film producer and company chairman George Lucas built a $350 million digital-arts studio in Presidio Park to house the creative geniuses behind *Star Wars: Episode III* and *Star Wars Galaxies*. The two divisions' animators and interactive designers now share not only the same office space, but also the same technological design tools and corporate culture. How do Lucas's planning and organizing decisions increase organizational efficiency and effectiveness at LucasFilm?

EXHIBIT 6.1   What Managers Do and Why

Good management consists of these four activities:		Which results in	And leads to
Planning • Set objectives and state mission • Examine alternatives • Determine needed resources • Create strategies to reach objectives **Organizing** • Design jobs and specify tasks • Create organizational structure • Staff positions • Coordinate work activities • Set policies and procedures • Allocate resources	**Leading** • Lead and motivate employees to accomplish organizational goals • Communicate with employees • Resolve conflicts • Manage change **Controlling** • Measure performance • Compare performance to standards • Take necessary action to improve performance	Organizational efficiency and effectiveness	Achievement of organizational mission and objectives

"A lot of success in this business," says Wagoner, "is having a big plan and implementing it better than the next guy."[3] As this example and Exhibit 6.1 show, good management uses the four management functions to increase a company's efficiency and effectiveness, which leads to the accomplishment of organizational goals and objectives. Let's look more closely at what each of the management functions entails.

CONCEPT check

Define the term *management*.

What are the four key functions of managers?

What is the difference between efficiency and effectiveness?

Planning

Planning begins by anticipating potential problems or opportunities the organization may encounter. Managers then design strategies to solve current problems, prevent future problems, or take advantage of opportunities. These strategies serve as the foundation for goals, objectives, policies, and procedures. Put simply, planning is deciding what needs to be done to achieve organizational objectives, identifying when and how it will be done, and determining by whom it should be done. Effective planning requires extensive information about the external business environment in which the firm competes, as well as its internal environment.

There are four basic types of planning: strategic, tactical, operational, and contingency. Most of us use these different types of planning in our own lives. Some plans are very broad and long term (more strategic in nature), such as planning to attend graduate school after earning a bachelor's degree. Some plans are much more specific and short term (more operational in nature), such as planning to spend a few hours in the library this weekend. Your short-term plans support your long-term plans. If you study now, you have a better chance of achieving some future goal, such as getting a job interview or attending graduate school. Like you, organizations tailor their plans to meet the requirements of future situations or events. A summary of the four types of planning appears in Exhibit 6.2 on the next page.

Strategic planning involves creating long-range (one to five years), broad goals for the organization and determining what resources will be needed to accomplish those goals. An evaluation of external environmental factors such as economic, technological, and social issues is critical to successful strategic planning. Strategic plans, such as the organization's long-term mission, are formulated by top-level managers and put into action at lower levels in the organization. For example, when Mickey Drexler took over as CEO of J. Crew, the company was floundering and had been recently purchased by a private equity group.[4] One of Drexler's first moves was to change the strategic direction of the company by moving it out of the crowded trend-following retail segment, where it was competing with stores like Gap, American Eagle, and Abercrombie & Fitch, and back into the preppie, luxury segment where it began. Rather than trying to sell abundant inventory to a mass market, J. Crew now cultivates scarcity, making sure items sell out early rather than hit the sale rack later in the season. The company is also limiting the number of new stores it opens for the next two years, but planning to double the number of stores in the next five to six years. Drexler is

2 What are the four types of planning?

planning
The process of deciding what needs to be done to achieve organizational objectives; identifying when and how it will be done; and determining by whom it should be done.

strategic planning
The process of creating long-range (one to five years), broad goals for the organization and determining what resources will be needed to accomplish those goals.

EXHIBIT 6.2   Types of Planning

Type of Planning	Time Frame	Level of Management	Extent of Coverage	Purpose and Goal	Breadth of Content	Accuracy/ Predictability
Strategic	1–5 years	Top management (CEO, vice presidents, directors, division heads)	External environment and entire organization	Establish mission and long-term goals	Broad and general	High degree of uncertainty
Tactical	Less than 1 year	Middle management	Strategic business units	Establish mid-range goals for implementation	More specific	Moderate degree of certainty
Operational	Current	Supervisory management	Geographic and functional divisions	Implement and activate specific objectives	Specific and concrete	Reasonable degree of certainty
Contingency	When an event occurs or a situation demands	Top and middle management	External environment and entire organization	Meet unforeseen challenges and opportunities	Both broad and detailed	Reasonable degree of certainty once event or situation occurs

even entertaining the idea of an initial public offering (IPO) of stock if revenues continue to soar. Strategic planning is not only for large companies, however. Learn how one small company changed its strategy and opened up a world of opportunity, described in the Catching the Entrepreneurial Spirit box on the next page.

mission
An organization's purpose and reason for existing; its long-term goals.

mission statement
A formal document that states an organization's purpose and reason for existing and describes its basic philosophy.

tactical planning
The process of beginning to implement a strategic plan by addressing issues of coordination and allocating resources to different parts of the organization; has a shorter time frame (less than one year) and more specific objectives than strategic planning.

An organization's **mission** is formalized in its **mission statement**, a document that states the purpose of the organization and its reason for existing. For example, Ben & Jerry's mission statement addresses three fundamental issues and states the basic philosophy of the company (see Exhibit 6.3).

In all organizations, plans and goals at the tactical and operational levels should clearly support the organization's mission statement.

Tactical planning begins the implementation of strategic plans. Tactical plans have a shorter (less than one year) time frame than strategic plans and more specific objectives designed to support the broader strategic goals. Tactical plans begin to address issues of coordinating and allocating resources to different parts of the organization.

Under Mickey Drexler, many new tactical plans were implemented to support J. Crew's new strategic direction. For example, he severely limited the number of stores opened each year, with only nine new openings in the first two years of his tenure (he closed seven). Instead, he is investing the company's resources in developing a product line that communicates J. Crew's new strategic direction. Drexler has dumped trend-driven apparel because it did not meet the company's new

---

EXHIBIT 6.3   Ben & Jerry's Mission Statement

"Ben & Jerry's is founded on and dedicated to a sustainable corporate concept of linked prosperity. Our mission consists of three interrelated parts:

Product Mission
To make, distribute & sell the finest quality all natural ice cream & euphoric concoctions with a continued commitment to incorporating wholesome, natural ingredients and promoting business practices that respect the Earth and the Environment.

Economic Mission
To operate the Company on a sustainable financial basis of profitable growth, increasing value for our stakeholders & expanding opportunities for development and career growth for our employees.

Social Mission
To operate the Company in a way that actively recognizes the central role that business plays in society by initiating innovative ways to improve the quality of life locally, nationally & internationally.

Central to the mission of Ben & Jerry's is the belief that all three parts must thrive equally in a manner that commands deep respect for individuals in and outside the company and supports the communities of which they are a part."

Source: "Our Mission Statement," **http://www.benjerry.com/our_company/our_mission**. Copyright © Ben & Jerry's Homemade, Inc. All rights reserved. Reproduced by permission.

Changing Strategy Can Change Your Opportunities

For more than 50 years, Gordon Bernard, a printing company in Milford, Ohio, has focused exclusively on printing fund-raising calendars for a variety of clients, like cities, schools, scout troops, and fire departments. The company's approximately 4,000 clients nationwide, 10 percent of which have been with the company since its inception, generated $4 million in revenue in 2006. In order to better serve customers, company president Bob Sherman invested $650,000 in the purchase of a Xerox iGEN3 digital color press so that the company could produce in-house a part of its calendar product that had been outsourced. The high-tech press has done more for the company than simply reduce costs, however.

The new press gives the company four-color printing capability for the first time in its history, and that has led the management of Gordon Bernard to rethink the company's strategy. The machine excels at short runs, which means that small batches of an item can be printed at a much lower cost than on a traditional press. The press also has the capability to customize every piece that rolls off the machine. For example, if a pet store wants to print 3,000 direct-mail pieces, every single postcard can have a personalized greeting and text. Pieces targeted to bird owners can feature pictures of birds, whereas the dog owners' brochure will contain dog pictures. Text and pictures can be personalized for owners of show dogs or overweight cats or iguanas.

Bob Sherman has created a new division to oversee the implementation, training, marketing, and creative aspects of the new production process. The company has even changed how it thinks of itself. No longer does Gordon Bernard consider itself a printing firm, but as a marketing services company with printing capabilities. That change in strategy is prompting the company to seek more commercial work. For example, Gordon Bernard will help clients of its new services develop customer databases from their existing information, and identify additional customer information they might want to collect. Even though calendar sales account for 97 percent of the firm's revenues, that business is seasonal and leaves large amounts of unused capacity in the off-peak periods. Managers hope to see the new division contribute 10 percent of total revenue in the next couple of years.[5]

Critical Thinking Questions

- What type of planning do you think Gordon Bernard is doing?
- Because Gordon Bernard's strategy changed only after it purchased the iGEN3, does the shift constitute strategic planning? Why or why not?

© Rubberball/Getty Images

---

image. He even cut some million-dollar-volume items. In their place, he has created limited editions of a handful of garments that he thinks will be popular, many of which fall into his new luxury strategy. For example, J. Crew now buys shoes directly from the same shoe manufacturers that produce footwear for designers like Prada and Gucci. In general, J. Crew has drastically tightened inventories, a move designed to keep reams of clothes from ending up on sale racks and to break its shoppers' habit of waiting for discounts.

This part of the plan is generating great results. Prior to Drexler's change in strategy, half of J. Crew's clothing sold at a discount. After implementing tactical plans aimed to change that situation, only a small percentage now does. The shift to limited editions and tighter inventory controls has not reduced the amount of new merchandise, however. On the contrary, Drexler has created a J. Crew bridal collection, a jewelry line, and Crew Cuts, a line of kids' clothing. The results of Drexler's tactical plans have been impressive. J. Crew saw same-store sales rise 17 percent in one year.[6]

Operational planning creates specific standards, methods, policies, and procedures that are used in specific functional areas of the organization. Operational objectives are current, narrow, and resource-focused. They are designed to help guide and control the implementation of tactical plans. For years, the motto of UPS was, "We run the tightest ship in the shipping business," and that's probably still the case today. Every day, UPS delivers 15 million packages around the world. That's more than twice as many as its key rival, FedEx. Handling that volume of goods requires a very smooth operations plan. One part of that is the company's detailed manual of rules and routines for drivers called "340 Methods." In addition to the 12-step process for deliveries, the manual contains prescribed routines and rules about things like:

- how to get in and out of the truck
- where to get gas (always in a station on the right side of the road)
- how to hold the truck key (on the ring finger)
- how to select packages in 15.5 seconds
- the pace you walk at for deliveries (walk briskly, never run)
- announce yourself (smile and give out a Hello? UPS!)

These and the rest of the methods in the manual help drivers move throughout the day in a focused manner, which enables them to handle the hundreds of packages that pass through their trucks each shift.[7]

operational planning
The process of creating specific standards, methods, policies, and procedures that are used in specific functional areas of the organization; helps guide and control the implementation of tactical plans.

Indra Nooyi made history recently by becoming PepsiCo's first woman CEO. Since joining Pepsi as vice president of strategic planning in the 1990s, the Indian-born executive has played a major role in leading the company beyond sugary soft drinks to healthier products. Nooyi's push to broaden PepsiCo's product line was nearly prescient, as the company's acquisition of Tropicana and Quaker Oats positioned the cola maker to capitalize on the healthy-foods trend. Which types of planning are associated with top management?

© MANPREET ROMANA/AFP/Getty Images

The key to effective planning is anticipating future situations and events. Yet even the best-prepared organization must sometimes cope with unforeseen circumstances such as a natural disaster, an act of terrorism, or a radical new technology. Therefore, many companies have developed **contingency plans** that identify alternative courses of action for very unusual or crisis situations. The contingency plan typically stipulates the chain of command, standard operating procedures, and communication channels the organization will use during an emergency.

An effective contingency plan can make or break a company. Consider the example of Northwest Airlines. Anticipating a strike by its mechanics, Andy Roberts, Northwest's executive vice president of operations, was the architect of the company's strike contingency plan, a key part of which was finding replacement workers. Managers developed and offered a six-week training seminar to veteran aviation mechanics who had been laid off during the recent industry downturn. Outside contractors were eligible as well. Northwest had no trouble lining up the 1,200 replacement mechanics the company estimated it would require to keep operating during a strike.[8] The company achieved its goal of being able to continue operations if its mechanics walked off the job, which did occur in August 2005. During the initial days of the strike, over half of Northwest flights continued to arrive on time, and the airline reported only minor glitches.[9] One month into the strike, the company began offering permanent jobs to its replacement workers.[10]

contingency plans
Plans that identify alternative courses of action for very unusual or crisis situations; typically stipulate the chain of command, standard operating procedures, and communication channels the organization will use during an emergency.

CONCEPT check

What is the purpose of planning, and what is needed to do it effectively?

Identify the unique characteristics of each type of planning.

Organizing

A second key function of managers is **organizing**, which is the process of coordinating and allocating a firm's resources in order to carry out its plans. Organizing includes developing a structure for the people, positions, departments, and activities within the firm. Managers can arrange the structural elements of the firm to maximize the flow of information and the efficiency of work processes. They accomplish this by doing the following:

- Dividing up tasks (*division of labor*)
- Grouping jobs and employees (*departmentalization*)
- Assigning authority and responsibilities (*delegation*)

These and other elements of organizational structure are discussed in detail in Chapter 7. In this chapter, however, you should understand the three levels of a managerial hierarchy. This hierarchy is often depicted as a pyramid as in Exhibit 6.4. The fewest managers are found at the highest level of the pyramid. Called **top management**, they are the small group of people at the head of the organization (such as the CEO, president, and vice president). Top-level managers develop *strategic plans* and address long-range issues such as which industries to compete in, how to capture market share, and what to do with profits. These managers design and approve the firm's basic policies and represent the firm to other organizations. They also define the company's values and ethics and thus set the tone for employee standards of behavior. For example, Ken Chenault, the CEO of American Express, has built an extensive program to establish a culture of leadership at Amex. Part of the program includes a high level of straight talk, or what Chenault calls constructive confrontation. He encourages his top managers to engage in open, frank discussions about facts and situations with each other and to give regular, informal feedback to their subordinates. As a result of the direction Chenault has set at American Express, retention of strong performers and scores from employee surveys are high, anchoring the culture of leadership and performance that sets the company apart from its competition.[11]

The second and third tiers of the hierarchy are called **middle management** and **supervisory (first-line) management**, respectively. Middle managers (such as division heads, departmental managers, and regional sales managers) are responsible for beginning the implementation of strategic plans. They design and carry out *tactical plans* in specific areas of the company. They begin the process of allocating resources to meet organizational goals, and they oversee supervisory managers throughout the firm. Supervisors, the most numerous of the managers, are at the bottom of the managerial pyramid. These managers design and carry out *operational plans* for the ongoing daily activities of the firm. They spend a great deal of their time guiding and motivating the employees who actually produce the goods and services.

3 What are the primary functions of managers in organizing activities?

organizing
The process of coordinating and allocating a firm's resources in order to carry out its plans.

top management
The highest level of managers; includes CEOs, presidents, and vice presidents, who develop strategic plans and address long-range issues.

middle management
Managers who design and carry out tactical plans in specific areas of the company.

supervisory (first-line) management
Managers who design and carry out operation plans for the ongoing daily activities of the firm.

CONCEPT check

Explain the managerial function of organizing.

What is the managerial pyramid?

EXHIBIT 6.4   The Managerial Pyramid

Middle management
Regional manager
Division head
Director
Plant manager
Sales manager

Top management
CEO,CFO,COO,CIO
President
Governor
General director

Supervisory (first-line) management
Supervisor
Team leader
Foreman

leadership
The process of guiding and motivating others toward the achievement of organizational goals.

power
The ability to influence others to behave in a particular way.

legitimate power
Power that is derived from an individual's position in an organization.

reward power
Power that is derived from an individual's control over rewards.

coercive power
Power that is derived from an individual's ability to threaten negative outcomes.

expert power
Power that is derived from an individual's extensive knowledge in one or more areas.

referent power
Power that is derived from an individual's personal charisma and the respect and/or admiration the individual inspires

Leading, Guiding, and Motivating Others

Leadership, the third key management function, is the process of guiding and motivating others toward the achievement of organizational goals. Managers are responsible for directing employees on a daily basis as the employees carry out the plans and work within the structure, created by management. Organizations need strong, effective leadership at all levels in order to meet goals and remain competitive.

To be effective leaders, managers must be able to influence others' behaviors. This ability to influence others to behave in a particular way is called **power**. Researchers have identified five primary sources, or bases, of power:

- **Legitimate power**, which is derived from an individual's position in an organization
- **Reward power**, which is derived from an individual's control over rewards
- **Coercive power**, which is derived from an individual's ability to threaten negative outcomes
- **Expert power**, which is derived from an individual's extensive knowledge in one or more areas
- **Referent power**, which is derived from an individual's personal charisma and the respect and/or admiration the individual inspires

Many leaders use a combination of all of these sources of power to influence individuals toward goal achievement. A. G. Lafley gets his legitimate power from his position as CEO of Procter & Gamble. His reward power comes from reviving the company and making the stock more valuable. Also, raises and bonuses for managers who meet their goals is another form of reward power. Lafley is also not hesitant to use his coercive power. He has eliminated thousands of jobs, sold underperforming brands, and killed weak product lines. With nearly 30 years of service to the company, Lafley has a unique authority when it comes to P&G's products, markets, innovations, and customers. He has captained the purchase of

4 How do leadership styles influence a corporate culture?

CONCEPT in action

Muhammad Yunus began a microcredit movement three decades ago when he began providing $27 loans to women in the Bangladeshi village of Jobra during a famine. Since that humble beginning, Yunus's Grameen Bank has grown internationally by providing microloans to more than 7 million people, most of whom are women from developing nations. The microlending revolution spawned a new category of banking and earned Dr. Yunus the Nobel Peace Prize as the "banker to the poor." What is Dr. Yunus's primary source of power?

© AP Images/Thanassis Stavrakis

CONCEPT in action

The Walt Disney Company's famous 1990s turnaround—one characterized by blockbuster animations like *The Lion King* and mega-acquisitions of ABC and ESPN—is widely credited to the leadership of former CEO Michael Eisner. But by 2004, Disney's prince charming was butting heads with shareholders and Disney relatives alike, as power struggles surfaced over stalled momentum and Eisner's micromanagement and autocratic leadership style. Mired in controversy, Eisner finally resigned, severing all ties with the company. Under what conditions can autocratic leadership become detrimental?

leadership style
The relatively consistent way that individuals in leadership positions attempt to influence the behavior of others.

autocratic leaders
Directive leaders who prefer to make decisions and solve problems on their own with little input from subordinates.

participative leaders
Leaders who share decision making with group members and encourage discussion of issues and alternatives; includes democratic, consensual, and consultative styles.

democratic leaders
Leaders who solicit input from all members of the group and then allow the members to make the final decision through a vote.

Clairol, Wella AG, and IAMS, as well as the multibillion-dollar merger with Gillette. As a result, Lafley has a substantial amount of referent power. Lafley is also widely respected, not only by people at P&G, but by the general business community as well. Ann Gillen Lefever, a managing director at Lehman Brothers, said, "Lafley is a leader who is liked. His directives are very simple. He sets a strategy that everybody understands, and that is more difficult than he gets credit for."[12]

Leadership Styles

Individuals in leadership positions tend to be relatively consistent in the way they attempt to influence the behavior of others, meaning that each individual has a tendency to react to people and situations in a particular way. This pattern of behavior is referred to as **leadership style**, and it has significant impact on the performance of an organization. The Customer Satisfaction and Quality box on the next page describes how one woman's unique leadership style is transforming the culture at T-Mobile. As Exhibit 6.5 shows, leadership styles can be placed on a continuum that encompasses three distinct styles: autocratic, participative, and free-rein.

Autocratic leaders are directive leaders, allowing for very little input from subordinates. These leaders prefer to make decisions and solve problems on their own and expect subordinates to implement solutions according to very specific and detailed instructions. In this leadership style, information typically flows in one direction, from manager to subordinate. The military, by necessity, is generally autocratic. When autocratic leaders treat employees with fairness and respect, they may be considered knowledgeable and decisive. But often autocrats are perceived as narrow-minded and heavy-handed in their unwillingness to share power, information, and decision making in the organization. The trend in organizations today is away from the directive, controlling style of the autocratic leader.

Instead, U.S. businesses are looking more and more for **participative leaders**, meaning leaders who share decision making with group members and encourage discussion of issues and alternatives. Participative leaders use a democratic, consensual, consultative style.

Democratic leaders solicit input from all members of the group and then allow the group members to make the final decision through a voting process. This approach works well with highly trained professionals. One company that takes democratic leadership to the extreme end of the spectrum is Ternary Software. The company's 13 employees vote on everything, even pay and incentives, and every decision must be unanimous. The company moved to a democracy

---

EXHIBIT 6.5	Leadership Styles of Managers	
Amount of authority held by the leader →←		
Autocratic Style	**Participative Style (democratic, consensual, consultative)**	**Free-Rein Style (laissez-faire)**
• Manager makes most decisions and acts in authoritative manner.	• Manager shares decision making with group members and encourages teamwork.	• Manager turns over virtually all authority and control to group.
• Manager is usually unconcerned about subordinates' attitudes toward decisions.	• Manager encourages discussion of issues and alternatives.	• Members of group are presented with task and given freedom to accomplish it.
• Emphasis is on getting task accomplished.	• Manager is concerned about subordinates' ideas and attitudes.	• Approach works well with highly motivated, experienced, educated personnel.
• Approach is used mostly by military officers and some production line supervisors.	• Manager coaches subordinates and helps coordinate efforts.	• Approach is found in high-tech firms, labs, and colleges.
	• Approach is found in many successful organizations.	
Amount of authority held by group members →		

Part 3: Managing Organizations

Working to Please

Before leaving Wal-Mart to run the sales and customer service at T-Mobile, Sue Nokes decided to tour a few of the telecommunication giant's call centers to get a sense of the job. She was horrified. Daily absenteeism was 12 percent, and annual turnover was 100 percent. Instead of having a regular desk, employees used hot desks, dragging their stuff from workstation to workstation depending on what was available when their shift started. Nonetheless, Nokes took the job, saying, "There's a new sheriff in town."

One of Nokes's first initiatives was a listening campaign. She asked employees what customers were complaining about. She asked employees what they thought should be improved in the workplace. She assigned employees to desks, raised salaries, and rolled out a robust training program. Understanding that attitude is not something you can teach, she began hiring for attitude rather than experience. She drafted standards and began measuring employee performance and call quality. Most important, she focused on the elements that were in the employees' control.

Employees responded favorably to the changes. Today, pep rallies pop up whenever Sue Nokes makes site visits. Representatives wear hot-pink clothes (hot pink is the company color), dye their hair hot pink, and write things like "I Love Sue Nokes"

on their faces with athletic paint. When Nokes arrived at one call center, an employee shouted from the crowd, "Marry me, Sue!"

Nokes uses basic principles to get her employees to care about their customers: she listens to her front-line employees; she develops clear career paths so those employees can achieve their personal goals; she provides training and coaching so employees can do their jobs better; and she celebrates success in terms of what the customer thinks is success. And Nokes's recipe is successful with customers as well as employees. Since Nokes joined the company, T-Mobile has won top place in J.D. Power's rankings of customer care in wireless communication six times in a row.[13]

Critical Thinking Questions
- What kind of leader is Sue Nokes? Explain.
- Do you think Sue Nokes's leadership style would work in any industry? Why or why not?

after frustrating attempts to use consensus to build a mission statement and a salary system. Employees like the democratic environment. One says, "You don't have to fight and claw to be heard."[14] **Consensual leaders** encourage discussion about issues and then require that all parties involved agree to the final decision. This is the general style used by labor mediators. **Consultative leaders** confer with subordinates before making a decision, but retain the final decision-making authority. This technique has been used to dramatically increase the productivity of assembly-line workers.

The third leadership style, at the opposite end of the continuum from the autocratic style, is **free-rein** or **laissez-faire** (French for "leave it alone") **leadership**. Managers who use this style turn over all authority and control to subordinates. Employees are assigned a task and then given free rein to figure out the best way to accomplish it. The manager doesn't get involved unless asked. Under this approach, subordinates have unlimited freedom as long as they do not violate existing company policies. This approach is also sometimes used with highly trained professionals as in a research laboratory. Gucci CEO Robert Polet uses this approach. He calls it "the art of letting go." Even though some core functional areas are controlled by the head office in London, individual brands are fully responsible for their products and their profits. But even though Polet has delegate control of individual brands, he expects the CEO of each brand to turn in regular reports and create a three-year strategic plan and revise it every year. Polet calls his particular variant of laissez-faire "freedom within a framework."[15]

Although one might at first assume that subordinates would prefer the free-rein style, this approach can have several drawbacks. If free-rein leadership is accompanied by unclear expectations and lack of feedback from the manager, the experience can be frustrating for an employee. Employees may perceive the manager as being uninvolved and indifferent to what is happening or as unwilling or unable to provide the necessary structure, information, and expertise.

There is no one best leadership style. The most effective style for a given situation depends on elements such as the characteristics of the subordinates, the complexity of the task, the source of the leader's power, and the stability of the environment.

Employee Empowerment

Participative and free-rein leaders use a technique called empowerment to share decision-making authority with subordinates. **Empowerment** means giving employees increased autonomy and discretion to make their own decisions, as

consensual leaders
Leaders who encourage discussion about issues and then require that all parties involved agree to the final decision.

consultative leaders
Leaders who confer with subordinates before making a decision, but who retain the final decision-making authority.

free-rein (laissez-faire) leadership
A leadership style in which the leader turns over all authority and control to subordinates.

empowerment
The process of giving employees increased autonomy and discretion to make decisions, as well as control over the resources needed to implement those decisions.

CONCEPT in action

What color is FedEx's corporate culture? Purple, of course. To ensure that its packages are delivered right every time, the express-delivery giant has created an awards program to recognize employees who go the extra mile in winning customers' loyalty. Dubbed the "Purple Promise," the program singles out workers who find creative ways to track lost packages, help overloaded couriers, and meet out-of-the-ordinary customer demands. Purple Promise winners receive exciting rewards, such as tours of Graceland. How does the Purple Promise promote a culture of empowerment at FedEx?

well as control over the resources needed to implement those decisions. When decision-making power is shared at all levels of the organization, employees feel a greater sense of ownership in, and responsibility for, organizational outcomes.

Management use of employee empowerment is on the rise. This increased level of involvement comes from the realization that people at all levels in the organization possess unique knowledge, skills, and abilities that can be of great value to the company. Managers at Infosys noticed that 20-something workers were keeping their opinions to themselves, so the company has started a program to reach out to younger employees. Top-performing younger workers now gain a seat on the company's management council, where they are expected to engage in frank discussions with older workers on all aspects of the company.[16]

corporate culture
The set of attitudes, values, and standards that distinguishes one organization from another.

CONCEPT in action

Like other Big Three automakers, Ford Motor Company is losing market share and hemorrhaging layoffs in the face of Toyota's astounding ascendancy. According to Chairman Bill Ford Jr., a thorough greening of Ford's corporate culture is the company's only hope. The famously granola-crunching CEO is pouring billions of dollars into eco-friendly factories and institutionalizing innovation-oriented processes around hybrids, biodegradable materials, and hydrogen-powered cars. Is a "greener" culture fronted by spokes-Muppet Kermit the Frog compatible with Ford's tradition-rich heritage that dates back to the Model T?

Corporate Culture

The leadership style of managers in an organization is usually indicative of the underlying philosophy, or values, of the organization. The set of attitudes, values, and standards of behavior that distinguishes one organization from another is called **corporate culture**. A corporate culture evolves over time and is based on the accumulated history of the organization, including the vision of the founders. It is also influenced by the dominant leadership style within the organization. Evidence of a company's culture is seen in its heroes (e.g., Andy Grove of Intel), myths (stories about the company that are passed from employee to employee), symbols (e.g., the Nike swoosh), and ceremonies. Corporate culture is critical for providers of service, especially luxury services, like five-star hotels. At the Four Seasons, the company has a solid culture of taking care of its employees as well as its guests. Every applicant, from laundry attendant to manager, goes through four interviews during which current employees assess the applicant's outlook. Founder Isadore Sharp says, "I can teach anyone to be a waiter, but you can't change an ingrained poor attitude. We look for people who say, 'I'd be proud to be a doorman.'"[17] One of the most powerful tools in strengthening the culture is guest stays. Every year, employees get free rooms (the number of nights depends on your years of service). Michelle De Rochemont, a Maui waitress for 17 years, says, "You're never treated like just an employee. You're a guest. You come back from those trips on fire. You want to do so much for the guest."[18] The result of Four Seasons management practices is a cultlike following, not only among its clientele, but more importantly, among its employees. Sometimes after an entrepreneur has created a successful company it is necessary to change both the corporate culture and strategy to successfully grow. Read the Managing Change box on the next page to see why a new CEO was hired at Zipcar.

CONCEPT check

How do leaders influence other people's behavior?

How can managers empower employees?

What is corporate culture?

Controlling

5 How do organizations control activities?

controlling
The process of assessing the organization's progress toward accomplishing its goals; includes monitoring the implementation of a plan and correcting deviations from the plan.

The fourth key function that managers perform is **controlling**. Controlling is the process of assessing the organization's progress toward accomplishing its goals. It includes monitoring the implementation of a plan and correcting deviations from that plan. As Exhibit 6.6 shows, controlling can be visualized as a cyclical process made up of five stages:

1. Setting performance standards (goals)
2. Measuring performance
3. Comparing actual performance to established performance standards
4. Taking corrective action (if necessary)
5. Using information gained from the process to set future performance standards

Performance standards are the levels of performance the company wants to attain. These goals are based on its strategic, tactical, and operational plans. The most effective performance standards state a measurable behavioral objective that can be achieved in a specified time frame. For example, the performance objective for the sales division of a company could be stated as "$100,000 in gross sales for the month of January." Each individual employee in that division would also have a specified performance goal. Actual firm, division, or individual performance can be measured against desired

© Stockbyte/Getty Images

Zipcar Zigs and Zags Before Setting its Pace

Unless you live in a major metropolitan area you may not have heard of Zipcar, but the new CEO hopes that doesn't last long. Zipcar members can reserve a car by phone or online for an hour, a day, or longer. Once a confirmation number and car have been assigned, members simply go to a Zipcar location (a parking lot or gas station) and use their membership access card to unlock the reserved car but only for the time period that corresponds to the reservation. Gas and insurance are included in the price. Once the rental period is over, the renter simply returns the car to its original location. No paperwork, no desks, nothing traditional about this rental process—which made Zipcar very successful with college students and city dwellers.

Started in Boston, Zipcar soon had fleets in New York and Washington, D.C., generating $2 million in annual sales. Founder Robin Chase started expansion plans to move into other cities, but for all of its success and appeal, Zipcar was losing money. Chase's board of outside investors asked her to step down as CEO, saying, "While we all think Robin did a fabulous job starting the company, the sense at the board level was that we needed a different type of manager for the next stage."

Zipcar hired Scott Griffith to be the new CEO. One of the first things Griffith did as CEO was halt Chase's expansion plans and focus first on getting things right in Boston. Griffith determined that, to be profitable, the city needed 150 to 200 cars, and at least 40 members per car. To support that membership volume, some things had to change. Before, Zipcar had simply been parking wherever there was a spot. Even though the system had been working, it would most certainly break down when 6,000 to 8,000 members were involved, so Griffith divided the city into 12 zones and arranged for regular parking areas for each. Then marketing teams began to target people in each zone on a very personal, neighborhood level. Griffith enlisted the technology team to develop a better system to generate data on car usage and to track when renters went over the mileage limits. And he also began changing the look of the fleet, buying models other than Mini Coopers and Jettas. Griffith expanded the fleet to include vehicles such as BMWs for baby boomers, four-wheel-drive cars for ski trips, and pickup trucks for weekend DIYers.

After only a few years at the helm, Griffith acquired Zipcar's biggest rival, Flexcar; grew the company to 15 cities and 200 employees; raised $35 million in venture capital; and is on track to hit $100 million in annual sales. Now that the company fundamentals are strong, he'll be able to shift his focus from setting strategy and obsessing over the numbers to managing his executives and developing the corporate culture.[19]

Critical Thinking Questions
- Most of Griffith's changes fall into which category of planning? Explain.
- What do you think is the difference between the leadership required to start a company and the management required to sustain a company?

performance standards to see if a gap exists between the desired level of performance and the actual level of performance. If a performance gap does exist, the reason for it must be determined and corrective action taken.

Feedback is essential to the process of control. Most companies have a reporting system that identifies areas where performance standards are not being met. A feedback system helps managers detect problems before they get out of hand. If a problem exists, the managers take corrective action. Toyota uses a simple but effective control system on its automobile assembly lines. Each worker

EXHIBIT 6.6   The Control Process

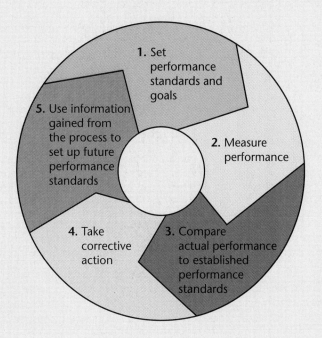

1. Set performance standards and goals
2. Measure performance
3. Compare actual performance to established performance standards
4. Take corrective action
5. Use information gained from the process to set up future performance standards

serves as the customer for the process just before his or her process. Each worker is empowered to act as a quality control inspector. If a part is defective or not installed properly, the next worker won't accept it. Any worker can alert the supervisor to a problem by tugging on a rope that turns on a warning light (i.e., feedback). If the problem isn't corrected, the worker can stop the entire assembly line.

Why is controlling such an important part of a manager's job? First, it helps managers to determine the success of the other three functions: planning, organizing, and leading. Second, control systems direct employee behavior toward achieving organizational goals. Third, control systems provide a means of coordinating employee activities and integrating resources throughout the organization.

CONCEPT check

Describe the control process.

Why is the control process important to the success of the organization?

Managerial Roles

6 What roles do managers take on in different organizational settings?

informational roles
A manager's activities as an information gatherer, an information disseminator, or a spokesperson for the company.

interpersonal roles
A manager's activities as a figurehead, company leader, or liaison.

decisional roles
A manager's activities as an entrepreneur, resource allocator, conflict resolver, or negotiator.

In carrying out the responsibilities of planning, organizing, leading, and controlling, managers take on many different roles. A role is a set of behavioral expectations, or a set of activities that a person is expected to perform. Managers' roles fall into three basic categories: *informational roles, interpersonal roles,* and *decisional roles*. These roles are summarized in Exhibit 6.7. In an **informational role**, the manager may act as an information gatherer, an information distributor, or a spokesperson for the company. For example, when Steve Jobs delivers his annual speech at Apple's shareholder meeting, he is fulfilling an informational role *(spokesperson)*. A manager's **interpersonal roles** are based on various interactions with other people. Depending on the situation, a manager may need to act as a figurehead, a company leader, or a liaison. When Jobs attends Comdex, the annual technology trade show, he is acting in the interpersonal role *(figurehead)*. When acting in a **decisional role**, a manager may have to think like an entrepreneur, make decisions about resource allocation, help resolve conflicts, or negotiate compromises. When Jobs decided to invest money and staff in developing the iPhone, he was fulfilling a decisional role *(resource allocator)*.

EXHIBIT 6.7	**The Many Roles That Managers Play in an Organization**	
Role	**Description**	**Example**
Informational Roles		
Monitor	Seeks out and gathers information relevant to the organization.	Finding out about legal restrictions on new product technology.
Disseminator	Provides information where it is needed in the organization.	Providing current production figures to workers on the assembly line.
Spokesperson	Transmits information to people outside the organization.	Representing the company at a shareholders' meeting.
Interpersonal Roles		
Figurehead	Represents the company in a symbolic way.	Cutting the ribbon at ceremony for the opening of a new building.
Leader	Guides and motivates employees to achieve organizational goals.	Helping subordinates to set monthly performance goals.
Liaison	Acts as a go-between among individuals inside and outside the organization.	Representing the retail sales division of the company at a regional sales meeting.
Decisional Roles		
Entrepreneur	Searches out new opportunities and initiates change.	Implementing a new production process using new technology.
Disturbance handler	Handles unexpected events and crises.	Handling a crisis situation such as a fire.
Resource allocator	Designates the use of financial, human, and other organizational resources.	Approving the funds necessary to purchase computer equipment and hire personnel.
Negotiator	Represents the company at negotiating processes.	Participating in salary negotiations with union representatives.

Managerial Decision Making

In every function performed, role taken on, and set of skills applied, a manager is a decision maker. Decision making means choosing among alternatives. Decision making occurs in response to the identification of a problem or an opportunity. The decisions managers make fall into two basic categories: programmed and nonprogrammed. **Programmed decisions** are made in response to routine situations that occur frequently in a variety of settings throughout an organization. For example, the need to hire new personnel is a common situation for most organizations. Therefore, standard procedures for recruitment and selection are developed and followed in most companies.

Infrequent, unforeseen, or very unusual problems and opportunities require **nonprogrammed decisions** by managers. Because these situations are unique and complex, the manager rarely has a precedent to follow. For example, when Hurricane Katrina was forecasted to make landfall, Thomas Oreck, CEO of the vacuum manufacturer that bears his name, had to make a series of nonprogrammed decisions. Oreck's corporate headquarters were in New Orleans and its primary manufacturing facility was in Long Beach, Mississippi. Before the storm hit, Oreck transferred its computer systems and call-center operations to backup locations in Colorado and planned to move headquarters to Long Beach. The storm, however, brutally hit both locations. Oreck executives began searching for lost employees, tracking down generators, assembling temporary housing for workers, and making deals with UPS to begin distributing its product (UPS brought food and water to Oreck from Atlanta and took vacuums back to the company's distribution center there). All of these decisions were made in the middle of a very challenging crisis environment.

Whether a decision is programmed or nonprogrammed, managers typically follow five steps in the decision-making process, as illustrated in Exhibit 6.8:

1. Recognize or define the problem or opportunity. Although it is more common to focus on problems because of their obvious negative effects, managers who do not take advantage of new opportunities may lose competitive advantage to other firms.
2. Gather information so as to identify possible solutions or actions.

© AP Images/Stuart Ramson

When A. G. Lafley took the helm at Procter & Gamble in 2000, the consumer-products leader was burdened with too many brands, slumping shares, and dizzying organizational change. Instead of trying to develop the next big thing, the P&G lifer retrained management's attention on dependable winners like Tide, Pampers, and Crest, employing a back-to-basics strategy that included the $57 billion acquisition of Gillette. The CEO's quiet-but-decisive demeanor is a hit with company managers. What roles and decisions are essential to good leadership?

programmed decisions
Decisions made in response to frequently occurring routine situations.

nonprogrammed decisions
Responses to infrequent, unforeseen, or very unusual problems and opportunities where the manager does not have a precedent to follow in decision making.

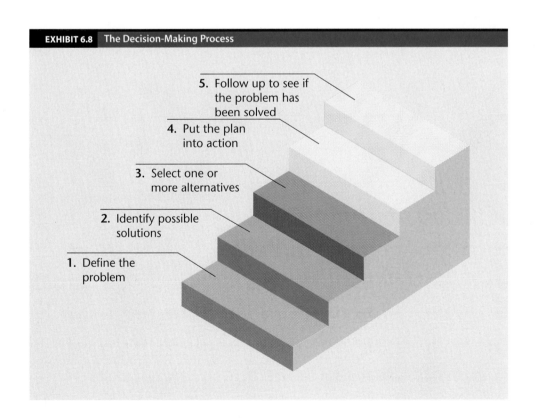

EXHIBIT 6.8   The Decision-Making Process

5. Follow up to see if the problem has been solved
4. Put the plan into action
3. Select one or more alternatives
2. Identify possible solutions
1. Define the problem

3. Select one or more alternatives after evaluating the strengths and weaknesses of each possibility.
4. Put the chosen plan into action.
5. Gather information to obtain feedback on the effectiveness of the chosen plan.

CONCEPT check

What are the three types of managerial roles?

Give examples of things managers might do when acting in each of the different types of roles.

List the five steps in the decision-making process.

It can be easy (and dangerous) for managers to get stuck at any stage of the decision-making process. For example, managers can become paralyzed while evaluating the options. For the United States Marines Corps (USMC), massaging the data too long can be risky, even deadly. To avoid "analysis paralysis," the USMC uses the 70 percent solution: if you have 70 percent of the information, have done 70 percent of the analysis, and feel 70 percent confident, then move.[20]

Managerial Skills

7 What set of managerial skills is necessary for managerial success?

In order to be successful in planning, organizing, leading, and controlling, managers must use a wide variety of skills. A *skill* is the ability to do something proficiently. Managerial skills fall into three basic categories: technical, human relations, and conceptual skills. The degree to which each type of skill is used depends on the level of the manager's position as seen in Exhibit 6.9. Additionally, in an increasingly global marketplace, it pays for managers to develop a special set of skills to deal with global management issues.

Technical Skills

technical skills
A manager's specialized areas of knowledge and expertise, as well as the ability to apply that knowledge.

Specialized areas of knowledge and expertise and the ability to apply that knowledge make up a manager's **technical skills**. Preparing a financial statement, programming a computer, designing an office building, and analyzing market research are all examples of technical skills. These types

| EXHIBIT 6.9 | The Importance of Managerial Skills at Different Management Levels |

	Conceptual Skills	Human Relations Skills	Technical Skills
Top Management			
Middle Management			
Supervisory Management			

Very important   Not as important

of skills are especially important for supervisory managers because they work closely with employees who are producing the goods and/or services of the firm. When Robert Polet was hired as the CEO of Gucci, many people wondered if he was the best choice. That's because not only did Polet have no experience in fashion, he was coming out of one of the biggest packaged consumer-goods companies in the world—Unilever. The lead story in the *New York Times* carried the lead "Can the emperor of ice cream survive under the hot lights of fashion?" (One of Unilever's brands is Ben & Jerry's.) One of Gucci's board members defends its hiring decision by saying, "There was a very important misunderstanding about the nature of the job. It wasn't about choosing someone to design dresses." Indeed, the job was about management, and Polet is succeeding. Since he took the helm at Gucci, sales are up 16 percent, brands had fewer markdowns for sales, and he's driven the operating margin from 3 to 15 percent.[21]

Conceptual Skills

Conceptual skills include the ability to view the organization as a whole, understand how the various parts are interdependent, and assess how the organization relates to its external environment. These skills allow managers to evaluate situations and develop alternative courses of action. Good conceptual skills are especially necessary for managers at the top of the management pyramid where strategic planning takes place.

Human Relations Skills

Human relations skills are the interpersonal skills managers use to accomplish goals through the use of human resources. This set of skills includes the ability to understand human behavior, to communicate effectively with others, and to motivate individuals to accomplish their objectives. Giving positive feedback to employees, being sensitive to their individual needs, and showing a willingness to empower subordinates are all examples of good human relations skills. Identifying and promoting managers with human relations skills is important for companies. A manager with little or no people skills can end up using an authoritarian leadership style and alienating employees.

Marvel Comics earned billions for Sony and Fox by licensing out Spider Man and the X-Men for box office success. Now the comic-book giant hopes to make bank on its famous characters with the launch of its own film company, Marvel Studios. Despite high expectations, it may take super strength for Marvel chief David Maisel to turn B-list superheroes like Iron Man and the Incredible Hulk into big-screen superstars. What managerial skills are needed to transform a book publisher into a Hollywood film studio?

CONCEPT check

Define the basic managerial skills.

How important is each of these skill sets at the different levels of the management pyramid?

Trends in Management and Leadership

Four important trends in management today are: crisis management, outside directors, the growing use of information technology, and the increasing need for global management skills.

Crisis Management

Crises, both internal and external, can hit even the best-managed organization. Sometimes organizations can anticipate crises, in which case managers develop contingency plans, and sometimes they can't. Take, for example, the sudden death of McDonald's CEO Jim Cantalupo. The company had a solid succession plan in place and immediately named Charlie Bell as new CEO. Only a few months later, Bell announced that he had terminal cancer. Even though the company had prepared for the event of its leader's untimely death, surely it couldn't have anticipated that his successor would also be stricken by a terminal illness at almost the same time.

Not all crises are unanticipated. Some crises are the result of inaction or a culminating effect of bad management. In 2008, the fraudulent actions of a young investment banker caused Société Générale, one of France's largest banks, to lose $7.2 billion. Managers had missed several opportunities to stop the trader. In the months leading up to his exposure, the trader, Jean-Pierre Mustier, was caught with some unusual investment holdings that managers questioned. Mustier would simply say the trades were mistakes. Once the magnitude of the fraudulent trading came to the attention of top executives, they decided to keep the knowledge of the problem to a tight circle of insiders. That only caused greater speculation that the bank would collapse. In the end the bank was able to absorb the financial losses, but it had a tougher task in saving its reputation.[22]

Regardless of whether crises are expected or unexpected, it's nearly impossible for a manager or executive to be completely prepared. Even in the case of Société Générale, where management had an idea of what was going on, it couldn't fully predict the public reaction. Nonetheless, how

8 What trends will affect management in the future?

conceptual skills
A manager's ability to view the organization as a whole, understand how the various parts are interdependent, and assess how the organization relates to its external environment.

human relations skills
A manager's interpersonal skills that are used to accomplish goals through the use of human resources.

a manager handles the situation could mean the difference between disaster, survival, or even financial gain. Ken Chenault, CEO of American Express, says, "We have to remember that reputations are won or lost in a crisis."[23] No matter what the crisis, there are some basic guidelines that managers should follow to minimize the negative outcomes. Managers should not become immobilized by the problem nor ignore it. Managers should face the problem head on. Managers should always tell the truth about the situation and then put the best people on the job to correct the problem. Managers should ask for help if they need it, and finally, managers must learn from the experience to avoid the same problem in the future.[24] Exhibit 6.10 shows what CEOs learned about crisis management in the aftermath of Katrina.

Managers and Information Technology

The second trend having a major impact on managers is the proliferation of information technology. An increasing number of organizations are selling technology, and an increasing number are looking for cutting-edge technology to make and market the products and services they sell. One particularly useful type of technology is dashboard software. Much like the dashboard in a car, dashboard software gives managers a quick look into the relevant information they need to manage their companies. Most large companies are organized in divisions (which you'll learn about in more detail in Chapter 7), and often each division relies on a particular type of application or database software. Dashboard software allows employees to access information from software they don't routinely use (for example, from an application used by a different division from their own). More important, however, is the ability of a dashboard to show up-to-the-minute information and to allow employees to see all the information they need—like financial and performance data—on a single screen.

Such integrated functionality is making dashboards extremely popular. A recent poll conducted by Riley Research Associates found that 35 percent of U.S. companies are already running dashboard software, and of those that aren't, 25 percent planned to buy dashboard software that year.[25] Despite the increasing

CONCEPT in action

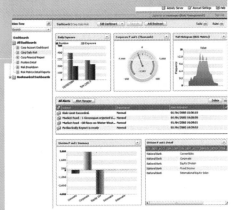

Marketing and sales professionals are increasingly turning to advanced software programs called "dashboards" to monitor business and evaluate performance. These computer tools help managers identify valuable customers, track sales, and align plans with company objectives—all in real time. A typical dashboard might include sales and bookings forecasts, monthly close data, customer satisfaction data, and employee training schedules. How does information technology influence managerial decision making?

Exhibit 6.10	**Lessons Learned by Fortune 500 Leaders about Crisis Management in the Aftermath of Hurricane Katrina**
Howard Schultz Chairman, Starbucks	**Learn from one crisis at a time.** After the Seattle earthquake of 2001, the company invested in a notification system that could handle text messaging. The night before Katrina hit, Starbucks sent out 2,300 phone calls to associates in the region, telling them about available resources.
Gary Loveman CEO, Harrah's Entertainment	**Make life easier for your employees.** Before the storm hit, Harrah's management announced that in the event of total disaster, employees would be paid for at least 90 days. The decision was meant to provide employees with some certainty during a very uncertain time.
J. W. Marriott CEO, Marriott International	**Communicate for safety.** Marriott moved its e-mail system out of New Orleans before Katrina hit. As a result, employees were able to communicate with each other and vendors to get food and water to affected areas. A massive publicity campaign (Dial 1–800-Marriott) helped the company find 2,500 of its 2,800 people in the region.
Bob Nardelli Former CEO, Home Depot	**Prepare for the next big one.** After each catastrophic event, Home Depot does a postmortem on its response efforts so that employees and managers can become more experienced and better prepared. Before Katrina hit, the company pre-staged extra supplies and generators, sent 1,000 relief associates to work in the stores in the Gulf Region, and made sure that area stores were overstocked with first-response items like insecticides, water, and home generators.
Scott Ford CEO, Alltel	**Take care of everybody.** When Katrina hit, Alltel was missing 35 employees. When the company had found all but one, managers used the company's network infrastructure to track her phone activity, contact the last person she had called, and work with the army to find her.
Paul Pressler CEO, Gap	**Empower the workforce.** Gap had 1,300 employees affected by Katrina, and one of the biggest problems the company faced was getting people their paychecks. The company, which had extended payroll by 30 days to affected employees, now encourages all employees to use direct deposit as a means to ensure access to their pay.
Jim Skinner CEO, McDonald's	**Be flexible with company assets.** McDonald's had 280 restaurants close in the immediate aftermath of the storm, but shortly afterward, 201 were already open. During the crisis, McDonald's converted its human resource service center into a crisis command center. The quickly formed help center fielded 3,800 calls.

Source: "New Lessons to Learn," *Fortune,* October 3, 2005, pp. 87–88. Copyright © 2005 by Time, Inc. All rights reserved. Reproduced by permission.

popularity of dashboard technology, the control tool has some drawbacks, like focusing too intently on short-term results and ignoring the overall progress toward long-term goals. And some employees might bristle at being monitored as closely as dashboard tools allow.

Nonetheless, companies are seeing real results from implementing dashboard software. At Capital One Financial Corp., Matt Schuyler, executive vice president in charge of human resources, uses dashboards to track headcount, attrition, and employment needs, so at any given time, his staff knows exactly which positions the company is looking to fill and the qualifications needed for each position. On a recruiting trip to Pennsylvania State University, Schuyler was able to give specific information to potential candidates, not just offer generalities like his competitors. As a result, Schuyler says, "we got a lot of résumés that night."[26]

global management skills
A manager's ability to operate in diverse cultural environments.

Managing Multinational Cultures

The increasing globalization of the world market, as discussed in Chapter 4, has created a need for managers who have **global management skills**, that is, the ability to operate in diverse cultural environments. With more and more companies choosing to do business in multiple locations around the world, employees are often required to learn the geography, language, and social customs of other cultures. It is expensive to train employees for foreign assignments and pay their relocation costs; therefore, choosing the right person for the job is especially important. Individuals who are open-minded, flexible, willing to try new things, and comfortable in a multicultural setting are good candidates for international management positions.

As companies expand around the globe, managers will face the challenges of directing the behavior of employees around the world. They must recognize that because of cultural differences, people respond to similar situations in very different ways. The burden, therefore, falls on the manager to produce results while adapting to the differences among the employees he or she manages.

How a manager gets results, wins respect, and leads employees varies greatly among countries, cultures, and individuals. For example, a Fortune 500 retailer based in the United States became frustrated with its Japanese division due to delays implementing a new computer system. When the division finally rolled out the new technology, it was overwhelmingly more effective than the average 65 percent success rate the retailer achieved elsewhere. U.S. management learned that the extra time the Japanese took was for developing internal ownership of the project among employees before executing it—quite a bit different from the "pull-the-trigger" approach used by many U.S. firms.[27] Despite differences like that (examples of which can be cited for every country in the world), managing within a different culture is only an extension of what managers do every day. That is working with differences in employees, processes, and projects.

CONCEPT in action

South by Southwest Music Festival (SXSW) began in 1987 as a grassroots concert series for unsigned indie-rock bands. Today the Austin, Texas, music-and-media conference showcases nearly 1,700 of the world's best-loved and emerging acts, from R.E.M. and Lou Reed to Paramore and Vampire Weekend. Coordination for the festival's international booking and promotions is handled through SXSW, Inc., a management company with offices in the United States, Europe, Asia, Australia, and New Zealand. What global management skills do the organizers of SXSW need to be successful?

CONCEPT check

How can information technology aid in decision making?

What are three principles of managing multinational cultures?

Describe several guidelines for crisis management.

Summary of Learning Goals

Management is the process of guiding the development, maintenance, and allocation of resources to attain organizational goals. Managers are the people in the organization responsible for developing and carrying out this management process. The four primary functions of managers are planning, organizing, leading, and controlling. By using the four functions, managers work to increase the efficiency and effectiveness of their employees, processes, projects, and organizations as a whole.

1 What is the role of management?

Planning is deciding what needs to be done, identifying when and how it will be done, and determining by whom it should be done. Managers use four different types of planning: strategic, tactical, operational, and contingency planning. Strategic planning involves creating long-range (one to five years), broad goals and determining the necessary resources to accomplish those goals. Tactical planning has a shorter time frame (less than one year) and more specific objectives that support the broader strategic goals. Operational planning creates specific standards, methods,

2 What are the four types of planning?

3 What are the primary functions of managers in organizing activities?

Organizing involves coordinating and allocating a firm's resources in order to carry out its plans. It includes developing a structure for the people, positions, departments, and activities within the firm. This is accomplished by dividing up tasks (division of labor), grouping jobs and employees (departmentalization), and assigning authority and responsibilities (delegation).

4 How do leadership styles influence a corporate culture?

Leading is the process of guiding and motivating others toward the achievement of organizational goals. Managers have unique leadership styles that range from autocratic to free-rein. The set of attitudes, values, and standards of behavior that distinguishes one organization from another is called corporate culture. A corporate culture evolves over time and is based on the accumulated history of the organization, including the vision of the founders.

5 How do organizations control activities?

Controlling is the process of assessing the organization's progress toward accomplishing its goals. The control process is as follows: (1) set performance standards (goals), (2) measure performance, (3) compare actual performance to established performance standards, (4) take corrective action (if necessary), and (5) use information gained from the process to set future performance standards.

6 What roles do managers take on in different organizational settings?

In an informational role, the manager may act as an information gatherer, an information distributor, or a spokesperson for the company. A manager's interpersonal roles are based on various interactions with other people. Depending on the situation, a manager may need to act as a figurehead, a company leader, or a liaison.

7 What set of managerial skills is necessary for managerial success?

Managerial skills fall into three basic categories: technical, human relations, and conceptual skills. Specialized areas of knowledge and expertise and the ability to apply that knowledge make up a manager's technical skills. Human relations skills include the ability to understand human behavior, to communicate effectively with others, and to motivate individuals to accomplish their objectives. Conceptual skills include the ability to view the organization as a whole, understand how the various parts are interdependent, and assess how the organization relates to its external environment.

8 What trends will affect management in the future?

Three important trends in management today are: preparing for crises management, the increasing use of information technology, and the need to manage multinational cultures. Crisis management requires quick action, telling the truth about the situation, and putting the best people on the task to correct the situation. Finally, management must learn from the crisis in order to prevent it from happening again. Using the latest information technology, like dashboard software, managers can make quicker, better-informed decisions. As more companies "go global," the need for multinational cultural management skills is growing. Managers must set a good example, create personal involvement for all employees, and develop a culture of trust.

policies, and procedures that are used in specific functional areas of the organization. Contingency plans identify alternative courses of action for very unusual or crisis situations.

Key Terms

autocratic leaders 162	empowerment 163
coercive power 161	expert power 161
conceptual skills 169	free-rein (laissez-faire) leadership 163
consensual leaders 163	global management skills 171
consultative leaders 163	human relations skills 169
contingency plans 160	informational roles 166
controlling 164	interpersonal roles 166
corporate culture 164	leadership 161
decisional roles 166	leadership style 162
democratic leaders 162	legitimate power 161
effectiveness 156	management 156
efficiency 156	middle management 160

Preparing for Tomorrow's Workplace: SCANS

1. Would you be a good manager? Do a self-assessment that includes your current technical, human relations, and conceptual skills. What skills do you already possess, and which do you need to add? Where do your strengths lie? Based on this exercise, develop a description of an effective manager. (**Resources, Information**)

2. Successful managers map out what they want to do with their time (planning), determine the activities and tasks they need to accomplish it in that time frame (organizing), and make sure they stay on track (controlling). How well do you manage your time? Do you think ahead, or do you tend to procrastinate? Examine how you use your time and identify at least three areas where you can improve your time management skills. (**Resources**)

3. Often researchers cast leadership in an inspirational role in a company and management in more of an administrative role. That tendency seems to put leadership and management in a hierarchy. Do you think one is more important than the other? Do you think a company can succeed if it has bad managers and good leaders? What about if it has good managers and bad leaders? Are managers and leaders actually the same? (**Systems**)

4. Today's managers must be comfortable using all kinds of technology. Do an inventory of your computer skills and identify any gaps. After listing your areas of weakness, make a plan to increase your computer competency by enrolling in a computer class on or off campus. You may want to practice using common business applications like Microsoft Excel by building a spreadsheet to track your budget, PowerPoint by creating slides for your next class project, and Outlook by uploading your semester schedule. (**Information, Technology**)

5. **Team Activity** One of the most common types of planning that managers do is operational planning, or the creation of policies, procedures, and rules and regulations. Assemble a team of three classmates and work as a team to draft an operational plan that addresses employee attendance (or absenteeism). (**Interpersonal, Systems**)

Ethics Activity

Are top executives paid too much? A study of CEO compensation revealed that CEO bonuses rose considerably—from 20 percent to 30 percent—even at companies whose revenues or profits dropped or those that reported significant employee layoffs. Such high pay for CEOs at underperforming companies, as well as CEO compensation at companies with stellar results, has raised many questions from investors and others. CEO pay has risen considerably in recent years; in 2004, for example, the average pay for a CEO at a public company was $11.4 million—versus just $27,000 for an average nonsupervisory production worker's pay. Under proposed regulations, the Securities and Exchange Commission (SEC) would require public companies to disclose full details of executive compensation, including salaries, bonuses, pensions, benefits, stock options, and severance and retirement packages.

Even some CEOs question the high levels of CEO pay. Edgar Woolard Jr., former CEO and chairman of DuPont, thinks so. "CEO pay is driven today primarily by outside consultant surveys," he says. Companies all want their CEOs to be in the top half, and preferably the top quarter, of all CEOs. This leads to annual increases. He also criticizes the enormous severance packages that company boards give to CEOs that fail. For example, Carly Fiorina of Hewlett-Packard received $20 million when she was fired.

Using a Web search tool, locate articles about this topic and then write responses to the following questions. Be sure to support your arguments and cite your sources.

ETHICAL DILEMMA: Are CEOs entitled to increases in compensation when their company's financial situation worsens, because their job becomes more challenging? If they fail, are they entitled to huge severance packages for their efforts? Should companies be required to divulge all details of compensation for their highest top managers, and what effect is such disclosure likely to have on executive pay?

Sources: "CEOs Are Overpaid, Says Former DuPont CEO Edgar Woolard Jr.," *PR Newswire*, February 9, 2006, **http://www.proquest.com/brand/umi.shtml** Elizabeth Souder, "Firm Questions Exxon CEO's Pay," *Dallas Morning News*, December 15, 2005, **http://galenet.cengagelearning.com**; "Weaker Company Performance Does Not Seem to Slow CEO Pay Increases," *Corporate Board*, September–October 2005, p. 27, **http://gale.cengage.com/**; "What Price CEO Pay?" *The Blade* (Toledo, Ohio), January 20, 2006, **http://www.toledoblade.com**.

Working the Net

1. Are you leadership material? See how you measure up at Magno Consulting, **http://www.magnoconsulting.com**. Click on "leadership" for a punch list of attributes for business leaders of the 21st century. Study the list and provide an example of how you would put each item into action.

2. Strategic Advantage, **http://www.strategy4u.com**, offers many reasons why companies should develop strategic plans, as well as a strategy tip of the month, assessment tools, planning exercises, and resource links. Explore the site to learn the effect of strategic planning on financial performance and present your evidence to the class. Then select a planning exercise and, with a group of classmates, perform it as it applies to your school.

3. Congratulations! You've just been promoted to your first supervisory position. However, you are at a loss as to how to actually manage your staff. About.com's guide to general management, **http://www.management.about.com**, brings together a variety of materials to help you. Check out the Essentials links such as Management 101 and How to Manage, as well as other resources. Develop a plan for yourself to follow.

4. How do entrepreneurs develop the corporate culture of their companies? Do a search of the term "corporate culture" on Inc., **http://www.inc.com**; Entrepreneur, **http://www.entrepreneur.com**; or Fast Company, **http://www.fastcompany.com**. Prepare a short presentation for your class that explains the importance of corporate culture and how it is developed in young firms.

5. Good managers and leaders know how to empower their employees. The Business e-Coach at **http://www.1000ventures.com** explains why employee empowerment is so important in today's knowledge economy. After reviewing the information at this site, prepare a brief report on the benefits of employee empowerment. Include several ideas you would like a manager to use to empower you.

6. Get some leadership tips from 7 Steps to Closure at the Learning Center, **http://www.learningcenter.net**. Complete the Closure Planning Form to develop your own personal Success-Oriented Action Plan.

Creative Thinking Case

Managing an Extreme Makeover

During a tour of a Toyota Corolla assembly plant located near their headquarters in Bangalore, India, executives of Wipro Ltd. hit on a revolutionary idea—why not apply Toyota's successful manufacturing techniques to managing their software development and clients' back-office operations business?

"Toyota preaches continuous improvement, respect for employees, learning, and embracing change," says T. K. Kurien, 45, head of Wipro's 13,600-person business-process outsourcing unit. "What we do is apply people, technology, and processes to solve a business problem."

Among the problems spotted early on by Kurien? Cubicles. They're normal for programmers but interrupt the flow for business-process employees. Deciding to position people side by side at long tables assembly-line style "was a roaring disaster," admits Kurien. "The factory idea concerned people." So based on feedback from his middle managers, Kurien arranged classes to explain his concepts and how they would ultimately make life easier for employees.

Wipro also adopted Toyota's kaizen system of soliciting employee suggestions. Priya, 28, who has worked for Wipro for nearly seven years, submitted several kaizen and was delighted when her bosses responded promptly to her suggestions. "Even though it's something small, it feels good. You're being considered," she says. Empowerment in the workplace washed over into her private life. As the first woman in her family to attend college, she told her parents they may arrange her marriage only to a man who will not interfere with her career.

Kurien and his managers work hard at boosting employee morale, offering rewards—pens, caps, or shirts—to employees who submit suggestions to kaizen boxes. And each week a top-performing employee receives a cake. Murthy, 25, an accountant who hopes to be Wipro's chief financial officer some day, spearheaded an effort to cut government import approval times from 30 to 15 days. He got a cake with his name written on it in honey. "I was surprised management knew what I was doing," he says. "Now I want to do more projects."

With $1.7 billion in revenues, 42,000 employees, and a U.S.-traded stock that has advanced 230 percent in two years, Wipro is a star of India's burgeoning information technology industry. Today, the company's paperwork-processing operations in Pune, Bangalore, and Chennai bear a clear resemblance to a Toyota plant. Two shifts of young men and women line long rows of tables. At the start of each shift, team leaders discuss the day's goals and divide up tasks. And just like in a Toyota factory, electronic displays mounted on the walls shift from green to red if things get bogged down.

This obsession with management efficiency has helped India become the back-office operation for hundreds of Western companies, resulting in the transfer of many thousands of jobs offshore. "If the Indians get this right, in addition to their low labor rates, they can become deadly competition," says Jeffrey K. Liker, a business professor at the University of Michigan and author of *The Toyota Way*, a book about Toyota's lean manufacturing techniques. If Kurien's management initiatives succeed, experts may soon be extolling the Wipro way.

Critical Thinking Questions

- What type of manager is T. K. Kurien? How would you characterize his leadership style?
- What managerial role does T. K. Kurien assume in his approach to attaining his division's goal of improved customer service?
- What management skill sets does he exhibit?

Sources: Steve Hamm, "Taking a Page from Toyota's Playbook," BusinessWeek Online, **http://www.businessweek.com**, August 22, 2005; Theodore Forbath, "Developing an Effective Global Sourcing Strategy," CIO Update, July 22, 2005, **http://www.cioupdate.com**; Toyota company Web site, **http://www.toyota.com**, December 29, 2005; Wipro company Web site, **http://www.wipro.com**, December 29, 2005.

Exploring Business Careers

You might ask, "How does one come to work in the world of online costume retail?" With a passion for holiday make-believe and dress-up? A keen eye for business potential? The drive to capitalize on a competitive advantage? If you're Jalem Getz, the answer is: all of these. Getz is the founder and CEO of BuyCostumes.com, the world's largest online costume and accessories retailer.

**Jalem Getz
BuyCostumes.com**

As with most businesses, BuyCostumes.com is the result of careful planning. It is a response to what Getz saw as inherent flaws of resource allocation with the business model of brick-and-mortar costume retailers. "As a brick-and-mortar business, we were the gypsies of retail, which caused scale problems since we started over every year. Because we only were in a mall four or five months a year, locations we had one year often were rented the next. So we had to find new stores to rent each year. Then we had to find management to run the stores, and train employees to staff them. We also had to shuffle the inventory around each year to stock them. It's almost impossible to grow a business like that." By turning to the Internet, however, Getz was able to bypass all of those issues. The virtual "space" was available year-round, and inventory and staff were centralized in a single warehouse location.

Today, BuyCostumes.com is a $30 million-a-year business that continues to grow with each passing holiday season. It has about 600 employees during its peak season. It carries more than 10,000 Halloween items and has upwards of 20 million visitors each holiday season. Last year, they shipped more than 1 million costumes across the world, including 45 countries outside the United States. "We say that our goal is to ensure that anytime anyone buys a costume anywhere in the world, it will be from BuyCostumes.com. And, although to some extent we're kidding, we're also very serious."

To keep track of all this action, Getz mixes ideals of a strong work ethic, a willingness to take risks, and an interest in having fun while making a profit. Given the size of the company, BuyCostumes.com organizes its management to help keep the company focused on the corporate goal of continued growth. For Getz, his role in the management hierarchy is to "hire excellent people who have similar goals and who are motivated the same way I am and then put them in a position where they can succeed." Beyond that? "Inspect what you expect." This maxim is a concise way to say that, although he does not believe in constantly watching over his employees' shoulders, he does believe in periodically checking in with them to ensure that both he and they are on the same page. By considering the process of management a conversation between himself and his employees, he exhibits a strong participative leadership style.

Getz will joke that he wishes he could say that he spent his childhood dreaming of the day he could work with costumes. The truth, though, is that he saw an opportunity, grabbed it, and hasn't let go since. And sometimes, especially during Halloween, truth can be even more satisfying than fiction.

Today's companies rely on managers to guide daily operations using human, technological, financial, and other resources to create a competitive advantage. For many beginning business students, being in "management" is an attractive, but somewhat vague, future goal. This vagueness is due in part to an incomplete understanding of what managers do and how they contribute to organizational success or failure.

Learning Goals

After reading this chapter, you should be able to answer these questions:

1 What are the five traditional forms of departmentalization?

2 What contemporary organizational structures are companies using?

3 Why are companies using team-based organizational structures?

4 What tools do companies use to establish relationships within their organizations?

5 How can the degree of centralization/decentralization be altered to make an organization more successful?

6 How do mechanistic and organic organizations differ?

7 How does the informal organization affect the performance of the company?

8 What trends are influencing the way businesses organize?

CHAPTER 7

Designing Organizational Structures

"Metro . . . Business . . . Foreign . . ."

Organizations do not run themselves. In fact, most organizations have a system of managers, assistant managers, department heads, and chief executives who ensure that it runs as efficiently as possible. Common sense dictates that there is a chain of command with the president or CEO of the organization maintaining the overall goals, mission, and direction of the organization at the top of the chain. But what lies below the CEO in that chain of command? In other words, what are the other links in that chain that allow for the successful and smooth operation of the organization, be it a manufacturer, a restaurant, a hospital, a movie company, a newspaper, or any other type of organization?

The Paper provides a brief glimpse into the world of newspaper publishing following metro editor Henry Hackett through a day in the life of a reporter. That day usually begins with a meeting of department heads where all involved discuss the faults and foibles of the most recent edition of the newspaper, the major stories of the day, and what each department is currently working on. As we can see, it is through this departmental meeting that the direction and format of the next edition is decided on.

In the meeting, Bernie White, the editor-in-chief of the *New York Sun,* first acknowledges that the most recent front-page headline was not necessarily the most appropriate headline for the paper to run as there was more important news in the city that needed to be covered. He then calls on the editor of the metro section—Henry Hackett—to provide him with an overview of what his department is currently working on. After Henry reports, he then calls on the business editor and the foreign editor to provide him with their information; all the while, the managing editor looks on making her notes. As the meeting begins to break up, the group decides that it is the subway story that metro is working on that will grace the front page of the next edition.

The organizational structure on display in *The Paper* hints at the specialization that comes with departmentalization. Each department is divided into a news specialty, three of which we see in the morning meeting. Metro handles news events that occur within the city such as subway wrecks and racial unrest; business specializes in all things business ranging from how well the Dow is performing to some sort of business scandal; and foreign manages the major stories that occur outside of America's borders such as a capsized ferry-boat in the Philippines or a coup in Bahrain, focusing, of course, on how those stories might in fact affect New York. This departmentalization ensures that all tasks are divided and subdivided so that the various stories and activities can be coordinated among the staff and so that no two reporters are working on the exact same story. Such departmentalization allows for the efficient operation of the newspaper.

The following chapter provides additional insight into departmentalization and how it helps to structure the organization and paves the way for the smooth operation of the organization. This structuring process begins with an understanding of how labor will be divided, which employees will undertake which tasks, and how authority and responsibilities will be delegated throughout the organization. The chapter then discusses various types of structures including a more in-depth examination of team structures before taking a closer look at authority and at the considerations one must make when developing an organizational design.

Discussion Questions

- Based on what you see in *The Paper,* what basic type of departmentalization best fits what you see on the screen and why?
- Describe how a contemporary organizational structure might also be on display in the film clip.
- How might teams assist in the operation of a newspaper? How might they hinder the operation of a newspaper?
- Based on what you see in *The Paper,* make a case that the *New York Sun* is a mechanistic or an organic structure.

The Paper/Corbis

Departmentalization—Building Organizational Structures

As you learned in Chapter 6, the key functions that managers perform include planning, organizing, leading, and controlling. This chapter focuses specifically on the organizing function. Organizing involves coordinating and allocating a firm's resources so that the firm can carry out its plans and achieve its goals. This organizing, or structuring, process is accomplished by:

- determining work activities and dividing up tasks (*division of labor*)
- grouping jobs and employees (*departmentalization*)
- assigning authority and responsibilities (*delegation*)

The result of the organizing process is a formal organizational structure. A **formal organization** is the order and design of relationships within the firm. It consists of two or more people working together with a common objective and clarity of purpose. Formal organizations also have well-defined lines of authority, channels for information flow, and means of control. Human, material, financial, and information resources are deliberately connected to form the business organization. Some connections are long lasting, such as the links among people in the finance or marketing department. Others can be changed at almost any time, as when a committee is formed to study a problem.

Companies also change their form of business organization when it becomes an obstacle to their success. For example, only two years after buying Sears and then Kmart, Eddie Lampert conceded that the turnaround plan he put in place for the retail giant had stalled. Lampert said he had put good managers in a structure that didn't work, so he reorganized the giant company into a five-unit holding company with divisions organized by brand and function—real estate (all those stores), brands (Kenmore, Craftsman, Diehard), operations (appliances, pharmacy, clothes, etc.), online (kmart.com, sears.com), and support (human resources, merchandising, and so on). The new structure was less centralized, and managers at individual units became responsible for decisions. Lampert says, "In a large company, the structure is very, very important. That's the thing, I feel, we haven't been able to get right."[1]

Every organization has some kind of underlying structure. Traditional structures are more rigid and group employees by function, products, processes, customers, or regions, as described in the next section. Contemporary and team-based structures are more flexible and assemble employees to respond quickly to dynamic business environments. Regardless of the structural skeleton a company chooses to implement, all managers must first consider what kind of work needs to be done within the firm.

1 What are the five traditional forms of departmentalization?

formal organization The order and design of relationships within a firm; consists of two or more people working together with a common objective and clarity of purpose.

CONCEPT in action

The eagerly anticipated merger between Sirius and XM has captivated the public since being announced in 2007. But the combination of the two satellite radio firms will involve more than bringing talk queen Oprah Winfrey and shock jock Howard Stern together under one roof. To achieve the billions of dollars in cost savings expected through the merger, XM and Sirius must integrate separate product lines, organizational units, and managerial hierarchies while eliminating redundancies. What determines how businesses are organized?

Division of Labor

The process of dividing work into separate jobs and assigning tasks to workers is called **division of labor**. In a fast-food restaurant, for example, some employees take or fill orders, others prepare food, a few clean and maintain equipment, and at least one supervises all the others. In an auto assembly plant, some workers install rearview mirrors, whereas others mount bumpers on bumper brackets. The degree to which the tasks are subdivided into smaller jobs is called **specialization**. Employees who work at highly specialized jobs, such as assembly-line workers, perform a limited number and variety of tasks. Employees who become specialists at one task, or a small number of tasks, develop greater skill in doing that particular job. This can lead to greater efficiency and consistency in production and other work activities. However, a high degree of specialization can also result in employees who are disinterested or bored due to the lack of variety and challenge. In Chapter 9, we will discuss ways managers can mitigate the disadvantages of a highly specialized workforce.

division of labor The process of dividing work into separate jobs and assigning tasks to workers.

specialization The degree to which tasks are subdivided into smaller jobs.

Traditional Structures

After a company divides into jobs the work it needs to do, managers then group the jobs together so that similar or associated tasks and activities can be coordinated. This grouping of people, tasks, and resources into organizational units is called **departmentalization** and it facilitates the planning, leading, and control processes.

departmentalization The process of grouping jobs together so that similar or associated tasks and activities can be coordinated.

organization chart
A visual representation of the structured relationships among tasks and the people given the authority to do those tasks.

An **organization chart** is a visual representation of the structured relationships among tasks and the people given the authority to do those tasks. In the organization chart in Exhibit 7.1, each figure represents a job, and each job includes several tasks. The sales manager, for instance, must hire salespeople, establish sales territories, motivate and train the salespeople, and control sales operations. The chart also indicates the general type of work done in each position. As Exhibit 7.2 shows, five basic types of departmentalization are commonly used in organizations:

functional departmentalization
Departmentalization that is based on the primary functions performed within an organizational unit.

1. **Functional departmentalization**, which is based on the primary functions performed within an organizational unit (marketing, finance, production, sales, and so on). Ethan Allen Interiors, a vertically integrated furniture manufacturer, switched to functional departmentalization when it reorganized into three functional subsidiaries: retail, operations and marketing, and financial reporting.[2]

product departmentalization
Departmentalization that is based on the goods or services produced or sold by the organizational unit.

2. **Product departmentalization**, which is based on the goods or services produced or sold by the organizational unit (such as outpatient/emergency services, pediatrics, cardiology, and orthopedics). For example, ITT Industries is organized into four product divisions: A Fluid Technology (pumps and wastewater treatment equipment), Defensive Electronics and Services, Motion and Flow Control products (like shock absorbers, pumps for Whirlpool spas, and beverage dispensers), and Electronic Components (like electromechanical switches, keypads, and more).[3]

process departmentalization
Departmentalization that is based on the production process used by the organizational unit.

3. **Process departmentalization**, which is based on the production process used by the organizational unit (such as lumber cutting and treatment, furniture finishing, and shipping). For example, the organization of Sibneft, a Russian oil company, reflects the activities the company needs to perform in order to extract oil from the ground and turn it into a final product: exploration and research, production (drilling), refining, and marketing and distribution.[4] Pixar, the animated-movie company, is divided into three parallel yet interactive process-based groups: technology development, which delivers computer-graphics tools; creative development, which concocts stories and characters and animates them; and production, which coordinates the filmmaking process.[5]

customer departmentalization
Departmentalization that is based on the primary type of customer served by the organizational unit.

4. **Customer departmentalization**, which is based on the primary type of customer served by the organizational unit (such as wholesale or retail purchasers). For example, PNC Bank restructured several lines of business within its banking operation. Now the company's banking business is divided into two units to reflect the customers it serves: consumer banking and institutional banking.

EXHIBIT 7.1	Organization Chart for a Typical Appliance Manufacturer

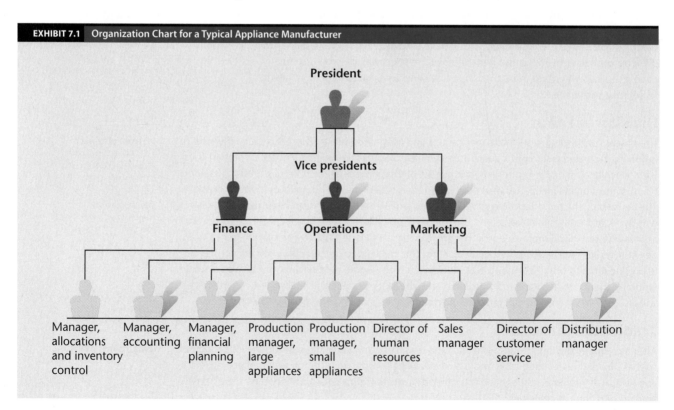

President

Vice presidents

Finance   Operations   Marketing

Manager, allocations and inventory control | Manager, accounting | Manager, financial planning | Production manager, large appliances | Production manager, small appliances | Director of human resources | Sales manager | Director of customer service | Distribution manager

EXHIBIT 7.2 **Five Traditional Ways to Organize**

Functional Departmentalization

President

Legal | Personnel | Manufacturing | Engineering | Marketing | Finance

Product Departmentalization

Administrator and CEO

Head of outpatient/emergency treatment | Head of pediatrics | Head of cardiology | Head of orthopedics | Head of obstetrics/gynecology

Process Departmentalization

Plant superintendent

Lumber cutting and treatment | Furniture assembly | Furniture finishing | Shipping

Customer Departmentalization

Vice president, marketing

Marketing manager, railroad customers | Marketing manager, aircraft customers | Marketing manager, automotive customers | Marketing manager, military customers

Geographic Departmentalization

Vice president, marketing

Director, U.S. and Canadian marketing | Director, European marketing | Director, South American marketing

5. **Geographic departmentalization**, which is based on the geographic segmentation of organizational units (such as U.S. and Canadian marketing, European marketing, and South American marketing). For example, under CEO Indra Nooyi, PepsiCo has reorganized geographically into three units: Americas food (North America and Latin America); Americas beverage; and international (the rest of the world) food and beverage. The impetus for the restructuring was to give top executives experience in developed and developing markets and encourage the sharing of best management practices from different regions.[6]

People are assigned to a particular organizational unit because they perform similar or related tasks, or because they are jointly responsible for a product, client, or market. Decisions about how

geographic departmentalization
Departmentalization that is based on the geographic segmentation of the organizational units.

Chapter 7: Designing Organizational Structures

line organization
An organizational structure with direct, clear lines of authority and communication flowing from the top managers downward.

line-and-staff organization
An organizational structure that includes both line and staff positions.

line positions
All positions in the organization directly concerned with producing goods and services and that are directly connected from top to bottom.

to departmentalize affect the way management assigns authority, distributes resources, rewards performance, and sets up lines of communication. Many large organizations use several types of departmentalization.

Line-and-Staff Organization

The **line organization** is designed with direct, clear lines of authority and communication flowing from the top managers downward. Managers have direct control over all activities, including administrative duties. An organization chart for this type of structure would show that all positions in the firm are directly connected via an imaginary line extending from the highest position in the organization to the lowest (where production of goods and services takes place). This structure with its simple design and broad managerial control is often well suited to small, entrepreneurial firms.

As an organization grows and becomes more complex, the line organization can be enhanced by adding staff positions to the design. Staff positions provide specialized advisory and support services to line managers in the **line-and-staff organization**, shown in Exhibit 7.3. In daily operations, individuals in **line positions** are directly involved in the processes used to create goods and services. Individuals in **staff positions** provide the administrative and support services that line employees need to achieve the firm's goals. Line positions in organizations are typically in areas such as production, marketing, and finance. Staff positions are found in areas such as legal counseling, managerial consulting, public relations, and human resource management.

CONCEPT check

How does specialization lead to greater efficiency and consistency in production?

What are the five types of departmentalization?

Contemporary Structures

2 What contemporary organizational structures are companies using?

staff positions
Positions in an organization held by individuals who provide the administrative and support services that line employees need to achieve the firm's goals.

Although traditional forms of departmentalization still represent how many companies organize their work, newer, more flexible organizational structures are in use at many firms. Let's look at matrix and committee structures, and how those two types of organizations are helping companies better leverage the diverse skills of their employees.

Matrix Structure

The **matrix structure** (also called the **project management** approach) is sometimes used in conjunction with the traditional line-and-staff structure in an organization. Essentially, this structure

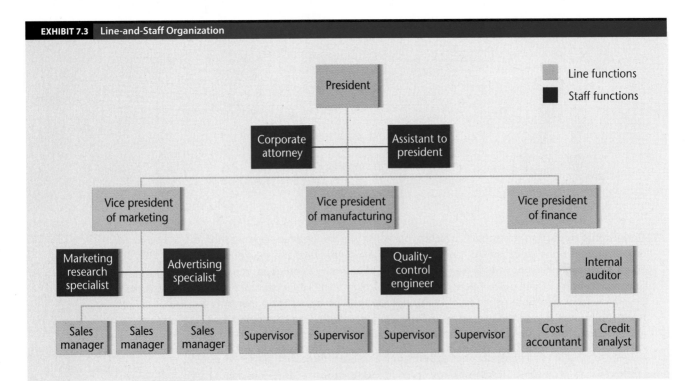

EXHIBIT 7.3   Line-and-Staff Organization

combines two different forms of departmentalization—functional and product—that have complementary strengths and weaknesses. The matrix structure brings together people from different functional areas of the organization (such as manufacturing, finance, and marketing) to work on a special project. Each employee has two direct supervisors: the line manager from her or his specific functional area and the project manager. Exhibit 7.4 shows a matrix organization with four special project groups (A, B, C, D), each with its own project manager. Because of the dual chain of command, the matrix structure presents some unique challenges for both managers and subordinates.

matrix structure (project management)
An organizational structure that combines functional and product departmentalization by bringing together people from different functional areas of the organization to work on a special project.

Advantages of the matrix structure include:

- *Teamwork*. By pooling the skills and abilities of various specialists, the company can increase creativity and innovation and tackle more complex tasks.
- *Efficient use of resources*. Project managers use only the specialized staff they need to get the job done, instead of building large groups of underused personnel.
- *Flexibility*. The project structure is flexible and can adapt quickly to changes in the environment; the group can be disbanded quickly when it is no longer needed.
- *Ability to balance conflicting objectives*. The customer wants a quality product and predictable costs. The organization wants high profits and the development of technical capability for the future. These competing goals serve as a focal point for directing activities and overcoming conflict. The marketing representative can represent the customer, the finance representative can advocate high profits, and the engineers can push for technical capabilities.
- *Higher performance*. Employees working on special project teams may experience increased feelings of ownership, commitment, and motivation.
- *Opportunities for personal and professional development*. The project structure gives individuals the opportunity to develop and strengthen technical and interpersonal skills.

CONCEPT in action

Like the futuristic characters trapped in a dizzying web of confusion in the movie *The Matrix Revolutions*, some managers experience chaos within a contemporary organizational structure known as the matrix. Advocates of matrix structures claim that combining the functional and product forms of departmentalization leads to greater innovation and responsiveness to markets, but others say having multiple supervisors and hierarchies invariably leads to power struggles and confusion among team members. Are workers capable of serving two masters?

Disadvantages of the matrix structure include:

- *Power struggles*. Functional and product managers may have different goals and management styles.
- *Confusion among team members*. Reporting relationships and job responsibilities may be unclear.

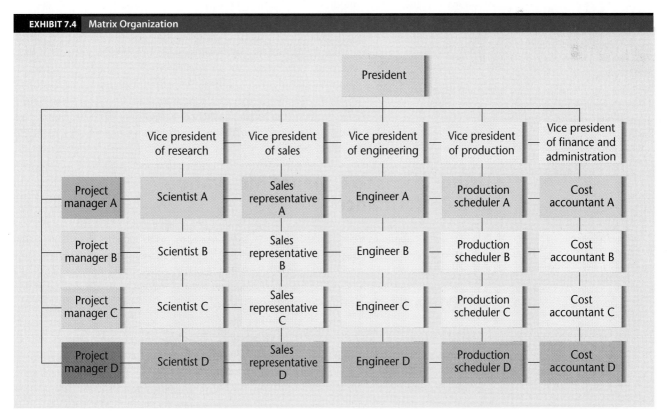

EXHIBIT 7.4   Matrix Organization

	Vice president of research	Vice president of sales	Vice president of engineering	Vice president of production	Vice president of finance and administration
Project manager A	Scientist A	Sales representative A	Engineer A	Production scheduler A	Cost accountant A
Project manager B	Scientist B	Sales representative B	Engineer B	Production scheduler B	Cost accountant B
Project manager C	Scientist C	Sales representative C	Engineer C	Production scheduler C	Cost accountant C
Project manager D	Scientist D	Sales representative D	Engineer D	Production scheduler D	Cost accountant D

(President at top, reporting to the five vice presidents)

- *Lack of cohesiveness.* Team members from different functional areas may have difficulty communicating effectively and working together as a team.

Although project-based matrix organizations can improve a company's flexibility and teamwork, some companies are trying to unravel complex matrix structures that create limited accountability. For example, during his first year as Hewlett-Packard CEO, Mark Hurd worked diligently to untangle the complex matrix structure implemented by his predecessor, Carly Fiorina. The reason Hurd gave for tossing out Fiorina's matrix management structure, which muddied responsibilities, was to give business heads more control of their units. "The more accountable I can make you, the easier it is for you to show you're a great performer," says Hurd. "The more I use a matrix, the easier I make it to blame someone else."[7]

Employees also recognize the limitations of the matrix system. One former employee of a packaging company that used a matrix system put it this way, "Everyone who could see himself in a mirror thought he was my boss."[8] Matrix structures were originally conceived of by NASA during the race to the moon in the mid-twentieth century. Dr. Richard Kilburg of Johns Hopkins notes, however, that when matrix structures are confined to a normal corporation, factional rivalries and other frictions make it backfire. "Inside companies, it fails more often than it succeeds," he says.[9]

Committee Structure

committee structure
An organizational structure in which authority and responsibility are held by a group rather than an individual.

In **committee structure**, authority and responsibility are held by a group rather than an individual. Committees are typically part of a larger line-and-staff organization. Often the committee's role is only advisory, but in some situations the committee has the power to make and implement decisions. Committees can make the coordination of tasks in the organization much easier. For example, Novartis, the huge Swiss pharmaceutical company, has a committee structure, which reports to its board of directors. Four permanent committees report to the board: the chairman's committee, the compensation committee, the audit and compliance committee, and a corporate governance committee. The chairman's committee deals with business matters that arise between board meetings and is responsible for high-level appointments and acquisitions. The compensation committee looks at the pay and expenses of board members, whereas the audit and compliance committee oversees accounting and financial reporting practices. The corporate governance committee's duties include focusing on board nominations, board performance evaluations, and possible conflicts of interest.[10]

Committees bring diverse viewpoints to a problem and expand the range of possible solutions, but there are some drawbacks. Committees can be slow to reach a decision and are

CONCEPT check

Why does the matrix structure have a dual chain of command?

How does a matrix structure increase power struggles or reduce accountability?

What are advantages of a committee structure? Disadvantages?

sometimes dominated by a single individual. It is also more difficult to hold any one individual accountable for a decision made by a group. Committee meetings can sometimes go on for long periods of time with seemingly little being accomplished. One example of an extreme committee structure is the U.S. Department of Homeland Security. More than 80 committees and subcommittees have some jurisdiction over the agency. Secretary Michael Chertoff says, "We're serving so many masters with so many inconsistent positions that it's very hard to do our job."[11]

Using Teams to Enhance Motivation and Performance

3 Why are companies using team-based organizational structures?

One of the most apparent trends in business today is the use of teams to accomplish organizational goals. Using a team-based structure can increase individual and group motivation and performance. This section gives a brief overview of group behavior, defines work teams as specific types of groups, and provides suggestions for creating high-performing teams. The growing importance of teams is discussed in the Managing Change box on the next page.

Understanding Group Behavior

Teams are a specific type of organizational group. Every organization contains groups, social units of two or more people who share the same goals and cooperate to achieve those goals. Understanding some fundamental concepts related to group behavior and group processes provides a good foundation for understanding concepts about work teams. Groups can be formal or informal in

Notable Companies Trade Tradition for Teams

It's becoming increasingly common to find companies that are throwing off the traditional management structures discussed earlier in the chapter in favor of innovative team structures that give more autonomy and responsibility to front-line workers. Two well-known companies at the forefront of this movement are Whole Foods Market and W. L. Gore, inventor of Gore-Tex fabric, Glide dental floss, and Elixir guitar strings.

At Whole Foods Market, the organizational unit does not contain any of the building blocks of the traditional management structures discussed so far. The building block of the Whole Foods organizational structure is the team. Each store is divided into roughly eight teams, each of which takes responsibility for a specific area of the store, from seafood to produce to checkout. New hires are assigned to a team, and after a four-week trial, the team votes on whether the newest member can stay. A two-thirds majority is needed to win a full-time position on the team. Teams at Whole Foods aren't responsible only for determining staffing, however. Teams also take responsibility for all key operating decisions, like pricing, ordering, promotions, and even product assortment. In contrast to the majority of national supermarket chains, Whole Foods does not have a staff of national product buyers. Rather, its stores are free to stock whatever their teams think will appeal to local markets. Team structures allow for a more customer-focused organization.

Like Whole Foods, W. L. Gore has long used a team structure. The company has no organizational chart and no management layers, few people have titles, and no one has a boss. Teams come together when a leader emerges. That is, there are no preset teams. If someone calls a meeting and people show up, that person is a leader, and the group that convenes is a team. Gore uses self-management in its most extreme to encourage grassroots innovation, but before those innovations are funded, they must pass muster financially. Team members must present a solid business case for their ideas. That combination of innovation and discipline keeps Gore a perennial success story.[12]

Critical Thinking Questions

- What challenges do you think face companies that trade a traditional organizational structure for one based on self-managing teams?
- How can self-managing teams better help companies manage change inside and outside of their organizations?

© Stockbyte/Getty Images

---

nature. Formal groups are designated and sanctioned by the organization; their behavior is directed toward accomplishing organizational goals. Informal groups are based on social relationships and are not determined or sanctioned by the organization.

Formal organizational groups, like the sales department at Dell Computers, must operate within the larger Dell organizational system. To some degree, elements of the larger Dell system, such as organizational strategy, company policies and procedures, available resources, and the highly motivated employee corporate culture, determine the behavior of smaller groups, like the sales department, within Dell. Other factors that affect the behavior of organizational groups are individual member characteristics (e.g., ability, training, personality), the roles and norms of group members, and the size and cohesiveness of the group. Norms are the implicit behavioral guidelines of the group, or the standards for acceptable and nonacceptable behavior. For example, a Dell sales manager may be expected to work at least two Saturdays per month without extra pay. Although this isn't written anywhere, it is the expected norm.

Group cohesiveness refers to the degree to which group members want to stay in the group and tend to resist outside influences (such as a change in company policies). When group performance norms are high, group cohesiveness will have a positive impact on productivity. Cohesiveness tends to increase when the size of the group is small, individual and group goals are similar, the group has high status in the organization, rewards are group based rather than individual based, and the group competes with other groups within the organization. Work group cohesiveness can benefit the organization in several ways including increased productivity, enhanced worker self-image because of group success, increased company loyalty, reduced employee turnover, and reduced absenteeism. The team that developed the "Priceless" advertising campaign for MasterCard was a highly cohesive and very small team. The ads feature a list of ordinary transactions, but the final item in the series of purchased items is described as "Priceless." Joyce Thomas, one of the three-member team that conceived of and created the ads, says, "We were very comfortable working together, so we debated everything."[13] On the other hand, cohesiveness can also lead to restricted output, resistance to change, and conflict with other work groups in the organization. The opportunity to turn the decision-making process over to a group with diverse skills and abilities is one of the arguments for using work groups (and teams) in organizational settings. For group decision making to be most effective, however, both managers and group members must understand its strengths and weaknesses (see Exhibit 7.5 on the next page).

group cohesiveness
The degree to which group members want to stay in the group and tend to resist outside influences.

CONCEPT in action

The RAZR, with its sleek design and superstar backing from soccer icon David Beckham, is the ultimate in cell phone fashions. A team of more than 20 Motorola engineers designed the trendy handset in secret, using materials and techniques well outside of normal company processes. The team's sometimes-combative brainstorm sessions, which centered on the trade-offs between Razr's functionality and thinness, produced the breakthrough idea of hiding the antenna in the unit's mouthpiece. Why are work teams well suited to the development of innovative products?

© Seokyong Lee/Bloomberg News/Landov

Chapter 7: Designing Organizational Structures

EXHIBIT 7.5   Strengths and Weaknesses of Group Decision Making

Strengths	Weaknesses
• Groups bring more information and knowledge to the decision process.	• Groups typically take a longer time to reach a solution than an individual takes.
• Groups offer a diversity of perspectives and, therefore, generate a greater number of alternatives.	• Group members may pressure others to conform, reducing the likelihood of disagreement.
• Group decision making results in a higher-quality decision than does individual decision making.	• The process may be dominated by one or a small number of participants.
• Participation of group members increases the likelihood that a decision will be accepted.	• Groups lack accountability, because it is difficult to assign responsibility for outcomes to any one individual.

Work Groups versus Work Teams

work groups
The groups that share resources and coordinate efforts to help members better perform their individual jobs.

We have already noted that teams are a special type of organizational group, but we also need to differentiate between work groups and work teams. **Work groups** share resources and coordinate efforts to help members better perform their individual duties and responsibilities. The performance of the group can be evaluated by adding up the contributions of the individual group members. **Work teams** require not only coordination but also *collaboration,* the pooling of knowledge, skills, abilities, and resources in a collective effort to attain a common goal. A work team creates *synergy,* causing the performance of the team as a whole to be greater than the sum of team members' individual contributions. Simply assigning employees to groups and labeling them a team does not guarantee a positive outcome. Managers and team members must be committed to creating, developing, and maintaining high-performance work teams. Factors that contribute to their success are discussed later in this section.

work teams
Like a work group but also requires the pooling of knowledge, skills, abilities, and resources to achieve a common goal.

Types of Teams

problem-solving teams
Usually members of the same department who meet regularly to suggest ways to improve operations and solve specific problems.

The evolution of the team concept in organizations can be seen in three basic types of work teams: problem-solving, self-managed, and cross-functional. **Problem-solving teams** are typically made up of employees from the same department or area of expertise and from the same level of the organizational hierarchy. They meet on a regular basis to share information and discuss ways to improve processes and procedures in specific functional areas. Problem-solving teams generate ideas and alternatives and may recommend a specific course of action, but they typically do not make final decisions, allocate resources, or implement change.

self-managed work teams
Teams without formal supervision that plan, select alternatives, and evaluate their own performance.

Many organizations that experienced success using problem-solving teams were willing to expand the team concept to allow team members greater responsibility in making decisions, implementing solutions, and monitoring outcomes. These highly autonomous groups are called **self-managed work teams**. They manage themselves without any formal supervision, taking responsibility for setting goals, planning and scheduling work activities, selecting team members, and evaluating team performance. When Motorola was pursuing an extremely important project dubbed "Thin Calm," it assembled a team of 20 members and gave it complete control over all aspects of the project. The team was well-funded, worked in secrecy, and delivered the Motorola RAZR, which since it hit the market, has sold nearly as many units as Apple has sold iPods.[14]

cross-functional team
Members from the same organizational level but from different functional areas.

An adaptation of the team concept is called a **cross-functional team**. These teams are made up of employees from about the same hierarchical level, but different functional areas of the organization. Many task forces, organizational committees, and project teams are cross-functional. Often the team members work together only until they solve a given problem or complete a specific project. Cross-functional teams allow people with various levels and areas of expertise to pool their resources, develop new ideas, solve problems, and coordinate complex projects. Both problem-solving teams and self-managed teams may also be cross-functional teams.

CONCEPT in action

© Ali Goldstein/NBC/Courtesy Everett Collection

Fans of NBC's *The Celebrity Apprentice* know all about the rewards of effective teamwork—and about the consequences of failure. Each season, millions tune in to watch teams of enterprising protégés compete for the approval of iconic real-estate tycoon Donald Trump. To the group demonstrating the best cohesiveness, collaboration, and resourcefulness, Trump offers beaucoup perks; but to the nonperformers, Donald offers his trademark "You're fired!" during the dramatic final boardroom scene. What are common characteristics of high-performance teams?

Building High-Performance Teams

A great team must possess certain characteristics, so selecting the appropriate employees for the team is vital. Employees who are more willing to work together to accomplish a common goal should be selected, rather than employees who are more interested in their own personal achievement. Team members should also possess a variety of skills. Diverse skills strengthen the overall effectiveness of the team, so teams should consciously recruit members to fill gaps in the collective skill set. To be effective, teams must also have clearly defined goals. Vague or unclear goals will not provide the necessary direction or allow employees to measure their performance against expectations. Next, high-performing teams need to practice good communication. Team members need to communicate messages and give appropriate feedback that seeks to correct any misunderstandings. Feedback should also be detached; that is, team members should be careful to critique ideas rather than criticize the person who suggests them. Nothing can degrade the effectiveness of a team like personal attacks. Lastly, great teams have great leaders. Skilled team leaders divide work up so that tasks are not repeated, help members set and track goals, monitor their team's performance, communicate openly, and remain flexible to adapt to changing goals or management demands.

CONCEPT check

What is the difference between a work team and a work group?

Identify and describe three types of work teams.

What are some ways to build a high-performance team?

Authority—Establishing Organizational Relationships

Once companies choose a method of departmentalization, they must then establish the relationships within that structure. In other words, the company must decide how many layers of management it needs and who will report to whom. The company must also decide how much control to invest in each of its managers and where in the organization decisions will be made and implemented.

Managerial Hierarchy

Managerial hierarchy (also called the *management pyramid*) is defined by the levels of management within an organization. Generally, the management structure has three levels: top, middle, and supervisory management. These three levels were introduced in Chapter 6. In a managerial hierarchy, each organizational unit is controlled and supervised by a manager in a higher unit. The person with the most formal authority is at the top of the hierarchy. The higher a manager, the more power he or she has. Thus, the amount of power decreases as you move down the management pyramid. At the same time, the number of employees increases as you move down the hierarchy.

Not all companies today are using this traditional configuration. One company that has eliminated hierarchy altogether is 5.11 Tactical, a Modesto, California, company that makes law enforcement uniforms. Like nearly every business around the world, 5.11 has a CEO and managers. Unlike nearly every business in the world, they are all on the same organizational line. The owner, Dan Costa, says, "Our management philosophy is that, unlike other management charts, our management is all on one line. I'm the CEO, and I am on that line. We don't have vice presidents, and we don't have directors. We have managers. There isn't a hierarchy in our company. Everybody feels very good and open about their positions and where they are within the company."[15]

An organization with a well-defined hierarchy has a clear **chain of command**, which is the line of authority that extends from one level of the organization to the next, from top to bottom, and makes clear who reports to whom. The chain of command is shown in the organization chart and can be traced from the CEO all the way down to the employees producing goods and services. Under the *unity of command* principle, everyone reports to and gets instructions from only one boss. Unity of command guarantees that everyone will have a direct supervisor and will not be taking orders from a number of different supervisors. Unity of command and chain of command give everyone in the organization clear directions and help coordinate people doing different jobs. In general, the chain of command flows from top to bottom, but Linden Labs, the creator of Second Life, has reversed that direction with tremendous results. Rather than having managers assign employees to jobs and tasks, the employees themselves figure out which projects are needed and which ones they are going to work on.[16]

Matrix organizations automatically violate the unity of command principle because employees report to more than one boss, if only for the duration of a project. For example, Unilever, the consumer-products company that makes Dove soap, Surf detergent, and Country Crock margarine, used to have a matrix structure with one CEO for North America and another for Europe. But employees in divisions that operated in both locations were unsure about which CEO's decisions took precedence.[17] Companies like Unilever and Hewlett-Packard tend to abandon matrix structures because of problems associated with unclear or duplicate reporting relationships, in other words, with a lack of unity of command.

4 What tools do companies use to establish relationships within their organizations?

managerial hierarchy
The levels of management within an organization; typically, includes top, middle, and supervisory management.

chain of command
The line of authority that extends from one level of an organization's hierarchy to the next, from top to bottom, and makes clear who reports to whom.

authority
Legitimate power, granted by the organization and acknowledged by employees, that allows an individual to request action and expect compliance.

delegation of authority
The assignment of some degree of authority and responsibility to persons lower in the chain of command.

span of control
The number of employees a manager directly supervises; also called span of management.

Individuals who are part of the chain of command have authority over other persons in the organization. **Authority** is legitimate power, granted by the organization and acknowledged by employees, that allows an individual to request action and expect compliance. Exercising authority means making decisions and seeing that they are carried out. Most managers *delegate*, or assign, some degree of authority and responsibility to others below them in the chain of command. The **delegation of authority** makes the employees accountable to their supervisor. *Accountability* means responsibility for outcomes. Typically, authority and responsibility move downward through the organization as managers assign activities to, and share decision making with, their subordinates. Accountability moves upward in the organization as managers in each successively higher level are held accountable for the actions of their subordinates. Delegating authority is not always easily done. Phil Knight, the charismatic founder of Nike, tried three times to delegate authority over the company to a successor, but each time, he was unable to fully relinquish control.[18] Former CEO William Perez puts Knight at the top of the list of CEOs who can't delegate. Perez says, "From virtually the day I arrived, Phil was as engaged in the company as he ever was. He was talking to my direct reports. It was confusing for the people and frustrating for me."[19]

Span of Control

Each firm must decide how many managers are needed at each level of the management hierarchy to effectively supervise the work performed within organizational units. A manager's **span of control** (sometimes called *span of management*) is the number of employees the manager directly supervises. It can be as narrow as 2 or 3 employees or as wide as 50 or more. In general, the larger the span of control, the more efficient the organization. Google tried to impose a traditional supervisory structure with a narrow span of control, but the company's culture became increasingly bureaucratic as a result. After only a few weeks, the structure was replaced with one that had a wider span of control. Today, the average manager in Google's product development group has 50 direct reports, and some managers have more than 100.[20] As Exhibit 7.6 shows, however, both narrow and wide spans of control have benefits and drawbacks.

If hundreds of employees perform the same job, one supervisor may be able to manage a very large number of employees. Such might be the case at a clothing plant, where hundreds of sewing machine operators work from identical patterns. But if employees perform complex and dissimilar tasks, a manager can effectively supervise only a much smaller number. For instance, a supervisor in the research and development area of a pharmaceutical company might oversee just a few research chemists due to the highly complex nature of their jobs.

The optimal span of control is determined by the following five factors:

1. *Nature of the task.* The more complex the task, the narrower the span of control.
2. *Location of the workers.* The more locations, the narrower the span of control.
3. *Ability of the manager to delegate responsibility.* The greater the ability to delegate, the wider the span of control.

CONCEPT check

How does the chain of command clarify reporting relationships?

What is the role of a staff position in a line-and-staff organization?

What factors determine the optimal span of control?

EXHIBIT 7.6	Narrow and Wide Spans of Control	
	Advantages	**Disadvantages**
Narrow span of control	• High degree of control. • Fewer subordinates may mean manager is more familiar with each individual. • Close supervision can provide immediate feedback.	• More levels of management, therefore more expensive. • Slower decision making due to vertical layers. • Isolation of top management. • Discourages employee autonomy.
Wide span of control	• Fewer levels of management means increased efficiency and reduced costs. • Increased subordinate autonomy leads to quicker decision making. • Greater organizational flexibility. • Higher levels of job satisfaction due to employee empowerment.	• Less control. • Possible lack of familiarity due to large number of subordinates. • Managers spread so thin that they can't provide necessary leadership or support. • Lack of coordination or synchronization.

4. *Amount of interaction and feedback between the workers and the manager.* The more feedback and interaction required, the narrower the span of control.
5. *Level of skill and motivation of the workers.* The higher the skill level and motivation, the wider the span of control.

Degree of Centralization

The final component in building an effective organizational structure is deciding at what level in the organization decisions should be made. **Centralization** is the degree to which formal authority is concentrated in one area or level of the organization. In a highly centralized structure, top management makes most of the key decisions in the organization, with very little input from lower-level employees. Centralization lets top managers develop a broad view of operations and exercise tight financial controls. It can also help to reduce costs by eliminating redundancy in the organization. After the dot-com crash, Cisco realized that it needed an organizational structure that would enable it to innovate faster. Previously, the company had been organized into product and geographic units that each had their own functional support team. But with this structure, the cost of support (marketing, sales, engineering, etc.) was over 50 percent of the total sales the company was making in a year. Today, all those functions are highly centralized, and when the company enters new markets or works on new products, managers must assemble a team from the people who report to the functional heads. This structure eliminated redundancies in the functional areas, and even though Cisco doubled in size between 2001 and 2007, its cost of support has dropped to 39 percent of annual sales.[21]

Like all organizational structures, centralization has its drawbacks. In highly centralized organizations, lower-level personnel may not get a chance to develop their decision-making and leadership skills, and the organization is less able to respond quickly to customer demands.

Decentralization is the process of pushing decision-making authority down the organizational hierarchy, giving lower-level personnel more responsibility and power to make and implement decisions. Benefits of decentralization can include quicker decision making, increased levels of innovation and creativity, greater organizational flexibility, faster development of lower-level managers, and increased levels of job satisfaction and employee commitment. But decentralization can also be risky. If lower-level personnel don't have the necessary skills and training to perform effectively, they may make costly mistakes. Additionally, decentralization may increase the likelihood of inefficient lines of communication, competing objectives, and duplication of effort.

Several factors must be considered when deciding how much decision-making authority to delegate throughout the organization. These factors include the size of the organization, the speed of change in its environment, managers' willingness to give up authority, employees' willingness to accept more authority, and the organization's geographic dispersion.

Decentralization is usually desirable when the following conditions are met:

- The organization is very large, like ExxonMobil, Ford, or General Electric.
- The firm is in a dynamic environment where quick, local decisions must be made, as in many high-tech industries.
- Managers are willing to share power with their subordinates.
- Employees are willing and able to take more responsibility.
- The company is spread out geographically, such as JCPenney, Caterpillar, or Ford.

As organizations grow and change, they continually reevaluate their structure to determine whether it is helping the company to achieve its goals.

Organizational Design Considerations

You are now familiar with the different ways to structure an organization, but as a manager, how do you decide which design will work the best for your business? What works for one company may

5 How can the degree of centralization/decentralization be altered to make an organization more successful?

centralization
The degree to which formal authority is concentrated in one area or level of an organization. Top management makes most of the decisions.

© Joe Raedle/Getty Images

The Federal Emergency Management Agency (FEMA), the U.S. agency responsible for responding to floods, hurricanes, and other natural disasters, was once an independent agency with a cabinet-level officer directly accountable to the president. But after 9/11, FEMA was placed under the Department of Homeland Security—a move that former director Michael D. Brown said interfered with communication, planning, and coordination during Hurricane Katrina. What degree of centralization is desirable for an emergency-response organization?

decentralization
The process of pushing decision-making authority down the organizational hierarchy.

CONCEPT check

What are the characteristics of a centralized organization?

What are the benefits of a decentralized organization?

What factors should be considered when choosing the degree of centralization?

6 How do mechanistic and organic organizations differ?

not work for another. In this section, we'll look at two generic models of organizational design and briefly examine a set of contingency factors that favor each.

Mechanistic versus Organic Structures

Structural design generally follows one of the two basic models described in Exhibit 7.7: mechanistic or organic. A **mechanistic organization** is characterized by a relatively high degree of job specialization, rigid departmentalization, many layers of management (particularly middle management), narrow spans of control, centralized decision making, and a long chain of command. This combination of elements results in what is called a tall organizational structure. The U.S. Armed Forces and the United Nations are typical mechanistic organizations.

In contrast, an **organic organization** is characterized by a relatively low degree of job specialization, loose departmentalization, few levels of management, wide spans of control, decentralized decision making, and a short chain of command. This combination of elements results in what is called a flat organizational structure. Colleges and universities tend to have flat organizational structures, with only two or three levels of administration between the faculty and the president. Exhibit 7.8 shows examples of flat and tall organizational structures.

Factors Influencing the Choice Between Mechanistic versus Organic Structures

Although few organizations are purely mechanistic or purely organic, most organizations tend more toward one type or the other. The decision to create a more mechanistic or a more organic structural design is based on factors such as the firm's overall strategy, the size of the organization, and the stability of its external environment, among others.

A company's organizational structure should enable it to achieve its goals, and because setting corporate goals is part of a firm's overall strategy-making process, it follows that a company's structure depends on its *strategy*. Recall the example of how Hewlett-Packard's CEO, Mark Hurd, is working to untangle the unwieldy organizational structure put in place by his predecessor. Hurd has flattened H-P's 14 layers of management to have more executive vice presidents reporting directly to the CEO. Business units will have more autonomy to execute their plans combined with increased accountability for their results. H-P has simply aligned its structure with its strategy.[22]

CONCEPT in action

The Walt Disney Company recently expanded its entertainment empire by acquiring Pixar studios, the animation powerhouse behind such blockbusters as *Ratatouille, Finding Nemo,* and *Toy Story.* The $7.4 billion purchase absorbed Pixar into the Disney Studio Entertainment division, one of Disney's four operating units, alongside Parks and Resorts, Consumer Products, and Media Networks. Why do some analysts believe that Disney's colossal organizational structure could engulf the smaller Pixar operation and stifle its creative output?

That alignment can be challenging for struggling companies trying to accomplish multiple goals. For example, a company with an innovation strategy will need the flexibility and fluid movement of information that an organic organization provides. But a company using a cost-control strategy will require the efficiency and tight control of a mechanistic organization. Often, struggling companies try to simultaneously increase innovation and rein in costs, which can mean organizational challenges for managers. Such is the case at Sony, whose CEO, Howard Stringer, cut 10,000 jobs, closed factories, and shuffled management in an attempt to control costs and improve efficiency. At the same time, he is also trying to encourage cross-divisional communication (like between the music and electronics divisions) and increase the pace of innovation. Stringer will need to balance these two strategies regardless of which organizational model he relies on most.[23]

Another factor that affects how mechanistic or organic a company's organizational structure is its *size*. Much research has been conducted that shows a company's size has a significant impact on its organizational structure.[24] Smaller companies tend to follow the more organic model, in part because they can. It's

EXHIBIT 7.7	Mechanistic versus Organic Structure	
Structural Characteristic	**Mechanistic**	**Organic**
Job specialization	High	Low
Departmentalization	Rigid	Loose
Management hierarchy (levels of management)	Tall (many levels)	Flat (few levels)
Span of control	Narrow	Wide
Decision-making authority	Centralized	Decentralized
Chain of command	Long	Short

EXHIBIT 7.8 Flat versus Tall Organizational Structures

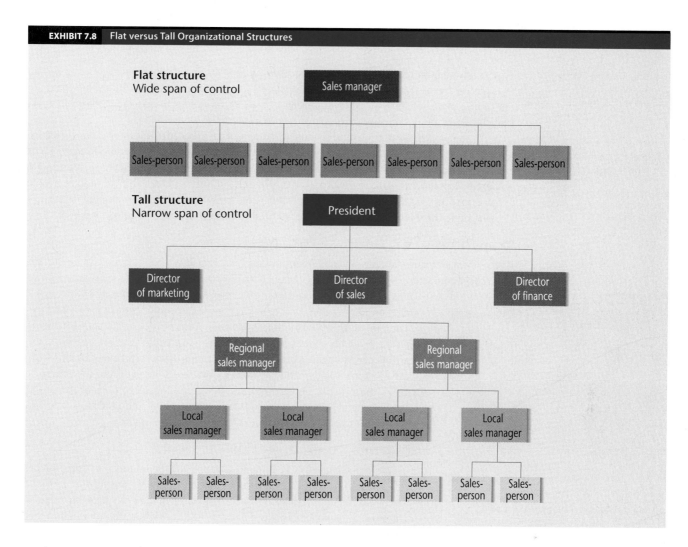

much easier to be successful with decentralized decision making, for example, if you have only 50 employees. A company with that few employees is also more likely, by virtue of its size, to have a lesser degree of employee specialization. That's because when there are fewer people to do the work, those people tend to know more about the entire process. As a company grows, it becomes more mechanistic as systems are put in place to manage the greater number of employees. Procedures, rules, and regulations replace flexibility, innovation, and independence.

Lastly, the industry in which a company operates has a significant impact on its organizational structure. In complex, dynamic, and unstable environments, companies need to organize for flexibility and agility. That is, their organizational structures need to respond to rapid and unexpected changes in the business environment. Linden Labs, the company that produces Second Life, the popular virtual world, has created an internal system that encourages team effort and helps the company respond quickly to its rapidly changing environment. Every week, employees are allocated a certain number of points to invest in internal projects they believe in. Employees are all given the same number of points and pledge those points to a project or projects that they feel will be the greatest benefit to the company. Employees can also give their points directly to the people they feel deserve the points. Phillip Rosedale, the founder of Linden Labs and Second Life, says, "The belief is that, in an environment with a high degree of transparency, it's likely under those conditions that encouraging people to make their own decisions on what to work on will result in a higher level of productivity and a higher success rate." In other words, the company's highly collaborative and extremely flat structure allows it to respond quickly—and successfully—to changes in its environment.[25] For companies operating in stable environments, however, the demands for flexibility and agility are not so great. The environment is predictable. In a simple, stable environment, therefore, companies benefit from the efficiencies created by a mechanistic organizational structure.

CONCEPT check

Compare and contrast mechanistic and organic organizations.

What factors determine whether an organization should be mechanistic or organic?

Chapter 7: Designing Organizational Structures

The Informal Organization

7 How does the informal organization affect the performance of the company?

informal organization
The network of connections and channels of communication based on the informal relationships of individuals inside an organization.

Up to this point in the chapter, we have focused on formal organizational structures that can be seen in the boxes and lines of the organization chart. Yet many important relationships within an organization do not show up on an organization chart. Nevertheless, these relationships can affect the decisions and performance of employees at all levels of the organization.

The network of connections and channels of communication based on the informal relationships of individuals inside the organization is known as the **informal organization**. Informal relationships can be between people at the same hierarchical level or between people at different levels and in different departments. Some connections are work related, such as those formed among people who carpool or ride the same train to work. Others are based on nonwork commonalties such as belonging to the same church or health club or having children who attend the same school.

Functions of the Informal Organization

The informal organization has several important functions. First, it provides a source of friendships and social contact for organization members. Second, the interpersonal relationships and informal groups help employees feel better informed about and connected with what is going on in their firm, thus giving them some sense of control over their work environment. Third, the informal organization can provide status and recognition that the formal organization cannot or will not provide employees. Fourth, the network of relationships can aid the socialization of new employees by informally passing along rules, responsibilities, basic objectives, and job expectations. Finally, the organizational grapevine helps employees to be more aware of what is happening in their workplace by transmitting information quickly and conveying it to places that the formal system does not reach.

CONCEPT in action

Smart managers understand that not all of a company's influential relationships appear on the organization chart. Off the chart there exists a web of informal personal connections between workers, across which vital information and knowledge pass constantly. By using social network analysis software and communication-tracking tools, managers are able to map and quantify the normally invisible relationships that form between employees. How might identifying a firm's informal organization aid managers in fostering teamwork, motivating employees, and boosting productivity?

Informal Communication Channels

The informal channels of communication used by the informal organization are often referred to as the *grapevine*, the *rumor mill*, or the *intelligence network*. Managers need to pay attention to the grapevines in their organization, because their employees increasingly put a great deal of stock in the information that travels along it. A recent survey found that many business leaders have their work cut out for them in the speeches and presentations they give employees. Survey participants were asked if they would believe a message delivered in a speech by a company leader or one that they heard over the grapevine. Forty-seven percent of those responding said they would put more credibility in the grapevine. Only 42 percent said they would believe senior leadership, and another 11 percent indicated they would believe a blend of elements from both messages.[26] Perhaps even more interesting is how accurate employees perceive their company grapevine to be. According to the Workplace Index Survey on the Nature of Work in 2007, 76 percent of employees said that office gossip is accurate always, usually, or some of the time.[27] One respondent on a similar survey said, "The grapevine may not be wholly accurate, but it is a very reliable indicator that something is going on."[28]

With this in mind, managers need to learn to use the existing informal organization as a tool that can potentially benefit the formal organization. An excellent way of putting the informal organization to work for the good of the company is to bring informal leaders into the decision-making process. That way, at least the people who use and nurture the grapevine will have more accurate information to send it.

CONCEPT check

What is the informal organization?

How can informal channels of communication be used to improve operational efficiency?

Trends In Organizational Structure

8 What trends are influencing the way businesses organize?

To improve organizational performance and achieve long-term objectives, some organizations seek to reengineer their business processes or adopt new technologies that open up a variety of organizational design options such as virtual corporations and virtual teams. Other trends that have strong footholds in today's organizations include outsourcing and managing global businesses.

© iStockphoto.com/Alex Slobodkin

Reengineering Organizational Structure

Periodically, all businesses must reevaluate the way they do business. This includes assessing the effectiveness of the organizational structure. To meet the formidable challenges of the future, companies are increasingly turning to **reengineering**—the complete redesign of business structures and processes in order to improve operations.

An even simpler definition of reengineering is "starting over." In effect, top management asks, "If we were a new company, how would we run this place?" The purpose of reengineering is to identify and abandon the outdated rules and fundamental assumptions that guide current business operations. Every company has many formal and informal rules based on assumptions about technology, people, and organizational goals that no longer hold. Thus, the goal of reengineering is to redesign business processes to achieve improvements in cost control, product quality, customer service, and speed. The reengineering process should result in a more efficient and effective organizational structure that is better suited to the current (and future) competitive climate of the industry. That is the hope of Guy Hands, CEO of the company that owns EMI Group Ltd., the record label of popular bands like the Rolling Stones and Coldplay. After spending millions of dollars to fight file sharing, the music industry is facing new threats to its traditional model of signing artists to contracts. Today, artists are making lucrative arrangements with retailers (like Starbucks), aligning with concert promoters, and even selling their music directly to consumers through Web sites. Bands like Radiohead and artists like Paul McCartney have left EMI and been so successful doing all of those things on their own that other bands and artists, including the Rolling Stones, are considering leaving as well. CEO Hands has determined that only a serious restructuring of EMI will stem the talent exodus and keep the label viable in the future. Historically, artists and repertoire (A&R) executives have been involved in all aspects of an album's creation, from working with the music to marketing, public relations, legal contracts, distribution, and artist pay. Hands's reengineering will pull all of the operational aspects of the business away from the A&R executives, who will now only be responsible for discovering new talent and connecting them to the record company. This change will call for 6,000 job cuts, which amounts to almost one-third of EMI's workforce, including its senior management, which will be replaced with executives from industries other than music. The goal is to use in the sale of music the same marketing and operational tools that are used to sell consumer products like toothpaste. Hands hopes that his massive restructuring will stop the erosion of EMI's market share and strengthen what many consider the weakest of the recording labels in the industry.[29]

Yahoo is shuffling its operations and management at a dizzying pace to keep up with search-rival Google and social-networking trendsetters MySpace and Twitter. In late 2006, former CEO Terry Semel announced that the company would reorganize into three groups that align with three customer segments of audiences, advertisers, and publishers. But by mid-2007, Semel resigned, and company cofounder Jerry Yang initiated a new plan to restructure departments and personnel. What are the main purposes for reengineering a business?

The Virtual Corporation

One of the biggest challenges for companies today is adapting to the technological changes that are affecting all industries. Organizations are struggling to find new organizational structures that will help them transform information technology into a competitive advantage. One alternative that is becoming increasingly prevalent is the **virtual corporation**, which is a network of independent companies (suppliers, customers, even competitors) linked by information technology to share skills, costs, and access to one another's markets. This network structure allows companies to come together quickly to exploit rapidly changing opportunities. The key attributes of a virtual corporation are:

- *Technology.* Information technology helps geographically distant companies form alliances and work together.
- *Opportunism.* Alliances are less permanent, less formal, and more opportunistic than in traditional partnerships.
- *Excellence.* Each partner brings its core competencies to the alliance, so it is possible to create an organization with higher quality in every functional area and increase competitive advantage.
- *Trust.* The network structure makes companies more reliant on each other and forces them to strengthen relationships with partners.
- *No borders.* This structure expands the traditional boundaries of an organization.

In the concept's purest form, each company that links up with others to create a virtual corporation is stripped to its essence. Ideally, the virtual corporation has neither a central office

Instant Companies—Keen!

Footwear companies can spend up to 10 months designing new styles, which retailers expect to see and touch long before stocking them. But just eight weeks before they would need samples for their summer line, Jim Van Dine and his three partners were still debating the merits of Mary Janes.

The four men were banging out the concept for Keen Footwear, their new shoe company. Everyone agreed on the core product, an athletic sandal with a protective cap at the toe. Van Dine, hoping to make Keen more than a one-shoe wonder, argued for a broader array of styles, including clogs, slip-ons, and the strap-and-buckle design known as a Mary Jane. "We had one shot to get it right," he says. "I didn't want to just be a sandal company."

Rolling out so many shoes at such a late date would have been unthinkable for an established shoemaker, let alone a brand-new one. Keen, however, had at its disposal resources far more powerful than what has traditionally been available to a start-up. One partner had already reserved capacity in two Chinese factories for massive production runs. Van Dine himself knew there were plenty of freelance shoe designers who could quickly translate his team's vision in to manufacturing specifications. And he believed that Keen could make its brand practically a household name while spending virtually nothing on advertising. In sum, four guys with a great idea, some good contacts, and a loan to cover initial inventory figured they could go head-to-head with Nike in just 60 days.

Two months later, a factory in China was churning out Keen clogs, slip-ons, and yes, Mary Janes—16 styles in all. Keen sold $30 million worth of shoes in its first year—around 700,000 pairs—with Mary Janes and other nonsandals accounting for 45 percent of the total. (It took Teva three years to reach just $1 million in annual sales.) Keen's overnight rise reflects marketing strength, but the company's swift transformation is just one of many product-oriented start-ups going from concept to contender at warp speed.

In every industry you can think of, small, savvy new companies are wedging themselves into established industries unburdened by the fixed costs of an organizational infrastructure. Resources like out-sourced manufacturing, Internet-powered publicity, and robust design tools have never before been available so cheaply to start-ups. To get to market fast, these virtual organizations farm out everything they can, from logistics and billing to sales and support. "This," says Timothy Faley, managing director of the University of Michigan's Institute for Entrepreneurial Studies, "is how the manufacturing moguls of the future are getting started."[30]

Critical Thinking Questions
- Do you think Keen's business model is sustainable? In other words, do you think virtual corporations can have long-term success? Why or why not?
- Can any type of company use the virtual corporation model? Explain your answer.

© Rubberball/Getty Images

nor an organization chart, no hierarchy, and no vertical integration. It contributes to an alliance only its core competencies, or key capabilities. It mixes and matches what it does best with the core competencies of other companies and entrepreneurs. For example, a manufacturer would only manufacture, while relying on a product design firm to decide what to make and a marketing company to sell the end result.

Although firms that are purely virtual organizations are still relatively scarce, many companies are embracing several characteristics of the virtual structure. One great example is Cisco Systems. Cisco has 34 plants that produce its products, but the company owns only 2 of them. Human hands touch only 10 percent of customer orders. Less than half of all orders are processed by a Cisco employee. To the average customer, the interdependency of Cisco's suppliers and inventory systems makes it look like one huge, seamless company. Virtual companies are not just for big entities like Cisco, however. Read the Catching the Entrepreneurial Spirit box above to find out how one member of the new generation of U.S. manufacturers built a company with millions of dollars in revenue with a bare-bones organizational structure.

Virtual Teams

Technology is also enabling corporations to create virtual work teams. Geography is no longer a limitation when employees are considered for a work team. When managers need to staff a project, all they need to do is make a list of required skills and a general list of employees who possess those skills. When the pool of employees is known, the manager simply chooses the best mix of people and creates the virtual team. According to management consultant Christopher Rice of Blessing White, one in four global managers works in the same location as his or her team and in three-quarters of large organizations, team members are dispersed by location and time zone.[31]

Virtual teams mean reduced travel time and costs, reduced relocation expenses, and utilization of specialized talent regardless of employee's location. Special challenges of virtual teams include keeping team members focused, motivated, and communicating positively despite their location. Rice says, "Team

CONCEPT in action

No more traffic jams, no time wasted on frivolous office chat, no need to dress up—alternative work arrangements are increasingly common among today's business professionals. However, individuals should think twice before leaving the traditional office cubicle for good. Interruptions from kids make working from home a challenge, and a lack of face-to-face interaction can be detrimental to building trustworthy business relationships. Moreover, the living room is no place to meet with clients. What are the pros and cons of alternative work arrangements?

© Botanica/Jupiterimages

leaders and members alike have to cope with time shifts and extra-long days." Because team members don't have informal opportunities to socialize, "misunderstandings are common and may erode the trust base," he continues. Therefore, leaders of virtual teams should take care to nurture trusting relationships.[32] If feasible, at least one face-to-face meeting during the early stages of team formation will help with these potential problems.

Once the team is established, Rice offers these tips to keep it productive and on track:

- *Make conversations more personal to build relationships.* When you don't see people casually in the halls and can't go to lunch together, it's difficult for teams to form the social bonds that help create cohesiveness. Tools like instant messaging and Twitter can help with this.
- *Be attuned to the mood and nuances of virtual meetings.* Because team members aren't face-to-face, leaders need to establish the mood of each meeting. Leaving time at the beginning of the meeting for small talk can set a positive mood as well as help build personal relationships.
- *Keep staff engaged and focused.* It's too easy to multitask during a teleconference, particularly when team members who are participating in the meeting during their nonbusiness hours (remember, virtual teams often work across time zones) may be doing things like helping kids with homework or getting dinner started. The team leader needs to make sure meetings stay focused and that team members engage in the discussion.
- *Establish one-on-one time with each member of the team.* That kind of personalized time with each member builds relationships, trust, and commitment to the team.[33]

Outsourcing

Another organizational trend that continues to influence today's managers is outsourcing. For decades, companies have outsourced various functions. For example, payroll functions like recording hours, benefits, wage rates, and issuing paychecks, have been handled for years by third-party providers. Today, however, outsourcing includes a much wider array of business functions: customer service, production, engineering, information technology, sales and marketing, janitorial services, maintenance, and more. Outsourcing is evolving from a trend to a way of doing business.

Companies outsource for two main reasons: cost reduction and labor needs. Often, to satisfy both requirements, companies will outsource work to firms in foreign countries. It seems that nearly every day an article in the business press mentions global outsourcing. That is because more and more companies are integrating global outsourcing into their business strategy. A recent survey conducted by Archstone, a Connecticut consulting firm, found that 73 percent of the *Fortune* 500 and *Forbes* 2000 companies it polled, with average annual revenues of $25 billion, see global outsourcing as an important part of their growth strategy and a way to cut administrative costs.[34] In addition, more than 65 percent of the companies in the Archstone survey indicated that their primary reason for outsourcing was labor needs.[35] Sometimes outsourcing is required for survival as discussed in the Expanding Around the Globe box on the next page.

CONCEPT in action

British luxury brands Jaguar and Land Rover are now under Indian ownership after operating for years beneath the umbrella of Michigan's Ford Motor Company. In 2008, Mumbai-based Tata Motors purchased the premium-auto firms for $2.3 billion—about half of what Ford paid for them originally. Despite Tata's pledge to pursue a hands-off approach to Jaguar-Land Rover's U.K. operations, the merger faces a range of challenges, from managing a multinational workforce to Tata's lack of experience in the luxury-car market. What structuring difficulties arise when global businesses combine?

© AP Images/Tony Ding

The attractiveness of outsourcing should not blind managers to its real challenges and limits. Companies in growing numbers are turning to offshore service providers as a way to cut costs, but a survey of more than 5,000 executives worldwide shows that savings aren't as high as typically expected. "Most people across the board think they're going to cut a third or half of their costs," says Phillip Hatch, president of offshoring consulting and market research firm Ventoro. "That simply isn't realistic."[36] Hatch found that companies achieve only a little better than 9 percent savings as a result of sending work overseas. Weeding out catastrophic failures increases the savings to only 19 percent.[37]

Another misconception about outsourcing is the size of the talent pool in developing nations. Shockingly enough, it isn't as large as you might think. Due to inadequate foreign-language proficiency, lack of practical skills, unwillingness to move for a job, and limited or no access to airports and other transportation networks, only a fraction of those dirt-cheap engineers, financiers, accountants, scientists, and other professionals in China, India, and elsewhere can be put to effective use by multinational corporations anytime soon.[38] Only 14 percent of the 33 million university graduates in low-wage countries who have up to seven years' experience are ready to work for multinational companies. That compares to 15 million young professionals in higher-wage nations.[39]

Lego Builds a New Business Model— Without Its Bricks

Since its invention in the 1940s, the iconic Lego brick has been manufactured in the town of Billund, Denmark. But changes in the external environment forced Lego to rethink its business model and to come to grips with the changing nature of play.

One of the strongest brands in the toy business, Lego built its business on a philosophy of inventive play. Its colorful bricks are sold in over 130 countries, everyone on earth has, on average, 52 of them, and with only six 8-sided bricks, 915,103,765 combinations are possible. Lego bricks are so meticulously made that in 1 million bricks, only 18 will be declared defective and removed from the set. What makes that quality rate even more impressive is the fact that Lego manufactures over 15 billion elements (bricks, tires, people) per year. In fact, Lego is the world's largest tire manufacturer.

Despite its reputation for quality and the nostalgia many people have for Legos, Lego began experiencing significant losses as children stopped spending as much time in inventive play and more time with electronic toys and games. For the company to survive, it needed to reduce the costs associated with producing its elements, and the only way the CEO could see to do that was by outsourcing. Choosing

a partner to maintain the quality standards was critical, so rather than rely on a supplier's technical capabilities, Lego decided to ship its proprietary manufacturing equipment to its new American outsource partner, Flextronics. Lego then closed all of its manufacturing facilities in Switzerland and Denmark and shifted its production to Flextronics locations in Mexico and Eastern Europe.

Outsourcing manufacturing, combined with job cuts, allowed Lego to fend off private equity companies that were looking to buy the classic toy-maker. Sales have increased, new-product development has blossomed, and Lego is again profitable.[40]

Critical Thinking Questions
- What are the risks to outsourcing Lego brick and element production?
- Do you think outsourcing to developing nations is inevitable? In other words, can companies avoid outsourcing, or will financial constraints ultimately force all companies to outsource to developing nations with lower labor costs?

Despite the challenges, global outsourcing programs can be effective. To be successful in outsourcing efforts, managers must do the following:

- Identify a specific business problem.
- Consider all possible solutions.
- Decide whether sending work offshore is the appropriate answer to the problem.
- Look for offshore providers that have high-caliber systems in place that will push clients to optimize their own internal processes.
- Find an offshore provider that understands their business.[41]

CONCEPT check

How does technology enable firms to organize as virtual corporations?

What are some organizational issues that must be addressed when two large firms merge?

Companies that follow these basic steps and manage their offshore projects well could surpass the average and realize savings of as much as 30 percent.[42]

Summary of Learning Goals

1 What are the five traditional forms of departmentalization?

To build an organizational structure, companies first must divide the work into separate jobs and tasks. Managers then group related jobs and tasks together into departments. Five basic types of departmentalization (see Exhibit 7.2) are commonly used in organizations:

- *Functional*. Based on the primary functions performed within an organizational unit.
- *Product*. Based on the goods or services produced or sold by the organizational unit.
- *Process*. Based on the production process used by the organizational unit.
- *Customer*. Based on the primary type of customer served by the organizational unit.
- *Geographic*. Based on the geographic segmentation of organizational units.

2 What contemporary organizational structures are companies using?

In recent decades, companies have begun to expand beyond traditional departmentalization methods and use matrix, committee, and team-based structures. Matrix structures combine two types of traditional organizational structures (for example, geographic and functional). Matrix structures bring together people from different functional areas of the organization to work on a special project. As such, matrix organizations are more flexible, but because employees report to two direct supervisors, managing matrix structures can be extremely challenging. Committee structures give authority and responsibility to a group rather than to an individual. Committees are part of a line-and-staff organization and often fulfill only an advisory role. Team-based structures also involve assigning authority and responsibility to groups rather than individuals, but different from committees, team-based structures give these groups autonomy to carry out their work.

Work groups share resources and coordinate efforts to help members better perform their individual duties and responsibilities. The performance of the group can be evaluated by adding up the contributions of the individual group members. Work teams require not only coordination but also collaboration, the pooling of knowledge, skills, abilities, and resources in a collective effort to attain a common goal. Four types of work teams are used: problem-solving, self-managed, cross-functional, and virtual teams. Companies are using teams to improve individual and group motivation and performance.

3 Why are companies using team-based organizational structures?

The managerial hierarchy (or the management pyramid) comprises the levels of management within the organization, and the managerial span of control is the number of employees the manager directly supervises. In daily operations, individuals in line positions are directly involved in the processes used to create goods and services. Individuals in staff positions provide the administrative and support services that line employees need to achieve the firm's goals. Line positions in organizations are typically in areas such as production, marketing, and finance. Staff positions are found in areas such as legal counseling, managerial consulting, public relations, and human resource management.

4 What tools do companies use to establish relationships within their organizations?

In a highly centralized structure, top management makes most of the key decisions in the organization with very little input from lower-level employees. Centralization lets top managers develop a broad view of operations and exercise tight financial controls. In a highly decentralized organization, decision-making authority is pushed down the organizational hierarchy, giving lower-level personnel more responsibility and power to make and implement decisions. Decentralization can result in faster decision making and increased innovation and responsiveness to customer preferences.

5 How can the degree of centralization/decentralization be altered to make an organization more successful?

A mechanistic organization is characterized by a relatively high degree of work specialization, rigid departmentalization, many layers of management (particularly middle management), narrow spans of control, centralized decision making, and a long chain of command. This combination of elements results in a tall organizational structure. In contrast, an organic organization is characterized by a relatively low degree of work specialization, loose departmentalization, few levels of management, wide spans of control, decentralized decision making, and a short chain of command. This combination of elements results in a flat organizational structure.

6 How do mechanistic and organic organizations differ?

The informal organization is the network of connections and channels of communication based on the informal relationships of individuals inside the organization. Informal relationships can be between people at the same hierarchical level or between people at different levels and in different departments. Informal organizations give employees more control over their work environment by delivering a continuous stream of company information throughout the organization, thereby helping employees stay informed.

7 How does the informal organization affect the performance of the company?

Reengineering is a complete redesign of business structures and processes in order to improve operations. The goal of reengineering is to redesign business processes to achieve improvements in cost control, product quality, customer service, and speed.

8 What trends are influencing the way businesses organize?

The virtual corporation is a network of independent companies (suppliers, customers, even competitors) linked by information technology to share skills, costs, and access to one another's markets. This network structure allows companies to come together quickly to exploit rapidly changing opportunities.

Many companies are now using technology to create virtual teams. Team members may be down the hall or across the ocean. Virtual teams mean that travel time and expenses are eliminated and the best people can be placed on the team regardless of where they live. Sometimes, however, it may be difficult to keep virtual team members focused and motivated.

Outsourcing business functions—both globally and domestically—is evolving from trend to regular business practice. Companies choose to outsource either as a cost-saving measure or as a way to gain access to needed human resource talent. To be successful, outsourcing must solve a clearly articulated business problem, and managers must closely match third-party providers with their company's actual needs.

Key Terms

Preparing for Tomorrow's Workplace: SCANS

1. When people talk of climbing the corporate ladder, they are referring to moving upward through the organizational structure. Many employees plot career paths that will take them to increasingly higher levels of management. Do you think you would be more interested in climbing higher in an organization, or being a middle-management bridge between the employees who do the work and the executives who set the strategy? Explain the reasons for your choice. (Resources, Interpersonal)

2. Teams are an increasingly popular method of organizing corporations, but not all people are suited for teamwork. As a manager, what do you do with employees who are talented but unapproachable? Can you think of a way to involve people who are uncomfortable in team settings so that your teams have the perspective of these employees as well? (Interpersonal)

3. Think about how gossip and rumors travel through a grapevine. Draw as many grapevines as you can think of that reflect the different ways rumors move through an organization. Can you think of information that a manager would want to disseminate through the grapevine? Is there information that is inappropriate to disseminate through informal channels? What? (Information)

4. Do you think that companies that outsource will inevitably become virtual corporations? Why or why not? (Resources, Systems)

5. It used to be that only high-level executives and CEOs were able to work on the road. Mobile corporate computing, however, is trickling down the organizational chart. In your opinion, is there a point in the organizational structure at which working remotely (at home, on the road) should stop? Should all employees in the hierarchy be allowed to work in a virtual environment, or should there be limits? Explain your reasoning. (Technology, Systems)

6. **Team Activity** Have you ever worked on a team with an underperforming member, like a slacker, a complainer, or a critic? Assemble a team of three to five students and brainstorm a list of "bad" team members you have experience working with. Once you have a list of types, discuss how that person affected the work of the team and the outcome the team produced. Brainstorm ways to better manage and mitigate the negative effects of "bad" team members. Share your results with the class. (Interpersonal, Systems)

Ethics Activity

In January 2006, St. Paul Travelers Insurance announced that it would lay off more than 100 technology employees and outsource their jobs to Indian workers. This change is part of a larger plan to increase its technology outsourcing. Currently the company outsources about 500 jobs and intends to double that number by 2008. As the insurer shifts responsibilities to the Indian contractors, it has asked its own employees to help with training. "We're sitting here training our India [counterparts] in what we do," said one St. Paul employee who no longer is employed. "The gall of the company. It's insulting."

According to company spokesman Shane Boyd, the main reason for outsourcing the technology jobs is to improve efficiency by using temporary workers for short-term projects or to find specially trained workers, rather than for cost savings. "We're going to use outsourcing when it makes sense for our business," he said.

Using a Web search tool, locate articles about this topic and then write responses to the following questions. Be sure to support your arguments and cite your sources.

ETHICAL DILEMMA: Is St. Paul Travelers justified in outsourcing technology jobs to India? Does it have any obligation to find other jobs or provide training for its displaced employees? Should it ask employees who were being laid off to train the contract labor?

Sources: Pete Engardio, "The Future of Outsourcing," *Business Week*, January 30, 2006, p. 50+; "Global Experts Favour Outsourcing of Jobs," *Press Trust of India Ltd.*, January 26, 2006, **http://www.gale.cengage.com/**; Sheryl Jean, "Travelers Outsources IT Jobs," *Saint Paul Pioneer Press* (St. Paul, Minnesota), January 27, 2006, **http://www.gale.cengage.com/**; Bernadette Starzee, "How to Decide Whether and What to Outsource," *Daily Record* (Kansas City, MO), February 9, 2006, **http://www.gale.cengage.com/**.

Working the Net

1. Using a search engine like Google or Yahoo! to search for the term "company organizational charts," find at least three examples of organizational charts for corporations, not-for-profits, or government agencies. Analyze each entity's organizational structure. Is it organized by function, product/service, process, customer type, or geographic location?

2. Search the archives at the *Business Week* (**http://www.businessweek.com**), *Fortune* (**http://money.cnn.com/magazines/fortune/**), or *Forbes* (**http://www.forbes.com**) Web site for stories about companies that have reorganized. Pick two examples and prepare a summary of their reorganization efforts, including the underlying reasons the company chose to reorganize, the key elements of the reorganization plan, and, if possible, how successful it has been.

3. Visit the *Inc.* magazine Web site, **http://www.inc.com**, and use the search engine to find articles about virtual corporations. Using a search engine, find the Web site of at least one virtual corporation and look for information about how the company uses span of control, informal organization, and other concepts from this chapter.

4. What are the challenges of being part of a virtual team, for both the leader and the participants? Go to **http://www.managementhelp.org/grp_skll/virtual/virtual.htm**. The site offers many resources on this topic. Explore the site to find articles about virtual collaboration and select two that interest you. Share your findings with your classmates and lead a discussion about the characteristics of a successful virtual team.

5. Managing change in an organization is no easy task, as you've discovered in your new job with a consulting firm that specializes in change management. To get up to speed, go to Bpubs.com, the Business Publications Search Engine, **http://www.bpubs.com**, and navigate to the Change Management section of the Management Science category. Select three articles that discuss how companies approached the change process and summarize their experiences.

6. After managing your first project team, you think you might enjoy a career in project management. The Project Management Institute is a professional organization for project managers. Its Web site, **http://www.pmi.org**, has many resources about this field. Explore the site to learn what project management is, then go to the Professional Development and Careers pages. What are the requirements to earn the Project Management Professional designation? Explore other free areas of the site to learn more about the job of project manager. Prepare a brief report on the career and its opportunities. Does what you've learned make you want to follow this career path?

7. Many companies are outsourcing portions of their information technology (IT) departments. Should they, and why? Develop a position on this issue using the resources at NetworkWorld's Outsourcing Research Center, **http://www.networkworld.com/topics/outsourcing.html**, and at InformationWeek's Outsourcing Tech Center, **http://www.informationweek.com/outsourcing/**. Then divide the class into two groups, those that support outsourcing and those that oppose it, and have a debate on this subject.

creative

Creative Thinking Case

Meet the Gore Family

Imagine an organization with more than 7,000 employees working at 45 facilities around the world—with no hierarchy structure. W. L. Gore & Associates, headquartered in Newark, Delaware, is a model of unusual business practices. Wilbert Gore, who left Dupont to explore new uses for Teflon, started the company in 1958. Best known for its breathable, weatherproof Gore-Tex fabric, Glide dental floss, and Elixir guitar strings, the company has no bosses, no titles, no departments, and no formal job descriptions. There is no managerial hierarchy at Gore, and top management treats employees, called associates, as peers.

In April 2005, the company named 22-year associate Terri Kelly its new chief executive officer. Unlike large public corporations, Gore's announcement was made without much fanfare. "It's never about the CEO," she says. "You're an associate, and you just happen to be the CEO. We don't like anyone to be the center of attention." She considers the idea that the CEO of W. L. Gore manages the company a misperception. "My goal is to provide the overall direction. I spend a lot of time making sure we have the right people in the right roles. . . . We empower divisions and push out responsibility. We're so diversified that it's impossible for a CEO to have that depth of knowledge—and not even practical."

The company focuses on its products and company values rather than individuals. Committees, composed of employees, make major decisions such as hiring, firing, and compensation. They even set top executives' compensation. Employees work on teams, which are switched around every few years. In fact, all employees are expected to make minor decisions instead of relying on the "boss" to make them. "We're committed to how we get things done," Kelly says. "That puts a tremendous burden on leaders because it's easier to say, 'Just do it,' than to explain the rationale. But in the long run, you'll get much better results because people are making a commitment."

The company tries to maintain a family-like atmosphere by dispersing its employees into 60 buildings, with no more than 200 employees in any one place. Because no formal lines of authority exist, employees can speak to anyone in the company at any time. This arrangement also forces employees to spend considerable time developing relationships. As one employee described it, instead of trying to please just one "boss," you have to please everyone.

The informal organizational structure is working well. With revenues of almost $2 billion, the company produces thousands of advanced technology products for the electronics, industrial, fabrics, and medical markets. Its corporate structure fosters innovation and has been a significant contributor to associate satisfaction. Employee turnover is a low 5 percent a year, and the company can choose new associates from the 38,000 job applications it receives annually. For the ninth consecutive year, W. L. Gore was near the top of the list of *Fortune's* "100's Best Companies to Work For."

Critical Thinking Questions

- Given the lack of formal structure, how important do you think the informal structure becomes? Does Gore's reliance on committee work slow processes down?
- Is W. L. Gore a mechanistic or an organic organization? Support your answer with examples from this case.
- How do you think Gore's organizational structure affects the division of labor?

Sources: Alan Deutschman, "What I Know Now: Terri Kelly, CEO, W. L. Gore & Associates," *Fast Company*, September 2005, p. 96; "Gore Marks 9th Year as One of Nation's Best, Company Earns #5 Position on FORTUNE Magazine '100 Best Companies to Work For' List," *W. L. Gore & Associates*, press release, January 9, 2006, **http://www.gore.com**; Robert Levering and Milton Moskowitz, "And the Winners Are . . . ," *Fortune*, January 23, 2006, p. 89; Sara J. Welch, "GORE The Fabric of Success," *Successful Meetings*, May 2005, pp. 49–51; and W. L. Gore & Associates Web site, **http://www.gore.com** (February 10, 2006).

knowledge, and abilities a person must have to fill a job are spelled out in a **job specification**. These two documents help human resource planners find the right people for specific jobs. A sample job description and specification is shown in Exhibit 8.2.

job specification
A list of the skills, knowledge, and abilities a person must have to fill a job.

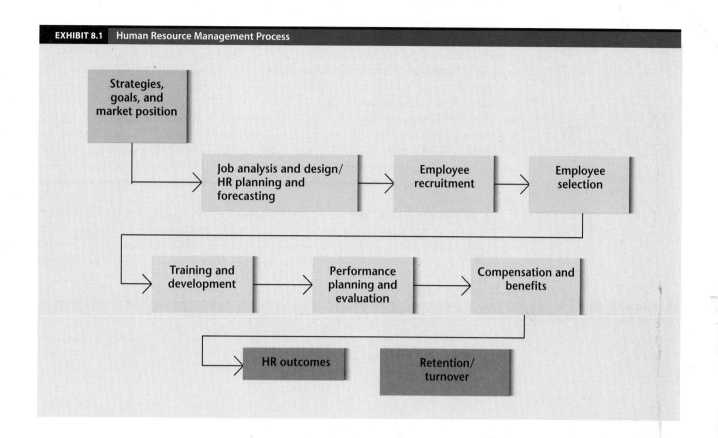

EXHIBIT 8.1   Human Resource Management Process

EXHIBIT 8.2   Job Description and Specification

Position: College Recruiter   **Location: Corporate Offices**
Reports to: Vice President of Human Resources   **Classification: Salaried/Exempt**

Job Summary: Member of HR corporate team. Interacts with managers and department heads to determine hiring needs for college graduates. Visits 20 to 30 college and university campuses each year to conduct preliminary interviews of graduating students in all academic disciplines. Following initial interviews, works with corporate staffing specialists to determine persons who will be interviewed a second time. Makes recommendations to hiring managers concerning best-qualified applicants.

Job Duties and Responsibilities:

Estimated time spent and importance

15%   Works with managers and department heads, determines college recruiting needs.
10%   Determines colleges and universities with degree programs appropriate to hiring needs to be visited.
15%   Performs college relations activities with numerous colleges and universities.
25%   Visits campuses to conduct interviews of graduating seniors.
15%   Develops applicant files and performs initial applicant evaluations.
10%   Assists staffing specialists and line managers in determining who to schedule for second interviews.
5%   Prepares annual college recruiting report containing information and data about campuses, number interviewed, number hired, and related information.
5%   Participates in tracking college graduates who are hired to aid in determining campuses that provide the most outstanding employees.

Job Specification (Qualifications):

Bachelor's degree in human resource management or a related field. Minimum of two years of work experience in HR or department that annually hires college graduates. Ability to perform in a team environment, especially with line managers and department heads. Very effective oral and written communication skills. Reasonably proficient in Excel, Word, and Windows computer environment and familiar with PeopleSoft software.

HR Planning and Forecasting

Forecasting an organization's human resource needs, known as an HR demand forecast, is an essential aspect of HR planning. This process involves two forecasts: (1) determining the number of people needed by some future time (in one year, for example), and (2) estimating the number of people currently employed by the organization who will be available to fill various jobs at some future time; this is an *internal supply forecast*.

The Advancement Planning process at Kraft Foods involves comparing human resource demand and supply forecasts that will reveal whether a surplus or shortage of HR talent exists and the actions required to match demand with the internal supply of HR professionals. The performance of HR professionals at Kraft is reviewed to identify people who can fill vacancies and be promoted, a process known as **succession planning**. According to Thomas Thurman, Kraft's Senior VP of Human Resources, "This process allows us to identify who is ready now for a position of higher responsibility, who will be ready in one to three years, and who will be ready in three to five years."[3] If Kraft has a temporary shortage of HR professionals, it can hire an experienced but possibly semiretired person as a temporary or **contingent worker**, someone who wants to work but not on a permanent, continuous basis. Exhibit 8.3 summarizes the process of planning and forecasting an organization's personnel needs.

An increasingly popular tool for managing staffing levels is the hiring freeze. In the past, when firms face uncertain financial futures, whether due to poor performance, changes in the competitive environment, or a generally softening economy, managers have needed to lay off workers in large numbers. Today, however, managers are becoming more proactive and

succession planning
Examination of current employees to identify people who can fill vacancies and be promoted.

contingent worker
Person who prefers temporary employment, either part-time or full-time.

| EXHIBIT 8.3 | Human Resource Planning Process |

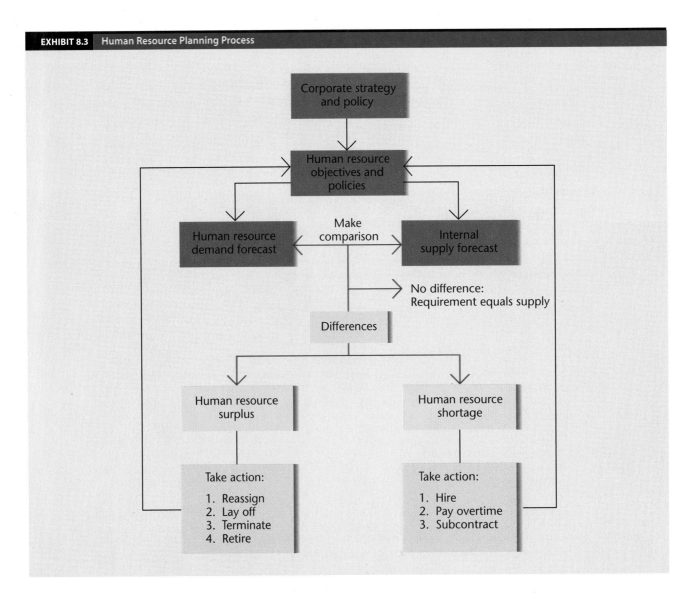

curtailing hiring until the company financials and work flow can support additional workers. According to John Silvia, chief economist at Wachovia Bank, "A lot of firms have simply said the risks are too great to add workers."[4] Hiring freezes can be applied across the company or to select functions. For example, Delta put a freeze on non-customer-facing positions (i.e., back office, administration, etc.) but will hire 1,000 flight attendants to support increases on the international side of its business.[5]

CONCEPT check

Define human resource management.

Distinguish between job analysis, job description, and the job specification.

Describe the human resource management process.

Employee Recruitment

When a firm creates a new position or an existing one becomes vacant, it starts looking for people with qualifications that meet the requirements of the job. Two sources of job applicants are the internal and external labor markets. The internal labor market consists of employees currently employed by the firm; the external labor market is the pool of potential applicants outside the firm. Recruiting is one of the most critical challenges facing today's managers. In a survey conducted by Deloitte & Touche of executives at fast-growing technology companies, 41 percent say their greatest operational challenge—more significant than increasing sales, maintaining strong cash flow, and building internal systems—is finding, hiring, and retaining workers. Sixty-six percent of the CEOs surveyed said that high-quality employees are the biggest contributors to growth, more so than even strategy and leadership.[6]

2 How do firms recruit applicants?

Internal Labor Market

Internal recruitment can be greatly facilitated by using a human resource information system containing a skills inventory, or computerized employee database of information about an employee's previous work experience, education and certifications, job and career preferences, performance, and attendance. Promotions and job transfers are the most common results of internal recruiting. BNSF Railway, Wal-Mart, Boeing Aircraft, Ritz-Carlton Hotels, and most other firms, large and small, promote from within and manage the upward mobility of their employees. Several high-profile companies like American Express, General Electric, and Procter & Gamble, have a reputation for developing leadership and management talent internally. Many firms have begun to develop their internal labor market in preparation for the transition in the executive suite. PepsiCo CEO Indra Nooyi reorganized the company and reassigned executives to broaden the experience of future candidates, all of whom currently work at PepsiCo; eBay's Meg Whitman did the same in preparation for her exit as the company's CEO.

External Labor Market

The external labor market consists of prospects to fill positions that cannot be filled from within the organization. **Recruitment** is the process of attracting qualified people to form an applicant pool. Numerous methods are used to attract applicants, including print, radio, Web, and television advertising. Hospitality and entertainment firms, such as the Ritz-Carlton and Six Flags, frequently use job fairs to attract applicants. A **job fair**, or *corporate open house,* is usually a one- or two-day event at which applicants are briefed about job opportunities, given tours, and encouraged to apply for jobs. Zappos, the online shoe retailer, hosts private job fairs to which it invites roughly 200 applicants. The company uses these fairs to staff positions in accounting, merchandising, customer service, and product information.[7] For firms needing accountants, engineers, chemists, and others for professional and scientific positions, college recruiting is very common. These firms (PricewaterhouseCoopers, Cisco Systems, Intel, Texas Instruments, and thousands of others) schedule on-campus interviews with graduating seniors.

recruitment
The attempt to find and attract qualified applicants in the external labor market.

job fair
An event, typically one day, held at a convention center to bring together job seekers and firms searching for employees.

Electronic Job Boards

Two relatively new aspects of employee recruitment involve use of the Internet. Monster.com and CareerBuilder.com are electronic job boards where applicants post their résumés and firms can post job openings. Companies can also use their Web sites to announce job openings and encourage candidates to apply online. Large firms may receive thousands of online applications per month. To review and evaluate thousands of online résumés and job applications, firms depend on software

Podcasting Goes Corporate

When global consulting firm Bain and Company was planning the opening of its first major Indian office, it knew it needed to recruit students from the Indian Institute of Management. Bain also knew it needed to do more than use traditional recruiting tools like campus visits, DVDs, brochures, and a Web site, so executives created a 20-minute podcast and posted it on the company Web site. Interested candidates could download the podcast at their convenience and listen to 20 minutes of material designed to introduce them to the company and help them prepare for the interview. The podcast featured three different Bain executives and an alumna from the Institute who actually works in Bain's London office.

Partners in India recognized that they needed a more aggressive way to attract talent and thought that using podcasting technology would enable them to better reach young job seekers. The podcasts, however, were not available to everyone but were used in conjunction with a written application process. Once managers reviewed written applications, they selected 100 students who were given access to the podcasts. Of those 100 students, 10 were hired. Despite the stiff competition for the openings, interviewers said that the applicant pool seemed more relaxed and confident during the interview process, something the company attributes to the podcast.

Bain plans on expanding its use of podcasting to more countries and more universities in the near future. Company executives say the technology helps the firm spread its message, bolsters communication with candidates, informs candidates of expectations, and makes the company look technology savvy.

Experts like Daniel Finnigan, the general manager at HotJobs, think podcasts are the next big thing in recruiting and job hunting because "they make the job description come alive." He expects that podcasts will lead to audio and video job listings in the not too distant future. But even though podcasting was a key element in Bain's India staffing strategy, not all those to whom the consultancy offered positions accepted. One student thought the podcast showed "Bain's commitment to recruiting and building a relationship" with the Indian Institute of Management, but nonetheless, he accepted a job at rival firm, McKinsey & Co.[8]

Critical Thinking Questions

- For what kind of job or company would podcasting be the most effective recruitment tool?
- Why do you think podcasting would be most useful for global recruiting efforts?

CONCEPT in action

Online recruiting is among the top Internet success stories of the past decade. Monster and CareerBuilder are hotspots for job hunters and recruiters seeking to establish a working relationship, while other sites like Netshare and JobCentral have a reputation for executive-level opportunities and ties to corporations that invest heavily in online recruitment. What are advantages and disadvantages of online recruiting compared to traditional forms of recruitment?

recruitment branding
Presenting an accurate and positive image of the firm to those being recruited.

to scan and track applicant materials and glean from them critical information for applicant selection. Another high-tech recruitment method, podcasting, is discussed in the Expanding Around the Globe box above.

Social Networking

Referrals and professional networking are traditional methods of identifying job prospects, particularity for managerial, professional, and technical positions. With the Internet, today's networks are bigger and more diverse than ever, and Web-based professional networks like LinkedIn help companies find candidates by navigating employees' network connections. LinkedIn is a giant electronic Rolodex or business card file. Membership involves online registering, providing basic information about one's professional experience, contact information, and current employment, and paying a monthly fee. A member can search through an extended network of contacts based on his or her professional acquaintances. The basis for a search can be job, company, zip code, or membership in a professional organization. LinkedIn uses the concept that there are no more than six degrees of separation between two people, or one person can be linked to any other individual through no more than six other people. With approximately 2 million members in 120 industries, LinkedIn has opened its database to HR professionals for purposes of posting job notices and searching for candidates.[9] A similar site, TheLadders. com, provides the same function but limits its job postings to executive positions that pay more than $100,000 a year.

Recruitment Branding

Recruitment branding combines the elements of recruitment and marketing to present an accurate and positive image of the firm to those being recruited. Typically, integrating HR and marketing allows the company to excel at attracting talent (by establishing it as a cool place to work) and customers (by establishing it as a cool place to do business). This is done by including current information about the firm in printed recruitment materials and Web-based job announcements. Razon Suzelman, founder of I Love Rewards, an incentive marketing company, decided to apply his talent for selling to the hiring process after realizing that the company was suffering from high turnover. He instituted group interviews during which he or other employees give job applicants a complete view of the company and treated them like customers. After only two years of this hiring practice, I Love Rewards saw turnover plummet to 10 percent, and recently the company received 1,700 résumés for seven openings. One candidate who was not offered a job went on to work for a well-known retailer. The candidate was so impressed with I Love Rewards that he convinced his new boss to sign on with I Love Rewards as a customer. That new client boosted annual revenue by 12 percent in a single year, showing that recruitment branding, when done well, can produce exceptional results.[10]

Realistic Job Previews

With the popularity of online job boards and recruitment sites, job descriptions have become laden with key words designed to increase the likelihood of a good person–job fit. Unfortunately, such descriptions can be cryptic and focused heavily on education and experience requirements. Offering little insight into what the advertised job actually entails, such job descriptions may ultimately increase the rate of employee turnover, as new hires realize the job isn't what they thought it would be. One way around this conundrum is to draft descriptions that give a realistic job preview. Aimco, an apartment management company, attributed its high rate of turnover to the fact that new hires hadn't understood what the job involved, so managers rewrote job descriptions in plain English (no jargon) and then tested the new descriptions in markets from Florida to Texas. In markets where the new ads ran, Aimco saw its turnover in the first 90 days of employment drop from 22 percent to 3 percent. Because its new requirements were more open, it attracted from a larger talent pool.[11] Exhibit 8.4 compares Aimco's old job descriptions with its new, more realistic job preview.

CONCEPT check

What are the two sources of job applicants?

What are some methods firms use to recruit applicants?

What is meant by recruitment branding?

Employee Selection

After a firm has attracted enough job applicants, employment specialists begin the selection process. **Selection** is the process of determining which people in the applicant pool possess the qualifications necessary to be successful on the job. The steps in the employee selection process are shown in Exhibit 8.5 on the next page. An applicant who can jump over each step, or hurdle, will very likely receive a job offer; thus, this is known as the successive hurdles approach to applicant screening. Alternatively, an applicant can be rejected at any step or hurdle. Selection steps or hurdles are described below:

1. *Initial screening.* During initial screening, an applicant completes an application form, and/or submits a résumé, and has a brief interview of 30 minutes or less. The job application includes information about educational background, previous work experience, and job duties performed.

3 How do firms select qualified applicants?

selection
The process of determining which persons in the applicant pool possess the qualifications necessary to be successful on the job.

EXHIBIT 8.4	Aimco's Realistic Job Preview	
Old	**New**
• "Responsible for all operations of the apartment community with the primary objectives of increasing net operating income of the community . . ."	• "Community Managers run the show, so to speak, . . ."
• "Has staff of at least one Leasing Consultant and/or at least one Service Technician."	• "A Community Manager is a team leader . . . motivates, challenges, delegates."
• "Bachelor's Degree or equivalent experience required. Typically 2–4 years related experience required."	• ". . . may not necessarily have previous apartment management experience . . . should have strong management, sales, customer service, and fiscal decision-making background."

Source: Erin White, "Job Ads Loosen Up, Get Real," *Wall Street Journal,* March 12, 2007, B3. © 2007 by Dow Jones & Company, Inc. Reproduced with permission of Dow Jones & Company, Inc. in the format Textbook via Copyright Clearance Center.

© AP Images/Richard Drew

Robert Irvine, the celebrity chef who rose to fame by preparing unbelievable meals on the Food Network series *Dinner: Impossible,* has proved yet again that it doesn't pay to pad one's résumé. The culinary conniver lost his network spot after word spread that many spectacular qualifications on his résumé, such as having cooked for U.S. presidents and Britain's royal family, proved untrue. The TV chef was caught spicing up other details of his past, like the claim of being a knight in England's Royal Victorian Order. How do employers screen candidates during the employee selection process?

selection interview
An in-depth discussion of an applicant's work experience, skills and abilities, education, and career interests.

The short, structured interview contains specific questions, such as "Do you have a valid diver's license for operating company vehicles? How many employees were in your work team? How many days did you miss work for illness last year?"

2. *Employment testing.* Following initial screening, the applicant may be asked to take one or more tests. According to Scott Erker, a human resources consultant, about 70 percent of entry- and midlevel jobs at big companies include some kind of testing.[12] Tests can measure special job skills (typing and data entry), aptitudes (numeric and spatial dimensions), and even personality characteristics. Sherri Merbach of Orange Lake Resorts finds personality tests particularly helpful in assessing some candidates. "You're less likely to make a bad hiring decision," she says.[13]

3. *Selection interview.* The tool most widely used in making hiring decisions is the **selection interview**, an in-depth discussion of an applicant's work experience, skills and abilities, education, and career interests. For managerial and professional positions, an applicant may be interviewed by several persons, including the line manager for the position to be filled. This interview is designed to determine a person's communication skills and motivation. During the interview, the applicant may be presented with realistic job situations, such as dealing with a disgruntled customer, and asked to describe how he or she would handle the problem. At the Container Store, interviewees are required to do an impromptu sales presentation that demonstrates their passion for organization.[14] Selecting new employees is a step-by-step process as shown in Exhibit 8.5.

4. *Background and reference check.* If applicants pass the selection interview, most firms examine their background and check their references. In recent years an increasing number of employers such as American Airlines, Disney, and Microsoft are carefully researching applicants' backgrounds, particularly their legal history, reasons for leaving previous jobs, and even creditworthiness. Retail firms, where employees have extensive contact with customers, tend to be very careful about checking applicant backgrounds.

5. *Physical exams and drug testing.* A firm may require an applicant to have a medical checkup to ensure he or she is physically able to perform job tasks. Drug testing is common in the transportation and health care industries. Southwest Airlines,

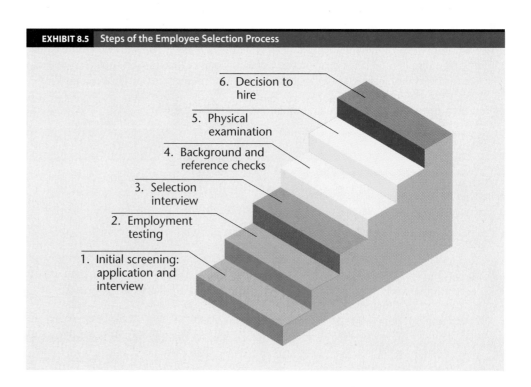

EXHIBIT 8.5   Steps of the Employee Selection Process

6. Decision to hire
5. Physical examination
4. Background and reference checks
3. Selection interview
2. Employment testing
1. Initial screening: application and interview

BNSF Railway, Texas Health Resources, and the U.S. Postal Service use drug testing for reasons of workplace safety, productivity, and employee health.

6. *Decision to hire.* If an applicant progresses satisfactorily through all the selection steps (or jumps all of the selection hurdles), a decision to hire the person is made; however, the job offer may be contingent on passing a physical exam and/or drug test. The decision to hire is nearly always made by the manager of the new employee.

CONCEPT check

Describe the employee selection process.

What are some of the ways that prospective employees are tested?

Employee Training and Development

To ensure that both new and experienced employees have the knowledge and skills to perform their jobs successfully, organizations invest in training and development activities. Recently, Merrill Lynch overhauled the training program for its financial advisers to ensure they could better serve their clients, most of whom are baby boomers who want more financial advice than simple stock tips. The new program includes classes in Monte Carlo analysis, a statistical sampling technique that helps predict the odds that a client will reach his or her financial goals; psychology and behavioral finance, to help clients avoid making catastrophic, impulsive decisions; and nontraditional financial planning elements like trusts and insurance. The company also encourages its new recruits to take classes outside of work to obtain a professional certification, such as certified financial planner.[15] **Training and development**, like that done at Merrill Lynch, involves learning situations in which the employee acquires additional knowledge or skills to increase job performance. Training objectives specify performance improvements, reductions in errors, job knowledge to be gained, and/or other positive organizational results. The process of creating and implementing training and development activities is shown in Exhibit 8.6. Training is done either on the job or off the job.

training and development
Activities that provide learning situations in which an employee acquires additional knowledge or skills to increase job performance.

4 What types of training and development do organizations offer their employees?

orientation
Presentation to get the new employee ready to perform his or her job.

On-the-Job Training

New employee training is essential and usually begins with **orientation**, which entails getting the new employee ready to perform on the job. Formal orientation (often a half-day classroom program) provides information about company policies, salary and benefits, and parking. Orientation sets the tone for the employer–employee relationship, so it needs to be carefully planned. At Gap, orientation starts with a video on the perils of employee theft (authoritarian tone); the Starbucks orientation handbook instructs employees to "Be authentic" (patronizing tone). By contrast, at Apple all employees receive business cards—even front-line store clerks—which communicates to employees that they are important as individuals and as part of the Apple team.[16] More important, however, is the specific job orientation by the new

CONCEPT in action

With over 15 manufacturing plants and 38,000 employees in North America, Toyota is becoming as American as baseball and apple pie. Bolstering the Japanese automaker's "American made" image is a new multimillion-dollar training center in Georgetown, Kentucky, that serves the company's North American plants. The 98,000-square-foot facility offers hands-on training simulations of Toyota manufacturing processes including production, maintenance, and supervisory management. How is technology helping companies develop skilled workers both on and off the job?

© Toyota Motor Engineering & Manufacturing North America, Inc. (TEMA)

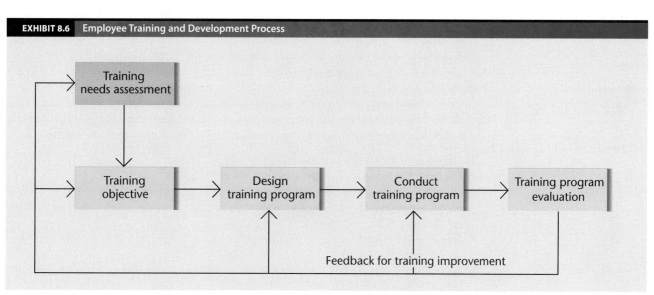

EXHIBIT 8.6   Employee Training and Development Process

Training needs assessment → Training objective → Design training program → Conduct training program → Training program evaluation

Feedback for training improvement

employee's supervisor concerning work rules, equipment, and performance expectations. This second briefing tends to be more informal and may last for several days or even weeks.

Beyond employee orientation, job training takes place at the job site or workstation and is directly related to the job. This training involves specific job instruction, coaching (guidance given to new employees by experienced ones), special-project assignments, or job rotation. **Job rotation** is the reassignment of workers to several different jobs over time. At Sears and Wal-Mart, management trainees rotate through three or more merchandizing departments, customer service, credit, and even the human resource department during the first year or two on the job.

Two other on-the-job forms of training are apprenticeship and mentoring. An **apprenticeship** usually combines specific on-the-job instruction with classroom training. It may last as long as four years and can be found in the skilled trades of carpentry, plumbing, and electrical work. **Mentoring** involves a senior manager or other experienced employee providing job- and career-related information to a mentee. Mentoring, which is inexpensive and provides instantaneous feedback, is becoming increasingly popular with many firms, including FedEx, Merrill Lynch, Dow Chemical, and Bank of America.

Off-the-Job Training

Even with the advantages of on-the-job training, many firms recognize that it is often necessary to train employees away from the workplace. With off-the-job training, employees learn the job away from the job. There are numerous popular methods of off-the-job training. Frequently, it takes place in a classroom where cases, role-play exercises, films, videos, lectures, and computer demonstrations are used to develop workplace skills.

Web-based technology is increasingly being used along with more traditional off-the-job training methods. *E-learning* and *e-training* involve online computer presentation of information for learning new job tasks. Union Pacific Railroad has tens of thousands of its employees widely dispersed across much of the United States so it delivers training materials electronically to save time and travel costs. Technical and safety training at Union Pacific are made available as **programmed instruction**, a computer-assisted, self-paced, and highly structured training method that presents trainees with concepts and problems using a modular format. Software provided by Plateau Systems can make sure that employees receive, undergo, and complete, as well as sign off on, various training modules.[17]

Computer-assisted training can also be done using a **simulation**, a scaled-down version of a manufacturing process or even a mock cockpit of a jet airplane. American Airlines uses a training simulator for pilots to practice hazardous flight maneuvers or learn the controls of a new aircraft in a safe, controlled environment with no passengers. The simulator allows for more direct transfer of learning to the job.

Performance Planning and Evaluation

Along with employee orientation and training, new employees learn about performance expectations through performance planning and evaluation. Managers provide employees with expectations about the job. These are communicated as job objectives, schedules, deadlines, and product and/or service quality requirements. As an employee performs job tasks, the supervisor periodically evaluates the employee's efforts. A **performance appraisal** is a comparison of actual performance with expected performance to determine an employee's contributions to the organization and to make decisions about training, compensation, promotion, and other job changes. The performance planning and appraisal process is shown in Exhibit 8.7 and described below.

1. The manager establishes performance standards.
2. The employee works to meet the standards and expectations.
3. The employee's supervisor evaluates the employee's work in terms of quality and quantity of output and various characteristics such as job knowledge, initiative, relationships with others, and attendance and punctuality.
4. Following the performance evaluation, reward (pay raise) and job change (promotion) decisions can be made.
5. Rewards are positive feedback and provide reinforcement, or encouragement, for the employee to work harder in the future.

job rotation
Reassignment of workers to several different jobs over time so that they can learn the basics of each job.

apprenticeship
A form of on-the-job training that combines specific job instruction with classroom instruction.

mentoring
A form of on-the-job training in which a senior manager or other experienced employee provides job- and career-related information to a mentee.

programmed instruction
A form of computer-assisted off-the-job training.

simulation
A scaled-down version or mock-up of equipment, process, or work environment.

CONCEPT check

Describe several types of on-the-job training.

What are the advantages of simulation training?

How is technology impacting off-the-job training?

5 How are performance appraisals used to evaluate employee performance?

performance appraisal
A comparison of actual performance with expected performance to assess an employee's contributions to the organization.

EXHIBIT 8.7   Performance Planning and Evaluation

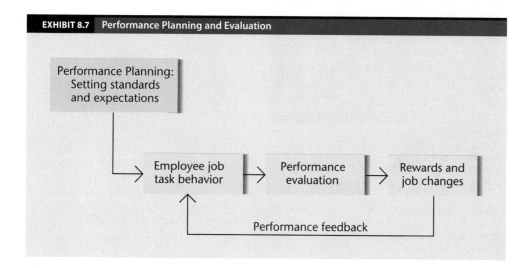

Information for performance appraisals can be assembled using rating scales, supervisor logs of employee job incidents, and reports of sales and production statistics. Regardless of the source, performance information should be accurate and a record of the employee's job behavior and efforts. Exhibit 8.8 illustrates a rating scale for one aspect of a college recruiter's job. A rating of "9" is considered outstanding job behavior and performance; a rating of "1" is viewed as very poor to unacceptable. Read more about how companies are revising their review processes in the Managing Change box on the next page.

CONCEPT check

What are the steps in the performance planning and appraisal process?

What purposes do performance appraisals serve?

Describe some sources of information for the performance appraisal.

EXHIBIT 8.8   Example of Behavior-Based Rating Scale for Performance Appraisal

Position: College Recruiter

Job Description: Visits campuses and conducts interviews of graduating seniors

Behavior Rated	Performance Rating	Explanation of Rating
Plans and organizes spring semester college recruiting schedule to minimize travel expenses and maximize the number of colleges visited and students interviewed.	9	
	8	Even with tight travel schedules between campuses, this recruiter completes each campus report before arrival at next campus.
	7	In making plans to visit a new campus, this recruiter might not have identified two or three faculty members for obtaining pre-visit information about degree programs.
	6	
Occasionally does not check with college placement office to request student résumés two days before arrival.	5	
	4	Sometimes this recruiter's notes are incomplete concerning a student's response to interview question.
	3	This recruiter is often several minutes late in starting interviews.
Frequently late in sending thank-you letters to students interviewed.	2	
	1	Recruiter is always late completing campus recruiting reports.

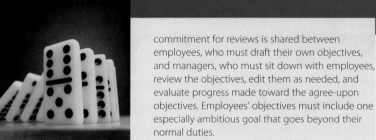

© Stockbyte/Getty Images

The New Review

The annual performance review has had its own performance appraisal at many companies, and the results haven't been good. Companies as diverse as National Cooperative Bank, forest-products firm Weyerhauser, electricity company KeySpan, Texas Children's Hospital, and appliance company Whirlpool have all revised their annual performance appraisal system to have a better understanding of what employees are actually contributing to the organization. Some companies, like Whirlpool, changed a couple of times before finding the system that worked for them.

In an effort to streamline what is widely considered a cumbersome process, Whirlpool moved much of its annual review process online. Managers had been complaining that the system they had been using was too time consuming, so the chief of human resources, David Binkley, developed a system in which employees filled out surveys and submitted them electronically. Managers and employees then traded comments online, and face-to-face review meetings were all but eliminated.

Although the new process helped reduce the time spent on performance appraisals, it did little to provide effective feedback. Employees voiced their concerns through focus groups and employee surveys, so David Binkley changed the process after only a couple of years. The new system, which is still in place today, requires quarterly meetings between managers and employees. The time commitment for reviews is shared between employees, who must draft their own objectives, and managers, who must sit down with employees, review the objectives, edit them as needed, and evaluate progress made toward the agree-upon objectives. Employees' objectives must include one especially ambitious goal that goes beyond their normal duties.

Overall, the new, more involved system has been embraced by managers and employees. Both groups like the fact that the new system encourages more regular and meaningful communication. Underlying issues come to the surface more frequently, so they can be resolved more effectively. And employees feel more ownership for their performance, which for Whirlpool is a definite change for the better.[18]

Critical Thinking Questions

- What role do performance reviews play in a company's overall business strategy?
- Some Whirlpool managers go beyond the required quarterly review and meet with each of their reports for 45 minutes every two weeks. Is more feedback always better, or can there be too much feedback?

Employee Compensation and Benefits

> **6** What are the types of compensation and methods for paying workers?

Compensation, which includes both pay and benefits, is closely connected to performance appraisal. Employees who perform better tend to get bigger pay raises. Several factors affect an employee's pay:

1. *Pay structure and internal influences.* Wages, salaries, and benefits usually reflect the importance of the job. The jobs that management considers more important are compensated at a higher rate; president, chief engineer, and chief financial officer are high-paying jobs. Likewise, different jobs of equal importance to the firm are compensated at the same rate. For instance, if a drill-press operator and a lathe operator are considered of equal importance, they may both be paid $21 per hour.

2. *Pay level and external influences.* In deciding how much to pay workers, the firm must also be concerned with the salaries paid by competitors. If competitors are paying higher wages, a firm may lose its best employees. Larger firms conduct salary surveys to see what other firms are paying. Wage and salary surveys conducted by the Chamber of Commerce and the U.S. Department of Labor can also be useful.

An employer can decide to pay at, above, or below the going rate. Most firms try to offer competitive wages and salaries within a geographic area or an industry. If a company pays below-market wages, it may not be able to hire skilled people. The level of a firm's compensation is determined by the firm's financial condition (or profitability), efficiency, and employee productivity, as well as the going rates paid by competitors. Miller Brewing Co. is considered a high-paying firm ($25–$28 per hour for production employees).

Types of Compensation or Pay

There are two basic types of compensation: direct and indirect. Direct pay is the wage or salary received by the employee; indirect pay consists of various employee benefits and services. Employees are usually paid directly on the basis of the amount of time they work, the amount they produce, or some combination of time and output. An hourly rate of pay or a monthly salary are considered base pay, or an amount of pay received by the employee regardless of output level. In many jobs, such as sales and manufacturing, an employee can earn additional pay as a result of an **incentive pay**

incentive pay
Additional pay for attaining a specific goal.

arrangement. The accelerated commission schedule for a salesperson shown below indicates that as sales increases, the incentive becomes increasingly more attractive and rewarding, and therefore, pay can function as a powerful motivator. In this example, a salesperson receives a base monthly salary of $1,000, then earns 3 percent on the first $50,000 of product sold, 4 percent on the next $30,000, and 5 percent on any sales beyond $80,000.

Base pay	$1,000
3% × 50,000	1,500
4% × 30,000	1,200
5% × 20,000	1,000
	$4,700

Two other incentive pay arrangements are bonuses and profit sharing. Employees may be paid bonuses for reaching certain monthly or annual performance goals or achieving a specific cost-saving objective. In this instance, employees are rewarded some portion of the amount of cost savings.

In a profit-sharing plan, employees may receive some portion of the firm's profit. Employee profit shares are usually based on annual financial performance and are therefore paid once a year. With either a bonus or a profit share, an important incentive pay consideration is whether the bonus or profit share is the same for all employees or whether it is differentiated by level in the organization, base pay, or some other criterion. Trufast, a manufacturer of fasteners, uses a point system to award bonuses. Each quarter, workers are graded by their managers, who can award up to 25 points in each of four categories: initiative, aptitude, flexibility, and attitude. Employees who earn 70 points or more receive incentive pay (bonus), and the higher the score, the higher the bonus. On average, workers receive 75¢ more per hour worked during the grading period, but exceptional performers can earn up to $1.50 more per hour. Employees who score less than 70 two quarters in a row are terminated.[19]

Indirect pay includes things like pensions, health insurance, and vacations. Some forms of indirect pay are required by law: unemployment compensation, worker's compensation, and Social Security, which are all paid in part by employers. **Unemployment compensation** provides former employees with money for a certain period while they are unemployed. To be eligible, the employee must have worked a minimum number of weeks, be without a job, and be willing to accept a suitable position offered by the state Unemployment Compensation Commission. Some state laws permit payments to strikers. **Worker's compensation** pays employees for lost work time caused by work-related injuries and may also cover rehabilitation after a serious injury. Social Security is mainly a government pension plan, but it also provides disability and survivor benefits and benefits for people undergoing kidney dialysis and transplants. Medicare (health care for the elderly) and Medicaid (health care for the poor) are also part of Social Security.

Many employers also offer benefits not required by law. Among these are paid time off (vacations, holidays, sick days, even pay for jury duty), insurance (health and hospitalization, disability, life, dental, vision, and accidental death and dismemberment), pensions and retirement savings accounts, and stock purchase options.

Some firms with numerous benefits allow employees to mix and match benefit items or select items based on individual needs. This is a cafeteria-style benefit plan. A younger employee with a family may desire to purchase medical, disability, and life insurance, whereas an older employee may want to put more benefit dollars into a retirement savings plan. All employees are allocated the same number of benefit dollars, but can spend these dollars on different items and in different amounts.

Pay and benefits are obviously important elements of human resource management and are frequently studied as aspects of employee job satisfaction. Pay can be very satisfactory or it can be a point of job dissatisfaction. In a study of job satisfaction conducted by the Society for Human Resource Management and CNN financial news, benefits and direct compensation were ranked one and two respectively as very important elements of job satisfaction by employees from various companies.[20] Read how benefits keep working moms on the job in the Customer Satisfaction and Quality box on the next page.

Quarterback Ben Roethlisberger is among the highest-paid athletes in NFL history. The Pittsburgh Steelers offensive leader joined the $100 Million Club recently when management and agents hammered out a deal to pay Big Ben $102 million over an eight-year term. The player contract, which includes more than $36 million in guarantees, places the Super Bowl–winning Roethlisberger alongside other top NFL fat cats such as Peyton Manning and Donovan McNabb. How can employers use different types of compensation to motivate employees toward higher performance?

unemployment compensation
Government payment to unemployed former workers.

worker's compensation
Pay for lost work time due to employment–related injuries.

CONCEPT check

How does a firm establish a pay scale for its employees?

What is the difference between direct and indirect pay?

Explain the concept of a cafeteria-style benefit plan.

Chapter 8: Managing Human Resources and Labor Relations

Benefits Make a Difference—Especially for Working Moms

Regardless of where working mothers fall on the corporate hierarchy, they all feel the relief (or strain) that their company benefits program provides (or doesn't). As *Yahoo! hotjobs* notes, at GlaxoSmithKline, the drug company's Flexible Working Policy is certainly designed for working mothers and having a rewarding career. There all working mothers can take advantage of six weeks' maternity leave and can customize a reduced-hours schedule or create a job-sharing arrangement when they return. When Azalea Manley, a factory worker who compresses pills for the pharmaceutical company, returned to work after having a baby, she changed to a schedule of three extended workdays followed by four days off. The company's on-site day care facilities further reduce stress for working moms.

Baptist Health South Florida, a hospital system, also offers help to working mothers. Employee Jennifer Wilson worked at a hospital that didn't have an on-site child care facility, and affordable day care for her two-year-old daughter required a daily three-and-a-half-hour commute to another hospital in the Baptist Health system that did. Exhausted by the long hours and effort to arrange her work life, Wilson was contemplating quitting. Then, one of her supervisors convinced the hospital to approve a $240 monthly reimbursement for child care expenses, which allowed Wilson to find high-quality care closer to her home. Wilson says, "To have my bosses help me is one of the best perks of working here. I feel valued and appreciated, despite the fact that I'm nowhere near the top of the hospital hierarchy."

Not all benefits for working mothers relate to scheduling and child care, however. Baptist Health also offers a tuition reimbursement program, which enables working mothers in entry-level positions to further their education. Sandra Chica, formerly a nurse practitioner supporting two children on $20,000 a year, took advantage of the program and earned a college degree. For a portion of her studies, she was even able to receive full salary and health benefits while going to school full-time. She was then promoted to nurse clinician and saw her salary triple. "I'm so thankful for the life I have now. Even when I was making very little, my employers listened to me and my concerns," Chica says.

Programs like those at GlaxoSmithKline and Baptist Health provide benefits that can mean the difference between keeping or losing an employee.[21]

Critical Thinking Questions

- Are there any drawbacks to tailoring benefit programs to the needs of parents (versus people with no children)? What are they? How could they be mitigated?
- Can a firm give its employees too much in terms of benefits and services? Explain.

The Labor Relations Process

7 What is a labor union and how is it organized?

labor union
An organization that represents workers in dealing with management.

collective bargaining
Negotiating a labor agreement.

Tens of thousands of American firms are unionized and millions of American workers belong to unions. Historically, the mining, manufacturing, construction, and transportation industries have been significantly unionized, but in recent years service-based firms, including health care organizations, have also become unionized.

A **labor union**, such as the International Brotherhood of Teamsters, is an organization that represents workers in dealing with management over disputes involving wages, hours, and working conditions. The labor relations process that produces a union-management relationship consists of three phases: union organizing, negotiating a labor agreement, and administering the agreement. In phase one, a group of employees within a firm may form a union on their own, or an established union (United Auto Workers, for example) may target an employer and organize many of the firm's workers into a local labor union. The second phase constitutes **collective bargaining**, which is the process of negotiating a labor agreement that provides for compensation and working arrangements mutually acceptable to the union and to management. Finally, the third phase of the labor relations process involves the daily administering of the labor agreement primarily through handling worker grievances and other workforce management problems that require interaction between managers and labor union officials.

The Modern Labor Movement

The basic structure of the modern labor movement consists of three parts: local unions, national and international unions, and union federations. There are approximately 60,000 local unions, 75 national and international unions, and 2 federations. Union membership has been declining for about three decades. According to the U.S. Bureau of Labor Statistics, currently about 12.1 percent of the American labor force are union members, or approximately 15.7 million workers.[22] Workers in the public sector are five times more likely to be union members than people working in the private sector, and union membership is more prevalent among older workers than younger and male workers than female.[23]

local union
Branch of a national union that represents workers in a specific plant or geographic area.

A **local union** is a branch or unit of a national union that represents workers at a specific plant or over a specific geographic area. Local 276 of the United Auto Workers represents assembly employees at the General Motors plant in Arlington, Texas. A local union (in conformance with its national union rules) determines the number of local union officers, procedures for electing officers, the schedule of local meetings, financial arrangements with the national organization, and the local's role in negotiating labor agreements.

The three main functions of the local union are collective bargaining, worker relations and membership services, and community and political activities. Collective bargaining takes place every three or four years. Local union officers and shop stewards in the plant oversee labor relations on a day-to-day basis. A **shop steward** is an elected union official who represents union members to management when workers have complaints. For most union members, his or her primary contact with the union is through union officials at the local level.

A national union can range in size from a few thousand members (Screen Actors Guild) to more than a million members (Teamsters). A national union may have a few to as many as several hundred local unions. The number of national unions has steadily declined since the early twentieth century. Much of this decline has resulted from union mergers. In 1999, for example, the United Papermakers International Union (UPICU) and the Oil, Chemical and Atomic Workers Union (OCAW) agreed to merge under the new name of PACE or Paper, Allied-Industrial, Chemical and Energy International Union. PACE has about 320,000 members.

For 50 years, one union federation (the American Federation of Labor-Congress of Industrial Organization, or AFL-CIO) dominated the American labor movement. A **federation** is a collection of unions banded together to further organizing, public relations, political, and other mutually agreed-upon purposes of the member unions. In the summer of 2005, several unions (Teamsters, Service Employees International Union, Laborers' International Union, United Farm Workers, Carpenters and Joiners, Unite Here, and the United Food and Commercial Workers Union) split from the AFL-CIO and formed a new federation named the Change to Win Coalition.[24] The new federation and its member unions represent more than 5 million union members. Change to Win Coalition member unions left the AFL-CIO over leadership disagreements and ineffective organizing strategies of the AFL-CIO; one of its primary goals is to strengthen union organizing drives and reverse the decline in union membership.[25]

Union Organizing

A nonunion employer becomes unionized through an organizing campaign. The campaign is started either from within, by unhappy employees, or from outside, by a union that has picked the employer for an organizing drive. Once workers and the union have made contact, a union organizer tries to convince all the workers to sign authorization cards. These cards prove the worker's interest in having the union represent them. In most cases, employers resist this card-signing campaign by speaking out against unions in letters, posters, and employee assemblies. However, it is illegal for employers to interfere directly with the card-signing campaign or to coerce employees into not joining the union.

Once the union gets signed authorization cards from at least 30 percent of the employees, it can ask National Labor Relations Board (NLRB) for a union certification election. This election, by secret ballot, determines whether the workers want to be represented by the union. The NLRB posts an election notice and defines the bargaining unit—employees who are eligible to vote and who will be represented by the particular union if it is certified. Supervisors and managers cannot vote. The union and the employer then engage in a preelection campaign conducted through speeches, memos, and meetings. Both try to convince workers to vote in their favor. Exhibit 8.9 on the next page lists benefits usually stressed by the union during a campaign and common arguments employers make to convince employees a union is unnecessary.

The election itself is conducted by the NLRB. If a majority vote for the union, the NLRB certifies the union as the exclusive bargaining agent for all employees who had been designated as eligible voters. The employer then has to bargain with the union over wages, hours, and other terms of employment. The complete organizing process is summarized in Exhibit 8.10 on the next page.

In some situations, after one year, if the union and employer don't reach an agreement, the workers petition for a decertification election, which is similar to the certification election but allows workers to vote out the union. Decertification elections are also held when workers become dissatisfied with a union that has represented them for a longer time. In recent years, the number of decertification elections has increased to several hundred per year.

© AP Images/Carlos Osorio

CONCEPT in action

The future of the labor movement grew uncertain recently when the United Auto Workers agreed to a radical transformation of the auto industry's North American workforce. To help stave off bankruptcy, GM, Ford, and Chrysler have begun offering up to $140,000 to unionized employees who voluntarily quit the company. The worker attrition plan, which began amid GM's stunning $38.7 billion loss in 2007, is a way for automakers to eliminate unionized wages-and-benefits packages averaging $73 an hour. Can the labor movement survive its shrinking membership?

shop steward
An elected union official who represents union members to management when workers have complaints.

federation
A collection of unions banded together to achieve common goals.

© AP Images/Carlos Osorio

EXHIBIT 8.9 Benefits Stressed by Unions in Organizing Campaigns and Common Employer Arguments Against Unions

Benefits Stressed by Unions:

Almost Always Stressed	Often Stressed	Seldom Stressed
Grievance procedures	More influence in decision making	Higher-quality products
Job security	Better working conditions	Technical training
Improved benefits	Lobbying opportunities	More job satisfaction
Higher pay	Increased production	

Employer Arguments Against Unionization:

- An employee can always come directly to management with a problem; a third party (the union) isn't necessary.
- As a union member, you will pay monthly union dues of $15 to $30.
- Merit-based decisions (promotions) are better than seniority-based.
- Pay and benefits are very similar to the leading firms in the industry.
- We meet all health and safety standards of the Federal Occupational Safety and Health Administration.
- Performance and productivity are more important than union representation in determining pay raises.

EXHIBIT 8.10 Union Organizing Process and Election

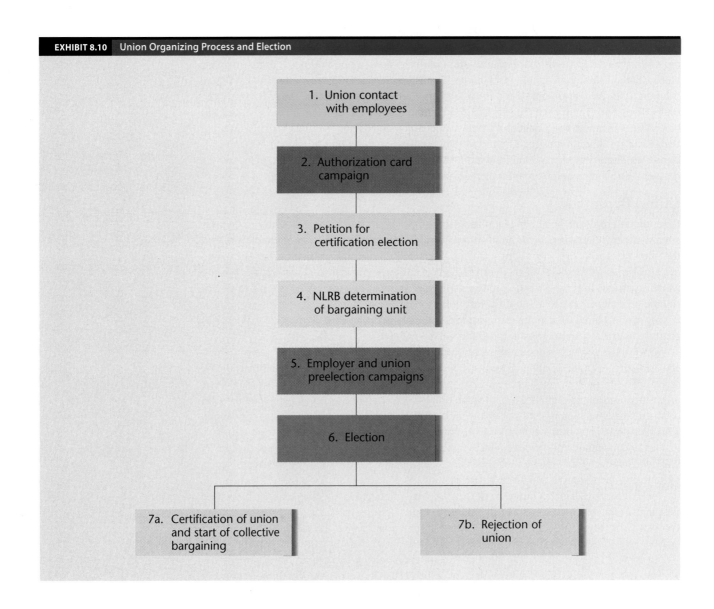

1. Union contact with employees
2. Authorization card campaign
3. Petition for certification election
4. NLRB determination of bargaining unit
5. Employer and union preelection campaigns
6. Election
7a. Certification of union and start of collective bargaining
7b. Rejection of union

Negotiating Union Contracts Through Collective Bargaining

A labor agreement, or union contract, is created through collective bargaining. Typically, both management and union negotiation teams are made up of a few people. One person on each side is the chief spokesperson. Bargaining begins with union and management negotiators setting a list of contract issues that will be discussed. Much of the bargaining over specific details takes place through face-to-face meetings and the exchange of written proposals. Demands, proposals, and counterproposals are exchanged during several rounds of bargaining. The resulting contract must be approved by top management and ratified by the union members. Once both sides approve, the contract is a legally binding agreement that typically covers such issues as union security, management rights, wages, benefits, and job security. The collective bargaining process is shown in Exhibit 8.11. We will explore some of the bargaining issues below.

8 What is collective bargaining, and what are some of the key negotiation issues?

Union Security

A union wants all employees to be union members. This can be accomplished by negotiating a union security clause. The most common union security arrangement is the **union shop** whereby

union shop
Nonunion workers can be hired but must join the union later.

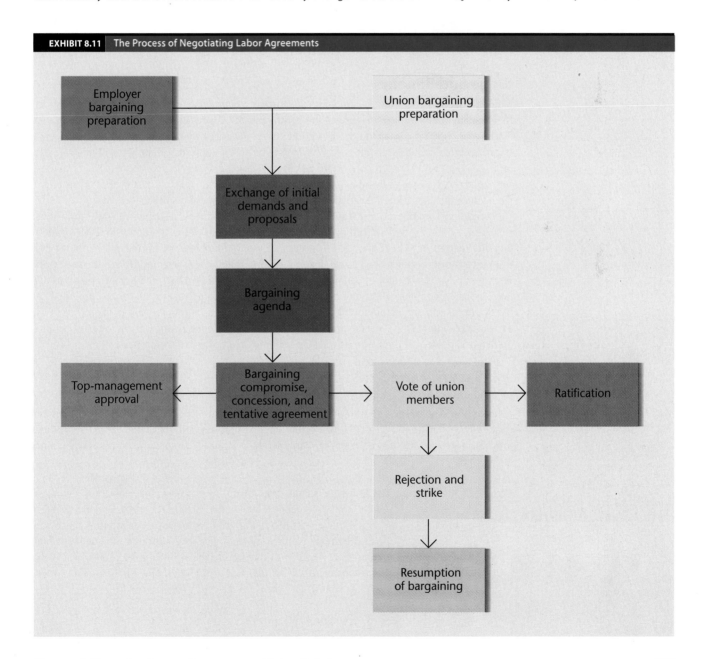

EXHIBIT 8.11   The Process of Negotiating Labor Agreements

agency shop
Workers don't have to join a union but must pay union dues.

right-to-work law
State law that an employee does not have to join a union.

open shop
Workers do not have to join the union or pay union dues.

management rights clause
Clause in a labor agreement that gives management the right to manage the business except as specified in the contract.

nonunion workers can be hired by the firm, but then they must join the union, normally within 30 to 60 days. An **agency shop** does not require employees to join the union, but in order to remain employees, workers must pay the union a fee (known as the agency fee) to cover the union's expenses in representing them. The union must fairly represent all workers, including those in the bargaining unit who do not become members.

Under the Taft-Hartley Act of 1947, a state can make any and all forms of union security illegal by enacting a **right-to-work law**. In the 21 states that have these laws, employees can work at a unionized company without having to join the union. This arrangement is commonly known as an **open shop**. Workers don't have to join the union or pay dues or fees to the union.

Management Rights

When a company becomes unionized, management loses some of its decision-making abilities. But management still has certain rights that can be negotiated in collective bargaining. One way to resist union meddling in management matters is to put a **management rights clause** in the labor agreement. Most union contracts have one. A typical clause gives the employer all rights to manage the business except as specified in the contract. For instance, if the contract does not specify the criteria for promotions, with a management rights clause managers will have the right to use any criteria they wish. Another way to preserve management rights is to list areas that are not subject to collective bargaining. This list might secure management's right to schedule work hours, hire and fire workers, set production standards, determine the number of supervisors in each department, and promote, demote, and transfer workers.

Wage and Benefits

Much bargaining effort focuses on wage adjustments and changes in benefits. Once agreed to, they remain in effect for the length of the contract. In 2003, the United Auto Workers negotiated a four-year contract containing modest hourly wage increases with American car manufacturers; pay hikes were about 3 percent each year for the four-year contract. Hourly rates of pay can also increase under some agreements when the cost of living increases above a certain level each year, say 4 percent. No cost-of-living adjustment is made when annual living cost increases are under 4 percent, which has been the experience for the early years of the twenty-first century.

In addition to requests for wage increases, unions usually want better benefits. In some industries, such as steel and auto manufacturing, benefits are 40 percent of the total cost of compensation. Benefits may include higher wages for overtime work, holiday work, and less desirable shifts; insurance programs (life, health and hospitalization, dental care); payment for certain nonwork time (rest periods, vacations, holiday, sick time); pensions; and income-maintenance plans. In the auto industry, supplementary unemployment benefits (income-maintenance) are provided by the employer and are in addition to state unemployment compensation given to laid-off workers. The unemployment compensation from the state and supplementary unemployment pay from the employer together maintain as much as 80 percent of an employee's normal pay.

Job Security and Seniority

Wage adjustments, cost-of-living increases, supplementary unemployment pay, and certain other benefits give employees under union contracts some financial security. But most financial security is directly related to job security—the assurance, to some degree, that workers will keep their jobs. Of course, job security depends primarily on the continued success and financial well-being of the company.

Seniority, the length of an employee's continuous service with a firm, is discussed in about 90 percent of all labor contracts. Seniority is a factor in job security; usually, unions want the workers with the most seniority to have the most job security. Seniority is often one of the largest issues the union deals with. For months, Delta and Northwest airlines held merger talks, and although management had come to a tentative arrangement, the pilots, represented by different branches of the same national union, threw up a roadblock. Despite weeks of discussion, pilots from the two airlines couldn't agree on a way to integrate their seniority. For pilots, seniority dictates not only pay, benefits, and advancement opportunities, but also which model of plane and which routes a pilot can fly.[26]

CONCEPT check

Discuss the modern labor movement.

What are the various topics that may be covered during collective bargaining?

Explain the differences among a union shop, agency shop, and an open shop.

Managing Grievances and Conflicts

In a unionized work environment, employees follow a step-by-step process for handling grievances or disputes between management and labor. Conflicts over contracts, however, are far more challenging to resolve and may result in the union or employer imposing economic pressure as described in this section.

9 How are grievances between management and labor resolved, and what tactics are used to force a contract settlement?

grievance
A formal complaint by a union worker that management has violated the contract.

Grievance Handling and Arbitration

The union's main way of policing the contract is the grievance procedure. A **grievance** is a formal complaint, by an employee or the union, that management has violated some part of the contract. Under a typical contract, the employee starts by presenting the grievance to the supervisor, either in person or in writing. The typical grievance procedure is illustrated in Exhibit 8.12. An example grievance is a situation in which an employee is disciplined with a one-day suspension (and loss of pay) for being late for work several times in one month.

If the problem isn't solved, the grievance is put in writing. The employee, one or more union officials, the supervisor, and perhaps the plant manager then discuss the grievance. If the matter still can't be resolved, another meeting takes place with higher-level representatives of both parties present. If top management and the local union president can't resolve the grievance, it goes to arbitration.

CONCEPT in action

Terrell Owens is a Dallas Cowboy—at least for now. The controversial NFL wide receiver lost a highly publicized arbitration case with former team the Philadelphia Eagles in which arbitrator Richard Bloch ruled Owens's behavior was destructive and a continuing threat to the organization. Despite protests from player agent Drew Rosenhaus, Bloch ruled that the Eagles' decision to suspend Owens did not violate the labor agreement. What options did Owens have after losing arbitration?

© ERIC ESPADA/CSM/Landov

EXHIBIT 8.12   Typical Grievance Procedure

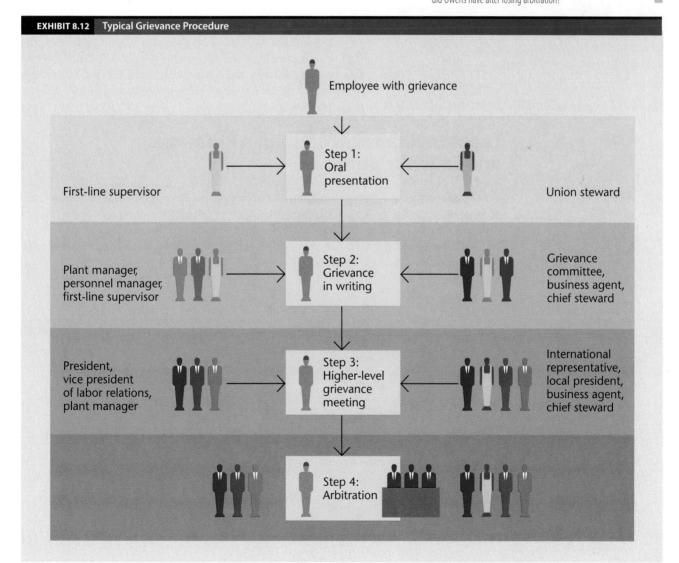

Employee with grievance

First-line supervisor → Step 1: Oral presentation ← Union steward

Plant manager, personnel manager, first-line supervisor → Step 2: Grievance in writing ← Grievance committee, business agent, chief steward

President, vice president of labor relations, plant manager → Step 3: Higher-level grievance meeting ← International representative, local president, business agent, chief steward

Step 4: Arbitration

arbitration
Settling labor–management disputes through a third party. The decision is final and binding.

Arbitration is the process of settling a labor–management dispute by having a third party—a single arbitrator or a panel—make a decision. The decision is final and binding on the union and employer. The arbitrator reviews the grievance at a hearing and then makes the decision, which is presented in a document called the award. In the one-day suspension mentioned above, the arbitration might rule that the discipline was improperly made because the employee's attendance record for the month was not accurately maintained by the firm. In the case of the Delta and Northwest pilots, the airlines could push their pilots' unions toward binding arbitration in an attempt to resolve the one outstanding item—seniority—on which they haven't come to consensus.[27]

Tactics for Pressuring a Contract Settlement

Virtually all labor agreements specify peaceful resolution of conflicts, usually through arbitration. However, when a contract expires and a new agreement has not been reached, the union is free to strike or engage in other efforts to exert economic pressure on the employer. A *strike* occurs when employees refuse to work. One of the most widely publicized strikes of recent years was the strike by the Writers Guild of America in 2007 and 2008. Lasting over three months, the strike against Hollywood studios and broadcast networks nearly destroyed the scripted television season, crippled a number of feature-film projects, and caused the cancellation of many of the industry's annual awards shows. The strike only ended after two weeks of intense negotiation and a vote by the union's members to end the strike and take a deal for a three-year contract.[28]

selective strike strategy
Strike at a critical plant that typically stops operations system wide.

In addition to a full strike, unions can implement a **selective strike strategy**, which involves striking only at a critical facility. For example, the United Auto Workers union decided to conduct a strike against General Motors, but only at a critical stamping and parts facility in Flint, Michigan, which supplied critical parts to other plants. The 54-day strike caused the company to stop production at many of its assembly plants because parts were not available from the Flint plant. General Motors lost approximately $2.2 billion during this dispute. Likewise, the employer can put pressure on the union through a lockout or hiring strike replacements if the union has called a strike. Exhibit 8.13 provides a summary of union and employer pressure strategies for forcing a contract settlement.

CONCEPT check

Describe the grievance procedure.

In what ways do arbitrators act like judges?

What are some tactics for pressuring for a contract settlement?

Legal Environment of Human Resources and Labor Relations

10 What are the key laws and federal agencies affecting human resource management and labor relations?

Federal laws help ensure that job applicants and employees are treated fairly and not discriminated against. Hiring, training, and job placement must be unbiased. Promotion and compensation decisions must be based on performance. These laws help all Americans who have talent, training, and the desire to get ahead. The key laws that currently impact human resource management and labor relations are listed in Exhibit 8.14.

EXHIBIT 8.13	Strategies of Unions and Employers		
Union Strategies		**Employer Strategies**	
Strike:	Employees refuse to work.	**Lockout:**	Employer refuses to let employees enter plant to work.
Boycott:	Employees try to keep customers and others from doing business with employer.	**Strike replacements:**	Employer uses nonunion employees to do jobs of striking union employees.
Picketing:	Employees march near entrance of firm to publicize their view of dispute and discourage customers.	**Mutual-aid pact:**	Employer receives money from other companies in industry to cover some of income lost because of strikes.
Corporate campaign:	Union disrupts stockholder meetings or buys company stock to have more influence over management.	**Shift production:**	Employer moves production to nonunion plant or out of country.

Several laws govern wages, pensions, and unemployment compensation. For instance, the Fair Labor Standards Act sets the minimum wage, which is periodically raised by Congress. Many minimum-wage jobs are found in service firms, such as McDonald's and car washes. The Pension Reform Act protects the retirement income of employees and retirees. Federal tax laws also affect compensation, including employee profit-sharing and stock purchase plans.

Employers must also be aware of changes to laws concerning employee safety, health, and privacy. The Occupational Safety and Health Act requires employers to provide a workplace free of health and safety hazards. For instance, manufacturers must require their employees working on loading docks to wear steel-toed shoes so their feet won't be injured if materials are dropped. Drug and AIDS testing are also governed by federal laws.

Another employee law that continues to affect the workplace is the Americans with Disabilities Act. To be considered disabled, a person must have a physical or mental impairment that greatly limits one or more major life activities. More than 54 million Americans fall into this category. Employers may not discriminate against disabled persons. They must make "reasonable accommodations" so that qualified employees can perform the job, unless doing so would cause "undue hardship" for the business. Altering work

CONCEPT in action

Television audiences were left out in the cold recently when a contract dispute between Hollywood studio bosses and the Writers Guild of America caused TV writers to strike. The 100-day-long walkout, which forced networks to rehash past seasons of scripted shows like *Saturday Night Live* and *The Tonight Show*, pressured the Alliance of Motion Picture and Television Producers to increase the compensation writers receive from new-media content. The strike cost an estimated $1.5 billion to the economy, as 50,000 employees lost their jobs and networks lost a quarter of their viewers. What developments can prolong or end a strike?

EXHIBIT 8.14	Laws Impacting Human Resource Management	
Law	**Purpose**	**Agency of Enforcement**
Social Security Act (1935)	Provides for retirement income and old age health care	Social Security Administration
Wagner Act (1935)	Gives workers the right to unionize and prohibits employer unfair labor practices	National Labor Relations Board
Fair Labor Standards Act (1938)	Sets minimum wage, restricts child labor, sets overtime pay	Wage and Hour Division, Department of Labor
Taft-Hartley Act (1947)	Obligates the union to bargain in good faith and prohibits union unfair labor practices	Federal Mediation and Conciliation Service
Equal Pay Act (1963)	Eliminates pay differentials based on gender	Equal Employment Opportunity Commission
Civil Rights Act (1964), Title VII	Prohibits employment discrimination based on race, color, religion, gender, or national origin	Equal Employment Opportunity Commission
Age Discrimination Act (1967)	Prohibits age discrimination against those over 40 years of age	Equal Employment Opportunity Commission
Occupational Safety and Health Act (1970)	Protects worker health and safety, provides for hazard-free workplace	Occupational Safety and Health Administration
Vietnam Veterans' Readjustment Act (1974)	Requires affirmative employment of Vietnam War veterans	Veterans Employment Service, Department of Labor
Employee Retirement Income Security Act (1974)—also called Pension Reform Act	Establishes minimum requirements for private pension plans	Internal Revenue Service, Department of Labor, and Pension Benefit Guaranty Corporation
Pregnancy Discrimination Act (1978)	Treats pregnancy as a disability, prevents employment discrimination based on pregnancy	Equal Employment Opportunity Commission
Immigration Reform and Control Act (1986)	Verifies employment eligibility, prevents employment of illegal aliens	Employment Verification Systems, Immigration and Naturalization Service
Americans with Disabilities Act (1990)	Prohibits employment discrimination based on mental or physical disabilities	Department of Labor
Family and Medical Leave Act (1993)	Requires employers to provide unpaid leave for childbirth, adoption, or illness	Equal Employment Opportunity Commission
Uniformed Services Employment and Reemployment Rights Act (USERRA) (1994)	Prohibits discrimination against members of the U.S. Armed Services and requires employers to reemploy reserve service members who return from active duty	U.S. Department of Labor

© James P. Blair/National Geographic/Getty Images

For some occupations, danger is part of the job description. Tallies of work-related casualties routinely identify loggers, pilots, commercial fishermen, and steel workers as holding the most deadly jobs in industry. Job fatalities are often linked to the use of heavy or outdated equipment. However, many work-related deaths also happen in common highway accidents or as homicides. What laws and agencies are designated to improve occupational safety?

Occupational Safety and Health Administration (OSHA)
Sets workplace safety and health standards and assures compliance.

Equal Employment Opportunity Commission (EEOC)
Processes discrimination complaints, issues regulations regarding discrimination, and disseminates information.

protected classes
The specific groups who have legal protection against employment discrimination; include women, African Americans, Native Americans, and others.

affirmative action programs
Programs established by organizations to expand job opportunities for women and minorities.

conciliator
Specialist in labor–management negotiations that acts as a go-between for management and the unions and helps focus on the problems.

schedules, modifying equipment so a wheelchair-bound person can use it, and making buildings accessible by ramps and elevators are considered reasonable. Two companies often praised for their efforts to hire the disabled are McDonald's and DuPont.

The Family and Medical Leave Act went into effect in 1993. The law applies to employers with 50 or more employees. It requires these employers to provide unpaid leave of up to 12 weeks during any 12-month period to workers who have been employed for at least a year and work a minimum of 25 hours a week. The reasons for the leave include the birth or adoption of a child; the serious illness of a child, spouse, or parent; or a serious illness that prevents the worker from doing the job. When the employee returns, he or she must be given back his or her former job.

The Wagner and Taft-Hartley Acts govern the relationship between an employer and union. Employees have the right to unionize and bargain collectively with the company. The employer must deal with the union fairly, bargain in good faith, and not discriminate against an employee who belongs to the union. The union must also represent all employees covered by a labor agreement fairly and deal with the employer in good faith.

Several federal agencies oversee employment, safety, compensation, and related areas. The **Occupational Safety and Health Administration (OSHA)** sets workplace safety and health standards, provides safety training, and inspects places of work (assembly plants, construction sites, and warehouse facilities, for example) to determine employer compliance with safety regulations.

The Wage and Hour division of the Department of Labor enforces the federal minimum-wage law and overtime provisions of the Fair Labor Standards Act. Employers covered by this law must pay certain employees a premium rate of pay (or time and one-half) for all hours worked beyond 40 in one week.

The **Equal Employment Opportunity Commission (EEOC)** was created by the 1964 Civil Rights Act. It is one of the most influential agencies responsible for enforcing employment laws. The EEOC has three basic functions: processing discrimination complaints, issuing written regulations, and gathering and disseminating information. An employment discrimination complaint can be filed by an individual or a group of employees who work for a company. The group may comprise a **protected class**, such as women, African Americans, or Hispanic Americans. The protected group may pursue a class action complaint that may eventually become a lawsuit. As a measure to prevent employment discrimination, many employers set up **affirmative action programs** to expand job opportunities for women and minorities.

Even with affirmative action and other company efforts to follow the law, each year the EEOC receives tens of thousands of complaints from current or former employees. The monetary benefits that the EEOC wins for employees has grown substantially during the past 10 years. Large monetary settlements often occur when the EEOC files a class action suit against an employer. For example, the $34 million paid by Mitsubishi Motor Manufacturing to settle several sexual harassment cases was distributed to nearly 500 former and current female employees (in addition to the lawyers). Also, Sears, Motorola, and AT&T have had to make large back-pay awards and to offer special training to minority employees after the court found they had been discriminated against.

The National Labor Relations Board (NLRB) was established to enforce the Wagner Act. Its five members are appointed by the president; the agency's main office is in Washington, DC, and regional and field offices are scattered throughout the United States. NLRB field agents investigate charges of employer and union wrongdoing (or unfair labor practices) and supervise elections held to decide union representation. Judges conduct hearings to determine whether employers and unions have violated the law.

The Federal Mediation and Conciliation Service helps unions and employers negotiate labor agreements. Agency specialists, who serve as impartial third parties between the union and company, use two processes: conciliation and mediation, both of which require expert communication and persuasion. As a **conciliator**, the specialist assists management and the union to focus on the issues in dispute and acts as a go-between or communication channel through which the union and employer send messages to and share information with each other. The specialist takes a stronger role as a **mediator** by suggesting compromises to the disputing organizations.

CONCEPT check

Discuss the laws that govern wages, pensions, and employee compensation.

Describe the Americans with Disabilities Act.

How do the Wagner and Taft-Hartley Acts impact labor–management relations?

Trends in Human Resource Management and Labor Relations

Some of today's most important trends in human resource management are using employee diversity as a competitive advantage, improving efficiency through outsourcing and technology, and hiring employees who fit the organizational culture. Although overall labor union enrollment continues to decline, a possible surge in membership in service unions is anticipated.

11 What trends and issues are affecting human resource management and labor relations?

mediator
Specialist that facilitates labor–management contract discussions and suggests compromises.

competitive advantage
A set of unique features of an organization that are perceived by customers and potential customers as significant and superior to the competition.

Employee Diversity and Competitive Advantage

American society and its workforce are becoming increasingly more diverse in terms of racial and ethnic status, age, educational background, work experience, and gender. A company with a demographic employee profile that looks like its customers may be in a position to gain a **competitive advantage**, which is a set of unique features of a company and its product or service that are perceived by the target market as superior to those of the competition. Competitive advantage is the factor that causes customers to patronize a firm and not the competition. Many things can be a source of competitive advantage: for Southwest Airlines it is route structure and high asset utilization; for the Ritz-Carlton it is very high quality guest services; for Toyota it is manufacturing efficiency and product durability; and for Starbucks it is location, service, and outstanding coffee products. For these firms, a competitive advantage is also created by their HR practices. Many firms are successful because of employee diversity, which can produce more effective problem solving, a stronger reputation for hiring women and minorities, greater employee diversity, quicker adaptation to change, and more robust product solutions because a diverse team can generate more options for improvement.[29]

In order for an organization to use employee diversity for competitive advantage, top management must be fully committed to hiring and developing women and minority individuals. *Pink* magazine does a yearly ranking of top companies for women, but instead of looking at what are considered traditional women's workplace issues (child care, flextime, etc.), the magazine evaluates things like how many women are among the top earners in the company, how well the company provides leadership and mentoring programs for women, how many women are in positions of power, and how well the corporate culture allows women to grow in their careers and remain authentic (that is, not have to act like men). In 2007, *Pink*'s study, conducted by KPMG, identified American Express, Heller Ehrman (legal services), and Kelly Services (temporary staffing services) as the top three companies for recruiting, hiring, promoting, and retaining talented women at all levels of the organization.[30]

Outsourcing HR and Technology

The role of the HR professional has changed noticeably over the past 20 years. One significant change has been the use of technology in handling relatively routine HR tasks, such as payroll processing, initial screening of applicants, and benefits enrollments. Large firms such as Nokia and Lockheed Martin purchase specialized software (SAP and Oracle/PeopleSoft) to perform the information processing aspects of many HR tasks. Other firms such as Carter and Burgess (a large engineering firm) outsource, or contract out these tasks to HR service providers, such as Hewitt Associates and Workforce Solutions.

According to a survey by Culpepper Compensation & Benefits, 53 percent of all companies outsource some portion of their HR tasks.[31] Some HR companies specialize in handling payroll and benefits; others can conduct recruiting, drug screening, preemployment testing, performance reviews, and even write handbooks; still others can build for clients an entire HR department from scratch.[32] HR outsourcing is done when another firm can perform a task better and more efficiently, thus cutting costs. Sometimes HR activities are outsourced because HR requirements are extraordinary and too overwhelming to execute in-house in a timely fashion. Frequently, HR activities are simply outsourced because a provider has greater expertise.

They're young, they're hip, they're pierced in unusual places— Generation Y graduates are entering the workforce, and businesses are wondering how best to tap their potential. Born between 1980 and the mid-1990s, Gen Y-ers have come of age in an Internet world. Early descriptions portray these Millennials as tech-savvy, team oriented, and entrepreneurial. They expect high-paying jobs and seek alternative employment arrangements that strike a balance between work and life. What corporate cultures might appeal to ambitious-yet-demanding Gen Y workers?

Organizational Culture and Hiring for Fit

Regardless of general business and economic conditions, many firms are expanding operations and hiring additional employees. For many growing firms, corporate culture can be a key aspect of developing employees into a competitive advantage for the firm. Corporate culture refers to the core values and beliefs that support the mission and business model of the firm and guide employee behavior. Many companies frequently hire for fit with their corporate cultures. This necessitates recruitment and selection of employees who exhibit the values of the firm. Online shoe retailer Zappos looks for people who are team oriented. Interview candidates who answer questions only by touting their own contributions are generally dismissed.[33]

Ari Weinzweig, founder and CEO of Zingerman's, offers some good advice for managers looking to determine if a job candidate will fit with the company culture. He suggests first identifying personal attributes that are important in the company. For example, he looks for people who strive for greatness, are willing to serve fellow employees in addition to customers, and have a passion for food. He also recommends sharing the company's vision for its future with interviewees, conducting the interview in a real-world situation, and allowing 8 to 10 employees to participate in the interview. According to Weinzweig, if the candidate understands the vision, is able to handle an interview in the middle of the shop floor, and gets approval by a group of his or her future peers, chances are greater for good person–organization fit.[34]

More Service Workers Joining Labor Unions

Organized labor has faced tumultuous times during the last several decades due to declining union membership, loss of factory jobs, dwindling political clout, and the shifting of jobs outside the United States. With union membership now down to 12.1 percent of the U.S. workforce, some wonder if labor unions, who organize as a united front against poor working conditions, still have a place in America.[35] Andrew Stern, president of Service Employees International Union (SEIU), is optimistic that unions are capable of resurgence by organizing the growing number of service workers into labor unions. The SEIU is the fastest-growing union in the nation—having jumped to 1.8 million members from 1.1 million a decade ago.[36]

Stern's goal is to focus on recruiting the millions of low-wage service workers that are filled by the bulk of the country's working poor. These workers are disproportionately women, immigrants, and members of minority groups that have all been traditionally more open to unionization.[37] If successful at recruiting these workers to the SEIU, Sterns believes that their wages and benefits would increase in much the same way unions brought factory workers into the middle class in the 1930s.[38]

The SEIU believes that the service industry provides a target of opportunity, with the largest expected employment growth through 2012 in low-paid local services:

CONCEPT check

How can employee diversity give a company a competitive advantage?

Explain the concept of hiring for fit.

Why does the service industry provide an opportunity for labor union growth?

Job	Projected Growth[39]
Cashier	13%
Customer Service	24%
Food preparation	23%
Janitorial	18%
Nursing aide	25%

Reversing labor's decline will be challenging, but the SEIU looks positively toward the future.[40]

Summary of Learning Goals

The human resource management process consists of a sequence of activities that begins with the job analysis and HR planning; progresses to employee recruitment and selection; then focuses on employee training, performance appraisal, and compensation; and ends when the employee leaves the organization.

1 What is the human resource management process, and how are human resource needs determined?

Creating a strategy for meeting human resource needs is called human resource planning, which begins with the job analysis. Job analysis is a process of studying a job to determine its tasks and duties for setting pay, determining employee job performance, specifying hiring requirements, and designing training programs. Information from the job analysis is used to prepare a job description, which lists the tasks and responsibilities of the job. A job specification describes the skills, knowledge, and abilities a person needs to fill the job described in the job description. By examining the human resource demand forecast and the internal supply forecast, human resource professionals can determine if the company faces a personnel surplus or shortage.

When a job vacancy occurs, most firms begin by trying to fill the job from within the ranks of its own employees, known as the internal labor market. If a suitable internal candidate is not available, the firm turns to the external labor market. Firms use local media to recruit nontechnical, unskilled, and nonsupervisory workers. To locate highly trained recruits, employers use college recruiters, executive search firms, job fairs, and company Web sites to promote job openings. During the job search process, firms present an accurate and positive image of the company to those being recruited, called recruitment branding.

2 How do firms recruit applicants?

The selection process helps identify the candidates in the applicant pool who possess the best qualifications for the open position. Typically, an applicant submits an application, or résumé, and then receives a short, structured interview. If an applicant makes it past the initial screening, he or she may be asked to take an aptitude, personality, or skills test. The next step is the selection interview, which is an in-depth discussion of the applicant's work experience, skills and abilities, education, and career interests. If the applicant passes the selection interview, most firms conduct background checks and talk with their references. Physical exams and drug testing may also be part of the selection process.

3 How do firms select qualified applicants?

Training and development programs are designed to increase employees' knowledge, skills, and abilities in order to foster job performance improvements. Formal training (usually classroom in nature and off-the-job) takes place shortly after being hired. Development programs prepare employees to assume positions of increasing authority and responsibility. Job rotation, executive education programs, mentoring, and special-project assignments are examples of employee development programs.

4 What types of training and development do organizations offer their employees?

A performance appraisal compares an employee's actual performance with the expected performance. Performance appraisals serve several purposes but are typically used to determine an employee's compensation, training needs, and advancement opportunities.

5 How are performance appraisals used to evaluate employee performance?

Direct pay is the hourly wage or monthly salary paid to an employee. In addition to the base wage or salary, direct pay may include bonuses and profit shares. Indirect pay consists of various benefits and services. Some benefits are required by law and include unemployment compensation, worker's compensation, and Social Security. Many employers also offer benefits not required by law. These include paid vacations and holidays, pensions, health and other insurance, employee wellness programs, and college tuition reimbursement.

6 What are the types of compensation and methods for paying workers?

A labor union is an organization that represents workers in dealing with management over disputes involving wages, hours, and working conditions. A company is unionized through an organizing drive that begins either inside, with a small group of existing employees, or outside, with an established union that targets the employer. When the union receives signed authorization cards from 30 percent of the firm's employees, the NLRB conducts a union certification election. A majority vote is needed to certify the union as the exclusive bargaining agent. The union and the employer then begin collective bargaining and have one year in which to reach an agreement.

7 What is a labor union and how is it organized?

Collective bargaining is the process of negotiating, administering, and interpreting labor agreements. Both union and management negotiators prepare a bargaining proposal. The two sides meet and exchange demands and ideas. Bargaining consists of compromises and concessions that lead to a tentative agreement. Top management then approves or disapproves the agreement for the management team. Union members vote to either approve or reject the contract. The key issues included in a union contract are wage increases, fringe benefits, and job security.

In most labor agreements the grievance procedure consists of three or four steps. In the initial step, the employee files a grievance; this is an oral and/or written presentation to the supervisor and may involve a union steward as representative of the grievant. Steps two and three involve meetings of the employee and one or more union officials and the appropriate supervisor and one or more management officials. If the grievance is not resolved at step three, either party (union or management) can request that an arbitrator, or neutral third party, hear and decide the grievance. The arbitrator reviews the grievance at a hearing and then makes the decision, which is presented in a document called the award.

When a union contract expires and a new agreement has not been reached, the union may impose economic pressure on the firm. These tactics may take the form of strikes, boycotts, picketing, or corporate campaigns. Similarly, employers may implement lockouts, hire replacements, or move production to another facility to place pressure on a union to accept a new contract.

A number of federal laws (listed in Exhibit 8.14) affect human resource management. Federal law prohibits discrimination based on age, race, gender, color, national origin, religion, or disability. The Americans with Disabilities Act bans discrimination against disabled workers and requires employers to change the work environment to accommodate the disabled. The Family and Medical Leave Act requires employers, with certain exceptions, to provide employees up to 12 weeks of unpaid leave a year. The leave can be for the birth or adoption of a child or due to serious illness of a family member.

Federal agencies that deal with human resource administration are the Equal Employment Opportunity Commission (EEOC), the Occupational Safety and Health Administration (OSHA), the Office of Federal Contract Compliance Programs (OFCCP), and the Wage and Hour Division of the Department of Labor. The EEOC and OFCCP are primary agencies for the enforcement of employment discrimination laws; OSHA enforces safety regulation; and the Wage and Hour Division enforces the minimum wage and related laws. Many companies employ affirmative action and safety officers to ensure compliance with antidiscrimination and workplace safety laws. The Wagner and Taft-Hartley Acts govern the union–management relationship, in part through the functions performed by the National Labor Relations Board. The law gives workers the right to form and join labor unions and obligates the employer to deal with the union fairly.

Human resource managers recognize that diverse workforces create an environment that nurtures creative decision making, effective problem solving, more agility in adapting to change, and a strong competitive advantage. Therefore, firms are becoming committed to recruiting and hiring a diverse workforce. To maximize efficiency, many firms are outsourcing HR functions and using technology to reduce costs and improve efficiency. Firms are also striving to hire employees that possess qualities that match those of the corporate culture. Although labor unions have faced declining membership in the last several decades, enrollment of service workers into labor unions may increase as low-wage earners seek improved working conditions, pay, and health benefits.

Key Terms

affirmative action programs 224

agency shop 220

apprenticeship 212

arbitration 222

collective bargaining 216

competitive advantage 225

conciliator 224

contingent worker 206

Equal Employment Opportunity
    Commission (EEOC) 224

federation 217

grievance 221

human resource (HR) management 204

human resources planning 204

incentive pay 214

job analysis 204

job description 204

job fair 207

job rotation 212

job specification 205

labor union 216

local union 216

management rights clause 220

mediator 225

mentoring 212

Occupational Safety and Health
    Administration (OSHA) 224

open shop 220

orientation 211

performance appraisal 212

programmed instruction 212

protected classes 224

recruitment 207

recruitment branding 208

right-to-work law 220

selection 209

selection interview 210

selective strike strategy 222

shop steward 217

simulation 212

succession planning 206

training and development 211

unemployment compensation 215

union shop 219

worker's compensation 215

Preparing for Tomorrow's Workplace: SCANS

1. Would an overseas job assignment be good for your career development? If you think so, what country would you prefer to live and work in for two or three years, and what type of job would you like to have in that country? (**Resources**)

2. The fringe benefit package of many employers includes numerous items such as health insurance, life insurance, pension plan, paid vacations, tuition reimbursement, employee price discounts on products of the firm, and paid sick leave. At your age, what are the three or four most important benefits? Why? Twenty years from now, what do you think will be your three or four most important benefits? Why? (**Resources**)

3. Assume you have been asked to speak at a local meeting of human resources and labor relations professionals. The topic is whether union membership will increase or decline in the next 50 years. Take either the increase or the decline position and outline your presentation. (**Information**)

4. Go to the government documents section in your college or university library and inspect publications of the Department of Labor (DOL), including *Employment and Earnings*, *Compensation and Working Conditions*, *Monthly Labor Review*, *Occupational Outlook Handbook*, and *Career Guide to Industries*. Alternatively, go to the DOL, Bureau of Labor Statistics Web site at **http://stats.bls.gov**. Access the most recent DOL publications and locate the following information. (**Information**)
   - Number of persons in the American workforce
   - Unemployment rate for last year
   - Demographic characteristics of the American workforce: race, ethnic status, age, marital status, and gender
   - Occupations where there are projected shortages for the next 5 or 10 years
   - Union membership by major industry category: manufacturing, banking and finance, health care, business and personal services, sports and entertainment, and any other area of interest to you

5. Assume you are a director of labor relations for a firm faced with a union certification election in 30 days. Draft a letter to be sent to your employees in which you urge them to vote "no union"; be persuasive in presenting your arguments against the union. (**Information**)

6. Using BCRC, research articles featuring a recent strike or a labor contract settlement. Report to your class the specifics of the strike or settlement. **(Technology, Resources)**
7. **Team Activity** Select two teams of five. One team will take the position that employees are simply a business expense to be managed. The second team will argue that employees are an asset to be developed to enable the firm to gain a competitive advantage. The remainder of the class will judge which team provided the stronger argument. **(Interpersonal)**
8. Have you or a family member ever been a union member? If so, name the union and describe it in terms of membership size, membership characteristics, strike history, recent bargaining issues, and employers under union contracts. **(Information)**
9. **Team Activity** Divide the class into two groups. One group will take the position that workers should be required to join unions and pay dues. The other group will take the position that workers should not be required to join unions. Hold a debate in which a spokesperson from each group is given 10 minutes to present the group's arguments. **(Interpersonal)**

Ethics Activity

More companies are installing global positioning systems (GPSs) in company vehicles and in cell phones. GPSs send location information to satellites that transmit the data to receivers at a computer. As the cost of GPSs drops and the number of mobile workers rises—an estimated 105 million in 2006—companies are depending on GPSs to monitor the movement of personnel and products. Companies find they improve customer service and help with time management. "I wanted to see how much time was spent on each job," says one small-business owner with a fleet of seven service vehicles. "We've had a few problems in the past—people weren't where they said they'd be. With GPS, we can defend ourselves to the customers. We know how fast the drivers drove, what route they took, and how long they spent on each job."

Many employees don't like the idea of Big Brother following their every move. In 2003, Boston road maintenance drivers demonstrated against the Massachusetts Highway Department, which was using their required GPS-enabled cell phones to measure employee productivity. Does it invade employee privacy, though? "It's a receive-only system. It just tells you a position. What the recipient wants to do with the information is another ballgame," says Michael Swiek, executive director of the U.S. GPS Industry Council.

Using a Web search tool, locate articles about this topic and then write responses to the following questions. Be sure to support your arguments and cite your sources.

ETHICAL DILEMMA: Do GPS devices constitute an invasion of employee privacy? Are there guidelines companies can develop for appropriate GPS use?

Sources: Diane Cadrain, "GPS on Rise; Workers' Complaints May Follow," *HR,* April 2005, pp. 32–33; and Cindy Waxer, "Navigating Privacy Concerns to Equip Workers with GPS," *Workforce Management,* August 1, 2005, p. 71.

Working the Net

1. Go to the Job Web site of the National Association of Colleges and Employers, **http://www.jobweb.com**, and click on Resumes & Interviews. Read the relevant articles to learn how to prepare an electronic résumé that will get results. Develop a list of rules for creating effective electronic résumés, and revise your résumé into electronic format. Now read about how to apply for a job online. What tips were the most useful to you?
2. Working as a contingent employee can help you explore your career options. Visit the Manpower Web site at **http://www.manpower.com**, and use the Job Search feature to look for several types of jobs that interest you. Choose your current city and one where you would like to live, either in the United States or abroad. What are the advantages of being a temporary worker? What other services does Manpower offer job seekers?
3. As a corporate recruiter, you must know how to screen prospective employees. The Integrity Center Web site at **http://www.integctr.com** offers a brief tutorial on preemployment screening, a glossary of key words and phrases, and related information. Prepare a short report that tells your assistant how to go about this process.
4. You've been asked to give a speech about the current status of affirmative action and equal employment to your company's managers. Starting with the Web site of the American Association for Affirmative Action (**http://www.affirmativeaction.org**) and its links to related

sites, research the topic and prepare an outline for your talk. Include current legislation and recent court cases.

5. Web-based training is becoming popular at many companies as a way to bring a wider variety of courses to more people at lower costs. The Web-Based Training Information Center site at **http://www.webbasedtraining.com** provides a good introduction. Learn about the basics of online training at its Primer page. Then link to the Resources section, try a demo, and explore other areas that interest you. Prepare a brief report on your findings, including the pros and cons of using the Web for training, to present to your class.

6. What are the key issues facing labor unions today? Visit the AFL-CIO Web site, **http://www.aflcio.org**, and Labornet, **http://www.labornet.org**. Select three current topics and summarize the key points for the class.

7. Not everyone believes that unions are good for workers. The National Right to Work Legal Defense Foundation offers free legal aid to employees whose "human and civil rights have been violated by compulsory unionism abuses." Read the materials on its site (**http://www.nrtw.org**) and prepare a short report on its position regarding the disadvantages of labor unions.

8. Although we tend to think of labor unions as representing manufacturing employees, many office and service industry employees, teachers, and professionals belong to unions. Visit the Web sites of two of the following nonmanufacturing unions and discuss how they help their members: the Office and Professional Employees International Union (**http://www.opeiu.org**), the American Federation of State, County and Municipal Employees (**http://www.afscme.org**), the National Education Association (**http://www.nea.org**), the Actor's Equity Association (**http://www.actorsequity.org**), and the American Federation of Musicians (**http://www.afm.org**). What are the differences, if any, between these unions and those in other industries?

Creative Thinking Case

Diversity and Discrimination in the Workplace

Although we live in enlightened times, a recent Gallup Poll found that 15 percent of American workers still experienced some form of workplace discrimination. The study was conducted to mark the anniversary of the Civil Rights Act of 1964, and the creation of the Equal Employment Opportunity Commission (EEOC). It was carried out in conjunction with the EEOC, and partially sponsored by Kaiser-Permanente, the Society for Human Resource Management (SHRM), and United Parcel Service (UPS).

The poll found that the two most frequently cited types of discrimination are gender (26 percent) and race/ethnicity (23 percent). Also mentioned were age, disability, sexual orientation, and religion. The work areas found to be most susceptible to discrimination are promotion and pay. Being selected for a job, and treatment in the workplace, were also cited.

The study discovered that women are twice as likely to report that they have been discriminated against than men. Among racial and ethnic groups, Asians (31 percent) and blacks (26 percent) are most likely to report experiences of discrimination, followed by Hispanics (18 percent) and whites (12 percent).

"We are grateful to The Gallup Organization and its sponsors for this important information," said EEOC chair, Cari M. Dominguez. "At the Commission we deal with concrete charges of discrimination that workers file, and this insight into the perceptions of discrimination by a sampling of the workforce will aid us as we continue our emphasis on proactive prevention, outreach, and law enforcement."

The survey, conducted via telephone interviews with 1,252 adults, measured employees' evaluation of their companies' efforts to provide diversity and protect against employee discrimination. The results show that employees' satisfaction with their company, their likelihood of retention, and their loyalty, are all highly related to their companies' Diversity Policy Scores. The Gallup Organization's Government Division Partner, Max Larsen, observes, "These data make it pretty clear that it makes good business sense to have operable diversity efforts in organizations."

"The survey results underscore the importance of Kaiser-Permanente's historical commitment to diversity and inclusion, to cultural competence in healthcare, and to the clear articulation of the business imperative that demands workforce diversity," said Kaiser-Permanente vice president and chief diversity officer, Ron Knox. "The survey strengthens Kaiser-Permanente's determination to make workplace discrimination a thing of the past."

"In today's global marketplace, workforce diversity is not a politically or morally correct obligation—it is also a business imperative," said Society for Human Resource Management (SHRM) president and CEO, Susan R. Meisinger, SPHR. "It simply makes good business sense to use the talents of all workers."

Critical Thinking Questions

- Why is workplace diversity so important in today's business environment?
- What are the major sources of workplace discrimination? Cite specific examples from the case.
- What steps are companies taking to ensure that employees are not discriminated against?

Sources: Frank Scanlan, Eric Nielsen, "Almost One in Six Americans Report Discrimination at Workplace in Past Year," SHRMOnline, **http://www.shrm.org** December 8, 2005; Robyn D. Clarke, "Workplace Bias Abounds: New Study Confirms the American Workplace Has Much Farther to Go to Achieve True Diversity," *Black Enterprise,* September 2005, **http://findarticles.com**; Francis Lora, "Diversity in the Workplace: How Much Have Things Really Changed?" *Latino Leaders: The National Magazine of the Successful American Latino,* August-September 2005, **http://findarticles.com**.

Andrea Herran
Human Resources
Consultant

Exploring Business Careers

In college, Andrea Herran studied business administration and minored in psychology. Always interested in a business career, she initially took psychology simply because it was interesting. Little did she know how applicable that minor would become. As a human resources (HR) consultant, she often benefits from her psychology background. "Studying human behavior really gave me the background necessary to put myself in the position of others, to see things from their point of view, which has definitely been helpful in my career in human resources."

Herran started out as an administrative assistant in the HR department of a hotel, and her career has run the gamut of human resources over the 17 years since she graduated from college. She has been an employment coordinator, focusing on employee recruitment and selection, and personnel manager, where she learned the skills necessary to maintain and evaluate employees. As a training manager, she sharpened her talent for developing, coordinating, and even administering staff training. Eventually, she became the director of human resources for companies both in the United States and abroad. Indeed, beyond the United States, she has worked in Mexico, Argentina, and South Africa. Today, she sees her varied employment history as key to her success. "Anyone interested in this field should experience as many possibilities within human resources as possible. You leave school with the theory, but only through experience do you really get to see what the potential of such a career is."

Consistent with her desire for a fast-paced, changing environment, both in terms of what she does and who she works with, she has made the move to consulting. "Consulting allows me to draw upon all my human resources skills. I have opened five HR departments in my career, so I bring my full experience to bear on the challenges each company has."

Herran has been working for about six months with her first client, Aquion Water Treatment Products (AWTP), which produces commercial and individual water treatment products such as water softeners and purifiers. She was brought on to update their department, which oversees 138 employees. The department has been using many of the same policies and practices for several years. For example, their performance reviews were very task-oriented. Performance reviews, however, have become much more behavior-oriented in the past 30 years. Instead of determining whether a task was completed, today's performance reviews seek to evaluate not only whether the person completed the task but also how he or she did so, especially examining the interactions involved in the task. Is an employee punctual at returning consumer request calls? How does he or she relate to customers? As a manager, does he or she express thoughts clearly? "By evaluating specific behaviors, you create an environment with clearly set qualifications for advancement and opportunities for targeted employee development. Without this, the human aspect of human resources can be overlooked."

This chapter looked at the role of human resources within an organization, from the general processes of developing and planning to the more specific tasks of employee evaluation and compensation.

Human resources management and labor relations involve acquisition, development, use, and maintenance of a human resource mix (people and positions) to achieve strategic organizational goals and objectives. Successful human resource management is based on a company's ability to attract and hire the best employees, equip them with the knowledge and skills they need to excel, compensate them fairly, and motivate them to reach their full potential and perform at high levels. Today's business environment presents numerous challenges to effectively managing employees:

- Technology continues to advance, which places great importance on knowledge workers, especially when demand outstrips the supply of high talent individuals.
- Global business operations involve rapid data transfer and necessitate accelerated decision making by executive and technical employees.
- The workforce is increasingly more diversified and multicultural, which places increased emphasis on communication and cultural understanding.
- Work life and family priorities are more difficult to balance as dual worker families populate the labor force.
- Employment and labor laws continue to greatly influence employee recruitment and hiring, compensation decisions, and employee retention and turnover in both union and nonunion organizations.

Each day, human resource experts and front-line supervisors deal with these challenges while sharing responsibility for attracting and retaining skilled, motivated employees. Whether faced with a large or small human resource problem, supervisors need some understanding of difficult employee relations issues, especially if there are legal implications.

In this chapter, you learned about the elements of the human resource management process, including human resource planning and job analysis and design, employee recruitment and selection, training and development of employees, performance planning and evaluation, and compensation of the workforce. The chapter also described labor unions and their representation of millions of American workers in construction, manufacturing, transportation, and service-based industries.

Motivating Employees

Learning Goals

After reading this chapter, you should be able to answer these questions:

1 What are the basic principles of Frederick Taylor's concept of scientific management?

2 What did Elton Mayo's Hawthorne studies reveal about worker motivation?

3 What is Maslow's hierarchy of needs, and how do these needs relate to employee motivation?

4 How are McGregor's Theories X and Y and Ouchi's Theory Z used to explain worker motivation?

5 What are the basic components of Herzberg's motivator-hygiene theory?

6 What four contemporary theories on employee motivation offer insights into improving employee performance?

7 How can managers redesign existing jobs to increase employee motivation and performance?

8 What initiatives are organizations using today to motivate and retain employees?

"Just Throw"

Anybody who has even a passing interest in baseball knows that a perfect game is a special thing. In fact, it's so special that only 17 men in professional baseball have accomplished the near-impossible feat of facing only 27 men and recording 27 outs while not allowing a single man to reach first or any other base through a walk, a hit, an error, a hit batsman, or any other possible means of reaching base. As such, the feat requires solid defense behind the pitcher and at the plate a solid catcher who not only calls the pitches appropriately but—since he's the only defensive player to see the whole field—also manages the team from behind home plate.

And sometimes managing the team requires managing the pitcher as well, as we see in *For Love of the Game*. In the movie, Billy Chapel is a longtime Detroit Tiger with Hall of Fame credentials who might just be pitching the final game of his career. Throughout the course of the game, his attention has been diverted to a variety of his past experiences including his baseball experience as well as his relationship with Jane Aubrey, his on-again, off-again girlfriend. His attention, needless to say, is divided; however, he has managed to enter the eighth inning of his game having allowed no one to reach first base or beyond. He is pitching a perfect game, and he is only now coming to realize it.

"Anybody been on base?" he asks his catcher, Gus Sinski, who informs him that nobody has. Billy steps off the mound shaking his head, informing Gus that he's not sure if he has anything left in his tank, meaning he's not sure he has the strength—mental, physical, or emotional—to continue. Gus steps up and performs a task that many managers, both on the field and off the field, must do when it comes to managing human resources: providing motivation.

Motivation is essentially the means through which an individual is prompted to move in a certain direction or perform in a certain way in order to fulfill a particular need or want. A need is best defined as the gap between what *is* and what is *required,* and the want is best defined as the gap between what *is* and what is *desired.* The needs or wants that need to be fulfilled may be directed by the overall firm strategy or organizational goals, or they may be held personally by the individual. Either way, individuals who are assigned to fulfill these needs and wants sometimes require some form of motivation to get their energy moving in the appropriate direction.

Gus steps up and provides that motivation to Billy. He recognizes that there are both individual goals—Billy's being credited with pitching a perfect game—as well as organizational goals—winning the game and not rolling over and letting the Yankees into the postseason easily. "Chappy," he says, "you just throw whatever you got. Whatever's left. The boys are all here for you. We'll back you up, we'll be there . . . 'cause Billy, we don't *stink* right now. We're the best team in baseball . . . right now, right this minute 'cause of you. You're the reason. We're not going to screw that up. We're going to be awesome for you right now. Just throw." He urges Billy Chapel to give it his best, motivating him to complete what he has started.

The following chapter explores a variety of theories of motivation, both past and present, ranging from Frederick Taylor's theory of scientific management to Maslow's hierarchy of needs to expectancy theory to reinforcement theory and many more in between. The chapter then provides an overview of how you might put theory into practice, exploring how you might redesign or modify existing jobs for motivational purposes, provide recognition and empowerment within the workforce, or even jump-start motivation through economic incentives. The chapter concludes with an overview of various trends in employee motivation.

Discussion Questions

- The chapter discusses several early theories of motivation. Pick one and explain how it best describes Gus's motivation of Billy Chapel on the pitcher's mound.

- The chapter also discusses several current theories of motivation. Again, pick one and explain how it best describes Gus's motivation of Billy Chapel on the pitcher's mound.
- Gus reveals that Billy has also motivated the team to succeed. Pick a motivational theory discussed in the chapter and use it to explain how you think Billy has motivated the team.
- Imagine you are the manager of a baseball team. How might you motivate a pitcher to pitch a perfect game? How might you motivate the team to win an individual game? How might you motivate the team to make it to the postseason?

This chapter details motivational theory, both historically and currently, and applies that theory to the business world, where motivation is key to success.

People can be a firm's most important resource. They can also be the most challenging resource to manage well. Employees who are motivated and work hard to achieve personal and organizational goals can become a crucial competitive advantage for a firm. The key then is understanding the process of motivation, what motivates individuals, and *how* an organization can create a workplace that allows people to perform to the best of their abilities. **Motivation** is the set of forces that prompt a person to release energy in a certain direction. As such, motivation is essentially a need- and want-satisfying process. A **need** is best defined as the gap between what *is* and what is *required*. Similarly, a **want** is the gap between what *is* and what is *desired*. Unsatisfied needs and wants create a state of tension that pushes (motivates) individuals to practice behavior that will result in the need being met or the want being fulfilled. That is, motivation is what pushes us to move from where we are to where we want to be because expending that effort will result in some kind of reward.

Rewards can be divided into two basic categories: intrinsic and extrinsic. Intrinsic rewards come from within the individual, things like satisfaction, contentment, sense of accomplishment, confidence, and pride. By contrast, extrinsic rewards come from outside the individual and include things like pay raises, promotions, bonuses, prestigious assignments, and so forth. Exhibit 9.1 illustrates the motivation process.

Successful managers are able to marshal the forces to motivate employees to achieve organizational goals. And just as there are many types of gaps between where organizations are and where they want to be, there are many motivational theories from which managers can draw to inspire employees to bridge those gaps. In this chapter, we will first examine motivational theories that grew out of the industrial revolution and early ideas of organizational psychology. Then we

motivation
Something that prompts a person to release his or her energy in a certain direction.

need
The gap between what is and what is required.

want
The gap between what is and what is desired.

EXHIBIT 9.1	Model of Motivation

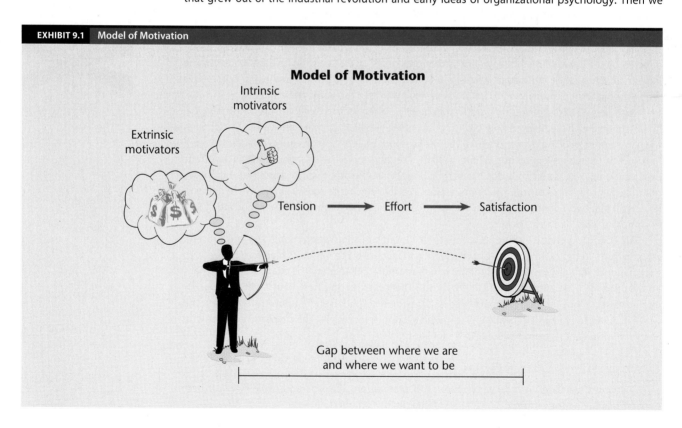

Model of Motivation

will examine needs-based theories and more contemporary ideas about employee motivation like equity, expectancy, goals, and reinforcement theories. Finally, we will show you how managers are applying these theories in real-world situations.

Early Theories of Motivation

How can managers and organizations promote enthusiastic job performance, high productivity, and job satisfaction? Many studies of human behavior in organizations have contributed to our current understanding of these issues. A look at the evolution of management theory and research shows how managers have arrived at the practices used today to manage human behavior in the workplace. A sampling of the most influential of these theorists and research studies are discussed in this section.

Frederick Taylor's Scientific Management

One of the most influential figures of the *classical era* of management, which lasted from about 1900 to the mid-1930s, was Frederick W. Taylor, a mechanical engineer sometimes called the "father of **scientific management**." Taylor's approach to improved performance was based on economic incentives and the premise that there is "one best way" to perform any job. As a manager at the Midvale and Bethlehem Steel companies in Philadelphia in the early 1900s, Taylor was frustrated at the inefficiency of the laborers working in the mills.

Convinced that productivity could be improved, Taylor studied the individual jobs in the mill and redesigned the equipment and the methods used by workers. Taylor timed each job with a stopwatch and broke down every task into separate movements. He then prepared an instruction sheet telling exactly how each job should be done, how much time it should take, and what motions and tools should be used. Taylor's ideas led to dramatic increases in productivity in the steel mills and resulted in the development of four basic principles of scientific management:

1. Develop a scientific approach for each element of a person's job.
2. Scientifically select, train, teach, and develop workers.
3. Encourage cooperation between workers and managers so that each job can be accomplished in a standard, scientifically determined way.
4. Divide work and responsibility between management and workers according to who is better suited to each task.

Taylor published his ideas in *The Principles of Scientific Management.* His pioneering work vastly increased production efficiency and contributed to the specialization of labor and the assembly-line method of production. Taylor's approach is still being used nearly a century later. Recall from Chapter 6 UPS's manual for drivers titled "340 Methods." Industrial engineers help the company maximize efficiency by carefully studying every step of the delivery process, looking for the quickest possible way to deliver packages to customers. Though Taylor's work was a giant step forward in the evolution of management, it had a fundamental flaw in that it assumed that all people are primarily motivated by economic means. Taylor's successors in the study of management found that motivation is much more complex than he envisioned.

The Hawthorne Studies

The classical era of management was followed by the *human relations era,* which began in the 1930s and focused primarily on how human behavior and relations affect organizational performance. The new era was ushered in by the Hawthorne studies, which changed the way many managers thought about motivation, job productivity, and employee satisfaction. The studies began when engineers at the Hawthorne Western Electric plant decided to examine the effects of varying levels of light on worker productivity—an experiment that might have interested Frederick Taylor. The engineers expected brighter light to lead to increased productivity, but the results showed that varying the level of light in either direction (brighter or dimmer) led to increased output from the experimental group. In 1927, the Hawthorne engineers asked Harvard professor Elton Mayo and a team of researchers to join them in their investigation.

scientific management
A system of management developed by Frederick W. Taylor and based on four principles: developing a scientific approach for each element of a job, scientifically selecting and training workers, encouraging cooperation between workers and managers, and dividing work and responsibility between management and workers according to who can better perform a particular task.

1 What are the basic principles of Frederick Taylor's concept of scientific management?

Danica Patrick is on a roll. The American racecar driver began racing go-karts at age 10 and quickly zoomed her way to multiple national championships. By the time she was old enough to obtain a state driver's license, Patrick was determined to make it in professional racing. In 2005 she was named the IndyCar Series Rookie of the Year, and in 2008 Patrick made history by becoming the first female driver to win an IndyCar race, taking the victory lap at the Indy Japan 300. What motivates people to achieve their personal best?

© Kyodo/Landov

2 What did Elton Mayo's Hawthorne studies reveal about worker motivation?

From 1927 to 1932, Mayo and his colleagues conducted experiments on job redesign, length of workday and workweek, length of break times, and incentive plans. The results of the studies indicated that increases in performance were tied to a complex set of employee attitudes. Mayo claimed that both experimental and control groups from the plant had developed a sense of group pride because they had been selected to participate in the studies. The pride that came from this special attention motivated the workers to increase their productivity. Supervisors who allowed the employees to have some control over their situation appeared to further increase the workers' motivation. These findings gave rise to what is now known as the **Hawthorne effect**, which suggests that employees will perform better when they feel singled out for special attention or feel that management is concerned about employee welfare. The studies also provided evidence that informal work groups (the social relationships of employees) and the resulting group pressure have positive effects on group productivity. The results of the Hawthorne studies enhanced our understanding of what motivates individuals in the workplace. They indicate that in addition to the personal economic needs emphasized in the classical era, social needs play an important role in influencing work-related attitudes and behaviors.

Maslow's Hierarchy of Needs

Another well-known theorist from the behavioral era of management history, psychologist Abraham Maslow, proposed a theory of motivation based on universal human needs. Maslow believed that each individual has a hierarchy of needs, consisting of physiological, safety, social, esteem, and self-actualization needs, as shown in Exhibit 9.2.

Maslow's theory of motivation contends that people act to satisfy their unmet needs. When you're hungry, for instance, you look for and eat food, thus satisfying a basic physiological need. Once a need is satisfied, its importance to the individual diminishes, and a higher-level need is more likely to motivate the person.

According to **Maslow's hierarchy of needs**, the most basic human needs are physiological needs, that is, the needs for food, shelter, and clothing. In large part, it is the physiological needs that

Hawthorne effect
The phenomenon that employees perform better when they feel singled out for attention or feel that management is concerned about their welfare.

3 What is Maslow's hierarchy of needs, and how do these needs relate to employee motivation?

Maslow's hierarchy of needs
A theory of motivation developed by Abraham Maslow; holds that humans have five levels of needs and act to satisfy their unmet needs. At the base of the hierarchy are fundamental physiological needs, followed in order by safety, social, esteem, and self-actualization needs.

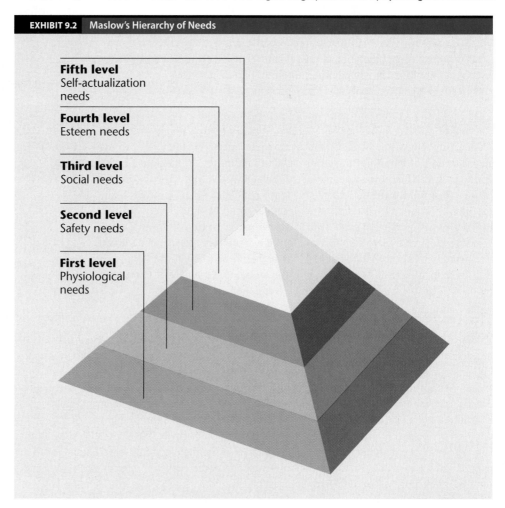

EXHIBIT 9.2   Maslow's Hierarchy of Needs

Fifth level
Self-actualization needs

Fourth level
Esteem needs

Third level
Social needs

Second level
Safety needs

First level
Physiological needs

© Rubberball/Getty Images

How Maslow Saved My Company

At the end of the 20th century, Chip Conley's small boutique hotel chain, Joie de Vivre, was generating $100 million in annual revenue. But after the dot-com bust, the September 11 terrorist attacks, the SARS outbreak, and the explosive growth of online travel sites, his revenue fell 25 percent. Conley didn't take a salary for three years and was about to declare bankruptcy when he came across Abraham Maslow's *Toward a Psychology of Being* in a bookstore.

Rereading the text he remembered from college reminded Conley why he had gone into business in the first place: he wanted to create for himself and others a sense of the joy of life in the workplace. Conley realized that his company was helping satisfy needs up and down Maslow's pyramid for many different groups: himself, his employees, his guests, and his investors. Rather than focus on things like compensation that live at the bottom of the pyramid, Conley began thinking of higher-level needs like meaning.

One way Conley makes his employees' work experience meaningful is by incorporating a large dose of recognition into company operations. Fifteen minutes of every executive meeting is devoted to people sharing examples of employees who did something really amazing. After the meeting, Conley assigns someone unrelated to the recognized employees to call them up and say thank you. For example, if a bellman is recognized for doing an outstanding job, Conley might assign the head of IT to call the bellman to say thanks.

Another way Conley helps his employees experience the meaning of their work is to do what he calls the "George Bailey" exercise, which he based on the movie

It's a Wonderful Life. For example, he might bring together housekeepers from the different Joie de Vivre locations and talk about what would happen if they weren't there each day. Usual answers include things like, "Trash would pile up. Carpets wouldn't be vacuumed. Bathrooms would be full of wet towels." Conley then uses these examples to help the group brainstorm alternative names for housekeeping ("clutter busters" and "serenity keepers" are only a few of the great ones). The exercise helps employees develop a very real sense that the customer experience would not be the same without their contribution.

By focusing on the higher-order needs on Maslow's pyramid, Conley was able to pull his company out of the doldrums and rekindle the *joie de vivre* at Joie de Vivre.[1]

Critical Thinking Questions

- Can companies thrive by focusing on only one or two levels of Maslow's hierarchy of needs? Why or why not?
- What impact do you think focusing on employees' higher-level needs has on the customer experience at Joie de Vivre? On Conley's business as a whole?

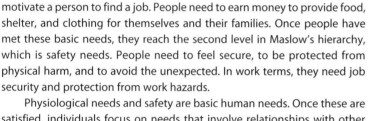

CONCEPT in action

motivate a person to find a job. People need to earn money to provide food, shelter, and clothing for themselves and their families. Once people have met these basic needs, they reach the second level in Maslow's hierarchy, which is safety needs. People need to feel secure, to be protected from physical harm, and to avoid the unexpected. In work terms, they need job security and protection from work hazards.

Physiological needs and safety are basic human needs. Once these are satisfied, individuals focus on needs that involve relationships with other people. At Maslow's third level are social needs, or needs for belonging (acceptance by others) and for giving and receiving friendship and love. Informal social groups on and off the job help people satisfy these needs. At the fourth level in Maslow's hierarchy are esteem needs, which are needs for the respect of others and for a sense of accomplishment and achievement. Satisfaction of these needs is reflected in feelings of self-worth. Praise and recognition from managers and others in the firm contribute to the sense of self-worth. Finally, at the highest level in Maslow's hierarchy are self-actualization needs, or needs for fulfillment, for living up to one's potential, and for using one's abilities to the utmost. Read how Maslow's theory helped one entrepreneur save his company from bankruptcy in the Catching the Entrepreneurial Spirit box above.

Maslow's theory is not without criticism, however. Maslow claimed that a higher-level need was not activated until a lower-level need was met. He also claimed that a satisfied need is not a motivator. A farmer who has plenty to eat is not motivated by more food (the physiological hunger need). Travelocity CEO Michelle Peluso puts it this way: "People internalize compensation for a few hours or days, but it doesn't fire them up to get out of bed every morning—unless of course it's bonus day."[2] Peluso is a believer that people are more motivated by higher-level needs. She says, "Seriously, you don't get up saying 'I've got great compensation.' You go to work because you believe in the people around you, your peers, your

© Kevin Winter/Getty Images

Simon Cowell has made a career out of snubbing vocally-challenged Mariah Carey wannabes on the ratings-busting reality show *American Idol*. But the British-born A&R rep-turned-TV star also produces a slew of entertainment ventures that are turning heads and shaping the industry. *Britain's Got Talent* and *The X-Factor* are his creations, as are Cowell-produced music groups Il Divo and Westlife. Fortunately for fans, Cowell still finds time to dish out cheeky, disgust-filled insults on *Idol*. What needs motivate individuals at the peak of their careers?

colleagues [*third level*], and when you believe your company does something great for your customers [*fifth level*]."[3]

Research has not verified these principles in any strict sense. The theory also concentrates on moving up the hierarchy without fully addressing moving back down the hierarchy. Despite these limitations, Maslow's ideas are very helpful for understanding the needs of people at work and for determining what can be done to satisfy them.

McGregor's Theories X and Y

Douglas McGregor, one of Maslow's students, influenced the study of motivation with his formulation of two contrasting sets of assumptions about human nature—Theory X and Theory Y.

The **Theory X** management style is based on a pessimistic view of human nature and assumes the following:

- The average person dislikes work and will avoid it if possible.
- Because people don't like to work, they must be controlled, directed, or threatened with punishment to get them to make an effort.
- The average person prefers to be directed, avoids responsibility, is relatively unambitious, and wants security above all else.

This view of people suggests that managers must constantly prod workers to perform and must closely control their on-the-job behavior. Theory X managers tell people what to do, are very directive, like to be in control, and show little confidence in employees. They often foster dependent, passive, and resentful subordinates.

In contrast, a **Theory Y** management style is based on a more optimistic view of human nature and assumes the following:

- Work is as natural as play or rest. People want to and can be self-directed and self-controlled and will try to achieve organizational goals they believe in.
- Workers can be motivated using positive incentives and will try hard to accomplish organizational goals if they believe they will be rewarded for doing so.
- Under proper conditions, the average person not only accepts responsibility but seeks it out. Most workers have a relatively high degree of imagination and creativity and are willing to help solve problems.

Managers who operate on Theory Y assumptions recognize individual differences and encourage workers to learn and develop their skills. An administrative assistant might be given the responsibility for generating a monthly report. The reward for doing so might be recognition at a meeting, a special training class to enhance computer skills, or a pay increase. In short, the Theory Y approach builds on the idea that worker and organizational interests are the same. At Travelocity, employees are asked to nominate coworkers they believe reflect the company's core values.[4] CEO Michelle Peluso circulates the list of nominees in a weekly e-mail to all staff members. In the newsletter, Peluso describes how the nominees' service ties back to the mission of the company. Peluso also makes quarterly office visits during which she discusses Travelocity's financial performance with the employees. That way, each employee understands how his or her individual performance contributes to the health of the whole team.[5]

Theory Z

William Ouchi (pronounced O Chee), a management scholar at the University of California, Los Angeles, has proposed a theory that combines U.S. and Japanese business practices. He calls it **Theory Z**. Exhibit 9.3 compares the traditional U.S. and Japanese management styles with the Theory Z approach. Theory Z emphasizes long-term employment, slow career development, moderate specialization, group decision making, individual responsibility, relatively informal control over the employee, and concern for workers. Theory Z has many Japanese elements. But it reflects U.S. cultural values.

In the past decade, admiration for Japanese management philosophy that centers on creating long-term relationships has declined. The cultural beliefs of groupthink, not taking risks, and employees not thinking for themselves are passé. Such conformity has limited Japanese competitiveness in the global marketplace. Today there is a realization that Japanese firms need to be more proactive and nimble in order to prosper. It was that realization that led Japanese icon Sony to name a foreigner as the CEO of Japan's most famous company. Over the years, Sony's performance

Theory X
A management style, formulated by Douglas McGregor, that is based on a pessimistic view of human nature and assumes that the average person dislikes work, will avoid it if possible, prefers to be directed, avoids responsibility, and wants security above all.

Theory Y
A management style, formulated by Douglas McGregor, that is based on a relatively optimistic view of human nature; assumes that the average person wants to work, accepts responsibility, is willing to help solve problems, and can be self-directed and self-controlled.

Theory Z
A theory developed by William Ouchi that combines U.S. and Japanese business practices by emphasizing long-term employment, slow career development, moderate specialization, group decision making, individual responsibility, relatively informal control over the employee, and concern for workers.

EXHIBIT 9.3   Differences in Management Approaches

Factor	Traditional U.S. Management	Japanese Management	Theory Z (Combination of U.S. and Japanese Management)
Length of employment	Relatively short term; worker subject to layoffs if business is bad	Lifetime; layoffs never used to reduce costs	Long term but not necessarily lifetime; layoffs "inappropriate"; stable, loyal workforce; improved business conditions don't require new hiring and training
Rate of evaluation and promotion	Relatively rapid	Relatively slow	Slow by design; manager thoroughly trained and evaluated
Specialization in a functional area	Considerable; worker acquires expertise in single functional area	Minimal; worker acquires expertise in organization instead of functional areas	Moderate; all experience various functions of the organization and have a sense of what's good for the firm rather than for a single area
Decision making	On individual basis	Input from all concerned parties	Group decision making for better decisions and easier implementation
Responsibility for success or failure	Assigned to individual	Shared by group	Assigned to individual
Control by manager	Very explicit and formal	More implicit and informal	Relatively informal but with explicit performance measures
Concern for workers	Focuses on work-related aspects of a worker's life	Extends to whole life of worker	Is relatively concerned with worker's whole life, including the family

Source: Comparison of traditional U.S. and Japanese management styles with the Theory Z approach. Based on information from Jerry D. Johnson, Austin College. Dr. Johnson was a research assistant for William Ouchi.

had declined until in April 2005, the company posted its biggest loss ever: Nobuki Idei, the former CEO who inherited Sony's massive debts and stagnant product lines, realized his strategy wasn't working, so he determined to appoint a successor who would be able to transform Sony from the lumbering giant it had become back into the forward-thinking company it had been. Idei tapped Sir Howard Stringer, a Welsh-born American who had been running Sony's U.S. operations. In doing so, Idei hoped to shock company insiders and industry analysts alike. "It's funny, 100 percent of the people around here agree we need to change, but 90 percent of them don't really want to change themselves," he says. "So I finally concluded that we needed our top management to quite literally speak another language."[6]

Herzberg's Motivator–Hygiene Theory

Another important contribution to our understanding of individual motivation came from Frederick Herzberg's studies, which addressed the question, "What do people really want from their work experience?" In the late 1950s Herzberg surveyed numerous employees to find out what particular work elements made them feel exceptionally good or bad about their jobs. The results indicated that certain job factors are consistently related to employee job satisfaction while others can create job dissatisfaction. According to Herzberg, **motivating factors** (also called *job satisfiers*) are primarily intrinsic job elements that lead to satisfaction. **Hygiene factors** (also called *job dissatisfiers*) are extrinsic elements of the work environment. A summary of motivating and hygiene factors appears in Exhibit 9.4.

One of the most interesting results of Herzberg's studies was the implication that the opposite of satisfaction is not dissatisfaction. Herzberg believed that proper management of hygiene factors

5 What are the basic components of Herzberg's motivator-hygiene theory?

motivating factors
Intrinsic job elements that lead to worker satisfaction.

hygiene factors
Extrinsic elements of the work environment that do not serve as a source of employee satisfaction or motivation.

EXHIBIT 9.4   Herzberg's Motivating and Hygiene Factors

Motivating Factors	Hygiene Factors
Achievement	Company policy
Recognition	Supervision
Work itself	Working conditions
Responsibility	Interpersonal relationships at work
Advancement	Salary and benefits
Growth	Job security

Employee Satisfaction Leads to Five-Star Service

Every morning, employees throughout the Ritz-Carlton chain of hotels meet for 15 minutes to share "Wow" stories. Employees of every department recount true stories of fellow employees' heroic measures to go above and beyond the conventional customer service duties. In one story, the hotel's laundry service failed to remove a stain on a guest's suit before the guest left. The hotel manager flew to the guest's house and personally delivered a reimbursement check for the cost of the suit. Stories like this are quickly spread throughout the organization and reinforce the customer service skill and experience the hotel chain is trying to instill in all its employees. Most important, though, the stories recognize and motivate.

Ritz-Carlton has 12 service values that it wants every employee to embody, not only with guests but with fellow employees. When attending a housekeeping staff meeting, for example, the head housekeeper arrives in a suit and tie with smartly polished shoes. His formal attire signals to his staff that he takes them and their job seriously. His outfit communicates respect. When he greets his staff enthusiastically and with all smiles, they return the greeting with equal if not greater enthusiasm.

At one meeting, the members of the housekeeping staff debated the merits of one cleaning product over another while the manager was in rapt attention.

The whole time his housekeepers discussed and debated, he maintained eye contact and asked questions. The respect he receives from his staff comes, he says, "because I listen to their concerns, and they know I will follow up." When he asked his staff, "Why do we go the extra mile?" one housekeeper replied, "It offers a personal touch that shows we care." Another adds, "It reflects our commitment to five-star service."

That service has been a hallmark of Ritz-Carlton since the company was founded and is summed up by its motto: Ladies and gentlemen serving ladies and gentlemen. Ritz-Carlton considers its employees on par with its customers, and that kind of employee respect creates employee *and* customer satisfaction to the highest levels.[7]

Critical Thinking Questions
- Is employee satisfaction entirely the responsibility of management? Why or why not?
- How well do you think the principles of Ritz-Carlton could extend to hotel chains like Motel 6 (which has a different customer) or even to another industry? Explain.

© Digital Vision/Getty Images

CONCEPT in action

© AP Images/Marcio Jose Sanchez

Being square has been a hip competitive advantage for on-site tech-support firm Geek Squad since 1994. The company's 24-hour computer-support taskforce consists of uniformed double agents in squad-car-painted geekmobiles on a critical mission: to save frantic customers from computer viruses, crashes, and the blue screen of death. According to Herzberg's Motivator-Hygiene theory, what effect might Geek Squad's artfully geeky work environment have on employee satisfaction?

CONCEPT check

What did Elton Mayo's studies reveal about employee productivity?

How can a manager use an understanding of Maslow's hierarchy to motivate employees?

How do the Theory X, Theory Y, and Theory Z management styles differ?

could prevent employee dissatisfaction, but that these factors could not serve as a source of satisfaction or motivation. Good working conditions, for instance, will keep employees at a job but won't make them work harder. But poor working conditions, which are job dissatisfiers, may make employees quit. According to Herzberg, a manager who wants to increase employee satisfaction needs to focus on the motivating factors, or satisfiers. A job with many satisfiers will usually motivate workers, provide job satisfaction, and prompt effective performance. But a lack of job satisfiers doesn't always lead to dissatisfaction and poor performance; instead, a lack of job satisfiers may merely lead to workers doing an adequate job, rather than their best.

Recognizing that business performance increases when employees are motivated to perform their best, Verizon implemented a series of initiatives that focus on motivating factors. Plan Your Career (PYC) combines Web resources, manager coaching, and classroom training to help employees outline career goals and draft action plans to improve in certain skill areas. Other programs focus on developing employees for promotion and lateral-movement opportunities. Surprisingly, Verizon has noticed an increased interest in lateral moves, because employees perceive them as helpful elements in their long-term career goals. Nearly half of Verizon's employees use PYC, and more than 60 percent have had career discussions with their managers.[8]

Although Herzberg's ideas have been widely read and his recommendations implemented at numerous companies over the years, there are some very legitimate concerns about Herzberg's work. Whereas his findings have been used to explain employee motivation, in fact his studies focused on job satisfaction, a different (though related) concept from motivation. Other criticisms focus on the unreliability of Herzberg's methodology, the fact that the theory ignores the impact of situational variables, and the assumed relationship between satisfaction and productivity. Nevertheless, the questions raised by Herzberg about the nature of job satisfaction and the effects of intrinsic and extrinsic factors on employee behavior have proved a valuable contribution to the evolution of theories of motivation and job satisfaction. Read how the Ritz-Carlton turns employee satisfaction into a five-star experience for its customers in the Customer Satisfaction and Quality box above.

Contemporary Views on Motivation

The early management scholars laid a foundation that enabled managers to better understand their workers and how best to motivate them. Since then, new theories have given us an even better understanding of worker motivation. Three of these theories are explained in this section: the expectancy theory, the equity theory, and the goal-setting theory.

Expectancy Theory

One of the best-supported and most widely accepted theories of motivation is expectancy theory, which focuses on the link between motivation and behavior. According to **expectancy theory**, the probability of an individual acting in a particular way depends on the strength of that individual's belief that the act will have a particular outcome and on whether the individual values that outcome. The degree to which an employee is motivated depends on three important relationships, shown in Exhibit 9.5.

1. The link between effort and performance, or the strength of the individual's expectation that a certain amount of effort will lead to a certain level of performance.
2. The link between performance and outcome, or the strength of the expectation that a certain level of performance will lead to a particular outcome.
3. The link between outcomes and individual needs, or the degree to which the individual expects the anticipated outcome to satisfy personal needs. Some outcomes have more valence, or value, for individuals than others do.

Based on the expectancy theory, managers should do the following to motivate employees:

- Determine the rewards valued by each employee.
- Determine the desired performance level and then communicate it clearly to employees.
- Make the performance level attainable.
- Link rewards to performance.
- Determine what factors might counteract the effectiveness of an award.
- Make sure the reward is adequate for the level of performance.

Recall from Chapter 8 how Trufast, the fastener manufacturer in Ohio, linked performance tightly to rewards. Each quarter, managers award their employees up to 25 points in four categories: initiative, attitude, aptitude, and flexibility. Employees must receive at least 70 points to receive incentive pay, and the higher the score, the higher the incentive pay, which can be up to an additional $1.50 per hour. Those who score under 70 points in two consecutive quarters, however, are terminated.[9]

Equity Theory

Another contemporary explanation of motivation, **equity theory**, is based on individuals' perceptions about how fairly they are treated compared with their coworkers. Equity means justice or fairness, and in the workplace it refers to employees' perceived fairness of the way they are treated and the rewards they earn. For example, imagine that after graduation you were offered a job that paid $55,000 a year and had great benefits. You'd probably be ecstatic. Even more so if you discovered that the coworker in the next cubicle was making $45,000 for the same job. But what if that same colleague

6 What four contemporary theories on employee motivation offer insights into improving employee performance?

expectancy theory
A theory of motivation that holds that the probability of an individual acting in a particular way depends on the strength of that individual's belief that the act will have a particular outcome and on whether the individual values that outcome.

CONCEPT in action

Winning all four major golf championships in a single year is the professional golfer's dream. Since Bobby Jones became the first to win four major golf events in 1930, no player has captured a single-year "Grand Slam." Tiger Woods won four majors within a two-year span—known as a "Tiger Slam"—and many golf greats have achieved a Career Grand Slam, winning four majors in the course of their careers. According to expectancy theory, why is the prospect of achieving a Grand Slam a powerful motivator for golfers?

© AP Images/Elise Amendola

equity theory
A theory of motivation that holds that worker satisfaction is influenced by employees' perceptions about how fairly they are treated compared with their coworkers.

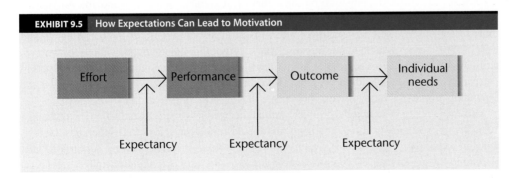

| EXHIBIT 9.5 | How Expectations Can Lead to Motivation |

Effort → Performance → Outcome → Individual needs

Expectancy · Expectancy · Expectancy

CONCEPT in action

Ben & Jerry's founders Ben Cohen and Jerry Greenfield firmly believe the maxim that companies "do well by doing good." This idealism led the founders to once famously swear that no Ben & Jerry's executive would ever make more than seven times that of the lowest paid worker. But when growth required attracting exceptional top-level management, the company abandoned its self-imposed ratio between its lowest and highest compensation rates. How might perceived inequities in pay affect worker satisfaction and motivation?

were making $59,000 for the same job? You'd probably think it unfair, particularly if the coworker had the same qualifications and started at the same time as you did. Your determination of the fairness of the situation would depend on how you felt you compared to the other person, or referent. Employees evaluate their own *outcomes* (e.g., salary, benefits) in relation to their *inputs* (e.g., number of hours worked, education, and training) and then compare the outcomes-to-inputs ratio to one of the following: (1) the employee's own past experience in a different position in the current organization, (2) the employee's own past experience in a different organization, (3) another employee's experience inside the current organization, or (4) another employee's experience outside the organization.

According to the theory, if employees perceive that an inequity exists, they will make one of the following choices:

- *Change their work habits* (exert less effort on the job).
- *Change their job benefits and income* (ask for a raise, steal from the employer).
- *Distort their perception of themselves* ("I always thought I was smart, but now I realize I'm a lot smarter than my coworkers").
- *Distort their perceptions of others* ("Joe's position is really much less flexible than mine").
- *Look at the situation from a different perspective* ("I don't make as much as the other department heads, but I make a lot more than most graphic artists").
- *Leave the situation* (quit the job).

Managers can use equity theory to improve worker satisfaction. Knowing that every employee seeks equitable and fair treatment, managers can make an effort to understand an employee's perceptions of fairness and take steps to reduce concerns about inequity. After the terrorist attacks of September 11, 2001, the 12,000 pilots at American Airlines voluntarily took a 23 percent pay cut, among other concessions, to keep the airline out of bankruptcy. But only four years after the attacks, top executives at the airline had received roughly $250 million in company stock while employees had received only small pay increases. When American had sufficiently recovered financially, pilots attempted to restore equity by demanding that their pay be reinstated to the same level as it had been well before the 9/11 attacks—in 1992—adjusted for inflation. According to the airline, doing so would cost $1.4 billion and be the equivalent of a 50 percent raise.[10]

Goal-Setting Theory

goal-setting theory
A theory of motivation based on the premise that an individual's intention to work toward a goal is a primary source of motivation.

Goal-setting theory is based on the premise that an individual's intention to work toward a goal is a primary source of motivation. Once set, the goal clarifies for the employee what needs to be accomplished and how much effort will be required for completion. The theory has three main components: (1) specific goals lead to a higher level of performance than do more generalized goals ("do your best"); (2) more difficult goals lead to better performance than do easy goals (provided the individual accepts the goal); and (3) feedback on progress toward the goal enhances performance. Feedback is particularly important because it helps the individual identify the gap between the *real* (the actual performance) and the *ideal* (the desired outcome defined by the goal). Given the trend toward employee empowerment in the workplace, more and more employees are participating in the goal-setting process.

Recent improvements in company performance at General Mills can be directly attributed to goal setting. In the mid-1990s, the company set the goal of having its products preferred by 60 percent of consumers in market tests; in the early 2000s, management added the goal that 20 percent of company sales should come from products that meet certain nutritional standards. An internal team of scientists set health targets, and then management linked individual bonuses to meeting those targets. Today even the executives' annual bonuses are tied to meeting the new health and wellness objectives. (By tying bonuses to health standards rather than sales goals, management was encouraging its employees to achieve longer-term goals. However, what motivates individuals in one country may be of little importance to that in other lands. This notion is further explained in the Expanding Around the Globe box on page 246).

To meet the new standards, products can either have a 10 percent reduction in fat, have a 10 percent increase in healthful ingredients, or meet FDA guidelines for health labels (like fat-free, reduced sodium, low fat, etc.). Initially, division heads were not enthusiastic and complained that increasing the health value of products would compromise taste and negatively affect sales. CEO Kendall Powell, says, "We said, 'You're just going to have to figure out a way to do both.'" The teams at General Mills did just that and earlier than expected. So, in 2006, management set a target of generating 20 percent of overall revenue from sales of the more-healthful products by 2010. General Mills surpassed its 2010 goal in early 2008, when 34 percent of the company's products met the new standards.[11] Setting and meeting goals has provided direction for General Mills employees on an individual, divisional, and corporate level.

Reinforcement Theory

Reinforcement theory says that behavior is a function of its consequences. In other words, people do things because they know other things will follow. So, depending on what type of consequences follows, people will either practice a behavior or refrain from it. There are three basic types of consequences: positive, negative, and none. In general, we think of positive consequences as rewards, but a **reward** is anything that increases the particular behavior. By contrast, **punishment** is anything that decreases the behavior.

Motivating with the reinforcement theory can be tricky because the theory is functional. All of its components are defined by their function rather than their structure. That is, consequences can operate differently for different people and in different situations. What is considered a punishment by one person may, in fact, be a reward for another. Nonetheless, managers can successfully use reinforcement theory to motivate workers to practice certain behaviors and avoid others. Often, managers use both rewards and punishment to achieve the desired results.

For example, hospitals have long offered surgeons the precious perk of scheduling elective surgeries in the middle of the week so that they can attend conferences, teach medical students, and leave early for the weekend. Although convenient for the surgeons, this scheduling system translates into overcrowding in hospital operating rooms and late starts that accrue throughout the day, causing patients' surgeries to be bumped for hours or even days. St. John's Regional Health Center in Springfield, Missouri, now spreads out its elective surgery schedule to cover five days instead of two. It wasn't easy, however, to convince surgeons to give up their long weekends or to start on time. To help change the pattern of late starts and bumped patient schedules, managers at St. John's used reinforcement theory to ease patient congestion in operating rooms. Now, doctors who are more than 10 minutes late 10 percent of the time are fined a portion of their fee (*punishment* for being late). Fines go into a kitty to reward those who are the best on-time performers (*reward* for being on time). Two years after the program was started, late starts for surgeries dropped from 16 percent to less than 1 percent.[12]

CONCEPT in action

With employees clocking longer hours at work, office romances have become more frequent and less taboo than in the past. Regular collaboration between dedicated colleagues can easily spill over into lunch breaks, happy hour, or even after-hours work assignments. While such tight teamwork raises fewer eyebrows today, companies concerned about workplace distractions and dramatic breakups often frown upon interoffice dating. How might managers utilize reinforcement theory to discourage employees from pursuing office trysts?

reinforcement theory
People do things because they know that certain consequences will follow.

reward
Anything that increases a specific behavior.

punishment
Anything that decreases a specific behavior.

CONCEPT check

Discuss the three relationships central to expectancy theory.

Explain the comparison process that is a part of equity theory.

How does goal-setting theory contribute to our understanding of motivation?

What are the main elements of reinforcement theory?

From Motivation Theory to Application

The material presented thus far in this chapter demonstrates the wide variety of theorists and research studies that have contributed to our current understanding of employee motivation. Now we turn our attention to more practical matters, to ways that these concepts can be applied in the workplace to meet organizational goals and improve individual performance.

7 How can managers redesign existing jobs to increase employee motivation and performance?

Motivational Job Design

How might managers redesign or modify existing jobs to increase employee motivation and performance? The following three options have been used extensively in the workplace:

Job Enlargement. The horizontal expansion of a job, increasing the number and variety of tasks that a person performs, is called **job enlargement**. Increasing task diversity can enhance job satisfaction, particularly when the job is mundane and repetitive in nature. A potential drawback to job enlargement is that employees may perceive that they are being asked to work harder and do more with no change in their level of responsibility or compensation. This can cause resentment and lead to dissatisfaction.

Job Enrichment. **Job enrichment** is the vertical expansion of an employee's job. Whereas job enlargement addresses the breadth or scope of a job, enrichment attempts to increase job depth

job enlargement
The horizontal expansion of a job by increasing the number and variety of tasks that a person performs.

job enrichment
The vertical expansion of a job by increasing the employee's autonomy, responsibility, and decision-making authority.

Motivation Is Culture Bound

Most motivation theories in use today were developed in the United States by Americans and about Americans. Of those that were not, many have been strongly influenced by American theories. But several motivation theories do not apply to all cultures. For example, Maslow's theory does not often hold outside the United States. In countries higher on uncertainty avoidance (such as Greece and Japan) as compared with those lower on uncertainty avoidance (such as the United States), security motivates employees more strongly than does self-actualization. Employees in high-uncertainty-avoidance countries often consider job security and lifetime employment more important than holding a more interesting or challenging job. Also contrasting with the American pattern, social needs often dominate the motivation of workers in countries such as Denmark, Norway, and Sweden that stress the quality of life over materialism and productivity.

When researchers tested Herzberg's theory outside the United States, they encountered different results. In New Zealand, for example, supervision and interpersonal relationships appear to contribute significantly to satisfaction and not merely to reducing dissatisfaction. Similarly, researchers found that citizens of Asia, Canada, Europe, Latin America, the Republic of Panama, and the West Indies cited certain extrinsic factors as satisfiers with greater frequency than did their American counterparts. In other words, the factors that motivate U.S. employees, summarized in Exhibit 9.4, may not spark the same motivation in employees in other cultures. Some of the major differences among the cultural groups include the following:

1. English-speaking countries rank higher on individual achievement and lower on the desire for security.
2. French-speaking countries, although similar to the English-speaking countries, give greater importance to security and somewhat less to challenging work.
3. Northern European countries have less interest in "getting ahead" and work recognition goals and place more emphasis on job accomplishment. In addition, they have more concern for people and less for the organization as a whole (it is important that their jobs not interfere with their personal lives).
4. Latin American and Southern European countries find individual achievement somewhat less important; Southern Europeans place the highest emphasis on job security, whereas both groups of countries emphasize fringe benefits.
5. Germany ranks high on security and fringe benefits and among the highest on "getting ahead."
6. Japan, although low on advancement, also ranks second highest on challenge and lowest on autonomy, with a strong emphasis on good working conditions and a friendly working environment.[13]

Critical Thinking Questions
- In today's global business environment, with its diversity of perspectives, can a manager ever successfully use equity theory? Why or why not?
- What impact, if any, do these cultural differences have on managers managing an entirely American workforce? Explain.

© Digital Vision/Getty Images

---

by providing the employee with more autonomy, responsibility, and decision-making authority. In an enriched job, the employee can use a variety of talents and skills and has more control over the planning, execution, and evaluation of the required tasks. In general, job enrichment has been found to increase job satisfaction and reduce absenteeism and turnover.

Job Rotation. Also called *cross-training*, **job rotation** is the shifting of workers from one job to another. This may be done to broaden an employee's skill base or because an employee has ceased to be interested in or challenged by a particular job. The organization may benefit from job rotation because it increases flexibility in scheduling and production, as employees can be shifted to cover for absent workers or changes in production or operations. It is also a valuable tool for training lower-level managers in a variety of functional areas. Drawbacks of job rotation include an increase in training costs and decreased productivity while employees are getting "up to speed" in new task areas.

Work-Scheduling Options

As companies try to meet the needs of a diverse workforce and retain quality employees, while remaining competitive and financially prosperous, managers are challenged to find new ways to keep workers motivated and satisfied. Increasingly popular are alternatives to the traditional work schedule, such as the compressed workweek, flextime, telecommuting, and job sharing.

One option for employees who want to maximize their leisure hours, indulge in three-day weekends, and avoid commuting during morning and evening rush hours, is the compressed workweek. Employees work the traditional 40 hours, but fit those hours into a shorter workweek. Most common is the 4–40 schedule, where employees work four 10-hour days a week. Organizations that offer this option claim benefits ranging from increased motivation and productivity to reduced absenteeism and turnover. According to the Society for Human Resource Management, over 32 percent of U.S. companies offer employees a compressed workweek.[14]

Another scheduling option, flextime, is even more popular, in use at 55 percent of U.S. companies.[15] Flextime allows employees to decide what their work hours will be. Employees

job rotation
The shifting of workers from one job to another; also called cross-training.

are generally expected to work a certain number of hours per week, but have some discretion as to when they arrive at work and when they leave for the day. Typically, flextime has been seen as a benefit primarily for female employees, but some companies are trying to transform that perception by pitching flextime as a quality-of-life benefit available also to male employees. Accounting firm Ernst & Young (E&Y) has been aggressively implementing flextime policies and practices for several years. The firm regularly surveys employees and tailors its programs based on employee feedback. Lisa Young, a partner at the firm, told employees she'd be unavailable one Friday morning until 10 a.m. because she was going to build gingerbread houses at her daughter's school. Before the big push for flextime, she says she would have described her absence as "an appointment." The firm's head of diversity, Anne Erni, believes that E&Y can retain more women and recruit younger workers by making flextime gender neutral. She says, "We're committed to destigmatizing flex schedules."[16]

Telecommuting is a work-scheduling option that allows employees to work from home via a computer that is linked with their office, headquarters, or colleagues. Although telecommuting, also called telework, has been around for years, it has been steadily increasing in popularity, especially among the younger generation of workers. A recent study conducted by Telework Exchange in which the participants' average age was 26 revealed that compressed workweeks and telecommuting were considered key perks. Participants even went so far as to say that telecommuting should be a priority.[17] Telework is not, however, without drawbacks. Timothy Golden, a professor at Rensselaer Polytechnic Institute, conducted a survey that showed a greater prevalence of teleworkers in a department or division has a negative impact on the attitude of those in the department or division who do *not* telecommute. His survey found that those in a department who work in the office may think their workload is heavier than their telecommuting colleagues and their work arrangement less flexible. They also report having difficulty managing relationships with their teleworking colleagues.[18]

Job sharing is a scheduling option that allows two individuals to split the tasks, responsibilities, and work hours of one 40-hour-per-week job. Though used less frequently than flextime and the compressed workweek, this option can also provide employees with job flexibility. The primary benefit to the company is that it gets "two for the price of one"—the company can draw on two sets of skills and abilities to accomplish one set of job objectives. Charlotte Schutzman and Sue Manix share the job of vice president of public affairs and communications at Verizon Communications. They have been a job-sharing team for an astonishing 16 years. Each woman works two days a week and on alternate Wednesdays. They talk by phone at least twice a week, and their close partnership has enabled them to stay on track professionally while raising their children—Manix has three; Schutzman has two. "It's been good for us; it's been good for the company," says Schutzman. "If we didn't jobshare, we might have left." Charlie Bowman, who oversees work–life programs for Verizon's 212,000 employees, says the biggest benefit in job sharing is that "it allows highly skilled, motivated employees to stay on when they want to work part time but their job must be done full time."[19]

Although each of these work-scheduling options may have some drawbacks for the sponsoring organizations, the benefits far outweigh the problems. For this reason, not only are the number of companies offering compressed work increasing, but so are the number of companies offering other options. Today, over 39 percent of the top companies offer telecommuting programs, 46 percent offer job sharing, and 31 percent offer flexible schedules. All of these figures are growing, and this trend is expected to continue.

Recognition and Empowerment

All employees have unique needs that they seek to fulfill through their jobs. Organizations must devise a wide array of incentives to ensure that a broad spectrum of employee needs can be addressed in the work environment, thus increasing the likelihood of motivated employees. A sampling of these motivational tools is discussed here.

Formal recognition of superior effort by individuals or groups in the workplace is one way to enhance employee motivation. Recognition serves as positive feedback and reinforcement, letting employees know what they have done well and that their contribution is valued by the

CONCEPT in action

In past decades, businesses have incentivized seniors to exit the workplace and make room for the next generation. But as 78 million baby boomers march toward retirement, employers are worrying about the inevitable loss of expertise and labor. With this shortage in view, many businesses are finding ways to delay the retirement of valued older workers. One effective strategy for retaining boomers and seniors is to offer alternatives to the traditional work schedule. Which scheduling options are most likely to appeal to seniors?

© Jose Luis Pelaez, Inc/Blend Images/Jupiterimages

job sharing
A scheduling option that allows two individuals to split the tasks, responsibilities, and work hours of one 40-hour-per-week job.

organization. Recognition can take many forms, both formal and informal. Some companies use formal awards ceremonies to acknowledge and celebrate their employees' accomplishments. Others take advantage of informal interaction to congratulate employees on a job well done and offer encouragement for the future. Recognition can take the form of a monetary reward, a day off, a congratulatory e-mail, or a verbal "pat on the back." Recognition does not have to come from superiors to be meaningful, however. At any time, for any reason, employees at Kimley-Horn, a big civil-engineering firm in North Carolina, can award a bonus of $50 to another employee. An employee who wants to award a bonus to a coworker downloads a form, fills it out, and often delivers it to the awardee in person. The awardee then redeems the form at the payroll department for a $50 check. The best part is that bonuses don't have to be approved by anyone, and there are no strings attached. Kimley-Horn employees give out more than 6,100 bonuses per year for a total corporate expense nearing $340,000.[20]

Employee empowerment, sometimes called employee involvement or participative management, involves delegating decision-making authority to employees at all levels of the organization. Employees are given greater responsibility for planning, implementing, and evaluating the results of decisions. Empowerment is based on the premise that human resources, especially at lower levels in the firm, are an underutilized asset. Employees are capable of contributing much more of their skills and abilities to organizational success if they are allowed to participate in the decision-making process and are given access to the resources needed to implement their decisions. At Zappos, the online shoe retailer, employees are completely empowered to solve customer problems. If customers can't find the shoes they want, Zappos agents are encouraged to recommend another store. The company has a wiki to which employees can post complaints and propose solutions. According to chairman and founder Nick Swinmurn, empowerment isn't just about solving customer problems, however. It's about giving employees the power to make the company better. The company's training manual is a 156-page handbook on Zappos culture—written entirely by the employees themselves. One of the entries in the handbook, written by an associate, reads, "I'm helping write the book. We all are."[21]

Economic Incentives

Any discussion of motivation has to include the use of monetary incentives to enhance performance. Currently, companies are using a variety of variable-pay programs such as piece-rate plans, profit sharing, gain sharing, stock options, and bonuses to encourage employees to be more productive. Unlike the standard salary or hourly wage, variable pay means that a portion of an employee's pay is directly linked to an individual or organizational performance measure. In *piece-rate pay plans,* for example, employees are paid a given amount for each unit they produce, directly linking the amount they earn to their productivity. *Profit-sharing plans* are based on overall company profitability. Using an established formula, management distributes some portion of company profits to all employees. *Gain-sharing plans* are incentive programs based on group productivity. Employees share in the financial gains attributed to the increased productivity of their group. This encourages employees to increase productivity within their specific work area regardless of the overall profit picture for the organization as a whole.

One well-known approach to monetary incentives is the award of *stock options*, or giving employees the right to purchase a given amount of stock at below-market prices. Stock can be a strong motivator because those who receive the options have the chance to make a lot of money. Lately companies have reduced the amount of equity (stock) they give to employees annually from 7 percent to roughly 2 percent, indicating that stock options are declining in popularity.[22]

One increasingly popular incentive is the *bonus*. A bonus is simply a onetime lump-sum monetary reward. According to a survey by Hewitt Associates, 80 percent of companies offer a bonus plan, and employers spend roughly 11 percent of their total payroll on bonuses for nonexecutive white-collar employees. In today's workplace, more employees than ever are eligible for bonuses, and employers have actually increased the share of their payroll devoted to variable pay.[23] One reason is that bonuses do not raise a company's fixed costs. Another is that variable pay is often tied to pay-for-performance measures. Ken Abosch of Hewitt notes that bonuses are "very effective in creating focus on business objectives."[24]

For those reasons and more, bonuses are replacing the merit raise as the way companies compensate employees for a job well done and motivate them to perform at even higher levels. That is because bonuses can vary according to outcomes. Financial incentives that allow variability in compensation to reflect an individual employee's contribution are generally known as *pay-for-performance programs*. Whirlpool, the appliance maker, recently overhauled its pay-for-performance system and increased the maximum bonus a high-performing employee can receive. A larger percentage of employees are eligible for the higher bonuses. Even though Whirlpool still awards merit raises, the company considers bonuses a more powerful motivator. Whirlpool's human relations chief, David Binkley, says, "It starts breaking away at the notion of entitlement. With merit pay, if you just spread it around, it just raises your costs."[25] Most often, larger bonuses carry with them the responsibility of higher performance. A survey by Watson Wyatt Worldwide found that 30 percent of employers are raising expectations for individual performance to earn bonuses.[26]

CONCEPT check

Explain the difference between job enlargement and job enrichment.

What are the four work-scheduling options that can enhance employee performance?

Are all employees motivated by the same economic incentives? Explain.

Trends in Employee Motivation

This chapter has focused on understanding what motivates people and how employee motivation and satisfaction affect productivity and organizational performance. Organizations can improve performance by investing in people. In reviewing the ways companies are currently choosing to invest in their human resources, we can spot three positive trends: (1) education and training, (2) employee ownership, and (3) work–life benefits. All of the companies making *Fortune's* annual list of the "100 Best Companies to Work For" know the importance of treating employees right. They all have programs that allow them to invest in their employees through programs such as these and many more. Today's businesses also face the challenge of increased costs of absenteeism. This section discusses each of these trends in motivating employees.

8 What initiatives are organizations using today to motivate and retain employees?

Praise

Today's companies are using compliments, prizes, and public displays of appreciation as motivation and retention tools. The trend toward extreme praise is in part prompted by the entrance of Generation Y into the workforce, which on the whole has been raised in a context of continual praise. As a result, younger workers expect regular feedback on the job and perceive an absence of regular praise as criticism. Many companies have implemented extreme programs to ensure a regular flow of motivational praise in the workplace. The Container Store has something called "Celebration Voice Mailboxes" especially for messages of praise. By company estimates, every 20 seconds, one of the Container Store's 4,000 employees receives praise. The Scooter Store, which sells power wheelchairs, has a "celebrations assistant" whose job it is to throw confetti at employees (she throws more than 25 pounds per week) and pass out celebratory helium balloons (she hands out 100 to 500 per week).[27]

CONCEPT in action

The Cheesecake Factory has grown from a small dessert shop in Detroit to a national chain of upscale casual-dining establishments. The idea of opening a cheesecake company originated in the 1940s with Evelyn Overton, a midwestern housewife with good baking skills and a coveted cheesecake recipe. As the Overtons added new recipes and a training program that rivals the finest restaurants and hotels, the family cheesecake business transformed into a billion-dollar enterprise with more than 130 locations. What message does a good training program send to employees?

Employee Ownership

A recent trend that seems to have leveled off is employee ownership, most commonly implemented as employee stock ownership plans, or ESOPs. ESOPs are not the same as stock options, however. In an ESOP, employees receive compensation in the form of company stock. Recall that stock options give employees the opportunity to purchase company stock at a set price, even if the market price of the stock increases above that point. Because employees are compensated with stock, over time they can become the owners of the company. Behind employee ownership programs is the belief that employees who think like owners are more motivated to take care of customers' needs, reduce unnecessary expenses, make operations smoother, and stay with the company longer.

According to the National Center for Employee Ownership, there are roughly 9,650 ESOPs in the United States, for a total of 10 million participants.[28] Although the number of overall ESOPs has declined roughly 20 percent since 2005, the number of employee stock ownership plans at small companies has grown steadily over the same time frame.[29] ESOPs, however, also have drawbacks. For example, employees in privately held ESOPs are not able to check the value of their stock on a daily basis and may have to wait a year or more between appraisals.[30] Likewise, some employees—of public and private companies alike—have so much of their nest eggs tied to their company's ESOP that if their company's performance starts to decline, they risk losing a significant portion of their wealth.

Still, many companies successfully implement ESOPs. Van Meter Industrial, an electrical-parts distributor in Iowa, had a rough start to its ESOP. Although Mick Slinger, the company's financial officer, thought the plan was great, an employee at a company meeting stood up and asked, "Why don't you just give me a couple hundred bucks for beer and cigarettes?" Slinger realized that many of the company's employees didn't know what stock was or what an employee owner was, so he set out to promote the ESOP program throughout the company. He assembled a committee to help him design training materials, marketing materials, anything to raise awareness of the ESOP. The committee developed the slogan "Work 10: get 5 for free" to help reinforce the math that an employee working 10 years for $30,000 a year can accumulate an ESOP account of $150,000, or the equivalent of 5 years of work. To get employees thinking like owners, managers encourage everyone to cut expenses, speed up debt collection, and make smart spending decisions. Slinger's efforts have paid off. Van Meter's stock is up 78 percent due to increased sales, decreases in debt, and improved cash flow. Employee turnover has also fallen to 8 percent from 18 percent before the ESOP education and promotion campaigns.[31]

Work–Life Benefits

In another growing trend in the workplace, companies are helping their employees to manage the numerous and sometimes competing demands in their lives. Organizations are taking a more active role in helping employees achieve a balance between their work responsibilities and their personal obligations. The desired result is employees who are less stressed, better able to focus on their jobs, and, therefore, more productive. One increasingly popular tool companies are using to help their employees achieve work–life balance is the paid sabbatical. Sabbaticals can be traced back to the need for an incentive that would attract potential faculty members to Harvard University in the late 1800s. Today, sabbaticals can mean paid time off anywhere from a month to a couple of years.[32] In today's business environment, companies are trying to juggle cutting costs and increasing profits, while simultaneously battling to keep employees motivated and positive about work. Sabbaticals can be an important tool to help managers achieve this balancing act.

Many of the companies on *Fortune's* list of the "100 Best Companies to Work For" offer paid sabbaticals for their employees. One reason for the growing popularity of sabbaticals is the increased pressures facing today's workforce. When companies have several rounds of layoffs, for example, fewer employees are left to take care of business, and those employees often feel the need to continually go above and beyond the call of duty in order to avoid receiving a pink slip themselves.

CONCEPT in action

Telecommuting has created a new type of worker who clocks in and out from virtually anywhere: the professional blogger. These busy Web writers, who opine on topics ranging from electronics to celebrity antics, work around the clock, often burning the midnight oil to scoop other bloggers. While most enjoy working from virtual offices, the 24-hour news cycle along with the competition for clicks have led many to report fatigue and burnout. How might paid bloggers achieve a better work–life balance?

About 75 percent of office employees feel that work has infiltrated their private lives. With more and more professions requiring 60-plus-hour workweeks, it is no wonder that there is a growing epidemic of work-related stress.[33] Another factor is the tremendous influx of women into the workforce in the past two decades. More than 45 percent of all employees are women, and 70 percent of married women with children under the age of 18 work outside the home.[34] A working mother often finds herself in a tight balancing act of handling the responsibilities of her family and career, and any unexpected problem can wreak havoc on her situation. And in general, a growing number of employees are already tired and depleted.

In that business environment, sabbaticals are an attractive option for companies hoping to rejuvenate their workforce. For example, Accenture allows its best employees to take a company-sponsored sabbatical to work with nonprofit groups. During the sabbatical, employees are paid half their regular salary, and the nonprofit receives consulting services at an extremely reduced fee. Soon after Accenture's program was launched, it became a huge draw for current and prospective employees. Accenture sabbatical employees have worked on disaster-relief projects in the United States and Indonesia, hunger-relief projects in India, and nursing projects in Africa. One sabbatical employee says the program "was one of the reasons I joined Accenture in the first place. It's a fantastic opportunity."[35]

Coping with the Rising Costs of Absenteeism

With today's companies trying to do more work with fewer employees, managers must be attentive to two major trends that affect the performance and morale of their employees: absenteeism and turnover. According to a survey by Harris Interactive, some 2.4 percent of workers at 305 for-profit and nonprofit entities nationwide called in sick each day. That amounted to a 50 percent increase over the same period the year before.[36] Absenteeism in the auto industry runs 10 percent, or more than three times that of other industries. General Motors is trying a unique approach to curbing employee absenteeism: a year of perfect attendance makes an employee eligible to win a new car.[37]

Long considered one of the main causes of high absenteeism is low employee morale. According to a February 2007 Conference Board survey, less than half of all Americans say they are satisfied with their jobs, down from 61 percent 20 years ago. The decline in satisfaction transcends age, income, and even residence. Additionally, a poll taken by CCH HR Management found that there was a direct association with absenteeism and employee morale. Nearly twice as many companies with "Poor/Fair" morale reported an increase in unscheduled absences in a recent two-year period compared to companies with "Good/Very Good" morale (33 percent vs. 17 percent). Moreover, 46 percent of companies with low morale reported that unscheduled absenteeism is a serious problem for them.[38]

Another survey showed that work–life programs that give employees more control over their schedules are the most successful in stemming unscheduled absences. The top four are alternative work arrangements, the ability to leave for children's school functions, telecommuting, and compressed workweeks.[39] See Exhibit 9.6 for a breakdown of the reasons employees give for unscheduled absences.

Another trend related to employee morale and absenteeism is turnover. After years of stability, the number of employees who are job-searching is on the rise. A survey from the Society of Human Resources Management and CareerJournal.com, 2004 U.S. Job Recovery and Retention, found that 35 percent of current employees are actively seeking a new job, and another 40 percent are passively looking for one.[40] Those figures are great cause for concern. A high rate of turnover can be expensive and dampen the morale of other employees who watch their colleagues leave the company. Both employees and human resource professionals agree on the biggest reasons behind increasing turnover rates: (1) better compensation elsewhere, (2) career opportunities elsewhere, and (3) dissatisfaction with potential for career development at the

In its quest to outmaneuver Blockbuster and Apple, online-movies giant Netflix is finding new ways to attract and retain employees who are among the industry's best and brightest. Netflix employees are scouted through headhunters, and once on board they receive lavish salaries, unlimited vacation, and à la carte compensation packages. In return they are expected to do the work of multiple employees—underperformers are quickly let go. Does Netflix's retention strategy address the root causes of employee turnover?

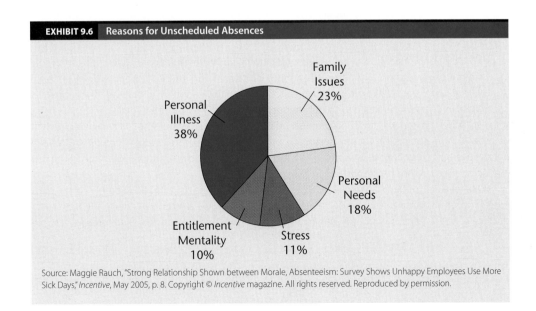

EXHIBIT 9.6 | **Reasons for Unscheduled Absences**

- Family Issues 23%
- Personal Needs 18%
- Stress 11%
- Entitlement Mentality 10%
- Personal Illness 38%

Source: Maggie Rauch, "Strong Relationship Shown between Morale, Absenteeism: Survey Shows Unhappy Employees Use More Sick Days," *Incentive*, May 2005, p. 8. Copyright © *Incentive* magazine. All rights reserved. Reproduced by permission.

What benefits can an organization derive from training and educational opportunities and stock ownership programs?

Why are sabbaticals growing in popularity as work-life balance tools?

Why are absenteeism and turnover rates increasing and what is the impact on companies?

current organization. Whereas human resource professionals think that burnout and feeling unappreciated are also major causes for leaving, employees cited "readiness for a new experience," boredom, and better benefits elsewhere as more pressing reasons.[41]

High rates of turnover (or absenteeism) at the management level can be destabilizing for employees, who need to develop specific strategies to manage a steady flow of new bosses. High rates of turnover (or absenteeism) at the employee level compromises the company's ability to perform at its highest levels. In order to stay competitive, companies need to have programs in place to motivate employees to come to work each day and to stay with the company year after year.

Summary of Learning Goals

1 What are the basic principles of Frederick Taylor's concept of scientific management?

Scientific management is based on the belief that employees are motivated by economic incentives and that there is "one best way" to perform any job. The four basic principles of scientific management developed by Taylor are as follows:

1. Develop a scientific approach for each element of a person's job.
2. Scientifically select, train, teach, and develop workers.
3. Encourage cooperation between workers and managers so that each job can be accomplished in a standard, scientifically determined way.
4. Divide work and responsibility between management and workers according to who is better suited to each task.

2 What did Elton Mayo's Hawthorne studies reveal about worker motivation?

The pride that comes from special attention motivates workers to increase their productivity. Supervisors who allow employees to have some control over their situation appeared to further increase the workers' motivation. The Hawthorne effect suggests that employees will perform better when they feel singled out for special attention or feel that management is concerned about employee welfare.

3 What is Maslow's hierarchy of needs, and how do these needs relate to employee motivation?

Maslow believed that each individual has a hierarchy of needs, consisting of physiological, safety, social, esteem, and self-actualization needs. Managers who accept Maslow's ideas attempt to increase employee motivation by modifying organizational and managerial practices to increase the likelihood that employees will meet all levels of needs. Maslow's theory has also helped managers understand that it is hard to motivate people by appealing to already satisfied needs.

4 How are McGregor's Theories X and Y and Ouchi's Theory Z used to explain worker motivation?

Douglas McGregor influenced the study of motivation with his formulation of two contrasting sets of assumptions about human nature—designated Theory X and Theory Y. Theory X says people don't like to work and will avoid it if they can. Because people don't like to work, they must be controlled, directed, or threatened to get them to make an effort. Theory Y says that people want to be self-directed and will try to accomplish goals that they believe in. Workers can be motivated with positive incentives. McGregor personally believed that Theory Y assumptions describe most employees and that managers seeking to motivate subordinates should develop management practices based on those assumptions.

William Ouchi's Theory Z combines U.S. and Japanese business practices. Theory Z emphasizes long-term employment, slow career development, and group decision making. The long-term decline of the Japanese economy has resulted in most U.S. firms moving away from Japanese management practices.

5 What are the basic components of Herzberg's motivator-hygiene theory?

Frederick Herzberg's studies indicated that certain job factors are consistently related to employee job satisfaction whereas others can create job dissatisfaction. According to Herzberg, motivating factors (also called satisfiers) are primarily intrinsic job elements that lead to satisfaction, such as achievement, recognition, the (nature of) work itself, responsibility, advancement, and growth.

What Herzberg termed hygiene factors (also called dissatisfiers) are extrinsic elements of the work environment such as company policy, relationships with supervisors, working conditions, relationships with peers and subordinates, salary and benefits, and job security. These are factors that can result in job dissatisfaction if not well managed. One of the most interesting results of Herzberg's studies was the implication that the opposite of satisfaction is not dissatisfaction. Herzberg believed that proper management of hygiene factors could prevent employee dissatisfaction, but that these factors could not serve as a source of satisfaction or motivation.

According to expectancy theory, the probability of an individual acting in a particular way depends on the strength of that individual's belief that the act will have a particular outcome and on whether the individual values that outcome. Equity theory is based on individuals' perceptions about how fairly they are treated compared with their coworkers. Goal-setting theory states that employees are highly motivated to perform when specific goals are established and feedback on progress is offered. Reinforcement theory states that behavior is a function of consequences; that is, people do things because they know other things will follow.

6 What four contemporary theories on employee motivation offer insights into improving employee performance?

The horizontal expansion of a job by increasing the number and variety of tasks that a person performs is called job enlargement. Increasing task diversity can enhance job satisfaction, particularly when the job is mundane and repetitive in nature. Job enrichment is the vertical expansion of an employee's job to provide the employee with more autonomy, responsibility, and decision-making authority. Other popular motivational tools include work-scheduling options, employee recognition programs, empowerment, and variable-pay programs.

7 How can managers redesign existing jobs to increase employee motivation and performance?

Today firms are using several key tactics to motivate and retain workers. First, companies are investing more in employee education and training, which makes employees more productive and confident in their jobs. Second, managers are giving employees the opportunity to participate in the ownership of the company, which can strongly increase employee commitment. Employers are providing more work–life benefits to employees, and a small but growing percentage of companies is offering employees paid sabbaticals in addition to regular vacation and sick time. Finally, managers in today's business environment need to pay special attention to managing absence rates and employee (and management) turnover.

8 What initiatives are organizations using today to motivate and retain employees?

Key Terms

equity theory 243
expectancy theory 243
goal-setting theory 244
Hawthorne effect 238
hygiene factors 241
job enlargement 245
job enrichment 245
job rotation 246
job sharing 247
Maslow's hierarchy of needs 238
motivating factors 241

motivation 236
need 236
punishment 245
reinforcement theory 245
reward 245
scientific management 237
Theory X 240
Theory Y 240
Theory Z 240
want 236

Preparing for Tomorrow's Workplace: SCANS

1. Are you motivated more by intrinsic rewards (satisfaction, sense of accomplishment, etc.) or by extrinsic rewards (money, bonuses, etc.)? Interview some friends and classmates to find out what motivates them. Discuss your differences in perspective. (**Interpersonal, Information**)

2. Think of a task or project you have completed recently that required a great deal of effort. What motivated you to exert so much energy to complete the task or project? Describe your motivation in terms of the theories presented in the chapter. (**Systems**)

3. Not all jobs are intrinsically motivating. For example, many entry-level jobs often involve repetitive and simple tasks that can become rapidly boring. (You may have worked a job that fits that description.) How can managers motivate front-line employees (like fast-food cashiers, trash collectors, supermarket cashiers, etc.) to perform at high levels? (**Systems, Interpersonal**)

4. If you were offered the opportunity to job share, would you need to have a partner who was motivated by the same things as you are? Why or why not? (**Interpersonal**)

5. **Team Activity** Assemble a team of three to five students. Imagine that you are the management team for a start-up business with limited resources but a need for a highly motivated, skilled workforce. Brainstorm ways you could motivate your employees other than large bonuses and high salaries. (**Resources**)

Ethics Activity

You join a large bank that encourages and promotes employee volunteerism, allowing employees 1 day a month, or up to 12 days a year, to volunteer for a cause of their choosing. Shortly after you start working there as a junior teller your boss's wife is diagnosed with a particularly aggressive form of breast cancer that carries a very poor prognosis. Realizing it will win you kudos with your boss, you choose the local chapter of the Susan B. Komen Foundation—a breast cancer charity that sponsors an annual Race for the Cure—for your company-sponsored volunteer work.

In addition to working at the foundation's office one day a month, you spend your own time actively soliciting other staffers at your firm to sign up for the charity walk in a few months' time. Impressed with your qualities of tireless dedication, your boss puts your name forward for promotion to junior bank officer, well before the customary two years of service normally required for being considered for promotion.

Using a Web search tool, locate articles about this topic and then write responses to the following questions. Be sure to support your arguments and cite your sources.

ETHICAL DILEMMA: Your company is generous in its approach to employee volunteerism. It gives you paid time off and you acquire enhanced job skills through your volunteer activities. Have you just been smart in recognizing the value of volunteering for a charity that you know will earn your boss's personal appreciation? Or are you taking unfair advantage of your boss's vulnerability and manipulating the situation?

Sources: Margarita Bauza, "Companies Find Volunteering Makes Good Business Sense," *Detroit Free Press*, November 20, 2005, **http://www.gale.cengage.com/**; "Deloitte Volunteer IMPACT Survey Reveals Link Between Volunteering and Professional Success," Internet Wire, June 3, 2005, **http://www.gale.cengage.com/**; Charley Hannagan, "Can Work Help?" *Post-Standard (Syracuse, NY)*, September 30, 2005, p. C1.

Working the Net

1. Looking for 1,001 ways to motivate or reward your employees? Bob Nelson can help. Visit his Nelson Motivation site at **http://www.nelson-motivation.com** to get some ideas you can put to use to help you do a better job, either as a manager or as an employee.

2. More companies are offering their employees stock ownership plans. To learn the differences between an employee stock ownership plan (ESOP) and stock options, visit the National Center for Employee Ownership (NCEO) at **http://www.nceo.org** and the Foundation for Enterprise Development (FED) at **http://www.fed.org**. Which stock plan would you rather have? Why?

3. Openbook management is one of the better-known ways to create a participatory work environment. Over 2,000 companies have adopted this practice, which involves sharing financial information with nonmanagement employees and training them to understand financial information. Does it really motivate employees and improve productivity? The National Center

for Employee Ownership (NCEO) Web site, **http://www.nceo.org**, has a number of articles on Open Book Management in its "Ownership Culture" section. Read several of the articles to get more insight into this practice and then develop your answers to these questions.

4. You've been asked to develop a staff recognition program for your company but don't have a clue where to start! Three sites with articles and other useful information are *Incentive* magazine, **http://www.incentivemag.com**, the National Association for Employee Recognition, **http://www.recognition.org**, and the U.S. Office of Personnel Management, **http://opm.gov/ perform/reward.asp**. Using the material you'll find there, outline the plan you would recommend for your company.

5. You have two great job opportunities. Both are equally attractive in terms of job content and offer the same salary. However, one offers year-end bonuses, whereas the other includes stock options for employees. How do you compare the offers? Learn how to evaluate stock options at the Money section of How Stuff Works, **http://money.howstuffworks.com/question436. htm**. Prepare a comparison of bonuses versus stock options and determine which appeals to you more. Explain your reasons.

6. Use a search engine to find companies that offer "work–life benefits." Link to several companies and review their employee programs in this area. How do they compare? Which benefits would be most important to you if you were job hunting, and why?

Creative Thinking Case

Motivating Employees: A Monster of a Problem

As mentioned in earlier chapters, American businesses will face a decrease in the available workforce due in part to a smaller generation of talented workers replacing retiring baby boomers. "Our study reveals that recruiters and hiring managers are not only cognizant of the issue but are concerned about its current and future impact on organizational growth," said Dr. Jesse Harriott, vice president of research at Monster.com (**http://www.monster.com**), the leading global online career and recruitment resource. "Businesses of all sizes and across all industries must develop and implement creative programs and strategies to attract and hire top candidates while retaining and motivating current employees. As the talent pool shrinks, it is imperative that immediate action is taken to ensure businesses are properly prepared and staffed for the future."

In a sampling of more than 600 human resource managers, Monster's survey showed that over 75 percent believe compensation is one of the top three motivators that prevent employees from leaving their jobs. The fact that money motivates top-performing employees is supported by almost half the human resources professionals surveyed for the 2005 Rewards Program and Incentive Compensation Survey released by the Society of Human Resource Management. The survey also found that neither monetary nor nonmonetary rewards were effective motivators for underperformers.

While compensation is clearly a significant issue, not all companies can offer this advantage. Other strategies that motivate employee loyalty and commitment are necessary. Some of these include making supervisors more accountable for worker retention; promoting work–life balance for employees; fostering a workplace where employee expectations are clearly articulated; learning and development programs that groom employees for future management roles; performance-based systems that identify and proactively manage top employees and when possible promote from within; mentoring programs that match new employees with seasoned veterans; monitoring sentiment throughout the employee life cycle; creating an employment brand "experience" that not only motivates and energizes employees, but also can be used to attract new talent.

Diana Pohly, president and owner of The Pohly Company, keeps vigilant watch over the morale of the office, ensuring that employees are satisfied. "Business owners of growing companies must possess strong leadership and management skills in order to solidify the foundation of their business," said Pohly. "Effective team leadership is imperative to sustain efficient team workflows and contribute to employee morale."

"Employees are the lifeblood of any organization. Building a positive work environment is an important strategy in attracting, retaining and motivating a team," says Michelle Swanda, corporate marketing manager of The Principal. Improving employee morale with creative and effective management tactics ultimately boosts employee productivity, and that goes straight to the bottom line.

Critical Thinking Questions

- How are social and economic factors influencing companies' approaches to hiring, motivating, and retaining employees?
- What are some of the nonmonetary strategies companies must develop to attract, reward, and keep employees motivated?
- What "reward factors" would be important to you when working for a company? List at least five in order of importance and your reasons for each.

Sources: "70 Percent of HR Managers Concerned about Workforce Retention, According to Monster Study," *Business Wire,* January 9, 2006, **http://findarticles.com;** "Poll Says Top-Performing Workers Motivated By Money," *Nation's Restaurant News,* April 25, 2005, **http://findarticles.com;** "Team Motivation: Women Business Owners Increase Productivity Through Effective Leadership," *Business Wire,* October 27, 2005, **http://findarticles.com.**

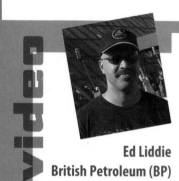

**Ed Liddie
British Petroleum (BP)**

Exploring Business Careers

At first glance, Ed Liddie might seem like a typical guy. A family man, he will tell you about his kids: four of them, ranging in ages from 8 to 16. Shift supervisor of the British Petroleum (BP) Carson refinery in California, he works hard and has been with BP for almost 20 years. He likes rock 'n roll and might tell you he even plays bass guitar occasionally. Oh, and did he mention he's played in the Rock and Roll Hall of Fame? How many "typical" people can say that?

Liddie is a member of the band OVP, along with fellow BP employees Hugh Parsons, Maribel Pegler, Lonnie Sumrall, and Mark and Elaine Rongers. The band formed after some of the members met in 2000 at Operation People, a global BP conference to foster employee motivation in their refineries. In an effort to increase employee satisfaction and retention, BP wanted to hear from the employees about the realities of the day-to-day work. "After all, petroleum is not always pretty," Liddie notes. Following days of intense discussions during the conference, a small group of people would gather in the evening to talk and to relax. "Soon we discovered no matter where we were from—California, Chicago, Scotland, London—we all loved music. It was a great barrier-breaker." Indeed, music was such a common theme, on a whim they decided to form a band to play at the next Operation People conference.

Considering the members of OVP were spread out across the globe, preparation for the conference proved a bit tricky. The group compiled a song list over e-mail, and each member rehearsed alone. "It was scary at first because we had to rely on each other so heavily. It forced us to really trust each other, though, which probably helped us even more. So that, even though we first met to practice the night before the conference, after the first song, we felt and sounded like we'd been together much longer." And apparently they weren't the only ones who thought they could really rock. Their performance the next night was a huge success, both musically and as an icebreaker for the conference participants. "After we played that night, you could just tell: For the rest of the conference, everyone was a lot more comfortable together and open with each other."

Looking back, Liddie views the performance as a very motivational event for both band members and conference participants. Indeed, the band itself came together as a team, inspired by the goal of sharing great music and helping others to open up. And at the conference, they were able to create a corporate culture in which people felt safe enough to share. BP had allowed OVP a space to flex their musical muscles, and the synergy that the band helped spark carried well past the end of the conference.

In 2004, the band had the opportunity to participate in a competition, the Fortune Battle of the Corporate Bands, at the Rock and Roll Hall of Fame. They competed alongside bands from Nextel and Wells-Fargo, among others, and walked away with the Best Lead Guitarist award. After their success as a band, a team, and a motivating force within BP, though, this almost pales in comparison. Did they make petroleum prettier?

Learning Goals

After reading this chapter, you should be able to answer these questions:

1 Why is production and operations management important in both manufacturing and service firms?

2 What types of production processes do manufacturers and service firms use?

3 How do organizations decide where to put their production facilities? What choices must be made in designing the facility?

4 Why are resource-planning tasks like inventory management and supplier relations critical to production?

5 How do operations managers schedule and control production?

6 How can quality management and lean-manufacturing techniques help firms improve production and operations management?

7 What roles do technology and automation play in manufacturing and service industry operations management?

8 What key trends are affecting the way companies manage production and operations?

CHAPTER 10

Achieving World-Class Operations Management

"Dreams for Cash"

Sam "Ace" Rothstein is an extremely successful sports handicapper working for mobsters who have decided that he has the skills to run the Tangiers Casino in Las Vegas. Sam jumps at the opportunity to make the move to Vegas, even claiming that the opportunity to make the move was a no-brainer. Anywhere else, he was essentially a criminal to be hassled by the police, always looking over his shoulder to make sure either the police or any enemies were not coming for him. In Las Vegas, however, he achieves a different level of success. "But here, I'm Mr. Rothstein," he states. "I'm not only legitimate, but running a casino, and that's like selling people dreams for cash." And he talks about the various Vegas attributes that result in those dreams: the bright lights, the comped rooms, the alcohol, the women, and everything else that ultimately feed the dreams of the individuals who come to Las Vegas.

The bright lights and the rooms and the "booze and the broads" are all essentially inputs that are converted into outputs that are the end result of the production process provided within Las Vegas. The type of conversion process that Sam describes is essentially an assembly process where the basic inputs are combined in such a way as to create the output, the dreams people come to Las Vegas to find. However, Sam also describes a second production process where raw materials and natural resources are broken down into one basic output, and that output is money. "This is the end result of all the bright lights, and all the comped trips . . . of all the champagne and free hotel suites," he says. Those natural resources are converted into the dollars that are then skimmed by the men who are running the Vegas of the 1970s. In short, Sam describes *process manufacturing*.

Achieving world-class operations management requires an understanding of both of these processes as depicted in *Casino*. We have to understand that there are often upstream and downstream processes that have an impact on the various entities within the supply chain, which includes the entire chain of transitions from one stage to the next. Sam's job as operations manager of the Tangiers is to ensure that the production process, in both directions, runs as smoothly as possible. He makes sure that the downstream customers of the Tangiers—the vacationers and the gamblers—are provided with the best possible experience so that they are willing to pay for the dreams he helps to create; and he also makes sure the cash moves smoothly "from the tables to our boxes, through the cage, and into the most sacred room in the casino . . . the place where they add up all the money . . . the holy of holies . . . the count room."

The following chapter takes you through the various and varied processes involved with operations management, ranging from the production line within the organization to the supply chain of which the organization is a link. We begin with a basic overview of the production process, describing production processes, facility design, resource planning, and keeping goods flowing through the supply chain. We then discuss how organizations can maintain control of such operations through routing and scheduling tasks; and then we explore methods for improving production and operations, focusing on quality control, trimming the fat from manufacturing, and ultimately putting technology to work during the production process. Finally, the chapter closes with an overview of the trends affecting operations management in today's global environment.

Discussion Questions

- Two types of production processes are described in this clip. Of the three production classifications described in this chapter, which best fits each of those production processes and why?
- Location is a key resource in the marketing and manufacturing of goods. What advantages does Las Vegas provide the casino industry that other locations do not?
- How do you think the Tangiers and Sam Rothstein exert production control over the various production processes in the casino?

Chapter 10 discusses how companies achieve world-class operations management, detailing the processes of production and operations management from planning to quality control.

Nearly every type of business organization needs to find the most efficient and effective methods of producing the goods or services it sells to its customers. Technological advances, ongoing competition, and consumer expectations force companies to rethink where, when, and how they will produce products or services.

Manufacturers have discovered that it is no longer enough to simply push products through the factory and onto the market. Consumers demand high quality at reasonable prices. They also expect manufacturers to deliver products in a timely manner. Firms that can't meet these expectations often face strong competition from businesses that can. To compete, many manufacturers are streamlining how they make their products—by automating their factories, developing new production processes, focusing on quality control techniques, and improving relationships with suppliers.

Service organizations also face challenges. Their customers are demanding better service, shorter waiting periods, and more individualized attention. Like manufacturers, service companies are using new methods to deliver what their customers need and want. Banks, for example, are using technology such as ATMs and the Internet to make their services more accessible to customers. Colleges offer evening, weekend, and online courses to accommodate the schedules of working students. Tax services file tax returns via computer.

This chapter examines how manufacturers and service firms manage and control the creation of products and services. We'll discuss production planning, including the choices firms must make concerning the type of production process they will use, the location where production will occur, the design of the facility, and the management of resources needed in production. Next, we'll explain routing and scheduling, two critical tasks for controlling production and operations efficiency. Then we will look at how firms can improve production and operations by employing quality management and lean-manufacturing techniques. Finally we will review some of the trends affecting production and operations management.

Production and Operations Management: An Overview

Production, the creation of products and services, is an essential function in every firm. Production turns inputs, such as natural resources, raw materials, human resources, and capital, into outputs, which are products and services. This process is shown in Exhibit 10.1. Managing this conversion process is the role of **operations management**.

The goal of customer satisfaction is an important part of effective production and operations. In the past, the manufacturing function in most companies was focused inwardly. Manufacturing had little contact with customers and didn't always understand their needs and desires. In the 1980s,

production
The creation of products and services by turning inputs, such as natural resources, raw materials, human resources, and capital, into outputs, which are products and services.

1 Why is production and operations management important in both manufacturing and service firms?

operations management
Management of the production process.

EXHIBIT 10.1 | **Production Process for Products and Services**

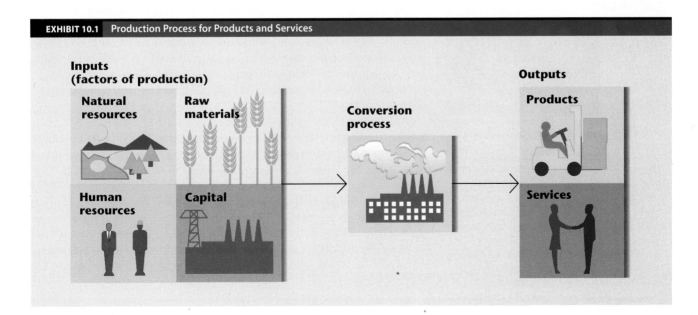

With oil reserves second only to Saudi Arabia, Canada's Alberta province is set to become a vast supplier of crude oil worldwide. Unlike the smooth petroleum that gushes from Arabian wells, however, Alberta's black gold has to be mined from oil-rich sands. The process is rigorous: 400-ton trucks transport excavated bitumen to crushers and mixers that separate the sands from the oil, and the resulting slurry travels miles of pipeline to North American refineries. What are key inputs in the mining of oil sands?

production planning
The aspect of operations management in which the firm considers the competitive environment and its own strategic goals in an effort to find the best production methods.

CONCEPT in action

From its storied creation in postwar Italy to its big-screen immortalization in movies like *Roman Holiday* and *Quadrophenia*, the Vespa scooter has a reputation for romance, rebellion, and style. Manufactured by Italy's Piaggio, the Vespa's svelte, stainless-steel chassis and aeronautic-inspired designs are seen everywhere in Europe and increasingly in the United States. The Piaggio Group presently operates factories in Italy, Spain, India, and China. What important production-planning decisions does Piaggio need to make as it considers expanding into overseas markets?

many U.S. industries, such as automotive, steel, and electronics, lost customers to foreign competitors because their production systems could not provide the quality customers demanded. As a result, today most American companies, both large and small, consider a focus on quality to be a central component of effective operations management.

Stronger links between marketing and manufacturing also encourage production managers to be more outwardly focused and to consider decisions in light of their effect on customer satisfaction. Service companies find that making operating decisions with customer satisfaction in mind can be a competitive advantage.

Operations managers, the personnel charged with managing and supervising the conversion process, play a vital role in today's firm. They control about three-fourths of a firm's assets, including inventories, wages, and benefits. They also work closely with other major divisions of the firm, such as marketing, finance, accounting, and human resources, to ensure that the firm produces its goods profitably and satisfies its customers. Marketing personnel help them decide which products to make or which services to offer. Accounting and human resources help them face the challenge of combining people and resources to produce high-quality goods on time and at reasonable cost. They are involved in the development and design of goods and determine what production processes will be most effective.

Production and operations management involve three main types of decisions, typically made at three different stages:

1. *Production planning.* The first decisions facing operations managers come at the planning stage. At this stage, managers decide where, when, and how production will occur. They determine site locations and obtain the necessary resources.
2. *Production control.* At this stage, the decision-making process focuses on controlling quality and costs, scheduling, and the actual day-to-day operations of running a factory or service facility.
3. *Improving production and operations.* The final stage of operations management focuses on developing more efficient methods of producing the firm's goods or services.

All three decisions are ongoing and may occur simultaneously. In the following sections, we will take a closer look at the decisions and considerations firms face in each stage of production and operations management.

Gearing Up: Production Planning

An important part of operations management is **production planning**. Production planning allows the firm to consider the competitive environment and its own strategic goals to find the best production methods. Good production planning has to balance goals that may conflict, such as providing high-quality service while keeping operating costs low, or keeping profits high while maintaining adequate inventories of finished products. Sometimes accomplishing all these goals is difficult.

Production planning involves three phases. *Long-term planning* has a time frame of three to five years. It focuses on which goods to produce, how many to produce, and where they should be produced. *Medium-term planning* decisions cover about two years. They concern the layout of factory or service facilities, where and how to obtain the resources needed for production, and labor issues. *Short-term planning*, which occurs within a one-year time frame, converts these broader goals into specific production plans and materials management strategies.

Four important decisions must be made in production planning. They involve the type of production process that will be used, site selection, facility layout, and resource planning.

The Production Process: How Do We Make It?

In production planning, the first decision involves which type of **production process**—the way a good or service is created—best fits with company goals and customer demand. An important consideration is the type of good or service being produced because different goods may require different production processes. In general, there are three types of production: mass production, mass customization, and customization. In addition to production type, operations managers also classify production processes in two ways: (1) how inputs are converted into outputs and (2) the timing of the process.

2 What types of production processes do manufacturers and service firms use?

production process
The way a good or service is created.

One for All: Mass Production **Mass production**, manufacturing many identical goods at once, was a product of the Industrial Revolution. Henry Ford's Model-T automobile is a good example of early mass production. Each car turned out by Ford's factory was identical, right down to its color. If you wanted a car in any color except black, you were out of luck. Canned goods, over-the-counter drugs, and household appliances are other examples of goods that are mass-produced. The emphasis in mass production is on keeping manufacturing costs low by producing uniform products using repetitive and standardized processes. As products became more complicated to produce, mass production also became more complex. Automobile manufacturers, for example, must now incorporate more sophisticated electronics into their car designs. As a result, the number of assembly stations in most automobile manufacturing plants has increased.

mass production
The manufacture of many identical goods at once.

Just for You: Customizing Goods In **mass customization**, goods are produced using mass-production techniques, but only up to a point. At that point, the product or service is custom-tailored to the needs or desires of individual customers. American Leather, a leather-furniture manufacturer, uses mass customization to produce couches and chairs to customer specifications within 30 days. The basic frames in the furniture are the same, but automated cutting machinery precuts the color and type of leather ordered by each customer. Using mass-production techniques, they are then added to each frame.

mass customization
A manufacturing process in which goods are mass-produced up to a point and then custom-tailored to the needs or desires of individual customers.

Customization is the opposite of mass production. In customization, the firm produces goods or services one at a time according to the specific needs or wants of individual customers. Unlike mass customization, each product or service produced is unique. For example, a print shop may handle a variety of projects, including newsletters, brochures, stationery, and reports. Each print job varies in quantity, type of printing process, binding, color of ink, and type of paper. A manufacturing firm that produces goods in response to customer orders is called a **job shop**.

customization
The production of goods or services one at a time according to the specific needs or wants of individual customers.

Some types of service businesses also deliver customized services. Doctors, for instance, must consider the illnesses and circumstances of each individual patient before developing a customized treatment plan. Real estate agents may develop a customized service plan for each customer based on the type of house the person is selling or wants to buy. The differences between mass production, mass customization, and customization are summarized in Exhibit 10.2. Read about one company

job shop
A manufacturing firm that produces goods in response to customer orders.

EXHIBIT 10.2	Classification of Production Types	
Mass Production	**Mass Customization**	**Customization**
Highly uniform products or services. Many products made sequentially.	Uniform standardized production to a point, then unique features added to each product.	Each product or service produced according to individual customer requirements.
Examples: Breakfast cereals, soft drinks, and computer keyboards.	**Examples:** Dell Computers, tract homes, and TaylorMade golf clubs.	**Examples:** Custom homes, legal services, and haircuts.

CONCEPT in action

Expressing yourself has never been easier. Mass customization is producing a thriving build-to-order society in which the compulsion to parade one's individuality is a hot commodity. Thanks to this revolution in manufacturing, consumers can now design a pair of sneakers with Vans Customs, build their own bags at Timbuk2, and create a snowboard using Burton's Series 13 customization program—all while munching a pack of personalized M&M's candies. What developments have made mass customization a viable method of production?

process manufacturing
A production process in which the basic input is broken down into one or more outputs (products).

assembly process
A production process in which the basic inputs are either combined to create the output or transformed into the output.

continuous process
A production process that uses long production runs lasting days, weeks, or months without equipment shutdowns; generally used for high-volume, low-variety products with standardized parts.

intermittent process
A production process that uses short production runs to make batches of different products; generally used for low-volume, high-variety products.

that produces highly customized products in the Catching the Entrepreneurial Spirit box on the next page.

Converting Inputs to Outputs As previously stated, production involves converting *inputs* (natural resources, raw materials, human resources, capital) into *outputs* (products or services). In a manufacturing company, the inputs, the production process, and the final outputs are usually obvious. Harley-Davidson, for instance, converts steel, rubber, paint, and other inputs into motorcycles. But the production process in a service company involves a less obvious conversion. For example, a hospital converts the knowledge and skills of its medical personnel, along with equipment and supplies from a variety of sources, into health care services for patients. Exhibit 10.3 provides examples of the inputs and outputs used by various other businesses.

There are two basic processes for converting inputs into outputs. In **process manufacturing**, the basic input (natural resources, raw materials) is broken down into one or more outputs (products). For instance, bauxite (the input) is processed to extract aluminum (the output). The **assembly process** is just the opposite. The basic inputs, like natural resources, raw materials, or human resources, are either *combined* to create the output or *transformed* into the output. An airplane, for example, is created by assembling thousands of parts, which are its raw-material inputs. Steel manufacturers use heat to transform iron and other materials into steel. In services, customers may play a role in the transformation process. For example, a tax preparation service combines the knowledge of the tax preparer with the client's information about personal finances in order to complete the tax return.

Production Timing A second consideration in choosing a production process is timing. A **continuous process** uses long production runs that may last days, weeks, or months without equipment shutdowns. This is best for high-volume, low-variety products with standardized parts, such as nails, glass, and paper. Some services also use a continuous process. Your local electric company is an example. Per-unit costs are low and production is easy to schedule.

In an **intermittent process**, short production runs are used to make batches of different products. Machines are shut down to change them to make different products at different times. This process is best for low-volume, high-variety products such as those produced by mass customization or customization. Job shops are examples of firms using an intermittent process.

EXHIBIT 10.3	Converting Inputs to Outputs	
Type of Organization	**Input**	**Output**
Airline	Pilots, crew, flight attendants, reservations system, ticketing agents, customers, airplanes, maintenance crews, ground facilities	Movement of customers and freight
Grocery store	Merchandise, building, clerks, supervisors, store fixtures, shopping carts, customers	Groceries for customers
High school	Faculty, curriculum, buildings, classrooms, library, auditorium, gymnasium, students, staff, supplies	Graduates, public service
Manufacturer	Machinery, raw materials, plant, workers, managers	Finished products for consumers and other firms
Restaurant	Food, cooking equipment, serving personnel, chefs, dishwashers, host, patrons, furniture, fixtures	Meals for patrons

Waiting for a Steelman

In an unassuming, and unmarked, warehouse in Redmond, California, Brent Steelman makes custom bikes—but only for a certain clientele. "There are certain people I get a wrong vibe from, and I just don't deal with them," Steelman says. If you are lucky enough to give off the right vibe, you can pass to the next stage: an interview that can take up to three hours.

Why does Steelman take such care selecting his customers? He fits each bike perfectly to each customer, so he spends a lot of time considering the person for whom he is building each bike, which ends up fitting a rider as well as a Savile Row suit. Steelman measures each client from the bottom of the foot to the base of the kneecap and from the upper reach of the arm to the wrist. He even measures shoe size. Only then does he begin cutting the frame's tubes to match the proportions of its future rider.

Rather than use high-tech materials, Steelman sticks with traditional steel because he wants his bikes to have the feel of a road-gripping Porsche rather than

a smooth-riding Lexus. (The comparison to luxury cars is apt, as a Steelman bike costs an average of $5,500.) To a traditionally constructed frame, he adds high-end component parts from companies like Campagnolo, Shimano, and Dedacciai. Not only does Steelman make bikes, he has also made the machinery he uses to make the bikes. Steelman's reputation for precision and care has created demand far in excess of his capacity. Steelman makes only about 50 bikes a year.[1]

Critical Thinking Questions
- Could Steelman retain his commitment to quality and precision *and* increase his capacity?
- Brent Steelman is a craftsman. Does it make sense to talk about him as a manufacturer? Why or why not?

© Rubberball/Getty Images

Although some service companies use continuous processes, most service firms rely on intermittent processes. For instance, a restaurant preparing gourmet meals, a physician performing physical examinations or surgical procedures, and an advertising agency developing ad campaigns for business clients, all customize their services to suit each customer. They use the intermittent process. Note that their "production runs" may be very short—one grilled salmon or one eye exam at a time.

Location, Location, Location: Where Do We Make It?

A big decision that managers must make early in production and operations planning is where to put the facility, be it a factory or a service office. The facility's location affects operating and shipping costs and, ultimately, the price of the product or service and the company's ability to compete. Mistakes made at this stage can be expensive, because moving a factory or service facility once production begins is difficult and costly. Firms must weigh a number of factors to make the right decision.

3 How do organizations decide where to put their production facilities? What choices must be made in designing the facility?

Availability of Production Inputs
As we discussed earlier, organizations need certain resources to produce products and services for sale. Access to these resources, or inputs, is a huge consideration in site selection. Executives must assess the availability of raw materials, parts, equipment, and available manpower for each site under consideration. The cost of shipping raw materials and finished goods can be as much as 25 percent of a manufacturer's total cost, so locating a factory where these and other costs are as low as possible can make a major contribution to a firm's success.

Companies that use heavy or bulky raw materials, for example, may choose to be located close to their suppliers. Mining companies want to be near ore deposits, oil refiners near oil fields, paper mills near forests, and food processors near farms. Bottlers are discovering that rural Western communities in need of an economic boost make rich water sources. In Sitka, Alaska, it made sense for True Alaska Bottling Company to produce glacier-fed bottled water on the grounds of a closed pulp sawmill.[2]

The availability and cost of labor are also critical to both manufacturing and service businesses, and the unionization of local labor is another point to consider in many industries. Payroll costs can vary widely from one location to another due to differences in the cost of living, the number of jobs available, and the size, skills, and productivity of the local workforce. Mississippi has been able to attract the interest of several manufacturers to the state because of the low cost of labor, but what most impressed officials from Toyota were the loyalty and work

© AP Images/Carlos Osorio

Faced with the meltdown of its once-dominant auto industry, Michigan is enticing new companies to come to The Automotive State. A marketing campaign operated through The Michigan Economic Development Corporation and fronted by actor Jeff Daniels explains the numerous benefits of locating operations on the state's double peninsula. Michigan's business tax structure, land availability, and educated workforce have attracted new facilities for Dow, BASF, and General Electric in recent years. What factors determine where businesses locate their operations?

ethic of Mississippians. Toyota visited other manufacturers in Mississippi, including Cooper Tire and Lane Furniture, before deciding to build a production facility in Blue Springs, Mississippi, for its Highlander SUV. Then the automaker quickly announced it would build an auto-body plant in northern Mississippi to act as a supplier to the Blue Springs facility.[3]

Marketing Factors A business must evaluate how its facility location will affect its ability to serve its customers. For some firms it may not be necessary to be located near customers. Instead, the firm will need to assess the difficulty and costs of distributing its goods to customers from its chosen location. Other firms may find that locating near customers can provide marketing advantages. When a factory or service center is close to customers, the firm can often offer better service at a lower cost. Other firms may gain a competitive advantage by locating their facilities so that customers can easily buy their products or services. The location of competitors may also be a consideration. And businesses with more than one facility may need to consider how far to spread their locations in order to maximize market coverage.

Manufacturing Environment Another factor to consider is the manufacturing environment in a potential location. Some localities have strong existing manufacturing bases. When a large number of manufacturers in a certain industry are already located in an area, that area is likely to offer greater availability of resources, such as manufacturing workers, better accessibility to suppliers and transportation, and other factors that can increase a plant's operating efficiency.

In 2008, Honda decided to locate its new North American factory in Indiana. The new Honda plant adds to the already established presence of Japanese automakers in Ohio (Honda), Kentucky (Toyota), and Indiana. The region is home to many mature manufacturing companies in a multitude of industries, which means that Honda will not have far to look for dozens of suppliers to meet all of its needs.

Local Incentives Incentives offered by countries, states, or cities may also influence site selection. Tax breaks are a common incentive. A locality may reduce the amount of taxes a firm must pay on income, real estate, utilities, or payroll. Local governments may offer financial assistance and/or exemption from certain regulations to attract or keep production facilities in their area. For example, several companies have relocated to Manatee County, Florida, to receive its Qualified Target Industry Tax Refund. Gammerler Corp., a German company that makes finishing equipment for commercial printers and newspapers, moved its North American headquarters from Chicago to Palmetto, Florida. By adding new manufacturing jobs that pay at least 115 percent more than the current average to the county's economic base, Gammerler will achieve tax savings of $280,000 a year.[4]

International Location Considerations There are often sound financial reasons for considering a foreign location. Labor costs are considerably lower in countries like Singapore, China, India, and Mexico. Foreign countries may also have fewer regulations governing how factories operate. A foreign location may also move production closer to new markets. Automobile manufacturers such as Honda, Toyota, and even BMW and Hyundai, are among many that build plants in the United States to reduce shipping costs. Other considerations in choosing an international location are the type and skills of the labor force in that country. When French luxury-goods company Louis Vuitton needed to increase production of its footwear, it decided to build a factory in Italy, a country with a deep tradition in high-quality shoe design and manufacture.[5]

Designing the Facility

After the site location decision has been made, the next focus in production planning is the facility's layout. The goal is to determine the most efficient and effective design for the particular production process. A manufacturer might opt for a U-shaped production line, for example, rather than a long, straight one, to allow products and workers to move more quickly from one area to another.

Service organizations must also consider layout, but they are more concerned with how it affects customer behavior. It may be more convenient for a hospital to place its freight elevators in the center of the building, for example, but doing so may block the flow of patients, visitors, and medical personnel between floors and departments.

There are three main types of facility layouts: process, product, and fixed-position. All three layouts are illustrated in Exhibit 10.4. Cellular manufacturing is another type of facility layout.

EXHIBIT 10.4   Facility Layouts

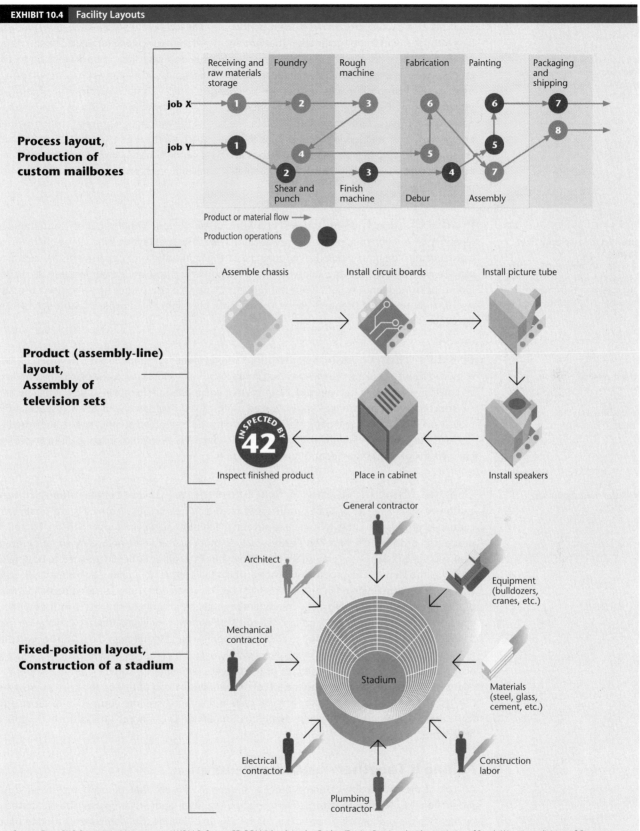

Process layout, Production of custom mailboxes

Receiving and raw materials storage | Foundry | Rough machine | Fabrication | Painting | Packaging and shipping

job X

job Y

Shear and punch | Finish machine | Debur | Assembly

Product or material flow →
Production operations

Product (assembly-line) layout, Assembly of television sets

Assemble chassis | Install circuit boards | Install picture tube

Inspect finished product | Place in cabinet | Install speakers

INSPECTED BY 42

Fixed-position layout, Construction of a stadium

General contractor

Architect

Equipment (bulldozers, cranes, etc.)

Mechanical contractor

Stadium

Materials (steel, glass, cement, etc.)

Electrical contractor

Construction labor

Plumbing contractor

Process Layout: All Welders Stand Here

The **process layout** arranges work flow around the production process. All workers performing similar tasks are grouped together. Products pass from one workstation to another (but not necessarily to every workstation). For example, all grinding would be done in one area, all assembling in another, and all inspection in yet another. The process layout is best for firms that produce small numbers of a wide variety of products, typically using general-purpose machines that can be changed rapidly to new operations for different product designs. For example, until the twenty-first century, Louis Vuitton used a process layout to make its iconic bags. Craftsmen specialized in one part of the production process: cutting leather; preparing, gluing, and sewing it; making pockets and stitching the lining; or assembling the bag. These specialists worked on one batch of bags at a time, and when they had completed their part of the process, they loaded the partially completed bags onto carts and moved them to the next process station.[6]

Product Layout: Moving Down the Line

Products that require a continuous or repetitive production process use the **product** (or **assembly-line**) **layout**. When large quantities of a product must be processed on an ongoing basis, the workstations or departments are arranged in a line with products moving along the line. Automobile and appliance manufacturers, as well as food-processing plants, usually use a product layout. Service companies may also use a product layout for routine processing operations. For example, overnight film processors use assembly-line techniques.

Fixed-Position Layout: Staying Put

Some products cannot be put on an assembly line or moved about in a plant. A **fixed-position layout** lets the product stay in one place while workers and machinery move to it as needed. Products that are impossible to move—ships, airplanes, and construction projects—are typically produced using a fixed-position layout. Limited space at the project site often means that parts of the product must be assembled at other sites, transported to the fixed site, and then assembled. The fixed-position layout is also common for on-site services like housecleaning services, pest control, and landscaping.

Cellular Manufacturing: A Start-to-Finish Focus

Cellular manufacturing combines some aspects of both product and fixed-position layout. Work cells are small, self-contained production units that include several machines and workers arranged in a compact, sequential order. Each work cell performs all or most of the tasks necessary to complete a manufacturing order. There are usually 5 to 10 workers in a cell, and they are trained to be able to do any of the steps in the production process. The goal is to create a team environment wherein team members are involved in production from beginning to end. To meet rising demand for its products, Louis Vuitton changed its manufacturing process from the process layout described above to a cell structure. Today, groups of 6 to 12 craftsmen work in a U-shaped workstation that contains all the equipment needed to complete an entire bag. Rather than move carts of partially finished goods through the factory, workers simply pass the pieces around the cell. Workers are now trained to do more than one part of the process (e.g., gluing, stitching, and finishing the edges of the pocket have become the job of one worker instead of three), so fewer workers are needed to complete a single bag. The cell system has increased the company's revenue and its flexibility—now it can reassign workers to different products according to the fluctuations of demand.[7]

Pulling It Together: Resource Planning

As part of the production-planning process, firms must ensure that the resources needed for production—such as raw materials, parts, equipment, and labor—will be available at strategic moments in the production process. This can be a huge challenge. The components used to build just one Boeing airplane, for instance, number in the millions. Cost is also an important factor. In many industries, the cost of materials and supplies used in the production process amounts to as much as half of sales revenues. Resource planning is therefore a big part of any firm's production strategy.

Resource planning begins by specifying which raw materials, parts, and components will be required, and when, to produce finished goods. To determine the amount of each item needed, the

---

process layout
A facility arrangement in which work flows according to the production process. All workers performing similar tasks are grouped together, and products pass from one workstation to another.

product (or **assembly-line**) **layout**
A facility arrangement in which workstations or departments are arranged in a line with products moving along the line.

fixed-position layout
A facility arrangement in which the product stays in one place and workers and machinery move to it as needed.

cellular manufacturing
Production technique that uses small, self-contained production units, each performing all or most of the tasks necessary to complete a manufacturing order.

4 Why are resource-planning tasks like inventory management and supplier relations critical to production?

expected quantity of finished goods must be forecast. A **bill of material** is then drawn up that lists the items and the number of each required to make the product. **Purchasing**, or *procurement*, is the process of buying production inputs from various sources.

Make or Buy? The firm must decide whether to make its own production materials or buy them from outside sources. This is the **make-or-buy decision**. The quantity of items needed is one consideration. If a part is used in only one of many products, buying the part may be more cost-effective than making it. Buying standard items, such as screws, bolts, rivets, and nails, is usually cheaper and easier than producing them internally. Purchasing larger components from another manufacturer can be cost-effective as well. When items are purchased from an outside source instead of being made internally, it is called **outsourcing**. Harley-Davidson, for example, purchases its tires, brake systems, and other motorcycle components from manufacturers that make them to Harley's specifications. However, if a product has special design features that need to be kept secret to protect a competitive advantage, a firm may decide to produce all parts internally.

In deciding whether to make or buy, a firm must also consider whether outside sources can provide the high-quality supplies it needs in a reliable manner. Having to shut down production because vital parts aren't delivered on time can be a costly disaster. Boeing made headlines with its best-selling 787 Dreamliner, but only a year after the company booked a record number of Dreamliner orders, it made headlines again, this time for several production delays that meant customers couldn't take delivery of their planes for up to a year after the date promised. Boeing had decided to outsource development and production of several key components to suppliers, many of whom fell behind in their work. To catch up, Boeing took some of the work back in-house but was still unable to get back on its original schedule.[8]

Just as bad are inferior parts or materials, which can damage a firm's reputation for producing high-quality goods. Therefore, firms that buy some or all of their production materials from outside sources should make building strong relationships with quality suppliers a priority.

Inventory Management: Not Just Parts A firm's **inventory** is the supply of goods it holds for use in production or for sale to customers. Deciding how much inventory to keep on hand is one of the biggest challenges facing operations managers. On the one hand, with large inventories, the firm can meet most production and customer demands. Buying in large quantities can also allow a company to take advantage of quantity discounts. On the other hand, large inventories can tie up the firm's money, are expensive to store, and can become obsolete.

Inventory management involves deciding how much of each type of inventory to keep on hand and the ordering, receiving, storing, and tracking of it. The goal of inventory management is to keep down the costs of ordering and holding inventories while maintaining enough on hand for production and sales. Good inventory management enhances product quality, makes operations more efficient, and increases profits. Poor inventory management can result in dissatisfied customers, financial difficulties, and even bankruptcy.

Failure to monitor and regulate inventory of finished goods can have as significant an impact on a firm as poor management of component parts inventory. The goal of a production system is to produce exactly the number of goods demanded by the market, but it is not uncommon that companies find themselves with either too little inventory (risking a stockout) or too much inventory (risking a glut). In 2008, automakers were experiencing the latter, as sales plummeted and car inventories began to pile up. (Throughout the first quarter of 2008, several automakers had over four months of inventory on hand.[9]) In response, Chrysler CEO Robert Nardelli announced the company would shut down all operations for a two-week period in the summer. Toyota also cut production at its San Antonio and Princeton, Indiana, plants because consumers weren't buying as many SUVs and pickup trucks as the company could produce.[10] By drawing down production levels, both companies were attempting to better regulate their finished-goods inventories and production capacities to market demands.

One way to determine the best inventory levels is to look at three costs: holding inventory, frequent reordering, and not keeping enough inventory on hand. Managers must measure all three costs and try to minimize them.

bill of material
A list of the items and the number of each required to make a given product.

purchasing
The process of buying production inputs from various sources; also called procurement.

make-or-buy decision
The determination by a firm of whether to make its own production materials or to buy them from outside sources.

outsourcing
The purchase of items from an outside source rather than making them internally.

inventory
The supply of goods that a firm holds for use in production or for sale to customers.

inventory management
The determination of how much of each type of inventory a firm will keep on hand and the ordering, receiving, storing, and tracking of it.

CONCEPT in action

With most of manufacturing, the goal is to ensure that quality parts are sourced from reliable suppliers and delivered just in time. When it comes to enriching uranium for Iran's nuclear weapons, however, many governments are working to throw a wrench in the machinery. Secret operatives infiltrating the black market as parts suppliers sell defective components that make finished nuclear weapons unusable. Disrupting production at the resource-planning level could potentially stop a nuclear program without military action. What makes resource planning vulnerable to industrial sabotage and quality breakdowns?

© AP Images/Hasan Sarbakhshian

Wal-Mart's retail dominance is built upon advanced logistics and inventory management. The company's vendor-managed inventory system puts the burden on suppliers to maintain stock until needed in stores and radio frequency identification tags (RFIDs) help automate the flow of goods. Wal-Mart's remarkable 2:1 sales-to-inventory ratio is expected to shrink further to a theoretical "zero inventory" state in which the retailer won't pay for products until they're purchased by consumers. What costs are associated with keeping too much or too little inventory?

To control inventory levels, managers often track the use of certain inventory items. Most companies keep a **perpetual inventory**, a continuously updated list of inventory levels, orders, sales, and receipts, for all major items. Today, companies mostly use computers to track inventory levels, calculate order quantities, and issue purchase orders at the right times.

Computerized Resource Planning Many manufacturing companies have adopted computerized systems to control the flow of resources and inventory. **Materials requirement planning (MRP)** is one such system. MRP uses a master schedule to ensure that the materials, labor, and equipment needed for production are at the right places in the right amounts at the right times. The schedule is based on forecasts of demand for the company's products. It says exactly what will be manufactured during the next few weeks or months and when the work will take place. Sophisticated computer programs coordinate all the elements of MRP. The computer comes up with materials requirements by comparing production needs to the materials the company already has on hand. Orders are placed so items will be on hand when they are needed for production. MRP helps ensure a smooth flow of finished products.

Manufacturing resource planning II (MRPII) was developed in the late 1980s to expand on MRP. It uses a complex computerized system to integrate data from many departments, including finance, marketing, accounting, engineering, and manufacturing. MRPII can generate a production plan for the firm, as well as management reports, forecasts, and financial statements. The system lets managers make more accurate forecasts and assess the impact of production plans on profitability. If one department's plans change, the effects of these changes on other departments are transmitted throughout the company.

Whereas MRP and MRPII systems are focused internally, **enterprise resource planning (ERP)** systems go a step further and incorporate information about the firm's suppliers and customers into the flow of data. ERP unites all of a firm's major departments into a single software program. For instance, production can call up sales information and know immediately how many units must be produced to meet customer orders. By providing information about the availability of resources, including both the human resources and materials needed for production, the system allows for better cost control and eliminates production delays. The system automatically notes any changes, such as the closure of a plant for maintenance and repairs on a certain date or a supplier's inability to meet a delivery date, so that all functions adjust accordingly. Both large and small organizations use ERP to improve operations.

Keeping the Goods Flowing: Supply Chain Management

In the past, the relationship between purchasers and suppliers was often competitive and antagonistic. Businesses used many suppliers and switched among them frequently. During contract negotiations, each side would try to get better terms at the expense of the other. Communication between purchasers and suppliers was often limited to purchase orders and billing statements.

Today, however, many firms are moving toward a new concept in supplier relationships. The emphasis is increasingly on developing a strong **supply chain**. The supply chain can be thought of as the entire sequence of securing inputs, producing goods, and delivering goods to customers. If any links in this process are weak, chances are customers—the end point of the supply chain—will end up dissatisfied.

Effective supply chain strategies reduce costs. For example, integration of the shipper's and customer's supply chains allows companies to automate more processes and save time. Technology also improves supply chain efficiency by tracking goods through the various supply chain stages and also helping with logistics. With better information about production and inventory, companies can order and receive goods at the optimal point to keep inventory holding costs low.

Companies also need contingency plans for supply chain disruptions. Is there an alternative source of supply if a blizzard closes the airport so that cargo planes can't land or if a drought causes crop failures in the Midwest? Being caught without an alternative can be costly. For example, in 2008, General Motors had to cut production because of a strike by a key supplier, American Axle & Manufacturing. Only a few weeks into the strike, GM was forced to shut down 28 of its facilities, which affected tens of thousands of workers at GM and its other suppliers.[11] By thinking ahead, companies can avert major losses. The length and distance involved in a supply line is also a consideration. Importing parts from or outsourcing manufacturing to Asia creates a long supply

---

perpetual inventory
A continuously updated list of inventory levels, orders, sales, and receipts.

materials requirement planning (MRP)
A computerized system of controlling the flow of resources and inventory. A master schedule is used to ensure that the materials, labor, and equipment needed for production are at the right places in the right amounts at the right times.

manufacturing resource planning II (MRPII)
A complex computerized system that integrates data from many departments to allow managers to more accurately forecast and assess the impact of production plans on profitability.

enterprise resource planning (ERP)
A computerized resource-planning system that incorporates information about the firm's suppliers and customers with its internally generated data.

supply chain
The entire sequence of securing inputs, producing goods, and delivering goods to customers.

Look Before You Leap into Global Sourcing

When Amber McCrocklin wanted to expand production of her popular line of gear for pet owners who like to take their dogs out to sea, she immediately thought of China. She hired an engineer from Shenzhen to redesign her products (boat ladders, life jackets, and waterproof leashes) for mass production. Once that was accomplished, McCrocklin increased production fivefold and watched her profit margin double—for a while, anyway.

It wasn't long before shipments were late, customers were returning defective products, and her contact in China was unresponsive. When she received 3,000 leashes with colors reversed and logos upside down, she finally put a halt to her outsourcing relationship.

Many companies around the globe have made China their number one destination for subcontract manufacturing. In 2007, however, enthusiasm for Chinese production was tempered by a large number of recalls. In the United States, 60 percent of product recalls in 2007 were products manufactured in China. Toys, toothpaste, tires, pet food, and more were on the list of recalled products.

Still, entrepreneurs see China as an opportunity to lower the cost of their goods (and increase their profit margins). Unlike large multinational companies, which are better able to control their supply chains, smaller companies don't have the human or financial resources to have someone on site in China monitoring their production processes. To have a better chance at a successful sourcing relationship, smaller businesses should take advantage of the services offered by a sourcing consultant. Not all sourcing consultants are equal, however, so research into a consultant's client list and background are critical. Also, it's important to negotiate for rigorous and copious product testing and draft a written quality and ethics agreement. Delays are commonplace, so companies need to plan for more time in production than they think. Finally, it pays to diversify. Having more than one supplier can reduce the likelihood of interruptions if faulty products become a problem.

After her first outsourcing fiasco, Amber McCrocklin found a different sourcing consultant, this time at a trade show. The consultant took over her account, including the manufacturing, quality control, and shipping of McCrocklin's pet gear. As a result, McCrocklin's costs have dropped an additional 30 percent, and she doesn't get late night calls from China anymore.[12]

Critical Thinking Questions

- Do you think outsourcing to Chinese manufacturers is worth the hidden costs? Why or why not?
- Can an American manufacturer remain competitive against Chinese competition? How?

---

chain for a manufacturer in Europe or the United States. Perhaps there are closer suppliers or manufacturers who can meet a company's needs at a lower overall cost. Companies should also reevaluate outsourcing decisions periodically. The Expanding Around the Globe box above shows the critical role of supply chain management when looking for overseas suppliers.

Strategies for Supply Chain Management

Ensuring a strong supply chain requires that firms implement supply chain management strategies. **Supply chain management** focuses on smoothing transitions along the supply chain, with the ultimate goal of satisfying customers with quality products and services. A critical element of effective supply chain management is to develop tight bonds with suppliers. This may mean reducing the number of suppliers used and asking them to offer more services or better prices in return for an ongoing relationship.

Ford Motor Company plans to pare down the number of its suppliers to give larger, longer-term contracts to a strategically selected group, providing the company with access to new technology and supplier expertise. Ford will involve its suppliers in the early stages of vehicle design, giving them money up front for engineering and development. And longer contracts mean suppliers can invest more and not worry that Ford will takes its business elsewhere. "I think we'll put ourselves in a much better position to be successful than the position we're in today," said Tony Brown, Ford's senior vice president for global purchasing.[13]

Instead of being viewed as "outsiders" in the production process, many suppliers play an important role in supporting the operations of their customers. They are expected to meet high quality standards, offer suggestions that can help reduce production costs, and even contribute to the design of new products.

Talk to Us: Improving Supplier Communications Effective supply chain management depends on strong communications with suppliers. Technology, particularly the Internet, is providing new ways to do this. **E-procurement**, the process of purchasing supplies and materials online using the Internet, is booming. Some manufacturing firms use the Internet to keep key suppliers informed about their requirements. Intel, for example, has set up a special Web site for its suppliers and potential suppliers. Would-be suppliers can visit the site to get information about doing business with Intel; once they are approved, they can access a secure area to make bids on Intel's current and future resource needs.

CONCEPT in action

Managing an efficient supply chain is critical for businesses, especially when the product being delivered is a bouquet of fresh-cut flowers. To ensure that only the freshest, most colorful floral arrangement arrives for that special someone, Internet florist ProFlowers ships directly from the flower fields, bypassing the middleman. This direct-from-the-grower strategy, combined with coordinated carrier scheduling and a 100 percent product-inspection policy, enables ProFlowers to deliver flowers twice as fresh as the competition's. What strategies help businesses create and maintain an effective supply chain?

supply chain management
The process of smoothing transitions along the supply chain so that the firm can satisfy its customers with quality products and services; focuses on developing tight bonds with suppliers.

e-procurement
The process of purchasing supplies and materials online using the Internet.

The Internet also streamlines purchasing by providing firms with quick access to a huge database of information about the products and services of hundreds of potential suppliers. Many large companies now participate in reverse auctions online, which can slash procurement costs. In a reverse auction, the manufacturer posts its specifications for the materials it requires. Potential suppliers then bid against each other to get the job. However, there are risks with reverse auctions. It can be difficult to establish and build ongoing relationships with specific suppliers using reverse auctions because the job ultimately goes to the lowest bidder. Therefore, reverse auctions may not be an effective procurement process for critical production materials. Other types of corporations can use these auctions as well. UMB Bank, headquartered in Kansas City, Missouri, uses this strategy for a variety of products, from paper to computers. Costs dropped by 15 percent to 50 percent, depending on the item. Only prequalified vendors are allowed to bid. "It isn't exclusively about lowest price," says the bank's chairman and CEO Peter deSilva. "We look for service after the sale. We look at shipping costs. We look at maintenance costs."[14]

Another communications tool is **electronic data interchange (EDI)**, in which two trading partners exchange information electronically. EDI can be conducted via a linked computer system or over the Internet. The advantages of exchanging information with suppliers electronically include speed, accuracy, and lowered communication costs. EDI plays a critical role in Ford Motor Company's efforts to produce and distribute vehicles worldwide. Ford and its major North American logistics partner, Penske Logistics, rely on EDI transmissions from its auto carriers for status updates as they strive to meet strict delivery schedules.[15]

electronic data interchange (EDI)
The electronic exchange of information between two trading partners.

CONCEPT check

What are the three types of decisions that must be made in production planning?

What factors does a firm consider when making a site selection decision?

How is technology being used in resource planning?

Production and Operations Control

5 How do operations managers schedule and control production?

Every company needs to have systems in place to see that production and operations are carried out as planned and to correct errors when they are not. The coordination of materials, equipment, and human resources to achieve production and operating efficiencies is called *production control*. Two of its key aspects are routing and scheduling.

Routing: Where to Next?

routing
The aspect of production control that involves setting out the work flow—the sequence of machines and operations through which the product or service progresses from start to finish.

Routing is the first step in production control. It sets out a work flow, the sequence of machines and operations through which a product or service progresses from start to finish. Routing depends on the type of goods being produced and the facility layout. Good routing procedures increase productivity and cut unnecessary costs.

One useful tool for routing is **value-stream mapping**, whereby production managers "map" the flow from suppliers through the factory to customers. Simple icons represent the materials and information needed at various points in the flow. Value-stream mapping can help identify where bottlenecks may occur in the production process and is a valuable tool for visualizing how to improve production routing.

value-stream mapping
Routing technique that uses simple icons to visually represent the flow of materials and information from suppliers through the factory to customers.

Electronics manufacturer Rockwell Collins used value-stream mapping to automate more of its purchasing operations. The company evaluated 23 areas to identify where process changes would improve efficiency. Based on the study, managers decided to automate three steps: request for quote, quote receipt and total purchase cost, and automated purchase order. The company implemented a new system that automatically sends requests for quotes to appropriate suppliers and evaluates the responses to determine which best meets Rockwell Collins's requirements. Once in place, the new systems allowed purchasing professionals to focus on strategic, rather than routine, activities.[16]

Scheduling: When Do We Do It?

scheduling
The aspect of production control that involves specifying and controlling the time required for each step in the production process.

Closely related to routing is **scheduling**. Scheduling involves specifying and controlling the time required for each step in the production process. The operations manager prepares timetables showing the most efficient sequence of production and then tries to ensure that the necessary materials and labor are in the right place at the right time.

Scheduling is important to both manufacturing and service firms. The production manager in a factory schedules material deliveries, work shifts, and production processes. Trucking companies schedule drivers, clerks, truck maintenance, and repairs in accordance with customer transportation needs. Scheduling at a college entails deciding when to offer which courses, in which classrooms, with which instructors. A museum must schedule special exhibits, ship works to be displayed, market its offerings, and conduct educational programs and tours. Scheduling can range from simple to complex. Giving numbers to customers waiting to be served in a bakery and making interview appointments with job applicants are examples of simple scheduling. Organizations that must produce large quantities of products or services, or service a diverse customer base, face more complex scheduling problems.

Three common scheduling tools used for complex situations are Gantt charts, the critical path method, and PERT.

Tracking Progress with Gantt Charts Named after their originator, Henry Gantt, **Gantt charts** are bar graphs plotted on a time line that show the relationship between scheduled and actual production.

In the example shown in Exhibit 10.5, the left side of the chart lists the activities required to complete the job or project. Both the scheduled time and the actual time required for each activity are shown, so the manager can easily judge progress.

Gantt charts are most helpful when only a few tasks are involved, when task times are relatively long (days or weeks rather than hours), and when job routes are short and simple. When projects are large and complex, however, Gantt charts reach the limits of their usefulness. At Nokia, the cell phone company, Gantt charts for complex projects would typically contain 2,000 tasks lined up step-by-step in chronological order. Former Nokia employee Anders Heie used to run those complex projects. When he wanted to update the Gantt chart, it could take a couple of days. Understandably, the charts were only updated once a month or so. Heie left Nokia and with a partner, developed KaDonk, a plug-in for Microsoft Project (project management software) that aims to simplify the project management process.[17]

One of the biggest shortcomings of Gantt charts, then, is that they are static. They also fail to show how tasks are related. These problems can be solved, however, by using two other scheduling techniques, the critical path method and PERT.

The Big Picture: Critical Path Method and PERT To control large projects, operations managers need to closely monitor resources, costs, quality, and budgets. They also must be able to see the "big picture"—the interrelationships of the many different tasks necessary to complete the project. Finally, they must be able to revise scheduling and divert resources quickly if any tasks fall behind schedule. The critical path method (CPM) and the program evaluation and review technique (PERT) are related project management tools that were developed in the 1950s to help managers accomplish this.

Gantt charts
Bar graphs plotted on a time line that show the relationship between scheduled and actual production.

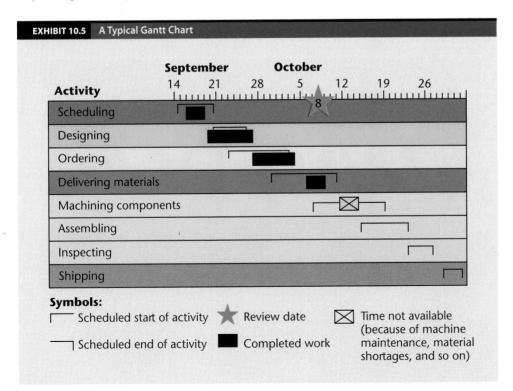

EXHIBIT 10.5   A Typical Gantt Chart

Symbols:
⌐ Scheduled start of activity   ★ Review date   ⊠ Time not available (because of machine maintenance, material shortages, and so on)
⌐ Scheduled end of activity   ■ Completed work

In the **critical path method (CPM)**, the manager identifies all of the activities required to complete the project, the relationships between these activities, and the order in which they need to be completed. Then, the manager develops a diagram that uses arrows to show how the tasks are dependent on each other. The longest path through these linked activities is called the **critical path**. If the tasks on the critical path are not completed on time, the entire project will fall behind schedule.

To better understand how CPM works, look at Exhibit 10.6, which shows a CPM diagram for constructing a house. All of the tasks required to finish the house and an estimated time for each have been identified. The arrows indicate the links between the various steps and their required sequence. As you can see, most of the jobs to be done can't be started until the house's foundation and frame are completed. It will take five days to finish the foundation and another seven days to erect the house frame. The activities linked by brown arrows form the critical path for this project. It tells us that the fastest possible time the house can be built is 38 days, the total time needed for all of the critical path tasks. The noncritical path jobs, those connected with black arrows, can be delayed a bit or done early. Short delays in installing appliances or roofing won't delay construction of the house because these activities don't lie on the critical path.

Like CPM, **program evaluation and review technique (PERT)** helps managers identify critical tasks and assess how delays in certain activities will affect operations or production. In both methods, managers use diagrams to see how operations and production will flow. PERT differs from CPM in one important respect: CPM assumes that the amount of time needed to finish a task is known with certainty; therefore, the CPM diagram shows only one number for the time needed to complete each activity. In contrast, PERT assigns three time estimates for each activity: an optimistic time for completion, the most probable time, and a pessimistic time. These estimates allow managers to anticipate delays and potential problems and schedule accordingly.

Looking for a Better Way: Improving Production and Operations

6 How can quality management and lean-manufacturing techniques help firms improve production and operations management?

Competing in today's business world is challenging. To compete effectively, firms must keep production costs down. At the same time, however, it's becoming increasingly complex to produce and

| EXHIBIT 10.6 | A CPM Network for Building a House |

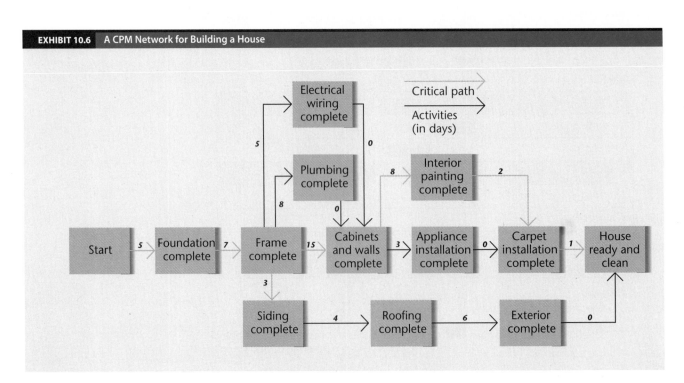

deliver the high-quality goods and services customers demand. Methods to help meet these challenges include quality management techniques, lean manufacturing, and technology and automation.

Putting Quality First

Successful businesses recognize that quality and productivity must go hand in hand. **Quality** goods and services meet customer expectations by providing reliable performance. Defective products waste materials and time, increasing costs. Worse, poor quality causes customer dissatisfaction, which usually results in lost sales.

A consumer measures quality by how well a product serves its purpose. From the manufacturer's point of view, quality is the degree to which the product conforms to a set of predetermined standards. **Quality control** involves creating quality standards, producing goods that meet them, and measuring finished goods and services against them. It takes more than just inspecting goods at the end of the assembly line to ensure quality control, however. Quality control requires a company-wide dedication to managing and working in a way that builds excellence into every facet of operations.

Dr. W. Edwards Deming, an American management consultant, was the first to say that quality control should be a company-wide goal. His ideas were adopted by the Japanese in the 1950s but largely ignored in the United States until the 1970s. Deming believed that quality control starts with top management, who must foster a company-wide culture dedicated to producing quality.

Deming's concept of **Total Quality Management (TQM)** emphasizes the use of quality principles in all aspects of a company's production and operations. It recognizes that all employees involved with bringing a product or service to customers—marketing, purchasing, accounting, shipping, manufacturing—contribute to its quality. TQM focuses on **continuous improvement**, a commitment to constantly seek better ways of doing things in order to achieve greater efficiency and improve quality. Company-wide teams work together to prevent problems and systematically improve key processes, instead of troubleshooting problems only as they arise. Continuous improvement continually measures performance using statistical techniques and looks for ways to apply new technologies and innovative production methods.

Another quality control method is the **Six Sigma** quality program. Six Sigma is a company-wide process that focuses on measuring the number of defects that occur and systematically eliminating them in order to get as close to "zero defects" as possible. In fact, Six Sigma quality aims to have every process produce no more than 3.4 defects per million. Six Sigma focuses on designing products that not only have fewer defects but that also satisfy customer needs. A key process of Six Sigma is called *DMAIC*. This stands for Define, Measure, Analyze, Improve, and Control. Employees at all levels define what needs to be done to ensure quality, then measure and analyze production results using statistics to see if standards are met. They are also charged with finding ways to improve and control quality.

General Electric was one of the first companies to institute Six Sigma throughout the organization. All GE employees are trained in Six Sigma concepts, and many analysts believe this has given GE a competitive manufacturing advantage. Service firms and government entities have applied Six Sigma to their quality initiatives as well.

Malcolm Baldrige National Quality Award Named for a former secretary of commerce, the **Malcolm Baldrige National Quality Award** was established by the U.S. Congress in 1987 to recognize U.S. companies that offer goods and services of world-class quality. The award promotes awareness of quality and allows the business community to assess which quality control programs are most effective.

Administered by the U.S. Department of Commerce's National Institute of Standards and Technologies (NIST), the award's most important criterion is a firm's effectiveness at meeting customer expectations, as well as demonstrating that it offers quality goods and services. To qualify for the award, a company must also show continuous improvement in internal operations. Company leaders and employees must be active participants in the firm's quality program and they must respond quickly to data and analysis.

Organizations in a wide variety of industries have won the Baldrige Award since it was first presented in 1987. Up to five awards can be given in the industries of manufacturing, health care, education, service, small business, and nonprofit. Since its creation, about 10 million copies of the Baldrige criteria have

Toyota's rise from a World War II Japanese truck maker to the world's top-selling auto manufacturer is owed to an innovative production philosophy known as "The Toyota Way." The Toyota Way includes the Japanese ideal of continuous improvement, or *kaizen*, which seeks new methods of efficiency and quality. Though *kaizen* is a never-ending pursuit, its ultimate purpose is to build automobiles without any defects. Toyota's approach has worked especially well in the United States, where the Toyota Camry and Prius are top-selling models. Why is quality essential to business success?

quality
Goods and services that meet customer expectations by providing reliable performance.

quality control
The process of creating quality standards, producing goods that meet them, and measuring finished goods and services against them.

Total Quality Management (TQM)
The use of quality principles in all aspects of a company's production and operations.

continuous improvement
A commitment to constantly seek better ways of doing things in order to achieve greater efficiency and improve quality.

Six Sigma
A quality control process that relies on defining what needs to be done to ensure quality, measuring and analyzing production results statistically, and finding ways to improve and control quality.

Malcolm Baldrige National Quality Award
An award given to recognize U.S. companies that offer goods and services of world-class quality; established by Congress in 1987 and named for a former secretary of commerce.

been distributed. Downloads currently number about 1 million annually. Additionally, more than 40 U.S. states and more than 45 countries worldwide have implemented programs based on the Baldrige criteria. The slate of 2007 award winners included two health care companies (Mercy Health Systems and Sharp Healthcare), two nonprofits (City of Coral Springs and the U.S. Army Armament Research, Development, and Engineering Center), and one small business (PRO-TEC Coating Company).[18]

Worldwide Excellence: International Quality Standards   The International Organization for Standardization (ISO), located in Belgium, is an industry organization that has developed standards of quality that are used by businesses around the world. **ISO 9000**, introduced in the 1980s, is a set of five technical standards designed to offer a uniform way of determining whether manufacturing plants and service organizations conform to sound quality procedures. To register, a company must go through an audit of its manufacturing and customer service processes, covering everything from how it designs, produces, and installs its products, to how it inspects, packages, and markets them. Over 500,000 organizations worldwide have met ISO 9000 standards.

ISO 14000, launched after ISO 9000, was designed in response to environmental issues like global warming and water pollution, and promotes clean production processes. To meet ISO 14000 standards, a company must commit to continually improving environmental management and reducing pollution resulting from its production processes.

Lean Manufacturing Trims the Fat

Manufacturers are discovering that they can better respond to rapidly changing customer demands, while keeping inventory and production costs down, by adopting lean-manufacturing techniques. **Lean manufacturing** streamlines production by eliminating steps in the production process that do not add benefits customers want. In other words, *non-value-added production processes* are cut so that the company can concentrate its production and operations resources on items essential to satisfying customers. Toyota was a pioneer in developing these techniques, but today manufacturers in many industries have adopted the lean-manufacturing philosophy.

A Japanese organizational tool often used in conjunction with lean manufacturing is called 5S. The five Ss are Sort, Set in Order, Shine, Standardize, and Sustain. Derived from five Japanese words that describe a process for organizing the workplace, a general translation might be "a place for everything and everything in its place." Sorting involves determining what is useful activity in the workplace, setting in order is finding a good place for everything and generally being uncluttered, and shining is keeping the workplace clean. Standardizing involves making orderliness standard operating procedure, and sustaining means embedding 5S into the fabric of the organization until 5S discipline becomes a way of life.[19]

The purpose of 5S is to spot problems quickly. For example, a shadow board in the kitchen of the San Francisco Bay Penitentiary shows outlines of each sharp knife in the kitchen. At a glance, a cook can see if a knife is missing—before it shows up in an inmate. The same idea of keeping things visually organized is also a key to efficiency on the factory floor.[20]

Another Japanese concept, **just-in-time (JIT)**, goes hand in hand with lean manufacturing. JIT is based on the belief that materials should arrive exactly when they are needed for production, rather than being stored on site. Relying closely on computerized systems such as MRP, MRPII, and ERP, manufacturers determine what parts will be needed and when, and then order them from suppliers so they arrive "just in time." Under the JIT system, inventory and products are "pulled" through the production process in response to customer demand. JIT requires close teamwork between vendors and purchasing and production personnel because any delays in deliveries of supplies could bring JIT production to a halt.

Unexpected events like the September 11 terrorist attacks or the shutdown of ports due to Hurricane Katrina can cause chaos in the supply chains of manufacturers, resulting in problems for firms relying on JIT. But if employed properly, and in spite of these risks, a JIT system can greatly reduce inventory-holding costs and smooth production highs and lows.

Transforming the Factory Floor with Technology

Technology is helping many firms improve their operating efficiency and ability to compete. Computer systems in particular are enabling manufacturers to automate factories in ways never

ISO 9000
A set of five technical standards of quality management created by the International Organization for Standardization to provide a uniform way of determining whether manufacturing plants and service organizations conform to sound quality procedures.

ISO 14000
A set of technical standards designed by the International Organization for Standardization to promote clean production processes to protect the environment.

lean manufacturing
Streamlining production by eliminating steps in the production process that do not add benefits customers want.

CONCEPT in action

© Kimimasa Mayama/Bloomberg News/Landov

Formerly the stuff of sci-fi thrillers, robots have arrived and are taking over our homes and businesses. iRobot has developed machines that sniff out terrorist bombs and wash floors. The da Vinci surgical robot performs live organ transplants in the operating room. Japan is experiencing a robotics revolution, as robots clean office corridors, spoon-feed the elderly, serve tea, and even perform "Pomp and Circumstance" on violin. How are new technologies transforming the factory floor?

just-in-time (JIT)
A system in which materials arrive exactly when they are needed for production, rather than being stored on site.

7 What roles do technology and automation play in manufacturing and service industry operations management?

before possible. Among the technologies helping to automate manufacturing are computer-aided design and manufacturing systems, robotics, flexible manufacturing systems, and computer-integrated manufacturing.

Computer-Aided Design and Manufacturing Systems

Computers have transformed the design and manufacturing processes in many industries. In **computer-aided design (CAD)**, computers are used to design and test new products and modify existing ones. Engineers use these systems to draw products and look at them from different angles. They can analyze the products, make changes, and test prototypes before manufacturing a single item. **Computer-aided manufacturing (CAM)** uses computers to develop and control the production process. These systems analyze the steps required to make the product, then automatically send instructions to the machines that do the work. **CAD/CAM systems** combine the advantages of CAD and CAM by integrating design, testing, and manufacturing control into one linked computer system. The system helps design the product, control the flow of resources needed to produce the product, and operate the production process.

Cardianove Inc., a Montreal-based manufacturer of medical and surgical equipment, used CAD software to develop the world's smallest heart pump. The company says using computer-aided design shaved two years off the normal design time for cardiac devices. The company's CAD program ran complex three-dimensional simulations to confirm that the design would function properly inside the human body. Using CAD software, Cardianove tested more than 100 virtual prototypes before the top three designs were produced for real-life testing.

Robotics

Robots are computer-controlled machines that can perform tasks independently. **Robotics** is the technology involved in designing, constructing, and operating robots. The first robot, or "steel-collar worker," was used by General Motors in 1961. Robots can be mobile or fixed in one place. Fixed robots have an arm that moves and does what the computer instructs. Some robots are quite simple, with limited movement for a few tasks such as cutting sheet metal and spot welding. Others are complex, with hands or grippers that can be programmed to perform a series of movements. Some robots are even equipped with sensing devices for sight and touch.

Robots usually operate with little or no human intervention. Replacing human effort with robots is most effective for tasks requiring accuracy, speed, or strength. Although manufacturers like Harley-Davidson are most likely to use robots, some service firms are also finding them useful. Hospitals, for example, may use robots to sort and process blood samples, freeing medical personnel from a tedious, sometimes hazardous, repetitive task. The Customer Satisfaction and Quality box on the next page describes other ways automation leads to better health care.

Adaptable Factories: Flexible and Computer Integrated Manufacturing Systems

A **flexible manufacturing system (FMS)** automates a factory by blending computers, robots, machine tools, and materials-and-parts-handling machinery into an integrated system. These systems combine automated workstations with computer-controlled transportation devices. Automatic guided vehicles (AGVs) move materials between workstations and into and out of the system.

Flexible manufacturing systems are expensive. But once in place, a system requires little labor to operate and provides consistent product quality. It can also be adjusted easily and inexpensively. FMS equipment can quickly be reprogrammed to perform a variety of jobs. These systems work well when small batches of a variety of products are required or when each product is made to individual customer specifications.

Computer-integrated manufacturing (CIM) combines computerized manufacturing processes (like robots and flexible manufacturing systems) with other computerized systems that control design, inventory, production, and purchasing. With CIM, when a part is redesigned in the CAD system, the changes are quickly transmitted both to the machines producing the part and to all other departments that need to know about and plan for the change.

Technology and Automation at Your Service

Manufacturers are not the only businesses benefiting from technology. Nonmanufacturing firms are also using automation to improve customer service and productivity. Banks now offer services to customers through automated teller machines (ATMs), via automated telephone systems, and even over the Internet. Retail stores of all kinds use point-of-sale (POS)

---

computer-aided design (CAD)
The use of computers to design and test new products and modify existing ones.

computer-aided manufacturing (CAM)
The use of computers to develop and control the production process.

CAD/CAM systems
Linked computer systems that combine the advantages of computer-aided design and computer-aided manufacturing. The system helps design the product, control the flow of resources needed to produce the product, and operate the production process.

robotics
The technology involved in designing, constructing, and operating computer-controlled machines that can perform tasks independently.

flexible manufacturing system (FMS)
A system that combines automated workstations with computer-controlled transportation devices—automatic guided vehicles (AGVs)—that move materials between workstations and into and out of the system.

computer-integrated manufacturing (CIM)
The combination of computerized manufacturing processes (like robots and flexible manufacturing systems) with other computerized systems that control design, inventory, production, and purchasing.

CONCEPT check

Describe total quality management and the role that Six Sigma, ISO 9000, and ISO 14000 play in it.

How can lean manufacturing and just-in-time inventory management help a firm improve its production and operations?

How are both manufacturing and nonmanufacturing firms using technology and automation to improve operations?

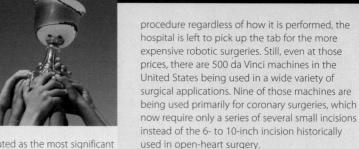

Can Technology Save Your Life?

Using robots to perform surgery once seemed like a futuristic fantasy, but not anymore. Tens of thousands of robotic procedures take place every year, from heart bypass surgeries to kidney transplants to prostate removals and gynecological surgeries. In fact, robot-assisted surgeries are being touted as the most significant development in 20 years in the field of minimally invasive surgeries.

One reason for the increased use of robotic technology in the operating room is improved outcomes for patients. Surgeons who use the da Vinci robotic system find that patients have less blood loss and pain, lower risks of complications, shorter hospital stays, and quicker recovery times than those who have open surgery.

In a typical robotic procedure, as many as three robotic arms hold surgical tools while a fourth holds a camera. Images from the camera are projected on a screen and are 10 times what a surgeon would see during an open surgery. From a few feet away from the patient, the surgeon looks through eye pieces at the three-dimensional images and operates the controls that determine the movement of the robotic arms, which can make up to 100 adjustments per second. "Human hands are remarkable, but they have limitations," said Russell H. Taylor, a professor of computer science and director of a Johns Hopkins research center devoted to designing robots for surgeries. "There are times when it would be useful to have a 'third hand,' and we can provide that. Sometimes a surgeon's fingers are too large to work in a small confined space within the body. We can help by building tools that act like unhumanly small and highly dexterous hands."

So what are the downsides? At a price of $1.8 million each, the cost of the robots can be a barrier. Because insurance companies pay a fixed amount for a

procedure regardless of how it is performed, the hospital is left to pick up the tab for the more expensive robotic surgeries. Still, even at those prices, there are 500 da Vinci machines in the United States being used in a wide variety of surgical applications. Nine of those machines are being used primarily for coronary surgeries, which now require only a series of several small incisions instead of the 6- to 10-inch incision historically used in open-heart surgery.

Taylor of Johns Hopkins sees even more integration—for example, pairing surgery robots with patients' electronic medical records. Algorithms could check how well patients responded to treatments, and so help doctors learn what protocols are most effective. "We could produce the equivalent of a flight-data recorder for the operating room," he said.[21]

Critical Thinking Questions
- In what other ways do you think technology can be used to streamline hospital operations, improve the quality of patient care, and provide better outcomes for patients?
- What criteria should hospitals use to evaluate whether these expensive technologies are worthwhile investments?

terminals that track inventories, identify items that need to be reordered, and tell which products are selling well. WalMart, the leader in retailing automation, has its own satellite system connecting POS terminals directly to its distribution centers and headquarters.

Trends in Production and Operations Management

8 What key trends are affecting the way companies manage production and operations?

What trends will impact U.S. production and operations management both now and in the future? Manufacturing employment stabilized after losing 3 million factory jobs over 43 consecutive months, down to a level of 14.3 million in February 2004. The economy has created 2.1 million new jobs, with unemployment in 2005 standing at 5 percent—the lowest level since September 2001. (Many economists consider 5 percent unemployment to represent a society with full employment.) Production continues to grow, as does productivity, which even increased 1.7 percent during the fourth quarter of 2007 when many considered the United States to be in recession.[22]

Yet rapid changes in technology and intense global competition—particularly from Asia—create anxiety about the future. Is technology replacing too many jobs? Or with qualified workers predicted to be in short supply, is the increased reliance on technology imperative to the United States' ability to compete in a global marketplace? Will the business environment in the United States jeopardize the manufacturing sector? Will anything be made in the United States in the future?

Recent surveys show finding qualified workers is a major concern facing U.S. industry today. In general, the business environment is a challenging one for today's U.S. manufacturers. And what of the increasingly crucial role of technology? These are some of the trends we will examine that companies are facing today.

Looming Workforce Crisis Threatens U.S. Competitiveness

According to the latest National Association of Manufacturers (NAM) Skills Gap Report, manufacturing executives rank a "high-performing workforce" as the most important factor in their firms' future success. This finding concurs with a recent study by the U.S. Department of Labor, which concluded that 85 percent of future jobs in the United States will require advanced training, an associate degree, or a four-year college degree. Minimum skills will be adequate for only 15 percent of future jobs. The 2007 NAM annual Labor Day report indicated that 97 percent of the workforce with at least some college coursework is already employed and that "trouble finding qualified workers" ranks only behind the "cost of health care" as the most serious problem facing manufacturers. The report also found that demand for skilled workers will continue to grow as manufacturers continue to innovate in order to remain competitive in the global economy.[23]

As demand for better-educated and more highly skilled workers begins to grow, troubling trends project a severe shortage of such workers. U.S. employers already struggling to find qualified workers will face an increasing shortage of such workers in coming years. To make matters worse, trends in U.S. secondary education suggest that even those future workers who stay in school to study math and science may not receive globally competitive educations.[24]

A global economy in which jobs and inputs are sourced overseas presents both opportunities and threats. Nowhere is this more evident than in U.S.–China trade. In 2007, toymaker Mattel was forced to recall almost 20 million items made in China due to the presence of deadly lead paint. The massive recall involved more than 80 toy types, including best-selling Barbie, Elmo, and Dora characters. The event was especially alarming since Mattel is considered to be a model of quality control. Do the benefits of global operations outweigh the risks?

A Challenging Domestic Business Environment

Domestic manufacturers are riddled by concerns about rising external costs that make manufacturing from a U.S. base difficult. These costs for corporate taxes, health care and pensions, regulation, energy, and tort litigation add up to a 31.7 percent cost disadvantage experienced by U.S. manufacturers. Federal regulations cost U.S. manufacturers roughly $10,000 per employee (nonmanufacturing companies face costs only half that), and health care costs for some manufacturers amount to about 30 percent of sales. Most small and medium-size manufacturers consider health care their most pressing cost exposure. Finally, the tax rates for businesses and the cost of litigation are higher in the United States than in many other developed nations, including the United Kingdom, Germany, France, Ireland, and others.[25] Between 1980 and 2005, the tax burden of small and medium-size companies jumped from $105 billion to $500 billion, with manufacturers paying the largest share! All of these factors combine to make U.S.-made goods more expensive than many imports.

Business Process Management (BPM)—The Next Big Thing?

The twenty-first century is the age of the scattered corporation. With an assortment of partners and an army of suppliers often spread across thousands of miles, many companies find themselves with global design, supply, and logistics chains stretched to the breaking point. Few firms these days can afford to go it alone—with their own raw materials, in–house production processes, and exclusive distribution systems.[26]

"**Business process management (BPM)** is the glue to bind it all together," says Eric Austvold, research director at AMR Research. "It provides a unified system for business." This new and exciting technology has the power to integrate and optimize a company's sprawling functions by automating much of what it does. The results speak for themselves. BPM has saved U.S. firms $117 billion a year on inventory costs alone. Defense contractor Lockheed Martin recently used a BPM system to resolve differences among the hundreds of businesses that it acquired, unifying them into a whole and saving $50 million per year by making better use of existing resources and data.

business process management (BPM)
A unified system that has the power to integrate and optimize a company's sprawling functions by automating much of what it does.

BPM is the key to the success of such corporate high-flyers as Wal-Mart and Dell, which collect, digest, and utilize all sorts of production, sales, and shipping data to continually hone their operations. So how does BPM actually work? When a Dell system is ordered online, rather than waiting for a person to get the ball rolling, a flurry of electronic traffic flows back and forth between suppliers so that every part arrives within a few hours and that the computer's assembly, as well as software loading and testing, are scheduled. Production runs like a well-oiled clock so customers get their computers quickly, and Dell can bill them on shipment. A well-thought-through BPM system can even reschedule production runs, reroute deliveries, or shift work to a plant out of harm's way if a typhoon off the coast of Thailand threatens freight shipments in and out of your factory.[27]

The amount of available data—business intelligence (BI), enterprise resource planning (ERP), customer relationship management (CRM), and other systems—is staggering. "Companies are flooded with information," says Jeanne Baker, director and chair of the industry support group, Business Process Management Initiative (BPMI), and vice president of technology at Sterling Commerce. "The challenge is to make sense of it all. How you leverage the value chain is the true competitive advantage of the twenty-first century."[28]

Summary of Learning Goals

1 Why is production and operations management important in both manufacturing and service firms?

In the 1980s, many U.S. manufacturers lost customers to foreign competitors because their production and operations management systems did not support the high-quality, reasonably priced products consumers demanded. Service organizations also rely on effective operations management in order to satisfy consumers. Operations managers, the personnel charged with managing and supervising the conversion of inputs into outputs, work closely with other functions in organizations to help ensure quality, customer satisfaction, and financial success.

2 What types of production processes do manufacturers and service firms use?

Products are made using one of three types of production processes. In mass production, many identical goods are produced at once, keeping production costs low. Mass production, therefore, relies heavily on standardization, mechanization, and specialization. When mass customization is used, goods are produced using mass-production techniques up to a point, after which the product or service is custom-tailored to individual customers by adding special features. When a firm's production process is built around customization, the firm makes many products one at a time according to the very specific needs or wants of individual customers.

3 How do organizations decide where to put their production facilities? What choices must be made in designing the facility?

Site selection affects operating costs, the price of the product or service, and the company's ability to compete. In choosing a production site, firms must weigh the availability of resources—raw materials, manpower, and even capital—needed for production, as well as the ability to serve customers and take advantage of marketing opportunities. Other factors include the availability of local incentives and the manufacturing environment. Once a site is selected, the firm must choose an appropriate design for the facility. The three main production facility designs are process, product, and fixed-position layouts. Cellular manufacturing is another type of facility layout.

4 Why are resource-planning tasks like inventory management and supplier relations critical to production?

Production converts input resources, such as raw materials and labor, into outputs, finished products and services. Firms must ensure that the resources needed for production will be available at strategic moments in the production process. If they are not, productivity, customer satisfaction, and quality may suffer. Carefully managing inventory can help cut production costs while maintaining enough supply for production and sales. Through good relationships with suppliers, firms can get better prices, reliable resources, and support services that can improve production efficiency.

5 How do operations managers schedule and control production?

Routing is the first step in scheduling and controlling production. Routing analyzes the steps needed in production and sets out a work flow, the sequence of machines and operations through which a product or service progresses from start to finish. Good routing increases productivity and can eliminate unnecessary cost. Scheduling involves specifying and controlling the time and resources required for each step in the production process. Operations managers use three methods to schedule production: Gantt charts, the critical path method, and program evaluation and review technique.

6 How can quality management and lean-manufacturing techniques help firms improve production and operations management?

Quality and productivity go hand in hand. Defective products waste materials and time, increasing costs. Poor quality also leads to dissatisfied customers. By implementing quality control methods, firms can reduce these problems and streamline production. Lean manufacturing also helps streamline production by eliminating unnecessary steps in the production process. When activities that don't add value for customers are eliminated, manufacturers can respond to changing market conditions with greater flexibility and ease.

7 What roles do technology and automation play in manufacturing and service industry operations management?

Many firms are improving their operational efficiency by using technology to automate parts of production. Computer-aided design and manufacturing systems, for example, help design new products, control the flow of resources needed for production, and even operate much of the production process. By using robotics, the time and effort spent by humans can be minimized. Factories are being automated by blending computers, robots, and machinery into flexible manufacturing systems that require less labor to operate. Service firms are also automating operations by using technology to cut labor costs and control quality.

Data show the U.S. economy steaming steadily ahead, but dramatic advances in technology, predicted worker shortages, and global competition create challenges for the future. How will companies balance their technology and workforce needs? Will the United States maintain its lead in the ongoing war for leadership in innovation? And what should it be doing to convert today's students into tomorrow's innovators and scientists? Surveys indicate that finding qualified workers is a major concern facing U.S. industry today. If the United States is to maintain its competitive edge, more federal investment is needed for science and research. And what of the increasingly crucial role of technology? These are some of the trends companies are facing today.

8 What key trends are affecting the way companies manage production and operations?

Key Terms

assembly process 262
bill of material 267
business process management (BPM) 277
CAD/CAM systems 275
cellular manufacturing 266
computer-aided design (CAD) 275
computer-aided manufacturing (CAM) 275
computer-integrated manufacturing (CIM) 275
continuous improvement 273
continuous process 262
critical path 272
critical path method (CPM) 272
customization 261
electronic data interchange (EDI) 270
e-procurement 269
enterprise resource planning (ERP) 268
fixed-position layout 266
flexible manufacturing system (FMS) 275
Gantt charts 271
intermittent process 262
inventory 267
inventory management 267
ISO 9000 274
ISO 14000 274
job shop 261
just-in-time (JIT) 274
lean manufacturing 274
make-or-buy decision 267

Malcolm Baldrige National Quality Award 273
manufacturing resource planning II (MRPII) 268
mass customization 261
mass production 261
materials requirement planning (MRP) 268
operations management 259
outsourcing 267
perpetual inventory 267
process layout 266
process manufacturing 262
product (or assembly-line) layout 266
production 259
production planning 260
production process 261
program evaluation and review technique (PERT) 272
purchasing 267
quality 273
quality control 273
robotics 275
routing 270
scheduling 270
Six Sigma 273
supply chain 268
supply chain management 269
Total Quality Management (TQM) 273
value-stream mapping 270

Preparing for Tomorrow's Workplace: SCANS

1. Tom Lawrence and Sally Zickle are co-owners of L-Z Marketing, an advertising agency. Last week, they landed a major aerospace manufacturer as a client. The company wants the agency to create its annual report. Tom, who develops the art for the agency, needs about a week to develop the preliminary report design, another two weeks to set the type, and three weeks to get the report printed. Sally writes the material for the report and doesn't need as much time: two days to meet with the client to review the company's financial information and about three weeks to write the report copy. Of course, Tom can't set type until Sally has finished writing the report. Sally will also need three days to proofread the report before it goes to the printer. Develop either a Gantt chart or a critical path diagram for Tom and Sally to use in scheduling the project. Explain why you chose the method you did. How long will it take Tom and Sally to finish the project if there are no unforeseen delays? (**Resources, Systems**)

2. Look for ways that technology and automation are used at your school, in the local supermarket, and at your doctor's office. As a class, discuss how automation affects the service you receive from each of these organizations. Does one organization use any type of automation that might be effectively used by one of the others? Explain. (**Interpersonal, Information**)

3. Pick a small business in your community. Make a list of the resources critical to the firm's production and operations. What would happen if the business suddenly couldn't acquire any of these resources? Divide the class into small groups and discuss strategies that small businesses can use to manage their supply chain. (**Resources, Information, Interpersonal**)

4. Broadway Fashions is a manufacturer of women's dresses. The company's factory has 50 employees. Production begins when the fabric is cut according to specified patterns. After being cut, the pieces for each dress style are placed into bundles, which then move through the factory from worker to worker. Each worker opens each bundle and does one assembly task, such as sewing on collars, hemming dresses, or adding decorative items like appliqués. Then, the worker puts the bundle back together and passes it on to the next person in the production process. Finished dresses are pressed and packaged for shipment. Draw a diagram showing the production process layout in Broadway Fashion's factory. What type of factory layout and process is Broadway using? Discuss the pros and cons of this choice. Could Broadway improve production efficiency by using a different production process or factory layout? How? Draw a diagram to explain how this might look. (**Resources, Systems**)

5. As discussed in this chapter, many American firms have moved their manufacturing operations to overseas locations in the past decade. Although there can be sound financial benefits to this choice, moving production overseas can also raise new challenges for operations managers. Identify several of these challenges and offer suggestions for how operations managers can use the concepts in this chapter to minimize or solve them. (**Resources, Information**)

6. **Team Activity** Reliance Systems, headquartered in Oklahoma City, is a manufacturer of computer keyboards. The company plans to build a new factory and hopes to find a location with access to low-cost but skilled workers, national and international transportation, and favorable government incentives. Working in teams, assign tasks and use the Internet and your school library to research possible site locations, both domestic and international. Choose a location you feel would best meet the company's needs. Make a group presentation to the class explaining why you have chosen this location. Include information about the location's labor force, similar manufacturing facilities already located there, availability of resources and materials, possible local incentives, political and economic environment at the location, and any other factors you feel make this an attractive location. After all teams have presented their proposed locations, as a class, rank all of the locations and decide the top two Reliance should investigate further. (**Interpersonal, Information**)

7. Your teacher has just announced a huge assignment, due in three weeks. Develop a Gantt chart to plan and schedule more effectively:

   - Break the assignment down into smaller tasks: Pick a topic, conduct research at the library or on the Internet, organize your notes, develop an outline, and write, type, and proofread the paper.
   - Estimate how much time each task will take.
   - Across the top of a piece of paper list all the days until the assignment is due. Along the side of the paper list all the tasks you've identified in the order they need to be done.

- Starting with the first task, block out the number of days you estimate each task will take. Include days that you won't be able to work on the project.
- Track the actual time spent on each task.

After you complete and submit your assignment, compare your time estimates to the actual time each task took. How can these findings help you with future assignments? (**Resources, Systems**)

Ethics Activity

A recent spate of mine disasters that caused numerous fatalities refocused national attention on the question: Is management doing enough to protect employees on the job? Recent serious OSHA (Occupational Safety and Health Administration) violations resulting in the deaths of two workers, from falls due to the lack of harnesses or guardrails, suggest there is still a long way to go.

Companies are responsible for providing a safe workplace for employees. So why do accidents like these continue to happen? In a word—money. It takes money to purchase harnesses, install guardrails, and otherwise ensure a safe and healthy work environment. And even more is needed to employ the staff necessary to enforce company safety policies. It is often less costly for a company to just pay the fines that are levied for violations.

As a supervisor at a company with frequent violations of OSHA regulations, you worry about your employees' safety. But each time your company needs to implement a new safety feature, end-of-year employee bonuses get smaller. The money has to come from somewhere, management claims.

Using a Web search tool, locate articles about this topic and then write a response to the following question. Be sure to support your arguments and cite your sources.

ETHICAL DILEMMA: Do you report safety violations to management in the hope they will be corrected before someone gets hurt, or do you stage a total work stoppage to force management's hand, knowing that either way you risk losing popularity at every level, and very possibly your job? Or, of course, you could say nothing and hope for the best. It is not a problem you created and you're just there to do a job, after all.

Sources: Susanne Nadeau, "Company Fined Thousands for Trench Collapse: Minnesota Contractor Fights OSHA Fine," *Grand Forks Herald* (Grand Forks, North Dakota), January 12, 2006, **http://galenet.thomsonlearning.com**; Jacqueline Seibel, "OSHA Fines 2 Firms in Pair of Workplace Deaths," *Milwaukee Journal Sentinel*, February 2, 2006, **http://galenet.thomsonlearning.com**; John J. Steuby, "Company Cited for Alleged Workplace Safety, Health Violations," *America's Intelligence Wire*, January 13, 2006, **http://galenet.thomsonlearning.com**.

Working the Net

1. Use the Google search engine, **http://www.google.com**, to conduct a search for "supplier information" and visit the Web sites of several firms (for example, Motorola, Northrop Grumman, Verizon, etc.). Compare the requirements companies set for their suppliers. How do they differ? How are they similar?
2. Visit Site Selection magazine, **http://www.siteselection.com**. Click on Area Demographics for information about the manufacturing environment in various U.S. locations. Pick three to four areas to read about. Using this information, identify the locations you would recommend for firms in the following industries: general services, telecommunications, automotive manufacturing, and electronics manufacturing. Explain.
3. Manufacturers face many federal, state, and local regulations. Visit the National Association of Manufacturers at **http://www.nam.org**. Pick two or three legislative or regulatory issues discussed under the "policy" sections and use a search engine like Yahoo! (**http://www.yahoo.com**) to find more information.
4. Using a search engine like Excite (**http://www.excite.com**) or AltaVista (**http://www.altavista.com**) search for information about technologies such as ERP, CAD/CAM systems, or robotics. Find at least three suppliers for one of these technologies. Visit their Web sites and discuss how their clients are using their products to automate production.
5. Research either the Malcolm Baldrige National Quality Award or the ISO 9000 Quality Standards program on the Internet. Write an executive summary that explains the basic requirements and costs of participating. What are the benefits of participating? Include a brief example of a company that has participated and their experiences. Include a list of relevant Web site links for further reading.

Creative Thinking Case

With sales of 12.5 million units in less than a year, no one is questioning why designers of the sleek new Razr, Motorola's ultra-light, half-inch-thick cell phone, broke some internal rules in bringing the phone to market. Leaving their cubicles at the company's traditional research facility in suburban Libertyville, Illinois, Motorola engineers joined with designers and marketers at the company's downtown Chicago innovation lab known as Moto City. Open space and waist-high cubicles—for even senior executives—fostered team spirit and a breaking down of barriers, which contributed to the project's success. Customary practices like running new-product ideas past regional managers were bypassed. "We did not want to be distracted by the normal inputs we get," says Gary R. Weis, senior director of mechanical engineering. "It would not have allowed us to be as innovative."

Innovation labs are fast becoming a key element in the effort to revamp old-style research and development (R&D). In the past, scientists and engineers toiled away for years in pursuit of patents, then handed their work over to product developers and marketers for eventual shipment to consumers. But today's sophisticated production and operations technology, as well as ferocious competition, can mean new innovations grow old quickly, so companies must work fast to get products to market. To keep pace with consumer demand, Motorola has already introduced new colors for the Razr, as well as follow-on phones like the candy-bar-shaped Slvr and the rounded Pebl.

But the need for speed in innovation stretches beyond high-tech companies. Businesses as varied as Mattel, Boeing, Wrigley, Procter & Gamble, and even the Mayo Clinic also use such labs to shatter the bureaucratic barriers that existed among inventors, engineers, researchers, designers, marketers, and others. Now teams of people from different disciplines gather to focus on a problem—brainstorming, tinkering, and toying with different approaches—and generate answers to test on customers. Successful products are then sped to the market.

Although innovation labs are typically created to generate new-product ideas, they are also used to improve manufacturing processes. Large organizations have discovered that innovation labs can be a powerful tool for cutting through bureaucratic bloat. At Boeing Company, for instance, nearly 3,000 engineers and finance and program management staffers from scattered locations in the Renton, Washington, area were moved last year to the factory that assembles 737 jetliners. To urge people to mingle, Boeing created common break areas where mechanics and engineers could talk shop over coffee or a snack, building informal relationships that improved both daily working processes and innovations.

But innovation labs are not panaceas. If ideas that emerge from these facilities are flawed, the products will undoubtedly be failures. And some older workers, especially baby boomers, may have a hard time giving up cherished perks such as private offices. Yet for companies in a creative rut, innovation labs can be places where something magical gets started.

Critical Thinking Questions

- How do innovation labs contribute to successful production and operations management?
- In what significant ways do they differ from a more traditional research and development approach?
- What market conditions lead companies to use innovation labs?

Sources: Joseph Weber, Stanley Holmes, and Christopher Palmieri, "'Mosh Pits' of Creativity," *Business Week*, November 7, 2005, **http://www.businessweek.com**; Rebecca Fannin, "Unlocking Innovation: CEOs Are Learning How to Better Tap University R & D," *The Chief Executive*, June 2005, **http://findarticles.com**; Innovation Labs Web site, **http://www.innovationlabs.com** (May 22, 2006).

Exploring Business Careers

Deborah Butler is a certified Master Black Belt, but don't expect to see her working with Jet Li anytime soon. In fact, her job has little to do with martial arts. Employed by Caterpillar, "the world's leading manufacturer of construction and mining equipment, diesel and natural gas engines, and industrial gas turbines," Butler's Master Black Belt status reflects her expertise in Six Sigma: the process Cat employees use to continually manage, improve, and create processes, products, and services. "Sigma" refers to the maximum number of defects tolerated in production or service delivery; Six Sigma is the highest level of quality control, demanding no more than 3.4 defects per million parts. That means if you were to use Six Sigma in your college career, you would miss only *one half of a single question* in over four years of taking tests!

**Deborah Butler
Caterpillar**

Caterpillar was the first corporation to take Six Sigma global, deploying it corporate-wide in 2001 not only to its almost 300 facilities, but also eventually to every dealer and over 400 key suppliers throughout the world. The corporation hails the process as a key element of its overall operations management, attributing increased profits, improved customer service, and supply chain efficiency to Six Sigma.

Caterpillar's more than 300 Master Black Belts lead projects that use Six Sigma and train the company's approximately 3,300 Black Belts in the principles of the process. Butler is currently in charge of updating and implementing *Our Values in Action: Caterpillar's Worldwide Code of Conduct*. Outlining the four core values of Integrity, Excellence, Teamwork, and Commitment, the updated code of conduct embodies two important aspects of Caterpillar's philosophy on Six Sigma.

First, Caterpillar recognizes that employees are the heart of any operation. Therefore, Caterpillar employees use Six Sigma to improve as people and workers, as much as to improve the products they produce. The core values, reflected in a series of action statements such as "We put Integrity in action when we compete fairly," are the product of a yearlong development process involving Butler's global team. As part of the project research, the team interviewed thousands of Caterpillar employees, from officers of the company to production and hourly workers, for the purpose of, as Butler says, "bringing to the surface the values that have made Caterpillar a successful enterprise, enhancing behavioral expectations, and accurately expressing Caterpillar's corporate culture."

Caterpillar is not content simply to produce *Our Values in Action* and leave it at that, however, and the second aspect of its Six Sigma philosophy is that employees must bring the process to their lives. Butler has worked to inject the code of conduct's values into employee's day-to-day work. If an employee writes about safety-related changes, for example, she would not just list the changes. Instead, she might write first: "According to *Our Values In Action*, we put Commitment in action when we protect the health and safety of others and ourselves. As such, we are implementing the following changes. . . ." In this way, the code becomes a living part of corporate culture, a critical component of operations management.

Apple, Inc.
continuing case
Part 3: Managing the Business of Apple, Inc.

Apple has experienced a tumultuous life. Its periods of boom or bust have made Apple one of the most talked-about and written-about companies in history. At the beginning of the 1980 banner years, Apple offered its first sale of stock to the public. Other significant events in the 1980s included the introduction of the Macintosh (1984), and the move to desktop publishing with the Mac Plus and the LaserWriter (1986). Jumping ahead to the twenty-first century, the world is awash with Apple's iPod and iTunes, and the Web-surfing iPhone has transformed the mobile handset industry. In between, there were the somewhat abysmal bust periods in which the Lisa flopped (1983) and, 10 years later, when the company experienced an 84 percent drop in earnings. A major player in the management of business at Apple has been Steve Jobs. However, the company did experience a rash of CEOs in its attempt to pull itself out of the mid-1990s slump.

Fragmented Leadership

In the formative years, Apple was led by Steve Jobs, Steve Wozniak, and Mike Markkula. Not particularly interested in the corporate world and worth more than $100 million, Wozniak left the company around 1985 and discovered a new calling—educating youth. While remaining active in the corporate world, Mike Markkula has focused considerable energy on the world of ethics. Markkula and his wife provided the seed funding and endowment for the Markkula Center for Applied Ethics at Santa Clara University in California. Of the three, Jobs is the only one who remained active in the company.

Jobs led the company until 1985. At that time, the board replaced him with John Sculley. Jobs went on to found NeXT and Pixar. Sculley remained as Apple's CEO until 1993. In 1993, the board appointed Michael Spindler as CEO. Spindler held the position for two years, and then the board appointed Gilbert Amelio to the position. Amelio's term lasted until mid-1997, and Steve Jobs again took the helm. After regaining the leadership position at Apple, Jobs reinvigorated the company, introducing such innovative products as the iMac, iPod, iPhone, and MacBook Air.

The board of directors at Apple is a showcase of prominent individuals, including former U.S. vice president Al Gore. In 2004, however, the company was noted as one of 27 California-based Fortune 500 companies that did not have a woman on its board. The company did, however, fare well on the Corporate Equality Index. This index rates large corporations on the basis of policies that affect gay, lesbian, bisexual, and transgender employees. Apple scored perfectly on this index.

Mixed Employee Satisfaction

As the company experienced its roller coaster ride in the product and financial markets, the same appeared to be happening internally. In a 2005 survey conducted by the New York–based research firm Vault, Apple employees expressed mixed reactions to their workplace experiences. Vault conducted interviews of Apple employees in four major areas:

- Workplace (e.g., corporate culture, diversity, hours, dress code, opportunities for advancement),
- Interview and recruiting (e.g., number of rounds of interviews, who conducts interviews, interview questions),
- Salary and compensation (e.g., base salary, signing bonus, year-end bonuses, stock options, vacation time, perks, reimbursements), and
- Business outlook (e.g., competition, distribution channels, products and services, morale).

Responses to the survey were generally positive, except with respect to salary and compensation. Passion, which has always been a hallmark at Apple, was evident in the findings. This passion was exemplified in responses about the company culture, particularly with respect to the dress code, diversity issues, task variety, and belief in the company's products. Findings from those surveyed suggested that employees (e.g., product managers) were less than pleased with the lack of bonuses, raises, and stock options, as well as the inherent difficulties of climbing the corporate ladder. Findings from the Vault survey tended to corroborate a 2003 news story that reported on an incentive bonus program for executives at the director level or higher. This report noted that, although the company failed to reach its stated objectives, a special recognition bonus was approved for 230 executives (director level or higher, but excluding senior executive officers). The failure to meet the stated objectives was attributed to external economic and business conditions rather than employee performance. It was reported that lower-ranking employees were also eligible for bonuses, but within a reduced pool because the company had missed its company-wide targets.

Operations Strategies

Apple Computer was generally known for its lenient business philosophy, which included a hands-off approach exemplified in all aspects of its operations. However, this operational style did not match the management philosophies of either Spindler or Amelio, who were both considered to be no-nonsense operational managers. As operational managers, Spindler and Amelio focused on cost-cutting measures and simplification.

Although Spindler and Amelio attempted operational savings, it was only after Jobs reclaimed the helm that true operational savings were achieved. Jobs recognized that he was not the person to oversee a much-needed operational overhaul, so he brought in an operations expert who had considerable experience at Compaq Computer. In the second half of the 1990s, the company decided to hire outside organizations to perform many of its major business functions that had originally been performed by Apple employees. Called *outsourcing*, these agreements were made with SCI Systems (USA), Quanta (Taiwan), LG (Korea, Mexico, Wales), Alpha Top/GVC (Taiwan), and Hon Hai/Foxconn (China, Czech Republic). With these outsourcing agreements in place, purchased parts, work in progress, and finished-goods inventories were reduced dramatically.

In late 1998, to facilitate a new supply chain that involved both build-to-order systems and outsourcing, Apple began using i2 Technologies' Rhythm software to help improve sales forecasting, optimize production, and reduce costs. Additionally, the company adopted an *ERP (enterprise resource planning)* system from SAP, a computerized resource-planning system that incorporates information about the firm's suppliers and customers with its internally generated data. An ERP would allow the company to further reduce operational costs while improving customer service and ultimately increasing revenue. These systems enabled Apple to better link daily production to weekly sales forecasts and provide employees with clear goals and measures for evaluation.

Critical Thinking Questions

- Describe the tumultuous environment as related to CEO turnover at Apple.
- What was Steve Jobs's role during both stints as CEO?
- Why do people enjoy working at Apple even with the apparent compensation problems revealed in the 2005 employee survey?
- Why was Apple hesitant to outsource and install supply chain systems?
- What is an ERP?

Sources: "Apple's Steve Wozniak Is Reprogrammed—As a Grade School Teacher," **http://www.woz.org**, accessed on March 21, 2006; David Bovet and Joseph Martha, "Change at the Core," *Business 2.0,* November 28, 2000, pp. 278–79; Elizabeth Brown, "California Leads Nation in Naming Women to Boards," *San Francisco Business Times,* February 26, 2004, **http://www.bizjournals.com**, accessed on February 6, 2006; Peter Burrows and Ronald Grover, "Steve Jobs' Magic Kingdom," *BusinessWeek*, February 6, 2006, pp. 63–69; Peter Cohen, "Gay Advocacy Group Gives Apple Perfect Score," *Macworld,* August 14, 2002, **http://www.macworld.com**, accessed on February 6, 2006; Ian Fried, "Top Apple Employees Take Home Bonuses," *CNET News*, March 24, 2003, **http://news.cnet.com**, accessed on February 6, 2006; **http://www.scu.edu/ethics**, accessed on March 21, 2006; **http://www.vault.com**, accessed on March 21, 2006; Kasper Jade and Katie Marsal, "Employees Offer Mixed Reactions to Apple Corporate Life," *AppleInsider,* March 30, 2005, **http://www.appleinsider.com**, accessed on February 6, 2006; Jenny C. McCune, "Polishing the Apple," *Management Review,* September 1996, pp. 43–48; Joel West, "Apple Computer: The iCEO Seizes the Internet," Center for Research on Information Technology and Organizations, Paper 348, 2002, **http://repositories.cdlib.org**, accessed on December 6, 2005; David B. Yoffie and Yusi Wang, *Apple Computer 2002,* (Boston: Harvard Business School Press, October 2005).

© PhotoAlto/Getty Images

Marketing Management

PART 4

Chapter 11
Creating Products and Pricing Strategies to Meet Customers' Needs

Chapter 12
Distributing and Promoting Products and Services

Creating Products and Pricing Strategies to Meet Customers' Needs

CHAPTER 11

© iStockphoto.com/Sam Poon

"Like a Better Person"

Many of us have a "what-if" story we might like to daydream about from time to time. What if I had asked that special person out in high school? What if I had decided to major in anthropology instead of business? What if I had purchased that lottery ticket that just won somebody $43 million? After a confrontation with an angel named Cash, Jack Campbell, a highly successful and rich bachelor living in New York City, wakes up one morning to find himself living his "what-if" story. He no longer has untold wealth and power. Instead, he is a married man with two kids living in a suburban neighborhood and working for his father-in-law selling tires. Unable to return to his former life, he begrudgingly starts going through the motions of being a family man.

That is, until he comes across the suit. While on a family outing to the mall, Jack stumbles onto a suit that, as the salesperson states, "fits" his frame perfectly. He tries it on, telling the salesperson that he "might want to take an inch out of the back . . . and lengthen the sleeve" just as his wife and daughter come walking up. After Kate, his wife, acknowledges just how "amazing" he looks in the suit, Jack looks at himself in the mirror and states in a very deadpan manner, "It's an unbelievable thing . . . wearing this suit actually makes me feel like a better person." A moment later, he decides that he's going to buy the suit, which prompts Kate to look at the $2,400 price tag. After she says no, an argument ensues that allows him to rant about how disappointing his life is.

Customers make decisions about what to buy and what not to buy for a variety of different reasons. As we see in *The Family Man,* Jack Campbell is willing to lay down $2,400 for a suit that makes him look and feel better about who he is and how his life seems to be turning out. It is a suit that allows him to escape from the routine of his life. "I wake up in the morning covered in dog saliva. I drop the kids off, spend eight hours selling tires retail . . . retail, Kate. I pick the kids up, walk the dog . . . which, by the way, carries the added bonus of carting away her monstrous . . ." Well, you get the picture. His purchasing decision, in large part, is based around his own psychological needs.

Kate, however, says no, taking a more practical approach to the purchasing decision. Even though the suit looks, in her own words, "amazing" on her husband, one glance at the price tag shuts any thoughts of amazing out of her head. She based her decision on price relative to the family income. Later, however, she relents . . . in a way. "The Jack Campbell I married," she states, "wouldn't need a two thousand and four hundred dollar suit to feel better about his life, but I'm telling you . . . if that's what it's going to take, then buy it. We'll take the money out of the kids' college fund." She points out the absurdity of his purchasing decision and then reminds him of the actual cost associated with the $2,400 price tag, the deprivation of the children.

This clip also provides an excellent example of how consumer decisions are not made in a vacuum. Husbands and wives often make decisions together about items ranging from an expensive suit to a house to something as simple as the groceries purchased for family meals. We actually witness this process where each individual starts at essentially the same point—Jack looks great in the suit—but come to very different conclusions on whether or not to purchase it. Then a negotiation begins with Jack equating his $2,400 suit to the $25 pair of shoes Kate just purchased for their daughter, and eventually, a compromise is reached with Jack not buying the suit.

The following chapter provides an overview of marketing and marketing strategy, stressing the importance of understanding your customers and how they make decisions in the marketplace. As such, you will be introduced to such strategic notions as the marketing concept, creating a marketing strategy, market segmentation, and the use of marketing research to help determine what customers want and need as well as how to best fulfill those wants and needs. Furthermore, the chapter introduces the first two of marketing's four Ps—product and price—providing an overview of the strategies businesses utilize when developing their products and the prices that they will charge for those products.

BIZ FLIX

- The salesperson steps up to Jack and tells him the suit is perfect for his frame. What do you think was his strategy for approaching Jack in such a way?
- What important facet of marketing strategy did the salesperson fail to recognize when attempting to make the sale of the suit to Jack? Explain.
- Describe Jack's experience with the suit in terms of the marketing concept, and then describe Kate's experience with it. Now, what's Kate's experience with the marketing concept as it concerns the $25 Mary Janes she just purchased for their daughter.
- Based upon Jack's perception, how would you classify the product he wants to purchase? How do you think his wife would classify the product? How would you classify that product? Why are all three different?
- There are several product pricing strategies described in the chapter. Which one do you think best fits the price of the suit and why? Kate has purchased a $25 dollar pair of shoes for their daughter; what pricing strategy do you think best fits the price of the shoes and why?

This chapter looks at the nature of marketing and the creation of product and pricing strategies to meet customers' needs.

Marketing plays a key role in the success of businesses. It is the task of marketing to generate sales for the firm. Sales revenue, in turn, pays workers' salaries, buys supplies, covers the costs of new buildings and equipment, and hopefully enables the company to earn a profit. In this chapter, you will learn about the marketing concept, marketing strategies, and consumer and business buying decisions. You will also see how the marketing mix is used to create sales opportunities. We discuss how new products are created and how they go through periods of sales growth and then decline. Next you will discover how managers set prices to reach organizational goals.

Marketing is the process of getting the right goods or services to the right people at the right place, time, and price, using the right promotion techniques. This concept is referred to as the "*right*" *principle*. We can say that **marketing** is finding out the needs and wants of potential buyers and customers and then providing goods and services that meet or exceed their expectations. Marketing is about creating exchanges. An **exchange** takes place when two parties give something of value to each other to satisfy their respective needs. In a typical exchange, a consumer trades money for a good or service.

To encourage exchanges, marketers follow the "right" principle. If your local Avon rep doesn't have the right lipstick for you when you want it, at the right price, you will not exchange money for a new lipstick from Avon. Think about the last exchange (purchase) you made: What if the price had been 30 percent higher? What if the store or other source had been less accessible? Would you have bought anything? The "right" principle tells us that marketers control many factors that determine marketing success.

The Marketing Concept

If you study today's best organizations, you'll see that they have adopted the **marketing concept**, which involves identifying consumer needs and then producing the goods or services that will satisfy them while making a profit. The marketing concept is oriented toward pleasing consumers by offering value. Specifically, the marketing concept involves the following:

- Focusing on customer wants so the organization can distinguish its product(s) from competitors' offerings.
- Integrating all of the organization's activities, including production, to satisfy these wants.
- Achieving long-term goals for the organization by satisfying customer wants and needs legally and responsibly.

Today, companies of every size in all industries are applying the marketing concept. Enterprise Rent-A-Car found that its customers didn't want to have to drive to its offices. Therefore, Enterprise began delivering vehicles to customers' homes or places of work. Disney found that some of its patrons really disliked waiting in lines. In response, Disney began offering FastPass at a premium price, which allows patrons to avoid standing in long lines waiting for attractions.

Despite the notion that the marketing concept is an important key to a firm's long-term success, not all companies follow it. A survey of executives in America, Europe, Asia, and Africa found that

marketing
The process of discovering the needs and wants of potential buyers and customers and then providing goods and services that meet or exceed their expectations.

exchange
The process in which two parties give something of value to each other to satisfy their respective needs.

1 What are the marketing concept and relationship building?

marketing concept
Identifying consumer needs and then producing the goods or services that will satisfy them while making a profit for the organization.

50 percent weren't truly committed to the customer![1] If a firm is not completely focused on the needs of its customers, it will often produce goods and services that can't be sold. For example, General Motors has lost its leadership in the U.S. market to Toyota. American car manufacturers have historically not built cars to suit customers' tastes. Instead, they produce vehicles that make sense for their plants and then use incentives and rebates to attract buyers.[2]

One large firm that fully understands the marketing concept is Tesco, one of the top three retailers in the world and the leading supermarket chain in the United Kingdom. Tesco accounts for approximately $1.80 out of every $14.44 spent at a UK retailer. The company didn't achieve its leading status by accident, but by intently focusing on its customers. Two core values govern how Tesco does business.

- No one tries harder for customers: This means understanding customers better than competitors and delivering unbeatable value. It requires being energetic and innovative, and taking care of staff so it can take care of customers.
- Treating people how we like to be treated: The members of a Tesco team trust, respect, and support each other, and make the very best effort for customers.[3]

Customer Value

Customer value is the ratio of benefits to the sacrifice necessary to obtain those benefits. The customer determines the value of both the benefits and the sacrifices. Creating customer value is a core business strategy of many successful firms. Customer value is rooted in the belief that price is not the only thing that matters. A business that focuses on the cost of production and price to the customer will be managed as though it were providing a commodity differentiated only by price. In contrast, businesses that provide customer value believe that many customers will pay a premium for superior customer service or accept fewer services for a value price. Southwest Airlines, the budget carrier, historically has delivered what it promises: on-time departures. In "service value" surveys, Southwest routinely beats the full-service airlines like American Airlines that actually provide passengers with luxuries like movies and food on selected long-haul flights. Yet times are changing and so must Southwest. Their new strategy is discussed in the Managing Change box on the next page.

CONCEPT **in action**

© Courtesy of GEICO

GEICO—the major auto insurer with the scaly mascot—famously boasts a 97 percent customer-satisfaction rating. Although the firm's claim may be exaggerated a bit, consumers get the message that GEICO delivers quality insurance coverage at low prices. In what way does the company's quirky and ubiquitous advertising—in which customers claim to have saved a bunch of money on car insurance by switching to GEICO—influence customers' service expectations?

Customer Satisfaction

Customer satisfaction is a theme that we have stressed throughout the text. **Customer satisfaction** is the customer's feeling that a product has met or exceeded expectations. Lexus consistently wins awards for its outstanding customer satisfaction. JD Powers and Associates surveys car owners two years after they make their purchase. The Customer Satisfaction Survey is made up of four measures that each describe an element of overall ownership satisfaction at two years: vehicle quality/reliability, vehicle appeal, ownership costs, and service satisfaction from a dealer. Lexus continues to lead the industry and has been America's top-ranked vehicle for five years in a row.[4]

Building Relationships

Relationship marketing is a strategy that focuses on forging long-term partnerships with customers. Companies build relationships with customers by offering value and providing customer satisfaction. Companies benefit from repeat sales and referrals that lead to increases in sales, market share, and profits. Costs fall because it is less expensive to serve existing customers than to attract new ones. Keeping a customer costs about one-fourth of what it costs to attract a new customer and the probability of retaining a customer is over 60 percent, whereas the probability of landing a new customer is less than 30 percent.

Customers also benefit from stable relationships with suppliers. Business buyers have found that partnerships with their suppliers are essential to producing high-quality products while cutting costs. Customers remain loyal to firms that provide them greater value and satisfaction than they expect from competing firms.

Frequent-buyer clubs are an excellent way to build long-term relationships. All major airlines have frequent-flyer programs. After you fly a certain number of miles you become eligible for

JetBlue and Southwest Airlines Target the Business Set

To enhance its appeal to business travelers, one airline began installing work desks with power outlets in boarding areas and created a new fare, dubbed Business Select, that lets business travelers buy their way to the best seats, even if booking at the last minute. Which carrier? Southwest Airlines Co., which used to pride itself on one-size-fits-all bare-bones service. Faced with slowing growth and higher costs, discount carriers like Southwest and JetBlue Airways Corp. are making a new push for business travelers, adding flights in heavily traveled business routes and even quietly offering special deals.

With the economy struggling, discounters see new opportunities among business travelers. Low-fare airlines have historically done well with corporate customers during recessions as travel budgets get pinched. At the same time, with fares higher because of fuel costs, Southwest and JetBlue can't stimulate as much leisure travel with low fares, so they have to resort to trying to grab customers from incumbent airlines. "When you can't rely as much on market stimulation and have to steal share from other airlines, you have to be relevant to business travelers," says Donald Uselmann, manager of sales products at JetBlue.

JetBlue recently began offering a fully refundable fare to attract more business-travel customers. Previously, all the airline's fares were nonrefundable, subject to a $25 change fee. But some companies told JetBlue they let employees travel only on refundable fares. Some road warriors change plans an average of four times before takeoff. "There's part of the market we hadn't been reaching," says Noreen Courtney-Wilds, JetBlue's vice president of sales. JetBlue also strengthened its relationship with corporate America. It rejoined the centralized computer reservation systems used by corporate travel departments. For a time, it had tried to route all bookings through its Web site. The airline also teamed up with American Express Co. to offer a small-business credit card with flight benefits. Later this year, JetBlue says it will launch a new incentive program aimed at midsize corporate accounts.

Southwest has also tweaked its boarding process to appeal to business travelers. The airline used to board passengers in three mass groups—a cattle-call system that irritated many road warriors. The new boarding system assigns customers a boarding number, holding back the lowest numbers for Business Select customers so they get first pick of seats. That's still a long way from assigned seating that many business travelers prefer, Michael Boyd, an aviation consultant, notes, "but is no longer as reminiscent of lunchtime at the feedlot." Southwest began selling Business Select tickets in late 2007. Besides giving buyers a spot at the front of a flight's boarding line, it also gives extra frequent-flier program credit and a coupon for a cocktail in-flight. Business Select tickets typically cost $30 to $50 more per round trip than Southwest's regular unrestricted, fully refundable fares. Southwest estimated Business Select generated $100 million in added revenue in 2009.[5]

Critical Thinking Questions
- Southwest has always done well with bare-bones service and low prices. Should they simply stick with the old strategy? Why or why not?
- Do you think that Southwest and JetBlue should begin flying to Europe? Why?

---

a free ticket. Now, cruise lines, hotels, car rental agencies, credit card companies, and even mortgage companies give away "airline miles" with purchases. Consumers patronize the airline and its partners because they want the free tickets. Thus, the program helps to create a long-term relationship with the customer. Southwest Airlines carries their loyalty program a bit further than most. Members get birthday cards and some even get profiled in the airline's in-flight magazine!

The hottest way to determine if a company is satisfying customers and building relationships is called the "net promoter score." It is explained in the Customer Satisfaction and Quality box on the next page.

CONCEPT check

Explain the marketing concept.

Explain the difference between customer value and customer satisfaction.

What is meant by relationship marketing?

Creating a Marketing Strategy

2 How do managers create a marketing strategy?

environmental scanning
The process in which a firm continually collects and evaluates information about its external environment.

Unless marketing managers understand the external environment, a firm cannot intelligently plan for the future. Thus, many organizations assemble a team of specialists to continually collect and evaluate environmental information, a process called **environmental scanning**. The goal in gathering the environmental data is to identify future market opportunities and threats.

Computer manufacturers understand the importance of environmental scanning to monitor rapidly changing consumer interests. Since the invention of the PC, techies have taken two things for granted: processor speeds will grow exponentially, and PCs will become indistinguishable from televisions—that there will be, in industry lingo, convergence. The first prediction obviously has come true, and the second is beginning. Apple has been a clear winner in the past few years. Continuous innovation will create new opportunities for firms such as Dell, HP, Lenovo, and others.

In general, six categories of environmental data shape marketing decisions:

- *Social forces* such as the values of potential customers and the changing roles of families and women working outside the home.

© Digital Vision/Getty Images

The Net Promoter Score Helps Measure Loyalty and Satisfaction

It has been called "the holy grail of business growth." What is it? A simple measure called the net promoter score (NPS). The theory says a firm can measure customer loyalty by asking one simple question rather than relying on lengthy satisfaction surveys: "On a scale of zero to 10, how likely is it that you would recommend us to your friends or colleagues?"

The article showed that "net promoter scores," which measure the difference between the percentage of customers who give high responses ("promoters") and those who give low ones ("detractors"), correlate closely with a company's revenue growth. Promoters are defined as customers who give the company 9 or 10, while detractors hand out 0 through 6. Customers who log 7 or 8 are deemed "passively satisfied" and aren't calculated in the final score.

Fred Reichheld, the creator of the NPS, has presented research data that shows that NPS is better than other measures in linking the firm to growth. In other words, high NPS equates to high growth and vice versa. Not only is NPS linked to growth of a firm, but it is also easy to understand and simple to measure. Some of America's biggest firms have jumped on the NPS bandwagon, including GE, Allianz, Intuit, eBay, Enterprise Rent-A-Car, Four Seasons Hotels, and many others. Some firms have even redesigned their executive compensation systems to reward managers for achieving higher NPSs.

General Electric has found that "promoters" had an 84 percent higher likelihood for repeat business. The firm uses NPS to drive process excellence for its customers. Procter & Gamble uses NPS to measure the health of its brands. Verizon Wireless uses it in its call centers and retail stores.

The net promoter score concept is not without its detractors. Some say that it is too easy and companies won't do follow-up research to understand what is going right or wrong. Other researchers say that they tried to replicate Reichheld's work and could not. They say that NPS is not an indicator or predictor of growth. Yet other researchers claim that they did find a fundamental relationship between NPS and competitive growth rates. And so the controversy continues.[6]

Critical Thinking Questions

- Do you think a company should only use NPS as its measure of loyalty and customer satisfaction? Why?
- Is it fair to tie an executive's compensation to NPS? Why or why not?

- *Demographic forces* such as the ages, birth and death rates, and locations of various groups of people.
- *Economic forces* such as changing incomes, inflation, and recession.
- *Technological forces* such as advances in communications and data retrieval capabilities.
- *Political and legal forces* such as changes in laws and regulatory agency activities.
- *Competitive forces* from domestic and foreign-based firms.

target market
The specific group of consumers toward which a firm directs its marketing efforts.

Defining the Target Market

Managers and employees focus on providing value for a well-defined target market. The **target market** is the specific group of consumers toward which a firm directs its marketing efforts. It is selected from the larger overall market. Quaker Oats targets its grits to blue-collar consumers in the South. The Limited, Inc. has several different types of stores, each for a distinct target market: Express for trendy younger women, Lerner for budget-conscious women, Lane Bryant and Roaman's for full-size women, and Henri Bendel's for upscale, high-fashion women. These target markets are all part of the overall market for women's clothes.

Correctly defining the target market is critical to creating a successful marketing strategy. Developing a marketing strategy for the wrong target market is a recipe for disaster. Robert Fisher, chief executive officer of Gap, notes that poor sales over the past few years was due to a vague definition of its target market.[7] Marka Hansen, president of the Gap brand, said, "The Gap brand had defined its customer as 18 to 35 years old, an overly broad target that confused designers and merchants within the company and didn't fit today's niche-focused marketplace."[8] She noted that "Gap will narrow the specific target market within the 18-to-35 range and it will clearly not be the 18-year-old."[9]

Concentrating on potential customers lets the firm use its resources efficiently. The target markets for Marriott International's lodging alternatives are shown in Exhibit 11.1 on the next page.

Creating a Competitive Advantage

A **competitive advantage**, also called a *differential advantage*, is a set of unique features of a company and its products that are perceived by the target market as significant and superior to those of the competition. As Andrew Grove, former CEO of Intel, says, "You have to understand what it is you are better at than anybody else and mercilessly focus your efforts on it." Competitive

CONCEPT in action

© Vanderlei Almeida/AFP/getty Images

Harley-Davidson is revving up efforts to attract women into its motorcycling ranks. To woo this formerly overlooked half of the population, the iconic manufacturer has begun producing smaller Harley models with narrower seats, softer clutches, and easy-adjust handlebars. Apparel lines have expanded beyond traditional black and orange to include bright colors with glitzy rhinestones. Even dealerships have received a makeover: motorcycle outlets now include child-play areas, attractive landscaping, clean bathrooms, and regular "garage parties." How might defining a target market lead to more effective marketing strategies?

competitive advantage
A set of unique features of a company and its products that are perceived by the target market as significant and superior to those of the competition; also called differential advantage.

EXHIBIT 11.1   The Target Markets for Marriott International

	Price Range	Target Market
Fairfield Inn	$45–65	Economizing business and leisure travelers
TownePlace Suites	$55–70	Moderate-tier travelers who stay three to four weeks
SpringHill Suites	$75–95	Business and leisure travelers looking for more space and amenities
Courtyard	$75–105	Travelers seeking quality and affordable accommodations designed for the road warrior
Residence Inn	$85–110	Travelers seeking a residential-style hotel
Marriott Hotels, Resorts, and Suites	$90–235	Grounded achievers who desire consistent quality
Renaissance Hotels and Resorts	$90–235	Discerning business and leisure travelers who seek creative attention to detail
Ritz-Carlton	$175–300	Senior executives and entrepreneurs looking for a unique, luxury, personalized experience

advantage is the factor or factors that cause customers to patronize a firm and not the competition. There are three types of competitive advantage: cost, product/service differentiation, and niche.

Cost Competitive Advantage

cost competitive advantage
A firm's ability to produce a product or service at a lower cost than all other competitors in an industry while maintaining satisfactory profit margins.

A firm that has a **cost competitive advantage** can produce a product or service at a lower cost than all its competitors while maintaining satisfactory profit margins. Firms become cost leaders by obtaining inexpensive raw materials, making plant operations more efficient, designing products for ease of manufacture, controlling overhead costs, and avoiding marginal customers.

Over time, the cost competitive advantage may fail. Typically, if one firm is using an innovative technology to reduce its costs, then other firms in the industry will adopt this technology and reduce their costs as well. For example, Bell Labs invented fiber-optic cables that reduced the cost of voice and data transmission by dramatically increasing the number of calls that could be transmitted simultaneously through a two-inch cable. Within five years, however, fiber-optic technology had spread through the industry and Bell Labs lost its cost competitive advantage. Firms may also lose their cost competitive advantage if competing firms match their low costs by using the same lower-cost suppliers. Therefore, a cost competitive advantage may not offer a long-term competitive advantage.

Product/Service Differentiation Competitive Advantage

differential competitive advantage
A firm's ability to provide a unique product or service with a set of features that the target market perceives as important and better than the competitor's.

A firm with **differential competitive advantage** is able to provide a unique product or service with a set of features that the target market perceives as important and better than the competition's. Because cost competitive advantages are subject to continual erosion, product/service differentiation tends to provide a longer lasting competitive advantage. The durability of a differential competitive advantage tends to make this strategy more attractive to many top managers. Common differential advantages are brand names (Tide detergent), a strong dealer network (Caterpillar Tractor for construction equipment), product reliability (Lexus cars), image (Neiman Marcus in retailing), and service (Four Seasons Hotels). Brand names such as Chanel, BMW, and Cartier stand for quality the world over. Through continual product and marketing innovations and attention to quality and value, managers at these organizations have created enduring competitive advantages.

Niche Competitive Advantage

niche competitive advantage
A firm's ability to target and effectively serve a single segment of the market, often within a limited geographic area.

A company with a **niche competitive advantage** targets and effectively serves a single segment of the market. For small companies with limited resources that potentially face giant competitors, "niche-ing" may be the only viable option. A market segment that has good growth potential but is not crucial to the success of major competitors is a good candidate for a niche strategy. Once a potential segment has been identified, the firm needs to make certain it can defend against challengers through its superior ability to serve buyers in the segment. For example, STI Music Private Bank follows a niche strategy with its concentration on country music stars and entertainment industry professionals in Nashville. Its office is in the heart of Nashville's music district. STI has decided to expand its niche strategy to Miami, the "epicenter" of Latin music, and Atlanta. The latter is a longtime rhythm-and-blues capital and now is the center of contemporary "urban" music. Both new markets have the kinds of music professionals—entertainers, record executives, producers, agents, and others—that have made STI so successful in Nashville.

Online dating is a huge and highly competitive business. For example, eHarmony has 17 million registered users. In 2008, there were more than 40 million people looking for love online. In order to compete, Spark Networks has followed a niche strategy. It offers online matchups for small groups that share certain affinities. For instance, Spark has sites for Jewish singles, Seventh-day Adventists, Mormons, Baptists, seniors, deaf singles, and heavyset persons.[10]

CONCEPT check

What is environmental scanning?

What is a target market, and why should a company have one?

Explain the three types of competitive advantages and provide examples of each.

Developing a Marketing Mix

Once a firm has defined its target market and identified its competitive advantage, it can create the **marketing mix**, that is, the blend of product offering, pricing, promotional methods, and distribution system that brings a specific group of consumers superior value. Distribution is sometimes referred to as *place*, so the marketing mix is based on the **four Ps**: product, price, promotion, and place. Every target market requires a unique marketing mix to satisfy the needs of the target consumers and meet the firm's goals. A strategy must be constructed for each of the four Ps and blended with the strategies for the other elements. Thus, the marketing mix is only as good as its weakest part. An excellent product with a poor distribution system could be doomed to failure. A successful marketing mix requires careful tailoring. For instance, at first glance you might think that McDonald's and Wendy's have roughly the same marketing mix. After all, they are both in the fast-food business. But McDonald's targets parents with young children through Ronald McDonald, heavily promoted children's Happy Meals, and playgrounds. Wendy's is targeted to a more adult crowd. Wendy's has no playgrounds but it does have carpeting in many stores (a more adult atmosphere) and has expanded its menu to include items for adult tastes.

3 What is the marketing mix?

marketing mix
The blend of product offering, pricing, promotional methods, and distribution system that brings a specific group of consumers superior value.

four Ps
Product, price, promotion, and place (distribution), which together make up the marketing mix.

Product Strategy

Marketing strategy typically starts with the product. You can't plan a distribution system or set a price if you don't know what you're going to market. Marketers use the term *product* to refer to both *goods*, such as tires, MP3 players, and clothing, and *services*, such as hotels, hair salons, and restaurants. Thus, the heart of the marketing mix is the good or service. Creating a **product strategy** involves choosing a brand name, packaging, colors, a warranty, accessories, and a service program.

Marketers view products in a much larger context than you might imagine. They include not only the item itself but also the brand name and the company image. The names Ralph Lauren and Gucci, for instance, create extra value for everything from cosmetics to bath towels. That is, products with those names sell at higher prices than identical products without the names. We buy things not only for what they do, but also for what they mean.

CONCEPT in action

With their computerized profile-matching capabilities, online dating services are a high-tech way to make a love connection. Today's date-seeking singles want more than automated personals, however. They want advice from experts. At Match.com, popular shrink Dr. Phil guides subscribers toward healthy relationships. At eHarmony.com, Dr. Neil Clark Warren helps the lovelorn find soul mates. How do Internet dating services use various elements of the marketing mix to bolster the effectiveness of their product strategies?

© Michael Caulfield/WireImage/Getty Images

Pricing Strategy

Pricing strategy is based on demand for the product and the cost of producing it. Some special considerations can also influence the price. Sometimes, for instance, a special introductory price is used to get people to try a new product. Some firms enter the market with low prices and keep them low, such as Carnival Cruise Lines and Suzuki cars. Others enter a market with very high prices and then lower them over time, such as producers of high-definition televisions and personal computers.

product strategy
Taking the good or service and selecting a brand name, packaging, colors, a warranty, accessories, and a service program.

pricing strategy
Setting a price based on the demand for and cost of a good or service.

Distribution Strategy

Distribution strategy is creating the means (the channel) by which a product flows from the producer to the consumer. One aspect of distribution strategy is deciding how many stores and which specific wholesalers and retailers will handle the product in a geographic area. Cosmetics, for instance, are distributed in many different ways. Avon has a sales force of several hundred thousand representatives who call directly on consumers. Clinique and Estée Lauder are distributed through selected department stores. Cover Girl and Del Laboratories use mostly chain drugstores

distribution strategy
Creating the means by which products flow from the producer to the consumer.

and other mass merchandisers. Redken sells through beauticians. Revlon uses several of these distribution channels.

Promotion Strategy

promotion strategy
The unique combination of personal selling, advertising, publicity, and sales promotion to stimulate the target market to buy a product or service.

Many people feel that promotion is the most exciting part of the marketing mix. **Promotion strategy** covers personal selling, advertising, public relations, and sales promotion. Each element is coordinated with the others to create a promotional blend. An advertisement, for instance, helps a buyer get to know the company and paves the way for a sales call. A good promotion strategy can dramatically increase a firm's sales.

Public relations plays a special role in promotion. It is used to create a good image of the company and its products. Bad publicity costs nothing to send out, but it can cost a firm a great deal in lost business. Good publicity, such as a television or magazine story about a firm's new product, may be the result of much time, money, and effort spent by a public relations department.

Sales promotion directly stimulates sales. It includes trade shows, catalogs, contests, games, premiums, coupons, and special offers. McDonald's discount coupons and contests offering money and food prizes are examples of sales promotions.

Not-for-Profit Marketing

Profit-oriented companies are not the only ones that analyze the marketing environment, find a competitive advantage, and create a marketing mix. The application of marketing principles and techniques is also vital to not-for-profit organizations. Marketing helps not-for-profit groups identify target markets and develop effective marketing mixes. In some cases, marketing has kept symphonies, museums, and other cultural groups from having to close their doors. In other organizations, such as the American Heart Association, marketing ideas and techniques have helped

CONCEPT check

What is meant by the marketing mix?

What are the components of the marketing mix?

How can marketing techniques help not-for-profit organizations?

managers do their jobs better. In the private sector, the profit motive is both an objective for guiding decisions and a criterion for evaluating results. Not-for-profit organizations do not seek to make a profit for redistribution to owners or shareholders. Rather, their focus is often on generating enough funds to cover expenses. For example, the Methodist Church does not gauge its success by the amount of money left in offering plates. The Museum of Science and Industry does not base its performance evaluations on the dollar value of tokens put into the turnstile.

Buyer Behavior

4 How do consumers and organizations make buying decisions?

buyer behavior
The actions people take in buying and using goods and services.

An organization cannot reach its goals without understanding buyer behavior. **Buyer behavior** is the actions people take in buying and using goods and services. Marketers who understand buyer behavior, such as how a price increase will affect a product's sales, can create a more effective marketing mix.

To understand buyer behavior, marketers must understand how consumers make buying decisions. The consumer decision-making process has several steps, which are shown in Exhibit 11.2. The entire process is affected by cultural, social, individual, and psychological factors. The buying process starts with need recognition. This may be as simple as running out of coffee. Yes, I need to purchase more coffee. Or perhaps you recently got married and recognize that you need to start building equity instead of paying rent. Perhaps you are also considering starting a family. Therefore, you decide to buy your first home (Step 1 in Exhibit 11.2).

Next, you begin to gather information about financing, available homes, styles, locations, and so forth (Step 2). After you feel that you have gathered enough information, you begin to evaluate alternatives (Step 3). For example, you might eliminate all homes that cost over $250,000 or are more than a 30-minute drive to your work. Then an offer is made and, if it is accepted, a purchase is made (Step 4). Finally, you assess the experience and your level of satisfaction with your new home (Step 5).

Influences on Consumer Decision Making

Cultural, social, individual, and psychological factors have an impact on consumer decision making from the time a person recognizes a need through postpurchase behavior. We will examine each of these in more detail.

culture
The set of values, ideas, attitudes, and other symbols created to shape human behavior.

Culture Purchase roles within the family are influenced by culture. **Culture** is the set of values, ideas, attitudes, and symbols created to shape human behavior. Culture is environmentally oriented.

EXHIBIT 11.2 Consumer Decision-Making Process

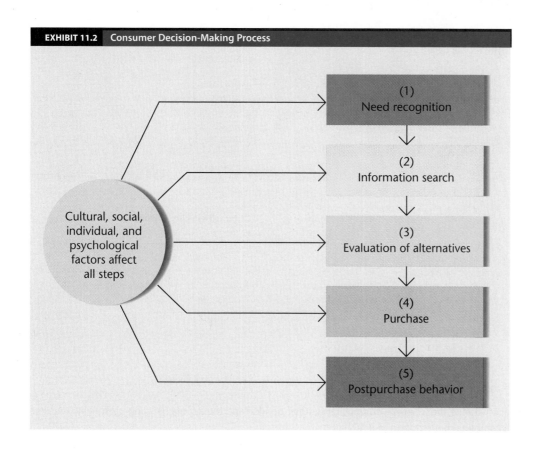

The nomads of Finland have developed a culture for Arctic survival. Similarly, the natives of the Brazilian jungle have created a culture suitable for jungle living.

Culture by definition is social in nature. It is human interaction that creates values and prescribes acceptable behavior. Thus, culture gives order to society by creating common expectations. Sometimes these expectations are codified into law; for example, if you come to a red light, you stop the car. As long as a value or belief meets the needs of society, it will remain part of the culture; if it is no longer functional, the value or belief recedes. The value that very large families are "good" is no longer held by a majority of Americans. Because Americans live in an urban rather than a rural environment, children are no longer needed to perform farm chores.

Understanding cultural factors when selling a product abroad can make or break a marketing strategy. We explain how in the Expanding Around the Globe box on the next page.

Social Factors

Most consumers are likely to seek out the opinions of others to reduce their search and evaluation effort or uncertainty, especially as the perceived risk of the decision increases. Consumers may also seek out others' opinions for guidance on new products or services, products with image-related attributes, or products where attribute information is lacking or uninformative. Specifically, consumers interact socially with reference groups, opinion leaders, and family members to obtain product information and decision approval. All the formal and informal groups that influence the buying behavior of an individual are that person's **reference groups**. Consumers may use products or brands to identify with or become a member of a group. They learn from observing how members of their reference groups consume, and they use the same criteria to make their own consumer decisions. A reference group might be a fraternity or sorority, a group you work with, or a club to which you belong.

Individual Influences on Consumer Buying Decisions

A person's buying decisions are also influenced by personal characteristics that are unique to each individual, such as gender and personality. Individual characteristics are generally stable over the course of one's life.

CONCEPT in action

© Charley Gallay/Getty Images

"Guitar Hero" is no mere game: it's a sensation. "Legends of Rock," the latest release in Activision's red-hot video game franchise, transforms the most unmusical of gamers into virtual rock gods. With guitar-shaped controllers firmly in hand, players hammer out solos against friends, trade licks with Slash from Guns N' Roses, and square off against that most diabolical of all axe masters, the Devil. Teens and adults alike host neighborhood Guitar Hero parties to see who can kick out the hottest jams. Why do some products develop into popular fads and crazes?

reference groups
Formal and informal groups that influence buyer behavior.

Chapter 11: Creating Products and Pricing Strategies to Meet Customers' Needs

Understanding Foreign Cultures Is a Key to Marketing Success

A U.S. luggage manufacturer found out that culture also affects thinking and perception. The company designed a new Middle East advertising campaign around the image of its luggage being carried on a magic flying carpet. Many of the participants in a group in a marketing research study thought they were seeing advertising for Samsonite *carpets*. Green Giant learned that it could not use its Jolly Green Giant in parts of Asia where wearing a green hat signifies that a man has an unfaithful wife.

Making successful sales presentations abroad requires a thorough understanding of the country's culture. Germans, for example, don't like risk and need strong reassurance. A successful presentation to a German client will emphasize three points: the bottom-line benefits of the product or service, that there will be strong service support, and that the product is guaranteed. In southern Europe, it is an insult to show a price list. Without negotiating, you will not close the sale. The English want plenty of documentation for product claims and are less likely to simply accept the word of the sales representative. Scandinavian and Dutch companies are more likely to approach business transactions as Americans do than are companies in any other country. Yet, sometimes Scandinavians will finish day-long meetings in the sauna—in the nude—in accordance with local custom.

The clothes that one wears can either enhance a relationship with a foreign client or, in some cases, insult him or her. For example, many Hindus in India may be offended by your finely tooled leather belt and briefcase. Some shades of yellow are reserved for the royal families to wear in Malaysia, and white is the color of mourning in parts of Asia.

Critical Thinking Questions
- Some consultants say that a firm should never enter a country without first understanding its culture. Would you agree? Why?
- Why might understanding the cultural impact of colors be important to a company like PepsiCo? Levi Strauss? Ikea?

© Digital Vision/Getty Images

For instance, most people do not change their gender, and the act of changing personality requires a complete reorientation of one's life.

Physiological differences between men and women result in different needs, such as health and beauty products. Just as important are the distinct cultural, social, and economic roles played by men and women and the effects that these have on their decision-making processes. Men and women also shop differently. Studies show that men and women share similar motivations in terms of where to shop—that is, seeking reasonable prices, merchandise quality, and a friendly, low-pressure environment—but they don't necessarily feel the same about shopping in general. Most women enjoy shopping; their male counterparts claim to dislike the experience and shop only out of necessity. Furthermore, men desire simple shopping experiences, stores with less variety, and convenience.

personality
A way of organizing and grouping how an individual reacts to situations.

Each consumer has a unique personality. **Personality** is a broad concept that can be thought of as a way of organizing and grouping how an individual typically reacts to situations. Thus, personality combines psychological makeup and environmental forces. It includes people's underlying dispositions, especially their most dominant characteristics. Although personality is one of the least useful concepts in the study of consumer behavior, some marketers believe that personality influences the types and brands of products purchased. For instance, the type of car, clothes, or jewelry a consumer buys may reflect one or more personality traits.

Psychological Influences on Consumer Buying Decisions
An individual's buying decisions are further influenced by psychological factors such as perception, beliefs, and attitudes. These factors are what consumers use to interact within their world. They are the tools consumers use to recognize their feelings, gather and analyze information, formulate thoughts and opinions, and take action. Unlike the other three influences on consumer behavior, psychological influences can be affected by a person's environment because they are applied on specific occasions. For example, you will perceive different stimuli and process these stimuli in different ways, depending on whether you are sitting in class concentrating on the instructor, sitting outside of class talking to friends, or sitting in your dorm room watching television.

Business-to-Business Purchase Decision Making

Business buyer behavior and business markets are different from consumer markets. Business markets include institutions such as hospitals and schools, manufacturers, wholesalers and retailers, and various branches of government. The key difference between a consumer product and a business product is the intended use. If you purchase a certain model of Dell computer for your home so you can surf the Internet, it is a consumer good. If a purchasing agent for MTV buys exactly the same computer for an MTV script writer, it is a business good. Why? The reason is that MTV is a business, so the computer will be used in a business environment.

Characteristics of the Business-to-Business Market
The main differences between consumer markets and business markets are as follows:

1. *Purchase volume.* Business customers buy in much larger quantities than consumers. Think how many truckloads of sugar Mars must purchase to make one day's output of M&Ms. Imagine the number of batteries Sears buys each day for resale to consumers. Think of the number of pens the federal government must use each day.

2. *Number of customers.* Business marketers usually have far fewer customers than consumer marketers. As a result, it is much easier to identify prospective buyers and monitor current needs. Think about how few customers for airplanes or industrial cranes there are compared to the more than 80 million consumer households in the United States.

3. *Location of buyers.* Business customers tend to be much more geographically concentrated than consumers. The computer industry is concentrated in Silicon Valley and a few other areas. Aircraft manufacturing is found in Seattle, St. Louis, and Dallas/Fort Worth. Suppliers to these manufacturers often locate close to the manufacturers to lower distribution costs and facilitate communication.

4. *Direct distribution.* Business sales tend to be made directly to the buyer because such sales frequently involve large quantities or custom-made items like heavy machinery. Consumer goods are more likely to be sold through intermediaries like wholesalers and retailers.

CONCEPT check

Explain the consumer decision-making process.

How do business markets differ from consumer markets?

Market Segmentation

The study of buyer behavior helps marketing managers better understand why people make purchases. To identify the target markets that may be most profitable for the firm, managers use **market segmentation**, which is the process of separating, identifying, and evaluating the layers of a market to identify a target market. For instance, a target market might be segmented into two groups: families with children and families without children. Families with young children are likely to buy hot cereals and presweetened cereals. Families with no children are more likely to buy health-oriented cereals. You can be sure that cereal companies plan their marketing mixes with this difference in mind. A business market may be segmented by large customers and small customers or by geographic area.

The five basic forms of consumer market segmentation are demographic, geographic, psychographic, benefit, and volume. Their characteristics are summarized in Exhibit 11.3 and discussed in the following sections.

Demographic Segmentation

Demographic segmentation uses categories such as age, education, gender, income, and household size to differentiate among markets. This form of market segmentation is the most

5 What are the five basic forms of market segmentation?

market segmentation
The process of separating, identifying, and evaluating the layers of a market in order to identify a target market.

demographic segmentation
The differentiation of markets through the use of categories such as age, education, gender, income, and household size.

EXHIBIT 11.3	Forms of Consumer Market Segmentation
Form	**General Characteristics**
Demographic segmentation	Age, education, gender, income, race, social class, household size
Geographic segmentation	Regional location (e.g., New England, Mid-Atlantic, Southeast, Great Lakes, Plains States, Northwest, Southwest, Rocky Mountains, Far West); population density (urban, suburban, rural); city or county size; climate
Psychographic segmentation	Lifestyle, personality, interests, values, attitudes
Benefit segmentation	Benefits provided by the good or service
Volume segmentation	Amount of use (light vs. heavy)

Wal-Mart customers have long been classified as value-price shoppers. But after extensive research in recent years, marketers have concluded that the retail giant's more than 200 million customers actually belong in three different groups. Wal-Mart's "value-price shoppers" continue to shop for low prices. "Brand aspirationals" are low-income consumers who seek after brand-name items. "Price-sensitive affluents" are wealthy shoppers who like good deals on pricey brand-name merchandise. What forms of consumer market segmentation does Wal-Mart use to help identify and understand its customers?

common. To help boost sales, Wal-Mart has recently dropped its cookie-cutter approach of having stores stocked largely with the same products. It is now customizing its merchandise mix based on demographics. The six groups that Wal-Mart uses are: the affluent, African Americans, empty-nesters, Hispanics, suburbanites, and rural consumers. The U.S. Census Bureau provides a great deal of demographic data. For example, marketing researchers can use census data to find areas within cities that contain high concentrations of high-income consumers, singles, blue-collar workers, and so forth.

Many products are targeted to various age groups. Most music CDs, Pepsi, Coke, many movies, the Dodge Neon, and thousands of other products are targeted toward teenagers and people under 25 years old. In contrast, most cruises, medical products, fine jewelry, vacation homes, Buicks, and denture products are targeted toward people 50 years old and up. Marketers target every age group. A few examples are shown in Exhibit 11.4 below.

Income is another popular way to segment markets. Income level influences consumers' wants and determines their buying power. Housing, clothing, automobiles, and alcoholic beverages are among the many markets segmented by income. Budget Gourmet frozen dinners are targeted to lower-income groups, whereas the Le Menu line and California Pizza Kitchen frozen pizzas are aimed at higher-income consumers.

Gender is also often very important in segmentation. Women, for example, make about 83 percent of consumer spending decisions.[11] Women purchase at least 60 percent of the new cars outright; they are influential in 85 percent of the car-buying decisions overall.[12] Why is this important? Because men and women differ on four key elements of the car buying decision: styling, speed, fuel efficiency, and safety:

- *Styling*. Both men and women care about it. But to him, styling is more about the lines and accents of the exterior. To her, styling is more about the design and finishes of the interior.
- *Speed*. He wants bragging rights about how many seconds it takes to get from zero to 60. She wants to feel secure that her car has enough acceleration to outrun the truck trying to squeeze past her on the expressway entrance ramp.
- *Safety*. For him, it's about features that help avoid an accident, such as antilock brakes and responsive steering. For her, it's about features that help to survive an accident: passenger airbags, reinforced side panels, or a drop-down engine.
- *The environment*. Women have always expressed interest in hybrids because of the environmental impact. Continued high gas prices will only increase her interest, resulting in potential category growth.[13]

Geographic Segmentation

geographic segmentation
The differentiation of markets by region of the country, city or county size, market density, or climate.

Geographic segmentation means segmenting markets by region of the country, city or county size, market density, or climate. *Market density* is the number of people or businesses within a certain area. Many companies segment their markets geographically to meet regional preferences and buying habits. Pizza Hut, for instance, gives easterners extra cheese, westerners more ingredients,

EXHIBIT 11.4	All Age Groups are Targets for Segmentation
Products and Services	**Targeted Age Group**
Fisher-Price "Grow-with-Me"	1.5 to 5 Years of Age
Sesame Street television	3 to 5 Years of Age
Guide to Babysitting (Book)	8 to 12 Years of Age
Juicy Couture Tote Bags	13 to 18 Years of Age
You're Not in Mom's Kitchen Anymore: College Cooking for the Dorming Gourmet (book)	17 to 24 Years of Age
Jitterbug No-Frills cell phone	51 Plus Years of Age

and midwesterners both. Both Ford and Chevrolet sell more pickup trucks and truck parts in the middle of the country than on either coast. The well-defined "pickup truck belt" runs from the upper Midwest south through Texas and the Gulf states. Ford has historically "owned" the northern half of this truck belt, and Chevrolet the southern half. Now, imports such as the Toyota Tundra are stealing market share.

Psychographic Segmentation

Race, income, occupation, and other demographic variables help in developing strategies but often do not paint the entire picture of consumer needs. Demographics provide the skeleton, but psychographics add meat to the bones. **Psychographic segmentation** is market segmentation by personality or lifestyle. People with common activities, interests, and opinions are grouped together and given a "lifestyle name." For example, Harley-Davidson divides its customers into seven lifestyle segments, from "cocky misfits" who are most likely to be arrogant troublemakers, to "laid-back camper types" committed to cycling and nature, to "classy capitalists" who have wealth and privilege.

Benefit Segmentation

Benefit segmentation is based on what a product will do rather than on consumer characteristics. For years Crest toothpaste was targeted toward consumers concerned with preventing cavities. Recently, Crest subdivided its market. It now offers regular Crest, Crest Tartar Control for people who want to prevent cavities and tartar buildup, Crest for kids with sparkles and a bubble gum flavor and another Crest that prevents gum disease. Another toothpaste, Topol, targets people who want whiter teeth—teeth without coffee, tea, or tobacco stains. Sensodyne toothpaste is aimed at people with highly sensitive teeth.

Volume Segmentation

The fifth main type of segmentation is **volume segmentation**, which is based on the amount of the product purchased. Just about every product has heavy, moderate, and light users, as well as nonusers. Heavy users often account for a very large portion of a product's sales. Thus, a firm might want to target its marketing mix to the heavy-user segment. For example, in the fast-food industry, the heavy user (a young, single male) accounts for only one in five fast-food patrons. Yet, this heavy user makes over 60 percent of all visits to fast-food restaurants.

Retailers are aware that heavy shoppers not only spend more, but also visit each outlet more frequently than other shoppers. Heavy shoppers visit the grocery store 122 times per year, compared with 93 annual visits for the medium shopper. They visit discount stores more than twice as often as medium shoppers, and they visit convenience/gas stores more than five times as often. On each trip, they consistently spend more than their medium-shopping counterparts.

Using Marketing Research to Serve Existing Customers and Find New Customers

How do successful companies learn what their customers value? Through marketing research, companies can be sure they are listening to the voice of the customer. **Marketing research** is the process of planning, collecting, and analyzing data relevant to a marketing decision. The results of this analysis are then communicated to management. The information collected through marketing research includes the preferences of customers, the perceived benefits of products, and consumer lifestyles. Research helps companies make better use of their marketing budgets. Marketing research has a range of uses from fine-tuning existing products to discovering whole new marketing concepts.

For example, everything at the Olive Garden restaurant chain from the décor to the wine list is based on marketing research. Each new menu item is put through a series of consumer taste tests before being added to the menu. Hallmark Cards uses marketing research to test messages, cover designs, and even the size of the cards. Hallmark's experts know which kinds of cards

CONCEPT in action

© iStockphoto.com/Fanelie Rosier

Are "shop for money" ads a gimmick? Can people really earn cash by grabbing a cup of coffee at Starbucks? It may sound suspicious, but marketers really do pay people to shop and evaluate businesses from a customer's perspective. With mystery shopping, undercover customers visit ice cream shops, department stores, and a host of other establishments to rate them on performance. It's a win-win situation: the buyer gets an excuse to go on sprees, and businesses get relevant market feedback in a natural consumer setting. What are advantages and limitations of using mystery shopping to gather research data?

survey research
A marketing research method in which data is gathered from respondents, either in person, by telephone, by mail, at a mall, or through the Internet to obtain facts, opinions, and attitudes.

observation research
A marketing research method in which the investigator monitors respondents' actions without interacting directly with the respondents; for example, by using cash registers with scanners.

experiment
A marketing research method in which the investigator changes one or more variables—price, packaging, design, shelf space, advertising theme, or advertising expenditures—while observing the effects of these changes on another variable (usually sales).

CONCEPT check

Define market segmentation.

List and discuss the five basic forms of market segmentation.

How does marketing research help companies make better use of their marketing budgets?

will sell best in which places. Engagement cards, for instance, sell best in the Northeast, where engagement parties are popular. Birthday cards for "Daddy" sell best in the South because even adult southerners tend to call their fathers Daddy.

There are three basic research methods: survey, observation, and experiment.

With **survey research**, data is gathered from respondents, either in person or at a mall, or through the Internet, by telephone, or via mail, to obtain facts, opinions, and attitudes. A questionnaire is used to provide an orderly and structured approach to data gathering. Face-to-face interviews may take place at the respondent's home, in a shopping mall, or at a place of business. The Internet is now the most popular mode of survey research. It is cost-effective and can reach respondents who are difficult to find.

Observation research is research that monitors respondents' actions without direct interaction. In the fastest-growing form of observation research, researchers use cash registers with scanners that read tags with bar codes to identify the item being purchased. Technological advances are rapidly expanding the future of observation research. Arbitron research has developed a portable people meter (P.P.M.) about the size of a cell phone, that research participants clip to their belts or any article of clothing. They agree to wear it during all waking hours. Before the study participants go to sleep, they put the P.P.M. in a cradle that automatically sends data back to Arbitron. The P.P.M. will tell the market research company exactly which television programs the person watched and for how long. It also records radio programs listened to, as well as any Web streaming, supermarket Muzak, or any other electronic media that the research participant encountered during the day.

In the third research method, **experiment**, the investigator changes one or more variables—price, package, design, shelf space, advertising theme, or advertising expenditures—while observing the effects of those changes on another variable (usually sales). The objective of experiments is to measure causality. For example, an experiment may reveal the impact that a change in package design has on sales.

What Is a Product?

6 What is a product, and how is it classified?

The goal of marketing research is to create products and services that are desired by the target market. In marketing, a **product** is any good or service, along with its perceived attributes and benefits, that creates value for the customer. Attributes can be tangible or intangible. Among the tangible attributes are packaging and warranties as illustrated in Exhibit 11.5. Intangible attributes are symbolic, such as brand image. People make decisions about which products to buy after considering both tangible and intangible attributes of a product. For example, when you buy a pair of jeans, you consider price, brand, store image, and style before you buy. These factors are all part of the marketing mix.

product
In marketing, any good or service, along with its perceived attributes and benefits, that creates value for the customer.

Classifying Consumer Products

Because most things sold are a blend of goods and services, the term *product* can be used to refer to both. After all, consumers are really buying packages of benefits that deliver value. The person who buys a plane ride on Continental Airlines is looking for a quick way to get from one city to another (the benefit). Providing this benefit requires goods (a plane, drinks) and services (ticketing, maintenance, piloting).

Marketers must know how consumers view the types of products their companies sell so that they can design the marketing mix to appeal to the selected target market. To help them define target markets, marketers have devised product categories. Products that are bought by the end user are called *consumer products*. They include electric razors, sandwiches, cars, stereos, magazines, and houses. Consumer products that get used up, such as Nexxus shampoo and Lay's potato chips, are called *consumer nondurables*. Those that last for a long time, such as Whirlpool washing machines and computers, are *consumer durables*.

Another way to classify consumer products is by the amount of effort consumers are willing to make to acquire them. The four major categories of consumer products are unsought products, convenience products, shopping products, and specialty products, as summarized in Exhibit 11.6. **Unsought products** are products unknown to the potential buyer or known products that the buyer does not actively seek.

unsought products
Products that either are unknown to the potential buyer or are known but the buyer does not actively seek them.

Part 4: Marketing Management

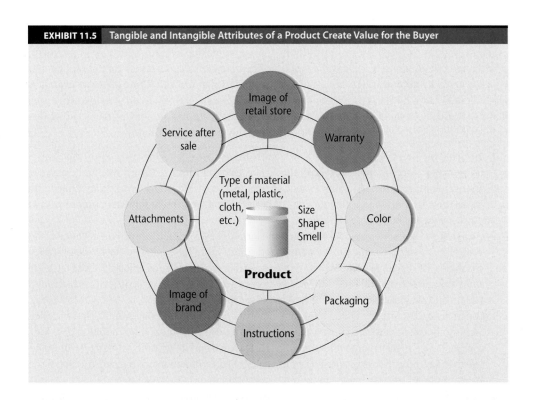

EXHIBIT 11.5   Tangible and Intangible Attributes of a Product Create Value for the Buyer

EXHIBIT 11.6   Classification of Consumer Products by the Effort Expended to Buy Them

Consumer Product	Examples	Degree of Effort Expended by Consumer
Unsought products	Life insurance Burial plots Time-share condos	No effort
Convenience products	Soft drinks Bread Milk Coffee	Very little or minimum effort
Shopping products	Automobiles Homes Vacations	Considerable effort
Specialty products	Expensive jewelry Gourmet restaurants Limited-production automobiles	Maximum effort

Convenience products are relatively inexpensive items that require little shopping effort. Soft drinks, candy bars, milk, bread, and small hardware items are examples. We buy them routinely without much planning. This does not mean that such products are unimportant or obscure. Many, in fact, are well known by their brand names—such as Pepsi-Cola, Pepperidge Farm breads, Domino's pizza, Sure deodorant, and UPS shipping.

In contrast to convenience products, **shopping products** are bought only after a brand-to-brand and store-to-store comparison of price, suitability, and style. Examples are furniture, automobiles, a vacation in Europe, and some items of clothing. Convenience products are bought with little planning, but shopping products may be chosen months or even years before their actual purchase.

Specialty products are products for which consumers search long and hard and for which they refuse to accept substitutes. Expensive jewelry, designer clothing, state-of-the-art stereo equipment, limited-production automobiles, and gourmet restaurants fall into this category. Because consumers are willing to spend much time and effort to find specialty products, distribution is often limited to one or two sellers in a given region, such as Neiman-Marcus, Gucci, or the Porsche dealer.

convenience products
Relatively inexpensive items that require little shopping effort and are purchased routinely without planning.

shopping products
Items that are bought after considerable planning, including brand-to-brand and store-to-store comparisons of price, suitability, and style.

specialty products
Items for which consumers search long and hard and for which they refuse to accept substitutes.

Chapter 11: Creating Products and Pricing Strategies to Meet Customers' Needs

Classifying Business Products

Products bought by businesses or institutions for use in making other products or in providing services are called *business* or *industrial products*. They are classified as either capital products or expense items. **Capital products** are usually large, expensive items with a long life span. Examples are buildings, large machines, and airplanes. **Expense items** are typically smaller, less expensive items that usually have a life span of less than a year. Examples are printer cartridges and paper. Industrial products are sometimes further classified in the following categories:

capital products
Large, expensive items with a long life span that are purchased by businesses for use in making other products or providing a service.

expense items
Items, purchased by businesses, that are smaller and less expensive than capital products and usually have a life span of less than one year.

1. *Installations.* These are large, expensive capital items that determine the nature, scope, and efficiency of a company. Capital products like General Motors' Saturn assembly plant in Tennessee represent a big commitment against future earnings and profitability. Buying an installation requires longer negotiations, more planning, and the judgments of more people than buying any other type of product.

2. *Accessories.* Accessories do not have the same long-run impact on the firm as installations, and they are less expensive and more standardized. But they are still capital products. Minolta copy machines, HP personal computers (PCs), and smaller machines such as Black & Decker table drills and saws are typical accessories. Marketers of accessories often rely on well-known brand names and extensive advertising as well as personal selling.

3. *Component parts and materials.* These are expense items that are built into the end product. Some component parts are custom-made, such as a drive shaft for an automobile, a chip for a computer, or a special pigment for painting U.S. Navy harbor buoys; others are standardized for sale to many industrial users. Intel's Pentium chip for PCs and cement for the construction trade are examples of standardized component parts and materials.

4. *Raw materials.* Raw materials are expense items that have undergone little or no processing and are used to create a final product. Examples include lumber, copper, and zinc.

5. *Supplies.* Supplies do not become part of the final product. They are bought routinely and in fairly large quantities. Supply items run the gamut from pencils and paper to paint and machine oil. They have little impact on the firm's long-run profits. Bic pens, Champion copier paper, and Pennzoil machine oil are typical supply items.

6. *Services.* These are expense items used to plan or support company operations; for example, janitorial cleaning and management consulting.

CONCEPT check

What is a product?

What are the classes of consumer goods?

Explain how business products are classified.

Creating Products that Deliver Value

7 How do organizations create new products?

New products pump life into company sales, enabling the firm not only to survive but also to grow. Companies like Allegheny Ludlum (steel), Dow (chemicals), Samsung (electronics), Campbell Soup (foods), and Stryker (medical products) get most of their profits from new products. Companies that lead their industries in profitability and sales growth get 49 percent of their revenues from products developed within the last five years. A recent survey found that 87 percent of top executives in the United States believed that their companies' success depended on new products.[14]

Marketers have several different terms for new products, depending on how the product fits into a company's existing product line. When a firm introduces a product that has a new brand name and is in a product category new to the organization, it is classified as a new product.

How New Products Are Developed

Developing new products is both costly and risky. New-product failure rates for household and grocery products approach 80 percent. The overall failure rate is approximately 75 percent.[15] Industrial goods failure rates tend to be lower than those for consumer goods. To increase their chances for success, most firms use the following product development process, which is also summarized in Exhibit 11.7.

1. *Set new-product goals.* New-product goals are usually stated as financial objectives. For example, a company may want to recover its investment in three years or less. Or it may want to earn at least a 15 percent return on the investment. Nonfinancial goals may include using existing equipment or facilities.

2. *Develop new-product ideas.* Smaller firms usually depend on employees, customers, investors, and distributors for new ideas. Larger companies use these sources and more structured marketing research techniques, such as focus groups and brainstorming. A **focus group** consists of 8 to 12 participants led by a moderator in an in-depth discussion on one particular topic or concept. The goal of focus group research is to learn and understand what people have to say and why. The emphasis is on getting people talking at length and in detail about the subject at hand. The intent is to find out how they feel about a product, concept, idea, or organization, how it fits into their lives, and their emotional involvement with it. Focus groups often generate excellent product ideas. A few examples of focus group–influenced products are the interior design of the Toyota Rav4, Stick-Up room deodorizers, Swiffer WetJet, and Wendy's Salad Sensations. In the industrial market, machine tools, keyboard designs, aircraft interiors, and backhoe accessories evolved from focus groups.

Brainstorming is also used to generate new-product ideas. With **brainstorming**, the members of a group think of as many ways to vary a product or solve a problem as possible. Criticism is avoided, no matter how ridiculous an idea seems at the time. The emphasis is on sheer numbers of ideas. Evaluation of these ideas is postponed to later steps of development.

3. *Screen ideas and concepts.* As ideas emerge, they are checked against the firm's new-product goals and its long-range strategies. Many product concepts are rejected because they don't fit well with existing products, needed technology is not available, the company doesn't have enough resources, or the sales potential is low.

4. *Develop the concept.* Developing the new-product concept involves creating a prototype of the product, testing the prototype, and building the marketing strategy. The type and amount of product testing vary, depending on such factors as the company's experience with similar products, how easy it is to make the item, and how easy it will be for consumers to use it.

© AP Images/Stefano Paltera

Nintendo Wii, the videogame console that allows players to get their whole bodies into the action, has a new role: exercise trainer. A recent spin-off version of the popular gaming console enables fitness enthusiasts and body trainers to perform activities ranging from calisthenics to yoga. Called Wii Fit, the new offshoot literally entertains individuals into tip-top shape. Why might product teams want to develop new variations of existing products instead of pursuing new-product ideas?

focus group
A group of 8 to 12 participants led by a moderator in an in-depth discussion on one particular topic or concept.

brainstorming
A method of generating ideas in which group members suggest as many possibilities as they can without criticizing or evaluating any of the suggestions.

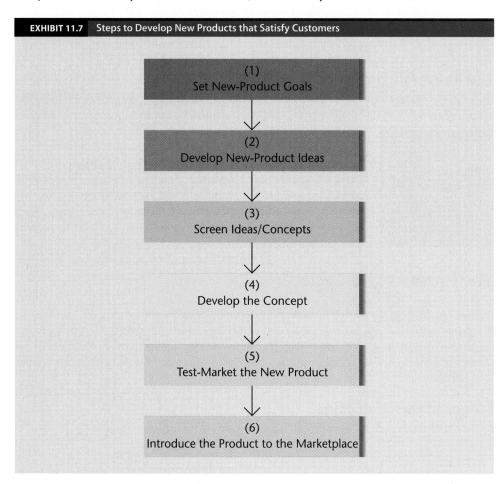

EXHIBIT 11.7 Steps to Develop New Products that Satisfy Customers

(1) Set New-Product Goals

↓

(2) Develop New-Product Ideas

↓

(3) Screen Ideas/Concepts

↓

(4) Develop the Concept

↓

(5) Test-Market the New Product

↓

(6) Introduce the Product to the Marketplace

© John MacNeill

The air travel of tomorrow may have little in common with today's passenger flights. Aerospace defense contractors have long tinkered with massive airships for potential military use, but now the private firm Worldwide Aeros Corporation plans to make its Aeroscraft cruise-liner the preferred travel of the future. Spanning two football fields and touted as a flying luxury hotel, Aeroscraft will ferry pampered passengers around the world with unprecedented comfort and style. At what stage of product development is the Aeroscraft airship?

test marketing
The process of testing a new product among potential users.

product manager
The person who develops and implements a complete strategy and marketing program for a specific product or brand.

product life cycle
The pattern of sales and profits over time for a product or product category; consists of an introductory stage, growth stage, maturity, and decline (and death).

Suppose that Kraft's Seven Seas is developing a new salad dressing flavor. The company already has a lot of experience in this area, so the new dressing will go directly into advanced taste tests and perhaps home-use tests. To develop a new line of soft drinks, however, Seven Seas would most likely do a great deal of testing. It would study many aspects of the new product before actually making it.

While the product is tested, the marketing strategy is refined. Channels of distribution are selected, pricing policies are developed and tested, the target market is further defined, and demand for the product is estimated. Management also continually updates the profit plan.

As the marketing strategy and prototype tests mature, a communication strategy is developed. A logo and package wording are created. As part of the communication strategy, promotion themes are developed, and the product is introduced to the sales force.

5. *Test-market the new product.* **Test marketing** is testing the product among potential users. It allows management to evaluate various strategies and to see how well the parts of the marketing mix fit together. Few new-product concepts reach this stage. For those that pass this stage, the firm must decide whether to introduce the product on a regional or national basis.

  Companies that don't test-market their products run a strong risk of product failure. In essence, test marketing is the "acid test" of new-product development. The product is put into the marketplace and then the manufacturer can see how it performs against the competition.

6. *Introduce the product.* A product that passes test marketing is ready for market introduction, called rollout, which requires a lot of logistical coordination. Various divisions of the company must be encouraged to give the new item the attention it deserves. Packaging and labeling in a different language may be required. Sales training sessions must be scheduled, spare parts inventoried, service personnel trained, advertising and promotion campaigns readied, and wholesalers and retailers informed about the new item. If the new product is to be sold internationally, it may have to be altered to meet the requirements of the target countries. For instance, electrical products may have to run on different electrical currents.

The Role of the Product Manager

When a new product enters the marketplace in large organizations, it is often placed under the control of a product or brand manager. A **product manager** develops and implements a complete strategy and marketing program for a specific product or brand. Product management first appeared at Procter & Gamble in 1929. A new company soap, Camay, was not doing well, so a young Procter & Gamble executive was assigned to devote his exclusive attention to developing and promoting this product. He was successful, and the company soon added other product managers. Since then, many firms—especially consumer products companies—have set up product management organizations.

The Product Life Cycle

8 What are the stages of the product life cycle?

Product managers create marketing mixes for their products as they move through the life cycle. The **product life cycle** is a pattern of sales and profits over time for a product (Ivory dishwashing liquid) or a product category (liquid detergents). As the product moves through the stages of the life cycle, the firm must keep revising the marketing mix to remain competitive and meet the needs of target customers.

Stages of the Life Cycle

As illustrated in Exhibit 11.8, the product life cycle consists of the following stages:

1. *Introduction.* When a product enters the life cycle, it faces many obstacles. Although competition may be light, the introductory stage usually features frequent product

modifications, limited distribution, and heavy promotion. The failure rate is high. Production and marketing costs are also high, and sales volume is low. Hence profits are usually small or negative.

2. *Growth.* If a product survives the introductory stage, it advances to the growth stage of the life cycle. In this stage, sales grow at an increasing rate, profits are healthy, and many competitors enter the market. Large companies may start to acquire small pioneering firms that have reached this stage. Emphasis switches from primary demand promotion to aggressive brand advertising and communicating the differences between brands. For example, the goal changes from convincing people to buy compact plasma TVs to convincing them to buy Sony versus Panasonic or Sharp.

Distribution becomes a major key to success during the growth stage, as well as in later stages. Manufacturers scramble to acquire dealers and distributors and to build long-term relationships. Without adequate distribution, it is impossible to establish a strong market position.

Toward the end of the growth phase, prices normally begin falling and profits peak. Price reductions result from increased competition and from cost reductions due to producing larger quantities of items (economies of scale). Also, most firms have recovered their development costs by now, and their priority is in increasing or retaining market share and enhancing profits.

3. *Maturity.* After the growth stage, sales continue to mount—but at a decreasing rate. This is the maturity stage. Most products that have been on the market for a long time are in this stage. Thus, most marketing strategies are designed for mature products. One such strategy is to bring out several variations of a basic product (**line extension**). Kool-Aid, for instance, was originally offered in three flavors. Today there are more than 10, as well as sweetened and unsweetened varieties.

4. *Decline (and death).* When sales and profits fall, the product has reached the decline stage. The rate of decline is governed by two factors: the rate of change in consumer tastes and the rate at which new products enter the market. Sony VCRs are an example of a product in the decline stage. The demand for VCRs has now been surpassed by the demand for DVD players.

line extension
A new flavor, size, or model using an existing brand name in an existing category.

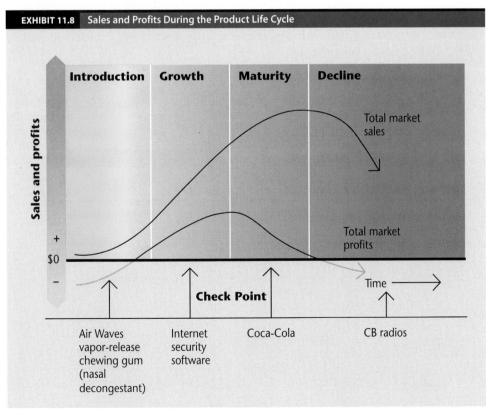

EXHIBIT 11.8   Sales and Profits During the Product Life Cycle

What is the product life cycle?

Describe each stage of the product life cycle.

What are the marketing strategies for each stage of the product life cycle?

The Product Life Cycle as a Management Tool

The product life cycle may be used in planning. Marketers who understand the cycle concept are better able to forecast future sales and plan new marketing strategies. Exhibit 11.9 is a brief summary of strategic needs at various stages of the product life cycle. Marketers must be sure that a product has moved from one stage to the next before changing its marketing strategy. A temporary sales decline should not be interpreted as a sign that the product is dying. Pulling back marketing support can become a self-fulfilling prophecy that brings about the early death of a healthy product.

Pricing Strategies

9 What strategies are used for pricing products?

An important part of the product development process is setting the right price. Price is the perceived value that is exchanged for something else. Value in our society is most commonly expressed in dollars and cents. Thus, price is typically the amount of money exchanged for a good or service. Note that *perceived value* refers to the time of the transaction. After you've used a product you've bought, you may decide that its actual value was less than its perceived value at the time you bought it. The price you pay for a product is based on the *expected satisfaction* you will receive and not necessarily the *actual satisfaction* you will receive.

Although price is usually a dollar amount, it can be anything with perceived value. When goods and services are exchanged for each other, the trade is called *barter*. If you exchange this book for a math book at the end of the term, you have engaged in barter.

CONCEPT in action

© Theo Wargo/WireImage/Getty Images

British rock group Radiohead made an unprecedented business decision in 2007 with the release of *In Rainbows,* the band's seventh album. Instead of offering the record in stores at standard industry prices, Radiohead offered *In Rainbows* online at "pay-what-you-want" prices. Despite the album's huge popularity—an estimated 1.2 million copies were downloaded on the first day—tracking surveys indicated that nearly two-thirds of the album's listeners paid nothing for the recording. Paying customers offered $6 on average for the songs. What do these results say about the perceived value of popular music in today's music industry?

Pricing Objectives

Price is important in determining how much a firm earns. The prices charged customers times the number of units sold equals the *gross revenue* for the firm. Revenue is what pays for every activity of the company (production, finance, sales, distribution, and so forth). What's left over (if anything) is profit. Managers strive to charge a price that will allow the firm to earn a fair return on its investment.

The chosen price must be neither too high nor too low. And the price must equal the perceived value to target consumers. If consumers think the price is too high, sales opportunities will be lost. Lost sales mean lost revenue. If the price is too low, consumers may view the product as a great value, but the company may not meet its profit goals.

Product Pricing

Managers use various pricing strategies when determining the price of a product, as this section explains. Price skimming and penetration pricing are strategies

EXHIBIT 11.9	Strategies for Success at Each Stage of the Product Life Cycle			
Category	**Introduction**	**Growth**	**Maturity**	**Decline**
Marketing objectives	Encourage trial, establish distribution	Get triers to repurchase, attract new users	Seek new users or uses	Reduce marketing expenses, keep loyal users
Product	Establish competitive advantage	Maintain product quality	Modify product	Maintain product
Distribution	Establish distribution network	Solidify distribution relationships	Provide additional incentives to ensure support	Eliminate trade allowances
Promotional	Build brand awareness	Provide information	Reposition product	Eliminate most advertising and sales promotion
Pricing	Set introductory price (skimming or penetration pricing)	Maintain prices	Reduce prices to meet competition	Maintain prices

used in pricing new products; other strategies such as leader pricing and bundling may be used for established products as well.

Price Skimming

The practice of introducing a new product on the market with a high price and then lowering the price over time is called **price skimming**. As the product moves through its life cycle, the price usually is lowered because competitors are entering the market. As the price falls, more and more consumers can buy the product.

Price skimming has four important advantages. First, a high initial price can be a way to find out what buyers are willing to pay. Second, if consumers find the introductory price too high, it can be lowered. Third, a high introductory price can create an image of quality and prestige. Fourth, when the price is lowered later, consumers may think they are getting a bargain. The disadvantage is that high prices attract competition.

Price skimming can be used to price virtually any new product such as high-definition televisions, new cancer drugs, and color computer printers. For example, the Republic of Tea has launched new Imperial Republic White Tea, which it says is among the rarest of teas. Because it is minimally processed, white tea is said to retain the highest level of antioxidants and has a lower caffeine content than black and green teas. The company says the tea is picked only a few days each year, right before the leaf opens, yielding a small harvest. The product retails for $14 per tin of 50 bags. Products don't have to cost hundreds of dollars to use a skimming strategy.

> **price skimming**
> The strategy of introducing a product with a high initial price and lowering the price over time as the product moves through its life cycle.

Penetration Pricing

A company that doesn't use price skimming will probably use **penetration pricing**. With this strategy, the company offers new products at low prices in the hope of achieving a large sales volume. Procter & Gamble did this with the SpinBrush toothbrush. Penetration pricing requires more extensive planning than skimming does because the company must gear up for mass production and marketing. When Texas Instruments entered the digital-watch market, its facilities in Lubbock, Texas, could produce 6 million watches a year, enough to meet the entire world demand for low-priced watches. If the company had been wrong about demand, its losses would have been huge.

Penetration pricing has two advantages. First, the low initial price may induce consumers to switch brands or companies. Using penetration pricing on its jug wines, Gallo has lured customers away from Taylor California Cellars and Inglenook. Second, penetration pricing may discourage competitors from entering the market. Their costs would tend to be higher, so they would need to sell more at the same price to break even.

> **penetration pricing**
> The strategy of selling new products at low prices in the hope of achieving a large sales volume.

Leader Pricing

Pricing products below the normal markup or even below cost to attract customers to a store where they wouldn't otherwise shop is **leader pricing**. A product priced below cost is referred to as a **loss leader**. Retailers hope that this type of pricing will increase their overall sales volume and thus their profit.

Items that are leader priced are usually well known and priced low enough to appeal to many customers. They also are items that consumers will buy at a lower price, even if they have to switch brands. Supermarkets often feature coffee and bacon in their leader pricing. Department stores and specialty stores also rely heavily on leader pricing.

> **leader pricing**
> The strategy of pricing products below the normal markup or even below cost to attract customers to a store where they would not otherwise shop.
>
> **loss leader**
> A product priced below cost as part of a leader pricing strategy.

Bundling

Bundling means grouping two or more related products together and pricing them as a single product. Marriott's special weekend rates often include the room, breakfast, and one night's dinner. Department stores may offer a washer and dryer together for a price lower than if the units were bought separately.

The idea behind bundling is to reach a segment of the market that the products sold separately would not reach as effectively. Some buyers are more than willing to buy one product but have much less use for the second. Bundling the second product to the first at a slightly reduced price thus creates some sales that otherwise would not be made. Aussie 3-Minute Miracle Shampoo is typically bundled with its conditioner because many people use shampoo more than conditioner so they don't need a new bottle of conditioner.

> **bundling**
> The strategy of grouping two or more related products together and pricing them as a single product.

Odd–Even Pricing

Psychology often plays a big role in how consumers view prices and what prices they will pay. **Odd–even pricing** (or **psychological pricing**) is the strategy of setting a price at an odd number to connote a bargain and at an even number to imply quality. For years, many retailers have priced their products in odd numbers—for example, $99.95 or $49.95—to make consumers feel that they are paying a lower price for the product.

> **odd–even (psychological) pricing**
> The strategy of setting a price at an odd number to connote a bargain and at an even number to suggest quality.

What is the difference between penetration pricing and price skimming?

Explain the concept of price bundling.

Describe odd–even pricing and prestige pricing.

Prestige Pricing The strategy of raising the price of a product so consumers will perceive it as being of higher quality, status, or value is called **prestige pricing**. This type of pricing is common where high prices indicate high status. In the specialty shops on Rodeo Drive in Beverly Hills, which cater to the super-rich of Hollywood, shirts that would sell for $15 elsewhere sell for at least $50. If the price were lower, customers would perceive them as being of low quality.

Trends in Developing Products and Pricing

10 What trends are occurring in products and pricing?

prestige pricing
The strategy of increasing the price of a product so that consumers will perceive it as being of higher quality, status, or value.

As customer expectations increase and competition becomes fiercer, perceptive managers will find innovative strategies to satisfy demanding consumers and establish unique products in the market. Satisfying customers requires the right prices. The Internet has delivered pricing power to both buyers and sellers. Another significant trend is the use of one-to-one marketing to create a customized marketing mix for each consumer.

The Impact of the Internet on Pricing

The Internet, corporate networks, and wireless setups are linking people, machines, and companies around the globe—and connecting sellers and buyers as never before. This link is enabling buyers to quickly and easily compare products and prices, putting them in a better bargaining position. At the same time, the technology enables sellers to collect detailed data about customers' buying habits, preferences, and even spending limits so that they can tailor their products and prices. For a time, all of these developments raised hopes for a more efficient marketplace.

Unfortunately, the promise of pricing efficiencies for Internet retailers and lower costs for consumers has run headlong into reality. Flawed pricing strategies have taken much of the blame for the implosion of many dot-coms. Too many merchants offered deep discounts that made profits all but impossible to achieve. Other e-retailers have felt the consumer backlash against price discrimination, because the Internet has given shoppers the ability to better detect price discrepancies and bargains. The e-retailers must now figure out how to take advantage of the Internet's unique capabilities to set dynamic prices, which would better reflect a customer's willingness to pay more under different circumstances.

Setting prices on the Internet was expected to offer retailers a number of advantages. To begin with, it would be far easier to raise or lower prices in response to demand, without the need for a clerk to run through a store with a pricing gun. Online prices could be changed in far smaller increments—even by just a penny or two—as frequently as a merchant desired, making it possible to fine-tune pricing strategies.

But the real payoff was supposed to be better information on exactly how price-conscious customers are. For instance, knowing that customer A doesn't care whether an Oscar-nominated DVD in her shopping basket costs $21.95 or $25.95 would leave an enterprising merchant free to charge the higher price on the spot. By contrast, knowing that customer B is going to put author John Le Carré's latest thriller back on the shelf unless it's priced at $20, instead of $28, would open an opportunity for a bookseller to make the sale by cutting the price in real time.

The idea was to charge exactly what the market will bear. But putting this into practice online has turned out to be exceptionally difficult, in part because the Internet has also empowered consumers to compare prices to find out if other merchants are offering a better deal or if other consumers are getting a bigger break.

Although the Internet helps drive down prices by making it easier for consumers to shop for the best bargain, it also makes it possible for online merchants to monitor each other's prices—whether higher or lower—and to adjust them in concert without overtly colluding. As long as the number of retailers in a given market is relatively small, it is now much simpler for merchants to signal each other by changing prices for short periods—long enough for their competitors to notice, but not so long that consumers do. Airlines have long used online reservation systems to signal fare changes to one another.

Online price-comparison engines, know as shopbots, are continuing to add new features. Smarter.com now includes coupons and additional retailer discounts in its price results. In the past, consumers would have had to click deep into a retailer's site to find out about these additional savings. Vendio Services, Inc. recently introduced a toolbar that people can download. If a person is on the Web page of a particular product—whether it's an iPod or a Canon digital camera—the toolbar flashes a blinking alert when it finds a lower price for that same item somewhere else. The person can then open a window on the side of the site to learn details of the cheaper price—or, simply ignore the alert. BuySafe, Inc. introduced a Web site last month that lets consumers search among about 1.5 million products that are backed by antifraud guarantees. If a buyer purchases one of the items and the seller fails to deliver, the buyer can be reimbursed for the full cost up to $25,000. Merchants on the site include those that sell on eBay and Overstock.com.

Use of these sites has boomed in the past few years as people have become more reliant on the Web both as a research tool and as a place to shop. About 70 percent of consumers have used a comparison-shopping Web site.[16] Much of the growth has come from the more-established sites such as Shopzilla, Bizrate, and Nextag, as well as the shopping sections of Yahoo, Inc., Microsoft Corp.'s MSN, and Google. The big attraction with comparison-shopping services, of course, is the hunt for a better bargain. Consumers save 18 to 20 percent on average by using comparison-shopping sites to buy products on the Web.

Merchants like the sites because they help drive consumer spending. Consumers who use comparison-shopping sites spend 25 to 30 percent more on the Web than those who don't, estimates market research firm Forrester Research.[17]

Brand/Product Line Extensions

A **product line extension**, or brand extension, is taking a product with a well-developed brand image and using that brand name for a new product in either the same product category or a different product category. Thus, the well-developed brand name Coke was extended to Diet Coke, Caffeine-free Coke, Vanilla Coke, Cherry Coke, and many others. Companies use this strategy to increase **brand equity**, which is value and long-term sustainability of a renowned brand name. The brand equity of Coca-Cola is estimated to be over $100 billion.[18]

A brand's "extendibility" depends on how consumers perceive a brand and the relationship, or lack of a relationship, with a new product. If Jell-O extends its product offerings to mango-flavored Jell-O, that is an easy extension. Ralph Lauren's Polo was successfully extended from clothes to bedding and towels. Stretching, or extending, a brand requires that the target market perceives either a logical or emotional relationship between the core brand and the new product. A few brands that have been successfully stretched in the past couple of years are: Mr. Clean windshield wash, Wheaties vitamins, Steinway furniture polish, Dannon Activia, and Charmin Basic toilet paper.

Sometimes firms try to extend a core brand too far and target customers simply don't see the connection. A few recent failures are: Trump steaks, Guinness bread, Hooters energy drink, Adidas deodorant, and Harley-Davidson cake-decorating kits. Overextending a core brand can damage the overall brand image.[19] KitKat, the chocolate-covered wafer, has been one of Britain's best-selling candies since the 1930s. Nestlé, KitKat's manufacturer, decided to extend the brand with new flavors and styles. The company rolled out a new array of KitKats. For the summer months, it launched strawberries and cream, passion fruit and mango, and even red-berry versions. In the winter came "Christmas pudding" and tiramisu, which contained real wine and mascarpone. Even though Britons never fully embraced the Atkins diet craze, the company launched a low-carb version. The brand extension failed because consumers were confused and upset. KitKat sales in the United Kingdom fell 18 percent in just two years.[20]

Private-Label Branding

Private-label branding, or simply private branding, is where a retailer, or wholesaler, has a manufacturer produce products and the retailer, or wholesaler, puts its own name on the item. There are far more retail private brands than wholesaler private brands.

Historically, private brands were mostly cheap and of questionable quality. Some private labels were packaged in plain brown paper to denote "low cost." Today, strategic private branding has completely changed. Many private labels today have fancy packaging and prices that approach the manufacturers' brands. Above all, the mantra of private branding today is "product quality." Traditionally, the price spread between a manufacturer's brand, such as Procter & Gamble's Tide and Costco's Kirkland laundry detergent, was about 30 percent. Now it is less, and often approaches parity.

product line (or brand) extension
Taking a product with a well-developed brand image and using that brand name for a new product in either the same product category or a different product category.

brand equity
Value and long-term sustainability of a renowned brand name.

private-label branding
Where a retailer, or wholesaler, has a manufacturer produce products and the retailer, or wholesaler, puts its own name on the item.

Private-label sales of food and nonalcoholic beverages is approaching $50 billion annually.[21] Savvy retailers know that a quality private brand ties the customer to their store. If you want a Diehard battery you must go to Sears. Also, private brands typically have a higher gross profit margin.

Major manufacturers often produce private brands to raise their profits. For example, Kimberly-Clark, which makes Huggies diapers, also produces training pants for Wal-Mart. Wal-Mart offers some of America's most popular private labels, including Great Value, Equate, Sam's Choice, Wal-Mart, and Member's Mark (Sam's Club). On the other hand, some manufacturers produce only private-label products. Menu Foods, from Ontario, Canada, produces more than 100 brand names ranging from Procter & Gamble Co.'s Iams and Eukanuba brands to Hill's Pet Nutrition Science Diet, owned by Colgate-Palmolive Co., to Ol' Roy pet food by Wal-Mart. To be sure, ingredients, designs, and quality can differ substantially among the labels. "We have more than 1,300 recipes," says Sam Bornstein, a spokesman for Menu Foods.[22]

CONCEPT check

How have online price-comparison engines helped consumers shop for the best price?

What is brand equity and why is it important to companies?

Summary of Learning Goals

1 What are the marketing concept and relationship building?

Marketing includes those business activities that are designed to satisfy consumer needs and wants through the exchange process. Marketing managers use the "right" principle—getting the right goods or services to the right people at the right place, time, and price, using the right promotional techniques. Today, many firms have adopted the marketing concept. The marketing concept involves identifying consumer needs and wants and then producing goods or services that will satisfy them while making a profit. Relationship marketing entails forging long-term relationships with customers, which can lead to repeat sales, reduced costs, and stable relationships.

2 How do managers create a marketing strategy?

A firm creates a marketing strategy by understanding the external environment, defining the target market, determining a competitive advantage, and developing a marketing mix. Environmental scanning enables companies to understand the external environment. The target market is the specific group of consumers toward which a firm directs its marketing efforts. A competitive advantage is a set of unique features of a company and its products that are perceived by the target market as significant and superior to those of the competition.

3 What is the marketing mix?

To carry out the marketing strategy, firms create a marketing mix—a blend of products, distribution systems, prices, and promotion. Marketing managers use this mix to satisfy target consumers. The mix can be applied to nonbusiness as well as business situations.

4 How do consumers and organizations make buying decisions?

Buyer behavior is what people and businesses do in buying and using goods and services. The consumer decision-making process consists of the following steps: recognizing a need, seeking information, evaluating alternatives, purchasing the product, judging the purchase outcome, and engaging in postpurchase behavior. A number of factors influence the process. Cultural, social, individual, and psychological factors have an impact on consumer decision making. The main differences between consumer and business markets are purchase volume, number of customers, location of buyers, direct distribution, and rational purchase decisions. Companies learn more about their target markets by conducting marketing research—the process of planning, collecting, and analyzing data relevant to a marketing decision.

5 What are the five basic forms of market segmentation?

Success in marketing depends on understanding the target market. One technique used to identify a target market is market segmentation. The five basic forms of segmentation are demographic (population statistics), geographic (location), psychographic (personality or lifestyle), benefit (product features), and volume (amount purchased).

6 What is a product, and how is it classified?

A product is any good or service, along with its perceived attributes and benefits, that creates customer value. Tangible attributes include the good itself, packaging, and warranties. Intangible attributes are symbolic like a brand's image. Products are categorized as either consumer products or industrial products. Consumer products are goods and services that are bought and used by the end users. They can be classified as unsought products, convenience products, shopping products, or specialty products, depending on how much effort consumers are willing to exert to get them.

Industrial products are those bought by organizations for use in making other products or in rendering services and include capital products and expense items.

To succeed, most firms must continue to design new products to satisfy changing customer demands. But new-product development can be risky. Many new products fail. The steps in new-product development are setting new-product goals, exploring ideas, screening ideas, developing the concept (creating a prototype and building the marketing strategy), test marketing, and introducing the product. When the product enters the marketplace, it is often managed by a product manager.

7 How do organizations create new products?

After a product reaches the marketplace, it enters the product life cycle. This cycle typically has four stages: introduction, growth, maturity, and decline (and possibly death). Profit margins usually are small in the introductory phase, reach a peak at the end of the growth phase, and then decline. Marketing strategies for each stage are listed in Exhibit 11.9.

8 What are the stages of the product life cycle?

Price indicates value, helps position a product in the marketplace, and is the means for earning a fair return on investment. If a price is too high, the product won't sell well and the firm will lose money. If the price is too low, the firm may lose money even if the product sells well. Prices are set according to pricing objectives.

The two main strategies for pricing a new product are price skimming and penetration pricing. Price skimming involves charging a high introductory price and then, usually, lowering the price as the product moves through its life cycle. Penetration pricing involves selling a new product at a low price in the hope of achieving a large sales volume.

9 What strategies are used for pricing products?

Pricing tactics are used to fine-tune the base prices of products. Sellers that use leader pricing set the prices of some of their products below the normal markup or even below cost to attract customers who might otherwise not shop at those stores. Bundling is grouping two or more products together and pricing them as one. Psychology often plays a role in how consumers view products and in determining what they will pay. Setting a price at an odd number tends to create a perception that the item is cheaper than the actual price. Prices in even numbers denote quality or status. Raising the price so an item will be perceived as having high quality and status is called prestige pricing.

The Internet has given pricing power to both buyers and sellers. A second trend is that many firms are using databases to create one-to-one marketing.

10 What trends are occurring in products and pricing?

Key Terms

benefit segmentation 301
brand equity 311
brainstorming 305
bundling 309
buyer behavior 296
capital products 304
competitive advantage 293
convenience products 303
cost competitive advantage 294
culture 296
customer satisfaction 291

customer value 291
demographic segmentation 299
differential competitive advantage 294
distribution strategy 295
environmental scanning 292
exchange 290
expense items 304
experiment 302
focus group 305
four Ps 295
geographic segmentation 300

PREPARING

Preparing for Tomorrow's Workplace: SCANS

1. Can the marketing concept be applied effectively by a sole proprietorship, or is it more appropriate for larger businesses with more managers? Explain. **(Information)**

2. Before starting your own business, you should develop a marketing strategy to guide your efforts. Choose one of the business ideas listed below and develop a marketing strategy for the business. Include the type of market research you will perform and how you will define your target market. **(Information, Systems)**
   - Crafts store to capitalize on the renewed interest in knitting and other crafts
   - Online corporate-training company
   - Ethnic restaurant near your campus
   - Another business opportunity that interests you

3. "Market segmentation is the most important concept in marketing." Why do you think some marketing professionals make this statement? Give an example of each form of segmentation. **(Systems)**

4. Pick a specific product that you use frequently, such as a cosmetic or toiletry item, a snack food, an article of clothing, a book, a computer program, or a music CD. What is the target market for this product, and does the company's marketing strategy reflect this? Now consider the broader category of your product. How can this product be changed and/or the marketing strategy adjusted to appeal to other market segments? **(Systems)**

5. Under what circumstances would a jeans maker market the product as a convenience product? A shopping product? A specialty product? **(Information)**

6. Go to the library and look through magazines and newspapers to find examples of price skimming, penetration pricing, and value pricing. Make copies and show them to the class. **(Information)**

7. Explain how something as obvious as a retail price can have a psychological dimension. **(Information)**

8. **Team Activity** Divide the class into teams. Create a single market list of products. Each team should go to a different supermarket chain store or an independent supermarket and write down the prices of the goods selected. Report your findings to the class. **(Interpersonal)**

9. How does the stage of a product's life cycle affect price? Give some examples. **(Informational)**

Ethics Activity

As cosmetics companies roll out line after line of products to satisfy consumers' quest for youth, the shelves are getting crowded. How can a company stand out? The new Cosmedicine line from Klinger Advanced Aesthetics, introduced at Sephora cosmetics stores in February 2006, promoted its affiliation with the prestigious Johns Hopkins Medicine to distinguish itself from its competition. Hopkins' professors worked with Klinger on product design and reviewed research. In return, Hopkins would receive fees (which could be sizable), Klinger stock, and a seat on Klinger's board. Klinger would be able to use the Johns Hopkins name in advertising and promotional materials. For example, the Sephora Web site displayed this ad: "Truth is, it will achieve your highest skin health possible. . . . Truth is, its performance is confirmed by Johns Hopkins Medicine." Other ads claimed that Cosmedicine was the only skin-care line tested "in consultation with Johns Hopkins Medicine."

Immediately, medical ethicists criticized Johns Hopkins for this arrangement. Hopkins defended its position, claiming that its consulting work does not imply any endorsement of Cosmedicine. "We have been pretty clear about our role," said Hopkins CEO Edward Miller. "We are reporting on the scientific validity of studies that were done by outside testing agencies." And Cosmedicine packaging includes a disclaimer that discloses the nature of the research and financial relationship between Hopkins and Klinger. Others, such as Mildred Cho, associate director of the Stanford Center for Biomedical Ethics; Dr. Peter Lurie of the Public Citizen Health Research Group; and Dr. Marcia Angell, a former editor

of The New England Journal of Medicine, believed the promotional materials could mislead consumers. "You can't evaluate the product that's made by a manufacturer that's hired you," said Dr. Angell. "The thing is riddled with conflict of interest."

The uproar caused Johns Hopkins Medicine to acknowledge that its role could be viewed as an endorsement and to refuse an equity position in or a board seat at Klinger. Klinger and Sephora removed references to Hopkins from future advertising and promotional materials.

Using a Web search tool, locate articles about this topic and then write responses to the following questions. Be sure to support your arguments and cite your sources.

ETHICAL DILEMMA: Johns Hopkins Medicine hoped to gain funds for research and teaching with its arrangement with Klinger Advanced Aesthetics. Was it wrong to enter into the relationship with Klinger? Should it have backed down? Could it have structured the deal differently to avoid a conflict of interest? What is an appropriate relationship between academic medical centers and private sector companies?

Sources: Julie Bell and Frank D. Roylance, "Hopkins Assailed for Tie to Product," *Baltimore Sun*, April 6, 2006, **http://galenet.thomsonlearning.com**; "COSMEDICINE™ in Sephora Stores Now," *PR Newswire*, February 21, 2006, **http://galenet.thomson learning.com**; "Klinger Advanced Aesthetics CEO Details Johns Hopkins Medicine's Consulting Role," *Business Wire*, April 13, 2006, **http://galenet.thomsonlearning. com**; Rhonda L. Rundle, "A New Name in Skin Care: Johns Hopkins," *Wall Street Journal*, April 5, 2006, p. B1; Rhonda L. Rundle, "Johns Hopkins Backs Off Pact for Skin Care," *Wall Street Journal*, April 11, 2006, p. B1.

Working the Net

1. You and a friend want to start a new magazine for people who work at home. Do a search of the U.S. Census database at **http://www.census.gov** to get information about the work-at-home market. Then visit **http://www.jbsba.com** to expand your research. Summarize your findings.

2. Visit the SRI Consulting site, **http://www.sric-bi.com**, and click on the VALS Survey link. First read about the VALS survey and how marketers can use it. Describe its value. Then take the survey to find out which psychographic segment you're in. Do you agree or disagree with the results? Why or why not?

3. How good was the marketing strategy you developed in Question 1 of Preparing for Tomorrow's Workplace? Using advice from the marketing section of *Entrepreneur* (**http://www.entrepreneur.com**) or other resources, revisit your marketing strategy for the business you selected and revise the plan accordingly. (*Entrepreneur's* article "Write a Simple Marketing Plan" is a good place to start.) What did you overlook? (If you didn't do this exercise, pick one of the businesses and draft a marketing strategy using online resources to guide you.)

4. Visit an online retailer such as Amazon.com (**http://www.amazon.com**), PCConnection.com (**http://www.pcconnection.com**), or Drugstore.com (**http://www.drugstore.com**). At the site, try to identify examples of leader pricing, bundling, odd–even pricing, and other pricing strategies. Do online retailers have different pricing considerations than "real-world" retailers? Explain.

5. Do a search on Yahoo! (**http://www.yahoo.com**) for online auctions for a product you are interested in buying. Visit several auctions and get an idea of how the product is priced. How do these prices compare with the price you might find in a local store? What pricing advantages or disadvantages do companies face in selling their products through online auctions? How do online auctions affect the pricing strategies of other companies? Why?

6. Pick a new consumer electronic product such as a digital camera, HDTV, or laptop computer. Then go to the following shopping bots: **http://www.dealio.com**, **http://www.become.com**, **http://www.smarter.com**, and **http://brilliantshopper.com**. Compare prices, information, and ease of use of the sites. Report your findings to the class.

Creative Thinking Case

Coca-Cola is promoting its new Full Throttle energy drink, PepsiCo, Inc. is marketing energy drinks under its SoBe and Mountain Dew brands, and smaller companies are challenging the soft-drink giants with products like Rockstar and FUZE Mega Energy.

But South African Rodney C. Sacks, chairman and chief executive of Hansen's Natural Corporation, believes there's plenty of room for all comers in the booming energy-drink market. "These are the new soft drinks of the world," he declares. Sacks and Hansen president and chief financial officer, Hilton H. Schlosberg, raised $6 million from family and friends and bought Hansen, which was doing about $17 million in sales, for $14.5 million in 1992.

The California-based company made wholesome beverages such as preservative-free natural sodas, low-carb peach smoothies, and fruit-flavored iced teas—until Sacks and Schlosberg decided to give Red Bull a run for its money. They had seen the product in Europe and timed the launch of Hansen's Energy to coincide with Red Bull's appearance on American store shelves in 1997. Carbonated, citrusy, heavy on sugar and caffeine, Hansens's Energy failed to strike any sparks with its target market of college students, truckers, and sports fans.

So Sacks and Schlosberg added even more sugar and caffeine to a new mixture they marketed as Monster. They sold it for the same price as Red Bull but in big black cans twice the size, decorated with neon-colored "claw M" logos. Monster's slogan, "Unleash the beast," its eye-catching packaging, and extreme-sports sponsorships quickly made it a force in the fast-growing $2 billion a year energy-drink market.

Hansen supported the Monster brand with clever marketing. Teams of Monster "ambassadors" distribute samples at concerts, beach parties, and other events. The company sponsors high-profile sporting events like motor cross, surfing, and skateboarding competitions. Hansen representatives in black Monster vans help assemble store displays and restock racks in convenience store coolers. "A lot of companies say they will do that; [Hansen] really delivers," says Daniel R. Perry, senior vice president of All-American Bottling Corporation, a Monster distributor based in Oklahoma City.

Sales of $248 million earned Hansen's the top spot on *Forbes's* "Top 200 Best Small Companies in 2005." Hansen's energy-drink sales increased 162 percent last year, three times Red Bull's growth, earning it the number 26 spot on *Business Week's* annual ranking of Hot Growth Companies. But even though Hansen's sales growth gave it an 18 percent share of the energy-drink market, Red Bull still leads with nearly half the market.

Undaunted, Sacks and Schlosberg are fighting back. "A small subset of consumers is going wild over these drinks," says Beverage Digest editor and publisher John Sicher. "Hansen is really riding a tiger." The company launched Joker, an energy drink sold exclusively in Circle K convenience stores; Rumba, a morning pick-me-up, caffeine-laced juice drink; and Monster Assault, which comes in a black-and-gray camouflage can that says "Declare war on the ordinary!" It is a catchphrase that captures the high-energy tactics of a formerly low-energy player.

Critical Thinking Questions

- Hansen's Natural made a bold move in developing a product that was the opposite of what the company was known for. What accounts for Monster's huge success?
- What types of unique marketing support helped to sustain the product's tremendous growth?
- How powerful a role did pricing play in pitting Monster against its competition?

Sources: Andrew Murr, "Monster vs. Red Bull," *Newsweek*, March 20, 2006, p. E22; Christopher Palmeri, "Hansen Natural: Charging at Red Bull with a Brawny Energy Brew," *Business Week*, June 6, 2005; Christopher Palmeri, "Online Extra: Fruitful Energy," *Business Week*, June 6, 2005: Hansen's Natural corporate Web site **http://www.hansens.com**, April 29, 2006.

Exploring Business Careers

August Schaefer, public safety officer for Underwriters Laboratories, Inc. (UL), describes his company as "a neat place to work." Not the most exciting description from someone who enjoys his work so much that he has stayed at UL for over 30 years. However, as he says this, he is in a laboratory where employees test protective equipment like bullet-resistant vests. In another testing facility, engineers try to break into a safe—by dropping it, smashing into it, and blowing it up. In fact, UL engineers test everything from flat-screen televisions to roofing shingles to drinking water in Iraq. All told, UL tests over 19,000 different products made in over 70,000 factories throughout the world, ensuring that each one conforms to quality and safety standards. The average American household has more than 125 UL-safety-certified products. As Schaefer says, "UL is all around us. We affect everybody's life, every single day."

**August Schaefer
Underwriters
Laboratories, Inc.**

Originally Underwriters' Electrical Bureau, UL was started in 1894 by William Henry Merrill, who was inspired to start the company after investigating a rash of fires caused by Thomas Edison's light bulb exhibit at the World's Columbian Exposition in Chicago. Today, UL refers to itself as "an independent, not-for-profit product safety certification organization." Being independent and not-for-profit allows them to focus on the safety standards—standards they both develop and test products against—instead of on corporate profits, shareholder interests, or other outside influences. The tests UL engineers conduct vary according to the standards developed for the product being tested, taking into account its intended use, potential misuses, and other possible dangers. Carrying out the rigorous testing each product undergoes makes UL as much a playground as a place of employment for engineers like Schaefer.

However, the product safety testing that UL conducts is not all fun and games, especially for the manufacturers whose products are tested. Although not required, UL certification has become a vital part of many products' development and often is a critical component of their successful introduction to the marketplace. Manufacturers strive for certification for several reasons: It is a mark of trust and integrity, assuring that a product has been tested thoroughly and that the manufacturer cares not only about the quality of its product but also the safety of its consumer. Beyond this, people interested in the product look for UL safety certification. When a consumer—whether a wholesaler, retailer, or end-user—sees the UL label, he or she can be confident that the product has been tested thoroughly and is compliant with the highest standards.

Ultimately, UL product safety certification provides peace of mind for both manufacturers and consumers. As Schaefer says, "When they buy a product, . . . they don't have to worry, 'Is it going to be a safe product?' They can expect it to be safe when they see the UL mark." And that makes both manufacturers and consumers happy—a "neat" concept, indeed.

Distributing and Promoting Products and Services

Learning Goals

After reading this chapter, you should be able to answer these questions.

1 What is the nature and function of distribution?

2 What is wholesaling, and what are the types of wholesalers?

3 What are the different kinds of retail operations?

4 How can supply chain management increase efficiency and customer satisfaction?

5 What is promotion, and what are the key elements of a promotional mix?

6 How are advertising media selected?

7 What is personal selling?

8 What are the goals of a sales promotion, and what are several types of sales promotion?

9 How does public relations fit into the promotional mix?

10 What are the trends in promotion and distribution?

BIZ FLIX

"Perfect for Your Frame"

In the previous chapter, we explored a clip from *The Family Man,* a movie that follows Jack Campbell through a "what if" story. He wakes up one morning to find himself in what he considers a suburban nightmare with a wife and two kids and a retail job selling tires. This is in stark contrast to his previous life as a wealthy investment banker living in New York City, becoming richer and more successful his only cares in the world. Now he's living the nuclear-family life, wandering through the mall until he stumbles upon a suit that makes him feel like a better person. On top of demonstrating a variety of strategic marketing elements, the clip also provides an overview of the four Ps of marketing—product, price, place, and promotion—which are discussed in greater detail throughout the chapter.

The suit that Jack is trying on in the clip is obviously the product. We often think of products as simple things that are bought and sold in the marketplace; however, products are much more than that. They are not only the physical thing (or the actual service), but they are also the attributes and benefits that the consumer perceives them to be. So, in Jack's eyes, the product is not just the cloth and material that make up the suit, but it also includes the added benefit of how it makes him feel about himself and who he is. Furthermore, it looks "amazing" on him according to his wife, so if he purchases it, he's purchasing the suit, how it makes him feel about himself, and how it makes his wife think about him as well. In such a way, Jack sees great value in the product.

But this value comes with a whopping $2,400 price tag. Many of us might look at that price tag and understand exactly where Kate is coming from when she tells her husband it is absurd to think of buying the suit. She does not see the value relative to the cost that Jack sees, and price is all about seeing the value in relationship to the thing received. Price in this sense is all about individual perception. Jack sees the suit as a bargain whereas Kate sees it as a drain on vital resources. Jack expects to receive an inordinate amount of satisfaction from the purchase, but Kate sees something completely different. In such a way, price and perception are inextricably linked when it comes to the value received in exchange for a product.

The product and price would not be an issue if Jack had never stumbled across the suit in the first place, which brings us to the third of the four Ps: place. By place, we mean distribution or, in other words, how we place the product within reach of our consumers. The suit did not just magically appear in front of Jack. It started as a set of raw materials in a manufacturer's plant and was converted into the product that was then sent through a chain of various entities, each adding value to the product in some way before finally arriving in the store where Jack happened to be shopping at the time. Without this distribution channel, Jack does not even see the product.

And without the promotional efforts of the salesperson, Jack might not even have tried on the suit. He steps right up to Jack and states, "It's perfect for your frame . . . why don't you try it on?" Promotion is the part of the marketing mix that informs consumers of a product, persuades them to try or purchase a product, and also reminds them of a product's benefits. In this case, the promotional tool in use is personal selling, where an actual salesperson works to inform and persuade Jack. He starts by identifying a prospect, approaches that prospect, and then presents and demonstrates the product, but then the process gets derailed by Kate. The total marketing mix was not strong enough to overcome Kate's objections.

The following chapter provides a more detailed overview of the nature and function of distribution and distribution channels as well as an understanding of the promotional efforts businesses undertake in an effort to sell goods to customers. The chapter covers various elements of the supply chain, including wholesalers and retailers as well as how companies go about managing the supply chain. Then, the authors discuss the various elements of the promotional mix including advertising, personal selling, sales promotion, and public relations. The chapter then concludes with various trends in promotion and distribution. As such, and coupled with the previous chapter, you should come away with a general understanding of the marketing mix and its importance in business.

319

Discussion Questions

- Describe the distribution channel you think the suit flowed through, making sure that you explain how each segment in that channel adds value to the end product.
- Describe the type of retailing operation Jack has entered into. If he really wants the suit but at a reduced price, what other retail outlet might he visit and why?
- In the clip, Jack states that he will take the suit, but Kate enters at that point and even though she thinks he looks amazing in the suit, she balks at the price tag. What might the salesman have done to counter Kate's objections to the price and closed the sale?
- Describe any other elements in the promotional toolkit that the salesperson might have used and how he might have used them to close the sale. Describe any other elements the manufacturer might have used and how they might have been used to close the sale.

The Nature and Functions of Distribution

1 What is the nature and function of distribution?

distribution (logistics)
Efficiently managing the acquisition of raw materials to the factory and the movement of products from the producer to industrial users and consumers.

manufacturer
A producer; an organization that converts raw materials to finished products.

distribution channel
The series of marketing entities through which goods and services pass on their way from producers to end users.

marketing intermediaries
Organizations that assist in moving goods and services from producers to end users.

Distribution (or logistics) is efficiently managing the acquisition of raw materials to the factory and the movement of products from the producer or **manufacturer** to industrial users and consumers. Logistics activities are usually the responsibility of the marketing department and are part of the large series of activities included in the supply chain. A supply chain is the connected chain of all business entities, both internal and external to the company, that performs or supports the marketing channel functions. As products move through the supply chain, channel members facilitate the distribution process. Exhibit 12.1 illustrates a supply chain. Supply chain management helps increase the efficiency of logistics service by minimizing inventory and moving goods efficiently from producers to the ultimate users.

On their way from producers to end users and consumers, goods and services pass through a series of marketing entities known as a **distribution channel**. We will look first at the entities that make up a distribution channel and then will examine the functions that channels serve.

Marketing Intermediaries in the Distribution Channel

A distribution channel is made up of **marketing intermediaries**, or organizations that assist in moving goods and services from producers to end users and consumers. Marketing intermediaries are in the middle of the distribution process between the producer and the end user. The following marketing intermediaries most often appear in the distribution channel:

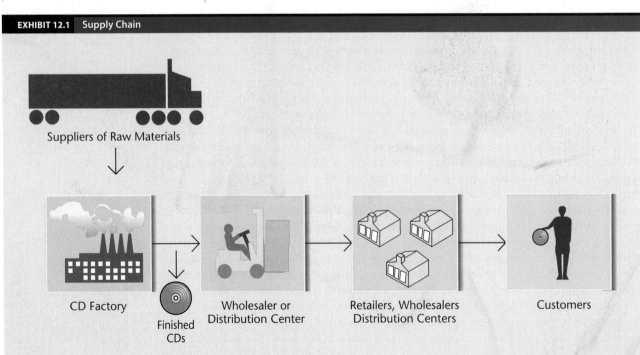

EXHIBIT 12.1 Supply Chain

Suppliers of Raw Materials

CD Factory

Finished CDs

Wholesaler or Distribution Center

Retailers, Wholesalers Distribution Centers

Customers

- *Agents and brokers.* **Agents** are sales representatives of manufacturers and wholesalers, and **brokers** are entities that bring buyers and sellers together. Both agents and brokers are usually hired on commission basis by either a buyer or a seller. Agents and brokers are go-betweens whose job is to make deals. They do not own or take possession of goods.
- *Industrial distributors.* **Industrial distributors** are independent wholesalers that buy related product lines from many manufacturers and sell them to industrial users. They often have a sales force to call on purchasing agents, make deliveries, extend credit, and provide information. Industrial distributors are used in such industries as aircraft manufacturing, mining, and petroleum.
- *Wholesalers.* **Wholesalers** are firms that sell finished goods to retailers, manufacturers, and institutions (such as schools and hospitals). Historically, their function has been to buy from manufacturers and sell to retailers.
- *Retailers.* **Retailers** are firms that sell goods to consumers and to industrial users for their own consumption.

At the end of the distribution channel are final consumers, like you and me, and industrial users. Industrial users are firms that buy products for internal use or for producing other products or services. They include manufacturers, utilities, airlines, railroads, and service institutions, such as hotels, hospitals, and schools.

Exhibit 12.2 shows various ways marketing intermediaries can be linked. For instance, a manufacturer may sell to a wholesaler that sells to a retailer that in turn sells to a customer. In any of these distribution systems, goods and services are physically transferred from one organization to the

agents
Sales representatives of manufacturers and wholesalers.

brokers
Go-betweens that bring buyers and sellers together.

industrial distributors
Independent wholesalers that buy related product lines from many manufacturers and sell them to industrial users.

wholesalers
Firms that sell finished goods to retailers, manufacturers, and institutions.

retailers
Firms that sell goods to consumers and to industrial users for their own consumption.

EXHIBIT 12.2 Channels of Distribution for Industrial and Consumer Products

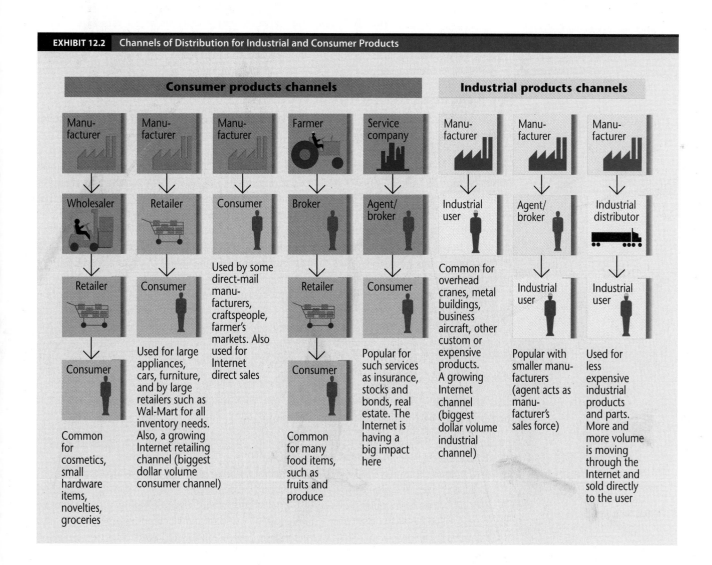

next. As each takes possession of the products, it may take legal ownership of them. As the exhibit indicates, distribution channels can handle either consumer products or industrial products.

Nontraditional Channels Often nontraditional channel arrangements help differentiate a firm's product from the competition. For example, manufacturers may decide to use nontraditional channels such as the Internet, mail-order channels, or infomercials to sell products instead of going through traditional retailer channels. Although nontraditional channels may limit a brand's coverage, they can give a producer serving a niche market a way to gain market access and customer attention without having to establish channel intermediaries. Nontraditional channels can also provide another avenue of sales for larger firms. For example, a London publisher sells short stories through vending machines in the London Underground. Instead of the traditional book format, the stories are printed like folded maps, making them an easy-to-read alternative for commuters.

Kiosks, long a popular method for ordering and registering for wedding gifts, disbursing cash through ATMs, and facilitating airline check-in, are finding new uses. Ethan Allen furniture stores use kiosks as a product locator tool for consumers and salespeople. Kiosks on the campuses of Cheney University allow students to register for classes, see their class schedule and grades, check account balances, and even print transcripts. The general public, when it has access to the kiosks, can use them to gather information about the university.

Small- and medium-size Louisiana food and beverage companies banded together to sell their goods over the Internet at **http://www.shoppinglouisiana. com**. They also have found that they can successfully sell their offerings through the QVC Shopping Network. With electronic media rapidly evolving, downloading first-run movies to cell phones may not be too far off! The changing world of electronics technology and the Internet opens many doors for new, nontraditional channels.

CONCEPT in action

Not since the invention of the printing press has the publishing industry had so many exciting possibilities for distributing content. With the recent arrival of electronic devices and digital downloading, traditional publishers can now digitize printed materials and send them to customers wirelessly, using simple cell phone technology. The product driving this new revolution is Kindle, a wireless reading device from Amazon.com that provides readers with instant access to its books, blogs, magazines, and newspapers. Kindle's electronic ink display even reads like real paper. How are electronic media transforming the traditional distribution channel?

The Functions of Distribution Channels

Why do distribution channels exist? Why can't every firm sell its products directly to the end user or consumer? Why are go-betweens needed? Channels serve a number of functions.

Channels Reduce the Number of Transactions Channels make distribution simpler by reducing the number of transactions required to get a product from the manufacturer to the consumer. Assume for the moment that only four students are in your class. Also assume that your professor requires five textbooks, each from a different publisher. If there were no bookstore, 20 transactions would be necessary for all students in the class to buy the books, as shown in Exhibit 12.3. If the bookstore serves as a go-between, the number of transactions is reduced to nine. Each publisher sells to one bookstore rather than to four students. Each student buys from one bookstore instead of from five publishers.

Dealing with channel intermediaries frees producers from many of the details of distribution activity. Producers are traditionally not as efficient or as enthusiastic about selling products directly to end users as channel members are. First, producers may wish to focus on production. They may feel that they cannot both produce and distribute in a competitive way. On the other hand, manufacturers are eager to deal directly with giant retailers, such as Wal-Mart. Wal-Mart offers huge sales opportunities to producers.

Channels Ease the Flow of Goods Channels make distribution easier in several ways. The first is by sorting, which consists of the following:

- *Sorting out.* Breaking many different items into separate stocks that are similar. Eggs, for instance, are sorted by grade and size.
- *Accumulating.* Bringing similar stocks together into a larger quantity. Twelve large grade A eggs could be placed in some cartons and 12 medium grade B eggs in other cartons.
- *Allocating.* Breaking similar products into smaller and smaller lots. (Allocating at the wholesale level is called **breaking bulk**.) For instance, a tank-car load of milk could be broken down into gallon jugs. The process of allocating generally is done when the goods are dispersed by region and as ownership of the goods changes.

breaking bulk
The process of breaking large shipments of similar products into smaller, more usable lots.

Part 4: Marketing Management

EXHIBIT 12.3   How Distribution Channels Reduce the Number of Transactions

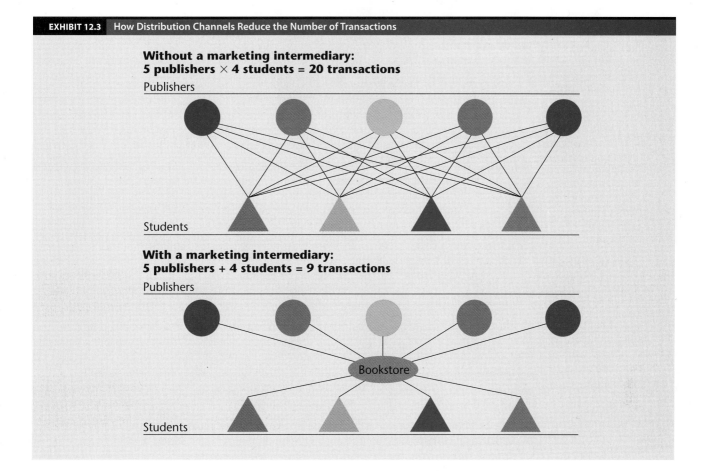

Without a marketing intermediary:
5 publishers × 4 students = 20 transactions

Publishers

Students

With a marketing intermediary:
5 publishers + 4 students = 9 transactions

Publishers

Bookstore

Students

Without the sorting, accumulating, and allocating processes, modern society would not exist. We would have home-based industries providing custom or semi-custom products to local markets. In short, we would return to a much lower level of consumption.

A second way channels ease the flow of goods is by locating buyers for merchandise. A wholesaler must find the right retailers to sell a profitable volume of merchandise. A sporting-goods wholesaler, for instance, must find the retailers who are most likely to reach sporting-goods consumers. Retailers have to understand the buying habits of consumers and put stores where consumers want and expect to find the merchandise. Every member of a distribution channel must locate buyers for the products it is trying to sell.

Channel members also store merchandise so that goods are available when consumers want to buy them. The high cost of retail space often means that many goods are stored by the wholesaler or the manufacturer.

Sometimes global manufacturers, like Procter & Gamble, must use drastically different channels of distribution from those used in the United States. The Expanding Around the Globe box on the next page explains why.

CONCEPT check

List and define the marketing intermediaries that make up a distribution channel.

Provide an example of a strategic channel alliance.

How do channels reduce the number of transactions?

Wholesaling

Wholesalers are channel members that buy finished products from manufacturers and sell them to retailers. Retailers in turn sell the products to consumers.

2 What is wholesaling, and what are the types of wholesalers?

Wholesalers also sell products to institutions, such as manufacturers, schools, and hospitals, for use in performing their own missions. A manufacturer, for instance, might buy computer paper from Nationwide Papers, a wholesaler. A hospital might buy its cleaning supplies from Lagasse Brothers, one of the nation's largest wholesalers of janitorial supplies.

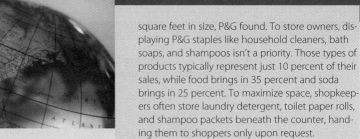

Procter & Gamble often Targets Tiny Stores in Its Global Distribution Strategy

Every day, Martina Pérez Díaz, who lives in Leon, Mexico, spends about five hours sewing 70 pairs of black loafers by hand for a wage of 120 pesos, or about $11. When she wants to wash her hair, she walks to he local *tiendita,* or "small store," to buy a 0.34-ounce, single-use packet of Procter & Gamble Co.'s Head & Shoulders shampoo. The price: two pesos, or about 19¢. "That I usually can afford," she says.

Shoppers like Ms. Díaz factor heavily into P&G's plan to conquer more of the globe. The consumer products giant has a goal of increasing total sales by 5 percent to 7 percent annually. As part of that mission, it is looking to tap roughly 1 billion additional consumers—most of them very poor women who live in developing countries.

Reaching these customers isn't easy. In emerging markets, P&G estimates that 80 percent of people buy their wares from mom-and-pop stores no bigger than a closet. Crammed with food and a hodgepodge of household items, these retailers serve as the pantries of the world's poorest consumers for whom both money and space are tight.

P&G calls such locally owned bodegas, stalls, and kiosks "high-frequency stores," because of the multiple times shoppers visit them during a single day or week. Though most are rudimentary, usually operating out of the owner's home, these shops are a vital route into developing markets, executives believe. But while P&G estimates there to be about 20 million high-frequency stores worldwide, so far just 2.5 million carry their products.

Product visibility, for instance, is one of the biggest challenges to selling in high-frequency stores. Shops tend to be poorly lit and in Latin America average just 250 square feet in size, P&G found. To store owners, displaying P&G staples like household cleaners, bath soaps, and shampoos isn't a priority. Those types of products typically represent just 10 percent of their sales, while food brings in 35 percent and soda brings in 25 percent. To maximize space, shopkeepers often store laundry detergent, toilet paper rolls, and shampoo packets beneath the counter, handing them to shoppers only upon request.

So P&G began lobbying for better shelf space, one tiny store at a time, by offering them special perks that rivals do not. P&G-employed merchandisers visit the stores about every two weeks to tidy the shelves of their products, post signs with the items' prices, and hand out promotional items, including posters. Also, sales representatives deliver inventory to stores themselves, often sparing owners a trip to the local distributor.[1]

Critical Thinking Questions
- Do you think that P&G is wasting its time with "high-frequency stores" because sooner or later Wal-Mart will put them out of business?
- Who are some other manufacturers that might target "high-frequency stores?" Why would they do so?

Sometimes wholesalers sell products to manufacturers for use in the manufacturing process. A builder of custom boats, for instance, might buy batteries from a battery wholesaler and switches from an electrical wholesaler. Some wholesalers even sell to other wholesalers, creating yet another stage in the distribution channel.

Types of Wholesaler Intermediaries

The two main types of wholesalers are merchant wholesalers and agents and brokers. Merchant wholesalers take title to the product (ownership rights); agents and brokers simply facilitate the sale of a product from producer to end user.

Merchant Wholesalers

merchant wholesaler
An institution that buys goods from manufacturers (takes ownership) and resells them to businesses, government agencies, other wholesalers, or retailers.

Merchant wholesalers make up 80 percent of all wholesaling establishments and conduct slightly less than 60 percent of all wholesale sales. A **merchant wholesaler** is an institution that buys goods from manufacturers and resells them to businesses, government agencies, other wholesalers, or retailers. All merchant wholesalers take title to the goods they sell.

Agents and Brokers

manufacturers' representatives (manufacturer's agent)
Salespeople who represent noncompeting manufacturers; function as independent agents rather than as salaried employees of the manufacturers.

As mentioned earlier, agents represent manufacturers and wholesalers. **Manufacturers' representatives** (also called **manufacturers' agents**) represent noncompeting manufacturers. These salespeople function as independent agents, rather than as salaried employees of manufacturers. They do not take title to or possession of merchandise. They get commissions if they make sales—and nothing if they don't. They are found in a variety of industries, including electronics, clothing, hardware, furniture, and toys.

Brokers bring buyers and sellers together. Like agents, brokers do not take title to merchandise, they receive commissions on sales, and they have little say over company sales policies. They are found in markets where the information that would join buyers and sellers is scarce. These markets include real estate, agriculture, insurance, and commodities.

CONCEPT check

Define wholesaling and describe what wholesalers do.

Describe merchant wholesalers.

Explain the difference between agents and brokers.

The Competitive World of Retailing

3 What are the different kinds of retail operations?

Some 30 million Americans are engaged in retailing. Of this number, almost 16 million work in service businesses like barber shops, lawyers' offices, and amusement parks. Although most retailers are involved in small businesses, most sales are made by the giant retail organizations, such as Sears, Wal-Mart, Target, and JCPenney. Half of all retail sales come from fewer than 10 percent of all retail businesses. This small group employs about 40 percent of all retail workers. Retailers feel the impact of changes in the economy more than many other types of businesses. Survival depends on keeping up with changing lifestyles and customer shopping patterns.

Types of Retail Operations

There is a great deal of variety in retail operations. The major types of retailers are described in Exhibit 12.4, which divides them into two main categories: in-store and nonstore retailing. Examples of in-store retailing include Sears, Wal-Mart, Target, Macy's, and Neiman Marcus. These retailers get most of their revenue from people who come to the store to buy what they want. Many in-store retailers also do some catalog and telephone sales.

Nonstore retailing includes vending, direct selling, direct-response marketing, home shopping networks, and Internet retailing. Vending uses machines to sell food and other items, usually as a convenience in institutions like schools and hospitals.

Creating an Image and Promotional Strategy

An important task in retailing is to create an image and a promotional strategy. Promotion combines with the store's merchandise mix, service level, and atmosphere to make up a retail image. Atmosphere refers to the physical layout and décor of the store. They can create a relaxed or busy feeling, a sense of luxury, a friendly or cold attitude, and a sense of organization or clutter.

These are the most influential factors in creating a store's atmosphere:

- *Employee type and density.* Employee type refers to an employee's general characteristics—for instance, neat, friendly, knowledgeable, or service

CONCEPT in action

Whether you're shopping for women's business apparel or chic back-to-school fashions, Kohl's is the place. Not only does the popular chain offer deep discounts on brand-name apparel like Vera Wang and Candie's, but Kohl's also offers an exclusive line of juniors' fashions inspired by pop diva Avril Lavigne. Named Abbey Dawn, the cross-category collection offers up Lavigne's trademark taste in plaids, stripes, and mix-and-match prints—with plenty of rock-n-roll attitude. What type of retailer is Kohl's, and what categories of merchandise does it offer?

EXHIBIT 12.4	Retailing Takes Many Forms	
Types of In-Store Retailing	**Description**	**Examples**
Department store	Houses many departments under one roof with each treated as a separate buying center to achieve economies of buying, promotion, and control	JCPenney, Saks, Bloomingdale's, Macy's
Specialty store	Specializes in a category of merchandise and carries a complete assortment	Toys "R" Us, Radio Shack, Zales Jewelers
Convenience store	Offers convenience goods with long store hours and quick checkout	7-Eleven, Circle K
Supermarket	Specializes in a wide assortment of food, with self-service	Safeway, Kroger, Winn-Dixie
Discount store	Competes on the basis of low prices and high turnover; offers few services	Wal-Mart, Target
Off-price retailer	Sells at prices 25 percent or more below traditional department store prices in spartan environment	Robs, T. J. Maxx, Clothestime
Factory outlet	Owned by manufacturer; sells close-outs, factory seconds, and canceled orders	Levi Strauss, Ship 'n Shore, Dansk
Catalog store	Sends catalogs to customers and displays merchandise in showrooms where customers can order from attached warehouse	Best, Lurias
Hypermart	Offers huge selection of food and general merchandise with very low prices; sometimes called "mall without a wall"	Hypermart USA, American Fare
Types of Nonstore Retailing	**Description**	**Examples**
Vending machine	Sells merchandise by machine	Canteen
Direct selling	Sells face-to-face, usually in the person's home	Fuller Brush, Avon, Amway
Direct-response marketing	Attempts to get immediate consumer sale through media advertising, catalogs, pop-up ads or direct mail	K-Tel, L. L. Bean, Ronco
Home shopping networks	Selling via cable television	Home Shopping Network, QVC
Internet retailing (e-retailing)	Selling over the Internet	Bluefly.com, landsend.com, gap.com, Amazon.com, Cheapstuff.com, Dell.com, overstock.com

Whether peering through department store windows, buying holiday gifts, or going on a spending spree, people love to shop. Shopping makes people feel good and a growing body of research suggests that shopping activates key areas of the brain, boosting one's mood—at least until the bill arrives. Feelings of pleasure and satisfaction derived from a buying binge may be linked to brain chemicals that produce a "shopping high." How might retailers use atmosphere to stimulate consumers' natural impulse to shop?

oriented. Density is the number of employees per 1,000 square feet of selling space. A discounter such as Target has a low employee density that creates a "do-it-yourself" casual atmosphere.

- *Merchandise type and density*. The type of merchandise carried and how it is displayed add to the atmosphere the retailer is trying to create. A prestigious retailer such as Saks or Bergdorf Goodman carries the best brand names and displays them in a neat, uncluttered arrangement.

- *Fixture type and density*. Fixtures can be elegant (rich woods), trendy (chrome and smoked glass), or old, beat-up tables, as in an antique store. The fixtures should be consistent with the general atmosphere the store is trying to create. By displaying its merchandise on tables and shelves rather than on traditional pipe racks, the Gap creates a relaxed and uncluttered atmosphere that enables customers to see and touch the merchandise more easily. In addition to traditional display racks, Bass Pro Shops feature shooting and archery ranges, 64,000-gallon aquariums stocked with trophy bass and other fish, huge rock fireplaces with trophy mounts, numerous ponds, and waterfalls. A typical Bass Pro Shop has several million customers a year. It is not unusual for someone to drive over 100 miles to get to a Bass Pro Shop.[2]

- *Sound*. Sound can be pleasant or unpleasant for a customer. Classical music at a nice Italian restaurant helps create ambiance, just as country and western music does at a truck stop. Music can also entice customers to stay in the store longer and buy more or encourage them to eat quickly and leave a table for others.

- *Odors*. Smell can either stimulate or detract from sales. The wonderful smell of pastries and breads entices bakery customers. Conversely, customers can be repulsed by bad odors, such as cigarette smoke, musty smells, antiseptic smells, and overly powerful room deodorizers.

A Spanish retailer is changing the way many clothing retailers manage their supply chains. Their strategy is explained in the Managing Change box on the next page.

Describe at least five types of in-store retailing and four forms of nonstore retailing.

What factors most influence a retail store's atmosphere?

Using Supply Chain Management to Increase Efficiency and Customer Satisfaction

4 How can supply chain management increase efficiency and customer satisfaction?

Distribution is an important part of the marketing mix. Retailers don't sell products they can't deliver, and salespeople don't (or shouldn't) promise deliveries they can't make. Late deliveries and broken promises may mean loss of a customer. Accurate order filling and billing, timely delivery, and arrival in good condition are important to the success of the product.

The goal of supply chain management is to create a satisfied customer by coordinating all of the activities of the supply chain members into a seamless process. Therefore, an important element of supply chain management is that it is completely customer driven. In the mass-production era, manufacturers produced standardized products that were "pushed" down through the supply channel to the consumer. In contrast, in today's marketplace, products are being driven by customers, who expect to receive product configurations and services matched to their unique needs. For example, Dell only builds computers according to its customers' precise specifications, such as the amount of RAM memory; type of monitor, modem, or CD drive; and amount of hard-disk space. The process begins by Dell purchasing partially-built laptops from contract manufacturers. The final assembly is done in Dell factories in Ireland, Malaysia, or China where microprocessors, software, and other key components are added. Those finished products are then shipped to Dell-operated distribution centers in the United States where they are packaged with other items and shipped to the customer.

Through the channel partnership of suppliers, manufacturers, wholesalers, and retailers along the entire supply chain who work together toward the common goal of creating customer value, supply chain management allows companies to respond with the unique product configuration and mix of services demanded by the customer. Today, supply chain management plays a dual role: first, as a communicator of customer demand that extends from the point of sale all the way back

© Stockbyte/Getty Images

Zara—Retailing at the Speed Of Light

Zara and "quick" are basically synonymous. No one controls its supply chain as well and as efficiently as Zara. Fashion is highly perishable, quickly influenced by the latest item seen at a Paris fashion show or on the back of a celebrity. Zara, with its in-house design team in La Coruna, Spain, follows fashion trends closely. Often tips are passed on from the managers of the almost 4,000 Zara stores around the globe. Also, if trend-setters spot, say, fashion leaders wearing white eyelet—cotton with tiny holes in it—Zara will confirm the trend with a quick telephone survey of Zara store managers. If it is a "go," the designers quickly get to work.

Using company-owned manufacturing plants in Spain, production is ramped up as soon as the designs are ready. The clothing is then delivered by truck to Europe and then by air to Zara stores all over the world. The total elapsed time: about two weeks. Zara produces new items in small batches. Unlike conventional retailers, Zara wants to run out of inventory. This only makes trendy shoppers want a "can't have" piece even more. The tight inventory accomplishes several things. It means that Zara shoppers won't all be wearing the same thing, thus preserving an air of exclusivity. "If you go in to Zara's on Monday and find something you like, you had better buy it because it won't be there on Friday." Also, shoppers return often because they

know the offerings will be fresh and new. Finally, Zara takes fewer markdowns because of white-hot demand and limited supply. Zara's objective is not that customers buy a lot, but that they buy often and will find something new every time they enter the store.

Zara avoids advertising and lets the stores speak for themselves. It uses spacious, minimalist outlets—more like an exclusive fashion house than a Target store. The firm also has no big-name designers, which helps hold down costs. Yet, these designers create around 40,000 new designs a year of which about a quarter are manufactured.[3]

Critical Thinking Questions

- Do you think that Zara has an efficient supply chain by manufacturing everything in Spain and surrounding countries? Would it be better to switch to low-cost countries like China for manufacturing?
- Do you think that management is correct by not spending money on advertising? Why?

to the supplier, and second, as a physical flow process that engineers the timely and cost-effective movement of goods through the entire supply pipeline.

Accordingly, supply chain managers are responsible for making channel strategy decisions, coordinating the sourcing and procurement of raw materials, scheduling production, processing orders, managing inventory, transporting and storing supplies and finished goods, and coordinating customer service activities. Supply chain managers are also responsible for the management of information that flows through the supply chain. Coordinating the relationships between the company and its external partners, such as vendors, carriers, and third-party companies, is also a critical function of supply chain management. Because supply chain managers play such a major role in both cost control and customer satisfaction, they are more valuable than ever.

CONCEPT check

What is the goal of supply chain management?

What does it mean for a supply chain to be customer driven?

Promotional Goals

Promotion is an attempt by marketers to inform, persuade, or remind consumers and industrial users to influence their opinion or elicit a response. Most firms use some form of promotion. Because company goals vary widely, so do promotional strategies. The goal is to stimulate action. In a profit-oriented firm, the desired action is for the consumer to buy the promoted item. Mrs. Smith's, for instance, wants people to buy more frozen pies. Not-for-profit organizations seek a variety of actions with their promotions. They tell us not to litter, to buckle up, to join the army, and to attend the ballet.

Promotional goals include creating awareness, getting people to try products, providing information, retaining loyal customers, increasing the use of products, and identifying potential customers. Any promotional campaign may seek to achieve one or more of these goals:

1. *Creating awareness*. All too often, firms go out of business because people don't know they exist or what they do. Small restaurants often have this problem. Simply putting up a sign and opening the door is rarely enough. Promotion through ads on local radio or television, coupons in local papers, flyers, the Internet, and so forth can create awareness of a new business or product.

   Large companies often use catchy slogans to build brand awareness. Dodge trucks' wildly successful ads where a guy yells over to another truck at a stoplight, "That thing got a HEMI?" has created a huge number of new customers for Dodge trucks. HEMI has become a brand within a brand. Now, DaimlerChrysler is extending the HEMI engine to the Jeep brand, hoping for the same success.

5 What is promotion, and what are the key elements of a promotional mix?

promotion
The attempt by marketers to inform, persuade, or remind consumers and industrial users to engage in the exchange process.

People who had never heard of Carl's Jr. were dramatically introduced to the California-based burger chain after a commercial for Carl's Spicy BBQ Burger featured socialite Paris Hilton. In the TV spot, a swimsuit-clad Hilton washes a sleek Bentley before stealing away to take a bite of the hefty sandwich. The $5 million ad generated enormous buzz and garnered millions in controversy-related publicity. Are risqué ads risky for advertisers?

© Fred Prouser/Reuters/Landov

2. *Getting consumers to try products.* Promotion is almost always used to get people to try a new product or to get nonusers to try an existing product. Sometimes free samples are given away. Lever, for instance, mailed over 2 million free samples of its Lever 2000 soap to target households. Coupons and trial-size containers of products are also common tactics used to tempt people to try a product. Celebrities are also used to get people to try products. Beyonce, for example, received $4.7 million from L'Oreal to promote its products. Peyton Manning makes over $11 million per year by endorsing MasterCard, Sprint Nextel, Sony, Reebok, and DirectTV.[4] After Eli Manning won the Super Bowl, his endorsement value skyrocketed.

3. *Providing information.* Informative promotion is more common in the early stages of the product life cycle. An informative promotion may explain what ingredients (like fiber) will do for your health, tell you why the product is better (plasma versus LCD television), inform you of a new low price, or explain where the item may be bought.

   People typically will not buy a product or support a not-for-profit organization until they know what it will do and how it may benefit them. Thus, an informative ad may stimulate interest in a product. Consumer watchdogs and social critics applaud the informative function of promotion because it helps consumers make more intelligent purchase decisions. Star-Kist, for instance, lets customers know that its tuna is caught in dolphin-safe nets.

4. *Keeping loyal customers.* Promotion is also used to keep people from switching brands. Slogans such as Campbell's Soups are "M'm! M'm! Good!" and Intel's new "Leap Ahead" remind consumers about the brand. Marketers also remind users that the brand is better than the competition. For years, Pepsi has claimed it has the taste that consumers prefer. Southwest Airlines brags of its improvement in on-time ratings. Such advertising reminds customers about the quality of the product.

   Firms can also help keep customers loyal by telling them when a product or service is improved. Marriott announced that it spent $190 million on new bedding.[5] It offers plusher mattresses, softer sheets, more pillows, and a new, fresh look.

5. *Increasing the amount and frequency of use.* Promotion is often used to get people to use more of a product and to use it more often. The National Cattlemen's Beef Association reminds Americans to "Eat More Beef." The most popular promotion to increase the use of a product may be frequent-flyer or -user programs. The Marriott Rewards program awards points for each dollar spent at a Marriott property. At the Platinum level, members receive a guaranteed room, an upgrade to their finest available accommodations, access to the concierge lounge, a free breakfast, free local phone calls, and a variety of other goodies.

6. *Identifying target customers.* Promotion helps find customers. One way to do this is to list a Web site. For instance, the *Wall Street Journal* and *Business Week* include Web addresses for more information on computer systems, corporate jets, color copiers, and other types of business equipment, to help target those who are truly interested. Fidelity Mutual Funds ads trumpet, "Solid investment opportunities are out there," then direct consumers to go to **http://www.fidelity.com**. A full-page ad in the *Wall Street Journal* for Sprint unlimited wireless e-mail invites potential customers to visit **http://www.sprint.com**. These Web sites typically will ask for your e-mail address.

The Promotional Mix

promotional mix
The combination of advertising, personal selling, sales promotion, and public relations used to promote a product.

The combination of advertising, personal selling, sales promotion, and public relations used to promote a product is called the **promotional mix**. Each firm creates a unique mix for each product. But the goal is always to deliver the firm's message efficiently and effectively to the target audience. These are the elements of the promotional mix:

- *Advertising.* Any paid form of nonpersonal promotion by an identified sponsor.
- *Personal selling.* A face-to-face presentation to a prospective buyer.

- *Sales promotion*. Marketing activities (other than personal selling, advertising, and public relations) that stimulate consumer buying, including coupons and samples, displays, shows and exhibitions, demonstrations, and other types of selling efforts.
- *Public relations*. The linking of organizational goals with key aspects of the public interest and the development of programs designed to earn public understanding and acceptance.

Ideally, marketing communications from each promotional-mix element (personal selling, advertising, sales promotion, and public relations) should be integrated. That is, the message reaching the consumer should be the same regardless of whether it comes from an advertisement, company blog, a salesperson in the field, a magazine article, or a coupon in a newspaper insert.

Integrated Marketing Communications

This unintegrated, disjointed approach to promotion has propelled many companies to adopt the concept of **integrated marketing communications (IMC)**. IMC involves carefully coordinating all promotional activities—media advertising, Internet advertising, sales promotion, personal selling, and public relations, as well as direct marketing, packaging, and other forms of promotion—to produce a consistent, unified message that is customer focused. Following the concept of IMC, marketing managers carefully work out the roles the various promotional elements will play in the marketing mix. Timing of promotional activities is coordinated, and the results of each campaign are carefully monitored to improve future use of the promotional mix tools. Typically, a marketing communications director is appointed to have overall responsibility for integrating the company's marketing communications.

Pepsi relied on IMC to launch Pepsi One. The $100 million program relied on personal selling in the distribution channels, a public relations campaign with press releases to announce the product, and heavy doses of advertising and sales promotion. The company toured the country's shopping malls setting up Pepsi One "lounges"—inflatable couches with plastic carpeting—for random taste tests. It also produced 11,000 end-cap displays for supermarket aisles and created stand-up displays for 12-packs to spark impulse purchases. It secured Oscar-winning actor Cuba Gooding Jr. as spokesperson for the ad campaign. The ads made their debut during the World Series. The tagline for the ad campaign was "Only One has it all."

The sections that follow examine the elements of the promotional mix in more detail.

integrated marketing communications (IMC)
The careful coordination of all promotional activities—media advertising, sales promotion, personal selling, and public relations, as well as direct marketing, packaging, and other forms of promotion—to produce a consistent, unified message that is customer focused.

CONCEPT check

What is the objective of a promotional campaign?

What is the promotional mix?

What are the features of an integrated marketing communications campaign?

The Huge Impact of Advertising

Most Americans are bombarded daily with advertisements to buy things. **Advertising** is any paid form of nonpersonal presentation by an identified sponsor. It may appear on television or radio; in newspapers, magazines, books, or direct mail; or on billboards, transit cards, or the Internet. In the United States, a child is exposed to more than 30,000 TV commercials a year. Adults are exposed to three times as many—more than 2 million commercials in a lifetime.

The money that big corporations spend on advertising is mind-boggling. Total advertising expenses in this country are estimated to be more than $200 billion in 2008. Global advertising expenditures are approximately $475 billion annually. Global Internet advertising reached $147 billion in 2008.[6] Super Bowl ads for 2008 cost $2.7 million for 30 seconds.[7]

Does advertising work? It depends on the media and the quality of the advertising. One study found that for every dollar pharmaceutical companies spend on advertising, it generates an additional $4.20 in revenue.[8]

6 How are advertising media selected?

advertising
Any paid form of nonpersonal presentation by an identified sponsor.

CONCEPT in action

In Apple's "Get a Mac" ad campaign, actor Justin Long (Mac) and humorist John Hodgman (PC) engage in lighthearted comparisons in which Mac outshines PC again and again. While crashes, viruses, and complex assembly plague the buttoned-up PC, hip and easygoing Mac is free of such problems. The message is powerful: Mac computers are more reliable and easier to use than PCs in almost every way. Apple's campaign is developed by TBWA—a creative firm recognized as the "Most-Awarded Advertising Agency in the World" in 2007. Is Apple's campaign changing the way people think about their computers?

CONCEPT in action

In addition to listing hundreds of scrumptious menu choices and cheesecakes, the Cheesecake Factory's magazine-size menus feature full-page glossy ads for Bebe, Macy's, Mercedes-Benz, and more. An increasingly popular media option, menu advertising offers many promotional benefits: huge readership by a captive audience, outstanding demographic selectivity, and great value—less than a penny per exposure. How do advertisers decide whether or not menu advertising is right for their promotional mixes?

advertising media
The channels through which advertising is carried to prospective customers; includes newspapers, magazines, radio, television, outdoor advertising, direct mail, and the Internet.

The Crazy New World of Advertising

Many new media are not hardwired or regulated, and digital technology is delivering content any time, anywhere. Cable, satellite, and the Internet have highly fragmented audiences, making them tougher than ever to reach. In the late 1950s, Gunsmoke on CBS captured a 65 percent share of the TV audience nearly every Saturday night. Only one event, the Super Bowl, has a chance to do that now.

Yesterday, Internet banner ads were the hottest thing around. Today, new companies such as Adzilla and Phorm are providing online advertisers tools that will enable them to track users and show them relevant ads. This is called behavioral targeting. For example, Internet user 98765 visited two online car-dealer sites yesterday. You don't know who 98765 is; you just know that he or she is looking at cars. Thus, Toyota can show 98765 an ad for its new offerings. This is but one of many new changes brought about by technology and creative thinking.

Here are a few examples of the new world of advertising:

- Conquesting, that is, taking out online ads right next to editorial content about their rivals, has become a new online advertising strategy. For example, Edmunds.com voted the Dodge Ram Pickup 5000 as their "best pick." Next to the glowing review was a prominent ad for the Chevy Silverado, which noted that the Silverado was *Motor Trend's* Truck of the Year.
- The growth of cell phone advertising. Terri Miller went to the NBA All-Star game in Las Vegas. She saw an ad on a Vegas billboard for Adidas and sent a text message to the number on the billboard. Adidas sent Ms. Miller a text message about the sale of 200 pairs of limited-edition All-Star basketball shoes.
- In-text online advertising is becoming a new phenomenon. Companies like Intel, Ford, and Microsoft are attaching ads to selected words on newspaper and other media Web sites. For example, words like "cell phone," "New York," and "global travel" can trigger a "pop-up ad" when a reader moves a cursor over highlighted, double-underlined words in a story. Pausing over a link produces a bubble containing written pitches, voiceover, or even video. It is estimated that up to 10 percent of all Web users click on in-text ads.[9]
- Bright, digital billboards are replacing old-fashioned billboards. Digital billboards can sequence 8 to 10 different ads for different companies one after the other. This multiplies the revenue for the billboard company. Cities are usually less critical of the new boards because in addition to ads, the digital boards can flash emergency messages.[10]
- Advertisers are entering the parallel online universe of Second Life. Second Life users (called "avatars") are encountering companies such as IBM, Starwood Hotels, and Toyota in the Second Life.[11]
- Digital video recorders (DVRs) and on-demand technologies allow viewers to skip through commercials. Most national advertisers worry that these technologies will reduce or destroy the effectiveness of 30-second spot TV advertising.
- People using global positioning systems (GPSs) to find their way along the nation's highways and byways may soon encounter advertising. Dunkin' Donuts, Cold Stone Creamery, and others have begun appearing on in-car GPS devices to alert drivers to nearby locations, and in some cases, offering special deals.

These are just a few of the ways that the landscape of advertising is evolving. We will discuss blogs and podcasts later in the chapter.

Choosing Advertising Media

The channels through which paid advertising is carried to prospective customers are the **advertising media**. Both product and institutional ads appear in all the major advertising media. Each company must decide which media are best for its products. Two of the main factors in making that choice are the cost of the medium and the audience reached by it.

Advertising Costs and Market Penetration Cost per contact is the cost of reaching one member of the target market. Naturally, as the size of the audience increases, so does the total cost. Cost per contact enables an advertiser to compare media vehicles, such as television versus radio, or magazine versus newspaper, or, more specifically, *Newsweek* versus *Time*. An advertiser debating whether to spend local advertising dollars for TV spots or radio spots could consider the cost per contact of each. The advertiser might then pick the vehicle with the lowest cost per contact to maximize advertising punch for the money spent. Often costs are expressed on a **cost per thousand (CPM)** contacts basis.

Reach is the number of different target consumers who are exposed to a commercial at least once during a specific period, usually four weeks. Media plans for product introductions and attempts at increasing brand awareness usually emphasize reach. For example, an advertiser might try to reach 70 percent of the target audience during the first three months of the campaign. Because the typical ad is short-lived and often only a small portion of an ad may be perceived at one time, advertisers repeat their ads so consumers will remember the message. **Frequency** is the number of times an individual is exposed to a message. Average frequency is used by advertisers to measure the intensity of a specific medium's coverage.

Media selection is also a matter of matching the advertising medium with the product's target market. If marketers are trying to reach teenage females, they might select *Seventeen* magazine. If they are trying to reach consumers over 50 years old, they may choose *AARP Magazine*. A medium's ability to reach a precisely defined market is its **audience selectivity**. Some media vehicles, like general newspapers and network television, appeal to a wide cross section of the population. Others— such as *Brides*, *Popular Mechanics*, *Architectural Digest*, MTV, ESPN, and Christian radio stations—appeal to very specific groups.

cost per thousand (CPM)
Cost per thousand contacts is a term used in expressing advertising costs; refers to the cost of reaching 1,000 members of the target market.

reach
The number of different target consumers who are exposed to a commercial at least once during a specific period, usually four weeks.

frequency
The number of times an individual is exposed to an advertising message.

audience selectivity
An advertising medium's ability to reach a precisely defined market.

CONCEPT check

How is technology impacting the way advertisers reach their markets?

What are the two main factors that should be considered when selecting advertising media?

The Importance of Personal Selling

Advertising acquaints potential customers with a product and thereby makes personal selling easier. **Personal selling** is a face-to-face sales presentation to a prospective customer. Sales jobs range from sales clerks at clothing stores to engineers with MBAs who design large, complex systems for manufacturers. About 6.5 million people are engaged in personal selling in the United States. Slightly over 45 percent of them are women. The number of people who earn a living from sales is huge compared, for instance, with the half a million workers employed in the advertising industry. Personal selling offers several advantages over other forms of promotion:

7 What is personal selling?

personal selling
A face-to-face sales presentation to a prospective customer.

- Personal selling provides a detailed explanation or demonstration of the product. This capability is especially desirable for complex or new goods and services.
- The sales message can be varied according to the motivations and interests of each prospective customer. Moreover, when the prospect has questions or raises objections, the salesperson is there to provide explanations. In contrast, advertising and sales promotion can respond only to the objections the copywriter thinks are important to customers.
- Personal selling can be directed only to qualified prospects. Other forms of promotion include some unavoidable waste because many people in the audience are not prospective customers.
- Personal selling costs can be controlled by adjusting the size of the sales force (and resulting expenses) in one-person increments. In contrast, advertising and sales promotion must often be purchased in fairly large amounts.
- Perhaps the most important advantage is that personal selling is considerably more effective than other forms of promotion in obtaining a sale and gaining a satisfied customer.

The Selling Process

Selling is a process that can be learned. Scholars have spelled out the steps of the selling process, shown in Exhibit 12.5 on the next page, and professional salespeople use them all the time. These steps are as follows:

1. *Prospecting and qualifying*. To start the process, the salesperson looks for **sales prospects**, those companies and people who are most likely to buy the seller's offerings. This activity is

sales prospects
The companies and people who are most likely to buy a seller's offerings.

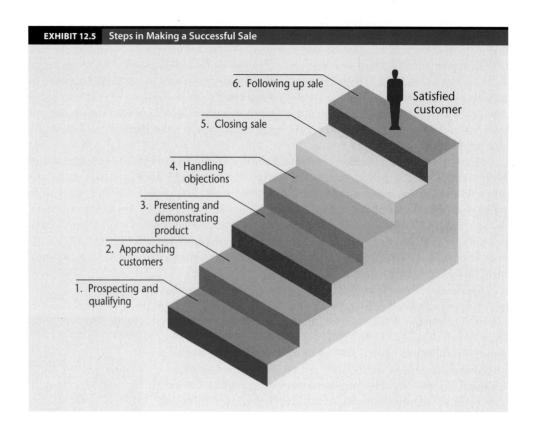

EXHIBIT 12.5 Steps in Making a Successful Sale

6. Following up sale

Satisfied customer

5. Closing sale

4. Handling objections

3. Presenting and demonstrating product

2. Approaching customers

1. Prospecting and qualifying

prospecting
The process of looking for sales prospects.

called **prospecting**. Because there are no surefire ways to find prospects, most salespeople try many methods.

For many companies, the inquiries generated by advertising and promotion are the most likely source of prospects. Inquiries are also known as sales leads. Leads usually come in the form of letters, cards, e-mail addresses, or telephone calls. Some companies supply salespeople with prospect lists compiled from external sources, such as Chamber of Commerce directories, newspapers, public records, club membership lists, Internet inquiries, and professional or trade publication subscription lists. Meetings, such as professional conventions and trade shows, are another good source of leads. Sales representatives attend such meetings to display and demonstrate their company's products and to answer the questions of those attending. The firm's files and records can be another source of prospects. Correspondence with buyers can be helpful. Records in the service department can identify people who already own equipment and might be prospects for new models. Finally, friends and acquaintances of salespeople can often supply leads.

One rule of thumb is that not all prospects are "real." Just because someone has been referred or has made an inquiry does not mean that the person is a genuine prospect. Salespeople can avoid wasting time and increase their productivity by qualifying all prospects. **Qualifying questions** are used to separate prospects from those who do not have the potential to buy. The following three questions help determine who is a real prospect and who is not:

qualifying questions
Inquiries used by salespeople to separate prospects from those who do not have the potential to buy.

- Does the prospect have a need for our product?
- Can the prospect make the buying decision?
- Can the prospect afford our product?

2. *Approaching customers.* After identifying a prospect, the salesperson explains the reason for wanting an appointment and sets a specific date and hour. At the same time, the salesperson tries to build interest in the coming meeting. One good way to do this is to impart an interesting or important piece of information—for instance, "I think my product can cut your shipping and delivery time by two days."

3. *Presenting and demonstrating the product.* The presentation and demonstration can be fully automated, completely unstructured, or somewhere in between. In a fully automated

Part 4: Marketing Management

presentation, the salesperson shows a movie, shows slides, or makes a PowerPoint presentation and then answers questions and takes any orders. A completely unstructured presentation has no set format. It may be a casual conversation, with the salesperson presenting product benefits that might interest the potential buyer.

4. *Handling objections*. Almost every sales presentation, structured or unstructured, meets with some objection. Rarely does a customer say "I'll buy it" without asking questions or voicing concerns. The professional salesperson tries to anticipate objections so they can be countered quickly and with assurance.

   Often employed in business, the "higher authority" objection is frequently used when one of the parties says, "This agreement looks good, but I'll have to run it by my committee" (or wife or any other "higher authority"). The result is that that sales presentation turns out to be just a preliminary, nonbinding round. After the higher authority responds, often disapproving the agreement, the sale goes into round two or starts all over again.

   The next time you buy a house, car, or anything expensive, watch carefully how the salesperson will say, "If we find the house (or car) that you really like, is there any reason you could not make the purchase today?" Once they get the green light, the salesperson will spend whatever time it takes to find you the right product. However, if you say your uncle has to give the final approval, because he will be loaning you the money, the salesperson will try and set up an appointment when the uncle can be present.

5. *Closing the sale*. After all the objections have been dealt with, it's time to close the sale. Even old pros sometimes find this part of the sales process awkward. Perhaps the easiest way to close a sale is to ask for it: "Ms. Jones, may I write up your order?" Another technique is to act as though the deal has been concluded: "Mr. Bateson, we'll have this equipment in and working for you in two weeks." If Mr. Bateson doesn't object, the salesperson can assume that the sale has been made.

6. *Following up on the sale*. The salesperson's job isn't over when the sale is made. In fact, the sale is just the start. The salesperson must write up the order properly and turn it in promptly. Often this part of the job is easy. But an order for a complex piece of industrial equipment may be a hundred pages of detail. Each detail must be carefully checked to ensure that the equipment is exactly what was ordered.

   After the product is delivered to the customer, the salesperson must make a routine visit to see that the customer is satisfied. This follow-up call may also be a chance to make another sale. But even if it isn't, it will build goodwill for the salesperson's company and may bring future business. Repeat sales over many years are the goal of professional salespeople.

CONCEPT check

What are the advantages of personal selling?

Explain the selling process.

Sales Promotion

Sales promotion helps make personal selling and advertising more effective. **Sales promotions** are marketing events or sales efforts—not including advertising, personal selling, and public relations—that stimulate buying. Today, sales promotion is a $300 billion industry and growing. Sales promotion is usually targeted toward either of two distinctly different markets. Consumer sales promotion is targeted to the ultimate consumer market. Trade sales promotion is directed to members of the marketing channel, such as wholesalers and retailers.

The goal of many promotion tactics is immediate purchase. Therefore, it makes sense when planning a sales promotion campaign to target customers according to their general behavior. For instance, is the consumer loyal to your product or to your competitor's? Does the consumer switch brands readily in favor of the best deal? Does the consumer buy only the least expensive product, no matter what? Does the consumer buy any products in your category at all?

Procter & Gamble Co. believes shoppers make up their mind about a product in about the time it takes to read this paragraph.

This "first moment of truth," as P&G calls it, is the three to seven seconds when someone notices an item on a store shelf. Despite spending billions on traditional advertising, the consumer-products giant thinks this instant is one of its most important marketing opportunities. It recently created a position titled Director of First Moment of Truth, or Director of FMOT (pronounced "EFF-mott"),

8 What are the goals of a sales promotion, and what are several types of sales promotion?

sales promotions
Marketing events or sales efforts—not including advertising, personal selling, and public relations—that stimulate buying.

to produce sharper, flashier in-store displays. There's a 15-person FMOT department at P&G headquarters in Cincinnati as well as 50 FMOT leaders stationed around the world.[12]

point of purchase (POP) display
A strategically placed visual display or product display that informs potential customers about a product or service.

A **point-of-purchase display (POP)** is a strategically placed visual display or product display that informs potential customers about a product or service. POP displays typically encourage impulse buying in grocery stores, drug stores, and other types of retailers. The POP trade association says that supermarket POP displays can increase sales from 1 to 20 percent depending on the product and type of display.[13] An unusual form of in-store and out-of-store promotion is scent promotion. Recently, a chain of 100 California service stations installed devices that resembled large coffee cups. When a customer lifted the handle to pump gas, the coffee device emitted a scent of fresh coffee. The idea is to get credit card purchasers to go inside and buy a cup of coffee. In San Francisco, bus shelters were equipped with chocolate chip cookie–fragranced strips for the "Got Milk" campaign.[14]

CONCEPT in action

Pet lovers want the best for their animals and choosing a proper diet is an essential part of raising happy, healthy pets. That's why Purina offers the Purina ONE 30-Day Challenge. To participate in the sales promotion, animal lovers transition their pets to Purina ONE premium brand food, track pet performance using an interactive scorecard, and evaluate the "before-and-after" results of their pet's health. What promotional objectives underlie the Purina ONE 30-Day Challenge?

Event marketing is growing in popularity as a form of sales promotion. Caterpillar is a $41.5 billion manufacturer of construction equipment. In the southwest United States, homes are built on concrete slabs, which require heavy equipment designed to level rough ground and prepare it for the laying of smooth concrete. Cat didn't produce a machine specifically for this purpose, so it designed and manufactured the 414E industrial loader. To publicize the machine in the Southwest, Cat sent invitations to home builders to try out the 414E by building a race track. Cat sponsors the number 22 car in NASCAR racing, so the race track was a natural fit. After the track was completed, builders then raced dune buggies on the track. Whoever registered the best race time would lead a parade lap around the California Speedway in Fontana, California, before the start of the Auto Club 500 NASCAR race.[15] Research has shown that when customers interact with a brand during event marketing, purchase intent rose 34 percent.[16]

The objectives of a promotion depend on the general behavior of target consumers as described in Exhibit 12.6. For example, marketers who are targeting loyal users of their product don't want to change behavior. Instead, they want to reinforce existing behavior or increase product usage. Frequent-buyer programs that reward consumers for repeat purchases can be effective in strengthening brand loyalty. Other types of promotions are more effective with customers prone to brand switching or with those who are loyal to a competitor's product. Cents-off coupons, free samples, or an eye-catching display in a store will often entice shoppers to try a different brand.

Two important areas of sales promotion are couponing and product placement. American consumers receive over $250 billion worth of coupons each year and redeem about $2.6 billion.[17] Almost 80 percent of all Americans redeem coupons. Sunday newspaper supplements remain the number one source, but there has been explosive growth of online or "consumer printed" coupons. General Mills, Kimberly-Clark, and General Electric like online coupons because they

EXHIBIT 12.6	Types of Consumers and Sales Promotion Goals	
Type of Behavior	**Desired Results**	**Sales Promotion Examples**
Loyal customers: People who buy your product most or all of the time	Reinforce behavior, increase consumption, change purchase timing	Loyalty marketing programs, such as frequent-buyer cards or frequent-shopper clubs
		Bonus packs that give loyal consumers an incentive to stock up or premiums offered in return for proof-of-purchase
Competitor's customers: People who buy a competitor's product most or all of the time	Break loyalty, persuade to switch to your brand	Sweepstakes, contests, or premiums that create interest in the product
Brand switchers: People who buy a variety of products in the category	Persuade to buy your brand more often	Sampling to introduce your product's superior qualities compared to their brand
Price buyers: People who consistently buy the least expensive brand	Appeal with low prices or supply added value that makes price less important	Trade deals that help make the product more readily available than competing products Coupons, cents-off packages, refunds, or trade deals that reduce the price of the brand to match that of the brand that would have been purchased

have a higher redemption rate. More than a million people have signed up to receive coupons over their cell phones, based on a service offered by Cellfire. Coupons are available from Domino's Pizza, Quiznos Subs, Virgin Megastores, and other retailers. To cash in the coupons, consumers show their cell phone screen—where the coupons are displayed—to a cashier at a checkout line. E-mailing the coupon's discount from the phone to the cash register isn't technologically available yet.[18]

Product placement is paid inclusion of brands in mass-media programming. This includes movies, TV, books, music videos, and video games. So when you see Ford vehicles in the latest James Bond movie or Tom Hanks drinking a Coke on-screen, that is product placement. Product placement has become a huge business. Toyota paid several million dollars to have its cars featured on the reality TV show *The Contender*. Many large companies are cutting their advertising budgets to spend more on product placements. One area of product placement that is raising ethical issues is so-called "experts" being paid to mention brands on the air. *Child* magazine's technology editor James Oppenheimer went on an ABC station to review educational toys. He praised *My ABCs Picture Book*, a personalized photo album from Eastman Kodak. What he didn't say was that Kodak paid him to mention the photo album. Similarly, Katleen de Monchy talked on *Good Morning America* about clothes worn by the stars at the Golden Globes. She mentioned Faviana, DSW, and retailer David's Bridal. All paid her to mention these products on TV.[19]

CONCEPT in action

Marketers of the television hit-series *American Idol* are masters at the art of product placement. In addition to mounting mega-size Cokes permanently atop the judges' table, *Idol* airs Ford music videos that feature performers in automobile adventures. Viewers of one recent season got a peek at Ford's latest Escape, Fusion, and Focus models as lovable contestants shot hoops to the tune of "It's Tricky" and played comic-book heroes in a Goth-inspired version of "Tainted Love." Does product placement blur the lines between content and advertising?

CONCEPT check

How does sales promotion differ from advertising?

Describe several types of sales promotion.

Public Relations Helps Build Goodwill

Like sales promotion, public relations can be a vital part of the promotional mix. **Public relations** is any communication or activity designed to win goodwill or prestige for a company or person. Its main form is **publicity**, information about a company or product that appears in the news media and is not directly paid for by the company. Publicity can be good or bad. Reports of children overeating fast food leading to obesity is an example of negative publicity.

Naturally, firms' public relations departments try to create as much good publicity as possible. They furnish company speakers for business and civic clubs, write speeches for corporate officers, and encourage employees to take active roles in such civic groups as the United Way and the Chamber of Commerce. The main tool of the public relations department is the press release, a formal announcement of some newsworthy event connected with the company, such as the start of a new program, the introduction of a new product, or the opening of a new plant. Public relations departments may perform any or all of the functions described in Exhibit 12.7.

9 How does public relations fit into the promotional mix?

public relations
Any communication or activity designed to win goodwill or prestige for a company or person.

publicity
Information about a company or product that appears in the news media and is not directly paid for by the company.

EXHIBIT 12.7	The Functions of a Public Relations Department
Public Relations Function	**Description**
Press relations	Placing positive, newsworthy information in the news media to attract attention to a product, a service, or a person associated with the firm or institution
Product publicity	Publicizing specific products or services
Corporate communications	Creating internal and external messages to promote a positive image of the firm or institution
Public affairs	Building and maintaining national or local community relations
Lobbying	Influencing legislators and government officials to promote or defeat legislation and regulation
Employee and investor relations	Maintaining positive relationships with employees, shareholders, and others in the financial community
Crisis management	Responding to unfavorable publicity or a negative event

© Steve Helber-Pool/Getty Images

The National Football League promotes goodwill through its community outreach programs and family-oriented sports entertainment. While the league generally benefits from the good reputation of its players, a recent dog-fighting scandal involving star quarterback Michael Vick created a public relations nightmare for the NFL and its sponsors. To assuage public outrage, the NFL placed Vick on permanent suspension. Likewise big sponsors such as Rawlings, Nike, and Reebok cut business ties with the pro athlete. What public relations tools can organizations use to soften the impact of bad publicity?

CONCEPT check

What is the role of public relations?

Explain the concept of buzz marketing.

Although companies try to avoid unpleasant situations, crises do happen. Southwest Airlines grounded 41 airplanes in 2008 after the FAA said the company made 60,000 flights without fuselage inspections. Evenflo Company recalled about a million Discovery Infant Car Seats because the seat could potentially separate from the base in high-impact side collisions. Bad publicity, such as those just mentioned, can scare away customers for good. One recent survey found that while 55 percent of people said they would switch brands temporarily in the case of a safety and health recall on a product they usually purchase, a full 15 percent said they'd never again purchase the recalled brand. Additionally, 21 percent of those polled said that they would avoid using any brand made by the manufacturer of the recalled product.[20]

Companies need a contingency plan that is well-thought-out in advance to handle potential negative publicity. Many companies, such as American Airlines and General Electric, have crisis management teams to handle a coordinated effort to blunt the impact of bad publicity. Crisis management ensures fast and accurate communication and actions in times of an emergency.

Trends in Promotion and Distribution

10 What are the trends in promotion and distribution?

Advances in technology are changing the marketing landscape. As you will see in this section, marketers are harnessing new technology to hone their marketing message and reach more customers.

Promotion through Blogs

Blogs provide marketers with a real-time dialogue with customers and an avenue to promote its products or services. A blog is an online journal with regularly updated content. This content is pushed to subscribers by RSS (really simple syndication) or e-mail and allows for response and discussion from site visitors. RSS enables users to automatically gather updates from various Web sites, especially news sites and blogs, and display headlines and a brief summary of those updates in a single location.

Well-run marketing blogs usually focus tightly on one niche area, product line, or vertical market segment. The aim is to provide the blogs' readers with a constantly renewing source of news and insight about that topic. While no one knows the exact number, it is estimated by your authors that there are over 70 million blogs worldwide.

Many companies are setting up their own blogs. A few of the new bloggers are General Motors, Apple, American Cancer Society, and Microsoft, to name a few. These companies blog because they: (1) get real-time input from customers and prospects, (2) create and maintain relationships, (3) can have a dialogue with their clients and prospects, and (4) can focus on specific marketing goals. Firms can also use emerging search tools like BlogPulse, Feedster, PubSub, and Technorati to monitor conversations about their company and brands. A public relations department might then decide to feed new product information to bloggers who are evangelists for their brand.

A number of companies send influential bloggers free samples hoping for a positive review. For example, David Ponce, author of OhGizmo.com, has received a $600 telephone from Nokia, a wireless weather station, and numerous other tech toys.[21] In addition to free products, some firms also pay for positive posts. Ron Des Groseilliers has recommended more than 260 products on his two blogs and has often been paid to do so.[22] The PayPerPost web site lets advertisers place "opportunities" listing what they want to promote and what they will pay.[23] Bloggers receive $5 to $10 per post if they put a positive spin on the firm's product.

Advertisers Jump on Podcasting

Podcasts are basically blogs with a multimedia file. The trend developed when iTunes software made it easy for people to create their own podcasts and post them on a Web site. Other podcasting software can be found at **http://www.podcastingalley.com**. There will be over 57 million podcasters in the United States by 2010.[24] Besides individuals, companies are beginning to do their own podcasts. ABC News is now offering a podcast of Nightline and other programs. For listeners, the advantage of a podcast is convenience. Their favorite programs download automatically from the Internet, usually free of charge, and they can listen to the programs any time they wish. They can also listen wherever they wish, if they have an iPod or other MP3 player to receive the downloads.

From a consumer's perspective, podcasts allow someone to download content into their MP3 player, personal computer, or other device and then shift when and where they will listen to or view the content. Unlike traditional media, podcasts have a strong element of consumer control. Advertisers love the podcasting audience because the audience tends to be young, well-educated, tech-smart, and have high incomes.[25] So far, brands like Volvo, Lexus, and Honda have sponsored podcasts. Other recent sponsorship deals include Dixie, which spent $100,000 for *Mommycast*, a podcast by two moms in northern Virginia. Nature's Cure, an acne product, sponsored *EmoGirltalk*, created by a 15-year-old San Francisco girl.[26]

Pet owners can go to **http://www.purina.com** and opt-in to receive Purina's podcasts. The products will offer advice ranging from animal training to pet insurance. Weekly tips will also be sent on things such as how to help your dog lose weight. Owners spend about $13.4 billion a year on pet food. The aim of the podcasts is to build brand loyalty with a soft sell. You can even download pet travel info to your cell phone.

It's All About Buzz

The hot topic in promotion today is about creating buzz. Buzz marketing (or viral marketing) is intense word-of-mouth marketing. Word-of-mouth is essentially a linear process with information passing from one individual to another, then to another. A marketer has successfully created a buzz when the interactions are so intense that the information moves in a matrix pattern rather than a linear one and everyone is talking about the topic. Leading edge firms now feel that they get more bang–for–their-buck using buzz marketing than other forms of promotion.

All information now has the opportunity to travel rapidly through the Internet using such venues as YouTube, MySpace, Epinions, and others. Creating positive buzz is not always easy. Companies often play a key role in initiating the buzz process. Phillips Norelco created a device called the Bodygroom for males to shave areas of the body other than the face. It wasn't a product that men were talking about. Phillips Norelco created an online campaign involving a video at a Web site called shaveeverywhere.com. The comic, and slightly risqué video, became a huge hit. The product has taken off in sales and over 60 percent of the purchasers claimed that they learned about the Bodygroom from the new Web site.[27] Armed with initial success, Phillips Norelco is now pushing a nose-hair trimmer and a new video and cartoon on the same Web site.

Buzz marketing is forecasted to reach $3.7 billion in 2011.[28] It is the fastest-growing alternative-media segment. Most buzz and word-of-mouth marketing still occurs offline. This can be face-to-face or telephone. Also, offline tends to be viewed as more credible and likely to create purchase intent. However, chat rooms and blogs will drive consumers to search for more information about a brand. As more and more consumers access online Web sites, the importance of online buzz will continue to grow.[29]

CONCEPT in action

Television has jumped on the podcasting craze in recent years, offering digital downloads of top-rated TV shows such as *24*, *The Tonight Show*, and *Desperate Housewives*. The Big Four networks' venture into podcasting delighted consumers but sent shockwaves across the advertising world. Initial podcasts priced at $1.99 generated high margins and talks of subscription and rental pricing models—but with no advertising. How will advertisers pitch brands if ad-free consumer-downloaded content eliminates the traditional 30-second TV commercial?

CONCEPT check

Why would a company such as Apple set up a blog?

What factors contribute to the Internet's soaring growth in retailing?

Summary of Learning Goals

1 What is the nature and function of distribution?

Distribution or logistics is efficiently managing the acquisition of raw materials to the factory and the movement of products from the producer or manufacturer, to industrial users and consumers. Logistics activities are usually the responsibility of the marketing department and are part of the large series of activities included in the supply chain.

Distribution channels are the series of marketing entities through which goods and services pass on their way from producers to end users. Distribution systems focus on the physical transfer of goods and services and on their legal ownership at each stage of the distribution process. Channels reduce the number of transactions and ease the flow of goods.

2 What is wholesaling, and what are the types of wholesalers?

Wholesalers typically sell finished products to retailers and to other institutions, such as manufacturers, schools, and hospitals. The two main types of wholesalers are merchant wholesalers, and agents and brokers. Merchant wholesalers buy from manufacturers and sell to other businesses. Agents and brokers are essentially independents who provide buying and selling services. They receive commissions according to their sales and don't take title (ownership) of the merchandise.

3 What are the different kinds of retail operations?

Some 30 million Americans are engaged in retailing. Retailing can be either in-store or nonstore. In-store retail operations include department stores, specialty stores, discount stores, off-price retailers, factory outlets, and catalog showrooms. Nonstore retailing includes vending machines, direct sales, direct-response marketing, and Internet retailing. The most important factors in creating a store's atmosphere are employee type and density, merchandise type and density, fixture type and density, sound, and odors.

4 How can supply chain management increase efficiency and customer satisfaction?

The goal of supply chain management is to coordinate all of the activities of the supply chain members into a seamless process, thereby increasing customer satisfaction. Supply chain managers have responsibility for main channel strategy decisions, coordinating the sourcing and procurement of raw materials, scheduling production, processing orders, managing inventory, transporting and storing supplies and finished goods, and coordinating customer service activities.

5 What is promotion, and what are the key elements of a promotional mix?

Promotion aims to stimulate demand for a company's goods or services. Promotional strategy is designed to inform, persuade, or remind target audiences about those products. The goals of promotion are to create awareness, get people to try products, provide information, keep loyal customers, increase use of a product, and identify potential customers.

The unique combination of advertising, personal selling, sales promotion, and public relations used to promote a product is the promotional mix. Advertising is any paid form of nonpersonal promotion by an identified sponsor. Personal selling consists of a face-to-face presentation in a conversation with a prospective purchaser. Sales promotion consists of marketing activities—other than personal selling, advertising, and public relations—that stimulate consumers to buy. These activities include coupons and samples, displays, shows and exhibitions, demonstrations, and other selling efforts. Public relations is the marketing function that links the policies of the organization with the public interest and develops programs designed to earn public understanding and acceptance. Integrated marketing communications (IMC) is being used by more and more organizations. It is the careful coordination of all of the elements of the promotional mix to produce a consistent, unified message that is customer focused.

6 How are advertising media selected?

Cost per contact is the cost of reaching one member of the target market. Often costs are expressed on a cost per thousand (CPM) basis. Reach is the number of different target customers who are exposed to a commercial at least once during a specific period, usually four weeks. Frequency is the number of times an individual is exposed to a message. Media selection is a matter of matching the advertising medium with the target audience.

7 What is personal selling?

About 6.5 million people in the United States are directly engaged in personal selling. Personal selling enables a salesperson to demonstrate a product and tailor the message to the prospect; it is effective in closing a sale. Professional salespeople are knowledgeable and creative. They also are familiar with the selling process, which consists of prospecting and qualifying, approaching customers, presenting and demonstrating the product, handling objections, closing the sale, and following up on the sale.

Immediate purchase is the goal of most sales promotion, whether it is aimed at consumers or the trade (wholesalers and retailers). The most popular sales promotions are coupons, samples, product placement, premiums, contests, and sweepstakes. Trade shows, conventions, and point-of-purchase displays are other types of sales promotion.

8 What are the goals of a sales promotion, and what are several types of sales promotion?

Public relations is mostly concerned with getting good publicity for companies. Publicity is any information about a company or product that appears in the news media and is not directly paid for by the company. Public relations departments furnish company speakers for business and civic clubs, write speeches for corporate officers, and encourage employees to take active roles in civic groups. These activities help build a positive image for an organization and create buzz, which is a good backdrop for selling its products.

9 How does public relations fit into the promotional mix?

The Internet and new technology are having a major impact on promotion and promotion expenditures. Traditional media are losing advertising funds to the Internet. Many companies are now creating blogs to get closer to customers and potential customers. Podcasts offer advertisers a new medium to reach consumers.

10 What are the trends in promotion and distribution?

A final trend is the huge growth in Internet retailing. The ease of use and ability to comparison shop is driving millions of people to the Internet to purchase goods and services. Huge retailers like Wal-Mart are quickly increasing their Web presence.

Key Terms

advertising 329
advertising media 330
agents 321
audience selectivity 331
breaking bulk 322
brokers 321
cost per thousand (CPM) 331
distribution (logistics) 320
distribution channel 320
frequency 331
industrial distributors 321
integrated marketing communications (IMC) 329
manufacturer 320
manufacturers' representatives (manufacturer's agent) 324

marketing intermediaries 320
merchant wholesaler 324
personal selling 331
point of purchase (POP) display 334
promotion 327
promotional mix 328
prospecting 331
public relations 335
publicity 335
qualifying questions 332
reach 331
retailers 321
sales promotions 333
sales prospects 331
wholesalers 321

Preparing for Tomorrow's Workplace: SCANS

1. **Team Activity** Divide the class into two groups with one taking the "pro" position and the other the "con" position on the following issue: "The only thing marketing intermediaries really do is increase prices for consumers. It is always best to buy direct from the producer." (**Interpersonal**)
2. Trace the distribution channel for some familiar product. Compose an e-mail that explains why the channel has evolved as it has and how it is likely to change in the future. (**Systems**)
3. You work for a small chain of department stores (six stores total) located within a single state. Write a memo to the president explaining how e-retailing may affect the chain's business. (**Technology**)
4. How does supply chain management increase customer value? (**Systems**)
5. Think of a product that you use regularly. Find several examples of how the manufacturer markets this product, such as ads in different media, sales promotions, and publicity. Assess each example for effectiveness in meeting one or more of the six promotional goals described in the chapter. Then analyze them for effectiveness in reaching you as a target consumer.

Consider such factors as the media used, the style of the ad, and ad content. Present your findings to the class. **(Information)**

6. Go to the blogging search sites listed in the text and find personal blogs, both positive and negative, for a brand. Also report on a consumer good manufacturer's blogging site. Was it appealing? Why or why not? **(Technology)**

7. The Internet and technology has changed the world of promotion forever. Explain the meaning of this sentence. **(Technology)**

8. What advantages does personal selling offer over types of promotion? **(Information)**

9. Choose a current advertising campaign for a beverage product. Describe how the campaign uses different media to promote the product. Which media is used the most, and why? What other promotional strategies does the company use for the product? Evaluate the effectiveness of the campaign. Present your results to the class. **(Information)**

10. The Promotional Products Association International is a trade association of the promotional-products industry. Its Web site, **http://www.ppa.org**, provides an introduction to promotional products and how they are used in marketing. Read its FAQ page and the Industry Sales Volume statistics (both reached through the Education link). Then go to the Resources and Technology section then case studies and link to the most recent Golden Pyramid Competition. Choose three to four winners from different categories. Now prepare a short report on the role of promotional products in the promotional mix. Include the examples you selected and explain how the products helped the company reach its objective. **(Technology)**

Ethics Activity

ethics

After working really hard to distinguish yourself, you've finally been promoted to a senior account executive at a major advertising agency and placed in charge of the agency's newest account, a nationally known cereal company. Their product is one you know contains excessive amounts of sugar as well as artificial colorings, and lacks any nutritional value whatsoever. In fact, you have never allowed your own children to eat it.

Your boss has indicated that the cereal company would like to use the slogan, "It's good for you," in their new television and print advertising campaign. You know that a $2 billion lawsuit has been filed against the Kellogg and Viacom corporations for marketing junk food to young children. The suit cited "alluring product packaging, toy giveaways, contests, collectibles, kid-oriented Web sites, magazine ads, and branded toys and clothes." In addition, two consumer groups have brought suit against children's television network, Nickelodeon, for "unfair and deceptive junk-food marketing."

Your new role at the agency will be tested with this campaign. Doing a good job on it will cement your position and put you in line for a promotion to vice president. But as a responsible parent you have strong feelings about misleading advertising targeted at susceptible children.

Using a Web search tool, locate articles about this topic and then write responses to the following questions. Be sure to support your arguments and cite your sources.

ETHICAL DILEMMA: Do you follow your principles and ask to be transferred to another account? Or do you help promote a cereal you know may be harmful to children in order to secure your career?

Sources: Stephanie Thompson, "Standing Still, Kellogg Gets Hit with a Lawsuit," *Advertising Age*, January 23, 2006; Stephanie Thompson, "Kellogg Co. Might as Well Have Painted a Bull's-eye on Itself," *Advertising Age*, January 23, 2006; and Abbey Klaassen, "Viacom Gets Nicked," *Advertising Age*, January 23, 2006 (all from **http://galenet.thomsonlearning.com**)

Working the Net

working

1. Visit *Industry Week's* Web site at **http://www.industryweek.com**. Under Archives, do a search using the search term "supply chain management." Choose an article from the results that describes how a company has used supply chain management to improve customer satisfaction, performance, or profitability. Give a brief presentation to your class on your findings.

2. What are some of the logistics problems facing firms that operate internationally? Visit the *Logistics Management* magazine Web site at **http://www.logisticsmgmt.com** and see if you can find information about how firms manage global logistics. Summarize the results.

3. Go to **http://www.w00t.com**. Why do you think that this e-retailer is successful? How can it expand its market? Why do you think that the site has such a cult following?

4. A beauty of the Internet is the ability to comparison shop like never before. To compare brands, features, and prices of products, go to three of these sites: **http://www1.bottomdollar.com**, **http://www.mysimon.com**, or **http://www.compare.net**. For the best bargains try

http://www.overstock.com, http://www.smartbargains.com, http://www.bluefly.com, http://www.smartshopper.com, http://www.nextag.com, or http://www.shopzilla.com. Which is easiest to use? Hardest? Which provides the most information?

5. The Zenith OptiMedia site at http://www.zenithoptimedia.com is a good place to find links to Internet resources on advertising. At the site, click on "Leading Corporate and Brand Sites." Pick three of the company sites listed and review them, using the concepts in this chapter.

6. Go to the *Sales and Marketing* magazine site at http://www.salesandmarketing.com. Read several of the free recent articles from the magazine as well as online exclusives and prepare a brief report on current trends in one of the following topics: sales strategies, marketing strategies, customer relationships, or training. Also check out their new blog "Soundoff." What is your opinion of this blog?

7. Entrepreneurs and small businesses don't always have big sales promotion budgets. The Guerrilla Marketing Web page at http://www.gmarketing.com has many practical ideas for those with big ideas but small budgets. After exploring the site, explain the concept of guerrilla marketing. Then list five ideas or tips that appeal to you and summarize why they are good marketing strategies.

8. Press releases are a way to get free publicity for your company and products. Visit several of the following sites to learn how to write a press release: http://www.press-release-examples.com, http://www.publicityinsider.com, or http://www.netpress.org/careandfeeding.html. Which sites were most helpful, and why? Develop a short "how-to" guide on press releases for your classmates. Then write a press release that announces the opening of your new health food restaurant, Zen Foods, located just two blocks from campus.

Creative Thinking Case

creative

Advertisers Score with the World Cup

What sporting event is televised in 213 countries and watched by more passionate fans than any other? If you guessed the Olympics, you'd be wrong. It's the World Cup football (soccer) matches, which last a month and are held every four years. An estimated 29 billion people watched the 2002 Cup matches, and Web surfers registered over 2 billion page views at http://www.FIFAworldcup.com. Even more viewers tuned in for the June 2006 games, held in Germany. Online venues such as chat rooms, blogs, and discussion boards added another media channel for fans to get more of the action.

Soccer's worldwide popularity makes it a prime advertising buy for many global companies, who want to get their message out to these large audiences. More than 240 million players on 1.4 million teams around the world play the game, supporting its claim to be the world's favorite sport. As the FIFA World Cup Web site explains, "The FIFA World Cup™ reaches an audience of a size and diversity that is unrivalled by any other single sports body. Add to this a passion for the game found in all corners of the world, and you have a sporting, social, and marketing phenomenon." As a result, companies vie to become Official Partners with global marketing rights as well as custom opportunities. The 2006 FIFA World Cup™ Official Partners were Adidas, Avaya, Budweiser, Coca-Cola, Continental, Deutsche Telekom, Emirates, Fujifilm, Gillette, Hyundai, MasterCard, McDonald's, Philips, Toshiba, and Yahoo!.

The World Cup's global nature presents major challenges as well as opportunities for its advertisers. Unlike the Super Bowl, which focuses on the United States, the World Cup requires even greater levels of creativity to produce ads that make a strong connection with soccer fans from very diverse cultures. Ads may have to appeal to viewers in countries as different as Ireland, Mexico, Malaysia, and Bangladesh.

Companies accomplish this task in various ways. They can select the countries that see their ads. Some have one ad for all countries, whereas others customize ads. MasterCard overcame the language barrier by showing soccer fans from many countries cheering. The only words appear at the end with the company logo: "Football fever. Priceless." Anheuser-Busch, which spent more for its 2006 World Cup ads than it did for its Olympics or Super Bowl ads, also opted for a visual rather than verbal ad: People in the stands at a sporting event do the "wave," holding cards that show beer flowing from a Budweiser bottle into a glass, which then empties. "If you get too complicated, you lose people with different cultures and perspectives," says Tony Ponturo, vice president of global sports marketing for the brewer. Gillette starts with the same ad but uses digital techniques so that each ad features the team colors for the country where the spot is showing.

Critical Thinking Questions

- What are some of the challenges global marketers encounter when developing advertising and promotion campaigns? How does the type of product affect the promotional strategies?
- You work for an ad agency that has a World Cup sponsor as a client. What approach would you recommend for your agency as it develops a campaign—universal, customized for each geographical region, or something else, and why?
- What types of companies could benefit from placing ads on the FIFA Web site, and how can they use the Internet effectively to promote their products?

Sources: Adapted from "Marketing & TV," *Fédération Internationale de Football Association*, **http://www.fifa.com**, May 3, 2006; Aaron O. Patrick, "World Cup's Advertisers Hope One Size Fits All," *Wall Street Journal*, March 28, 2006, p. B7; "The Wave, " TV Commercials, *Budweiser.com*, **http://www.Budweiser.com**, May 3, 2006; "World Cup Advertising Analysis," *Analyst Wire*, March 3, 2006, **http://galenet.cengagelearning.com**.

Video

**Steve Piehl
Harley-Davidson**

Exploring Business Careers

A road not taken is the next adventure waiting. Live to ride; ride to live. These are just a few of the creeds that Harley riders live by. Whether it's the vision of the open road, the shine of chrome, or the smell of dust mixed with exhaust, people are drawn to Harley-Davidson motorcycles. How often do you see someone with "Honda" tattooed on their chest? Harleys are the stuff that dreams and identities are made of.

Steve Piehl, the Director of Communications at Harley-Davidson, has been shaping people's dreams for over 25 years. He uses traditional marketing channels such as print, radio, and television advertising; however, Harley also, understandably, approaches marketing nontraditionally.

The focus of Harley marketing is not selling a product, but selling an experience. Piehl explains, "The difference of that experience is what has given us success. We don't categorize what that experience is. We leave it up to people to make it their own." For some, a Harley is a ticket to freedom, for others it is a knockout ride to work. Harley's promotion of accessories supports this idea. As Piehl says, "No two Harleys on the street are the same." A part of the purchasing process is a meeting with a "chrome consultant" who can help with customizing and accessorizing your bike. In this way, the bike becomes part of one's identity.

Part of Harley's focus on experience is its support of motorcycle riding as a sport. On their Web site and at the dealerships, they provide tips and classes for rider improvement. Through the Harley Owner's Group (HOG), a membership group of Harley owners, Harley promotes events and rallies where owners can get together and ride. They form what Piehl calls "brothers and sisters of the road."

It is with this focus on the "sport" that Harley creates its most powerful marketing tool: the motorcycle mentor. Through the nature of the Harley community, previous owners coach new owners on buying a more advanced bike, taking an overnight trip, or packing for long-distance rides. Piehl says, "We would be doing a disservice if we said we reach everyone with our product announcements. But when we put it out, it works its way through the customer base. Our owners sell our products. They encourage people to get more involved in the sport." And tools like chat rooms on the Harley Web site or magazines like *HOGtales* or *Motorcycle Enthusiast* facilitate that sharing.

So how does Harley-Davidson measure its marketing success? They participate in Customer Satisfaction Index studies to measure satisfaction for people who purchase new motorcycles. But it is the statistic that over 90 percent of Harley owners will repurchase a Harley that carries the weight. Piehl laughs, "When we get a customer, we can pretty much keep them. Our marketing is to get new customers and to keep existing [customers] happy."

It is just another part of Harley's creed: We believe life is what you make it, and we make it one heck of a ride.

Chapter 12 revealed the role of marketing, starting with a discussion of the distribution system and concluding with a look at traditional and nontraditional marketing channels.

This chapter explored how organizations use a distribution system to enhance the value of a product and examined the methods used to move products to locations where consumers wish to buy them. First, we looked at the members of a distribution system and then explored the role of wholesalers and retailers in delivering products to customers. After learning how the supply chain works to increase efficiency and customer satisfaction, we took a look at promotion, the last element of the marketing mix. You also learned about advertising and how personal selling and public relations fit into the promotional mix.

Apple, Inc.
continuing case
Part 4: Marketing at Apple, Inc.

To marketers, the name "Apple" might seem an odd name for a computer company. But the name represented everything that the company's founders wanted to project—personal, healthy, and in the home. Over time, this storyline led to Apple's lifestyle branding strategy. Another benefit of the name was that Apple was always at the top of the alphabetical list when computer magazines identified new microcomputers that were slated to hit the market.

Unfortunately, by the mid-1990s industry experts had begun suggesting that Apple was passive and ignoring the changing business environment. They claimed that Apple did not have a competitive advantage in either its offering or pricing. Essentially, customers began asking, "Why should I pay a higher price for Apple products that only work with other Apple products when the components of competing computers (PCs) work with each other?" Astute shoppers could buy the "best" computer, the "best" monitor, the "best" printer, and the "best" software (or even cheapest of any of these) from different vendors and feel assured that they would all work together. This definitely was not the case for Apple products. However, a quick turnaround in perception occurred. By the next decade, Apple was being lauded as one of the most innovative companies in corporate America. Some would suggest that Apple's innovation is driven by the company's product design, that marketing at Apple begins with this innovative product design, and that great business is derived from great products.

Product Models and Target Markets

When Apple's sales and market share collapsed in the mid-1990s, Steve Jobs reappeared as its savior. One of his earliest moves was to frame the company's computer product strategy within a two-by-two matrix. Within this matrix, the company would have two different product models (desktop and laptop) for two different market segments (professional and consumer). The professional market would be offered the PowerMac and the PowerBook models, and the consumer market would have the iMac and the iBook. In both markets, these products would come to represent a lifestyle brand, and this lifestyle branding strategy meant that Apple consumers would be offered more than just computers.

Ultimately, Apple crossed professional, consumer, and generational boundaries with the iPod, currently the world's best-selling digital audio player. The 2007 release of the iPhone likewise transformed the company into a serious competitor in the cellular handsets market. Using its strategy surrounding innovative product design, Apple was able to merge its products into an all-encompassing strategy that hinged on the digital world. The focus on a digital hub took the world into the third phase of personal computing. In the first phase, users were seeking utility (word processing, spreadsheets, and graphics). The second phase was about the Internet. In the third phase, the emphasis is on digital products (cameras, MP3 players, cell phones, and PDAs) that have entered into the mainstream of everyday life.

In this digital environment, Apple introduced the iPod, one of the most significant "disruptive innovations" in history. With the introduction of the iPod, Apple became deeply rooted in consumer lifestyle and become a cultural phenomenon. Whereas competitors were also offering their own versions of portable media players, the iPod quickly became synonymous for MP3 players and a huge success for the company. Within a five-year time period, the company created multiple versions of the iPod, with the iPod Nano introduced in the fall of 2005 amid much fanfare. Quarterly sales of the various iPod models hovered just above 10 million units in 2007, and Apple sold a record-high 22.1 million iPods in the fiscal first quarter of 2008, earning the company $9.6 billion in revenue.

According to some experts, Apple provided three signature product innovations in its 30-plus years of existence: the Apple II, the Macintosh, and the iPod. Yet Apple has also delivered a broad range of product line extensions and cutting-edge applications. In hardware, Apple unleashed the trend-setting iMac desktop computer and produced the world's thinnest notebook, MacBook Air. Apple's programming effort gave consumers the OS X operating system, complete with award-winning stability and speedy "Leopard" interface. Homegrown applications like iTunes, iMovie, GarageBand, and iWeb, with their point-and-click simplicity, transformed even novice computer users into multimedia wizards. And on the digital retail front, Apple delivered the online iTunes Music Store.

Distribution through Retail Stores

When crafting the marketing mix, Apple chose a unique distribution plan to satisfy the needs of the target consumers and meet the firm's goals. Although Apple did some innovative advertising at various points when promoting its Macintosh computers, its foray into retail stores has been a key driver in generating product interest and sales. But, its retail success did not come without some ups and downs. Originally, the company partnered with retail chains such as BusinessLand, ComputerLand, Sears Business Centers, ComputerWare, Circuit City, and

CompUSA. When sales were in the depths of decline in the mid-1990s, the company phased out many of its dealers and focused on CompUSA's Apple store-in-a-store concept. This concept was later adopted at other retail chains (e.g., Fry's Electronics and Micro Center). The bottom line was that Apple recognized that it needed to make its products readily available to the mass market if it was to become a branded consumer product.

Much to the disappointment of its Apple resellers, the company announced that it would begin opening and operating its own Apple stores. In doing so, Steve Jobs conveyed his concern that resellers had been unsuccessful at making Apple's stylish products appealing at the consumer level. The first Apple Store opened on May 19, 2001, with well-trained Apple salespeople. Computer and retail experts predicted the failure of the specialty stores, citing that Apple users already knew where to buy Apple products so Apple did not need to invest in retail stores with high fixed costs. They argued that the high-priced Apple products would have limited appeal to the mass consumer, and that a company not known for its customer service would be unable to provide assistance to the average consumer.

Yet, a mere three years after opening its first retail store, Apple was attaining around one-seventh of its revenue from Apple Stores. Interestingly, customers in these Apple Stores were not just current Apple users. Rather, half of the Macs sold at the Apple Stores were to first-time Mac buyers. When the iPod was introduced, consumers could easily visit an Apple Store and make their MP3 purchase. Additionally, having its own retail outlet made it easy for Apple to offer a variety of iPod accessories such as carrying cases, portable stereos, and adapters. Essentially, Apple was locking consumers into Apple-supported add-ons rather than sending consumers to competitors' add-on products. By the end of 2007, Apple operated more than 200 stores, including locations in the United States, Canada, Japan, the United Kingdom, and Rome.

Critical Thinking Questions

- How was Apple's market segmented?
- Why was the iPod referred to as a disruptive innovation?
- Where did pricing fit into Apple's marketing program? Why were channel partners unhappy when Apple opened its own stores?
- Why has the company been more successful attracting new Apple users through its Apple Stores instead of through innovative advertising?

Sources: Peter Burrows, "Can the iPod Keep Leading the Brand?" *BusinessWeek*, November 8, 2004, p. 54; Peter Burrows and Ronald Grover, "Steve Jobs' Magic Kingdom," *BusinessWeek*, February 6, 2006, pp. 63–69; Amanda Cantrell, "Mac Sales May Juice Apple's Earnings," *CNN Money*, October 10, 2005, **http://money.cnn.com**, accessed on March 21, 2006; Alice A. Cuneo, Tobi Elkin, Hank Kim, and T. L. Stanley, "Apple Transcends as Lifestyle Brand," *Advertising Age*, December 15, 2003, pp. S2–S6; Cliff Edwards, "Sorry, Steve: Here's Why It Won't Work," *BusinessWeek*, May 21, 2001, pp. 44–45; Lev Grossman, "How Apple Does It," *Time Canada*, October 24, 2005, pp. 42–46; Carleen Hawn, "If He's So Smart . . . Steve Jobs, Apple, and the Limits of Innovation," *Fast Company*, January 2004, **http://pf.fastcompany.com**, accessed on December 6, 2005; Jenny C. McCune, "Polishing the Apple," *Management Review*, September 1996, pp. 43–48; Gregory Quick, "Apple Blossoming from New Consumer Strategy," *Computer Retail Week*, July 6, 1998, p. 3; Josh Quittner and Rebecca Winters, "Apple's New Core," *Time South Pacific*, January 14, 2002, pp. 46–53; Jason Snell, "Geniuses Behind Bars," *Macworld*, May 2004, p. 9; Stephen Wozniak, "Homebrew and How the Apple Computer Came to Be," **http://www.atariarchives.org**, accessed on March 20, 2006; Joel West, "Apple Computer: The iCEO Seizes the Internet," Center for Research on Information Technology and Organizations, Paper 348, 2002, **http://repositories.cdlib.org**, accessed on December 6, 2005; Tom Yager, "Into the Mac Trap," *Infoworld.com*, January 31, 2005, p. 56; **http://finance.yahoo.com/q/pr?s5AAPL**, accessed on February 6, 2006; Ken Mingis and Michael DeAgonia, "Apple's Leopard Leaps to New Heights," *Computerworld*, October 25, 2007, **http://www.computerworld.com**, accessed February 11, 2008; Dan Moren, "Inside Apple's iPod Sales Figures: Slowing Growth Rate Doesn't Tell the Whole Story for iPod's Prospects," *Macworld*, January 31, 2008, **http://www.macworld.com**, accessed February 11, 2008; "Apple Nearing Milestone Opening," ifoAppleStore, October 16, 2007, **http://www.ifoapplestore.com**, accessed February 11, 2008.

Technology and Information

PART 5

Using Technology to Manage Information

Learning Goals

After reading this chapter, you should be able to answer these questions:

1 How has information technology transformed business and managerial decision making?

2 Why are computer networks an important part of today's information technology systems?

3 What types of systems make up a typical company's management information system?

4 How can technology management and planning help companies optimize their information technology systems?

5 What are the best ways to protect computers and the information they contain?

6 What are the leading trends in information technology?

"Houston, We Have a Problem"

Talk about your understatements. When Commander James Lovell very calmly tells NASA, "Houston, we have a problem," it seems like a major understatement. He and his crew are piloting the Apollo 13 space mission, which is headed toward the moon. Two days into the journey from Earth to the moon and just a bit shy of 200,000 miles away from the nearest service station, an explosion in the number two oxygen tank caused a host of problems to occur, including damage to the number one oxygen tank which, in turn, caused a drain on the electrical system. Three men, literally, were trapped inside a faulty machine heading farther and farther away from Earth with all its systems going haywire and no apparent way out of it. If that's not the definition of a problem, I simply don't know what is.

However, the situation faced by these astronauts and the individuals on Earth charged with bringing them home safely, also demonstrates the key attributes and issues associated with information technology. Information technology is, very simply, the equipment and the techniques used to manage and process information. In the clip, we see nothing but information technology. We have the spaceship with all its sensors and alarms telling the astronauts about all the problems occurring at that point in time. We have the astronauts relaying that information to the people on the ground via their headsets, and then the mission controllers on the ground are relaying information back to the astronauts in much the same manner.

And these mission controllers are simply surrounded by information technology. One man is monitoring the heart rates of the astronauts via a long-distance EKG. Another is connected directly to the oxygen data and is getting conflicting information. Another is keyed into the flight systems, and another is tapped into communications. Still another is managing the entire process and trying to assimilate all the information he receives into a useable form. In other words, information technology is actually the key to the entire situation, and the men in the space capsule will actually live or die based on how that technology is managed.

Management information systems, or MIS, are quite similar to NASA's mission control in that they assist in providing as much information as possible about the parameters associated with whatever task they are designed to monitor, allowing individuals to make decisions and act accordingly. In this case, MIS provides information about the mission parameters, letting people know what is wrong with the Apollo 13 space module and also providing the men with the means to solve the problem or, at the very least, work around the problem to bring James Lovell and his crew home safely.

In business, MIS may not always involve such dire circumstances, but it can provide you with the information you need to act accordingly on decisions that are as well-informed as possible. The following chapter takes you through an overview of how technology and information are used and managed within the workplace. It begins with a discussion of how information is used in business and then moves into the technologies used to store and disseminate that information. It then discusses in greater detail different types of management information systems such as decision support systems, expert systems, and transaction-processing systems. Finally, it takes you through key issues in technology planning and management before providing an overview of current trends in information technology. As such, it will provide you with a foundation that can help you solve problems that you might face in business.

Discussion Questions

- Describe the system of computer networks at work in the Apollo 13 mission and how they might be improved.
- Describe the management information systems that are on display during the Apollo 13 mission, and describe any not on display that could help the situation.
- Besides those mentioned above, what lessons about MIS can managers take away from the Apollo 13?

This chapter focuses on IT's role in business, examining the details of management information system (MIS) organization, as well as the challenges companies encounter in an increasingly technological world. **Information technology (IT)** includes the equipment and techniques used to manage and process information.

Information is at the heart of all organizations. Without information about the processes of and participants in an organization—including orders, products, inventory, scheduling, shipping, customers, suppliers, employees—a business cannot operate.

Transforming Businesses through Information

1 How has information technology transformed business and managerial decision making?

In less than 60 years, we have shifted from an industrial society to a knowledge-based economy driven by information. Businesses depend on information technology for everything from running daily operations to making strategic decisions. Computers are the tools of this information age, performing extremely complex operations as well as everyday jobs like word processing and creating spreadsheets. The pace of change has been rapid since the personal computer became a fixture on most office desks. Individual units became part of small networks, followed by more sophisticated enterprise-wide networks. Exhibits 13.1 and 13.2 summarize the types of computer equipment and software, respectively, most commonly used in business management information systems (MIS) today.

Although most workers spend their days at powerful desktop computers, other groups tackle massive computational problems at specialized supercomputer centers. Tasks that would take years on a PC can be completed in just hours on a supercomputer. With their ability to perform complex calculations quickly, supercomputers play a critical role in national security research, such as analysis of defense intelligence; scientific research, from biomedical experiments and drug development to simulations of earthquakes and star formations; demographic studies such as analyzing and predicting voting patterns; and weather and environmental studies. Businesses, too, put supercomputers to work improving inventory and production management and for product design. For example, Pringles potato chips are so light that they would catch air and fly off the high-speed production line. To curb this waste problem, Procter & Gamble, makers of the chips, used supercomputers to model the airflow patterns over Pringles production lines. Armed with the data from these simulations, product designers modified the shape of the chips to keep them from floating off the production line.[1] In the 15 years that Goodyear Tire & Rubber has used supercomputing, the company has reduced the time to develop a new tire from three years to one.[2]

EXHIBIT 13.1	Business Computing Equipment	
Computer Type	**Description**	**Comments**
Desktop personal computers (PCs)	Self-contained computers on which software can reside. These PCs can also be linked into a network over which other programs can be accessed.	Increasing power, speed, memory, and storage make these computers the dominant computer for many business processes. Can handle text, audio, video, and complex graphics.
Laptop computers	Portable computers similar in power to desktop computers.	Smaller size and weight make mobile computing easier for workers.
Minicomputers	Medium-sized computers with multiple processors, able to support from 4 to about 200 users at once.	The distinction between the larger minicomputers and smaller mainframes is blurring.
Mainframe computers	Large machines about the size of a refrigerator; can simultaneously run many different programs and support hundreds or thousands of users. Greatest storage capacity and processing speeds.	Extremely reliable and stable, used by companies and governments to process large amounts of data. More secure than PCs. Not subject to crashes; can be upgraded and repaired while operating.
Supercomputers	Most powerful computers, now capable of operating at speeds of 280 trillion calculations per second.	Companies can rent time to run projects from special supercomputer centers.

EXHIBIT 13.2   Business and Personal Software Applications

Application Type	Description
Word processing software	Used to write, edit, and format documents such as letters and reports. Spelling and grammar checkers, mail merge, tables, and other tools simplify document preparation.
Spreadsheet software	Used for preparation and analysis of financial statements, sales forecasts, budgets, and similar numerical and statistical data. Once the mathematical formulas are keyed into the spreadsheet, the data can be changed and the solution will be recalculated instantaneously.
Database management programs	Serve as electronic filing cabinets for records such as customer lists, employee data, and inventory information. Can sort data based on various criteria to create different reports.
Graphics and presentation programs	Create tables, graphs, and slides for customer presentations and reports. Can add images, video, animation, and sound effects.
Desktop publishing software	Combines word processing, graphics, and page layout software to create documents. Allows companies to design and produce sales brochures, catalogs, advertisements, and newsletters in-house.
Communications programs	Translate data into a form for transmission and transfer it across a network to other computers. Used to send and retrieve data and files.
Integrated software suites	Combine several popular types of programs, such as word processing, spreadsheet, database, graphics presentation, and communications programs. Component programs are designed to work together.
Groupware	Facilitates collaborative efforts of work groups so that several people in different locations can work on one project. Supports online meetings and project management (scheduling, resource allocation, document and e-mail distribution, etc.).
Financial Software	Used to compile accounting and financial data and create financial statements and reports.

chief information officer (CIO)
An executive with responsibility for managing all information resources in an organization.

knowledge worker
A worker who develops or uses knowledge, contributing to and benefiting from information used to perform planning, acquiring, searching, analyzing, organizing, storing, programming, producing, distributing, marketing, or selling functions.

In addition to a business's own computers and internal networks, the Internet increasingly offers companies opportunities for collaboration on a global scale. A manager can share information with hundreds of thousands of people worldwide as easily as with a colleague on another floor of the same office building. The Internet and the Web have become indispensable business tools that facilitate communication within companies as well as with customers. The rise of electronic trading hubs, discussed in the Expanding Around the Globe box on the next page is just one example of how technology is facilitating the global economy.

Many companies entrust an executive called the **chief information officer (CIO)** with the responsibility of managing all information resources. The importance of this responsibility is immense. As Jerry McElhatton, the retired CIO of MasterCard, points out, "Next to actual cash itself, data is probably the most precious asset a financial institution has. And for good reason." Companies such as MasterCard, banks, and insurance companies don't sell tangible products. "There is nothing to look at in a showroom, nothing to ship, nothing that will make a noise if you drop it. There is simply an agreement that something will happen, such as funds will become available if the customer signs on the dotted line. That's what makes data so precious to us and why we're more protective of it than the average mother lioness is with her cubs," McElhatton explains.[3]

Today most of us are **knowledge workers** who develop or use knowledge. Knowledge workers contribute to and benefit from information they use to perform planning, acquiring, searching, analyzing, organizing, storing, programming, producing, distributing, marketing, or selling functions. We must know how to gather and use information from the many resources available to us.

Because most jobs today depend on information—obtaining, using, creating, managing, and sharing it—this chapter begins with the role of information in decision making and goes on to discuss computer networks and management information systems. The management of information technology—planning and

CONCEPT in action

© Bob Schatz

In today's high-tech world, CIOs must possess not only the technical smarts to implement global IT infrastructures, integrate communications systems with partners, and protect customer data from insidious hackers, but most also have strong business acumen. FedEx's acclaimed tech chief Rob Carter manages the technology necessary to deliver more than 6 million packages daily, with an eye toward greater business efficiency, growth, and profits. Why is it important for CIOs to possess both technological and business expertise?

Electronic Hubs Integrate Global Commerce

Thanks to the wonders of technological advancement, global electronic trading now goes far beyond the Internet retailing and trading that we are all familiar with. Special Web sites known as trading hubs, or e-marketplaces, facilitate electronic commerce between businesses in specific industries such as automotive manufacturing, retailing, telecom provisioning, aerospace, financial products and services, and more. In 2005 approximately 6 percent of business-to-business trade in the European Union was done via trading hubs, a level unheard of even several years before.

The trading hub functions as a means of integrating the electronic collaboration of business services. Each hub provides standard formats for the electronic trading of documents used in a particular industry, as well as an array of services to sustain e-commerce between businesses in that industry. Services include demand forecasting, inventory management, partner directories, and transaction settlement services. And the payoff is significant—lowered costs, decreased inventory levels, and shorter time to market—resulting in bigger profits and enhanced competitiveness. For example, large-scale manufacturing procurement can amount to billions of dollars. Changing to "just-in-time purchasing" on the hub can save a considerable percentage of these costs.

Electronic trading across a hub can range from the collaborative integration of individual business processes to auctions and exchanges of goods (electronic barter). Global content management is an essential factor in promoting electronic trading agreements on the hub. A globally consistent view of the "content" of the hub must be available to all. Each participating company handles its own content, and applications such as *content managers* keep a continuously updated master catalog of the inventories of all members of the hub. The *transaction manager* application automates trading arrangements between companies, allowing the hub to provide aggregation and settlement services.

Ultimately, trading hubs for numerous industries could be linked together in a global e-commerce Web—an inclusive *"hub of all hubs."* One creative thinker puts it this way: "The traditional linear, one-step-at-a-time supply chain is dead. It will be replaced by parallel, asynchronous, real-time marketplace decision-making. Take manufacturing capacity as an example. Enterprises can bid their excess production capacity on the world e-commerce hub. Offers to buy capacity trigger requests from the seller for parts bids to suppliers who in turn put out requests to other suppliers, and this whole process will all converge in a matter of minutes."[4]

Critical Thinking Questions
- How do companies benefit from participating in an electronic trading hub?
- What impact does electronic trading have on the global economy?

© Digital Vision/Getty Images

protection—follows. Finally, we'll look at the latest trends in information technology. Throughout the chapter, examples show how managers and their companies are using computers to make better decisions in a highly competitive world.

Data and Information Systems

Information systems and the computers that support them are so much a part of our lives that we almost take them for granted. These **management information systems (MIS)**, methods and equipment that provide information about all aspects of a firm's operations, provide managers with the information they need to make decisions. They help managers properly categorize and identify ideas that result in substantial operational and cost benefits.

Businesses collect a great deal of *data*—raw, unorganized facts that can be moved and stored—in their daily operations. Only through well-designed IT systems and the power of computers can managers process these data into meaningful and useful *information* and use it for specific purposes, such as making business decisions. One such form of business information is the **database**, an electronic filing system that collects and organizes data and information. Using software called a *database management system* (DBMS), you can quickly and easily enter, store, organize, select, and retrieve data in a database. These data are then turned into information to run the business and to perform business analysis.

Databases are at the core of business information systems. For example, a customer database containing name, address, payment method, products ordered, price, order history, and similar data provides information to many departments. Marketing can track new orders and determine what products are selling best; sales can identify high-volume customers or contact customers about new or related products; operations managers need order information to obtain inventory and schedule production of the ordered products; and finance needs sales data to prepare financial statements. American Airlines uses software to link its AAdvantage frequent-flier program and its AA.com Web site. The airline can track who buys tickets online, the fare paid, the method of payment, and how much profit each customer generates in a given year. American can also find out about its customers' spending habits at the airline's partners, like 1–800-Flowers and audio-equipment maker Bose.[5] Later in the chapter we will see how companies use very large databases called data warehouses and data marts.

management information system (MIS)
The methods and equipment that provide information about all aspects of a firm's operations.

database
An electronic filing system that collects and organizes data and information.

Companies are discovering that they can't operate well with a series of separate information systems geared to solving specific departmental problems. Company-wide *enterprise resource planning (ERP)* systems that bring together human resources, operations, and technology are becoming an integral part of business strategy. So is managing the collective knowledge contained in an organization, using data warehouses and other technology tools. Technology experts are learning more about the way the business operates, and business managers are learning to use information systems technology effectively to create new opportunities and reach their goals.

Another challenge that businesses face is transforming thousands of paper documents into digital format, to make the information accessible to databases and other information systems.

Linking Up: Computer Networks

Today most businesses use networks to deliver information to employees, suppliers, and customers. A **computer network** is a group of two or more computer systems linked together by communications channels to share data and information. Today's networks often link thousands of users and can transmit audio and video as well as data.

Networks include clients and servers. The *client* is the application that runs on a personal computer or workstation. It relies on a *server* that manages network resources or performs special tasks such as storing files, managing one or more printers, or processing database queries. Any user on the network can access the server's capabilities.

By making it easy and fast to share information, networks have created new ways to work and increase productivity. They provide more efficient use of resources, permitting communication and collaboration across distance and time. With file sharing, all employees, regardless of location, have access to the same information. Shared databases also eliminate duplication of effort. Employees at different sites can "screen share" computer files, working on data as if they were in the same room. Their computers are connected by phone or cable lines, they all see the same thing on their display, and anyone can make changes that are seen by the other participants. The employees can also use the networks for videoconferencing.

Networks make it possible for companies to run enterprise software, large programs with integrated modules that manage all of the corporation's internal operations. Enterprise resource planning systems run on networks. Typical subsystems include finance, human resources, engineering, sales and order distribution, and order management and procurement. These modules work independently and then automatically exchange information, creating a company-wide system that includes current delivery dates, inventory status, quality control, and other critical information. Let's now look at the basic types of networks companies use to transmit data—local area networks and wide area networks—and popular networking applications like intranets and virtual private networks.

Connecting Near and Far with Networks

Two basic types of networks are distinguished by the area they cover. A **local area network (LAN)** lets people at one site exchange data and share the use of hardware and software from a variety of computer manufacturers. LANs offer companies a more cost-effective way to link computers than linking terminals to a mainframe computer. The most common uses of LANs at small businesses, for example, are office automation, accounting, and information management. LANs can help companies reduce staff, streamline operations, and cut processing costs. LANs can be set up with wired or wireless connections.

A **wide area network (WAN)** connects computers at different sites via telecommunications media such as phone lines, satellites, and microwaves. A modem connects the computer or a terminal to the telephone line and transmits data almost instantly, in less than a second. The Internet is essentially a worldwide WAN. Long-distance telephone companies, such as AT&T, MCI, and Sprint, operate very large WANs. Companies also connect LANs at various locations into WANs. WANs make it possible for companies to work on critical projects around the clock by using teams in different time zones.

2 Why are computer networks an important part of today's information technology systems?

computer network
A group of two or more computer systems linked together by communications channels to share data and information.

CONCEPT in action

© Kimberly White/Reuters/Landov

The Internet has been in public use for less than two decades, but analysts say its lightning-speed replacement is already on the horizon. A future worldwide network called "the Grid" will connect through fiber-optic cables and operate 10,000 times faster than today's broadband connections. This astounding data-transmission capability will enable high-definition video telephony, the use of 3-D holographic images, and full-length movie downloads in seconds. How might the Grid's unprecedented metacomputing power affect the efficiency and productivity of business?

local area network (LAN)
A network that connects computers at one site, enabling the computer users to exchange data and share the use of hardware and software from a variety of computer manufacturers.

wide area network (WAN)
A network that connects computers at different sites via telecommunications media such as phone lines, satellites, and microwaves.

Several forms of WANs—intranets, virtual private networks (VPNs), and extranets—use Internet technology. Here we'll look at intranets, internal corporate networks that are widely available in the corporate world, and VPNs. Extranets are discussed in the online enrichment chapter, "Using the Internet for Business Success," at **www.cengage.com/introbusiness/gitman**.

Although wireless networks have been around for more than a decade, they are increasing in use because of falling costs, faster and more reliable technology, and improved standards. They are similar to their wired LAN and WAN cousins, except they use radio frequency signals to transmit data. You probably use a wireless WAN (WWAN) regularly when you use your cellular phone. WANs' coverage can span several countries. Telecommunications carriers AT&T Wireless, Cingular Wireless, Sprint PCS, T-Mobile, and Verizon operators use wireless WANs.

Wireless LANs (WLANs) that transmit data at one site offer an alternative to traditional wired systems. WLANs' reach is a radius of 500 feet indoors and 1,000 feet outdoors and can be extended with antennas, transmitters, and other devices. The wireless devices communicate with a wired access point into the wired network. WLANs are convenient for specialized applications where wires are in the way or when employees are in different locations in a building. Hotels, airports, restaurants, hospitals, retail establishments, universities, and warehouses are among the largest users of WLANs.

An Inside Job: Intranets

Like LANs, **intranets** are private corporate networks. Many companies use both types of internal networks. However, because they use Internet technology to connect computers, intranets are WANs that link employees in many locations and with different types of computers. Essentially mini-Internets that serve only the company's employees, intranets operate behind a *firewall* that prevents unauthorized access. Employees navigate using a standard Web browser, which makes the intranet easy to use. They are also considerably less expensive to install and maintain than other network types and take advantage of the Internet's interactive features such as chat rooms and team work spaces. Many software providers now offer off-the-shelf intranet packages so that companies of all sizes can benefit from the increased access to and distribution of information.

Although intranets have been around for years, forward-thinking companies have recognized the power of intranets to connect employers to employees and, more important, employees to each other, as the Managing Change box on the next page describes.

Enterprise Portals Open the Door to Productivity

Intranets that take a broader view serve as sophisticated knowledge management tools. One such intranet is the **enterprise portal**, an internal Web site that provides proprietary corporate information to a defined user group. Portals can take one of three forms: business to employee (B2E), business to business (B2B), and business to consumer (B2C). Unlike a standard intranet, enterprise portals allow individuals or user groups to customize the portal home page to gather just the information they need for their particular job situations into one place and deliver it through a single Web page. Because of their complexity, enterprise portals are typically the result of a collaborative project that brings together designs developed and perfected through the collaborative effort of HR, corporate communications, and information technology departments.

More companies are turning to portal technology to provide:

- A consistent, simple user interface across the company
- Integration of disparate systems and multiple sets of data and information
- A single source for accurate and timely information that integrates internal and external information
- A shorter time to perform tasks and processes
- Cost savings through the elimination of "information intermediaries"
- Improved communications within the company and with customers, suppliers, dealers, and distributors

At Intercontinental Hotels Group (IHG), a new enterprise portal will connect staff at the group's 3,500 hotels around the world and support marketing, human resources, finance, and IT functions. A major goal is to eliminate duplication of efforts. "All of these departments are tackling similar problems independently," says David House, IHG's senior vice president for global human resources. "For example, you might have marketing efforts going on in one part of the world and someone doing a similar kind of thing in another without knowing it." The portal will facilitate collaboration

© Stockbyte/Getty Images

Unlocking the Power of Social Networking

Most company intranets are still so twentieth century. Even though companies continue to commit resources to maintaining them, often, the company intranet is nothing more than a series of mass-distribution communication tools. Unless, that is, the intranet is at one of the growing number of forward-looking companies embracing a range of Web 2.0 tools, like wikis and social networking, as foundational elements of their intranets and enterprise portals.

The World Wide Web has evolved from a worldwide publishing medium to a collaborative environment. Many intranets are still based on the former iteration of the Web, meaning intranets that function as a repository for company missives and an archive for forms, templates, and other documentation. Companies that appreciate the Web as a social resource, however, are the ones that are able to transform their intranets into extremely useful information and knowledge-sharing tools.

At Motorola, 70,000 employees span 70 countries, yet social-media tools allow them all to publish and share information. The company's intranet includes blogs (around 5,400 of them), wilds, a social-bookmarking utility (which employees have used to create about 65,000 bookmarks), wikis (4,500 or so), and shared documents (numbering approximately 30 million). Every day, Motorola employees add about 100,000 new documents to the shared pool of information. Although this sounds like a lot, the volumes of information are more than just spreadsheets and reports. These postings represent conversational interactions among the company's 70,000 employees who are reaching out to each other to help solve problems, share best practices, and identify future business opportunities. To date, 92 percent of Motorola employees have tapped into the common pool of resources.

Technology companies aren't the only ones incorporating social networking and Web 2.0 tools into their intranets. Accenture uses a search function made popular by YouTube to help its employees find training videos. Before the company added tagging capabilities, employees could only find a video they had in mind if they knew the exact name of the file. Now, any employee who watches the video can tag it and comment on it. Other employees can search for videos by title, tags, and comments.

McDonald's CEO Mike Roberts used blogging tools to upload pictures and stories from a trip he took to Dubai. Because employees responded so positively to his casual personal tone, Roberts let everyone know he'd be at his "virtual desk" during a certain time of day. A group from Canada joined the conversation to ask about why they hadn't received bonuses. Roberts was able to explain that bonuses were given for performance, and remind them that they hadn't met their goals. Blogging tools allowed McDonald's employees to have a personal conversation with the CEO.

Beyond increasing the functionality and effectiveness of company intranets, social-networking capabilities help reconcile the technologies employees are using in their personal life with those to which they have access in their professional life. Employees are accustomed to using sites like YouTube, MySpace, Wikipedia, and so on, in their personal lives and so have become accustomed to the efficiency and performance these tools bring to communication. Company intranets that don't include any of these tools will become increasingly frustrating to use and outdated.[6]

Critical Thinking Questions

- Given the amount of information in the Motorola intranet, don't intranets enhanced with Web 2.0 functionalities contribute to information overload? Why or why not?
- Beyond the differences in technology, how do you think communication in an old-style intranet differs from communication in a Web 2.0 intranet that includes social-networking tools?

and teamwork throughout the organization. "We want people to use the intranet to bridge these gaps, to improve availability of information, and to better exploit the intellectual capital in the organization," explains House.[7]

No More Tangles: Wireless Technologies

Wireless technology has become commonplace today. We routinely use devices such as cellular phones, personal digital assistants (PDAs), garage door openers, and television remote controls—without thinking of them as examples of wireless technology. Businesses use wireless technologies to improve communications with customers, suppliers, and employees. You may have seen the term Wi-Fi, which refers to wireless fidelity. When products carry the "Wi-Fi Certified" designation, they have been tested and certified to work with each other, regardless of manufacturer.

Companies in the package delivery industry, such as UPS and FedEx, were among the first users of wireless technology. Delivery personnel use handheld computers to send immediate confirmation of package receipt. You may also have seen meter readers and repair personnel from utility and energy companies send data from remote locations back to central computers.

Bluetooth short-range wireless technology is a global standard that improves personal connectivity for users of mobile phones, portable computers, stereo headsets, and MP3 players. Bluetooth wirelessly connects keyboards and mice to computers and headsets to phones and music players. A Bluetooth-enabled mobile phone, for example, provides safer hands-free cell phone use while driving. The technology is finding many applications in the auto industry as well. "Bluetooth

© Thomas Barwick/Getty Images

CONCEPT in action

PDAs (personal digital assistants) are revolutionizing the way people work. The BlackBerry, with its mini-keyboard interface and easy integration with corporate networks, is a staple of business users. But the iPhone—a triple-threat cell phone, iPod, and Web browser in one—is proving to be a serious challenger. PDAs represent a leap forward in wireless innovation, combining hardware, software, and network technologies in stylish handheld devices. What impact is wireless technology having on the traditional office?

wireless technology will start to become standard in cars in the near future," predicts David McClure, head of Telematics Research at SBD automotive technology consultants. Many car and cell phone manufacturers—among them Audi, BMW, Honda, Mercedes, Saab, Toyota, Volkswagen, Motorola, and Nokia—already offer Bluetooth hands-free solutions. Other uses include simplifying the connection of portable digital music players to the car's audio system and of transferring music to the system.[8]

Perhaps the newest venue for wireless technology is in the air. Read the Catching the Entrepreneurial Spirit box on the next page to find out how Aircell is bringing wireless Internet access to a flight near you.

Private Lines: Virtual Private Networks

virtual private networks (VPNs)
Private corporate networks connected over a public network, such as the Internet. VPNs include strong security measures to allow only authorized users to access the network.

Many companies use **virtual private networks (VPNs)** to connect two or more private networks (such as LANs) over a public network, such as the Internet. VPNs include strong security measures to allow only authorized users to access the network and its sensitive corporate information. Companies with widespread offices may find that a VPN is a more cost-effective option than creating a network using purchased networking equipment and leasing expensive private lines. This type of private network is more limited than a VPN, because it doesn't allow authorized users to connect to the corporate network when they are at home or traveling.

As Exhibit 13.3 shows, the VPN uses existing Internet infrastructure and equipment to connect remote users and offices almost anywhere in the world—without long-distance charges. In addition to saving on telecommunications costs, companies using VPNs don't have to buy or maintain special networking equipment and can outsource management of remote access equipment. VPNs are useful for salespeople and telecommuters, who can access the company's network as if they were on-site at the company's office. On the downside, the VPN's availability and performance, especially when it uses the Internet, depends on factors largely outside of an organization's control.

VPNs are popular with many different types of organizations. Global law firm Baker & McKenzie, with 3,300 attorneys in 38 countries, uses a VPN to connect lawyers and clients. It outsourced the VPN to Equant, a provider that offers service in 145 countries, making it easy to expand into new locations. Equant operates its own private network, which gives Baker & McKenzie a higher level of quality, security, and reliability.[9] The Abilene, Texas, Independent School District developed a cost-effective VPN for distance learning and educational software applications that will save as much as $875,000 over a five-year period. Instead of having to install software on individual computers, the district distributes them to students and teachers through the VPN. Chief technical officer Martin Yarborough says that without the system, he would need five more technical support staff to maintain all the computers.[10]

Software on Demand: Application Service Providers

application service providers (ASPs)
A service company that buys and maintains software on its servers and distributes it through high-speed networks to subscribers, for a set period and price.

As software developers release new types of application programs and updated versions of existing ones every year or two, companies have to analyze whether they can justify buying or upgrading to the new software—in terms of both cost and implementation time. **Application service providers (ASPs)** offer a different approach to this problem. Companies subscribe, usually on a monthly basis, to an ASP and use the applications much like you'd use telephone voice mail, the technology for which resides at the phone company. Other names for ASPs include on-demand software, hosted

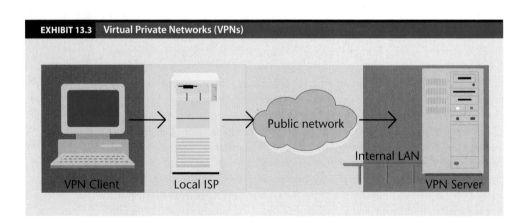

EXHIBIT 13.3   Virtual Private Networks (VPNs)

VPN Client   Local ISP   Public network   Internal LAN   VPN Server

Surfing the Internet at 40,000 Feet

© Rubberball/Getty Images

Every airline passenger knows that electronic devices need to be turned off during takeoff and landing. Once passengers on American, JetBlue, and Virgin America hit cruising altitude, however, chances are they are able to surf the Internet. That's because in 2008, Aircell received approval from the Federal Aviation Administration (FAA) to operate its air-to-ground (ATG) communication network, and those airlines were the first to sign up for the new service.

Aircell has created a network of 92 ground towers across the United States that, like cell phone towers, radiate wireless signals. Whereas cell phone towers send their signals toward the ground, Aircell towers send signals skyward. Planes outfitted with Aircell antennas can receive the signals and transmit them to wireless access points, or repeaters, in the cabin.

Passengers on Aircell-equipped planes will pay about $10 to access the Web, which they can do either from their own device or from the in-flight entertainment system. American first rolled out the service on 15 of its jets, each of which had three access points able to handle 256 users at a time. Virgin committed to roll out the service on its entire fleet. Aircell's system supports full corporate and personal e-mail, VPN access, and Web surfing, and the company boasts that its network is the first to provide seamless Internet connectivity coast to coast.

Aircell is not the only company offering in-flight data transmission capabilities. AeroMobile has its service in Quantas and Emirates. Another firm, OnAir, is in trials at Air France and Ryanair. And yet another service, Row44, is available on Alaskan and Southwest Airlines flights.

Why have wireless communications only now begun to flood the skies? The cost of outfitting a plane with the ability to receive communications has dropped significantly. It used to cost $1,000,000 to outfit a single plane; today, Aircell can install three specialized antennas on a jet for $100,000. In addition, today's consumers are demanding full-time access to their e-mail and text-messaging services—on the ground and in the air.[11]

Critical Thinking Questions

- Can you think of other industries that might be poised to roll out wireless Internet capabilities, or do you think the airlines are the last to provide this service to their customers?
- Do you think people will pay $10 to $15 to access the Internet in the air?
- If you were the CEO of an airline, would you roll out wireless on your entire fleet, like Virgin America, or would you outfit only a handful of planes in your fleet, like American Airlines? Explain your choice. If you would outfit only a portion of your fleet, how would you decide which planes and routes would get the new wireless capabilities?

applications, and software-as-a-service. Exhibit 13.4 shows how the ASP interfaces with software and hardware vendors and developers, the IT department, and users.

The simplest ASP applications are automated—for example, a user might use one to build a simple e-commerce site. ASPs provide three major categories of applications to users:

- Enterprise applications, including customer relationship management, enterprise resource planning (ERP), e-commerce, and data warehousing.
- Collaborative applications for internal communications, e-mail, groupware, document creation, and management messaging.
- Applications for personal use—for example, games, entertainment software, and home-office applications.

EXHIBIT 13.4 Structure of an ASP Relationship

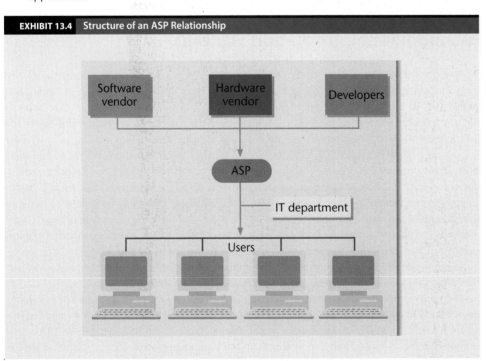

Salesforce.com dominates the customer-relationship-management market by offering more than 800 on-demand software applications developed by Adobe, Google, Skype, and others. The company's software-as-a-service platform, AppExchange, is enormously popular with small businesses—and even big ones like Ryder and Expedia.com—that don't want the hassle or expense of buying and maintaining conventional licensed applications. Salesforce.com reached 1 million subscribers in 2008. What are the benefits and risks of using software hosted remotely by ASPs?

According to recent surveys, about one-third of U.S. companies currently use an ASP, and another third indicate that they will take the ASP route. AMR Research estimates that revenues from subscriptions to on-demand software products were about $2 billion in 2006. Although this represents less than 10 percent of the total software market, this sector is growing much more rapidly—more than 20 percent a year—while traditional software sales are rising at about 6 to 8 percent.[12] As this market grows, more companies are adding on-demand offerings to their traditional software packages. SAP, one of the world's largest software companies, recently joined the ranks of ASPs such as Salesforce.com and Siebel to offer on-demand customer relationship management (CRM) software. CRM has been an especially successful on-demand software category, and SAP hopes that customers who begin with on-demand CRM will buy the software to run in-house once they become familiar with its capabilities.[13]

Until recently, many companies were reluctant to outsource critical enterprise applications to third-party providers. As ASPs improved their technologies and proved to be reliable and cost-effective, attitudes have changed. Companies, both large and small, that seek cost advantages like the convenience ASPs provide. The basic idea behind subscribing to an ASP is compelling. Users can access any of their applications and data from any computer, and IT can avoid purchasing, installing, supporting, and upgrading expensive software applications. ASPs buy and maintain the software on their servers and distribute it through high-speed networks. Subscribers rent the applications they want for a set period and price. The savings in licensing fees, infrastructure, time, and staff are significant.[14]

Managed service providers (MSPs) represent the next generation of ASPs, offering greater customization and expanded capabilities that include business processes and complete management of the network servers. For example, Checkpoint is one of the largest MSPs in the industry. One of its products, Youniquely 4U (Y4U) was designed for use by libraries. When patrons of a library enrolled in Y4U to check out books, information about community and library events on the same topics is e-mailed to them. For example, someone checking out a book on parenting might receive coupons for a family fun center, information on a local parenting seminar, or a list of pediatricians in the area. Using an MSP like Y4U can help a library connect with its patrons without having to incur the expense of building such detailed data and software capabilities from scratch.[15]

CONCEPT check

What is a computer network? What benefits do companies gain by using networks?

How do a LAN and a WAN differ? Why would a company use a wireless network?

What advantages do VPNs offer a company? ASPs and MSPs?

Management Information Systems

3 What types of systems make up a typical company's management information system?

managed service providers (MSPs)
Next generation of ASPs, offering customization and expanded capabilities such as business processes and complete management of the network servers.

Whereas individuals use business productivity software such as word processing, spreadsheet, and graphics programs to accomplish a variety of tasks, the job of managing a company's information needs falls to *management information systems*: users, hardware, and software that support decision making. Information systems collect and store the company's key data and produce the information managers need for analysis, control, and decision making.

As we learned in Chapter 10, factories use computer-based information systems to automate production processes and order and monitor inventory. Most companies use them to process customer orders and handle billing and vendor payments. Banks use a variety of information systems to process transactions such as deposits, ATM withdrawals, and loan payments. Most consumer transactions also involve information systems. When you check out at the supermarket, book a hotel room using a toll-free hotel reservations number, or buy CDs over the Internet, information systems record and track the transaction and transmit the data to the necessary places.

Companies typically have several types of information systems, starting with systems to process transactions. Management support systems are dynamic systems that allow users to analyze data to make forecasts, identify business trends, and model business strategies. Office automation systems improve the flow of communication throughout the organization. Each type of information system serves a particular level of decision making: operational, tactical, and strategic. Exhibit 13.5 shows the relationship between transaction processing and management support systems as well as

EXHIBIT 13.5   A Company's Integrated Information System

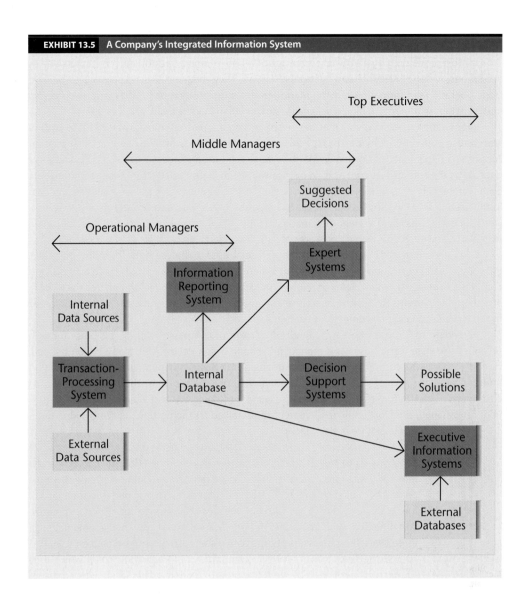

the management levels they serve. Let's now take a more detailed look at how companies and managers use transaction processing and management support systems to manage information.

Transaction-Processing Systems

A firm's integrated information system starts with its **transaction-processing system (TPS)**. The TPS receives raw data from internal and external sources and prepares these data for storage in a database similar to a microcomputer database but vastly larger. In fact, all the company's key data are stored in a single huge database that becomes the company's central information resource. As noted earlier, the *database management system* tracks the data and allows users to query the database for the information they need.

The database can be updated in two ways: **batch processing**, where data are collected over some time period and processed together, and **online**, or **real-time, processing**, which processes data as they become available. Batch processing uses computer resources very efficiently and is well suited to applications such as payroll processing that require periodic rather than continuous processing. Online processing keeps the company's data current. When you make an airline reservation, the agent enters your reservation directly into the airline's computer and quickly receives confirmation. Online processing is more expensive than batch processing, so companies must weigh the cost versus the benefit. For example, a factory that operates round-the-clock may use real-time processing for inventory and other time-sensitive requirements but process accounting data in batches overnight.

transaction-processing system (TPS)
An information system that handles the daily business operations of a firm. The system receives and organizes raw data from internal and external sources for storage in a database using either batch or online processing.

batch processing
A method of updating a database in which data are collected over some time period and processed together.

online (real-time) processing
A method of updating a database in which data are processed as they become available.

Decisions, Decisions: Management Support Systems

Transaction-processing systems automate routine and tedious back-office processes such as accounting, order processing, and financial reporting. They reduce clerical expenses and provide basic operational information quickly. **Management support systems (MSSs)** use the internal master database to perform high-level analyses that help managers make better decisions.

Information technologies such as data warehousing are part of more advanced MSSs. A **data warehouse** combines many databases across the whole company into one central database that supports management decision making. With a data warehouse, managers can easily access and share data across the enterprise, to get a broad overview rather than just isolated segments of information. Data warehouses include software to extract data from operational databases, maintain the data in the warehouse, and provide data to users. They can analyze data much faster than transaction-processing systems. Data warehouses may contain many **data marts**, special subsets of a data warehouse that each deal with a single area of data. Data marts are organized for quick analysis.

Companies use data warehouses to gather, secure, and analyze data for many purposes, including customer relationship management systems, fraud detection, product line analysis, and corporate asset management. Retailers might wish to identify customer demographic characteristics and shopping patterns to improve direct-mailing responses. Banks can more easily spot credit card fraud, as well as analyze customer usage patterns.

According to Forrester Research, about 60 percent of companies with $1 billion or more in revenues use data warehouses as a management tool. Union Pacific (UP), a $12 billion railroad, turned to data warehouse technology to streamline its business operations. By consolidating multiple separate systems, UP achieved a unified supply chain system that also enhanced its customer service. "Before our data warehouse came into being we had stovepipe systems," says Roger Bresnahan, principal engineer. "None of them talked to each other. . . . We couldn't get a whole picture of the railroad."

UP's data warehouse system took many years and the involvement of 26 departments to create. The results were well worth the effort: UP can now make more accurate forecasts, identify the best traffic routes, and determine the most profitable market segments. The ability to predict seasonal patterns and manage fuel costs more closely has saved UP millions of dollars by optimizing locomotive and other asset utilization and through more efficient crew management. In just three years, Bresnahan reports, the data warehouse system had paid for itself.[16]

At the first level of an MSS is an *information-reporting system*, which uses summary data collected by the TPS to produce both regularly scheduled and special reports. The level of detail would depend on the user. A company's payroll personnel might get a weekly payroll report showing how each employee's paycheck was determined. Higher-level managers might receive a payroll summary report that shows total labor cost and overtime by department and a comparison of current labor costs with those in the prior year. Exception reports show cases that fail to meet some standard. An accounts receivable exception report that lists all customers with overdue accounts would help collection personnel focus their work. Special reports are generated only when a manager requests them; for example, a report showing sales by region and type of customer can highlight reasons for a sales decline.

CONCEPT in action

Decision support systems help businesses by providing quantitative data and predictive models that aid decision making. Now the health care industry wants this problem-solving technology in hospitals to improve the practice of medicine. Spearheading the effort for a clinical decision-support system is the American Medical Informatics Association, which believes a national DSS could assist physicians in diagnosing and treating illnesses. What are pros and cons to having medical professionals rely on a DSS for help in treating patients?

© Mike Kemp/Rubberball/Jupiterimages

Decision Support Systems

A **decision support system (DSS)** helps managers make decisions using interactive computer models that describe real-world processes. The DSS also uses data from the internal database but looks for specific data that relate to the problems at hand. It is a tool for answering "what if" questions about what would happen if the manager made certain changes. In simple cases, a manager can create a spreadsheet and try changing some of the numbers. For instance, a manager could create a spreadsheet to show the amount of overtime required if the number of workers increases or decreases. With models, the manager enters into the computer the values that describe a particular situation, and the program computes the results. Marketing executives at a furniture company could run DSS models that use sales data and demographic assumptions to develop forecasts of the types of furniture that would appeal to the fastest-growing population groups.

Athletic apparel and footwear manufacturer PUMA turned to a predictive analytics program to improve its North American real-time inventory management system. Its existing ERP system lacked the flexibility to provide new types of reports required by the rapidly changing industry, requiring PUMA to call the vendor to make all changes. With the new software, Karen King, the company's data warehouse specialist, creates and generates the reports she needs, as she needs them. Instead of taking a day or more, she can produce a report in an hour or less.[17]

Executive Information Systems

Although similar to a DSS, an **executive information system (EIS)** is customized for an individual executive. These systems provide specific information for strategic decisions. For example, a CEO's EIS may include special spreadsheets that present financial data comparing the company to its principal competitors and graphs showing current economic and industry trends.

Expert Systems

An **expert system** gives managers advice similar to what they would get from a human consultant. Artificial intelligence enables computers to reason and learn to solve problems in much the same way humans do, using what-if reasoning. Although they are expensive and difficult to create, expert systems are finding their way into more companies as more applications are found. Lower-end expert systems can even run on PDAs like the PalmPilot. Top-of-the-line systems help airlines appropriately deploy aircraft and crews, critical to the carriers' efficient operations. The cost of hiring enough people to do these ongoing analytical tasks would be prohibitively expensive. Expert systems have also been used to help explore for oil, schedule employee work shifts, and diagnose illnesses. Some expert systems take the place of human experts, whereas others assist them.

Office Automation Systems

Today's **office automation systems** assist all levels of employees and enable managers to handle most of their own communication. Many of the newer devices now combine multiple functions. The key elements, many of which have been around for years and others that are fairly new, include:

- Word processing systems for producing written messages.
- E-mail systems for communicating directly with other employees and customers and transferring computer files.
- Departmental scheduling systems for planning meetings and other activities.
- Cell phones for providing telephone service away from the office, as in cars. Newer models can receive and send e-mail and text messages, graphics, and browse the Web.
- Personal digital assistants (PDAs) such as PalmPilots that replace paper personal planners and address books; these can also transfer data to and from the user's PC and run some software. Newer models can also handle e-mail and Web browsing, and some include cell phones.
- Wireless e-mail devices, such as the BlackBerry.
- Pagers that notify employees of phone calls. Some pagers can display more extensive written messages sent from a computer network.
- Voice-mail systems for recording, storing, and forwarding phone messages.
- Facsimile (fax) systems for delivering messages on paper within minutes.
- Electronic bulletin boards and computer conferencing systems for discussing issues with others who are not present.

Office automation systems also make telecommuting and home-based businesses possible. An estimated 8 million people work at home, using microcomputers and other high-tech equipment to keep in touch with the office. Instead of spending time on the road twice a day, telecommuters work at home two or more days a week.

CONCEPT in action

E-mail continues to be the Internet's "killer app." The speed and convenience with which people send e-mail messages is unlike anything businesses have ever experienced using traditional forms of written communication. Moreover, electronic messages provide a record of conversations that is digitally stored and easily retrieved. But the technology also has downsides. Many professionals report spending up to two hours a day checking inboxes, and a majority of employers admit to monitoring the electronic communications of workers. How can organizations maximize the benefits of e-mail while limiting pitfalls?

© iStockphoto.com/Kristian Sekulic

CONCEPT check

What are the main types of management information systems, and what does each do?

Differentiate between the types of management support systems, and give examples of how companies use each.

How can office automation systems help employees work more efficiently?

Technology Management and Planning

4 How can technology management and planning help companies optimize their information technology systems?

With the help of computers, people have produced more data in the last 30 years than in the previous 5,000 years combined. Companies today make sizable investments in information technology to help them manage this overwhelming amount of data, convert the data into knowledge, and deliver it to the people who need it. In many cases, however, the companies do not reap the desired benefits from these expenditures. Among the typical complaints from senior executives are that the company is spending too much and not getting adequate performance and payoff from IT investments, these investments do not relate to business strategy, the firm seems to be buying the latest technology for technology's sake, and communications between IT specialists and IT users are poor.

Optimize IT!

Managing a company's enterprise-wide IT operations, especially when those often stretch across multiple locations, software applications, and systems, is no easy task. IT managers must deal not only with on-site systems, they must also oversee the networks and other technology—such as PDAs and cell phones that handle e-mail messaging—that connect staff working at locations ranging from the next town to another continent. At the same time, IT managers face time constraints and budget restrictions, making their jobs even more challenging.

At most companies, IT is managed by one segment of the organization. The rationale is that such centralization allows for tighter security and greater standardization. Growing companies, however, may find themselves with a decentralized IT structure that includes many separate systems and duplication of efforts. At Google, decentralization isn't a by-product of growth but an intentional IT structure. Because nearly everyone at Google is a technologist, employees are allowed to manage their own IT system to optimize their own performance. As such, employees can choose from a broad selection of computers, operating systems, and even applications. Rather than managing machines and installing approved software, the central IT department at Google performs a support and service function. Google employees can go to tech stops, areas at the company where IT workers provide tech support, or they can download software on their own from the company's internal Web site.[18]

Whether a firm specializes in technology or not, its goal should be to develop an integrated, company-wide technology plan that balances business judgment, technology expertise, and technology investment. IT planning requires a coordinated effort among a firm's top executives, IT managers, and business-unit managers to develop a comprehensive plan. Such plans must take into account the company's strategic objectives and how the right technology will help managers reach those goals.

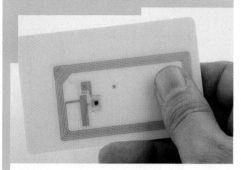

CONCEPT in action

Radio frequency identification (RFID) has transformed the supply-chain management of companies like Gillette and Wal-Mart. However, new uses are emerging for these tiny computer tags that transmit data when scanned. RFID tags are turning up in store clothing, credit cards, automotive transponder keys, and library books. The technology could soon be embedded in everything we buy, wear, drive, and read—providing companies with comprehensive awareness of consumer activities. Aside from the privacy issues raised by RFID technology, how can businesses turn the raw data collected by RFID tags into useful, actionable knowledge?

© iStockphoto.com/Albert Lozano

Managing Knowledge Resources

As a result of the proliferation of information, we are also seeing a major shift from information management to a broader view that focuses on finding opportunities in and unlocking the value of intellectual rather than physical assets. Whereas *information management* involves collecting, processing, and condensing information, the more difficult task of **knowledge management (KM)** focuses on researching, gathering, organizing, and sharing an organization's collective knowledge to improve productivity, foster innovation, and gain competitive advantage. Some companies are even creating a new position, *chief knowledge officer*, to head up this effort.[19]

knowledge management (KM) The process of researching, gathering, organizing, and sharing an organization's collective knowledge to improve productivity, foster innovation, and gain competitive advantage.

Companies use their IT systems to facilitate the physical sharing of knowledge. But better hardware and software are not the answer to KM. KM is not technology based but rather a business practice that uses technology. Technology alone does not constitute KM, nor is it the solution to KM. Rather, it facilitates KM. Executives with successful KM initiatives understand that KM is not a matter of buying a major software application that serves as a data depository and coordinates all of a company's intellectual capital. Instead, KM is an investment that, if nurtured, will reap benefits over time.

Effective KM calls for an interdisciplinary approach that coordinates all aspects of an organization's knowledge. It requires a major change in behavior as well as technology to leverage the power of information systems, especially the Internet, and a company's human capital resources.

The first step is creating an information culture through organizational structure and rewards that promotes a more flexible, collaborative way of working and communicating. However, moving an organization toward KM is no easy task, but well worth the effort in terms of creating a more collaborative environment, reducing duplication of effort, and increasing shared knowledge. The benefits can be significant in terms of growth, time, and money.

Such is the case at Caterpillar, the manufacturer of heavy equipment. Since 2000, Caterpillar has invested $5 million in its knowledge network and projects savings through 2008 to reach $75 million. A pillar of the company's KM program is the **community of practice**, or **CoP**, which is a group of people who share a concern, problem, or passion about a topic, and who deepen their knowledge and expertise in this area by interacting on an ongoing basis. Caterpillar has over 4,300 CoPs in which more than 18,000 employees participate. Each CoP is organized around a specific business topic, and people post information, ask questions, share tips, and so on. All entries in a CoP are accessible to the users, but a community manager must verify the knowledge before adding it to a community. In that way, the quality of the information available stays high.[20]

community of practice (CoP)
A group of people who share a concern, problem, or passion about a topic, and who deepen their knowledge and expertise in this area by interacting on an ongoing basis.

Technology Planning

A good technology plan provides employees with the tools they need to perform their jobs at the highest levels of efficiency. The first step is a general needs assessment, followed by a ranking of projects and the specific choices of hardware and software. Exhibit 13.6 poses some basic questions departmental managers and IT specialists should ask when planning technology purchases.

Once managers identify the projects that make business sense, they can choose the best products for the company's needs. The final step is to evaluate the potential benefits of the technology, in terms of efficiency and effectiveness. For a successful project, you must evaluate and restructure business processes, choose technology, develop and implement the system, and manage the change processes to best serve your organizational needs. Installing a new IT system on top of inefficient business processes is a waste of time and money!

CONCEPT check

What are some ways a company can manage its technology assets to its advantage?

Differentiate between information management and knowledge management. What steps can companies take to manage knowledge?

List the key questions managers need to ask when planning technology purchases.

Protecting Computers and Information

Have you ever lost a term paper you'd worked on for weeks because your hard drive crashed or you deleted the wrong file? You were upset, angry, and frustrated. Multiply that paper and your feelings hundreds of times over, and you can understand why companies must protect computers, networks, and the information they store and transmit from a variety of potential threats. For example, security breaches of corporate information systems—from human hackers or electronic versions like viruses and worms—are increasing at an alarming rate. The ever-increasing dependence on computers requires plans that cover human error, power outages, equipment failure—and, since September 11, 2001, terrorist attacks. To withstand natural disasters such as major fires, earthquakes, and floods, many companies install specialized fault-tolerant computer systems.

5 What are the best ways to protect computers and the information they contain?

EXHIBIT 13.6 | Questions for IT Project Planning

- What are the company's overall objectives?
- What problems does the company want to solve?
- How can technology help meet those goals and solve the problems?
- What are the company's IT priorities, both short and long term?
- What type of technology infrastructure (centralized or decentralized) best serves the company's needs?
- Which technologies meet the company's requirements?
- Are additional hardware and software required? If so, will they integrate with the company's existing systems?
- Does the system design and implementation include the people and process changes, in addition to the technological ones?
- Do you have the in-house capabilities to develop and implement the proposed applications, or should you bring in an outside specialist?

Disasters are not the only threat to data. A great deal of data, much of it confidential, can easily be tapped or destroyed by anyone who knows about computers. Keeping your networks secure from unauthorized access—from internal as well as external sources—requires formal security policies and enforcement procedures. The increasing popularity of mobile devices—laptops, handheld computers, PDAs, and digital cameras—and wireless networks requires calls for new types of security provisions.

In response to mounting security concerns, companies have increased spending on technology to protect their IT infrastructure and data. Along with specialized hardware and software, companies need to develop specific security strategies that take a proactive approach to prevent security and technical problems before they start. Until recently, retailers that accepted a selection of credit cards were forced to comply with the security standards of each card company. To make things simpler and more secure, the industry consolidated the best security practices into a single, unified code called Payment Card Industry Security Standards Council (PCI). Standards require things like masking customer data, restricting access to card data, data encryption, and more. Retailers that fail to meet the standards can be fined. Credit card fraud was about $5.5 billion in 2007, and it's not surprising that companies like Visa saw a surge in merchants complying with PCI standards: 77 percent of large merchants and 62 percent of midsize merchants were compliant, up from 12 and 15 percent in 2006.[21]

Data Security Issues

Unauthorized access into a company's computer systems can be expensive, and not just in monetary terms. The FBI estimates that computer crime costs U.S. businesses more than $67 billion in 2005, compared to just $450 million in 2001. The most costly categories of threats were worms, viruses, and Trojan horses (defined later in this section), computer theft, financial fraud, and unauthorized network access. The 2005 FBI Computer Crime Survey also reports that almost all U.S. businesses reported at least one security issue, and almost 20 percent incurred 20 or more incidents.[22] In the 13-year period from 1995 through 2007, the number of vulnerabilities (susceptibility to security deficiencies) reported to the CERT Coordination Center, a federally financed information center for computer security information, climbed from 171 to 7,236 in 2007.[23]

Computer crooks are becoming more sophisticated all the time, finding new ways to get into ultrasecure sites. "As companies and consumers continue to move towards a networked and information economy, more opportunity exists for cybercriminals to take advantage of vulnerabilities on networks and computers," says Chris Christiansen, program vice president at technology research firm IDC.[24] Whereas early cybercrooks were typically amateur hackers working alone, the new ones are more professional and often work in gangs to commit large-scale Internet crimes for large financial rewards. The Internet, where criminals can hide behind anonymous screen names, has increased the stakes and expanded the realm of opportunities to commit identity theft and similar crimes. Catching such cybercriminals is difficult, and fewer than 5 percent are caught.[25] (We discuss Internet crime in more detail in the online enrichment chapter, "Using the Internet for Business Success," at **www.cengage.com/introbusiness/gitman**.)

Firms are taking steps to prevent these costly computer crimes and problems, which fall into several major categories:

- *Unauthorized access and security breaches.* Whether from internal or external sources, unauthorized access and security breaches are a top concern of IT managers. These can create havoc with a company's systems and damage customer relationships. Unauthorized access also includes employees, who can copy confidential new-product information and provide it to competitors or use company systems for personal business that may interfere with systems operation. About 45 percent of respondents to the 2005 FBI Computer Crime Survey experienced such internal intrusions.[26] Networking links also make it easier for someone outside the organization to gain access to a company's computers.

One new form of unauthorized access is called *sidejacking*. Sidejackers obtain unauthorized access to computers on wireless networks at places like hotels, coffee shops, airports, and other public Wi-Fi areas. Sidejackers then can infiltrate e-mails, view confidential e-mail, and generally take control over

CONCEPT in action

To gauge the overall security of today's computer systems one needn't look any further than the Pentagon. Hard-core hackers try to penetrate the U.S. Department of Defense hundreds of times each day. Though most high-tech attempts at espionage fail, a 2007 attack on the computer network serving Defense Secretary Robert Gates was successful, compromising sensitive information and forcing 1,500 computers to be taken offline. What's at stake if data security experts are unable to stop hackers from disrupting business, financial, and government organizations around the world?

a user's computer and screen without the user's knowledge.[27] Another form of security breach comes from *botnets*, short for "robot networks." In a botnet, one computer hides behind and commands a network of infected PCs, and typically, when the commanding computer starts sending orders to the network of bots, it becomes identifiable, or visible, to computers not in the network. Computer criminals have figured out how to remain hidden even when controlling the network. They do this by constantly changing the domain name server (DNS) of the network, making it nearly impossible to catch them. Botnets using this so-called fast-flux technique are commonly used to breach online security at banks and host phishing sites.[28] The Storm Trojan used botnet technology and was responsible for 1 out of every 12 computer virus infections only a week after its release.[29]

- *Computer viruses, worms, and Trojan horses.* Computer viruses and related security problems such as worms and Trojan horses are among the top threats to business and personal computer security. A **computer virus**, a computer program that copies itself into other software and can spread to other computer systems, can destroy the contents of a computer's hard drive or damage files. Another form is called a *worm* because it spreads itself automatically from computer to computer. Unlike a virus, a worm doesn't require e-mail to replicate and transmit itself into other systems. It can enter through valid access points. In January 2006, for example, two mass-mailing worms were discovered: Email-Worm.Win32.Nyxem.e and Email-Worm.Win32.VB.bi. These worms delete certain types of files and attempt to disable security-related and file-sharing software.

  Trojan horses are programs that appear to be harmless and from legitimate sources but trick the user into installing them. When run, they damage the user's computer. For example, a Trojan horse may claim to get rid of viruses but instead infects the computer. Other forms of Trojan horses provide a "trapdoor" that allows undocumented access to a computer, unbeknownst to the user. Trojan horses do not, however, infect other files or self-replicate.[30]

  Viruses can hide for weeks or months before starting to damage information. A virus that "infects" one computer or network can be spread to another computer by sharing disks or by downloading infected files over the Internet. To protect data from virus damage, virus protection software automatically monitors computers to detect and remove viruses. Program developers make regular updates available to guard against newly created viruses. In addition, experts are becoming more proficient at tracking down virus authors, who are subject to criminal charges.

- *Deliberate damage to equipment or information.* For example, an unhappy employee in the purchasing department could get into the computer system and delete information on past orders and future inventory needs. The sabotage could severely disrupt production and the accounts payable system. Willful acts to destroy or change the data in computers are hard to prevent. To lessen the damage, companies should back up critical information.

- *Spam.* Although you might think that *spam*, or unsolicited and unwanted e-mail, is just a nuisance, it also poses a security threat to companies. Viruses spread through e-mail attachments that can accompany spam e-mails. On most days, spam accounts for 70 to 80 percent of all e-mail sent, according to Postini, a message-filtering company. In contrast, mail that carries viruses represents just 1.5 percent of all messages on average. The volume of spam has increased five times since just 2003. Spam is now clogging blogs, instant messages, and cell phone text messages as well as e-mail inboxes. Spam presents other threats to a corporation: lost productivity and expenses from dealing with spam—like opening the messages to search for legitimate messages that special spam filters keep out. The cost of spam is more than $50 billion worldwide and $17 billion a year for U.S. businesses. Spam filters can greatly reduce the amount of spam that gets through, but spammers continually find new ways to bypass them.[31]

- *Software and media piracy.* The copying of copyrighted software programs, games, and movies by people who haven't paid for them is another form of unauthorized use. Piracy, defined as using software without a license, takes revenue away from the company that developed the program at great cost. It includes making counterfeit CDs to sell as well as personal copying of software to share with friends. The Business Software Alliance estimates that the global software piracy rate is 35 percent and the cost to software manufacturers is more than $33 billion a year worldwide. Of that amount, U.S. firms accounted for $6.6 billion. The highest rates of piracy, ranging from 92 percent to 87 percent, are in Vietnam, Ukraine, China, Indonesia, and Russia. In the United States, it is 21 percent.

computer virus
A computer program that copies itself into other software and can spread to other computer systems.

Software firms take piracy seriously and go after the offenders. Countries are also becoming more vigilant in cracking down on pirates. In February 2006, 19 people in the United States, Australia, and Barbados were charged with illegally distributing copyrighted computer software, games, and movies valued at more than $6.5 million over the Internet. Microsoft recently filed lawsuits against eight eBay sellers who sold counterfeit versions of Windows and Office.[32] Many software firms also make special arrangements so that large companies can get multiple copies of programs at a lower cost rather than use illegal copies. Companies are continually adding features such as anti-piracy codes and "shells" to limit the use of the software on other computers and prevent unauthorized copying of CDs. Recent versions of Microsoft's Windows Vista and Office require "activation" to get full use and limit the user in the number of times he or she can start up a system without registering the software. Other companies like Intuit and Adobe require customers to obtain a special product activation number before using their software. See Exhibit 13.7 for a list of the top cyber security threats identified for 2008.

Preventing Problems

Creating formal written information security policies to set standards and provide the basis for enforcement is the first step in a company's security strategy. Unfortunately, a recent survey of 8,200 IT executives worldwide revealed that only 37 percent have such policies, and just 24 percent of the other companies intend to develop one within a year. Without information security strategies in place, companies spend too much time in a reactive mode—responding to crises—and don't focus enough on prevention.[33]

Security policies should have the support of top management, and then follow with procedures to implement the security policies. Because IT is a dynamic field with ongoing changes to equipment and processes, it's important to review security policies often. Some security policies can be handled automatically, by technical measures, whereas others involve administrative policies that rely on humans to perform them. Examples of administrative policies are "Users must change their

EXHIBIT 13.7	Top 10 Cyber Security Threats of 2008
Threat	**Reason**
Attacks on Web browsers and plug-in components	Plug-ins are widely distributed and not automatically updated, so they're more vulnerable.
Botnets	Botnets operate through encrypted peer-to-peer channels; fast-flux techniques make them difficult to block.
Cyber espionage	Successful penetration in 2007 of United States defense data by other nations will only encourage additional and more sophisticated attacks.
Breaches of mobile phones	Open mobile platforms and developer toolkits—particularly for smart phones—give easy access to hackers.
Insider attacks	Rising value of data and the interconnectedness of today's systems make it easy for discontented employees and contractors to steal trade secrets and personal identities.
Advanced identity theft	Bots that stay on machines for three to five months collecting enough personal information to pass basic security checks.
Malware	Trend is toward more insidious and more aggressive Trojans.
Web application vulnerabilities	Criminals are looking to exploit vulnerabilities in Web programming for financial gain.
Blended attacks	Combining elements makes it more likely that a target will be duped. For example, a phishing attack combined with an inducement to reveal the personal information only over the phone might be more successful than a simple phishing attack.
Supply-chain attacks	Many stores have a no-questions-asked return policy, making it easy to buy an external device, like a USB or flash drive, infect it, and return it. Easy for pranksters.

Source: The SANS Institute, "Top Ten Cyber Security Menaces for 2008," SANS.org; and Thomas Claburn, "Top 10 Cybersecurity Menaces For 2008 Listed," InformationWeek.com, January 15, 2008.

passwords each quarter" and "End users will update their virus signatures at least once a week." Exhibit 13.8 shows the types of security measures companies use to protect data.

Preventing costly problems can be as simple as regularly backing up applications and data. Companies should have systems in place that automatically back up the company's data every day and store copies of the backups off-site. In addition, employees should back up their own work regularly. Another good policy is to maintain a complete and current database of all IT hardware, software, and user details to make it easier to manage software licenses and updates and diagnose problems. In many cases, IT staff can use remote access technology to automatically monitor and fix problems, as well as update applications and services.

Companies should never overlook the human factor in the security equation. One of the most common ways that outsiders get into company systems is by posing as an employee, first getting the staffer's full name and username from an e-mail message, then calling the help desk to ask for a forgotten password. Crooks can also get passwords by viewing them on notes attached to a desk or computer monitor, using machines that employees leave logged on when they leave their desks, and leaving laptop computers with sensitive information unsecured in public places.

Portable devices, from handheld computers and PDAs to tiny plug-and-play flash drives and other storage devices (including MP3 players), pose security risks as well. They are often used to store sensitive data such as passwords, bank details, and calendars. PDAs can spread viruses when users download virus-infected documents to their company computers. Research firm Gartner Inc. reports that only about 10 percent of companies have policies covering security for these portable devices. "It's actually a fairly big problem," says Eric Ouellet, Gartner's vice president of research for security. "You've got so much space on these things now. You can go for an iPod or MP3 player and you've got 60 GB or more on them. You can put a small database on them. It's just a matter of time before we hear about someone losing data because of this."[34]

Imagine the problems that could arise if an employee saw a calendar entry on a PDA like "meeting re: layoffs," an outsider saw "meeting about merger with ABC Company," or an employee lost a flash drive containing files about marketing plans for a new product. Manufacturers are responding to IT managers' concerns about security by adding password protection and encryption to flash drives. Companies can also use flash drive–monitoring software that prevents unauthorized access on PCs and laptops.

Companies have many ways to avoid an IT meltdown, as Exhibit 13.9 on the next page demonstrates. Further discussion of protecting confidential data is covered in the online chapter, "Using the Internet for Business Success," at **www.cengage.com/introbusiness/gitman**.

Keep IT Confidential: Privacy Concerns

The very existence of huge electronic file cabinets full of personal information presents a threat to our personal privacy. Until recently, our financial, medical, tax, and other records were stored in separate computer systems. Computer networks make it easy to pool these data into data warehouses. Companies also sell the information they collect about you from sources like warranty

The first computer hackers were mostly harmless techno-geeks and curious experimenters testing the limits of a new electronic medium. Today the world of computing is brimming with cybercriminals—sophisticated computer experts who defraud millions by exploiting network security holes. Cybercrimes may involve phishing, pharming, scumware, spyware, spam, viruses and other threats to sensitive personal and corporate data. What can businesses and individuals do to avoid becoming victims of cybercrime?

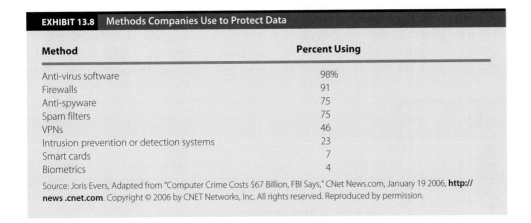

EXHIBIT 13.8	Methods Companies Use to Protect Data

Method	Percent Using
Anti-virus software	98%
Firewalls	91
Anti-spyware	75
Spam filters	75
VPNs	46
Intrusion prevention or detection systems	23
Smart cards	7
Biometrics	4

Source: Joris Evers, Adapted from "Computer Crime Costs $67 Billion, FBI Says," CNet News.com, January 19 2006, **http:// news .cnet.com**. Copyright © 2006 by CNET Networks, Inc. All rights reserved. Reproduced by permission.

- Develop a comprehensive plan and policies that include portable as well as fixed equipment.
- Protect the equipment itself with stringent physical security measures on the premises.
- Protect data using special *encryption* technology to encode confidential information so only the recipient can decipher it.
- Stop unwanted access from inside or outside with special authorization systems. These can be as simple as a password or as sophisticated as fingerprint or voice identification.
- Install *firewalls*, hardware or software designed to prevent unauthorized access to or from a private network.
- Monitor network activity with intrusion-detection systems that signal possible unauthorized access, and document suspicious events.
- Conduct periodic IT audits to catalog all attached storage devices as well as computers.
- Use technology that monitors ports for unauthorized attached devices and turn off those that are not approved for business use.
- Train employees to troubleshoot problems in advance, rather than just react to them.
- Hold frequent staff-training sessions to teach correct security procedures, such as logging out of networks when they go to lunch and changing passwords often.
- Make sure employees choose sensible passwords, at least six and ideally eight characters long, containing numbers, letters, and punctuation marks. Avoid dictionary words and personal information.
- Establish a database of useful information and FAQs (frequently asked questions) for employees so they can solve problems themselves.
- Develop a healthy communications atmosphere.

CONCEPT in action

© iStockphoto.com/Pali Rao

At the heart of the computer-privacy dilemma is the trade-off between confidentiality and convenience. Today's tech-savvy consumers are increasingly willing to give out personal information in exchange for greater shopping, download, and user benefits. Entrusting personal data to online merchants eliminates repeat data entry, enables greater personalization of Web sites, and produces remarkably relevant cross-selling and search results. Can consumers have both convenience and privacy, or will they ultimately have to choose one or the other?

data mining
Sophisticated database applications that look for hidden patterns in a group of data to help track and predict future behavior.

registration cards, credit card records, registration at Web sites, personal data forms required to purchase online, and grocery store discount club cards. Telemarketers can combine data from different sources to create fairly detailed profiles of consumers.

The September 11, 2001, tragedy raised additional privacy concerns. In its aftermath, the government began looking for ways to improve domestic-intelligence collection and analyze terrorist threats within the United States. Sophisticated database applications that look for hidden patterns in a group of data, a process called **data mining**, increase the potential for tracking and predicting people's daily activities. Legislators and privacy activists worry that such programs as this and ones that eavesdrop electronically could lead to excessive government surveillance that encroaches on personal privacy. The stakes are much higher as well: errors in data mining by companies in business may result in a consumer being targeted with inappropriate advertising, whereas a governmental mistake in tracking suspected terrorists could do untold damage to an unjustly targeted person.

Increasingly, consumers are fighting to regain control of personal data and how that information is used. Privacy advocates are working to block sales of information collected by governments and corporations. For example, they want to prevent state governments from selling driver's license information and supermarkets from collecting and selling information gathered when shoppers use bar-coded plastic discount cards. With information about their buying habits, advertisers can target consumers for specific marketing programs.

The challenge to companies is to find a balance between collecting the information they need while at the same time protecting individual consumer rights. Most registration and warranty forms that ask questions about income and interests have a box for consumers to check to prevent the company from selling their names. Many companies now state their privacy policies to ensure consumers that they will not abuse the information they collect. At Google, the approach to security might well be summed up by the saying "trust, but verify." According to Douglas Merrill, Google's CIO, "very few employees have access to consumer data, and those who do have to go through background checks." More than 150 security engineers at the company do nothing but security, and automated tools check every engineer's code.[35] We'll return to the topic of protecting consumer privacy in the online chapter, "Using the Internet for Business Success," at **www.cengage.com/introbusiness/gitman**.

CONCEPT check

Describe the different threats to data security.

How can companies protect information from destruction and unauthorized use?

Why are privacy rights advocates alarmed over the use of techniques such as data warehouses and data mining?

Trends in Information Technology

Information technology is a continually evolving field. The fast pace and amount of change, coupled with IT's broad reach, make it especially challenging to isolate industry trends. From the time we write this chapter to the time you read it—as little as six months—new trends will appear and those that seemed important may fade. However, some trends that are reshaping today's IT landscape are virtualization, Web-based applications, and the increasing use of grid computing.

6 What are the leading trends in information technology?

Virtualization

Even though virtualization has been around for decades, it wasn't until the 2007 launch of VMWare that the possibilities of virtualization began to be realized. The "VM" in VMWare stands for "virtual machine." The software tricks servers and other computers into running multiple operating systems and multiple applications simultaneously, even though they're designed to run just one operating system and one version of an application at a time. One computer, then, is transformed into several "virtual machines." A company can get 5, 10, even a dozen "machines" for the price of 1, which can represent a huge cost savings. At the time of this writing, VMWare was the only company with a viable virtualization platform, reflected in the fact that it had an estimated 90 percent market share. Researchers estimate, however, that the virtualization industry will double in the next four years to $12 billion.[36]

Web-Based Applications

It used to be (and still generally is) that companies buy software in packages. Whether uploaded from purchased CDs or downloaded directly from the Web, a preponderance of software resides on the user's computer. In certain areas, however, such as financial planning software, the trend looks to be moving toward smaller Web-based applications. Although this sounds like ASPs, which were discussed earlier, Web apps, as they are often called, are free. Intuit's Quicken has long held a firm grip on the market, but several smaller competitors with names like Geezeo, Wesabe, Yodlee, and Mint have started to make inroads. Mint started in 2007, and by early 2008, it already had 100,000 members.[37] In office management and work flow, Google Apps are hoping to displace Microsoft Office software. After seeing how popular its Gmail and Google Docs are in consumer markets, the company realized that its suite of easy-to-use tools might be attractive in the business market as well. The tools are intuitive (you don't need to know Web programming to insert dynamic documents into Web pages), and thousands of employees can migrate their work to Google Apps at a time. Google is reframing software and office tools as a service rather than a product, and companies like Procter & Gamble and General Electric have already begun using Google Apps.[38] ASP Salesforce.com is distributing the software by weaving it into its own proprietary software. That way, customers using Salesforce.com products will be able to easily migrate information back and forth between their Salesforce.com software and Google Apps.[39] Adobe is even offering Photoshop Express via the Web. Express works entirely within the Web browser of your choice; there's no need to download anything.[40]

Grid Computing Offers Powerful Solutions

How can smaller companies that occasionally need to perform difficult and large-scale computational tasks find a way to accomplish their projects? They can turn to *grid computing*, also called *utility computing* or *peer-to-peer computing*. Grid technology provides a way to divide the job into many smaller tasks and distribute them to a virtual supercomputer consisting of many small computers linked into a common network. Combining multiple desktop machines results in computing power that exceeds supercomputer speeds. A hardware and software infrastructure clusters and integrates computers and applications from multiple sources, harnessing unused power in existing PCs and networks. The grid structure distributes computational resources but maintains central control of the process. A central server acts as a team leader and traffic monitor. The controlling cluster server divides a task into subtasks, assigns the work to computers on the grid with surplus processing power, combines the results, and moves on to the next task until the job is finished. Exhibit 13.10 on the next page shows how a typical grid setup works.

With utility computing, any company—large or small—can access the software and computer capacity on an as-needed basis.

EXHIBIT 13.10 How Grid Computing Works

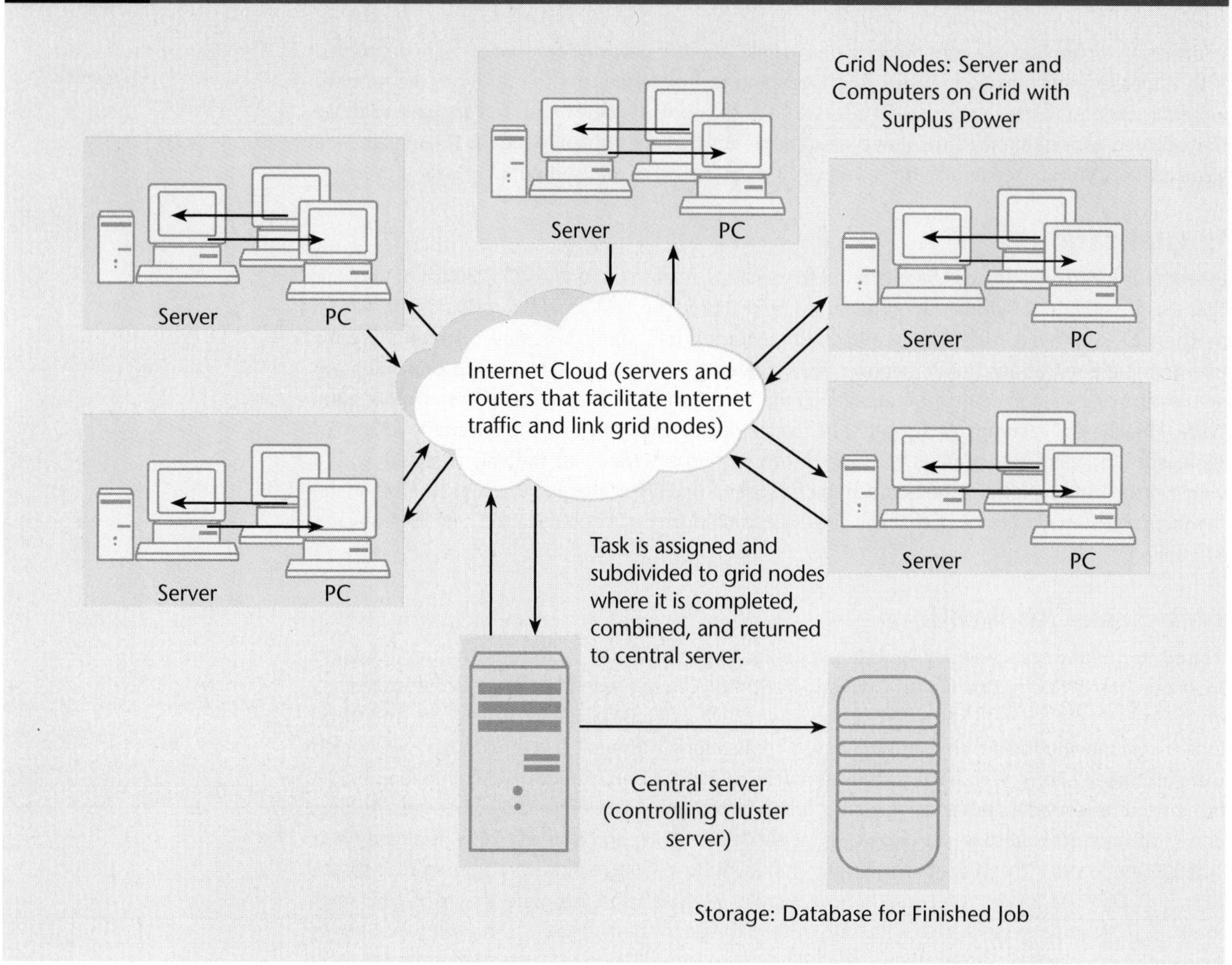

Grid Nodes: Server and Computers on Grid with Surplus Power

Server   PC

Server   PC

Server   PC

Server   PC

Server   PC

Internet Cloud (servers and routers that facilitate Internet traffic and link grid nodes)

Task is assigned and subdivided to grid nodes where it is completed, combined, and returned to central server.

Central server (controlling cluster server)

Storage: Database for Finished Job

IBM, Sun Microsystems, and Hewlett-Packard are among the companies providing as-needed grid services. Although grid computing appears similar to outsourcing or on-demand software from ASPs, it has two key differences:

- Pricing is set per-use, whereas outsourcing involves fixed-price contracts.
- Grid computing goes beyond hosted software and includes computer and networking equipment as well as services.

Grids provide a very cost-effective way to provide computing power for complex projects in areas such as weather research and financial and biomedical modeling. Because the computing infrastructure already exists—grids tap into computer capacity that is otherwise unused—the cost is quite low. The increased interest in grid technology will contribute to high growth.

The online auction company eBay wants to make its site easier to manage, quicker to upgrade, and even more scalable than it already is. On any given day (or hour), eBay lists 106 million active auctions in which any number of the company's 243 million registered users can participate. Those users add approximately 6 million new items to the site each day, so finding an off-the-shelf software that can handle that volume of information is impossible. "Historically we have tended to break most of what we have used," says Paul Strong, distinguished research scientist who helps design and manage eBay's massive IT structure. To manage that tremendous volume of data, eBay uses grid computing. More than

CONCEPT check

What is virtualization and how does it benefit companies that use it? Are many companies offering viable virtualization platforms?

How are Web-based applications helping to reframe software and office tools as a service rather than a product?

What advantages does grid computing offer a company? What are some of the downsides to using this method?

600 databases are organized into about 100 computing clusters in six different data centers. Fifteen thousand servers power the site. Despite that tremendous scale, when eBay technicians want to upload new code, they can run it over a 100-node test network and upload a final version in less than 30 minutes.[41]

Summary of Learning Goals

Businesses depend on information technology (IT) for everything from running daily operations to making strategic decisions. Companies must have management information systems that gather, analyze, and distribute information to the appropriate parties, including employees, suppliers, and customers. These systems are comprised of different types of computers that collect data and process it into usable information for decision making. Managers tap into databases to access the information they need, whether for placing inventory orders, scheduling production, or preparing long-range forecasts. They can compare information about the company's current status to its goals and standards. Company-wide enterprise resource planning systems that bring together human resources, operations, and technology are becoming an integral part of business strategy.

1 How has information technology transformed business and managerial decision making?

Today companies use networks of linked computers that share data and expensive hardware to improve operating efficiency. Types of networks include local area networks (LANs), wide area networks (WANs), and wireless local area networks (WLANs). Intranets are private WANs that allow a company's employees to communicate quickly with each other and work on joint projects, regardless of their location. Companies are finding new uses for wireless technologies like handheld computers, cell phones, and e-mail devices. Virtual private networks (VPNs) give companies a cost-effective secure connection between remote locations by using public networks like the Internet.

2 Why are computer networks an important part of today's information technology systems?

A management information system consists of a transaction processing system, management support systems, and an office automation system. The transaction processing system (TPS) collects and organizes operational data on the firm's activities. Management support systems help managers make better decisions. They include an information-reporting system that provides information based on the data collected by the TPS to the managers who need it, decision support systems that use models to assist in answering "what if" types of questions, and expert systems that give managers advice similar to what they would get from a human consultant. Executive information systems are customized to the needs of top management. All employees benefit from office automation systems that facilitate communication by using word processing, e-mail, fax machines, and similar technologies.

3 What types of systems make up a typical company's management information system?

To get the most value from IT, companies must go beyond simply collecting and summarizing information. Technology planning involves evaluating the company's goals and objectives and using the right technology to reach them. IT managers must also evaluate the existing infrastructure to get the best return on the company's investment in IT assets. Knowledge management (KM) focuses on sharing an organization's collective knowledge to improve productivity and foster innovation. Some companies establish the position of chief knowledge officer to head up KM activities.

4 How can technology management and planning help companies optimize their information technology systems?

Because companies are more dependent on computers than ever before, they need to protect data and equipment from natural disasters and computer crime. Types of computer crime include unauthorized use and access, software piracy, malicious damage, and computer viruses. To protect IT assets, companies should prepare written security policies. They can use technology such as virus protection, firewalls, and employee training in proper security procedures. They must also take steps to protect customers' personal privacy rights.

5 What are the best ways to protect computers and the information they contain?

IT is a dynamic industry, and companies must stay current on the latest trends to identify ones that help them maintain their competitive edge, such as virtualization, Web-based applications, and grid computing. Virtualization allows companies to transform one piece of hardware into

6 What are the leading trends in information technology?

Chapter 13: Using Technology to Manage Information

371

multiple machines using software that allows multiple operating systems and applications to run simultaneously. Similar to ASPs, Web-based applications are allowing companies to replace traditional software with *free* programs and storage capacity maintained by a third party. Many Web-based applications are transforming the simple yet highly functional tools from consumer applications and transitioning them to business applications. Grid computing harnesses the idle power of desktop PCs and other computers to create a virtual supercomputer. A company can access the grid on an as-needed basis instead of investing in its own supercomputer equipment. Outsourcing a portion of the company's computing needs provides additional flexibility and cost advantages. Companies can also set up internal grids.

Key Terms

application service providers (ASPs) 356

batch processing 359

chief information officer (CIO) 351

community of practice (CoP) 363

computer network 353

computer virus 365

data mart 360

data mining 368

data warehouse 360

database 352

decision support system (DSS) 360

enterprise portal 354

executive information system (EIS) 361

expert system 361

information technology (IT) 350

intranet 354

knowledge management (KM) 362

knowledge worker 351

local area network (LAN) 353

managed service providers (MSPs) 358

management information system (MIS) 352

management support systems (MSSs) 360

office automation system 361

online (real-time) processing 359

transaction-processing system (TPS) 359

virtual private networks (VPNs) 356

wide area network (WAN) 353

Preparing for Tomorrow's Workplace: SCANS

1. How has information technology changed your life? Describe at least three areas (both personal and school/work related) where having access to better information has improved your decisions. Are there any negative effects? What steps can you take to manage information better? (**Information, Technology**)

2. Visit or conduct a phone interview with a local small-business owner about the different ways her or his firm uses information technology. Prepare a brief report on your findings that includes the hardware and software used, how it was selected, benefits of technology for the company, and any problems in implementing or using it. (**Interpersonal, Information**)

3. Your school wants to automate the class registration process. Prepare a memo to the dean of information systems describing an integrated information system that would help a student choose and register for courses. Make a list of the different groups that should be involved and questions to ask during the planning process. Include a graphic representation of the system that shows how the data becomes useful information. Indicate the information a student needs to choose courses and its sources. Explain how several types of management support systems could help students make better course decisions. Include ways the school could use the information it collects from this system. Have several students present their plans to the class, which will take the role of university management in evaluating them. (**Resources, Systems, Technology**)

4. You recently joined the IT staff of a midsize consumer products firm. After a malicious virus destroys some critical files, you realize that the company lacks a security strategy and policies. Outline the steps you'd take to develop a program to protect data and the types of policies you'd recommend. How would you present the plan to management and employees to encourage acceptance? (**Resources, Technology**)

5. **Team Activity** Should companies outsource IT? Some executives believe that IT is too important to outsource and that application service providers (ASPs) don't have a future. Yet spending for ASP subscriptions, MSPs, and other forms of IT outsourcing continues to grow. What's your position? Divide the class into groups designated "for" or "against" outsourcing and/or ASPs. Have them research the current status of ASPs using publications like *CIO* and *Computerworld* and Web sites like ASPnews.com, **http://www.aspnews.com**. (**Interpersonal, Information**)

Ethics Activity

As the owner of a small but growing business, you are concerned about employees misusing company computers for personal matters. Not only does this cost the company in terms of employee productivity, but it also ties up bandwidth that may be required for company operations and exposes the firm's networks to increased risks of attacks from viruses, spyware, and other malicious programs. Installing e-mail monitoring and Web security and filtering software programs would allow you to track e-mail and Internet use, develop use policies, block access to inappropriate sites, and limit the time employees can conduct personal online business. At the same time, the software will protect your IT networks from many types of security concerns, from viruses to Internet fraud. You are concerned, however, that employees will take offense and consider such software an invasion of privacy.

Using a Web search tool, locate articles about this topic and then write responses to the following questions. Be sure to support your arguments and cite your sources.

ETHICAL DILEMMA: Should you purchase employee-monitoring software for your company, and on what do you base your decision? If you install the software, do you have an obligation to tell employees about it? Explain your answers and suggest ways to help employees understand your rationale.

Sources: Lindsay Gerdes, "You Have 20 Minutes to Surf. Go," *BusinessWeek,* December 26, 2005, p. 16; "Nothing Personal," *Global Cosmetic Industry,* August 2005, p. 19; and "Tips on Keeping Workplace Surveillance from Going to Far," *HR Focus,* January 2006, p. 10.

Working the Net

1. Enterprise resource planning (ERP) is a major category of business software. Visit the site of one of the following companies: SAP (**http://www.sap.com**); Oracle and Peoplesoft, which Oracle acquired, (**http://www.oracle.com**); or SSA Global (**http://www.ssaglobal.com**). Prepare a short presentation for the class about the company's ERP product offerings and capabilities. Include examples of how companies use the ERP software. What are the latest trends in ERP?
2. What can intranets and enterprise portals accomplish for a company? Find out by using such resources as Brint.com's Intranet Portal, **http://www.brint.com/Intranets.htm**, and Intranet Journal, **http://www.intranetjournal.com/**. Look for case studies that show how companies apply this technology. Summarize the different features an intranet or enterprise portal provides.
3. Learn more about the CERT Coordination Center (CERT/CC), which serves as a center of Internet security expertise. Explore its Web site, **http://www.cert.org**. What are the latest statistics on incidents reported, vulnerabilities, security alerts, security notes, mail messages, and hotline calls? What other useful information does the site provide to help a company protect IT assets?
4. Research the latest developments in computer security at Computerworld's site, **http://computerworld.com/securitytopics/security**. What types of information can you find there? Pick one of the categories in this area (Cybercrime, Encryption, Disaster Recovery, Firewalls, Hacking, Privacy, Security Holes, Viruses and Worms, and VPN) and summarize your findings.
5. How can someone steal your identity? Using information at the Federal Trade Commission's identity theft Web site **http://www.ftc.gov/bcp/edu/microsites/idtheft/**, compile a list of the ways thieves can access key information to use your identity. What steps should you take if you've been a victim of identity theft? Summarize key provisions of federal laws dealing with this crime and the laws in your state.

Creative Thinking Case

Novartis's Prescription for Invoice Processing

What do you do when you have more than 600 business units operating through 360 independent affiliates in 140 countries around the world—processing complex invoices in various languages and currencies? You seek out the best technology solution to make the job easier.

At global pharmaceutical giant Novartis, the IT department is a strategic resource, a community of 2,000 people serving 63,000 customers in 200 locations and 25 data centers. Because most of the company's invoices come from international suppliers, they have differences in design, language, taxes, and currency. Consequently, many ended up as "query items" requiring manual resolution by Novartis accounting staff—which delayed payments and made those invoices extremely costly to process. In fact, finance personnel spent so much of their time resolving queried invoices that other work suffered. A solution was badly needed.

To maximize its investment, Novartis needed a flexible solution that would meet its current and future needs and function in other business departments in a variety of geographic locations. It should provide fast accurate document capture, multi-language support, and extend to other types of information—such as faxes and electronic data—in addition to paper documents. Finally, in order to obtain financing for the project, return on investment (ROI) was required within nine months of project implementation.

Input*Accel* for Invoices from Captiva Software Corporation was the answer. The software extracts data from paper documents, applies intelligent document recognition (IDR) technology to convert them to digital images, and sends relevant data to enterprise resource planning (ERP), accounts payable (A/P), and other back-end management systems. The specialized Input*Accel* server manages output by recognizing and avoiding holdups in the work flow process. It also ensures that if a server goes offline, others will carry on functioning, thus avoiding downtime.

Now Novartis scans incoming invoices at a centrally located site, and the images are transmitted to the Input*Accel* for Invoices server for image improvement. Invoice data is then extracted and validated against supplier information. Most invoices are transferred directly for payment, with relatively few invoices requiring transfer to one of three accounts payable clerks who deal with queries manually.

Thanks to IT, overall efficiency has increased, processing errors are reduced, and accounting personnel can use their time and expert knowledge for more meaningful tasks than resolving invoice errors. For Novartis it is "mission accomplished."

Critical Thinking Questions

- What factors contributed to Novartis's invoice processing being so complex?
- How did IT help the company solve that problem?
- What other uses and functions does Input*Accel* serve and how will this be useful to Novartis over the long term? (You may want to visit the Captiva Software Web site, **http://www.captiva software.com**, for more information on Input*Accel's* capabilities.)

Sources: Adapted from Kathryn Balint, "Captiva's Paper Chase Paying Off," *San Diego Union-Tribune*, December 9, 2005, pp. C1, C5. Captiva Software corporate Web site, **http://www.captivasoftware.com**, March 22, 2006; "Processing Invoices from Around the World," *Captiva Software*, **http://www.captivasoftware.com**, February 2, 2006; Novartis corporate Web site, **http://www. novartis.com**, March 20, 2006.

Exploring Business Careers

Rebekah Krupski A.G. Edwards

When meeting with an A.G. Edwards (**http://www.agedwards.com**) financial consultant, most likely you are thinking about money, your money. Whether you seek a short-term investment or a retirement nest egg, money will be your focus. You probably will not be thinking about the technological infrastructure required to transmit information throughout a multibillion dollar, nationwide institution like A.G. Edwards—information that often is private and financial in nature. Luckily for you, however, the company employs many people to think about just that—people like Rebekah Krupski, who works in its Information Technology (IT) division.

Starting with A.G. Edwards as a systems analyst eight years ago, Krupski is currently the manager of the IT Vendor Management Office, which focuses on the hardware and software vendors with whom A.G. Edwards does business. Her position involves not only fostering relationships with vendors, but also keeping abreast of the newest IT trends and evaluating cutting-edge products. Additionally, Krupski must ensure that the equipment the company currently uses is performing as promised by the vendors. "One of my main roles is to make sure that A.G. Edwards, and ultimately the client, are getting the IT performance that they expect and that they are paying for."

Given the company's size, A.G. Edwards's management information system (MIS) is necessarily large. The IT Vendor Management Office is located within the IT Business Management department, which oversees the IT division's business aspects. The division includes four other departments that each have a different focus: the division's financial targeting and planning, its human resource management needs, compliance issues related to information sharing and financial regulations, and the training and evaluation of IT division members. Together these five departments manage the company's extensive IT needs.

Computer and Internet technologies have impacted the way financial institutions conduct business. No longer are firms reliant on phone transactions and paper trails. Instead businesses today operate at lightning speed in a real-time environment of electronic transactions and computer-based information storage. At A.G. Edwards, IT is critical for both employees and clients. One of the IT division's most important functions is security. As regulations controlling personal information tighten and the technology to infiltrate security systems evolves, A.G. Edwards's protection of its own information and that of its clients is increasingly a priority. However, that is not its only function. Internally, the company's MIS provides vital reporting functionality, such as what allows financial consultants to track client interests and needs. Clients rely on the system for financial information, whether they want to access the day's stock quotes as the markets close or their own retirement plan at three in the morning. As Krupski states, "The main factors differentiating any company's IT management are its processes, the services it offers clients and how those services are run, and its time-to-market with any new services." To stay competitive, A.G. Edwards has focused efforts on making its MIS as flexible and responsive as possible. In this way, the company can respond to its own needs, as well as the needs of its clients and the markets.

Using Financial Information and Accounting

Learning Goals

After reading this chapter, you should be able to answer these questions:

1 Why are financial reports and accounting information important, and who uses them?

2 What are the differences between public and private accountants, and are public accountants subject to new regulations?

3 What are the six steps in the accounting cycle?

4 In what terms does the balance sheet describe the financial condition of an organization?

5 How does the income statement report a firm's profitability?

6 Why is the statement of cash flows an important source of information?

7 How can ratio analysis be used to identify a firm's financial strengths and weaknesses?

8 What major trends affect the accounting industry today?

© iStockphoto.com/H-Gall

"I Can't See, Charlie"

Lieutenant Colonel Frank Slade is a retired U.S. Army officer who was blinded just prior to his retirement. Charlie Simms has been hired to watch over him for a weekend while Slade's family goes on a brief vacation, but things start to go a bit haywire for Charlie when Lieutenant Colonel Slade decides to take a trip to New York City to live the high life one last time, including staying at the Waldorf-Astoria, eating at a five-star restaurant, and other pursuits before committing suicide. During the trip, almost as an afterthought, Slade informs Charlie that he always appreciated the look and feel of a Ferrari. In an attempt to prevent Slade from actually going through with his suicide plans, Charlie entices Slade with an opportunity to drive a Ferrari.

Slade accepts that offer with enthusiasm, and Charlie actually finds a back-street area with no traffic that the Lieutenant Colonel can drive on. Slade starts out slow at first, just barely pressing the gas and keeping the wheel steady, but he quickly starts to speed up, popping the car into another gear. Charlie begins to panic as the Ferrari moves faster and faster and obstacles appear in their path. Then, the blind Slade decides he wants to "see how this baby corners." Charlie protests, but Slade insists. He will turn the car with Charlie's help or without. Finally, Charlie relents, and he gauges each of the passing streets until he tells the blind man he can turn. Slade does in a skid and a screech of tires that culminates in a successful turn. The Ferrari handles like the fine piece of machinery that it is, Slade is happy, and Charlie has successfully done his duty.

Now, you might find yourself asking, what in the world does this movie *Scent of a Woman* have to do with accounting, especially considering that accounting is all about processing the financial activities of the firm. However, if you think of the financial activities as information, then the relationship becomes a little bit clearer. Think of a company's decision makers as a blind man driving a Ferrari. They know what the firm can do and how it can handle, and can keep it on track moving straight ahead. In a sense, that's simply business as usual as long as they can navigate any roadblocks. But they may not have the information necessary to steer the firm in a new direction or onto a new path.

Enter the accountants. Accountants take the financial activities of the firm, summarize them into usable data, and then analyze that data, producing financial reports that are then used by the firm to help make decisions. Charlie is, in a sense, the accounting arm of Slade's driving enterprise. He cautions Slade based on available information, assesses the situation in light of new information, and then makes a recommendation that allows the blind man to make a turn at a fairly high speed. Accountants do much the same thing, ultimately providing information that is then used to make decisions.

In the following chapter, we will explore accounting in a little more detail, starting with an understanding of the basics of accounting and the accounting profession. We will outline how accounting reports are used and who uses them, and we will describe the changing environment for accountants in the modern era. Then we will take you through some of the basic accounting procedures, including the accounting equation and the accounting cycle. Finally, this chapter will cover some of the basic financial statements like the balance sheet, the income statement, and the statement of cash flows, closing with some of the current trends in accounting. Such information is important because, even though you may not become an accountant, an understanding of basic accounting information will allow you to make better decisions for and about your business.

Discussion Questions

- After the Enron scandal in 2001, ethics in accounting procedures have been an issue at the forefront of business. In what way does the scenario described above deal with the ethics associated with accounting?
- Assuming that Charlie and Slade work for a firm, how does the Ferrari fit into the balance sheet? Explain your answer.

Accounting: More than Numbers

1 Why are financial reports and accounting information important, and who uses them?

Prior to 2001, accounting topics rarely made the news. That changed when Enron Corp.'s manipulation of accounting rules to improve its financial statements hit the front pages of newspapers. The company filed bankruptcy in 2001, and its former top executives were charged with multiple counts of conspiracy and fraud. Arthur Andersen, Enron's accounting firm, was indicted and convicted of obstruction of justice and in 2002, the once respected firm went out of business. Since then, dozens of other companies and their executives have faced criminal charges stemming from financial abuses. Most recently:

CONCEPT in action

While serving as attorney general of New York, Eliot Spitzer prosecuted corporate executives, exposed shady accounting practices, shut down call-girl services, and even sued the former chairman of the New York Stock Exchange. But Spitzer recently became the focus of corruption when the *New York Times* exposed the "Sheriff of Wall Street" as a client of the Emperor's Club, a big-money prostitution ring. Ensnared by the same shady financial-accounting methods he once prosecuted, Spitzer set off bookkeeping alarms by making suspicious cash withdrawals to pay for club services—a money-laundering technique called "structuring." How does good accounting practice promote a more ethical society?

- Charles Wang, founder, former chairman, and CEO of CA (Computer Associates) was accused of directing and participating in fraudulent accounting procedures that ultimately forced the company to restate its earnings by $2.2 billion. Wang's successor, Sanjay Kumar, was also found guilty, sentenced to 12 years in prison, and according to the terms of a settlement arrangement, will pay $800 million in restitution to shareholders over his lifetime.[1]
- Accounting fraud at Metropolitan Mortgage & Securities in Seattle wiped out nearly $500 million in shareholder value. The company president was charged with two felony counts of making false and misleading statements to accountants of a publicly traded company and one felony count of material omissions to accountants.[2]
- Film director Peter Jackson sued New Line Cinema over alleged accounting frauds related to the profits from *The Lord of the Rings*, the first movie in Jackson's film trilogy based on the work of J. R. R. Tolkien. Jackson contends that accounting "tricks" cheated him out of millions of dollars in profits. At the time of this writing, the suit was as yet unsettled.[3]

These and other cases raised critical concerns about the independence of those who audit a company's financial statements, questions of integrity and public trust, and issues with current financial reporting standards. Investors suffered as a result, because the crisis in confidence sent stock prices tumbling, and companies lost billions in value.

So it's no surprise that more people are paying attention to accounting topics! We now recognize that accounting is the backbone of any business, providing a framework to understand the firm's financial condition. Reading about accounting irregularities, fraud, audit (financial statement review) shortcomings, out-of-control business executives, and bankruptcies, we have become very aware of the importance of accurate financial information and sound financial procedures. In the wake of regular publicity about accounting scandals, companies are taking proactive measures to head off allegations of fraud. Dell Computer uncovered accounting irregularities in its books in 2007, and after the Securities and Exchange Commission (SEC) began investigating (a serious signal), Dell assembled hundreds of forensic accountants to pore over its books to identify, publicize, and correct any errors they found before the SEC did. The computer maker even created its own software tool to identify potentially questionable journal entries.[4] Dell ultimately restated four years' worth of earnings, which represented a drop in profits of $92 million.[5]

As these examples show, all of us—whether we are self-employed, work for a local small business or a multinational Fortune 100 firm, or are not currently in the workforce—benefit from knowing the basics of accounting and financial statements. We can use this information to educate ourselves about companies before interviewing for a job or buying a company's stock or bonds. Employees at all levels of an organization use accounting information to monitor operations. They also must decide which financial information is important for their company or business unit, what those numbers mean, and how to use them to make decisions.

This chapter starts by discussing why accounting is important for businesses and for users of financial information. Then it provides a brief overview of the accounting profession and the post-Enron regulatory environment. Next it presents an overview of basic accounting procedures, followed by a description of the three main financial statements—the balance sheet, the income statement, and the statement of cash flows. Using these statements, we then demonstrate how ratio analysis of financial statements can provide valuable information about a company's financial condition. Finally, the chapter explores current trends affecting the accounting profession.

Accounting Basics

Accounting is the process of collecting, recording, classifying, summarizing, reporting, and analyzing financial activities. It results in reports that describe the financial condition of an organization. All types of organizations—businesses, hospitals, schools, government agencies, and civic groups—use accounting procedures. Accounting provides a framework for looking at past performance, current financial health, and possible future performance. It also provides a framework for comparing the financial positions and financial performances of different firms. Understanding how to prepare and interpret financial reports will enable you to evaluate two computer companies and choose the one that is more likely to be a good investment.

The accounting system shown in Exhibit 14.1 converts the details of financial transactions (sales, payments, purchases, and so on) into a form that people can use to evaluate the firm and make decisions. Data become information, which in turn becomes reports. These reports describe a firm's financial position at one point in time and its financial performance during a specified period. Financial reports include financial statements, such as balance sheets and income statements, and special reports, such as sales and expense breakdowns by product line.

Who Uses Financial Reports?

The accounting system generates two types of financial reports, as shown in Exhibit 14.2: internal and external. Internal reports are used within the organization. As the term implies, **managerial accounting** provides financial information that managers inside the organization can use to

accounting
The process of collecting, recording, classifying, summarizing, reporting, and analyzing financial activities.

managerial accounting
Accounting that provides financial information that managers inside the organization can use to evaluate and make decisions about current and future operations.

EXHIBIT 14.1 **The Accounting System**

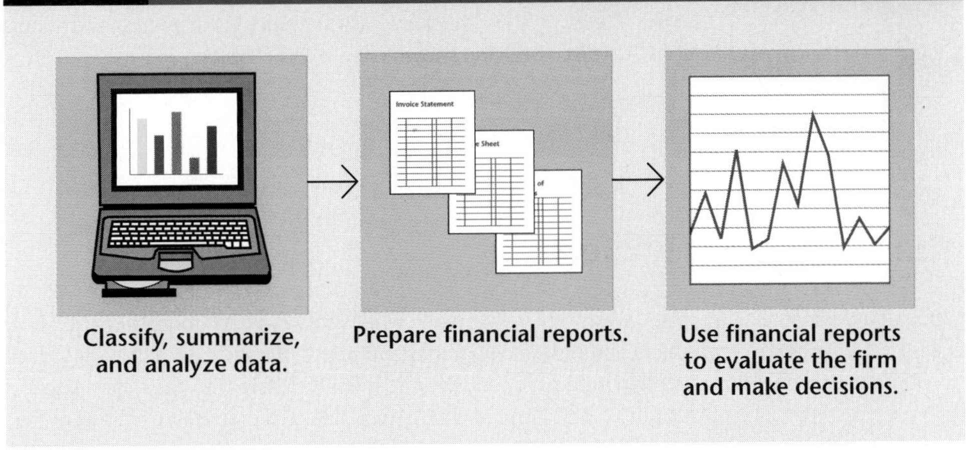

Classify, summarize, and analyze data.

Prepare financial reports.

Use financial reports to evaluate the firm and make decisions.

EXHIBIT 14.2 **Reports Provided by the Accounting System**

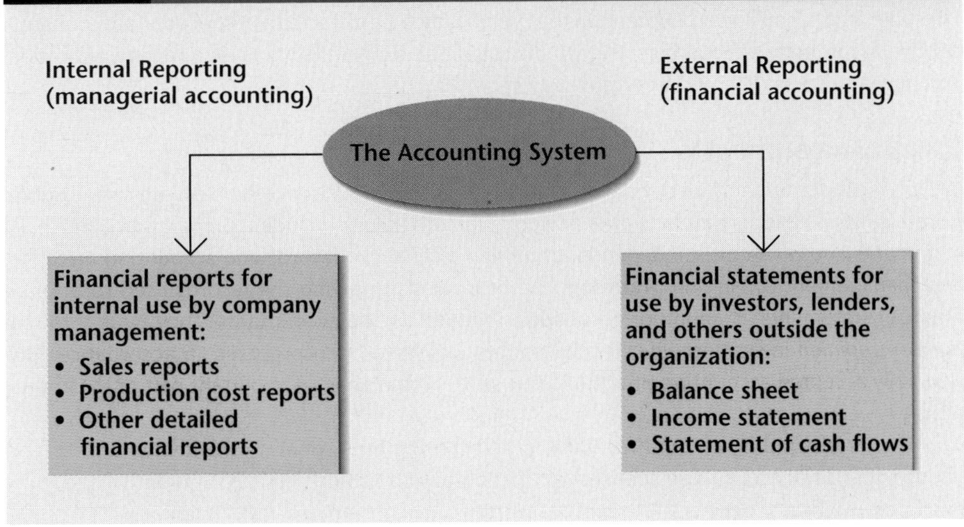

Internal Reporting (managerial accounting)

External Reporting (financial accounting)

The Accounting System

Financial reports for internal use by company management:
- Sales reports
- Production cost reports
- Other detailed financial reports

Financial statements for use by investors, lenders, and others outside the organization:
- Balance sheet
- Income statement
- Statement of cash flows

---

financial accounting
Accounting that focuses on preparing external financial reports that are used by outsiders such as lenders, suppliers, investors, and government agencies to assess the financial strength of a business.

generally accepted accounting principles (GAAP)
The financial accounting standards followed by accountants in the United States when preparing financial statements.

Financial Accounting Standards Board (FASB)
The private organization that is responsible for establishing financial accounting standards in the United States.

annual report
A yearly document that describes a firm's financial status and usually discusses the firm's activities during the past year and its prospects for the future.

CONCEPT check

Explain who uses financial information.

Differentiate between financial accounting and managerial accounting.

How do GAAP, FASB, and the IASB influence the accounting field?

---

evaluate and make decisions about current and future operations. For instance, the sales reports prepared by managerial accountants show how well marketing strategies are working. Production cost reports help departments track and control costs. Managers may prepare very detailed financial reports for their own use and provide summary reports to top management.

Financial accounting focuses on preparing external financial reports that are used by outsiders, that is, people who have an interest in the business but are not part of management. Although these reports also provide useful information for managers, they are used primarily by lenders, suppliers, investors, and government agencies to assess the financial strength of a business.

To ensure accuracy and consistency in the way financial information is reported, accountants in the United States follow **generally accepted accounting principles (GAAP)** when preparing financial statements. The **Financial Accounting Standards Board (FASB)** is a private organization that is responsible for establishing financial accounting standards in the United States.

At the present time, there are no international accounting standards. Because accounting practices vary from country to country, a multinational company must make sure that its financial statements conform to both its own country's accounting standards and those of the parent company's country. Often another country's standards are quite different from U.S. GAAP. The U.S. Financial Accounting Standards Board (FASB) and the International Accounting Standards Board (IASB) are currently working together to develop global accounting standards that make it easier to compare financial statements of foreign-based companies. The Expanding Around the Globe box on the next page discusses the challenges involved in this effort.

Financial statements are the chief element of the **annual report**, a yearly document that describes a firm's financial status. Annual reports usually discuss the firm's activities during the past year and its prospects for the future. Three primary financial statements included in the annual report are discussed and shown later in this chapter:

- The balance sheet
- The income statement
- The statement of cash flows

The Accounting Profession

2 What are the differences between public and private accountants, and are public accountants subject to new regulations?

When you think of accountants, do you picture someone who works in a back room, hunched over a desk, wearing a green eye shade and scrutinizing pages and pages of numbers? Although today's accountants still must love working with numbers, they now work closely with their clients to not only prepare financial reports but also help them develop good financial practices. Computers have taken the tedium out of the number-crunching and data-gathering parts of the job and now offer powerful analytical tools as well. Therefore, accountants must keep up with information technology trends. The accounting profession has grown due to the increased complexity, size, and number of businesses and the frequent changes in the tax laws. Accounting is now a $40-plus billion industry. The more than 1.2 million accountants in the United States are classified as either public accountants or private (corporate) accountants. They work in public accounting firms, private industry, education, and government, and about 10 percent are self-employed.

Public Accountants

public accountants
Independent accountants who serve organizations and individuals on a fee basis.

auditing
The process of reviewing the records used to prepare financial statements and issuing a formal *auditor's opinion* indicating whether the statements have been prepared in accordance with generally accepted accounting principles.

Independent accountants who serve organizations and individuals on a fee basis are called **public accountants**. Public accountants offer a wide range of services, including preparation of financial statements and tax returns, independent auditing of financial records and accounting methods, and management consulting. **Auditing**, the process of reviewing the records used to prepare financial statements, is an important responsibility of public accountants. They issue a formal *auditor's opinion* indicating whether the statements have been prepared in accordance with generally accepted accounting principles. This written opinion is an important part of the annual report.

The largest public accounting firms, called the Big Four, operate worldwide and offer a variety of business consulting services in addition to accounting services. In order of size, they are PricewaterhouseCoopers (PWC), Deloitte & Touche Tohmatsu International (DTT), KPMG

Moving toward One World of Numbers

Imagine being the controller of a major multi-national company with significant operations in 10 other countries. Because the accounting rules in those countries don't conform to GAAP, your staff has to prepare ten sets of financial reports that comply with the host country's rules, and translate the figures to GAAP for consolidation into the parent company's statements. It's a massive undertaking.

The rapidly growing and increasingly interrelated global economy prompted the U.S. Financial Accounting Standards Board (FASB) and the International Accounting Standards Board (IASB) to work together to develop international accounting standards that will remove disparities between national and international standards, improve the quality of financial information worldwide, and simplify comparisons of financial statements across borders for both corporations and investors.

In February 2006, the FASB and the IASB jointly published a Memorandum of Understanding (MOU) reaffirming the two organizations' desire to create uniform global accounting standards. As they worked toward convergence, the board members decided to develop a new set of common standards, rather than try to reconcile the two standards. These new standards must do more than simply eliminate differences—they must be better than the existing standards. Merging GAAP and IFRS into a consistent set of international accounting standards has proven to be very difficult because of different approaches used in the two sets: GAAP is more rigid; IFRS is more flexible.

According to Dr. Charles Mulford, professor of accounting at Georgia Tech's College of Management, "Under GAAP, we are very reliant on rules and we try to restrict flexibility in reporting. We have very specific ways of doing things." By contrast, IFRS uses a more principles-based approach, which is more flexible. Mulford believes that as companies used to reporting using GAAP start to move to the blended system, the risk for accounting impropriety may increase, and not necessarily because of an increase in wrongdoing. The convergence of the two sets of standards would mean replacing rules with abstract principles that are open to more interpretation and variation. "Even without doing things wrong, even without an intent to mislead, there's going to be much more flexibility in reporting, and it's going to make it that

much harder to compare results with companies, across competitors, and within industries," he says.

The convergence of GAAP and IFRS methods into one set of globally accepted accounting practices would mean some significant changes for U.S. firms. For example, the new standards would make use of fair-value accounting, in which assets and liabilities are valued at their market values during each accounting cycle. Because fair value of an item fluctuates, corporate earnings statements will be more volatile. Rules relating to what even counts as an asset or a liability would change, as would the definition of what constitutes shareholder equity.

Two years after the initial MOU, the FASB and IASB were still working on the new set of standards and working out the inevitable kinks that have surfaced as they try to create a single method out of two foundationally different approaches. Even when the new standards are complete, accountants around the world will need to reeducate themselves. Some level of turmoil is also anticipated as companies transition to the new methods. "Once we get through all that, we get to the final end result and there's one set of accounting standards for all companies," says Dr. Mulford. "That will be a plus."[6]

Critical Thinking Questions

- Is it important to have a single set of international accounting standards for at least publicly owned companies? Defend your answer.
- If a blended set of standards is more principles-based and flexible, can it really achieve the desired goal of allowing for more accurate comparisons between companies? Explain.

International, and Ernst & Young (E&Y). A former member of this group, Arthur Andersen, disbanded in 2002 as a result of the Enron scandal.

To become a **certified public accountant (CPA)**, an accountant must complete an approved bachelor's degree program and pass a test prepared by the American Institute of Certified Public Accountants (AICPA). Each state also has requirements for CPAs such as several years' on-the-job experience and continuing education. Only CPAs can issue the auditor's opinion on a firm's financial statements. Most CPAs first work for public accounting firms and later may become private accountants or financial managers. The majority of the about 350,000 accountants who belong to the AICPA work in public accounting firms (39 percent) and business and industry (also 39 percent).[7]

Private Accountants

Accountants employed to serve one particular organization are **private accountants**. Their activities include preparing financial statements, auditing company records to be sure employees follow accounting policies and procedures, developing accounting systems, preparing tax returns, and providing financial information for management decision making. Whereas some private accountants hold the CPA designation, managerial accountants also have a professional certification program. Requirements to become a **certified management accountant (CMA)** include passing an examination.

Reconfiguring the Accounting Environment

Although our attention was focused on big-name accounting scandals, an epidemic of accounting irregularities was also taking place in the wider corporate arena. The number of companies restating annual financial statements grew at an alarming rate, tripling between 1997 and 2002. In the wake of the numerous corporate financial scandals, Congress and the accounting profession took major

certified public accountant (CPA)
An accountant who has completed an approved bachelor's degree program, passed a test prepared by the American Institute of Certified Public Accountants, and met state requirements. Only a CPA can issue an auditor's opinion on a firm's financial statements.

private accountants
Accountants who are employed to serve one particular organization.

certified management accountant (CMA)
A managerial accountant who has completed a professional certification program, including passing an examination.

© Tim Shaffer/Reuters /Landov

America's charities are under increasing scrutiny from watchdogs and donors alike, as high-profile scandals and lax financial reporting continue to hit chapters of groups including the United Way and the Red Cross. Executive scandals, bookkeeping irregularities, fraud, and misappropriation of donations have shaken donors' confidence in recent years and contributed to declines in giving. What can be done to foster greater financial transparency and tighter accounting practices in nonprofit organizations?

steps to prevent future accounting irregularities. These measures targeted the basic ways, cited by a report from the AICPA, that companies massaged financial reports through creative, aggressive, or inappropriate accounting techniques, including:

- Committing fraudulent financial reporting.
- Unreasonably stretching accounting rules to significantly enhance financial results.
- Following appropriate accounting rules, but using loopholes to manage financial results.

Why did companies willfully push accounting to the edge—and over it—to artificially pump up revenues and profits? Looking at the companies involved in the recent scandals, some basic similarities have emerged:

- A company culture of arrogance and above-average tolerance for risk.
- Interpretation of accounting policies to their advantage and manipulation of the rules to get to a predetermined result and conceal negative financial information.
- Compensation packages tied to financial or operating targets, making executives and managers greedy and pressuring them to find sometimes questionable ways to meet what may have been overly optimistic goals.
- Ineffective checks and balances, such as audit committees, boards of directors, and financial control procedures, that were not independent from management.
- Centralized financial reporting that was tightly controlled by top management, increasing the opportunity for fraud.
- Financial performance benchmarks that were often out of line with the companies' industry.
- Complicated business structures that clouded how the company made its profits.
- Cash flow from operations that seemed out of line with reported earnings. (You'll learn about this important difference between cash and reported earnings in the sections on the income statement and statement of cash flows.)
- Acquisitions made quickly, often to show growth rather than for sound business reasons; management focused more on buying new companies than making the existing operations more profitable.[8]

Companies focused on making themselves look good in the short term, doing whatever was necessary to top past performance and to meet the expectations of investment analysts, who project earnings, and investors, who panic when a company misses the analysts' forecasts. Executives who benefited when stock prices rose had no incentive to question the earnings increases that led to the price gains.

These number games raised serious concerns about the quality of earnings and questions about the validity of financial reports. Investors discovered to their dismay that they could neither assume that auditors were adequately monitoring their clients' accounting methods nor depend on the integrity of published financial information.

Better Numbers Ahead

Since 2002 a number of accounting reforms have been put in place to set better standards for accounting, auditing, and financial reporting. Investors, now aware of the possibility of various accounting shenanigans, are avoiding companies that use complicated financial structures and off-the-books financing.

On July 30, 2002, the **Sarbanes-Oxley Act** went into effect. This law, one of the most extensive pieces of business legislation ever passed by Congress, was designed to start the economy on the road to recovery and address the investing public's lack of trust in corporate America. It redefines the public corporation–auditor relationship and restricts the types of services auditors can provide to clients. The act clarifies auditor-independence issues, places increased accountability on a company's senior executives and management, strengthens disclosure of insider transactions (an employee selling stock based on information not known by the public), and prohibits loans to executives.

Sarbanes-Oxley Act
Act passed in 2002 that sets new standards for auditor independence, financial disclosure and reporting, and internal controls; establishes an independent oversight board; and restricts the types of nonaudit services auditors can provide their clients.

An independent five-member Public Company Accounting Oversight Board (PCAOB) holds the authority to set and amend auditing, quality control, ethics, independence, and other standards for audit reports. The act specifies that all PCAOB members be financially literate. Two members must have their CPA designation, and the other three cannot be or have been CPAs. Appointed and overseen by the Securities and Exchange Commission (SEC), the PCAOB can also inspect accounting firms; investigate breaches of securities law, standards, competency, and conduct; and take disciplinary action. The Board registers public accounting firms, as the act now requires. Altering or destroying key audit documents now carries felony charges and increased penalties.

Other key provisions of the act cover the following areas:

- *Auditing standards.* The Board must include in its standards several requirements, such as maintaining audit work papers and other documentation for audit reports for seven years, the review and approval of audit reports by a second partner, and audit standards for quality control and review of internal control procedures.
- *Financial disclosure.* Companies must clearly disclose all transactions that may have a material current or future effect on their financial condition, including those that are off the books or with unconsolidated entities (related companies whose results the company is not required to combine with its own financial statements under current accounting rules). Management and major stockholders must disclose transactions such as sales of company stock within two days of the transaction. The company must disclose its code of ethics for senior financial executives. Any significant changes in a company's operations or financial condition must be disclosed "on a rapid and current basis."
- *Financial statement certification.* Chief executive officers and chief financial officers must certify company financial statements, or face severe criminal and civil penalties for false certification. If securities fraud results in restatement of financial reports, these executives will lose any stock-related profits and bonuses they received prior to the restatement.
- *Internal controls.* Each company must have appropriate internal control procedures in place for financial reporting, and its annual report must include a report on implementation of those controls to assure the integrity of financial reports.
- *Consulting work.* The act restricts the nonauditing work auditors may perform for an auditing client. In the past, the large accounting firms had expanded their roles to include a wide range of advisory services that went beyond their traditional task of validating a company's financial information. Conflicts of interest arose when the same firm earned lucrative fees for both audit and consulting work for the same client.[9]

Other regulatory organizations also took steps to prevent future abuses. In September 2002, the AICPA Auditing Standards Board (ASB) issued expanded guidelines to help auditors uncover fraud while conducting audits. The New York Stock Exchange stiffened its listing requirements so that the majority of directors at listed companies must be independent and not employees of the corporation. Nor can auditors serve on clients' boards for five years. Companies listed in the Nasdaq marketplace cannot hire former auditors at any level for three years.

In response to the passage of Sarbanes-Oxley and other regulations, companies implemented new control measures and improved existing ones. The burdens in both cost and time have been considerable. Many companies had to redesign and restructure financial systems to improve efficiency. More than 60 percent of financial executives believe that their investment in increased controls has improved shareholder perceptions of their company's ethics. However, about one-third reported that costs would depress earnings and negatively affect stock prices.[10]

Has Sarbanes-Oxley (often called SarbOx) been effective in reducing financial statement fraud? Results from a 2008 survey conducted by Financial Executives International indicate that executives tend to think so. Nearly 44 percent of the survey participants agreed that compliance with SarbOx has helped prevent or detect fraud. (The same survey in 2007 found that only 33 percent thought the same.) Roughly half of the respondents agreed that financial reports are

CONCEPT in action

With hundreds of billions of dollars being lost to corporate fraud and abuse each year, it's not surprising that forensic accounting is one of the fastest-growing sectors in the world of work. A forensic accountant is a specialist who combines CPA know-how and investigative prowess to sort out tricky or even criminal financial situations. Businesses and government agencies hire these financial sleuths to follow the money trail of potentially explosive cases, from partnership disputes and corporate accounting fraud to money laundering. What conditions in the accounting environment have led to the need for forensic accountants?

CONCEPT in action

The Sarbanes-Oxley Act has done much to redeem the public's trust in corporate financial reporting, but it may not do enough to recover bonuses bestowed on CEOs undeservedly. Because the act's provision on executive forfeiture of bonuses is vague and doesn't allow shareholder lawsuits, many ex-chiefs of publicly traded companies have not been required to pay back multimillion-dollar rewards acquired through fraudulent accounting. Should the government increase federal regulation of accounting practices, or can business resolve such issues through self-regulation?

© iStockphoto.com/Rob Friedman

© iStockphoto.com/Terraxplorer

more accurate and 56 percent thought that financial reports were more reliable than before the implementation of the act. Accuracy comes at a price, however. The average cost of complying with all the provisions of the act is staggering: more than 12,300 hours of work and on average $1.6 million ($3.6 million for companies with over $75 million market capitalization) per year. Still, a positive outlook about SarbOx comes through the results: nearly 7 out of 10 respondents said that compliance has resulted in more investor confidence in their financial reports.[11] The best strategies to prevent fraud are executives who promote a top-down tone of integrity, prosecution of those who commit fraud, and implementation of strict internal controls.

CONCEPT check

Compare the responsibilities of public and private accountants. How are they certified?

Summarize the major changes affecting accounting and corporate reporting and the reasons for them.

Basic Accounting Procedures

3 What are the six steps in the accounting cycle?

Using generally accepted accounting principles, accountants record and report financial data in similar ways for all firms. They report their findings in financial statements that summarize a company's business transactions over a specified time period. As mentioned earlier, the three major financial statements are the balance sheet, income statement, and statement of cash flows.

People sometimes confuse accounting with bookkeeping. Accounting is a much broader concept. *Bookkeeping*, the system used to record a firm's financial transactions, is a routine, clerical process. Accountants take bookkeepers' transactions, classify and summarize the financial information, and then prepare and analyze financial reports. Accountants also develop and manage financial systems and help plan the firm's financial strategy.

The Accounting Equation

The accounting procedures used today are based on those developed in the late fifteenth century by an Italian monk, Brother Luca Pacioli. He defined the three main accounting elements as assets, liabilities, and owners' equity. **Assets** are things of value owned by a firm. They may be tangible, such as cash, equipment, and buildings, or intangible, such as a patent or trademarked name. **Liabilities**—also called *debts*—are what a firm owes to its creditors. **Owners' equity** is the total amount of investment in the firm minus any liabilities. Another term for owners' equity is *net worth*.

assets
Things of value owned by a firm.

liabilities
What a firm owes to its creditors; also called *debts*.

owners' equity
The total amount of investment in the firm minus any liabilities; also called *net worth*.

The relationship among these three elements is expressed in the accounting equation:

$$\text{Assets} - \text{Liabilities} = \text{Owners' equity}$$

The accounting equation must always be in balance (that is, the total of the elements on one side of the equals sign must equal the total on the other side).

Suppose you start a bookstore and put $10,000 in cash into the business. At that point, the business has assets of $10,000 and no liabilities. This would be the accounting equation:

$$\text{Assets} = \text{Liabilities} + \text{Owners' equity}$$
$$\$10,000 = \$0 \qquad + \$10,000$$

The liabilities are zero and owners' equity (the amount of your investment in the business) is $10,000. The equation balances.

To keep the accounting equation in balance, every transaction must be recorded as two entries. As each transaction is recorded, there is an equal and opposite event so that two accounts or records are changed. This method is called **double-entry bookkeeping**.

Suppose that after starting your bookstore with $10,000 cash, you borrow another $10,000 from the bank. The accounting equation will change as follows:

double-entry bookkeeping
A method of accounting in which each transaction is recorded as two entries so that two accounts or records are changed.

Assets	=	Liabilities	+	Owners' equity	
$10,000	=	$0	+	$10,000	Initial equation
$10,000	=	$10,000	+	$0	Borrowing transaction
$20,000	=	$10,000	+	$10,000	Equation after borrowing

Now you have $20,000 in assets—your $10,000 in cash and the $10,000 loan proceeds from the bank. The bank loan is also recorded as a liability of $10,000 because it's a debt you must repay. Making two entries keeps the equation in balance.

The Accounting Cycle

The *accounting cycle* refers to the process of generating financial statements, beginning with a business transaction and ending with the preparation of the report. Exhibit 14.3 shows the six steps in the accounting cycle. The first step in the cycle is to analyze the data collected from many sources. All transactions that have a financial impact on the firm—sales, payments to employees and suppliers, interest and tax payments, purchases of inventory, and the like—must be documented. The accountant must review the documents to make sure they're complete.

Next, each transaction is recorded in a *journal*, a listing of financial transactions in chronological order. The journal entries are then recorded in *ledgers*, which show increases and decreases in specific asset, liability, and owners' equity accounts. The ledger totals for each account are summarized in a *trial balance*, which is used to confirm the accuracy of the figures. These values are used to prepare financial statements and management reports. Finally, individuals analyze these reports and make decisions based on the information in them.

Computers in Accounting

Computerized accounting programs do many different things. Most accounting packages offer six basic modules that handle general ledger, sales order, accounts receivable, purchase order, accounts payable, and inventory control functions. Tax programs use accounting data to prepare tax returns and tax plans. Computerized point-of-sale terminals used by many retail firms automatically record sales and do some of the bookkeeping. The Big Four and many other large public accounting firms develop accounting software for themselves and for clients.

CONCEPT in action

Sage Software is a well-known software developer that provides business-management solutions to small and midsize companies. The firm's accounting software tools benefit professionals by automating a broad range of accounting tasks. Sage Software installations like Peachtree, Sage MAS 90, and BusinessVision are standards in the accounting field—aiding managerial decision making and streamlining bookkeeping and accounting processes. What accounting functions are usually incorporated into basic accounting software programs?

EXHIBIT 14.3   The Accounting Cycle

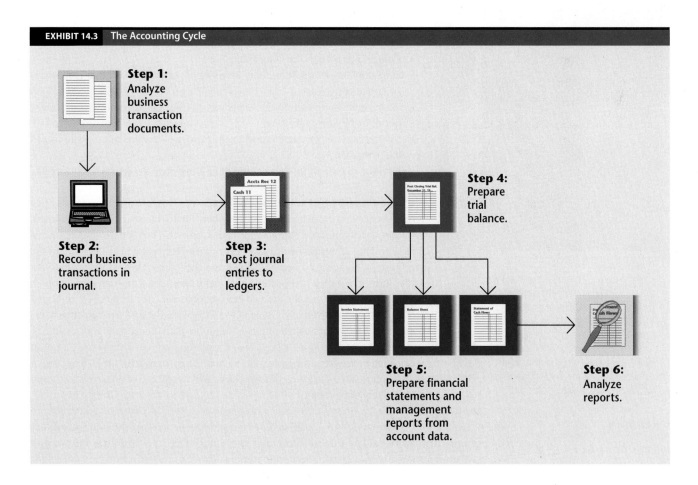

Step 1: Analyze business transaction documents.

Step 2: Record business transactions in journal.

Step 3: Post journal entries to ledgers.

Step 4: Prepare trial balance.

Step 5: Prepare financial statements and management reports from account data.

Step 6: Analyze reports.

Accounting and financial applications typically represent one of the largest portions of a company's software budget. Accounting software ranges from off-the-shelf programs for small businesses to full-scale customized enterprise resource planning systems for major corporations. Small CPA firms are now using sophisticated IT applications like data mining to provide better service to clients.

The Balance Sheet

4 In what terms does the balance sheet describe the financial condition of an organization?

balance sheet
A financial statement that summarizes a firm's financial position at a specific point in time.

liquidity
The speed with which an asset can be converted to cash.

The **balance sheet**, one of three financial statements generated from the accounting system, summarizes a firm's financial position at a specific point in time. It reports the resources of a company (assets), the company's obligations (liabilities), and the difference between what is owned (assets) and what is owed (liabilities), or owners' equity.

The assets are listed in order of their **liquidity**, the speed with which they can be converted to cash. The most liquid assets come first, and the least liquid are last. Because cash is the most liquid asset, it is listed first. Buildings, on the other hand, have to be sold to be converted to cash, so they are listed after cash. Liabilities are arranged similarly: liabilities due in the short term are listed before those due in the long term.

The balance sheet as of December 31, 2010, for Delicious Desserts, Inc., an imaginary bakery, is illustrated in Exhibit 14.4. The basic accounting equation is reflected in the three totals highlighted on the balance sheet: assets of $148,900 equal the sum of liabilities and owners' equity ($70,150 + $78,750). The three main categories of accounts on the balance sheet are explained below.

Assets

Assets can be divided into three broad categories: current assets, fixed assets, and intangible assets. **Current assets** are assets that can or will be converted to cash within the next 12 months. They are important because they provide the funds used to pay the firm's current bills. They also represent the amount of money the firm can quickly raise. Current assets include:

- *Cash.* Funds on hand or in a bank.
- *Marketable securities.* Temporary investments of excess cash that can readily be converted to cash.
- *Accounts receivable.* Amounts owed to the firm by customers who bought goods or services on credit.
- *Notes receivable.* Amounts owed to the firm by customers or others to whom it lent money.
- *Inventory.* Stock of goods being held for production or for sale to customers.

Fixed assets are long-term assets used by the firm for more than a year. They tend to be used in production and include land, buildings, machinery, equipment, furniture, and fixtures. Except for land, fixed assets wear out and become outdated over time. Thus, they decrease in value every year. This declining value is accounted for through depreciation. **Depreciation** is the allocation of the asset's original cost to the years in which it is expected to produce revenues. A portion of the cost of a depreciable asset—a building or piece of equipment, for instance—is charged to each of the years in which it is expected to provide benefits. This practice helps match the asset's cost against the revenues it provides. Because it is impossible to know exactly how long an asset will last, estimates are used. They are based on past experience with similar items or IRS guidelines for assets of that type. Notice that, through 2010, Delicious Desserts has taken a total of $16,000 in depreciation on its bakery equipment.

Intangible assets are long-term assets with no physical existence. Common examples are patents, copyrights, trademarks, and goodwill. *Patents* and *copyrights* shield the firm from direct competition, so their benefits are more protective than productive. For instance, no one can use more than a small amount of copyrighted material without permission from the copyright

CONCEPT in action

© AP Images/Richard Drew

In 2008 the Federal Reserve made an unprecedented offer of emergency loans to financial firms in hopes of easing the nation's credit crisis. Big Wall Street investment companies like Goldman Sachs quickly made use of the Fed's short-term lending mechanism, borrowing nearly $33 billion from the government. This onetime lending event—which represented the government's broadest use of its lending authority since the 1930s—drew comparisons to the Fed's "discount window" for banks and was offered as a source of short-term cash. Where on the balance sheet do business loans appear?

current assets
Assets that can or will be converted to cash within the next 12 months.

EXHIBIT 14.4   Balance Sheet for Delicious Desserts

Delicious Desserts, Inc.
Balance Sheet as of December 31, 2010

Assets

Current assets:			
Cash		$15,000	
Marketable securities		4,500	
Accounts receivable	$45,000		
Less: Allowance for doubtful accounts	1,300	43,700	
Notes receivable		5,000	
Inventory		15,000	
Total current assets			$ 83,200
Fixed assets:			
Bakery equipment	$56,000		
Less: Accumulated depreciation	16,000	$40,000	
Furniture and fixtures	$18,450		
Less: Accumulated depreciation	4,250	14,200	
Total fixed assets			54,200
Intangible assets:			
Trademark		$ 4,500	
Goodwill		7,000	
Total intangible assets			11,500
Total assets			**$148,900**

Liabilities and Owners' Equity

Current liabilities:			
Accounts payable	$30,650		
Notes payable	15,000		
Accrued expenses	4,500		
Income taxes payable	5,000		
Current portion of long-term debt	5,000		
Total current liabilities		$60,150	
Long-term liabilities:			
Bank loan for bakery equipment	$10,000		
Total long-term liabilities		10,000	
Total liabilities			**$ 70,150**
Owners' equity:			
Common stock (10,000 shares outstanding)		$30,000	
Retained earnings		48,750	
Total owners' equity			78,750
Total liabilities and owners' equity			$148,900

holder. *Trademarks* are registered names that can be sold or licensed to others. One of Delicious Desserts' intangible assets is a trademark valued at $4,500. *Goodwill* occurs when a company pays more for an acquired firm than the value of its tangible assets. Delicious Desserts' other intangible asset is goodwill of $7,000.

Liabilities

Liabilities are the amounts a firm owes to creditors. Those liabilities coming due sooner—current liabilities—are listed first on the balance sheet, followed by long-term liabilities.

Current liabilities are those due within a year of the date of the balance sheet. These short-term claims may strain the firm's current assets because they must be paid in the near future. Current liabilities include:

fixed assets
Long-term assets used by a firm for more than a year such as land, buildings, and machinery.

depreciation
The allocation of an asset's original cost to the years in which it is expected to produce revenues.

intangible assets
Long-term assets with no physical existence, such as patents, copyrights, trademarks, and goodwill.

current liabilities
Short-term claims that are due within a year of the date of the balance sheet.

Chapter 14: Using Financial Information and Accounting

- *Accounts payable.* Amounts the firm owes for credit purchases due within a year. This account is the liability counterpart of accounts receivable.
- *Notes payable.* Short-term loans from banks, suppliers, or others that must be repaid within a year. For example, Delicious Desserts has a six-month, $15,000 loan from its bank that is a note payable.
- *Accrued expenses.* Expenses, typically for wages and taxes, that have accumulated and must be paid at a specified future date within the year although the firm has not received a bill.
- *Income taxes payable.* Taxes owed for the current operating period but not yet paid. Taxes are often shown separately when they are a large amount.
- *Current portion of long-term debt.* Any repayment on long-term debt due within the year. Delicious Desserts is scheduled to repay $5,000 on its equipment loan in the coming year.

long-term liabilities
Claims that come due more than one year after the date of the balance sheet.

retained earnings
The amounts left over from profitable operations since the firm's beginning; equal to total profits minus all dividends paid to stockholders.

Long-term liabilities come due more than one year after the date of the balance sheet. They include bank loans (such as Delicious Desserts' $10,000 loan for bakery equipment), mortgages on buildings, and the company's bonds sold to others.

Owners' Equity

Owners' equity is the owners' total investment in the business after all liabilities have been paid. For sole proprietorships and partnerships, amounts put in by the owners are recorded as capital. In a corporation, the owners provide capital by buying the firm's common stock. For Delicious Desserts, the total common stock investment is $30,000. **Retained earnings** are the amounts left over from profitable operations since the firm's beginning. They are total profits minus all dividends (distributions of profits) paid to stockholders. Delicious Desserts has $48,750 in retained earnings.

CONCEPT check

What is a balance sheet?

What are the three main categories of accounts on the balance sheet, and how do they relate to the accounting equation?

How do retained earnings relate to owners' equity?

The Income Statement

5 How does the income statement report a firm's profitability?

income statement
A financial statement that summarizes a firm's revenues and expenses and shows its total profit or loss over a period of time.

The balance sheet shows the firm's financial position at a certain point in time. The **income statement** summarizes the firm's revenues and expenses and shows its total profit or loss over a period of time. Most companies prepare monthly income statements for management and quarterly and annual statements for use by investors, creditors, and other outsiders. The primary elements of the income statement are revenues, expenses, and net income (or net loss). The income statement for Delicious Desserts for the year ended December 31, 2010, is shown in Exhibit 14.5. The Catching the Entrepreneurial Spirit box on the next page shows how many of the elements of accounting work together in starting a business.

Major League Baseball topped $6 billion in revenue in 2007, placing the sport in a dead heat with the National Football League. This doubling of baseball's revenues since 2000 is owed to improved attendance in smaller markets as well as to new revenue streams like online ticket sales and satellite radio, which supplement traditional ticket sales and television broadcasting. What are some examples of baseball's operating expenses that must be deducted from revenues to determine the league's profitability?

Revenues

Revenues are the dollar amount of sales plus any other income received from sources such as interest, dividends, and rents. The revenues of Delicious Desserts arise from sales of its bakery products. Revenues are determined starting with **gross sales**, the total dollar amount of a company's sales. Delicious Desserts had two deductions from gross sales. *Sales discounts* are price reductions given to customers who pay their bills early. For example, Delicious Desserts gives sales discounts to restaurants that buy in bulk and pay at delivery. *Returns and allowances* is the dollar amount of merchandise returned by customers because they didn't like a product or because it was damaged or defective. **Net sales** is the amount left after deducting sales discounts and returns and allowances from gross sales. Delicious Desserts' gross sales were reduced by $4,500, leaving net sales of $270,500.

Expenses

Expenses are the costs of generating revenues. Two types are recorded on the income statement: cost of goods sold and operating expenses.

The **cost of goods sold** is the total expense of buying or producing the firm's goods or services. For manufacturers, cost of goods sold includes all costs directly related to production: purchases of raw materials and parts, labor, and factory

Starting a Barbershop Means Brushing Up on Accounting

Everyone—well, almost everyone—needs a haircut from time to time. That's why barbershops offer a good business opportunity for entrepreneurs. "Even in the worst economic times, you have a strong chance of survival in the hair business," says Joe Grondin, a barbering business consultant and owner of the 23-store barber franchise Roosters Men's Grooming Centers. Indeed, according to the latest U.S. Census data, the barbering industry grew from $500 million to $2 billion between 2002 and 2005, and the amount of money men spend on grooming is increasing at a rate of 9 to 10 percent annually.

That growth is part of the reason Corey Lee Bell Jr. decided to open a barbershop after graduating from the University of North Carolina, Chapel Hill. Today, he owns three shops. What does it take to start a barber shop? An enterprising barber can expect to pay start-up costs in the neighborhood of $100,000 to $150,000:

$50,000–$80,000	Building or renovating the space (floors, electric, lighting, etc.)
$50,000–$70,000	Furniture and fixtures (chairs, countertops, reception desk, etc.)

Running a business, however, isn't only a matter of start-up expenditures. The following is a good estimate of ongoing expenses associated with running a barbershop each month:

$3,000–$4,000	Rent, utilities, maintenance fees (say, a broken chair)
$250	Cleaning supplies, products used on clients

Typically barbershop owners rent the chairs in the shop to stylists on a monthly basis. With his first two stores, Bell followed that model, but for his newest shop,

The Renaissance Barbershop, he decided to use a commission model. He pays his barbers 50 percent of the profits they generate each month. Although pay is now variable, Bell says it's better for the barbers and better for the business.

Calvin Hudson, another enterprising barber, uses a blend of the traditional chair rental model and Bell's profit-based model. Hudson charges the barbers at his Classic Cuts shop in Las Vegas $250 per week for a chair (average rates are $160) or he retains 20 percent of their profits. The annual revenue for the basketball-themed Classic Cuts is $200,000. Hudson prefers the commission style because, he says, "the more heads you cut, the more money you make." [12]

Critical Thinking Questions

- How can a service company, like a barbershop, calculate the cost of goods sold?
- Barber and consultant Joe Grondin recommends pricing haircuts at least as much as the cost of the lease by the square foot. For example, if the lease is $20 a square foot, the haircut should cost at least $20. From an accounting perspective, why do you think he recommends this?
- Should Bell run financial statements for each of his three shops or for his company as a whole? Explain your reasoning.

© Rubberball/Getty Images

EXHIBIT 14.5 Income Statement for Delicious Desserts

Delicious Desserts, Inc.
Income Statement for the Year Ending December 31, 2010

Revenues

Gross sales	$275,000	
Less: Sales discounts	2,500	
Less: Returns and allowances	2,000	
Net sales		$270,500

Cost of Goods Sold

Beginning inventory, January 1	$ 18,000	
Cost of goods manufactured	109,500	
Total cost of goods available for sale	$127,500	
Less: Ending inventory December 31	15,000	
Cost of goods sold		112,500

Gross profit		$158,000

Operating Expenses

Selling expenses

Sales salaries	$31,000	
Advertising	16,000	
Other selling expenses	18,000	
Total selling expenses		$ 65,000

General and administrative expenses

Professional and office salaries	$20,500	
Utilities	5,000	
Office supplies	1,500	
Interest	3,600	
Insurance	2,500	
Rent	17,000	
Total general and administrative expenses	50,100	
Total operating expenses		115,100

Net profit before taxes		$ 42,900
Less: Income taxes		10,725
Net profit		$ 32,175

revenues
The dollar amount of a firm's sales plus any other income it received from sources such as interest, dividends, and rents.

gross sales
The total dollar amount of a company's sales.

net sales
The amount left after deducting sales discounts and returns and allowances from gross sales.

expenses
The costs of generating revenues.

cost of goods sold
The total expense of buying or producing a firm's goods or services.

Chapter 14: Using Financial Information and Accounting

gross profit
The amount a company earns after paying to produce or buy its products but before deducting operating expenses.

operating expenses
The expenses of running a business that are not directly related to producing or buying its products.

net profit (net income)
The amount obtained by subtracting all of a firm's expenses from its revenues, when the revenues are more than the expenses.

net loss
The amount obtained by subtracting all of a firm's expenses from its revenues, when the expenses are more than the revenues.

overhead (utilities, factory maintenance, machinery repair). For wholesalers and retailers, it is the cost of goods bought for resale. For all sellers, cost of goods sold includes all the expenses of preparing the goods for sale, such as shipping and packaging.

Delicious Desserts' cost of goods sold is based on the value of inventory on hand at the beginning of the accounting period, $18,000. During the year, the company spent $109,500 to produce its baked goods. This figure includes the cost of raw materials, labor costs for bakery workers, and the cost of operating the bakery area. Adding the cost of goods manufactured to the value of beginning inventory, we get the total cost of goods available for sale, $127,500. To determine the cost of goods sold for the year, we subtract the cost of inventory at the end of the period:

$$\$127{,}500 - \$15{,}000 = \$112{,}500$$

The amount a company earns after paying to produce or buy its products but before deducting operating expenses is the **gross profit**. It is the difference between net sales and cost of goods sold. Because service firms do not produce goods, their gross profit equals net sales. Gross profit is a critical number for a company because it is the source of funds to cover all the firm's other expenses.

The other major expense category is **operating expenses**. These are the expenses of running the business that are not related directly to producing or buying its products. The two main types of operating expenses are selling expenses and general and administrative expenses. *Selling expenses* are those related to marketing and distributing the company's products. They include salaries and commissions paid to salespeople and the costs of advertising, sales supplies, delivery, and other items that can be linked to sales activity, such as insurance, telephone and other utilities, and postage. *General and administrative expenses* are the business expenses that cannot be linked to either cost of goods sold or sales. Examples of general and administrative expenses are salaries of top managers and office support staff; utilities; office supplies; interest expense; fees for accounting, consulting, and legal services; insurance; and rent. Delicious Desserts' operating expenses totaled $115,100.

CONCEPT in action

Accounting rule makers in the United States and internationally are seeking a major overhaul of financial statements. One possible change includes the elimination of net profit, the bottom-line statistic on income statements that indicates what an organization has left after expenses and taxes. The suggested move is one of many proposed changes associated with the push for a global set of accounting standards. How will investors and the general public gauge the financial health of businesses if dramatic changes are made to traditional financial statements?

Net Profit or Loss

The final figure—or bottom line—on an income statement is the **net profit** (or **net income**) or **net loss**. It is calculated by subtracting all expenses from revenues. If revenues are more than expenses, the result is a net profit. If expenses exceed revenues, a net loss results.

Several steps are involved in finding net profit or loss. (These are shown in the right-hand column of Exhibit 14.5.) First, cost of goods sold is deducted from net sales to get the gross profit. Then total operating expenses are subtracted from gross profit to get the net profit before taxes. Finally, income taxes are deducted to get the net profit. As shown in Exhibit 14.5, Delicious Desserts earned a net profit of $32,175 in 2010.

It is very important to recognize that profit does not represent cash. The income statement is a summary of the firm's operating results during some time period. It does not present the firm's actual cash flows during the period. Those are summarized in the statement of cash flows, which is discussed briefly in the next section.

CONCEPT check

What is an income statement? How does it differ from the balance sheet?

Describe the key parts of the income statement. Distinguish between gross sales and net sales.

How is net profit or loss calculated?

The Statement of Cash Flows

6 Why is the statement of cash flows an important source of information?

statement of cash flows
A financial statement that provides a summary of the money flowing into and out of a firm during a certain period, typically one year.

Net profit or loss is one measure of a company's financial performance. However, creditors and investors are also keenly interested in how much cash a business generates and how it is used. Read in the Managing Change box on the next page the story of a Minnesota moving company that reengineered its billing processes to increase its cash flow during the recent housing downturn. The **statement of cash flows**, a summary of the money flowing into and out of a firm, is the financial statement used to assess the inflows and outflows of cash during a certain period, typically one year. All publicly traded firms must include a statement of cash flows in their financial reports to stockholders. The statement of cash flows tracks the firm's cash receipts and cash payments. It gives financial managers and analysts a way to identify cash flow problems and assess the firm's financial viability.

Increasing Cash Flow Helps Company Navigate a Turbulent Economy

Even though Beltmann Group, a Minnesota moving company, was on track to match its previous year's sales of $100 million, CEO Dana Battina was still concerned about the economy. In response to general volatility in the consumer housing markets and the resulting tightening of the credit markets, Battina wanted a larger cash cushion in the bank. Unfortunately, at any given point, his sales outstanding amounted to $16.7 million. That meant the amount of time between a sale and payment of the related invoice was 61 days!

Instead of simply tightening payment terms, for example by changing from a 45-day term to a 30-day term, Battina wanted to understand why it was taking the company so long to get paid. So, he hired three consultants who spent two months analyzing the company's billing process. Not only did they conduct interviews with employees and visit branches, they compiled all of the billing errors they uncovered into a master spreadsheet. What they discovered was this: not only were customers late, it was taking Beltmann an average of 10 days to even send out the invoices for services rendered. And during those 10 plus days, documents were mishandled over 40 percent of the time!

Part of the reason was that Beltmann's 300 subcontractors would deliver paperwork to one of the company's 13 branches around the country. From those branches, the paperwork took over a week to travel through three departments. At each step, forms and signatures were often missing and errors needed fixing. Sometimes incomplete paperwork would make it all the way through the process, only to be returned to the branch office for a missing form.

A simple cover form was all it took to simplify the process. The new quality control form lists every process along the invoicing route; as employees complete their part of the process, they check off all the elements for which they are responsible. After implementing the fix, the time to invoice dropped to six days. Increased speed and accuracy in the invoicing process has increased the company's cash flow. After only a year using the new process, Beltmann had freed up an extra $1.1 million—a nice cushion until things in the real estate markets start moving again.[13]

Critical Thinking Questions
- What kind of cash flow did Beltmann increase with its new process?
- Is managing cash flow only critical in difficult economic environments?
- What ways can you think of for fast-growing companies to increase their cash flow? Aren't high growth and large cash reserves mutually exclusive situations?

Using income statement and balance sheet data, the statement of cash flows divides the firm's cash flows into three groups:

- *Cash flow from operating activities*. Those related to the production of the firm's goods or services.
- *Cash flow from investment activities*. Those related to the purchase and sale of fixed assets.
- *Cash flow from financing activities*. Those related to debt and equity financing.

Delicious Desserts' statement of cash flows for 2010 is presented in Exhibit 14.6. It shows that the company's cash and marketable securities

CONCEPT check

What is the purpose of the statement of cash flows?

Why has cash flow become such an important measure of a firm's financial condition?

What situations can you cite from the chapter that support your answer?

EXHIBIT 14.6	Statement of Cash Flows for Delicious Desserts

Delicious Desserts, Inc.
Statement of Cash Flows for 2010

Cash Flow from Operating Activities		
Net profit after taxes	$32,175	
Depreciation	2,500	
Decrease in accounts receivable	2,140	
Increase in inventory	(3,500)	
Decrease in accounts payable	(4,065)	
Decrease in accruals	(1,035)	
Cash provided by operating activities		$28,215
Cash Flow from Investment Activities		
Increase in gross fixed assets	($ 5,000)	
Cash used in investment activities		($5,000)
Cash Flow from Financing Activities		
Decrease in notes payable	($ 3,000)	
Decrease in long-term debt	(5,000)	
Cash used by financing activities		($8,000)
Net increase in cash and marketable securities		$15,215

have increased over the last year. And during the year the company generated enough cash flow to increase inventory and fixed assets and to reduce accounts payable, accruals, notes payable, and long-term debt.

Analyzing Financial Statements

7 How can ratio analysis be used to identify a firm's financial strengths and weaknesses?

Individually, the balance sheet, income statement, and statement of cash flows provide insight into the firm's operations, profitability, and overall financial condition. By studying the relationships among the financial statements, however, one can gain even more insight into a firm's financial condition and performance.

Ratio analysis involves calculating and interpreting financial ratios using data taken from the firm's financial statements in order to assess its condition and performance. A financial ratio states the relationship between financial data on a percentage basis. For instance, current assets might be viewed relative to current liabilities or sales relative to assets. The ratios can then be compared over time, typically three to five years. A firm's ratios can also be compared to industry averages or to those of another company in the same industry. Period-to-period and industry ratios provide a meaningful basis for comparison, so that we can answer questions such as, "Is this particular ratio good or bad?"

It's important to remember that ratio analysis is based on historical data and may not indicate future financial performance. Ratio analysis merely highlights potential problems; it does not prove that they exist. However, ratios can help managers monitor the firm's performance from period to period, to understand operations better and identify trouble spots.

Ratios are also important to a firm's present and prospective creditors (lenders), who want to see if the firm can repay what it borrows and assess the firm's financial health. Often loan agreements require firms to maintain minimum levels of specific ratios. Both present and prospective shareholders use ratio analysis to look at the company's historical performance and trends over time.

Ratios can be classified by what they measure: liquidity, profitability, activity, and debt. Using Delicious Desserts' 2010 balance sheet and income statement (Exhibits 14.4 and 14.5), we can calculate and interpret the key ratios in each group. Exhibit 14.7 summarizes the calculations of these ratios for Delicious Desserts. We'll now discuss how to calculate the ratios and, more important, how to interpret the ratio value.

CONCEPT in action

For giant retailers like Macy's, the high expense of operating a store counters the elevated markup on merchandise, resulting in slim profit margins. Since competition forces marketers to keep prices low, it is often a retailer's cost-cutting strategy, not markup or sales volume, that determines whether the business will be profitable. What expenses other than payroll and the cost of merchandise affect a retailer's net profit margin?

© Michael Nagle/Bloomberg News/Landov

ratio analysis
The calculation and interpretation of financial ratios using data taken from the firm's financial statements in order to assess its condition and performance.

liquidity ratios
Ratios that measure a firm's ability to pay its short-term debts as they come due.

current ratio
The ratio of total current assets to total current liabilities; used to measure a firm's liquidity.

acid-test (quick) ratio
The ratio of total current assets excluding inventory to total current liabilities; used to measure a firm's liquidity.

Liquidity Ratios

Liquidity ratios measure the firm's ability to pay its short-term debts as they come due. These ratios are of special interest to the firm's creditors. The three main measures of liquidity are the current ratio, the acid-test (quick) ratio, and net working capital.

The **current ratio** is the ratio of total current assets to total current liabilities. Traditionally, a current ratio of 2 ($2 of current assets for every $1 of current liabilities) has been considered good. Whether it is sufficient depends on the industry in which the firm operates. Public utilities, which have a very steady cash flow, operate quite well with a current ratio well below 2. A current ratio of 2 might not be adequate for manufacturers and merchandisers that carry high inventories and have lots of receivables. The current ratio for Delicious Desserts for 2010, as shown in Exhibit 14.7, is 1.4. This means little without a basis for comparison. If the analyst found that the industry average for small bakeries was 2.4, Delicious Desserts would appear to have low liquidity.

The **acid-test (quick) ratio** is like the current ratio except that it excludes inventory, which is the least-liquid current asset. The acid-test ratio is used to measure the firm's ability to pay its current liabilities without selling inventory. The name acid-test implies that this ratio is a crucial test of the firm's liquidity. An acid-test ratio of at least 1 is preferred. But again, what is an acceptable value varies by industry. The acid-test ratio is a good measure of liquidity when inventory cannot easily be converted to cash (for instance, if it consists of very specialized goods with a limited market). If inventory is liquid, the current ratio is better. Delicious Desserts' acid-test ratio for 2010 is 1.1. Because the bakery's products are perishable, it does not carry large inventories. Thus, the values of its acid-test

EXHIBIT 14.7

EXHIBIT 14.7 Ratio Analysis for Delicious Desserts at Year-End 2010

Ratio	Formula	Calculation	Result
Liquidity Ratios			
Current ratio	$\dfrac{\text{Total current assets}}{\text{Total current liabilities}}$	$\dfrac{\$83{,}200}{\$60{,}150}$	1.4
Acid-test (quick) ratio	$\dfrac{\text{Total current assets} - \text{inventory}}{\text{Total current liabilities}}$	$\dfrac{\$83{,}200 - \$15{,}000}{\$60{,}150}$	1.1
Net working capital	Total current assets − Total current liabilities	$\$83{,}200 - \$60{,}150$	$23,050
Profitability Ratios			
Net profit margin	$\dfrac{\text{Net profit}}{\text{Net sales}}$	$\dfrac{\$32{,}175}{\$270{,}500}$	11.9%
Return on equity (ROE)	$\dfrac{\text{Net profit}}{\text{Total owners' equity}}$	$\dfrac{\$32{,}175}{\$78{,}750}$	40.9%
Earnings per share (EPS)	$\dfrac{\text{Net profit}}{\text{Number of shares of common stock outstanding}}$	$\dfrac{\$32{,}175}{10{,}000}$	$3.22
Activity Ratio			
Inventory turnover	$\dfrac{\text{Cost of goods sold}}{\text{Average inventory}}$		
	$\dfrac{\text{Cost of goods sold}}{(\text{Beginning inventory} + \text{Ending inventory})/2}$	$\dfrac{\$112{,}500}{(\$18{,}000 + \$15{,}000)/2}$	
		$\dfrac{\$112{,}500}{\$16{,}500}$	6.8 times
Debt Ratio			
Debt-to-equity ratio	$\dfrac{\text{Total liabilities}}{\text{Owners' equity}}$	$\dfrac{\$70{,}150}{\$78{,}750}$	89.1%

and current ratios are fairly close. At a manufacturing company, however, inventory typically makes up a large portion of current assets, so the acid-test ratio will be lower than the current ratio.

Net working capital, though not really a ratio, is often used to measure a firm's overall liquidity. It is calculated by subtracting total current liabilities from total current assets. Delicious Desserts' net working capital for 2010 is $23,050. Comparisons of net working capital over time often help in assessing a firm's liquidity.

net working capital
The amount obtained by subtracting total current liabilities from total current assets; used to measure a firm's liquidity.

Profitability Ratios

To measure profitability, a firm's profits can be related to its sales, equity, or stock value. **Profitability ratios** measure how well the firm is using its resources to generate profit and how efficiently it is being managed. The main profitability ratios are net profit margin, return on equity, and earnings per share.

profitability ratios
Ratios that measure how well a firm is using its resources to generate profit and how efficiently it is being managed.

The ratio of net profit to net sales is the **net profit margin**, also called *return on sales*. It measures the percentage of each sales dollar remaining after all expenses, including taxes, have been deducted. Higher net profit margins are better than lower ones. The net profit margin is often used to measure the firm's earning power. "Good" net profit margins differ quite a bit from industry to industry. A grocery store usually has a very low net profit margin, perhaps below 1 percent, whereas a jewelry store's net profit margin would probably exceed 10 percent. Delicious Desserts' net profit margin for 2010 is 11.9 percent. In other words, Delicious Desserts is earning 11.9 cents on each dollar of sales.

net profit margin
The ratio of net profit to net sales; also called *return on sales*. It measures the percentage of each sales dollar remaining after all expenses, including taxes, have been deducted.

The ratio of net profit to total owners' equity is called **return on equity (ROE)**. It measures the return that owners receive on their investment in the firm, a major reason for investing in a company's stock. Delicious Desserts has a 40.9 percent ROE for 2010. On the surface, a 40.9 percent ROE seems quite good. But the level of risk in the business and the ROE of other firms in the same industry must also be considered. The higher the risk, the greater the ROE investors look for. A firm's ROE can also be compared to past values to see how the company is performing over time.

return on equity (ROE)
The ratio of net profit to total owners' equity; measures the return that owners receive on their investment in the firm.

earnings per share (EPS)
The ratio of net profit to the number of shares of common stock outstanding; measures the number of dollars earned by each share of stock.

activity ratios
Ratios that measure how well a firm uses its assets.

inventory turnover ratio
The ratio of cost of goods sold to average inventory; measures the speed with which inventory moves through a firm and is turned into sales.

debt ratios
Ratios that measure the degree and effect of a firm's use of borrowed funds (debt) to finance its operations.

debt-to-equity ratio
The ratio of total liabilities to owners' equity; measures the relationship between the amount of debt financing (borrowing) and the amount of equity financing (owner's funds).

Earnings per share (EPS) is the ratio of net profit to the number of shares of common stock outstanding. It measures the number of dollars earned by each share of stock. EPS values are closely watched by investors and are considered an important sign of success. EPS also indicates a firm's ability to pay dividends. Note that EPS is the dollar amount earned by each share, not the actual amount given to stockholders in the form of dividends. Some earnings may be put back into the firm. Delicious Desserts' EPS for 2010 is $3.22.

Activity Ratios

Activity ratios measure how well a firm uses its assets. They reflect the speed with which resources are converted to cash or sales. A frequently used activity ratio is inventory turnover. The **inventory turnover ratio** measures the speed with which inventory moves through the firm and is turned into sales. It is calculated by dividing cost of goods sold by the average inventory. (*Average inventory* is estimated by adding the beginning and ending inventories for the year and dividing by 2.) Based on its 2010 financial data, Delicious Desserts' inventory, on average, is turned into sales 6.8 times each year, or about once every 54 days (365 days ÷ 6.8). The acceptable turnover ratio depends on the line of business. A grocery store would have a high turnover ratio, maybe 20 times a year, whereas the turnover for a heavy equipment manufacturer might be only 3 times a year.

Debt Ratios

Debt ratios measure the degree and effect of the firm's use of borrowed funds (debt) to finance its operations. These ratios are especially important to lenders and investors. They want to make sure the firm has a healthy mix of debt and equity. If the firm relies too much on debt, it may have trouble meeting interest payments and repaying loans. The most important debt ratio is the debt-to-equity ratio.

The **debt-to-equity ratio** measures the relationship between the amount of debt financing (borrowing) and the amount of equity financing (owners' funds). It is calculated by dividing total liabilities by owners' equity. In general, the lower the ratio, the better. But it is important to assess the debt-to-equity ratio against both past values and industry averages. Delicious Desserts' ratio for 2010 is 89.1 percent. The ratio indicates that the company has 89 cents of debt for every dollar the owners have provided. A ratio above 100 percent means the firm has more debt than equity. In such a case, the lenders are providing more financing than the owners.

CONCEPT check

How can ratio analysis be used to interpret financial statements?

Name the main liquidity and profitability ratios and explain what they indicate.

What kinds of information do activity ratios give? Why are debt ratios of concern to lenders and investors?

Trends in Accounting

8 What major trends affect the accounting industry today?

The post–Sarbanes-Oxley business environment has brought many changes to the accounting profession. The public accounting industry could no longer regulate itself and became subject to formal regulation for the first time. The new regulatory environment set higher standards for audit procedures—and at the same time created uncertainty in how to interpret the rules. Once again the core auditing business, rather than financial advisory and management consulting services, became their primary focus, which caused the relationship between accountants and their clients to change. Another significant trend in accounting is the development of standards to create tagged electronic financial reports. The FASB is pushing for major changes in GAAP, such as the shift to principles-based accounting and separate procedures for private and small companies.

Reevaluating SarbOx

In the period following the enactment of Sarbanes-Oxley, auditors had no experience with how to apply and interpret the act. Many took a conservative view and went to extremes in following the provisions of Section 404 of the act (audits of internal controls). The PCAOB subsequently criticized such practices and acknowledged that they unnecessarily raised compliance costs. "The criticisms are valid, and the profession needs to transition to a risk-based, judgment approach," commented Kelly Dreishpoon, manager at Rothstein Kass, a New Jersey CPA firm. "However, a lot of the initial approach [to Section 404] was predicated by the first-time-through nature of the implementation. What other guidance was there outside the strict interpretation of what was written?"

Both the PCAOB and AICPA issued guidance that covered these concerns and helped auditors increase the effectiveness of their audits. Overall, the guidance explained to accountants how to determine what is required to audit and test internal control procedures effectively and at an appropriate cost.[14] The AICPA's Auditing Standards Board (ASB) addressed similar issues in its March 2006 Risk Assessment Standards, which included eight Statements on Auditing Standards.[15] After those clarifications, the cost of compliance with Section 404 began to follow a downward trend.

Regulators continue to investigate ways to keep the rudiments of the act and limit the requirements it imposes, which are onerous to small and medium publicly traded companies. An independent, bipartisan committee on Capital Markets Regulation found that implementing SarbOx cost $15–20 billion, or more than 35 times what was estimated when the law was passed.[16] Proposed legislation in Congress would make SarbOx reporting optional for companies with less than $700 million in market capitalization and limit the costs of audits. Even though the proposal was initiated by Republicans in Congress, Democrats like Speaker of the House Nancy Pelosi also appreciate the burdens on smaller companies. Her agenda calls for "specifically tailored guidelines for small public companies to ensure Sarbanes-Oxley requirements are not overly burdensome."[17] Seeming proof that the SarbOx requirements are, at present, overly burdensome is the trend of small and medium publicly traded companies going private or offering private equity companies stakes in their firms in place of pursuing an initial public offering (IPO).[18] After much bipartisan urging, SEC Chairman Christopher Cox announced plans to delay the December 2008 deadline by which small public firms comply with SarbOx in the same way that the large publicly traded companies do. During the extended delay, the Commmission's economists will conduct a study of costs of compliance.[19]

CONCEPT in action

While the enactment of Sarbanes-Oxley has pressured executives to fly right in financial matters, the legislation has also produced unintended consequences that may require reevaluation. The number of American companies to deregister from U.S. stock exchanges has nearly tripled since the passing of the new restrictions. Moreover, many small businesses are staying private to avoid the act's high compliance costs, which average millions of dollars annually for publicly traded companies. SarbOx's proposed jail time for inadvertent accounting errors is also having a chilling effect on business leadership and risk. How might legislators reassess the pros and cons of specific accounting regulations?

Accountants Stick to the Numbers

During the 1980s, accountants moved beyond their traditional task of auditing a company's financial information to provide additional services. Their first steps were financial services that were a logical extension of their audit assignments, such as tax, legal, and investment advisory services. As they moved further afield from their core businesses, they developed huge consulting units that provided a wide range of information technology, business strategy, human resources, and similar management services.

Nonaudit fees soon dwarfed revenues from audits. Especially at the largest firms, accountants became more involved in the operations of their clients. This raised the question of potential conflicts of interest: Can auditors serve both the public and the client? Auditors' main purpose is to certify financial statements. Could they maintain sufficient objectivity to raise questions while auditing a client that provides significant consulting revenues? Can they review systems and methods that they designed and implemented?

Sarbanes-Oxley brought an end to the days when accountants could serve as both auditor and adviser to a client. Auditors may no longer provide eight specific types of nonaudit services to their audit clients. These include services (like bookkeeping) related to the client's accounting records or financial statements, design and implementation of financial information systems, internal auditing, management functions, human resources, investment services, and legal services. "They'll give you information, but they won't give you a recommendation," sums up Peter Kruse, CFO of Nissan Forklift.[20]

The relationship between financial executives and their outside accountants has become increasingly formal, in part because of lawsuits against audit firms as well as the new regulations. "The consultative advice that auditors had been able to provide in the past has now changed to 'You tell me what you think the answer is, and I'll get back to you on that,'" explains Patrick Scannell, CFO at Netezza Corp., a Massachusetts data-warehousing firm. One CFO summed it up by saying she was paying more for her audit but getting much less for her money, because her auditors no longer provided accounting advice, which she considered the most valuable component of audits past.[21]

Tagging Data in Financial Reports

Data tagging has long been a common feature in Web site development, database management, banking reporting, and even academic testing software, and soon it will be an integrated element of financial reporting. Extensible Business Reporting Language, or XBRL, will be the language for the electronic communication of business data. Using XBRL, companies will tag each item in a business report with information regarding various attributes of the data. For example, a company can tag data with information regarding the calendar year, the company's reporting cycle, if the data has been audited (or not), currency (dollars, euros, yen, etc.), and so forth.[22]

One of the main advantages of reports tagged in XBRL is the ability of a single report to be understood by readers around the world. That is, the tagging structure allows a Japanese executive to read in Japanese a report drafted in French by an executive of a French company. Another expected advantage is the reduction of errors introduced when companies rekey data from accounting spreadsheets into word processing software before publication of the reports.[23]

For such tagging procedures to be effective, businesses need to use a common set of tags. To help in this regard, the SEC engaged the services of XBRL US, a nonprofit consortium of more than 500 organizations worldwide working to build XBRL language and design XBRL business reporting standards. To start, XBRL US drafted a taxonomy (a dictionary of tags which represents a comprehensive collection of financial and business terms) and posted it online for review. Feedback was incorporated before the final taxonomy of roughly 350 tags was rolled out.[24]

Initially, only the first 500 largest U.S. public companies would be required to tag their financial documents, but the eventual goal is for all public companies over a certain size to submit XBRL-tagged reports to the SEC.[25] Even though U.S. banks have been submitting XBRL-tagged reports to the Federal Deposit Insurance Company (FDIC) for years, U.S. businesses in general lag other countries, especially those in Europe, in developing a program for using XBRL in accounting. Some expect that by 2013, the SEC will require XBRL-tagged financial reports from all public U.S. companies.[26]

Closing the GAAP

Many accounting industry experts place some of the blame for recent accounting fraud on the complexity of GAAP, among them Robert Herz, who is now head of the FASB. The FASB supports a shift from rules-based accounting to the principles-based accounting system used by the International Accounting Standards Board. Instead of asking if the accounting follows the rules, executives and auditors would look at how it shows a transaction's underlying economics. "A principles-based system is one where the accounting standard simply lays out objectives of good reporting in an area," explains Herz. Standards would be broader, simpler, and more concise—12 pages instead of 200 pages.

CONCEPT check

What issues have surfaced since the Sarbanes-Oxley Act went into effect, and how is the accounting industry resolving them? How has the relationship between public accounting firms and their clients changed in recent years?

What role do data tagging and XBRL play in financial reports? What is the outlook for data tagging using XBRL?

What changes is the FASB considering for GAAP?

However, Herz anticipates much resistance to such a change. "Fundamental structural, institutional, cultural, and behavioral forces have caused, and continue to cause, complexity in the system and impede transparent financial reporting," he says. These forces include an overemphasis on short-term earnings, which leads to using accounting "tricks" to boost quarterly results. Another obstacle is that relying on principles, which are open to interpretation, could result in problems with regulators. This uncertainty does not exist with standards and rules.

No easy answers are on the horizon. "Everyone is in favor of simplification," says former FASB chairman Dennis Beresford, who currently teaches accounting at the University of Georgia. But "everyone also wants rules—just in case."[27]

Summary of Learning Goals

Accounting involves collecting, recording, classifying, summarizing, reporting, and analyzing a firm's financial activities according to a standard set of procedures. The financial reports resulting from the accounting process give managers, employees, investors, customers, suppliers, creditors, and government agencies a way to analyze a company's past, current, and future performance. Financial accounting is concerned with the preparation of financial reports using generally accepted accounting principles. Managerial accounting provides financial information that management can use to make decisions about the firm's operations.

1 Why are financial reports and accounting information important, and who uses them?

Public accountants work for independent firms that provide accounting services—such as financial report preparation and auditing, tax return preparation, and management consulting—to other organizations on a fee basis. Private accountants are employed to serve one particular organization and may prepare financial statements, tax returns, and management reports.

The bankruptcies of companies like Enron, plus widespread abuses of accounting practices, raised critical issues of auditor independence and the integrity and reliability of financial reports. To set better standards for accounting, auditing, and financial reporting and prevent future accounting irregularities, Congress passed the Sarbanes-Oxley Act in 2002. This act establishes an independent board to oversee the accounting profession, sets stricter auditing and financial disclosure standards, and places increased accountability on a company's senior executives and management. It restricts auditors from providing certain types of consulting services to clients. Other organizations such as the SEC, the New York Stock Exchange, and accounting industry professional associations issued new regulations and guidelines related to compliance with the act.

2 What are the differences between public and private accountants, and are public accountants subject to new regulations?

The accounting cycle refers to the process of generating financial statements. It begins with analyzing business transactions, recording them in journals, and posting them to ledgers. Ledger totals are then summarized in a trial balance that confirms the accuracy of the figures. Next the accountant prepares the financial statements and reports. The final step involves analyzing these reports and making decisions. Computers have simplified many of these labor-intensive tasks.

3 What are the six steps in the accounting cycle?

The balance sheet represents the financial condition of a firm at one moment in time, in terms of assets, liabilities, and owners' equity. The key categories of assets are current assets, fixed assets, and intangible assets. Liabilities are divided into current and long-term liabilities. Owners' equity, the amount of the owners' investment in the firm after all liabilities have been paid, is the third major category.

4 In what terms does the balance sheet describe the financial condition of an organization?

The income statement is a summary of the firm's operations over a stated period of time. The main parts of the statement are revenues (gross and net sales), cost of goods sold, operating expenses (selling and general and administrative expenses), taxes, and net profit or loss.

5 How does the income statement report a firm's profitability?

The statement of cash flows summarizes the firm's inflows and outflows of cash during a financial-reporting period. It breaks the firm's cash flows into those from operating, investment, and financing activities. It shows the net change during the period in the firm's cash and marketable securities.

6 Why is the statement of cash flows an important source of information?

Ratio analysis is a way to use financial statements to gain insight into a firm's operations, profitability, and overall financial condition. The four main types of ratios are liquidity ratios, profitability ratios, activity ratios, and debt ratios. Comparing a firm's ratios over several years and comparing them to ratios of other firms in the same industry or to industry averages can indicate trends and highlight financial strengths and weaknesses.

7 How can ratio analysis be used to identify a firm's financial strengths and weaknesses?

Under the more stringent regulations of Sarbanes-Oxley, higher standards are being applied to audits. However, when the Sarbanes-Oxley Act was passed, accountants were unsure of how strictly to interpret the rules. Many were too rigid, and this increased the costs of audits significantly. In response, the PCAOB and AICPA published guidance to help auditors use risk assessments. Accountants returned to their core auditing business, rather than financial advisory and management consulting services. The relationship between accountants and their clients has changed, as the threat of lawsuits made accountants less willing to offer advice. A set of XBRL standards and tags

8 What major trends affect the accounting industry today?

are in development to help companies increase the accuracy and the accessibility of their financial reports. Although initially only large, publicly traded companies will be required to submit XBRL-tagged financial documents, experts expect that all publicly traded companies in the United States will need to comply with XBRL standards by 2013. We could also see some major changes in GAAP from a shift to principles-based rather than rules-based accounting. FASB is also considering simplifying GAAP for private and small companies.

Key Terms

accounting 379

acid-test (quick) ratio 392

activity ratios 394

annual report 380

assets 384

auditing 380

balance sheet 386

certified management accountant (CMA) 381

certified public accountant (CPA) 381

cost of goods sold 388, 389

current assets 386

current liabilities 387

current ratio 392

debt ratios 394

debt-to-equity ratio 394

depreciation 386, 387

double-entry bookkeeping 384

earnings per share (EPS) 394

expenses 388, 389

financial accounting 380

Financial Accounting Standards Board (FASB) 380

fixed assets 386, 387

generally accepted accounting principles (GAAP) 380

gross profit 390

gross sales 388, 389

income statement 388

intangible assets 386, 387

inventory turnover ratio 394

liabilities 384

liquidity 386

liquidity ratios 392

long-term liabilities 388

managerial accounting 379

net loss 390

net profit margin 393

net profit (net income) 390

net sales 388, 389

net working capital 393

operating expenses 390

owners' equity 384

private accountants 381

profitability ratios 393

public accountants 380

ratio analysis 392

retained earnings 388

return on equity (ROE) 393

revenues 388, 389

Sarbanes-Oxley Act 382

statement of cash flows 390

Preparing for Tomorrow's Workplace: SCANS

1. Your firm has been hired to help several small businesses with their year-end financial statements.

    a. Based on the following account balances, prepare the Marbella Design Enterprises balance sheet as of December 31, 2010:

Cash	$30,250
Accounts payable	28,500
Fixtures and furnishings	85,000
Notes payable	15,000
Retained earnings	64,450
Accounts receivable	24,050
Inventory	15,600
Equipment	42,750
Accumulated depreciation on fixtures and furnishings	12,500
Common shares (50,000 shares at $1)	50,000
Long-term debt	25,000
Accumulated depreciation on equipment	7,800
Marketable securities	13,000
Income taxes payable	7,500

b. The following are the account balances for the revenues and expenses of the Windsor Gift Shop for the year ending December 31, 2010. Prepare the income statement for the shop. **(Resources, Information)**

Rent	$ 15,000
Salaries	23,500
Cost of goods sold	98,000
Utilities	8,000
Supplies	3,500
Sales	195,000
Advertising	3,600
Interest	3,000
Taxes	12,120

2. During the year ended December 31, 2010, Lawrence Industries sold $2 million worth of merchandise on credit. A total of $1.4 million was collected during the year. The cost of this merchandise was $1.3 million. Of this amount, $1 million has been paid, and $300,000 is not yet due. Operating expenses and income taxes totaling $500,000 were paid in cash during the year. Assume that all accounts had a zero balance at the beginning of the year (January 1, 2010). Write a brief report for the company controller that includes calculation of the firm's (a) net profit and (b) cash flow during the year. Explain why there is a difference between net profit and cash flow. **(Information, Systems)**

3. A friend has been offered a sales representative position at Draper Publications, Inc., a small publisher of computer-related books, but wants to know more about the company. Because of your expertise in financial analysis, you offer to help analyze Draper's financial health. Draper has provided the following selected financial information:

Account balances on December 31, 2010:	
Inventory	$ 72,000
Net sales	450,000
Current assets	150,000
Cost of goods sold	290,000
Total liabilities	180,000
Net profit	35,400
Total assets	385,000
Current liabilities	75,000
Other information	
Number of common shares outstanding	25,000
Inventory at January 1, 2010	48,000

Calculate the following ratios for 2010: acid-test (quick) ratio, inventory turnover ratio, net profit margin, return on equity (ROE), debt-to-equity ratio, and earnings per share (EPS). Summarize your assessment of the company's financial performance, based on these ratios, in a report for your friend. What other information would you like to have to complete your evaluation? **(Information, Systems)**

4. Use the Internet and business periodicals to research how companies and accounting firms are implementing the provisions of the Sarbanes-Oxley Act. What are the major concerns they face? What rules have other organizations issued that relate to Act compliance? Summarize your findings. **(Information)**

5. **Team Activity** Two years ago, Rebecca Mardon started a computer consulting business, Mardon Consulting Associates. Until now, she has been the only employee, but business has grown enough to support an administrative assistant and another consultant this year. Before she adds staff, however, she wants to hire an accountant and computerize her financial record keeping. Divide the class into small groups, assigning one person to be Rebecca and the others to represent members of a medium-size accounting firm. Rebecca should think about the type of financial information systems her firm requires and develop a list of questions for the firm. The accountants will prepare a presentation making recommendations to her as well as explaining why their firm should win the account. **(Resources, Interpersonal)**

6. One of the best ways to learn about financial statements is to prepare them. Put together your personal balance sheet and income statement, using Exhibits 14.4 and 14.5 as samples. You will have to adjust the account categories to fit your needs. Here are some suggestions:
   - Current assets—cash on hand, balances in savings and checking accounts.
   - Investments—stocks and bonds, retirement funds.
   - Fixed assets—real estate, personal property (cars, furniture, jewelry, etc.).
   - Current liabilities—credit card balances, loan payments due in one year.
   - Long-term liabilities—auto loan balance, mortgage on real estate, other loan balances that will not come due until after one year.
   - Income—employment income, investment income (interest, dividends).
   - Expenses—housing, utilities, food, transportation, medical, clothing, insurance, loan payments, taxes, personal care, recreation and entertainment, and miscellaneous expenses.

   After you complete your personal financial statements, use them to see how well you are managing your finances. Consider the following questions:
   a. Should you be concerned about your *debt ratio*?
   b. Would a potential creditor conclude that it is safe or risky to lend you money?
   c. If you were a company, would people want to invest in you? Why or why not? What could you do to improve your financial condition? (**Information**)

Ethics Activity

As the controller of a medium-size manufacturing company, you take pride in the accounting and internal control systems you have developed for the company. You and your staff have kept up with changes in the accounting industry and have been diligent in updating the systems to meet new accounting standards. Your outside auditor, which has been reviewing the company's books for 15 years, routinely complimented you on your thorough procedures.

The passage of the Sarbanes-Oxley Act, with its emphasis on testing internal control systems, has initiated several changes. You have studied the law and made adjustments to ensure you comply with the regulations, even though it has created additional work. Your auditors, however, have chosen to interpret SarbOx very aggressively—too much so, in your opinion. The auditors have recommended that you make costly improvements to your systems and also enlarged the scope of the audit engagement, raising their fees. When you question the partner in charge,

he explains that the newness of the law means that it is open to interpretation and it is better to err on the side of caution than risk noncompliance. You are not pleased with this answer, as you believe that your company is in compliance with SarbOx, and consider changing auditors.

Using a Web search tool, locate articles about this topic and then write responses to the following questions. Be sure to support your arguments and cite your sources.

ETHICAL DILEMMA: Should you change auditors because your current one is too stringent in applying the Sarbanes-Oxley Act? What other steps could you take to resolve this situation?

Sources: Laurie Brannen, "Sarbanes-Oxley's Footprint on Finance Deepens," *Business Finance*, March 2005, **http://www.businessfinancemag.com**; Eric Krell, "Sarbanes Fatigue Strikes the Boardroom," *Business Finance*, May 2005, **http://www.businessfinancemag.com**; Michael Rapoport, "SEC Panel to Turn In Report on Sarbanes Debate," *Wall Street Journal*, April 17, 2006, p. C3; Tim Reason, "Feeling the Pain," *CFO*, May 1, 2005, **http://cfo.com**; and Helen Shaw, "Donaldson, Levitt Diverge on Convergence," *CFO*, February 22, 2006, **http://cfo.com**.

Working the Net

1. Visit the Web site of one of the following major U.S. public accounting firms: Deloitte & Touche, **http://www.deloitte.com**; Ernst & Young, **http://www.ey.com**; KPMG, **http://www.kpmg.com**; PricewaterhouseCoopers, **http://www.pwc.com**; Grant Thornton, **http://www.grantthornton.com**; or BDO Seidman, **http://www.bdo.com**. Explore the site to learn the services the firm offers. What other types of resources does the firm have on its Web site? How well does the firm communicate via the Web site with existing and prospective clients? Summarize your findings in a brief report.
2. Do annual reports confuse you? Many Web sites can take the mystery out of this important document. See IBM's "Guide to Understanding Financials" at **http://www.prars.com/ibm/ibmframe.html**. Moneychimp's "How to Read an Annual Report" features an interactive diagram that provides a big picture view of what the report's financial information tells you: **http://www.moneychimp.com/articles/financials/fundamentals.htm**. Which site was more helpful to you, and why?

3. Corporate reports filed with the SEC are now available on the Web at the EDGAR (Electronic Data Gathering, Analysis, and Retrieval system) Web site, **http://www.sec.gov/edgar.shtml**. First, read about the EDGAR system; then go to the search page **http://www.sec.gov/edgar/searchedgar/webusers.htm**. To see the type of information that companies must file with the SEC, use the search feature to locate a recent filing by Microsoft. What types of reports did you find, and what was the purpose of each report?

4. Can you judge an annual report by its cover? What are the most important elements of a top annual report? Go to Sid Cato's Official Annual Report Web site, **http://www.sidcato.com**, to find his 15 standards for annual reports and read about the reports that receive his honors. Then get a copy of an annual report and evaluate it using Cato's 135-point scale. How well does it compare to his top picks?

5. Go to the Web site of the company whose annual report you evaluated in Question 4. Find the Web version of its annual report and compare it to the print version. What differences do you find, if any? Do you think companies should put their financial information online? Why or why not?

Creative Thinking Case

Compliance Conundrum

The Sarbanes-Oxley Act of 2002 placed new compliance and disclosure burdens on corporate executives. Not only must top executives certify their firms' financial statements, but they must also quickly publicize "on a current basis" such matters as insider transactions in the company's stock, events that require certain SEC filings, and "any material changes in their financial condition."

No wonder, then, that a company's Web site has become a critical component of its investor-relations efforts. Both investors and analysts now turn first to corporate Web sites as a major source of information for quarterly earnings releases, press releases other than earnings, annual reports, SEC filings such as the 10K or 10Q, Webcasts of current conference calls with security analysts and archives of past Webcasts, and other financial and investment-related information. Companies often outsource their online investor relations initiatives to specialized companies such as Thomson/CCBN IR Web Hosting and Thomson/CCBN Webcasting.

Because the Web has become such an important way to reach individual and institutional investors, most major companies today also use their corporate Web sites to communicate compliance with the act and rebuild investor confidence. Their Web sites now include corporate governance information such as composition of the board of directors and its committees, governance policies, alerts to changes in corporate governance, and related information. Companies can also set up governance reporting procedures and hotlines to record complaints, as Section 301 of Sarbanes-Oxley requires. An additional benefit of providing ready access to materials on corporate governance and regulatory compliance is an increase in investor confidence in the organization's credibility.

Technology is helping companies with other compliance solutions as well. For example, specialized software from companies such as Compliance 360 and OpenPages provides corporations with comprehensive governance, risk, and compliance management programs for Sarbanes-Oxley and other regulatory agencies. Together, all compliance-related data streamlines the compliance process across the enterprise, eliminates redundancy, identifies risks, and reduces the cost of compliance. Duke University Hospital implemented Compliance 360's software to track thousands of constantly changing regulations, standards, codes, and accreditations. "Our corporate compliance management solution automates many of those processes and provides an enterprise-wide view of corporate compliance through a single interface," says Steve McGraw, CEO of Compliance 360.

Critical Thinking Questions

- How does the Web help companies manage compliance with the Sarbanes-Oxley Act?
- Why are companies turning to firms like Compliance 360 and Open Pages to improve compliance procedures?

- Visit the investor relations pages of the corporate Web sites for two of the following companies: ExxonMobil, IBM, Dell, Microsoft, Pfizer, Bank of America, AT&T, Verizon, Gilette, or Procter & Gamble. How well does each company use the Web to present information? Where does corporate governance information appear, and what does it tell you about the company?

Sources: Adapted from Compliance 360 Web site, **http://www.compliance360.com**, April 16, 2006; "Duke University Hospital Selects Compliance 360 for Regulatory Management," *PRNewswire*, July 27, 2005, **http://galenet.cengagelearning.com**; "Multicare Health System Selects Open Pages SOXExpress for Sarbanes-Oxley Compliance," *Internet Wire*, February 13, 2006, **http://galenet.cengagelearning.com**; and "Thomson/CCBN's Corporate Governance Online Disclosure Solution," *Thomson Financial*, 2004, **http://www.thomson.com/financial**, April 17, 2006.

video

Evie Wexler
The Little Guys

Exploring Business Careers

Wexler describes the early days of The Little Guys, the home electronics business she and her husband started in the mid-1990s, as "days of rapid weight gain." "We were so busy we didn't lunch until four o'clock. By that time we were starving so, you know, we'd eat like twelve hot dogs. It was crazy hours." Like many entrepreneurs, the Wexlers brought in a few key people early on, and that core group handled every aspect of the fledgling business. From constructing individual "living rooms" that allow their customers to better envision a particular home theater setup in their own homes to raising capital for start-up costs, they soon became experts in all facets of running a business. One area that required expertise, and quickly, was accounting. As you know, a business cannot survive without money and to prosper, business owners must use that money wisely.

Since the beginning of The Little Guys, the Wexlers, who are both involved in the business's finances, have worked with a public accountant who provides the financial experience. Initially, when they were most concerned with cultivating trust in their manufacturers and the buying public, he gave them the financial tools and background necessary to keep the cash flow steady, making the business a successful venture. As the business developed and they became more comfortable with the workings of the financial world, the accountant's role shifted. Once the Wexlers knew the ins and outs of balance sheets, and assets and liabilities, he became more of a consultant on issues of financial forecasting. Today, they meet with him at least once a quarter to review the financials. He continues to handle the more complex financial calculations, such as figuring adjustments based on depreciation of their assets; however, much of the time, she says with a laugh, he just "reassures us that we're doing okay" and that their financial decisions are sound.

For the day-to-day bookkeeping, the Wexlers use QuickBooks, a common accounting software package. They use it to prepare the reports that then allow them to conduct daily financial essentials such as paying bills and calculating payroll. In addition, the software has extensive reporting capabilities that provide the Wexlers with an up-to-date snapshot of the business's finances. These reports allow them to evaluate the financial health of the company and make decisions based on that evaluation. They can capture trends and adjust their spending or inventory based on those results. Ultimately, they can be responsive to changes in the business as those changes affect their finances.

In the years since the Wexlers first took The Little Guys from dream to reality, they have grown steadily into one of the most well-known home electronics dealers in the Chicago area. It hasn't always been easy, with many of the early days stretching on more than 16 hours a day. But sound financial practices have made them a success, allowing them to develop relationships with both their suppliers and their customers.

This chapter examined the role of accounting in business, how accounting contributes to a company's overall success, the three primary financial statements, and careers in accounting.

Financial information is central to every organization. To operate effectively, businesses must have a way to track income, expenses, assets, and liabilities in an organized manner. Financial information is also essential for decision-making. Managers prepare financial reports using accounting, a set of procedures and guidelines for companies to follow when preparing financial reports. Unless you understand basic accounting concepts, you will not be able to "speak" the standard financial language of businesses.

Apple, Inc.
continuing case
Part 5: Information Technology at Apple, Inc.

Apple is in the business of information and technology. The company focuses on using innovative technology to improve the way information is accumulated and shared. As one of the earliest entries into the information age, Apple has been at the forefront of technological innovation and is one of the leaders in the information age.

Early Developments in Technological Innovation

AppleLink was the worldwide computer network that electronically connected Apple's employees, sales force, dealers, and third-party developers. The initial use of AppleLink was for electronic mail. Apple employees were encouraged to use AppleLink at work and at home. Encouraging home usage was a critical step in obtaining buy-in to what Apple executives thought was the future of electronic mail—being in touch regardless of time and location. After going online in 1985, AppleLink opened up a new avenue of communication within the company. As a new phenomenon, Apple employees began to share opinions, ideas, thoughts, and concerns using electronic communication. Employees debated company issues as well as worldwide events in this new format. Some suggest that AppleLink was a precursor to today's e-mail. AppleLink also provided dealers with the ability to quickly and easily communicate with the company. From the perspective of external software developers, AppleLink was a direct connection for internal company support.

Eventually, Apple aligned with Quantum Computer Services to develop AppleLink Personal Edition, which led to the development of e-mail exchanges among personal computer users. Apple Computer, with its AppleLink software, became infamous in 1991 with the first e-mail message from space. On August 28, 1991, the crew of the space shuttle STS-43 *Atlantis* sent e-mail greetings using a Mac Portable and specially configured AppleLink software. *Atlantis* astronauts Shannon Lucid and James C. Adamson sent this message: "Hello Earth! Greetings from the STS-43 Crew. This is the first AppleLink from space. Having a GREAT time, wish you were here . . . send cryo and RCS! Hasta la vista, baby . . . we'll be back!"

The AppleLink Personal Edition software was a forerunner for America Online, which was developed by Quantum (Apple retained ownership of the AppleLink name). After Quantum launched the original AOL software, Apple premiered its own eWorld program in 1994. eWorld was to be a competitor to AOL and was developed for Macintosh computer users. However, eWorld was discontinued in 1996 when Apple and America Online, Inc. partnered to distribute AOL to Apple customers.

In its continued quest to develop better internal communication programs, Apple developed AppleTalk. AppleTalk enabled multiple users to share files, applications, and printers. With the introduction of AppleTalk, new computer vocabulary such as "servers" and "clients" became commonplace. The device that allowed users to share services was referred to as the *server*, and the users of the services were called *clients* (for example, a desktop computer was usually the user or client). AppleTalk was one of the earliest uses of a distributed client/server network. AppleTalk Phase 1 was developed in the early 1980s and was for use in local workgroups. AppleTalk Phase 2 was then developed for use in larger Internet workgroups.

Advanced Technologies and Later Developments

The rapid rise of the Internet led to massive changes in Apple's internal and external information technology environments. Internally, technological advances inspired new modes of training both for the company workforce and Apple users. The means of reaching current and potential Apple users also changed dramatically. From an external environmental perspective, the products ultimately developed and offered by Apple led to new and intriguing uses of technology.

Apple uses its information technology in its training and development programs. Apple University, home of the company's training and development program, engages executives in interactive electronic forums in which the executives can exchange insight and information about changes in the business environment. The University also uses its vast electronic network as a library of both company- and industry-wide information. This electronic campus allows information to be exchanged quickly among interested parties.

With a twist on training and development, Apple offers programs to professional educators who use Apple computers in the classroom. The intent of the Apple Professional Development program is to help educators make the best use of classroom technologies and to raise student achievement. The company's online resources are available with a subscription to Apple Digital School Community. The subscription makes available online tutorials, libraries of articles and resources, and an interactive environment for professional development.

Advances in information technology, as well as changes in the competitive environment (particularly involving that of Dell Computer), led to dramatic changes in the way Apple reached its customer base. Apple began phasing out many of its resellers and moved to a more direct, online sales program. In the mid-1990s, the company began using its vast technological resource to debut a Web site that allowed customers to make online purchases. This direct-sales model has helped Apple improve its forecasting and became a forerunner to the Apple Stores that began opening in 2001.

Apple's e-commerce strategies evolved into a wide array of product offerings that reached customers around the world. The company developed a set of revolutionary "i" products that essentially changed the way customers thought about products, services, capabilities, and connections. Probably the most popular and revolutionary product has been iTunes—a digital music library for organizing and playing digital music and video files. Used in connection with the iPod and iTunes Music Store, customers can purchase and download songs onto their MP3 players. This product combination has been extremely successful for Apple, with more than 4 billion iTunes songs sold as of January 2008. iPhone, the company's recent foray into the Web-enabled mobile-phone market, is also winning critical acclaim and consumer dollars; in addition to being named *Time* magazine's Invention of the Year in 2007, the cellular super-gadget sold a total of 5 million units by early 2008. iChat is an instant text-messaging application that supports both AOL and Jabber Instant Messenger services, and iChat AV allows ease of use in videoconferencing. iCal is a personal calendar that allows for sharing schedules over the Internet. In conjunction with iSync, the iCal can be synchronized with an iPhone, PDA, or iPod. Apple tapped into the digital-picture marketplace with its iLife series that includes iPhoto, iMovie HD, and iDVD. With these types of product development, Apple Computer used advances in information technology to improve internal and external communication and to make revolutionary changes in long-standing product communities—essentially moving normal, everyday aspects of life onto the computer for sharing worldwide.

Critical Thinking Questions

- What early advances in information technology did Apple Computer develop?
- How were these early advances precursors to later developments at Apple?
- What new developments occurred at Apple in response to new advanced technologies, including the Internet?
- Why did AOL survive whereas Apple's electronic programs, such as AppleLink and eWorld, did not?
- How can advances in information technology help employees in different locations and different business units communicate and work together more effectively?

Sources: Anonymous, "Apple Computer Launches eWorld, Its New Online Community," *PR Newswire*, June 20, 1994, **http://scottconverse.com/apple's_eworld.htm**, accessed on April 5, 2006; Anonymous, "Apple PR: Cupertino, CA/Vienna, VA," March 7, 1996, **http://scottconverse.com/apple's_eworld.htm**, accessed on April 5, 2006; Owen Linzmayer and Bryan Chaffin, "This Week in Apple History," The *Mac Observer*, October 31, 2004, **http://www.macobserver.com**, accessed on April 6, 2006; Judy D. Olian, Cathy C. Durham, Amy L. Kristof, Kenneth G. Brown, Richard M. Pierce, and Linda Kunder, "Designing Management Training and Development for Competitive Advantage: Lessons from the Best," *Human Resource Planning* 21 (1), 1998, pp. 20–31; Gregory C. Rogers, *Apple Computer (A) (Abridged): Corporate Strategy and Culture* (Boston: Harvard Business School Press, February 1997); Joel West, "Apple Computer: The iCEO Seizes the Internet," Center for Research on Information Technology and Organizations, Paper 348, 2002, **http://repositories.cdlib.org**, accessed on December 6, 2005; **http://www.apple.com**, accessed on April 6, 2006; **http://www.cisco.com/univercd/cc/td/doc/cisintwk/ito_doc/applet.htm**, accessed on April 5, 2006; Peter Kafka, "Hope For Amazon? iTunes Sales Flat," *Silicon Alley Insider*, January 15, 2008, **http://www.alleyinsider.com**, accessed February 11, 2008; Cleve Nettles, "Apple Expected to Announce Sales of 5 Million iPhones at Macworld," *9-to-5 Mac*, December 21, 2007, **http://9to5mac.com/5-million-iphones-4235654546345**, accessed February 11, 2008; Lev Grossman, "Invention of the Year: The iPhone," *Time*, October 31, 2007, **http://www.time.com**, accessed February 11, 2008.

Finance

Chapter 15
Understanding Money and
Financial Institutions

Chapter 16
Understanding Financial
Management and Securities
Markets

© PhotoAlto/Getty Images

Understanding Money and Financial Institutions

Learning Goals

After reading this chapter, you should be able to answer these questions:

1 What is money, what are its characteristics and functions, and what are the three parts of the U.S. money supply?

2 How does the Federal Reserve manage the money supply?

3 What are the key financial institutions, and what role do they play in the process of financial intermediation?

4 How does the Federal Deposit Insurance Corporation (FDIC) protect depositors' funds?

5 What role do U.S. banks play in the international marketplace?

6 What trends are reshaping financial institutions?

"Dirt"

On a postapocalyptic Earth where the oceans have risen to cover all but the highest peaks and civilization is reduced to floating outposts, traders have developed the necessary skills and mutations to dive to the lowest reaches of the oceans to scavenge for the detritus left behind in the submerged cities and towns. The Mariner is one such trader, living a solitary life aboard his boat and scavenging for items to trade. Having amassed a tradable haul, he approaches a gated atoll that floats somewhere in the middle of the ocean. At first, he is turned away by the men guarding the gate, stating they have enough traders; however, he then shows them a big jar of dirt, eliciting gasps and awe from the atoll dwellers.

In a world of water, dirt is a scarce commodity. Soil of any kind is a scarce commodity, and its value increases as a result of its scarcity. Because it is scarce, dirt becomes a form of money in a waterworld. But other characteristics of the dirt also pave the way for it to become part of the monetary system. It needs to be durable in that it will not spoil or whither away and will withstand as much wear and tear as possible. Dirt is certainly durable. Even if you mix it with water, it just becomes mud, which will then dry out. It also has to have some degree of portability, meaning that it can be easily moved around. The Mariner keeps his in a glass jar, which he can then move from one place to another. Finally, the dirt can be divided into smaller amounts of dirt so that one can use it for a variety of different transactions, large and small.

The Mariner is brought before a "banker" of sorts who weighs his dirt, tests it by tasting a sample of it, and proclaims that it is "pure dirt." After asking the Mariner where he got the dirt, the banker announces that they will honor its value with "62 chits." (A chit is essentially a bank note or a receipt of a deposit made.) However, instead of simply accepting the banker's offer of 62 chits, the Mariner demands twice that amount and the barter is successful. A third man, behind the banker, looks at the Mariner and then nods his head, agreeing to the transaction.

What we see in *Waterworld* is not necessarily some strange reality in which dirt has become a tradable commodity. In fact, we see it even today. Real estate, especially when dealing with farmland, is all about the value of a plot of dirt. *Waterworld* has simply taken that dirt and placed it into a jar in an effort to show how much value the dirt has taken on. Ultimately, the point of the film clip is to show that financial systems exist regardless of access to or need for paper money. During World War II, American and British prisoners of war developed a rather complex economic system based around cigarettes; and even today, similar economic systems exist. *Waterworld* simply makes the logical connection between a world composed almost entirely of water and the value that dirt and soil then take on.

The following chapter further explores the financial systems that *Waterworld* introduces. It begins with a discussion of money, including what it is, what its functions are, and its various forms in the United States. The chapter then moves into an overview of the various institutions that comprise the financial system in the United States, including the Federal Reserve System and what it does, as well as various depository and nondepository financial institutions. Bank deposit insurance and international banking are then explored before the chapter concludes with various trends in banking. In short, this chapter is designed to provide you with a basic understanding of financial systems and how they work.

Discussion Questions

- The Mariner takes his dirt to a central "banker" instead of simply bartering with each of the traders at the atoll and dividing the dirt among them. Based on the functions that money serves, why does he do this?
- In the clip, we know of two exchange mediums: dirt and chits. How do these two forms of exchange media compare to the U.S. money supply?

- In detail, what is "the banker's" role in the financial transaction that occurs with the Mariner's dirt? What is the role of the man behind the banker in this financial transaction?
- In the clip, the Mariner mentions "Smokers," another group of individuals who travel around in packs and, like the prisoners of war during World War II, use cigarettes as a medium of exchange. How do cigarettes fit into the monetary system?

Chapter 15 focuses on the role of financial institutions in U.S. and international economies. It discusses different types of financial institutions, how they are set up and function internally, and government oversight of their operations.

Advanced technology, globalization of markets, and the relaxation of regulatory restrictions are accelerating the pace of change in the financial services industry. These changes are giving businesses and consumers new options for conducting their financial transactions. The competitive landscape for financial institutions is also changing, creating new ways for these firms to increase their market share and boost profits.

Because financial institutions connect people with money, this chapter begins with a discussion of money, its characteristics and functions, and the components of the U.S. money supply. Next, it explains the role of the Federal Reserve System in managing the money supply. Then it describes different types of financial institutions and their services and the organizations that insure customer deposits. The chapter ends with a discussion of international banking and trends in the financial institutions.

Show Me the Money

1 What is money, what are its characteristics and functions, and what are the three parts of the U.S. money supply?

money
Anything that is acceptable as payment for goods and services.

Money is anything that is acceptable as payment for goods and services. It affects our lives in many ways. We earn it, spend it, save it, invest it—and often wish we had more of it. Business and government use money in similar ways. Both require money to finance their operations. By controlling the amount of money in circulation, the federal government can promote economic growth and stability. For this reason, money has been called the lubricant of the machinery that drives our economic system. Our banking system was developed to ease the handling of money.

Characteristics of Money

For money to be a suitable means of exchange, it should have these key characteristics:

- *Scarcity*. Money should be scarce enough to have some value but not so scarce as to be unavailable. Pebbles, which meet some of the other criteria, would not work well as money because they are widely available. Too much money in circulation increases prices (inflation, as discussed in Chapter 1). Governments control the scarcity of money by limiting the quantity of money in circulation.
- *Durability*. Any item used as money must be durable. A perishable item such as a banana becomes useless as money when it spoils. Even early societies used durable forms of money, such as metal coins and paper money, which lasted for a long time.
- *Portability*. Money must be easily moved around. Large or bulky items, such as boulders or heavy gold bars, cannot be transported easily from place to place.
- *Divisibility*. Money must be capable of being divided into smaller parts. Divisible forms of money help make transactions of all sizes and amounts possible.

  Exhibit 15.1 provides some interesting facts about our money.

Functions of Money

Using a variety of items as money would be confusing. Thus, societies develop a uniform money system to measure the value of goods and services. For money to be acceptable, it must function as a medium of exchange, as a standard of value, and as a store of value.

As a *medium of exchange*, money makes transactions easier. Having a common form of payment is much less complicated than having a barter system, wherein goods and services are exchanged for other goods and services. Money allows the exchange of products to be a simple process.

CONCEPT in action

Supermodel Gisele Bündchen made financial headlines recently when news outlets reported that the Brazilian beauty prefers receiving payment in currencies other than the U.S. dollar. The world's top-paid model appears to have joined a growing throng of billionaires like Warren Buffett who expect the dollar's value to continue to depreciate relative to other currencies. The dollar has fallen sharply in recent years—most notably against the euro, which press reports claimed to be the currency Bündchen received for her work with Pantene hair products. What determines the value of money?

EXHIBIT 15.1   Fantastic Facts about Money

Did you know that:

- Currency paper is composed of 25 percent linen and 75 percent cotton.
- About 4,000 double folds (first forward and then backward) are required before a note will tear.
- The Bureau of Engraving and Printing produces 38 million notes a day with a face value of approximately $750 million.
- Ninety-five percent of the notes printed each year are used to replace notes already in circulation.
- Forty-five percent of the notes printed are $1 notes.
- The largest note ever printed by the Bureau of Engraving and Printing was the $100,000 Gold Certificate, Series 1934.
- During fiscal year 2007, it cost approximately 6.2 cents per note to produce 9.1 billion U.S. paper currency notes.
- A stack of currency one mile high would contain more than 14 million notes.
- The Department of the Treasury redeems approximately $30 million in mutilated currency each year.
- If you had 10 billion $1 notes and spent 1 every second of every day, it would take 317 years for you to go broke.

Source: "Money Facts," Bureau of Engraving and Printing, **http://www.moneyfactory.gov**, May 9, 2008.

Money also serves as a *standard of value*. With a form of money whose value is accepted by all, goods and services can be priced in standard units. This makes it easy to measure the value of products and allows transactions to be recorded in consistent terms.

As a *store of value*, money is used to hold wealth. It retains its value over time, although it may lose some of its purchasing power due to inflation. Individuals may choose to keep their money for future use rather than exchange it today for other types of products or assets.

The U.S. Money Supply

The U.S. money supply is composed of currency, demand deposits, and time deposits. **Currency** is cash held in the form of coins and paper money. Other forms of currency are travelers' checks, cashier's checks, and money orders. The amount of currency in circulation depends on public demand. Domestic demand is influenced primarily by prices for goods and services, income levels, and the availability of alternative payment methods such as credit cards. Until the mid-1980s nearly all U.S. currency circulated only domestically. Today domestic circulation totals only a small fraction of the total amount of U.S. currency in circulation.

In the past 20 years, the amount of U.S. currency has grown more than 300 percent to $792.2 billion and is now held widely outside the country.[1] Foreign demand is influenced by the political and economic uncertainties associated with some foreign currencies, and recent estimates show that between one-half and two-thirds of the value of U.S. currency in circulation is held abroad.[2] Some residents of foreign countries hold dollars as a store of value, whereas others use it as a medium of exchange.

Federal Reserve notes make up more than 99 percent of all U.S. currency in circulation. Each year the Federal Reserve Board determines new currency demand and submits a print order to the Treasury's Bureau of Engraving and Printing (BEP). The order represents the Federal Reserve System's estimate of the amount of currency the public will need in the upcoming year and reflects estimated changes in currency usage and destruction rates of unfit currency. Exhibit 15.2 on the next page shows how long we can expect our money to last on average.

Demand deposits consist of money kept in checking accounts that can be withdrawn by depositors on demand. Demand deposits include regular checking accounts as well as interest-bearing and other special types of checking accounts. **Time deposits** are deposits at a bank or other financial institution that pay interest but cannot be withdrawn on demand. Examples are certain savings accounts, money market deposit accounts, and certificates of deposit. Economists use two terms to report on and discuss trends in the U.S. monetary system: M1 and M2. **M1** (the M stands for money) is used to describe the total amount of readily available money in the system and includes currency and demand deposits. As of December 2007, the M1 monetary supply was $1.4 trillion. **M2** includes all M1

CONCEPT in action

© AP Images/Ross D. Franklin

The housing market, which sizzled in the low-interest economic climate following 9/11, froze in subsequent years, sending chills throughout the U.S. economy. During the boom, lenders began extending credit to high-risk "subprime" borrowers, often at low introductory teaser rates that later adjusted upward significantly. Inevitable payment defaults by these borrowers led to record numbers of foreclosures, a glut of home sales, and a credit crunch that sent lending giants like American Home Mortgage into bankruptcy. How does a housing crisis affect other sectors of the economy?

currency
Cash held in the form of coins and paper money.

demand deposits
Money kept in checking accounts that can be withdrawn by depositors on demand.

time deposits
Deposits at a bank or other financial institution that pay interest but cannot be withdrawn on demand.

M1
The total amount of readily available money in the system and includes currency and demand deposits.

M2
A term used by economists to describe the U.S. monetary supply. Includes all M1 monies plus time deposits and other money that are not immediately accessible.

Have you ever wondered how quickly money wears out from being handled or damaged? Not surprisingly, smaller denominations have a shorter life span.

$1 bill	21 months
$5 bill	16 months
$10 bill	18 months
$20 bill	24 months
$50 bill	4.6 years
$100 bill	8.5 years
coins	25 years

Source: "Money Facts," Bureau of Engraving and Printing, **http://www.moneyfactory.gov**, May 9, 2008.

monies plus time deposits and other money that is not immediately accessible. In December 2007, the M2 monetary supply was $7.5 trillion.[3]

CONCEPT check

What is money, and what are its characteristics?

What are the main functions of money?

What are the three main components of the U.S. money supply? How do they relate to M1 and M2?

Credit cards, sometimes referred to as "plastic money," are routinely used as a substitute for cash and checks. Credit cards are not money; they are a form of borrowing. When a bank issues a credit card to a consumer, it gives a short-term loan to the consumer by directly paying the seller for the consumer's purchases. The consumer pays the credit card company after receiving the monthly statement. Credit cards do not replace money; they simply defer payment. U.S. consumers are currently deferring payment of $915 billion. That is, they hold $915 in credit card debt.[4]

The Federal Reserve System

2 How does the Federal Reserve manage the money supply?

CONCEPT in action

© Kevin Dietsch/UPI /Landov

In the two years prior to Ben Bernanke's appointment as Federal Reserve Chairman, the Federal Reserve raised interest rates more than a dozen consecutive times. The incoming chief initially tightened rates further to guard against inflation. But the Fed reversed course late in 2007, lowering the federal funds rate more than three percentage points over a nine-month period. Analysts viewed the abrupt policy shift as the Fed's attempt to avert an economic meltdown stemming from the national banking crisis. How do interest rates affect economic activity?

Before the twentieth century, there was very little government regulation of the U.S. financial or monetary systems. In 1907, however, several large banks failed, creating a public panic that led worried depositors to withdraw their money from other banks. Soon, many other banks had failed and the U.S. banking system was near collapse. The panic of 1907 was so severe that Congress created the Federal Reserve System in 1913 to provide the nation with a more stable monetary and banking system.

The **Federal Reserve System** (commonly called the **Fed**) is the central bank of the United States. The Fed's primary mission is to oversee the nation's monetary and credit systems and to support the ongoing operation of America's private-banking system. The Fed's actions affect the interest rates banks charge businesses and consumers, help keep inflation under control, and ultimately stabilize the U.S. financial system. The Fed operates as an independent government entity. It derives its authority from Congress but its decisions do not have to be approved by the president, Congress, or any other government branch. However, Congress does periodically review the Fed's activities and the Fed must work within the economic framework established by the government.

The Fed consists of 12 district banks, each located in a major U.S. city and covering a specific geographic area. Exhibit 15.3 shows the 12 districts of the Federal Reserve. Each district has its own bank president who oversees operations within that district.

Originally, the Federal Reserve System was created to control the money supply, act as a borrowing source for banks, hold the deposits of member banks, and supervise banking practices. Its activities have since broadened, making it the most powerful financial institution in the United States. Today, four of the Federal Reserve System's most important responsibilities are carrying out monetary policy, setting rules on credit, distributing currency, and making check clearing easier.

Federal Reserve System (Fed)
The central bank of the United States; it consists of 12 district banks, each located in a major U.S. city.

Carrying Out Monetary Policy

The most important function of the Federal Reserve System is carrying out monetary policy. The Federal Open Market Committee (FOMC) is the Fed policy-making body that meets eight times a year to make monetary policy decisions. It uses its power to change the money supply in order to control

EXHIBIT 15.3   Federal Reserve Districts and Banks

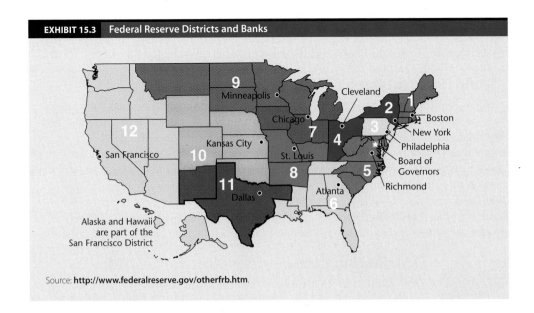

Source: **http://www.federalreserve.gov/otherfrb.htm**.

inflation and interest rates, increase employment, and influence economic activity. Three tools used by the Federal Reserve System in managing the money supply are open market operations, reserve requirements, and the discount rate. Exhibit 15.4 summarizes the short-term effects of these tools on the economy.

Open market operations—the tool most frequently used by the Federal Reserve—involve the purchase or sale of U.S. government bonds. The U.S. Treasury issues bonds to obtain the extra money needed to run the government (if taxes and other revenues aren't enough). In effect, treasury bonds are long-term loans (five years or longer) made by businesses and individuals to the government. The Federal Reserve buys and sells these bonds for the Treasury. When the Federal Reserve buys bonds, it puts money into the economy. Banks have more money to lend so they reduce interest rates, which generally stimulates economic activity. The opposite occurs when the Federal Reserve sells government bonds.

Banks that are members of the Federal Reserve System must hold some of their deposits in cash in their vaults or in an account at a district bank. This **reserve requirement** ranges from 3 to 10 percent on different types of deposits. When the Federal Reserve raises the reserve requirement, banks must hold larger reserves and thus have less money to lend. As a result, interest rates rise and economic activity slows down. Lowering the reserve requirement increases loanable funds, causes banks to lower interest rates, and stimulates the economy; however, the Federal Reserve seldom changes reserve requirements.

The Federal Reserve is called "the banker's bank" because it lends money to banks that need it. The interest rate that the Federal Reserve charges its member banks is called the **discount rate**. When the discount rate is less than the cost of other sources of funds (such as certificates of deposit), commercial banks borrow from the Federal Reserve and then lend the funds at a higher rate to customers. The banks profit from the *spread*, or difference, between the rate they charge

open market operations
The purchase or sale of U.S. government bonds by the Federal Reserve to stimulate or slow down the economy.

reserve requirement
Requires banks that are members of the Federal Reserve System to hold some of their deposits in cash in their vaults or in an account at a district bank.

discount rate
The interest rate that the Federal Reserve charges its member banks.

Tool	Action	Effect on Money Supply	Effect on Interest Rates	Effect on Economic Activity
Open market operations	Buy government bonds	Increases	Lowers	Stimulates
	Sell government bonds	Decreases	Raises	Slows Down
Reserve Requirements	Raise reserve requirements	Decreases	Raises	Slows Down
	Lower reserve requirements	Increases	Lowers	Stimulates
Discount Rate	Raise discount rate	Decreases	Raises	Slows Down
	Lower discount rate	Increases	Lowers	Stimulates

Chapter 15: Understanding Money and Financial Institutions

their customers and the rate paid to the Federal Reserve. Changes in the discount rate usually produce changes in the interest rate that banks charge their customers. The Federal Reserve raises the discount rate to slow down economic growth and lowers it to stimulate growth.

Setting Rules on Credit

selective credit controls
The power of the Federal Reserve to control consumer credit rules and margin requirements.

Another activity of the Federal Reserve System is setting rules on credit. It controls the credit terms on some loans made by banks and other lending institutions. This power, called **selective credit controls**, includes consumer credit rules and margin requirements. *Consumer credit rules* establish the minimum down payments and maximum repayment periods for consumer loans. The Federal Reserve uses credit rules to slow or stimulate consumer credit purchases. *Margin requirements* specify the minimum amount of cash an investor must put up to buy securities or investment certificates issued by corporations or governments. The balance of the purchase cost can be financed through borrowing from a bank or brokerage firm. By lowering the margin requirement, the Federal Reserve stimulates securities trading. Raising the margin requirement slows trading.

CONCEPT in action

© AP Images/US Mint

In 2007 the United States Mint unveiled a shiny new coin with an old familiar face. Timed for the arrival of President's Day, the President Washington $1 Coin began circulating as part of a congressional decision to create dollar coins with portraits of former U.S. presidents like John Adams shown above. The Statue of Liberty appears on the coin's reverse, along with the inscription "United States of America." Why does the Department of the Treasury produce dollar coins, which rarely catch on with the general public?

Distributing Currency: Keeping the Cash Flowing

The Federal Reserve distributes to banks the coins minted and the paper money printed by the U.S. Treasury. Most paper money is in the form of Federal Reserve notes. Look at a dollar bill and you'll see "Federal Reserve Note" at the top. The large letter seal on the left indicates which Federal Reserve Bank issued it. For example, bills bearing a *D* seal are issued by the Federal Reserve Bank of Cleveland, and those with an *L* seal are issued by the San Francisco district bank.

Making Check Clearing Easier

Another important activity of the Federal Reserve is processing and clearing checks between financial institutions. When a check is cashed at a financial institution other than the one holding the account on which the check is drawn, the Federal Reserve system lets that financial institution—even if distant from the institution holding the account on which the check is drawn—quickly convert the check into cash. Checks drawn on banks within the same Federal Reserve district are handled through the local Federal Reserve Bank using a series of bookkeeping entries to transfer funds between the financial institutions. The process is more complex for checks processed between different Federal Reserve districts.

The time between when the check is written and when the funds are deducted from the check writer's account provides float. Float benefits the check writer by allowing it to retain the funds until the check clears; that is, when the funds are actually withdrawn from its accounts. Businesses open accounts at banks around the country that are known to have long check-clearing times. By "playing the float," firms can keep their funds invested for several extra days, thus earning more money. To reduce this practice, in 1988 the Fed established maximum check-clearing times. However, as credit cards and other types of electronic payments have become more popular, the use of checks is declining. Responding to this decline, the Federal Reserve scaled back its check-processing facilities by closing five sites and cutting several hundred jobs. Although check volume continues to decline overall, the number of transactions paid by check is still around 30 billion per year.[5]

CONCEPT check

What are the four key responsibilities of the Federal Reserve System?

What three tools does the Federal Reserve System use to manage the money supply, and how does each affect economic activity?

U.S. Financial Institutions

3 What are the key financial institutions, and what role do they play in the process of financial intermediation?

The well-developed financial system in the United States supports our high standard of living. The system allows those who wish to borrow money to do so with relative ease. It also gives savers a variety of ways to earn interest on their savings. For example, a computer company that wants to build a new headquarters in Atlanta might be financed partly with the savings of families in California. The Californians deposit their money in a local financial institution. That institution looks for a profitable and safe way to use the money and decides to make a real estate loan to the computer company. The transfer of funds from savers to investors enables businesses to expand and the economy to grow.

Households are important participants in the U.S. financial system. Although many households borrow money to finance purchases, they supply funds to the financial system through their purchases and savings. Overall, businesses and governments are users of funds. They borrow more money than they save.

Sometimes those who have funds deal directly with those who want them. A wealthy realtor, for example, may lend money to a client to buy a house. Most often, financial institutions act as intermediaries—or go-betweens—between the suppliers and demanders of funds. The institutions accept savers' deposits and invest them in financial products (such as loans) that are expected to produce a return. This process, called **financial intermediation**, is shown in Exhibit 15.5. Households are shown as suppliers of funds, and businesses and governments are shown as demanders. However, a single household, business, or government can be either a supplier or a demander, depending on the circumstances.

Financial institutions are the heart of the financial system. They are a convenient vehicle for financial intermediation. They can be divided into two broad groups: depository institutions (those that accept deposits) and nondepository institutions (those that do not accept deposits).

Depository Financial Institutions

Not all depository financial institutions are alike. Most people call the place where they save their money a "bank." Some of those places are indeed banks, but other depository institutions include thrift institutions and credit unions.

financial intermediation
The process in which financial institutions act as intermediaries between the suppliers and demanders of funds.

CONCEPT in action

According to the U.S. Department of the Treasury, nearly three-fourths of senior citizens use direct deposit for receiving Social Security, SSI, and other federal benefits. Baby boomers are less comfortable with direct-deposit services, however, preferring standard paper deposits to their electronic counterpart. Banks promote the electronic transfer of funds because it eliminates paper and mail costs; seniors like the convenience and aren't fretting over cybercrime. Are electronic banking services the wave of the future?

EXHIBIT 15.5   The Financial Intermediation Process*

Financial intermediaries
Commercial banks
Savings and loan
  associations
Savings banks
Credit unions
Life insurance
  companies
Pension funds

Suppliers of funds
Households

$

Bank accounts
Life insurance
Retirement income

Demanders of funds
Businesses
Governments

$

Loans
Securities

*Only the dominant suppliers and demanders are shown here. Clearly, a single household, business, or government can be either a supplier or demander, depending on circumstances.

Commercial Banks

A **commercial bank** is a profit-oriented financial institution that accepts deposits, makes business and consumer loans, invests in government and corporate securities, and provides other financial services. Commercial banks vary greatly in size from the "money center" banks located in the nation's financial centers, to smaller regional and local community banks. As a result of consolidations, small banks are decreasing in number. A large share of the nation's banking business is now held by a relatively small number of big banks. There are 7,400 commercial banks in the United States, accounting for $10 trillion in assets and more than $9 trillion in total liabilities.[6] Banks hold a variety of assets, as shown in the diagram in Exhibit 15.6.

Exhibit 15.7 lists the top 10 insured U.S.-chartered commercial banks, based on their consolidated assets.

Customers' deposits are a commercial bank's major source of funds, the main use for which is loans. The difference between the interest the bank earns on loans and the interest it pays on deposits, plus fees it earns from other financial services, pays the bank's costs and provides a profit.

Commercial banks are corporations owned and operated by individuals or other corporations. They can be either national or state banks and to do business, they must get a **bank charter**—an operating license—from the federal or state government. *National banks* are chartered by the Comptroller of the Currency, who is part of the U.S. Treasury Department. These banks must belong

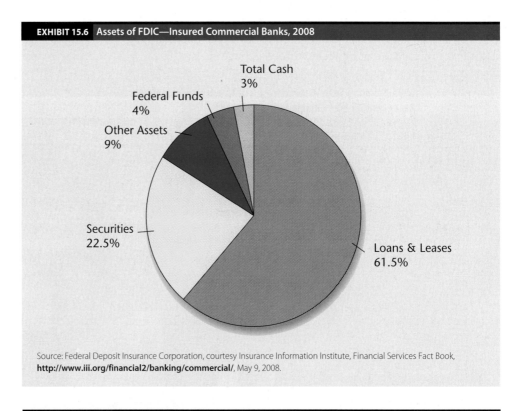

EXHIBIT 15.6 Assets of FDIC—Insured Commercial Banks, 2008

- Total Cash 3%
- Federal Funds 4%
- Other Assets 9%
- Securities 22.5%
- Loans & Leases 61.5%

Source: Federal Deposit Insurance Corporation, courtesy Insurance Information Institute, Financial Services Fact Book, **http://www.iii.org/financial2/banking/commercial/**, May 9, 2008.

EXHIBIT 15.7 Top 10 Insured U.S.-Chartered Commercial Banks, Based on Consolidated Assets, 2007

Bank	Consolidated Assets
1. J. P. Morgan Chase & Co.	$1,318,888,000
2. Bank of America Corp.	1,312,794,000
3. Citigroup, Inc.	1,251,715,000
4. Wachovia Corp.	653,269,000
5. Wells Fargo & Co.	467,861,000
6. U.S. Bancorp	232,760,000
7. HSBC Bank USA NA	184,493,000
8. SunTrust Bank Inc.	175,108,000
9. Bank of America Corp.	161,692,000
10. National City Corp.	138,755,000

Source: Federal Reserve Statistical Release, December 31, 2007 **http://www.federalreserve.gov**.

© Digital Vision/Getty Images

Who Gives Better Service—Big or Small Banks?

Customer satisfaction is critical because it holds the key to increased deposits. According to a J.D. Power and Associates survey, a bank with 1 million customers could generate an additional $1 billion in deposits with only a slight increase in the number of customers shifting from being moderately to highly committed to their bank. That accounts for the interest banks take in the results of the annual surveys conducted by the American Customer Satisfaction Institute (ACSI) at the University of Michigan and J.D. Power and Associates to determine how satisfied consumers are with their banks. ACSI surveys roughly 18,000 customers who bank at one of about 190 institutions and then identifies the best performers and how the industry is perceived overall. ACSI surveys about 250 customers at each of the 190 banks on its list. By contrast, J.D. Power surveys individual households (20,898 of them in 2007) about their experiences with their primary banking provider and then identifies the banks that provide the best service.

In 2007, J.D. Power's survey showed winners by region: Commerce Banc (Midatlantic); Bank of America (Southeast); Woodforest National Bank (Southwest); and Washington Mutual (Midwest and West Pacific regions). Even though ACSI looks at 190 banks, it only discloses the details on the top biggest banks on its list. For 2007, those were Wachovia, J.P. Morgan Chase, Bank of America, Citibank, and Wells Fargo. Wachovia is usually the leader, and it was again in 2007. How does Wachovia stay on top year after year?

One way is by looking at best practices in nonbanking industries. That is, managers at Wachovia research how hotels, car rentals, retailers, and other industries improve customer service. "We are always looking at how others might do it differently or better," says Andrea Bierce, director of customer experience and loyalty at Wachovia. In addition, the different divisions at Wachovia share their internal best practices. The wealth management division recently implemented a 14-step process for new customers, which includes things like calling the customers 60 days after they sign up for Wachovia's services to inquire about their satisfaction. The 14-step procedure for new clients may be adopted by the general banking division for all new Wachovia customers.

Other banks use different methods to improve their customer satisfaction. Citibank introduced electronic kiosks in all of its branches to survey customer experiences. The company received over 60,000 responses the first year the kiosks were in place.

Even though ACSI reports details on only the biggest of the banks in its surveys, it is the smaller community banks that have the highest customer satisfaction, according to J.D. Power's survey. Craig Buford, the president and CEO of the Community Bankers Association of Oklahoma, attributes that to the fact that smaller banks know their customers better. He says, "You see the mega-banks coming in, and it's not that they don't have good people working for them, but our community banks know those customers and take a personal interest in them. They're in Rotary club with them, in church with them—those bankers live in that community."[7]

Critical Thinking Questions:

- What kind of services could a bank offer to increase customer satisfaction? Are some services more feasible for large banks? Smaller banks?
- What role do you think self-service banking (ATMs, online and mobile banking, kiosks, etc.) plays in customer satisfaction?

---

to the Federal Reserve System and must carry insurance on their deposits from the Federal Deposit Insurance Corporation. *State banks* are chartered by the state in which they are based. Generally, state banks are smaller than national banks, are less closely regulated than national banks, and are not required to belong to the Federal Reserve System. The Customer Satisfaction and Quality box above describes some of what it takes for banks to keep their customers happy and attract new ones.

Thrift Institutions A **thrift institution** is a depository institution formed specifically to encourage household saving and to make home mortgage loans. Thrift institutions include *savings and loan associations (S&Ls)* and *savings banks*. S&Ls keep large percentages of their assets in home mortgages. Compared with S&Ls, savings banks focus less on mortgage loans and more on stock and bond investments. Thrifts are declining in number. At their peak in the late 1960s, there were more than 4,800. But a combination of factors has reduced their ranks significantly, including sharp increases in interest rates in the late 1970s and increased loan defaults during the recession of the early 1980s. An early 2008 report by the Office of Thrift Supervision, which is a division of the Department of the Treasury, reported that there were only 826 regulated thrifts in the United States at the end of 2007.[8]

thrift institutions
Depository institutions formed specifically to encourage household saving and to make home mortgage loans.

Credit Unions A **credit union** is a not-for-profit, member-owned financial cooperative. Credit union members typically have something in common: they may, for example, work for the same employer, belong to the same union or professional group, or attend the same church or school. The credit union pools their assets, or savings, in order to make loans and offer other services to members. The not-for-profit status of credit unions makes them tax-exempt, so they can pay good interest rates on deposits and offer loans at favorable interest rates. Like banks, credit unions can have either a federal or state charter.

credit unions
Not-for-profit, member-owned financial cooperatives.

The 8,266 credit unions in the United States have nearly 89 million members and roughly $770 billion in assets.[9] The five largest credit unions in the United States are shown in Exhibit 15.8 on the next page. However, recent data from the Credit Union National Association (CUNA) economic

EXHIBIT 15.8	Five Largest U.S. Credit Unions

1. Navy Federal Credit Union, Merrifield, Virginia
2. State Employees' Credit Union, Raleigh, North Carolina
3. Pentagon Federal Credit Union, Alexandria, Virginia
4. Boeing Employees Credit Union, Tukwila, Washington
5. SchoolsFirst Federal Credit Union, Santa Ana, California

Source: NCUA and CUNA E & S, **http://webapps.ncua.gov/customquery/**, May 12, 2008.

forecast indicate that even though credit union savings growth is expected to rise through 2008, credit union loan growth is expected to have the lowest growth rate in decades. A slowing economy, falling consumer confidence, higher underwriting standards, and falling consumer demand will reduce members' demand for loans.[10]

Services Offered Commercial banks, thrift institutions, and credit unions offer a wide range of financial services for consumers and businesses. Typical services offered by depository financial institutions are listed in Exhibit 15.9. Some financial institutions specialize in providing financial services to a particular type of customer, such as consumer banking services or business banking services. Online banking is an increasingly popular bank service. According to a Gartner survey conducted in 2008, 71 million Americans used online banking, indicating that online banking has transitioned into being adopted by the mainstream.[11]

Nondepository Financial Institutions

Some financial institutions provide certain banking services but do not accept deposits. These nondepository financial institutions include insurance companies, pension funds, brokerage firms, and finance companies. They serve both individuals and businesses.

EXHIBIT 15.9	Services Offered by Depository Financial Institutions
Service	**Description**
Savings accounts	Pay interest on deposits
Checking accounts	Allow depositors to withdraw any amount of funds at any time up to the amount on deposit
Money market deposit accounts	Savings accounts on which the interest rate is set at market rates
Certificates of deposit (CDs)	Pay a higher interest rate than regular savings accounts, provided that the deposit remains for a specified period
Consumer loans	Loans to individuals to finance the purchase of a home, car, or other expensive items
Business loans	Loans to businesses and other organizations to finance their operations
Money transfer	Transfer of funds to other banks
Electronic funds transfer	Use of telephone lines and computers to conduct financial transactions
Automated teller machine (ATM)	Allows bank customers to make deposits and withdrawals from their accounts 24 hours a day
Debit cards	Allow customers to transfer money from their bank account directly to a merchant's account to pay for purchases
Smart card	Card that stores monetary value and can be used to buy goods and services instead of using cash, checks, and credit and debit cards
Online banking	Allows customers to conduct financial transactions via the Internet

Insurance Companies Insurance companies are major suppliers of funds. Policyholders make payments (called *premiums*) to the insurance company to buy financial protection. Insurance companies invest the premiums in stocks, bonds, real estate, business loans, and real estate loans for large projects. The insurance industry is discussed in detail in the Online Appendix called "Managing Risk and Insurance" at **www.cengage.com/introbusiness/gitman**.

Pension Funds Corporations, unions, and governments set aside large pools of money for later use in paying retirement benefits to their employees or members. These **pension funds** are managed by the employers or unions themselves or by outside managers, such as life insurance firms, commercial banks, and private investment firms. Pension plan members receive a specified monthly payment when they reach a given age. After setting aside enough money to pay near-term benefits, pension funds invest the rest in business loans, stocks, bonds, or real estate. They often invest large sums in the stock of the employer. U.S. pension fund assets, including both private and state and local government employee retirement funds, comprise nearly $10.8 trillion of total retirement assets. Of that total, about $4.9 trillion are private pension funds.[12]

Brokerage Firms A *brokerage firm* buys and sells securities (stocks and bonds) for its clients and gives them related advice. Many brokerage firms offer some banking services. They may offer clients a combined checking and savings account with a high interest rate and also make loans, backed by securities, to them. Chapter 16 explains the activities of brokerage firms in more detail.

Finance Companies A *finance company* makes short-term loans for which the borrower puts up tangible assets (such as an automobile, inventory, machinery, or property) as security. Finance companies often make loans to individuals or businesses that cannot get credit elsewhere. Promising new businesses with no track record and firms that can't get more credit from a bank often obtain loans from *commercial finance companies. Consumer finance companies* make loans to individuals, often to cover the lease or purchase of large consumer goods such as automobiles or major household appliances. To compensate for the extra risk, finance companies usually charge higher interest rates than banks. Read the Catching the Entrepreneurial Spirit box on the next page to learn about a new type of lender that commercializes loans between friends and family.

Insurance companies hurt by billions of dollars in unforeseen payouts are rethinking their reliance on catastrophe-risk modelers, whose risk estimates failed to anticipate cataclysmic storms like Hurricane Katrina. Catastrophe-risk businesses forecast potential weather-related expenses for insurers through sophisticated computer models that analyze historical meteorological data. Inaccurate modeling has led to massive losses for insurers like Allstate. How do frequent natural disasters affect insurance companies and their policyholders?

© AP Images/Reed Saxon

pension funds
Large pools of money set aside by corporations, unions, and governments for later use in paying retirement benefits to their employees or members.

CONCEPT check

What is the financial intermediation process?

Differentiate between the three types of depository financial institutions and the services they offer.

What are the four main types of nondepository financial institutions?

Insuring Bank Deposits

The U.S. banking system worked fairly well from when the Federal Reserve System was established in 1913 until the stock market crash of 1929 and the Great Depression that followed. Business failures caused by these events resulted in major cash shortages as people rushed to withdraw their money from banks. Many cash-starved banks failed because the Federal Reserve did not, as expected, lend money to them. The government's efforts to prevent bank failures were ineffective. Over the next two years, 5,000 banks—about 20 percent of the total number—failed.

President Franklin D. Roosevelt made strengthening the banking system his first priority. After taking office in 1933, Roosevelt declared a bank holiday, closing all banks for a week so he could take corrective action. Congress passed the Banking Act of 1933, which empowered the Federal Reserve System to regulate banks and reform the banking system. The act's most important provision was the creation of the **Federal Deposit Insurance Corporation (FDIC)** to insure deposits in commercial banks. The 1933 act also gave the Federal Reserve authority to set reserve requirements, ban interest on demand deposits, regulate the interest rates on time deposits, and prohibit banks from investing in specified types of securities. In 1934 the Federal Savings and Loan Insurance Corporation (FSLIC) was formed to insure deposits at S&Ls. When the FSLIC went bankrupt in the 1980s, the FDIC took over responsibility for administering the fund that insures deposits at thrift institutions.

4 How does the Federal Deposit Insurance Corporation (FDIC) protect depositors' funds?

Federal Deposit Insurance Corporation (FDIC)
An independent, quasi-public corporation backed by the full faith and credit of the U.S. government that insures deposits in commercial banks and thrift institutions for up to a ceiling of $100,000 per account.

Easy Money between Family and Friends

Billionaire and perennial entrepreneur Richard Branson knows what it means to start small. His first two attempts at starting a business involved selling Christmas trees and raising parakeets. Both failed. Then he quit school, started a magazine, and began selling records out of the trunk of his car. From that came a record store, then a record label, then the signing of a block-buster recording act, the Sex Pistols. Virgin is now the name of a variety of companies, from airlines to a cell phone service provider to bridal gowns. One of the latest entries in the Virgin family is Virgin Money.

Going from Christmas tree seller to record mogul took some money. Richard Branson borrowed thousands of pounds from his mother, and recognizing that family and friends are often major lenders in any entrepreneurial venture, Branson launched a company specifically designed to facilitate those personal loans. Although in other countries, Virgin Money offers a full range of banking products, its operations in the United States are starting small (like Branson did) and focusing only on lending services.

Technically, Virgin Money organizes and administers private loans. CEO of Virgin Money USA, Asheesh Advani, explains it this way: "Your mom would give you the money, and we would document it and manage all the payments. All the money would flow on a monthly or quarterly basis and be managed just like a car loan. It saves the borrower money, and keeps the money in the family." Virgin Money, then, simply handles all the administrative elements of the transaction: repayment plans,

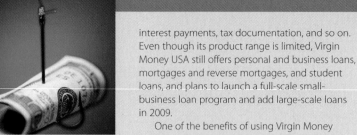

interest payments, tax documentation, and so on. Even though its product range is limited, Virgin Money USA still offers personal and business loans, mortgages and reverse mortgages, and student loans, and plans to launch a full-scale small-business loan program and add large-scale loans in 2009.

One of the benefits of using Virgin Money as a broker in loan transactions between friends and family members is that the loan default rate decreases to 5 percent from 14 percent. Formalizing the transaction also allows the borrower to build good credit even while borrowing from a friendly lender (for example, parents). Once the borrower's good credit is established, Virgin Money will match business loans and provide entrepreneurs with another way to build credit and secure funding for their startup.[13]

Critical Thinking Questions:
- Is Virgin Money a depository or a nondepository financial institution? Explain.
- If you were an entrepreneur, would you be more inclined to use Virgin Money to broker a family loan, just ask your parents to invest, or max out your credit cards as a means of securing capital to start your business?

Today, the major deposit insurance funds include the following:

- *The Bank Insurance Fund (BIF).* Administered by the FDIC, this fund provides deposit insurance to commercial banks.
- *The Savings Association Insurance Fund (SAIF).* Administered by the FDIC, this fund provides deposit insurance to thrift institutions.
- *The National Credit Union Share Insurance Fund.* Administered by the National Credit Union Administration, this fund provides deposit insurance to credit unions.

Role of the FDIC

The FDIC is an independent, quasi-public corporation backed by the full faith and credit of the U.S. government. It examines and supervises about 5,250 banks and savings banks, more than half the institutions in the banking system. It insures about $3 trillion of deposits in U.S. banks and thrift institutions against loss if the financial institution fails.[14] The FDIC insures all member banks in the Federal Reserve System. The ceiling on insured deposits is $100,000 per account. Each insured bank pays the insurance premiums, which are a fixed percentage of the bank's domestic deposits. In 1993, the FDIC switched from a flat rate for deposit insurance to a risk-based premium system because of the large number of bank and thrift failures during the 1980s and early 1990s. Some experts argue that certain banks take too much risk because they view deposit insurance as a safety net for their depositors—a view many believe contributed to earlier bank failures.

While essential to global business, the international banking system is subject to economic and political uncertainties. In 2008, number-two French bank Société Générale sent shockwaves through global financial markets by disclosing a massive fraud. A junior employee in the company's Corporate and Investment Banking Division squandered $7.1 billion of the bank's money through a series of bogus futures trades. This largest-ever fraud case forced the bank to seek emergency financing from other world banks to cover the lost sum. What are the benefits and risks of international banking?

Enforcement by the FDIC

To ensure that banks operate fairly and profitably, the FDIC sets guidelines for banks and then reviews the financial records and management practices of member banks at least once a year. Bank examiners perform these reviews during unannounced visits, rating banks on their compliance with banking regulations (for example, the Equal Credit Opportunity Act, which states that a bank cannot refuse to lend money to people because of their color, religion, or national origin). Examiners also rate a bank's overall financial condition, focusing on loan quality, management practices, earnings, liquidity, and whether the bank has enough capital (equity) to safely support its activities.

When bank examiners conclude that a bank has serious financial problems, the FDIC can take several actions. It can lend money to the bank, recommend that the bank merge with a stronger bank, require the bank to use new management practices or replace its managers, buy loans from the bank, or provide extra equity capital to the bank. The FDIC may even cover all deposits at a troubled bank, including those over $100,000, to restore the public's confidence in the financial system.

International Banking

The financial marketplace spans the globe, with money routinely flowing across international borders. U.S. banks play an important role in global business by providing loans to foreign businesses and governments. Multinational corporations need many special banking services, such as foreign-currency exchange and funding for overseas investments. U.S. banks also offer trade-related services, like global cash management, that help firms manage their cash flows, improve their payment efficiency, and reduce their exposure to operational risks. Sometimes consumers in other nations have a need for banking services that banks in their own countries don't provide. Therefore, large banks often look beyond their national borders for profitable banking opportunities.

Many U.S. banks have expanded into overseas markets by opening offices in Europe, Latin America, and Asia. They often provide better customer service than local banks and have access to more sources of funding. Citibank, for example, was the first bank to offer banking-by-phone and 24-hour-a-day ATM service in Japan. It earns approximately 50 percent of its net income from operations outside North America.[15] The Expanding Around the Globe box on the next page illustrates how Wal-Mart entered the international banking industry after its efforts to enter the U.S. banking industry were endlessly rejected by multiple constituencies.

For U.S. banks, expanding internationally can be difficult. Banks in other nations are often subject to fewer regulations than U.S. banks, making it easier for them to undercut American banks on the pricing of loans and services. Some governments also protect their banks against foreign competition. The Chinese government imposes high fees and limits the amount of deposits that foreign banks can accept from customers. It also controls foreign-bank deposit and loan interest rates, limiting the ability of foreign banks to compete with government-owned Chinese banks.

U.S. banks aren't alone in extending their presence abroad. At the end of 2007, the Federal Reserve counted banks from 60 countries conducting banking operations inside the United States. International banks operating within the U.S. have a substantial impact on the economy through job creation (they employ more than 250,000 people in the U.S. and over 90 percent of them are U.S. citizens), operating and capital expenditures, taxes, and other contributions.[16] According to September 2007 Federal Reserve data, the combined banking and non-banking assets of the U.S. operations of international banks totaled $5.7 trillion.[17]

The United States has three banks listed in the top 10 world's biggest banks as shown in Exhibit 15.10.

5 What role do U.S. banks play in the international marketplace?

CONCEPT in action

While world banks play a central role in global economic development, they also play a part in global counterterrorism. The Society for Worldwide Interbank Financial Telecommunication (SWIFT), an international banking cooperative that oversees financial transactions in more than 200 countries, began monitoring the wire transfers of suspected terrorists after 9/11. SWIFT's financial surveillance, in coordination with U.S. Treasury Department initiatives, has led to the interruption of terror networks worldwide. Why do world banks have an interest in combating terrorism?

© iStockphoto.com/Ilya Genkin

EXHIBIT 15.10	The World's Biggest Banks, 2007
Citigroup	United States
Bank of America	United States
Industrial and Commercial Bank of China	China
HSBC	United Kingdom
J.P. Morgan Chase	United States
Bank of China	China
China Construction Bank	China
UBS	Switzerland
Royal Bank of Scotland	Scotland
Mitsubishi UFJ Financial Group	Japan

Source: "The World's Biggest Banks 2007," *CBC Canada*, **http://www.cbc.ca/news/interactives/who-top10-banks/** May 12, 2008.

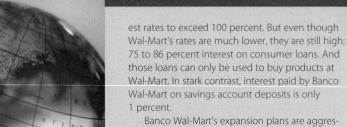

Wal-Mart Finally Gets Approval to Open a Bank, but It's in Mexico

After spending years trying to win approval to begin operating banks in the United States, Wal-Mart gave up in 2007. It pulled its application after staunch opposition from domestic retail banks, unions, grocery store owners, and both Republicans and Democrats in Congress. Even then-Federal Reserve Chairman Alan Greenspan was opposed. Although Wal-Mart abandoned, even if only temporarily, its desire to enter the U.S. banking business, it didn't give up on banking altogether. It just went to Mexico.

Every day 2.5 million people shop at a Wal-Mart in Mexico, and now those people, along with the company's 155,000 employees and 12,000 Mexican suppliers, are potential customers of Banco Wal-Mart. Roughly 44 million medium- and low-income Mexicans are considered unbanked (don't use banks) and make up the core target market for Banco Wal-Mart. "What you find in Mexico is the type of people who shop [at Wal-Mart] often don't have the regular checking accounts," says Refugio Rochin, a professor of Chicana/Chicano studies and an economist at the University of California at Davis. In fact, only 24 percent of Mexican households have a savings account. Early information indicates Banco Wal-Mart is indeed reaching the 76 percent of Mexicans without a savings account: according to the manager at the first Banco Wal-Mart, 40 percent of the new savings account clients have never had a savings account before.

Different from the chilly reception it received in the United States, Wal-Mart has been warmly supported in Mexico. The president of Mexico's central bank credits the mega-retailer with helping drive inflation to the low single digits. And Mexican regulators hope Wal-Mart can bring competition to the banking sector, which drives down the cost of consumer credit. Currently, it's common for annual consumer inter-

est rates to exceed 100 percent. But even though Wal-Mart's rates are much lower, they are still high: 75 to 86 percent interest on consumer loans. And those loans can only be used to buy products at Wal-Mart. In stark contrast, interest paid by Banco Wal-Mart on savings account deposits is only 1 percent.

Banco Wal-Mart's expansion plans are aggressive. In a country that averages only eight bank branches for 100,000 people, Wal-Mart is planning to put a Banco Wal-Mart in 1 out of 10 of its nearly 1,000 Mexican stores. With a more favorable regulatory environment than the one in its home country, combined with new Mexican legislation that makes it easier for low-income consumers to open bank accounts, Wal-Mart sees tremendous opportunity to offer banking services to its unbanked store customers. That strategy must be attractive: other international banks like Britain's HSBC are also looking into it.[18]

Critical Thinking Questions

- Why do you think U.S. regulators and other stakeholders were so vehemently opposed to Wal-Mart opening a bank?
- Were Banco Wal-Mart to offer low interest rates on consumer loans (along the lines of American rates), what do you think the impact would be on its stores? On the Mexican banking system? On the Mexican economy overall?

Political and economic uncertainty in other countries can make international banking a high-risk venture. In the late 1990s, for example, Asian banks underwrote loans to finance highly speculative real estate ventures and corporate expansions that fueled booming economies in several Pacific Rim countries, which attracted many foreign investors. The bank loans and foreign investments made the balance sheets of the Asian banks and their customers look better than they actually were, which encouraged United States, German, French, and other European banks to make billions of dollars worth of loans to Thailand, Indonesia, Malaysia, and Korea. When investors started taking their money out of the Asian banks, the banks' assets plummeted, forcing currency devaluations. The situation severely injured the economies of several Asian countries, resulting in high inflation and deep debt. Lacking capital, Asian banks could not get loans to conduct business, and companies couldn't get loans to finance the production and export of their products. The crisis also hurt many U.S. banks.

CONCEPT check

What is the role of U.S. banks in international banking?

What challenges do U.S. banks face in foreign markets?

Trends in Financial Institutions

6 What trends are reshaping financial institutions?

After a dismal 2007, during which lenders lost tremendous value after being forced to write down defaulted mortgage loans, what factors will influence financial institutions in the years ahead? Technology will continue to create trends in banking, from online and mobile banking options for consumers to electronic payment and deposit options for businesses. One of the hottest trends in financial institutions is microlending, also called microfinance, which involves nontraditional loans of small sums to people who otherwise couldn't get a loan. These and other banking trends are illustrated in Exhibit 15.11.

Direct Banking

When the Internet was primarily accessible through dial-up modems and broadband was in its infancy, many banks pursued online banking, or offering customers access to their accounts through

EXHIBIT 15.11   Top 10 Banking Industry Trends in 2007

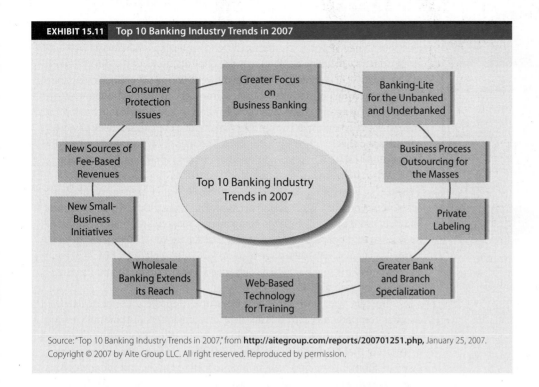

Top 10 Banking Industry Trends in 2007

- Consumer Protection Issues
- Greater Focus on Business Banking
- Banking-Lite for the Unbanked and Underbanked
- New Sources of Fee-Based Revenues
- Business Process Outsourcing for the Masses
- New Small-Business Initiatives
- Private Labeling
- Wholesale Banking Extends its Reach
- Web-Based Technology for Training
- Greater Bank and Branch Specialization

the Internet. Because connections were slow and the value unclear, many banks abandoned online banking. Some banks even failed as a result of their attempts at online banking.

Not so today. With nearly universal access to broadband, not only are traditional banks aggressively adding online capabilities to their services, some banks are going direct with no–or nearly no–branches. Called *direct banking*, this model gives customers access to their accounts on a 24-hour basis (no more banking hours) and tends to pay higher yields on savings accounts. Even though banks still rely heavily on the traditional banking model, the direct model is gaining traction. One of the pioneers in direct banking is ING Direct, which boasts more than $60 billion in deposits.[19]

The nearly exclusively online bank had little competition when it started in the United States several years ago, but today it faces a wave of competition, not only from other online banks (like HSBC Direct, EmigrantDirect), but now from insurance companies (MetLife) and brokerage firms (eTrade, Univest, Charles Schwab).[20] Even though only 40 percent of U.S. households take advantage of online banking, its popularity is expected to continue growing and online deposits to swell to $377 billion by 2010.[21]

Direct and online banking present significant challenges to the traditional banks. That's because hybrid banks, those that offer both physical branches and robust online-banking options, may be their own toughest competition. For example, within the first year of starting CitiDirect, Citi amassed $11 billion in deposits, or the equivalent of opening 150 branches. Unfortunately, roughly 20 percent of CitiDirect's deposits have come from its existing customers.[22] Washington Mutual announced it would close 4 percent of its branches because it had been so successful gathering deposits online.[23]

Mobile Banking

Although in its early stages, banking through mobile devices is a trend to watch. The year 2007 saw the introduction of significant numbers of mobile banking and payment applications, but unfortunately for the companies that funded these products, mobile banking continues to be attractive to only a small segment of the market: the young and already mobile-savvy. This market does count millions of members, but overall it represents only a fraction of the mass market. Many of the mobile-banking products unveiled in 2007 failed because they didn't offer a compelling reason for those not "into" cell phones to begin using them for banking. Nonetheless, as cell phones evolve into personal computing devices, mobile banking may be adopted on a large scale.[24]

For the millions of consumers who can't live without their BlackBerrys, RAZRs, iPhones, and other mobile communication devices, banks now offer services that make paying bills and transferring cash possible on the go. Fast-growing mobile banking services keep customers connected to their finances anytime, anywhere—with only a handset. Despite the early success of mobile banking, many customers worry that cybercriminals could hack online systems and empty accounts in seconds. What can banks do to ease consumer fears about cybercrime?

Operational Technologies

Electronic-banking options represent a trend for business bankers as well. Just as consumers use online banking to make deposits (think of the direct deposit of your paycheck) and pay bills (like paying your phone bill online), companies use similar technologies to affect business transactions. Throughout the history of business, companies have received payments for their services in the form of checks. The accountant or comptroller makes out a deposit slip daily or weekly and takes the check and the slip to the bank. The majority of business transactions still occur this way, but a growing trend in this area is remote deposit capture (RDC). When Company A pays Company B using RDC, Company B never receives a check. The payment is transferred electronically from Company A's checking account to Company B's checking account. This technology, which previously had been used primarily by large companies, is gaining acceptance with small businesses and home-based businesses (SOHO). By 2007, 10 percent of small businesses and SOHOs were already using RDC or had plans to, but 50 percent were aware of the technology, causing analysts to anticipate sharp increases in the adoption rate of RDC.

Generally speaking, for every electronic deposit a company makes, another company has sent out an electronic payment. Automated clearing house (ACH) payments are also growing in popularity. For example, consider a magazine that contracts with a freelance writer. Because the writer travels a lot on assignment, she may have trouble collecting checks and taking deposits to the bank in a timely fashion. Her clients could pay her using ACH. The client essentially sends an e-check that is received like a direct deposit in the writer's checking account. As with RDC, large companies have been the largest adopters of ACH, but 10 percent of small businesses and SOHOs have as well. (Keep in mind that a single percentage point represents hundreds of thousands of small businesses, so even though the percentage seems small, it is a slice of a pie comprising millions of businesses.) Even though checks still dominate the payment landscape, e-payments and deposits are trends that over time are likely to become common practice in business banking. It's just a question of when.[25]

Microlending

Arguably the hottest trend in banking comes from outside traditional financial institutions: microlending. When Maria Guadalupe Licona of Mexico needed money to expand her herd, she borrowed $100 from a microlender to purchase additional sheep and pigs. In additional to repaying the principal, Licona would pay 40 percent interest.[26] Although that rate might sound usurious, microfinance interest rates typically reach as high as 85 percent, which is still a bargain compared to the alternatives (a village money lender who charges three times as much). The size of microloans varies. In India the average is $100, but in Bolivia, the average microloan is $1,530.[27]

The concept of making miniscule loans to small businesses in poor countries started more than 30 years ago when Muhammad Yunus started Grameen Bank in Bangladesh. (Grameen had $521 million in outstanding loans in 2008.) Today, there are over 12,000 microfinance institutions issuing loans.[28] In developed nations, the microfinance phenomenon has been translated into peer-to-peer lending (P2P) networks. In addition to small businesses seeking loans, borrowers may ask for a loan to pay for a vacation, college tuition, or surgeries.

Different from regulated institutions, peer-to-peer networks like Prosper, Zopa, and LoanBack connect individuals who need loans, sometimes as small as $50, with individuals willing to make small loans for interest. (Virgin Money USA, discussed previously, is also a P2P microlender.) Both parties bypass the traditional banks and each gets better rates: lenders get a better rate of return, and borrowers get a better rate than if they had borrowed from a bank. Even though traditional financial institutions may dismiss P2P lending as a fad, the growth of P2P networks is too fast and substantial to ignore. Prosper's loan volume reached $130 million in 2008 after only a few years in business, and because Prosper is a microlender, that sum represents millions of individual loans. Experts anticipate that P2P microlending loans will hit $9 billion by 2017.[29]

The P2P phenomenon has revealed gaps in the product and service offerings of traditional banks. Borrowers want more say regarding the terms and conditions of their loans. They want more flexible products, better pricing, and longer terms. Going forward, traditional banks may find it more advantageous to watch clear market segments emerge (as happens in P2P lending) rather than trying to name them and then find them.[30]

Dirty Money—New Focus on Money Laundering

In today's world of international terrorism and the relatively easy and "invisible" electronic transfer of funds, the current focus on money laundering is here to stay says Boston, Massachusetts–based Aite Group, which anticipates increased emphasis on *money laundering* compliance. The International Monetary Fund (IMF) estimates that money laundering, the process drug traffickers use to introduce proceeds gained from the sale or distribution of controlled substances into the legitimate financial market, amounts to between 2 and 5 percent of the world's gross domestic product, or about $600 billion annually.[31] The potential impact of money laundering on firms and individuals on a global, economic, and social scale makes analyzing the stream of funds moving in and out of financial institutions an ongoing priority.

Money laundering allows the true source of the funds gained through the sale and distribution of drugs to be concealed and converts the funds into assets that appear to have a legitimate legal source. Tracking and intercepting the illegal flow of drug money is an important tool to identify and dismantle international drug-trafficking organizations. Regulators are continuously checking that criminals are not using financial products for objectives other than those for which they were meant. The Financial Action Task Force (FATF) is an intergovernmental body that develops and promotes national and international policies to combat money laundering and terrorist financing. It is responsible for legislative and regulatory reform.

"There is universal agreement that the fight against money laundering will be a priority from here on out," says Eva Weber, an Aite Group analyst. "Institutions should be asking themselves the same questions that regulators are asking: Am I consistently applying anti-money laundering [AML] policies and procedures? Are those policies and procedures appropriate to the risks my business faces? Can I demonstrate compliance fairly readily?"

AML vendors are offering improved technology in response to financial firms' requirements. Key AML functions are list checking, transaction monitoring, and reporting. Weber observes that there is no "right" answer when it comes to preventing money laundering. "Regulators are unlikely to penalize institutions for isolated oversights, as long as those institutions have given appropriate thought to their anti-money laundering programs."[32]

Summary of Learning Goals

Money is anything accepted as payment for goods and services. For money to be a suitable means of exchange, it should be scarce, durable, portable, and divisible. Money functions as a medium of exchange, a standard of value, and a store of value. The U.S. money supply consists of currency (coins and paper money), demand deposits (checking accounts), and time deposits (interest-bearing deposits that cannot be withdrawn on demand).

1 What is money, what are its characteristics and functions, and what are the three parts of the U.S. money supply?

The Federal Reserve System (the Fed) is an independent government agency that performs four main functions: carrying out monetary policy, setting rules on credit, distributing currency, and making check clearing easier. The three tools it uses in managing the money supply are open market operations, reserve requirements, and the discount rate.

2 How does the Federal Reserve manage the money supply?

Financial institutions can be divided into two main groups: depository institutions and nondepository institutions. Depository institutions include commercial banks, thrift institutions, and credit unions. Nondepository institutions include insurance companies, pension funds, brokerage firms, and finance companies. Financial institutions ease the transfer of funds between suppliers and demanders of funds.

3 What are the key financial institutions, and what role do they play in the process of financial intermediation?

The Federal Deposit Insurance Corporation insures deposits in commercial banks through the Bank Insurance Fund and deposits in thrift institutions through the Savings Association Insurance Fund. Deposits in credit unions are insured by the National Credit Union Share Insurance Fund, which is administered by the National Credit Union Administration. The FDIC sets banking policies and practices and reviews banks annually to ensure that they operate fairly and profitably.

U.S. banks provide loans and trade-related services to foreign businesses and governments. They also offer specialized services such as cash management and foreign-currency exchange.

Various economic and social factors mean banks face challenges ahead, not the least of which is figuring out how to deploy online banking without jeopardizing their traditional branches. Online and direct banking have grown in popularity as broadband Internet access becomes nearly ubiquitous. Young, mobile-savvy consumers are using mobile devices to conduct their banking, but it may take a while for mobile banking to be attractive to the masses. Technology trends may be realized more quickly on the business side of banking through remote deposit capture (direct deposits) and automated clearing house transactions (e-checks). Microlending is an increasingly viable alternative to fund socially responsible investments and small businesses in developing nations. Microlending has migrated from developing nations to developed nations, where it has manifested as a peer-to-peer network of lenders and borrowers. Banks and federal agencies are placing greater emphasis on regulations to fight money laundering so that funds do not fall into the wrong hands. The Financial Action Task Force (FATF) is an intergovernmental body that develops and promotes national and international policies to combat the illegal flow of drug money.

key terms

Key Terms

bank charter 414	M1 409
commercial banks 414	M2 409
credit unions 415	money 408
currency 409	open market operations 411
demand deposits 409	pension funds 417
discount rate 411	reserve requirement 411
Federal Deposit Insurance Corporation (FDIC) 417	selective credit controls 412
	thrift institutions 415
Federal Reserve System (Fed) 410	time deposits 409
financial intermediation 413	

PREPARING

Preparing for Tomorrow's Workplace: SCANS

1. How much does a checking account cost? Call or visit several local banks and weigh prices and services. Take into consideration how you use your checking account, how many checks a month you write, and the average balances you keep. On the Internet, BankRate.com (http://www.bankrate.com) lets you digitally compare bank products. Could you pay lower fees elsewhere? Could you earn interest on your checking account at a credit union? Would you be better off paying a monthly fee with unlimited check-writing privileges? Crunch the numbers to find the best deal. (Resources, Information)

2. You are starting a small business selling collectible books over the Internet and need to establish a business banking account that will provide the following services: business checking, credit card processing, a business savings account, and perhaps a line of credit. Call or visit at least three local banks to gather information about their business banking services, including data about fees, service options, and other features of interest to entrepreneurs. Write a short summary of each bank's offerings and benefits and make a recommendation about which bank you would choose for your new business. (Interpersonal, Information)

3. If you watch the news, you've undoubtedly heard mention that the Fed is going to raise or lower interest rates. What exactly does this mean? Explain how the Fed's decision to raise and lower its discount rate might affect (a) a large manufacturer of household appliances, (b) a midsize software firm, (c) a small restaurant, (d) a family hoping to purchase their first home, and (e) a college student. **(Information)**

4. Research the banking system of another country and write a report on your findings by answering these questions: Is there a central banking system similar to the U.S. Federal Reserve System in place? Which government agency or department controls it and how does it operate? How stable is the country's central banking system? How does it compare in structure and operation to the Federal Reserve System? How much control does the government have over banks operating in the country? Are there any barriers to entry specifically facing foreign banks? What would this mean to a foreign business attempting to do business in this country? **(Information)**

5. Banks use databases to identify profitable and unprofitable customers. Bankers say they lose money on customers who typically keep less than $1,000 in their checking and savings accounts and frequently call or visit the bank. Profitable customers keep several thousand dollars in their accounts and seldom visit a teller or call the bank. To turn unprofitable customers into profitable ones, banks have assessed fees on almost 300 services, including using a bank teller, although many of the fees are waived for customers who maintain high account balances. Bankers justify the fees by saying they're in business to earn a profit. Discuss whether banks are justified in treating profitable and unprofitable customers differently. Defend your answers. **(Information, Systems)**

6. **Team Activity** During its regular meetings, the Federal Open Market Committee, the Federal Reserve's monetary policy-making body, considers a number of economic indicators and reports before making decisions. The decisions made by the Fed include: whether to sell or purchase Federal treasury bonds, whether to raise or lower bank reserve requirements, and whether to raise or lower the Federal Reserve discount rate. Divide your class into groups (if possible, try to use seven members, the size of the FOMC) and assign each group one of these decisions. As a group, identify the types of information used by the Fed in making their assigned decision and how that information is used. Find the most recent information (sources may include newspapers, business publications, online databases, etc.) and analyze it. Based on this information and your group's analysis, what should the Fed do now? Present your findings and recommendations to the class. **(Interpersonal, Information)**

Ethics Activity

You are a loan officer with Sweet Home Mortgage Company. The senior vice president in charge of your area sets new loan quotas for your group and suggests that courting more subprime borrowers would make the new quotas easier to meet. He reminds you that the company can justifiably charge higher interest rates, loan fees, and servicing costs for these higher-risk loans. He also points out that the loans will earn you and your team larger commissions as well. "Everyone wins," he tells you. "We help people who might otherwise not be able to get the financing they need, the company makes money, and so do you."

But you are uneasy about the company's focus on subprime borrowers, low-income applicants with blemished or limited credit histories, many of whom are also minorities. You suspect the company's tactics could be considered "predatory lending" or "reverse redlining." You are also convinced that the cost of Sweet Home's subprime loans isn't tied to the increased risk factor at all, but to how much profit the company can squeeze from a group of unsophisticated borrowers with few other options.

Using a Web search tool, locate articles about this topic and then write a response to the following question. Be sure to support your arguments and cite your sources.

ETHICAL DILEMMA: Should you seek out subprime loans, knowing that you will have to charge borrowers the high fees your company demands, while believing they may not be totally justified?

Sources: Kimberly Blanton, "Dark Side of Subprime Loans," *The Boston Globe*, August 3, 2005, **http://www.boston.com**; Sue Kirchhoff, "Minorities Depend on Subprime Loans," *USA Today*, March 16, 2005, **http://www.usatoday.com**; "Subprime Lending," HUD Web site, **http://www.hud.gov**, June 8, 2006.

1. Banking on a great career? Go to **http://www.careerbank.com** to explore what positions are available. Use the Salary Wizard to estimate what you can earn and make a presentation on the type of job you might choose and its location.
2. Visit the International Money Laundering Network Services Association (**http://www.imolin. org**) for the latest information on what organizations are doing to ensure that international monetary transfers remain out of terrorists' hands. Summarize your findings.
3. Find out everything you want to know about financial institutions and banking from the latest edition of the U.S. Census Bureau Statistical Abstract of the United States. Visit the U.S. Census Bureau Web site at **http://www.census.gov** to access the Banking, Finance, and Insurance section of this publication. Explain why this information is important to you.
4. Using an Internet search engine such as Google (**http://www.google.com**) or Yahoo! (**http://www.yahoo.com**), research information on the bank branch renaissance. Make a presentation describing the merits of this trend to your class.
5. There is a current move to increase the security of financial transactions with credit cards that generate a onetime passcode for every transaction. Go to **http://www.dogpile.com** to research articles on the pros and cons. Write up your findings and recommendations.
6. What are your rights to privacy when dealing with financial institutions? Research the specific privacy provisions related to banking and financial services using the Internet and write a paper on how you can use this information to protect your privacy and financial identity.

Creative Thinking Case

Banking Industry Goin' Mobile

In the 1990s, the introduction of the Internet enabled consumers to shop, communicate, and even manage finances using only a desktop computer. But now a more recent technological development is taking the usefulness of the Internet a step further. The recent marriage of Internet technology and wireless connectivity in the form of PDAs, smart phones, and other handheld gadgets is transforming business and changing the way people live. Although the implications for this "Wi-Fi revolution" are boundless, perhaps no sector is better positioned to benefit from a world without wires than the financial-services industry.

For the millions of wireless users who appear almost surgically attached to their BlackBerrys, RAZRs, and iPhones, banks have begun offering services that make paying bills and checking balances possible on the go. Leading the pack is Mobile Banking from Bank of America, a free service that keeps customers connected to their finances anytime, anywhere, through only a handset. "We've created a pocket-sized bank that can be taken anywhere," remarks Sanjay Gupta, an executive in Bank of America's e-commerce division. Wireless gurus at the Charlotte-based financial institution foresee a brave new world in which individuals will manage finances and transfer payments while commuting to work or taking a cruise.

With its more than one million online customers, Bank of America is in the pole position of a wireless-banking race that has just received the green flag. Research firm Celent estimates that 35 percent of online banking households will use mobile banking services by 2010. The firm also predicts that as much as 70 percent of all bank-center call volume will come from mobile phones. This shifting consumer pattern is generating excitement among industry leaders, as 23 of the 80 largest U.S. financial institutions view mobile banking as a product-development priority for the next few years, according to an Aite Group survey.

Despite rosy predictions by market researchers, there is one major dilemma that threatens the future of all online financial services: cybercrime. Identity theft and credit card data breaches make headline news with alarming regularity, and sinister schemes like phishing and pharming lurk within cyberspace's often-untraceable digital pathways, ready to empty savings accounts in seconds. In fact, data attacks have snatched away the financial data of hundreds of thousands of Bank of America customers in recent years. In one high-profile incident, the bank lost the personal data of 1.2 million federal employees, including that of some U.S. senators.

If these data breaches were not cause enough for worry, cyber-terror prevention experts foresee an all-out assault on the Internet that could bring worldwide networks to a screeching halt. In one bizarre incident occurring early in 2008, multiple undersea Internet cables were mysteriously cut, leaving millions of Web users in Egypt and India without service. Likewise, successful penetrations of Pentagon computers by international cyber warfare groups have led some experts to predict a computer-triggered economic Armageddon.

Though such dangers loom on the horizon, Bank of America believes that its customers are safe. The bank's state-of-the-art encryption system helps prevent hackers from digital safecracking, and the company's "zero liability online banking guarantee" acts as a financial safety net—just in case cybercriminals stage a successful heist.

At the end of the day, consumer demand for mobility may trump all fears of a cyber meltdown. The palpable spirit of freedom driving many consumers to leap headlong into the wireless era is captured in a recent television commercial: two expert rock climbers, while scaling a treacherous canyon and dangling hundreds of feet up in the air, pause to transfer funds on their cell phones. That's the promise of mobility.

Critical Thinking Questions

- What impact do you think mobile banking will have on the traditional retail services that banks offer through their local branch offices?
- Does the switch to digital banking leave the financial-services industry vulnerable to a worldwide economic attack triggered by cyber warfare groups? Explain.
- What demographic groups are most likely to embrace mobile banking, and why?

Sources: Riley McDermid, "Banks Turn to Mobile Access as the Next Big Thing," *MarketWatch*, May 15, 2008, **http://www. marketwatch.com**, accessed May 31, 2008; John Vause, "Chinese Hackers: No Site Is Safe," CNN, March 11, 2008, **http://www. cnn.com/2008/TECH/03/07/china.hackers/index.html**, accessed June 1, 2008; John R. Quain, "Cellphone Banking Is Coming of Age," *The New York Times*, May 24, 2007, p. C7; "Bank of America's Mobile Banking Now Available Anytime, Anywhere to More Than 20 Million Online Customers Across the U.S.," *Payments News*, May 22, 2007, **http://www.paymentsnews.com/2007/05/ bank_of_america.html**, accessed May 31, 2008; Paul Nowell, "Bank of America Says Tapes with Customer Data Lost," *USA Today*, February 27, 2005, **http://www.usatoday.com**, accessed May 31, 2008; "US Mobile Banking: Beyond the Buzz—Mobile Banking Will Be a Significant Financial Services Channel That Will Be Used By 35% of Online Banking Households by 2010," Celent Web site, **http://www.celent.com**, May 17, 2007, accessed May 31, 2008; "Third Internet Cable Cut in Middle East," *Associated Press*, February 1, 2008, **http://www.foxnews.com/story/0,2933,327588,00.html**, accessed June 1, 2008; Michael Hanlon, "Attack of the Cyber Terrorists," *Mail Online*, May 24, 2007, **http://www.dailymail.co.uk**, accessed May 31, 2008.

Exploring Business Careers

**Michael Cleary
JP Morgan Chase**

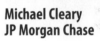

We live in a world of giants—not of the Jack and the Beanstalk variety, but giants who tempt us with fast food, develop our computer technology, or sell us our groceries and just about everything else under one expansive roof. As companies expand, consistency is an issue. A McDonald's hamburger in San Diego needs to taste the same as one in Miami. Along with this, differentiation also becomes more critical. Think about it: when you order a Coke at a restaurant, does it much matter if the waiter asks you, "Is Pepsi all right?" For most people, it doesn't. A company needs to set themselves apart, while maintaining the consistent quality that makes them successful. And financial institutions are no exception.

Therefore, when the directors of JP Morgan Chase decided to revamp their 200-year-old institution, they looked for a dynamic, forward-thinking leader. They found Michael Cleary. A constant innovator, Cleary had cut his teeth in the oil and gas exploration business before moving to banking as president of First Chicago's online banking venture, Wingspan. When JP Morgan Chase bought First Chicago, they were impressed with Cleary's knowledge and ideas about the banking industry and promoted him to chief operating officer of Chase, the brand of their U.S. commercial banking services.

Cleary quickly saw the need to differentiate Chase. Within a nationwide field of banking choices, why would a customer choose Chase? His vision for delineating Chase focused more on customer experience than on who had the best rate. As he says, "This is a commodity industry and you can either differentiate yourself on rate, which I think is a very difficult thing to do, or you can differentiate yourself on customer experience. And we focus on customer experience."

Cleary's strategy is straightforward: treat each customer as an individual with unique needs that Chase can meet. To do this, he stresses the importance of having all the financial services in one place for the customer to access and providing the trained staff and sophisticated technology to assure that these services efficiently satisfy the customer's financial wants. "That's what we're here to do. Can we help them get their first mortgage? Can we talk to them about consolidating debt with a home equity loan instead of using their credit cards? But it's really about individual answers. And it really is that my needs are very different than someone else's needs."

One simple yet revolutionary change he made was to remove the word "Bank" from their name. The company's commercial banking brand is "Chase." As Cleary explains, the term "bank" is too limiting. People think of it as checking and savings accounts. The new Chase needed to provide the entire gamut of financial services and individualize that service to the needs of each customer.

© Ryan McVay/Digital Vision/Getty Images

Understanding Financial Management and Securities Markets

CHAPTER 16

Learning Goals

After reading this chapter, you should be able to answer these questions:

1 How do finance and the financial manager affect the firm's overall strategy?

2 What types of short-term and long-term expenditures does a firm make?

3 What are the main sources and costs of unsecured and secured short-term financing?

4 What are the key differences between debt and equity, and the major types and features of long-term debt?

5 When and how do firms issue equity, and what are the costs?

6 How do securities markets help firms raise funding, and what securities trade in the capital markets?

7 Where can investors buy and sell securities, and how are securities markets regulated?

8 What are the current developments in financial management and the securities markets?

"In the End . . ."

After taking over the Tangiers casino and resort in Las Vegas, Sam "Ace" Rothstein, in the movie *Casino*, has proven himself to be a more than capable manager and an enterprising pillar of the casino business. The main task he has been assigned as manager is to maximize the value of the casino to its owner, and he has taken that task to heart. In particular, he has taken a special interest in the whales that come through the casino, understanding in full one of the elemental rules of business. That rule is the 80/20 rule, which basically argues that 80 percent of a company's business (and subsequent profits) come from about 20 percent of the company's customers. In the casino business, that 20 percent lies within the hands of the whales like Ichikawa.

Ichikawa is a successful Japanese billionaire who can literally affect the bottom line of a casino with one night of gambling. He bets $30,000 a hand on a high stakes game called baccarat, where the risk versus return ratio is relatively high. In financial terms, risk is associated with the potential for monetary loss, whereas a return is the potential reward associated with financial decisions. When Ichikawa places a bet for $30,000, he is actually risking that amount of money for the potential reward associated with winning the hand. The greater the risk, the greater the amount of return that is required. Ichikawa risked quite a bit of his own money, and the return was two million dollars of the casino's money, along with robes, towels, soap, and shampoo pilfered from his comped hotel room.

But Sam Rothstein is a very savvy casino manager. In fact, he knows that such an outflow of cash can hurt the casino and his chances to retain his position as the manager of the casino. As such, his activities include maintaining a basic understanding of the influx and outflow of cash from the casino, projecting how various activities—such as the loss of two million dollars—will affect the casino over a given period, and what needs to be invested in order to provide a higher return for the casino. He makes the necessary investments to get Ichikawa back into the casino—including a whole floor of rooms to himself—so that he will play again.

Sam is also banking on the risk versus return. He knows that he is taking a huge risk with a player of Ichikawa's magnitude because the two million the man has already won could escalate to double or even triple that amount. But the return on such a risk is high, and it proves to be well worth it. Ichikawa returns to the casino and begins playing only $1,000 a hand with a $10,000 return on his risk. Sam knows, however, that Ichikawa will not be satisfied with such "winnings" for long because he is used to winning $100,000 a hand. Ultimately, Ichikawa loses back the two million he won the previous night but also a million dollars of his own money. "In the end," Sam says, "we get it all."

This chapter provides you with the basic information that should assist you in making financial decisions on your own as well as a basic understanding of how financial managers protect and serve the company's financial interests. It starts with an overview of the roles of finance and financial managers in a company, and then focuses on how companies use the funds they acquire. It then moves into a discussion of gaining financing in the short and long term. The chapter also takes a look into securities markets as well as buying and selling securities before considering current trends in financial management and financing. In the end, you should have a basic understanding of how individuals like Sam Rothstein and even Ichikawa make basic financial decisions and how you can make them in the future.

Discussion Questions

- Sam Rothstein, in essence, is acting like the casino's financial manager. In what ways is he doing so?
- The casino is faced with both short-term and long-term expenses that it must deal with. Given what you've seen in the clip, describe which are short-term and which are long-term expenses and why.

- In what ways is a casino like the Tangiers similar to a securities market?
- What are the ethical considerations that Sam makes that probably would be called into question in true financial markets?

In today's fast-paced global economy, managing a firm's finances is more complex than ever. For financial managers, a thorough command of traditional finance activities—financial planning, investing money, and raising funds—is only part of the job. Financial managers are more than number crunchers. As part of the top-management team, chief financial officers (CFOs) need a broad understanding of their firm's business and industry, as well as leadership ability and creativity. They must never lose sight of the primary goal of the financial manager: *to maximize the value of the firm to its owners*.

Financial management—spending and raising a firm's money—is both a science and an art. The science of it is analyzing numbers and flows of cash through the firm. The art is answering questions: Is the firm using its financial resources in the best way? Aside from costs, why choose a particular form of financing? How risky is each option? Another important concern for both business managers and investors is understanding the basics of securities markets and the securities traded on them, which affect both corporate plans and investor pocketbooks. More than half of adult Americans now own stocks, compared to just 25 percent in 1981.[1]

This chapter focuses on the financial management of a firm and the securities markets in which firms raise funds. We'll start with an overview of the role of finance and of the financial manager in the firm's overall business strategy. Discussions of short- and long-term uses of funds and investment decisions follow. Next, we'll examine key sources of short- and long-term financing. Then we'll review the function, operation, and regulation of securities markets. Finally, we'll look at key trends affecting financial management and securities markets.

The Role of Finance and the Financial Manager

1 How do finance and the financial manager affect the firm's overall strategy?

Any company, whether it's a two-attorney law partnership or General Motors, needs money to operate. To make money, it must first spend money—on inventory and supplies, equipment and facilities, and employee wages and salaries. Therefore, finance is critical to the success of all companies. It may not be as visible as marketing or production, but management of a firm's finances is just as critical to the firm's success.

financial management
The art and science of managing a firm's money so that it can meet its goals.

Financial management—the art and science of managing a firm's money so that it can meet its goals—is not just the responsibility of the finance department. All business decisions have financial consequences. Managers in all departments must work closely with financial personnel. If you are a sales representative, for example, the company's credit and collection policies will affect your ability to make sales. The head of the IT department will need to justify any requests for new systems.

Revenues from sales of the firm's products should be the chief source of funding. But money from sales doesn't always come in when it's needed to pay the bills. Financial managers must track how money is flowing into and out of the firm (see Exhibit 16.1). They work with the firm's other department managers to determine how available funds will be used and how much money is needed. Then they choose the best sources from which to obtain the required funding.

For example, a financial manager will track day-to-day operational data such as cash collections and disbursements to ensure that the company has enough cash to meet its obligations. Over a longer time horizon, the manager will thoroughly study whether and when the company should open a new manufacturing facility. The manager will also suggest the most appropriate way to finance the project, raise the funds, and then monitor the project's implementation and operation.

Financial management is closely related to accounting. In most firms, both areas are the responsibility of the vice president of finance or the chief financial officer (CFO). But the accountant's main function is to collect and present financial data. Financial managers use financial statements and other information prepared by accountants to make financial decisions. Financial managers focus on **cash flows**, the inflows and outflows of cash. They plan and monitor the firm's cash flows to ensure that cash is available when needed.

cash flows
The inflows and outflows of cash for a firm.

The Financial Manager's Responsibilities and Activities

Financial managers have a complex and challenging job. They analyze financial data prepared by accountants, monitor the firm's financial status, and prepare and implement financial plans.

EXHIBIT 16.1 How Cash Flows through a Business

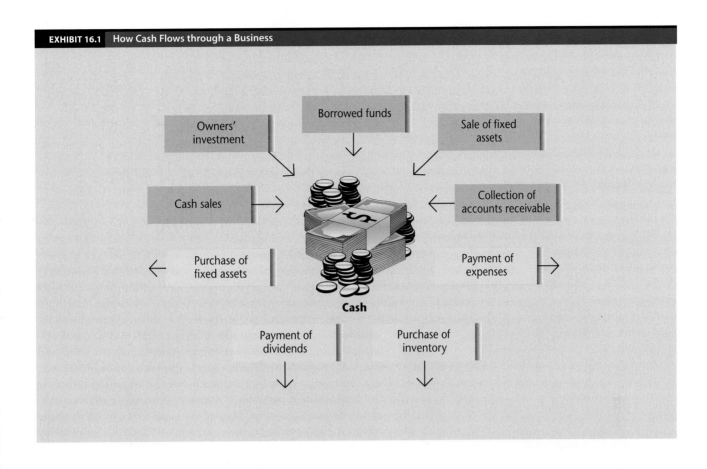

One day they may be developing a better way to automate cash collections, the next they may be analyzing a proposed acquisition. The key activities of the financial manager are:

- *Financial planning.* Preparing the financial plan, which projects revenues, expenditures, and financing needs over a given period.
- *Investing (spending money).* Investing the firm's funds in projects and securities that provide high returns in relation to their risks.
- *Financing (raising money).* Obtaining reasonably priced funding for the firm's operations and investments, and seeking the proper balance between debt (borrowed funds) and equity (funds raised through the sale of ownership in the business).

The Goal of the Financial Manager

How can financial managers make wise planning, investment, and financing decisions? The main goal of the financial manager is *to maximize the value of the firm to its owners.* The value of a publicly owned corporation is measured by the share price of its stock. A private company's value is the price at which it could be sold.

To maximize the firm's value, the financial manager has to consider both short- and long-term consequences of the firm's actions. Maximizing profits is one approach, but it should not be the only one. Such an approach favors making short-term gains over achieving long-term goals. What if a firm in a highly technical and competitive industry did no research and development? In the short run, profits would be high because research and development is very expensive. But in the long run, the firm might lose its ability to compete because of its lack of new products.

This is true regardless of a company's size or point in its life cycle. At Corning, a company founded more than 150 years ago, CEO Wendell Weeks believes in taking the long-term view and not managing for quarterly earnings to satisfy Wall Street's expectations. The company, once known

Financial mismanagement reached unprecedented levels recently, as a housing slump and cascading mortgage defaults triggered a lending crisis in the banking sector. Bear Stearns, one of the largest investment banks in the world, fell victim to the crisis in 2008, when fears about the company's financial troubles led to a massive run on the bank. As creditors began demanding their money, Bear's stock plummeted, dropping to less than $3 per share from $90 earlier in the year. The Federal Reserve arranged an emergency buyout by JP Morgan Chase, preventing a domino effect. Are some banks too large to manage financially?

to consumers mostly for kitchen products such as Corelle dinnerware and Pyrex heat-resistant glass cookware, is today a technology company that manufactures specialized glass and ceramic products. It is a leading supplier of flat glass panels for LCD displays used in large-screen televisions and other electronic products and was the inventor of optical fiber and cable for the telecommunications industry. These product lines require large investments during their long research and development (R&D) cycles and for plant and equipment once they go into production.

This can be risky in the short term, but staying the course can pay off. The LCD glass unit reported losses for 14 years. Now it provides 38 percent of total revenues and most of the profits. As major telecommunications companies built up their fiber-optic networks in the late 1990s and early 2000s, Corning expanded its capacity to meet that demand. Profits rose—and then fell just as quickly in 2001 as the telecommunications sector collapsed. "We lost half our revenues in a year," recalls Weeks. He and company leaders quickly revamped the business model to channel new business and R&D investments to several product lines, rather than focusing too heavily on one. And when the telecommunications sector regained its footing in 2004 and began a new push to install fiber-optic lines to customer homes, Corning was right there to supply the cable. Annual sales rose almost 50 percent from 2003 to 2005, and the company was again profitable for the first year since 2000.[2]

As the Corning situation demonstrates, financial managers constantly strive for a balance between the opportunity for profit and the potential for loss. In finance, the opportunity for profit is termed **return**; the potential for loss, or the chance that an investment will not achieve the expected level of return, is **risk**. A basic principle in finance is that the higher the risk, the greater the return that is required. This widely accepted concept is called the **risk-return trade-off**. Financial managers consider many risk and return factors when making investment and financing decisions. Among them are changing patterns of market demand, interest rates, general economic conditions, market conditions, and social issues (such as environmental effects and equal employment opportunity policies).

return
The opportunity for profit.

risk
The potential for loss or the chance that an investment will not achieve the expected level of return.

risk-return trade-off
A basic principle in finance that holds that the higher the risk, the greater the return that is required.

CONCEPT check

What is the role of financial management in a firm?

How do the three key activities of the financial manager relate?

What is the main goal of the financial manager? How does the risk-return trade-off relate to the financial manager's main goal?

How Organizations Use Funds

2 What types of short-term and long-term expenditures does a firm make?

To grow and prosper, a firm must keep investing money in its operations. The financial manager decides how best to use the firm's money. Short-term expenses support the firm's day-to-day activities. For instance, athletic-apparel maker Nike regularly spends money to buy such raw materials as leather and fabric and to pay employee salaries. Long-term expenses are typically for fixed assets. For Nike, these would include outlays to build a new factory, buy automated manufacturing equipment, or acquire a small manufacturer of sports apparel.

Short-Term Expenses

Short-term expenses, often called operating expenses, are outlays used to support current production and selling activities. They typically result in current assets, which include cash and any other assets (accounts receivable and inventory) that can be converted to cash within a year. The financial manager's goal is to manage current assets so the firm has enough cash to pay its bills when due and to support its accounts receivable and inventory.

cash management
The process of making sure that a firm has enough cash on hand to pay bills as they come due and to meet unexpected expenses.

Cash Management: Assuring Liquidity Cash is the lifeblood of business. Without it, a firm could not operate. An important duty of the financial manager is **cash management**, or making sure that enough cash is on hand to pay bills as they come due and to meet unexpected expenses.

Businesses estimate their cash requirements for a specific period. Many companies keep a minimum cash balance to cover unexpected expenses or changes in projected cash flows. The financial manager arranges loans to cover any shortfalls. If the size and timing of cash inflows closely match the size and timing of cash outflows, the company needs to keep only a small amount of cash on hand. A company whose sales and receipts are fairly predictable and regular throughout the year needs less cash than a company with a seasonal pattern of sales and receipts. A toy company, for instance, whose sales are concentrated in the fall, spends a great deal of cash during the spring and summer to build inventory. It has excess cash during the winter and early spring, when it collects on sales from its peak selling season.

Because cash held in checking accounts earns little, if any, interest, the financial manager tries to keep cash balances low and to invest the surplus cash. Surpluses are invested temporarily in **marketable securities**, short-term investments that are easily converted into cash. The financial manager looks for low-risk investments that offer high returns. Three of the most popular marketable securities are Treasury bills, certificates of deposit, and commercial paper. (**Commercial paper** is unsecured short-term debt—an IOU—issued by a financially strong corporation.) Today's financial managers have new tools to help them find the best short-term investments. For instance, online trading platforms save time and provide access to more types of investments. These have been especially useful for smaller companies who don't have large finance staffs. "We don't have enough to invest that we can chase money market [funds] or commercial paper," says Bob DiAntonio of Arbella Insurance Group, a Massachusetts company that provides property and casualty insurance. By using an online money market platform to invest between $20 million and $35 million each day, he has access to about 30 different investments. The portal allows him to move Arbella's cash into the marketable securities offering the highest interest rates in just a few minutes. "We don't have to waste half the morning doing short-term investments," he says.[3]

Companies with overseas operations face even greater cash management challenges. Developing the systems for international cash management may sound simple in theory, but in practice it's extremely complex. In addition to dealing with multiple foreign currencies, treasurers must understand and follow banking practices and regulatory and tax requirements in each country. Regulations may impede their ability to move funds freely across borders. Also, issuing a standard set of procedures for every office may not work because local business practices differ from country to country. Furthermore, local managers may resist the shift to a centralized structure, because they don't want to give up control of cash generated by their units. Corporate financial managers must be sensitive to and aware of local customs and adapt the centralization strategy accordingly.

In addition to seeking the right balance between cash and marketable securities, the financial manager tries to shorten the time between the purchase of inventory or services (cash outflows) and the collection of cash from sales (cash inflows). The three key strategies are to collect money owed to the firm (accounts receivable) as quickly as possible, to pay money owed to others (accounts payable) as late as possible without damaging the firm's credit reputation, and to minimize the funds tied up in inventory.

Managing Accounts Receivable

Accounts receivable represent sales for which the firm has not yet been paid. Because the product has been sold but cash has not yet been received, an account receivable amounts to an outflow of funds. For the average manufacturing firm, accounts receivable represent about 15 to 20 percent of total assets.

The financial manager's goal is to collect money owed to the firm as quickly as possible, while offering customers credit terms attractive enough to increase sales. Accounts receivable management involves setting credit policies, guidelines on offering credit, credit terms, and specific repayment conditions, including how long customers have to pay their bills and whether a cash discount is given for quicker payment. Another aspect of accounts receivable management is deciding on collection policies, the procedures for collecting overdue accounts.

Setting up credit and collection policies is a balancing act for financial managers. On the one hand, easier credit policies or generous credit terms (a longer repayment period or larger cash discount) result in increased sales. On the other hand, the firm has to finance more accounts receivable. The risk of uncollectible accounts receivable also rises. Businesses consider the impact on sales, timing of cash flow, experience with bad debt, customer profiles, and industry standards when developing their credit and collection policies.

Companies that want to speed up collections actively manage their accounts receivable, rather than passively letting customers pay when they want to. The Credit Research Foundation (CRF) measures the efficiency of receivables collection processes by collecting data on the median days sales outstanding (DSO), a key measure of accounts receivable performance. DSO measurements are taken every quarter. For example, in the third quarter of 2007, average DSO was 42.30 days, an increase over the 41.37 days the year prior. Another metric the CRF tracks is the collections effectiveness index (CEI), or how many receivables are collected compared to the amount available to collect. Even though the DSO increased in the third quarter of 2007, the CEI actually increased. That indicates that companies are working to improve their overall collections process.[4] Monitoring DSO is especially important during rough economic times. Recall from Chapter 14 how Beltmann Group,

© AP Images/Jim R. Bounds

Cash is king when it comes to financial management of an organization. Therefore, smart cash-flow management means delaying payouts while speeding up collection cycles. Strategies for going after overdue accounts range from sending simple past-due e-mail notices to hiring a collection attorney. Implementing technology to automate accounts receivable is also effective—payment-tracking software helped Duke University Health System recover $4.5 million in managed care underpayments in one year. Why is setting collection policies a balancing act for financial managers?

the moving company based in Minnesota, had a DSO of 61 days and needed to increase its cash flow to navigate an economic downturn. Management implemented a variety of new processes and trained employees to understand the importance of reducing the company's DSO. Improved collections processes translated to millions more dollars in cash on hand.[5]

Other companies chose to outsource financial and accounting business processes to specialists rather than develop their own systems. The availability of cutting-edge technology and specialized electronic platforms that would be difficult and expensive to develop in-house is winning over firms of all sizes. Giving up control of finance to a third party has not been easy for CFOs. The risks are high when financial and other sensitive corporate data are transferred to an outside computer system: data could be compromised or lost, or rivals could steal corporate data. It's also harder to monitor an outside provider than your own employees. One outsourcing area that has attracted many clients is international trade, which has regulations that differ from country to country and requires huge amounts of documentation. With specialized IT systems, providers can track not only the physical location of goods, but also all the paperwork associated with shipments. Processing costs for goods purchased overseas are about twice that of domestic goods, so more efficient systems pay off.[6]

Inventory Another outflow of funds is buying inventory needed by the firm. In a typical manufacturing firm, inventory is nearly 20 percent of total assets. The cost of inventory includes not only its purchase price, but also ordering, handling, storage, interest, and insurance costs.

Production, marketing, and finance managers usually have differing views about inventory. Production managers want lots of raw materials on hand to avoid production delays. Marketing managers want lots of finished goods on hand so customer orders can be filled quickly. But financial managers want the least inventory possible without harming production efficiency or sales. Financial managers must work closely with production and marketing to balance these conflicting goals. Techniques for reducing the investment in inventory—inventory management, the just-in-time system, and materials requirement planning—were described in Chapter 10.

For retail firms, inventory management is a critical area for financial managers, who closely monitor inventory turnover ratios. As we learned in Chapter 14, this ratio shows how quickly inventory moves through the firm and is turned into sales. "If the turnover number goes too low, it adversely affects our working capital and we have to borrow money to cover the excess inventory," says Andrew Demott, CFO of Superior Uniform Group, a wholesale apparel company. Holding purchased inventory in the warehouse increases inventory costs and takes up financial resources that could be used more effectively elsewhere. At the same time, Dermott explains, a high inventory turnover ratio may indicate that goods may not be available for customers, who will take their business to another firm.[7] Read the Managing Change box on the next page to find out how some companies are using inventory management to gain a competitive advantage in the apparel industry.

Long-Term Expenditures

A firm also invests funds in long-lived assets such as land, buildings, machinery, equipment, and information systems. These are called **capital expenditures**. Unlike operating expenses, which produce benefits within a year, the benefits from capital expenditures extend beyond one year. For instance, a printer's purchase of a new printing press with a usable life of seven years is a capital expenditure and appears as a fixed asset on the firm's balance sheet. Paper, ink, and other supplies, however, are expenses. Mergers and acquisitions, discussed in Chapter 4, are also considered capital expenditures.

Firms make capital expenditures for many reasons. The most common are to expand, to replace or renew fixed assets, and to develop new products. Most manufacturing firms have a big investment in long-term assets. The Boeing Company, for instance, puts millions of dollars a year into airplane-manufacturing facilities.

Because capital expenditures tend to be costly and have a major effect on the firm's future, the financial manager uses a process called **capital budgeting** to analyze long-term projects and select those

capital expenditures
Investments in long-lived assets, such as land, buildings, machinery, equipment, and information systems, that are expected to provide benefits over a period longer than one year.

capital budgeting
The process of analyzing long-term projects and selecting those that offer the best returns while maximizing the firm's value.

CONCEPT check

Distinguish between short- and long-term expenses.

What is the financial manager's goal in cash management? List the three key cash management strategies.

Describe a firm's main motives in making capital expenditures.

© Stockbyte/Getty Images

Turning Fashion on a Dime

Efficiencies in supply chain management have become a new source of competitive advantage, and nowhere is this more clear than in the fashion industry. Companies like Zara and H&M are seamlessly integrating their design cycles with inventory control, resulting in a strong combination of controlling short-term expenses while focusing on long-term performance goals.

Zara is the second-largest clothing store in the world (behind GAP). The fast-fashion company introduces more than 11,000 products per year, which translates to 300,000 stock-keeping units (styles times sizes), and can get each of those products from concept to racks in its 600 plus stores in only two weeks. From the minute a garment is ready for production, each of its pieces are tracked by bar code. Tracking continues through production until the garment is on the rack in the store, but it doesn't stop there.

Store clerks carry PDAs that they use to transmit inventory information back to a centralized computer network. If a design is not selling, production teams will stop making the garment immediately. That means inventory expenditures for poor-selling items are stopped much sooner than in a traditional fashion business model. Zara can do this effectively because it manufactures garments in small, frequent batches.

Likewise, if a design is selling well, information from the store floor will allow production to redirect resources into a new design. To avoid stockouts, Zara uses sophisticated optimization software. Sometimes the store would rather move a set of products out of the store if some pieces or sizes are out of stock, rather than have an incomplete offering. For example if half of a two-piece outfit was out of stock, managers might opt to remove the more plentiful half from the shop floor to prevent customers from getting frustrated. The optimization software enables Zara to evaluate what items are needed in each store to meet dynamic demand fluctuations. Store managers can reorder best sellers in under an hour.

At its core, however, Zara is a finance-driven business. In design, Zara starts with the price of the garment to the consumer and works back to the most efficient production process. In staffing, it uses software to create worker schedules around peak sales times each day. In operations, it has alarm tags attached to garments at the factory (that frees up 12 hours per shop for employees to be selling). Always the goal is to grow sales faster than costs, and to date Zara has been so successful doing just that that industry icons like Gucci and Burberry are moving closer to faster fashion cycles.[8]

Critical Thinking Questions
- How is Zara's strategy of fast inventory turns related to a cash management strategy?
- Are there any disadvantages to such an aggressive inventory cycle?

---

that offer the best returns while maximizing the firm's value. Decisions involving new products or the acquisition of another business are especially important. Managers look at project costs and forecast the future benefits the project will bring to calculate the firm's estimated return on the investment.

Obtaining Short-Term Financing

How do firms raise the funding they need? They borrow money (debt), sell ownership shares (equity), and retain earnings (profits). The financial manager must assess all these sources and choose the one most likely to help maximize the firm's value.

Like expenses, borrowed funds can be divided into short- and long-term loans. A *short-term loan* comes due within one year; a *long-term loan* has a maturity greater than one year. Short-term financing is shown as a current liability on the balance sheet, and is used to finance current assets and support operations. Short-term loans can be unsecured or secured.

3 What are the main sources and costs of unsecured and secured short-term financing?

Unsecured Short-Term Loans

Unsecured loans are made on the basis of the firm's creditworthiness and the lender's previous experience with the firm. An unsecured borrower does not have to pledge specific assets as security. The three main types of unsecured short-term loans are trade credit, bank loans, and commercial paper.

Trade Credit: Accounts Payable When Goodyear sells tires to General Motors, GM does not have to pay cash on delivery. Instead, Goodyear regularly bills GM for its tire purchases, and GM pays at a later date. This is an example of **trade credit**: the seller extends credit to the buyer between the time the buyer receives the goods or services and when it pays for them. Trade credit is a major source of short-term business financing. The buyer enters the credit on its books as an **account payable**. In effect, the credit is a short-term loan from the seller to the buyer of the goods and services. Until GM pays Goodyear, Goodyear has an account receivable from GM, and GM has an account payable to Goodyear.

Bank Loans Unsecured bank loans are another source of short-term business financing. Companies often use these loans to finance seasonal (cyclical) businesses. Unsecured bank loans include lines of credit and revolving credit agreements. A **line of credit** specifies the maximum

unsecured loans
Loans for which the borrower does not have to pledge specific assets as security.

trade credit
The extension of credit by the seller to the buyer between the time the buyer receives the goods or services and when it pays for them.

accounts payable
Purchases for which a buyer has not yet paid the seller.

line of credit
An agreement between a bank and a business that specifies the maximum amount of unsecured short-term borrowing the bank will allow the firm over a given period, typically one year.

revolving credit agreement
A guaranteed *line of credit* whereby a bank agrees that a certain amount of funds will be available for a business to borrow over a given period, typically two to five years.

secured loans
Loans for which the borrower is required to pledge specific assets as collateral, or security.

factoring
A form of short-term financing in which a firm sells its accounts receivable outright at a discount to a factor.

CONCEPT in action

For businesses with steady orders but a lack of cash to make payroll or other immediate payments, factoring is a popular way to obtain financing. In factoring, a firm sells its invoices to a third-party funding source for cash. The factor purchasing the invoices then collects on the due payments over time. Trucking companies with voluminous accounts receivable in the form of freight bills are good candidates for factoring. Why might firms choose factoring instead of loans?

CONCEPT check

Distinguish between unsecured and secured short-term loans.

Briefly describe the three main types of unsecured short-term loans.

Discuss the two ways that accounts receivable can be used to obtain short-term financing.

amount of unsecured short-term borrowing the bank will allow the firm over a given period, typically one year. The firm either pays a fee or keeps a certain percentage of the loan amount (10 to 20 percent) in a checking account at the bank. Another bank loan, the **revolving credit agreement**, is basically a guaranteed line of credit that carries an extra fee in addition to interest. Revolving credit agreements are often arranged for a two- to five-year period. At the end of 2007, Bank of America had more than $400 billion outstanding for business loans alone (not counting lines of credits to consumers and homeowners). Indeed, before credit tightened in 2007, banks had pledged to make available to companies roughly $1 trillion in credit agreements. Most of these revolving lines were put in place before the credit crunch in summer 2007 and offered very low interest rates. As the economy tightened, more companies were looking to tap into their low-interest credit lines for cash, which caused banks to face the real possibility of not having the capacity to support all those loans *at the same time*. In drastic cases, banks tried to renegotiate credit amounts or the terms of the loans. Radian, a Philadelphia bond insurance company, agreed to have its credit line reduced from $400 million to $250 million.[9]

Commercial Paper   As noted earlier, *commercial paper* is an unsecured short-term debt—an IOU—issued by a financially strong corporation. Thus, it is both a short-term investment and a financing option for major corporations. Corporations issue commercial paper in multiples of $100,000 for periods ranging from 3 to 270 days. Many big companies use commercial paper instead of short-term bank loans because the interest rate on commercial paper is usually 1 to 3 percent below bank rates.

Secured Short-Term Loans

Secured loans require the borrower to pledge specific assets as collateral, or security. The secured lender can legally take the collateral if the borrower doesn't repay the loan. Commercial banks and commercial finance companies are the main sources of secured short-term loans to business. Borrowers whose credit is not strong enough to qualify for unsecured loans use these loans. Typically, the collateral for secured short-term loans is accounts receivable or inventory. Because accounts receivable are normally quite liquid (easily converted to cash), they are an attractive form of collateral. The appeal of inventory—raw materials or finished goods—as collateral depends on how easily it can be sold at a fair price.

Another form of short-term financing using accounts receivable is **factoring**. A firm sells its accounts receivable outright to a *factor*, a financial institution (often a commercial bank or commercial finance company) that buys accounts receivable at a discount. Factoring is widely used in the clothing, furniture, and appliance industries. Factoring is more expensive than a bank loan, however, because the factor buys the receivables at a discount from their actual value. At its origin, factoring was a fairly simple loan strategy, but factoring is becoming increasingly complex. According to J. Michael Stanley, managing director at Rosenthal & Rosenthal Inc.'s factoring division, one of the country's larger factoring firms, today's firms are borrowing against more than receivables: they're borrowing against inventory, letters of credit, in-transit inventory, intellectual property and trademarks, and receivables.[10]

Raising Long-Term Financing

A basic principle of finance is to match the term of the financing to the period over which benefits are expected to be received from the associated outlay. Short-term items should be financed with short-term funds, and long-term items should be financed with long-term funds. Long-term financing sources include both debt (borrowing) and equity (ownership). Equity financing comes either from selling new ownership interests or from retaining earnings. Financial managers try to select the mix of long-term debt and equity that results in the best balance between cost and risk.

Debt versus Equity Financing

Say that the Boeing Company plans to spend $2 billion over the next four years to build and equip new factories to make jet aircraft. Boeing's top management will assess the pros and cons of both

4   What are the key differences between debt and equity, and the major types and features of long-term debt?

debt and equity and then consider several possible sources of the desired form of long-term financing.

The major advantage of debt financing is the deductibility of interest expense for income tax purposes, which lowers its overall cost. In addition, there is no loss of ownership. The major drawback is **financial risk**: the chance that the firm will be unable to make scheduled interest and principal payments. The lender can force a borrower that fails to make scheduled debt payments into bankruptcy. Most loan agreements have restrictions to ensure that the borrower operates efficiently.

Equity, on the other hand, is a form of permanent financing that places few restrictions on the firm. The firm is not required to pay dividends or repay the investment. However, equity financing gives common stockholders voting rights that provide them with a voice in management. Equity is more costly than debt. Unlike the interest on debt, dividends to owners are not tax-deductible expenses.

In the 1970s, when Mel Zuckerman decided to open what he termed a "fat farm" resort, he went to the bank to finance his venture. Because he had been a successful homebuilder who had borrowed (and repaid) up to $200 million at a time for prior projects, he didn't anticipate any hurdles getting debt financing for his Canyon Ranch resort. The bankers, who didn't understand the concept, however, told Zuckerman he had lost his mind. Rather than abandon the idea, Zuckerman shifted from thinking about debt financing to equity financing. He and his wife liquidated their own assets to get start-up money. Eight months later, Canyon Ranch opened, and today Canyon Ranch's two resort spas, three SpaClubs, and three Canyon Ranch Living condominium developments generate $150 million in annual revenue.[11]

Exhibit 16.2 summarizes the major differences between debt and equity financing.

Debt Financing

Long-term debt is used to finance long-term (capital) expenditures. The initial maturities of long-term debt typically range between 5 and 20 years. Three important forms of long-term debt are term loans, bonds, and mortgage loans.

A **term loan** is a business loan with a maturity of more than one year. Term loans generally have 5- to 12-year maturities and can be unsecured or secured. They are available from commercial banks, insurance companies, pension funds, commercial finance companies, and manufacturers' financing subsidiaries. A contract between the borrower and the lender spells out the amount and maturity of the loan, the interest rate, payment dates, the purpose of the loan, and other provisions such as operating and financial restrictions on the borrower, which are used to control the risk of default. The payments include both interest and principal, so the loan balance declines over time. Borrowers try to arrange a repayment schedule that matches the forecast cash flow from the project being financed.

Bonds are long-term debt obligations (liabilities) issued by corporations and governments. A bond certificate serves as proof of the obligation. The issuer of a bond must pay the buyer a fixed amount of money—called **interest**, stated as the *coupon rate*—on a regular schedule, typically every

financial risk
The chance that a firm will be unable to make scheduled interest and principal payments on its debt.

term loan
A business loan with a maturity of more than one year; can be unsecured or secured.

bonds
Long-term debt obligations (liabilities) issued by corporations and governments.

interest
A fixed amount of money paid by the issuer of a bond to the bondholder on a regular schedule, typically every six months; stated as the *coupon rate*.

EXHIBIT 16.2	Major Differences between Debt and Equity Financing	
	Debt Financing	**Equity Financing**
Voice in management	Creditors typically have none, unless the borrower defaults on payments. Creditors may be able to place restrictions on management in the event of default.	Common stockholders have voting rights.
Claim on income and assets	Debt holders rank ahead of equity holders. Payment of interest and principal is a contractual obligation of the firm.	Equity owners have a residual claim on income (dividends are paid only after paying interest and any scheduled principal) and the firm has no obligation to pay dividends.
Maturity	Debt has a stated maturity and requires repayment of principal by a specified maturity date.	The firm is not required to repay equity, which has no maturity date.
Tax treatment	Interest is a tax-deductible expense.	Dividends are not tax-deductible and are paid from after-tax income.

principal
The amount borrowed by the issuer of a bond; also called *par value*.

mortgage loan
A long-term loan made against real estate as collateral.

six months. The issuer must also pay the bondholder the amount borrowed—called the **principal**, or *par value*—at the bond's maturity date (due date). Bonds are usually issued in units of $1,000—for instance, $1,000, $5,000, or $10,000—and have initial maturities of 10 to 30 years. They may be secured or unsecured, include special provisions for early retirement, or be convertible to common stock.

A **mortgage loan** is a long-term loan made against real estate as collateral. The lender takes a mortgage on the property, which lets the lender seize the property, sell it, and use the proceeds to pay off the loan if the borrower fails to make the scheduled payments. Long-term mortgage loans are often used to finance office buildings, factories, and warehouses. Life insurance companies are an important source of these loans. They make billions of dollars worth of mortgage loans to businesses each year.

Equity Financing

5 When and how do firms issue equity, and what are the costs?

Equity refers to the owners' investment in the business. In corporations, the preferred and common stockholders are the owners. A firm obtains equity financing by selling new ownership shares (external financing), or by retaining earnings (internal financing), or for small and growing, typically high-tech, companies through venture capital (external financing).

common stock
A security that represents an ownership interest in a corporation.

Selling New Issues of Common Stock
Common stock is a security that represents an ownership interest in a corporation. A company's first sale of stock to the public is called an *initial public offering (IPO)*. Going public is the dream of many small-company founders and early investors, who hope to recoup their investments and become instant millionaires. Google, which went public in 2004 at $85 a share and soared to $580 in mid-2008, is one of the most successful IPOs. The largest IPO in history, however, was that of Visa, the operator of the world's largest credit-card payment network, in 2008. With an offering price of $44 per share, Visa generated $17.9 billion from its IPO, and a mere month later the stock was trading at double that. At its first profit reporting as a public company, Visa boasted annual revenue of $1.45 billion and annual free cash flow of $1 billion.[12] An IPO often enables existing stockholders, usually employees, family, and friends who bought the stock privately, to earn big profits on their investment. (Companies that are already public can issue and sell additional shares of common stock to raise equity funds.)

CONCEPT in action

Visa Inc., the world's biggest credit card network, set a record for U.S. initial public offerings, raising $17.9 billion during its 2008 IPO. The San Francisco-based company sold 406 million shares at $44 apiece, eclipsing the previous IPO record set by AT&T eight years earlier. Trading under the "V" ticker symbol, Visa shares jumped an additional 22 percent on the first day of public trading, closing at $56.50 on the New York Stock Exchange. What are the advantages and disadvantages of going public?

But going public has some drawbacks. For one thing, there is no guarantee an IPO will sell. It is also expensive. Big fees must be paid to investment bankers, brokers, attorneys, accountants, and printers. Once the company is public, it is closely watched by regulators, stockholders, and securities analysts. The firm must reveal such information as operating and financial data, product details, financing plans, and operating strategies. Providing this information is often costly. In 2007, Ernst and Young conducted a survey in which 91 percent of the executive participants believed they were prepared to take their companies public, yet nearly 40 percent of those companies announced earnings below market expectations, leading to sharp drops in stock prices.[13]

Some companies choose to remain private. Cargill, Hallmark Cards, Levi Strauss, Mars, Publix Super Markets, and Toys "R" Us are among the largest U.S. private companies.

dividends
Payments to stockholders from a corporation's profits.

stock dividends
Payments to stockholders in the form of more stock; may replace or supplement cash dividends.

Dividends and Retained Earnings
Dividends are payments to stockholders from a corporation's profits. Dividends can be paid in cash or in stock. **Stock dividends** are payments in the form of more stock. Stock dividends may replace or supplement cash dividends. After a stock dividend has been paid, more shares have a claim on the same company, so the value of each share often declines. A company does not have to pay dividends to stockholders. But if investors buy the stock expecting to get dividends and the firm does not pay them, the investors may sell their stocks.

At their quarterly meetings, the company's board of directors (typically with the advice of its CFO) decides how much of the profits to distribute as dividends and how much to reinvest. A firm's basic approach to paying dividends can greatly affect its share price. A stable history of dividend payments indicates good financial health. In November 2007, Xerox paid its first dividend in six years. The company had been on the verge of bankruptcy when Anne Mulcahy took over as CEO, and the cessation of the dividend was a means to retain the earnings required to turn the company around. She embarked on a massive restructuring, which returned the company to profitability and allowed the reinstatement of the dividend.[14]

If a firm that has been making regular dividend payments cuts or skips a dividend, investors start thinking it has serious financial problems. The increased uncertainty often results in lower stock prices. Thus, most firms set dividends at a level they can keep paying. They start with a relatively low dividend payout ratio so that they can maintain a steady or slightly increasing dividend over time.

Retained earnings, profits that have been reinvested in the firm, have a big advantage over other sources of equity capital: They do not incur underwriting costs. Financial managers strive to balance dividends and retained earnings to maximize the value of the firm. Often the balance reflects the nature of the firm and its industry. Well-established and stable firms and those that expect only modest growth—like public utilities, financial-services companies, and large industrial corporations—typically pay out much of their earnings in dividends. For example, in the 12-month period ending March 31, 2006, Altria Group paid dividends of $3.20 per share, Bank of America paid $2.00 per share, Chevron paid $2.08 per share, Dominion Resources paid $2.76 per share, Merck paid $1.52 per share, and Wachovia Bank paid $2.04 per share.

Most high-growth companies, like those in technology-related fields, finance much of their growth through retained earnings and pay little or no dividends to stockholders. As they mature, many decide to begin paying dividends, as did Microsoft and Qualcomm, in 2003. One highly visible, high-growth company that still retains its earnings is Starbucks. Not paying dividends has given the company access to the capital needed to open more stores—more than 8,500 of them. The annual number of new stores the company opened increased each year through 2007. In that year Starbucks opened 1,342 new stores.[15]

McDonald's upped its annual dividend by 50 percent in 2007, to $1.50 per share. The move is expected to put $15 billion to $17 billion in the pockets of company shareholders by 2010. Chief Executive Jim Skinner said that the financial decision was indicative of the burger giant's business momentum and stable cash flow. Some analysts disagreed, however, claiming that McDonald's would require $5 billion in new debt to pay out the cash dividends. Why do some companies pay dividends?

Preferred Stock

Another form of equity is **preferred stock**. Unlike common stock, preferred stock usually has a dividend amount that is set at the time the stock is issued. These dividends must be paid before the company can pay any dividends to common stockholders. Also, if the firm goes bankrupt and sells its assets, preferred stockholders get their money back before common stockholders do.

Like debt, preferred stock increases the firm's financial risk because it obligates the firm to make a fixed payment. But preferred stock is more flexible. The firm can miss a dividend payment without suffering the serious results of failing to pay back a debt.

Preferred stock is more expensive than debt financing, however, because preferred dividends are not tax-deductible. Also, because the claims of preferred stockholders on income and assets are second to those of debtholders, preferred stockholders require higher returns to compensate for the greater risk.

Venture Capital

As we learned in Chapter 5, *venture capital* is another source of equity capital. It is most often used by small and growing firms that aren't big enough to sell securities to the public. This type of financing is especially popular among high-tech companies that need large sums of money.

Venture capitalists invest in new businesses in return for part of the ownership, sometimes as much as 60 percent. They look for new businesses with high growth potential, and they expect a high investment return within 5 to 10 years. By getting in on the ground floor, venture capitalists buy stock at a very low price. They earn profits by selling the stock at a much higher price when the company goes public. Venture capitalists generally get a voice in management through seats on the board of directors.

Getting venture capital is difficult, even though there are hundreds of private venture-capital firms in this country. Most venture capitalists finance only about 1 to 5 percent of the companies that apply. Venture-capital investors, many of whom experienced losses during recent years from their investments in failed dot-coms, are currently less willing to take risks on very early stage companies with unproven technology. As a result, other sources of venture capital, including private foundations, state governments, and wealthy individuals (called *angel investors*), are helping start-up firms find equity capital. These private investors are motivated by the potential to grow a significant business and earn a high return on their investment.

retained earnings
Profits that have been reinvested in a firm.

preferred stock
An equity security for which the dividend amount is set at the time the stock is issued and the dividend must be paid before the company can pay any dividends to common stockholders.

CONCEPT **check**

Compare the advantages and disadvantages of debt and equity financing.

Discuss the costs involved in issuing common stock.

Briefly describe these sources of equity: retained earnings, preferred stock, venture capital.

Securities Markets

6 How do securities markets help firms raise funding, and what securities trade in the capital markets?

securities
Investment certificates issued by corporations and governments that represent either *equity* or *debt*.

institutional investors
Investment professionals who are paid to manage other people's money.

primary market
The securities market where *new* securities are sold to the public.

secondary market
The securities market where *old* (already issued) securities are bought and sold, or traded, among investors; includes broker markets, dealer markets, the over-the-counter market, and the commodities exchanges.

investment bankers
Firms that act as intermediaries, buying securities from corporations and governments and reselling them to the public.

underwriting
The process of buying securities from corporations and governments and reselling them to the public; the main activity of investment bankers.

stockbroker
A person who is licensed to buy and sell securities on behalf of clients.

Stocks, bonds, and other securities trade in securities markets. These markets streamline the purchase and sales activities of investors by allowing transactions to be made quickly and at a fair price. **Securities** are investment certificates that represent either *equity* (ownership in the issuing organization) or *debt* (a loan to the issuer). Corporations and governments raise capital to finance operations and expansion by selling securities to investors, who in turn accept a certain amount of risk with the hope of receiving a profit from their investment.

Securities markets are busy places. On an average day, individual and institutional investors trade billions of shares of stock in more than 10,000 companies through securities markets. *Individual investors* invest their own money to achieve their personal financial goals. **Institutional investors** are investment professionals who are paid to manage other people's money. Most of these professional money managers work for financial institutions, such as banks, mutual funds, insurance companies, and pension funds. Institutional investors control very large sums of money, often buying stock in 10,000-share blocks. They aim to meet the investment goals of their clients. Institutional investors are a major force in the securities markets, accounting for about half of the dollar volume of equities traded.

Types of Markets

Securities markets can be divided into primary and secondary markets. The **primary market** is where *new* securities are sold to the public, usually with the help of investment bankers. In the primary market, the issuer of the security gets the proceeds from the transaction. A security is sold in the primary market just once—when the corporation or government first issues it. The Visa IPO described earlier in this chapter is an example of a primary-market offering.

Later transactions take place in the **secondary market**, where *old* (already issued) securities are bought and sold, or traded, among investors. The issuers generally are not involved in these transactions. The vast majority of securities transactions take place in secondary markets, which include broker markets, dealer markets, the over-the-counter market, and the commodities exchanges. You'll see *tombstones*, announcements of both primary and secondary stock and bond offerings, in the *Wall Street Journal* and other newspapers.

The Role of Investment Bankers and Stockbrokers

Two types of investment specialists play key roles in the functioning of the securities markets. **Investment bankers** help companies raise long-term financing. These firms act as intermediaries, buying securities from corporations and governments and reselling them to the public. This process, called **underwriting**, is the main activity of the investment banker, which acquires the security for an agreed-upon price and hopes to be able to resell it at a higher price to make a profit. Investment bankers advise clients on the pricing and structure of new securities offerings, as well as on mergers, acquisitions, and other types of financing. Well-known investment banking firms include Goldman, Sachs & Co., Merrill Lynch & Co., Morgan Stanley, UBS, Crédit Suisse, and Citi Smith Barney (a division of Citigroup).

A **stockbroker** is a person who is licensed to buy and sell securities on behalf of clients. Also called *account executives* or *financial advisors,* these investment professionals work for brokerage firms and execute the orders customers place for stocks, bonds, mutual funds, and other securities. Investors are wise to seek a broker who understands their investment goals and can help them pursue their objectives. We'll discuss how individuals make securities transactions in the online enrichment chapter, "Managing Your Personal Finances."

Brokerage firms are paid commissions for executing clients' transactions. Although brokers can charge whatever they want, most firms have fixed commission schedules for small transactions. These commissions usually depend on the value of the transaction and the number of shares involved. All investment decisions should be based on sound information, but the availability of accurate information is often limited or clouded by conflicts of interest. A new company profiled in the Customer Satisfaction and Quality box on the next page is setting out to improve the quality of corporate information used by investors.

CONCEPT in action

Courtesy of E*Trade

In E*Trade's popular TV ads, a talking baby executes stock trades with a single mouse click, showing audiences that even an infant with reflux issues can trade online. Internet brokerages have turned millions of financial amateurs into informed self-directed investors. Like the baby in the ads, these "do-it-yourselfers" take their financial futures into their own hands, buying and selling stocks over the Internet for a fraction of the cost associated with traditional brokerage firms. What professional-class services do online brokerages offer customers to help them invest on their own?

Crowdsourced Investment Information

While attending Harvard, Mike Sha and Parker Conrad were also day-trading. Buoyed by great success, the pair was caught off guard when their investment gains began to dissipate in the wake of accounting or management oversights. Watching their upside erode caused them to question the quality of the research and analysis on which they based their investment choices. What they ultimately realized was that as a company's performance begins to slip, the bank or analysts covering it refrain from commenting on it. Noticing this shift, the company itself stops sharing information in an attempt to conceal its troubles. As performance spirals downward, there is less and less current and frank information about the company.

At least that's the opinion of Sha and Conrad, who are using a favorite Web 2.0 tool, the wiki, to combat this opaque curtain. Their start-up, Wikinvest.com, is inspired by the success of Wikipedia, the online collaborative encyclopedia. Sha and Conrad hope to bring scope to investment information in the same way that Wikipedia brought scope to the encyclopedia—by involving thousands of people in the collaborative building and maintenance of the information. To date, Wikinvest has 100,000 contributors who have been assigned a grade based on their contributions (volume and quality). Because contributors post biographies, a visitor can better weigh their credentials. The site shows the latest additions and edits in company profiles, industry synopses, and concept tutorials. Sha and Conrad have retained a measure of editorial control over the site, and with one click, they can erase all edits that occurred on a given day if needed or desired.

The tools at Wikinvest are designed to allow a multifaceted view of each company profiled. The site hopes to incorporate information moderated by the interests of as many people as possible as a guard against information curated by the few. The result is a site that contains information an investor would have tremendous difficulty finding elsewhere. Contributors build out dynamic charts and include information beyond just financial metrics. For example, the Starbucks entry contains information on coffee and dairy futures and cannibalization risks. The full profile for Starbucks contains more detailed and more synthetic information than what can be found for free on other sites, including press and brokerage sites.

Designed as an information and analysis tool for investors, Wikinvest has already secured its own investors in the form of $2.25 million in venture capital. Soon, it could find its own profile on Wikinvest.[16]

Critical Thinking Questions

- Would you rather have a great deal of information available about a potential investment, or would you rather have a few key statistics on which to base an investment decision?
- Do you think Wikinvest can play a role in the corporate world, or do you see it becoming a tool primarily for consumers and day traders?

Online Investing

Improvements in Internet technology have made it possible for investors to research, analyze, and trade securities online. Today almost all brokerage firms offer online-trading capabilities. Online brokerages are popular with "do-it-yourself" investors who choose their own stocks and don't want to pay a full-service broker for these services. Lower transaction costs are a major benefit. Fees at online brokerages range from about $4 to $20, depending on the number of trades a client makes and the size of a client's account. Although there are many online brokerage firms, the five largest—Charles Schwab, Fidelity.com, TD Ameritrade, E*Trade, and Scottrade—account for about 80 percent of all trading volume and about $1.3 trillion in assets in customer accounts.[17] The Internet also offers investors access to a wealth of investment information.

Investing in Bonds

When many people think of financial markets, they picture the equity markets. However, the bond markets are huge—the Securities Industry and Financial Markets Association estimates that the global bond market is $47 trillion. The United States is the largest participant, with a $25 trillion bond market.[18]

Bonds can be bought and sold in the securities markets. However, the price of a bond changes over its life as market interest rates fluctuate. When the market interest rate drops below the fixed interest rate on a bond, it becomes more valuable and the price rises. If interest rates rise, the bond's price will fall. *Corporate bonds*, as the name implies, are issued by corporations. They usually have a par value of $1,000. They may be secured or unsecured (called *debentures*), include special provisions for early retirement, or they may be convertible to common stock. Corporations can also issue *mortgage bonds*, bonds secured by property such as land, buildings, or equipment. Approximately $1.13 trillion in new corporate bonds were issued in 2007, an increase of 6.6 percent over 2006 offerings.[19]

In addition to regular corporate debt issues, investors can buy *high-yield bonds* (also called *junk bonds*), which are high-risk, high-return bonds often

CONCEPT in action

Investors have placed trillions of dollars into companies aligned with political causes since the 1990s. These so-called socially responsible investors avoid companies that have controversial products or practices. Instead, they fill their investment portfolios with firms that have politically safe business models—such as those with clean-energy usage or humane treatment of animals. What investment vehicles are available for individuals who want to participate in socially responsible investing?

used by companies whose credit characteristics would not otherwise allow them access to the debt markets. They generally earn 3 percent or more above the returns on high-quality corporate bonds. Corporate bonds may also be issued with an option for the bondholder to convert them into common stock. These *convertible bonds* generally allow the bondholder to exchange each bond for a specified number of shares of common stock.

U.S. Government Securities and Municipal Bonds

Both the federal government and local government agencies also issue bonds. The U.S. Treasury sells three major types of federal debt securities: Treasury bills, Treasury notes, and Treasury bonds. All three are viewed as default-risk-free because they are backed by the U.S. government. Treasury bills mature in less than a year and are issued with a minimum face value of $1,000. Treasury notes have maturities of 10 years or less, and Treasury bonds have maturities as long as 25 years or more. Both notes and bonds are sold in denominations of $1,000 and $5,000. The interest earned on government securities is subject to federal income tax but is free from state and local income taxes. According to the Securities Industry and Financial Markets Association (SIFMA), at the end of 2007 there was $4.5 trillion outstanding marketable Treasury debt and a total of $752 billion in U.S. treasuries were issued in 2007, down 4.6 percent from 2006.[20]

municipal bonds
Bonds issued by states, counties, cities, and other state and local government agencies.

Municipal bonds are issued by states, counties, cities, and other state and local government agencies. In 2007, municipal bond markets reached $2.6 trillion.[21] These bonds typically have a par value of $5,000 and are either general obligation or revenue bonds. *General obligation bonds* are backed by the full faith and credit (and taxing power) of the issuing government. *Revenue bonds*, on the other hand, are repaid only from income generated by the specific project being financed. Examples of revenue bond projects include toll highways and bridges, power plants, and parking structures. Because the issuer of revenue bonds has no legal obligation to back the bonds if the project's revenues are inadequate, they are considered more risky and therefore have higher interest rates than general obligation bonds.

Municipal bonds are attractive to investors because interest earned on them is exempt from federal income tax. For the same reason, the coupon interest rate for a municipal bond is lower than for a similar-quality corporate bond. In addition, interest earned on municipal bonds issued by governments within the taxpayer's home state is exempt from state income tax as well. In contrast, all interest earned on corporate bonds is fully taxable.

Bond Ratings

Bonds vary in quality, depending on the financial strength of the issuer. Because the claims of bondholders come before those of stockholders, bonds are generally considered less risky than stocks. However, some bonds are in fact quite risky. Companies can default (fail to make scheduled interest or principal payments) on their bonds. Investors can use **bond ratings**, which are letter grades assigned to bond issues to indicate their quality or level of risk. Ratings for corporate bonds are easy to find. The two largest and best-known rating agencies are Moody's and Standard & Poor's (S&P), whose publications are in most libraries and in stock brokerages. Exhibit 16.3 lists the

bond ratings
Letter grades assigned to bond issues to indicate their quality or level of risk; assigned by rating agencies such as Moody's and Standard & Poor's (S&P).

EXHIBIT 16.3	Moody's and Standard & Poor's Bond Ratings	
Moody's Ratings	**S&P Ratings**	**Description**
Aaa	AAA	**Prime-quality investment bonds:** Highest rating assigned; indicates extremely strong capacity to pay.
Aa A	AA A	**High-grade investment bonds:** Also considered very safe bonds, although not quite as safe as Aaa/AAA issues; Aa/AA bonds are safer (have less risk of default) than single As.
Baa	BBB	**Medium-grade investment bonds:** Lowest of investment-grade issues; seen as lacking protection against adverse economic conditions.
Ba B	BB B	**Junk bonds:** Provide little protection against default; viewed as highly speculative.
Caa Ca C	CCC CC C D	**Poor-quality bonds:** Either in default or very close to it.

letter grades assigned by Moody's and S&P. A bond's rating may change if a company's financial condition changes.

Other Popular Securities

In addition to stocks and bonds, investors can buy mutual funds, a very popular investment category, or exchange-traded funds (ETFs). Futures contracts and options are more complex investments for experienced investors.

Mutual Funds

Suppose that you have $1,000 to invest but don't know which stocks or bonds to buy, when to buy them, or when to sell them. By investing in a mutual fund, you can buy shares in a large, professionally managed portfolio, or group, of stocks and bonds. A **mutual fund** is a financial-service company that pools its investors' funds to buy a selection of securities—marketable securities, stocks, bonds, or a combination of securities—that meet its stated investment goals. Each mutual fund focuses on one of a wide variety of possible investment goals, such as growth or income. Many large financial-service companies, such as Fidelity Investments and The Vanguard Group, sell a wide variety of mutual funds, each with a different investment goal. Investors can pick and choose funds that match their particular interests. Some specialized funds invest in a particular type of company or asset: in one industry such as health care or technology, in a geographical region such as Asia, or in an asset such as precious metals.

Mutual funds are one of the most popular investments for individuals today: 50.6 million American households own mutual funds, and the number of shareholder accounts tops 300 million.[22] Mutual funds appeal to investors for three main reasons:

- They are a good way to hold a diversified, and therefore less risky, portfolio. Investors with only $500 or $1,000 to invest cannot diversify much on their own. Buying shares in a mutual fund lets them own part of a portfolio that may contain 100 or more securities.
- Mutual funds are professionally managed.
- Mutual funds may offer higher returns than individual investors could achieve on their own.

Exchange-Traded Funds

A relatively new type of investment, the **exchange-traded fund (ETF)**, has become very popular with investors. ETFs are similar to mutual funds because they hold a broad basket of stocks with a common theme, giving investors instant diversification. ETFs trade on stock exchanges (most trade on the American Stock Exchange, AMEX), so their prices change throughout the day, whereas mutual fund share prices, called net asset values (NAVs), are calculated once a day at the end of trading. Between early 2006 and year-end 2007, ETF assets had more than quadrupled, growing from roughly $313 billion to an astounding $1.4 trillion.[23]

Investors can choose from more than 200 ETFs that track almost any market sector, from a broad market index such as the S&P 500 (described later in this chapter), industry sectors such as health care or energy, and geographical areas such as a particular country (Japan) or region (Latin America). ETFs have very low expense ratios. However, because they trade as stocks, investors pay commissions to buy and sell these shares.

Futures Contracts and Options

Futures contracts are legally binding obligations to buy or sell specified quantities of commodities (agricultural or mining products) or financial instruments (securities or currencies) at an agreed-upon price at a future date. An investor can buy commodity futures contracts in cattle, pork bellies (large slabs of bacon), eggs, coffee, flour, gasoline, fuel oil, lumber, wheat, gold, and silver. Financial futures include Treasury securities and foreign currencies, such as the British pound or Japanese yen. Futures contracts do not pay interest or dividends. The return depends solely on favorable price changes. These are very risky investments because the prices can vary a great deal.

Options are contracts that entitle holders to buy or sell specified quantities of common stocks or other financial instruments at a set price during a specified time. As with futures contracts, investors must correctly guess future price movements in the underlying financial instrument to earn a positive return. Unlike futures contracts, options do not legally obligate the holder to buy or sell, and the price paid for

mutual fund
A financial-service company that pools investors' funds to buy a selection of securities that meet its stated investment goals.

exchange traded fund (ETF)
A security similar to a *mutual fund* that holds a broad basket of stocks with a common theme but trades on a stock exchange so that its price changes throughout the day.

futures contracts
Legally binding obligations to buy or sell specified quantities of commodities or financial instruments at an agreed-upon price at a future date.

options
Contracts that entitle holders to buy or sell specified quantities of common stocks or other financial instruments at a set price during a specified time.

CONCEPT check

Distinguish between primary and secondary securities markets. How does an investment banker work with companies to issue securities?

Describe the types of bonds available to investors and the advantages and disadvantages they offer.

Why do mutual funds and exchange-traded funds appeal to investors? Discuss why futures contracts and options are risky investments.

an option is the maximum amount that can be lost. However, options have very short maturities, so it is easy to quickly lose a lot of money with them.

Buying and Selling at Securities Exchanges

7 Where can investors buy and sell securities, and how are securities markets regulated?

When we talk about stock markets, we are typically referring to secondary markets, which handle most of the securities trading activity. The two segments of the secondary markets are broker markets and dealer markets, as Exhibit 16.4 shows. The primary difference between broker and dealer markets is the way each executes securities trades. Securities trades can also take place in alternative trading systems and globally on foreign securities exchanges.

The securities markets both in the United States and around the world are in flux and undergoing tremendous changes. We present the basics of securities exchanges in this section and discuss the latest trends in the global securities markets later in the chapter.

Broker Markets

broker markets
National and regional securities exchanges that bring buyers and sellers together through brokers on a centralized trading floor.

The **broker market** consists of national and regional securities exchanges that bring buyers and sellers together through brokers on a centralized trading floor. In the broker market, the buyer purchases the securities directly from the seller through the broker. Broker markets account for about 60 percent of the total dollar volume of all shares traded in the U.S. securities markets.

New York Stock Exchange
The oldest and most prestigious broker market is the *New York Stock Exchange (NYSE)*, which has existed since 1792. Often called the Big Board, it is located on Wall Street in downtown New York City. The NYSE, which lists the shares of over 2,800 corporations, had a total domestic market capitalization of $15.7 trillion at year-end 2007. (Its total global market capitalization, which includes non-U.S. companies, was about $27.1 trillion.) On a typical day, more than 2.6 billion shares of stock, valued at $139 billion, are traded on the NYSE.[24] It represents 90 percent of the trading volume in the U.S. broker marketplace. Major companies such as IBM, Coca-Cola, AT&T, Procter & Gamble, Ford Motor Co., and Chevron list their shares on the NYSE. In 2007, total share volume on the NYSE was more than 556 billion shares, a record for the exchange. Companies that list on the NYSE must meet stringent listing requirements and annual maintenance requirements, which give them creditability.

The NYSE is also popular with non-U.S. companies. More than 420 foreign companies with a total global market capitalization of almost $11.4 trillion now list their securities on the NYSE.[25]

Until recently, all NYSE transactions occurred on the vast NYSE trading floor. Each of the companies traded at the NYSE is assigned to a trading post on the floor. When an exchange member

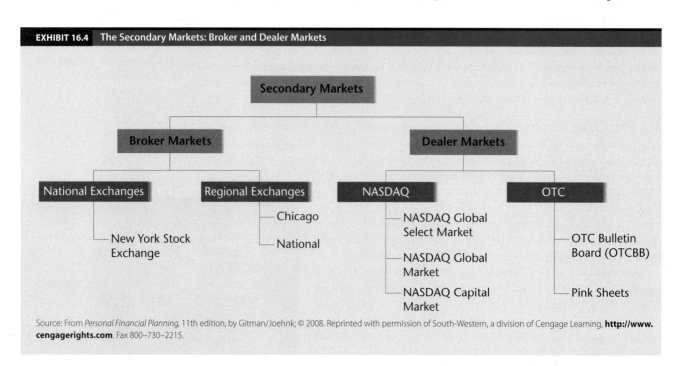

EXHIBIT 16.4   The Secondary Markets: Broker and Dealer Markets

Source: From *Personal Financial Planning*, 11th edition, by Gitman/Joehnk; © 2008. Reprinted with permission of South-Western, a division of Cengage Learning, **http://www. cengagerights.com**. Fax 800–730–2215.

receives an order to buy or sell a particular stock, the order is transmitted to a floor broker at the company's trading post. The floor brokers then compete with other brokers on the trading floor to get the best price for their customers.

In response to competitive pressures from electronic exchanges, the NYSE created a Hybrid Market that combines features of the floor auction market and automated trading. Its customers now have a choice of how they execute trades. In the trends section we'll discuss other changes the NYSE is making to maintain a leadership position among securities exchanges.

For over 165 years, the NYSE and the American Stock Exchange (AMEX) were ardent rivals. Because the AMEX's rules were less strict than those of the NYSE, most AMEX firms were smaller and less well known than NYSE-listed corporations. Still, the AMEX stood out as a pioneer of exchange-traded funds and a major market for options trading. In January 2008, the NYSE acquired AMEX for $260 million in stock. By May 2008, the Securities and Exchange Commission (SEC) had approved the deal and the NYSE had already begun implementing plans to move the AMEX into the NYSE building.[26]

CONCEPT in action

The New York Stock Exchange (NYSE) is the oldest and most prestigious of the broker markets. Its market capitalization dwarfs both foreign and domestic challengers. For more than a century, the NYSE traded exclusively through human specialists, but the need to compete with computer-automated exchanges has recently forced the Big Board to embrace an electronic trading system. The switch has all but eliminated the iconic pandemonium associated with NYSE floor-brokers. What benefits does an automated trading system provide to the investing public?

Regional Exchanges For centuries, the United States had robust regional markets in addition to the larger, New York–based markets. Exchanges in Boston, Chicago, Cincinnati, and Philadelphia made up the balance of annual share volume and focused on the securities of firms located in their geographic area. An electronic network linked the NYSE and many of the regional exchanges and allowed brokers to make securities transactions at the best prices.

The regional exchanges have struggled to compete, and now only Chicago and the National Stock Exchange (NSX, formerly the Cincinnati exchange) are independent regional exchanges. The NSX benefited from the passage of the SEC's Regulation NMS (National Market System), which became fully effective in 2007. Regulation NMS makes price the most important factor in making securities trades, and all orders must go to the trading venue with the best price.[27] This has transformed equity markets into commodity markets and accelerated the pace of consolidation in exchange markets.[28]

Dealer Markets

Unlike broker markets, **dealer markets** do not operate on centralized trading floors but instead use sophisticated telecommunications networks that link dealers throughout the United States. Buyers and sellers do not trade securities directly, as they do in broker markets. They work through securities dealers called "market makers," who make markets in one or more securities and offer to buy or sell securities at stated prices. A security transaction in the dealer market has two parts: the selling investor sells his or her securities to one dealer, and the buyer purchases the securities from another dealer (or in some cases, the same dealer).

dealer markets
Securities markets where buy and sell orders are executed through dealers, or "market makers" linked by telecommunications networks.

NASDAQ The largest dealer market is the **National Association of Securities Dealers Automated Quotation system**, commonly referred to as NASDAQ. The first electronic-based stock market, the NASDAQ is a sophisticated telecommunications network that links dealers throughout the United States. Founded in 1971 with origins in the over-the-counter (OTC) market, today NASDAQ is a separate securities exchange that is no longer part of the OTC market. The NASDAQ lists more companies than the NYSE (3,900 to 2,805), but the NYSE has an edge on daily exchange share volume (2.6 billion shares daily to the NASDAQ's 2 billion) and still leads in total market capitalization. The average daily trading volume of the NASDAQ in early 2008 was $85.2 billion.[29] The NASDAQ's sophisticated electronic communication system provides faster transaction speeds than traditional floor markets and is the main reason for the popularity and growth of the OTC market.

In January 2006 the SEC approved NASDAQ's application to operate as a national securities exchange. As a result, the NASDAQ Stock Market LLC began operating independently in August 2006 and is no longer part of the National Association of Securities Dealers, its primary regulator. This removes possible conflicts of interest between the market and its regulatory arm.[30]

The securities of many well-known companies, some of which could be listed on the organized exchanges, trade on the NASDAQ. Examples include Amazon.com, Apple Computer, Coors, Dell Computer, Google, Intel, Microsoft, Panera Bread, Qualcomm, and Starbucks. The stocks of most

National Association of Securities Dealers Automated Quotation (NASDAQ) system
The largest dealer market and the first electronic stock market, which is a sophisticated telecommunications network that links dealers throughout the United States.

commercial banks and insurance companies also trade in this market, as do most government and corporate bonds. About 315 foreign companies also trade on the NASDAQ.

NASDAQ is structured as a three-tier market:

- The NASDAQ Global Select Market has "financial and liquidity requirements that are higher than those of any other market," according to NASDAQ. More than 1,000 NASDAQ companies qualify for this group.
- The NASDAQ Global Market (formerly the NASDAQ National Market), which lists about 1,650 companies.
- The NASDAQ Capital Market (formerly the NASDAQ Small Cap Market) lists about 550 companies.

All three market tiers adhere to NASDAQ's rigorous listing and corporate governance standards.[31]

over-the-counter (OTC) market
Markets, other than the organized exchanges, on which small companies trade; includes the *Over-the-Counter Bulletin Board* (*OTCBB*) and the *Pink Sheets*.

The Over-the-Counter Market The **over-the-counter (OTC) markets** refer to those other than the organized exchanges described above. There are two OTC markets: The *Over-the-Counter Bulletin Board (OTCBB)* and the *Pink Sheets*. These markets generally list small companies and have no listing or maintenance standards, making them attractive to young companies looking for funding. OTC companies do not have to file with the SEC or follow the costly provisions of Sarbanes-Oxley. Investing in OTC companies is therefore highly risky and should be for experienced investors only. With dollar volumes doubling between 2005 and 2007, the Pink Sheets became the third-largest trading venue behind the NYSE and the NASDAQ by January 2008.[32]

Alternative Trading Systems

electronic communications networks (ECNs)
Private trading networks that allow institutional traders and some individuals to make direct transactions in the *fourth market*.

In addition to broker and dealer markets, alternative trading systems such as **electronic communications networks (ECNs)** make securities transactions. ECNs are private trading networks that allow institutional traders and some individuals to make direct transactions in what is called the *fourth market*. ECNs bypass brokers and dealers to automatically match electronic buy and sell orders. They are most effective for high-volume, actively traded stocks. Money managers and institutions such as pension funds and mutual funds with large amounts of money to invest like ECNs because they cost far less than other trading venues.

As ECNs began to compete with the NYSE and NASDAQ, the exchanges themselves acquired their own ECNs. Archipelago is now part of the NYSE, and the NASDAQ acquired INET ECN from Instinet Group. Prominent independent ECNs are BATS, DirectEdge, Track, Lava-Flow (part of Citi), and Bloomberg Tradebook. In addition, advances in technology have made it possible for brokerage firms and other financial institutions to develop their own ECNs.[33]

Global Trading and Foreign Exchanges

Improved communications and the elimination of legal barriers are helping the securities markets go global. The number of securities listed on exchanges in more than one country is growing. Foreign securities are now traded in the United States. Likewise, foreign investors can easily buy U.S. securities.

Stock markets also exist in foreign countries: Over 100 countries operate their own securities exchanges. Exhibit 16.5 contains a ranking of the top global exchanges by market capitalization. Other important foreign stock exchanges include those in Toronto, Frankfurt, Hong Kong, Zurich, Buenos Aires, Sydney, Paris, and Taiwan. The number of big U.S. corporations with listings on foreign exchanges is growing steadily, especially in Europe. For example, significant activity in NYSE-listed stocks also occurs on the London Stock Exchange (LSE). The LSE is also getting a growing share of the world's IPOs. Emerging markets such as India, whose economy has been growing 6 percent or more a year, are also attracting investor attention. The Sensex, the benchmark index of the Bombay Stock Exchange, tripled between 2003 and 2006 as foreign investors pumped more than $10 billion into Indian stocks.[34]

Why should U.S. investors pay attention to international stock markets? As we've discussed throughout this book, the world's economies are increasingly interdependent. Businesses must look beyond their own national borders to find materials to make their goods and to find markets for foreign goods and services. The same is true for investors, who may find that they can earn

EXHIBIT 16.5   Ranking of Global Securities Exchanges, 2007

By Market Capitalization

Ranking	Exchange	Market Capitalization (in billions of U.S. dollars)
1	NYSE Group	15,650.8
2	Tokyo SEGroup	4,330.9
3	Euronext	4,222.7
4	NASDAQ	4,013.7
5	London SE	3,851.7
6	Shanghai SE	3,694.3
7	Hong Kong Exchanges	2,654.4
8	TSX Group	2,186.6
9	Deutsche Börse	2,105.2
10	Bombay SE	1,819.1

By Number of Listed Companies

Ranking	Exchange	Companies Listed
1	Bombay SE	4,887
2	TSX Group	3,951
3	BME Spanish Exchange	3,537
4	London SE	3,307
5	NASDAQ	3,069
6	Tokyo SE Group	2,414
7	NYSE Group	2,297
8	Australian SE	1,998
9	Korea Exchange	1,757
10	National Stock Exchange India	1,330

Source: World Federation of Securities, **http://www.world-exchanges.org**, Annual Statistics, 2007.

higher returns in international markets. E*Trade recognizes that there is money to be made in foreign markets, as the Expanding Around the Globe box on the next page explains.

Regulation of Securities Markets

Both state and federal governments regulate the securities markets. The states were the first to pass laws aimed at preventing securities fraud. But most securities transactions occur across state lines, so federal securities laws are more effective. In addition to legislation, the industry has self-regulatory groups and measures.

Securities Legislation   Congress passed the Securities Act of 1933 in response to the 1929 stock market crash and subsequent problems during the Great Depression. It protects investors by requiring full disclosure of information about new securities issues. The issuer must file a *registration statement* with the SEC, which must be approved by the SEC before the security can be sold.

The *Securities Exchange Act of 1934* formally gave the SEC power to regulate securities exchanges. The act was amended in 1964 to give the SEC authority over the dealer markets as well. The amendment included rules for operating the stock exchanges and granted the SEC control over all participants (exchange members, brokers, dealers) and the securities traded in these markets.

The 1934 act also banned **insider trading**, the use of information that is not available to the general public to make profits on securities transactions. Because of lax enforcement, however, several big insider trading scandals occurred during the late 1980s. The *Insider Trading and Fraud Act of 1988* greatly increased the penalties for illegal insider trading and gave the SEC more power to investigate and prosecute claims of illegal actions. The meaning of insider was expanded beyond a company's directors, employees, and their relatives to include anyone who gets private information about a company.

CONCEPT in action

France's highest court recently upheld a ruling that billionaire investor and Democratic Party financier George Soros illegally bought and sold shares of Société Générale after receiving information about a planned corporate raid on the bank. In addition to incurring a multimillion-dollar fine for Soros, the insider trading conviction expanded the list of billionaires who have unfairly gamed securities markets while cheating ordinary investors. What regulations help prevent insider trading in the United States?

insider trading
The use of information that is not available to the general public to make profits on securities transactions.

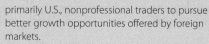
E*Trade Builds a Network—of Brokers

When E*Trade launched in 1982, it was one of the first online discount brokers. As market tools became more accessible to the masses, E*Trade grew in both customers and deposits. The company ran humorous ad campaigns during the Super Bowl and added online-banking services to its mix of offerings. But for all the success and adaptations, the one thing an E*Trade customer (or any discount broker-age customer) couldn't do was purchase foreign stocks.

In 2007, however, that changed when E*Trade rolled out its Global Trading Platform. E*Trade's new capability allows customers to buy, hold, and sell stocks from Canada, France, Germany, Hong Kong, Japan, and the United Kingdom. In addition, the company began offering broker-assisted trading in 36 other countries. Traders pay for the foreign stock in their own currency and are charged a currency conver-sion fee and a commission.

E*Trade's new platform comes at what many could argue is a perfect time. While the dollar is dropping in value and U.S. markets are growing at a 13 percent annual-ized rate, markets in developing nations are exploding. For example, a consensus forecast on China expects that country's markets to achieve 19 percent annualized growth over a three- to five-year period. The Shanghai Composite Index returned 182 percent in a single year! E*Trade's new platform allows North American, and primarily U.S., nonprofessional traders to pursue better growth opportunities offered by foreign markets.

Global expansion doesn't stop at the Global Trading Platform. E*Trade also has sites and opera-tions in 16 other countries and has been moving aggressively to increase the number of its overseas branded Web sites, like those in Hong Kong and Singapore. E*Trade Australia even made a bid to purchase Australia's online stockbroker IWL, and even though the takeover offer was not accepted, E*Trade Australia's stock price rose on the attempt. E*Trade has also solicited bids from marketing companies to help it re-create itself as a more recognizable brand across Europe so that it can expand its presence in that region.[35]

Critical Thinking Questions:
- Are there risks to creating an online global trad-ing network accessible to consumers?
- E*Trade competitors Charles Schwab and Ameritrade have explicitly stated that they will not follow E*Trade's lead into global markets. Why do you think that is so?

© Digital Vision/Getty Images

Other important legislation includes the *Investment Company Act of 1940*, which gives the SEC the right to regulate the practices of investment companies (such as mutual funds), and the *Investment Advisers Act of 1940*, which requires investment advisers to disclose information about their background. The *Securities Investor Protection Corporation (SIPC)* was established in 1970 to protect customers if a brokerage firm fails by insuring each customer's account for up to $500,000.

In response to corporate scandals that hurt thousands of investors, the SEC passed new regulations designed to restore public trust in the securities industry. It issued *Regulation FD* (for Fair Disclosure) in October 2000. Regulation FD requires public companies to share information with all investors at the same time, leveling the information playing field. The *Sarbanes-Oxley Act of 2002*, introduced in Chapter 14, has given the SEC more power when it comes to regulating how securities are offered, sold, and marketed.

circuit breakers
A corrective measure that, under certain conditions, stops trading in the securities markets for a short cooling-off period to limit the amount the market can drop in one day.

Self-Regulation The investment community also regulates itself, developing and enforcing ethical standards to reduce the potential for abuses in the financial marketplace. The National Association of Securities Dealers (NASD) oversees the nation's 5,600 brokerage firms and more than half a million registered brokers. It develops rules and regulations, provides a dispute resolution forum, and conducts regulatory reviews of member activities for the protection and benefit of investors.

In response to "Black Monday"—October 19, 1987, when the Dow Jones Industrial Average plunged 508 points and the trading activity severely overloaded the exchange's computers—the securities markets instituted corrective measures to prevent a repeat of the crisis. Now, under certain conditions, **circuit breakers** stop trading for a short cooling-off period to limit the amount the market can drop in one day. The NYSE circuit breaker levels are set quarterly based on the Dow Jones Industrial Average closing values of the previous month, rounded to the nearest 50 points.

CONCEPT check

How do the broker markets differ from dealer markets, and what organizations compose each of these two markets?

Why is the globalization of the securities markets important to U.S. investors? What are some of the other exchanges where U.S companies can list their securities?

Briefly describe the key provisions of the main federal laws designed to protect securities investors. What is insider trading, and how can it be harmful? How does the securi-ties industry regulate itself?

Trends in Financial Management and Securities Markets

8 What are the current developments in financial management and the securities markets?

Many of the key trends shaping the practice of financial management echo those in other disciplines. For example, technology is improving the efficiency with which financial managers run their operations. In the wake of a slowing economy and corporate scandals, the SEC assumed a stronger role and implemented additional regulations to protect investors from fraud and misinformation. A wave of merger mania hit the global securities markets as the securities exchanges themselves have begun to consolidate to capture larger shares of the world's trading volume in multiple types of securities. Technology is playing an ever increasing role in securities markets, and the transition to completely electronic trading means shifting to automated algorithmic computing.

Consolidation Continues

Although the markets could be nearing the end of consolidation, it's still a trend that's having tremendous impact on global securities exchanges. Within a single year, the NASDAQ bought the regional Philadelphia exchange and the regional Boston exchange, and entered a joint agreement with Borse Dubai to buy the Nordic exchange OMX. (Before combining forces, Borse Dubai and NASDAQ were in a heated bid battle for the acquisition of the OMX. Borse Dubai ultimately agreed to step back from challenging NASDAQ and instead acquired a nearly 20 percent stake in NASDAQ. In return, NASDAQ took a stake in Borse Dubai.) In roughly the same time period, the NYSE bought Euronext and the American Stock Exchange, and the Qatar Investment Authority bought a significant stake in the London Stock Exchange.[36]

Not all areas of the world are actively interested in consolidating their exchanges, however. Despite talks about a single Middle Eastern exchange, big discrepancies in the economic situations of the countries in the region makes the development of a single unified exchange less likely. For example, the Gulf Cooperative Countries (GCC) of Bahrain, Kuwait, Oman, Qatar, Saudi Arabia, and the United Arab Emirates have markets that are pulling away from the rest of the Middle East.[37] Even though GCC countries would face political and economic hurdles to creating a merged market, future consolidation seems likely. The fact that global economic turmoil in early 2008 had an effect on the GCC markets illustrates that perhaps the GCC markets are more tightly linked to—and in tighter competition with—world markets than previously thought.[38]

Trade-Cycle Automation

In 2007, the SEC's long-planned goal to automate market exchanges was realized as the Regulation National Market System (Reg NMS) went into full effect. Reg NMS requires that the best electronic bid or offer in a market be protected. That means that traders can't undercut the pricing to beat a competitor. The requirement for an automated quote forced the NYSE to abandon its traditional manual trading system and switch to online trading, and that move had put the NYSE in full and direct competition with entities against which it had previously held an advantage (for example, the online brokerage houses).

The full implementation of Reg NMS is a response to the dynamic and complex trading and technological environment in which exchanges are operating. As a result of Reg NMS, the volume of electronic trade transmissions skyrocketed in 2007. Even four months before the transition to Reg NMS requirements was complete, the data traffic had increased sixfold from the year prior. That means that the networks transmitting the data are getting clogged. So much data is flowing through the pipes that the information could be old by the time a trader receives it. Chris Keeling, partner in Accuity Risk Management explains, "There can actually be movements in the market price between the time at which the button is pushed and the time the final result comes back."[39] Another trader put it this way: "By the time you see it, it could be a second old, it could be a minute old."[40] In addition, quote updates are changing at nano speeds—up to 100,000 updates a second.[41]

To compete in this data frenzy, companies need more high-powered software running on the most powerful computers, servers, and networks. A vital tool for all traders is the computer algorithm. Widely used to help institutional investors (those traders who buy large quantities of stocks and bonds for pension funds, mutual funds, and so forth) determine certain aspects of the order (like timing, price, and even final order quantity), algorithms allow traders to shave seconds off the time required to complete a transaction. The buy or sell order is implemented automatically (and nearly instantly). Even though many standard algorithmic programs exist, companies are increasingly requesting that software providers create algorithms that behave differently under different conditions. In essence, the greater the customization of algorithms, the closer the mathematical models get to combining the flexibility of the human traders they replace with the speed of electronic communications.[42] Spending on electronic algorithm programs is expected to rise to $469 billion by 2009.[43]

CONCEPT check

How has the role of CFO changed since the passage of the Sarbanes-Oxley Act?

Describe the major changes taking place in the U.S. securities markets. What trends are driving these changes?

Summary of Learning Goals

1 How do finance and the financial manager affect the firm's overall strategy?

Finance involves managing the firm's money. The financial manager must decide how much money is needed and when, how best to use the available funds, and how to get the required financing. The financial manager's responsibilities include financial planning, investing (spending money), and financing (raising money). Maximizing the value of the firm is the main goal of the financial manager, whose decisions often have long-term effects.

2 What types of short-term and long-term expenditures does a firm make?

A firm incurs short-term expenses—supplies, inventory, and wages—to support current production, marketing, and sales activities. The financial manager manages the firm's investment in current assets so that the company has enough cash to pay its bills and support accounts receivable and inventory. Long-term expenditures (capital expenditures) are made for fixed assets such as land, buildings, equipment, and information systems. Because of the large outlays required for capital expenditures, financial managers carefully analyze proposed projects to determine which offer the best returns.

3 What are the main sources and costs of unsecured and secured short-term financing?

Short-term financing comes due within one year. The main sources of unsecured short-term financing are trade credit, bank loans, and commercial paper. Secured loans require a pledge of certain assets, such as accounts receivable or inventory, as security for the loan. Factoring, or selling accounts receivable outright at a discount, is another form of short-term financing.

4 What are the key differences between debt and equity, and the major types and features of long-term debt?

Financial managers must choose the best mix of debt and equity for their firm. The main advantage of debt financing is the tax-deductibility of interest. But debt involves financial risk because it requires the payment of interest and principal on specified dates. Equity—common and preferred stock—is considered a permanent form of financing on which the firm may or may not pay dividends. Dividends are not tax-deductible.

The main types of long-term debt are term loans, bonds, and mortgage loans. Term loans can be unsecured or secured and generally have 5- to 12-year maturities. Bonds usually have initial maturities of 10 to 30 years. Mortgage loans are secured by real estate. Long-term debt usually costs more than short-term financing because of the greater uncertainty that the borrower will be able to make the scheduled loan payments.

5 When and how do firms issue equity, and what are the costs?

The chief sources of equity financing are common stock, retained earnings, and preferred stock. The cost of selling stock includes issuing costs and potential dividend payments. Retained earnings are profits reinvested in the firm. For the issuing firm, preferred stock is more expensive than debt because its dividends are not tax-deductible and its claims are secondary to those of debtholders, but less expensive than common stock. Venture capital is often a source of equity financing for young companies.

6 How do securities markets help firms raise funding, and what securities trade in the capital markets?

Securities markets allow stocks, bonds, and other securities to be bought and sold quickly and at a fair price. New issues are sold in the primary market. After that, securities are traded in the secondary market. Investment bankers specialize in issuing and selling new security issues. Stockbrokers are licensed professionals who buy and sell securities on behalf of their clients.

In addition to corporate securities, investors can trade U.S. government Treasury securities and municipal bonds, mutual funds, futures, and options. Mutual funds are financial-service companies that pool the funds of many investors to buy a diversified portfolio of securities. Investors choose mutual funds because they offer a convenient way to diversify and are professionally managed. Exchange-traded funds (ETFs) are similar to mutual funds but trade on stock exchanges similar to common stock. Futures contracts are legally binding obligations to buy or sell specified quantities of commodities or financial instruments at an agreed-upon price at a future date. They are very risky investments because the price of the commodity or financial instrument may change drastically. Options are contracts that entitle the holder the right to buy or sell specified quantities of common stock or other financial instruments at a set price during a specified time. They, too, are high-risk investments.

7 Where can investors buy and sell securities, and how are securities markets regulated?

Securities are resold in secondary markets, which include both broker markets and dealer markets. The broker market consists of national and regional securities exchanges such as the New York Stock Exchange that bring buyers and sellers together through brokers on a centralized trading floor. Dealer markets use sophisticated telecommunications networks that link dealers throughout the United States. The NASDAQ and over-the-counter markets are examples of dealer markets. In addition to broker and dealer markets, electronic communications networks (ECNs) can be used to make securities transactions. In addition to the U.S. markets, more than 100 countries have securities exchanges. The largest non-U.S. exchanges are the Tokyo, Euronext, London, Shanghai, and Hong Kong exchanges.

The Securities Act of 1933 requires disclosure of important information regarding new securities issues. The Securities Exchange Act of 1934 and its 1964 amendment formally empowered the Securities and Exchange Commission and granted it broad powers to regulate the securities exchanges and the dealer markets. The Investment Company Act of 1940 places investment companies such as mutual funds under SEC control. The securities markets also have self-regulatory groups such as the NASD and measures such as "circuit breakers" to halt trading if the Dow Jones Industrial Average drops rapidly.

The effect of globalization on securities markets is manifest in the wave of domestic market mergers as well as international market mergers. Increasingly, exchanges are buying stakes in competing or complementary exchanges as a way to remain competitive.

8 What are the current developments in financial management and the securities markets?

Intense competition in exchange markets has been fueled by the full implementation of Regulation National Market System (Reg NMS) which requires the best (lowest) bid be protected. (The regulation prevents the undercutting of a bid by a competitor.) Exchanges protect bids by further automating the trade cycle, thereby reducing the time it takes to effect the transaction. Automated trading and algorithms reduce latency, or the time between when the trader sends the data (buy, sell) and when the action actually takes place. Increasingly, traders are asking software providers to create customized algorithms.

Key Terms

accounts payable 435
accounts receivable 433
bond ratings 442
bonds 437
broker markets 444
capital budgeting 434
capital expenditures 434
cash flows 430
cash management 432
circuit breakers 448
commercial paper 433
common stock 438
dealer markets 445
dividends 438
electronic communications networks (ECNs) 446
exchange traded fund (ETF) 443
factoring 436
financial management 430
financial risk 437
futures contracts 443
insider trading 447
institutional investors 440
interest 437
investment bankers 440
line of credit 435

marketable securities 433
mortgage loan 438
municipal bonds 442
mutual fund 443
National Association of Securities Dealers Automated Quotation (NASDAQ) system 445
options 443
over-the-counter (OTC) market 446
preferred stock 439
primary market 440
principal 438
retained earnings 439
return 432
revolving credit agreement 436
risk 432
risk-return trade-off 432
secondary market 440
secured loans 436
securities 440
stockbroker 440
stock dividends 438
term loan 437
trade credit 435
underwriting 440
unsecured loans 435

Preparing for Tomorrow's Workplace: SCANS

1. The head of your school's finance department has asked you to address a group of incoming business students about the importance of finance to their overall business education. Develop an outline with the key points you would cover in your speech. (**Information**)

2. You are the chief financial officer of Discovery Labs, a privately held, five-year-old biotechnology company that needs to raise $3 million to fund the development of a new drug. Prepare a report for the board of directors that discusses the types of long-term financing available to the firm, their pros and cons, and the key factors to consider in choosing a financing strategy. (**Information**)

3. **Team Activity** Does paying dividends enhance the value of a company? Some financial experts caution companies to look long and hard before beginning to pay dividends. They believe that committing yourself to a regular dividend curtails financial flexibility and reduces debt capacity. Dividends might also signal that the company doesn't have good growth opportunities in which to invest its excess cash. Others counter that dividends can help a company's stock by making it less volatile. Data from Standard & Poor's support this; typically, dividend-paying stocks in the S&P 500 outperform nonpayers. Divide the class into two teams to debate whether dividends add value to a company's stock. (**Interpersonal, Information**)

4. Research the trends in the IPO marketplace from 1998 to 2007. Then select two IPO success stories and two failures. Prepare a report for the class on their performance. What lessons about the securities markets can you learn from these stories? (**Information**)

5. While having dinner at a Manhattan restaurant, you overhear two investment bankers at the next table. They are discussing the takeover of Bellamco Industries by Gildmart Corp., a deal that has not yet been announced. You have been thinking about buying Bellamco stock for a while, so the next day you buy 500 shares for $30 each. Two weeks later, Gildmart announces its acquisition of Bellamco at a price of $45 per share. Have you fairly earned a profit, or are you guilty of insider trading? What's wrong with insider trading? (**Information**)

6. **Team Activity** Is joining an investment club a good way to learn about investing in the stock market? Divide the class into groups of five to eight students to develop a strategy to form their own investment club. Use the National Association of Investors Corporation (NAIC) Web site at **http://www.better-investing.org** to learn how investment clubs operate and the investment strategy the NAIC teaches. Each group should then set up guidelines for their investment club and present their plan to the class. After the presentations, the class members should discuss whether they would prefer to start investing through an investment club or on their own. (**Resources, Interpersonal, Information**)

Ethics Activity

In June 2006, the SEC opened an investigation into the stock option practices of Cyberonics, a Houston medical-devices manufacturer. As defined by the SEC, stock options give a company's employees the right to buy a specific number of shares at a fixed price within a certain period of time. Holders of stock options hope that the price of the stock will rise by the time they exercise their options so that they make a profit. Companies use stock options to compensate, retain, attract, and motivate executives and other employees.

The issue at Cyberonics was the timing of options grants to three executives in 2004, to buy stock at $19.58, the June 14, 2004 closing price—just after the company received FDA approval of one of its devices. This positive news was expected to raise its share price and all but guarantee the executives profits if they exercised the options. On June 16, 2004, a press release issued by Cyperonics announced the FDA approval to the public, and the stock price jumped 62 percent to close at $31.70.

This practice of issuing stock options in advance of good news is called *spring-loading*. Whether spring-loading is illegal was unclear, however, and became the focus of more than 40 SEC inquiries. Some experts believe that timing options grants in this manner is a form of insider trading, although they concede that proving that the good news would in fact raise the share price could be tricky.

Cyberonics' CFO Pamela B. Westbrook maintained that the options were "properly approved, priced, and granted at fair market value." In addition, the executives receiving the options had not yet exercised the options. At the end of July 2006, Cyberonics shares were trading between $20 and $22.

Using a Web search tool, locate articles about this topic and then write a response to the following question. Be sure to support your arguments and cite your sources.

ETHICAL DILEMMA: Is it legal for a company to grant stock options to its executives just before it releases good news, or does this constitute insider trading?

Sources: "Dates from Hell: Executive Share Options," *Economist*, July 22, 2006, p. 68; "Employee Stock Options Plans," Securities and Exchange Commission, **http://www.sec.gov/answers/empopt.htm**; Jane Sasseen, "Another Dodgy Way to Dole Out Options," *Business Week*, June 26, 2006, p. 40; and "SEC Probing Cyberonics Stock Options," *Houston Business Journal*, June 13, 2006, **http://biz.yahoo.com**.

Working the Net

1. If factoring accounts receivable is still a mystery to you, visit the 21st Financial Solutions site, **http://www.21stfinancialsolutions.com**. Follow the links on the home page to answer these questions: What are factoring's advantages? What are the additional benefits, and what types of companies can use factoring to their advantage? Then summarize the factoring process.

2. Go to vfinance.com, **http://www.vfinance.com**, and link to three different venture capital firms. Compare the firms' investment strategies (industry specialization, age of companies in which they invest, etc.). Also do an AngelSearch to check out two angel investor firms. How do their requirements differ from the venture firms?

3. Compare the listing requirements of the NYSE, NASDAQ, and AMEX using the information at their Web sites: **http://www.nyse.com**, **http://www.nasdaq.com**, and **http://www.amex.com**. Search the sites for listing requirements. What types of companies qualify for listing on each exchange? Why do the NASDAQ and AMEX offer alternative listing standards?

4. Choose a company currently traded on the NYSE (**http://www.nyse.com**). Find the company's Web site using a search engine such as Google.com. At the Web site, find the firm's investor relations information. Review the information, including, if available, the most recent online annual report. Follow up by researching if any SEC actions have been taken against the firm at the SEC Web site, **http://www.sec.gov**. Summarize your findings in a brief report that discusses whether you would recommend this company's stock as an investment.

5. Using the information and links available at the Securities Industry and Financial Markets Association's (SIFMA's) Web site, **http://www.sifma.org**, write a brief paper explaining the pros and cons of investing in corporate bonds. In your paper, provide at least three examples of currently available corporate bonds from a site such as **http://www.investinginbonds.com**, and explain why they would be good investments.

6. The MaxFunds University, **http://www.maxfunds.com/?q=node/35**, offers courses on investing and mutual funds. Choose either MAXuniversity–Part I, Investing Basics, or MAXuniversity–Part II, Everything You Wanted to Know about Mutual Funds. Prepare a presentation for the class based on the course materials.

7. Research the job responsibilities of a corporate Investor Relations Officer (IRO). If possible, try to interview an IRO, by either phone or e-mail. The National Investor Relations Institute (**http://www.niri.org**), a trade association for IROs, is an alternate source of information. What types of experience and education does an IRO need in order to perform effectively? How are their roles changing? Write a paper summarizing your findings.

Creative Thinking Case

Investors Hang Up on Vonage

Founded in 2002, Vonage quickly became a major player in Voice over Internet Protocol (VoIP) phone service. Using Internet connections instead of traditional phone lines, it offered customers an attractive flat rate of about $25 a month for calls to the United States, Canada, and many European countries. By the time of its May 2006 IPO, Vonage had 1.7 million customers and more than half the U.S. market for Internet phone service. Vonage claimed to be the fastest-growing phone company in the United States. Revenues in 2005 were almost triple 2004 levels.

Management thought the time was right to go public and raise funds for expansion. Investors were again interested in IPOs after several years of low demand. So on May 24, 2006, it sold 31.25 million shares and raised $531 million. It also offered its individual customers—usually closed out of high-profile IPOs—the chance to buy 100 shares at the IPO price, an unusual move. So why was the Vonage IPO the worst in two years?

Timing is everything, and Vonage's timing was off. The market fell sharply on inflation concerns. The shares opened on the New York Stock Exchange at $17, fell to $14.85 by the end of the first day, and were trading below $7 by September 2006.

The offer to individual investors worked against Vonage, sending a message to some analysts that institutions were not interested in buying the stock and that Vonage needed help from its customers. Chad Brand of Peridot Capital Management considered this a "huge red flag. . . . If that's not a sign that nobody else wanted their stock, I don't know what is," he posted on his Web site.

Several factors negatively affected the Vonage offering. Increased competition created pricing pressure. Rivals ranged from small VoIP players similar to Vonage to Internet powerhouses including Google, Yahoo, and MSN. Cable companies such as Time Warner, who offer phone service bundled with television and broadband services, and Verizon and other traditional providers were lowering prices as well. Vonage's sales were already falling, while costs-per-subscriber were rising. The company's marketing costs were very high, and the per-line cost of providing service was also rising at the same time that customer complaints about service quality were mounting.

Regulatory uncertainty added another layer of complexity. Telecommunications providers were campaigning to charge for carrying other company's calls. This would add to Vonage's costs. As Vonage grows, it will be required to collect sales tax and other fees, pushing customer bills well above the $25 flat rate they were expecting to pay and removing pricing advantages.

These are just a few of the issues that stand in the way of Vonage's profitability—currently projected for 2009. In fact, Vonage's IPO prospectus said that it will focus on growth rather than profitability and went so far as to say that it might never become profitable. As a public company, Vonage was under greater pressure to execute its business plan and also faces close scrutiny from its investors. Only time will tell if investors hang up when Vonage calls.

Critical Thinking Questions

*   What issues should executives of a company such as Vonage consider before deciding to go public? In your opinion, was the company ready for an IPO, and why?
*   How else could Vonage have raised funds to continue to grow? Compare the risks of raising private equity to going public.
*   Use a search engine and a site such as Yahoo! Finance to learn about Vonage's current situation. Prepare a brief summary, including its current financial situation. Is it still a public company, and how has its stock fared? Would you invest in it, and why?

Sources: David A. Gaffen, "Tale of Two IPOs," *Wall Street Journal Online*, May 24, 2006, **http://www.wsj.com**; Olga Kharif, "Vonage's Iffy IPO," *Business Week Online*, February 9, 2006, **http://www.businessweek.com**; Timothy J. Mullaney, "Vonage's Lackluster IPO," *Business Week Online*, May 24, 2006, **http://www.businessweek.com**; Shawn Young and Li Yuan, "Vonage Faces User Complaints as IPO Looms," *Wall Street Journal*, May 18, 2006, p. B1; Shawn Young and Lynn Cowan, "Vonage Lacks Voltage in Its IPO, with Weakest Debut in 2 Years," *Wall Street Journal*, May 25, 2006, p. C4; Shawn Young and Randall Smith, "How Vonage's High-Profile IPO Stumbled on the Stock Market," *Wall Street Journal*, June 3, 2006, p. A1.

video

**Scott Swanson
JP Morgan Chase**

Exploring Business Careers

Many people dream of working for themselves and owning their own small business. But this involves a large investment of time, dedication, creativity, and money. Even the best ideas fall flat without strong financial backing and fiscal management. Most small businesses don't have a chief financial officer, so a partnership with a reliable financial institution is crucial to ensuring viability.

Scott Swanson, the national executive for Business Bank at JP Morgan Chase, feels strongly about the need to support small businesses. "We have always been an entrepreneurial nation. Small business is the core of our economy. Our Business Bank provides us with an opportunity to support this business segment." Chase helps small-business owners by loaning them money or helping them collect money to further invest in the business.

© South-Western, *Exploring Business Careers*

Unlike corporations, small businesses cannot rely on the sale of stock shares to help them raise capital to purchase equipment, raw materials, real estate, or to pay employees. And often a "time lag" exists between when products are sold and when payments come in. That is where Swanson and Chase come in. "We help bridge that gap between accounts payable and accounts receivable, to help businesses run more smoothly." Chase uses two mechanisms to do this: loans and lines of credit. Long-term loans are lump sums that can be used for purchases of buildings, equipment, or inventory. Payments of the loan go toward the interest and the principal. In contrast, lines of credit are sums of money available to the business owner as he or she needs them. Only the interest must be paid off monthly. Lines of credit can be used to smooth out cash flow and pay for daily business needs, such as utilities and wages, until payments for products sold come in. As customers pay the company, those funds are used to pay down the line of credit.

Swanson believes that in order to support small-business owners, Chase must develop strong relationships with them. "In order to be an effective partner, we need to share information. We need to understand what a business owner sees as their business's future, so we can be proactive in providing solutions and opportunities to maximize future growth." To achieve this, Swanson ensures his bankers are constantly trained in the services Chase provides and have the necessary resources to best understand their customer's business. In this way, the bankers can adapt as the needs of the company change.

Scott Swanson has a commitment to supporting small businesses. Through Chase's many services and products, Swanson is ensuring that this vital sector of our economy stays vibrant. And he is helping more business owners realize their dream.

Apple, Inc.
continuing case
Part 6: Financial Management at Apple, Inc.

In the early days of the company's history, Apple's founders and venture capitalists maintained tight control of the company and its shares. As the company began to grow, however, an initial public offering (IPO) was planned. This is an example of a company *going public*—selling its first shares of stock to the public. The company successfully completed a $96.8 million initial public stock issue in December of 1980. The company went public on December 12, 1980, at $22 per share.

The company experienced a rise of more than 30 percent on its 1980 IPO, a precursor to several boom years. Despite ups and downs, Apple's stock rose continuously between 1985 and 1991. However, 1991 was the beginning of both internal and external problems for Apple. Company stock moved up and down considerably beginning in 1991, with the company hitting rock bottom in July of 1997, resulting in a profitability crisis and, ultimately, a viability crisis. By March of 2000, however, the stock price had skyrocketed again and hit an all-time high. According to some analysts, Apple had pioneered the get-rich-quick IPO and had also epitomized the boom-and-bust cycle of technology companies.

Apple's common stock is traded on the NASDAQ Stock Market under the ticker symbol AAPL and on the Frankfurt Stock Exchange under the symbol APCD. The company does not have any preferred stock outstanding, and there have been three stock splits since the company went public in 1980—in May of 1987, June of 2000, and February of 2005. When a company declares a *stock split*, the price of the stock decreases and the number of shares increases proportionately. By reducing the price of the stock, companies try to make their stock more affordable to investors. Quarterly financial results are released on the third Wednesday of each quarter, with the fiscal year beginning the first of October.

Share Prices Plummet

Apple had steadily taken itself into near oblivion by the mid-1990s. By the beginning of 1996, the company had basically fallen into the category of sad stories about high-tech companies that had gone broke. At the end of the first quarter in 1996, the company reported a loss of $740 million and its market share had shrunk to 5.4 percent. With cash reserves dwindling, new CEO Gilbert Amelio was seeking additional financing. Rather than continuing to adhere to what was referred to as a developer-led culture, Amelio promised investors that the company was going to concentrate on products with good profit margins (a premium-priced, differentiation strategy). This meant a shift to a competitive market focus, as well as a more structured organization with processes and management systems that enabled checks and balances.

According to Apple's chief financial officer during this time, the company had spent 10 years responding to financial crisis after financial crisis with only short-term solutions. The initial step in finding the cure for such growing pains was to find the cash to keep the company running, followed by adding managerial discipline to all functions of the company. The managerial discipline adhered to by Amelio was that of streamlining the product and reducing the payroll through staff cuts. However, Amelio's high-priced, cost-cutting efforts were unsuccessful. Apple's shares hit their all-time low and he was forced out in 1997—only one year after taking the company's helm.

Jobs's Return and Apple's Rebound

The July day in 1997 that Amelio left Apple was the same day that Steve Jobs returned. Unlike Amelio, who had attributed Apple's problems to a lax developer-led culture, Jobs attributed Apple's problems to new-product development that resulted in products without passion. Thus, Jobs began a drastic turnaround of the company.

This turnaround took Apple from a beleaguered computer company to a top performer in about three years. By 2000, Apple was experiencing notably improved stock performance. While the company did experience a slump in the late 1990s, the slump was industry-wide, and Apple began pulling out of the slump before its competitors. As such, the company's stock was of interest to investors who were focused more on valuation than rapid growth in earnings. These value investors specialize in bargain shopping, purchasing stock at a low point and sticking with it for the longer term. Apple's stock hit an all-time high of $72.10 in March of 2000.

Five years later, Apple set another new stock market high. The company's stock finished trading on January 31, 2005, at $76.80. This trading price valued the company around $30 billion. In October of 2005, the company reported its highest revenue and earnings in company history to that date. It shipped around 1.2 million Macintosh computers and 6.5 million iPods during fiscal 2005 fourth quarter. This was a 48 percent increase in Mac sales and a 220 percent increase in iPod sales compared to fiscal 2004 fourth quarter. Full-year numbers for fiscal 2005 were $14 billion in sales (a 68 percent one-year sales growth), $1.3 billion net income (a 384 percent one-year net income growth), and 13,426 employees (a 23 percent one-year employee growth).

Macintosh and iPod sales continued to rise steadily, all the way into the first fiscal quarter of 2008. Apple's first-quarter 2008 revenue of $9.6 billion constituted a 35 percent increase year-over-year. The company's quarterly net profit of $1.58 billion, or $1.76 per share, was up from $1 billion in the year-earlier quarter. The robust figures were indicative of the shipment of 2.3 million Macintosh computers and a record 22.1 million iPods. iPhone sales reached 2.3 million units in the same three-month period. Apple's early 2008 success came on the heels of the company's annual earnings report for fiscal year 2007, in which Apple reported full-year revenue of $24 billion and $3.5 billion in net income. On the NASDAQ, Apple's stock reflected the company's economic and technological growth, closing at $155.64 per share on January 22, 2008.

Critical Thinking Questions

- Describe a value investor.
- Would value investors be interested in purchasing Apple shares today?
- Why did Apple reduce the price of its stock through stock splits?
- What impact did Apple's February 2005 stock split have on the performance of shares in subsequent years?
- Are there indications that Apple's rapid growth is beginning to level off?
- Which Apple products can be expected to drive revenue growth in 2008 and beyond?

Sources: Roy A. Allan, *A History of the Personal Computer* (London, Ontario, Canada: Allan Publishing, 2001); Anonymous, "Apple Seeks Cash," *Information Week,* May 6, 1996, p. 30; Anonymous, "Apple Sells 661 Million Dollars' Worth of Notes, Common Stock," *Agence France-Presse,* June 10, 1996, **http://global.factiva.com**, accessed on December 6, 2005; Anonymous, "Buyers Bite at Apple Offer," *Electronic News,* June 17, 1996, p. 12; Peter Burrows and Ronald Grover, "Steve Jobs' Magic Kingdom," *BusinessWeek,* February 6, 2006, pp. 63–69; Thomas Claburn, "Financial Analyst Sees Windows Users Going Mac," *InternetWeek,* November 8, 2005, **http://www.internetweek.com**, accessed on December 6, 2005; Dow Jones &. Co., Inc., "Apple Computer Shares Sold Out; Nautilus Fund Skids on Sale," *DowJones Newswires,* December 12, 1980, **http://global.factiva.com**, accessed on December 6, 2005; Benny Evangelista, "Preaching Beyond the Mac Faithful iPod Phenomenon Could Have Halo Effect on Apple's Mac Products," *San Francisco Chronicle,* December 5, 2004, **http://www.sfgate.com**, accessed on April 7, 2006; Robert Paul Leitao, "Welcome," *ATPM,* February 2005, **http://www.atmp.com**, accessed on April 5, 2006; Reuters, "Apple Profit Nearly Doubles but Forecast Disappoints," *USA Today,* January 18, 2006, **http://www.usatoday.com**, accessed on April 7, 2006; Pui-Wing Tam, "Value Investors Go Apple (Computer) Picking," *Wall Street Journal,* March 29, 2001, p. C1; Chris Ward, "The Apple Crumble That Was Saved by Dr. Amelio's Recipe," *The Times,* July 31, 1996, **http://global.factiva.com**, accessed on December 6, 2005; Joel West, "Apple Computer: The iCEO Seizes the Internet," Center for Research on Information Technology and Organizations, Paper 348, 2002, downloaded from **http://repositories.cdlib.org**, accessed on December 6, 2005; **http://www.apple.com/investor**, accessed on April 7, 2006; **http://www.hoovers.com**, accessed on February 6, 2006; Agam Shah, "Record iPhone, Mac Sales Boost Apple's Earnings: A 35 Percent Year-over-Year Revenue Increase Topped Analysts' Projections for the Quarter," *Infoworld,* January 22, 2008, **http://www.infoworld.com**, accessed February 11, 2008; Apple Inc., "Apple Reports Fourth Quarter Results," Apple.com, October 22, 2007, **http://www.apple.com/pr/library/2007/10/22results.html**, accessed February 12, 2008.

glossary

A

absolute advantage The situation when a country can produce and sell a product at a lower cost than any other country or when it is the only country that can provide the product.

accounting The process of collecting, recording, classifying, summarizing, reporting, and analyzing financial activities.

accounts payable Purchase for which a buyer has not yet paid the seller.

accounts receivable Sales for which a firm has not yet been paid.

acid-test (quick) ratio The ratio of total current assets excluding inventory to total current liabilities; used to measure a firm's liquidity.

acquisition The purchase of a target company by another corporation or by an investor group, typically negotiated with the target company board of directors.

activity ratios Ratios that measure how well a firm uses its assets.

actual cash value The market value, determined by subtracting the amount of depreciation from its replacement cost, of personal property; the amount paid by standard homeowners and renters insurance policies.

administrative law The rules, regulations, and orders passed by boards, commissions, and agencies of government (local, state, and federal).

advertising Any paid form of nonpersonal presentation by an identified sponsor.

advertising media The channels through which advertising is carried to prospective customers; includes newspapers, magazines, radio, television, outdoor advertising, direct mail, and the Internet.

affirmative action programs Programs established by organizations to expand job opportunities for women and minorities.

agency shop Workers don't have to join a union but must pay union dues.

agents Sales representatives of manufacturers and wholesalers.

angel investors Individual investors or groups of experienced investors who provide financing for start-up businesses by investing their own funds.

annual report A yearly document that describes a firm's financial status and usually discusses the firm's activities during the past year and its prospects for the future.

antitrust regulation Laws that prevent companies from entering into agreements to control trade through a monopoly.

appellate courts (courts of appeals) The level of courts above the trial courts; the losing party in a civil case and the defendant in a criminal case may appeal the trial court's decision to an appellate court.

application service providers (ASPs) A service company that buys and maintains software on its servers and distributes it through high-speed networks to subscribers, for a set period and price.

apprenticeship A form of on-the-job training that combines specific job instruction with classroom instruction.

arbitration A method of settling disputes in which the parties agree to present their case to an impartial third party and are required to accept the arbitrator's decision.

assembly process A production process in which the basic inputs are either combined to create the output or transformed into the output.

assets Things of value owned by a firm.

audience selectivity An advertising medium's ability to reach a precisely defined market.

auditing The process of reviewing the records used to prepare financial statements and issuing a formal auditor's opinion indicating whether the statements have been prepared in accordance with accepted accounting rules.

authority Legitimate power, granted by the organization and acknowledged by employees, that allows an individual to request action and expect compliance.

autocratic leaders Directive leaders who prefer to make decisions and solve problems on their own with little input from subordinates.

automobile liability insurance Insurance that protects the insured from financial losses caused by automobile-related injuries to others and damage to their property.

automobile physical damage insurance Insurance that covers damage to or loss of the policyholder's vehicle from collision, theft, fire, or other perils; includes collision coverage and comprehensive (other-than-collision) coverage.

B

balance of payments A summary of a country's international financial transactions showing the difference between the country's total payments to and its total receipts from other countries.

balance of trade The difference between the value of a country's exports and the value of its imports during a specific time.

balance sheet A financial statement that summarizes a firm's financial position at a specific point in time.

bank charter An operating license issued to a bank by the federal government or a state government; required for a commercial bank to do business.

bankruptcy The legal procedure by which individuals or businesses that cannot meet their financial obligations are relieved of their debt.

barriers to entry Factors, such as technological or legal conditions, that prevent new firms from competing equally with an existing firm.

batch processing A method of updating a database in which data are collected over some time period and processed together.

benefit segmentation The differentiation of markets based on what a product will do rather than on customer characteristics.

bill of material A list of the items and the number of each required to make a given product.

board of directors A group of people elected by the stockholders to handle the overall management of a corporation, such as setting major corporate goals and policies, hiring corporate officers, and overseeing the firm's operations and finances.

bond ratings Letter grades assigned to bond issues to indicate their quality, or level of risk; assigned by rating agencies such as Moody's and Standard & Poor's (S&P).

bonds Long-term debt obligations (liabilities) issued by corporations and governments.

brainstorming A method of generating ideas in which group members suggest as many possibilities as they can without criticizing or evaluating any of the suggestions.

brand equity Value and long-term sustainability of a known brand name.

breach of contract The failure by one party to a contract to fulfill the terms of the agreement without a legal excuse.

breaking bulk The process of breaking large shipments of similar products into smaller, more usable lots.

broker markets National and regional securities exchanges that bring buyers and sellers together through brokers on a centralized trading floor.

brokers Go-betweens that bring buyers and sellers together.

browsers Software that allows users to access the Web with a graphical point-and-click interface.

budgets Formal written forecasts of revenues and expenses that set spending limits based on operational forecasts; include cash budgets, capital budgets, and operating budgets.

bundling The strategy of grouping two or more related products together and pricing them as a single product.

business An organization that strives for a profit by providing goods and services desired by its customers.

business cycles Upward and downward changes in the level of economic activity.

business law The body of law that governs commercial dealings.

business plan A formal written statement that describes in detail the idea for a new business and how it will be carried out; includes a general description of the company, the qualifications of the owner(s), a description of the product or service, an analysis of the market, and a financial plan.

Business Process Management (BPM) A unified system that has the power to integrate and optimize a company's sprawling functions by automating much of what it does.

business-to-business e-commerce (B2B) Electronic commerce that involves transactions between companies.

business-to-consumer e-commerce (B2C) Electronic commerce that involves transactions between businesses and the end user of the goods or services; also called e-tailing.

buyer behavior The actions people take in buying and using goods and services.

buyer cooperative A group of cooperative members who unite for combined purchasing power.

buy-national regulations Government rules that give special privileges to domestic manufacturers and retailers.

C

C corporation Conventional or basic form of corporate organization.

CAD/CAM systems Linked computer systems that combine the advantages of computer-aided design and computer-aided manufacturing. The system helps design the product, control the flow of resources, and operate the production process.

capital The inputs, such as tools, machinery, equipment, and buildings, used to produce goods and services and get them to the customer.

capital budgeting The process of analyzing long-term projects and selecting those that offer the best returns while maximizing the firm's value.

capital budgets Budgets that forecast a firm's outlays for fixed assets (plant and equipment), typically covering a period.

capital expenditures Investments in long-lived assets, such as land, buildings, machinery, and equipment, that are expected to provide benefits that extend beyond one year.

capital products Large, expensive items with a long life span that are purchased by businesses for use in making other products or providing a service.

capitalism An economic system based on competition in the marketplace and private ownership of the factors of production (resources); also known as the private enterprise system.

cash budgets Budgets that forecast a firm's cash inflows and outflows and help the firm plan for cash surpluses and shortages.

cash flow plan A cash management tool that includes a plan for managing income and expenses, and the savings and investment contributions needed to accomplish one's financial goals; often called a budget.

cash flows The inflows and outflows of cash for a firm.

cash management For a firm, the process of making sure that it has enough cash on hand to pay bills as they come due and to meet unexpected expenses. For individuals, the day-to-day handling of their liquid assets.

cash value The dollar amount paid to the owner of a life insurance policy if the policy is canceled before the death of the insured; term life insurance has no cash value.

cellular manufacturing Production technique that uses small, self-contained production units, each performing all or most of the tasks necessary to complete a manufacturing order.

centralization The degree to which formal authority is concentrated in one area or level of an organization. Top management makes most of the decisions.

certified management accountant (CMA) A managerial accountant who has completed a professional certification program, including passing an examination.

certified public accountant (CPA) An accountant who has completed an approved bachelor's degree program, passed a test prepared by the American Institute of Certified Public Accountants, and met state requirements. Only a CPA can issue an auditor's opinion on a firm's financial statements.

chain of command The line of authority that extends from one level of an organization's hierarchy to the next, from top to bottom, and makes clear who reports to whom.

chief information officer (CIO) An executive with responsibility for managing all information resources in an organization.

circuit breakers Corrective measures that, under certain conditions, stop trading in the securities markets for a short cooling-off period to limit the amount the market can drop in one day.

circular flow The movement of inputs and outputs among households, businesses, and governments; a way of showing how the sectors of the economy interact.

COBRA A federal regulation that allows most employees and their families to continue group health insurance coverage at their own expense for up to 18 months after leaving an employer.

code of ethics A set of guidelines prepared by a firm to provide its employees with the knowledge of what the firm expects in terms of their responsibilities and behavior toward fellow employees, customers, and suppliers.

coercive power Power that is derived from an individual's ability to threaten negative outcomes.

coinsurance (participation) A percentage of covered expenses that the holder of a major medical insurance policy must pay.

collective bargaining Negotiating a labor agreement.

commercial banks Profit-oriented financial institutions that accept deposits, make business and consumer loans, invest in government and corporate securities, and provide other financial services.

commercial paper Unsecured short-term debt—an IOU—issued by a financially strong corporation.

committee structure An organizational structure in which authority and responsibility are held by a group rather than an individual.

common law The body of unwritten law that has evolved out of judicial (court) decisions rather than being enacted by a legislature; also called case law.

common stock A security that represents an ownership interest in a corporation.

communism An economic system characterized by government ownership of virtually all resources, government control of all markets, and economic decision making by central-government planning.

community of practice (CoP) A group of people who share a concern, problem, or passion about a topic, and who deepen their knowledge and expertise in this area by interacting on an ongoing basis.

competitive advantage A set of unique features of a company and its products that are perceived by the target market as significant and superior to those of the competition; also called differential advantage.

comprehensive (other-than-collision) insurance Automobile insurance that covers damage to or loss of the policyholder's vehicle due to perils such as fire, floods, theft, and vandalism; part of automobile physical damage insurance.

computer network A group of two or more computer systems linked together by communications channels to share data and information.

computer virus A computer program that copies itself into other software and can spread to other computer systems.

computer-aided design (CAD) The use of computers to design and test new products and modify existing ones.

computer-aided manufacturing (CAM) The use of computers to develop and control the production process.

computer-integrated manufacturing (CIM) The combination of computerized manufacturing processes (like robots and flexible manufacturing systems) with other computerized systems that control design, inventory, production, and purchasing.

conceptual skills A manager's ability to view the organization as a whole, understand how the various parts are interdependent, and assess how the organization relates to its external environment.

conciliation The process whereby a specialist in labor-management negotiations acts as a go-between for management and the unions and helps focus on the problems.

conciliator Specialist in labor–management negotiations that acts as a go-between for management and the unions and helps focus on the problems.

conglomerate merger A merger of companies in unrelated businesses; done to reduce risk.

consensual leaders Leaders who encourage discussion about issues and then require that all parties involved agree to the final decision.

consultative leaders Leaders who confer with subordinates before making a decision, but who retain the final decision-making authority.

consumer price index (CPI) An index of the prices of a "market basket" of goods and services purchased by typical urban consumers.

consumerism A social movement that seeks to increase the rights and powers of buyers vis-à-vis sellers.

contingency plans Plans that identify alternative courses of action for very unusual or crisis situations; typically stipulate the chain of command, standard operating procedures, and communication channels the organization will use during an emergency.

contingent worker Person who prefers temporary employment, either part-time or full-time.

continuous improvement A commitment to constantly seek better ways of doing things in order to achieve greater efficiency and improve quality.

continuous process A production process that uses long production runs lasting days, weeks, or months without equipment shutdowns; generally used for high-volume, low-variety products with standardized parts.

contract An agreement that sets forth the relationship between parties regarding the performance of a specified action; creates a legal obligation and is enforceable in a court of law.

contract manufacturing The practice in which a foreign firm manufactures private-label goods under a domestic firm's brand name.

contractionary policy The use of monetary policy by the Fed to tighten the money supply by selling government securities or raising interest rates.

controlling The process of assessing the organization's progress toward accomplishing its goals; includes monitoring the implementation of a plan and correcting deviations from the plan.

convenience products Relatively inexpensive items that require little shopping effort and are purchased routinely without planning.

cooperative A legal entity typically formed by people with similar interests, such as suppliers or customers, to reduce costs and gain economic power. A cooperative has limited liability, an unlimited life span, an elected board of directors, and an administrative staff; all profits are distributed to the member-owners in proportion to their contributions.

copyright A form of protection established by the government for creators of works of art, music, literature, or other intellectual property; gives the creator the exclusive right to use, produce, and sell the creation during the lifetime of the creator and for 50 years thereafter.

corporate culture The set of attitudes, values, and standards that distinguishes one organization from another.

corporate philanthropy The practice of charitable giving by corporations; includes contributing cash, donating equipment and products, and supporting the volunteer efforts of company employees.

corporation A legal entity with an existence and life separate from its owners, who are not personally liable for the entity's debts. A corporation is chartered by the state in which it is formed and can own property, enter into contracts, sue and be sued, and engage in business operations under the terms of its charter.

cost competitive advantage A firm's ability to produce a product or service at a lower cost than all other competitors in an industry while maintaining satisfactory profit margins.

cost of goods sold The total expense of buying or producing a firm's goods or services.

cost per thousand (CPM) Cost per thousand contacts is a term used in expressing advertising costs; refers to the cost of reaching 1,000 members of the target market.

cost-push inflation Inflation that occurs when increases in production costs push up the prices of final goods and services.

costs Expenses incurred from creating and selling goods and services.

countertrade A form of international trade in which part or all of the payment for goods or services is in the form of other goods and services.

credit life insurance Insurance that will repay a loan if the borrower dies while the loan is still outstanding.

credit unions Not-for-profit, member-owned financial cooperatives.

critical path In a critical path method network, the longest path through the linked activities.

critical path method (CPM) A scheduling tool that enables a manager to determine the critical path of activities for a project—the activities that will cause the entire project to fall behind schedule if they are not completed on time.

cross-functional team Members from the same organizational level but from different functional areas.

crowding out The situation that occurs when government spending replaces spending by the private sector.

culture The set of values, ideas, attitudes, and other symbols created to shape human behavior.

currency Cash held in the form of coins and paper money.

current assets Assets that can or will be converted to cash within the next 12 months.

current liabilities Short-term claims that are due within a year of the date of the balance sheet.

current ratio The ratio of total current assets to total current liabilities; used to measure a firm's liquidity.

customer departmentalization Departmentalization that is based on the primary type of customer served by the organizational unit.

customer satisfaction The customer's feeling that a product has met or exceeded expectations.

customer value The ratio of benefits to the sacrifice necessary to obtain those benefits, as determined by the customer; reflects the willingness of customers to actually buy a product.

customization The production of goods or services one at a time according to the specific needs or wants of individual customers.

cyclical unemployment Unemployment that occurs when a downturn in the business cycle reduces the demand for labor throughout the economy.

D

data mart Special subset of a data warehouse that deals with a single area of data and is organized for quick analysis.

data mining Sophisticated database applications that look for hidden patterns in a group of data to help track and predict future behavior.

data warehouse An information technology that combines many databases across a whole company into one central database that supports management decision making.

database An electronic filing system that collects and organizes data and information.

dealer markets Securities markets where buy and sell orders are executed through dealers, or "market makers," linked by telecommunications networks.

debt A form of business financing consisting of borrowed funds that must be repaid with interest over a stated time period.

debt ratios Ratios that measure the degree and effect of a firm's use of borrowed funds (debt) to finance its operations.

debt-to-equity ratio The ratio of total liabilities to owners' equity; measures the relationship between the amount of debt financing and the amount of equity financing (owner's funds).

decentralization The process of pushing decision-making authority down the organizational hierarchy.

decision support system (DSS) A management support system that helps managers make decisions using interactive computer models that describe real-world processes.

decisional roles A manager's activities as an entrepreneur, resource allocator, conflict resolver, or negotiator.

deductible The portion of a claim for which the insured, not the insurer, is responsible for paying.

delegation of authority The assignment of some degree of authority and responsibility to persons lower in the chain of command.

demand The quantity of a good or service that people are willing to buy at various prices.

demand curve A graph showing the quantity of a good or service that people are willing to buy at various prices.

demand deposits Money kept in checking accounts that can be withdrawn by depositors on demand.

demand-pull inflation Inflation that occurs when the demand for goods and services is greater than the supply.

democratic leaders Leaders who solicit input from all members of the group and then allow the members to make the final decision through a vote.

demographic segmentation The differentiation of markets through the use of categories such as age, education, gender, income, and household size.

demography The study of people's vital statistics, such as their age, gender, race and ethnicity, and location.

deontology A person who will follow his or her obligations to an individual or society because upholding one's duty is what is ethically correct.

departmentalization The process of grouping jobs together so that similar or associated tasks and activities can be coordinated.

depreciation The allocation of an asset's original cost to the years in which it is expected to produce revenues.

deregulation The removal of rules and regulations governing business competition.

devaluation A lowering of the value of a nation's currency relative to other currencies.

differential competitive advantage A firm's ability to provide a unique product or service with a set of features that the target market perceives as important and better than the competitor's.

direct foreign investment Active ownership of a foreign company or of manufacturing or marketing facilities in a foreign country.

disability income insurance Insurance that will replace a portion of your earnings, typically 60 to 70 percent of your monthly income, if you are unable to work due to illness or accident.

discount rate The interest rate that the Federal Reserve charges its member banks.

distribution (logistics) Efficiently managing the acquisition of raw materials to the factory and the movement of products from the producer to industrial users and consumers.

distribution channel The series of marketing entities through which goods and services pass on their way from producers to end users.

distribution strategy Creating the means by which products flow from the producer to the consumer.

diversification An investment strategy that involves investing in different classes of assets, such as cash equivalents, stocks, bonds, and real estate, and purchasing securities with different risk patterns and rates of return.

dividend reinvestment plan (DRIP) A program in which dividends paid by a stock are automatically reinvested in that stock along with any additional stock purchases submitted by the stockholder.

dividends Payments to stockholders from a corporation's profits.

division of labor The process of dividing work into separate jobs and assigning tasks to workers.

double-entry bookkeeping A method of accounting in which each transaction is recorded as two entries so that two accounts or records are changed.

dumping The practice of charging a lower price for a product in foreign markets than in the firm's home market.

E

earned income Income that is earned from employment such as wages, tips, and self-employment income.

earnings per share (EPS) The ratio of net profit to the number of shares of common stock outstanding; measures the number of dollars earned by each share of stock.

economic growth An increase in a nation's output of goods and services.

economic system The combination of policies, laws, and choices made by a nation's government to establish the systems that determine what goods and services are produced and how they are allocated.

economics The study of how a society uses scarce resources to produce and distribute goods and services.

effectiveness The ability to produce the desired result or good.

efficiency Using the least amount of resources to accomplish the organization's goals.

electronic commerce (e-commerce) The entire process of selling a product or service via the Internet; also called electronic business (e-business).

electronic communications networks (ECNs) Private trading networks that allow institutional traders and some individuals to make direct transactions in the fourth market.

electronic data interchange (EDI) The electronic exchange of information between two trading partners.

embargo A total ban on imports or exports of a product.

emergency fund Liquid assets that are available to meet emergencies.

empowerment The process of giving employees increased autonomy and discretion to make decisions, as well as control over the resources needed to implement those decisions.

enterprise portal A customizable internal Web site that provides proprietary corporate information to a defined user group, such as employees, supply chain partners, or customers.

enterprise resource planning (ERP) A computerized resource-planning system that incorporates information about the firm's suppliers and customers with its internally generated data.

enterprise risk management (ERM) A company-wide, strategic approach to identifying, monitoring, and managing all elements of a company's risk.

entrepreneurs People who combine the inputs of natural resources, labor, and capital to produce goods or services with the intention of making a profit or accomplishing a not-for-profit goal.

environmental scanning The process in which a firm continually collects and evaluates information about its external environment.

e-procurement The process of purchasing supplies and materials online using the Internet.

Equal Employment Opportunity Commission (EEOC) Processes discrimination complaints, issues regulations regarding discrimination, and disseminates information.

equilibrium The point at which quantity demanded equals quantity supplied.

equity A form of business financing consisting of funds raised through the sale of stock (i.e., ownership) in a business.

equity theory A theory of motivation that holds that worker satisfaction is influenced by employees' perceptions about how fairly they are treated compared with their coworkers.

ethical issue A situation where a person must choose from a set of actions that may be ethical or unethical.

ethics A set of moral standards for judging whether something is right or wrong.

European integration The delegation of limited sovereignty by European Union member states to the EU so that common laws and policies can be created at the European level.

European Union Trade agreement among 25 European nations.

exchange The process in which two parties give something of value to each other to satisfy their respective needs.

exchange controls Laws that require a company earning foreign exchange (foreign currency) from its exports to sell the foreign exchange to a control agency, such as a central bank.

exchange-traded fund (ETF) A security similar to a mutual fund that holds a broad basket of stocks with a common theme, but trades on a stock exchange so that its price changes throughout the day.

excise taxes Taxes that are imposed on specific items such as gasoline, alcoholic beverages, airline tickets, and guns.

executive information system (EIS) A management support system that is customized for an individual executive; provides specific information for strategic decisions.

expansionary policy The use of monetary policy by the Fed to increase the growth of the money supply.

expectancy theory A theory of motivation that holds that the probability of an individual acting in a particular way depends on the strength of that individual's belief that the act will have a particular outcome and on whether the individual values that outcome.

expense items Items, purchased by businesses, that are smaller and less expensive than capital products and usually have a life span of less than one year.

expenses The costs of generating revenues.

experiment A marketing research method in which the investigator changes one or more variables—price, packaging, design, shelf space, advertising theme, or advertising expenditures—while observing the effects of these changes on another variable (usually sales).

expert power Power that is derived from an individual's extensive knowledge in one or more areas.

expert system A management support system that gives managers advice similar to what they would get from a human consultant; it uses artificial intelligence to enable computers to reason and learn to solve problems in much the same way humans do.

exporting The practice of selling domestically produced goods to buyers in another country.

exports Goods and services that are shipped and sold to buyers in other countries.

extranet A private computer network that uses Internet technology and a browser interface but is accessible only to authorized outsiders with a valid username and password.

F

factoring A form of short-term financing in which a firm sells its accounts receivable outright at a discount to a factor.

factors of production The resources used to create goods and services.

federal budget deficit The condition that occurs when the federal government spends more for programs than it collects in taxes.

Federal Deposit Insurance Corporation (FDIC) An independent, quasi-public corporation backed by the full faith and credit of the U.S. government that insures deposits in commercial banks and thrift institutions for up to a ceiling of $100,000 per account.

Federal Reserve System (the Fed) The central bank of the United States; it consists of 12 district banks, each located in a major U.S. city.

federation A collection of unions banned together to achieve common goals.

filing status The marital status of a taxpayer specified on the income tax return.

financial accounting Accounting that focuses on preparing external financial reports that are used by outsiders such as lenders, suppliers, investors, and government agencies to assess the financial strength of a business.

Financial Accounting Standards Board (FASB) The private organization that is responsible for establishing financial accounting standards in the United States.

financial intermediation The process in which financial institutions act as intermediaries between the suppliers and demanders of funds.

financial management The art and science of managing a firm's money so that it can meet its goals.

financial risk The chance that a firm will be unable to make scheduled interest and principal payments on its debt.

fiscal policy The government's use of taxation and spending to affect the economy.

fixed assets Long-term assets used by a firm for more than a year such as land, buildings, and machinery.

fixed-cost contribution The selling price per unit (revenue) minus the variable costs per unit.

fixed-position layout A facility arrangement in which the product stays in one place and workers and machinery move to it as needed.

flexible manufacturing system (FMS) A system that combines automated workstations with computer-controlled transportation devices—automatic guided vehicles (AGVs)—that move materials between workstations and into and out of the system.

floating exchange rates A system in which prices of currencies move up and down based on the demand for and supply of the various currencies.

focus group A group of 8 to 12 participants led by a moderator in an in-depth discussion on one particular topic or concept.

formal organization The order and design of relationships within a firm; consists of two or more people working together with a common objective and clarity of purpose.

four Ps Product, price, promotion, and place (distribution), which together make up the marketing mix.

franchise agreement A contract setting out the terms of a franchising arrangement, including the rules for running the franchise, the services provided by the franchisor, and the financial terms. Under the contract, the franchisee is allowed to use the franchisor's business name, trademark, and logo.

franchisee In a franchising arrangement, the individual or company that sells the goods or services of the franchisor in a certain geographic area.

franchising A form of business organization based on a business arrangement between a franchisor, which supplies the product or service concept, and the franchisee, who sells the goods or services of the franchisor in a certain geographic area.

franchisor In a franchising arrangement, the company that supplies the product or service concept to the franchisee.

free trade The policy of permitting the people and businesses of a country to buy and sell where they please without restrictions.

free-rein (laissez-faire) leadership A leadership style in which the leader turns over all authority and control to subordinates.

free-trade zone An area where the nations allow free, or almost free, trade among each other while imposing tariffs on goods of nations outside the zone.

frequency The number of times an individual is exposed to an advertising message.

frictional unemployment Short-term unemployment that is not related to the business cycle.

full employment The condition when all people who want to work and can work have jobs.

functional departmentalization Departmentalization that is based on the primary functions performed within an organizational unit.

futures contracts Legally binding obligations to buy or sell specified quantities of commodities or financial instruments at an agreed-on price at a future date.

G

Gantt charts Bar graphs plotted on a time line that show the relationship between scheduled and actual production.

general partners Partners who have unlimited liability for all of the firm's business obligations and who control its operations.

general partnership A partnership in which all partners share in the management and profits. Each partner can act on behalf of the firm and has unlimited liability for all its business obligations.

generally accepted accounting principles (GAAP) The financial accounting standards followed by accountants in the United States when preparing financial statements.

geographic departmentalization Departmentalization that is based on the geographic segmentation of the organizational units.

geographic segmentation The differentiation of markets by region of the country, city or county size, market density, or climate.

global management skills A manager's ability to operate in diverse cultural environments.

global vision The ability to recognize and react to international business opportunities, be aware of threats from foreign competition, and effectively use international distribution networks to obtain raw materials and move finished products to customers.

goal-setting theory A theory of motivation based on the premise that an individual's intention to work toward a goal is a primary source of motivation.

goods Tangible items manufactured by businesses.

grace period The period of time after a purchase is made on a credit card during which interest is not owed if the entire balance is paid on time.

grievance A formal complaint by a union worker that management has violated the contract.

gross domestic product (GDP) The total market value of all final goods and services produced within a nation's borders in each year.

gross profit The amount a company earns after paying to produce or buy its products but before deducting operating expenses.

gross sales The total dollar amount of a company's sales.

group cohesiveness The degree to which group members want to stay in the group and tend to resist outside influences.

H

Hawthorne effect The phenomenon that employees perform better when they feel singled out for attention or feel that management is concerned about their welfare.

health maintenance organizations (HMOs) Managed care organizations that provide comprehensive health care services for a fixed periodic payment.

horizontal merger A merger of companies at the same stage in the same industry; done to reduce costs, expand product offerings, or reduce competition.

human relations skills A manager's interpersonal skills that are used to accomplish goals through the use of human resources.

human resource (HR) management The process of hiring, developing, motivating, and evaluating employees to achieve organizational goals.

human resources planning Creating a strategy for meeting current and future human resource needs.

hygiene factors Extrinsic elements of the work environment that do not serve as a source of employee satisfaction or motivation.

hypertext A file or series of files within a Web page that links users to documents at the same or other Web sites.

I

import quota A limit on the quantity of a certain good that can be imported.

imports Goods and services that are bought from other countries.

incentive pay Additional pay for attaining a specific goal.

income statement A financial statement that summarizes a firm's revenues and expenses and shows its total profit or loss over a period of time.

income taxes Taxes that are based on the income received by businesses and individuals.

indemnity (fee-for-service) plans Health insurance plans that reimburse the insured for medical costs covered by the insurance policy. The policyholder selects the health care providers.

industrial distributors Independent wholesalers that buy related product lines from many manufacturers and sell them to industrial users.

inflation The situation in which the average of all prices and goods is rising.

informal organization The network of connections and channels of communication based on the informal relationships of individuals inside an organization.

information technology (IT) The equipment and techniques used to manage and process information.

informational roles A manager's activities as an information gatherer, an information disseminator, or a spokesperson for the company.

infrastructure The basic institutions and public facilities on which an economy's development depends.

insider trading The use of information that is not available to the general public to make profits on securities transactions.

institutional investors Investment professionals who are paid to manage other people's money.

intangible assets Long-term assets with no physical existence, such as patents, copyrights, trademarks, and goodwill.

integrated marketing communications (IMC) The careful coordination of all promotional activities—media advertising, sales promotion, personal selling, and public relations, as well as direct marketing, packaging, and other forms of promotion—to produce a consistent, unified message that is customer focused.

interest A fixed amount of money paid by the issuer of a bond to the bondholder on a regular schedule, typically every six months; stated as the coupon rate.

intermittent process A production process that uses short production runs to make batches of different products; generally used for low-volume, high-variety products.

International Monetary Fund (IMF) An international organization, founded in 1945, that promotes trade, makes short-term loans to member nations, and acts as a lender of last resort for troubled nations.

Internet A worldwide computer network that includes both commercial and public networks and offers various capabilities including e-mail, file transfer, online chat sessions, and newsgroups.

Internet service providers (ISPs) Commercial services that connect companies and individuals to the Internet.

interpersonal roles A manager's activities as a figurehead, company leader, or liaison.

intranet An internal corporate-wide area network that uses Internet technology to connect computers and link employees in many locations and with different types of computers.

intrapreneurs Entrepreneurs who apply their creativity, vision, and risk-taking within a large corporation, rather than starting a company of their own.

inventory The supply of goods that a firm holds for use in production or for sale to customers.

inventory management The determination of how much of each type of inventory a firm will keep on hand and the ordering, receiving, storing, and tracking of inventory.

inventory turnover ratio The ratio of cost of goods sold to average inventory; measures the speed with which inventory moves through a firm and is turned into sales.

investing The process of committing money to various investment instruments in order to obtain future financial returns.

investment bankers Firms that act as intermediaries, buying securities from corporations and governments and reselling them to the public.

ISO 9000 A set of five technical standards of quality management created by the International Organization for Standardization to provide a uniform way of determining whether manufacturing plants and service organizations conform to sound quality procedures.

ISO 14000 A set of technical standards designed by the International Organization for Standardization to promote clean production processes to protect the environment.

J

job analysis A study of the tasks required to do a particular job well.

job description The tasks and responsibilities of a job.

job enlargement The horizontal expansion of a job by increasing the number and variety of tasks that a person performs.

job enrichment The vertical expansion of a job by increasing the employee's autonomy, responsibility, and decision-making authority.

job fair An event, typically one day, held at a convention center to bring together job seekers and firms searching for employees.

job rotation Reassignment of workers to several different jobs over time so that they can learn the basics of each job.

job sharing A scheduling option that allows two individuals to split the tasks, responsibilities, and work hours of one 40-hour-per-week job.

job shop A manufacturing firm that produces goods in response to customer orders.

job specification A list of the skills, knowledge, and abilities a person must have to fill a job.

joint venture Two or more companies that form an alliance to pursue a specific project usually for a specified time period.

judiciary The branch of government that is responsible for settling disputes by applying and interpreting points of law; consists of the court system.

justice What is considered fair according to the prevailing standards of society; an equitable distribution of the burdens and rewards that society has to offer.

just-in-time (JIT) A system in which materials arrive exactly when they are needed for production, rather than being stored on site.

K

knowledge The combined talents and skills of the workforce.

knowledge management (KM) The process of researching, gathering, organizing, and sharing an organization's collective knowledge to improve productivity, foster innovation, and gain competitive advantage.

knowledge worker A worker who develops or uses knowledge, contributing to and benefiting from information used in performing planning, acquiring, searching, analyzing, organizing, storing, programming, producing, distributing, marketing, or selling functions.

L

labor union An organization that represents workers in dealing with management.

laws The rules of conduct in a society, created and enforced by a controlling authority, usually the government.

leader pricing The strategy of pricing products below the normal markup or even below cost to attract customers to a store where they would not otherwise shop.

leadership The process of guiding and motivating others toward the achievement of organizational goals.

leadership style The relatively consistent way that individuals in leadership positions attempt to influence the behavior of others.

lean manufacturing Streamlining production by eliminating steps in the production process that do not add benefits that customers are willing to pay for.

legitimate power Power that is derived from an individual's position in an organization.

leveraged buyout (LBO) A corporate takeover financed by large amounts of borrowed money; can be started by outside investors or the corporation's management.

liabilities What a firm owes to its creditors; also called debts.

licensing The legal process whereby a firm agrees to allow another firm to use a manufacturing process, trademark, patent, trade secret, or other proprietary knowledge in exchange for the payment of a royalty.

limited liability company (LLC) A hybrid organization that offers the same liability protection as a corporation but may be taxed as either a partnership or a corporation.

limited partners Partners whose liability for the firm's business obligations is limited to the amount of their investment. They help to finance the business, but do not participate in the firm's operations.

limited partnership A partnership with one or more general partners who have unlimited liability, and one or more limited partners whose liability is limited to the amount of their investment in the company.

line extension A new flavor, size, or model using an existing brand name in an existing category.

line of credit For a business, an agreement with a bank that specifies the maximum amount of unsecured short-term borrowing the bank will make available to the firm over a given period, typically one year. For credit cards, the maximum amount the cardholder can have outstanding on the card at any one time.

line organization An organizational structure with direct, clear lines of authority and communication flowing from the top managers downward.

line positions All positions in the organization directly concerned with producing goods and services and that are directly connected from top to bottom.

line-and-staff organization An organizational structure that includes both line and staff positions.

liquidity The speed with which an asset can be converted to cash.

liquidity ratios Ratios that measure a firm's ability to pay its short-term debts as they come due.

local area network (LAN) A network that connects computers at one site, enabling the computer users to exchange data and share the use of hardware and software from a variety of computer manufacturers.

local union Branch of a national union that represents workers in a specific plant or geographic area.

long-term liabilities Claims that come due more than one year after the date of the balance sheet.

loss leader A product priced below cost as part of a leader pricing strategy.

M

M1 The total amount of readily available money in the system, that includes currency and demand deposits.

M2 A term used by economists to describe the U.S. monetary supply; includes all M1 monies plus time deposits and other money that are not immediately accessible.

macroeconomics The subarea of economics that focuses on the economy as a whole by looking at aggregate data for large groups of people, companies, or products.

major medical insurance Health insurance that covers a wide range of medical costs with few exclusions and high maximum limits. The insured pays a deductible and a coinsurance portion.

make-or-buy decision The determination by a firm of whether to make its own production materials or buy them from outside sources.

Malcolm Baldrige National Quality Award An award given to recognize U.S. companies that offer goods and services of world-class quality; established by Congress in 1987 and named for a former secretary of commerce.

managed care plans Health insurance plans that generally pay for services provided only by doctors and hospitals that are part of the plan.

managed service providers (MSPs) Next generation of ASPs, offering customization and expanded capabilities such as business processes and complete management of the network servers.

management The process of guiding the development, maintenance, and allocation of resources to attain organizational goals.

management information system (MIS) The methods and equipment that provide information about all aspects of a firm's operations.

management rights clause Clause in a labor agreement that gives management the right to manage the business except as specified in the contract.

management support system (MSS) An information system that uses the internal master database to perform high-level analyses that help managers make better decisions.

managerial accounting Accounting that provides financial information that managers inside the organization can use to evaluate and make decisions about current and future operations.

managerial hierarchy The levels of management within an organization; typically, includes top, middle, and supervisory management.

manufacturer A producer; an organization that converts raw materials to finished products.

manufacturers' representatives Salespeople who represent noncompeting manufacturers; function as independent agents rather than as salaried employees of the manufacturers.

manufacturing resource planning II (MRPII) A complex computerized system that integrates data from many departments to allow managers to better forecast and assess the impact of production plans on profitability.

market segmentation The process of separating, identifying, and evaluating the layers of a market in order to identify a target market.

market structure The number of suppliers in a market.

marketable securities Short-term investments that are easily converted into cash.

marketing The process of discovering the needs and wants of potential buyers and customers and then providing goods and services that meet or exceed their expectations.

marketing concept Identifying consumer needs and then producing the goods or services that will satisfy them while making a profit for the organization.

marketing database Computerized file of customers' and potential customers' profiles and purchase patterns.

marketing intermediaries Organizations that assist in moving goods and services from producers to end users.

marketing mix The blend of product offering, pricing, promotional methods, and distribution system that brings a specific group of consumers superior value.

marketing research The process of planning, collecting, and analyzing data relevant to a marketing decision.

Maslow's hierarchy of needs A theory of motivation developed by Abraham Maslow; holds that humans have five levels of needs and act to satisfy their unmet needs. At the base of the hierarchy are fundamental physiological needs, followed in order by safety, social, esteem, and self-actualization needs.

mass customization A manufacturing process in which goods are mass-produced up to a point and then custom tailored to the needs or desires of individual customers.

mass production The ability to manufacture many identical goods at once.

materials requirement planning (MRP) A computerized system of controlling the flow of resources and inventory. A master schedule is used to ensure that the materials, labor, and equipment needed for production are at the right places in the right amounts at the right times.

matrix structure (project management) An organizational structure that combines functional and product departmentalization by bringing together people from different functional areas of the organization to work on a special project.

mechanistic organization An organizational structure that is characterized by a relatively high degree of job specialization, rigid departmentalization, many layers of management, narrow spans of control, centralized decision making, and a long chain of command.

mediation A method of settling disputes in which the parties submit their case to an impartial third party but are not required to accept the mediator's decision.

mediator Specialist that facilitates labor-management contract discussions and suggests compromises.

mentoring A form of on-the-job training in which a senior manager or other experienced employee provides job- and career-related information to a mentee.

merchant wholesaler An institution that buys goods from manufacturers (takes ownership) and resells them to businesses, government agencies, other wholesalers, or retailers.

Mercosur Trade agreement between Peru, Brazil, Argentina, Uruguay, and Paraguay.

merger The combination of two or more firms to form one new company.

microeconomics The subarea of economics that focuses on individual parts of the economy, such as households or firms.

middle management Managers who design and carry out tactical plans in specific areas of the company.

mission An organization's purpose and reason for existing; its long-term goals.

mission statement A formal document that states an organization's purpose and reason for existing and describes its basic philosophy.

mixed economies Economies that combine several economic systems; for example, an economy where the government owns certain industries but others are owned by the private sector.

monetary policy A government's programs for controlling the amount of money circulating in the economy and interest rates.

money Anything that is acceptable as payment for goods and services.

monopolistic competition A market structure in which many firms offer products that are close substitutes and in which entry is relatively easy.

mortgage loan A long-term loan made against real estate as collateral.

motivating factors Intrinsic job elements that lead to worker satisfaction.

motivation Something that prompts a person to release his or her energy in a certain direction.

multinational corporations Corporations that move resources, goods, services, and skills across national boundaries without regard to the country in which their headquarters are located.

multipreneurs Entrepreneurs who start a series of companies.

municipal bonds Bonds issued by states, cities, counties, and other state and local government agencies.

mutual fund A financial-service company that pools its investors' funds to buy a selection of securities that meet its stated investment goals.

N

National Association of Securities Dealers Automated Quotation (NASDAQ) system The first and largest electronic stock market, which is a sophisticated telecommunications network that links dealers throughout the United States.

national debt The accumulated total of all of the federal government's annual budget deficits.

nationalism A sense of national consciousness that boosts the culture and interests of one country over those of all other countries.

need The gap between what is and what is required.

net loss The amount obtained by subtracting all of a firm's expenses from its revenues, when the expenses are more than the revenues.

net profit (net income) The amount obtained by subtracting all of a firm's expenses from its revenues, when the revenues are more than the expenses.

net profit margin The ratio of net profit to net sales; also called return on sales. It measures the percentage of each sales dollar remaining after all expenses, including taxes, have been deducted.

net sales The amount left after deducting sales discounts and returns and allowances from gross sales.

net working capital The amount obtained by subtracting total current liabilities from total current assets; used to measure a firm's liquidity.

net worth An individual's wealth at a given point in time, calculated as total assets minus total liabilities.

niche competitive advantage A firm's ability to target and effectively serve a single segment of the market within a limited geographic area.

nonprogrammed decisions Responses to infrequent, unforeseen, or very unusual problems and opportunities where the manager does not have a precedent to follow in decision making.

North American Free Trade Agreement (NAFTA) A 1993 agreement creating a free-trade zone including Canada, Mexico, and the United States.

not-for-profit organization An organization that exists to achieve some goal other than the usual business goal of profit.

O

observation research A marketing research method in which the investigator monitors respondents' actions without interacting directly with the respondents; for example, by using cash registers with scanners.

Occupational Safety and Health Administration (OSHA) Sets workplace safety and health standards and assures compliance.

odd-even (psychological) pricing The strategy of setting a price at an odd number to connote a bargain and at an even number to suggest quality.

office automation system An information system that uses information technology tools such as word processing systems, e-mail systems, cell phones, PDAs, pagers, and fax machines to improve communications throughout an organization.

oligopoly A market structure in which a few firms produce most or all of the output and in which large capital requirements or other factors limit the number of firms.

one-to-one marketing Creating a unique marketing mix for every customer.

on-line (real-time) processing A method of updating a database in which data are processed as they become available.

open market operations The purchase or sale of U.S. government bonds by the Federal Reserve to stimulate or slow down the economy.

open shop Workers do not have to join the union or pay union dues.

open-end credit Any type of credit where the borrower applies for the credit and then, if approved, is allowed to use it over and over again; for example, credit cards.

operating budgets Budgets that combine sales forecasts with estimates of production costs and operating expenses in order to forecast profits.

operating expenses The expenses of running a business that are not directly related to producing or buying its products.

operational planning The process of creating specific standards, methods, policies, and procedures that are used in specific functional areas of the organization; helps guide and control the implementation of tactical plans.

operations management Management of the production process.

options Contracts that entitle holders to buy or sell specified quantities of common stocks or other financial instruments at a set price during a specified time.

organic organization An organizational structure that is characterized by a relatively low degree of job specialization, loose departmentalization, few levels of management, wide spans of control, decentralized decision making, and a short chain of command.

organization chart A visual representation of the structured relationships among tasks and the people given the authority to do those tasks.

organizing The process of coordinating and allocating a firm's resources in order to carry out its plans.

orientation Presentation to get the new employee ready to perform his or her job.

outsourcing The purchase of items from an outside source rather than producing the goods and services internally. Often the goods and services are purchased from less expensive sellers in foreign countries.

over-the-counter (OTC) markets Markets, other than exchanges, on which small companies trade; includes the Over-the-Counter Bulletin Board (OTCBB) and the Pink Sheets.

owners' equity The total amount of investment in the firm minus any liabilities; also called net worth.

P

participative leadership A leadership style in which the leader shares decision making with group members and encourages discussion of issues and alternatives; includes democratic, consensual, and consultative styles.

partnership An association of two or more individuals who agree to operate a business together for profit.

patent A form of protection established by the government for inventors; gives an inventor the exclusive right to manufacture, use, and sell an invention for 17 years.

payroll taxes The employer's share of Social Security taxes and federal and state unemployment taxes.

penetration pricing The strategy of selling new products at low prices in the hope of achieving a large sales volume.

pension funds Large pools of money set aside by corporations, unions, and governments for later use in paying retirement benefits to their employees or members.

perfect (pure) competition A market structure in which a large number of small firms sell similar products, buyers and sellers have good information, and businesses can be easily opened or closed.

performance appraisal A comparison of actual performance with expected performance to assess an employee's contributions to the organization.

perpetual inventory A continuously updated list of inventory levels, orders, sales, and receipts.

personal balance sheet A summary of a person's financial position on a given day; provides information about assets, liabilities, and net worth.

personal exemptions Deductions that reduce the amount of income on which income tax is paid. Each taxpayer is entitled to a personal exemption, for himself, his spouse, and each of his dependents; a personal exemption can be used only once.

personal financial planning The process of managing one's own finances to achieve financial goals.

personal selling A face-to-face sales presentation to a prospective customer.

personality A way of organizing and grouping how an individual reacts to situations.

planning The process of deciding what needs to be done to achieve organizational objectives; identifying when and how it will be done; and determining by whom it should be done.

point-of-purchase (POP) display A strategically placed visual display or product display that informs potential customers about a product or service.

portfolio A collection of investments.

power The ability to influence others to behave in a particular way.

preferential tariff A tariff that is lower for some nations than for others.

preferred provider organizations (PPOs) Networks of health care providers who enter into a contract to provide services at discounted prices; combines major medical insurance with a network of health care providers.

preferred stock An equity security for which the dividend amount is set at the time the stock is issued; the dividend amount must be paid before the company can pay dividends to common stockholders.

prepayment penalties Additional fees that may be owed if a loan is repaid early.

prestige pricing The strategy of increasing the price of a product so that consumers will perceive it as being of higher quality, status, or value.

price skimming The strategy of introducing a product with a high initial price and lowering the price over time as the product moves through its life cycle.

pricing strategy Setting a price based upon the demand for and cost of producing a good or service.

primary market The securities market where new securities are sold to the public.

principal The amount borrowed by the issuer of a bond; also called par value. On loans, the amount borrowed.

principle of comparative advantage The concept that each country should specialize in the products that it can produce most readily and cheaply and trade those products for those that other countries can produce more readily and cheaply.

private accountants Accountants who are employed to serve one particular organization.

private-label branding Where a retailer, or wholesaler, has a manufacturer produce products and the retailer, or wholesaler, puts its own name on the item.

problem-solving teams Usually members of the same department who meet regularly to suggest ways to improve operations and solve specific problems.

process departmentalization Departmentalization that is based on the production process used by the organizational unit.

process layout A facility arrangement in which work flows according to the production process. All workers performing similar tasks are grouped together, and products pass from one workstation to another.

process manufacturing A production process in which the basic input is broken down into one or more outputs (products).

producer price index (PPI) An index of the prices paid by producers and wholesalers for commodities such as raw materials, partially finished goods, and finished products.

product In marketing, any good or service, along with its perceived attributes and benefits, that creates value for the customer.

product departmentalization Departmentalization that is based on the goods or services produced or sold by the organizational unit.

product (assembly-line) layout A facility arrangement in which workstations or departments are arranged in a line with products moving along the line.

product liability The responsibility of manufacturers and sellers for defects in the products they make and sell.

product life cycle The pattern of sales and profits over time for a product or product category; consists of an introductory stage, growth stage, maturity, and decline (and death).

product line (or brand) extension Taking a product with a well-developed brand image and using that brand name for a new product in either the same product category or a different product category.

product manager The person who develops and implements a complete strategy and marketing program for a specific product or brand.

product strategy Taking the good or service and selecting a brand name, packaging, colors, a warranty, accessories, and a service program.

production The creation of products and services by turning inputs, such as natural resources, raw materials, human resources, and capital, into outputs, which are products and services.

production planning The aspect of operations management in which the firm considers the competitive environment and its own strategic goals in an effort to find the best production methods.

production process The way a good or service is created.

productivity The amount of goods and services one worker can produce.

profit The money left over after all costs are paid.

profitability ratios Ratios that measure how well a firm is using its resources to generate profit and how efficiently it is being managed.

program evaluation and review technique (PERT) A scheduling tool that is similar to the CPM method but assigns three time estimates for each activity (optimistic, most probable, and pessimistic); allows managers to anticipate delays and potential problems and schedule accordingly.

programmed decisions Decisions made in response to frequently occurring routine situations.

programmed instruction A form of computer-assisted off-the-job training.

progressive tax An income tax that is structured so that the higher a person's taxable income, the higher the percentage of income paid in taxes.

promotion The attempt by marketers to inform, persuade, or remind consumers and industrial users to engage in the exchange process.

promotion strategy The unique combination of personal selling, advertising, publicity, and sales promotion to stimulate the target market to buy a product or service.

promotional mix The combination of advertising, personal selling, sales promotion, and public relations used to promote a product.

property taxes Taxes that are imposed on real and personal property based on the assessed value of the property.

prospecting The process of looking for sales prospects.

protected classes The specific groups who have legal protection against employment discrimination; include women, African Americans, Native Americans, and others.

protectionism The policy of protecting home industries from outside competition by establishing artificial barriers such as tariffs and quotas.

protective tariffs Tariffs that are imposed in order to make imports less attractive to buyers than domestic products are.

psychographic segmentation The differentiation of markets by personality or lifestyle.

public accountants Independent accountants who serve organizations and individuals on a fee basis.

public relations Any communication or activity designed to win goodwill or prestige for a company or person.

publicity Information about a company or product that appears in the news media and is not directly paid for by the company.

punishment Anything that decreases a specific behavior.

purchasing The process of buying production inputs from various sources; also called procurement.

purchasing power The value of what money can buy.

pure monopoly A market structure in which a single firm accounts for all industry sales and in which there are barriers to entry.

Q

qualifying questions Inquiries used by salespeople to separate prospects from those who do not have the potential to buy.

quality Goods and services that meet customer expectations by providing reliable performance.

quality control The process of creating standards for quality, producing goods that meet them, and measuring finished products and services against them.

quality of life The general level of human happiness based on such things as life expectancy, educational standards, health, sanitation, and leisure time.

R

ratio analysis The calculation and interpretation of financial ratios using data taken from the firm's financial statements in order to assess its condition and performance.

reach The number of different target consumers who are exposed to a commercial at least once during a specific period, usually four weeks.

recession A decline in GDP that lasts for at least two consecutive quarters.

recruitment The attempt to find and attract qualified applicants in the external labor market.

recruitment branding Presenting an accurate and positive image of the firm to those being recruited.

reengineering The complete redesign of business structures and processes in order to improve operations.

reference groups Formal and informal groups that influence buyer behavior.

referent power Power that is derived from an individual's personal charisma and the respect and/or admiration the individual inspires.

reinforcement theory People do things because they know that certain consequences will follow.

relationship management The practice of building, maintaining, and enhancing interactions with customers and other parties to develop long-term satisfaction through mutually beneficial partnerships.

relationship marketing A strategy that focuses on forging long-term partnerships with customers by offering value and providing customer satisfaction.

replacement cost coverage Homeowners and renters insurance that pays enough to pay lost and damaged personal property.

reserve requirement Requires banks that are members of the Federal Reserve System to hold some of their deposits in cash in their vaults or in an account at a district bank.

retailers Firms that sell goods to consumers and to industrial users for their own consumption.

retained earnings Profits that have been invested in a firm.

return The opportunity for profit.

return on equity (ROE) The ratio of net profit to total owners' equity; measures the return that owners receive on their investment in the firm.

revenue The dollar amount of a firm's sales plus any other income it received from sources such as interest, dividends, and rents.

revolving credit agreement A guaranteed line of credit whereby a bank agrees that a certain amount of funds will be available for a business to borrow over a given period, typically two to five years.

revolving credit cards Credit cards that do not require full payment upon billing.

reward Anything that increases a specific behavior.

reward power Power that is derived from an individual's control over rewards.

right-to-work law State law that an employee does not have to join a union.

risk The potential for loss or the chance that an investment will not achieve the expected level of return.

risk-return trade-off A basic principle in finance that holds that the higher the risk, the greater the return that is required.

robotics The technology involved in designing, constructing, and operating computer-controlled machines that can perform tasks independently.

routing The aspect of production control that involves setting out the work flow—the sequence of machines and operations through which the product or service progresses from start to finish.

S

S corporation A hybrid entity that is organized like a corporation, with stockholders, directors, and officers, but taxed like a partnership, with income and losses flowing through to the stockholders and taxed as their personal income.

sales promotions Marketing events or sales efforts—not including advertising, personal selling, and public relations—that stimulate buying.

sales prospects The companies and people who are most likely to buy a seller's offerings.

sales taxes Taxes that are levied on goods when they are sold; calculated as a percentage of the price.

Sarbanes-Oxley Act Act passed in 2002 that sets new standards for auditor independence, financial disclosure and reporting, and internal controls; establishes an independent oversight board; and restricts the types of nonaudit services auditors can provide audit clients.

savings bonds Government bonds issued in relatively small denominations.

scheduling The aspect of production control that involves specifying and controlling the time required for each step in the production process.

scientific management A system of management developed by Frederick W. Taylor and based on four principles: developing a scientific approach for each element of a job, scientifically selecting and training workers, encouraging cooperation between workers and managers, and dividing work and responsibility between management and workers according to who can better perform a particular task.

seasonal unemployment Unemployment that occurs during specific seasons in certain industries.

secondary market The securities market where old (already issued) securities are bought and sold, or traded, among investors.

secured loans Loans for which the borrower is required to pledge specific assets as collateral, or security.

securities Investment certificates issued by corporations or governments that represent either equity or debt.

security requirements Provisions that allow a lender to take back the collateral if a loan is not repaid according to the terms of the agreement.

selection The process of determining which persons in the applicant pool possess the qualifications necessary to be successful on the job.

selection interview An in-depth discussion of an applicant's work experience, skills and abilities, education, and career interests.

selective credit controls The power of the Federal Reserve to control consumer credit rules and margin requirements.

selective strike strategy Strike at a critical plant that typically stops operations systemwide.

self-managed work teams Teams without formal supervision that plan, select alternatives, and evaluate their own performance.

seller cooperative Individual producers who join together to compete more effectively with large producers.

servicemark A symbol, name, or design that identifies a service rather than a tangible object.

services Intangible offerings of businesses that can't be held, touched, or stored.

shop steward An elected union official that represents union members to management when workers have complaints.

shopping products Items that are bought after considerable planning, including brand-to-brand and store-to-store comparisons of price, suitability, and style.

short-term forecasts Projections of revenues, costs of goods, and operating expenses over a one-year period.

simulation A scaled-down version or mock-up of equipment, process, or work environment.

Six Sigma A quality control process that relies on defining what needs to be done to ensure quality, measuring and analyzing production results statistically, and finding ways to improve and control quality.

small business A business with under 500 employees that is independently managed, is owned by an individual or a small group of investors, is based locally, and is not a dominant company in its industry.

Small Business Administration (SBA) A government agency that speaks on behalf of small business; specifically it helps people start and manage small businesses, advises them in the areas of finance and management, and helps them win federal contracts.

Small Business Investment Companies (SBICs) Privately owned and managed investment companies that are licensed by the Small Business Administration and provide long-term financing for small businesses.

social investing The practice of limiting investments to securities of companies that behave in accordance with the investor's beliefs about ethical and social responsibility.

social responsibility The concern of businesses for the welfare of society as a whole; consists of obligations beyond those required by law or contracts.

socialism An economic system in which the basic industries are owned either by the government itself or by the private sector under strong government control.

socialization process The passing down of cultural norms and values to children.

sole proprietorship A business that is established, owned, operated, and often financed by one person.

span of control The number of employees a manager directly supervises; also called span of management.

specialization The degree to which tasks are subdivided into smaller jobs.

specialty products Items for which consumers search long and hard and for which they refuse to accept substitutes.

spyware Software downloaded without the user's consent that controls all or part of a computer's operation for the benefit of a third party.

staff positions Positions in an organization held by individuals who provide the administrative and support services that line employees need to achieve the firm's goals.

stakeholders Individuals or groups to whom a business has a responsibility; include employees, customers, the general public, and investors.

standard deduction An amount that most taxpayers can automatically deduct from their gross income in computing their income tax; as an alternative the taxpayer is permitted to itemize deductions.

standard of living A country's output of goods and services that people can buy with the money they have.

statement of cash flows A financial statement that provides a summary of the money flowing into and out of a firm during a certain period, typically one year.

statutory law Written law enacted by a legislature (local, state, or federal).

stock dividends Payments to stockholders in the form of more stock; may replace or supplement cash dividends.

stockbroker A person who is licensed to buy and sell securities on behalf of clients.

stockholders (or shareholders) The owners of a corporation who hold shares of stock that carry certain rights.

strategic alliance A cooperative agreement between business firms; sometimes called a strategic partnership.

strategic giving The practice of tying philanthropy closely to the corporate mission or goals and targeting donations to regions where a company operates.

strategic planning The process of creating long-range (one to five years), broad goals for the organization and determining what resources will be needed to accomplish those goals.

strict liability A concept in product liability law under which a manufacturer or seller is liable for any personal injury or property damage caused by defective products or packaging even though all possible care was used to prevent such defects.

structural unemployment Unemployment that is caused by a mismatch between available jobs and the skills of available workers in an industry or region; not related to the business cycle.

succession planning Examination of current employees to identify people who can fill vacancies and be promoted.

supervisory (first-line) management Managers who design and carry out operation plans for the ongoing daily activities of the firm.

supply The quantity of a good or service that businesses will make available at various prices.

supply chain The entire sequence of securing inputs, producing goods, and delivering goods to customers.

supply chain management The process of smoothing transitions along the supply chain so that the firm can satisfy its customers with quality products and services; focuses on developing tighter bonds with suppliers.

supply curve A graph showing the quantity of a good or service that businesses will make available at various prices.

survey research A marketing research method in which data is gathered from respondents, either in person, by telephone, by mail, at a mall, or through the Internet to obtain facts, opinions, and attitudes.

T

tactical planning The process of beginning to implement a strategic plan by addressing issues of coordination and allocating resources to different parts of the organization; has a shorter time frame (less than one year) and more specific objectives than strategic planning.

target market The specific group of consumers toward which a firm directs its marketing efforts.

tariff A tax imposed on imported goods.

technical skills A manager's specialized areas of knowledge and expertise, as well as the ability to apply that knowledge.

technology The application of science and engineering skills and knowledge to solve production and organizational problems.

term loan A business loan with an initial maturity of more than one year; can be unsecured or secured.

term life insurance Life insurance that covers the insured's life for a fixed amount and a specified time period and has no cash value; provides the maximum amount of life insurance coverage for the lowest premium.

test-marketing The process of testing a new product among potential users.

theft insurance A broad insurance coverage that protects business against losses for an act of stealing.

Theory X A management style, formulated by Douglas McGregor, that is based on a pessimistic view of human nature and assumes that the average person dislikes work, will avoid it if possible, prefers to be directed, avoids responsibility, and wants security above all.

Theory Y A management style, formulated by Douglas McGregor, that is based on a relatively optimistic view of human nature; assumes that the average person wants to work, accepts responsibility, is willing to help solve problems, and can be self-directed and self-controlled.

Theory Z A theory developed by William Ouchi that combines U.S. and Japanese business practices by emphasizing long-term employment, slow career development, moderate specialization, group decision making, individual responsibility, relatively informal control over the employee, and concern for workers.

thrift institutions Depository institutions formed specifically to encourage household saving and to make home mortgage loans.

time deposits Deposits at a bank or other financial institution that pay interest but cannot be withdrawn on demand.

top management The highest level of managers; includes CEOs, presidents, and vice presidents, who develop strategic plans and address long-range issues.

tort A civil, or private, act that harms other people or their property.

Total Quality Management (TQM) The use of quality principles in all aspects of a company's production and operations.

trade credit The extension of credit by the seller to the buyer between the time the buyer receives the goods or services and when it pays for them.

trade deficit An unfavorable balance of trade that occurs when a country imports more than it exports.

trade surplus A favorable balance of trade that occurs when a country exports more than it imports.

trademark A design, name, or other distinctive mark that a manufacturer uses to identify its goods in the marketplace.

training and development Activities that provide learning situations in which an employee acquires additional knowledge or skills to increase job performance.

transaction processing system (TPS) An information system that handles the daily business operations of a firm. The system receives and organizes raw data from internal and external sources for storage in a database using either batch or online processing.

transmission control protocol/Internet protocol (TCP/IP) A communications technology that allows different computer platforms to communicate with each other to transfer data.

trial courts The lowest level of courts, where most cases begin; also called courts of general jurisdiction.

U

underwriting The process of buying securities from corporations and governments and reselling them to the public, hopefully at a higher price; the main activity of investment bankers.

unearned income Income that is not earned through employment such as interest, dividends, and other investment income.

unemployment compensation Government payment to unemployed former workers.

unemployment rate The percentage of the total labor force that is not working but is actively looking for work.

Uniform Commercial Code (UCC) A model set of rules that apply to commercial transactions between businesses and between businesses and individuals; has been adopted by all states except Louisiana, which uses only part of it.

union shop Nonunion workers can be hired but must join the union later.

universal life insurance A combination of term life insurance and a tax-deferred savings plan. Part of the premium is invested in securities, so the cash value earns interest, at current market rates, that contributes to the policy's cash value.

unsecured loans Loans for which the borrower does not have to pledge specific assets as security.

unsought products Products that either are unknown to the potential buyer or are known but the buyer does not actively seek them.

Uruguay Round A 1994 agreement by 117 nations to lower trade barriers worldwide.

utilitarianism A philosophy that focuses on the consequences of an action to determine whether it is right or wrong; holds that an action that affects the majority adversely is morally wrong.

V

value-stream mapping Routing technique that uses simple icons to visually represent the flow of materials and information from suppliers through the factory and to customers.

venture capital Financing obtained from venture capitalists, investment firms that specialize in financing small, high-growth companies and receive an ownership interest and a voice in management in return for their money.

vertical merger A merger of companies at different stages in the same industry; done to gain control over supplies of resources or to gain access to different markets.

virtual corporation A network of independent companies linked by information technology to share skills, costs, and access to one another's markets; allows the companies to come together quickly to exploit rapidly changing opportunities.

virtual private networks (VPNs) Private corporate networks connected over a public network, such as the Internet. VPNs include strong security measures to allow only authorized users to access the network.

volume segmentation The differentiation of markets based on the amount of the product purchased.

W

waiting period (elimination period) In disability income insurance, the length of time the insurance coverage payments will continue.

want The gap between what is and what is desired.

Web sites Locations on the World Wide Web consisting of a home page and, possibly, other pages with documents and files.

whole life (straight life, cash value, continuous pay) insurance Life insurance that covers the insured for his or her entire life, as long as the premiums are paid; has a cash value that increases over the life of the policy.

wholesalers Firms that sell finished goods to retailers, manufacturers, and institutions.

wide area network (WAN) A network that connects computers at different sites via telecommunications media such as phone lines, satellites, and microwaves.

withholding allowances Allowances claimed with an employer that determine the amounts that are withheld from each of the employees' paychecks.

work groups The groups that share resources and coordinate efforts to help members better perform their individual jobs.

work teams Like a work group but also requires the pooling of knowledge, skills, abilities, and resources to achieve a common goal.

worker's compensation Pay for lost work time due to employment-related injuries.

World Bank An international bank that offers low-interest loans, as well as advice and information, to developing nations.

World Trade Organization (WTO) An organization established by the Uruguay Round in 1994 to oversee international trade, reduce trade barriers, and resolve disputes among member nations.

World Wide Web (WWW) A subsystem of the Internet that consists of an information retrieval system composed of Web sites.

endnotes

Chapter 1

1. "2007 World-Wide Quality of Life Survey," http://www.mercer.com, April 2, 2007.
2. Phred Dvorak, "Sony to Cut 10,000 Jobs, Reduce Costs by $1.8 Billion," *Wall Street Journal,* September 22, 2005, p. A3; and Adam Lashansky, "Saving Face at Sony," *Fortune,* February 21, 2005, pp. 79–86.
3. http://www.heart.org, January 22, 2008.
4. "The Brains Business," *Economist,* September 10, 2005, pp. 3–4.
5. Allan E. Alter, "Knowledge Workers Need More Supervision," *CIO Insight,* August 5, 2005, http://www.cioinsight.com; and Edward H. Baker, "How to Manage Smart People," *CIO Insight,* August 5, 2005, http://www.cioinsight.com.
6. Jim Carroll, "E-Commerce Is Alive and Well," *CA Magazine,* January/February 2008, p. 18; "New Words Such As 'w00t' Worth a <G>," *Dayton Daily News,* December 17, 2007, p. D5; "Web Watch," *The Florida Times-Union,* March 6, 2007, p. C-3; Melissa Campanelli, "Seize the Day," *Entrepreneur,* May 2007, pp. 46–47; "W00t," *Wikipedia,* January 22, 2008; and "Gadgets Brief—Internet: Late Night Shoppers Need to be Wary of Discounts," *The Wall Street Journal,* July 5, 2007, p. 31.
7. "Minority Population Tops 100 Million," *US Fed News,* May 17, 2007.
8. "K-Mart Stacks Shelves with Multicultural Dolls," *The Grand Rapids Press,* August 13, 2007, p. B4.
9. "Sarkozy's Free Market Muscle," *Business Week,* July 9, 2007, p. 42.
10. "As China Rises, Pollution Soars," *International Herald Tribune,* August 25, 2007, p. 1.
11. Tom Wright, "Firms Back a Plan to Put the Green in 'Green Gold,'" *Wall Street Journal,* January 18, 2008, pp. B1, B2. Copyright 2008 by Dow Jones & Company, Inc. Reproduced with permission of Dow Jones & Company, Inc. in the format Textbook via Copyright Clearance Center.
12. Michael Mandel, "The Economics Fueling the French Riots," *Business Week Online,* November 7, 2005, http://www.businessweek.com, and Carol Matlack, "Crisis in France," *Business Week,* November 21, 2005, http://www.businessweek.com.
13. "Endangered Species: Factory Jobs," *Automotive News,* November 26, 2007, p. 1.

14. http://www.aneki.com, January 23, 2008.
15. "Fed Rate Cut Halts Market Free Fall, but Recession Fears Are Mounting," *Wall Street Journal,* January 23, 2008, p. A1.
16. Ibid.
17. http://www.treasurydirect.gov, January 23, 2008.
18. Joseph De Avila, "A Beer and a Game of Pool With That Manicure?" *Wall Street Journal,* January 3, 2008, p. B7. Copyright 2008 by Dow Jones & Company, Inc. Reproduced with permission of Dow Jones & Company, Inc. in the format Textbook via Copyright Clearance Center.
19. Section based on Peter Coy, "Old. Smart. Productive." *Business Week,* June 27, 2005, http://www.businessweek.com; Kitchen, "The 4 Generation Workplace," p. A52; and Jennifer J. Salopek, "The New Brain Drain," *T + D,* June 2005, pp. 23–24.
20. Ellen M. Heffes, "Dramatic Workforce Trends Require Planning Now," *Financial Executive,* July/August 2005, pp. 18–21; Patricia Kitchen, "The 4 Generation Workplace, It's Not What It Used to Be," *Newsday,* August 14, 2005, p. A52.
21. "The Impact of Baby Boomer Retirement on Corporate America," http://www.capgemini.com, January 24, 2008.
22. Nelson D. Schwartz, "Why China Scares Big Oil," *Fortune,* July 25, 2005, pp. 33–36; and "The World's Number One: Saudi Oil," *Economist,* November 12, 2005, p. 83.
23. Gregory L. White and Chip Cummins, "Gas Dispute Pinches Europe," *Wall Street Journal,* January 2, 2006, http://www.online.wsj.com.
24. Robert Bryce, "Five Myths About Energy Independence," *Fort Worth Star Telegram,* January 22, 2008, p. 15B. Special to *Washington Post.* Copyright © 2008 by Robert Bryce.
25. Pui-Wing Tam and Ann Zimmerman, "Wal-Mart's H-P Elves," *Wall Street Journal,* December 15, 2005, pp. B1, B4.

Chapter 2

1. "BAE: Ethics Review Unrelated to Kickback Allegations," *Dow Jones Newswires,* June 15, 2007.
2. "An Uptick in Untruths," *Business Week,* December 17, 2007, p. 17.
3. From JENNINGS. *Case Studies in Business Ethics,* 2E. © 1995 South-Western, a part

of Cengage Learning, Inc. Reproduced by permission. www.cengage.com/permissions.
4. "Tyco Trial Jurors Say Defendants Weren't Credible," *Wall Street Journal,* June 20, 2005, pp. A1, A10; and "When Charity Begins at Home," *Business Week,* November 9, 2004, p. 76.
5. "100 Best Corporate Citizens," Reprinted from CRO Today, February 14, 2007.
6. Reprinted from Bruce Weinstein, "The Customer Isn't Always Right; Business Ethics Isn't Just About What Businesses Owe Customers-It's Also About What Customers Owe in Return," *Business Week Online,* March 15, 2007 by special permission, Copyright © 2007 by the McGraw-Hill Companies, Inc.
7. "Attorney General Stumbo Announces $7.4 million Settlement with Louisville J.D. Byrider and Corporate Franchises," *States News Service,* January 31, 2006; and Brian Grow and Keith Epstein, "The Poverty Business," *Business Week,* May 21, 2007, pp. 57–64.
8. "State Makes Bid to End Costly Tax-Refund Loans," *The New York Times,* January 18, 2008, p. 2; and "The Poverty Business," p. 64.
9. "We're Good Guys, Buy from Us," *Business Week,* November 22, 2004, p. 74.
10. "The Debate over Doing Good," *Business Week,* August 15, 2005, p. 77.
11. Helen Coster, "Mexican Maverick," *Forbes.com,* 29 October 2007. Reprinted by permission of Forbes Magazine © 2008 Forbes LLC.
12. http://www.business-ethics.com.
13. Stacy Perman, "Tiny Outfits, Big Hearts," *Business Week Online,* February 7, 2005, www.businessweek.com. Copyright © The McGraw-Hill Companies, Inc. All rights reserved. Reproduced by permission.
14. "Bayer USA Foundation Refocuses Charitable Giving Areas," *Science Letter,* January 22, 2008.
15. "Creative Capitalism: Profit from Helping the Poor," *The Globe and Mail,* January 25, 2008, p. A17.
16. "Keeping Up with the Gateses," *Financial Times,* December 11, 2007, p. 5.
17. Reprinted from Steve Hamm, "The Electric Car Acid Test: Shai Agassi's audacious effort to end the era of gas-powered autos," *BusinessWeek.com,* 24 January 2008 by

special permission, copyright © 2008 by the McGraw-Hill Companies, Inc.

18. "Shopping Can Boost Donations to Charity," *Augusta Chronicle,* May 29, 2007, p. C7.

19. Larry Chiagouris and Ipshita Ray, "Saving the World with Cause-Related Marketing," *Marketing Management,* July/August 2007, pp. 48–51.

20. "Op-Ed: Cause Efforts Go Deeper Than Dollars," *PR Week,* April 16, 2007, p. 8.

21. Source: Jaclyne Badal, "Checking On Charities," *Wall Street Journal,* December 10, 2007, p. B5. Copyright 2007 by Dow Jones & Company, Inc.. Reproduced with permission of Dow Jones & Company, Inc. in the format Textbook via Copyright Clearance Center.

22. "Christmas Ornaments Made in China Sweatshop–Report," *Reuters News,* December 12, 2007.

Chapter 3

1. Yahoo.brand.edgar-online.com (January 30, 2008).

2. http://townhall-talk.edmunds.com (January 16, 2008).

3. *Trade and American Jobs: The Impact of Trade on U.S. and State Level Employment* (Washington, DC: Business Roundtable, February 2007).

4. "Strategic Alliances Help U.S. Firms Export," http://trade.gov (February 5, 2008).

5. http://www.census.gov/foreign-trade/statistics (February 4, 2008).

6. "Revaluation by Stealth," http://www.economist.com (January 10, 2008).

7. David Wesell and Bob Davis, "Pain from Free Trade Spurs Second Thoughts," *Wall Street Journal,* March 28, 2007, pp. A1, A14.

8. Ibid.

9. "Protect US from Protectionists," *Wall Street Journal,* April 25, 2005, p. A14.

10. Ibid.

11. "Global Market Is Good to U.S. Firms," *Wall Street Journal* (April 15, 2005), p. A14.

12. "Ethanol: Castro Was Right," *Economist,* April 7, 2007, pp. 13–14.

13. "Brazil to Seek Lower US Tariffs, Accord on Ethanol," *Reuters News,* February 28, 2007).

14. "Just Try Selling Half a Pantsuit," *Business Week,* August 22, 2005, p. 12.

15. "Dour Hope for Doha," *The Weekly Times,* February 6, 2008, p. 26.

16. James Kanter and Gary Rivlin, "Antigua Wins Freedom to Violate U.S. Copyrights," *International Herald Tribune,* December 22–23, 2007, p. 13. Copyright © 2007 The New York Times Corp.

17. "Most Canadians, Americans Support NAFTA: Poll," *Xinhua News Agency,* October 1, 2007).

18. http://europa.eu.int (February 5, 2008).

19. "Intel Raided in EU Antitrust Investigation," *The Globe and Mail,* July 13, 2005, p. B8.

20. "EU Limits Coke's Sales Tactics in Settlement of Antitrust Case," *Wall Street Journal,* June 23, 2005, p. B6.

21. Jonathan Bensky, "World's Biggest Market: European Union Offers Great Opportunities for U.S. Companies," *Shipping Digest,* July 30, 2007.

22. Ibid.

23. Tux Turkel, "Maine's Big Cheese of Global Marketing; The Portland Firm's Task: Sell Americans on Cheese from France," *Portland Press Herald,* February 9, 2007, p. C1.

24. "GM's China Partner Looms as a New Rival," *Wall Street Journal,* April 20, 2007, pp. A1, A8.

25. "GM Splits with Creator of Its Success in China," *International Herald Tribune* (August 9, 2005), p. 13.

26. "Pernod Boss Slams French Protectionism," *Associated Press Newswires,* August 1, 2005.

27. Geoffrey A. Fowler, "Main Street, H.K.: Disney Localizes Mickey to Boost Its Hong Kong Theme Park," *Wall Street Journal,* January 23, 2008. B1. Copyright 2008 by Dow Jones & Company, Inc.. Reproduced with permission of Dow Jones & Company, Inc. in the format Textbook via Copyright Clearance Center.

28. "Haves and Have Nots of Globalization," *New York Times.com,* July 8, 2007.

29. "Foreign Investors Face New Hurdles Across the Globe," *Wall Street Journal,* July 6, 2007, pp. A1, A7.

30. Anil Gupta and Haiyan Wang, "How to Get China and India Right," *Wall Street Journal,* April 28–29, 2007, p. R9.

31. Ibid.

Chapter 4

1. "Case Study: The Furniture Company Wanted to Sell Him Its Buildings—and Close Down. Should He Buy the Company, Too?" *Inc.,* November 2007, pp. 60–62.

2. Jena Wuu, "Work–Life Not an Issue for Owners," *Inc. Online,* August 10, 2005, http://www.inc.com; Christina Galoozis, "Employees View Leadership Through Lens of Work–Life Balance," *Inc. Online,* June 8, 2005, http://www.inc.com.

3. Linda Ravden, personal interview by author, May 25, 2006.

4. Meredith Derby, "Debating Crocs' Future; Analysts Weigh in on Clog Company's Jibbitz Buy and Its Overall Growth Strategies," *Footwear News,* October 6, 2006, p. 2; Eric Newman, "Winning Ugly: How This Marketing Director Kicked Off a Viral Phenomenon and Created an Attractive Footprint for an 'Ugly' Brand," *Brandweek,* October 8, 2007, p. S22; Jillian Lloyd, "Crocs: The Ugly Footling," *Christian Science Monitor,* August 22, 2007, p. 20; "Crocs Inc. Named 2005 Brand of the Year by Footwear News," *PRNewswire,* November 21, 2005; Alicia Wallace, "On the Verge of Possible IPO, Crocs Battles Knock-Offs, Its Own Popularity," *Daily Camera,* September 6, 2005.

5. "Definition of Cooperatives," University of Wisconsin Online, Center for Cooperatives, http://www.wisc.edu/uwcc/info/i_pages/prin.htpm (May 24, 2006).

6. "Ace Hardware Reports Second Quarter Sales Surge of 9.5%," Ace Hardware Press Release, August 10, 2006, and Ace Hardware 2004 Annual Report, both at http://www.acehardware.com.

7. "Sony BMG Music Entertainment and Dada Form Joint Venture to Create a Leading U.S. Direct to Consumer Digital and Mobile Entertainment Service," *PRNewswire,* July 16, 2007.

8. Sara Wilson, "Got Laid Off? Buy a Franchise," *Entrepreneur,* December 2006, http://www.entrepreneur.com/franchises/buyingafranchise/successstories/article170800-2.html.

9. "Economic Impact of Franchised Businesses, Volume 2," *International Franchise Association,* http://www.franchise.org.

10. "Dairy Queen in Suit with Franchisees," *Ice Cream Reporter,* February 20, 2008, p. 2.

11. Sheridan Prasso, "India's Pizza Wars," *Fortune,* October 1, 2007, pp. 61–63; Lisa Takeuchi Cullen, "When East Meets West," *Time,* January 28, 2008, p. 44.

12. Chuck Carlton, "Merger Gives Hope for Open-Wheel Revival at TMS," *Dallas Morning News,* February 29, 2008, http://www.dallasnews.com/sharedcontent/dws/spt/motorsports/stories/022908dnspotmsbriefs.1d18e56.html; Shawn Courchesne, "Indy-Style Racing on a New Track: Single Series After Merger," *Hartford Courant,* February 28, 2008, http://blogs.courant.com/autoracing/2008/02/back-from-the-dead-indycar-ser.html.

13. William M. Bulkeley, "Staples Offers $3.6 Billion for Dutch Rival," *Wall Street Journal,* February 20, 2008, p. A8; Kevin Delaney, Matthew Karnitschnig, and Heidi Moore, "Microsoft Stands by Yahoo Bid," *Wall Street Journal,* February 12, 2008, p. B4; Nick Wingfield, "Electronic Arts Offers $2 Billion for Take-Two," *Wall Street Journal,* February 25, 2008, p. B1.

14. Matthew Karnitschnig, "For Deal Makers, Tale of Two Halves," *Wall Street Journal,* January 2, 2008, p. R10.

15. Timothy Aeppel, "A Hot Commodities Market Spurs Buying Spree by Manufacturers," *Wall Street Journal,* August 14, 2006, pp. A1, A7.

16. Bolaji Ojo and Patrick Mannion, "Freescale's Public Musings—Debt-Laden IC Vendor Weighing Return to Markets," *Electronic Engineering Times,* July 2, 2007, p. 1.

17. Sandra M. Jones, "Macy's to Eliminate Marshall Field's Headquarters, Consolidate Regional Offices, *Chicago Tribune,* February 6, 2008; "Macy's, Inc. Approves 2-for-1 Stock Split," http://www.macysinc.com/company/stocksplit.asp.

18. "Why Murdoch Wants the WSJ," *The Economist,* May 5, 2007, p. 78.

19. Ken Belson, "eBay to Buy Internet Phone Provider Skype," *San Diego Union-Tribune,* September 13, 2005, p. C1.

20. Andy Serwer, "A Marriage of Inconvenience," *Fortune,* December 13, 2004, p. 50.

21. Ben Steverman, "Why M&A Is Back, for Now; What's Behind the New Urge to Merge? The November Election, for Starters," *BusinessWeek Online,* February 25, 2008.

22. Jeanette Borzo, "Follow the Money: More Businesses Are Starting to Cater to an Affluent—and Discriminating—'Mature Market,'" *Wall Street Journal,* September 26, 2005, p. R9; and Sara Wilson, "All the 'Rage,'" *Entrepreneur,* January 2005, http://www.entrepreneur.com.

23. Home Instead Corporate Web site, http://www.homeinstead.com (May 4, 2006).

24. "Sarah Adult Day Services," *Franchise Zone,* http://www.entrepreneur.com/franzone/ (May 31, 2006).

25. Karnitschnig, "For Deal Makers, Tale of Two Halves."

26. Ibid.

27. Dennis K. Berman, "Big Deals Put Europe at M&A Center Stage," *Wall Street Journal,* April 3, 2006, p. C9.

28. Greg Hitt, "U.S. Foreign-Investment Debate Goes Global," *Wall Street Journal,* May 30, 2006, p. A4.

29. Ibid.

30. Judy Ettenhofer, "Organic Valley a Big Success," *The Capital Times,* July 29, 2004, http://www.madison.com; Craig Maier, "Duckworth's Part of Organic Valley Success Story," *Juneau County Star-Times,* January 22, 2005, http://www.star-times.scwn.com (September 28, 2005); Organic Valley corporate Web site, http://www.organicvalleycoop.com (May 26, 2006).

Chapter 5

1. Joe Truini, "You Make Products Out of What? Dropout Makes His Mark Making Fertilizer from Worm Droppings," *Waste News,* July 23, 2007, p. 38; Rob Walker, "The Worm Turns." *The New York Times Magazine,* May 20, 2007, p. 32.

2. Andrew Morse, "An Entrepreneur Finds Tokyo Shares Her Passion for Bagels," *Wall Street Journal,* October 18, 2005, p. B1.

3. Teri Agins, "Tory Burch Fashioned a Business Model First," *Wall Street Journal,* February 5, 2008, p. B1.

4. Gwendolyn Bounds, Kelly K. Spors, and Raymund Flandez, "The Secrets of Serial Success: How Some Entrepreneurs Manage to Score Big Again and Again and . . . ," *Wall Street Journal,* August 20, 2007, pp. R1, R4. Copyright 2007 by Dow Jones & Company, Inc.. Reproduced with permission of Dow Jones & Company, Inc. in the format Textbook via Copyright Clearance Center.

5. Max Chafkin, "Electric Sports Cars. Solar Power. Space Travel. Finally an Entrepreneur Who's Not Afraid to Think Really, Really Big," *Inc.,* December 2007, p. 115.

6. "IBM Research Unveils 3D Avatar to Help Doctors Visualize Patient Records and Improve Care," *Internet Wire,* September 26, 2007.

7. Keith McFarland, "What Makes Them Tick," Inc. 500, October 19, 2005, http://www.inc.com.

8. Traci Purdum, "Teaming, Take 2: Once a Buzzword, Teaming Today Is One of the Fundamentals of Manufacturing," *Industry Week,* May 2005, p. 41.

9. Gregory Katz, "Her Daily Bread," *American Way Magazine,* July 15, 2005, p. 34; Poilane Web site http://www.poilane.com (October 27, 2005).

10. Joel Spolsky, "Why I Decided to Take My Product to 34 Cities, from L.A. to Amsterdam," *Inc.,* December 2007, pp. 99–100.

11. Olga Kharif, "A Cellular Call for Simplicity," *Business Week Online,* July 17, 2005, http://www.businessweekonline.com (October 27, 2005).

12. McFarland, "What Makes Them Tick."

13. David H. Freeman, "The Secret Life of a Serial CEO," *Inc.,* January 2008, p. 83.

14. http://www.sba.gov/advo/stats/sbfaq.pdf.

15. Timothy Aeppel, "U.S. Shoe Factory Finds Supplies Are Achilles' Heel," *Wall Street Journal,* March 3, 2008, p. B1, B2.

16. Phred Dvorak, "Board of Advisers Can Help Steer Small Firms to Right Tack," *Wall Street Journal,* March 3, 2008, p. B4.

17. Chuck Salter, "Girl Power: No Rich Relatives? No Professional Mentors? No Problem. Ashley Qualls, 17, Has Built a Million-Dollar Web Site. She's LOL All the Way to the Bank." *Fast Company,* September 2007, pp. 104–112; and Kevin Sites, "Teen Millionaire," *Yahoo! News: People on the Web,* October 30, 2007, http://potw.news.yahoo.com/s/potw/52250/teen-millionaire.

18. Michelle Prather, "Talk of the Town," *Entrepreneur* magazine, February 2003, http://www.entrepreneur.com. Little Log Company, Inc. Web site, http://www.littlelog.com (May 31, 2006).

19. Matthew Bandyk, "Small Businesses Go Global," *U.S. News & World Report,* February 22, 2008, http://www.usnews.com/articles/business/small-business-entrepreneurs/2008/02/22/small-businesses-go-global.htmlp.

20. Don Debelak, "Rookie Rules," *Business Start-Ups Magazine,* http://www.entrepreneur.com (March 2, 2006).

21. Leigh Buchanan, "The Way I Work: Kim Kleeman," *Inc.,* October 2007, pp. 111–114.

22. Much of the statistical information for the SBA section is from the Small Business Administration Web site, http://www.sba.gov.

23. "Small Businesses Receive Nearly 100,000 SBA-Backed Loans in FY 2005, a Fifth Consecutive Record," Small Business Administration, press release, October 5, 2005, http://www.sba.gov/news.

24. Samantha Marshall, "Incorporating the Cause: Gen Y Entrepreneurs Pair Profits with Philanthropy," *Crain's New York Business,* January 14, 2008, p. 47.

25. "Agents of Change: Social Entrepreneurs," *The Economist,* February 2, 2008, p. 94.

26. Nicholas D. Kristof, "The Age of Ambition," *New York Times,* January 27, 2008, p. 18.

27. "Boomers Lead Trend as Job Security Wanes," Challenger, Gray & Christmas, Inc., May 31, 2007.

28. Angus Loten, "Why 80 Is the New 30," *Inc.com,* November 2007, online at http://www.inc.com/8over80/2007/why-80-is-the-new-30.html.

29. Ibid.

30. "Boomers Lead Trend as Job Security Wanes," p. 4.

31. Jeff Cornwall, "We Will Not Go Quietly," *The Entrepreneurial Mind,* June 22, 2004, http://www.belmont.edu (October 27, 2005).

32. "Demand for SBA-Backed Loans Continues at Record Pace Through Third Quarter of FY 2005," SBA News Release, July 6, 2005, http:// www.sba.gov (October 28, 2005).

33. Daniel Del'Re, "Entrepreneurship Grows in All Market Conditions," *Inc.,* September, 27, 2005, http://www.inc.com (October 30, 2005).

34. "Minority and Women Business Ownership Increasing Faster than National Average" SBA News Release, July 29, 2005, http://www.sba.gov.

35. Stacy Zhao, "Web-Based Companies Significant Part of U.S. Small Business," Inc.com, June 7, 2005, http://www.inc.com.

Chapter 6

1. Chris Isidore, "Doomed GM Plant Is Most Productive," *CNNMoney.com,* May 31, 2007, http://money.cnn.com/2007/05/31/news/companies/autoplant_productivity/index.htm.

2. "GM Pushes New Models during UAW Strike," *Edmunds Auto Observer,* September 25, 2007, http://www.autoobserver.com/2007/09/gm-tries-to-boo.html.

3. Alex Taylor III, "Gentlemen, Start Your Turnaround," *Fortune,* January 21, 2008, pp. 71–78.

4. Julia Boorstin. "Mickey Drexler's Second Coming," *Fortune,* May 2, 2005, p. 101.

5. Karen Bells, "Hot Off the Press; Milford Printer Spends Big to Fill New Niche," *Cincinnati Business Courier,* July 15, 2005, pp. 17–18.

6. Boorstin, "Mickey Drexler's Second Coming."

7. Nadira A. Hira, "The Making of a UPS Driver," *Fortune,* November 12, 2007, pp. 118–29.

8. Janet Adamy, "One Mechanic's Journey to Aid Northwest Air," *Wall Street Journal,* August 26, 2005, p. B1.

9. Avery Johnson, Susan Carey, and Chris Maher, "Delays Frustrate Air Travelers, but

Carrier Reports Few Glitches," *Wall Street Journal,* August 22, 2005, online.

10. Susan Carey, "With Talks at End, Northwest to Offer Jobs to Stand-Ins," *Wall Street Journal,* September 12, 2005, p. B2.

11. Geoff Colvin, "Leader Machines," *Fortune,* October 1, 2007, pp. 98–106.

12. Nancy Brumback, "6. A. G. Lafley, Chairman and CEO, Procter & Gamble Company," *Supermarket News,* July 25, 2005.

13. Jennifer Reingold, "You Got Served," *Fortune,* October 1, 2007, pp. 55–58. © 2007 Time Inc. All rights reserved.

14. Jaclyne Badal, "Can a Company Be Run as a Democracy?" *Wall Street Journal,* April 23, 1007, p. B1.

15. Peter Gumbel, "Galvanizing Gucci," *Fortune,* January 21, 2008, pp. 81–88.

16. "How They Do It," *Fortune,* October 1, 2007, p. 114.

17. Jeffrey M. O'Brien, "A Perfect Season," *Fortune,* February 4, 2008, pp. 62–66.

18. Ibid.

19. Stephanie Clifford, "How Fast Can This Thing Go, Anyway?" *Inc.,* March 2008, pp. 94–101. Copyright 2008 by Mansueto Ventures LLC. Reproduced with permission of Mansueto Ventures LLC in the format Textbook via Copyright Clearance Center.

20. Michael Useem and Jerry Useem, "Great Escapes: Nine Decision-Making Pitfalls— And Nine Simple Devises to Beat Them," *Fortune,* June 27, 2005, p. 98.

21. Peter Gumbel, "Galvanizing Gucci," p. 86.

22. David Gauthier-Villars, "Société Générale's Damage Control: After Alleged Fraud, French Bank Strives to Save Reputation," *Wall Street Journal,* January 26–27, 2008, p. A3.

23. Geoff Colvin, "Leader Machines," p. 103.

24. This section is adapted from David Henry, Mike France, and Louis Lavelle, "The Boss on the Sidelines: How Auditors, Directors, and Lawyers Are Asserting Their Power," *Business Week,* April 25, 2005, pp. 88–96.

25. "Dashboard Use Rising," *Intelligent Enterprise,* March 2005, p. 18.

26. Carol Hymowitz, "Dashboard Technology: Is It a Helping Hand or a New Big Brother?" *Wall Street Journal,* September 26, 2005, p. B1.

27. Diane Nilsen, Brenda Kowske, and Kshanika Anthony, "Managing Globally—Managing a Diverse Global Environment Is Critical Today. How You Do It Depends on Where You Are," *HR Magazine,* August 2005, p. 111.

Chapter 7

1. Gary McWilliams and Gregory Zuckerman, "Lampert Admits Flubs, Sees Sears Turnaround," *Wall Street Journal,* January 30, 2008, p. B1; Gary McWilliams and Joann Lublin, "Flagging Sears Plans Shakeup in Latest Bid at Turnaround," *Wall Street Journal,* January 19–20, 2008, p. A1.

2. "Ethan Allen Restructures, Creates 3 Subsidiaries," *HFN, the Weekly Newspaper for the Home Furnishing Network,* August 8, 2005, p. 3.

3. ITT Industries Annual Report 2004 Fact Sheet, http://www.itt.com/downloads/ITT_2004_ENGLISH.pdf, October 19, 2005.

4. Sibneft.com, http://www.sibneft.ru/pages.php?lang=1&page=25, October 19, 2005.

5. Brent Schlender, "Incredible: The Man Who Built Pixar's Innovation Machine," *Fortune,* November 15, 2004, p. 212.

6. Betsy McKay, "Pepsi Revamps, with Eye on Succession," *Wall Street Journal,* November 6, 2007, p. A15.

7. Peter Burrows, "HP Says Goodbye to Drama; Five Months in, CEO Mark Hurd's No-nonsense Approach Is Being Felt in a Big Way— and the Street Has Taken Notice," *Business Week Online,* September 1, 2005.

8. Jared Sandberg, "Office Democracies: How Many Bosses Can One Person Have?" *Wall Street Journal,* November 22, 2005, p. B1.

9. Ibid.

10. http://www.novartis.com/about_novartis/en/board_directors.shtml.

11. Pam Fessler, "Experts Challenge Homeland Security Strategy," *NPR,* January 16, 2008.

12. Gary Hamel, "Breaking Free!" *Fortune,* October 1, 2007, 119–26.

13. E. Levenson, "The Power of an Idea," *Fortune,* June 12, 2006, p. 131.

14. Adam Lashinsky, "RAZR's Edge: How a Team of Engineers and Designers Defied Motorola's Own Rules to Create the Cellphone that Revived Their Company," *Fortune,* June 12, 2006, pp. 124–32.

15. Kristina Seward, "5.11 Tactical CEO Keeps His Employees Busy," *Modesto Bee,* September 28, 2005.

16. "A Conversation with Scott Cook," *Inc.,* September 2007, p. 214.

17. "Unilever UK Gets Its House in Order," *Grocer,* February 12, 2005, p. 8; "From Rivalry to Mergers; Anglo-Dutch Companies," *The Economist* (U.S.), February 12, 2005, p. 61.

18. S. Holmes, "Inside the Coup at Nike," *BusinessWeek Online,* January 26, 2006.

19. S. Holmes, "Nike CEO Gets the Boot," *BusinessWeek Online,* January 24, 2006.

20. Hamel, "Break Free."

21. Rik Kirkland, "Cisco's Display of Strength," *Fortune,* November 21, 2007, p. 94.

22. "Re-Inventing H-P the Hurd Way," *Information Age,* September 10, 2005.

23. Hiroshi Ikematsu, "Sony's Restructuring No Easy Task," *The Yomiuri Shimbun,* September 23, 2005; Cliff Edwards with Tom Lowry, Moon Ihlwan, and Kenji Hall, "The Lessons for Sony at Samsung," *Business Week,* October 10, 2005, p. 37.

24. See R. Z. Gooding and J. A. Wagner III, "A Meta-Analytic Review of the Relationship Between Size and Performance: The Productivity and Efficiency of Organizations and Their Subunits," *Administrative Science Quarterly,* December 1985, pp. 462–81.

25. "One-On-One with Second Life Creator Philip Rosedale," *Information Week,* March 18, 2008.

26. "New Study Shows That Workers Believe the Office Grapevine More Than They Do Management," *M2 Presswire,* September 14, 2005.

27. Andrea V. Hernandez, "Controlling the Rumor Mill: Office Gossip Can Hurt Employees and Businesses," *Columbus Ledger-Enquirer,* October 16, 2007.

28. "New Study Shows that Workers Believe the Office Grapevine More Than They Do Management," *M2 Presswire,* September 14, 2005.

29. Ethan Smith and Aaron O. Patrick, "Can New EMI Owner Strike a Chord?" *Wall Street Journal,* January 22, 2008, pp. B1–B2.

30. Michael V. Copeland, "The New Instant Companies" *BUSINESS 2.0,* June 1, 2005, pp. 82–83. ©2005 Time Inc. All rights reserved.

31. "Virtual Reality: Most Teams Work Remotely, Increasing Need for Different Processes," *Employee Benefit News,* February 1, 2008.

32. Ibid.

33. Ibid.

34. Richard Lee, "More Firms Move Manufacturing Overseas, Connecticut Study Shows," *Stamford Advocate,* October 20, 2005.

35. Karin Rives, "Cost, Better Worker Access Drive Companies to Send Jobs Offshore, Survey Shows," *The News & Observer,* October 12, 2005.

36. Jennifer Mears, "Offshore Use on the Rise but Savings Lag," *Network World,* July 25, 2005, p. 13.

37. Ibid.

38. Rives, "Cost, Better Worker Access Drive Companies to Send Jobs Offshore."

39. Ibid.

40. John Tagliabue, "Taking Their Blocks and Playing Toymaker Elsewhere," *New York Times,* November 20, 2006, p. A4; "Picking Up the Pieces," *The Economist,* October 28, 2006, p. 76; Joseph Pisani, "The Making of a Lego," *BusinessWeek Online,* November 29, 2006, p. NA; Matt Defosse, "Toy Industry's Essential Block: Outsourcing," *Modern Plastics Worldwide,* August 2006, pp. 20–22.

41. Rives, "Cost, Better Worker Access Drive Companies to Send Jobs Offshore."

42. Ibid.

Chapter 8

1. Maria M. Perotin, "New Alcon Soft Lens Solutions Approved," *Fort Worth Star-Telegram,* October 13, 2005, p. 2C.

2. Robert Rodriguez, "Filling the HR Pipeline," *HR Magazine,* vol. 49 (September 2004), pp. 78–84.

3. Ibid.

4. Kris Maher, "Hiring Freezes Cushion New Layoffs," *Wall Street Journal,* January 24, 2008, p. A1.

5. Ibid.

6. J. Badal, "Surveying the Field," *Wall Street Journal,* June 26, 2006, p. B5.

7. Sarah E. Needleman, "Speed Interviewing Grows as Skills Shortage Looms," *Wall Street Journal,* November 6, 2007, p. B15.

8. Aman Singh, "Podcasts Extend Recruiters' Reach," *Wall Street Journal,* April 24, 2007, p. B3. Copyright 2007 by Dow Jones & Company, Inc. Reproduced with permission of Dow Jones & Company, Inc. in the format Textbook via Copyright Clearance Center.

9. Jennifer C. Berkshire, "Social Network Recruiting," *HR Magazine,* vol. 50 (April 2005), pp. 95–98.

10. Ryan McCarthy, "'Help Wanted' Meets 'Buy It Now': Why More Companies Are Integrating Marketing and Recruiting," *Inc.,* November 2007, pp. 51–52.

11. Erin White, "Job Ads Loosen Up, Get Real," *Wall Street Journal,* March 12, 2007, p. B3.

12. Erin White, "Personality Tests Aim to Stop Fakers," *Wall Street Journal*, November 6, 2006, p. B3.

13. Ibid.

14. Alex Frankel, "Magic Shop: Are Your Frontline Employees Going to Save or Kill Your Most Important Quarter?" *Fast Company,* November 2007, p. 47.

15. Victoria Knight, "Brokerage Houses Broaden Their Training Programs," *Wall Street Journal,* September 6, 2006, p. B6B.

16. Frankel, "Magic Shop," p. 47.

17. Eric Krell, "Budding Relationships," *HR Magazine,* vol. 50 (Jun, 2005), pp. 11418.

18. Erin White, "For Relevance, Firms Revamp Worker Reviews," *Wall Street Journal,* July 17, 2006, pp. B1, B5. Copyright 2006 by Dow Jones & Company, Inc.. Reproduced with permission of Dow Jones & Company, Inc. in the format Textbook via Copyright Clearance Center.

19. Scott Westcott, "Putting an End to End-of-Year Reviews," *Inc.,* December 2007, pp. 58–59.

20. Pamela Babcock, "Find What Workers Want," *HR Magazine,* vol. 50 (April, 2005), pp. 50–56.

21. "GlaxoSmithKline named to Working Mother Hall of Fame," GlaxoSmithKiline press release, September 25, 2006; Michelle Roberts, "Second Tier, Not Second Class," *Working Mother,* October 2007, pp 126-128; and Caroline M. Levchuck, "Five Hot Jobs for Working Mothers," Yahoo! hotjobs, http://hotjobs.yahoo.com.

22. "Union Members Summary," U.S. Bureau of Labor Statistics, January 25, 2008, http://www.bls.gov/news.release/union2.nr0.htm.

23. Ibid.

24. Jill Lawrence, "Unions Break off from AFL-CIO," *USA Today,* July 26, 2005, pp. 5A, 6A.

25. Kris Maher, "Breakaway Unions to Organize Themselves First," *Wall Street Journal*, September 26, 2005, p. A6.

26. Susan Carey, "Delta, Northwest Pilots Fail to Reach Deal," *Wall Street Journal,* March 18, 2008, p. B5.

27. Ibid.

28. Peter Sanders and Merissa Marr, "Writers Vote to End Their Workout," *Wall Street Journal,* February 13, 2008, p. B14.

29. Taylor Cox and Stacy Blake, "Managing Cultural Diversity: Implications for Organizational Competitiveness," *Academy of Management Executive,* vol. 5 (1991), pp. 45–56.

30. Della De Lafuente, "The Elite Eight," *Pink,* August/September 2007, pp. 67–73.

31. Taylor Mallory, "May I Handle That for You? Companies That Will Take Payroll—and the Rest of Your HR Department—Off Your Plate," *Inc.,* March 2008, pp. 40–42.

32. Ibid.

33. Needleman, "Speed Interviewing Grows."

34. "Ask Ari Weinzwieg," *Inc.,* November 2007, http://www.inc.com/magazine/20071201/ask-ari-weinzweig.html.

35. Aaron Bernstein and Joseph Weber, "So Long, AFL-CIO. Now What?" *Business Week,* August 8, 2005, p. 35.

36. Steven Greenhouse, "Splintered, but Unbowed," *New York Times,* July 30, 2005, p. C1.

37. Bernstein and Weber, "So Long, AFL-CIO. Now What?"

38. Ibid.

39. Projections of job growth from 2002 to 2012 Data: Bureau of Labor Statistics.

40. Greenhouse, "Splintered, but Unbowed."

Chapter 9

1. Mike Hofman, "The Idea that Saved My Company: Embattled Hotelier Chip Conley Found Inspiration from an Unlikely Source: Psychologist Abraham Maslow," *Inc.,* October 2007, pp. 43–44. Copyright 2007 by Mansueto Ventures LLC. Reproduced with permission of Mansueto Ventures LLC in the format Textbook via Copyright Clearance Center.

2. Carmine Gallo, "Bringing Passion to Starbucks, Travelocity; Two Companies Are Trying to Take Employee Engagement and Customer Service to New Levels," *Business Week Online,* January 10, 2008.

3. Ibid.

4. Ibid

5. Ibid.

6. Brent Schlender, "Inside the Shakeup at Sony: The Surprising Selection of Howard Stringer as Sony's CEO Was a Classic Boardroom Tale of Executive Intrigue and Dashed Ambitions," *Fortune,* April 4, 2005, p. 94.

7. "Tom Donovan – Ritz Carlton," Colorado Company, January–February 2007; Carmine Gallo, "Employee Motivation the Ritz-Carlton Way: The Upscale Hotelier's Staff Meetings Rely on Techniques Designed to Engage Staffers. Here's How You Can Incorporate Them in Your Own Shop," *Business Week Online,* March 3, 2008; and Melissa Yen, "Living Values the Ritz-Carlton Way, Human Resources (Australia)," 5 September 2006.

8. Lorri Freifeld, "It's the Network: Verizon," *Training,* February 6, 2008.

9. Scott Westcott, "Putting an End to End-of-Year Reviews," *Inc.,* December 2007, pp. 58–59.

10. Barry Gimbel, "Anger at 30,000 Feet," *Fortune,* December 10, 2007, p. 32.

11. Julie Jargon, "General Mills Sees Wealth via Health," *Wall Street Journal,* February 25, 2008, p. A9.

12. Laura Landro, "Unsnarling Traffic Jams in the O.R.," *Wall Street Journal,* August 10, 2005, p. D1.

13. From Nancy J. Adler, *International Dimensions of Organizational Behavior,* 4th ed. (South-Western Thomson Learning, 2002) pp. 174–81.

14. Susan Kelly, "Give Us a Break! The Benefit That Employees Want Most—That Is Besides More Money—Is More Time," *Treasury and Risk Management,* June 2004.

15. Ibid.

16. Jaclyne Badal, "To Retain Valued Women Employees, Companies Pitch Flextime as Macho," *Wall Street Journal,* December 11, 2006, p. B1.

17. "Generation 'Y' Loves Google, Telecommuting, Survey Finds," *InformationWeek,* November 30, 2007.

18. "Division of Labor: Telework Programs Can Strain Relations Between In-Office, At-Home Workers, Researcher Finds," *Employee Benefit News,* April 1, 2008.

19. Carolyn Hirschman, "Share and Share Alike: Job Sharing Can Boost Productivity and Help Retain Vital Workers, but It Can't Work Effectively Without Help from HR," *HRMagazine,* September 2005, p. 52.

20. A. C. Pasquariello, "Grant Makers," *Fast Company,* April 2007, p. 32.

21. C. Thomson, "The See-Through CEO," *Wired,* April 2007, http://www.wired.com/wired/archive/15.04/wired40_ceo.html.

22. Alan Deutschman, "Can Google Stay Google?" *Fast Company,* August 2005, p. 66.

23. Erin White, "Employers Increasingly Favor Bonuses to Raises," *Wall Street Journal,* August 26, 2006, p. B3.

24. Ibid.

25. Ibid.

26. Ibid.

27. J. Zaslow, "The Most-Praised Generation Goes to Work," *Wall Street Journal,* April 20, 2007, online.wsj.com/article_print/SB11702894815776259.html.

28. Simona Covel, "How to Get Workers to Think and Act Like Owners," *Wall Street Journal,* February 7, 2008, p. B6.

29. Ibid.; Kathy Bergen, "SmithBucklin Becomes Wholly Owned by Employees," *Chicago Tribune,* June 28, 2005, pp. 1, 7.

30. Brent Hunsberger, "Counting on the Company," *The Oregonian,* June 5, 2005.

31. Covel, "How to Get Workers to Think and Act Like Owners."

32. Andrew E. Carr and Thomas Li-Ping, "Sabbaticals and Employee Motivation: Benefits, Concerns, and Implications," *Journal of Education for Business,* January-February 2005, pp.160–65.

33. Ibid.

34. Ibid.

35. Loretta Chao, "Sabbaticals Can Offer Dividends for Employers," *Wall Street Journal,* July 17, 2006, p. B5.

36. David Wessel, "Motivating Workers by Giving Them a Vote," *Wall Street Journal,* August 25, 2005, p. A2.

37. Harry Maurer and Cristina Linblad, "Come to Work, Win a Car," *BusinessWeek,* November 26, 2007, p. 8.

38. Nancy Hatch Woodward, "Uplifting Employees: Raising and Maintaining Employee Morale Takes Sincere Communications and Respect," *HRMagazine,* August 2007, pp. 81–84.

39. Maggie Raunch, "Strong Relationship Shown Between Morale, Absenteeism: Survey Shows Unhappy Employees Use More Sick Days," *Incentive,* May 2005, p. 8.

40. "Surveys Reveal Turnover Rates Are on the Rise," *Report on Salary Surveys,* May 2005, pp. 1–6.

41. Ibid.

Chapter 10

1. Jessi Hempel, "Life at the Top: Silicon Valley's Cult Ride," *Fortune,* March 17, 2008, pp. 51–54.

2. Jim Carlton, "Can a Water Bottler Invigorate One Town?" *Wall Street Journal,* June 9, 2005, p. B1.

3. Jonathan Katz, "Toyota's Eco-Friendly Plan for New Plant: Mississippi Plant Will Have Green Features," *Industry Week,* March 2008, p. 20; Dennis Seid, "Business Newsmaker of the Year: The Northeast Mississippi Worker," *Northeast MS Daily Journal* (Tupelo, MS), December 30, 2007, http://www.industryweek.com/ReadArticle.aspx?ArticleID=15777.

4. Tilde Herrera, "Manatee Tax Cuts Lure New Company," *Bradenton Herald* (FL), May 4, 2005, p. 1B.

5. Christina Passariello, "Louis Vuitton Tries Modern Methods on Factory Lines," *Wall Street Journal*, October 9, 2006, pp. A1, A13.

6. Ibid.

7. Ibid.

8. August Cole, "Boeing Blames Latest Delay in 787 Jet on Supplier Issues," *Wall Street Journal,* January 17, 2008, p. A13.

9. "Stockpiles by Brand; Days Supply on January 1, 2008," *Automotive News,* January 14, 2008, p. 17; "Stockpiles by Brand; Days Supply on March 1, 2008," *Automotive News,* March 17, 2008, p. 24.

10. John D. Stoll and Josée Valcourt, "Woes Continue to Thwart Automakers," *Wall Street Journal,* March 14, 2008, p. A13.

11. Norihiko Shirouzu, Mike Spector, and Josée Valcourt, "Auto Sales Fall Steeply; Toyota Faces Overcapacity," *Wall Street Journal,* April 2, 2008, pp. A1, A11; Michael Cowden,

"AAM Strike Drives GM to Shut First Car Plants," *American Metal Market,* March 31, 2008, pp. 1–2.

12. Mina Kimes, "The New China Price," *Fortune,* November 12, 2007, p. F-1; Alex Salkever, "Manufacturing in the Middle Kingdom: How to Build a Product in China, Without Recalls, Defects, Missed Deadlines . . ." *Inc.,* December 2007, p. 56.

13. Dee-Ann Durbin, "Ford Announces Plans to Use Fewer Suppliers," *San Diego Union-Tribune,* September 30, 2005, p. C3.

14. Erik Sherman, "Supply Chain Alchemy," *Chief Executive,* March 1, 2005, p. 46.

15. Neil Shister, "Redesigned Supply Chain Positions Ford for Global Competition," *World Trade,* May 2005, p. 20.

16. Maria Varmazis, "Automation Frees Time for Strategic Activities," *Purchasing,* September 2005, p. 40.

17. Brad Graves, "KaDonk Helping to Chart Work Flows for Complicated Office Projects; Three Founders Invest $400k in Time, Money for Niche Software," *San Diego Business Journal,* October 15, 2007, pp. 8–10.

18. http://www.nist.gov/public_affairs/releases/2007baldrigerecipients.htm.

19. Robert Hemmant, "The 5Ss to Keeping Lean on Course: Without a Robust 5S Discipline, a Lean System Is Rendered Ineffective," *Circuits Assembly,* August 2007, p. 30.

20. Jamie Flinchbaugh, "Planning 5S? First Know Why!" *Assembly,* June 2006, p. 96.

21. David Pittman, "Robots Advance Surgery Techniques," *Amarillo Globe-News,* August 5, 2007, http://www.amarillo.com/stories/080507/bus_7912332.shtml; M. L. Baker, "Robots: Surgeons' Little Helpers," *eWeek,* December 27, 2006, http://www.channelinsider.com/c/a/News/Robots-Surgeons-Little-Helpers/; "Surgeons Use Robots During Heart Surgery," *UPI NewsTrack,* April 9, 2008, http://www.upi.com/NewsTrack/Science/2008/04/09/surgeons_use_robots_during_heart_surgery/4190/.

22. http://www.bls.gov; "2005 Annual Labor Day Report: The Looming Workforce Crisis—Preparing American Workers for 21st Century Competition," National Association of Manufacturers Web site, http://www.nam.org (May 30, 2006), http://www.nam.org/s_nam/bin.asp?CID=201825&DID=235064&DOC=FILE.PDF.

23. http://www.nam.org/hidden/pdf/2007_labor_report.pdf.

24. "2005 Annual Labor Day Report."

25. "Domestic Environment for Manufacturers," National Association of Manufacturers, http://www.nam.org/s_nam/bin.asp?CID=201507&DID=227168&DOC=FILE.PDF.

26. Elizabeth Millard, "Is Your Company Ready for BPM?" *CIO,* May 15, 2006, http://www.ciotoday.com.

27. Hollis Bischoff, "Teetering on the BPM Strategy Edge," http://www.bpminstitute.org (May 29, 2006).

28. "2005 Annual Labor Day Report."

Chapter 11

1. "Customer Is King—Says Who?" *Marketing News,* April 15, 2007, p. 4.

2. "Big Dealer to Detroit: Fix How You Make Cars," *Wall Street Journal,* February 9, 2007, pp. A1, A8.

3. Marianne Seiler, "High Performance," *Marketing Management,* November/December 2005, pp. 19–23.

4. http://www.theautochannel.com (February 22, 2008).

5. Scott McCartney, "The Middle Seat—Unusual Route: Discount Airlines Woo Business Set," *Wall Street Journal,* February 19, 2008, p. D1. Copyright 2008 by Dow Jones & Company, Inc.. Reproduced with permission of Dow Jones & Company, Inc. in the format Textbook via Copyright Clearance Center.

6. "Net Promoter Conference 2007 Blog," http://www.netpromoter.com (February 22, 2008); "Would You Recommend Us?" *Business Week,* January 30, 2006, pp. 94–95; Randall Brandt, "For Good Measure," *Marketing Management,* January/February 2007, pp. 21–25; Timothy Keiningham, Lerzan Aksoy, Bruce Cooil, and Tor Andreassen, "The Galileo Effect," *Marketing Management,* January/February 2008, pp. 48–51; and Paul Marsden, Alain Samson, and Neville Upton, "Advocacy Drives Growth," http://www.listening.co.uk.

7. "Gap Chief Offers Harsh Diagnosis," *Wall Street Journal,* March 2, 2007, p. B4.

8. Ibid.

9. Ibid.

10. "Getting Couples to Click," *Forbes,* May 22, 2006, pp. 68–69.

11. Marti Barletta, "Who's Really Buying That Car? Ask Her." *Brandweek,* September 4, 2006, p. 20.

12. Ibid.

13. Ibid.

14. "Brand Managers Struggle with Product Launches: Survey," *PROMO Xtra,* July 14, 2005.

15. "Surveyor of the Fittest," *Marketing Management,* September/October 2007, pp. 39–44.

16. "The Informed Consumer," *BusinessWeek,* December 17, 2007, p. 51.

17. "The Next Generation of Price-Comparison Sites," *Wall Street Journal,* September 14, 2005, pp. D1, D13.

18. http://www.1000ventures.com (February 27, 2008).

19. "Line Extensions That Crossed the Line in '07," *Brandweek,* December 10, 2007, p. 4.

20. "Flavor Experiment for KitKat Leaves Nestle with a Bad Taste," *Wall Street Journal,* July 6, 2006, p. A1.

21. "From Cheap Stand-in to Shelf Star," *Wall Street Journal,* August 29, 2007, pp. B1, B3.

22. "101 Brand Names, 1 Manufacturer," *Wall Street Journal,* May 9, 2007, pp. B1, B2.

Chapter 12

1. Ellen Byron, "P&G's Global Target: Shelves of Tiny Stores," *Wall Street Journal,* July 16, 2007, pp. A1, a10. Copyright 2007 by Dow Jones & Company, Inc.. Reproduced with permission of Dow Jones & Company, Inc. in the format Textbook via Copyright Clearance Center.

2. "Luring 'Em In," *Business 2.0,* March 2005, pp. 44–46.

3. "Uncovering Zara," *Apparel Magazine,* January 2006; "Fashion Conquistador," *Business Week,* September 4, 2006, pp. 38–39; "Zara: Taking the Lead in Fast-Fashion," *Business Week Online,* August 29, 2006; "Pace-Setting Zara Seeks More Speed to Fight Its Rising Cheap-Chic Rivals," *Wall Street Journal,* February 20, 2008, pp. B1–B2.

4. "Payday for Peyton," *cnnmoney.com,* January 26, 2007.

5. "Marriott Hotel Owners and Franchisees Investing $190 Million in New Bedding," *Hotel Online,* January 25, 2005, http://www.hotel-online.com/news/pr2005 (October 22, 2005).

6. http://www.marketingcharts.com (March 11, 2008).

7. "Super Bucks," *Fortune,* February 4, 2008, p. 8.

8. "Drug Firms Find That Ad Blitzes Pay," *International Herald Tribune,* August 17, 2007, p. 13.

9. "Pitching Between the Lines," *Business Week,* December 3, 2007, p. 60.

10. "In Billboard War, Digital Signs Spark a Truce," *Wall Street Journal,* February 3–4, 2007, pp. A1, A9.

11. "Test Ride," *Emerging Media Report,* April 2, 2007, pp. 21–24.

12. "In a Shift, Marketers Beef Up Ad Spending Inside Stores," *Wall Street Journal,* September 21, 2005, pp. A1, A8.

13. "Point of Purchase Displays," *Marketing News,* November 1, 2007, p. 8.

14. "How to Sell with Smell," *Business 2.0,* April 2007, p. 36.

15. "Eat My Dust," *Marketing News,* February 1, 2008, pp. 20–21.

16. "Study: Purchase Intent Grows with Each Event," *Brandweek,* January 28, 2008, p. 4.

17. "The Coupon King," *Wall Street Journal,* February 16–17, 2008, pp. A1, A12.

18. "Coupons Gain New Market on Cellphones," *Wall Street Journal,* September 11, 2007, p. B8.

19. "How Companies Pay TV Experts for On-Air Product Mentions," *Wall Street Journal,* April 19, 2005, pp. A1, A12.

20. "Study: Product Recalls Scare Some Away, Forever," *Brandweek,* June 11, 2007, pp. 12–13.

21. "Romancing the Bloggers," *Smart Money,* November 2007, pp. 92–96.

22. "This Blog for Hire," http://www.pcworld.com (February 2007), p. 28.

23. Ibid.

24. http://www.mediaconnection.com (March 11, 2008).

25. Daniel Haygood, "A Status Report on Podcast Advertising," *Journal of Advertising Research,* December 2007, pp. 517–23.

26. "Podcasting Ads Reel in $80M," *Brandweek,* March 6, 2006, p. 16.

27. "Buzz Marketing," *The New York Times,* August 5, 2007, p. 16.

28. "The Buzz on Word of Mouth & Consumer Generated Media," a presentation to the University of Texas at Arlington Marketing Research Advisory Board by Sandy Eubank, Director of U.S. Research and Communication Insights, OMD Worldwide (March 6, 2008).

29. Ibid.

Chapter 13

1. Jim Mackinnon, "Polymer Firms Offered Tech Help," *Akron Beacon-Journal,* September 12, 2007.

2. Ibid.

3. Jerry McElhatton, "Data BPO Can End Restless Nights for CIOs," *Bank Technology News,* February 2006, p.31.

4. "Electronic Trading Hubs," http://www.com-met2005.org.uk, April 4, 2006; David Luckham, "The Global Information Society and the Need for New Technology," http://www.informit.com, April 4, 2006; "Trading Hubs," http://www.investni.com, April 4, 2006; "Trading Hubs in Asia," *Oikono,* December 6, 2005, http://www.oikono.com.

5. Suzanne Marta, "American Follows Data Trail of Fliers: Airline Uses Info from AAdvantage, Web sites to Tailor Customer Offers," *Dallas Morning News,* January 2, 2007.

6. Shel Holtz, "Bring Your Intranet into the 21st Century: Social Media Can Make an Outdated Intranet Easier to Use—and Make Your Employees More Productive in the Process," *Communication World,* January/February 2008, pp. 14–18; Mike Reid and Christian Gray, "Online Social Networks, Virtual Communities, Enterprises, and Information Professionals: Part 2, Stories," *Searcher,* October 2007, pp. 23–33.

7. James Brown, "Hotel Group Installs Global Staff Intranet," *Computing,* October 20, 2005, http://www.computing.co.uk.

8. "Bluetooth® Wireless Technology Becoming Standard in Cars," Bluetooth SIG, February 13, 2006, http://www.bluetooth.com.

9. "Abilene Independent School District Installs AEP Networks' SSL VPN, Saves Up to $875,000 in Tech Support Costs over Five Years," *Internet Wire,* February 14, 2006, http://galenet.thomsonlearning.com.

10. Jessi Hempel, "Battle for the Wi-Fi Skies," *Fortune,* January 21, 2008, p. 16; "American Airlines to Introduce AirCell's In-Flight Internet Connectivity," *Telecomworldwire,* December 27, 2007; Mary Kirby, "Open Channels," *Airline Business,* December 17, 2007; Suzanne Marta, "Aircell Gets OK to Offer In-Flight Broadband on American Airlines, Virgin America Flights," *Dallas Morning News,* April 2, 2008; Mark R. Madler, "Surfing in the Friendly Skies: Satellite-Based Broadband Being Tested by Alaska, Southwest," *San Fernando Valley Business Journal,* March 3, 2008, p. 1; "Aircell Completes Coast-to-Coast Flight, Test of In-Flight Mobile Broadband Service," *Wireless News,* March 30, 2008.

11. "Leading Global Law Firm Extends Contract with Equant to Ensure Seamless Service," *Business Wire,* January 10, 2006, http://galenet.thomsonlearning.com.

12. Mitch Betts, "Application Service Providers Are Back for a Second Act," Computerworld, November 14, 2005, http://www.computerworld.com; Jeffrey Kaplan, "Software-as-a-Service Myths," *BusinessWeek,* April 17, 2006, http://www.businessweek.com; and Sarah Lacy, "The On-Demand Software Scrum," *BusinessWeek,* April 17, 2006, http://www.businessweek.com.

13. Richard Waters, "SAP Ventures into On-Demand Software Field," *Financial Times,* February 3, 2006, p. 28.

14. Kaplan, "Software-as-a-Service Myths."

15. "Checkpoint Patron Services Launches Groundbreaking 'Youniquely 4 U' Service at ALA Annual Meeting," *Internet Wire,* June 22, 2007.

16. Kathleen Hickey, "Data Warehouses Integrate Supply Chains," *World Trade,* February 1, 2006, p. 42.

17. Aaron Dalton, "Better Data with Business Intelligence," *Industry Week,* July 1, 2005, p. 54.

18. Vauhini Vara, "Pleasing Google's Tech-Savvy Staff," *Wall Street Journal,* March 18, 2008, p. B6.

19. Section based on "Executive Guides: Knowledge Management," *Darwin Executive Guides,* http://guide.darwinmag.com/technology/enterprise/knowledge/index.html (April 3, 2006).

20. Mike Reid and Christian Gray, "Online Social Networks."

21. Josh Pereira, "Credit-Card Security Falters," *Wall Street Journal,* April 29, 2008, p. A9.

22. Joris Evers, "Computer Crime Costs $67 Billion, FBI Says," CNet News.com, January 16 2006, http://www.news.com.

23. "Vulnerabilities Reported," CERT/CC Statistics, May 7, 2008, http://www.cert.org/stats/vulnerability_remediation.html.

24. "Cybercrime Cost about $400 Billion," *Computer Crime Research Center,* July 6, 2005, http://www.crime-research.org.

25. Ibid.

26. Evers, "Computer Crime Costs $67 Billion, FBI Says."

27. "AnchorFree Rolls Out Hotspot Shield," *Wireless News,* April 28, 2008.

28. Gavin Knight, "Cyber Crime Is in a State of Flux," *Guardian UKI,* March 29, 2008, http://www.crime-research.org/articles/cybercrime0308/.

29. "Top 10 Cybersecurity Menaces for 2008 Listed; Expect Increased Attacks on Web

Browsers, More Botnets, and Sophisticated Cyberespionage, According to the Annual SANS Institute Report," *InformationWeek*, January 15, 2008.

30. "The Difference Between a Virus, Worm and Trojan Horse?" *Webopedia*, http://www. webopedia.com (April 1, 2006).

31. "Spam Costs World Businesses $50 Billion," *InternetWeek*, February 23, 2005; and "Spam Rates Rebound," *InternetWeek*, March 7, 2006.

32. "Microsoft Files Piracy Charges Against Eight," *InternetWeek*, March 15, 2006; Megan Reichgott, "19 People Indicted in Alleged $6.5 Million Software Piracy Plot," *San Diego Union-Tribune*, February 1, 2006, http://www.signonsandiego.com; and Bill Roberts, "Pirates, Beware: EDA Goes on the Offensive against Software Piracy," *Electronic Business*, March 2006, p. 26.

33. Berinato, "The Global State of Information Security 2005."

34. Lucas Mearian, "IT Managers See Portable Storage Device Security Risk," *Computerworld*, March 17, 2006, http://www.computerworld.com.

35. Vara, "Pleasing Google's Tech-Savvy Staff."

36. Michael V. Copeland and Jon Fortt, "Tech Stocks for Tough Times," *Fortune*, January 21, 2008, p. 42; Adam Lashinsky, "Full Speed Ahead," *Fortune*, October 15, 2007, pp. 134–38.

37. Jon Fortt, "Got Cash? Apple, Google, and Microsoft Do. And Silicon Valley Is Full of Promising Startups," *Fortune*, February 4, 2008, p. 22.

38. Brad Kenney, "IT-as-a-Service: Google Apps and Sites Fit In with the Search Company's Overall Business Application Strategy: Taking the Mystery out of the IT Department," *Industry Week*, May 2008, pp. 64–66.

39. Jay Greene, "Google and Salesforce.com: A Tighter Bond," *BusinessWeekOnline*, April 16, 2008.

40. Stephen H. Wildstrom, "Photoshop's Little Online Brother," *BusinessWeek*, April 28, 2008, p. 128.

41. "How eBay Manages Its Data Centers; The Company Is a Third of the Way Through a Major Three-Year Grid Computing Initiative and Is Hoping to Move Toward Automatic Service Level Management," *InformationWeek*, February 29, 2008; Miya Knights, "Get More Power with Grid Computing," *Computer Weekly*, July 17, 2007.

Chapter 14

1. "CA Special Committee Accuses Ex-Chairman Charles Wang of Fraud," *InformationWeek*, April 14, 2007.

2. John Stucke, "Met Trial Set to Begin: Former Executive Charged in Accounting Scandal," *Spokesman-Review* (Spokane, WA), May 27, 2007.

3. Matthew Belloni, "One 'Rings' Penalty to Rule Them All: New Line Cinema Corp's Case

of Accounting Fraud on Lord of the Rings' Profit," *Hollywood Reporter*, October 5, 2007, p. 12.

4. Bolaji Ojo, "Dell's Costly Financial Restatement," *Electronic Engineering Times*, September 10, 2007, p. 25.

5. Andrew D. Smith, "Dell Restates More than 4 Years of Results," *Dallas Morning News*, October 31, 2007.

6. Jacob Barron, "In the Drop Zone: Regulators Continue to Work Toward One Global Set of Accounting Standard, but as IFRS and GAAP Are Converged, It's Not How You Land, It's How You Fall," *Business Credit*, March 2008, pp. 58–62; Glenn Cheney, "FASB, IASB Agree to Push on with Convergence Effort," *Accounting Today*, April 3, 2006, http://ask.elibrary.com; "FASB and IASB Reaffirm Commitment to Enhance Consistency, Comparability and Efficiency in Global Capital Markets," *Financial Accounting Standards Board*, February 27, 2006, http://www.fasb.org/news/; "FASB Issues Accounting Standard That Improves the Reporting of Accounting Changes as Part of Convergence Effort with IASB," *Financial Accounting Standards Board*, June 1, 2005, http://www.fasb.org/news.

7. "Sources and Occupations of AICPA Membership," AICPA Web site, http://www.aicpa.org (May 7, 2008).

8. Robert Durak, *Audit Risk Alert—2002/03: Current Risks* (New York: American Institute of Certified Public Accountants, Inc., 2002), p. 14; Eric Krell, "What Triggers Financial Restatements?" *Business Finance*, October 2005, http://www.businessfinacemag.com.

9. "In the Name of the Dollar: A Closer Look at the Sarbanes-Oxley Act of 2002," *California CPA*, September 2002, http://www.findarticles.com.

10. Laurie Brannen, "Sarbanes-Oxley's Footprint on Finance Deepens," *Business Finance*, March 2005, http://www.businessfinancemag.com; Laurie Brannen, "Sarbanes-Oxley's Impact on Shareholders," *Business Finance*, February 2005, http://www.businessfinancemag.com.

11. Stephen Taub, "Audit-Rate Spurt Tempers Sarbox Savings," *CFO*, April 20, 2008, http://www.cfo.com.

12. Kingsley Kanu Jr. and Aisha Sylvester, "The Cutting Edge: What Does It Take to Turn a Barbershop into a Booming Business?" *Black Enterprise*, May 2008, pp. 76–79; "V's Barbershop Franchise Expansion Continues—Fifth Location Opens in Chandler, Arizona; Scottsdale, AZ–Based Franchise V's Barbershop Continues Rapid Expansion with Opening of Fifth Location in Chandler, AZ—Nostalgic Environment and Classic Service Offerings Appeal to Broad Demographics," *Internet Wire*, October 4, 2007.

13. Shivani Vora, "Need Cash? Try Looking Inward," *Inc.*, May 2008, pp. 43–44. Copyright 2008 by Mansueto Ventures LLC. Reproduced with permission of Mansueto

Ventures LLC in the format Textbook via Copyright Clearance Center.

14. Laurie Brannen, "PCAOB Issues Audit Guidance," *Business Finance*, July 2005, http://businessfinancemag.com.

15. "AICPA Issues New Risk Assessment Auditing Standards," AICPA press release, February 22, 2006, http://www.aicpa.org.

16. Jim Manzi, "A Pox on SarbOx: The Unintended and Rotten Consequences of the Sarbanes-Oxley Law," *National Review*, May 14, 2007, p. 34.

17. Ibid.

18. Richard A. Epstein, "Scrapping Sarbox: Voluntary Measures Offer Efficient and Efficient and Effective Protection without Hobbling Management," *Chief Executive*, January–February 2008, pp. 56–59.

19. Floyd Norris, "S.E.C. Planning to Delay Accounting Rules for Small Companies for Another Year," *New York Times*, December 12, 2007, p. C4.

20. Kate O'Sullivan, "Can This Relationship Be Saved? Auditors and CFOs Aren't the Friends They Once Were, but They're Working Out Their Differences," *CFO*, May 1, 2008, http://www.cfo.com.

21. Ibid.

22. Mary E. Phillips, Tammy E. Bahmanziari, and Robert G. Colvard, "Six Steps to XBRL: Learn How to Translate Your Income Statement into Tagged Format," *Journal of Accountancy*, February 2008, pp. 34–38.

23. Nicholas Rummell, "SEC to Make Big Push for XBRL," *Financial Week*, April 21, 2008, p. 1.

24. "XBRL US Finalizes US GAAP Taxonomies and Preparers Guide with Delivery to SEC," *PR Newswire*, May 2, 2008.

25. Rummell, "SEC to Make Big Push for XBRL."

26. Ibid.

27. Marie Leone, "FASB Calls for a Cultural Change," *CFO*, March 7, 2006, http://www.cfo.com; Amey Stone and Robert Herz, "It's Like When Someone Robs a Bank," *Business Week Online*, August 19, 2002, http://www.businessweek.com.

Chapter 15

1. The Federal Reserve Board, "Currency in Circulation: Value (In Billions of Dollars, Updated December 31 Each Year)," http://www.federalreserve.gov/paymentsystems/coin/currcircvalue.htm.

2. "United States Dollar," http://en.wikipedia.org. June 3, 2006.

3. "Money Stock Measures," Federal Reserve Statistical Release, March 2008, http://www.federalreserve.gov.

4. Peter Gumbel, "The Bomb in Your Wallet," *Fortune*, November 12, 2007, p. 19.

5. Karen Epper Hoffman, "Retailer's Role in the Demise of the Check," Bank Administration Institute (BAI) Web site, http://www.bai.org (June 3, 2006); Kenneth Kerr and Leon Majors, "Five Payments Myths Debunked," *Banking Strategies*, January–February 2008, online at the Bank

Administration Institute (BAI) Web site, http://www.bai.org.

6. "Financial Services Fact Book—Commercial Banks," Insurance Information Institute Web site, http://www.financialservicesfacts.org (May 9, 2008).

7. "NCR Survey: Consumers Appreciate Self-Service Banking and Are Frustrated When It's Not Available," *Wireless News*, April 16, 2008; Matthias Rieker, "Bank-Client Satisfaction Up a Bit Despite Crunch," *American Banker*, February 19, 2008, p. 1; Don Mecoy, "Pleased Customers Stick Around," *Daily Oklahoman*, June 7, 2007; http://www.acsi.org; http://www.jdpower.com.

8. "Fourth Quarter 2007 Thrift Industry Report Data," Office of Thrift Regulation, Department of the Treasury, February 20, 2008, http://www.ots.treas.gov/docs/1/177400.pdf.

9. "U.S. Credit Union Profile: Year-End 2007," prepared by the Credit Union National Association, February 21, 2008, online at http://advice.cuna.org/download/uscu_profile_4q07.pdf.

10. Ibid.

11. "One Third Of Americans Regularly Bank Online; In a Survey of 2,000 Consumers Last Summer, Gartner Extrapolated that 71 Million U.S. Adults Use Online Banking Regularly," *InformationWeek*, February 19, 2008.

12. "Asset Management and Pension Sector, 2007," U.S. Department of Commerce, International Trade Association, http://trade.gov/investamerica/asset_mgmt_pensions.asp (May 9, 2008).

13. Katie Zezima, "Virgin Starting U.S. Lender Aimed at Family and Friends," *The New York Times*, October 15, 2007, p. C6; Jessica Harris, "Easy Money," *Fortune*, December 10, 2007, p. F2; Chris Taylor, "The Next Little Thing 2008," *Fortune Small Business*, December 2007, p. 68.

14. "Who Is the FDIC?" Federal Deposit Insurance Corporation Web site, http://www.fdic.gov (May 9, 2008).

15. "Economic Benefits to the United States from the Activities of International Banks," Institute of International Bankers, p. 6, http://www.iib.org/associations/6316/files/2008EcoBenefitStudy.pdf (May 10, 2008).

16. "Economic Benefits to the United States from the Activities of International Banks," p. 9.

17. "Economic Benefits to the United States from the Activities of International Banks," p. 7.

18. Geri Smith and Keith Epstein, "Wal-Mart Banks on 'the Unbanked'; Its New Mexican Lending Arm Taps a Fresh Source of Growth," *BusinessWeek*, December 24, 2007, p. 42; Carolyn Whelan, "Wal-Mart Gets Its Bank—In Mexico," *Fortune*, February 4, 2008, p. 16; Tricia Juhn, "Wal-Mart: Mexico's New Bank," *Latin Business Chronicle*, July 23, 2007, http://www.latinbusinesschronicle.com; Karen Willoughby, "Wal-Mart Begins Banking in Mexico," *Food International*, March 4, 2008, online at http://www.foodinternational.net.

19. "Top 10 Banking Industry Trends in 2006," Aite Group, January 9, 2006, http://www.aitegroup.com.

20. "Bricks 'n' Clicks: Internet Banking," *The Economist*, February 3, 2007, p. 76.

21. Jane Bryant Quinn, "Easy Money, A Click Away," *Newsweek*, May 21, 2007, p. 41.

22. Glen Fest, "Internet Banking: Luring the Laggards Will Require Enhancements," *Bank Technology News*, May 2007, p. 18; "Bricks 'n' Clicks."

23. Ibid.

24. Ibid.

25. Kenneth Kerr and Leon Majors, "Five Payments Myths Debunked," *Banking Strategies*, January/February 2008, http://www.bai.org; Leon Majors, "Unexpected Disruption in Payments Technology," *Banking Strategies*, January/February 2007, http://www.bai.org.

26. Matthew Swibel, "Microfinance Fever," *Forbes*, January 7, 2008, http://www.forbes.com.

27. Swibel, "Microfinance Fever."

28. Matthew Swibel, "The World's Top Microfinance Institutions," *Forbes*, December 20, 2007, http://www.forbes.com.

29. Amy Feldman, "How I Became a Little Guy Lender," *BusinessWeek*, May 5, 2008, p. 60.

30. Michael Sisk, "Peer-to-Peer Lending: The Rise of Lending Communities," *US Banker*, February 2008, p. 18.

31. "Money Laundering," U.S. Drug Enforcement Web site, http://www.dea.gov (June 2, 2006).

32. "Anti-Money Laundering Technology: Automating the Haystack Search," May 12, 2006, Aite Group Web site, http://www.aitegroup.com.

Chapter 16

1. Stephen Moore, "Guess Who Really Pays the Taxes?" *The American*, November–December 2007, pp. 58–64; Beth Piskora, "Tax Avoidance: Will Taxes Go Up with a New President?" *BusinessWeek Online*, May 12, 2008; Finlay Lewis, "Bush to Focus on Healthy Economy in Effort to Recharge His Agenda," San Diego Union-Tribune, January 6, 2006, http://www.signonsandiego.com.

2. Corning Inc. Web site, http://www.corning.com (June 3, 2006); Jonathan Fahey, "Glass Menagerie," Forbes, April 24, 2006, pp. 87–90; and Kevin Maney, "Corning CEO Insists on Keeping His Eye on the Long-Term Ball," USA Today, May 11, 2005, p. 3B.

3. Karen M. Kroll, "The Changing Face of Treasury Investments," Business Finance, March 2006, http://businessfinancemag.com.

4. "3rd Quarter 2007 NSDTR Shows Credit Pros Exercising Discipline," *Managing Credit, Receivables & Collections*, January 2008, p. 2.

5. Shivani Vora, "Need Cash? Try Looking Inward," *Inc.*, May 2008, pp. 43–45.

6. John Edwards, "BPO: Is Wider Better?" CFO.com, February 21, 2006, http://www.cfo.com; Susan Kelly, "Up Against Stiff Trade Winds? Boost Your Tech Power," Treasury & Risk Management, September 2005, http://www.treasuryandrisk.com; Dave Lindorff, "Trusting Others with Your Data," Treasury & Risk Management, May 2006, http://www.treasuryandrisk.com.

7. Helen Shaw, "Trimming Hemlines and Deadlines," CFO, April 24, 2006, http://www.cfo.com.

8. Wing S. Chow, Christian N. Madu, Chu-Hua Kuei, et al., "Supply Chain Management in the U.S. and Taiwan: An Empirical Study," Omega, October 2008, pp. 665–80; Miya Knights, "Fit-For-Purpose IT Breeds Profits," *Computer Weekly*, January 9, 2007; Connie Robbins Gentry, "European Fashion Stores Edge Past U.S. Counterparts: Zara Masters Replenishment Using Optimization Models," *Chain Store Age*, December 2007, p. 100; Bridget McCrea, "2007 Global Supply Chain Conference," *Supply Chain Management Review*, December 2007, pp. 37–43; Cecilie Rohwedder and Keith Johnson, "Pace-Setting Zara Seeks More Speed to Fight Its Rising Cheap-Chic Rivals," *Wall Street Journal*, February 20, 2008, p. B1.

9. Louise Story, "A Fear of Big Demand for Corporate Loans," *The New York Times*, May 9, 2008, p. C7.

10. Liza Casabona, "An Executive Take on Factoring's Global Future," *WWD*, September 17, 2007, p. 16.

11. Daniel McGinn, "A Fat-Farm Dropout Makes Good: How I Did It, Mel Zuckerman, Chairman, Canyon Ranch," *Inc.*, December 2007, pp. 140–41.

12. Ben Steverman, "IPOs: Back from the Dead?" *BusinessWeek Online*, May 9, 2008; Maria Aspan, "Visa Solid in First Post-IPO Profit Report," *American Banker*, April 29, 2008, p. 20.

13. Sara Hansard, "First Comes the IPO, Then Comes the Bad News: Investors Punish Companies for Failure to Prepare for Poor Earnings and Staff Defections," *Investment News*, December 10, 2007, p. 17.

14. "Xerox Declares First Common Stock Dividend in Six Years," *M2 Presswire*, November 19, 2007.

15. Starbucks annual report, 2007, p. 2.

16. Jeff D. Opdyke, "Nest Egg: Everybody's an Analyst Investment Research + Wiki = a Potentially Very Different Kind of Web Site," *Wall Street Journal*, December 17, 2007, p. R8; Carleen Hawn, "A Free Alternative to Alternative Research," Financial Week, April 28, 2008, p. 13; "About Wikinvest," http://www.wikinvest.com/site/About_Wikinvest.

17. Jeff D. Opdyke and Jane J. Kim, "The New Landscape of Online Trading," Wall Street Journal, August 9, 2005, pp. D1–D2.

18. Statistics from http://www.economywatch.com/market/bond-market/international.html (May 20, 2008).

19. Securities Industry and Financial Markets Association Web site, http://www.sifma.org/research/pdf/overall_issuance.pdf, accessed July 24, 2008.

20. http://www.sifma.org/research/pdf/Overall_Outstanding.pdf and http://www.sifma.org/research/pdf/Overall_Issuance.pdf.

21. http://www.sifma.org/research/pdf/Overall_Outstanding.pdf.

22. *2008 Investment Company Fact Book,* 48th ed. (Washington, DC: Investment Company Institute, May 2008), p. 42.

23. Selena Maranjian, "Are ETFs Getting Out of Control?" Fool.com, April 12, 2006, http://www.fool.com.

24. NYSE corporate Web site, http://www.nyse.com (May 20, 2008), online at http://www.nyse.com/press/1199444909934.html.

25. Ibid.

26. John Hintze, "NYSE Expands Offerings with Amex Acquisition: Deal Affirms Concept of a Bifurcated Options Market," *Securities Industry News,* January 21, 2008.

27. Tom Groenfeldt, "Gearing Up for Greater Volume," Institutional Investor, April 2006, p. 55; and Ivy Schmerken, "Resurrecting the Regionals," Wall Street & Technology, November 2005, p. A38.

28. Peter Chapman, "Another Bullseye?" *Traders,* March 1, 2007.

29. NASDAQ Web site, http://www.NASDAQ.com (May 20, 2008).

30. "SEC Approves NASDAQ's Exchange Registration Application," NASDAQ press release, January 16, 2006, http://www.NASDAQ.com.

31. "NASDAQ Creates New Market Tier with Highest Listing Standards in the World," NASDAQ press release, February 15, 2006, http://www.NASDAQ.com; "NASDAQ Global Select Fact Sheet," NASDAQ, http://www.NASDAQ.com (June 12, 2006).

32. "Pink Sheets Electronic OTC Markets Announces Record Trading Volume in 2007," *Internet Wire,* January 17, 2008.

33. Peter Chapman, "ECNs Packing Their Bags: Saying Sayonara to NASDAQ," Traders Magazine, May 2006, http://www.tradersmagazine.com; Ivy Schmerken, "Reg NMS Turns 1," Wall Street & Technology, March 2006, p. 48.

34. Yukari Iwatani Kane and Eric Bellman, "Japan, India Take a Beating," Wall Street Journal, June 1, 2006, p. C12.

35. Steve Kichen, "Global Supermarket," *Forbes,* July 23, 2007, p. 96; "E*Trade Eyes Digital Shop for Euro Drive," *Campaign,* June 1, 2007, p. 2; "Broker Justifies Play for E*Trade," *Australasian Business Intelligence,* March 15, 2007; Alejandro Bodipo-Memba, "E*Trade to Make Online Trading Simpler," *Detroit Free Press,* February 20, 2007; "E*Trade Goes Global: U.S. Discount Brokerage Is the First to Let Customers Trade Foreign-Listed Stocks Online," *Investment Dealer's Digest,* February 26, 2007.

36. "NASDAQ to Add an Exchange," *The New York Times,* November 8, 2007, p. C7; Quentin Carruthers, "OMX Rivalry Turns into Alliance: In the Latest Twist to the Store of Global Stock Exchange Consolidation, Rival Bidders Borse Dubai and NASDAQ Have Come to Terms over Their Target," *Acquisitions Monthly,* October 2007, pp. 12–14; Victoria Robson, "Stock Exchanges Around the World Are Looking to Their Neighbours for Merger Opportunities. But in the Gulf, a Single, Merged GCC Market Is Increasingly Unlikely," *Middle East Economic Digest,* November 16, 2007, pp. 64–67.

37. Robson, "Marketing Integration Off the Agenda."

38. Victoria Robson, "Volatility Spreads to Regional Bourses: Steep Falls on Middle East Exchanges Reveal Increasing Correlation with International Stock Markets," *Middle East Economic Digest,* January 25, 2008, p. 12.

39. Michelle Price, "Trading: Business Continuity," *The Banker,* April 1, 2008, p. NA.

40. Ivy Schmerken, "Is Hardware Acceleration the Next Data-Latency Killer? A Surge in Data Message Traffic Is Leading the Industry to Examine Hardware Acceleration to Reduce Data Latency," *Wall Street & Technology,* September 2007, pp. 15–18.

41. Ibid.

42. "The Year in Trading," *Traders,* December 1, 2007.

43. Christina McEachern, "Algorithmic Spending to Slow: Algo Spending Hits a Plateau in the United States, More Sophisticated Tools Are on the Horizon," *Wall Street & Technology,* December 2007, pp. SS29–SS32.

subject index

Job analysis, 204
Job descriptions, 204–205
    realistic job previews, 209–210
Job design, motivational, 245–246
Job dissatisfiers, 241
Job enlargement, 245
Job enrichment, 245–246
Job fairs, 207
Job rotation, 212, 246
Job satisfiers, 241
Job security and collective bargaining,
    220–221
Job sharing, 246, 247
Job shop, 261
Job specification, 205
Jobs, Steve, 42, 95, 129, 150, 166–167, 284–285,
    344, 345, 456
John, Daymond, 136
Joint ventures, 82–83, 110
Jones, Bobby, 243
Jones, Nathan, 133
Jospin, Lionel, 12
Journals in accounting cycle, 385
Judiciary, 58–59. *See also* Courts
Junk bonds, 441
Jury service pay, 215
Justice, 40
Just-in-time (JIT) system, 274

K

Kant, Immanuel, 44
Kapalka, Jason, 133
Kauffman Foundation Index for Entrepreneurial
    Activity, 144
Keeling, Chris, 449
Kilburg, Richard, 184
Kindle, Amazon.com, 322
King, Karen, 361
Kiosks, 322
Kleenan, Kim, 141
Knowledge, 6
*Knowledge: Confronting the Threat of an Aging
    Workforce* (DeLong), 27
Knowledge management (KM), 362–363
Knowledge workers, 6, 350
Knox, Ron, 231
Korea Exchange, 447
Kovacs, Myles, 133
Kozlowski, Dennis, 41
Krupski, Rebekah, 375
Kruse, Peter, 395
Kumar, Sanjay, 378
Kurien, T. K., 174–175
Kyoto Protocol, 57

L

Labor, Department of, 15
    on labor force crisis, 277
    Wage and Hour division of, 224
Labor force, 5. *See also* Employees
    crisis of, 276–277
    external labor market, 207
    internal labor market, 207
    location of production and, 263–264
    older workers in, 27
    outsourcing and, 195
Labor relations, 216–225. *See also* Collective
    bargaining
    arbitration, 222
    grievances, managing, 221–222
    legal environment and, 222–225
    modern labor movement, 216–217
    strikes, 222
    trends in, 225–226
Labor unions, 216
    arbitration, 222
    benefits of, 218

grievances, managing, 221–222
local unions, 216–217
national unions, 217
organizing by, 217–218
and service workers, 226
strategies of, 222
Lafley, A. G., 161–162, 166
Lagarde, Christine, 12
Laissez-faire leadership, 162–163
Lampert, Eddie, 117, 179
Language as trade barrier, 74
LANs (local area networks), 353–354
Laptop computers, 350
Latin America, 246
Lavigne, Avril, 325–326
Laws. *See* Legal issues; specific acts
Lawson, Lance, 133
Lawton, Mike, 94
Layout of facilities, 265
Le Gette, Brian, 147–148
Leader pricing, 309
Leadership, 160–164
    at Apple Computers, 284
    authority and, 162
    empowerment and, 163–164
    and management, 157
    styles of, 162–163
    trends in, 169–171
Leading by example, 42
Lean manufacturing, 274
Lee, Young, 113
Lefever, Ann Gillen, 162
Legal issues, 53–54, 58. *See also* Copyrights;
    Courts; Trademarks
    arbitration, 59
    bankruptcy laws, 53, 63–64
    business law, 8, 58
    environmental scanning and, 292
    and ethics, 41
    of human resource (HR) management,
        222–225
    of labor relations, 222–225
    mediation, 59
    patents, 62, 386
    product liability laws, 53, 63
    sexual harassment, 40, 224
    sources of, 58
    tort laws, 53, 62–63
    warranties, 61–62
Legal profession careers, 123
Legal responsibility, 45–46
"Legends of Rock," 297
Legitimate power, 161
Leveraged buyouts (LBOs), 116
Levy, Sarah, 130
Liabilities, 384
    on balance sheets, 387–388
    long-term liabilities, 388
Liability
    of corporations, 106
    of partnerships, 104
    product liability laws, 53, 63
    of sole proprietorships, 101
    strict liability, 63
Library of Congress, 62
Licensing, 82
    multinational corporations and, 87
Liddie, Ed, 256
Life insurance, 215
Lifestyles and psychographic
    segmentation, 301
Limited liability companies (LLCs), 100, 108
Limited partnerships, 103
Line extensions, 307, 311
Line of credit, 435–436
Line organization, 182
Line positions, 182

Line-and-staff organization, 182
Lippitt, Robb, 139
Liquidity, 386
    cash management and, 432–433
    ratios, 392–393
Litow, Stan, 49
Live Earth concert, 48
Loans
    business loans, 416
    consumer loans, 416
    ethical issues, 425
    for franchises, 115
    between friends and family, 418
    microlending, 422–423
    to minorities, 143–144
    revolving credit agreements, 436
    secured short-term loans, 436
    short-term loans, 435–436
Lobbying, 8
Local area networks (LANs), 353–354
Local unions, 216–217
Location
    and business-to-business market, 299
    international considerations, 264
    local incentives and, 264
    marketing factors and, 264
    production and, 263–264
Lockouts, 222
London Stock Exchange (LSE), 446, 447, 449
Long-term expenditures, 434–435
Long-term financing, 436–439
Long-term liabilities, 388
Long-term production planning, 260
Loss leaders, 309
Loveman, Gary, 170
Loyal customers, 334
Lucas, George, 156
Lucid, Shannon, 403
Lying and ethics, 39

M

M1, 409–410
M2, 409–410
Macintosh sales, 456–457
MacLean, Jessica, 123
Macroeconomics, 12
    fiscal policy and, 18–20
    and full employment, 14–15
    goals, achieving, 17–20
    growth and, 14
    monetary policy and, 17–18
    prices, steadiness of, 16–17
Magnuson-Moss Warranty Act, 66
Maguire, Tobey, 87
Mail Fraud Act, 66
Maine International Trade Center, 81
Mainframe computers, 350
Maisel, David, 167
Make-or-buy decision, 267
Malcolm Baldridge National Quality Award,
    273–274
Malware, 366
Managed service providers (MSPs), 358
Management
    conceptual skills, 169
    controlling function, 164–166
    crisis management, 169–170
    decision making and, 167–168
    entrepreneurship and, 130–131
    global management, 171
    good management, 157
    human relations skills, 169
    and information technology, 170
    leadership, 160–164
    organizing and, 160–161
    planning and, 157–160
    role of, 156–157, 166–168

National Association of Securities Dealers (NASD), 448
National banks, 414–415
National Cattlemen's Beef Association, 328
National Center for Employee Ownership, 249–250
National Credit Union Insurance Fund, 418
National debt, 19–20
National Environmental Policy Act, 58
National Federation of Independent Businesses, 140
National Institute of Standards and Technologies (NIST), 273–274
National Labor Relations Board (NLRB), 217
and Wagner Act, 224
National Market System (NMS), 445
National Stock Exchange India, 447
National Stock Exchange (NSX), 444, 445
Nationalism and global trade, 84
Natural resources, 5
Navistar, 201
Needs
defined, 236
Maslow's hierarchy of needs, 238–240
Negligence, 63
Net profit margin, 393
Net profit or loss figure, 390
Net promoter score (NPS), 293
Net sales, 388
Net working capital, 393
Net worth, 384
Networks. See also Computer networks
Electronic communications networks (ECNs), 446
peer-to-peer lending (P2P) networks, 422–423
New York Stock Exchange (NYSE), 444–445, 447
reforms, 383
New-product goals, 304–305
Newspaper tombstone ads, 440
Niche competitive advantage, 294–295
Nichols, Ed, 133
Nickell, Jake, 133
Niewulis, Steve, 141
Night, Phil, 188
Nokes, Sue, 163
Noncompete clauses, 137
Nondepository financial institutions, 416–417
Nonprogrammed decisions, 167
Nontraditional distribution channels, 322
Non-value-added production processes, 274
Nooyi, Indra, 156, 181, 207
North American Free Trade Agreement (NAFTA), 77–78
Notes payable, 388
Notes receivable, 386
Not-for-profit organizations, 5. See also Charities
careers in, 35–36
marketing by, 296
Nutrition Labeling and Education Act, 66

O

Objects in sales presentations, 333
Obligations and ethics, 41
Observation research, 302
Occupational safety, 224. See also OSHA (Occupational Safety and Health Administration)
Occupational Safety and Health Act, 222, 223
Odd-even pricing, 309–310
Odors in stores, 326
Office automation systems, 361
Office of Minority Enterprise Development (SBA), 142

Office of Thrift Supervision, 415
Office romances, 245
Officers of corporation, 106, 107
Off-price retailers, 325
Off-the-job training, 212
Oil and gas, reliance on, 28–29
Okosi, Alex, 93
Oligopolies, 25–26
Olsen, Ashley, 130
Olsen, Mary-Kate, 130
"100 Best Companies to Work For," 250
Online banking, 416
Online investing, 440–441
Online processing, 359
On-site child care, 216
On-the-job training, 211–212
Open market operations, 411
Open source companies, 80
Operating activities, cash flow from, 391
Operating expenses, 390
Operational planning, 159
middle management and, 160
Operations management, 259–260. See also Production
at Apple Computers, 284–285
trends in, 276–278
Oppenheimer, James, 335
Opportunism and virtual corporations, 193
Options trading, 443–444
Oral contracts, 61
Oreck, Thomas, 167
Organic farmers, 122–123
Organic organizations, 190–191
Organization charts, 180–181
Organization for Economic Co-operation and Development (OECD), 6
Organizational abuse, 40
Organizational structures, 180–182. See also Authority; Matrix structure
business environment and, 191
centralization, degree of, 189
committee structure, 184
contemporary structures, 182–184
decentralization, 189
design considerations, 189–191
flat structures, 190–191
informal organization, 192
line organization, 182
line-and-staff organization, 182
mechanistic organization, 190–191
organic organizations, 190–191
outsourcing, 195–196
reengineering, 192–193
tall structures, 190–191
teams, working as, 184–187
traditional structures, 179–182
trends in, 192–196
virtual corporations, 193–194
Organizing, 160–161
and management, 157
Orientation of employees, 211, 213
OSHA (Occupational Safety and Health Administration), 224
mine employees, protections for, 281
OTC (over-the-counter) markets, 445, 446
Ouchi, William, 240–241
Ouellet, Eric, 367
Outputs. See Inputs and outputs
Outsourcing, 73, 195–196
by Apple Computers, 285
to China, 269
ethical issues, 199
financial management, 434
global economy and, 277
human resource (HR) management, role of, 225–226

in manufacturing process, 267
by small businesses, 138
Overextension of product line, 311
Over-the-Counter Bulletin Board (OTCBB), 446
Owens, Terrell, 220
Owner's equity, 384
on balance sheets, 388
Ownership
capitalism and, 11
communism and, 11
employee stock ownership plans (ESOPs), 249–250
socialism and, 11

P

Pacific Rim countries, banking in, 420
Pacioli, Brother Luca, 384
Page, Larry, 6
Palm oil, 15
Par value
of bonds, 438
of corporate bonds, 441
Paramore, 171
Participative leaders, 162–163, 248
Partnerships, 100, 102–104. See also Small businesses
advantages of, 103, 109
disadvantages of, 103–104, 109
qualities of partner, 103
types of, 103
written agreements, 102–103
Patents, 62, 386
Patrick, Danica, 237
Pay structure. See Compensation and benefits
Pay-for-performance programs, 249
Payment Card Industry Security Standards Council (PCI), 364
Payroll costs, 263–264
Payroll taxes, 67
PDAs (personal data assistants), 355
expert systems and, 361
and office automation systems, 361
security issues, 367
Peer-to-peer computing, 369–371
Peer-to-peer lending (P2P) networks, 422–423
Pelosi, Nancy, 395
Peluso, Michelle, 238
Penetration pricing, 309
Pension Reform Act, 222, 223
Pensions, 215
laws governing, 222
nondepository financial institutions, pension funds as, 417
The Pentagon, 364
Perez, William, 188
Perfect competition, 24, 25
Performance
appraisals, 212–214
and matrix structure, 183
motivation and, 242
standards, 164–165
Perpetual inventory, 267–268
Personal behavior and ethics, 40
Personal selling, 331–333
process, 331–333
in promotional mix, 328
Personality
buyer behavior and, 298
and entrepreneurship, 130
psychographic segmentation, 301
testing, 210
PERT (program evaluation and review technique), 271–272
Pettitte, Andy, 39
Pharmaceutical business, 8
Philanthropy. See Corporate philanthropy

Razrs, 421
Reach, 331
Real-time processing, 359
Recession, 14
Recognition and motivation, 247–248
Recording Industry Association of America
  (RIAA), 65
Recreational vehicles (RVs), 6
Recruitment branding, 208–209
Recruitment of employees, 207–209
  podcasting and, 208
  realistic job previews, 209–210
  social networking, 208
Reed, Lou, 171
Reengineering organizational structure,
  192–193
Reference checks, 210
Reference groups, 297
Referent power, 161
Regional exchanges, 444, 445
Regulation FD (Fair Disclosure), 448
Regulation National Market System
  (Reg NMS), 449
Reichheld, Fred, 293
Reinforcement theory, 245
Relationship management, 29–30
Relationship marketing, 291–292
R.E.M., 171
Remington, John, 46
Remote deposit capture (RDC), 422
Research and development (R&D) cycles, 432
Reserve requirement, 411
Resource allocator role, 167
Resource planning, 266–267
  computerized planning, 268
  enterprise resource planning (ERP), 277
Resources, 4
  and matrix structure, 183
  natural resources, 5
Restitution for breach of contract, 61
Restraint of trade, 64
Retailers, 324–326
  Apple Computers, distribution by,
    344–345
  in distribution channel, 321
  types of, 325–32
Retained earnings, 388, 438, 439
Retirement. See also Pensions
  and baby boomer generation, 26–27
  savings accounts, 215
Return, 432
Return on equity (ROE), 393
Return on sales, 393
Returns and allowances, 388
Revenue, 4, 388
  taxes as, 18
Revenue bonds, 442
Reverse auctions, 270
Revolving credit agreements, 436
Rewards, 236
  power, 161
  in reinforcement theory, 245
Rhythm software, 285
Rice, Christopher, 194–195
Rifkin, Devon, 133
Rigas, John, 41
Right-to-work laws, 220
Risk, 4, 432
  debt financing and, 437
  entrepreneurship and, 127–128
  of small businesses, 137–138
Risk-return trade-off, 432
Roberts, Andy, 160
Roberts, Mike, 355
Robinson-Patman Act of 1936, 64–65
Robotics, 275, 276
Roedy, Bill, 93

Roethlisberger, Ben, 215
Roomba vacuum cleaner, 7
Rooney, Andy, 44
Roosevelt, Franklin D., 417
Rosedale, Phillip, 191
Rosenthal, Mort, 134
Roundtable on Sustainable Palm Oil
  (RSPO), 15
Routing, 270
RSS (really simple syndication), 336
Ruh, Duane, 139
Rule violations, 40
Rules-based accounting, 396
Rumor mills, 192
Rutan, Burt, 131
Rutledge, Matt, 7

S

S corporations, 108. See also Small businesses
Sabbaticals, 250–251
Sacks, Rodney C., 315–316
Safety. See also Workplace safety
  ethical issues, 281
  needs, 238–239
Salaries. See Compensation and benefits
Sales discounts, 388
Sales promotions, 296, 333–335
  event marketing, 334
  in promotional mix, 329
Sales prospects, 331–332
Sales taxes, 67
Sanchez, Ana, 130
Sandberg, Anthony, 138
Sarbanes-Oxley Act of 2002, 382–384, 448
  compliance issues, 401
  ethical issues, 400
  reevaluating, 394–395
Sarkozy, Nicolas, 12
Sarrazin, Juliette, 131
Satisfaction. See Customer satisfaction;
  Employee satisfaction
Sauve, John, 81
Savings accounts, 416
Savings and loan associations (S&Ls), 415
Savings Association Insurance Fund (SAIF), 418
Savings banks, 415
Savings bonds, 20
SBA (Small Business Administration),
  141–142
  Active Corps of Executives (ACE), 142
  Angel Capital Electronic Network, 142
  business plan samples from, 135
  E-Business Institute, 142
  on entrepreneurship, 127
  financial assistance programs, 141–142
  global trade, support for, 81
  New Markets Venture Capital Program, 142
  Office of International trade, 140
  Service Corps of Retired Executives
    (SCORE), 142
Scarcity of money, 402
Schaefer, August, 316–317
Scheduling and production control, 260–261
Schlosberg, Hilton H., 315–316
Schmidt, Eric, 42
Schultz, Howard, 113, 170
Schutzman, Charlotte, 247
Schuyler, Matt, 171
Scientific management, 237
SCORE (Service Corps of Retired
  Executives), 142
Scott, Tom, 129
Seasonal unemployment, 16
SEC (Securities and Exchange Commission)
  accounting fraud and, 378
  creation of, 447
  and executive compensation packages, 173

and Extensible Business Reporting
  Language (XBRL), 396
and NASDAQ, 445
National Market System (NSM) regulations,
  445
Public Company Accounting Oversight
  Board (PCAOB) and, 383
Regulation National Market System
  (Reg NMS), 449
and Sarbanes-Oxley Act, 395
Second Life users, 330
Secondary markets, 444
Secondary securities market, 440
Secretaries of corporations, 106, 107
Secured short-term loans, 436
Securities. See also Bonds
  defined, 440
  exchange-traded funds (ETFs), 443
  futures contracts, 443
  mutual funds, 443
  options, 443–444
  U.S. government securities, 442
Securities Act of 1933, 447
Securities Exchange Act of 1934, 447
Securities exchanges, 444–448
  alternative trading systems, 446
  consolidation of, 449
  dealer markets, 445–446
  global trading, 446–447
  Regulation National Market System
    (Reg NMS), 449
  self-regulation of, 448
Securities Industry and Financial Markets
  Association (SIFMA), 442
Securities Investor Protection Corporation
  (SIPC), 448
Securities markets, 440–444
  bonds, investing in, 441
  consolidation of, 449
  electronic communications networks
    (ECNs), 446
  online investing, 440–441
  Regulation National Market System
    (Reg NMS), 449
  regulation of, 446–447
  self-regulation, 448
  trade-cycle automation, 449
  trends in, 448–449
  types of, 440
Security for computers, 363–368
Seid, Michael H., 113
Selection of employees, 209–211
  interviews, 211
Selective credit controls, 412
Selective strike strategy, 222
Self-actualization needs, 238–239
Self-managed work teams, 186
Seller cooperatives, 109
Selling expenses, 390
Semel, Terry, 193
Seniority and collective bargaining,
  220–221
Sensex, 446
September 11th attacks, 368
Service Corps of Retired Executives
  (SCORE), 142
Service Employees International Union (SEIU),
  17, 226
Service workers
  labor unions and, 226
  minimum wage and, 222
  Service Employees International Union
    (SEIU), 17, 226
Services, 304
  defined, 4
  Uruguay Round on, 76
Sexual harassment, 40, 224

company index

Kohls, 325
Kool-Aid, 307
KPMG International, 380–381
Kraft Foods, 116, 204–206, 306
Krispy Kreme, 49
Kroger, 325
K-Tel, 325

L

Laborers' International Union, 217
The Ladders.com, 208
Lagasse Brothers, 323
Land O'Lakes, 108, 109
Land Rover, 195
Lands' End, 325
Lane Bryant, 293
Lane Furniture, 264
Lava-Flow, 446
Lay's, 302
Lego, 196
Lehman Brothers, 162
Le Menu, 300
Lenevo, 292
Lerner, 293
Lever, 328
Levi Strauss, 40, 42, 82, 325, 438
Lexus, 291, 294, 337
LG, 285
Liberty Tax Service, 113
The Limited, Inc., 293
Linden Labs, 187, 191
LinkedIn, 208
The Little Guys Home Electronics, 141, 402
Little Log Co., 139
L.L. Bean, 325
LoanBack, 422
Lockheed Martin, 225, 277
L'Oreal, 328
Louis Vuitton, 264, 266
Lowe's, 109
LucasFilm Ltd., 156
Lurias, 325

M

Macy's, 116, 325, 330, 392
Marriott Hotels, 328
Mark Matthew Fine Gentlemen's Grooming Club, 26
Marriott International, 170, 293, 294, 309
Mars Corp., 14, 299, 438
Marvel Comics, 169
Massage Envy, 113
MasterCard, 144, 185, 328, 341, 351
Mathnasium Learning Centers, 113
Mattel, 277, 282
May Company, 116
Mayo Clinic, 282
McDonald's, 4, 55, 70, 82, 111, 112, 169, 170, 222, 224, 295, 296, 329, 341, 355, 439
MCI, 26, 353
McKinsey & Co., 208
Menu Foods, 63, 312
Mercedes-Benz, 330, 356
Merck, 439
Mercy Health Systems, 274
Merriam-Webster, 7
Merrill Lynch & Co., 211, 212, 440
Methodist Hospital System, 47
MetLife, 421
Metropolitan Mortgage & Securities, 378
Michael H. Seid & Associates, 113
Micro Center, 346
Microsoft, 4, 6, 12, 74, 80, 104, 115, 210, 311, 330, 336, 366, 439, 445
Midvale Steel Co., 237
Miller Brewing Co., 116, 214
Minolta, 304

Mint, 369
Mitsubishi, 224, 419
Monster.com, 207, 255
Moon Valley Rustic Furniture, 100
Morgan Stanley, 440
Motorola, 44, 48, 89, 116, 185, 224, 282, 355, 356
Mr. Clean, 311
MSN, 454
MTV Networks, 93, 298–299, 331
Murjani Group, 89
MySpace, 139, 193, 337, 355

N

Nabisco, 116
National City Corp., 414
National Cooperative Bank, 214
National Energy Technology Laboratory, 27
Nationwide Papers, 323
Nature's Cure, 337
Navistar, 201
Navy Federal Credit Union, 416
Neiman Marcus, 294, 303, 325
Nescafe, 86
Nestlé, 15, 89, 311
Netezza Corp., 395
Netflix, 251
Netshare, 207
New Line Cinema, 378
News Corp., 116
Newsweek, 331
NeXT, 284
Nextage, 311
Nexxus, 302
N-Hance, 113
Nike, 25, 44, 164, 188, 336, 432
Nimbit, 136
Nintendo, 305
Nissan Motor Company, 51, 395
Nokia, 225, 271, 336, 356
Nordstrom, 34
North Face, 23
Northwest Airlines, 160, 220–221, 222
Novartis, 184, 374

O

O.C. Sailing Club, 138
Ocean Spray, 109, 129
OffThePathMedia.com, 130
OhGizmo.com, 336
Oil, Chemical and Atomic Workers Union (OCAW), 217
Olive Garden, 301
OnAir, 357
1-800-Flowers, 352
One Hour Air Conditioning & Heating, 113
OpenPages, 401
Oracle/PeopleSoft, 225
Orange Lake Resorts, 210
Oreck Vacuum Co., 167
Organon Biosciences, 116
Orkin Pest Control, 41
Otis Elevator, 88
Overstock.com, 311, 325

P

Pacific Gas & Electric Company, 5
Palm Harbor Enterprises, 6
Palm, 361
Pampers, 86
Panasonic, 307
Panera Bread, 445
Pantene, 408
Paper, Allied-Industrial, Chemical and Energy International Union (PACE), 217
Parents of Invention, 102
PayPal, 128
PayPerPost, 336

Pennzoil, 304
Penske Logistics, 270
Pentagon Federal Credit Union, 416
Pepperidge Farm, 303
PepsiCo, 74, 83, 84, 86, 159, 181, 207, 300, 303, 315, 328, 329
Perdue Farms, 84
Peridot Capital Management, 454
Pernod Ricard, 84
Pfizer, 8, 50
Philips, 341
Philip Morris Company, 116
Philips Norelco, 337
Phorm, 330
Piaggio, 260
Pinkberry, 113
Pixar, 180, 190
Pizza Hut, 111, 112, 114, 301
Plan B Entertainment, 104
Plan Your Career (PYC), 242
Plateau Systems, 212
Play N Trade Franchise Inc., 113
PNC Bank, 180
The Pohly Company, 255
Poilâne Bakery, 130–131
Polaroid, 24–25
PopCap Games, 133
Popular Mechanics, 331
Porsche, 303
Postini, 365
PostNet, 110
Prada, 159
PricewaterhouseCoopers (PWC), 45, 207, 380
The Principal, 255
Procter & Gamble, 88, 161–162, 167, 207, 282, 306, 309, 311, 312, 323, 324, 334, 350, 369, 444
ProFlowers, 269
Prosper, 422
Publix Super Markets, 438
PUMA, 361
Purina, 333, 337

Q

Qantas, 357
Quaker Oats, 159, 293
Qualcomm, 47, 439, 445
Quanta, 285
Quantum Computer Services, 403
Quicken Loans, 47
Quiznos, 112, 121
QVC Shopping Network, 148, 322, 325

R

Radio Shack, 95, 325
Rainforest Café, 82
Ralph Lauren, 295, 311
Rawlings, 336
RecycleBank, 142–143
Red Cross, 382
Redken, 295
Reebok, 328, 336
REI, 56
RE/MAX Int'l. Inc., 111, 113
Renaissance Barbershop, 389
Renaissance Hotels and Resorts, 294
Renault SA, 51
Republic of Tea, 309
Residence Inn, 294
Reuters, 116
Revlon, 295
Ritz-Carlton Hotels, 207, 225, 242, 294
Roaman's, 293
Robs, 325
Roc-A-Fella Records, 143
Rockford Corporation, 7
Rockwell Collins, 270
Rolex, 75